W9-CTW-130

DATE DUE

			PRINTED IN U.S.A.

Literature Criticism from 1400 to 1800

Guide to Gale Literary Criticism Series

For criticism on	Consult these Gale series
Authors now living or who died after December 31, 1959	*CONTEMPORARY LITERARY CRITICISM (CLC)*
Authors who died between 1900 and 1959	*TWENTIETH-CENTURY LITERARY CRITICISM (TCLC)*
Authors who died between 1800 and 1899	*NINETEENTH-CENTURY LITERATURE CRITICISM (NCLC)*
Authors who died between 1400 and 1799	*LITERATURE CRITICISM FROM 1400 TO 1800 (LC)* *SHAKESPEAREAN CRITICISM (SC)*
Authors who died before 1400	*CLASSICAL AND MEDIEVAL LITERATURE CRITICISM (CMLC)*
Black writers of the past two hundred years	*BLACK LITERATURE CRITICISM (BLC)*
Authors of books for children and young adults	*CHILDREN'S LITERATURE REVIEW (CLR)*
Dramatists	*DRAMA CRITICISM (DC)*
Hispanic writers of the late nineteenth and twentieth centuries	*HISPANIC LITERATURE CRITICISM (HLC)*
Native North American writers and orators of the eighteenth, nineteenth, and twentieth centuries	*NATIVE NORTH AMERICAN LITERATURE (NNAL)*
Poets	*POETRY CRITICISM (PC)*
Short story writers	*SHORT STORY CRITICISM (SSC)*
Major authors from the Renaissance to the present	*WORLD LITERATURE CRITICISM, 1500 TO THE PRESENT (WLC)*

ISSN 0740-2880

Volume 28

Literature Criticism from 1400 to 1800

Excerpts from Criticism of the Works
of Fifteenth-, Sixteenth-, Seventeenth-, and
Eighteenth-Century Novelists, Poets, Playwrights,
Philosophers, and Other Creative Writers, from
the First Published Critical Appraisals
to Current Evaluations

James E. Person, Jr., Editor

Jennifer Brostrom
Michael Magoulias
Associate Editors

Gale Research Inc.

An International Thomson Publishing Company

Changing the Way the World Learns

NEW YORK • LONDON • BONN • BOSTON • DETROIT • MADRID
MELBOURNE • MEXICO CITY • PARIS • SINGAPORE • TOKYO
TORONTO • WASHINGTON • ALBANY NY • BELMONT CA • CINCINNATI OH

STAFF

James E. Person, Jr., *Editor*

Dana Ramel Barnes, Jennifer Brostrom, Catherine C. Dominic,
Denise Kasinec, Jelena O. Krstović, Michael Magoulias, *Associate Editors*

Marlene H. Lasky, *Permissions Manager*
Margaret A. Chamberlain, Linda M. Pugliese, *Permissions Specialists*
Susan Brohman, Diane Cooper, Maria Franklin, Arlene Johnson, Josephine M. Keene,
Michele Lonoconus, Maureen Puhl, Shalice Shah,
Kimberly F. Smilay, Barbara A. Wallace, *Permissions Associates*
Edna Hedblad, Tyra Y. Phillips, *Permissions Assistants*

Victoria B. Cariappa, *Research Manager*
Donna Melnychenko, Eva M. Felts, Mary Beth McElmeel, Tracie A. Richardson, Norma Sawaya, *Research Associates*
Melissa E. Brown, Maria E. Bryson, Shirley Gates, Michele P. Pica,
Amy Terese Steel, Amy Beth Wieczorek, *Research Assistants*

Mary Beth Trimper, *Production Director*
Mary Kelley, *Production Associate*

Cynthia Baldwin, *Product Design Manager*
Sherrell Hobbs, *Macintosh Artist*
Willie Mathis, *Camera Operator*

∞™ This book is printed on acid-free paper that meets the minimum requirements of American National Standard for Information Sciences—Permanence Paper for Printed Library Materials, ANSI Z39.48-1984.

Library of Congress Catalog Card Number 94-29718
ISBN 0-8103-8944-4
ISSN 0740-2880
Printed in the United States of America
Published simultaneously in the United Kingdom
by Gale Research International Limited
(An affiliated company of Gale Research Inc.)

I(T)P™   Gale Research Inc., an International Thomson Publishing Company.
ITP logo is a trademark under license.

10 9 8 7 6 5 4 3 2 1

Contents

Preface   vii

Acknowledgments   xi

Preface

L *iterature Criticism from 1400 to 1800 (LC)* presents criticism of world authors of the fifteenth through eighteenth centuries. The literature of this period reflects a turbulent time of radical change that saw the rise of drama equal in stature to that of classical Greece, the birth of the novel and personal essay forms, the emergence of newspapers and periodicals, and major achievements in poetry and philosophy. Much of modern literature reflects the influence of these centuries. Thus the literature treated in *LC* provides insight into the universal nature of human experience, as well as into the life and thought of the past.

Scope of the Series

LC is designed to serve as an introduction to authors of the fifteenth through eighteenth centuries and to the most significant interpretations of these authors' works. The great poets, dramatists, novelists, essayists, and philosophers of this period are considered classics in every secondary school and college or university curriculum. Because criticism of this literature spans nearly six hundred years, an overwhelming amount of critical material confronts the student. *LC* therefore organizes and reprints the most noteworthy published criticism of authors of these centuries. Readers should note that there is a separate Gale reference series devoted to Shakespearean studies. For though belonging properly to the period covered in *LC*, William Shakespeare has inspired such a tremendous and ever-growing corpus of secondary material that the editors have deemed it best to give his works extensive coverage in a separate series, *Shakespearean Criticism*.

Each author entry in *LC* attempts to present a historical survey of critical response to the author's works. Early criticism is offered to indicate initial responses, later selections document any rise or decline in literary reputations, and retrospective analyses provide students with modern views. The size of each author entry is intended to reflect the author's critical reception in English or foreign criticism in translation. Articles and books that have not been translated into English are therefore excluded. Every attempt has been made to identify and include the seminal essays on each author's work and to include recent commentary providing modern perspectives.

The need for *LC* among students and teachers of literature was suggested by the proven usefulness of Gale's *Contemporary Literary Criticism (CLC)*, *Twentieth-Century Literary Criticism (TCLC)*, and *Nineteenth-Century Literature Criticism (NCLC)*, which excerpt criticism of works by nineteenth- and twentieth-century authors. Because of the different time periods covered, there is no duplication of authors or critical material in any of these literary criticism series. An author may appear more than once in the series because of the great quantity of critical material available and because of the aesthetic demands of the series's *thematic organization*.

Thematic Approach

Beginning with Volume 12, all the authors in each volume of *LC* are organized in a thematic scheme. Such themes include literary movements, literary reaction to political and historical events, significant eras in literary history, and the literature of cultures often overlooked by English-speaking readers.

Organization of the Book

Each entry consists of the following elements: author or thematic heading, introduction, list of principal works (in author entries only), annotated works of criticism (each followed by a bibliographical citation), and a bibliography o further reading. Also, most author entries contain author portraits and others illustrations.

- The **Author Heading** consists of the author's full name, followed by birth and death dates. If an author wrote consistently under a pseudonym, the pseudonym is used in the author heading, with the real name given in parentheses on the first line of the biographical and critical introduction. Also located here are any name variations under which an author wrote, including transliterated forms for authors whose native languages use nonroman alphabets. Uncertain birth or death dates are indicated by question marks. The **Thematic Heading** simply states the subject of the entry.

- The **Biographical and Critical Introduction** contains background information designed to introduce the reader to an author and to critical discussion of his or her work. Parenthetical material following many of the introductions provides references to biographical and critical reference series published by Gale in which additional material about the author may be found. The **Thematic Introduction** briefly defines the subject of the entry and provides social and historical background important to understanding the criticism.

- Most *LC* author entries include **Portraits** of the author. Many entries also contain illustrations of materials pertinent to an author's career, including author holographs, title pages, letters, or representations of important people, places, and events in an author's life.

- The **List of Principal Works** is chronological by date of first book publication and identifies the genre of each work. In the case of foreign authors whose works have been translated in to English, the title and date of the first English-language edition are given in brackets beneath the foreign-language listing. Unless otherwise indicated, drama are dated by first performance, not first publication.

- **Criticism** is arranged chronologically in each author entry to provide a useful perspective on changes in critical evaluation over the years. For the purpose of easy identification, the critic's name and the composition or publication date or the critical work are given at the beginning of each piece of criticism. Unsigned criticism is preceded by the title of the source in which it appeared. All titles by the author featured in the critical entry are printed in boldface type. Publication information (such as publisher names and book prices) and parenthetical numerical references (such as footnotes or page and line references to specific editions of works) have been deleted at the editors' discretion to provide smoother reading of the text.

- Critical essays are prefaced by **Annotations** as an additional aid to students using *LC*. These explanatory notes may provide several types of useful information, including: the reputation of a critic, the importance of a work of criticism, the commentator's individual approach to literary criticism, the intent of the criticism, and the growth of critical controversy or changes in critical trends regarding an author's work. In some cases, these notes cross-reference the work of critics within the entry who agree or disagree with each other.

- A complete **Bibliographical Citation** of the original essay or book follows each piece of criticism.

- An annotated bibliography of **Further Reading** appears at the end of each entry and suggests resources for additional study of authors and themes. It also includes essays for which the editors could not obtain reprint rights.

Cumulative Indexes

Each volume of *LC* includes a cumulative **Author Index** listing all the authors that have appeared in *Contemporary Literary Criticism, Twentieth-Century Literary Criticism, Nineteenth-Century Literature Criticism, Literature Criticism from 1400 to 1800, and Classical and Medieval Literature Criticism,* along with cross-references to the Gale series *Short Story Criticism, Poetry Criticism, Children's Literature Review, Authors in the News, Contemporary Authors, Contemporary Authors Autobiography Series, Contemporary Authors Bibliographical Series, Dictionary of Literary Biography, Concise Dictionary of Literary Biography, Something about the Author, Something about the Author Autobiography Series, and Yesterday's Authors of Books for Children.* Readers will welcome this cumulative author index as a useful tool for locating an author within the various series. The index, which includes authors' birth and death dates, is particularly valuable for those authors who are identified with a certain period but whose death dates cause them to be placed in another, or for those authors whose careers span two periods. For example, F. Scott Fitzgerald is found in *TCLC,* yet a writer often associated with him, Ernest Hemingway, is found in *CLC.*

Beginning with Volume 12, *LC* includes a cumulative **Topic Index** that lists all literary themes and topics treated in *LC, NCLC* Topics volumes, *TCLC* Topics volumes, and the *CLC* Yearbook. Each volume of *LC* also includes a cumulative **Nationality Index** in which authors' names are arranged alphabetically under their respective nationalities and followed by the numbers of the volumes in which they appear.

Each volume of *LC* also includes a cumulative **Title Index,** an alphabetical listing of the literary works discussed in the series since its inception. Each title listing includes the corresponding volume and page numbers where criticism may be located. Foreign-language titles that have been translated followed by the tiles of the translation—for example, *El ingenioso hidalgo Don Quixote de la Mancha (Don Quixote).* Page numbers following these translated titles refers to all pages on which any form of the titles, either foreign-language or translated, appear. Title of novels, dramas, nonfiction books, and poetry, short story, or essays collections are printed in italics, while individual poems, short stories, and essays are printed in roman type within quotation marks.

A Note to the Reader

When writing papers, students who quote directly from any volume in the Literary Criticism Series may use the following general forms to footnote reprinted criticism. The first example pertains to material drawn from periodicals, the second to material reprinted from books.

T. S. Eliot, "John Donne," *The Nation and the Athenaeum,* 33 (9 June 1923), 321-32; excerpted and reprinted in *Literature Criticism from 1400 to 1800,* Vol. 10, ed. James E. Person, Jr. (Detroit: Gale Research, 1989), pp. 28-9.

Clara G. Stillman, *Samuel Butler: A Mid-Victorian Modern* (Viking Press, 1932); excerpted and reprinted in *Twentieth-Century Literary Criticism,* Vol. 33, ed. Paula Kepos (Detroit: Gale Research, 1989), pp. 43-5.

Suggestions Are Welcome

In response to various suggestions features have been added to *LC* since the series began, including a nationality index, a Literary Criticism Series topic index, thematic entries, a descriptive table of contents, and more extensive illustrations.

Readers who wish to suggest new features, themes or authors to appear in future volumes, or who have other suggestions, are cordially invited to write to the editor.

Acknowledgments

The editors wish to thank the copyright holders of the excerpted criticism included in this volume and the permissions managers of many book and magazine publishing companies for assisting us in securing reprint rights. We are also grateful to the staffs of the Detroit Public Library, the Library of Congress, the University of Detroit Mercy Library, Wayne State University Purdy/Kresge Library Complex, and the University of Michigan Libraries for making their resources available to us. Following is a list of the copyright holders who have granted us permission to reprint material in this volume of *LC*. Every effort has been made to trace copyright, but if omissions have been made, please let us know.

Pierre Corneille

1606-1684

French dramatist, poet, and essayist.

INTRODUCTION

Corneille was the first great tragic dramatist of France. Although many of his thirty-four plays are comedies or works of mixed type, he is particularly known for creating the genre of French classical tragedy with his innovative and controversial masterpiece, *Le Cid* (1636-37; *The Cid*). This play and those that followed feature central characters of heroic stature who are torn by conflicting definitions of honor. Corneille's intense focus on human will, its striving for freedom, and the fashioning of one's own destiny distinguishes his tragedies from classical Greek dramas, in which humans are depicted as helpless victims of fate. While his theatrical career was marked by both triumphs and defeats, he was recognized in his lifetime as among his country's foremost dramatists and was commonly designated by the appellation "le grand Corneille."

Biographical Information

Little is known of Corneille's life. He was born into a middle-class family in Rouen and seems to have lived a quiet, retired, bourgeois existence all his life. His brother Thomas was also a playwright; his works, though very popular in their day, are now largely forgotten. Pierre studied law and joined the bar, but showed little aptitude for the profession. As a student he had written poetry and won prizes for his Latin versification. In 1629 he offered his first play, the comedy *Mélite, ou Les fausses lettres* (*Melite; or, The False Letters*), to a theatrical troupe led by the acclaimed actor Montdory during the group's stop in Rouen. The play was a great success when staged in Paris, and Corneille's theatrical career was effectively launched. Over the next several years, Corneille wrote five comedies—including *Clitandre, La galerie du palais, ou L'amie rivale* (1631; *The Palace Corridor; or, The Rival Friend*), and *La place royale, ou l'amoureux extravagant* (1633-34; *Place Royale; or, The Extravagant Lover*)—and the tragedy *Medée* (1634-35; *Medea*). During this period he attracted the attention of the powerful and influential Cardinal Richelieu, who enlisted him as a member of the "Society of Five Authors," a group of acclaimed writers who composed plays under Richelieu's direction, and whose number included (besides Corneille) François de Boisrobert, Guillaume Colletet, Claude de L'Estoile, and Jean de Rotrou. Although he contributed the third act to a joint effort, *La comédie des tuileries* (1635; *The Comedy of the Tuileries*), Corneille reportedly became involved in disputes with the Cardinal and soon resigned from the group.

Composed and first staged around 1636-37, *The Cid* was

a great popular success but gave rise to a heated controversy known as "la Querelle du *Cid*." The play's numerous violations of the neoclassical "rules" of tragic design prompted published attacks by Corneille's rivals as well as defenses by Corneille and his supporters. The rules demanded that the action of the play must transpire within a twenty-four-hour timeframe and must be noble in style. The matter of *The Cid* was eventually submitted by Richelieu to the newly formed Académie Française, which issued a judgment siding with Corneille's opponents. Wounded and discouraged, Corneille ceased writing plays for three years. After his return to the theater in 1640, he entered a very fertile period, producing at least three comedies and nine tragedies, including *Horace* (1640; *Horatius*), *Cinna, ou La clémence d'Auguste* (1640-41; *Cinna; or, The Clemency of Augustus*), and *Polyeucte* (1641-42; *Polyeuctes*), which are considered among his greatest.

In 1652 the signal failure of the tragedy *Pertharite, roi des Lombards* (*Pertharites, King of the Lombards*) led Corneille once again to leave the theater, this time for seven years. Although he attempted to regain his stature with *Oedipe* (*Oedipus*) in 1659, neither this tragedy nor

1

the works that followed were nearly so successful as his former triumphs. Furthermore, the heroic mode of characterization that Corneille employed was giving way in public favor to the more firmly classical and Jansenist work of his younger contemporary and rival, Jean Racine. With a style that has been described as simple yet polished, smooth yet natural, Racine created dramatic characters, who—like their forerunners in classical Greek drama—are undone by their passions, driven to ruin by ungovernable impulses. Corneille, his own works paling beside Racine's, retired from the theater in 1674 and died in obscurity ten years later.

Major Works

The Cid is considered one of the masterpieces of French drama, one which reflected the spirit of the age. Corneille's was an age of a growing French middle class and shrinking nobility, centralized government, and economic growth. As John Gassner has written, "Although he respected the new autocratic France, he was an independent spirit and not yet the complete courtier who became the ideal of the age. His *Cid* paid tribute to the ideals of 'honor' or duty, and to this extent it reflected the new age which set social responsibility above personal impulses. . . . Nevertheless, the play also celebrated the claims of individuality by the intensely heroic quality of its leading characters and the strength of their emotions." In *The Cid*, Corneille offered token regard to the neoclassical "rules," but his plot foreshadows the more elaborate plotting of the Elizabethan stage: within twenty-four hours the protagonist falls in love, fights a duel, kills his beloved's father, leads his outnumbered military force to a smashing victory over the Moors, and is vindicated in trial by combat, all while alternately losing and then regaining favor with both his beloved and his nation's king. In his later plays, Corneille focused less on celebrating individual heroism and more on classical themes: conflicts between patriotic duty and love, the call for mercy contrasted with the need for disinterested justice. Among Corneille's later works, *Horatius, Polyeuctes,* and *Suréna* (1674; *Surenas*) are often named as masterworks of French drama. In addition, Corneille's comedies, from his early *Mélite* through *Le menteur* (1643; *The Liar*) and regarded as clever, well-crafted works.

Critical Reception

Comparing Corneille and Racine, Jean de La Bruyère wrote that "the former paints men as they should be, the latter paints men as they are." Like La Bruyère, many critics compare the intents and accomplishments of Corneille with those of Racine, often to Racine's advantage. "Unlike Corneille," wrote Irving Babbitt, "Racine moved with perfect ease among all the rules that the neo-classic disciplinarians had imposed upon the stage," here speaking of the unities of time, space, and action prescribed by neoclassical theorists—those rules by which Corneille was judged in "la Querelle du *Cid.*" The judgment of the Académie aside, Corneille's work is noted for its great diversity, brilliant versification, and complexity of plot and situation. Critics and students of drama have extolled his depiction of humans as exalted beings, capable of

greatness; they have also praised the playwright's freeing of tragedy from the confinement and artificiality of neoclassical strictures. Although his reputation's decline, begun in his own lifetime, continued throughout the eighteenth century, the nineteenth saw a reappraisal of Corneille's place in literary history, and today he is situated in the front rank of French dramatists.

PRINCIPAL WORKS

Mélite, ou les fausses lettres [*Mélite; or, The False Letters*] (drama) 1630

Clitandre (drama) 1631

La veuve, ou Le traître trahi [*The Widow; or, The Betrayer Betrayed*] (drama) 1631?

La galerie du palais, ou L'amie rivale [*The Palace Corridor; or, The Rival Friend*] (drama) 1632

La Suivante [*The Maidservant*] (drama) 1633

Médée [*Medea*] (drama) 1634-35

La place royale, ou l'amoureux extravagant [*Place royale; or, The Extravagant Lover*] (drama) 1633-34

L'illusion comique [*The Comic Illusion*] (drama) 1635

Le Cid [*The Cid*] (drama) 1636-37

Horace [*Horatius*] (drama) 1640

Cinna, ou La clémence d'Auguste [*Cinna; or, The Clemency of Augustus*] (drama) 1640-41

Polyeucte [*Polyeuctes*] (drama) 1641-42

La mort de Pompée [*The Death of Pompey*] (drama) 1642

Le menteur [*The Liar*] (drama) 1643

Rodogune, Princesse des Parthes [*Rodogune, Princess of Parthia*] (drama) 1644

La suite du menteur [*Sequel to The Liar*] (drama) 1644

Théodore, vierge et martyre [*Theodora, Virgin and Martyr*] (drama) 1645

Héraclius [*Heraclius*] (drama) 1646

Dom Sanche d'Aragon [*Don Sancho of Aragon*] (drama) 1649

Andromède [*Andromeda*] (drama) 1650

Nicomède [*Nicomedes*] (drama) 1650

Pertharite, roi des Lombards [*Pertharites, King of the Lombards*] (drama) 1651

Oedipe [*Oedipus*] (drama) 1659

La toison d'or [*The Golden Fleece*] (drama) 1660

Sertorius (drama) 1662

Sophonisbe [*Sophonisba*] (drama) 1663

Othon [*Otho*] (drama) 1664

Agésilas [*Agesilaus*] (drama) 1666

Attila (drama) 1667

Tite et Bérénice [*Titus and Berenice*] (drama) 1670

Pulchérie [*Pulcheria*] (drama) 1672

Suréna [*Surenas*] (drama) 1674

Œuvres de P. Corneille, avec leas commentaires de Voltaire. 12 vols. (dramas, poetry, prose) 1817

CRITICISM

Charles de Saint-Evremond (essay date 1672?)

SOURCE: "To an Author Who Asked My Opinion of a Play Where the Heroine Does Nothing But Lament Herself," in *The Continental Model: Selected French Critical Essays of the Seventeenth Century, in English Translation,* edited by Scott Elledge and Donald Schier, Carleton College and the University of Minnesota Press, 1960, pp. 153-55.

[*In the following excerpt from an essay originally written in approximately 1672, Saint-Evremond decries Corneille's descent from the effective illumination of character to lachrymose sentimentality.*]

Corneille has had the misfortune to disgust the generality of his spectators in his latter days, because he must needs discover that which is most hidden in our hearts, that which is most exquisite in the passions and most delicate in the thoughts. After he had, as it were, worn out the ordinary passions with which we are agitated, he was in hopes of gaining a new reputation if he touched our most concealed tendernesses, our nicest jealousies, and our most secret griefs. But this studied penetration being too delicate for great assemblies, so precious and painful a discovery has made him lose some esteem in the world, whereas it ought to have procured him new applauses.

It is certain that no man understood nature better than Corneille, but he has described it differently according to the different periods of his life. When he was young, he contented himself with describing its motions; when he was old, he was for discovering its most secret springs. Formerly he ascribed everything to the sentiment; at present, penetration does everything with him; now he opens the heart and its most concealed recesses, whereas he formerly represented it with all its anxieties and agitations. Other authors have succeeded better in complying with the present humor of the age, which loves nothing but grief and tenderness upon the theatre.

C. A. Sainte-Beuve (essay date 1855)

SOURCE: "Corneille," in *Portraits of the Seventeenth Century: Historic and Literary,* translated by Katharine P. Wormeley, G. P. Putnam's Sons, 1904, pp. 29-54.

[*Sainte-Beuve is considered the foremost French literary critic of the nineteenth century. Of his extensive body of critical writings, the best known are his "lundis"—weekly newspaper articles which appeared over a period of several decades, in which he displayed his knowledge of literature and history. While Sainte-Beuve began his career as a champion of Romanticism, he eventually formulated a psychological method of criticism. Asserting that the critic cannot separate a work of literature from the artist and from the artist's historical milieu, Sainte-Beuve considered an author's life and character integral to the comprehension of his work. In the following excerpt from an essay originally published in 1855, he provides a capsule overview of Corneille's career and discusses his dramatic style, influences, and characterizations, among other concerns.*]

From 1629, the period when Corneille first came to Paris,

to 1636, when **The Cid** was first acted, he completed his literary education, which was merely sketched-out in the provinces. He put himself into connection with the wits and poets of his time, especially with those of his own age, Mairet, Scudéry, Rotrou: he learned then what he had not known hitherto, that Ronsard was a little out of fashion, that Malherbe, dead within a year, had dethroned him in public opinion; that Théophile, also dead, had disappointed all hopes and left but a questionable memory behind him; that the stage was growing nobler and purer under the care of Cardinal de Richelieu; that Hardy was no longer by any means its sole supporter, for a troop of young rivals were judging him, to his great displeasure, rather freely, and disputing his heritage. Above all, Corneille learned that there were rules of which he had never dreamed in Rouen, but about which the brains of Paris were keenly excited: such as keeping five acts in one place or getting out of it; to be, or not to be within the space of twenty-four hours, etc. The learned men and the rule-lovers made war on these points against the lawless and the ignorant. Mairet held with the former; Claveret declared against them; Rotrou cared little; Scudéry discussed emphatically.

In the various plays that Corneille composed during this

Corneille's reputation among his contemporaries:

Corneille, unlike many of the great writers of the world, was not driven to wait for "the next age" to do him justice. The cabal or clique which attacked the *Cid* had no effect whatever on the judgment of the public. All his subsequent masterpieces were received with the same ungrudging applause, and the rising star of Racine, even in conjunction with the manifest inferiority of Corneille's last five or six plays, with difficulty prevailed against the older poet's towering reputation. . . . [It] should not be forgotten that Racine, in discharge of his duty as respondent at the Academical reception of Thomas Corneille, pronounced upon the memory of Pierre perhaps the noblest and most just tribute of eulogy that ever issued from the lips of a rival. Boileau's testimony is of a more chequered character; yet he seems never to have failed in admiring Corneille whenever his principles would allow him to do so. Questioned as to the great men of Louis XIV.'s reign, he is said to have replied: "I only know three,—Corneille, Molière and myself." "And how about Racine?" his auditor ventured to remark. "He was an extremely clever fellow to whom I taught the art of elaborate rhyming" (*rimer difficilement*). It was reserved for the 18th century to exalt Racine above Corneille.

George Saintsbury, in French Literature and Its Masters, *edited by Huntington Cairns, Alfred A. Knopf, 1946.*

---

space of five years, he applied himself to understand thoroughly the habits of the stage and the taste of the public; I shall not try to follow him in this tentative course. . . .

During this time, Corneille made frequent excursions to

Rouen. In one of these journeys he visited the house of a M. de Châlons, former secretary of the queen-mother, now retired from old age:

> "Monsieur," the old man said to him, "the style of comedy which you have taken up can give you only ephemeral fame. You can find among the Spaniards subjects which, if treated according to our taste by hands like yours, would produce great effects. Learn their language, it is easy; I offer to teach you all I know of it, and, until you are able to read for yourself, I will translate to you parts of Guillen de Castro."

This meeting was great good luck for Corneille; no sooner had he set foot into the noble poesy of Spain than he felt at ease, as if in a country of his own. Loyal spirit, full of honour and morality, walking with uplifted head, he could not fail to feel a sudden and deep affection for the chivalrous heroes of that brave nation. His impetuous warmth of heart, his childlike sincerity, his inviolable devotion in friendship, his melancholy resignation in love, his religion of duty, his nature wholly unveiled, naïvely grave and sententious, noble with pride and *prud' homie*— all inclined him strongly to the Spanish style. He embraced it with fervour, adapted it, without much considering how, to the taste of his nation and his age, and created for himself a unique originality in the midst of the commonplace imitations that were being made around him. No more tentatives, no slow progressive advance, as in his preceding comedies. Blind and rapid in his instinct, he went at one stroke to the sublime, the glorious, the pathetic, as if to things familiar; producing them in splendid, simple language that all the world can understand, and which belongs to him alone. From the night of the first representation of *The Cid* our theatre was truly founded; France possessed the great Corneille; and the triumphant poet, who, like his own heroes, spoke openly of himself as he thought, had the right to exclaim, without fear of denial:

> "I know what I am; I believe what is said of me."

The dazzling success of *The Cid* and the very legitimate pride felt and shown by Corneille raised all his past rivals and all the authors of tragedy, from Claveret to Richelieu, against him. I shall not dwell here on the details of this quarrel, which is one of the best-illuminated spots in our literary history. The effect produced on the poet by this outbreak of criticism was such as might be expected from the character of his talent and his mind. Corneille, as I have said, was a pure, instinctive, blind genius, of free, spontaneous impulse, and well-nigh devoid of those medium qualities which accompany, and second efficaciously, the gift divine in a poet. He was neither adroit nor skilful in details, his taste was little delicate, his judgment not sure, his tact obtuse, and he gave himself small account of his methods as an artist; he piqued himself, however, on his shrewdness and reserve. Between his genius and his good sense there was nothing, or nearly nothing; and that good sense, which did not lack subtlety or logic, had to make strong efforts, especially if provoked, to goad itself up to the level of the genius, to

grasp it in hand, comprehend it, and train it. If Corneille had come earlier, before the Academy and Richelieu, in place of Alexandre Hardy, for example, he would doubtless not have been exempt from falls, errors, and mistakes; perhaps, indeed, other enormities might be found in him than those against which our present taste revolts in certain of his worst passages; but at least his failures would have been solely according to the nature and trend of his genius; and when he rose out of them, when he obtained sight of the beautiful, the grand, the sublime, he would have rushed to it as into his own region, without dragging after him the baggage of rules, cumbersome and puerile scruples, and a thousand petty hindrances to a vast and soaring flight. The quarrel of *The Cid,* arresting him at his first step, forcing him to return upon himself and confront his work with rules, disturbed for the future that prolonged growth, full of chances, that sort of potent, unconscious vegetation, so to speak, for which nature seemed to have destined him. He took umbrage, he was indignant at first at the cavillings of criticism; but he inwardly reflected on the rules and precepts imposed upon him, and ended, finally, by adapting himself to them, and believing them.

The mortifications that followed closely on the triumph of *The Cid* carried him back to his family in Rouen, which place he did not leave again until 1639, when he returned to Paris with *Horace* and *Cinna* in hand. To quit Spain the instant he had set foot in it, to push no farther that glorious victory of *The Cid,* to renounce, in gaiety of heart, all those magnanimous heroes who stretched their arms to him, and turn aside to fasten upon a Castilian Rome on the faith of Lucan and Seneca, Spanish burghers under Nero, was, for Corneille, not to profit by his advantages and to misinterpret the voice of his genius at the very moment when it spoke so clearly. But at that time fashion, vogue, carried minds more toward ancient Rome than toward Spain. Besides the amorous gallantries and noble, conventional sentiments attributed to those old republicans, special occasion was given, by producing them on the stage, to apply the maxims of State, and all the political and diplomatic jargon that we find in Balzac and in Gabriel Naudé, and to which Richelieu himself gave currency. Probably Corneille allowed himself to be seduced by these reasons of the moment; nevertheless, out of his very error came masterpieces.

I will not follow him through the various successes that marked his career during its fifteen finest years. *Polyeucte, Pompée, Le Menteur, Rodogune, Héraclius, Don Sanche,* and *Nicomède* are its enduring landmarks. He returned to imitation of the Spanish in *Le Menteur,* a comedy in which the comic (which Corneille did not understand) is much less to be admired than the *imbroglio,* the movement, and the fancy. Again he returned to the Castilian genius in *Héraclius,* but above all in *Nicomède* and *Don Sanche,* those two wonderful creations, unique upon our stage, which, coming in the midst of the Fronde, with their singular mixture of romantic heroism and familiar irony, stirred up innumerable malignant or generous allusions, and won universal applause. Yet it was shortly after these triumphs, in 1653, that

Corneille, wounded by the non-success of *Pertharite,* and touched perhaps by Christian sentiments and remorse, resolved to renounce the theatre. He was then forty-seven years of age; he had just translated in verse the first chapters of the *Imitation of Jesus Christ,* and he desired henceforth to devote the remainder of his vigour to pious subjects. . . .

Corneille imagined, in 1653, that he renounced the stage. Pure illusion! That withdrawal, could it have been possible, would no doubt have been better for his peace of mind, and perhaps for his fame. But he had not the kind of poetic temperament that could impose upon itself at will a continence of fifteen years—as Racine did later. Encouragement and a gratuity from Fouquet sufficed to bring him back to the stage, where he remained a score of years longer, till 1674, waning, day by day, under numberless mistakes and cruel griefs. . . .

Corneille's dramatic form has not the freedom of fancy that Lope de Vega and Shakespeare gave themselves; neither has it the exactly regular severity to which Racine subjected himself. If he had dared, if he had come before d'Aubignac, Mairet, or Chapelain, he would, I think, have cared very little for graduating and marshalling his acts, connecting his scenes, concentrating his effects on a single point of space and duration; he would have written haphazard, tangling and untangling the threads of his plot, changing the locality as it suited him, delaying on the way, and pushing his personages pell-mell before him to marriage or death. In the midst of this confusion beautiful scenes, admirable groups would have detached themselves here and there; for Corneille understands grouping very well, and, at essential moments, he poses his personages most dramatically. He balances one against the other, defines them vigorously with a brief and manly saying, contrasts them by cutting repartees, and presents to the spectator's eye the masses of a skilful structure. But he had not a genius sufficiently artistic to extend over an entire drama that concentric configuration which he has realized in places; at the same time, his fancy was not free or alert enough to create for itself a form, moving, undulating, diffuse, multiplied, but not less real, less beautiful than the other, such as we admire in certain plays of Shakespeare, such as the Schlegels admire so much in Calderon. Add to these natural imperfections the influence of a superficial and finical poetic art, about which Corneille overconcerned himself, and you will have the secret of what is ambiguous, undecided, and incompletely reckoned in the making of his tragedies.

His *Discours* and his *Examens* give us numerous details on this point, in which we find revealed the most hidden recesses of his great mind. We see how the pitiless unity of place frets him, and how heartily he would say to it: "Oh! you hamper me!" and with what pains he tries to combine it with "decorum." He does not always succeed. "Pauline," he writes, "comes to an antechamber to meet Severus whose visit she ought to await in her private apartment." Pompey seems to disregard the prudence of the general of an army, when, trusting to Sertorius, he goes to confer with him in a town where the latter is master; "but it was impossible," says Corneille, "to keep the unity of place without making him commit this blunder." But when there was absolute necessity for the action to be carried on in two different places, the following is the expedient that Corneille invents to evade the rule:

> These two places have no need of different scenery, and neither of the two should ever be named, but only the general region in which both are situated, such as Paris, Rome, Lyons, Constantinople, etc. This will help to deceive the audience, who, seeing nothing to mark the diversity of place, will not perceive it—unless by malicious and critical reflection, of which few are capable; most of them attending eagerly to the action they see represented before them.

He congratulates himself like a child on the complexity of *Héraclius* because "that poem is so involved it requires marvellous attention"; and requests us to notice in *Othon* that "never was a play seen in which so many marriages were proposed and none concluded."

Corneille's personages are grand, generous, valiant, frank, lofty of head, and noble of heart. Brought up for the most part under austere discipline, the maxims by which they rule their lives are for ever on their lips; and as they never depart from those maxims we have no difficulty in recognising them; a glance suffices: which is almost the contrary of Shakespeare's personages and of human beings in life. The morality of his heroes is spotless: as fathers, lovers, friends, or enemies, we admire and honour them; in pathetic parts their tone is sublime, it lifts the soul and makes us weep. But his rivals and his husbands have sometimes a tinge of the ridiculous: so has Don Sancho in *The Cid,* also Prusias and Pertharite. His tyrants and his step-mothers are all of a piece like his heroes, wicked from one end to the other; nevertheless, at sight of a fine action it sometimes happens that they face about suddenly to virtue, like Grimoald and Arsinoé.

Corneille's men have formal and punctilious minds: they quarrel about etiquette; they argue at length and wrangle loudly with themselves, even in their passions. There is something of the Norman in them. Auguste, Pompée and others seem to have studied logic at Salamanca, and to have read Aristotle with the Arabs. His heroines, his "adorable furies," nearly all resemble one another; their love is subtle, over-refined, with a purpose; coming more from the head than the heart. We feel that Corneille knew little of women. Nevertheless, he succeeded in expressing in Chimène and Pauline that virtuous power of self-sacrifice that he himself had practised in his youth. Strange as it may seem, after his return to the theatre in 1659, and in all the numerous plays of his decadence—*Attila,* Bérénice, *Pulchérie, Suréna,*—Corneille had a mania for mingling love in everything, just as La Fontaine had for introducing Plato. It seems as though the successes of Quinault and Racine enticed him to that ground, and that he wanted to read a lesson to "those tender ones" as he called them. He imagined that in his day he had been still more gallant and amorous than those "young flaxen wings," and he never spoke of other times without shaking his head like an elderly swain.

Corneille's style is, to my thinking, the merit by which he excels. Voltaire, in his commentary, exhibits on this point, as on others, a sovereign injustice, and also what may be called great ignorance of the origins of our language. He blames his author at every turn for having neither grace nor elegance nor clearness; he measures, pen in hand, the height of the metaphors, and when they exceed somewhat he calls them gigantic. He translates and disguises in prose Corneille's lofty and sonorous phrases, which suit so finely the bearing of his heroes, and asks if *that* is speaking and writing French. He churlishly calls "solecism" what he ought to describe as "idiom"—namely the construction, or form of speech peculiar to a special language; a thing that is completely lacking to the narrow, symmetrical, abbreviated French language of the eighteenth century. Corneille's style, with all its negligences, seems to me one of the greatest manners of the century that had Molière and Bossuet. The touch of the poet is rough, severe, vigorous. I compare him to a sculptor, who, working the clay to express heroic portraiture, employs no instrument but his thumb, and, kneading thus his work, gives it a supreme character of life itself with all the jostling incidents that accompany and complete it; but all such proceeding is incorrect, it is not polished, not "proper," as they say. There is little painting or colour in Corneille's style; it is warm rather than brilliant; it turns willingly to the abstract; imagination and fancy give way to thought and to reasoning. It ought to please statesmen, geometricians, soldiers, and others who enjoy the styles of Demosthenes, Pascal, and Caesar.

In short, Corneille, pure genius but incomplete, with his lofty aspects and his defects, gives me the impression of those great trees that are bare, rugged, sad, monotonous as to their trunk, with brunches and sombre foliage at their summit only. They are strong, powerful, gigantic, with little verdure; sap in abundance rises; but expect neither shelter, shade, nor bloom. They leaf out late, their leaves fall early, yet they live on, half-despoiled; but when their hoary brow has cast its last leaves to the autumn wind their perennial nature puts out, here and there, belated branches and green twigs. And when at last they die, their groans, the cracking of their fissures, remind one of that armoured trunk to which Lucan compared the great Pompey.

Lee Davis Lodge (essay date 1891)

SOURCE: "Final Estimate of Corneille: Fall of Classicism and Rise of Romanticism, Latest Developments," in *A Study in Corneille,* 1891. Reprint by Burt Franklin, 1970, pp. 281-313.

[*In the following excerpt from the major nineteenth-century treatment of Corneille in English, Lodge determines and assesses Corneille's contribution to French drama.*]

If it be asked what was the historic function that Corneille performed, we may answer that he banished bad taste from the theatre, that he quickened with the touch of life the chaotic theatrical materials which he found at his

coming, that he divined, developed and determined the classical drama, and that he peopled the French stage with heroic characters whom he idealized from real life, bestowing true passions upon them and causing them to give to the age object lessons in ethical science. He exerted a powerful influence upon both departments of dramatic art.

By writing *Le Cid,* he created the true classical tragedy; by writing "*Le Menteur*" he created the comedy of manners and gave the cue which brought upon the stage an author worthy to stand with covered head as an equal in the presence of such masters of the comedian's art as Aristophanes and Shakspeare.

Molière himself freely acknowledged his great debt to Corneille. Speaking, in a letter to Boileau, of *Le Menteur,* the great comedian said: "When it was first performed, I had already a wish to write, but was in doubt as to what it should be. My ideas were still confused, but this piece determined them. In short, but for the appearance of *Le Menteur,* though I should no doubt have written comedies of intrigue, like *l'Étourdi* or *le Dépit amoureux,* I should perhaps never have written *le Misanthrope.*"

This frank acknowledgment does as much honor to Molière as to Corneille. Only a truly great heart would be so generous.

The style of Corneille is remarkable for its inequality. This peculiarity has never been more happily indicated than by Molière. "My friend Corneille," said he, "has a familiar who inspires him with the finest verses in the world. But sometimes the familiar leaves him to shift for himself and then he fares very badly." Nothing could be more delicate or more apt.

Corneille was a great admirer of Lucan, whose *Pharsalia* he had, when a young man, translated in whole or in part. His careful study of that poem has left an indelible impress upon his own works. He was undoubtedly attracted to the Roman bard by the subtle affinity of similar genius. So marked are the resemblances between the styles of the two authors that many of the adjectives employed in a brief enumeration of the qualities of one must be used in epitomizing the qualities of the other.

Does Quintilian speak of Lucan as "ardens et concitatus et sententiis clarissimus?" We can say the same of Corneille. Is Lucan unequal, declamatory, sometimes bombastic? So is Corneille. Is the critical reader of *Pharsalia* offended at the Roman poet's evident straining after effect? Examples of the same overwrought rhetoric may be found in *La Mort de Pompée.* . . .

Corneille's genius was a limited genius—limited in its innate powers, limited by the clanking chains of the unities, and limited by the poet's own action in choosing all his subjects from one small segment in the great circle of human passions. He loved to represent upon the stage not the weak and yielding elements of our nature, but the strong, the firm, the resisting elements. Hence he is always appealing to the sentiment of admiration. Is this a proper principle on which to base a tragedy? Boileau says not. Critics, in plenty, after Boileau say not. But it is, perhaps, quite sufficient in reply to them all to say that admiration in the form of hero-worship has time and time again proved itself a powerful factor in the history of the world; that the roots of this hero-worship are entwined with our strongest passions; and that the sentiment of admiration aroused by the perusal of biographies of the world's great has kindled in the hearts of the young in every land and every age an intense desire to imitate the high exploits of which they have read. It would seem that the excitation of such an emotion was well adapted to produce the noblest effects of tragedy. At any rate these heroic themes were exactly suited to the genius of Corneille. He belongs by nature to the ideal school of dramatists. He has abstracted from human nature, as concreted in the actual, all those noble qualities that glorify our race, and has, by the exercise of his creative imagination, recombined them into sublime characters whose colossal figures tower above all the weakness and wickedness and weariness of real life. His writings are thus in the highest degree wholesome. We can not conceive how an intelligent person can attentively peruse one of our poet's masterpieces without experiencing emotions which themselves exert an influence at once purifying and fructifying upon the moral nature.

The majestic personality of Corneille pervades his works. In them we find a sublime man uttering his sublime thoughts in sublime words. The nervous vigor of his descriptions is worthy of the highest praise. He intuitively selects the essential elements of a scene, transfers them to his canvas with a few rapid strokes of his brush, and in a moment the whole is pictured before us with a fidelity to nature, a clearness of outline, and a vividness of color that bespeak the master.

Yet Corneille had his defects. There is sometimes too much of the hyper-heroic, too much of the super-human in his characters. They would be a good deal greater, if they were not quite so great. They are like Dante's tower which

> firmly set,
> Shakes not its top for any blast that blows.

Perhaps we should like them better, if they resembled more the giant oak which bends and groans, but breaks not beneath the wild power of the tempest.

Often, also, these characters are too self-conscious. They have a full appreciation of their own bravery, magnanimity and virtue. Their frequent assertion of their various excellencies jars upon the reader like a sharp discord in a soul-stirring symphony. Excessive self-consciousness is manifested in another way by Corneille's characters. In moments when we should expect to see them convulsed and contorted with passion, we find them in comparative calmness dissecting and defining their emotions according to the introspective method of the rational psychologists and with the precision of trained logicians. Thus

long sections of conscious declamation frequently usurp the place that should be occupied by the "disjecta membra" of passionate speech. The declamatory passages, it is true, are of the finest quality, "Sed nunc non erat his locus." Instead of these critical analyses of emotion, the poet should have given us the concussion and conflagration of emotion in synthesis.

We shall mention only one other fault of our author. He never succeeded in completely purging his writings of the affected gallantry, the fantastic euphuism, the "faux brillant" of his times. As we behold him struggling to burst the earthy bondage of bad taste, it makes us think of Milton's lion, "pawing to get free." The spectacle is one to excite admiring sympathy rather than contemptuous criticism.

Often the question is asked, which was the greater dramatist, Corneille or Racine? One may answer in metaphor. As we cast our eyes over the famous fields of French literature, we see yonder a silvery winding river, reflecting in its crystal flood the fleecy clouds, and singing a love song to the flowers on its banks, as it glides onward. And over there we see a majestic mountain towering up above all things near, rugged; sublime; with deep precipices and jagged peaks; girt round anon with storm-clouds in which the lightnings flash and the thunders crash and roll; but bearing aloft, above the storm, his kingly head with its jewelled diadem which glitters and glows in heaven's own light. The winding river is Jean Racine; the majestic mountain is *Le Grand Corneille*. And so we take our leave of him.

Martin Turnell (essay date 1938)

SOURCE: "The Great and Good Corneille," in *The Classical Moment: Studies of Corneille, Molière and Racine*, 1948. Reprint by Greenwood Press, 1971, pp. 18-43.

[*Turnell has written widely on French literature and has made significant translations of the works of Jean-Paul Sartre, Guy de Maupassant, Blaise Pascal, and Paul Valèry. In the following essay, originally published in 1938 in* Scrutiny, *he presents a broad overview of the principal themes, characters, and verse style of Corneille's dramas, comparing them to their counterparts in the works of Racine.*]

1

It is Corneille's misfortune that no English writer has done for him what Lytton Strachey did for Racine. Whatever the short-comings of Strachey's criticism, it did much to dispose of academic prejudice and to present Racine as a *poet*. It is true that Corneille has never aroused the same antipathy as Racine once did and that he has his place among the immortals on the Albert Memorial; but it is also true that he has never enjoyed the relative popularity which came to Racine with the publication of Strachey's essays. The insistence of living critics that Racine is not merely a great poet, but a great *contemporary* poet, has brought him closer to us, while the figure of Corneille has receded farther and farther into the past. For many of us he has become a sort of historical monument, the lonely representative of a vanished civilization. His poetry suggests Versailles with its vast porticoes and the rigid stone figures hiding coyly among the *bosquets* of its trim gardens or, more formidable still, a scratch troupe from the Comédie Française dressed in those strange, those impossible accoutrements which seem inseparable from the performance of high tragedy, declaiming the *Cid* to an audience of schoolgirls armed with the Hachette plain text. It is ironical to think that the veteran Rodrigue, a little hoarse of voice, a little "gone in the knees," who rants and stamps through five acts for the edification of the School Certificate class, should have become the symbol of the great writer who was all his life the champion of youth in revolt against the corruption and pretence of an older generation.

It is perhaps reassuring to find that this impression is not due entirely to insular prejudice and that Corneille's own countrymen have experienced similar difficulties. The most striking thing about the distinguished French critics of the last century is their profound dislike for the great masters of their own literature. Of Racine they could scarcely bring themselves to speak with patience. *"Bérénice,"* wrote Sainte-Beuve in a characteristic sally, "peut être dite une charmante et mélodieuse faiblesse dans l'œuvre de Racine, comme la Champmeslé le fut dans sa vie." In spite of Stendhal's timely championship of "the great and good Corneille," Corneille himself fared no better. "I admire his characters," said Taine, "but from a distance: I should not care to live with any of them." "C'est beau, admirable, sublime, ce n'est ni humain, ni vivant, ni réel," said Brunetière.

That was the verdict of the nineteenth century. Corneille was widely recognized as "the Father of French Tragedy," but he had become the professor's poet, a "classic" whose proper place was not the playbill, but the examination syllabus. Racine has long since come into his own in France, but it has been left to the younger French critics of our own day to discover in this staid classic, whose *Horace* delights or was supposed to delight the populace at the free matinée on Armistice Day, a much more exciting figure. According to one of the latest of his critics, Corneille's world is not a world of flourishes and lofty feelings. It is a world of corruption and intrigue inhabited by doddering, time-serving fathers and criminal stepmothers plotting the ruin of their children who are drawn with a ferocity that is worthy of Racine [Robert Brasillach, *Pierre Corneille*, 1938].

There is, perhaps, a danger of exaggerating the sensational element in Corneille and the reason is not hard to discover. Contemporary admirers are a little too anxious to profit by the popularity of Racine and to discover similarities between the two writers, though it is clearly the differences which ought to detain us. One of the most important of these differences is brought out in the first chapter of M. Jean Schlumberger's valuable study when he speaks of the contrast between

an heroic art and an art which aims at entertainment or pure knowledge, an art which builds up an exemplary picture of man and an art which destroys this picture by analysis and excessive refinement. [*Plaisir à Corneille: Promenade anthologique*, 1936]

It is a curious fact that few French critics manage to be fair to both poets and that their "rivalry," which is merely of historical interest, still influences critical opinion. Stendhal spoilt his defence of Corneille by declaring roundly that he was "immensely above Racine"; and it is one of the drawbacks of M. Schlumberger's study that he is inclined to diminish Racine's greatness in order to make his defence of Corneille more convincing. This is surely a mistake. No one seriously believes that he is as great a poet as Racine, but they are not "rivals" and they are not interchangeable. Without Corneille there would be a gap in French literature which Racine could never have filled.

Racine belongs to an age of transition from the old order to the new, from the old social solidarity to the new individualism. His impact on French poetry produced what was virtually a change of direction—a movement away from all that Corneille had stood for—and for this reason he seems to me to be much more the predecessor of Baudelaire than the successor of Corneille. Corneille is not in himself a difficult poet, but an appreciation of his poetry has been made difficult by changing circumstances. He is more than most other great poets the test of catholic taste in poetry, because to enjoy him it is necessary to realize that poetry may be "sublime" *and* "human, living and real." He wrote heroic plays and it is as an heroic poet that he stands or falls. A criticism of his work is primarily an elucidation of this uncomfortable term. M. Schlumberger's suggestion that an appreciation of Corneille involves an appreciation of Hugo and Claudel seems to me a strategic error, and Croce's invitation to us to discard Corneille's four most famous tragedies and to discover the true Corneille—Corneille the Poet—in the final plays simply shirks all the difficulties.

2

Corneille's achievement becomes more comprehensible when we consider it in relation to his own age. The reign of Louis XIII opened appropriately with an assassination. France was governed by a despotism, but an uneasy despotism. The first part of the century is dominated by Richelieu. The spectacle of Richelieu entering La Rochelle at the head of the King's troops to celebrate the Mass of thanksgiving for the fall of the town is a symbol of the contradictions of the age and of its strange mixture of piety and opportunism. It was an age of rival factions and incredible intrigues, an age that delighted in great exploits and violent actions. France had been shaken to the core by the religious wars of the previous century; and though the worst of them were over, the country was still split in two by the conflict between Catholic and Protestant. It was also a period of intense religious revival in which the chief figures were St. François de Sales and St. Vincent de Paul. Although it has seemed to later generations that theology and philosophy parted company in the seventheenth century, Corneille's contemporaries saw no conflict between the old religion and the "new philosophy." Descartes and the theologians were at one in their interest psychology and their preoccupation with moral problems; and Pascal and Bossuet were both admirers of the Cartesian philosophy.

In Corneille's poetry all these different and sometimes contradictory elements found a place. The interest that he shows in family feuds in the *Cid,* in political intrigue in *Cinna* and religious dissensions in *Polyeucte,* is clearly a reflection of events that were going on around him. The relation of a great poet to his time, however, is primarily a matter of temper, and it was left to Sainte-Beuve to define it in a sympathetic moment in his description of the famous *journée du guichet* in *Port-Royal:*

> It is the same struggle, the same triumph; if *Polyeucte* moves us and carries us away it is because something of the kind is and remains possible to human nature when assisted by grace. I will go further than this. If the genius of Corneille was capable of producing *Polyeucte* at this time, it was because there was still something in his surroundings (whether Corneille himself was aware of it or not) which matched its spirit and achieved the same miracles.

The fact that internally France was in a state of turmoil undoubtedly produced a considerable effort towards consolidation. In spite of its contradictions, Corneille's age was in many ways an age of reconstruction. A sense of effort, a striving towards a moral end, seems to me to be the deepest thing in his poetry. It is well expressed in a characteristic couplet from one Auguste's last speeches in *Cinna:*

> Je suis maître de moi comme de l'univers;
> Je le suis, je veux l'être.

In the first line we notice that the personal problem is related to the social one, and in the second that the statement is significantly followed by the aspiration.

A direct preoccupation with morality and the constant recurrence of words denoting moral qualities like *honneur, gloire, grand coeur* and *mâle assurance* are usually a sign of literary decadence—a sign that society is becoming self-conscious about qualities that it is in the process of losing. With Corneille this is not so. Much of his work—particularly the heroic element—is sixteenth-century in feeling, but it also marks the transition from the wild and extravagant sixteenth century to the reasonable seventeenth century. In his poetry, as surely as in Pope's the words represent "robust moral certitudes" which were the product of centuries of civilization and the common heritage of the people. France was engaged in setting her house in order, in trying to work out a fresh code after the upheavals of the previous century, and this produces a literature of great vitality. Corneille's heroes are not, as they are sometimes said to be, mere abstractions or metaphysical entities, but the embodiment of all that was best in the middle class from which the poet came. They are human beings realizing their aspirations in *action*. It is the integrity of this middle class—*la solide vertu,* as Horace calls it—which gives his poetry its personal idiom and its peculiar strength. For this reason Corneille's poetry, in spite of a certain narrowness, possesses a maturity of outlook which makes the lesser Elizabethans in England seem crude and immature by comparison.

The political triumphs of the latter part of Louis XIII's reign made possible the *external* stability of the reign of Louis XIV. They also account for some of the main differences in the poetry of the two periods. M. Schlumberger suggests that Corneille's work is the product of an age in which civilization was threatened and Racine's the product of an age of security, an age which encouraged disinterested speculation without the necessity of translating thought into action. Racine's elegance . . . belonged to a civilization which had reached its zenith, but a civilization which had within it the seeds of its own dissolution. Corneille's verse sometimes appears clumsy in comparison; but it is a clumsiness which comes from living in a difficult age and not the clumsiness of a man who is not the master of his medium. Racine's age did not possess the same internal stability and its moral fibre was less fine. I think that one might defend the view that Racine made greater poetry out of a poorer philosophy.

When we compare

> Il est doux de revoir les murs de la patrie
>
> (*Sertorius*)

with

> Dans le fond des forêts votre image me suit
>
> (*Phèdre*)

or

> Tous les monstres d'Égypte ont leurs temples
> dans Rome
>
> (*Polyeucte*)

with

> Dans l'Orient désert quel devint mon ennui!
>
> (*Bérénice*)

or

> . . . sur mes passions ma raison souveraine
> Eût blâmé mes soupirs et dissipé ma haine
>
> (*Polyeucte*)

with

> Il n'est plus temps. Il sait mes ardeurs insensées.
> De l'austère pudeur les bornes sont passées
>
> (*Phèdre*),

we may think that though Racine's lines are finer, they are not obviously more "poetical." It is clear, however, that the lines are the product of two very different sensibilities. Corneille limits and defines and finally sets a particular feeling against its background. Racine's method is a process of infinite suggestion; the lines seem to expand in the mind, to set up waves of feeling which become more and more subtle and elusive. In the first line *patrie* has a precise geographical connotation and limits the emotion to a definite area. In the second there is no barrier; *fond* suggests an infinite extension which has no limit and no term. In the third line—a description of the perverse Eastern cults which are tolerated in Rome while Christianity is persecuted—Corneille deliberately strips the East of the glamour with which Racine's *Orient désert* invests it. The squalor and degeneracy of the East are set against the moral integrity which Rome so often suggests in Corneille's poetry. In the last example, the "barrier" is purely a moral one; but the *raison souveraine* (which is deliberately placed after *passions*) is so vividly apprehended by the poet that it gives us a sense of physical repression. In Racine's couplet, on the contrary, the "limit" is only mentioned in order to tell us that it has long since been exceeded.

The differences become still more pronounced when we compare longer passages:

> Quoique pour ce vainqueur mon amour
>   s'intéresse,
> Quoiqu'un peuple l'adore et qu'un roi le caresse,
> Qu'il soit environné des plus vaillants guerriers,
> J'irai sous mes cyprès accabler ses lauriers.

> *(Le Cid.)*

> Je le vis, je rougis, je pâlis à sa vue;
> Un trouble s'éleva dans mon âme éperdue;
> Mes yeux ne voyaient plus, je ne pouvais parler,
> Je sentis tout mon corps et transir et brûler.

> *(Phèdre.)*

The speakers in these passages are both victims of a conflict between what might provisionally be called "duty" and "inclination." In Racine, Phèdre's personality crumbles and disintegrates at once; the emotion of the passage is split up into its component parts, but though there is analysis there is no synthesis. Chimène's character is different. She is not passive, but active. The two conflicting impulses are balanced against one another and the conflict is resolved by the will acting in obedience to a principle. There is nothing specious about it; the solution springs necessarily from the *données*. . . .

[The] four lines from the *Cid* seem to me to be one of the glories of Corneille's poetry. The first three lines have an extraordinary lyrical élan which is intensified by the obvious sexual connotation of *intéresse, adore, caresse,* and the suggestion of "action" and "vitality" contained in *vainqueur* and *guerriers*. This feeling of expansion, this sense of personal liberation which comes from the mo-

mentary identification of Chimène with Rodrigue and his exploits, is suddenly checked by something altogether impersonal in the last line. The spreading foliage of the cypresses, with their sinister hint of darkness and death, comes down like a pall and stifles the "life" which is now concentrated in *lauriers*. The final effect of the passage, however, is not negative. The emotion of the first three lines is skilfully transformed so that the last line has behind it the force of the whole passage. It will be seen that there is no casuistry and no argument here: Corneille's method is a purely poetic one and depends on the opposition of *cyprès* and *lauriers* and the triumphant use of the word *accabler*. The image in the last line is fully adequate to the emotion; it stands out against the sober background of Corneille's verse and glows with a sombre splendour.

I hope that these comparisons have given some indication of the structure of Corneille's world. It is a finite world whose geographical boundaries are marked with such clarity that we sometimes have a feeling of almost physical oppression in reading him. His conception of the nature of man is defined with the mathematical precision of Descartes' *Traité des passions de l'âme* which gives his poetry its certainty and forthrightness. He is only interested in a few aspects of human nature and therefore only master of a limited range of emotion. Within these limits he is a great writer, but when he ventures outside them the results are disastrous. He is, it need hardly be said, a more pedestrain writer than Racine, and the hard, metallic clang of his verse is in strong contrast to Racine's sensuous, flexible rhythms. There are no surprises in his poetry, none of those sudden glimpses into a subconscious world of primitive instinct that we get in Racine. For Corneille's aim was to bring that world of primitive instinct under the dominion of reason before reason was overthrown by it and society reduced to a state of chaos. Corneille's vocabulary was no smaller than Racine's, but it is probable that his language has less power of suggestion than that of any other great French poet. Words are scientific terms which mean exactly what they say. He did not possess Racine's gift of revealing mysterious depths with the most commonplace words as, for example, when Hippolyte says:

> Je me suis engagé trop avant.

> Je vois que la raison cède à la violence.

Corneille's four most famous plays are really variations on the same theme. They show the Cornelian hero in relation to the code of chivalry, to patriotism, to politics and finally to religion. In the later plays there is no doubt that Corneille was sometimes inclined to play the showman and to write without any inner compulsion and it is this, perhaps, which has led critics to say that his characters are artful mechanical contrivances without contact with living experience. The simplicity of his psychology and the ease with which he could define his position have undoubtedly lent currency to this view. In a remarkable passage in the Epistle Dedicatory to *La Place Royale* he wrote:

> It is from you that I learnt that the love of an *honnête homme* must always be voluntary; that we must never allow our love to reach the point at which we cannot stop loving; that if we do, love becomes a tyranny whose yoke must be shaken off; and, finally, that the person whom we love is under a much greater obligation to us when our love is the result of our own choice and of her merit than when it is the result of a blind impulse and is forced on us by some influence of birth which we are unable to resist.

This is a statement of principle which underlies the whole of Corneille's work, and our opinion of him as a poet depends on whether it is a living principle which produced vital poetry or an assumed position which led to a frigid formalism. It is plain that we have here a conception of love which is completely opposed to the one that dominates the poetry of Racine and of almost every great French poet who has since written. Hostile critics have always maintained that Corneille's was an artificial system deliberately imposed on living experience. Its authenticity can only be fully tested by an examination of Corneille's verse, but there are two reservations, both more or less theoretical, which should be made. The first is that the view of passion contained in Racine's poetry has become so much a part of our consciousness that we are no longer capable of approaching Corneille with an open mind. And the second is that although the code of honour on which the *Cid* is based may no longer seem valid, the quality of the poetry it once inspired is not affected by changed moral standards.

3

Corneille's poetry has been variously described as a conflict between "love and honour," as a "drama of the will" or as mere stoicism. All these views have been challenged at one time or another; but though it is true that a great poet's work can never be summed up in a single formula, these views may serve as pointers in examining his work so long as they are not too rigidly interpreted. "Love and honour" was a favourite theme in the literature of chivalry and it is interesting to see how Corneille extends its significance. The central fact in the *Cid* is a duel—the single combat between two "men of honour." It has not been sufficiently remarked that far from being a picturesque incident, the duel is a symbol of the whole play and indeed of all Corneille's poetry:

> D. RODRIGUE:
>   A moi, Comte, deux mots.
> LE COMTE:
>   Parle.
> D. RODRIGUE:
>   Ote-moi d'un doute.
>   Connais-tu bien don Diègue?
> LE COMTE:
>   Oui.
> D. RODRIGUE:
>   Parlons bas; écoute.

> Sais-tu que ce vieillard fut la même vertu,
> La vaillance et l'honneur de son temps? le sais-tu? . . .
> LE COMTE:
>   Que m'importe?
> D. RODRIGUE:
>   A quatre pas d'ici je te le fais savoir.
> LE COMTE:
>   Jeune présomptueux!
> D. RODRIGUE:
>   Parle sans témouvoir.
>   Je suis jeune, il est vrai; mais aux âmes bien nées
>   La valeur n'attend point le nombre des années. . . .
> LE LOMTE:
>   Retire-toi d'ici.
> D. RODRIGUE:
>   Marchons sans discourir.
> LE COMTE:
>   As-tu si las de vivre?
> D. RODRIGUE:
>   As-tu peur de mourir?

In this admirable scene we hear the thrust and parry of the rapiers—the hiss of steel in

> Sais-tu que c'est son sang? le sais-tu?

and we hear it all through the play. It is the duel that is evoked at the height of the drama in Chimène's

> Dedans mon ennemi je trouve mon amant;
> Et je sens qu'en dépit de toute ma colère,
> Rodrigue dans mon cœur combat encor mon père:
> Il l'attaque, il le presse, il cède, il se défend,
> Tantôt fort, tantôt faible, et tantôt triomphant;
> Mais, en ce dur combat de colère et de flamme,
> Il déchire mon cœur sans partager mon âme. . . .

The thrust and parry of the duel merges into the movement of consciousness, into the conflict between *amour* and *devoir* and this gives the play its unity. These passages reflect the movement of all Corneille's verse—a simple movement befitting a simple psychology. We feel it again, for example, in these lines from *Polyeucte* where the "duel" is purely an interior one:

> POLYEUCTE:
>   C'est peu d'aller au ciel, je vous y veux conduire.
> PAULINE:
>   Imaginations!
> POLYEUCTE:
>   Célestes vérités!
> PAULINE:
>   Étrange aveuglement!
> POLYEUCTE:
>   Éternelles clartés!

It is possible now to see how Corneille extends the significance of love and honour. The movement of his verse is not a destructive movement and the conflict does not end, as it usually does in tragedy, in the destruction of the characters. Nor is it true to say, as Lemaître and other French critics have said, that Corneille's poetry is simply a glorification of will and power for their own sake. There is always a definite aim in view, a process in which new values are forged, the human material reshaped and given a fresh direction. Honour is not merely a symbol of reason, it stands for the principle of order which has to be imposed on the chaos of unruly desires, on the whole of the instinctive life which Corneille constantly refers to as *les sens.* The real theme of his poetry, therefore, is not a simple clash between duty and inclination, but the subordination of one set of values to another which leads to the creation of a fresh order.

The background of Corneille's drama is aristocratic, the life of the court. In each of his major works the even flow of this life is disturbed by a shock—by a duel in the *Cid,* a conspiracy in *Cinna,* a conversion in *Polyeucte.* The effect of the shock and the conflict thus set up is to reveal the Cornelian hero to himself in a new way. The court life is seen to be conventional and unreal; and it is only when the convention is disturbed that the characters come into contact with the vital experience which is hidden beneath the outer husk, and that the mechanical code of honour is transformed into something living.

Corneille's drama, particularly the *Cid,* is always a drama of initiation. Fresh claims are made on human nature and it undergoes a change. In the opening scene of the *Cid* Chimène says to her *confidente:*

Dis-moi donc, je te prie, une seconde fois
Ce qui te fait juger qu'il approuve mon choix.

It is the voice of a child asking to be told over again that her father approves of her young man. In the second act she says to the Infanta:

Maudite ambition, détestable manie,
Dont les plus généreux souffrent la tyrannie!

This time it is the voice of the mature woman criticizing the values she is called upon to accept; and the alexandrine registers the change with remarkable delicacy.

The sudden contact with life produces in the Cornelian heroes a peculiar self-knowledge:

Je *sais* ce que je suis, et que mon père est mort,

cries Chimène.

Mon père, je suis femme, et je *sais* ma faiblesse,

says Pauline. This clairvoyance—this insight into their own feelings—gives Corneille's characters a poise, a centrality which are perhaps unique in European drama. The hero is always in imminent danger of being betrayed by the uprush of *les sens* which threaten to overturn reason

and plunge him into chaos and disaster.

La surprise des sens n'abat point mon courage,

says one of them, and it is precisely these *surprises* which are the condition of heroic virtue, of the *grand cœur:*

Une femme d'honneur peut avouer sans honte
Ces surprises des sens que la raison surmonte;
Ce n'est qu'en ces assauts qu'éclate la vertu,
Et l'on doute d'un cœur qui n'a point combattu.

The theme of the *Cid* is the clash between two generations, the dilemma of youth thrown into a world made by its parents and called upon to accept its standards. It is one of the signs of Corneille's maturity that these standards are never accepted passively; his attitude towards them is always critical. Honour is in constant danger of becoming inhuman and mechanical unless it is accompanied by a profound humanity which is always referred to by the word *généreux.* When Don Diègue says:

Nous n'avons qu'un honneur, il est tant de
    maîtresses!
L'amour n'est qu'un plaisir, l'honneur est un
    devoir.

the cynical slickness of the lines and the facile epigram are certainly ironic. *Honneur* and *devoir* are turned into counters which no longer correspond to any moral experience. For Don Diègue expresses something which is incompatible with the Cornelian view of life. The combat does not destroy *les sens,* it dominates them in order to incorporate them into a definite hierarchy—a hierarchy which would be ruined if they were predominant, but which would be hollow and incomplete without them, as the world of Don Diègue and the Horaces is hollow and incomplete.

The criticism in *Horace* is of a far more drastic order. The play becomes in the person of Camille—one of Corneille's most extraordinary creations—a harsh and angry indictment of the whole system:

Rome, l'unique objet de mon ressentiment!
Rome, à qui vient ton bras d'immoler mon
    amant!
Rome qui t'a vu naître, et que ton cœur adore!
Rome enfin que je hais parce qu'elle t'honore!
Puissent tous ses voisins ensemble conjurés
Saper ses fondements encor mal assurés!

The heavy, monotonous verse suggests the terrible machine remorselessly sacrificing humanity to an empty phantom. It is not easy to decide how far Corneille ever accepted his own sanctions, but it seems clear that they were only acceptable as a means to a richer and fuller life, not as an end in themselves.

The struggle towards a new synthesis produces some of Corneille's finest and subtlest verse:

Ma raison, il est vrai, dompte mes sentiments;
Mais quelque autorité que sur eux elle ait prise,
Elle n'y règne pas, elle les tyrannise;
Et quoique le dehors soit sans émotion,
Le dedans n'est que trouble et que sédition.
Un je ne sais quel charme encor vers vous
   m'emporte;
Votre mérite est grand, si ma raison est forte:
Je le vois encor tel qu'il alluma mes feux,
D'autant plus puissamment solliciter mes vœux,
Qu'il est environné de puissance et de gloire . . .
Mais ce même devoir qui le vainquit dans Rome,
Et qui me range ici dessous les lois d'un
   homme,
Repousse encor si bien l'effort de tant d'appas,
Qu'il déchire mon âme et ne l'ébranle pas.

This passage with its inversions, its verbs deliberately piled at the end of the lines, is a remarkable example of the pitiless self-inquisition to which the Cornelian heroes are subjected. There is a deliberate and calculated clumsiness about the verse which admirably expresses the immense effort that the speaker is making to dominate her feelings. The passage gets its life from the constant alteration of tone, the change from a note of defiance and determination to the half-whispered reflection of lines 6-8. The merits of Sévère are carefully catalogued and balanced against the claims of reason until one has the feeling that Pauline is being gradually engulfed in a vast stream which threatens to dislodge her at any moment. In the line

D'autant plus puissamment solliciter mes feux

the hiss of the s's suggests the voluptuous element, the tug of *les sens*. Then, at the moment when she seems lost, there is a sudden shifting of the tension in the victorious

Repousse encor si bien l'effort de tant d'appas,
Qu'il déchire mon âme et ne l'ébranle pas.

The Cornelian "will" is not an abstract principle. The *déchire* and the *ne l'ébranle pas* are both deeply *felt* and express a genuine tension between two conflicting tendencies. The antithesis, so far from being an artificial literary device, is dynamic and corresponds to a deep division in Pauline's mind. When we compare Corneille's lines with Racine's

. . . la raison cède à la violence

we see that while in Racine the accent falls on the destructive word *cède*, in Corneille it falls unmistakably on the words expressing opposition and resistance—*repousse* and *ne l'ébranle pas*. The will to resist temptation and the "inclination" for one's lover are sources of energy and vitality. Man cannot live without the energy derived from *amour*, but neither can he resist dissolution and collapse if it is allowed to become predominant. The conflict thus becomes a method of psychological revelation.

The dramatic assertion of the will is, as I have already

suggested, one of the most striking characteristics of Corneille's poetry; and it seems to me that it is here rather than in the famous *Qu'il mourût!* that we detect the authentic heroic note. It is a note that we hear not once, but many times in every play. It does not lower the tension or resolve the conflict, but produces a marked increase of life and vitality that enables the Cornelian hero to "carry on."

From this we may turn to Pauline's speech at the beginning of Act III:

Que de soucis flottants, que de confus nuages
Présent à mes yeux d'inconstantes images!
Douce tranquillité, que je n'ose espérer,
Que ton divin rayon tarde à les éclairer!
Mille agitations, que mes troubles produisent,
Dans mon cœur ébranlé tour à tour se détruisent:
Aucun espoir n'y coule où j'ose persister;
Aucun effroi n'y règne où j'ose m'arrêter.
Mon esprit, embrassant tout ce qu'il s'imagine,
Voit tantôt mon bonheur, et tantôt ma ruine,
Et suit leur vaine idée avec si peu d'effet,
Qu'il ne peut espérer ni craindre tout à fait.
Sévère incessamment brouille ma fantaisie:
J'espère en sa vertu, je crains sa jalousie;
Et je n'ose penser que d'un œil bien égal
Polyeucte en ces lieux puisse voir son rival.

"This is half-way to poetry," remarks a university lecturer patronizingly [*Poetry in England and France,* Jean Stewart, 1931]. It seems to me to be a good deal more than that. It seems to me to be not dramatically effective, but something to which we can hardly refuse the title of great poetry. The same writer complains that "the metaphors and images are confused," but the confusion does not seem to me to lie in Corneille's imagery. For the success of the passage depends very largely on the skill with which the poet presents "a whole of tangled feelings." The focal point of the passage is the image of the conflicting feelings dissolving into and destroying one another. The words *soucis flottants, confus nuages, inconstantes images* suggest a state of complete instability which is accompanied by a desperate longing for the elusive stability promised by *douce tranquillté, persister, arrêter;* but there is no security anywhere. Whatever Pauline tries to cling on to dissolves into mere *fantaisie*. For here the words "seem to do what they say" as surely as in the finest English poetry of the same period. Pauline's mind is battered into a state of immobility. She is acutely aware of what she feels, but in the midst of the tumult of warring impulses she is passive and unable to act. Only a dumb determination to "hang on" persists and gives the poetry its vitality. The tension does not depend, as it does in Racine, on the sickening sense of complete collapse, but on a contrast between the rigid immobility—the numbness between the metal walls of the alexandrine—which prevents action, and the swirl of the rapidly changing feelings.

Although the passages I have discussed come from different plays, they illustrate the stages in the evolution of Corneille's characters which scarcely varies from one play to another. It is evident that this evolution is as different from the one we find in Racine as it could well be. In Racine there is a violent conflict, but it does not end in the creation of fresh moral values or the renewal of life; it ends in the reversal of all moral values. Corneille is inferior to Racine as a psychologist, but he seems to me to reveal a greater range of what is commonly described as "character." Racine concentrates the whole of his attention on the moral crisis and there is nothing in his work which is comparable to the moral growth that takes place in Corneille's characters. We can, I think, sum up the differences between the two by saying that Corneille's characters are people *qui se construisent* and Racine's people *qui se défont*. The "shock," of which I have already spoken, shatters the complacency of Corneille's characters and reveals their own perplexity and confusion to them. But it also reveals the goal towards which they must strive, and by their immense determination they overcome this perplexity and confusion and achieve a new unity. Racine's characters, on the other hand, start their career as unified or apparently unified beings, and the drama lies in the dissolution of that inner unity.

The final change in Corneille's characters, when it does come, appears as a flash of illumination which transcends all the separate acts of the individual and the different phases of the drama which lead up to it. One is Auguste's sudden realization of his place in the existing order:

> Je suis maître de moi comme de l'univers;
> Je le suis, je veux l'être.

Another is the description of a conversion in *Polyeucte:*

> Je m'y trouve forcé par un secret appas;
> Je cède à des transports que je ne connais pas. .
> . .

I should be shirking a difficulty if I failed to mention the celebrated encounter between Rodrigue and Chimène in Act III. Sc. iv. This scene—too long to set out here— seemed to Corneille's age to be a masterpiece of pathos. M. Schlumberger cannot resist the temptation to quote it and Brasillach subjects it to an enthusiastic analysis. My own opinion is that Corneille was not a master of pathos and that though the scene contains good passages, the most admired parts are tiresome and embarrassing. They are an example of what happens when Corneille ventures outside his limited field. It must, of course, be remembered that his verse was written to be declaimed and that lines which are embarrassing in the study may sound well enough on the stage, and I have myself seen a good company "carry" what appear to be the weaker parts of this scene. It is one of the shortcomings of the grand manner that it does allow the poet to "fake" emotion, to rely on the sweep of the alexandrine when there is no correspondence between his personal sensibility and the emotion that he is staging.

4

The *Cid* has always been Corneille's most popular play

and it possesses the peculiar beauty which belongs to the first work of a great writer's maturity; but the plays which followed also possess a vision, a complexity, that we do not find in the *Cid*. It has been pointed out that the discovery of Rome was an event of the first importance in Corneille's development, but its importance is not always understood. Corneille wrote of Rome at several different periods of her history and his attitude towards her varied, but the most impressive of the Roman plays is perhaps *Cinna*. The *Cid* is the most individualistic, the most "romantic," of his works. It does not posses, that is to say, any coherent view of society. There is simply the life of the Court with its etiquette and conventions. *Cinna* is far from being a faultless play, but there does emerge from it a definite conception of society, something which can, I think, not unreasonably be called a social order. We must not expect to find in French drama the sort of picture of contemporary life that we get in the English drama of the same period. French tragedy was essentially the product of an intellectual aristocracy. There was no place for *le peuple* whom Corneille regarded as creatures of instinct in whose life reason played little part. The social order which emerges from *Cinna* is therefore concerned with the problems of the ruling class, for it is assumed—

Corneille and John Dryden compared as drama critics:

The difference between [Dryden's] essays and Corneille's discourses is very much the same as that between Horace's *Ars Poetica* and *Aristotle's Poetics.* Dryden's prose is almost as charming as Horace's verse; Corneille's prose is almost as heavy as Aristotle's. The Frenchman's critical works are mere adjuncts to his dramatic works; the Englishman's prefaces survive the plays for which they were written; and, as [W. P.] Ker says, 'their fault is that they make one disappointed with his plays when one comes to them after his criticisms'. So that it would not be quite unfair to reverse his own epigram: 'The French are as much better critics than the English, as they are worse poets', and say: 'Dryden is as much more living a dramatic critic than Corneille, as he is a less living dramatic poet.'

Pierre Legouis, in Seventeenth Century Studies Presented to Sir Herbert Grierson, *Octagon Books, Inc., 1967.*

---

not unnaturally—that reconstruction starts from above. The advance in Corneille's art is apparent from the great speech of Auguste who in the second act significantly displaces Cinna as the hero:

> Cet empire absolue sur la terre et sur l'onde,
> Ce pouvoir souverain que j'ai sur tout le monde,
> Cette grandeur sans borne et cet illustre rang,
> Qui m'a jadis coûté tant de peine et de sang,
> Enfin tout ce qu'adore en ma haute fortune
> D'un courtisan flatteur la présence importune,
> N'est que de ces beautés dont l'éclat éblouit,
> Et qu'on cesse d'aimer sitôt qu'on en jouit.
> L'ambition déplaît quand elle est assouvie,

D'une contraire ardeur son ardeur est suivie;
Et comme notre esprit, jusqu'au dernier soupir,
Toujours vers quelque objet pousse quelque
        désir,
Il se ramène en soi, n'ayant plus où se prendre,
Et monté sur le faîte, il aspire à descendre.
J'ai souhaité l'empire, et j'y suis parvenu;
Mais en le souhaitant, je ne l'ai pas connu:
Dans sa possession j'ai trouvé pour tous
        charmes
D'effroyables soucis, d'éternelles alarmes,
Mille ennemis secrets, la mort à tout propos,
Point de plaisir sans trouble, et jamais de repos.

It is one of the finest examples of Corneille's handling of the grand style. Without any rhetoric, the *ampleur* of the style and the regular thud of the end-rhymes contrive to suggest a stable order. For there are two voices speaking here—the voice of the lonely, harassed individual debating whether or not to give up his throne, and what one may call the public voice. It is no longer simply a matter of coming to terms with oneself or of satisfying accepted standards of honour, but of playing a part in society. *Cinna* is a drama of adjustment. The individual experience has to fit in with the experience of the community and the drama is only complete when this is accomplished. In *Cinna,* therefore, there is a blending of the political and the moral problems. It is not simply that all political problems are seen to involve a moral problem, but that in transforming moral problems into political problems Corneille gives them a wider context and immensely increases the import of his poetry. It is this which makes his approach extremely actual today. In the great political discussion at the beginning of Act II one is aware of a straightening out of the emotions, and order, which is so often discussed and so rarely defined, becomes something almost tangible.

Although Corneille's contemporaries thought of him as the author of *Cinna,* many modern critics consider that *Nicomède*—a much later work—is the finest of the political plays. It is not, perhaps, surprising that the Latin mind with its passion for the "well made play" should be more aware of *Cinna*'s faults than its virtues, and no doubt some writers have suspected that the defence of absolute monarchy implied a defence of the monstrous injustices associated with it. *Cinna,* however, is not important as a defence of a particular system of government, but for the passion for order which inspires it. The very violence with which the *individual* conspirators are swept into that order shows that Corneille was fully conscious of these difficulties—conscious of them *as a poet.* For his poetry marks the end of an epoch and he may have felt that the order for which he had fought was doomed to destruction by its inherent rigidity and its inability to provide a bulwark against chaos.

Nicomède is an extraordinary ironic *tour de force* which deserves to be better known in England. "Tenderness and passion have no part in it," said Corneille in his Dedication. "My chief aim has been to paint Rome's politics in her relations with other states." He sets his "cool and

efficient hero"—the language of the best-seller is somehow appropriate—against the background of political intrigue and proceeds, very skilfully, to "debunk" the large pretensions of Rome and her predatory designs on smaller countries. Nicomède's ruthless sardonic humour gives the play its peculiar flavour. Ostensibly he is trying to bolster up his father and make him resist the demands of Rome; but there is an undercurrent of resentment which spares neither Prusias' inefficiency nor his senile passion for his second wife.

PRUSIAS:
                    Quelle bassesse d'âme,
        Quelle fureur t'aveugle en faveur d'une
femme?
            Tu la préfères, lâche! à ces prix glorieux
            Que ta valeur unit au bien de tes aïeux! . .

NICOMÈDE:
            Je crois que votre exemple est glorieux à
suivre . . .

            Pardonnez-moi ce mot, il est fâcheux à
dire,
            Mais un monarque enfin comme un autre
homme expire . . .

He carefully points the contrast between the office of king and its present occupant. *Expire,* with its suggestions of the funeral cortège, the vast mausoleum with the appropriate inscriptions, reveals the fatuity of the person who will be buried there. The wit reaches its peak in the last act after Prusias' attempted flight:

ATTALE:
            J'ai couru me ranger auprès du Roi mon
père . . .
            . . . ce monarque étonné . . .
            Avait pris un esquif pour tâcher de
rejoindre
            Ce Romain, dont l'effroi peut-être n'est
pas moindre.
                                (*Prusias entre*)

PRUSIAS:
Non, non; nous revenons l'un et l'autre en ces
        lieux
Défendre votre gloire, ou mourir à vos yeux.

Prusias is a richly comic creation and has a definite place in Corneille's survey of seventeenth-century society. In the *Cid* and in *Horace* he exposed an "honour" which had become mechanical and inhuman. Through Félix in *Polyeucte* and Prusias in *Nicomède* he makes the essential criticisms of middle-class complacency, of the moral corruption which prevents the attainment of Cornelian honour.

A word must be said about a more debatable side of Corneille's work—the religious side. Some critics have denied that he is properly speaking a religious poet at all, while others have described *Polyeucte,* which is certainly his greatest play, as a masterpiece of religious poetry. It must be recorded with gratitude that it is refreshingly free from the incorrigibly romantic attitude towards sin that we find in certain living Catholic writers; but in spite of its subject it is neither more nor less religious than any of Corneille's other works. What is religious in all Corneille's best work is not the subject or the setting, but his sense of society as an ordered whole and of man as a member of this hierarchy. If he tried to round off the picture in *Polyeucte* by presenting the natural order in the light of the supernatural, it seems to me that he failed. It is significant that in this play the fable was modified to fit the usual Cornelian formula and we are left with the feeling that the religion was not inevitable, but that any other *motif* might have produced an equally great play. Corneille's world remains a circumscribed world and his religion does not extend the field of his experience as it clearly ought to have done.

It should be apparent by now in what sense Corneille is an heroic poet. It has nothing to do with declamation and bombast (though there is plenty of both in his work), or with the misleading theory that his characters are "supermen." It simply means that by a combination of insight and will power the moral values which Corneille derived from close contact with his class are raised in his plays to a high level of poetic intensity. He was a great poet because he expressed something that is permanent in human nature and because he had behind him the whole weight of what was best in contemporary society. One has only to compare him for a moment with Dryden to see the difference. For Dryden's age was not an heroic age and in trying to write heroic plays he was simply going against the spirit of his time. His drama is an example of the false sublime, of the stucco façade which ill conceals the viciousness and corruption beneath.

5

Corneille's later plays have been the subject of considerable controversy. Contemporary apologists like M. Schlumberger take up their stand against the traditional view which regards the later plays, in Lytton Strachey's words, as "miserable failures." Pierre Lièvre's introduction to his admirable edition of the plays [*Théâtre complet,* 2 vols., 1934] is an eloquent plea that Corneille's work should be treated as a whole, as a steady development from the early comedies to the final tragedies. I confess that I find it difficult to accept this view. Plays like *Rodogune* and *Pompée,* which belong to the third period that lasts from 1644 to 1669, contain fine things, but compared with Corneille's best work they seem to me to show a pronounced falling off. There is, perhaps, a greater breadth of characterization, but the poetry is less impressive. The fact that Corneille never stood still and never repeated himself may be the reason for the difficulty. With *Polyeucte* the Cornelian hero is complete and there is no room for further development along those lines. The poet loses interest in his hero who degenerates into a mechanical warrior—*Attila* provides the worst example—and concentrates on the people who surround him.

The main interest of the plays of this period lies in the amazons like Rodogune, Cornélie and the two Cléopâtres. This produces an alteration in the quality of the verse. Corneille develops the vein of rhetoric which is already visible in the *Cid:*

> Paraissez, Navarrois, Mores et Castillans,
> Et tout ce que l'Espagne a nourri de vaillants;
> Unissez-vous ensemble, et faites une armée,
> Pour combattre une main de la sorte animée. . .

In *Rodogune* this becomes the staple of the whole play:

> Serments fallacieux, salutaire contrainte,
> Que m'imposa la force et qu'accepta ma crainte,
> Heureux déguisements d'un immortel courroux,
> Vains fantômes d'État, évanouissez-vous.

There is a natural tendency to rhetoric in French poetry, to use words as mere labels and to rely for the "poetry" on the drive of the alexandrine. Certainly there is no lack of drive in *Rodogune,* but there is a loss of subtlety and a marked coarseness of texture in the verse.

Although M. Schlumberger has apparently abandoned the view that the last plays of all are the crown of Corneille's work, he still gives *Pulchérie* and *Suréna* a high place in it. In these plays there is a return to the old Cornelian formula which was to some extent abandoned in the plays of the middle period. He sees in them a tenderness and serenity which he does not find in any of Corneille's other work. This may be so, but one cannot help wondering whether they deserve all the praise they get. Consider, for example, the opening speech of *Pulchérie:*

> Je vous aime, Léon, et n'en fais point mystère:
> Des feux tels que les miens n'ont rien qu'il
>   faille taire.
> Je vous aime, et non point de cette folle ardeur
> Que les yeux éblouis font maîtresse du cœur,
> Non d'un amour conçu par les sens en tumulte,
> A qui l'âme applaudit sans qu'elle se consulte,
> Et qui ne concevant que d'aveugles désirs,
> Languit dans les faveurs, et meurt dans les
>   plaisirs:
> Ma passion pour vous, généreuse et solide,
> A la vertu pour âme, et la raison pour guide,
> La gloire pour objet, et veut sous votre loi
> Mettre en ce jour illustre et l'univers et moi.

According to Croce this passage marks the summit of Corneille's poetry and, with a lofty assumption of philosophical detachment, he proceeds to commend Pulchérie's attitude to physical love. It is not difficult to see why these lines appeal to one whose criterion is evidently "simple, sensuous and passionate." It is by no means a negligible piece of verse, but it owes its charm to a subtle flavour of dissolution. The difficulty that one feels might be expressed by saying that honour wins altogether too easily. It is clear from the looseness of texture, the slackness of the versification, that we are a long way from the poet of **Polyeucte**. It is the work of an old man, of a great poet in decline. Nor can one share Croce's enthusiasm for the content. For who but a survival of nineteenth-century romanticism can feel any sympathy for the bloodless spinster high-mindedly giving up her love to contract a "chaste" alliance with her father's aged counsellor?

What is to be the final estimate? "Corneille," answers M. Schlumberger, "does not ask the supreme questions, neither does he answer them. If I give him a high place in my æsthetic, there remains a vast region of myself in which I feel the need of other poets besides him." It is clear that he lacks many of the qualities that we have come to expect of poetry. Certain fundamental truths were grasped with the clarity and the tenacity of genius; he was a penetrating critic of the evils of the existing order; but his own vision was partial and incomplete and the order towards which he was striving seems somehow indistinct. Yet his central experience—his sense of society as an ordered whole and of man as a part of that hierarchy—has an important place in European literature and without him it would be incomplete. Of all the great masters Corneille is the most limited, but that he is a master we cannot doubt.

Wallace Fowlie (essay date 1948)

SOURCE: "Second Cycle: Corneille, the Sexuality of *Le Cid*," in *Love in Literature: Studies in Symbolic Expression,* Indiana University Press, 1965, pp. 37-44.

[*Fowlie is among the most respected and comprehensive scholars of French literature. His work includes translations of major poets and dramatists of France (Molière, Charles Baudelaire, Arthur Rimbaud, Paul Claudel, Saint-John Perse) and critical studies of the major figures and movements of modern French letters (Stephane Mallarmé, Marcel Proust, Andre Gidé, the Surrealists, among many others). Broad intellectual and artistic sympathies, along with an acute sensitivity for French writing and a firsthand understanding of literary creativity (he is the author of a novel and poetry collections in both French and English), are among the qualities that make Fowlie an indispensable guide for the student of French literature. In the following excerpt from an essay originally published in 1948, he examines* Le Cid *as a drama emblematic of Corneille's conception of tragedy as the domain of spirituality, reflecting the triumph of divine grace.*]

Like the philosophers of the Middle Ages, the great writers of the seventeenth century in France studied man, but from a different viewpoint. The medieval study was based on man as the son of Adam, as the victim of the fall, as the creature eminently free but who is caught in the eternal debate between good and evil, and who, through his own will power, determines his salvation or his damnation. The study of the Middle Ages was theological man whose characteristics were first traced by Plato and Aristotle. But the classical study, although not forgetful of the Christian conception of man, was based on the mystery of

the human spirit, on the meaning of his spiritual and corporeal destiny, on the celestial and infernal struggle for the possession of a soul. The study of the seventeenth century was tragic man, whose characteristics were first traced by Sophocles and Euripides.

The Middle Ages explain and illustrate man's anthropology, and the classical period explains the meaning of human tragedy. This tragedy which so purely concerns the spirit of man and his total destiny is enacted in a domain untouched by the explanations of psychology, of biology, and of sociology. To know oneself, for the writer of the seventeenth century, implies much more than knowing oneself psychologically, biologically, sociologically. For them, man is not a fragment of the whole, but rather it is he who contains the universe. All spheres meet in him. In his enigmatical, contradictory, and weak nature, he is able to surpass himself. This is Corneille's vision: of man in the cosmos and of the cosmos in man. His art is a new cosmic life. The common tendency of man is to humanize the concept of God, but the hero of Corneille tends to divinize the concept of man. Thus, in a certain sense, these two periods of French history are distinct and even contradictory: the Middle Ages consider theological man: namely, man according to his origin and his destiny; the seventeenth century considers tragic man: namely, man in conflict with the world and in conflict with himself.

What is the domain of tragedy? We can see first that it is the domain felt and explained above all by the artists, in comparison with the domain of theological man measured above all by the theologians and the mystics. (But it must be remembered that tragic man has been understood by some theologians, such as Saint Augustine, and by some thinkers, such as Kierkegaard and Freud.) The two essential acts of God for a Christian are (1) the creation of man; and (2) the gift of His grace. Between these two divine and gratuitous acts extends the domain of tragedy, more profoundly tragic as it is more equally separated from the two acts of God. Christian philosophy lovingly safeguards not only the dogma of man created by the Divine Creator, but cherishes the belief that man, thus created, becomes, in his turn, creator of his vast and measureless liberty. We like to say today, with our impoverished and insufficient vocabulary, that the entire history of the human race is the history of democracy. This is true enough in a limited sense. But it would perhaps be more exact to say that our history is our effort to understand our freedom hidden in the mystery of those abysses which existed before historical time.

Corneille is the initiator of a movement of ideas and of a chapter in art which begin roughly with the birth of the seventeenth century and which are perhaps destined to terminate in the cataclysms and the global revolutions of our own age. But since he was initiator, Corneille didn't progress very far in the domain of tragedy. He makes us feel it, however, in all his plays, and especially in **Le Cid** which we are going to use as example, by his persistent use of the triumph of grace. Corneille violates tragedy by insisting on the large amount of spirituality which inhabits each one of his great heroes. Rodrigue and Chimène are two children who announce all the forms of modern tragedy without succeeding in incarnating them explicitly. Markedly absent in them is any expression of terror, the sentiment which Kierkegaard defines in the nineteenth century as the eminent sign of spirituality in man. Even the women in *Le Cid* do not feel terror. Chimène isn't terrorized by the murder of her father and the appearance of Rodrigue in her own house. She feigns terror, as an actress would, but the primitive vigour of her joy and her love wins out over all the inferior sentiments. The Infanta, more purely tragic than Chimène, doesn't discover terror in herself, but rather that form of despair which henceforth will be the vice of modern spirituality.

No terror, then, in the virginal world of Corneille because purity abounds there. It is almost as if the Creation had just taken place, and that at the end of the twenty-four hours with all their fatiguing peripetiæ, joy would be reborn, greater still because it would be the joy of grace after having been the joy of creation. In the middle of the Corneilian play there occurs the tragic moment which is rapid and immediately over. It is the moment of the fall, the return to the void which existed before the creation. The moment of vengence felt by Rodrigue and Chimène, even if it is at once annihilated and surpassed by them, is sufficient to make out of this poem of love, a tragedy. Vengence is called by anthropologists the oldest of moral emotions, and can be traced back to the most primitive periods of history. Vengence exists because man is not only a being created by God, he is also a personality. Our personality is our oneness, that part of ourselves opposed to what is mortal in us. Christianity teaches us that personality exists because of the sentiment of love. The sentiment of vengence breaks out in man, only to hurl him toward the void of the fall, because of the collective personality of the clan which is innate in primitive man. This sentiment, which is very concealed but real in Hamlet, is born instinctively in Rodrigue and threatens his happiness in accordance with the formal law of tragedy. For a moment in the life of Rodrigue and Chimène, they forget themselves in order to sacrifice to the cult of the family and the clan, because of some primitive blood mysticism, their personal happiness and their love. This ancient instinct of collective responsibility toward the social group or the race has been converted by Christianity into the dogma of personal responsibility for the sins of all men and into the universal love of Christ in his mystical body.

Therefore, the principle of paternity, oldest of all principles, against which Oedipus had fought, is the first principle in *Le Cid*. The primitive character of this tragedy is clearly drawn in the effortlessness with which Rodrigue abandons and surpasses the principle of paternity which had engaged him during the first two acts. In the third act, he becomes a man in love, tormented by the drama of passion and sexuality, incapable of finding peace because the principle of sex divides man against himself and fills him with horror. In the fourth act, Rodrigue becomes a creator and enters upon his destiny. He channels all his sexual force and surpasses it in one great act of heroism. The triumph of the battle with the Moors is the triumph

of sexual sublimation in Rodrigue, as a great creative work in someone else, in a Leonardo for example, is the same kind of triumph. The principle of man is always an effort to deceive his sexuality, to do without woman, to remain faithful to his 'solar' principle, which is his principle of creation and fecundation. But Chimène doesn't renounce as willingly as Rodrigue the principle of paternity. She is clearly the woman who safeguards the communal idea and the perpetuity of the race. What is for Rodrigue a question of honour, is, for Chimène, the instinct of a woman, the instinct of maternity and procreation. The sun, a phallic symbol in its evolution and its force, is opposed to the earth, symbol of woman: of her maternal flesh and of her cosmic meaning. Whereas Rodrigue traverses the work of Corneille with the sword of his spirit and the solar force of his youth, Chimène remains stable during the entire play as the antithetic principle of man, as the symbol of matter and the collective unity of the earth.

Man doesn't succeed in destroying the sexual urge of his nature. If he doesn't give himself over to a free expression of his *libido,* he can hide it and suppress it in the obscure and sometimes dangerous recesses of his subconscious, or he can surpass it, sublimate it in a great spiritual act of creation or heroism. Thus, the hero, like the creative artist, transforms his sexual *libido* into an expression of power which the theologians call *libido excellendi.* Rodrigue in the second act, in his victory over the Count, and in the fourth act, in his victory over the Moors, struggles not only against his love for Chimène but against the very principle of woman. He affirms himself in the play as a single personality who opposes the maternal element, the earth, the community, and the primordial instinct of sexuality in his being. Rodrigue goes against everything once he discovers the fathomless liberty of human nature, once he discovers in his own subconscious that the principle of man is that of the logos and the creation and is eternally opposed to the principle of woman which is that of the earth, of procreation, and reproduction. Rodrigue, like all heroes and all great artists, has to struggle against the sexuality of his nature, not because of some point of honour, which critics explain so often and so insufficiently in the tragedies of Corneille, but because of a much more profound reason. He knows, at least in his subconscious, that sexual satisfaction is the source of life and death, and that there is in man a more imperious desire than that of life and death: it is the desire to triumph over life and death (desire which women do not know), to preserve and keep intact all of his sexual vigour.

If Rodrigue struggles for the freedom of his male spirit, in order to free himself by surpassing woman, and if he fights the Moors not through patriotism but in order to escape the monotony of domestic quarrels and forget himself in an adventure of danger and chance, Chimène renounces every struggle once she has chosen her rôle of matriarch representative of the clan, in order to throw into relief Rodrigue's struggle. She stabilizes the earth and the cosmos, and then she patiently waits for the prodigal to return to her arms, as to the source of life and to the maternal centre from which he tried to escape in the rantings of his youth as well as in the very passion of his love. Rodrigue is the eternal man pointing out the possible ways of the future and all the circular movements of the sun and of the spirit, who affirms his personality in the very presence of Chimène. She is the eternal woman revealing the vast and solid shelter of matter and community, the tranquil site of our genesis, the earth and the womb, the final repose of man devoured by restlessness.

'Je ne t'accuse point, je pleure nos malheurs', Chimène says to Rodrigue in their great scene of the third act, and her conscience is almost at ease. But in her subconscious she favours a sadism, which is another feminine principle. (If Descartes, at the time of Corneille and *Le Cid,* taught the psychology of consciousness and reason, Freud has shown since then the far greater importance of the conflict between the conscious and the subconscious faculties in man). Chimène torments others and rejoices in tormenting them, not through some point of honour, but because of a very ancient origin of primitive suffering. Rodrigue, more masochistic than Chimène, as most men are, knows that happiness is not the conscious goal of men. In loving Chimène, Rodrigue loves sorrow; he loves a good and not a happiness. Woman holds unto the past and prays for the present to stop. She opposes time and change because she is eternity, whereas man represents the triumph of time over eternity through his autonomous acts of heroism and violence which, once they are committed, die and disappear in that past he wants to create-and from which he hopes to liberate himself.

Each human being has an androgynous nature and develops through the union of the masculine and feminine principles, through the simultaneous existence of personal passion and communal sentiment. In that nature where equilibrium between man and woman is quite sustained, the effort to realize oneself and surpass oneself is sharper, more uninterrupted, more necessary. Tragic sentiment is easily created in it because this nature, conscious both of its personality and of the cosmos, favours so equal a struggle between the two principles that no triumph is assured. This kind of human nature lives under the threat of itself, anxious over the responsibilities it feels toward the entire world and toward its own heart. *Le Cid* offers to us in Rodrigue and Chimène two beings fashioned very lucidly in accordance to the two principles of man and woman, but in the character of the Infanta, Corneille depicts a more purely tragic nature in which the two worlds of man and woman face one another and devastate one another. Chimène and Rodrigue speak only of blood, of swords, and of immolation: blood to avenge and blood to shed are the two constant themes of their speeches which make of *Le Cid* a kind of mediaeval tournament. But the voice of the Infanta heard as early as the second scene of the first act and not silenced until the second scene of the fifth act, that is, the voice heard just after the beginning of the play and silenced just before the end, is the voice of modern times and of our heroines today. Her voice gives the work its true tragic colour because she is alone in the labyrinthic complexity of her heart. She is indifferent to vengences and thrones, to the sportive and youthful struggle

between Chimène and Rodrigue. They don't cease for a moment loving one another: they remain therefore very near to the creation of their love and they await impatiently the moment of grace destined to consecrate their love. They traverse so rapidly the domain of tragedy and with so much exuberance so weakly controlled, that they hardly perceive the domain itself. For them, the story is a bad day in their lives which will be quickly forgotten. But the Infanta, each time she appears on the stage, performs the eternal gesture of tragedy: she opens on herself the gates of death. Because she is not loved, she possesses all the cruel leisure necessary to understand the double principle of love: its expression of life and death, of life which, for her, is death, and of death, which is life. The Infanta, in the eternity of her waiting, of her despair, of her courage, and of her goodness, is a counterpart of the Blessed Virgin who is the eternity of grace, the awareness and the fecundity of grace. There are traits of Héloise in the Infanta in the image of her long fidelity, and traits of Hamlet in the restlessness of his nature, and traits also of Phèdre in the potency of an impossible love.

In a sense then, the Infanta came into being in spite of chronology, because Cornelian tragedy is the triumph of grace. Even *Le Cid,* because, of course, *Polyeucte* is a more obvious example. *Le Cid* is the story of Chimène who symbolizes the plenitude of the cosmos and the female element of the earth; and then, *Le Cid* is the story of Rodrigue who returns to Chimène after leaving her. He symbolizes the return of the sun to the maternal principle of the cosmos, to the principle which sustains and renews the earth. Thus, the Cornelian solution resembles a philosophic love which rediscovers the equilibrium between man and woman, and which, after arousing sentiments of theatric fright, arouses in their place sentiments of veneration and calms the impermanent virtues. The earth absorbs the heat of the sun in much the same way that Chimène envelops the intrepid passions of Rodrigue. The plenitude of the cosmos ends by covering the principle which pierces it and fecundates it.

Allardyce Nicoll (essay date 1949)

SOURCE: "Racine and the Tragedy of Sentiment," in *World Drama: From Aeschylus to Anouilh,* George G. Harrap & Company Ltd., 1949, pp. 299-315.

[Called "one of the masters of dramatic research," Nicoll is best known as a theater historian whose works have proven invaluable to students and educators. Nicoll's World Drama: From Aeschylus to Anouilh *(1949) is considered one of his most important works; theater critic John Gassner has stated that it was "unquestionably the most thorough [study] of its kind in the English language [and] our best reference book on the world's dramatic literature." Another of his ambitious theater studies is the six-volume* A History of English Drama, 1660-1900 *(1952-59), which has been highly praised for its perceptive commentaries on drama from the Restoration to the close of the nineteenth century. In the following excerpt from his* World Drama, *Nicoll places Corneille's work in the*

context of French literary history.]

The drama that first gave distinction to the French tragic stage was *Le Cid* (1636), the work of Pierre Corneille. Its author, a lawyer of Rouen, had been impelled towards the theatre by the visit to his native city of the Marais troupe, and when, in 1629, Mondory returned to Paris he carried with him the manuscript of a comedy, **Mélite**, by the young author. During the succeeding years Corneille trained himself in the penning of comedy, and then set all literary Paris in an uproar with his heroic drama on a Spanish theme.

At the time that this drama appeared classic theory and practice had not as yet fully established itself. Tragi-comedies were still being produced by men such as Rotrou and Benserade, and for some years these dramatists were to remain moderately popular. Along with their vogue was a vogue for dramas on English history—a kind of gesture on the part of romantic playwrights to the claims of tragedy. Here came La Calprenède's *Jeanne, Royne d'Angleterre* (printed 1638) and Regnault's *Marie Stuard, Royne d'Ecosse* (printed 1639). Already, however, the classical style was making headway. In 1634 Jean Mairet came forward with his *Sophonisbe*, the first tragedy in France truly based on the rules, and it was followed by a series of dramas which treated ancient themes in accordance with the critical precepts supposed to be found in Aristotle's *Poetics*. Mairet himself followed his *Sophonisbe* with *Marc Antoine, ou la Cléopâtre* (c. 1635), Scudéry produced his *La mort de César* (*The Death of Cæsar*, 1635) and Pierre Corneille his **Médée** (**Medea**, 1634-35).

At the same time the critics were eagerly discussing the precepts that should be followed. Some men of independent judgment followed François Ogier in objecting to the stricter application of the rules, but the majority welcomed Mairet as the leader of the classical legion. As yet, however, the debate was rather abstract, since no really important tragic drama, whether classically inclined or the reverse, had appeared to provide a concrete issue. It was precisely such a concrete issue that *Le Cid* gave to Parisian society. No one could deny its power; the question was whether that power was secured by legitimate means.

The plot of Corneille's drama was derived from a Spanish source. Chimène is the daughter of Don Gomès, and is the love of the gallant Rodrigue. Unfortunately Don Gomès insults and strikes Rodrigue's father, and the young man, at the very moment of his wedding, is forced to challenge the former; in the ensuing duel Don Gomès is slain. Chimène now is in turn forced to wish Rodrigue's death, and he, rather than commit suicide, takes command of a small troop of soldiers prepared to attempt the apparently forlorn hope of preventing the advance of a great Moorish army. Instead of perishing on the field, however, Rodrigue is triumphant, and returns home in glory. Still impelled by her sense of loyalty to her dead father, Chimène causes Don Sanche, who seeks her hand in marriage, to challenge Rodrigue, but, on hearing that

he proposes to let himself be killed, she herself bids him to use his strength in order to obtain victory—even although (or because) she is aware that by the King's order she must marry the survivor. Rodrigue wins the duel, and the lovers are united.

The storm that broke around this drama may at first seem inexplicable; but consideration of *Le Cid* in its setting dissipates all difficulty. Its brilliant, forceful verse and its bold, arresting presentation of character marked it out as a tremendous achievement. Here was a literary effort that could not be ignored, and in this period when men were so eagerly searching for the true road the question as to whether Corneille, by his very genius, might not be leading the world astray became a theme of profound significance.

Externally the author keeps the rules. All the action is supposed to take place within a period of twenty-four hours, and the entire action is pursued near the royal palace. Yet the five acts of the drama are crowded with incident, straining dangerously our sense of probability, and the end, instead of being tragic, bears a happy conclusion. Several questions were paramount for the dramatic authors of that time: Was probability or retention of the rules the more important? Could these two be reconciled, and, if so, in what way? What was the true end of the tragic drama? *Le Cid* provided a practical test for the establishing of opinion.

Anyone who wades through the spate of controversy which flooded upon *Le Cid* at that time may well deem that the critical comments are frequently weak, absurd, and beside the point; yet a general understanding of the situation shows that, although the authors were frequently arguing about problems of lesser import, their passionate advocating of even trivial views sprang from a consciousness of the ultimate importance of the quarrel.

Almost immediately following its presentation on the stage, Mairet (perhaps stung by jealousy) and others started debating its merits, and so bitter did the debate prove that within a few months the Academy was formally asked to judge the issue, with the result that Jean Chapelain, assisted by the learned institution to which he belonged, soon published the famous *Sentimens de l'Académie Françoise sur la tragi-comédie du Cid*.

Much space is taken up in the *Sentimens* with criticism of minor points, and even more with what seems utterly futile—the moral questions involved. In particular, the authors of that essay fix their attention on the impropriety of causing Chimène to marry the man who has slain her father, of allowing her to permit love to sway her heart above the dictates of duty. Unquestionably this appears to be but foolish criticism, yet, perhaps unconsciously, the *Sentimens* here have, although rather crudely, concentrated their attention upon what is ultimately the core of the entire controversy. Corneille, while he bows formally to the unities, has in reality a romantic soul. There is a strength about him that rebels against restraint: into the age of classicism he carries a bold, truculent individualism. But individualism of this sort is exactly that which the age was seeking to restrain, and in the criticisms directed at Chimène's conduct the Academy was, in effect, testifying to its desire for order, restraint, and social unity. Marlowes and their like could find place in the Renaissance; in this later age no room might be allowed to them.

The emphasis laid upon the improbabilities of the action of *Le Cid* also has deeper implications. The old tragicomedies had extended actions, but their structure was formless. Form was needed, hence the inculcation of the unities. At the same time form must harmonize with content, and the truth is that Corneille, despite the vigour and beauty of his work, failed to secure such harmony. In plays of romantic structure it may be proper to have variety of incident; in plays of classical restraint the subject-matter, and the passions, must be so conceived as to accord with the conventions employed. The Academy, rightly, recognized that what Corneille aimed at was a type of drama which could not provide the age with what it needed. Some of its members may have been animated by personal jealousies, some may have been too academic to recognize true genius when it appeared; but basically the general criticism of the *Sentimens,* in the light of what was then demanded of the theatre, must be deemed fully justified. The path indicated by Corneille could have led to nothing but chaos; the way of the *Sentimens* leads towards the work of Racine.

That Corneille himself took the lesson to heart is indicated in his later dramas. In *Horace* (1640) he selects a classical subject and attempts to deal with it more simply than he had treated the content of *Le Cid*. Basically this tragedy deals with conflicting loyalties. Rome is at war, and against the background of the conflict the dramatist sets Horace, the patriot of untroubled mind; Sabine, his wife, and a native of the enemy country; Camille, his sister, in love with a soldier, Curiace, also of that country. Each character, clearly etched, is presented without any inner conflict. Horace is so assured of the rightness of his views that he slays his sister when he finds her cursing her own country; for Camille nothing matters save love of Curiace. There is a noble grandeur about the entire conception; and with subtle sensitivity Corneille has been able to hammer out lines of almost Roman brevity, pith, and grandeur: "Qui veut mourir ou vaincre est vaincu rarement"; "Et qui veut bien mourir peut braver les malheurs"; "Mais Rome ignore encor comme on perd des batailles"—these and other epigrammatic lines linger in the memory.

Yet *Horace,* even although its author has taken the *Sentimens* to heart, still fails to point in the true direction. Its very boldness is too strong for the temper of the age, and its lack of inner conflict causes it to miss an opportunity such as Racine knew later how to embrace.

In *Cinna, ou la clémence d'Auguste* (*Cinna; or, The Clemency of Augustus, c.* 1641) Corneille turned once more to a tragedy with a happy ending, but, as in *Horace,* simplified the contents of the work. Auguste is the all-

powerful Emperor, and among his closest protégés are Emilie, burning with a desire to avenge her father's death; Cinna, induced to join in a conspiracy against Auguste because of his love for Emilie; and Maxime, another member of the conspiracy and also secretly in love with the heroine. With admirable conciseness and economy of means Corneille reveals these characters in their relations with the Emperor, and rises to a magnificent conclusion in Auguste's decision to pardon the offenders. Peculiarly effective is the monarch's soliloquy in the fourth act, which might be regarded as the classical equivalent of the romantic soliloquy put into the mouth of Henry V by Shakespeare:

> O Heaven, to whom is it your will that I
> Entrust my life, the secrets of my soul?
> Take back the power with which you have
>   endowed me,
> If it but steals my friends to give me subjects,
> If regal splendours must be fated ever,
> Even by the greatest favours they can grant,
> To foster only hate, if your stern law
> Condemns a king to cherish only those
> Who burn to have his blood. Nothing is certain.
> Omnipotence is bought with ceaseless fear. . . .

Polyeucte (*c.* 1642) carries us into a different world, for here Corneille moved from pagan character to Christian. Polyeucte is a descendant of Armenian princes who has accepted the material power of Rome and is married to the daughter of the Governor, Pauline. A quality of mystical faith enters in here, for the author is intent upon showing how this man, becoming dedicate to a higher law, is forced to a way of life different from that of his companions. The contrast is well revealed in his relations with Pauline. This Roman lady has married him only at her father's command; in reality her heart has been given to a fellow-Roman, Sévère. Faithful to her husband, the other love cannot be stilled, but when, towards the close of the tragedy, she finds Polyeucte, recognizing her passion, offering her happiness with Sévère when he himself is dead, while Sévère tacitly accepts the proposal, a sudden new light floods in upon her. She becomes a Christian in order that, even in death, she may be with the heroic soul whose virtues have thus been revealed to her.

The qualities displayed in these dramas are reproduced in the succeeding tragedies of Corneille—*Pompée* (1642), *Rodogune, Princesse des Parthes* (printed 1646), *Héraclius* (1646), and *Nicomède* (1650-51), as well as the later works, *Œdipe* (1659), *Sertorius* (1662), and *Sophonisbe* (1663)—but the times were rapidly leaving him as a monument of the past. His stalwart figure, strayed out of the Renaissance, stood somewhat awkwardly among the polite and delicate gallantries of the age. His characters were rough-hewn, bold in their proportions, massive; what the ladies and gentlemen of the Paris Court desired was something subtler and more polished. These audiences had the power to be aroused by "greatness of soul," as Charles Saint-Évremond expressed it, but even more they sought "tender admiration." There is a rugged masculinity about Corneille; more appropriate to the age were

Racine's sensitive heroines.

P. J. Yarrow (essay date 1963)

SOURCE: "The Realism of Corneille (1) Characters," in *Corneille,* St Martin's Press, 1963, pp. 178-229.

[*In the following excerpt, Yarrow provides a close study of Corneille's characterization.*]

Epithets derived from names of writers sometimes suffer a strange fate. Some are merely used with the sense of 'like or pertaining to the writer in question', as 'Shakespearean'. Others, however, take on a different shade of meaning and imply, not 'like the writer', but 'like some popular misconception of the writer'. The word 'Machiavellian', for instance, has acquired undertones and overtones of meaning which make the reading of *The Prince* something of a surprise to the reader who expects it to be 'Machiavellian'. 'Cartesianism' is only a part of Descartes, as 'marivaudage' is only a part of Marivaux. In the same way, the adjective 'Cornelian' has acquired implications, based on an over-simple, if not erroneous, interpretation of Corneille, which make it difficult to approach his plays with an open mind.

Corneille is often regarded as lacking in humanity, as the creator of a false psychology. Corneille, said La Bruyère in a famous phrase, 'peint les hommes comme ils devraient être.' 'Corneille est presque toujours hors de la nature,' wrote Voltaire. 'L' observation de la nature ne l'occupait point,' asserted Guizot. In more recent times, we find Faguet saying that 'rien ne ressemble moins à la vie que le théâtre de Corneille,' and Barrère that 'il a aimé l'humanité inhumaine'. His characters, it is said, are over-simplified, and get less and less convincing as time goes on:

> Drama of this kind must, it is clear, lack many of the qualities which are usually associated with the dramatic art; there is no room in it for variety of character-drawing, for delicacy of feeling, or for the realistic presentation of the experiences of life. Corneille hardly attempted to produce such effects as these; and during his early years his great gifts of passion and rhetoric easily made up for the deficiency. As he grew older, however, his inspiration weakened; his command of his material left him; and he was no longer able to fill the figures of his creation with the old intellectual sublimity. His heroes and his heroines became mere mouthing puppets, pouring out an endless stream of elaborate, high-flown sentiments, wrapped up in a complicated jargon of argumentative verse. His later plays are miserable failures. (Lytton Strachey)

Corneille, indeed, has even come to be regarded as a moralist, a creator of supermen. The Cornelian hero is often described as a being whose will is capable of executing whatever course he has selected by the exercise of his reason and whose passions are rational; a magnanimous being, following the path of duty whatever temptations beset him, and fond of abnegation for its own sake. His essential nature, it is said, is expressed in lines such as:

> Je le ferais encor, si j'avais à le faire.
>
> (*Le Cid,* III, 4; *Polyeucte,* V, 3)

> Je suis maître de moi comme de l'univers. . . .
>
> (*Cinna,* V, 3)

> *Antiochus.* Le pourrez-vous, mon frère?
> *Séleucus.*   Ah! que vous me pressez!
>   Je le voudrai du moins, mon frère, et c'est assez;
>   Et ma raison sur moi gardera tant d'empire
>   Que je désavouerai mon cœur, s'il en soupire.
>
> (*Rodogune,* I, 3)

> Voilà quelle je suis, et quelle je veux être.

The Cornelian hero has been seen as the dramatic equivalent of the *généreux* of Descartes, and Corneille has been described as 'le poète de la volonté,' 'professeur d'énergie nationale'. These views have been challenged by some recent writers, such as Bénichou and Nadal, for whom the Cornelian hero is motivated, not by virtue and reason, but by the passion for *gloire,* which makes him ambitious of heroism, magnanimity, or rank. Even this, however, does not clear Corneille of the imputation of lacking humanity; and, in any case, the older view is still current—even such a great Cornelian scholar as M. Couton talks of 'l'idée cornélienne de l'homme, éclairé par la raison, doué d'une volonté capable de dompter les passions.'

Now, Corneille began by writing comedies which, besides their comic elements, were distinguished by their use of baroque themes and characteristics and by realism of various kinds. Neither the baroque characteristics nor the comic elements disappeared from Corneille's work when he turned from tragedy to comedy, so that it would seem unlikely, on the face of it, that he abandoned his psychological realism and became a creator of supermen. Indeed, the presence of a comic element in his tragedies seems almost to be a guarantee of their realism. Certainly, in his theoretical writings, Corneille shows that he was no less concerned with realism in tragedy than in comedy:

> Le poème dramatique est une imitation, ou pour en mieux parler, un portrait des actions des hommes; et il est hors de doute que les portraits sont d'autant plus excellents, qu'ils ressemblent mieux à l'original. (*Troisième Discours*)

The same preoccupation with realism is evident in his views about the characters of tragedy:

> Le poète doit considérer l'âge, la dignité, la naissance,

l'emploi et le pays de ceux qu'il introduit: il faut qu'il sache ce qu'on doit à sa patrie, à ses parents, à ses amis, à son roi; quel est l'office d'un magistrat, ou d'un général d'armée, afin qu'il puisse y conformer ceux qu'il veut faire aimer aux spectateurs, et en éloigner ceux qu'il leur veut faire haïr; car c'est une maxime infaillible que, pour bien réussir, il faut intéresser l'auditoire pour les premiers acteurs. (***Premier Discours***)

He is no less concerned with the *vraisemblance* of the action: even in his first tragedy, ***Médée,*** he attempts to make the events more probable than they are in his original. As for style, he insists that it should be as natural as is compatible with writing in verse:

Il y a cette différence pour ce regard entre le poète dramatique et l'orateur, que celui-ci peut étaler son art, et le rendre remarquable avec pleine liberté, et que l'autre doit le cacher avec soin, parce que ce n'est jamais lui qui parle, et que ceux qu'il fait parler ne sont pas des orateurs [. . .] le langage doit être net, les figures placées à propos et diversifiées, et la versification aisée et élevée au-dessus de la prose, mais non pas jusqu'à l'enflure du poème épique, puisque ceux que le poète fait parler ne sont pas des poètes.

(***Premier Discours***)

His dislike of asides, his reluctance to let a monologue be overheard by another character, his aversion from moral discourses and maxims of a general nature, his insistence that narrations must be introduced realistically or not at all, his blend of comedy and tragedy, and his invention of the *comédie héroïque* are all evidence of the same tendency. It is clear that Corneille's conception of tragedy by no means excludes realism.

The Cornelian superman is certainly not to be found in the four most commonly read plays, ***Le Cid, Horace, Cinna*** and ***Polyeucte.***

In ***Le Cid,*** what is exceptional is the situation, not the characters. Rodrigue obeys the claims of family honour and kills the Count, who has insulted his father; but he makes the point clearly that this is the only course open to him, since, whatever he does, he is bound to lose Chimène:

Allons, mon bras, sauvons du moins l'honneur,
Puisqu'après tout il faut perdre Chimène.

(I, 6)

Once he has fought and killed the Count, there is no going back. The initiative passes to Chimène—and, in fact, in Chimène, as Corneille's critics pointed out in the *Querelle du Cid,* love is stronger than duty.

She easily strays from the course of action she thinks she ought to follow; her protestations of firmness cover up a fundamental indecision and weakness. After every effort

A Comédie-Française production of Le Cid.

to do what she thinks she ought, she makes, in reaction, increasingly greater concessions to her love, until the final concession of all, the acceptance of the marriage, is only the logical conclusion of the series.

She demands vengeance (II, 8). Subsequently, however, she refuses Don Sanche's offer of summary justice (III, 2), admits that she loves Rodrigue and is pursuing him unwillingly (III, 3), and, in an interview with her lover, not merely refuses to kill him, but confesses that she still loves him—

Va, je ne te hais point.—Tu le dois.—Je ne puis.

—and that she does not want vengeance:

Je ferai mon possible à bien venger mon père;
Mais malgré la rigueur d'un si cruel devoir,
Mon unique souhait est de ne rien pouvoir.

(III, 4)

When she hears of his exploits against the Moors, she immediately asks:

Mais n'est-il point blessé?

(IV, 1)

She then screws her courage up to the sticking-point once more and goes to the King to demand vengeance again; but, believing Rodrigue to be dead, she reveals her true feelings by fainting in the King's presence (IV, 5). The duel between Rodrigue and Don Sanche, Chimène's champion, is arranged, and the King tells her that she must marry the victor; all she can say in protest is:

> Quoi! Sire, m'imposer une si dure loi!
>
> (IV, 5)

Indeed, as Léonor points out, Chimène has chosen a weak champion:

> Chimène aisément montre par sa conduite
> Que la haine aujourd'hui ne fait pas sa
>   poursuite.
> Elle obtient un combat, et pour son combattant
> C'est le premier offert qu'elle accepte à l'instant:
> Elle n'a point recours à ces mains généreuses
> Que tant d'exploits fameux rendent si glorieuses;
> Don Sanche lui suffit. . . .
>
> (V, 3)

From this moment on, her resistance grows weaker. In Act V, scene I, she urges Rodrigue to fight and win her:

> Sors vainqueur d'un combat dont Chimène est le
>   prix.
> Adieu: ce mot lâché me fait rougir de honte.

Later, she does, it is true, say to Elvire:

> Quand il sera vainqueur, crois-tu que je me
>   rende?
> . . . . .
> Mon honneur lui fera mille autre ennemis.
>
> (V, 4)

But this is merely a momentary reaction: the King has already forbidden her to 'faire mille autre ennemis;' so that we cannot take the remark very seriously. Moreover, a few lines later, Elvire having suggested that perhaps Don Sanche might win and become her husband, she bursts out:

> Elvire, c'est assez des peines que j'endure,
> Ne les redouble point de ce funeste augure.
> Je veux, si je le puis, les éviter tous deux;
> Sinon, en ce combat Rodrigue a tous mes vœux.
>
> (V, 4)

Mistakenly believing Don Sanche to be the victor, she publicly admits her love for Rodrigue (V, 6), and in the final scene she agrees to marry him:

> Rodrigue a des vertus que je ne puis haïr;
> Et quand un roi commande, on lui doit obéir.
>
> (V, 7)

The Infante resembles Chimène: indeed, one of the functions of her rôle may well be to set another example of feminine sub-servience to passion by the side of Chimène and so lend credibility to the portrayal. Like Chimène, she is unable to master her love for Rodrigue:

> A combien de soupirs
>   Faut-il que mon cœur se prépare,
> Si jamais il n'obtient sur un si long tourment
> Ni d'éteindre l'amour, ni d'accepter l'amant!
>
> (V, 2)

She hopes until the last that the marriage of Rodrigue and Chimène will not take place: there is even a suggestion that she would not hesitate to use foul means to prevent it:

> Si Rodrigue combat sous ces conditions,
> Pour en rompre l'effet, j'ai trop d'inventions.
> L'amour, ce doux auteur de mes cruels
>   supplices,
> Aux esprits des amants apprend trop d'artifices.
>
> (V, 3)

In **Horace,** there is only one possible 'Cornelian hero', Horace. Curiace does his duty with reluctance; Sabine and Camille try to deter their menfolk from fighting; and Camille is all love:

> Je le vois bien, ma sœur, vous n'aimâtes jamais;
> Vous ne connaissez point ni l'amour ni ses
>   traits:
> On peut lui résister quand il commence à naître,
> Mais non pas le bannir quand il s'est rendu
>   maître. . . .
> . . . . .
> Et quand l'âme une fois a goûté son amorce,
> Vouloir ne plus aimer, c'est ce qu'elle ne peut,
> Puisqu'elle ne peut plus vouloir que ce qu'il
>   veut. . . .
>
> (III, 4)

She is, as Sarcey says, neither reasonable nor strong-willed, but 'une personne toute de premier mouvement, incapable de se maîtriser elle-même, l'esclave de ses nerfs toujours agités'. Horace alone masters his feelings and puts his duty to his country before his personal affections. But is he a 'Cornelian hero'?

There is certainly no question of reason and will getting the better of passion: the most that one can say is that one passion gets the better of another—for Horace, in contrast to Curiace, cares very much more about his *gloire* than his duty. Moreover, it is very doubtful whether Horace is an ideal character. The play is clearly a study of a Roman patriot, but it is by no means certain that Corneille shares his point of view. A man who, after seeing both his brothers killed, can remark:

> Quand la perte est vengée, on n'a plus rien
>   perdu.
>
> (IV, 5)

—who, having killed his wife's brothers, can greet her with the words:

> Sèche tes pleurs, Sabine, ou les cache à ma vue. . . .
>
> . . . . .

Participe à ma gloire au lieu de la souiller.

(IV, 7)

—who, having just killed his sister's lover, can adjure her:

Songe à mes trophées:
Qu'ils soient dorénavant ton unique entretien.

(IV, 5)

and who kills her because she cannot control her anguish, seems, on the face of it, to be too lacking in humanity, too self-centred, to be an ideal character. Of course, we may like to think that Corneille admired him, even if we do not; but it is striking that, in taking the law into his own hands in this way, in avenging a personal insult by violence, he places himself on a level with the Count in *Le Cid,* and that no one in the play condones his action: Tulle in his closing speech condemns it explicitly. Curiace calls Horace 'barbare',—

Mais votre fermeté tient un peu du barbare. . . .

(II, 3)

—and reproaches him with his inhumanity:

J'ai le cœur aussi bon, mais enfin je suis
    homme.

(II, 3)

Camille also calls him 'barbare' (IV, 5), and Corneille seems to share her attitude, for, in the *Examen,* he refers to the 'vertu farouche' of his hero and calls him 'criminel'. Moreover, the tragedy opens with a statement that human weakness and emotion are right and proper, which seems to strike the keynote of the play:

Approuvez ma faiblesse, et souffrez ma douleur;
Elle n'est que trop juste en un si grand malheur:
Si près de voir sur soi fondre de tels orages,
L'ébranlement sied bien aux plus fermes courages;
Et l'esprit le plus mâle et le moins abattu
Ne saurait sans désordre exercer sa vertu.

(I, 1)

The exponents of this point of view dominate the middle of the play. It is not easy to see Horace as the expression of Corneille's ideal.

It is no easier to find a 'Cornelian hero' in *Cinna.* In Emilie, as in the women of the two previous plays, love is the strongest passion:

J'aime encor plus Cinna que je ne hais Auguste,
Et je sens refroidir ce bouillant mouvement
Quand il faut, pour le suivre, exposer mon
    amant.

(I, 1)

In the following scene, she says:

Mon esprit en désordre à soi-même s'oppose:
Je veux et ne veux pas, je m'emporte et je
    n'ose;
Et mon devoir confus, languissant, étonné,
Cède aux rébellions de mon cœur mutiné. . . .

(I, 2)

The truth of her words is borne out subsequently. In Act I, scene 4, when Auguste sends for Cinna, she is filled with unreasoning apprehension: there is no real likelihood that the plot has been discovered, and even Cinna calls her alarm a 'terreur panique'. She urges him to flee, and only changes her mind when she reflects that flight would be useless.

Cinna is a most interesting character study, but a most unheroic hero. He is a hypocrite and a liar, who makes eloquent speeches to his fellow-conspirators, urging them to kill Auguste and restore the glories of Republican Rome—

Avec la liberté Rome s'en va renaître. . . .

(I, 3)

—and who says precisely the opposite to dissuade Auguste from abdicating—

la liberté ne peut plus être utile
Qu'à former les fureurs d'une guerre civile. . . .

(II, 1)

In neither case is he concerned in the least about the interests of Rome. He is full of illusions, about himself and his allies. The enthusiastic account he gives of his fellow-conspirators in Act I, scene 3—the falsity of which is surely revealed by the absurd

par un effet contraire,
Leur front pâlir d'horreur et rougir de colère

—is in marked contrast to that of Auguste in Act V, scene 1:

Le reste ne vaut pas l'honneur d'être nommé:
Un tas d'hommes perdus de dettes et de crimes,
Que pressent de mes lois les ordres légitimes,
Et qui désespérant de les plus éviter,
Si tout est renversé, ne sauraient subsister.

As for himself, he tells Emilie that, if he is betrayed:

Ma vertu pour le moins ne me trahira pas:
Vous la verrez, brillante au bord des précipices,
Se couronner de gloire en bravant les supplices,
Rendre Auguste jaloux du sang qu'il répandra,
Et le faire trembler alors qu'il me perdra.

(I, 4)

—a prophecy which his later conduct does not justify. When Auguste, having learned of the plot against his life, accuses Cinna of being involved in it, Cinna immediately denies it:

> Moi, Seigneur! moi, que j'eusse une âme si
>   traîtresse;
> Qu'un si lâche dessein. . . .
>
>   (V, 1)

Above all, Cinna is exclusively motivated by self-interest, and 'ne forme qu'en lâche un dessein généreux'. To kill Auguste is the only way to marry Emilie, and so Auguste must be killed—must not even be allowed to abdicate, because, if Auguste abdicates, though the freedom of Rome would be achieved, his marriage with Emilie would be impossible. But when Auguste promises him Emilie, he sees the possibility of getting Emilie without murdering Auguste and feels remorse as the result of Auguste's trust in him and generosity towards him. As the moment for action approaches, his purpose weakens and his hostility to Auguste diminishes. By Act III, scene 2, he has forgotten Auguste's crimes; by scene 3, Auguste has become a 'prince magnanime'; and by scene 4, he considers that it is honourable to be enslaved by Auguste. He is assailed by doubts and misgivings—

> On ne les sent aussi que quand le coup
>   approche.
>
>   (III, 2)

He is irresolute. When Emilie justly denounces him for succumbing to Auguste's promises—

> Je vois ton repentir et tes vœux inconstants:
> Les faveurs du tyran emportent tes promesses;
> Tes vœux et tes serments cèdent à ses caresses;
> Et ton esprit crédule ose s'imaginer
> Qu'Auguste, pouvant tout, peut aussi me donner.
> Tu me veux de sa main plutôt que de la mienne. . . .
>
>   (III, 4)

—he replies:

> J'obéis sans réserve à tous vos sentiments.

But by the end of the scene, finding that Emilie is intransigent and still expects him to fulfil his promises, he rails at her resentfully:

> Eh bien! vous le voulez, il faut vous satisfaire
> . . . . .
> Mais apprenez qu'Auguste est moins tyran que
>   vous,
> S'il nous ôte à son gré nos biens, nos jours, nos
>   femmes,
> Il n'a point jusqu'ici tyrannisé nos âmes . . .

Fortinbras says of Hamlet that

> he was likely, had he been put on,
> To have proved most royally.

Cinna, being put on, proves rather shabbily, and justifies Auguste's low opinion of him:

> Ta fortune est bien haut, tu peux ce que tu veux;
> Mais tu ferais pitié même à ceux qu'elle irrite,
> Si je t'abandonnais à ton peu de mérite.
> Ose me démentir, dis-moi ce que tu vaux,
> Conte-moi tes vertus, tes glorieux travaux,
> Les rares qualités par où tu m'as dû plaire,
> Et tout ce qui t'élève au-dessus du vulgaire.
> Ma faveur fait ta gloire, et ton pouvoir en vient. . . .
>
>   (V, 1)

Auguste, like Cinna, is a most interesting study, but scarcely heroic. He has fulfilled his ambition by becoming Emperor, but found no satisfaction; he is tired of conspiracies and rebellions, of oppression and bloodshed, and thinks seriously of abdicating. The discovery of Cinna's plot brings his dissatisfaction to a head. He is inclined to punish Cinna and kill himself. His wife suggests that he might try a new policy, that of clemency; but he rejects her advice. The successive revelations of the complicity of Emilie and the treachery of Maxime strip him of his last illusions. In his complete disillusionment, his course at last becomes clear, and he forgives them all:

> Je suis maître de moi comme de l'univers.
>
>   (V, 3)

But if that is true, it is true for the first time in the play.

Why does Auguste choose to be merciful? The failure of his policy and the need to try another course is the obvious reason; but Corneille seems to mean us to believe that inspiration from above was the deciding factor. After rejecting his wife's advice, he says:

> Le ciel m'inspirera ce qu'ici je dois faire.
>
>   (IV, 3)

Moreover, Emilie, learning that Cinna has been sent for, feels none of the alarm she had felt earlier (I, 3): something assures her that all will be well:

> Mon cœur est sans soupirs, mes yeux n'ont
>   point de larmes,
> Comme si j'apprenais d'un secret mouvement
> Que tout doit succéder à mon contentement!
>
>   (IV, 4)

It is to the gods that she attributes the cessation of her hatred for Auguste (V, 3). Disillusionment and divine inspiration: we are far from reason and will.

Pauline, in **Polyeucte,** is of the same lineage as Chimène, the Infante, Camille and Emilie. In her, too, emotion is stronger than reason. We first see her unreasonably worried by a dream, not only one with apparently no possibility of fulfilment, but one which is itself unreasonable, since Sévère is the last man in the world to appear,

> La vengeance à la main, l'œil ardent de colère. . . .
>
>   (I, 3)

Polyeucte talks of 'Pauline, sans raison dans la douleur plongée,' and adds that, to keep him at home,

> Elle oppose ses pleurs au dessein que je fais,
>
> (I, 1)

a feminine, rather than a rational, line of argument. So far from being a purely rational being, she has a certain amount of amour-propre and possessiveness. Though she does not love Polyeucte—at the beginning of the play, at least—his love for her flatters her amour-propre, and her amour-propre is wounded if she thinks he no longer loves her. She is unhappy because Polyeucte leaves her and will not tell her his secret, and attributes the change in him to the effects of marriage (I, 2-3); and later she complains:

> Je te suis odieuse après m'être donnée!
> . . . . .
> Tu préfères la mort à l'amour de Pauline!
> Va, cruel, va mourir: tu ne m'aimas jamais.
>
> (IV, 3)

When she prevails on Sévère to do his best to save Polyeucte, even that 'parfait amant' remarks:

> vos douleurs avec trop de rigueur
> D'un amant tout à vous tyrannisent le cœur.
>
> (IV, 6)

Her feminine, emotional nature betrays itself particularly in Act IV, scene 3, and in Act V, scene 3. Pauline feels a real affection for her husband; she has been filled with forebodings and fears on his account all day; she already thinks that marriage may have put an end to his love. In short, she is in a more or less hysterical state. And now, to crown everything, her husband not merely persists in his mistaken beliefs, but refuses to do anything to save himself. She at last control of herself and gives vent to her feelings:

> Cruel, car il est temps que ma douleur éclate. . . .
>
> (IV, 3)

In Act V, scene 3, she is stung—irrationally—by Polyeucte's bringing up her own words against her. Earlier, Pauline had told him, referring to her love for Sévère:

> Depuis qu'un vrai mérite a pu nous enflammer,
> Sa présence toujours a droit de nous charmer.
>
> (II, 4)

Now, trying to persuade her to marry Sévère after his death, Polyeucte reminds her:

> Puisqu'un si grand mérite a pu vous enflammer,
> Sa présence toujours a droit de vous charmer.

And this taunt causes her to burst out:

> Que t'ai-je fait, cruel, pour être ainsi traitée. . . .

She reminds him that she did violence to her feelings and over-came her love for Sévère in order to marry him, and suggests that it is time he made a sacrifice in his turn for her sake. To be wounded by being reminded of one's own words is intensely human, but not rational. The conversion of Pauline is entirely in keeping with her emotional nature.

One or two passages are sometimes quoted in support of the view that Pauline is rational:

> Ces surprises des sens que la raison surmonte. . . .
>
> (I, 3)

> jamais ma raison
> N'avoua de mes yeux l'aimable trahison.
>
> (I, 3)

> Et sur mes passions ma raison souveraine
> Eût blâmé mes soupirs et dissipé ma haine.
>
> (II, 2)

The first two of these passages occur in Act I, scene 3, in which Pauline talks all the more complacently about her reason because she thinks that her love of Sévère, which is dormant, is dead; and she changes her tune considerably in the very next scene. The third quotation is particularly interesting. Pauline, at the beginning of her interview with Sévère—that interview which she has dreaded so much—tries to make it clear that she no longer loves him, that she loves her husband:

> Oui, je l'aime, Seigneur, et n'en fais point
> d'excuse.

She adds that, whatever husband her father had chosen, and even if Sévère had been never so suitable a match,

> J'en aurais soupiré, mais j'aurais obéi,
> Et sur mes passions ma raison souveraine
> Eût blâmé mes soupirs et dissipé ma haine.

This, she says, is what *would* have happened; she is not necessarily to be believed—any more than Cinna's opinion of what would happen if the conspiracy were betrayed is confirmed by the event. In fact, a touch of ironical reproach from Sévère melts her; she discards this attitude of cold disdain, and tells Sévère just how little power reason had over her, how much she has suffered and still suffers:

> si mon âme
> Pouvait bien étouffer les restes de sa flamme,
> Dieux, que j'éviterais de rigoureux tourments!
> Ma raison, il est vrai, dompte mes sentiments;
> Mais quelque autorité que sur eux elle ait prise,
> Elle n'y règne pas, elle les tyrannise;
> Et quoique le dehors soit sans émotion,
> Le dedans n'est que trouble et que sédition.

Of Sévère, it is perhaps enough to quote a recent critic's opinion of him as 'weak and ineffectual'. As for Polyeucte, he is more like the conventional conception of a Cornelian hero, in so far as he loses his life rather than betray his faith, despite the entreaties of his wife. But there are some reservations to be made. Polyeucte is a saint and a martyr, i.e. one in whom, by definition, worldly affections and considerations of personal safety come second to his religion. Any martyr would resemble Polyeucte; there is nothing peculiar to Corneille in such a portrait. Moreover, his actions are the result of grace rather than of his own free will. Indeed, he wants to postpone his baptism, and it is only after he has been baptized that he is filled with fervour and zeal, with the desire to testify publicly to his new religion. Further, Polyeucte is certainly not rational, any more than Horace. The most one can say is that he is torn between two passions, love for his wife and religious zeal, and that the latter triumphs over the former.

The first play in which characters who might be called 'Cornelian' appear is *Pompée,* where the magnanimity of Cléopâtre, Cornélie and César leads them to behave in unexpected ways. Cléopâtre, who loves César, urges her brother Ptolomée to fight for Pompée; César allows Cornélie, Pompée's widow to go free, even though she is resolved to overthrow him; and Cornélie, whose chief desire is to avenge her husband's death, nevertheless gives César warning of a plot against his life.

'Cornelian' characters do in fact occur in Corneille, but chiefly in the plays from *Pompée* to *Pertharite* or *Oedipe.* In *Héraclius,* Martian and Héraclius vie in magnanimity, and the strong-minded Pulchérie, on learning that her lover is really her brother, is undismayed:

> Ce grand coup m'a surprise et ne m'a point
> troublée;
> Mon âme l'a reçu sans en être accablée;
> Et comme tous mes feux n'avaient rien que de
> saint,
> L'honneur les alluma, le devoir les éteint.
>
> (III, 1)

Pulchérie certainly verges on the inhuman: she is less concerned with her brother's fate than that he should not demean himself:

> Moi, pleurer! moi, gémir, tyran! J'aurais pleuré
> Si quelques lâchetés l'avaient déshonoré,
> S'il n'eût pas emporté sa gloire toute entière,
> Si quelque infâme espoir qu'on lui dût
> pardonner
> Eût mérité la mort que tu lui vas donner.
>
> (III, 2)

She refuses to marry the son of the tyrant Phocas, because, if she did, filial duty would prevent her from hating him:

> Mais durant ces moments unie à sa famille,
> Il deviendra mon père, et je serai sa fille:
> Je lui devrai respect, amour, fidélité;
> Ma haine n'aura plus d'impétuosité;

> Et tous mes vœux pour vous seront mols et
> timides,
> Quand mes vœux contre lui seront des
> parricides.
>
> (III, 1)

In subsequent plays, Don Sanche, Nicomède and Laodice, Grimoald and Rodelinde, Dircé, Thésée and Oedipe show no sign of weakness. Rodelinde (in *Pertharite*) carries self-abnegation to the point of agreeing to marry Grimoald only if he puts her son to death. Dircé is prepared to die to save Thebes:

> Je meurs l'esprit content, l'honneur m'en fait la
> loi. . . .
>
> (III, 1)

Her father's blood, she says,

>   ne peut trouver qu'on soit digne du jour,
> Quand aux soins de sa gloire on préfère l'amour.
>
> (III, 2)

As for Oedipe, after the discovery that he has killed his father and married his mother, he says:

> Ce revers serait dur pour quelque âme commune;
> Mais je me fis toujours maître de ma fortune.
>
> (V, 2)

And we are told:

> Parmi de tels malheurs que sa constance est rare!
> Il ne s'emporte point contre un sort si barbare;
> La surprenante horreur de cet accablement
> Ne coûte à sa grande âme aucun égarement;
> Et sa haute vertu, toujours inébranlable,
> Le soutient au-dessus de tout ce qui l'accable.
>
> (V, 7)

Even in this middle period, however, *Rodogune, Théodore,* and *Andromède* are exceptions. In *Rodogune,* the ambitious, crafty, and unscrupulous Cléopâtre, comparable with Lady Macbeth, might as well be called 'Shakespearean' as 'Cornelian'; and her two sons—a delicate portrayal of brotherly affection—alike, yet admirably differentiated, are certainly not 'Cornelian'. They are unanimous in putting love before ambition, in preferring Rodogune to the throne and their own unity to either. In *Théodore,* apart from the generosity with which Placide decides to succour his rival, Didyme, who has rescued Théodore from ignominy, and the contest between Didyme and Théodore in Act V, each demanding to be martyred in place of the other, there is little that is 'Cornelian'. The same is true of *Andromède,* in which the heroine fears death:

>   que la grandeur de courage
> Devient d'un difficile usage
> Lorsqu'on touche au dernier moment!
>   . . . . .
> Je pâme au moindre vent, je meurs au moindre

bruit. . . .

(III, 1)

Moreover, there are reservations to be made even about the other plays. Laodice and Nicomède show no sign of weakness; but equally there is no sign either of any conflict between love and duty; at no time have they to choose between each other and their *gloire*. Grimoald, similarly, is virtuous and generous, but again there is no question of any conflict.

Despite a common misconception, the plays of the last period contain few 'Cornelian' heroes and heroines, though there are one or two, or at least one or two who show some 'Cornelian' traits—such as Pompée, who, in *Sertorius,* destroys the letter containing the names of the Romans in correspondence with his enemy (a historical detail), or Viriate in the same play:

> Je sais ce que je suis, et le serai toujours,
> N'eussé-je que le ciel et moi pour mon secours.

(V, 3)

In fact, in this last period, the internal conflict, which had been relatively rare in the middle period, becomes common again and is resolved with more and more difficulty, and more and more frequently by the triumph of passion over duty.

All, then, is not false in the conventional conception of the Cornelian hero. Such characters are found in Corneille—magnanimous, strong-minded creatures, who put their duty or their *gloire* before their personal inclinations. But such characters are not found by any means in all the plays: they are found chiefly, almost exclusively, in the plays of the middle period. Moreover, even they do not entirely coincide with the conventional image of Corneille's heroes. There is in them all a strong element of emotion or passion—they are usually motivated, not by reason or duty, but by the passion for *gloire,* the desire for vengeance (Pulchérie in *Héraclius*), ambition, amour-propre, or the dislike of being subservient to another, of being second (Nicomède and Attale, Dircé who resents Oedipe's having usurped her throne and wants another, Sertorius, Pompée, Viriate, etc.). Nor is it true to describe these characters as 'les hommes comme ils devraient être'. Not only are they often far from ideal, but they are either men and women like the contemporaries of Corneille, or— if they outdo the men and women of Corneille's day— they show the influence of Corneille's conception of the character of Romans and Kings. For Corneille, like his contemporaries, regarded magnanimity as a Roman trait, and considered that Kings and Queens, more than their subjects, are obliged to master their inclinations.

Corneille's views on the obligations of persons of royal blood are constantly expressed from *Pompée* onwards:

> Plus la haute naissance approche des couronnes,
> Plus cette grandeur même asservit nos personnes;
> Nous n'avons point de cœur pouraimer ni haïr:

Toutes nos passions ne savent qu'obéir.

(*Rodogune,* III, 3)

Je sais ce que je suis, et ce que je me dois.
(Doña Elvire in *Don Sanche,* I, 1)

Madame, je suis reine, et dois régner sur moi.
(Doña Isabelle in *Don Sanche,* I, 2)

> Comptable de moi-même au nom de souveraine,
> Et sujette à jamais du trône où je me voi,
> Je puis tout pour tout autre et ne puis rien pour moi.
>
> . . . . .
> . . . Tu verras avec combien d'adresse
> Ma gloire de mon âme est toujours maîtresse.
(Doña Isabelle in *Don Sanche,* II, 1)

> Et si je n'étais pas, Seigneur, ce que je suis,
> J'en prendrais quelque droit de finir mes ennuis;
> Mais l'esclavage fier d'une haute naissance,
> Où toute autre peut tout, me tient dans l'impuissance;
> Et victime d'Etat, je dois sans reculer
> Attendre aveuglément qu'on me daigne immoler.
(Ildione in *Attila,* II, 6)

This is not to say that all these characters fulfil their obligations easily. Many, in fact, do not act in accordance with their principles, and there are plenty of undutiful princesses and weak or unvirtuous Kings in Corneille— Ptolomée, Prusias, and Eurydice and Orode (in *Suréna*), in whom mistrust and *raison d'état* overcome gratitude.

The identification of Corneille's heroes with the *généreux* of Descartes is not easy. The *généreux* controls his passions by means of the will using reason as its instrument; he is detached, aiming only at what it is in his power to achieve without the aid of external circumstances—such things as virtue, freedom, detachment. He is humble and esteems himself for nothing but self-mastery and will-power; he is not interested in *gloire* or ambition. . . .

The characters of Corneille are not usually subject to fear, but that is about the only respect in which they resemble the *généreux*. They are passionate, ambitious, egoistical, proud, amorous, subject to hatred, anger and jealousy; they are irrational, though they are good reasoners; above all, they are far from the philosophical detachment of the *généreux*.

They differ from the Cartesian character in another way: they are not usually rational in their love affairs. The conception of love as rational, as based on some positive quality (though it may only be good looks) in the loved one, is found in Descartes.

> Lorsqu'on remarque quelque chose en une [person of the opposite sex] qui agrée davantage que ce qu'on remarque au même temps dans les autres, cela détermine l'âme à sentir pour celle-là seule toute l'inclination que la nature lui donne à rechercher le

bien qu'elle lui représente comme le plus grand qu'on
puisse posséder . . .

The idea that love is based on 'mérite' does occur in
Corneille, too—though it is important to realize that
'mérite' often means personal attractions, not moral worth:

>Voyez-la donc, Seigneur, voyez tout son mérite. . . .
>
>>(*Sophonisbe,* IV, 5)

This conception of love is first expressed in *La Galerie
du Palais:*

>Nous sommes hors du temps de cette vieille
> erreur
>Qui faisait de l'amour une aveugle fureur,
>Et l'ayant aveuglé, lui donnait pour conduite
>Le mouvement d'une âme et surprise et séduite.
>Ceux qui l'ont peint sans yeux ne le
> connaissaient pas;
>C'est par les yeux qu'il entre et nous dit vos
> appas:
>Lors notre esprit en juge; et suivant le mérite,
>Il fait croître une ardeur que cette vue excite.
>
>>(III, 6)

But the speaker here is not sincere: he is paying court to
a lady whom he does not love in order to arouse his
mistress's jealousy. There are, however, examples in the
tragedies of love based on rational grounds. Chimène and
the Infante in *Le Cid* love Rodrigue because he is worthy
of their love, and Pauline in *Polyeucte* fell in love with
Sévère for his good qualities:

>Je l'aimai, Stratonice: il le méritait bien. . . .
>
>>(I, 3)

Carlos loves Doña Isabelle for her beauty:

>Lorsque je vois en vous les célestes accords
>Des grâces de l'esprit et des beautés du corps,
>Je puis, de tant d'attraits l'âme toute ravie,
>Sur l'heur de votre époux jeter un œil d'envie. . . .
>
>>(*Don Sanche,* II, 2)

Laodice loves Nicomède because he is worthy of her:

>Vous devez le connaître; et puisqu'il a ma foi,
>Vous devez présumer qu'il est digne de moi.
>Je le désavouerais s'il n'était magnanime,
>S'il manquait à remplir l'effort de mon estime,
>S'il ne faisait paraître un cœur toujours égal.
>
>>(*Nicomède,* V, 9)

Viriate's love for Sertorius (if it can be called love) is
rational:

>Ce ne sont pas les sens que mon amour consulte:
>Il hait des passions l'impétueux tumulte;
>Et son feu, que j'attache aux soins de ma
> grandeur,
>Dédaigne tout mélange avec leur folle ardeur.

>J'aime en Sertorius ce grand art de la guerre
>Qui soutient un banni contre toute la terre;
>J'aime en lui ces cheveux tous couverts de
> lauriers,
>Ce front qui fait trembler les plus braves
> guerriers,
>Ce bras qui semble avoir la victoire en partage.
>L'amour de la vertu n'a jamais d'yeux pour
> l'âge:
>Le mérite a toujours des charmes éclatants;
>Et quiconque peut tout est aimable en tout
> temps.
>
>>(*Sertorius,* II, 1)

But a different conception of love is much more common in Corneille—that of love as something quite irrational and instinctive. Isabelle, in *L'Illusion comique,*
rejects the suitor favoured by her father on these
grounds:

>Je sais qu'il est parfait,
>Et que je réponds mal à l'honneur qu'il me fait;
>Mais si votre bonté me permet en ma cause,
>Pour me justifier, de dire quelque chose,
>Par un secret instinct, que je ne puis nommer,
>J'en fais beaucoup d'état, et ne le puis aimer.
>Souvent je ne sais quoi que le ciel nous inspire
>Soulève tout le cœur contre ce qu'on désire,
>Et ne nous laisse pas en état d'obéir,
>Quand on choisit pour nous ce qu'il nous fait
> haïr.
>Il attache ici-bas avec des sympathies
>Les âmes que son ordre a là-haut assorties:
>On n'en saurait unir sans ses avis secrets;
>Et cette chaîne manque où manquent ses décrets.
>Aller contre les lois de cette providence,
>C'est le prendre à partie, et blâmer sa prudence,
>L'attaquer en rebelle, et s'exposer aux coups
>Des plus âpres malheurs qui suivent son
> courroux.
>
>>(III, 3)

Créuse, in *Médée,* rejects Ægée for similar reasons:

>Souvent je ne sais quoi qu'on ne peut exprimer
>Nous surprend, nous emporte, et nous force
> d'aimer;
>Et souvent, sans raison, les objects de nos
> flammes
>Frappent nos yeux ensemble et saisissent nos
> âmes.
>
>. . . . .
>
>Je vous estimai plus, et l'aimai davantage.
>
>>(II, 5)

In this last line, Créuse makes a sharp distinction between
love and esteem: one may love without esteem and esteem without love. Mélisse, in *La Suite du Menteur,* sees
love as the result of a heaven-created sympathy; for her,
love precedes esteem:

Quand les ordres du ciel nous ont faits l'un pour
　l'autre,
Lyse, c'est un accord bientôt fait que le nôtre:
Sa main entre les cœurs, par un secret pouvoir,
Sème l'intelligence avant que de se voir;
Il prépare si bien l'amant et la maîtresse,
Que leur âme au seul nom s'émeut et s'intéresse.
On s'estime, on se cherche, on s'aime en un
　moment:
Tout ce qu'on s'entre-dit persuade aisément;
Et sans s'inquiéter d'aucunes peurs frivoles,
La foi semble courir au-devant des paroles:
La langue en peu de mots en explique beaucoup;
Les yeux, plus éloquents, font tout voir tout
　d'un coup;
Et de quoi qu'à l'envi tous les deux nous
　instruisent,
Le cœur en entend plus que tous les deux n'en
　disent.

Rodogune, like Créuse, separates love and esteem: of two young princes, twin brothers, she loves one and not the other:

Comme ils ont même sang avec pareil mérite,
Un avantage égal pour eux me sollicite;
Mais il est malaisé, dans cette égalité,
Qu'un esprit combattu ne penche d'un côté.
Il est des nœuds secrets, il est des sympathies
Dont par le doux rapport les âmes assorties
S'attachent l'une à l'autre et se laissent piquer
Par ces je ne sais quoi qu'on ne peut expliquer.
C'est par là que l'un d'eux obtient la préférence:
Je crois voir l'autre encore avec indifférence;
Mais cette indifférence est une aversion
Lorsque je la compare avec ma passion.
Etrange effet d'amour! Incroyable chimère!
Je voudrais être à lui si je n'aimais son frère;
Et le plus grand des maux toutefois que je
　crains,
C'est que mon triste sort me livre entre ses
　mains.

(I, 5)

Placide complains of

la tyrannie ensemble et le caprice
Du démon aveuglé qui sans discrétion
Verse l'antipathie et l'inclination.

(*Théodore*, I, 1)

Andromède, wondering why she should so suddenly transfer her affections from Phinée to her rescuer, Persée, is told that the gods are responsible: it is they who control our sympathies and antipathies (IV, 2). Lysander in *Agésilas* is another who sees love as irrational, an 'aveugle sympathie' independent of beauty and 'vrai mérite' (II, 2). So are Spitridate in the same play (V, 3) and Domitian in *Tite et Bérénice* (II, 2).

Persée in *Andromède* sees love as irrational in another

way: though he has no hope of marrying Andromède, he cannot stop loving her; a lover cannot think of the future:

Vouloir que la raison règne sur un amant,
C'est être plus que lui dedans l'aveuglement.
Un cœur digne d'aimer court à l'objet aimable,
Sans penser au succès dont sa flamme est
　capable;
Il s'abandonne entier, et n'examine rien;
Aimer est tout son but, aimer est tout son bien;
Il n'est ni difficulté ni péril qui l'étonne.

(I, 4)

Camille, in *Othon,* complains that love makes one believe what one wants to believe:

Hélas! que cet amour croit tôt ce qu'il souhaite!
En vain la raison parle, en vain elle inquiète,
En vain la défiance ose ce qu'elle peut,
Il veut croire, et ne croit que parce qu'il le veut.
Pour Plautine ou pour moi je vois du stratagème,
Et m'obstine avec joie à m'aveugler moi-même.

(III, 1)

Albin, in *Tite et Bérénice,* expatiates on the essential selfishness of love:

L'amour-propre est la source en nous de tous les
　autres:
C'en est le sentiment qui forme tous les nôtres;
Lui seul allume, éteint, ou change nos désirs:
Les objets de nos vœux le sont de nos plaisirs.
Vous-même, qui brûlez d'une ardeur si fidèle,
Aimez-vous Domitie, ou vos plaisirs en elle?
Et quand vous aspirez à des liens si doux,
Est-ce pour l'amour d'elle, ou pour l'amour de
　vous?

(I, 3)

This passage no doubt owes something to the *Maximes* of La Rochefoucauld, but the essential idea is contained already in *L'Illusion comique:*

Ne me reproche plus ta fuite ni ta flamme:
Que ne fait point l'amour quand il possède une
　âme?
Son pouvoir à ma vue attachait tes plaisirs,
Et tu me suivais moins que tes propres désirs.

(V, 3)

Finally, in *La Toison d'Or,* written several years before Racine's *Andromaque,* there is a conception of love very close to that usually associated with Racine. Love in this play is an irrational, overriding passion, stronger than will or reason:

Je veux ne t'aimer plus, et n'en ai pas la force,

(II, 2)

says Médée. As in Racine, love changes easily into its opposite, hatred:

Tout violent qu'il est, l'amour l'a fait naître;
Il va jusqu'à la haine, et toutefois, hélas!
Je te haïrais peu, si je ne t'aimais pas.

(II, 2)

The action of the play is admirably summarized in a speech of Aæte, Médée's father, to her brother, Absyrte:

Ah! que tu connais mal jusqu'à quelle manie
D'un amour déréglé passe la tyrannie!
Il n'est rang, ni pays, ni père, ni pudeur,
Qu'épargne de ses feux l'impérieuse ardeur.
Jason plut à Médée, et peut encore lui plaire;
Peut-être es-tu toi-même ennemi de ton père
Et consens que ta sœur, par ce présent fatal,
S'assure d'un amant qui serait ton rival.
Tout mon sang révolté trahit mon espérance:
Je trouve ma ruine où fut mon assurance;
Le destin ne me perd que par l'ordre des miens,
Et mon trône est brisé par ses propres soutiens.

(V, 2)

If it seems rash to assert—as Lanson does, for example—that Corneille conceives of love as a rational preference based on merit, it is no less rash to say—as Lemaitre does—that *Le Cid* is the only play in which love gets the better of duty. In fact, it is remarkable how often in Corneille love triumphs over honour, ambition, duty, prudence, desire for revenge, and reason. This is already true of Alidor in *La Place Royale*. It is true, not only of Chimène and the Infante, of Camille and Emilie, of Médée in *La Toison,* but of most of the characters in the later plays.

Gloire is no more the mainspring of Corneille's characters than reason and will. In this respect, Corneille reflects the contradictory tendencies of his age—his characters often talk of *gloire,* but they mean very different things by it, they do not always live up to their ideal, and many are not animated by a desire for *gloire* at all.

There are characters who are concerned above all with *gloire.* Cléopâtre, in *Pompée,* says of princes:

Leur générosité soumet tout à leur gloire,

(II, 1)

—a remark which is certainly true of herself. For her, *gloire* consists of marrying César and becoming mistress of the world, but it must be achieved by honourable means; and, though she loves César, she wants her brother to treat Pompée magnanimously. César is a kindred spirit, though it is interesting to see that the point is twice made that for him *gloire* and self-interest point the same way. On having Pompée's head presented to him, we are told:

par un mouvement commun à la nature,
Quelque maligne joie en son cœur s'élevait,
Dont sa gloire indignée à peine le sauvait.

(III, 1)

And Cornélie points out that, in avenging Pompée, he is

also serving his own interests—ensuring his own safety ('le Roi le veut perdre, et son rival est mort'), and defending Cléopâtre too. Laodice in *Nicomède,* similarly, knows no conflict between love and another passion. *Gloire* and love alike keep her faithful to Nicomède: Attale, his rival, is a subject, has not distinguished himself, and has been educated in Rome, so that to prefer him to Nicomède would be a 'frénésie'. The best example of a character for whom *gloire* is all-important is Horace, who puts *gloire* before *devoir,* in contrast to Curiace, who is primarily concerned with *devoir.*

contre qui que ce soit que mon pays m'emploie,
J'accepte aveuglément cette gloire avec joie,

says Horace; whereas Curiace's attitude is different:

Encor qu'à mon devoir je coure sans terreur,
Mon cœur s'effarouche, et j'en frémis d'horreur.
. . .

(II, 3)

But Horace, as we have tried to show above, is in no sense an ideal character, and Sabine finds fault with him precisely because he is over-preoccupied with *gloire* to the exclusion of more human feelings:

Prenons part en public aux victoires publiques;
Pleurons dans la maison nos malheurs
   domestiques,
Et ne regardons point des biens communs à tous,
Quand nous voyons des maux qui ne sont que
   pour nous.
Pourquoi veux-tu, cruel, agir d'une autre sorte?
Laisse en entrant ici tes lauriers à la porte;
Mêle tes pleurs aux miens.

(IV, 7)

To these characters, there are few others to add—Don Alvar and Don Sanche in *Don Sanche,* and Rodelinde in *Pertharite,* are the chief.

It is easier to find examples of characters who act in the interests of their *gloire,* but only after a struggle—though often *gloire* is not the only motive. Rodrigue, in *Le Cid,* fights and kills the father of Chimène, but there is a struggle within him, and the conflict is resolved only by the realization that, whether he avenges his father or not, he is bound to lose Chimène. Emilie is similarly torn between duty and *gloire,* on the one hand, and love for Cinna on the other. With her, one might associate Sévère, in *Polyeucte,* in whom there is no particular struggle, but whose motives are mixed. In deciding to try to save Polyeucte, he says:

Et contentons ainsi, d'une seule action,
Et Pauline, et ma gloire, et ma compassion.

For him, *gloire* is being worthy of Pauline:

La gloire de montrer à cette âme si belle

Que Sévère l'égale, et qu'il est digne d'elle. . . .

(IV, 6)

He is also motivated by honour—'l'honneur m'oblige'.

Doña Isabelle in **Don Sanche** belongs to this group. Though *gloire* forbids her to marry except for *raison d'état,* she is deeply in love with Carlos, and her love influences her behaviour. She is so much preoccupied with Carlos that she gives him the responsibility of choosing a husband for her, and that her other suitors, not unreasonably, complain at one point: 'Toujours Carlos.' *Gloire* does not win easily in Doña Isabelle. Dircé, in *Oedipe,* despite the entreaties of her lover, Thésée, and her own regrets, is determined to die in obedience to the oracle, both to save her people and to achieve *gloire.* One is unworthy to live, she says,

Quand aux soins de sa gloire on préfère l'amour.

(III, 2)

Nevertheless, she is regretful:

Mais j'aurais vécu plus contente,
Si j'avais pu vivre pour toi.

(III, 1)

Mandane, in *Agésilas,* though she loves someone else, is prepared reluctantly to marry Agésilas, partly because this is the means of saving her brother and herself, but partly out of *gloire.* Domitie, in *Tite et Bérénice,* is similarly torn between love for Domitian and the *gloire* of being Empress, as Pulchérie is between love for Léon and the *gloire* of making a responsible choice of a husband.

Other characters, after a struggle, do not follow their *gloire.* Chimène, for example, admits:

Mon unique souhait est de ne rien pouvoir.

(III, 4)

For Othon, *gloire* means that he must remain faithful to Plautine and Plautine to him; but circumstances are too strong, and he agrees to pay court to Camille, as Plautine consents to marry Martian. In *Attila,* Honorie says firmly that she will not marry Valamir, who is merely a puppet-king:

. . . rien ne m'est sensible à l'égal de ma gloire.

(II, 2)

But—like Doña Isabelle—she is jealous of the happiness of Ildione and Ardaric, and, what is more, she later offers the hand of Flavie to Octar if he will bring about her marriage with Valamir—a change of heart which Flavie points out. Tite is prepared to abdicate in order to marry Bérénice:

Ma gloire la plus haute est celle d'être à vous.

(III, 5)

In other words, love matters more to him than *gloire.*

Cinna talks much of *gloire,* but his conception of it changes in the course of the play. In Act I, scene 3, he identifies *gloire* with the success of his conspiracy; two acts later, he tells Emilie that, after killing Auguste, he means to kill himself:

Et par cette action dans l'autre confondue,
Recouvrera ma gloire aussitôt que perdue.

(III, 4)

The murder of Auguste, from being *gloire,* has come to be its antithesis. One might class Félix with Cinna. For him, in Act III, scene 5, *gloire* means *not* sacrificing Polyeucte, whom he is tempted to put to death out of self-interest. In Act V, scene 4, *gloire* means shedding Polyeucte's blood and emulating the ancient Roman heroes, Brutus or Manlius. In fact, however, *gloire* is not his main motive. His decision to execute Polyeucte is due to self-interest, fear of Sévère, determination to carry out his *devoir* (his orders, the obligations of his official position), and revulsion from Polyeucte's new religion:

sans l'horreur de ses derniers blasphèmes,
Qui m'ont rempli soudain de *colère et d'effroi,*
J'aurais eu de la peine à *triompher de moi.*

(V, 4)

His self-domination results from wrath and fear: there is almost a burlesque contrast here between his words and

---

Characterization of Corneille and Racine compared:

Racine's world is full of men and women who give up all for love: Phèdre, Roxane, Pyrrhus, Hermione. No doubt this is a reason for his greater popularity. But how many such heroines or heroes do we meet in daily twentieth-century life? Corneille shows us his lovers as balancing the rewards of the world against the rewards of passion and the nobility of power against the nobility of love. The Carthaginian heroine of **Sophonisbe,** who repudiates one husband when he becomes a prisoner of war, marries another to carry on the battle, and finally swallows poison to avoid being led in triumph through Rome, can still boast that the greatest pleasure of her life has been in stealing a lover from a rival. The noble Pompée, in **Sertorius,** demands that his wife submit to the humiliation of divorce so that he may marry the daughter of the dictator, Sulla, fully intending to repudiate the latter after Sulla's anticipated demise. And the Eastern empress in **Pulcherie** solves her problem of choosing an imperial consort who will not dominate her politically by selecting a general who has loved her for a decade on condition that the marriage be not consummated. What made Corneille's characters grotesque to Voltaire is precisely what makes them real today; they are always trying to have their cake and eat it. They want the power *and* the glory, and in the long run this is not possible. They are greedy, but they are true.

Louis Kronenberger, in Life, Law and Letters:
Essays and Sketches, *Houghton Mifflin Company,*
1979.

their meaning.

Then there are characters for whom *gloire* is entirely divorced from honour or morals. The Infante, in *Le Cid,* begins by combating her love for Rodrigue in the interests of her *gloire* (i.e. because he is her inferior in station); but when later she decides that his *gloire* is the equivalent of her rank, she says that she will stop at nothing to prevent the marriage of Rodrigue with Chimène:

> Pour en rompre l'effet, j'ai trop d'inventions.
> L'amour, ce doux auteur de mes cruels
>   supplices,
> Aux esprits des amants apprend trop d'artifices.
>
> (V, 3)

For Cléopâtre in *Rodogune* and Aspar in *Pulchérie, gloire* is merely the throne. When Jason, in *La Toison,* says 'Il y va de ma gloire' (III, 3), he means that for him *gloire* is the achievement of the golden fleece, and that he can only win it by paying his addresses to Médée, whom he does not love. For Vinius in *Othon, gloire* means power; and when he says that he is prepared to die for his *gloire,* he means that he will commit suicide in order to avoid serving an emperor who is hostile to him.

Finally, there is a very large group of characters who do not seem to be motivated by the desire for *gloire*—i.e. there is nothing in the play to suggest that this is the motive for their actions. In *Horace,* Sabine and Curiace talk of *devoir,* not *gloire,* and Camille cares for nothing but love. There is nothing in *Cinna* to suggest a desire for *gloire* as the motive for Auguste's clemency. Polyeucte is animated by religious fervour, by grace, by the desire for permanent happiness; and, when he uses the word *gloire,* he uses it—the context makes it clear—in the sense of 'heaven', a perfectly normal sense of the word in the seventeenth century. Pauline uses the word *devoir* at least as much as the word *gloire,* and a convincing case has been made out for regarding her as a heroine of duty, the embodiment of the doctrines of the neostoical philosophers rather than of the *éthique de la gloire.* What matters for her, whether she calls it *gloire* or *devoir,* is obedience to her father, and obedience and fidelity to her husband:

> Je l'aimai par devoir: ce devoir dure encore.
>
> (III, 2)

For Séleucus and Antiochus in *Rodogune*—one of the plays in which the word *gloire* occurs least—love and their own unity are more important than anything else. It is true that Antiochus does once use the word, equating it with renunciation of the throne. Ptolomée and his advisers in *Pompée* care nothing for *gloire:* Ptolomée does say (III, 2) that he has 'immolé sa gloire' to César, but he seems at no time to have been deterred by the prospect of losing his *gloire.*

Gloire has little place in *Théodore.* Marcelle is animated by maternal love and the desire for vengeance. Valens's facile optimism leads him to a policy of masterly inactivity. At one point he does, it is true, claim that this will increase his *gloire*—

> cette illusion de ma sévérité
> Augmentera ma gloire et mon autorité,
>
> (V, 7)

—but it is difficult to take this very seriously. Didyme rescues Théodore out of Christian zeal. Théodore herself says that martyrdom will ensure her *gloire,* and protests that the particular martyrdom chosen will endanger her *gloire,* and Placide is eager to save Théodore's *gloire,* which—since he loves her—is also his own; but it is hard to see *gloire* as the fundamental principle of either—Théodore is primarily a Christian, and Placide a lover.

The word *gloire* is not much used in *Héraclius.* Phocas, the tyrant, is not interested in *gloire,* and Héraclius wants the throne only in order to give it to Eudoxe. Pulchérie says that marriage with Phocas would be fatal to her *gloire;* but, whenever she shows fortitude or does anything more positive, she talks more of her *devoir.* She is chiefly actuated by hatred of the tyrant, which she carries to extremes: she is prepared to acknowledge a false claimant, and, though she will not marry Martian to save her brother, she professes her willingness to marry anyone who will kill Phocas. Léontine, though she is gratified by the *gloire* of having sacrificed her own son to save her Emperor's, is chiefly animated by the desire for vengeance. It is, perhaps, significant that the only character in the play who cares about *gloire* is Martian: he is eager to have the *gloire* of dying as Héraclius (who, of course, he is not).

Gloire is unimportant in subsequent plays. In *Nicomède,* uprightness, independence, magnanimity, *générosité* and *vertu* are contrasted with Machiavellian principles. We cannot take Arsinoé very seriously when she claims that her *gloire* is 'souillée' by the false accusations of two informers, since they are in her pay, and the whole thing is a ruse. In *Pertharite,* Grimoald only once uses *gloire* so as to suggest that he cares for it: love and virtue are his pre-eminent characteristics. Pertharite returns from his place of concealment, not to win *gloire,* but to have the pleasure of seeing his wife. Eduige, after wanting the *gloire* of marrying a king, decides that in the last resort she prefers virtue to rank, and *gloire* has no significance for the scheming, selfish Garibalde. It is true that the play ends with the line:

> . . . des hautes vertus la gloire est le seul prix,

but (except in Rodelinde), it is virtue that is stressed in the play. In *Attila,* when Ardaric talks of dying to preserve his *gloire,* Ildione is unimpressed:

> Cette immortalité qui triomphe en idée
> Veut être, pour charmer, de plus loin regardée;
> Et quand à notre amour ce triomphe est fatal,
> La gloire qui le suit nous en console mal.
>
> (IV, 6)

Léon in **Pulchérie** is moved only by love of the Empress, not by ambition or *gloire,* and Martian by love, duty and virtue. In **Suréna,** Eurydice, Orode and Suréna care little for *gloire.* Eurydice tries to conceal her feelings—

> Mon intrépidité n'est qu'un effort de gloire,
> Que, tout fier qu'il paraît, mon cœur n'en veut
> 　　pas croire,
>
> 　　　　　　　　　　　　(IV, 2)

—but her behaviour is that of one for whom love is everything. *Gloire* has little part in **Andromède, Oedipe, Sophonisbe, Sertorius, Othon** and **Tite et Bérénice.**

The word *gloire* occurs frequently in Corneille's plays—some thirty times in each play (much less in **Rodogune** and **Héraclius**)—but too much must not be made of this. For one thing, not all the uses of the word are significant—it occurs quite often in the phrase 'faire gloire de', for example, which is an ordinary expression of the period for 'to be proud of', and sometimes, like the word 'honneur', it merely means 'glory' in the sense in which the word might be used to-day. Moreover, it is used in a variety of contexts and with a variety of meanings. It may mean military glory. Sometimes it is equated with honour and duty and virtue. For Pulchérie in **Héraclius** it means fortitude. For Emilie in **Cinna** it includes avenging her father and freeing Rome from a tyrant, but does not exclude crime:

> Pour qui venge son père il n'est point de
> 　　forfaits. . . .
>
> 　　　　　　　　　　　　(I, 2)

When Sophonisbe says that she 'prend pour seul objet ma gloire à satisfaire,' she means that *gloire* requires her to separate her fortunes from those of her vanquished husband. Polyeucte uses the word in the sense of Heaven. For Antiochus in **Rodogune** it means giving up the throne. Théodore uses the word to mean martyrdom and chastity. Elsewhere it means fidelity in love. It may be used without any idea of duty or honour. For many, such as Aspar, it means gaining a throne, or marrying a king. For Palmis in **Suréna** it means keeping one's lovers. Camille uses it in protest:

> C'est gloire de passer pour un cœur abattu,
> Quand la brutalité fait la haute vertu.
>
> 　　　　　　　　　　**(Horace,** IV, 4)

The variety of senses is admirably illustrated by a passage in **Agésilas.** Aglatide says that she wants the *gloire* of marrying a king, but Elpinice, with sisterly candour, points out that that is the only kind of *gloire* she wants, that the *gloire* of marrying a suitor of lesser rank in obedience to her father's wishes does not appeal to her:

> La gloire d'obéir à votre grand regret
> 　　Vous faisait pester en secret. . . .
>
> 　　　　　　　　　　　　(II, 6)

One wonders whether a word which can be used in so many senses can be a useful guide to the motivation of Corneille's characters. It can describe any aim or ambition, and is often very hard to distinguish from self-interest.

Even when characters are actuated by a desire for *gloire* without self-interest, they often have other motives as well. When they make sacrifices or renunciations, *gloire* is seldom, if ever, the motive. It is not for *gloire* that the Infante decides to let Chimène marry Rodrigue:

> Je me vaincrai pourtant, non de peur d'aucun
> 　　blâme,
> Mais pour ne troubler pas une si belle flamme. . . .
>
> 　　　　　　　　　　　　(V, 3)

The supreme example of a sacrifice in Corneille is that of Rodelinde in **Pertharite,** and Rodelinde is one of the characters who talks most of her *gloire;* but when she proposes that Grimoald should kill her child, the word disappears from her vocabulary, and she justifies her proposition on severely practical grounds. Since the usurper is certain to put her son to death sooner or later, it is better that he should do it now, when he will show himself in his true colours at the outset, and when his action may well be the signal for rebellion. Her attitude is not very human, but at least *gloire* has nothing to do with it. Agésilas, after a struggle, decides to marry Aglatide, though he prefers Mandane. The desire for *gloire* is not absent from his decision, but it is due mainly to more concrete motives. He has just learnt that Mandane loves another; he knows, and has just been reminded, that Mandane is not acceptable to Sparta; and he is aware that to marry Aglatide and contract an alliance with Lysander is the best means of consolidating his authority. Mandane, though she loves someone else, is prepared, reluctantly, to marry Agésilas, partly out of a desire for *gloire,* but also because this is the only means of saving her brother and herself. Bérénice leaves Tite because she has solid grounds for fearing that his safety would be endangered by marriage with her. Pulchérie renounces Léon, because marriage with him would endanger the Empire. If she marries Léon, Martian, the mainstay of her Empire, will go into retirement, and she is afraid both of weakening her Empire and of giving cause for revolts. Hence her determination to marry Léon only at the command of the Senate.

In short, although the word *gloire* is often on the lips of Corneille's characters, it covers a multitude of senses; and Corneille, in depicting the variety of motives which influence men and women, in depicting all kinds of men and women, from the noblest to the basest, reflects the complex reality both of his own age and of all others. His psychology is profoundly human.

There are, then, in Corneille, particularly in the plays of the middle period, magnanimous and intrepid characters, practically all of royal rank, who have a strong sense of their duty or the exigencies of their *gloire.* But they are much rarer than is generally supposed, much rarer than a cursory reading of the tragedies might lead one to suppose; for the characters of Corneille must not always be taken at their face value, and their words are not always plain statements of fact. Not only are they fond of using irony and double-entendre but they are often insincere. 'Il n'y a pas de théâtre,' says Rousset, 'dont les héros se mentent davantage les uns aux autres.'

Sometimes they delude themselves. Horace, on the point of murdering his sister, says:

> C'est trop, ma patience à la raison fait place. . . .
>
> (IV, 5)

'Raison' of course may not mean 'reason' in the modern sense; it can also mean 'tout ce qui est de devoir, de droit, d'équité, de justice' (*Dictionnaire de l' Académie*). But there is nothing rational or just in Horace's murder of his sister: he is deluding himself in his passion. Very frequently the actions of Corneille's characters belie their words and make their self-deception clear. Doña Isabelle in **Don Sanche,** for all her talk of her duties as a princess, cannot help betraying to Don Sanche her love for him. Médée, in **La Toison,** says:

> Je suis prête à l'aimer, si le Roi le commande;
> Mais jusque-là, ma sœur, je ne fais que souffrir
> Les soupirs et les vœux qu'il prend soin de m'offrir.
>
> (II, 2)

> Je ferai mon devoir, comme tu fais le tien.
> L'honneur doit m'être cher, si la gloire t'est chère:
> Je ne trahirai point mon pays et mon père. . . .
>
> (II, 2)

In fact, love is too strong for her:

> Silence, raison importune;
> Est-il temps de parler quand mon cœur s'est donné?
>
> (IV, 2)

She betrays her father, and helps Jason to win the fleece:

> Du pays et du sang l'amour rompt les liens,
> Et les dieux de Jason sont plus forts que les miens.
>
> (V, 5)

Nothing could be more apparently 'Cornelian' than some of Sophonisbe's lines:

> Je sais ce que je suis et ce que je dois faire,
> Et prends pour seul objet ma gloire à satisfaire.
>
> (III, 5)

> De tout votre destin vous êtes la maîtresse:
> Je la serai du mien. . . .
>
> (V, 4)

She tells Massinisse that she is only marrying him to avoid being taken in triumph to Rome (II, 4); she explains, too, that she is marrying him in order to gain an ally for her country:

> Il est à mon pays, puisqu'il est tout à moi.
> A ce nouvel hymen, c'est ce qui me convie,
> Non l'amour, non la peur de me voir asservie.
>
> (II, 5)

But she is motivated neither by the desire for *gloire* nor by patriotism, but by love and jealousy:

> c'est pour peu qu'on aime, une extrême douceur
> De pouvoir accorder sa gloire avec son cœur;
> Mais c'en est une ici bien autre, et sans égale,
> D'enlever, et sitôt, ce prince à ma rivale,
> De lui faire tomber le triomphe des mains,
> Et prendre sa conquête aux yeux de ses Romains.
>
> (II, 5)

> Ce n'était point l'amour . . .
> C'était la folle ardeur de braver ma rivale;
> J'en faisais mon suprême et mon unique bien.
> Tous les cœurs ont leur faible, et c'était là le mien.
> La présence d'Eryxe aujourd'hui m'a perdue;
> Je me serais sans elle un peu mieux défendue;
> J'aurais su mieux choisir et les temps et les lieux.
> Mais ce vainqueur vers elle eût pu tourner les yeux. . . .
>
> (V, 1)

Perpenna tells Sertorius:

> Oui, sur tous mes désirs je me rends absolu . . .
> J'en veux, à votre exemple, être aujourd'hui le maître.
>
> (IV, 3)

He is probably speaking ironically; if not, he is deluding himself, as the course of the rest of the play shows. Honorie, in **Attila,** says:

> . . . rien ne m'est sensible à l'égal de ma gloire,
>
> (II, 2)

but never lives up to her principles. Tite, in **Tite et Bérénice,** says, speaking of Domitie, 'Je veux l'aimer, je l'aime. . . . ' But he has no such power over his emotions:

> Je souffrais Domitie, et d'assidus efforts
> M'avaient malgré l'amour, fait maître du dehors.
> La contrainte semblait tourner en habitude;
> Le joug que je prenais m'en paraissait moins rude. . . .
>
> (III, 5)

He also says (II, 1) that, if Bérénice were to come to

Rome, he would still marry Domitie; but he is deceiving himself, as subsequent events show. Indeed, Tite admits that what he says and what he feels are two different things.

> Je sais qu'un empereur doit parler ce langage;
> Et quand il l'a fallu, j'en ai dit davantage;
> Mais de ces duretés que j'étale à regret,
> Chaque mot à mon cœur coûte un soupir secret;
> Et quand à la raison j'accorde un tel empire,
> Je le dis seulement parce qu'il le faut dire,
> Et qu'étant au-dessus de tous les potentats,
> Il me serait honteux de ne le dire pas.
>
>   (V, 1)

We have seen already how Corneille's characters often feign a calmness or indifference which they are far from feeling, like Eryxe. Similarly, they sometimes say one thing in public, for the sake of appearances, and another in private. Eryxe, for example, recognizes in public that 'l'hymen des rois doit être au-dessus de l'amour,' but in private she confesses that she does not share this view:

> Mais je suis au-dessus de cette erreur commune:
> J'aime en lui sa personne autant que sa fortune. . . .
>
>   (II, 1)

Pulchérie tells Léon that she loves him with a calm, rational love:

> Je vous aime, et non pas de cette folle ardeur
> Que les yeux éblouis font maîtresse du cœur,
> Non d'un amour conçu par les sens en tumulte,
> A qui l'âme applaudit, sans qu'elle se consulte,
> Et qui ne concevant que d'aveugles désirs,
> Languit dans les faveurs, et meurt dans les
>   plaisirs.
> Ma passion pour vous généreuse et solide
> A la vertu pour âme, et la raison pour guide,
> La gloire pour objet . . .
>
>   (I, 1)

But her real passion comes out in her confession to Irène:

> Léon seul est ma joie, il est mon seul désir. . . .
>   (III, 2)

Sometimes, too, Corneille's characters are simply untruthful or hypocritical. Chimène, when she faints on hearing that Rodrigue has been wounded, gives a false explanation of her emotion. Cinna denies his complicity in the plot against Auguste's life. Jason tells Aæte that his love for Médée is genuine:

> Et mon amour n'est pas un amour politique.
>   (III, 1)

But a few minutes later, he says precisely the opposite to Hypsipyle:

>   entendez-le, Madame,
> Ce soupir qui vers vous pousse toute mon âme;

> Et concevez par là jusqu'où vont mes malheurs,
> De soupirer pour vous, et de prétendre ailleurs.
>
>   (III, 3)

Othon tells Camille:

> C'est votre intérêt seul qui fait parler ma
>   flamme.
>
>   (III, 5)

In fact, he is only interested in obtaining the Empire. Suréna, when Orode asks him if he knows whom the princess Eurydice loves, does not answer truthfully.

In other words, to understand a character of Corneille—as of any other dramatist—it is not enough to consider isolated passages. What he says on one occasion, must be related with what he says elsewhere; what he says in public, must be taken in conjunction with what he says in private. Due allowance must always be made for irony, double-entendre and hypocrisy. Actions are a safer guide to character than words. Nor must the opinion of other characters in the play be overlooked—it is from Léonor that we learn that Chimène has chosen the weakest champion possible. We must beware, above all, of taking lines out of their context. One or two examples of the way in which this can distort the meaning have been encountered already. Here is one more. Sophonisbe's line,

> Sur moi, quoi qu'il en soit, je me rends absolue,
>
>   (V, 1)

is often quoted as an instance of the strength of will of Corneille's characters. Looked at in its context it is less convincing. In fact, it merely means that Sophonisbe is determined to commit suicide; and the rest of the speech shows that she is less resolute than that single line suggests. She continues:

> Contre sa dureté j'ai du secours tout prêt,
> Et ferai malgré lui moi seule mon arrêt.
>   Cependant de mon feu l'importune tendresse
> Aussi bien que ma gloire en mon sort
>   s'intéresse,
> Veut régner en mon cœur comme ma liberté;
> Et n'ose l'avouer de toute sa fierté.
> Quelle bassesse d'âme! ô ma gloire! ô Carthage!
> Faut-il qu'avec vous deux un homme la partage?
> Et l'amour de la vie en faveur d'un époux
> Doit-il être en ce cœur aussi puissant que vous?
>   (V, 1)

Although Corneille is almost always his best critic, what he says about his plays in his ***Discours*** and ***Examens*** is not *always* a safe guide to their interpretation. Of Sophonisbe, for example, he says this:

> Je lui prête un peu d'amour, mais elle règne sur lui, et ne daigne l'écouter qu'autant qu'il peut servir à ces passions dominantes qui règnent sur elle, et à qui elle sacrifie toutes les tendresses de son cœur, Massinisse, Syphax, sa propre vie. (*Avis au lecteur*)

As has been shown above, the text of the play contradicts him. Sophonisbe is less single-minded than this passage suggests; she herself admits that her downfall is the result of her jealousy and her desire to spite her rival.

Corneille's characters are not, then, remarkable for will-power or self-mastery. Moreover, if they often lack the will to carry out what they conceive to be their duties, will-power sometimes occurs divorced from any moral sense at all. Cléopâtre, in *Rodogune,* is the supreme example of a strong, immoral or amoral, character; but Médée (in *Médée*) and Arsinoé are her sisters, and Dircé in *Oedipe* is not strikingly dutiful.

Not only are Corneille's characters unable to master their passions, but they are far from ideal in other respects. Weak or vacillating or mediocre characters are not rare in Corneille. The King in *Le Cid;* Cinna, Auguste and Maxime in *Cinna;* Félix in *Polyeucte,* irresolute, pusillanimous, worldly and selfish; the vacillating Ptolomée of *Pompée* and his Machiavellian advisers; Antiochus and Séleucus in *Rodogune;* the indulgent but weak Valens in *Théodore,* who is dominated by his wife, allows her to act for him, and will not intervene even between her and his son; Prusias in *Nicomède,* timid, dominated by *his* wife, devoid of gratitude to his son, whom he mistrusts and who, he fears, is scheming to supplant him; Attale in the same play; the selfish Garibalde of *Pertharite,* who says:

> Je t'aime, mais enfin je m'aime plus que toi,
>
> (II, 2)

and who is Grimoald's evil counsellor, who is responsible for Grimoald's love for Rodelinde, and who persuades Grimoald to threaten the life of Rodelinde's son because he wants Grimoald to be hated: none of these is ideal; some are ordinarily human, others more than ordinarily weak and selfish.

Of the characters in the later plays, the same is true. In *La Toison d'Or,* there is Jason, the fickle opportunist, untruthful but possessed of a quick, subtle brain, for whom love is a means to an end, and who is prepared to make love to any woman if it suits his interests. There is Médée, who betrays her father for love, and who is jealous, violent, and cruel:

> Je ne croirai jamais qu'il soit douceur égale
> A celle de se voir immoler sa rivale. . . .
>
> (IV, 3)

There is her brother, Absyrte, for whom love takes precedence over every other consideration, who does not hesitate, with Médée's help to play a trick on Hypsipyle to make her love him, and who roundly declares:

> Et je ne suis pas homme à servir mon rival. . . .
>
> (V, 1)

There is Hypsipyle, too, who, devoid of any amour-propre, pursues her faithless lover, Jason, cannot resolve to give him up—

> Prince, vous savez mal combien charme un
>   courage
> Le plus frivole espoir de reprendre un volage,
> De le voir malgré lui dans nos fers retombé,
> Echapper à l'objet qui nous l'a dérobé,
> Et sur une rivale et confuse et trompée
> Ressaisir avec gloire une place usurpée,
>
> (II, 5)

—implores him to return to her, and finally marries someone else.

Sertorius opens with the words of Perpenna:

> D'où me vient ce désordre, Aufide, et que veut
>   dire
> Que mon cœur sur mes vœux garde si peu
>   d'empire?

—words which characterize not only Perpenna, but almost everyone else in the play. Aristie asks:

> Qu'importe de mon cœur, si je sais mon devoir?
>
> (I, 3)

but her state of mind is not so simple as that. Although her husband, Pompée, has divorced her and remarried, she cannot overcome her love for him:

> je hais quelquefois,
> Et moins que je ne veux et moins que je ne
>   dois.
>
> (III, 2)

She offers her hand to Sertorius from resentment, jealousy and wounded amour-propre. Love, in Sertorius himself, is stronger than political prudence. He decides to marry Viriate, whom he loves himself, to Perpenna, his lieutenant, in order to avoid dissensions in his army, but he lacks strength to carry out his resolution:

> Je m'étais figuré que de tels déplaisirs
> Pourraient ne me coûter que deux ou trois
>   soupirs;
> Et pour m'en consoler, j'envisageais l'estime
> Et d'ami généreux et de chef magnanime;
> Mais près d'un coup fatal, je sens par mes
>   ennuis
> Que je me promettais bien plus que je ne puis.
>
> (IV, 1)

He tries to evade discussing the matter with Perpenna, in order to avoid committing himself. It is by no means certain that he is telling the truth when he says to Perpenna:

> Non, je vous l'ai cédée, et vous tiendrai parole.
> Je l'aime, et vous la donne encor malgré mon
>   feu. . . .
>
> (IV, 3)

Certainly, the arguments he uses to dissuade Perpenna from marrying Viriate do not all appear to be sincere: it seems unlikely, for example, that Viriate would treat with her enemies if Sertorius were to keep his promise to Perpenna. It is because Sertorius cannot convince Perpenna of his sincerity that he is assassinated. Perpenna plots against Sertorius from envy and jealousy; yet in so doing he is conscious that he is doing wrong. He murders Sertorius, but his deed fills him with remorse.

Othon is by no means an ideal character. His love for Plautine originated in self-interest (like the love of Rastignac for Delphine de Nucingen in *Le Père Goriot*). Though it has become genuine, he agrees to relinquish her, albeit reluctantly. Having paid court to Camille, Galba's niece, in order to gain the Empire, he finds himself engaged to the princess but excluded from the succession, and has to try to dissuade her from marrying him, but without daring to confess the truth. He is hypocritical, virtuous under a good emperor, depraved under a bad one. Plautine, who urges Othon to make love to Camille, cannot help being jealous when he does so (like Atalide in *Bajazet,* later). Her father, Vinius, is another Félix, eager above all to maintain his power. Galba describes him thus:

> Voyez ce qu'en un jour il m'a sacrifié:
> Il m'offre Othon pour vous, qu'il souhaitait pour
>   gendre;
> Je le rends à sa fille, il aime à le reprendre;
> Je la veux pour Pison, mon vouloir est suivi;
> Je vous mets en sa place, et l'en trouve ravi;
> Son ami se révolte, il presse ma colère;
> Il donne à Martian Plautine à ma prière. . . .
>
>   (V, 1)

Galba is weak. Camille, his niece, is intelligent and shrewd, but jealous and vindictive. She is determined to marry Plautine, her rival in Othon's affections, to Martian, whom Plautine loathes, in order to be revenged upon her; and, when Othon places himself at the head of a revolt, she says:

> Allons presser Galba pour son juste supplice
>   . . . . .
> Du courroux à l'amour si le retour est doux,
> On repasse aisément de l'amour au courroux.
>
>   (IV, 7)

In *Agésilas,* Cotys, who is betrothed to Elpinice but does not love her, refuses to give her up to Spitridate:

> Je serai malheureux, vous le serez aussi.
>
>   (I, 4)

Spitridate is equally selfish in proposing to his sister that she should overcome her love for Cotys and marry Agésilas in order that he should be happy with Elpinice. Agésilas himself says:

> . . . Je ne suis pas assez fort
> Pour triompher de ma faiblesse.
>
>   (III, 4)

Attila is a most interesting study. He is an able politician, excelling rather at sowing dissension amongst his enemies than at military conquest, shrewd and suspicious, wily and cruel. He devises one scheme after another to torment the wretched kings and princesses in his power, playing with them like a cat with mice. But he is at the same time irresolute, and allows love to get the better of political prudence. Though Honorie is the more suitable match, he cannot overcome his preference for Ildione:

> Moi qui veux pouvoir tout, sitôt que je vous voi,
> Malgré tout cet orgueil, je ne puis rien pour
>   moi.
>
>   (III, 2)

Ildione and Honorie do not love Attila, but they are jealous of his favour and speak spitefully to each other. Honorie is particularly interesting. In situation, and to some extent in character, she resembles Racine's Hermione. She is unbalanced, and lacks self-control; jealousy makes her mean and spiteful. In a fit of pique, she refuses Attila, and, against her principle that a puppet-king is unworthy of her, agrees to marry Valamir. Wounded by Ildione's taunts, she seeks an unworthy revenge by betraying to Attila Ildione's love for Ardaric and suggesting that she should be made to marry a subject. She imprudently betrays the secret of her own love for Valamir:

> Que n'ai-je donc mieux tu que j'aimais Valamir!
> Mais quand on est bravée et qu'on perd ce
>   qu'on aime,
> Flavie, est-on si peu maîtresse de soi-même?
>
>   (IV, 2)

She sinks her pride and asks Attila to marry her.

Domitie, in *Tite et Bérénice,* finds that her ambition to be Empress is not strong enough to overcome her love for Domitian:

> Si l'amour quelquefois souffre qu'on le
>   contraigne,
> Il souffre rarement qu'une autre ardeur l'éteigne;
> Et quand l'ambition en met l'empire à bas,
> Elle en fait son esclave, et ne l'étouffe pas.
> Mais un si fier esclave ennemi de sa chaîne,
> La secoue à toute heure, et la porte avec gêne,
> Et maître de nos sens, qu'il appelle au secours,
> Il échappe souvent, et murmure toujours.
> Veux-tu que je te fasse un aveu tout sincère?
> Je ne puis aimer Tite, ou n'aimer pas son frère;
> Et malgré cet amour, je ne puis m'arrêter
> Qu'au degré le plus haut où je puisse monter.
>   . . . . .
> Hélas! plus je le vois, moins je sais que lui dire.
> Je l'aime, et le dédaigne, et n'osant m'attendrir,
> Je me veux mal des maux que je lui fais
>   souffrir.
>
>   (I, 1)

She cannot prevent herself from feeling jealous when she sees Domitian paying court to Bérénice; though, on the other hand, when she thinks that Tite prefers Bérénice, her pride is hurt and she wants to be revenged on him. Corneille's Tite, unlike Racine's Titus, is weak and vacillating—

> Maître de l'univers sans l'être de moi-même. . .

> (II, 1)

—and is prepared to abdicate to win Bérénice. His brother, Domitian, is not magnanimous. Finding Domitie determined to marry Tite, he expresses the wish that Bérénice would return and prevent the marriage and exults in her discomfiture:

> Que je verrais, Albin, ma volage punie,
> Si de ces grands apprêts pour la cérémonie,
> Que depuis si longtemps on dresse à si grand
>   bruit,
> Elle n'avait que l'ombre, et qu'une autre eût le
>   fruit!
> Qu'elle serait confuse! et que j'aurais de joie!

> (I, 3)

For Eurydice and Suréna, love is the only thing that matters.

> Je veux, sans que la mort ose me secourir,
> Toujours aimer, toujours souffrir, toujours
>   mourir,

says Eurydice, and Suréna echoes her words:

>   où dois-je recourir,
> O ciel! s'il faut toujours aimer, souffrir, mourir.

> (I, 3)

For Suréna,

> le moindre moment d'un bonheur souhaité,
> Vaut mieux qu'une si froide et vaine éternité.

> (I, 3)

There is nothing rational about Eurydice, who is all fears and jealousy, and who touchingly strikes up a friendship with Suréna's sister, as a way of being near him vicariously. Though her duty requires her to marry Pacorus, not only does she not love him, but she makes no pretence of doing so, reminds him that he has loved another, postpones her marriage with him, and does not conceal that she loves someone else. Nor can she bring herself to allow Suréna to obey the king and marry Mandane, so that she is directly responsible for his death. Pacorus, too, is another character who cannot master his love: Suréna tells him:

> l'amour jaloux de son autorité,
> Ne reconnaît ni rois ni souveraineté.
> Il hait tous les emplois où la force l'appelle:
> Dès qu'on le violente, on en fait un rebelle;
> Et je suis criminel de n'en pas triompher,
> Quand vous-même, Seigneur, ne pouvez
>   l'étouffer!

> (IV, 4)

Palmis is yet another:

> *Pacors.* Ah! vous ne m'aimez plus.

> *Palmis.*   Je voudrais le
>   pouvoir,
>   Mais pour ne plus aimer que sert de le
>   vouloir?

> (II, 3)

The women of Corneille are often spiteful, jealous and possessive. Doña Isabelle, who suspects that Don Sanche loves Doña Elvire, is determined that if she cannot marry him herself, her rival shall not be happier than she. If she should have to marry Doña Elvire's brother, she says:

>   devenant par là reine de ma rivale,
> J'aurai droit d'empêcher qu'elle ne se ravale,
> Et ne souffrirai pas qu'elle ait plus de bonheur
> Que ne m'en ont permis ces tristes lois
>   d'honneur.

> (**Don Sanche,** III, 6)

If Don Sanche must marry someone else, it must be a woman she has chosen for him, not one he has chosen himself:

> Qu'il souffre autant pour moi que je souffre
>   pour lui. . . .

> (III, 6)

Mandane, in **Agésilas,** expresses similar views; so do Bérénice and Eurydice. Sophonisbe is more openly possessive:

> Un esclave échappé nous fait toujours rougir.

> (I, 2)

Albin, in **Tite et Bérénice,** discourses in general terms on this feminine characteristic:

> Seigneur, telle est l'humeur de la plupart des
>   femmes.
> L'amour sous leur empire eût-il rangé mille
>   âmes,
> Elles regardent tout comme leur propre bien,
> Et ne peuvent souffrir qu'il leur échappe rien.
> Un captif mal gardé leur semble une infamie:
> Qui l'ose recevoir devient leur ennemie;
> Et sans leur faire un vol on ne peut disposer
> D'un cœur qu'un autre choix les force à refuser:
> Elles veulent qu'ailleurs par leur ordre il soupire,
> Et qu'un don de leur part marque un reste
>   d'empire.

> (IV, 4)

Several of Corneille's heroines, besides Domitie, illustrate his remarks.

Corneille's portrayal of human nature, then, is much more varied and subtle than is often supposed. His characters are for the most part unable to subdue their passions by their reason or their will; relatively few place honour or duty before inclination. They are not supermen or ideal creatures, but real men and women. Nearly all have their moments of weakness and indecision; nearly all have human faults and weaknesses. Above all, they are more complex in their motivation than they are often considered to be.

They are very varied. There are some strong characters, with some of the traits we think of as 'Cornelian', though they are far less numerous than is often imagined, and are by no means always virtuous. But such characters are relatively few and untypical, and confined to a certain number of plays. By their side are to be found a host of ordinary or weak or erring characters. Corneille's plays, indeed, constitute a wonderful and varied gallery of portraits. In *Polyeucte,* for example, we have Polyeucte, Sévère, Pauline, and Félix, all different types of humanity, admirably differentiated one from the other. To take another example, in *Nicomède* Corneille gives us—by the side of the self-confident, honourable, plain-speaking, tactless, ironical Nicomède and his feminine counterpart, Laodice—the wily Arsinoé, ambitious for her son, Attale, rather than for herself, adept at winding round her little finger her husband, the timid, mistrustful, uxorious Prusias. There are, too, the admirably portrayed diplomat, Flaminius, shrewd and subtle, skilfully concealing the iron hand beneath the velvet glove, making his will known by reasoned advice and hints, an excellent ambassador, and Attale, the brother of Nicomède, young and inexperienced, somewhat *précieux,* but intelligent and endowed with sound instincts, so that he gradually learns to distinguish between the world as he has been brought up to believe that it is and the world as it really is. Or, ranging over the whole work of Corneille, Rodrigue, Horace, Curiace, Auguste, Cinna, Polyeucte, César, Don Sanche, Nicomède, Othon, Martian and Suréna are not the same type of hero, any more than Chimène, Camille, Sabine, Pauline, Cléopâtre, Rodogune, Laodice, Dircé, Sophonisbe, Camille (in *Othon*), Ildione, Honorie, Pulchérie or Eurydice are one type of heroine. Maxime, Garibalde and Perpenna are three quite different types of weak character or villain. Again, Corneille shows many different types of older men—the count and Don Diègue, old Horace, Félix, Valens, Prusias, Vinius, Attila, Martian, and Suréna have little in common.

Corneille is excellent, too, at depicting family life. There is great variety in his fathers, for example: Don Diègue and old Horace, both affectionate and proud of their sons, but the former a little out of sympathy with his son's inner conflict, Félix, Valens, Prusias, Aæte. . . . Two deserve a particular mention: Phocas, in *Héraclius,* suffering because neither of the two young men will acknowledge him as father; and Martian, in *Pulchérie,* guessing the secrets of his daughter's heart and betraying his own in a touching scene. Then the mothers: Marcelle, in *Théodore,* full of fierce, maternal affection; Arsinoé, in *Nicomède,* like her a good mother but a bad stepmother; Jocaste, in *Oedipe,* who, though she has remarried, is thoughtful for her daughter's welfare; Cléopâtre, in *Rodogune,* devoid of any affection for her sons; Cassiope,

in *Andromède,* whose excessive maternal pride has brought misfortune to her country and her daughter. Perhaps Corneille is at his best in portraying the relationships between brothers and sisters. Leaving aside the comedies, we think of the sisterly bickering of Chalciope and Médée; of the delicate affection between Antiochus and Séleucus in *Rodogune;* of the dawning affection between the two half-brothers, Nicomède and Attale; of Mandane, in *Agésilas,* resisting the entreaties of her brother, Spitridate, who wants her to marry Agésilas, whom she does not love, so that Agésilas may let him be happy with Elpinice; of the eagerness of Irène in *Pulchérie* to help Léon; of the loyalty and affection of Palmis in *Suréna*. It is clear that no attempt to reduce Corneille's characters to a single formula can do justice to the range and variety of his characterization.

Nor is there any evidence that Corneille wrote with the object of inculcating a moral lesson of any kind. He himself, in the *Discours,* expressly denies that drama should have a moral aim; and it is difficult to feel that in any play we are being shown ideal characters on whom Corneille wishes us to model ourselves. Let us rather say, with Vedel: 'Il reste aussi invisible derrière son œuvre que Shakespeare.' The truth is surely that Corneille was concerned with studying human nature, with portraying different types of men and women, of fathers and sons and mothers and daughters, of lovers and their mistresses, of kings and tyrants and diplomats and politicians, of soldiers and adventurers, with studying their behaviour in different situations, their problems, their sufferings. Indeed, a contemporary anecdote, recently unearthed by Professor Lough, shows us a Corneille who—like Balzac—closely identified himself with his characters:

> M'a dit qu'étant à table avec M. l'Abbé de Cerisy, M. de Corneille, et avec d'autres honnêtes gens à Rouen, M. Corneille qu'était assis auprès de lui à mi-repos, lui donna un coup de poing sur l'épaule avec un cri, qui fut suivi de paroles, qui témoignèrent assez qu'il songeait ailleurs: Ah! que j'ai de la peine à faire mourir cette fille! Comme il avait surpris la compagnie, il fut obligé à dire la vérité, et en leur demandant pardon, il les assurait, qu'il n'était propre pour la conversation, et qu'il ne saurait s'empêcher rêver sur quelqu'une de ses comédies qu'il avait sur les mains, et qui fut l'occasion de ses paroles.

Claude Abraham (essay date 1972)

SOURCE: "The Comic Illusion," in *Pierre Corneille,* Twayne Publishers, Inc., 1972, pp. 32-47.

[*In the excerpt below from his book-length study of Corneille and his plays, Abraham surveys the dramatist's early comedies, from* Mélite *to* L'Illusion comique.]

"Such disorder, such irregularity!" Racine may or may not have thought of the very first plays of Corneille but there is no doubt that comedy in the late 1620's was of the lowest order, and Corneille was quite right in boasting, as he did in the *Examen* of *Mélite* which he penned decades later, that this play was really the first to be written for *honnestes gens* (gentlemen and ladies) and that, if it at times seemed to violate rules and unities, that was because they had not yet been established.

These early plays are a strange mixture of influences and independence. The influence of Hardy, one of Corneille's most prolific contemporaries, is readily seen in the violent melodrama of *Clitandre,* or in the numerous amorous deceptions scattered throughout all the early comedies. The effects of Italian comedy and of the pastoral vogue on Corneille cannot be denied either; witness the very names of the protagonists—Tirsis, Cloris, Lisis, Mélite, and so on. These influences, however, tend to be rather superficial, and even though Corneille did little to revolutionize the world of drama in the early 1630's, he did much to further the most salutary trends. To be sure, Corneille is a child of his times, and the ostentation, the illusion, the metamorphoses, the instability, all the commonplaces of Baroque literature are omnipresent in these early works. This is not only true of the content of the plays but of their form as well. It can truly be said that from *Mélite* to *Le Cid,* a period of some seven years during which he produced ten plays, Corneille was in constant search of a form. The fact that *Le Cid* was first called "tragicomedy" (an error that Corneille quickly corrected) is further indication of that. Call it Baroque or Romanesque, until *Le Cid* there is a certain exaltation, a youthful brio in these early plays which Corneille will never again be able to capture, not even in the verbal exuberance of later comedies such as *Le Menteur.* Thus, Corneille in search of Corneille is many things, unafraid as he is to borrow from everyone and everything that surrounds him. But he is above all, even in these early days, a man of taste. The psychological realism of *Clitandre* more than overshadows the borrowings from Hardy's shallow melodramas. Whereas Hardy had relied heavily on visual effects, Corneille used them but sparingly. The names of the first protagonists may recall those of the pastoral, but *Mélite,* as well as the later plays, is populated by gentle people who do not feel the need to disguise themselves in the ubiquitous shepherd's clothes, and for that alone Corneille deserves our gratitude. By the same token all the banal and gratuitous tricks of the theatrical trade are present in the plays—false letters; scenes of madness, real or feigned; commonplaces of words, plot, and character—but they are invariably enhanced by a grace and elegance of language and a psychological insight previously unknown in France.

I *Mélite*

Racine, when it came to plots, prided himself on "making something of nothing"; the same cannot be said of Corneille, as can be seen by the synopsis of *Mélite,* his first play. Eraste introduces Mélite, whom he loves, to his friend Tirsis, only to become jealous. To remedy the situation he sends some love letters (supposedly from Mélite) to Philandre, who is betrothed to Cloris, the sister of Tirsis. Philandre, thanks to the artifice and the persuasive powers of Eraste, decides to leave Cloris for Mélite and shows the letters of Tirsis. In despair the latter withdraws to the

home of a friend, Lisis, who spreads false rumors of Tirsis' death. Mélite faints at the news. Thus assured of Mélite's true feelings, Lisis reunites the two lovers. However Cliton, having seen Mélite in a faint, believes her dead too, and spreads the news of this "double death" to Eraste, who goes mad with remorse. Brought back to his senses by the Nourrice, he asks forgiveness and obtains from the two lovers not only his pardon but the hand of Cloris, who has rejected Philandre because of his fickleness.

The complexities of the plot are at times aggravated by a language that has often been characterized as overly distilled and ostentatious. While there is much truth in that, it must be kept in mind that the language is not Corneille's but that of the fashionable dandy of the era and thus contributes no little to the verisimilitude of the characters. In this respect, it is rather unfortunate that in later years Corneille, responding to criticism prompted either by jealousy or by changing taste, toned down the language of his earlier days, and in so doing eradicated the very essence of the gallant world of the 1620's and 1630's that he had so beautifully depicted. While the secondary characters are seldom imbued with any relief and seem rather flat, the four main ones sparkle. Of particular interest is Tirsis. The world of *Mélite* is a highly mercurial one in which few things are certain and in which a protagonist might be readily forgiven for not wanting to involve himself with his fellow creatures. But while a Philandre wallows in a cowardly and self-indulging narcissism, Tirsis is saved by his love. Upon the backdrop of constant interplay between truth and sham, between appearance and reality—in words and deeds—Tirsis moves not toward deception and eventually self-deception, but away from it. In the first scene Tirsis appears as a man who seeks only tangible gains, who deceives so as not to be deceived, and who is sure that all a woman's beauty will not turn him against the notion that constancy is a folly (135-36). But this gay young blade's notions are soon reduced to nothing when he is dazzled by Mélite. What exactly has he seen? "I saw I know not what." Mélite has but to appear for Tirsis to realize that it is the tangible gain that is an illusion. The new evidence, the new truth is in her beauty. This is not a metamorphosis of sham into verity or being opposed to appearance; rather, it is being expressed in appearance. Tirsis, at the beginning, opposed beauty to his "truth." He now sees that truth and beauty are but one and the same thing, that "to see Mélite is to love her" [Robert J. Nelson, *Corneille: His Heroes and Their Worlds,* 1963]. Henceforth for Tirsis, as for Mélite, there can be no deception. The dazzlement is not the result of trickery nor does it lead to it;—it leads to a new, deeper vision of reality which brings about the inevitable defeat of trickery and deception.

II *Clitandre*

Corneille had no sooner found success with the formula of *Mélite* than he sought to shine in an entirely different vein. *Clitandre* is a tragicomedy, the most popular dramatic genre at the time. Why did Corneille, so successful with a true comedy, write something so foreign to that initial accomplishment? Most likely it was, as Antoine Adam suggests [in *Histoire de la littérature française au XVIIe siecle,* 1962], not because he courted facile success but because he wanted to leave no challenge unanswered, because he wanted to be the successful rival of the stars of the day. In short, the same notion that made him write a "Racinian" play later on in his life now made him try a tragicomedy replete with all the Romanesque traits then in fashion.

Insofar as plot is concerned, *Mélite* is rather complex. Yet Corneille had synopsized it in less than twenty lines. For *Clitandre,* he wrote an "argument" of over three hundred lines, poking gentle fun at the critics of *Mélite*'s plot by exaggerating the complexities of this one. Reduced to its minimum, the story of *Clitandre* is as follows: Caliste and Dorise both love Rosidor who disdains the latter and loves the former. Dorise tries to kill her rival, fails, and is in turn attacked by a jilted lover, Pymante, who had also ambushed Rosidor. A rejected lover of Caliste, Clitandre, is blamed for the ambush, but he is finally recognized as innocent. He winds up in a joyless union with Dorise while Rosidor and Caliste live happily ever after. In the play the plot is anything but simple, and Corneille readily admitted in the preface that the least lapse in attention would result in the viewer, or reader, losing complete track of things.

Such a plot, of course, is typical of most of the tragicomedies of the era. Equally typical is the explicit brutality both in speech and deed: mad transports of anger, attempted murder and rape, an eye put out, and, to cap it off, nature as a whole matching the human violence with a storm of its own. In short, *Clitandre* is full of the type of physical and dithyrambic outbursts that the public was about to reject. For some time yet, this public was to keep its love of declamation, and many plays owed their success as much to great lyrical passages as to dramatic qualities—Tristan L'Hermite's *Mariane* is an excellent example of that—but the monologues of *Clitandre* are extremely passionate, verging on the brutal, and the play was far from successful. Its premiere passed unrecorded, and it had only three separate editions, the first in 1632, the last in 1689. As of 1644 it was included by Corneille in his collected works, but much reworked. In its revised version the play is somewhat toned down, but it remains a strange mixture of unexpected bedfellows, the most incongruous juxtaposition deriving from two tendencies that Corneille was to maintain in his work for a long time and which are, to some extent, hallmarks. On the one hand, as will be seen in plays such as *Médée, Horace,* and *Théodore,* Corneille kept a certain taste for brutality. On the other hand, *Clitandre* is already replete with those cameos of Cornelian expression, the brief passages that strike or spellbind, whose echoes remain long after the initial perception, and which every Frenchman knows by heart and loves to quote.

III *La Veuve*

With *La Veuve* Corneille returned to true comedy, though it must be clearly understood that in all of these plays laughter is evoked far less frequently than sophisticated smiles. *La Veuve*'s resemblance to *Mélite,* however, goes well beyond that broad trait. As Corneille himself acknowledged, both in inspiration and in plot, this, his third play, owed much to the first. Sensing that the public was growing tired of the type of play exemplified by *Clitandre,* Corneille returned to comedy which to him had less to do with laughter than with "a portrayal of our actions and of our speeches." The plot, as can be seen from Corneille's own *argument,* is not unlike that of *Mélite:* "Alcidon, in love with Clarice, widow of Alcandre and mistress of Philiste, his good friend, fearing that the latter notice this love, feigns to love Philiste's sister Doris who, however, is not taken in by the stratagem and consents to marry Florange, as proposed by her mother. The false friend, under the pretext of avenging the insult that this newly proposed union is to him, gets Celidan to agree to kidnap Clarice and to bring her to his castle. Philiste, taken in by the false resentment of his friend, breaks up the proposed union with Florange, upon which Celidan tries to convince Alcidon to go back to Doris and to give Clarice back to her lover. Unsuccessful in his persuasion, he suspects an act of treachery and, deceptive in turn, gets the truth out of Clarice's nurse (who had been a willing accomplice of Alcidon) and, turning against the traitor, he brings Clarice back to Philiste and obtains Doris in return."

The parallel of structure is obvious, as are the literary commonplaces already found in the previous places (character of the Nurse, the betrayed betrayer, truth not being truth, and so on). There are, however, some major steps forward insofar as the dramatic canon of Corneille is concerned. Whereas the first two plays were very loosely knit and had little unity of action (to all intents and purposes, the first love problem is settled at the end of Act I of each of the first two plays), *La Veuve* shows a determined effort on Corneille's part to cope with the problem. It is true that there are two actions, but they are properly connected. The first three acts are fairly well linked with only a slight difficulty in the last two. Still, we are a long way from Racine's concept, as enunciated in the preface to *Bérénice,* of a plot involving a minimal action taking place in a single locale in a few hours. For the unity of time Corneille chose to compromise, allowing one act a day. As for the locale, there is no indication whatsoever in the original edition, and, ten years later (1644), Corneille clarified the situation but slightly by adding that the action took place "in Paris."

Another aspect of the unity of action deserves comment. Not only is the plot more unified but the style of the entire play is closely linked with the dramatic development. Long speeches that have little to recommend them outside of their undeniable lyrical qualities and that advance neither action nor character of development are far less frequent than in the two previous plays, resulting in a greater sense of continuity in *La Veuve.* As Robert Nelson has suggested, "*Mélite* was a body of lyrics and *Clitandre* a tone poem. *La Veuve* is much more of an action." This new awareness undoubtedly had much to do with the fact that *La Veuve* underwent relatively few changes in later editions, most of them involving the quality of the vocabulary, the propriety of certain expressions or manners—in other words, changes made naturally necessary by evolutionary processes in the realm of language and behavior.

This new awareness is also visible in Corneille's handling of the characters. Perhaps the most important scene of the play, as far as the study of the development of Corneille's psychological insight is concerned, is the one in which Clarice declares her feelings for Philiste (II, 4). In order to get the bashful swain to declare his own feelings, she goes as far as she can without violating the laws of propriety in a sense that is a masterpiece of delicacy and of psychological realism, a perfect wedding of preciosity and profundity. The author's insight is further demonstrated in the way he has the two lovers address each other. The first time they meet (I, 5) she uses the familiar *tu* while he uses the more polite *vous*. The next meeting occurs while the Nurse is present (II, 4), and so both use *vous* until Philiste dares declare his love openly, at which point Clarice, sure of herself, switches triumphantly to *tu* in a speech that also includes the then bold epithet "my Philiste." They do not see each other again on stage until V, 7, and by then Philiste is so torn between sorrow and joy, so insecure—can he believe his fortune? Does she really love him?—that he still insists on the more formal address while Clarice, sure of his love—"Do you see any signs of doubt in me concerning your love?" (1814)—never stops using *tu*. Of course, there are many reasons for this difference in expression. Clarice is a widow, that is to say a woman of a certain experience and knowledge, and so it is proper and natural that she display greater maturity, certainty, and even boldness. Her advantage in this respect is made greater by the fact that in social standing she is slightly above her suitor, if not enough to cause a scandal and make a union unbelievable, at least enough to make him doubt his good fortune. In *Mélite,* there had also been a *tutoiement,* a use of the familiar *tu,* a momentary lapse by Mélite immediately taken up by Tircis made sufficiently bold by it to ask for more tangible rewards. By 1648, however, Corneille considered this move too improper, and Tirsis, like his creator, learned how to keep his passion in check and to use the polite form of address under all circumstances. Clarice did not have to suffer from this unjust fettering, undoubtedly because Corneille felt that the ground had been well laid for her *tutoiement.* There is little doubt that much of *La Veuve*'s success was due to these flashes of psychological brilliance which are demonstrated not only in the above display of finesse but also in the creation of the many cameos that dot the play. Unfortunately, these are but oases, for Corneille had not yet learned to maintain the quality of his insight or his expression. Nevertheless, they give a very good indication of things to come.

IV *La Galerie du Palais*

The sub-titles of Corneille's early plays—*The False Letters* for *Mélite, Innocence Delivered* for *Clitandre, The Traitor Betrayed* for *La Veuve,* and now *The Rival Friend* for *La Galerie du Palais*—are always more indicative of the content of the plays than the titles themselves, and so it is indeed ironic that any mention of *amie rivale* is dropped from all the editions of the play as of 1644. As a matter of fact, the subtitle of this play, as of all the previous ones, should have been *The Dissimilations,* with an emphasis on the plural.

The plot, for once, is relatively simple: Célidée and Lysandre are about to be engaged while Dorimant loves Hippolyte who, in turn, secretly loves Lysandre. Célidée suddenly begins to yearn for Dorimant, making it a nearly perfect quadrangle. Taking advantage of this new infatuation Hippolyte suggests that her friend Célidée put Lysandre to the test by feigning indifference. Paid by Hippolyte, Lysandre's servant advises Lysandre to pretend to court Hippolyte to make Célidée jealous, but he is too righteous to keep up such a sham. In fact, both male leads are so steadfast in their virtue and love that the inevitable is brought about, the union of Célidée with Lysandre and of Hippolyte with Dorimant.

After the success of *La Veuve* it was to be expected that Corneille would keep many of the features of that play for his next venture, and indeed he did, improving on several of them. He continued, for instance, in the portrayal of life as the mainstay of comedy. As the title of the play indicates, the locale of the play is real, and realistically described. Other authors had previously described shops, or merchants, or the language of the lower classes, but never had the French stage seen all of these elements combined, and so well. The descriptions and illustrations of the speech, the mentality, and the general behavior of the shopkeepers; the incisive portrayal of types such as the cowardly swashbucklers—changed in later editions to rogues, attacking a passerby; the delightful commentaries on tastes ranging from clothes to literature; the description of a rowdy theater crowd (at the rival Hôtel de Bourgogne, of course)—all these now, for the first time, were introduced not as colorless background but as a vivid part of the play itself.

Like *La Veuve, La Galerie* is a step away from tragicomedy and its ploys. While there is little frank laughter, and while there are many changes of fortune, there is never any danger of seeing the plays lapse into the maudlin melodrama of tragicomedy. Over-excitement and excessive adventures are carefully avoided, there being but one duel, a common event in those days. The language is quite simple, even in scenes of precious debate, and the unforeseen turns of event allow for a multiplicity of tone quite becoming a comedy. The only strong derogations to this otherwise favorable picture of the physical makeup of the play are the facts that the characters have little relief and the unity of time is still not too well applied, Corneille again allowing five days for the action to take place.

Of primary interest in *La Galerie du Palais* are some major innovations. There are four principals, paired off, with no "outside agitator." Whatever changes of fortune occur do so, not because of external forces, but because of the stengths and weaknesses of the characters themselves. As Philip Koch points out, if there is to be any treachery, it "must come from one of the four principal lovers" [*PMLA* 78 (June 1963)]. By the same token, there is no outside reconciler either, and so if the problem is from within, so is the solution, the former coming from the fickleness (Célidée) or the treachery (Hippolyte) of the women, the latter from the righteousness and willingness to act of the men. This "interiorization" of the action is of paramount importance to the comprehension of the evolutionary pattern of Corneille's dramatic technique. While secondary characters will continue to abound in his plays, their effect on the central action of the play will never again be of any consequence.

Perhaps of greatest interest is a concept of love destined to play a major role in later works and first introduced in *La Galerie*—though in the mouth of an insincere lover— namely, the concept of the importance of merit and esteem in the birth of love. When Lysandre, at the end of III, 6, claims that love as a blind passion is a thing of the past and that merit perceived intellectually gives rise to passion (916-18), he is not mocking a concept that later tragic heroes will exemplify. He, like so many comic antiheroes, believes that in matters of love, fraud is legitimate, whereas a Rodrigue will tell his father that there is but one honor, be it in love or in battle. But, and this is of paramount importance, Lysandre is a hypocrite, not an autohypocrite, and his statement is for public consumption, not to fool himself. He is, at the time of the utterance, not parodying but stating a valid concept, though he has not the slightest intention of fulfilling its promise.

V *La Suivante*

Late in life, Corneille stated that basically all his comedies had been predicated on a single theme: two young people in love, separated for a while, then reunited. Of all the plays examined so far, *La Suivante* is probably the one that would suffer least from such an oversimplification. To be sure, a plot synopsis could easily be made as long as the play, because this is basically a comedy of errors, and if each one of these errors were to be related it would be a long synopsis indeed. Nevertheless, the story can be told quite simply. Fundamentally, there are two

sets of characters: on the one hand Géraste, his daughter Daphnis, and her lover Florame; on the other, Théante, also in love with Daphnis, and the latter's *suivante*, Amarante. The first trio is fundamentally in agreement since Géraste wants the union of the other two, who love each other. The difficulties are introduced by the scheming pair, Théante and Amarante. After numerous misunderstandings, the true lovers are united while the schemers are not, the play ending with a bitter tirade by Amarante whose ambition has been thwarted. This last tirade, in alexandrine quatrains, shows her to be completely bewildered by all the misunderstandings, quid pro quos, and lies.

Outwardly, this is the most regular of the plays studied so far, with few innovations or surprises. The leading role is given for the first time to an attendant, but the Nurse as an old standby has already been replaced by a *suivante* in *La Galerie*. There is only one other innovation, one that will be of utmost importance in subsequent plays, and Robert Nelson has capsulized it to perfection: "The soliloquies do not merely recapitulate events or remind us of a character's role in a rapidly developing action, but serve rather to develop the character himself." That is indeed a step forward, as are a rigorously maintained balance between the acts (each one of which has 340 lines) and the strictly enforced unities, though the unity of action is forced by the presence of some lengthy episodes that keep the interest from being properly sustained.

In our days, it is fashionable to speak of "antiheroes," comic or other. The term could very properly be applied to the protagonists of this play in which supposedly "honest" people act out of the worst of intentions. Whereas in previous comedies men's enterprises were either prompted by good intentions or were doomed to failure, here they are prompted by bad intentions and succeed. In an effort to simplify the plot, I have categorized the protagonists in such a way as to possibly suggest that only two of them were treacherous, but that is not quite so. Deception is not entirely limited to Amarante and Théante since both young men enter the house of Géraste under the pretext of courting Amarante. This simultaneous seduction of the mistress and the servant is a commonplace that can be traced as far back as Ovid's *Art of Love,* and as Clindor of *L'Illusion comique* will say, "Love and marriage use different methods" (789). Théante, confessing his feelings to a friend who will only too readily betray him to his rival, puts it equally well: "However attractive she may be, she is only a servant, and my ambition is stronger than my love" (9-12). It is this calculating cold realism that bewilders Amarante more than anything else, and it is particularly the misfortune of pretty but poor women betrayed by greedy men desiring wealthy wives that she bemoans. In short, we are right back to the basic question of honor in love. In that sense, Florame is no better than Théante, and keeping this in mind one reaches the inevitable conclusion that, while Amarante is a schemer, to be sure, she is a defensive one, as she is more victim—or even tool—than sinister plotter. Once more, a comedy ends, leaving the reader with the mixed feelings that perforce result from the perversion of the old axiom into "all is fair in the war of love."

VI *La Place Royalle*

The mood at the end of *La Suivante* is, if anything, amplified in the following play, *La Place Royalle*. Except for a few lighthearted moments, the humor of this play is grating. Even the plot gives an indication of the indistinct nature of the play: Angélique and Alidor are in love, but he wants to break with her in order to assert his freedom, and tries to "give" her to his friend Cléandre. Angélique receives a letter supposedly from Alidor to a rival, confronts him with it, and receives mocking insults in answer to her queries. Doraste, taking advantage of the rift, asks for the hand of Angélique. Considering his glory at stake Alidor asks for forgiveness so that Angélique might run

A scene from L'illusion comique, *presented by the Théâtre National de Belgique.*

away with him, planning to allow Cléandre to take his place at the last moment. This elopement, occurring at night, in the darkness Cléandre takes Phylis, sister of Doraste, by mistake. Horrified by all this, Angélique escapes to a cloister, a solution that satisfies Alidor who now feels free again.

Throughout the play Angélique is very close to being a tragic figure, mocked, tortured, finally seeking refuge in God, but not really sure or satisfied as a result of that decision. The reader may well ask himself whether Corneille, tired of the genre, had worked himself into a rut, or whether, perhaps, the play is nothing less than the logical outcome of the evolution we have witnessed so far, namely, if the comic protagonist insists on an immoral or amoral pursuit and succeeds, what is one to expect? Just as Alidor's ancestors are to be found in the previous plays, so are hints of the black comedy that develops here. In this respect, then, *La Place Royalle* offers nothing new to the reader. By the same token, while Alidor and Philis are marvelously drawn characters, beautifully delineated, Corneille had succeeded in doing that before, though the exact degree of such a success is debatable. The exterior realism—the Place Royalle is today's Place

des Vosges—is not new either to the author, and the unities are observed no better or worse than before. In what sense then does the play deserve attention? Its importance resides, in part at least, in the fact that the action is more than ever the result of inner forces, in this case the struggle between two feelings within the breast of the protagonist.

From the first line of the play, a rapid tempo is established, though this rapidity is often verbal, not involving the advancement of the plot or character development. Soon the attentive reader perceives that this breathless rush is indeed deceptive, and the play grinds to a teeth-gnashing end. But does all that matter? The plot is, as a matter of fact, well conceived, and the unity of action fairly well kept, but all that is nothing more than a framework for the real play, the inner struggle within Alidor, one whose ups and downs no doubt have much to do with the varying tempos of the "outer" play. In that respect there is a certain harmony between décor, subject, and characters which overrides all other considerations. Alidor is forever torn between a genuine love and an equally genuine, and eventually much stronger, desire for freedom which might easily be construed as a misguided sense of self-respect. He wants to love because he chooses to, not because of an obligation due to the lady's own attentions. He demands to be master of his love, not its slave (209-32). As Koch puts it, Alidor is thus simultaneously the hero and the *"fourbe,"* the protagonist and the antagonist. He strives to be extraordinary, to rise above social norms (209-10). Here, as in previous plays, the subtitle, "L'Amoureux extravagant" or the "Extragavant Lover," helps immensely in the understanding of what the play is all about. The word *extravagant,* in the Cotgrave dictionary (1611), is defined as "astray, out of the way." Alidor, whatsoever his concept of self may be, is a comic antihero. Although he does not lack in will to act, he is quite incapable of doing anything about it, thus forever allowing the situation to backfire and turning any potential sympathy one might have for him into derision. He seeks freedom above all else, yet constantly depends on others, mostly on Angélique. Concerning his relationship with the latter, he does not even have the strength of character to abandon her, and must therefore behave so that she will reject him. It is precisely this divorce between the concept he has of himself and his actual being that makes Alidor comic and, in an anachronistic way, a parody of the real Cornelian hero. Alidor's "extravagance" is further demonstrated by his lack of a true sense of values, and therefore of a goal. The few values that he manages to enunciate are negative, as if the author had wished to warn us against these before proposing more valid ones. Wandering aimlessly Alidor thus stumbles into victory, unaware not only of the misery he has created for others, but also of the emptiness of what seems a triumph to him, but is nothing more than utter failure. It is precisely what he states that "henceforth I live, since I live for myself" (1579), that one feels like asking him "why?" What is this *"moy"* for which he so wants to live? The best that can be said for it, the most that he can guarantee for himself at the time of that last tirade is that he will never again be caught or hurt by love. Poor victory indeed, and not much of a career. It may well be, as Octave Nadal has suggested, that Alidor "announces Rodrigue," but hardly in any positive manner [*Le sentiment de l'amour dans l'œvre de Pierre Corneille,* 1948].

VII *L'Illusion comique*

With *La Place Royalle,* Corneille must have felt that he had exhausted the vein that had brought him great fame and some fortune and he turned to tragedy, a form that was enjoying a tremendous revival at the time. Still, he did not abandon comedy entirely, and within months of the creation of *Médée,* in the summer of 1635, *L'Illusion comique* was performed for the first time. Insofar as the plot and the characters are concerned, *L'Illusion* is a radical departure from the previous plays.

Pridamant, a good burgher, alienated his son Clindor through excessive severity ten years previously. To obtain some news of him, he consults the magician Alcandre who proposes to show him, magically, some of his son's many adventures. As the play within the play begins, we see Clindor—who has had many adventures and jobs in the ten years—in the employ of a swashbuckling Mata-

more. Both love Isabelle who is further admired by Adraste, while Lise, the maid of Isabelle, loves Clindor. While Matamore boasts of imaginary exploits and flees at the slightest danger, Clindor and Isabelle confess their love to each other. Jealous, Adraste fights Clindor who wounds him and is cast in jail for it. He is about to be condemned to death, but Lise conspires to allow him to escape by offering herself to the jailer, who loves her. The four are about to escape when the magician interrupts his evocation to show something even more startling to Pridamant. As the last act begins we see Clindor, who has obviously forsaken Isabelle, courting a princess whose husband sends men to kill Clindor for his boldness. But this tragic scene is an illusion in every way: we have just been allowed to witness a play within the play within the play, in that Clindor and Isabelle, after their successful escape, had joined a troupe of actors and were merely performing this fragment of tragedy. Pridamant, impressed by his son's success, goes to join him in Paris.

As can readily be seen from this plot summary, *L'Illusion* is indeed a departure from the vein previously mined by Corneille. This departure, however, concerns only the story and the main characters, for in theme, *L'Illusion* is the culmination, not the rejection, of the earlier plays. Until this play Corneille had shown a deftly controlled verve which he now let loose in what Garapon had called "verbal fantasy," concentrated in the person of Matamore, the *miles gloriosus* of antiquity, brilliantly revived by Corneille. More important still is the idea, not that Matamore lives in a world of fantasy (in that his exploits are imaginary), but that his world is literally an illusion which is not to be taken seriously. *L'Illusion* not only contains a very eloquent apology for the theater—culminating in the scene that sends father to rejoin son—but it is the embodiment of Corneille's dicta. The people creating illusions, be they magicians or actors, and illusion itself are the real heroes of the play. Appearances forever preempt reality, and Alcandre is not unlike Corneille himself in that respect. One might well ask why Alcandre does not, as requested, satisfy the father by giving him news of his son in a straightforward manner. If he did, of course, there would be no play, but the real reason is more complex for, as Clifton Cherpack points out, Alcandre, like a playwright, is compelled by the very presence of a captive audience to "demonstrate his talents" [*Modern Language Notes* 81 (1966)]. For all their supposedly realistic descriptions, the early plays revolve around the reality-fantasy dichotomy. At the end of *L'Illusion* the realistic father who, by his own confession, had been too harsh with his son, runs to escape into that son's newly found never-never world.

Nor is this the only way in which *L'Illusion* caps off the early plays of Corneille. The Machiavellian lover, not averse to wooing both servant and mistress, is again found in Clindor, courting both Isabelle and Lise. The father cast in the role of benevolent despot because of his desire to impose a reasoned will on rebellious lovers is the remorseful spectator of his son's adventures. In *La Place Royalle* a young man was willing to sacrifice his love for the sake of an inner peace. In *L'Illusion* the young people constantly remind the older "spectators" that such is precisely their quest. Isabelle intends to be absolute mistress of her destiny (906, 515-16, and so on) in her search for "happiness and inner calm" (664). The father realizes soon enough that when he opposed his paternal authority to his son's quest for freedom (26), he invited disaster. But most important is the idea, implicit in all the plays from *Mélite* to *La Place Royale,* explicit here, that all the world is a stage. *L'Illusion comique* deserves its complete title not only in that it ends well, but because "illusion" is the basic characteristic of "comedy," a word frequently used in the seventeenth century in its broader sense, denoting "drama" or "theater." *L'Illusion comique* is, in fact, the triumph of theatrical illusion.

If these early plays had to be reduced to one or two central ideas or themes, it would have to be the very Baroque ones of instability and illusion. All the titles or subtitles, from *Les Fausses letters* to *L'Illusion comique* bear witness to that. The world of these plays is, in the words of *La Veuve*'s Philiste, chaotic beyond remedy (919-20), and is ruled by fickle fate with only "uneven order" (*L'Illusion,* 1725-28). To make matters worse, men contribute to this chaos, so that nothing is really as it seems: letters are not letters, friends are foes, confidants are spies, reality is a dream, and dreams are real. Small wonder then that many characters, like Philis of *La Place Royale,* reject fidelity as a "vanity" (47-48), believing that steadfastness in an unstable world can only lead to unhappiness. Freedom, to these characters, is thus not a goal sought for its intrinsic value, or a sine qua non of self-attainment, but a protective wall saving the "hero" from involvement. Nowhere is this more evident than in *La Place Royale* where the walls that imprison Angélique not only protect her from an unreliable world but also save Alidor from a dreaded servitude; it is no less apparent in *L'Illusion,* where all escape into the make-believe world of the theater. It is this world of marionettes on a treadmill that Médée, the first truly tragic heroine of Corneille, rejected, because she was essentially a stranger in it, and by so doing gave the theater audience of 1635 a preview of what we have come to call Cornelian drama.

Gordon Pocock (essay date 1973)

SOURCE: "'Suréna'," in *Corneille and Racine: Problems of Tragic Form,* Cambridge at the University Press, 1973, pp. 141-54.

[*In the following essay, Pocock examines Corneille's* Suréna, *a drama "loved by those who value formal perfection."*]

1

Steiner has been tempted to call *Suréna* Corneille's masterpiece. Whatever value we assign it, it stands apart from the other plays. Its characters are few, its plot simple, love predominates over politics, it exhales a languorous pessimism. There are not qualities we call Cornelian, and we might suspect the influence of Racine: *Suréna* was,

after all, written later than most of Racine's plays. Nevertheless, the general impression left by *Suréna* is not at all Racinian. We are on former ground if we look at *Suréna* by itself and ask ourselves two questions: what is Corneille trying to express? and are the means of expression appropriate?

The key to *Suréna* is its language. Corneille's verse is usually forthright: we expect simply rhythms, sonorous abstract words, clear antitheses, straightforward heroics, irony or invective. The verse of *Suréna* is consistently unlike this. Its vocabulary is in general that of neoclassical tragedy, but some of the words it uses with relatively unusual frequency for Corneille: 'mystère', 'secret', 'soupçon'; 'craindre', 'deviner', 'murmurer', 'taire'. The constructions are also characteristic: the conditional, negative, subjunctive, pluperfect; 's'il', 'il n'y a que', 'ce n'est que', 'trop de'. The rhythms are unusual in Corneille: sometimes elegiac, often hesitant or broken, as if uncertain of their direction. The verse has a fluidity, a suggestiveness, unique in Corneille, yet quite without the luminous directness that accompanies these qualities in Racine.

I will take a short passage from Act III, Scene ii. Orode, King of Parthia, owes his throne to Suréna, and wonders how to reward him. At the same time, Orode not only is anxious at having such a powerful subject, but also suspects that Suréna hopes to marry Eurydice, a princess who for political reasons must marry Pacorus, Orode's son and heir. Orode decides that the only solutions are to kill Suréna or to offer him his daughter Mandane in marriage. If Suréna accepts Mandane, he obviously does not love Eurydice, and the marriage will both reward him and bind him more closely to Orode. If Suréna refuses Mandane, it will be clear that he loves Eurydice, and is thus a danger to Orode. When Suréna comes in, Orode addresses him thus:

> Suréna, vos services
> (Qui l'aurait osé croire?) ont pour moi des
>   supplices;
> J'en ai honte, et ne puis assez me consoler
> De ne voir aucun don qui les puisse égaler.
> Suppléez au défaut d'une reconnaissance
> Dont vos propres exploits m'ont mis en
>   impuissance;
> Et s'il en est un prix dont vous fassiez état,
> Donnez-moi les moyens d'être un peu moins
>   ingrat.

What are we to make of this? The verse is indirect, even slow. Is this clumsiness and fatigue, an inability to force the words and sense into a clear form? Apparently not. There is undoubted skill in the way in which the lines express Orode's convoluted thought by the careful placing of the clause in parentheses and the complicated manipulation of negatives and subjunctives. The lines express exactly the deviousness behind the king's attitude: he cannot make up his mind whether to kill or reward Suréna, and is quite unsure of Suréna's real attitude. Two qualities in the lines are notable. The first is ambiguity. It is notoriously difficult, in a sentence that contains several negatives, to be certain whether the sentence means what it seems to mean or the exact opposite. Corneille makes full use of this. After Orode's first sentence, we may well wonder whether the king is expressing gratitude or hostility: Corneille not only presents Orode as not knowing, but also leaves the audience and Suréna in doubt about the king's intentions. The use of language, then, reflects and expresses by literary means the immediate dramatic situation.

The second feature is paradox. Orode is king, Suréna is a subject, but Orode approaches Suréna with deference ('J'en ai honte, et ne puis . . . ', 'Suppléez au défaut'). Suréna has served the king well and returned him to power; but these 'services' are 'supplices', these 'exploits' 'm'ont mis en impuissance'. The king wishes to reward Suréna, but cannot see a gift that is sufficient: he therefore asks Suréna to give him the means with which to give (though this is just what Suréna has done in restoring the king to his throne, and this is why Orode wishes to reward him). This paradoxical quality, reinforced by the ambiguity, gives the lines a resonance which is audible at many levels: it expresses the immediate situation; it points to a paradoxical quality in the play as a whole; and it evokes suggestions of a mysterious significance beyond the immediate prose sense of the lines or the immediate (rather banal) situation. Nor does the ambiguity end here. The situation is on the face of it political: it could easily be accommodated in *Nicomède*. But the treatment points to something quite different. There are definite, if muted, sexual undertones. 'Ingrat', in seventeenth-century French tragedy, is the regular word for a loved one who does not return or appreciate the love bestowed on him. 'Services', 'supplices', 'reconnaissance' are words which, though ordinary in themselves, are often found with specialised meanings in the conventional language of *galanterie*. 'Consoler' and 'impuissance' have obvious sexual connotations. This undertone is relevant, not just to the immediate situation, but to the whole pattern of the play. Nor is the relevance just a vague fitting-in with the general mood. Some of the words ('supplice', 'impuissance', 'ingrat') have a very precise significance in the pattern. To examine what the pattern is, we shall review briefly some of the main features of the play.

First, plot. As has often been remarked, the plot is extremely simple. Orode has decided that Pacorus, who has loved and is loved by Suréna's sister Palmis, shall marry Eurydice for political reasons. Eurydice loves Suréna, and is manifestly reluctant to marry Pacorus. Orode and Pacorus realise that this is because she loves Suréna. Orode therefore has Suréna murdered. Eurydice dies (whether of grief or by suicide is not clear from the text, but, as we shall see, the significance in either case is the same). The plot material is as slight as in *Bérénice*. But Corneille handles it in a way which is very unlike Racine's.

In Act I, Eurydice tells Ormène, her confidante, that she must marry Pacorus, though she loves Suréna. She is jealous of Mandane, whom she thinks Suréna is likely to marry. Several points call for comment. Although Eury-

dice dwells lyrically on her love for Suréna, she never questions that she will in fact marry Pacorus; her grief springs hardly more from her impending marriage than from her jealousy of Mandane; this premonition that Mandane is intended to marry Suréna is so far quite unconfirmed; and Ormène says plainly that Eurydice's grief has a self-inflating quality:

Votre douleur, Madame, est trop ingénieuse.

Palmis appears, and Eurydice confesses her love for Suréna. Palmis in turn confesses her love for Pacorus. Suréna comes in, and he and Eurydice express their love for each other. Again, the precise manner in which these banal exchanges are treated is illuminating. Eurydice does not exactly reveal her secret: it is communicated to Palmis without actually being put into words:

Savez-vous mon secret?
   —Je sais celui d'un frère.
—Vous savez donc le mien.

Nor do Suréna and Eurydice exactly express their love, still less propose to do anything about it. Eurydice is mainly concerned that Suréna shall not marry Mandane, though she is quite willing for him to marry someone else; and when Suréna is about to react to this strange requirement, she cannot even let him finish:

  N'achevez point: l'air dont vous commencez
Pourrait à mon chagrin ne plaire pas assez . . .
Mais adieu; je m'égare.

Act I, then, is characterised by simplicity only if we think of the plot-material. The emotional content and the verse are characterised by over-refinement and inconclusiveness.

The same goes for Act II. Pacorus asks Suréna whether Eurydice loves someone else. Suréna evades the question. Pacorus asks Eurydice. She agrees that she loves someone else, but refuses to say whom. Pacorus asks Palmis to tell him, and she refuses. In Act III, Orode tries to find out whether Suréna is the mysterious lover; Suréna evades him and Palmis rebuffs him. By the beginning of Act IV, Orode has presumably made up his mind, as he has the palace gates closed and guarded. Palmis also seems to assume that the secret is out, as she begs Eurydice to marry Pacorus immediately and so divert suspicion from Suréna. Pacorus himself is now convinced that Suréna is his unknown rival, though no-one has told him so. Suréna still refuses to commit himself. By the beginning of Act V, everyone assumes that Orode will now kill Suréna, though still nothing definite has been revealed about any of the characters' intentions. At the same time, it seems to be assumed that Eurydice could save Suréna by marrying Pacorus, or by allowing Suréna to marry Mandane. Nevertheless, we feel that Suréna is doomed. Sure enough, he is killed—no doubt by order of Orode, but the assassin is not named:

A peine du palais il sortait dans la rue,
Qu'une flèche a parti d'une main *inconnue;*
Deux autres l'ont suivie; et j'ai vu ce vainqueur,
Comme si toute trois l'avaient atteint au coeur,
Dans un ruisseau de sang tomber mort sur la
    place.

Eurydice dies (presumably through suicide): that is, she says she is dying and according to the usual convention is carried off-stage, but no doubt we are meant to assume that she dies. We may certainly say that the plot of **Suréna** is simple, but the effect it makes is not: Corneille elaborately surrounds even the simplest action with ambiguities: it is not so much that nothing happens as that the action advances in spite of the fact that nothing happens.

Let us now look at the characters. The central oppositions are clear enough: Orode suspects Suréna of loving Eurydice; Eurydice loves Suréna but is required to marry Pacorus. Having said this, immediate doubts arise. What is Orode's attitude, and what are his reasons for it? He appears at first as, above all, anxious:

Qu'un tel calme, Sillace, a droit d'inquiéter
Un roi qui lui doit tant qu'il ne peut
    s'acquitter!

                (III.i)

Suréna is too great for a subject, and Orode fears him—yet his fear (like Eurydice's jealousy) is 'trop ingénieuse'. There is no sign that Suréna is disloyal: what worries Orode is 'un tel calme'—that is, that there is no apparent cause for worrying. Orode tyrannically draws the conclusion that he must either marry Suréna to Mandane or kill him. Then, immediately, he revolts against the thought:

Son trépas . . . Ce mot seul me fait pâlir
    d'effroi;
Ne m'en parlez jamais: que tout l'Etat périsse . .

Avant que je défère à ces raisons d'Etat
Qui nommeraient justice un si lâche attentat!

When he meets Suréna, he wavers between gratitude and threats. Suréna refuses to marry Mandane, and Orode veers. He explains frankly that Suréna is dangerous to him:

Vous êtes mon sujet, mais un sujet si grand,
Que rien n'est malaisé quand son bras
    l'entreprend.
Vous possédez sous moi deux provinces entières,
De peuples si hardis, de nations si fières,
Que sur tant de vassaux je n'ai d'autorité
Qu'autant que votre zèle a de fidélité.
Ils vous ont jusqu'ici suivi comme fidèle;
Et, quand vous le voudrez, ils vous suivront
    rebelle . . .
Et s'il faut qu'avec vous tout à fait je
    m'explique,
Je ne vous saurais croire assez en mon pouvoir,

Scene from a Comédie-Française production of Nicomède.

Si les noeuds de l'hymen n'enchaînent le devoir.

Frank speaking, for once in the play. But is it? Orode is presented here as a man ruled by political realism, but he is not quite like this in most of the play. In this very scene he is shown on the one hand firmly announcing that Pacorus must marry Eurydice ('La paix de l'Arménie à ce prix est jurée'), and then plaintively asking Suréna to confirm that the decision is right and that he cannot now break off the marriage:

Mais, Suréna, le puis-je après la foi donnée? . . .
Que dira la princesse, et que fera son père?

Is Orode a cynical statesman, caressing his victims to disarm their resistance, or is he, as this passage suggests, a much put-upon man doing his best in difficult circumstances? The answer is that he is both, and these two attitudes are held in suspense throughout the play. When in Act V he makes his last appearance, his attitude is still ambiguous. On the one hand, he is preparing to murder Suréna; on the other, he seems sincerely anxious to find a solution:

Empêchez-la [the murder], Madame, en vous
    donnant à nous;

Ou faites qu'à Mandane il s'offre pour époux.
Cet ordre exécuté, mon âme satisfaite
Pour ce héros si cher ne veut plus de retraite.

Nor are Orode's actions and motives just obscure; Corneille presents them as obscure by choice:

Ne me l'avouez point; en cette conjoncture,
Le soupçon m'est plus doux que la vérité sûre;
L'obscurité m'en plaît, et j'aime à n'écouter
Que ce qui laisse encor liberté d'en douter.

(V.i)

To the very last, Orode's motives and actions are left ambiguous. Suréna is killed—and by Orode's orders, though we are never told so explicitly. He is killed for disobeying the king—but we are told so in the most oblique way possible, by what a confidante thought she heard an (unknown) person say:

Et je pense avoir même entendu quelque voix
Nous crier qu'on apprît à dédaigner les rois.

In Orode's character, then, we have ambiguities in plenty: we are as far as possible from the clear-cut marionettes which nineteenth-century critics alleged populated Corneille's later plays. But the point is certainly not that Orode is presented 'in the round' (as the phrase goes) as a man who must also act as a king. The vacillation is part of the design of the play, not a part of a naturalistic character-study.

If this is true of Orode, it is doubly true of Eurydice and Suréna. Undoubtedly they love each other, but their actions are curiously oblique. Will Eurydice marry Pacorus? Of course:

Epousez-moi, Seigneur, et laissez-moi me taire . . .
Je ferais ce que font les coeurs obéissants . . .
Ce que je fais enfin.

(II.ii)

But she will not marry him yet:

Il (Pacorus) se verrait, Seigneur, dès ce soir mon
   époux,
S'il n'eût point voulu voir dans mon coeur plus
   que vous . . .
Pour peine il attendra l'effort de mon devoir . . .
Le devoir vient à bout de l'amour le plus ferme.

(V.i)

She is willing that Suréna should marry anyone else but Mandane; she is willing that he should save himself by marrying Mandane, providing he does not ask her permission:

Qu'il s'y donne, Mandame, et ne m'en dise rien.

(IV.ii)

She repeatedly (and justly) vows to kill herself if Suréna is killed, yet she refuses on the following grounds to save

him by telling him to marry Mandane:

Savez-vous qu'à Mandane envoyer ce que
   j'aime,
C'est de ma propre main m'assassiner moi-
   même?

(V.iv)

Eurydice loves Suréna, yet she will not save him (as Palmis tells her in V.iv, 'Il court à son trépas, et vous en serez cause'). In obeying her 'devoir' she agrees to give him up, but by refusing to give him up she kills him. The paradox is carried down from the broad design to the details. In Act I, Scene ii, she tells Palmis that Suréna can hardly love her, because he avoids her:

Mais dites-moi, Madame, est-il bien vrai qu'il
   m'aime?
Dites; et s'il est vrai, pourquoi fuit-il mes yeux?

Four lines later, when he has come in, she says to him:

Je vous ai fait prier de ne me plus revoir,
Seigneur: votre présence étonne mon devoir.

In a different play, this might be psychological subtlety ('Ah! je ne croyais pas qu'il fût si près d'ici'). Here, it is so only incidentally: it is a local manifestation of an all-pervading paradox. This comes out most clearly in the presentation of the hero. Suréna is a hero in all senses: brave, virile, a warrior. But here he appears in a passive rôle. He takes the true heroic stand:

J'ai vécu pour ma gloire autant qu'il fallait
   vivre,
Et laisse un grand exemple à qui pourra me
   suivre.

(IV.iv)

The threats and hints of Pacorus do not move him:

Je fais plus, je prévois ce que j'en dois attendre;
Je l'attends sans frayeur; et quel qu'en soit le
   cours,
J'aurai soin de ma gloire; ordonnez de mes
   jours.

(IV.iv)

Nevertheless, he is adept at evading the issue (Orode complains of this: Suréna m'a surprise, et je n'aurais pas dit Qu'avec tant de valeur il eût eu tant d'esprit), and he is capable of equivocation, even lies, when Pacorus asks him if Eurydice had any suitors:

Durant tout mon séjour rien n'y blessait ma vue;
Je n'y rencontrais point de visite assidue,
Point de devoirs suspects, ni d'entretiens si doux
Que, si j'avais aimé, j'en dusse être jaloux.

(II.i)

Again, this ambiguity is not to be taken as a personal trait showing his lack of heroic qualities: Suréna is a hero, because we are told so in verse that is unmistakably serious. He is not a king:

> Mais il sait rétablir les rois dans leurs Etats.
> Des Parthes le mieux fait d'esprit et de visage,
> Le plus puissant en biens, le plus grand en
>   courage,
> Le plus noble.
>
> (I.i)

> Il n'est rien d'impossible à la valeur d'un
>   homme
> Qui rétablit son maître et triomphe de Rome.
>
> (III.ii)

The point of the contrast is that it is paradoxical. The paradox is sustained to the end. In the last two acts, it becomes suffocatingly certain that Suréna will die. The gates of the palace are shut, and we can only wait for the murder. In Act V, Scene iii, it is quite obvious that Orode has decided to kill him, and that there is no escape from the palace save through death. But Suréna does not see this:

> Non, non, c'est d'un bon oeil qu'Orode me
>   regarde;
> Vous le voyez, ma soeur, je n'ai pas même un
>   garde.

Corneille is not trying to manipulate alternatives of hope and fear so as to generate suspense. Nor is he indulging in psychological byplay about the obtuseness of heroes. Even as Suréna speaks, we know that escape is hopeless. What we have is the supreme paradox, the trapped animal who cries, 'Je suis libre'.

Suréna leaves the palace, and even this detail has its significance in the close tissue of the play. Corneille usually avoids mentioning the rooms in which the actions of his plays take place, lest we should accuse him of infringing the unity of place. In his third **Discours,** he introduces the concepts of a *lieu théâtral* in which it is assumed that characters can tell their secrets as they would in their own apartments. As he points out, this is no more than an arbitrary convention. Nevertheless, the *lieu théâtral* in principle represents a place where the characters could, in real life, reasonably carry out their business, as the strict critics of the time demanded. Usually we can make out which concrete place it represents at any one time. A clear example is *Tite et Bérénice*. Act I takes place in Domitie's apartment: she voices her secret thoughts there, and Domitian comes to visit her. Act II is in Tite's audience chamber: Domitan, Domitie and Bérénice all come to him there. Tite expressly sends Bérénice to her apartment, and Domitie resolves to visit her there. Act III, then, is set in Bérénice's apartment, and the others come to visit her. In these three acts, we have three different rooms in the palace, and the reasons for the characters' comings and goings between them are plainly accounted for, as in any naturalistic play. They could be represented by three different sets, and the fact that they were all represented by one *palais à volonté* is purely a conces-

sion to the exigencies of stage-setting and the demands of the critics for exact unity of place. In Acts IV and V, however, Corneille cannot manage so neatly: the complications of the plot demand too much coming and going. He therefore takes refuge in vagueness. But this vagueness is due to embarrassment about the unity of place: we feel he would set his scenes in a definite room if he could.

There is nothing of this feeling in *Suréna*. The action takes place in an ideal space: a palace with gates that can be closed and with a street outside, but with no precise geography. Here the lovers meet, here the king consults his counsellor, here the king comes to visit Eurydice, but the place is impossible to define realistically. It is at once an open space to which all can come, a prison from which there is no escape, and an enclosure which anyone leaves at his peril: when Suréna leaves, he dies. It is not a series of physical rooms: it is a *lieu vague;* a place where dreams cross.

We can now perhaps look back at some of the features of the verse. It is full of the seventeenth-century jargon of love—'feux', 'flammes', 'soupirs'. What is extraordinary is how Corneille gives life and vigour to these banalities. Pacorus says he cannot marry Eurydice if she loves someone else:

> Que sera-ce, grands dieux! si toute ma tendresse
> Rencontre un souvenir plus cher à ma princesse,
> Si le coeur pris ailleurs ne s'en arrache pas,
> Si pour un autre objet il soupire en mes bras!
>
> (II.i)

The first two lines are insipid enough, but with the last two the dead metaphors revive. 'Arrache', with its cruel tearing sound; its association with 'coeur' (a key word in the play); the way in which the abstract 'objet' takes on a new significance by association with the physical reality of a woman 'sighing' (another word that comes in again and again) actually in the arms of her husband; these catch up the dull jargon into the more intense life of poetry.

We may find a controlling purpose in the apparent clumsiness of some of the verse. Ormène reports to Eurydice:

> Oui, votre intelligence à demi découverte
> Met votre Suréna sur le bord de sa perte.
> Je l'ai su de Sillace; et j'ai lieu de douter
> Qu'il n'ait, s'il faut tout dire, ordre de l'arrêter.
>
> (IV.i)

Even in this fragment the themes of the play appear: 'à demi découvert' (the secret throughout is revealed without being revealed—nothing is unambiguously stated); 'votre Suréna . . . sa perte' (Eurydice is causing the death of her lover); 'j'ai lieu de douter / Qu'il n'ait . . . ordre de l'arrêter' (the characteristic doubt again); 's'il faut tout dire' (the reluctance to speak directly which characterises the play and allows the action to proceed without proceeding); and the placing of the last phrase, where the sentence is checked, like a current running back on itself (the theme of paradox that runs through the play). And what follows this speech is significant. After the ambiguities and the check to the forward movement, we have a decisive lunge forward: 'On n'oserait, Ormène; on n'oserait.' This juxtaposition of contraries is also characteristic of the play, and even here the paradoxical form is maintained: the verb 'to dare' appears in the negative and the conditional.

It should now be clear that Corneille is following a consistent method. The consistency with which indirectness and paradox are expressed at every level—the plot, the setting, the characters, the language; the avoidance of any temptation to set up peripheral centres of interest; the lack of any neat 'meaning' that can be formulated in prose terms; above all, the completeness with which the action is controlled by and embodied in the verse: all these confirm abundantly that *Suréna* is poetic in method. Why, more than thirty years after *Cinna,* should Corneille return to the poetic form? And what shall we call the result?

2

The clue can be found only if we listen carefully to the verse:

Ne me parle plus tant de joie et d'hyménée.

(I.i)

Ma flamme dans mon coeur se tenait renfermée.

(I.i)

L'amour, sous les dehors de la civilité

(I.i)

Plus je hais, plus je souffre, et souffre autant
    que j'aime.

(I.ii)

Mais qui cherche à mourir doit chercher ce qui
    tue.

(I.iii)

  Il est hors d'apparence
Qu'il fasse un tel refus sans quelque préférence,
Sans quelque objet charmant, dont l'adorable
    choix
Ferme tout son grand coeur au pur sang de ses
    rois.

(III.iii)

Happiness is refused; love, though greatly desired, is held back from expression; the pleasure of love is therefore pain. In the last line quoted, we have an almost physical enactment of the central image: the heart, the seat of life and passion, is closed against the blood, as though the symbol of life itself refused to live (which is what Eurydice and Suréna both do). Moreover, this refusal is the result of a conscious effort. This comes up strongly in [a passage already quoted], where Orode refuses to learn the

secret he desires to learn. Its fullest development is in the lovers' scene at the end of Act I. Suréna will die of grief, but Eurydice (symbolic name!) adjures him:

Vivez, Siegneur, vivez, afin que je languisse,
Qu'à vos feux ma langueur rende langtemps
    justice.
Le trépas à vos yeux me semblerait trop doux,
Et je n'ai pas encore assez souffert pour vous.
Je veux qu'un noir chagrin à pas lents me
    consume,
Qu'il me fasse à longs traits goûter son
    amertume;
Je veux, sans que la mort ose me secourir,
Toujours aimer, toujours souffrir, toujours
    mourir.

It is this deliberate holding-back which forbids escape:

    Où dois-je recourir,
O ciel! s'il faut toujours aimer, souffrir, mourir!

The sexual imagery is obvious enough, and is carried forward to the end. Suréna dies, and immediately Eurydice dies:

Non, je ne pleure point, Madame, mais je meurs.

Whether she swoons or kills herself, the erotic parallel is plain. The tension is discharged, and in Palmis's last words the normal pattern of Cornelian energy reasserts itself. There is nothing languid about the last lines of Corneille's last play:

Suspendez ces douleurs qui pressent de mourir,
Grands dieux! et, dans les maux où vous m'avez
    plongée,
Ne souffrez point ma mort que je ne sois
    vengée!

Corneille is of course not merely exploiting the sexual suggestiveness of his theme. Still less is he imitating Racine: his theme is based on the image of refusal to become directly conscious of passion, which is very different from what we find in Racine. We must look for a deeper reason for his use of this imagery. The reason is that he is writing tragedy.

Tragedy demands a sense of the inevitable, of a daemonic and perhaps malevolent power beyond conscious human control. Corneille as a poet had never admitted such a power; his plays, however harsh, leave men's destinies either in the hands of men, or at least formally in the hands of a benevolent providence. In *Suréna,* perhaps because Racine had shown that such a conception was possible, he turns inwards to find this ineluctable fate. To be sure, it is not embodied in the instincts themselves— this is not Corneille's view of human nature—but in the conscious effort to control these impulses. But—and this is the distinctive feature of *Suréna*—this conscious effort has become merged with the automatisms it suppresses. Hence this curious paradox, this flowing back of the stream upon itself, which gives the play its inner tension. This is a difficult conception to render, and one which is equally far removed from optimistic metaplay and the ritual and public tragedy of the Greeks. In *Suréna,* fate is inevitable, yet private and human: it is still caught and held 'sous les dehors de la civilité'.

3

Suréna is the most difficult of Corneille's plays to judge. The best starting point is perhaps the critique by Steiner, who, though he sees the high merit of the play, finally decides that it fails by a small margin to achieve greatness. His reasons are three: the verse is uneven because of the attempt to express things for which the heroic couplet is not suited ('Sometimes the complex motion—the attempt to maintain a free impulse beneath a rigid surface—produces in the verse a curious sag or concavity'); there is a softness about the play which is elegiac rather than dramatic ('Corneille's purpose . . . I take it, was the creation of a kind of dramatic elegy—a drama of lament rather than of conflict'); and the action is too weak ('Perhaps the action is too slight to sustain the elaboration and the complexity of the poetic means').

The overall judgment is hard to fault, and the adverse criticisms obviously have substance. Nevertheless, if the reading suggested in this chapter is correct, we might formulate them rather differently. *Suréna* is a poetic play, and the poetry is of a high order. The occasional weaknesses of the verse—by which Steiner perhaps means the awkwardness of such passages as Ormène's speech [already quoted, which begins with the words "Oui, votre intelligence à demi découverte"]—are not weaknesses of expression at all: they result from the thoroughness with which the overall design of the play is made to inform every detail. Nor is it quite fair to complain of the elegiac softness of the plot: the indirectness and ambiguity spring from the rigour with which the form of every element is dictated by the central meaning of the play. In my view it is also slightly misleading to speak of the action as being too slight to sustain the elaboration and complexity of the poetic means: in *Suréna,* to a quite remarkable extent, the poetic means *are* the drama. Rather than saying that the action will not sustain the poetry, we might say that the action and the verse, each in their own mode, are the exact expression of the meaning of the play. It is not as though directness and slowness of action in themselves make a play undramatic. There are many works of the highest quality which in their several ways are more tenous, more obscure, more lacking in plot, than *Suréna: Prometheus Bound, The Trojan Women, En Attendant Godot, Long Day's Journey into Night, The Caretaker, La Guerre Civile.* In each of these, we feel that the apparent lack of action is appropriate, because the simple structure of incidents is exactly what is needed to express the underlying theme; in each of them, we feel the action is dramatic, because the underlying theme is dramatic. Where we might legitimately find *Suréna* lacking is in the dramatic quality of its central idea. The tragic quality of the play depends very much on the concept that in complicity with our unconscious desires we may consciously seek our own destruction. This may strike us as true, and profound. But on the stage, it will nearly always seem that a conscious drive can be reversed, and if the drive is not reversed the destructiveness appears merely wilful. It is for this reason, if at all, that the play seems to lack essential strength.

I have said 'if at all' and 'seems to lack'. We have no opportunity to see the play's effect in the theatre. In the absence of this vital evidence, we cannot reach a firm conclusion about *Suréna.* It lacks the sweep and energy of *Sertorius,* just as *Sertorius* lacks the purity and concentration of *Suréna.* In Corneille's work, only *Cinna* combines formal perfection and strength. It is a matter of choice whether we place energy before purity of form. In our more wide-awake moments we must prefer *Sertorius.* But *Suréna* will always be loved by those who value formal perfection.

John Cairncross (essay date 1975)

SOURCE: An introduction to *The Cid, Cinna, The Theatrical Illusion* by Pierre Corneille, translated by John Cairncross, Penguin Books, 1975, pp. 11-19.

[*A longtime correspondent for the* Observer, *the* Economist, *and the Canadian Broadcasting Corporation, Cairncross has translated several plays by Racine, Molière, and Corneille into English. In the following essay, he surveys the principal attributes of Cornelian drama, particularly its themes, characterization, and preoccupations.*]

Fate has dealt unkindly with the great seventeenth-century French dramatist, Pierre Corneille, even in his native land. 'As a result of an over-simple and restrictive tradition,' writes Raymond Picard in his admirable analysis of the writer [*Two Centuries of French Literature*], 'it has long been contended that, of all Corneille's plays, only a handful of tragedies such as *Le Cid, Horace, Cinna,* or *Pompée* (1637-43) deserve to survive. By disregarding all the rest, critics have had no trouble in reducing Corneille's genius to a few dramatic devices, some psychological stances and a certain lofty tone, and thus, by an obvious over-simplification, they have frozen the founder of the classical theatre in a pose of exaggerated sublimity.' But in fact 'his thirty-two plays show a prodigious range of talent. Far from having worked to a formula, Corneille again and again struck out in original directions, renewing his strength and genius over forty long years of writing. His work pulsates with an extraordinary creative vitality. A tragedy follows a comedy or a tragicomedy; a tragedy-ballet comes after a heroic comedy; and within the same genre there are profound differences between the plays.'

His first plays are poles apart from the stereotype of the bombastic tragedies he is represented as having written. 'With such works as *Mélite, La Galerie du Palais* and *La Place Royale* (1629-34), he created an original type of five-act comedy in verse.' They are remarkable for 'the naturalness, the freshness and the grace of the young people [portrayed], the badinage and the wit, the truth to life of the attitudes, the penetrating observation of the manners of the age—all in a simple colloquial style'. As Corneille himself pointed out (in 1634), 'My vein . . . often combines the lofty buskin with the comic sock, and . . . pleases the audience by striking contrasting notes.'

'But, at about the same time as Corneille wrote these three "contemporary" comedies, he produced in *Clitandre* an Elizabethan play in which fantasy runs wild. The stage changes from a wood to a prison, and then to a cave. Before the spectator's eyes, Pymantes tries to rape Dorisa who in her turn puts out one of his eyes. Frenzied, utterly impossible actions are enacted in an entirely fanciful world.' *The Theatrical Illusion* (*L'Illusion Comique*), dated 1636, also takes place in this world of fantasy, as readers will see from the Preface and translation of the play in the present volume; the irrepressible Corneille even parodies the martial sentiments of *The Cid* before that play was written.

What is more, though he 'appealed much more to the mind than to the eye in four or five of the finest tragedies of the seventeenth century, . . . he continued to delight and astonish visually . . . "My main aim," he wrote of the musical play of *Andromède*, "has been to satisfy the visual sense by the gorgeousness and the variety of the scenery and not to appeal to the intellect by cogent arguments or to touch the heart by delicate representations of the passions." '

The second obstacle to Corneille's demummification is the old but tenacious fallacy that his plays represent a school-book conflict, especially in *The Cid,* between 'love which is alleged to be a passion replete with weaknesses and honour which dictates duty. The carefully pondered love, which one feels for and claims from someone whom one deems worthy of it, is also a duty. Rodrigo goes so far as to affirm in a lyrical meditation at the end of the first act

> Duty's not only to my mistress. It
> Is also to my father.

Moreover, the two types of duty do not really conflict. If he does not avenge the insult done to his father, Rodrigo will draw down on himself the contempt of Ximena and will thereby forfeit her love for that love implies esteem and even admiration. Paradoxically it is his love for her, as well as his honour, that forces him to kill his sweetheart's father and thus to raise an obstacle between the two lovers which might to some appear insurmountable. As soon as Rodrigo has transcended the basic option between cowardice which would have involved the loss of everything—honour and love—and heroism, which is his vocation, he has no alternative but to fulfil his destiny as a hero. In this as in other tragedies, what is *cornélien* is the intolerable and sometimes agonizing situation in which the character is trapped and from which he can free himself only by shouldering his responsibility as a hero.

'Now, as it happens, Corneille's characters are nothing if not heroes. Rodrigo, Horace, Augustus and Nicomedes are of more than human stature. Endowed with extraordinary moral strength, they possess to the utmost degree the virtue of *générosité* (nobility of soul); they are ready to devote all their inner resources to the task of incarnating their sublime image of themselves. Will-power, self-control, courage and judgement, all these enhance man's powers and his greatness. In the humanist world in which they live, it would seem that nothing—misfortune, suffering or catastrophe—can undermine their overweening integrity. Fortified by their energy and stoicism, they have nothing to fear at the hands of Destiny. They will parry its blows, or bear them uncomplainingly. Fate may dog their steps. For them, it is nothing but a congeries of external accidents and mishaps, and it is powerless to force an entry into their hearts and alter their resolve. Man is entirely free and fully responsible. He has no grounds for dreading the gods. When treating the most sombre theme in Greek tragedy, Corneille in his *Oedipe* (1659) radically transforms the spirit of the legend and does not shrink from writing

> The heavens, fair in reward and punishment,
> To give to deeds their penalty or meed
> Must offer us their aid, then let us act.

This concept of free will is clearly borrowed from the Jesuits and the humanist tradition. The tragic element in Corneille, then, is not to be sought in the pathetic helplessness of the characters but in the harrowing circumstances in which a wicked fate has placed them. What we have, in a way, is a tragedy of circumstances, over which the hero must rise superior, relying on his own forces.

'But he does so only after exacting and grievous efforts. Corneille's characters are no cardboard supermen. For them, heroism is not a second nature to which they need merely abandon themselves. They are not sublime automata. They know what suffering is, and they sometimes vent their feelings in lyrical stanzas and in monologues. They are tugged this way and that. They are rent by inner conflicts, and they admit as much. Ximena confesses that Rodrigo "tears [her] heart to pieces"; but she adds, it is "without dividing [her] soul" (III, 3); Pauline also, in *Polyeucte,* recognizes that her duty "tears her soul" although it "does not alter its resolve" (II, 2). There is no doubt that we must jettison the half-baked concept of the swashbuckling Cornelian hero, always sure of himself and unhesitatingly sublime, whose greatness is manifested primarily in a swaggering boastfulness. Even Augustus (in *Cinna*) complains of having "a wavering heart" (IV, 3). It is only at the end of the play when he proves victorious over himself that he exclaims (and this is more wishful thinking than actual fact):

> I'm master of myself as of the world.

> (V, 3)

There is a quivering sensitivity at loggerheads with itself, a three-dimensional reality, in these characters who are too readily described as being all of a piece. Heroism is not something already conferred on them. It is conquered stage by stage as the action unfolds. The hero takes shape before the spectator's eyes. People are not born heroes, they become heroes. Corneille's Theatre is, in the literal sense of the phrase, "a school of moral greatness".

'This greatness is not always synonymous with goodness and virtue. A great crime is also a great deed. Moral power and energy are important in their own right and not only because of the enterprises on which they are brought to bear. Thus, Cleopatra's crimes in *Rodogune* (1644) "are accompanied by a moral greatness which has something so grandiose about it," notes Corneille, "that, at the same time as we detest her actions, we admire the source from which they spring" (*First Discourse*). What one has to do is to arouse in the spectators' hearts a feeling of astonishment, indeed a transport, whether of horror or admiration, at the deeds of which man is capable at the summit of his powers. Now in Corneille the hero arrives at this paroxysm only when the society in which he lives and his place in it are challenged, when his *gloire*—that is, his dignity, his reputation, his honour—are at stake, as well as the safety of the state. Political interests are regarded as providing the hero with the best opportunity and means for their fulfilment. Hence their important role in this theatre. Love, as against this, remains in the background, for tragedy "calls for some great issue of state . . . and seeks to arouse fears for setbacks which are more serious than the loss of one's mistress". In *Sertorius* (1662), one character asks

> When plans of such importance are conceived,
> Can one put in the balance thoughts of love?
>
> (I, 3)

And in the same play, another character gives the following advice:

> Let us, my lord, let's leave for petty souls
> This lowly give and take of amorous sighs.
>
> (I, 3)

Love, which is convincingly portrayed in many guises in such a host of characters, may prove their downfall. It cannot shape their destiny.'

It could be added . . . that the particular type of heroism analysed by Picard is not to be found in the early works. It is only in *The Place Royale* (1634) that we find the first traces of the conviction which was to pervade all his later plays—that the hero must retain his inner, moral independence, especially in love. The dominant note until then is 'a joyous lust for life, a certain cruelty, a pronounced taste for women in their simplest and most sensual aspects, a love for sword play and adventure'. There is no trace, for example, of his subsequent ideals in *The Theatrical Illusion*, which has the same freshness and fantasy as some of Shakespeare's comedies. In the same way, Corneille was uninhibited by the famous three unities which demanded that the central subject be closely knit, the scene unchanging, and the action confined to the space of twenty-four hours.

In *The Cid,* on the contrary, the new heroic ideal is the driving force in the minds and acts of the main characters, as Picard has so lucidly shown. But in that play there is such a powerful charge of youthful passion and excitement and such a balance between richness of episode and tautness of construction that the work is free from pompousness, unreal heroism or contrivance.

However, *The Cid,* though universally popular and the first masterpiece of the classical French stage, came under heavy fire from the playwright's rivals and was later submitted (in 1637) by Cardinal Richelieu to the newly founded French Academy (the literary establishment of the day) which was to act as an arbiter between the opposing factions. The Academy, though it tried hard to be fair, was in the main composed of 'the learned' who, while able to see the formal weaknesses of the work, were blind to its elemental greatness. Their findings praised Corneille warmly, but agreed with the critics that he had not observed the rules. Corneille was deeply hurt by the verdict, and his friend, Chapelain, found him two years later still obsessed by this issue and working out arguments to refute the Academy's strictures. Even in 1660, he was still trying in his critical writings to win a retrospective battle on this debate.

And hence, when he emerged from a three-year silence and produced *Horatius* and *Cinna* (in 1640), his craftsmanship, his choice of subject and his views had suffered a sea-change. True, he was always to maintain that he accepted the rules only to the extent that they suited him (but, as a modern writer has put it neatly, only once he had established what the rules were), but all his life, as far as he possibly could, he tried to stick to them, and often with the most disturbing results. For his innate tendency was to cram his five acts with the most varied action, whereas the three unities are suited to the spare psychological tragedy where external action is reduced to the absolute minimum (as in Racine's works).

The same switch in emphasis is reflected in his subjects. Whereas both *The Cid* and *The Theatrical Illusion* are Spanish by inspiration and source, *Horatius* and *Cinna* (for the first time in Corneille's theatre) take place in ancient Rome. Of course, the change was not an absolute one, for Corneille by no means abandoned Spain as a quarry for dramatic themes. But that he veered in a different direction is clear.

And lastly, there is a difference in the political values underlying his work. In *The Cid,* even if we make the fullest allowances for the fact that the action takes place at the height of the Middle Ages in Spain when kings were by no means absolute, there is a distinct contrast between the image of the monarch in, say, *The Cid* and in *Cinna.* In the former play, the king is still very much *primus inter pares.* He is dependent on, and is defied by, his general (the Count) to a far greater degree than any other prince in Corneille's theatre, and certainly than Augustus. What is more, the spotlight in *The Cid* is focused on a mere knight—and a twenty-year-old stripling at that. On the other hand, the men who challenge the limitless power of Caesar (Cinna, Maximus and the rest) would be ignominiously swept into the discard of history were they not rescued by the equally limitless nobility of soul of the emperor. Here again, of course, it is not a question of a complete volte-face. Corneille retains his belief in the superiority of the concept of the king as a Christian knight, firm but merciful, as against that of the centralized monarchy and its Machiavellian ethos which was being sponsored by Richelieu. And the heroism which, from *The Cid* on, is a constant of his work is not only based on grandeur of soul, but is placed at the service of the romanesque ideal of honour.

'Romanesque', as the form of the word indicates, stands for the type of literature and ethos derived from the medieval romance, and hence impregnated with its spirit. The romanesque thus meant the far-fetched, the unusual, the adventurous, the ideal, often with a touch of the supernatural. The typical subjects were the exploits of knights errant—single combats and abductions. The guiding principle was that of honour and a romantic devotion to the beloved, and the ending was always a happy one. Much of the material for romanesque novels or plays was taken from Spain. (There was, it has been noted, a large Spanish colony in Corneille's native Rouen.) In this largely feudal world, nobility of soul and nobility of rank are broadly identical. If abstraction is made of this equation, however, the romanesque ethos of the early seventeenth century is disconcertingly similar to that of the cinema. There are also close analogies with the works of Shakespeare, and it is perhaps in this perspective that Corneille can best be appreciated by an Anglo-Saxon public. In fact, in the rare cases where the language barrier has been surmounted, the reaction of English and American readers is usually one of incredulous delight at finding a French classical dramatist in whose plays events actually happen and which do not consist simply of endless discussions.

Of Corneille the man, only the briefest account is called for. He was born of sound bourgeois stock in 1606 in the Norman town of Rouen, and, after studies with the Jesuits (who at the time had most of pre-University education in their hands), he entered the legal profession and practised till 1662 when he moved to Paris with his brother and fellow writer, Thomas. He was a model father to his seven children, though perhaps somewhat over-keen in soliciting pensions and favours, for example by obsequious dedications. He was also the first dramatist to treat his works as an important source of income, which shocked many of his contemporaries. He was awkward in speech and manner, but was always attracted, though within respectable limits, by women. He was justifiably proud of his works and fiercely aggressive in defending them against criticism. As Adam puts it, he had an unfortunate way of proving that he was right. He resented competition and used the 'Norman clan' (his brother and Donneau de Visé, who controlled much of the press at the time) to suppress his competitors such as the up-and-coming Racine, who referred to him waspishly as 'an ill-intentioned old playwright'. Corneille had small cause for such defensiveness, for he was the uncontested master of the dramatic scene. In 1663, a collected edition of his plays was published in two folio volumes—an honour usually reserved for the classics such as Virgil. He lived modestly, but there is no truth in the assertion that he died in poverty (1684, at the age of 78).

There is no obvious link between Corneille's life and theatre, unless we regard the latter as an escape from his relatively modest social position in an aristocratic world. He was a typical representative of his age in his attitudes, but he was highly untypical in his literary craftsmanship. To his inventive and inexhaustible dramatic genius must be added an infinite capacity for going over his works again and again, usually, but not always, with felicitous results, which, however, improved the clarity and impact of the lines rather than the music. If he lacks the harmony of Racine, he has a power and sonority which often, in the original, remind the listener of the finer flights of Elizabethan tragedy.

Sharon Harwood-Gordon (essay date 1989)

SOURCE: An introduction to *The Poetic Style of Corneille's Tragedies: An Aesthetic Interpretation,* The Edwin Mellen Press, 1989, pp. vii-xi.

[In the essay below, Harwood-Gordon examines Corneille's poetic style.]

Perhaps no other writer of the classical age of French literature has undergone such dramatic swings in public acceptance and appreciation as Pierre Corneille. Enthusiastically received by his contemporaries at the time of the première of *Le Cid* and acclaimed as a genius of theatrical invention for several seasons to follow, Corneille felt for the first time in 1645, with the production of *Théodore,* the sting of rejection. A series of plays that met with sharp disapproval from both the critics and the public ensued, and, finally, with the failure of *Pertharite* in 1652 after only one performance, the weary dramatist acknowledged his passing from favor with theatre audiences and withdrew from dramatic production for seven years. However, when he returned to the stage in 1659 with the production of *Oedipe,* he once again found audiences willing to accept his particular style of tragedy. But his newly recovered mastery proved to be short-lived, for his moment of glory was soon dimmed by the brilliance of a young rival whose style and mood seemed more in harmony with that of audiences in the 1660's. During the remaining years of the seventeenth century Corneille was recognized as the talented author of the famous quartet of tragedies—*Le Cid, Horace, Polyeucte,* and *Cinna*—but the other plays of his repertory were generally ignored. The eighteenth century was particularly harsh in its attitude toward Corneille's dramatic compositions, which were scorned for their grandiloquent and unnatural style and ridiculed for their ponderous debates on the hierarchy of duties that forms the basis of so many Cornelian conflicts. Although Corneille began to find favor again with the Romantics, he was never as highly esteemed as his younger colleague, Racine. An ambivalent attitude toward the genius of Corneille and the literary merits of his work has persisted to the present day. Even though the universal themes of duty, honor, love, faith, and patriotism remain as true today as they were more than three hundred years ago, the modern reader feels at times bewildered and occasionally frustrated by the ornate linguistic style of Cornelian tragedy. However, we [can] see that the use of such a complex and embellished manner of speech contributes significantly to the definition of the characters' individual psyches and to the establishment of an appropriate psychological atmosphere for the tragedies.

The tragedies of Pierre Corneille have been criticized since the time of Voltaire for their grandiloquence, bombast, and excessive ornamentation; they are frequently characterized as being unrealistic and unnatural in both content and form. Critics have renounced the plays of Corneille for their failure to reflect the natural manner of expression of ordinary human beings, and this observation is quite accurate. But one must remember that Corneille's heroes and antagonists are *not* ordinary human beings who speak and act according to the codes of modern society; Corneille's personages are, on the contrary, extraordinary, superhuman creatures who belong to a rarefied heroic universe to which the conventional, everyday mortal, filled as he is with doubts, uncertainties, and trepidations, does not have access.

The exuberance and lyrical majesty of Corneille's style in his early tragedies is due at least partially to the writer's acquaintance with the declamatory grandiloquence of Renaissance tragedy. As a student in Rouen the young Corneille undoubtedly read the works of Jodelle, Montchrestien, Desmasures, La Taille, and Grevin whose works frequently echo the lyrical harmony of the Pléiade. The lengthy and ornate monologues coupled with the presence of lyrical choruses that serve as a commentary and elaboration of the action no doubt inspired the young dramatist to model the dramatic discourses of his early tragedies on the Renaissance style.

During the early years of the seventeenth century, especially in provincial centers such as Rouen, the philosophical heritage of the Renaissance still lived. The humanistic ideals that proclaimed man's innate goodness, probity, and strength of character had not, during the formative years of Corneille's education and training, yielded to the pessimistic view of human nature that would shadow the moral atmosphere of Corneille's later years. In the first few decades of the seventeenth century man continued to be seen as a powerful and virtuous creature whose will could triumph over most obstacles of human invention. And the individual was free to espouse the loftiest of ideals, which he was quite capable of defending and promulgating. Paul Bénichou has observed that Corneille has not in modern times been generally appreciated because of the "inhumaine bienséance morale" of his work [*Morales du grand siècle,* 1948]. Modern readers often feel uncomfortable with the uncompromising commitment to a sublime ideal that is made by so many Cornelian heroes; these readers dismiss as vainglorious, pompous, even absurd the Cornelian dedication to virtue, honor, and duty. Corneille's contemporaries, however, did not share this sentiment, for they greatly admired the passion, fire, and vigor of Cornelian tragedy. Mme de Sévigné spoke for the majority of her contemporaries when she wrote of her admiration for "ces tirades . . . qui font frissoner." During the age of Louis XIII the humanistic ideals still prevailed, particularly among the aristocracy who were, during this epoch, making a last heroic effort to affirm their supremacy with respect to the king. Under the ineffectual Louis XIII and during the minority of Louis XIV the power and influence of the nobility were aggrandized to the point that the aristocrats maintained for the last time the illusion that they were in control of France. During this period, which coincides with the composition of Corneille's most noble and grandiloquent tragedies, the nobility clung ferociously to the last vestiges of their feudal supremacy. The heroic stoicism and lofty eloquence of such heroes as Rodrigue, Horace, Polyeucte, and Auguste seem quite natural in the "atmosphère de la gloire, de la générosité et du romanesque aristocratiques, telle qu'on la respirait en France pendant le règne de Louis XIII . . . " [Benichou]. The grandiloquent monologues, tirades, and stances spoken by Cornelian heroes and heroines in the early tragedies thus mirror the prevailing moral and psychological atmosphere of the times. And Corneille was not alone in glorifying the super-human hero whose will was stronger than his passions and whose polished discourse echoes the sublimity of his nature; exceptional individuals who are strong in soul and sublime in speech abound in the tragedies of Corneille's contemporaries such as Tristan l'Hermite, Rotrou, Mairet, Scudéry, and Du Ryer.

Corneille's style is thus a faithful mirror of the psychological, philosophical, and social attitudes of his day. Corneille's heroes belong to the rarefied universe of the French aristocracy at the crucial moment of its last undaunted assertion of political authority. Corneille creates a lofty and grandiloquent parlance for heroes who are larger than life, whose passions, ideals, and aspirations are noble, august, defiant, and majestic. Their speech is the somewhat pompous, ostentatious style appropriate to the aristocratic cavaliers who saw themselves as the appointed instigators of all movement in French society—a right to which they were entitled by their illustrious ancestry. And yet their manner of speech is not the mere braggadocio of a swaggering *miles gloriosus;* Corneille's heroes, like many of their real counterparts, were firmly committed to illustrious ideals and lofty aspirations that could be expressed only in extraordinary language. In this context, the elaborate discourses so brilliantly colored with highly ornate figures of speech and thought are in perfect accord with the lofty ideals of the hero who strives constantly to subjugate his base passions to his will and reason.

FURTHER READING

Ault, Harold C. "The Tragic Genius of Corneille." *The Modern Language Review* XLV, No. 2 (April 1950): 164-76. Examination of *The Cid, Horatius, Cinna,* and *Polyeuctes* in order to "consider in what way they are still tragedies to an audience very different from that for which Corneille wrote. It is an audience more interested in humanity than in heroism, an audience ignorant of what he was attempting to do and careless as to why he did it in such a particular way, an audience with a cultural background completely changed from that of his."

Barnwell, H. T. *The Tragic Drama of Corneille and Racine: An Old Parallel Revisited.* Oxford: Clarendon Press, 1982, 275 p.

Investigates various aspects of plot in the dramas of Corneille and Racine with the aim of seeing more clearly "both the parallels and the divergences between the two dramatists, not only in their technique itself (what they called their art) but also in its implication in the presentation of their tragic vision."

Borgerhoff, E. B. O. "The Liberalism of Pierre Corneille." In his *The Freedom of French Classicism*, pp. 46-81. Princeton, N.J.: Princeton University Press, 1950.

Discusses Corneille as being among those artists who are "full of contradictions: they are split against themselves. They are very good artists, but perhaps not of the greatest."

Brereton, Geoffrey. "The Comedies of Pierre Corneille." In his *French Comic Drama, from the Sixteenth to the Eighteenth Century*, pp. 12-43. London: Methuen & Co., 1977.

Surveys and expounds upon the comedies, from *Mélite* to *Le Menteur*, from a technical, historical, biographical, and literary viewpoint.

Croce, Benedetto. "The Poetry of Corneille." In his *Ariosto, Shakespeare and Corneille*, translated by Douglas Ainslie, pp. 408-30. New York: Henry Holt and Co., 1920.

Discusses Corneille's dramatic poetry as the key to the playwright's success in "generating those beings, so warm with passion, who insinuate themselves into us and take possession of our imagination, who grow in it and eventually become so familiar to us that we seem to have really met them. . . . "

Gassner, John. "The Heroic Drama of Corneille." In his *Masters of the Drama*, 3d ed., pp. 267-73. New York: Dover Publications, 1954.

Broad survey of Corneille's career, with significant discussion of the dramatic unities as they relate to *The Cid*.

Greenberg, Mitchell. *Corneille, Classicism and the Ruses of Symmetry.* Cambridge: Cambridge Universitiy Press, 1986, 189 p.

Series of discourses on the tragedies through which the critic is enabled "to dialogue with Corneille where he is most compelling and most problematical. In a study that wishes to trace those shifting borders of power and pleasure that allow Corneille's tragedies to continue to speak to us, to involve us in their world, to make, in other words, their past present, these discourses seem

the most apt at engaging Corneille's texts where they engage us, in the unstable margins defining and undermining our articulaton of ourselves in the world."

Hawcroft, Michael. "Corneille's *Clitandre* and the Theatrical Illusion." *French Studies* 47, No. 2 (2 April 1993): 142-55.

Examines *Clitandre* as a play "in which the dramatist self-consciously plays with the notion of illusionist theatre."

Koch, Philip. "Cornelian Illusion." *Symposium* XIV, No. 2 (Summer 1960): 85-99.

Studies Corneille's conception of "illusion," holding that the dramatist "relied heavily on the techniques of illusion in plot development often to embody the major conflicts of the characters and always to sustain the public's interest."

Knight, R. C. *Corneille's Tragedies: The Role of the Unexpected.* New York: Barnes & Noble Books, 1991, 144 p.

Discusses the playwright's conception of tragedy, stressing the importance of the novel and striking in Corneille's works.

Matthews, Brander. "The Development of the French Drama." *International Quarterly* VII, No. 3 (March 1903): 14-31.

Contains an overview of Corneille's significance and the nature of his accomplishment, comparing Corneille to Racine in many areas.

Mueller, Martin. "*Oedipus Res* as Tragedy of Fate: Corneille's *Oedipe* and Schiller's *Di Braut von Messina*." In his *Children of Oedipus, and Other Essays on the Imitation of Greek Tragedy, 1500-1800*, pp. 105-52. Toronto: University of Toronto Press, 1980

Traces patterns of response by Corneille to Sophocles' tragedy and identifies his strategies of transformation used in adapting elements of the older material to the neoclassical French stage.

Nelson, Robert J. *Corneille: His Heroes and Their Worlds.* Philadelphia: University of Pennsylvania Press, 1963, 322 p.

Critical study of Corneille's complete dramatic canon. Nelson provides a résumé of each play discussed, and concludes with a summary chapter, "The Cornelian Universe."

Picard, Raymond. "Corneille's Tragedies." In his *Two Centuries of French Literature*, edited by John Cairncross, pp. 66-82. New York: McGraw-Hill Book Co., 1970.

Discursive survey of the tragedies.

Sellstrom, A. Donald. *Corneille, Tasso and Modern Poetics.* Columbus: Ohio State University Press, 1986, 166 p.

Close study of Torquato Tasso's influence upon Corneille.

Spitzer, Leo. "Corneille's *Polyeucte* and the *Vie de Saint Alexis*." In *Essays on Seventeenth-Century French Literature*, pp. 145-67. Cambridge: Cambridge University Press, 1983.

Spirited defense of *Polyeucte* by means of the medieval legend of Saint Alexis.

Vincent, Leon H. *Corneille*. Boston: Houghton Mifflin, 1901, 197 p.

Biographical and critical introduction to Corneille, written in a familiar style and covering both the plays and their critical reception over the centuries.

Claude Prosper Jolyot de Crébillon (*fils*)

1707-1777

French novelist, short story writer, and dramatist.

INTRODUCTION

The following entry presents a selection of criticism from 1962 to the present. For additional information on Crébillon's life and works see *Literature Criticism from 1400-1800, Volume 1.*

Crébillon's works examine the psychology and ethics of sexuality in the aristocratic society of eighteenth-century France. Scientific advances during the Enlightenment, along with the belief that reason could free humanity from superstition and prejudice, led to an age of broad intellectual tolerance and cosmopolitanism; for the aristocracy, it was also a relatively peaceful and prosperous era during which they were left with few pursuits besides social gatherings, conversation, and dilettantish diversions. Crébillon's characters are aristocrats who fill their time with amateur interests in art and science, and with the pursuit of sensual pleasures. Consistent with the Enlightenment desire to study all aspects of human experience, Crébillon attempted to reconcile pleasure with virtue, and depicted the power and attraction of eroticism without suggesting it as proof of man's fallen nature. Because interest in sexual relations pervaded his world, Crébillon's dissections of the game of seduction reveal as much about his society, in all its aspects, as they do about the psychology of sex.

Biographical Information

Crébillon was the son of Prosper Jolyot de Crébillon (père), a tragic dramatist whose reputation, in his day, rivalled that of Voltaire's. Although the younger Crébillon's first literary works were also written for the theater, he was drawn to dramatic burlesque and farces rather than tragedy. Following this early theatrical work Crébillon turned to short fiction: his first success, *L'Ecumoire; ou, Tanzaï et Néadarné* (1734; *The Skimmer; or, The History of Tanzaï and Néadarné*), is a collection of satirical tales based on the lives of prominent social figures. Because the work was considered slanderous, Crébillon was imprisoned for a short time. The stories in this and his next satirical work, *Le Sopha* (1740; *The Sofa*), which has been called "the most elegantly immoral of all French books," are based on the format of the *Arabian Nights*. *The Sofa* also scandalized court society and earned Crébillon a brief exile from Paris. Throughout his career Crébillon was prominent in social and literary circles, and relied on his knowledge of both in the composition of his witty and penetrating novels. Except for the publication and wide popularity of his novels, there was little

of significance in the remainder of Crébillon's long life; ironically, though, the writer who scandalized Paris early in his career was made royal literary censor in 1759.

Major Works

As the innovator of the elegantly erotic novel of fashionable manners, Crébillon helped create a genre—the memoir novel—that was popular in France from about 1730 to 1770. His masterpiece of the form, *Les Egarements du coeur et de l'esprit* (1736-38; *The Wayward Head and Heart*), is the study of a young man's introduction to sexuality and the sexual mores of his society. More than just a novel of initiation, *The Wayward Head and Heart* also portrays the difficulty of resolving the conflicts between reason and passion. Even though Crébillon never adopted a formal moral philosophy, there is implicit in the book serious criticism of his society's shallowness and callousness—criticism that is especially effective because it does not depend solely on didactic statement, but is demonstrated through the behavior of characters who condemn themselves by their own actions. Crébillon also wrote several Oriental romances, of which *The Skimmer* and *The Sofa*, both full of satire and sexual themes, are regarded as his best. *The Skimmer* deals with the young couple Tanzaï and Néadarné and their search for an understanding of their love. *The Sofa* focuses on the experience of the narrator, a Hindu whose soul has been forced to move from one sofa to another until it finds one upon which two virgins will consummate their desire. P. L. M. Fein has noted, "The main intention in writing those tales that have a fashionable oriental setting seems to have been to satirize French social conventions in an exotic milieu."

Critical Reception

Contemporary criticism of Crébillon has been primarily favorable. He has been praised for his psychological insight, wit, and brilliant description of early eighteenth-century society. Nineteenth-century English critics, who in general found the French novel inferior to the English, criticized Crébillon as a defective observer of the social scene with an insufficient command of the techniques of novel writing; however, critics now believe that Crébillon's merit has been obscured by moral prejudice, and many consider his works misunderstood and underrated by earlier critics. Most modern critics focus their attention on Crébillon's masterpiece, *The Wayward Head and Heart*; they find it a brilliantly understated examination of the immorality of popular conceptions of love in the author's time, not an immoral work concerned solely with erotic titillation. Crébillon's fiction has been the subject of several excellent critical studies in recent years. Vivienne Mylne has asserted that "it seems clear that Crébillon deserves serious attention as a literary craftsman," and Thomas M. Kavanagh has stated, "The pleasure of reading Crébillon lies in admiring how his characters find new ways to surprise, parry, and elude the rhetorical traps they continually set for one another." Martin Turnell and Peter Brooks, in particular, have written lengthy, perceptive essays on the author's work. In addition to the light Crébillon throws upon the age in which he lived, these critics argue that he provides an important and compelling study of the various conflicts surrounding the nature of love and lust, and the games of social intercourse.

PRINCIPAL WORKS

Le Sylphe; ou, Songe de Madame de R*** Ecrit par Elle-meme a Madame de S*** (novel) 1730

Lettres de la Marquise de M*** au Comte de R*** (novel) 1732

L'Ecumoire; ou, Tanzaï et Néardarné [The Skimmer; or The History of Tanzaï and Néardarné] (novel) 1734

Les Egarements du coeur et de l'esprit [The Wayward Head and Heart] (novel) 1736-38

Le Sopha [The Sofa] (novel) 1740

Les Heureux Orphelins (novel) 1754

La Nuit et le moment; ou, Les matines de Cythere [The Night and the Moment] (novel) 1755

Le Hasard du coin du feu, dialogue moral [The Opportunities of the Fireside] (novel) 1763

Les Lettres de la Duchese de *** au Duc de *** (novel) 1768

Lettres Athéniennes, extraites du porte-feuille d'Alcibiade (novel) 1771

CRITICISM

Clifton Cherpack (essay date 1962)

SOURCE: "The Ways of Love," in *An Essay on Crébillon fils*, Duke University Press, 1962, pp. 15-33.

[*In the essay below, Cherpack studies the views on love and sex found in Crébillon's works.*]

> Voilà, repliqua-t-il, une distinction que je n'entends pas; quelle valeur attachez-vous actuellement au mot d'aimer? Celle qu'il a, repartit-elle, je ne lui en connais qu'une. . . . (III)

For Crébillon's characters, this is not a very satisfactory answer to an absorbing question. What is love?

> Je ne connais point, comme vous savez, ce que l'on nomme amour, puisqu'enfin on a décidé qu'il n'est pas vrai qu'un goût, quelque vif qu'il soit, dés qu'il n'est pas durable, soit ce sentiment. . . . (VI)

At times, a fuller and apparently decisive answer is given to this question:

> Ce qu'alors les deux sexes nommaient amour, était une sorte de commerce où l'on s'engageait, souvent même sans goût, où la commodité était toujours préférée à la sympathie, l'intérêt au plaisir, et le vice au sentiment. (I)

But even this positive answer does not begin to describe the varieties of love found in Crébillon's works. The trouble with defining love for his characters is that it is so difficult to separate it from other emotions:

> Je sais que ne vous aime pas: serait-il possible que je m'abusasse? et si je me trompe à mes propres mouvements, pourrais-je espérer de connaître jamais les vôtres? (II)

What appears to be love may be simply desire:

> il avait cette impatience, cette ardeur qui, sans être amour, produit en nous des mouvements qui lui ressemblent, et que les femmes regardent toujours comme les symptômes d'une vrai passion. . . . (II)

Or it may be vanity:

> j'ai compris depuis, par l'impression qu'elle me faisait alors, qu'il est bien plus important pour les femmes de flatter notre vanité que de toucher notre cœur. (I)

Or it may well be only egotism:

l'amour-propre est toujours en nous plus susceptible
de reconnaissance que le cœur. (III)

L'amour-propre est de toutes leurs passions celles que
les femmes songent le moins à combattre, et de laquelle
elles craignent le moins; et celle-là, cependant, est
souvent pour elles plus dangereuse que l'amour. (V)

Love must also, as we have seen, be distinguished from
what is called "goût":

Il n'y a donc, à votre avis, aucune différence entre
l'amour et ce mouvement que nous appelons le goût .
. . ? (III)

Je rencontrais assez souvent ce mouvement vif et
passager, que l'on honore du nom de goût, mais je ne
retrouverais nulle part cet amour, cette délicatesse, cette
tendre volupté qui chez Phénime avait fait si longtemps
mon admiration et mes plaisirs. (III)

ce mouvement léger et capricieux, que l'on appelle le
goût, suffit-il au bonheur? La tranquillité qui
l'accompagne est-elle préférable à ce délicieux délire
où plonge une véritable passion? C'est ce qu'il serait
difficile de décider. (V)

Obviously, the question is complex. Perhaps it would be
helpful to discover how what might be called love starts
in Crébillon's fictional world. The texts already cited hint
that this elusive passion may have its beginning in another emotion. Desire may become true love. *Amour-propre*,
if properly flattered, may turn one's attention towards
another person, and may then become *amour*. Jealousy
may impel one to establish a liaison which may ultimately become a love affair, or it may force the revelation of
hidden love:

je voulais la rendre jalouse. C'est de tous les
mouvements, celui qui agite le plus, et que l'on peut
cacher le moins; et qui, par conséquent, décèle le plus
des sentiments que l'on condamne encore au silence.
(V)

Curiosity is a natural source of enterprises which may
lead to love:

Une si belle persévérance me toucha enfin; la curiosité
s'y joignit; les femmes doivent à ce mouvement plus
de complaisances de notre part qu'elles ne pensent. .
. . (V)

But the psychological state which most typically precedes
what students of Petrarch like to call "enamorment" is,
for Crébillon's characters, a state of nothingness. This
emptiness, this state of boredom, acts like Locke's uneasiness in provoking psychological action, for the void must
be filled. In a young man, this void may be a period
which precedes the first real affair:

Au milieu du tumulte et de l'éclat qui m'environnaient
sans cesse, je sentis que tout manquait à mon cœur: je

désirais une félicité dont je n'avais pas une idée bien
distincte. . . . Je voulais m'étourdir en vain sur l'ennui
intérieur dont je me sentais accablé; le commerce des
femmes pouvait seul les dissiper. (I)

Often it is a state which follows a terminated affair:

Ce vide affreux qui succède à une passion, et si pénible
pour quelqu'un qui vient d'en goûter les charmes. . .
. (III)

Pourrait-il l'apprendre et supporter ce vide affreux qui
allait succéder à ces tendres mouvements . . . ? (IV)

Or it may strike a man after he has wronged a woman:

quelque perfidie, que vous aviez peut-être faite, vous avait
laissé le cœur vide; vous cherchiez à le remplir. . . . (II)

Obviously, one has a right to suspect the genuineness and
spontaneity of a passion which is deliberately sought out
as a way of filling an unpleasant emotional vacuum. Yet,
at times, this void may not be recognized for what it is,
or may not even be felt at all, and love can come to
Crébillon's characters with typical romantic suddenness.
It can be a classic example of love at first sight:

Je ne sais quel mouvement singulier et subit m'agita à
cette vue: frappé de tant de beautés, je demeurais
comme anéanti. Ma surprise allait jusqu'au transport.
(I)

The victim of such a passion may not understand what
has happened to him:

Mais que vous ne vous offriez à mes yeux que sous la
forme de toutes la moins faite pour plaire, et que dans
le même instant, je sois plus vivement frappé que je ne
croyais pas possible d'être; c'est, je vous l'avoue, ce
que je ne puis comprendre. (IV)

Unfortunately, or, perhaps, fortunately, this kind of love
is not common, and is regarded with more and more suspicion in Crébillon's later works:

Clélie: "Quoi! Vous proscrivez ce mouvement dont la
cause nous est inconnue, et qui nous entraîne avec une
violence à laquelle on voudrait vainement résister vers
l'objet qui nous enchante . . . ?"

La Marquise: "Non: en le croyant infiniment plus rare
qu'on ne dit, je sais qu'il existe. . . ." (III)

With the mention of mysterious, irresistible attractions,
we are coming close to the kind of magic, sympathetic
love which Corneille described in his famous "je ne sais
quoi" passage in *Rodogune*. Strangely enough, just this
kind of attraction can be found occasionally in Crébillon's fiction:

un je ne sais quel charme, trop faible dans sa naissance
pour que je crusse avoir besoin de le combattre,

m'attachait à vos discours. (I)

un mouvement secret que l'amour lui inspirait sans doute, le fit s'obstiner à y porter les pas. (IV)

un penchant secret qui nous entraîne vers lui, souvent avant qu'il ait parlé. . . . (VII)

But other things the author says about sympathetic love, as well as love at first sight, suggest that a certain cynicism is more typical of his attitude:

je retournai chez moi, d'autant plus persuadé que j'étais vivement amoureux que cette passion naissait par un de ces coups de surprise qui caractérisent dans les romans les grandes aventures. (I)

Mais, soit qu'il eût l'esprit gâté par la lecture des anciens romans, ou qu'il fût né romanesque, il croyait qu'une véritable passion est toujours prédite à notre cœur . . . que l'on n'aime point lorsque l'on ne se sent pas entraîné par un penchant irrésistible. . . . (IV)

And his male characters are equally unimpressed by women who claim to seek voluptuousness which transcends that of the senses, since "les Platoniciennes ne sont pas conséquentes" (I).

More common in Crébillon's works is a kind of involuntary love based upon a passive psychology, popular in the eighteenth century, in which the autonomous emotions inevitably conquer reason even under the most adverse circumstances:

Ce qui m'a longtemps étonnée, et qu'encore aujourd'hui je ne conçois pas, c'est que ce trouble qui s'empare des sens et les confond, soit indépendant de nous-mêmes: cent fois il m'a surpris dans les occupations les plus sérieuses, et qui naturellement devaient y rendre mon âme moins accessible. (III)

Emotions are dominant in man because, unlike learned codes of conduct, they are the authentic manifestations of nature in man. So reasoned the partisans of the movement of ideas in the eighteenth century called *sensibilité*. That Crébillon contributed to this rationale is shown by a passage which deserves to stand as a *locus classicus:*

Puis-je répondre des mouvements de la nature; sa sensibilité est-elle mon ouvrage? Si l'âme devait être indépendante des sentiments du corps, pourquoi n'a-t-on pas distingué leurs fonctions? Pourquoi les ressorts de l'un sont-ils les ressorts de l'autre? Ah, sans doute! cette bizarrerie n'est pas de la nature, et nous ne devons qu'à des préjugés ces distinctions frivoles. Si elles étaient véritablement en nous, soumises à nos volontés, dépendantes d'elles, elles ne nous domineraient pas. Pourquoi cette lumière, qui nous fait apercevoir le bien ou le mal, n'est-elle pas assez puissante pour nous guider? Quel avantage est-ce pour moi que ce discernement qu'elle me procure, si me laissant toujours en liberté de choisir, son impulsion ne me détermine pas; et si ce choix n'est pas en ma puissance, pourquoi

m'oblige-t-on aux remords? (II)

But at times, in love, the psychological direction is reversed, and the mind, or, more properly, one of the "faculties" of the mind, arouses and influences the emotions:

sans qu'on s'en apperçoive, l'imagination s'échauffe, la tête se frappe, on se trouve amoureux de ce qu'on croyait détester, et le cœur partage enfin le désordre de l'esprit. (I)

Here the agent is "cette imagination déréglée qui souvent tient lieu de sentiments et même de vices . . . " (V). As such, this kind of imagination is usually found in cold, dispassionate persons. Speaking of a woman of this sort, a character says:

Il est aussi aisé d'embraser son imagination, qu'il serait difficile de lui donner l'idée du sentiment. . . . (V)

In other circumstances the imagination can work together with the senses to produce an amorous state which is not quite that of genuine passion:

Je me suis, sans doute, méprise trop souvent aux mouvements de mon cœur; trop souvent ou l'imagination, ou des sens trop faciles à s'émouvoir, m'en ont tenu lieu. . . . (VI)

Brought to its logical conclusion, this passive psychology views man as a machine which reacts purely mechanically as the proper buttons are pushed from outside. Crébillon, although he does not theorize like La Mettrie, occasionally hints at this conclusion:

je ne sais par quelle fatalité elle ne m'inspire que ce mouvement machinal, aussi souvent en nous, pour le moins, l'effet du caprice que l'ouvrage de la beauté, et qui n'est même pas le goût. (V)

Les transports d'un amant, ses larmes, ses caresses, doivent-ils, peuvent-ils même, laisser sa machine dans l'inaltérable tranquillité qu'elle lui prescrit? (V)

Can one say, then, that, according to Crébillon, people are completely helpless in the grip of passion, or of *goût,* or of imagination, or of the senses? Certainly, some of Crébillon's women know the difference between right and wrong, and are frequently reminded of it by that mysterious inner voice of conscience that Rousseau made so famous:

J'en crois aussi mes mouvements secrets: avec un mot vous me persuadiez autrefois que vous m'aimiez, aujourd'hui avec toutes les peines que vous vous donnez, vous augmentez ma défiance. (II)

Je ne sais quelle voix, plus forte que celle que je venais d'entendre, criait contre lui au fond de mon cœur. . . . (IV)

In accord with the doctrine of *sensibilité,* however, these voices are usually too weak in a corrupt age to affect the ladies' actual conduct:

> je n'avais pas encore pu parvenir à étouffer cette voix importune qui criait au fond de mon cœur, et qui n'ayant pu m'arracher à ma faiblesse, continuait de me la reprocher. . . . (III)

> une voix intérieure, qu'en vain je voulais étouffer, me faisait sur mon indigne faiblesse, les reproches les plus cruels; mais la combattit sans succès. (IV)

As a matter of fact, Crébillon's male characters often think of virtue as a *post-eventum* phenomenon:

> elles font consister la vertu moins dans la privation que dans le repentir. (III)

They do, of course, find it politic to give lip service to woman's virtue:

> Il faut toujours parler aux femmes comme si on leur croyait de la vertu, et agir avec elles comme ne leur en croyant pas . . . parce que s'il n'est pas vrai que la vertu soit pour toutes un état forcé, il l'est bien moins encore qu'elle soit pour toutes un état naturel. (V)

But most of them believe that the only real function of virtue in women is to make their surrender more pleasurable.

This is not to say that Crébillon's women do not want to be virtuous. Most of them are convinced, and say so time after time, that their surrender will earn only their lover's scorn. But surrender they usually do. Only two or three times are we shown a woman who is able to say, much like the Princess de Clèves:

> il n'a point dépendu de moi de ne vous pas aimer; les mouvements du cœur ne sont pas soumis à la réflexion: mais il dépend de moi d'être vertueuse, et l'on ne cesse pas de l'être malgré soi. (II)

And, in sad fact, the woman in Crébillon's works who most notably represents the ability of virtue to resist passion, would, as we shall see, have found her virtue ineffective without considerable help from external circumstances.

We have noted how a complex of affective reactions comes suddenly, or, more commonly, in a gradual way, to fill a psychological void in Crébillon's characters. Nothing about this process of falling in love is original or peculiar to Crébillon or even to the eighteenth century. But, as it happens, there are some aspects of love as he sees it which seem to him peculiar to the eighteenth century, and, more particularly, to eighteenth-century France. He makes it clear that love is not what it used to be in France:

> Si nous en croyons d'anciens mémoires, les femmes étaient autrefois plus flattées d'inspirer le respect, que le désir; et peut-être y gagnaient-elles. A la vérité, on leur parlait d'amour moins promptement; mais, celui

qu'elles faisaient naître n'en était que plus satisfaisant, et que plus durable. (I)

And he is equally certain that eighteenth-century love seems quite different when one crosses the English Channel. An Englishman writes this to a French friend:

> En France, une femme que le simple désir conduit et détermine, a la bonne foi de ne pas exiger plus qu'elle ne donne. . . . La tête seule fait tous les frais du sentiment qu'on se croit, ou que l'on feint de se croire. Le délire n'est pas long, mais il suffit au caprice ou aux sens. (V)

> Quelle différence de nos femmes aux vôtres, et qu'il s'en faut qu'elles soient aussi philosophes! . . . Sensibles, mais scrupuleuses, tendres, mais décentes, nos Anglaises ne sont pas assez heureuses pour connaître ce mouvement léger que vous appelez le goût. . . . (V)

The reason for these differences is made clear in another noteworthy passage which must figure in any discussion of the kind of love and the amorous milieu which Crébillon chose most often as the subject of his realistic fiction. Speaking of "la philosophie moderne," a character in *La Nuit et le moment* says:

> Je croirais bien aussi qu'en cela, comme en beaucoup d'autres choses, elle a rectifié nos idées; mais qu'elle nous a plus appris à connaître les motifs de nos actions, et à ne plus croire que nous agissons au hasard, qu'elle ne les a déterminées. Avant, par example, que nous sussions raisonner si bien, nous faisions sûrement tout ce que nous faisons aujourd'hui; mais nous le faisions, entraînés par le torrent, sans connaissance de cause, et avec cette timidité que donnent les préjugés. Nous n'étions pas plus estimables qu'aujourd'hui; mais nous voulions le paraître, et il ne se pouvait pas qu'une prétention si absurde ne gênât beaucoup les plaisirs. Enfin, nous avons eu le bonheur d'arriver au vrai: eh! que n'en résulte-t-il pas pour nous? Jamais les femmes n'ont mis moins de grimaces dans la société; jamais l'on n'a moins affecté la vertu. On se plaît, on se prend. S'ennuie-t-on l'un avec l'autre? on se quitte avec tout aussi peu de cérémonie que l'on s'est pris. Revient-on à se plaire? on se prend avec autant de vivacité que si c'était la première fois qu'on s'engageât ensemble. On se quitte encore, et jamais on ne se brouille. Il est vrai que l'amour n'est entré pour rein dans tout cela; mais l'amour, qu'était-il qu'un désir que l'on se plaisait à s'exagérer, un mouvement des sens, dont il avait plû à la vanité des hommes de faire une vertu? On sait aujourd'hui que le goût seul existe, et si l'on se dit encore qu'on s'aime, c'est bien moins parce qu'on le croit, que parce que c'est une façon plus polie de se demander réciproquement ce dont on sent qu'on a besoin. (I)

Obviously the speaker does not take the "anciens mémoires" and old-fashioned love very seriously. The modern philosophy which has effected the change in attitudes, according to him, is not necessarily the body of progressive ideas and attitudes which *philosophes* like Voltaire,

Diderot, Helvétius and others were busy disseminating in the eighteenth century. Crébillon also uses the word "philosophie" to mean the study of the formal philosophers (II), or, more commonly, any consecutive and reasoned way of looking at life. In this case, he seems to mean the view of life which was characteristic of the Régence. One detects a slight note of irony and, perhaps, bitterness under the cool nonchalance of this description of the new social attitude towards love. Or, perhaps, one is inclined to read bitterness and irony into the passage because of the pejorative way in which Crébillon refers to his philosophic century in other passages, like this one in which a character is describing a discussion he has had:

> j'avais trouvé d'assez belles choses contre mon siècle, ce siècle si faussement appelé, à ce qu'il me semble, le siècle, des lumières, et de la philosophie. Je croyais avoir vu que nous avons plus sacrifié aux passions qu'à la raison, plus immolé de principes, que nous n'avons extirpé de préjugés. Je me flattais même d'avoir prouvé que jamais nous n'avons été moins éclairés, puisque jamais nous n'avons été plus vicieux, ou que du moins, nous ne l'avons jamais été avec plus d'éclat, et moins de retenue. (V)

The varieties of love's vicissitudes, once an affair has begun in the corrupt society that Crébillon is pleased to paint for us, can best be treated in the discussion of his individual works, but it would be safe to say that all these affairs tend towards and are built around the sexual act. Hence the author's reputation as a pornographer. Yet it must seem to many a reader of his works that his erotic passages fail as pornography. A reader used to the explicit love scenes found in contemporary historical or detective novels will probably find Crébillon's seduction scenes either too satirical and light-hearted, or too vague and indirect.

A typical seduction scene in Crébillon runs something like this. After a good deal of talking about love, and, perhaps, some rubbing of knees under the gaming or dinner table (V), the lover sinks to his knees, and begins to kiss the lady's hand. Then, usually encountering some resistance, at least of the token variety, as he goes along, the lover allows his hands to wander. The lady, it must be understood, is seated on a sofa or "un de ces grands fauteuils qui sont aussi favorables à la témérité que propres à la complaisance . . ." (III). At this point, she modestly covers her eyes with one hand and permits the other one to be captured, which enables the lover to expose her physical charms.

This, the *voyeur* stage, is the one most emphasized by Crébillon, and, given such a predilection, it is remarkable that there are no detailed descriptions in his works of these coveted charms. Usually, the author is content to say that "mille beautés" were offered to the man's gaze. At other times, the account of what the lover sees is more prolonged, but still no more concrete or specific, as is indicated by this passage:

> Je choisis avec soin l'endroit d'où je pouvais le mieux observer les charmes de Zéïmis, et je me mis à les contempler. . . . Ciel! que de beautés s'offrirent à mes regards. . . . Je m'occupai alors à détailler tous les charmes qu'il me restait à examiner, et à revenir sur ceux que j'avais déjà parcourus . . . chaque mouvement qu'elle faisait, dérangeant sa tunique, offrit à mes avides regards de nouvelles beautés. (III)

Sometimes, the next and climactic phase of the seduction is rendered with a clever effacing of the key words and considerable reliance on suspension points:

> Que vous me donnez de transports, s'écria-t-elle! je sens tous les vôtres passer dans mon cœur, ils le remplissent, le troublent, le pénètrent! vous seul! . . . Oui, vous seul! . . . Mais Nassès! Ah! cruel!. . . . (III)

More often, the author depends on his reader's imagination, occasionally requesting his co-operation directly in less passionate moments:

> En cet endroit Clitandre doit à Cidalise les plus tendres remerciments, et les lui fait. Comme on ne peut supposer qu'il y ait parmi nos lecteurs quelqu'un qui ne se soit, ou n'ait été dans le cas d'en faire, ou d'en recevoir, ou de lire et d'entendre ces choses flatteuses et passionnées que suggère l'amour reconnaissant, ou que dicte quelquefois la nécessité d'être poli, l'on supprimera ce que les deux amants se disent ici, et l'on ose croire que le lecteur a d'autant moins à s'en plaindre, que l'on ne le prive que de quelques propos interrompus, qu'il aura plus de plaisir à composer lui-même d'après ses sentiments, qu'il n'en trouverait à les lire. (I)

The reader can usually follow Crébillon's circumspect periphrasis. One knows, for example, that when a woman says joyfully that a man is "digne d'être aimé," she is referring, to use Crébillon's own indirectness, to a certain thing. But occasionally it takes considerable imagination and experience to ferret out his meaning. Once, in discussing a beautiful fairy who, in an exposed position, finds it necessary to deflate the ardor (to use Crébillon's style again) of an inflamed young man without having actually to repulse him by force, he tells us that she finds just the right thing to do:

> Se venger de lui, de la même façon précisément, qu'elle en était offensée, lui parut donc le seul moyen qui lui restât pour échapper au péril qu'elle courait. Vengeance, en effect, d'autant plus adroite, qu'elle ne pouvait paraître qu'une preuve d'amour, à celui qui en était l'objet, et que quelque envie qu'il pût avoir de s'en plaindre, il ne pouvait point ne l'en pas remercier. (IV)

This obliqueness so annoys our old friend the Sultan that he is forced to interrupt the story:

> Un moment, je vous prie, dit le Sultan d'un air fâché, c'est que ceci devient d'une force qu'il faut que je meure, ou que j'y mette ordre. Je demande d'abord si tout ce qu'on vient de me dire s'entend, et si je suis dans mon tort quand je ne l'entends pas? (IV)

One wonders how many other readers have found themselves equally in the dark, and if those who can imagine meanings for this and similar passages do not find that co-operation with the author is more stimulating than the passive reception of, let us say, the franker passages in *Lady Chatterly's Lover.*

It is possible to glimpse, from time to time, in the treatment of these many amorous skirmishes, a certain limited hierarchy of values, a kind of amoral eighteenth-century French version of *buen amor* and *loco amor.* On one hand there is sophisticated education, conducted with style, taste, and urbanity:

> L'amour, comme dit La Fontaine, est nu, mais il n'est pas crotté. Et lorsqu'il se présente aux yeux sous une forme qui l'avilit, on est en droit de le méconnaître. (III)

The lover speaks with elegance and imagination:

> Quoi que le Prince ne me redît, peut-être, que les mêmes choses, il savait leur prêter tant de grâces, et leur donner une face si nouvelle! (IV)

The lady yields, but gracefully, intelligently, and according to her principles:

> nous n'en cédons pas moins, mais nous en cédons avec plus de noblesse. Tout ce qui nous heurte ne nous fait pas tomber. Si, comme il n'est que trop vrai, les principes ne triomphent point de la sensibilité du cœur, ils ont, du moins le pouvoir de dissiper les illusions de l'amour-propre; de maîtriser l'imagination, de commander aux sens. . . . (III)

On the other hand, there is a kind of vulgar, inexperienced amorous commerce which Crébillon's characters despise. This, for example, is how a slave makes love to his mistress:

> Il me parut peu délicat, peu tendre, mais vif et ardent, dévoré de désirs, ne connaissant point l'art de les satisfaire par degrés, ignorant la galanterie, ne sentant point de certaines choses, ne détaillant rien, mais s'occupant essentiellement de tout. (III)

And if vulgar love is revolting, inexperienced timidity is almost as bad:

> L'autre, sans usage, sans politesse, sans imagination, ne savait, dans des situations difficiles, que rester dans un étonnement stupide, semblait ignorer quel est quelquefois le prix des bagatelles. . . . (IV)

There is another kind of reprehensible seduction in Crébillon's novels, or so it may seem to the modern reader, which is practiced by those very experienced and polished lovers who can speak so cleverly of love. This occurs when they cold-bloodedly use the sexual act to degrade and punish the women they despise. These women may have offended by lack of taste, or of beauty, or because of their irritating reputations for prudery. What happens to them is usually quite cruel, in spite of the nobility of the lover:

> Je croyais en sentir redoubler mon mépris pour elle; cependant nous étions seuls, elle était belle, et je la savais sensible. Elle ne m'inspirait plus ni passion ni respect: je ne la craignais plus, mais je ne l'en désirai que davantage. (I)

Many of these more skilled ladies' men are not above using in their affairs a judicious amount of brutality at the proper moment, rationalizing these little "coups d'autorité" with a cynical doctrine borrowed from Ovid:

> croyez que ce n'est pas sans raison que les anciens ont dit qu'il vaut toujours mieux mettre une femme dans le cas d'avoir à se plaindre hautement de trop de témérité, que d'avoir, en secret, à vous reprocher de l'avoir trop respectée. (III)

These, then, are the paradoxical ways of eighteenth-century French love, according to Crébillon: it was witty, cruel, polished, brutal, dignified, and unprincipled. But there is also another aspect of his conception of love which was typical of his century, yet so much a part of it that he was undoubtedly unaware of its characteristic nature. Love, as he portrays it, is an intensely temporal phenomenon. That is, it not only starts at a given moment, endures more or less long, and dies, but also corresponds, with remarkable fidelity, with the age's conception of time itself. For the eighteenth century in France, as Georges Poulet has shown [in his *Etudes sur le temps humain,* n.d.], time seemed to be a discontinuous succession of instants, since man was conscious of time only as a discontinuous succession of sensations which came to draw him from a state of psychological nothingness. There could be a kind of duration, but only through affective variety: "L'intensité de la sensation fonde l'instant, la multiplicité des sensations fonde la durée." There was thus a yearning in eighteenth-century man to heighten at all costs the intensity of the moment, and to pass from stimulus to stronger stimulus: "La promptitude avec laquelle les états sensibles se succèdent, rend la vie plus riche, la durée plus longue, l'existence plus large."

We have already seen some evidence of the analogy between Crébillon's conception of love and the eighteenth-century conception of time. Love comes along to pull one out of a state of nothingness, and brings one into life, and, thus, into time. When told that her love is reciprocated, a woman says:

> Il me semblait que je ne commençais à vivre que de cet instant, qui me paraissait le seul heureux de ma vie. . . . (IV)

The instant figures large in Crébillon's works. Love, like life itself, proceeds from instant to instant. Each instant is fertile in possibilities. It can be the desired *instant de plénitude,* charged to the ultimate with life-assuring sensations. It can, as we have seen, be the start of a new passion, although there may be a hint of satire in such expressions as: "en fait d'amour, on dépend d'une seconde" (II). It can be the end of an affair, a *moment de rupture,* usually a welcome one, since for life to be filled with sensation, new loves must supplant weakening ones. Duration weakens sensation less than weakening sensation saps duration, and violence in passion is necessarily ephemeral:

> Mes goûts, j'en conviens, ressemblent assez à des fureurs, pour que l'on puisse d'abord s'y méprendre; mais personne n'ignore qu'ils sont d'aussi peu de durée qu'ils ont de violence; et si je donne quelquefois à mes amis sujet de craindre qu'ils me mènent trop loin, du moins, ne dois-je, jamais leur laisser à redouter qu'ils m'emportent trop longtemps. (VI)

To want love to be other than the way nature has made it has been one of man's follies:

> Il nous suffisait de plaire: nous avons voulu être aimés; et qu'une simple préférence qui devait être aussi momentanée que le désir qui la fait naître, devînt un sentiment, et même un sentiment suivi. (VI)

In Crébillon's works, love is regarded as a temporal phenomenon in still another way. We have seen that the vulgar slave did not know the art of satisfying "par degrés." Many passages show that skill in love is displayed by the ability of the lover to proceed by degrees through a subtle, carefully timed series of affective gradations:

> De là, en homme qui connaît le prix des gradations, il la prit dans ses bras, l'y serra voluptueusement. . . . (II)

This skill must be painfully learned by the neophyte:

> Elle ajouta à cela mille choses finement pensées, et me fit entrevoir de quelle nécessité était les gradations. Ce mot, et l'idée qu'il renfermait, m'étaient totalement inconnus. . . . (I)

At times, the success of this technique may even bring sorrow with it:

> se retraçant tout ce qu'il avait fait pour séduire Almaïde, combien sa criminelle passion l'avait aveuglé, avec quel art il l'avait corrompue par degrés, il tomba dans la douleur la plus amère. (III)

For, if a woman is carefully subjected to this technique, her defeat is progressive, and then suddenly climactic:

> Nous allons d'égarements en égarements, sans les prévoir ni les sentir; nous périssons vertueuses encore, sans être présentes, pour ainsi dire, au fatal moment de notre défaite. . . . (I)

Above all, Crébillon's successful lovers are able to recognize love's important moments as they occur in the course of an affair. The beginning of an affair, for example, has its own special symptoms:

> en êtes-vous encore à ignorer combien, dans les premiers temps d'une passion, une femme s'exagère ce qu'elle sent, et même tout le besoin que, pour pouvoir se reprocher moins ce qu'elle lui a sacrifié, elle a de l'exagérer? (VI)

> De quel bonheur ne jouit-on pas! Combien dans ces premiers et délicieux instants ne s'en promet-on point! (V)

But the most important moment of all for men to recognize is the "instant de fragilité" in which even the most principled woman finds herself helplessly vulnerable to love:

> Elle avouait cependant qu'il y avait pour la femme la plus ferme sur ses principes d'assez dangereuses occasions. . . . (I)

> Un de ces moments qui confondent toutes les idées des femmes, saisi par moi avec la dernière audace, vient de me rendre le plus heureux des hommes. (V)

Even the wrong man can succeed at the right moment:

> On ne peut répondre du moment: il en est où la nature agit seule et où l'on se trouve précisément dans le cas d'un songe qui offre à vos sens les objets qu'il veut, et non ceux que vous voudriez. (II)

Yet we should not pity women excessively for this involuntary weakness. Crébillon often shows that it can be a handy means of self-exculpation when a lady has been guilty of poor judgment.

As a matter of fact, the "moment de fragilité" is so common and so important in Crébillon's works that he went to the trouble of creating two rather thorough discussions of it by his fictional characters. It is succinctly defined by the Duke in *Le Hasard du coin du feu* when he is explaining to a lady how one can love involuntarily:

> Une certaine disposition des sens aussi imprévue qu'elle est involontaire, qu'une femme peut voiler, mais qui, si elle est aperçue, ou sentie par quelqu'un qui ait intérêt d'en profiter, la met dans le danger du monde le plus grand d'être un peu plus complaisante qu'elle ne croyait ni devoir ni pouvoir l'être. (III)

And Alcibiades, a very eighteenth-century French Alcibiades, treats the phenomenon at greater length in the *Lettres Athéniennes* as he advises a friend about an unsatisfactory affair. A woman, he begins, logically, is either naturally passionate or she is not. If she is not, she will banish a lover

> qui pouvant ne pas s'en tenir à une première témérité, pouvait aussi, malgré tous les obstacles que lui opposait en elle la nature, l'indifférence, et un système de conduite toujours très-dangereux à rencontrer dans une

femme, trouver le moment, et en ne le méconnaissant plus, le rendre décisif. (V)

In spite of this, we can afford to mistake this sensitive moment only when we are dealing with the naturally passionate woman, because such moments are not frequent or predictable. Women may deny that they exist at all, but it would be folly to believe that. If, Alcibiades adds, it were only a question of the so-called "surprise des sens," he would have to admit that lovers awaiting such an event would be wasting their time. Vanity, habit, and a lover's ability to dramatize his ardor are what wear a woman down:

> Enfin, n'arrive-t-il pas un moment où elle est si violemment agitée, que si elle se défend encore, ce n'est plus qu'avec une mollesse qui décèle tout le besoin que, souvent, et sans qu'elle le sache ellemême, elle a d'être vaincue? Quelquefois même cet instant critique arrive lorsque l'amant songeait le moins à le faire naître, s'en flattait le moins, et qu'elle s'en croyait aussi le plus éloignée. (V)

It would not be worthy of a philosopher, he thinks, to seek the cause of this "caprice de la nature," and to explain why a woman can resist with tiresome tenacity the most ardent wooing, and then find herself aroused in the least promising situations.

> Est-ce un mouvement du sang, aussi subit qu'il paraît involontaire, auquel le sentiment, la présence de l'objet aimé, une réflexion tendre, donnent une puissance qu'il n'aurait pas sans tout cela? C'est ce que j'ignore; mais, quelle que puisse être la cause du moment, il est certain, non seulement qu'il existe, mais encore que celles des femmes qui voudraient bien n'y pas céder, nous le dérobant le plus qu'elles peuvent, un homme n'a pas moins besoin de sagacité pour le saisir que de fermeté pour refuser aux prières, aux pleurs, aux cris même de la pudeur gémissante, et alarmée, ou aux ruses de la coquetterie désespérée de se voir près d'être vaincue, un répit que l'on a vu très-rarement n'être pas funeste à ceux qui le leur accordent. (V)

Obviously, the emotions which conquer a woman in this much-discussed moment are hardly lofty ones, and what the alert lover hopes to win at this instant is not her heart. In fact, having reviewed the most salient and characteristic ways of love in Crébillon's fiction, one might be justified in concluding that his view of love can be reduced, in the final analysis, to sexual desire. This is not to say that his reputation as a pornographer and insipid precursor of the Marquis de Sade is justified. Actually, Crébillon is not much interested in sex. That is, he does not stress the act itself, and, unlike Diderot, he is no sexologist, lacking Diderot's medical, scientific preoccupation with sex practices and aberrations. Homosexuality, for example, was common enough among both sexes in his day, and it figures in the works of Laclos, Diderot, and, of course, the Marquis de Sade, but we find none of it in Crébillon. He may muse briefly over the physiology behind the "moment," and concern himself in several works with impotence, but these phenomena interest him only in the effects they have on *social* relations between the sexes. Love for him, fundamentally, is interesting as a social, rather than a psychological or physical force, although these factors are, of course, interconnected. Sex is the brass ring on the carrousel of society. Or perhaps it might be more suitable and accurate to say that sex is for Crébillon like a bridge prize—a thing of little value in itself, but worth getting as a symbol of skilful action within a complex set of rules, a sign of a game well played. More than in sex, Crébillon is interested in men and women, and how they act in society.

Rayner Heppenstall (essay date 1963)

SOURCE: An introduction to *The Wayward Head and Heart* by Claude Prosper Jolyot de Crébillon, translated by Barbara Bray, 1963. Reprint by Greenwood Press, Inc., 1978, pp. vii-xiv.

[*Heppenstall was an English novelist, critic, and autobiographer who wrote extensively of his experiences with such literary figures as George Orwell and Dylan Thomas. In the following excerpt from an essay first published in 1963, he gives an overview of Crébillon's works.*]

In the course of our general reading we somehow contrive to pick up the name of Crébillon *fils*. It may be from *Antic Hay,* or it may be from the letters of Horace Walpole. Claude-Prosper Jolyot de Crébillon, son of Prosper Jolyot, Sieur de Crébillon, was, we gather, a witty but licentious minor French novelist of the eighteenth century. As to Crébillon *père,* it is understood that he wrote unreadable classical tragedies, which some people in his time thought better than Voltaire's.

To put his hand on an actual book by Crébillon *fils* is not so easy for the English reader. In general, 'licentious' authors are more known about than read. The most obvious case is no doubt the Marquis de Sade, but how many of us have read Aretino? And in fact, without recourse to a great library, it is difficult enough for a Frenchman to lay hold of Crébillon. Only the original of the present work is normally to be found in print in France. To find much else, you have to go back to Pierre Lièvre's five volumes of 1929, and we ourselves, going back only two years more, may at least find Bonamy Dobrée's translation of *The Sofa.*

Until the publication in 1930 of the Tchémerzine bibliography, it was even rather difficult to discover just how much Crébillon had written, for no two earlier lists of his books agree. Three or four of the dozen or so unprinted by Lièvre rouse one's interest by their mere titles, but I have not read them. To me, what is printed by Lièvre is canonical. In addition to *The Wayward Head and Heart* (1736-38) and *The Sofa* (written during those years but unpublished till 1742), Lièvre gives us an early story, *The Sylph* (1730), a novel in epistolary form, *The Letters of the Marquise de M———to the Comte de R———* (1732), *The Skimmer* (1734), and two dialogues, *Night and the Moment* (published 1755, but written as much as seventeen years earlier) and *The Opportunities of the Fireside* (1763). Like *The Sofa, The Skimmer* is an Oriental romance with contemporary satirical reference. For publishing *The Skimmer,* Crébillon, then aged twenty-seven, was imprisoned for a week or more at Vincennes, as, eight years later, he was to be rusticated for *The Sofa.*

The skimmer of the title is held to have represented the papal bull, *Unigenitus,* which had led to much persecution of Jansenists, Protestants, and Quietists in the previous reign and of which the effects had again been felt in the early years of the reign of Louis XV, who is himself recognizably present as the unfortunate young Tanzai, the hideous fairy Cucumber being, it was understood, the Duchesse du Maine. The skimmer has to be licked, its broad handle rammed into certain mouths. The satire in *The Skimmer* is a good deal tougher than it was to be in *The Sofa,* whose main theme, at any rate, is merely saucy, the teller of the various tales being a Hindu whose soul had been forced to transmigrate from one sofa to another until it found one upon which two virgins should yield each other the first-fruits of their love.

The Skimmer and *The Sofa* were evidently not Crébillon's only Oriental romances, but they stand apart from the rest of his work in the Lièvre canon. To my mind, that kind of thing, even when it is by Voltaire or Dr. Johnson, soon palls, however amusing it may be piecemeal. But so, I find, nowadays do all those early works of fiction whose form is purely serial and episodic, including true *picaresque,* including Sorel and Le Sage and even Cervantes. The nineteenth-century novel accustomed us to the overall structure, the organization of material, the careful plotting of incident and placing of dialogue, from one end of a book to the other, which keep our responses and expectations steady. The importance of Crébillon lies, I suggest, in those of his writings which bear directly on the development of the novel in Europe.

His first recorded work, the story *The Sylph,* is told in the form of a letter from one noble lady to another. His first novel, *The Letters of the Marquise de M———to the Comte de R———,* is wholly conceived in epistolary form. It ante-dates Richardson's *Pamela* by eight years, *Clarissa* by sixteen and *Dangerous Acquaintances* by fifty years. *Pamela* was translated into French by the Abbé Prévost, author of *Manon Lescaut.* That makes a nice little pocket of Anglo-French influences. The important point is, however, that *The Letters of the Marquise de M———to the Comte de R———* was, if not quite the first novel of sensibility to be told in the form of letters, yet the first altogether confident and successful exercise in the form. There had, of course, been the *Portuguese Letters* and Montesquieu's *Persian Letters,* but they were not at all the same thing.

The novel by exchange of letters did not remain long in fashion. At the beginning of the present century, Swinburne returned to it in *Love's Cross Currents.* Thriller-writers, American humourists, and M. Michel Butor have all toyed with it. The masterpiece in the form I take to be

still *Dangerous Acquaintances.* Formally, it seems likely that Choderlos de Laclos took as his model *Clarissa,* Richardson was not a well-read man, and I do not suppose that he knew *The Letters of the Marquise de M———to the Comte de R———* at first hand. He may have heard of it, but a modest project of his own, to compose model letters for the daughters of tradesmen, seems to have led him on to attempt a first novel. In any case, Richardson added something of his own. The Crébillon *Letters* are all from the Marquise. Though spaced in time, the narrative is unilateral, as it is, say, in *The Tenant of Wildfell Hall,* which is really in diary form, an offshoot which has thrived more effectively into our time, especially in France.

The *Letters,* in fact, lack the polyphony which has become so rich, so carefully managed and timed, in *Dangerous Acquaintances* and which makes the epistolary form so challengingly difficult to handle (hence, perhaps, its early demise). And so a direct cross-Channel transmission of impulses, from Crébillon *fils* to Samuel Richardson, from Richardson to Laclos, is not perhaps to be thought of. I do not underestimate the importance of purely formal innovation. As a practising novelist and as the friend of practising novelists, I think that it produces sharper effects, and is thus more important in literary history, than mere critics (who at present make rather a point of playing-down literary history) like to admit. I attach, for instance, far more importance to Édouard Dujardin's *We'll to the Woods No More* than any Joyce authority will admit (I charitably assume that they have read it). But the debt to Crébillon of *Dangerous Acquaintances* seems to me to be of a more general nature and markedly to concern the present work, as well as the two later dialogues.

There are fairly distinct indications that *The Wayward Head and Heart* was never finished according to its author's original plan. It is an incomplete work in that sense. It is also, I suggest, incomplete in this sense, that the preoccupations of Crébillon, in *The Wayward Head and Heart* and in the dialogues, require *Dangerous Acquaintances* to complete them, to show where they lead. I further suggest that Laclos, a man of the highest intelligence but not, in any large sense, a man of letters, had studied Crébillon *fils* and was concerned to show where *that* led rather than where the observed customs of his own day led. True, the observed customs of his own day may well have included much reading of Crébillon *fils* and some attempt to apply his principles to the noble art of seduction, which in Crébillon never leads to horrid consequences.

There is, to begin with, a similarity in the grouping of characters. We need not find exact parallels, of Madame de Lursay with the Présidente, of Versac with Valmont, of Hortense with Cécile, of Madame de Senanges with Madame de Merteuil and so on, but the grouping is similar. In the greater part of half a century, the society in which the two sets of characters flourish has not much changed. In Crébillon's world, very little but vanity is hurt. Laclos was the severer moralist.

Crébillon may perhaps be described as a sentimental amoralist, like, for instance, Mr. Kingsley Amis. Certainly, there is no lack of sentiment, underneath all that hard stuff, underneath all that intelligent systematization. There is a hierarchy of human feelings. We must more highly value *'amour'* than mere *'goût'* (*'amour-passion'*, Stendhal would later say, than *'amour-goût'*), but *'goût'* itself is friendly, pleasant, and considerate, even steady, not simply crude *'désir'*. We should certainly hope for *'plaisir'*, but cannot guarantee it and may have to make do with *'transports'* or mere *'volupté'*. A woman who is *'sensible'* is, as we should say, sexually responsive and thus alone capable of *'plaisir'*. Many a woman is more than usually *'galante'* (*i.e.*, promiscuous) precisely from a lack of sensibility (*i.e.*, as we should say, because she is frigid). The psychology seems almost post-Freudian. The hierarchy of sentiments is markedly different from the romantic one. It may not have been worse or less kind.

But love or, rather, gallantry is a game played according to rules, which are systematically discussed in the two later dialogues. These are decidedly licentious, but they are also extremely brilliant. Most of the discussion in **Night and the Moment** takes place, between one set-to and another, in the bed of Cidalise, into which Clitandre has introduced himself without permission. In **The Opportunities of the Fireside,** the hurly-burly on the *chaise longue* takes place between the Duc and Célie during the absence of the Marquise who is Célie's close friend and who is loved (with *'amour'*) by the Duc, Célie's point of honour being to make the Duc say that he loves herself and the Duc's being not to say it, since it is untrue. The Duc wins, of course.

The Wayward Head and Heart, as the reader will discover, is not so very licentious. But, indeed, neither in the dialogues nor in **The Sofa** is there any of that rhapsodical description with which nowadays the Home Secretary is teased. The nearest we ever come to physical detail is that a *'jambe'* is commended, a *'gorge'* admired, further *'charmes'* revealed. When nowadays the question arises, as it so frequently does, about the distinction between pornography and serious literature, lavish and minute description of the act of sex usually gets by as literature. It is the 'suggestive' which is always frowned upon. The eighteenth century would have found this surprising. Anything beyond mere suggestion would have been thought vulgar in the extreme.

In some ways, this is a pity. After all, when a nineteenth-century dairymaid was seduced by the young squire, she had a baby. The ladies of the eighteenth-century French upper classes were clearly subject to no such inconvenience. Little is known about what made the game so unflaggingly possible. But indeed, in Crébillon *fils,* as generally in eighteenth-century novels, there is not much local colour of any kind. We know little enough about real-life conversation at that time. Perhaps the ladies and gentlemen of that world spoke pretty well as Crébillon makes them speak. It seems more likely that his dialogue was conceived rather as Miss Compton-Burnett conceives hers. The reader will certainly find that the great scenes

in this novel are pure dialogue.

Vivienne Mylne (essay date 1965)

SOURCE: "Crébillon: Innovations in Points of View," in *The Eighteenth-Century French Novel: Techniques of Illusion,* second edition, Cambridge University Press, 1981, pp. 125-43.

[*In the following essay, first published in 1965, Mylne assesses Crébillon's treatment of the memoir-novel, particularly* Les Egarements.]

It was after the memoir-novel had become established as the predominant form of French fiction that a fresh form, the letter-novel, came into vogue in the mid-eighteenth century. Crébillon *fils* is an exception to this general pattern. His first novel was the **Letters de la Marquise de M*** au Comte de R***,** published in 1732, and it was not until 1736 that he began publishing **Les Egarements du cœur et de l'esprit, ou Mémoires de M. de Meilcour.** . . .

In his two editions of **Les Egarements,** Etiemble makes high claims for Crébillon, and maintains that he has been treated unfairly by generations of critics and teachers: **L'Ecumoire** and **Le Sopha** have overshadowed the real merits of his other works. There is a good deal of truth in this claim. It is usually these two quasi-Oriental *contes,* with their associations of obscenity, which receive first mention in any criticism of Crébillon, and all too rarely are we reminded that both stories contain an element of political and religious satire, so that obscenity itself was not their only aim. They represent, moreover, only a small part of Crébillon's writings, and it seems unjust that they should play such a disproportionate rôle in the customary verdicts on his work.

On the positive side, and quite apart from the intrinsic

Fraser's Magazine **analyzes "the genius of Crébillon":**

It cannot be denied that Crébillon was one of the remarkable men of his century. That untutored genius, so striking in the boldness and brilliancy of certain of its creations, but which more frequently repels through its own native barbarity, was eminently the genius of Crébillon. But what, above all, characterizes the genius of the French nation—wit, grace, and polish—Crébillon never possessed; consequently, with all his vigour and all his force, he never succeeded in creating a living work. He has depicted human perversity with a proud and daring hand—he has shown the fratricide, the infanticide, the parricide, but he never succeeded in attaining the sublimity of the Greek drama. And yet J. J. Rousseau affirmed that of all the French tragic poets, Crébillon alone had recalled to him the grandeur of the Greeks. If so, it was only through the nudity of terror, for the 'French Æschylus' was utterly wanting in what may be termed human and philosophical sentiment.

"Crébillon, The French Aeschylus," in Fraser's
Magazine, *September, 1851.*

qualities of his writings, Crébillon should receive credit for originality. He was the first French author to exploit the resources of the letter-novel for portraying character and motives in a full-length work—and well before Richardson in England. *Les Egarements* follows the more familiar memoir-novel tradition, but contains innovations which deserve notice. With *Les Heureux Orphelins* he found an even more unusual method of conveying the interplay of feeling between two characters. And in *La Nuit et le moment* (1755) and *Le Hasard du coin du feu* (1763), he adapted the literary *dialogue* to the ends of fiction. Even if one does not share to the full the admiration expressed by Etiemble, it seems clear that Crébillon deserves serious attention as a literary craftsman.

Already in the preface of *Les Egarements,* where he touches on the matter of 'truth' in the memoir-novel, one can see Crébillon moving away from the standards accepted by an earlier generation. He not only abstains from any claims to authenticity, but goes so far as to admit that these *mémoires* may be invented: 'soit qu'on doive les regarder comme un ouvrage purement d'imagination, ou que les aventures qu'ils contiennent soient réelles.' Lesage had denied writing a *roman à clef* but had finished by plunging Gil Blas into history; Prévost and Marivaux, in differing degrees, had both paid lip-service to the notion of authenticity. Crébillon explicitly puts aside truth and/ or history as being irrelevant to his ends, and in so doing shows a greater respect for fiction *per se.*

He goes on to defend the novel as a means of instruction, and to describe ways in which it could be improved. This manifesto is worth quoting at some length; its edifying approach may help to counter-balance the cynicism usually attributed to Crébillon, and it cites, with wit and clarity, the kind of undesirable features which had kept the genre in such low repute.

> Le Roman, si méprisé des personnes sensées, et souvent avec justice, serait peut-être celui de tous les genres qu'on pourrait rendre le plus utile, s'il était bien manié, si, au lieu de le remplir de situations ténébreuses et forcées, de Héros dont les caractères et les aventures sont toujours hors du vraisemblable, on le rendait, comme la Comédie, le tableau de la vie humaine, et qu'on y censurât les vices et les ridicules.

> Le Lecteur n'y trouverait plus à la vérité ces événements extraordinaires et tragiques qui enlèvent l'imagination, et déchirent le cœur; plus de Héros qui ne passât les Mers que pour y être â point nommé pris des Turcs, plus d'aventures dans le Sérail, de Sultane soustraite à la vigilance des Eunuques, par quelque tour d'adresse surprenant; plus de morts imprévues, et infiniment moins de souterrains. Le fait, préparé avec art, serait rendu avec naturel. On ne pécherait plus contre les convenances et la raison. Le sentiment ne serait point outré; l'homme enfin verrait l'homme tel qu'il est; on l'éblouirait moins, mais on l'instruirait davantage.

> J'avoue que beaucoup de Lecteurs, qui ne sont point

touchés des choses simples, n'approuveraient point qu'on dépouillât le Roman des puérilités fastueuses qui le leur rendent cher; mais ce ne serait point à mon sens une raison de ne le point réformer.

In his plea for *vraisemblance* and his attack on exaggerated characters and events, Crébillon might seem to do no more than echo seventeenth-century theorists such as Sorel. There is a difference, however: writers of serious novels in the seventeenth century relied on history as the basis of their *vraisemblance,* that is they dealt, ostensibly, in particular truths, or facts. In this they followed the pattern of contemporary tragedy. But although Crébillon is here referring to the serious novel, as we can see from his examples, he has transferred to it the standards which had hitherto been largely confined to the comic novel and comedy. (His own mention of censuring 'les vices et les ridicules' brings out this parallel.) The serious novelist can still carry out his function of moral improvement, but in Crébillon's view he will win the reader's belief by observing the probabilities of everyday life rather than by depending on specific historical or contemporary events. And the demand for natural portrayal—'Le fait, préparé avec art, sera rendu avec naturel'—would, if satisfied, have done away with the larger-than-life emotions and actions of characters like those of Prévost.

One should not over-estimate Crébillon's originality in drawing this parallel. With the decline of the idealized heroic novel, one or two critics had already perceived the possible similarity of function between realistic fiction and comedy. And among the novelists themselves writers such as Lesage and Marivaux had done much to bridge the gulf between the comic or satiric novel and the more elevated novel of serious feeling. In so doing they had also drawn nearer to a naturalistic or realistic portrayal of human behaviour. Nevertheless some credit is surely due to Crébillon for clearly formulating the concept of a serious novel which would not need to rely on the supposed 'truth' of specific events, and whose 'naturalness' would allow sensible people to enjoy and admire the genre.

The preface of *Les Egarements* closes with an outline of the complete story to be unfolded in these memoirs, an outline all the more useful in that Crébillon never got beyond Part III, published in 1738. The general scope of the novel was to be the portrayal of an *éducation sentimentale* in three stages: first the hero's initiation in matters of love, then a period of dissipation and false standards, and finally the discovery of virtue and peace of mind through the good graces of 'une femme estimable'. This programme would presumably have run into a dozen or more parts, as Meilcour is still pretty much of a novice at the end of Part III. As it is, apart from the opening pages which cover a period of several months, these three parts deal with only twelve days of Meilcour's life when he is seventeen. Crébillon's handling of time shows, indeed, a distinct resemblance to Marivaux's: devoted to detail, both authors fall into a pattern of closely succeeding events which fill the hours of each day.

The 'events' of the novel are, in essence, the variations of thought and feeling which Meilcour undergoes in relation to three women. Mme de Lursay, the first of these to appear, dominates the book and also, to a large extent, Meilcour. She is a woman of nearly forty, still attractive, and now respectable and careful of her reputation. Meilcour is attracted to her less from any strong attachment than because there is, to begin with, no woman he likes better. But he is timid and inept, and Mme de Lursay has to lead him on to declare his feelings. Although she is quite ready to yield, she has to proceed cautiously so as not to shatter his illusions about the respect he thinks is due to her.

The affaire is still in its early stages when Versac, a fashionable young roué, gossips maliciously about Mme de Lursay in front of Meilcour, who thus discovers that his idol is by no means as pure as he had believed:

> et je courus chez Mme de Lursay, dans l'intention de me venger, par ce que le mépris a de plus outrageant, du ridicule respect qu'elle m'avait forcé d'avoir pour elle.

This ends Part I.

Meilcour's vengeance is to take the form of winning Mme de Lursay and then throwing her over. But she is more skilled in manœuvres of this kind than he. His first attempt to put his new boldness into practice is rebuffed, but after regaining her ascendency over him, she relents and begins to initiate him into 'l'étude des gradations', a study which is however interrupted by the arrival of callers.

Under the pressure of fresh interests Meilcour's renewed affection for Mme de Lursay begins to decline. At first she reacts with pain and anger. After a few days, however, she appears no longer to care, and one evening she seems to be on the verge of starting an affaire with another young man. Meilcour's wounded vanity prompts him to return after the other guests have left, and demand an explanation. Mme de Lursay again wins him over, and this time he is granted complete satisfaction:

> Grâces aux bienséances que Madame de Lursay observait sévèrement, elle me renvoya enfin, et je la quittai en lui promettant, malgré mes remords, de la voir le lendemain de bonne heure, très déterminé, de plus, à lui tenir parole.

On this note the book ends.

Woven into the main plot, and affecting its progress at various points, are Meilcour's reactions to Hortense de Théville, a beautiful young girl whom he first sees in the box next to his own at the Opera. Her effect on him is immediate:

> Je ne sais quel mouvement singulier et subit m'agita à cette vue: frappé de tant de beautés, je demeurai comme anéanti. Ma surprise allait jusqu'au transport. Je sentis dans mon cœur un désordre qui se répandit sur tous mes sens.

When Meilcour at length discovers the identity of this girl he learns, too, that she is on terms of such friendly familiarity with the Marquis de Germeuil that he, Meilcour, would seem to have no hope. It is in moments of despair over this situation that he returns to Mme de Lursay, and it is because of Hortense that he feels remorse even while enjoying Mme de Lursay's favours.

The older woman knows nothing of Meilcour's feelings for Hortense, but becomes jealous of Mme de Senanges, an ageing coquette who openly sets her cap at Meilcour. He speaks of her, when she first enters the story, as the person 'à qui . . . j'ai eu le malheur de devoir mon éducation', but their association has scarcely begun in the novel as it stands. However, it is strongly favoured by Versac, who, towards the end of Part III, has become Meilcour's mentor and model.

From this description it can be seen that the action of the novel consists almost entirely of changes and developments in personal relationships. There are certainly no 'événements extraordinaires et tragiques' of the kind Crébillon deprecated. What we have here is a novel of purely psychological interest, a *roman d'analyse*. Nor was it Crébillon's first effort in this type of work; . . . his letter-novel of 1732 can be described in the same terms.

The characters in **Les Egarements,** then, are observed not under the stress of exceptional and fantastic events, but in the course of their everyday activities: paying social calls, holding dinner-parties, going to the opera, walking in the Tuileries. Yet in the midst of these ordinary pursuits they are still at the mercy of chance. However *vraisemblable* Crébillon has made his characters and the scenes they enact, he has still relied heavily on coincidence for the operation of his plot. Before Meilcour has learnt the identity of his fair Unknown, he happens to hear her talking to a companion in a secluded path in the Tuileries. The conversation on which he then eavesdrops happens to concern a young man, never named, who seems to have aroused Hortense's interest and who might, from the way she refers to him, even be himself. Later it turns out that Hortense's mother happens to be not only a friend of Mme de Lursay, but also a distant cousin of Meilcour's mother. Add to all this the pat arrival of a new character each time there is some need to give the story a fresh impetus—Versac, Mme de Senanges, etc.—and it becomes clear that in matters of plot-construction Crébillon is still far from respecting everyday standards of probability.

The same accusation could be made, if we think of the book as memoirs, concerning the way the plot unfolds, day by detailed day, and even, on occasion, with supplementary accounts of Meilcour's night thoughts. It is simply not to be believed that an elderly man, looking back on himself when young, could recall with such precision the events of one fortnight when he was seventeen. The convention of the autobiographer's powers of recall is here strained beyond its limits.

Crébillon oversteps the convention in another and possibly a more interesting way. Instead of keeping strictly to the narrator's point of view, describing his own thoughts and feelings but confining himself to an external view of others, he frequently enters the mind of these other characters. It is permissible, of course, for the first-person narrator to infer intentions and reactions from the behaviour that he observes, but Crébillon goes beyond this. During the whole course of the novel, Meilcour is in the position of a naïve youth who does not understand the desires and machinations of Mme de Lursay. He does not say, nor can we reasonably suppose, that at some later stage of his life she explained to him exactly how she decided to lead him on, or to out-manœuvre him in the conduct of their affaire. Yet Crébillon repeatedly makes Meilcour speak in definite and precise terms about Mme de Lursay's thoughts and intentions. A passage like the following shows the procedure clearly:

> Elle avait toujours espéré qu'elle me reverrait, mais sûre enfin que je l'évitais, elle commença à craindre de me perdre, et se détermina à me faire essuyer moins de rigueurs. Sur le peu que je lui avais dit, elle avait cru ma passion décidée: cependant je n'en parlais plus. Quel parti prendre? Le plus décent était d'attendre que l'amour, qui ne peut longtemps se contraindre, surtout dans un cœur aussi neuf que l'était le mien, me forçât encore à rompre le silence; mais ce n'était pas le plus sûr. Il ne lui vint pas dans l'esprit que j'eusse renoncé à elle: elle pensa seulement que, certain de n'être jamais aimé, je combattais un amour qui me rendait malheureux. . . . Mais comment me faire comprendre son amour, sans blesser cette décence à laquelle elle était si scrupuleusement attachée?

The presentation of feelings is complete, and is made even more vivid by the use of *style indirect libre* for the questions she put to herself: 'Quel parti prendre?' etc.

This insight into other people's minds is not confined to Mme de Lursay. In spite of his naïveté at the time of the events, Meilcour now shows an omniscient penetration into the thoughts of those he met, and only occasionally does Crébillon remember the conventional limits of his hero's knowledge, in a phrase such as, 'Ces réflexions, *que vraisemblablement il fit,* le calmèrent.' At such moments the artifice is all too obvious. But for most of the time Crébillon is moving away from the point of view of the first-person narrator to that of the omniscient third person.

The rise of the memoir-form meant that the *roman* came to be associated with first-person narrative, while third-person narrative was viewed as a characteristic of the *conte* and the independent *nouvelle*. By the second half of the century this association was so firmly established that we can find a writer [Mme Benoist, *Agathe et Isidore*, 1768] explaining, in the preface of her novel, why she has written in 'le style du conte', that is, in third-person narrative. Generally speaking, such narrative was offered in a quasi-historical manner. The writer could describe actions, but only infer thoughts and feelings. Crébillon himself outlines the historical method accurately, if sarcastically:

> Vous ne me montrez que l'extérieur de l'homme, ou ne m'offrez, pour percer plus loin, que des conjectures que je puis, si je veux, ne pas adopter, et qui, quelques fines qu'elles puissent être, n'en sont peut-être pas mieux fondées.

However, neither the historians nor the writers of third-person fiction had ever clung slavishly to this convention. As well as deducing the emotions and mental processes which 'must have' led to certain decisions and actions, they also, occasionally, presented inner debates which did *not* lead to action, and which were therefore not strictly within the scope of historical narrative, even allowing for inference. Such 'illegitimate' discussions of a character's inner life occur not only in *La Princesse de Clèves,* but in the heroic novels of, for instance, Mlle de Scudéry. What is noticeable in such cases, however, is that the usage is limited in extent and, as it were, surreptitious. In the serious novel, at least, writers generally attempted to preserve the appearance of an historical approach.

The authors of comic or burlesque novels enjoyed greater freedom. Their stories did not as a rule lay claim to historicity, and when such claims were made, they were obviously facetious. So there were no barriers of *vérité* to stop these writers moving into the minds of their characters and describing ideas or emotions as they saw fit. Cervantes, for instance, displays such omniscience in *Don Quixote,* and Sorel took advantage of it in *Francion.* By the eighteenth century, therefore, the omniscient narrator was nothing new in the novel as a genre. The fresh development came when this approach was exploited fully and unashamedly by writers of serious novels, a stage which was not reached until the early nineteenth century.

Crébillon's procedure in *Les Egarements* does however present a variant which had not, to my knowledge, occurred before. When first-person narrative began to be utilized for fiction, the novelists who adopted this method obeyed its conventions strictly. They did not enter the minds of any character except their narrator, or describe any incidents at which he was not present. (This, as we have seen, sometimes entailed excessive reliance on devices such as eavesdropping.) We can therefore view Crébillon's contraventions of the 'rules' of first-person narrative either as a reversion to the freedom enjoyed by seventeenth-century comic novelists—and *Les Egarements* does, after all, contain elements of satire—or else as a foreshadowing of the nineteenth-century omniscient narrator.

He was, one might judge, forced into such omniscience by his preoccupation with the analysis of feelings, and by the very nature of his story. After the ironical remarks cited above, on the 'external' historical method, he goes on to say:

> Moi, c'est le cœur que je développe, son délire particulier, le manège de la vanité, de la fausseté dans la plus intéressante des passions que j'expose à vos yeux.

This aim is attributed to one of his characters, but could

very well be taken as Crébillon's own. And one can see its consequences in the case of **Les Egarements**. The duplicity, scheming and secret intentions of the characters surrounding Meilcour are vital to the plot and, in Crébillon's eyes, interesting in themselves. They must therefore be conveyed to the reader. Meilcour is the only mouthpiece of the novel, so that even if he is supposedly too young and simple to know what his associates are thinking, it is still through him that this information must reach us. In the circumstances, it is hardly surprising that Crébillon has slipped over the brink into omniscience.

The author's occasional attempts to revert to the rules of memoir-writing, in phrases such as 'que vraisemblablement il fit', only remind us of a situation we could otherwise happily ignore. He is wiser in the matter of conversations, where he makes no attempt to explain how or why he can recall every word. Dialogue does play an extremely important part in the work, occupying about half the text. In most cases it is decisive in producing some new development of feeling, and is therefore intrinsic to the plot; the conversations count as events in themselves. In **Le Sopha** which, according to Crébillon's own account, was written at the same period as **Les Egarements,** he discusses and defends conversations both as being a kind of event and as providing a method of characterization:

> Vous avez tort de vous plaindre, lui dit la Sultane; cette conversation qui vous ennuie est pour ainsi dire un fait par ellemême. Ce n'est point une dissertation inutile et qui ne porte sur rien, c'est un fait . . . n'est-ce pas 'dialogué' qu'on dit? demanda-t-elle à Amanzéi en souriant.
>
> Oui, Madame, répondit-il.
>
> Cette façon de traiter les choses, reprit-elle, est agréable; elle peint mieux et plus universellement les caractéres que l'on met sur la scène.

These are the kinds of arguments which Marivaux too uses to defend both a conversational style and conversations as such, though in the latter case his main interest was to justify the use of lower-class speech. Crébillon, by contrast, keeps firmly to the upper levels of society. Within this more limited range he produces varied and individual styles of talk which are usually quite convincing. Mme de Lursay's veiled encouragement to Meilcour is in well-bred contrast to the vapid provocations of Mme de Senanges. The insolence and malice of Versac's remarks make it clear why he is both feared and admired. Most of these conversations are vivid and keep the story moving, though occasionally they do fall into the minutiae which Crébillon himself saw as one of their possible drawbacks. They are usually clearer and more interesting than the passages where Meilcour simply describes his feelings.

One conversation in particular calls for special comment, the long passage towards the end of the book in which Versac outlines his philosophy of action to Meilcour. The tone, of advice and persuasion, is that of Vautrin to Eu-

gène de Rastignac in *Le Père Goriot,* but Versac is not an outlaw from society. Having come to understand the factors which make for success in *la bonne compagnie,* he has not rejected the vice and hypocrisy they involve, but has learnt to handle them as a master.

> Entré de bonne heure dans le monde, j'en saisis aisément le faux. J'y vis les qualités solides proscrites, ou du moins ridiculisées, et les femmes, seuls juges de notre mérite, ne nous en trouver qu'autant que nous nous formions sur leurs idées. Sûr que je ne pourrais, sans me perdre, vouloir résister au torrent, je le suivis. Je sacrifiai tout au frivole; je devins étourdi pour paraître plus brillant; enfin, je me créai les vices dont j'avais besoin pour plaire: une conduite si ménagée me réussit.
>
> Je suis né si différent de ce que je parais, que ce ne fut pas sans une peine extrême que je parvins à me gâter l'esprit.

This account of a conscious change of character in order to fall in with the requirements of society suggests not Vautrin but Mme de Merteuil of *Les Liaisons dangereuses,* and she can indeed be seen as a feminine counterpart of Versac. Thinking of men as instruments for her power and of her pleasure, she obviously aspires to the same kind of ends as Versac. He states his aims to Meilcour:

> Je suppose d'abord, et avec assez de raison, ce me semble, qu'un homme de notre rang, et de votre âge, ne doit avoir pour object que de rendre son nom célèbre. Le moyen le plus simple et en même temps le plus agréable pour y parvenir, est de paraître n'avoir dans tout ce qu'on fait que les femmes en vue, de croire qu'il n'y a d'agrément que ce qui les séduit et que le genre d'esprit qui leur plaît, quel qu'il soit, est en effet le seul qui doive plaire.

We are dealing here with the type of person for whom sexual relationships are the chief, perhaps the only, interest in life. And this kind of sex-warfare—for it is success, not happiness, which is at stake—necessarily involves secret negotiations, bluff and hypocrisy. Marivaux's Jacob, using his physical attractions for social advancement, seems honest and practical in comparison with these creatures for whom a 'conquest' is an end in itself. According to the standards of most modern readers, the life led by Meilcour and Versac seems strangely empty. Meilcour himself, at the beginning of his story, sums up the various reasons—economic, social and political—which are partly responsible for such behaviour:

> L'idée du plaisir fut, à mon entrée dans le monde, la seule qui m'occupa. La paix qui régnait alors me laissait dans un loisir dangereux. Le peu d'occupation que se font communément les gens de mon rang et de mon âge, le faux air, la liberté, l'exemple, tout m'entraînait vers les plaisirs.

Apart from the two mothers, Mme de Meilcour and Mme de Théville, all the characters in the book appear to spend most of their time thinking about love and love-making. Versac brings out into the open, and analyses, the assumptions and motives which govern their behaviour. His treatment of the subject, which Crébillon obviously found an absorbing one, takes on almost the proportions of a lecture—or a tutorial.

Crébillon's view of sexual relations in the upper reaches of French society is very similar to that of Laclos. But while *Les Liaisons dangereuses* provides an effective treatment of this subject, **Les Egarements** is, for various reasons, a less satisfactory novel. The plot, first of all, has a see-saw regularity: Mme de Lursay wins Meilcour's attention, he breaks free; she wins him back, he breaks free again—and so on. And while Prévost managed to vary the equally repetitive pattern of *Manon Lescaut* by the development of the Chevalier's character, Meilcour scarcely grows up at all, and could hardly be expected to in the time covered by the novel. If Crébillon had fulfilled his plan for the whole work, a different impression might have emerged, but the three parts we have are weak in this respect.

Secondly, Crébillon has a tendency to envisage his theme in an abstract and theoretical fashion. There is a particular danger here, that of coming to consider the human race merely as two opposing masses, Men and Women. Writers who fall into this trap tend to generalize widely and even wildly, and Crébillon is no exception. 'Une femme, quand elle est jeune,' he begins, 'est plus sensible au plaisir d'inspirer des passions, qu'à celui d'en prendre.' The idea is developed, and followed by a further paragraph on the woman who has reached 'cet âge où ses charmes commencent à décroître'. This kind of generalization has several drawbacks. It is difficult, for instance, to produce observations of any complexity which really apply to the behaviour of every man, or every woman, in love. While reading, we may therefore be brought up short by the patent falsity of some of Crébillon's comments, judged in the light of our own experience. The trouble here is that instead of merely describing how certain kinds of people may act in certain situations, Crébillon has been tempted, by his fondness for theorizing, into writing of them as though they were typical of all mankind.

The habit of generalizing about the two halves of humanity even leads him into seeing some actions as typically masculine or feminine when they could as well be considered as typically human: 'Les femmes adorent souvent en nous nos plus grands ridicules, quand elles peuvent se flatter que c'est notre amour pour elles qui nous les donne.' Surely this comment would be equally true if it ran, *mutatis mutandis,* 'Les hommes adorent souvent . . . '? Feminine readers may have special cause to notice, and be annoyed by, this tendency, since it would seem to be *la Femme* who is the more frequent subject of such generalizations-by-sex. However, it is not merely the quality of such remarks which can be criticized in Crébillon—many a novelist gets away with generalizations which do not bear close consideration—it is their sheer quantity, and the space they occupy, which may become wearisome. **Les Egarements** might have been a better novel had we been shown more of the interplay between characters, and heard less of the narrator's abstract theorizing.

Crébillon's tendency to abstraction goes even deeper, and is inherent in his very vocabulary. It seems to be his natural mode of expression to deal in abstract nouns and general terms rather than in the concrete and specific. A passage like the following is typical of his discursive manner:

> Cependant il resait encore à Madame de Lursay bien des ressources contre moi, si elle eût voulu s'en servir. Ce caractère de sévérité qu'elle s'était donné, et qui, tout faux qu'il était en lui-même, l'arrêtait sur ses propres désirs, la honte de céder trop promptement, surtout avec quelqu'un qui, ne devinant jamais rien, lui laisserait tout le désagrément des démarches; la crainte que je ne fusse indiscret, et que mon amour découvert ne la chargeât d'un ridicule d'autant plus grand qu'elle avait affiché plus d'éloignement pour ces sortes de faiblesses; sa coquetterie même, qui lui faisait trouver plus de plaisir à s'amuser de mon ardeur qu'à la satisfaire, et qui avait vraisemblablement causé ses inégalités, plus encore que tout le reste. . . .

In description he follows the same pattern of abstractions. Here is how Hortense de Théville appeared to Meilcour on their first meeting:

> Qu'on se figure tout ce que la beauté la plus régulière a de plus noble, tout ce que les grâces ont de plus séduisant, en un mot, tout ce que la jeunesse peut répandre de fraîcheur et d'éclat; à peine pourra-t-on se faire une idée de la personne que je voudrais dépeindre. . . . Elle était mise simplement mais avec noblesse. Elle n'avait pas en effet besoin de parure: en était-il de si brillante qu'elle ne l'eût effacée; était-il d'ornement si modeste qu'elle ne l'eût embelli? Sa physionomie était douce et réservée. Le sentiment et l'esprit me paraissaient briller dans ses yeux.

Now it would be foolish to suggest that abstraction and lack of visual detail are, in themselves, major faults in a novelist; Prévost shares these characteristics with Crébillon, and we find Manon no less fascinating because her character is discussed with abstract nouns and we do not know the shape of her nose. The fondness for the general and the abstract goes back, of course, to the seventeenth century. *La Princesse de Clèves,* for instance, in its descriptions and discussions, has much in common with this aspect of Crébillon's style. But when such a style is combined with the theoretical, generalizing tendencies we have already observed, the overall effect may well be excessively remote and intellectual.

With his abstract approach Crébillon combines a liking for analysis. Nuances of feeling are distinguished and classified, motives are brought out into the light and carefully examined. Mme de Lursay denies that she is afraid of Meilcour falling in love with her:

> Non, reprit-elle, ce n'est pas que j'en aie peur; craindre de vous voir amoureux serait avouer à demi que vous pourriez me rendre sensible: l'Amant que l'on redoute le plus est toujours celui que l'on est le plus près d'aimer; et je serais bien fâchée que vous me crussiez aussi craintive avec vous.

She is of course playing a part, so that the passage has

overtones of dramatic irony. Even without this, the notion is complex enough, and Crébillon, one feels, is sometimes too subtle by half.

Finally, despite all this reflection and analysis, the moral and emotional values of the book remain curiously equivocal. From the preface and his general comments on characters like Versac and Mme de Senanges, Crébillon seems to condemn the futility of devoting all one's time to the pursuit of love. Yet he describes Meilcour's struggles with patient detail, thereby implying that they are worthy of interest and attention. A character like Mme de Meilcour, who receives explicit praise for her virtue and for devoting herself to bringing up her son, not only plays a minimal rôle in the action, but would seem to have left Meilcour ignorant both of the conventional moral principles and of the hazards of society life.

On the emotional side, we are first led to believe that Mme de Lursay's affection for Meilcour may be sincere; it is she who gives rise to the remark: 'Ce qu'on croit la dernière fantaisie d'une femme est bien souvent sa première passion'. Yet she is later portrayed as no more than a schemer, motivated by pride and physical desire rather than by *tendresse*. As for the one supposedly profound emotional situation of the novel, Meilcour's love for Hortense, this is likewise attenuated and ridiculed, by ironical references to love-affairs in novels. The hero speaks of himself as 'd'autant plus persuadé que j'étais vivement amoureux que cette passion naissait dans mon cœur par un de ces coups de surprise qui caractérisent dans les Romans les grandes aventures'. And when she is leaving the Tuileries he observes—with a passing thrust for Marivaux:

> Je me rappelai alors toutes les occasions que j'avais lues dans les Romans de parler à sa Maîtresse, et je fus surpris qu'il n'y en eût pas une dont je pusse faire usage. Je souhaitai mille fois qu'elle fît un faux pas, qu'elle se donnât même une entorse. . . .

The general effect of the traits we have noticed is to give an abstract and artificial air to Crébillon's world. His characters react, like puppets, to each fresh move of their manipulator, and their feelings are fully explained to us. But conceived and presented as they are in general analytical terms, they tend to remain mere creatures of the intellect, without emotional consistency. Crébillon does not even succeed in making them appear to care wholeheartedly about the loves and intrigues which are ostensibly the main interest of their existence. It is scarcely surprising, then, if the reader, however willing he may be to co-operate, finds it difficult to accord to such tenuous beings a continuous measure of imaginative belief. In spite of Crébillon's enlightened literary theories, in spite of his technical innovations, this memoir-novel does not wholly fulfil its promise.

It is even more unlikely that a modern reader will enjoy the curious hotch-potch of *Les Heureux Orphelins* (1754), though here again Crébillon's handling of the story is of considerable interest from a technical point of view. Part I of the novel is translated from Mrs Eliza Haywood's *The Fortunate Foundlings* (1744). The heroine, Lucy, runs away from home because of the attentions of her adoptive father. She is seen, in London, by a rich nobleman who plans to seduce her, but she manages to escape, and ends up in Bristol under the protection of the Duchess of Suffolk. Part I ends with Lady Suffolk declaring to Lucy:

> Je me sens un besoin extrême de parler, et de mon amour et de mes malheurs; et je crois ne pouvoir pas entretenir quelqu'un qui veuille bien s'y intéresser autant que vous.

Part II, where Crébillon begins to invent for himself, turns out to be Lady Suffolk's account of how she fell a victim to the wiles of Lord Durham, an unprincipled young rake brought up in France. Since the Duchess is virtuous and deeply in love with Durham, the effect is rather as though we were to hear about Valmont's seduction of Mme de Tourvel from the latter's point of view. When Durham has abandoned her, Lady Suffolk still feels some affection for him. In order to disabuse her completely, the Queen sends her a packet of Durham's letters, intercepted in the post to France. These letters take up the remaining two Parts of the novel.

The work thus consists, ostensibly, of a third-person narrative, a story in memoir-form, and a sequence of letters. In reality, these letters are merely another first-person account of past events, since they retail, firstly, Durham's plan to win the favours of three court ladies, and then his progress in these intrigues. Lady Suffolk is one of the three, and her sincerity and virtue are contrasted with the other two victims, an experienced coquette and a *fausse prude*. Durham's manœuvres show him to be as lucid and pitiless as Laclos's Valmont, and rather more successful, since he remains unpunished.

From a technical point of view, the interest of these letters lies in the way that Durham presents us with his version of events which we have already seen through the eyes of the Duchess. Crébillon seems to have worked over the two accounts with some care. The details are accurately correlated, and we repeatedly find that one narrative provides elements not available in the other, so that the two versions are truly complementary. Lady Suffolk, for instance, repeats verbatim her first conversation with Durham. He in his turn reports:

> Quoiqu'elle parût se prêter peu à la conversation, et qu'elle ne me laissât ni lui dire tout ce que j'aurais voulu, ni lui parler aussi longtemps que j'aurais désiré, il ne me fut pas difficile de juger, moins encore à son embarras, qui fut extrême, qu'à la promptitude avec laquelle elle termina notre entretien, de l'impression qu'il faisait sur elle.

On other occasions it is Durham who fills in the details of a scene to which the Duchess has merely alluded. Similarly, she tells how he looked and behaved, and how this affected her, while he reveals the motives for his conduct and his diagnosis of her reactions.

A further parallel between the accounts is that in each case there is a sympathetic 'listener', and this fictional audience affects the way the story is presented. Lucy does not yet know what it is like to be in love, and Lady Suffolk therefore comments on her own feelings and behaviour in remarks intended to warn the girl about the pitfalls of passion. Durham, on the other hand, is writing to a French nobleman who has been his tutor and guide in sexual intrigue. His 'progress reports' refer to the theories on which he acts, describe in detail the practical outcome of his manoeuvres, and include passing reflections on subjects such as the differences between society women in France and in England. Like Marivaux, Crébillon makes his narrator's tone depend on the fictional listener or reader, so that we are offered the story in two versions which are differentiated not only by the point of view but by overall distinctions of tone and attitude.

As in *Les Egarements,* Crébillon apparently wishes us to penetrate fully into the thoughts and feelings of both participants in the love-affair. In *Les Heureux Orphelins* he manages to do this without infringing the conventions of his chosen form of narrative; neither the Duchess nor Durham exceeds the limits of what each could be expected to know. (In this context I am accepting, as conventionally possible knowledge, the narrator's memories of long conversations, letters, etc.) But the two narratives together provide us with a double version of events, from the point of view of the deceived and the deceiver. This method is unusual, and shows Crébillon's desire to extend the author's resources in describing both the 'truth' of a given set of events, and also his characters' inner life.

The main plot of *Les Heureux Orphelins* reaches no conclusion, though it turns out that the nobleman who pursued Lucy in London was Durham himself, under his new title of Count of Chester. Crébillon's weakness in plot-construction has already been noticed. Clearly the linking together of events to form a complete and coherent structure was an aspect of his craft which he found unimportant. The chief interest of his memoir-novels lies not in the story as such, but in his efforts to grasp nuances of thought and feeling, and to find adequate and if necessary new methods of conveying them to his readers. For these aims, if not always for their execution, Crébillon still merits serious consideration.

P. L. M. Fein (essay date 1972)

SOURCE: "Crébillon fils, Mirror of His Society," in *Studies on Voltaire and the Eighteenth Century,* Vol. LXXX-VIII, 1972, pp. 485-91.

[Here, Fein contends that the actions of Crébillon's characters reflect their own desires, others' desires, and the desires of society.]

The mirror, together with the mask, is one of the chief symbols of 18th century society. As Gaston Bachelard has said, 'les miroirs sont des objects trop civilisés, trop maniables, trop géométriques, ils sont avec trop d'évidence des outils de rêve pour s'adapter d'eux-mêmes à la vie onirique'. So in reality the mirror creates a dream-world. Crébillon makes use of the dream itself as a mirror in his first work *Le Sylphe ou songe de mme. de R———,* demonstrating that the comment is capable of inversion.

The sylph is an ideal man for mme de R., and he can read her thoughts, her eyes mirror her heart. What he sees there is the reflection of her own desire and his recognition of this gives him the knowledge to exercise control over her. What he sees is only the reflection of herself, her gaze turned inwards to her own desire, but the dream gives her no control over the other and the sylph exploits his superior position through language. The conversation that ensues between them is a demonstration of the way that language becomes a weapon of control over the other. It is used to show mastery of social convention and limit the freedom of the other. To reject the arguments used by the seducer would involve rejection of the social conventions of that society because the arguments are expressed as self-evident truths about human behaviour and particularly about the normal behaviour of men and women within that society. The conflict between virtue and inclination is dismissed as an irrelevance and this expresses an attitude that Crébillon will continue to express and satirize in later works. The sylph uses the language of the 'amant courtois', but the lady fears, with reason, the physical brutality that may underlie it, she fears that the sous-entendus latent in the argumentation of the sylph, and which constitute her moral victimisation, will in due course become physical victimisation. Crébillon will express this more bluntly in later works as the theory from the *Ars amatoris* of Ovid that the lady prefers the use of physical force to the timidity of her admirer because it avoids her own moral questioning. But even if the physical culmination to the conversation is not achieved by force, as indeed it rarely is in Crébillon's work, it is nevertheless an expression of the control over one individual by another, an attempt to limit the latter's freedom. With all his theorising, and indeed because of it, as the lady will conform to the accepted values of her world, the Sylph achieves his conquest of mme de R., for her dream mirrors her own heart's desire and her mind is seduced by the language of the seducer. Crébillon's demonstration is that the mirror is multifaceted, the dream centred on the ego encompasses the dream centred on the ideal other that she has created.

This creative element is also found in the one-sided *Letters de la marquise de M——— au comte de R———,* for the marquise creates in her lover the ideal of her imagination, she never recognises him to be as he is and the mirror distorts for the benefit of her desire. The reader can imagine her sitting writing these letters at such a desk as the one given to the comtesse Du Barri by Louis XV and of which she writes: 'C'était un composé de vermeille et de plaques de porcelaine admirablement peintes. Lorsque je l'ouvrais, une glace se levait pour réfléchir mes traits'. In these letters language has a seductive effect, for while writing, the marquise is seducing herself into believing that she needs her lover and the portrait she gives of her husband establishes in her mind the normal conventions of her society. This is the only work in which Crébillon bluntly gives a tragic outcome to a novel. The marquise dies because of the sincerity of her own feelings, her image is a true reflection of that sincerity and those of the other characters are distorted. In this way, the marquise becomes a victim of her society, whose values cause her death. The truth of her reflection implies the falsehood of society.

The dialogue is particularly well suited to Crébillon's purpose, indeed almost all his work is a series of dialogues in different guises. In the conversation between Clitandre and Cidalise, the protagonists of *La Nuit et le moment,* the reader sees reflected, through the words spoken, an intimate game of attack and defence. The language of 'galanterie' and the anecdotes relating past seductions here conceal a situation in which both actors are equally willing to remove their masks, equally experienced in the attempt to satisfy their desires and equally aware that they are giving nothing and taking nothing, the relationship remains ephemeral and has no reason to last. The two mirrors of their personalities reflect themselves alone, their own inner desire, there is no movement outwards, they remain opaque, self-absorbed, narcissistic. At the same time, there is no control exercised over the other, they are partners in a dance of set movements and an anticipated conclusion.

The conversation between the duke and Célie in *Le Hasard du coin du feu* is different in form and in intention and it is far more complex. Célie wishes to gain control over the duke and remove him from the marquise. She reflects only desire and her conversation, allied with her gestures in the stage-directions included in the dialogue, show that her intention is to exercise control through her physical charms. The duke recognises this from the beginning and plays his part. In the final gesture, the act of love, there is a mingling of knowledge, each has reflected the mirror-image of the other's desire. But desire on Célie's part is unsatisfied. Crébillon writes elsewhere of women bringing to the sexual encounter 'plus de sentiment que de désir'. Control eludes her because she is not loved and the duke has expressed no feeling of love for her, by remaining silent he has retained mastery over himself. So that Célie expresses clearly her disillusionment: 'Ah! toujours des éloges! pensez-vous qu'ils me tiennent lieu de ce que vous ne m'avez pas encore dit? S'ils suffisent à la vanité, qu'ils sont peu faits pour contenter le cœur!' In the mingling of knowledge, the attempted satisfaction of desire, has come for her the dissatisfaction of seeing that the mirror held only her own desire, it reflected no feeling for her on the part of the other and she is as much alone, separated as she was before. What was acceptable to Cidalise is not acceptable to Célie and she cries out against the opaque reflection of the mirror. The duke is then able to exercise control on his own terms. The pretext he gives for this is once again the conventions of their society, which she cannot deny without excluding herself from it. He will not give up the marquise for her, but accepts to continue with Célie. It is at her suggestion

that he does this, but there is constantly an attempt on her part to force an admission of feeling from him: 'Puis-je raisonnablement me flatter que le goût que vous avez pour moi devienne jamais un sentiment?' The pathos of her inquiry, underlined by his negative reply, shows the weakness of her position and her recognition of it. An arrangement is made by which she will take an extra lover of both their choice and she cannot activate his jealousy on that count. The conclusion of the duke is that there is little difference between 'goût' and 'sentiment'. Crébillon comments as author in conclusion on the 'différence trop réelle qu'il y a, quoi qu'il en dise, entre ces deux mouvements,' for the language conceals the emptiness of the heart that lies beneath that 'contact de deux épidermes'. There are moments in this scene, however, where the language does become brutal, the truth of indifference is revealed and the delicate glass of the mirror reflects a heart that could break if pressed too far to recognise that truth.

The main intention in writing those tales that have a fashionable oriental setting seems to have been to satirize French social conventions in an exotic milieu. The repetitive form of *Le Sopha* comes from putting together a series of dialogues between couples abandoned to the pleasure of being alone, but secretly observed. The watcher holds the mirror that gives him total observation, but he can see and cannot be controlled. The double aspect of this mirror has been shown by Michel Foucault. The watcher sees only his own desire, the secret of his own heart, the mirror merely reflects.

The language of the protagonists in the dialogues and the report of the observer are imbued with the obscure feeling that the watcher does not know he sees only himself, the participants know they are alone and yet have the sense of being watched. The adult fairy-tale that ridicules the duc de Richelieu is on another level an erotic demonstration that desire remains unsatisfied even at the point where the two sides of the mirror meet, the observer and the observed, for what is desired cannot in the final gesture, the act of love, be controlled and escapes, as does Zéïnis from the soul of the sopha.

The allegory with the Japanese setting satirizes the political machinations in France surrounding the papal bull *Unigenitus,* but from another viewpoint the story is concerned with the young couple Tanzaï and Néadarné and their journey to gain experience of the meaning of loyalty and fidelity to each other as an essential concomitant of their love. The ridicule directed at the young prince is a social attack he must overcome, for nothing is more important to him than the truth of their reciprocated love. Their infidelities to each other with Concombre and Moustache are shown as relatively unimportant because they had no other choice and because their own feelings were not involved. Crébillon gives in this tale a rare example of the mirror reflecting a single image for the young couple, one in which they could see each other's reflection.

The Athenian letters describe a strange, perhaps subconsciously homosexual world in which Alcibiade discusses his conquests with his companions in his letters, thus achieving a more truly erotic pleasure. We rejoin the comments of Jean Luc Seylaz [in his *La Création romanesque chez Laclos*, 1958] on Laclos: 'Un être érotique ne s'abandonne jamais dans le plaisir; au contraire tout se passe comme s'il se dédoublait sans cesse et que ce fût à la partie de lui qui est en quelque sorte spectatrice de l'autre que dût être réservé le plaisir. L'amour est chez lui perpétuellement pensé et 'cérébralisé.' The letters here depict the exercise of control over victims and the reflection is an image of loneliness, a constantly repeated seduction process that seeks to prove ad infinitum the virility of the 'grand-maître'. The social attack is often explicit in this work: ' . . . si nous avons encore le même orgueil, qu'il s'en faut que nous ayons ces vertus que nous admirons dans nos pères et que peut-être nous n'y révérons tant que parce que nous nous sentons moins en nous-mêmes la possibilité de les égaler!' The attack on sexual pretence is expressed to Alcibiade by Némée: ' . . . vous m'avez, vous, dégoûtée du goût.' The association of Athenian and French decadence is an obvious one and the characters are left at the end of this work in an image of sadness. Alcibiade himself comments: 'si les hommes les plus jaloux de ma gloire savaient, et ce qu'elle me coûte, et combien souvent elle m'ennuie, ils cesseraient bientôt de m'envier une si onéreuse célébrité.' The Athenian is saying the same as Versac, as lord Durham, in the **Heureux orphelins,** indeed as any of the accomplished masters depicted by Crébillon. The letter-form acts as a mirror reflecting the purposelessness of the fictional writer's existence, the fictional writer comes to reflect his society.

Les Egarements du cœur et de l'esprit is a novel of initiation into society. The narrator recounts his initiation and reveals to himself the distance between what he was then and what he has become. The mirror here is turned to reflect the past and to reinterpret for Meilcour the circumstances and people that formed him. From his past come the conversation and behaviour of the only people he knew, his equals in society. It is striking that the most highly developed scene is Versac's set of instructions to the youth, which will enable him to exercise control over women and establish the reputation that they will make for him. The pathos of his situation, even at 17, is revealed to himself and to the reader at the outset: 'Je voulais m'étourdir en vain sur l'ennui intérieur dont je me sentais accablé; le commerce des femmes pouvait seul le dissiper.' The love of reciprocal feeling represented by Hortense is not developed, it remains unreal in the memory of the narrator, who sees his unrealised happiness through a glass darkly. Her place is taken in all realism by the woman who is all desire and who responds to the desire that motivates most strongly the thoughts and behaviour of the youth. Yet even she, at their moment of truth, looses the cri de cœur 'et je suis perdue, si je ne suis pas heureuse.' Desire remains unsatisfied and his initiation marks the prelude to a career that makes him into a second Versac. In this case the dissatisfaction moves beyond the inability to find satisfaction in the senses, for the narrator, in measuring the distance he has traversed, is dissatisfied with what he is, what his Society has made

of him. In this novel, the mirror-image reaches its ideal profundity, the distance between intention and achievement in a human life.

Les Lettres de la duchesse de ——— au duc de ——— is filled with sadness. The letters reflect the fears of the duchess and the final letter is an echo of the *Princesse de Clèves*: 'le ton de cette lettre doit vous dire que, quelque pouvoir que vous y avez encore, rien ne peut me déterminer jamais à accepter l'offre que vous me faites de votre main . . . votre façon de penser que rien, même le voulussiez-vous sincèrement, ne peut réformer'. The duchess has realised to her cost that the duke, whom she loves, is nothing more than an accomplished seducer, he is the replica of the duke of the dialogue, of Versac, of lord Durham in the **Heureux orphelins,** of so many others. He has been formed by his society to mirror in his thinking and his behaviour the libertin ethic of that society. The paradox of love within his society that Crébillon expresses with sadness is that through control there is no possession, there is only the destructive force of separation and loneliness.

Thomas R. Vessely (essay date 1981)

SOURCE: "Innocence and Impotence: The Scenario of Initiation in *L'Ecumoire* and in the Literary Fairy Tale," in *Eighteenth Century Life,* Vol. VII, October, 1981, pp. 71-85.

[*In the essay below, Vessely focuses on the sexuality of Tanzaï in Crébillon's French literary fairy tale* L'Ecumoire.]

The overriding literary project of Crébillon *fils* was to explore "The Ways of Love," and particularly, according to Clifton Cherpack [in his *An Essay on Crébillon 'fils'*, 1962], the ways in which love shapes the social relations between the sexes. Crébillon's premise, best illustrated by Versac's famous "Traité de morale" in **Les Egarements du coeur et de l'esprit**, is that the study of social dynamics constitutes a science which can be learned and then manipulated to one's personal advantage. Crébillon was concerned with the here and now, with the trajectories of social fortunes in the upper reaches of Parisian society, with the relation between social and sexual intercourse.

These observations are as pertinent to **L'Ecumoire,** which is cast in the mold of a fairy tale, as they are to **Les Egarements.** However, critics intent on showing the unity and continuity in Crébillon's thinking have tended to neglect or to diminish the importance of the *merveilleux* as a vehicle of meaning in **L'Ecumoire.** "This story," writes Cherpack, "has four notable features: naughtiness, social and political satire, an analysis of human jealousy, and the famous *pastiche* of Marivaux." What is absent from Cherpack's analysis is any developed consideration of the text against the backdrop of the French literary fairy tale. And yet, like all such stories **L'Ecumoire** involves temporal displacement, schematic characterization, and fantastic causality. Although it is ostensibly set in the Orient, this "histoire japonaise" is devoid of local color. Despite many thinly veiled references to important people and to recent political events in France, at the basic level of narrative coherence *L'Ecumoire* reveals no marks of historicity. Neither Parisian, nor oriental, nor actual, the implausible story unfolds in the deliberate vagueness of the far away and the long ago.

In the introduction and notes to his excellent critical edition of *L'Ecumoire,* Ernest Sturm broaches the subject of the conventions of the *merveilleux* in the text. The advantage which he sees in the fairy-tale features of *L'Ecumoire* lies in the opening they provide for "un systéme de projections symboliques," and Sturm is attentive to Crébillon's "exploration de la partie inavouée de l'être." However, unduly influenced by Mary Elizabeth Storer's argument ["Un Episode littéraire de la fin du dix-septième

---

Crébillon's dedication, to his father, of *Les Égarements du coeur et de l'esprit* (1736):

Sir,

I ought doubtless to have waited, before doing you public homage, until I might have offered you a work more worthy of you; but I dare to hope that in what I do today you will have the goodness to regard nothing but my zeal. Attached to one another by the closest bonds of kinship, we are, if I may venture to say so, united even more by the most sincere and tender friendship. . . . I, who have always seen myself the sole object of your fondness and concern, have no fear that you, my friend, my solace, my support, will see anything to detract from the respect I have for you in the titles I now lend you and you have so justly earned. Nay, I should not deserve to have been the object of your virtues if I failed to bestow on you their names. And if the public ever honours my humble talents with any small esteem; if posterity, in speaking of you, can succeed in calling to mind that I existed, I shall owe that glory only to the generous care with which you formed me, and to the desire I have always had that you might one day acknowledge me without undue regret.

I am, Monsieur, with the deepest respect,
Your most humble and obedient servant, and son.
        Crébillon.

Crébillon, in The Wayward Head and Heart, *translated by Barbara Bray, Oxford University Press, 1963.*

---

siècle: la mode des contes de fées," *Bibliothèque de la revue de littérature comparée,* Vol. 48, 1928] that the literary fairy tale was worn thin from overproduction by the early years of the eighteenth century, Sturm is reluctant to follow these threads of meaning very far into the fabric of the text. He is too quickly convinced that in this pseudo-oriental *conte merveilleux,* "Le genre n'aboutit en

fin de compte qu'à des ouvertures décevantes: l'irréalisme qu'il introduit risque de submerger l'intention du romancier sous une fantaisie assez vide." In spite of many penetrating remarks which would seem to indicate the contrary, Sturm nevertheless concludes that Crébillon's intention is at odds with the forms and *topoi* of the fairy tale.

The suggestion here is that there is no contradiction between "l'intention du romancier" and the conventions of the *conte merveilleux.* It is quite true that the genre of the fairy tale had attracted *conteurs* of dubious talent and had lost some of its early popularity, but the genre remained a vital mode of expression until well into the eighteenth century. Moreover, in part because of the association of fairy tales with children and with uneducated rustics, French authors had consistently felt the need to adapt the genre to the tastes of sophisticated urbanites: Perrault by his irony, Mme d'Aulnoy and Mme de Murat by their *précieux* conceits, Hamilton and Crébillon *fils* himself by the devices of the burlesque. The distance between the narrator and the narration is more apparent, but no greater, in *L'Ecumoire* than in Perrault's tales; and *L'Ecumoire* is no less able to elicit the reader's response to the important lessons conveyed by fairy tales. The central theme of *L'Ecumoire,* according to Sturm, is "la découverte de soi-même et du monde que tout être doit accomplir pour accéder à l'âge adulte." *L'Ecumoire,* like all the other literary fairy tales, relates the coming of age of a child. By drawing on the conventions of the genre, Crébillon asserts that a true knowledge of the world proceeds from the discovery of the self. In this tale, just as in those, happiness is not the lot of the innocent.

L'Ecumoire opens with a brief reference to the generation of the parents followed by a rapid shift of focus to the generation of the children. King Céphaès, ruler of the long-lost kingdom of Chéchianée, "ne se voyait pour succéder à sa vaste puissance qu'un seul fils." This abbreviated genealogy echoes the beginning of countless fairy tales. "Il était une fois un Roi et une Reine" are the first words of Perrault's *La Belle au bois dormant,* which continues four lines later, "Enfin pourtant la Reine devint grosse, et accoucha d'une fille." In the telescopic view of the literary fairy tale the adult world is represented by the couple. Two becomes two plus one in the introduction; the hero or heroine is married in the conclusion. The narrative develops in the period of isolation and instability whose beginning and end are marked by the destruction and re-creation of the figure of the pair. The broad structural outlines of the fairy tale thus relate the maturation of the child to the cyclical renewal of the social order. By encouraging the readers to make the appropriate generic association, Crébillon's introduction leads us to anticipate this connection between the hero's initiation to psycho-sexual maturity and his accession to "la vaste puissance" of his future social role. The same generic association invites notice of any changes in the usual scenario: no mention is made of the female figure, of Céphaès' wife. In *L'Ecumoire* the initial pair is incomplete, divested of sexuality. As we shall see, the boy reaches adolescence with no real knowledge of sex. If the story is to have a fairy-tale ending, the hero will first have to come to terms with this critical lack in his perception of himself and his world.

The reader of a fairy tale is rarely left to construe the personality of the main character on the basis of his actions and interactions. Rather, a complete portrait is presented at the outset. Following this principle of organization and using a stock device, Crébillon immediately introduces the hero to the reader. Tanzaï, heir to the throne of the Chéchianiens, is endowed at birth by Barbacela, his fairy-protectress:

> Elle donna au jeune prince, à cause de sa grande beauté, le nom Hiaouf-Zéles-Tanzaï (rival du soleil), et le doua en même temps de tous les avantages qui peuvent élever un mortel à la plus haute perfection. Il savait tout sans avoir rien appris.

By the time the boy is eighteen, his literary works are read by all, his music is performed often, his paintings hang everywhere. But, we are told, Destiny had decreed that Tanzaï should not marry before his twenty-first year, and Barbacela is helpless to change the dictates of Destiny.

Tanzaï's talents may seem frivolous and quite unlike those we have come to expect in the hero of a fairy tale. Yet, exception made for a definite difference in narrative tone, this portrait is conventional when viewed in the light of the earlier literary fairy tales. There are, for example, eight fairies present at the baptism of Sleeping Beauty; and the girl is endowed with beauty, grace, wit, the ability to dance, to sing like a nightingale, and to play all kinds of musical instruments. The evil fairy then casts the curse of death. The eighth fairy, unable to undo entirely what her elder sister had done, modifies the curse to one hundred years of sleep. The young heroine of Mme d'Aulnoy's *La Princesse Printanière* is similarly endowed with beauty, wit, and various artistic talents before the evil fairy casts her spell:

> Je doue cette petite créature,
>   De guignon guigonnant,
> Jusqu'à l'âge de vingt ans.

A good fairy intervenes to assure that the girl will enjoy a long and happy life after her twentieth birthday. These descriptions of Tanzaï, Sleeping Beauty, and the Princess are very much alike with respect to their contribution to the narrative logic of the stories.

The epithets included in these and many other similar portraits form an image of human perfection, exactly as Crébillon indicates in the passage quoted above. High-born, handsome, and possessed of all moral and social virtues, the main character of a fairy tale is thoroughly deserving of the happiness promised by the narrative form. At times the meritorious nature of the character is even translated into an explicit principle of causality. In Perrault's *Les Fées,* for example, a fairy says to the heroine, "Vous êtes si belle, si bonne, et si honnête, que je ne puis

m'empêcher de vous faire un don." In Mme d'Aulnoy's *L'Oiseau bleu,* Prince Charmant refuses to believe the malicious lies that are spread about Princess Florine because, he says, "il est impossible que le ciel ait mis une âme si mal-faite dans le chef-d'oeuvre de la nature." Happiness in the world is, so to speak, the birthright of the hero or heroine of a fairy tale. And yet, the initial portrait also contains a problematic feature, an impediment to happiness.

Because the perfections are coexistent with the character, this impediment appears to be artificial and imposed from the outside. It is Sleeping Beauty's father, after all, who neglects to invite the spiteful old fairy to the baptism; the lovely girl is born into a world in which the sins of the father are visited on the children. The mother of Princess Printanière refuses to choose an ugly old fairy as a nurse for her newborn daughter, and the punishment befalls the daughter. Princess Florine is persecuted by a stepmother whom she did not choose. Tanzaï's fate is shaped by a mysterious and apparently arbitrary force called "Destiny." The reader's search for the cause of unhappiness is deflected away from the character and toward the world. On first reading, these characters seem innocent and deserving, yet condemned to suffer, at least temporarily, from causes beyond their reach. This quasi-moral (and false) paradox is the first level of organization of the French literary fairy tale.

The impediment, however, is often explicitly limited in time—one hundred years in *Sleeping Beauty,* twenty-one years in **L'Ecumoire,** twenty in *La Princesse Printanière,* seven in *L'Oiseau bleu.* Long or short, this limitation is a cue which allows the reader to recognize the second level of organization: the real impediment to happiness is not situated in the world, but in the character of the young prince or princess. Among the dozens of fairy tales which appeared in France between 1690 and the publication of **L'Ecumoire** in 1734, there was a wide range of explicitness in the development of this psychological register. Sleeping Beauty, at one extreme, pricks her finger on a spindle and falls asleep. She awakens one hundred years later, her talents, her beauty, and her social status entirely unaltered; but she has been discovered by the world. There is almost no observable sign of change in the heroine. It is not her marriage which makes her a queen in any but the most literal sense. Sleeping Beauty is already beautiful, good, and queenly; and it seems that she is condemned to wait until the imperfect world has been enlightened. What is remarkable about this tale is the total lack of psychological development in the heroine. We know that Sleeping Beauty dreams, but no insight is offered into the content of her dreams. The implication of the absence of a psychological dimension is that the innocent suffer because the world has gone astray. It is only through considerable abstraction that the reader comes to realize that her very innocence is the impediment to Sleeping Beauty's happiness.

Other authors were less intent than Perrault on hiding the child's acquisition of emotional and sexual maturity behind the facade of a passive wait for deliverance. In

L'Oiseau bleu, Princess Florine emerges from her prison to wander through the mysterious world where she must submit to a series of trials. There is still little psychological development in this tale, but between the beginning and the end the reader glimpses that what is really at issue is Florine's emergence from childhood. Mme d'Aulnoy's heroines, as Renée Riese Hubert has written [in "Le Sens du voyage dans quelques contes de Mme d'Aulnoy," *French Review,* 46 (1973)], are far more complex than Perrault's:

> Madame d'Aulnoy, par les pérégrinations mystérieuses de ses héroines, a animé le monde où l'enfance et l'âge adulte, la conscience et l'inconscience, se croisent. Le voyage au sortir de l'enfance, la forêt obscure, constituent aussi des données du "Petit Chaperon Rouge." Mais Perrault, par le ton ironique, par le style "ma mère l'oye," se met à l'abri des problèmes complexes qui touchent à l'âme fèminine et des initiations rituelles par lesquelles elle doit passer.

In Mlle L'Héritier's *L'Adroite Princesse,* a king who is obliged to leave his daughters closes them up in a tower after charging them to protect and preserve the glass distaffs that a fairy has given to each. A young prince, however, manages to enter the tower and to "marry" two of the three girls. Only Finette resists with strength and intelligence. When the king returns, only Finette's fragile *quenouille* remains intact. Although it is possible, even in these tales, to attribute the heroine's final happiness to some change in the world, it is much more convincing to look for the changes in the heroines themselves.

Almost perfectly dissimulated in *La Belle au bois dormant* and just suggested in *L'Oiseau bleu* and *L'Adroite Princesse,* the determining psychological drama is brought to the forefront in Crébillon's ***L'Ecumoire.*** When Tanzaï decides to brave Destiny by marrying before the appointed time, Barbacela gives him a huge kitchen skimmer and describes his last hope to avoid disaster. On his way to the temple, she says, he will see an old lady by the door. He must *force* the handle of the skimmer into her mouth. Then, if successful, he must *persuade* the high priest to accept the handle in his mouth. The instructions are very clear, but Tanzaï is not up to the test: he first graciously asks the old lady to grant his request and resorts to force only when she refuses; he then impatiently tries to persuade the high priest, but quickly turns to force. The young man is obliged to abandon the effort when the high priest threatens to delay the wedding ceremony. To forestall his fate, Tanzaï is required to demonstrate his worthiness to marry through interaction with the world, represented by a woman and a religious authority, and he fails the test miserably. His bungling is symptomatic of his immaturity. It is immediately apparent in ***L'Ecumoire*** that the world is the unchanging factor, the hero the one who must adapt. In spite of his endowed perfections, Tanzaï is incomplete and incapable of acceding to adulthood.

Along with the nouns "force" and "persuasion," the dominant verb in this text is *voir.* Sleeping Beauty, once ready, had only to "be seen" to find happiness, while Florine,

Finette, and especially Tanzaï, must learn "to see." Tanzaï's education begins when he sees what he lacks. In the conjugal bed, just as his marriage is about to be consummated, he discovers that his penis has vanished:

> Mais quel fut son étonnement, quand implorant le secours d'une main si chère, il vit que ce serait inutilement qu'il voudrait l'employer! Il ne s'offrait plus à ses yeux d'objet sur qui pussent tomber les bontés de sa princesse.

Because of his refusal to heed, and his inability to circumvent, the injunction of Destiny, Tanzaï finds himself married but sexually immature, sexless in fact. His anguish is understandable as he is forced to confront himself and his situation. Typically, however, Tanzaï refuses to assume any responsibility. He clings to what he thinks is his unalienable right to happiness, and he says to his wife:

> Je suis de tous les hommes, celui qui devait le moins s'attendr
>
> e à ce qui m'arrive aujourd'hui. Barbacela m'avait doué d'une f
>
> açon si surprenante que ce qui m'étonne le plus, est que ce pré
>
> sent devenu cher à mes yeux par la part que vous alliez y prend
>
> re, ait disparu sans que j'en aie rien senti.

This heretofore unreported endowment is no more a guarantee of sexual satisfaction than were the others of social power. In desperation Tanzaï rubs himself with the talisman, and the skimmer immediately attaches itself between his legs. On the advice of the sacred oracle, the hero sets out to seek his cure, the skimmer balanced between the ears of his horse.

This voyage is actually the second time in the story that Tanzaï quits his home at the court. Shortly after Barbacela had informed him of the dangers should he marry without regard for his destiny, the hero withdrew to an isolated palace by the edge of the sea and forbade entry to all women. Tanzaï's strategy, involving retreat and an attempt to take shelter behind an interdiction, is found in many fairy tales. Although such separations from the world are usually imposed rather than voluntary, in all cases they end in failure. Sleeping Beauty's father attempts to "protect" his daughter by issuing a ban on spindles (=penes), but the fatal time arrives nonetheless. The girl ascends into the tower, going from room to room, until at last she finds a spindle, her blood flows, and she lapses into the long, healing sleep. In Mme de Murat's *Peine perdue,* a fairy gives birth to a child and, "sa science lui ayant appris tous les malheurs que l'amour préparait à cette chère, fille," she removes the girl to an island where no men are allowed. The girl's innocence lasts until, at fifteen, she happens to find a portrait of Prince Isabel. The fairy should have known, comments Mme de Murat, that it is impossible to avoid or to change the order of destiny. No father or mother, not even a fairy, can forestall the fate of a child. The lesson in these scenes is always the same: there is no place to hide from impending adulthood, no retreat so perfect that the advance of time is suspended. After just three months Tanzaï is bored in his palace: "moins il connaissait le plaisir d'aimer, plus il s'en formait une image flatteuse." The young man abandons his retreat to pursue his fate actively.

This first sojourn by the sea reveals the futility of trying to cling to childhood. As we have seen, however, Tanzaï fails to learn the more important lesson—that his destiny is written within himself. He charges ahead and marries too soon. Still psychologically immature, the boy is unable to bear the weight of the conjugal union; and his fears rise to the surface to cause impotence, represented by the absence of a penis. Forcing matters still more, Tanzaï falls deeper into the psychological abyss, and his own sexuality now appears to him as something monstrous. To reverse the effects of this psychological collapse, Tanzaï must return to the sea.

The second voyage includes a brief halt "dans une forêt fort sombre," where Tanzaï encounters an old woman who is boiling herbs in a cauldron. Readers nourished on fairy tales will recognize this forest, the same one in which Little Red Riding Hood is accosted by the wolf, in which the beautiful princess happens upon Riquet. It is in a comparable setting that Mme d'Auneuil's Princess Philonice observes a young girl who is in love with a huge and horrible dragon. The very next evening the Princess herself falls in love with a man asleep in the same woods. Ernest Sturm suggests that Crébillon may have drawn inspiration from Antoine Hamilton's *Histoire de Fleur d'Epine,* in which the hero similarly meets an ugly old fairy preparing a brew in the heart of the forest. As Sturm also notes, however, the forest is a traditional *locus* in stories of initiation. The advance into the forest represents the child's advance toward the dark and dangerous mysteries with which he must come to terms in order to pass to a new and better mode of existence. Tanzaï notices that the Fée au Chaudron is in need of a skimmer, and he offers his services. He plunges the skimmer into the caldron, "et le prince se mit à écumer de toutes ses forces, en conduisant l'instrument avec ses mains." Tanzaï lets out "un cri de surprise et de joie" as the skimmer detaches itself from between his legs.

The skimmer had originally attached itself when the hero, "se frottant de toute sa force," was desperately trying to convince himself and his wife that he was capable of sexual intercourse. In the forest Tanzaï confidently begins to "écumer de toutes ses forces." The difference between these two scenes is in Tanzaï's frame of mind, and the contrast suggests that the skimmer is the external sign of the adolescent's debilitating lack of self-assurance in his own sexual power. However, whereas for Tanzaï the metamorphosis of his penis is terrifying, for the reader it is comic. There is something not very serious about Tanzaï's handicap, something juvenile; and the similarity between the two scenes is that they both present acts of autoeroticism. In the forest Tanzaï sets to skimming only after asking the old woman to turn aside. The caldron is, one might say, disembodied; now as before the hero acts

alone. Although Tanzaï frees himself of the phantasm of the monstrous penis, he has still not been initiated to heterosexuality. The hero remains sexless, still consumed by a dread of impotence.

Tanzaï continues to the "Ile des Cousins" where, he had learned, a lady is awaiting him in her bed. The young man's imagination runs wild as he is bathed and fed—"il crut enfin qu'une divinité brillante lui accordait l'honneur de sa couche"—and his anxieties dissipate at the thought of the pleasures which will be his. This state of excited self-satisfaction lasts until Tanzaï approaches the bed to find the Fée Concombre, the same old woman who had suffered his violence at the door of the temple! No "divinité brillante," Concombre is bald and toothless, her warty nose is enormous, her breasts hang down over her belly. Even though Concombre is provocatively dressed in lace and annointed with perfumes, Tanzaï draws back in disgust at the sight and stench of the old hag.

Ernest Sturm, in his reading of this passage, emphasizes the role of the fairy as the "initiatrice":

> Si Crébillon s'attache à peindre Concombre avec un réalisme aussi caricatural, c'est pour faire mieux ressortir le caractère de l'initiatrice, empreint à la fois de bestialité insatiable et de minauderie apprise à l'usage du monde. L'adolescent ingénu doit inéluctablement apprendre à ce contact à dépouiller ses dernières réticences et à vaincre la répulsion que l'âge et la corruption lui inspirent.

Sturm's interpretation of the scene serves to highlight the "découverte du monde" which is part of the boy's initiation, but it neglects the "découverte de soi-même." Concombre is not only or even primarily the experienced "initiatrice," not only a substitute for the feminine figure that was missing from the initial configuration of the text. Con/c/ombre is both the phallic "cucumber" and the "shadow(y) *con.*" Tanzaï's rendezvous is with sexuality itself. The reticence which the boy must now overcome is inspired not only by the age and corruption of the woman, but by the physical reality of sexual contact. Having already rehearsed this scene in his imagination, that is with the skimmer and the caldron in the dim light of the forest, Tanzaï must now project his sexual identity into the world. He must learn to comprehend his own sexuality in relation to that of others, and Tanzaï manages this last step in his initiation very imperfectly.

In the state of feverish anticipation which preceded Tanzaï's encounter with Concombre, all thought of Néadarné, his wife, was banished from his imagination:

> Il se flattait même que sa princesse, qui était ce que les Dieux avaient formé de plus parfait, n'approcherait pas des beautés qui allaient se trouver en proie à ses désirs: son amour pour elle en diminua, et s'il se sentit quelques transports, ils furent tous pour la Déesse.

When Tanzaï then enters the bedroom and sees Concombre, the image of his wife suddenly returns to his mind:

"O Néadarné! c'est donc ce que la nature a formé de plus hideux qui vous a balancée, que dis-je? qui vous a anéantie dans mon coeur." Tanzaï is absolutely unable to integrate the Beauty and the Beast in a single view of human nature. His mind shifts from Néadarné, "ce que les Dieux avaient formé de plus parfait," to Concombre, "ce que la Nature a formé de plus hideux." The hero's problem in this moment of crisis is not so much that he cannot hold Néadarné and their mutual interests in his mind while he holds Concombre in his arms, but rather that he cannot comprehend that Concombre is part of his wife and part of himself.

Tanzaï is about to flee from the bedroom when he stops short at the sound of a familiar voice. He looks back toward the bed to see Néadarné in the place of Concombre. Néadarné berates her astonished husband for his failure to perceive that it was she who had appeared to him as the Fée au Chaudron and as Concombre. Tanzaï rushes to embrace his wife, but she vanishes and he finds himself alone with Concombre's attendant. The boy now seems to realize dimly that more is at stake than the consummation of his marriage:

> Malheureuse condition des rois, d'être soumis, malgré leur pouvoir, aux injustices des fées! Y a-t-il rien de si bizarre que ce qui m'arrive? Ma destinée dépend d'une vile écumoire!

Tanzaï is right: both his happiness as a husband and his power as king depend on the skimmer. As long as Tanzaï cannot overcome the psychological need to skim the divine from the natural, the spiritual from the sexual, the pure from the impure, he will remain the same ineffectual adolescent. As Sturm says, "Dans le rapport de l'être au monde extérieur, le rôle du sexe apparaît donc prédominant." Social and sexual impotence are effects of the same cause.

Tanzaï begs Concombre for a second chance, and she grants his request on the condition that he must make love to her thirteen times before Néadarné will appear in her place. The young man does what he must: "Alors se bouchant le nez, fermant les yeux, il tâcha de s'acquitter du mieux qu'il pourrait du devoir préscrit." Now as always Tanzaï keeps his eyes closed. His performance is heroic, but it is no more than a formalistic fulfillment of the rite of initiation. Tanzaï's cure is equally formalistic. Although he does recover his penis, Néadarné does not appear and he does not overcome the disgust that sex inspires in him. He attacks Concombre who flies away after pronouncing her sentence:

> Ne compte point, lui dit-elle, vaincre jamais ma fureur. Je serai ta persécutrice éternelle. Les malheurs que je t'ai fait éprouver ne sont ni les derniers, ni les plus cruels de ta vie. Je t'ai à la vérité rendu ce que tu désirais avec tant d'ardeur; mais prends garde qu'il ne te soit inutile, et souviens-toi longtemps de ton infernale écumoire.

Tanzaï returns home, anatomically complete, but psychologically fractured. His first decision is to be ever faithful to his wife, the second is to lie to Néadarné by telling her that his recovery occurred in a dream. Néadarné is not entirely convinced: "Seigneur, dit alors Néadarné, ce songe est bien suivi et son effet me paraît admirable. Croyez-vous que ce ne soit qu'une illusion?" Néadarné suspects that the dream might be real; the attentive reader realizes that it is "son effet" which is at least partially illusory.

Lest the readers overlook the flaws in Tanzaï's initiation, the narrative elements are redoubled to provide a contrasting example of a perfect initiation to sexuality. Again in the conjugal bed, Tanzaï and Néadarné again fail to consummate their marriage. Just at the critical moment, Néadarné's sex vanishes and is replaced by an impenetrable wall of flesh. Because Néadarné has done nothing to incur Concombre's wrath, this "chatiment" leads Sturm to conclude: "que l'innocence, loin de détourner les agressions réalistes de la vie, peuvent au contraire les provoquer." Sturm's interpretation is solid so long as one assumes that innocence *ought* to serve as a mantle of protection against misfortune, that there is something unjust about Néadarné's inability. Although this reading is encouraged by many literary fairy tales, one cannot, as we have seen, neglect the other level of organization. Néadarné's misfortune is no more unjust than Sleeping Beauty's. It is not in spite of Néadarné's innocence that she is subject to the same fate as Tanzaï, but rather because of it.

On the advice of the sacred oracle, Néadarné leaves to seek relief at the island home of the handsome enchanter Jonquille, whose reputation allows no doubt as to the nature of her cure. Yet Jonquille, like Concombre, represents something more than simply the experienced seducer. Jonquille is both male and female, a "jonquil" but also a *jonc* and a *quille*. Like Concombre, his name suggests a vegetal, natural element. The girl is at first reluctant and steadfast in her refusal of the enchanter's skillful advances, but slowly she is overcome by Jonquille's charms. She smiles as he carries her off to bed where, "enivrée de volupté," she remarks a resemblance between Jonquille and Tanzaï. Surprised that she had not noticed this earlier, she responds fully to the ardor of the enchanter.

Né/adar/né is, as her name indicates, twice-born. Through her initiation the innocent child has been born again as an adult. She emerges from Jonquille's bed, dresses in the new clothes he has provided for her, then pauses briefly to admire his great beauty before slipping away. Néadarné has succeeded where Tanzaï failed. By fusing the image of her husband with that of Jonquille, she has included sex in her view of humankind and human affairs. In one night of pleasure she was able to integrate her social self as wife and her physical self as woman; and since Jonquille has promised to return from time to time, disguised as Tanzaï, to share her bed, the lesson will not be forgotten. Néadarné can love and be loved, while Tanzaï will always remain "Tant (de fois) sailli."

Néadarné is no fool and has no illusions about her husband. She assures Tanzaï that her cure, like his own, occurred in a dream and that he was ever-present in her mind. Néadarné knows that Tanzaï is most concerned with appearances, and she takes care to restore the physical signs of her virginity by means of a secret which a fairy had taught her. It is this "incontrovertible" proof that assuages Tanzaï's jealousy as the marriage is finally consummated. Barbacela arrives and convinces the high priest to lick the skimmer by appealing to his ambition to succeed the recently deceased patriarch. Céphaès cedes the throne to his son; and, as expected, Tanzaï and Néadarné are reported to live happily and to have many children.

"One wonders," says Cherpack, "if they really could have lived happily ever after." Although the happy ending is the *sine qua non* of the fairy tale, the conclusion of *L'Ecumoire* is not entirely satisfying. The figure of the pair has indeed been established, but the harmony of the conventional ending covers imperfectly the imbalance in this particular couple. It is as if the complexity of *L'Ecumoire* strains against the limits of the fairy tale.

This tension is not due to the superficiality of the fairy-tale features of *L'Ecumoire,* but to the specificity of the psychological drama which these elements evoke. Tanzaï's detailed encounter with Concombre, along with Néadarné's equally detailed evening with Jonquille, serve exactly the same narrative function as Sleeping Beauty's sleep: they both portray the passage from childhood to adulthood. However, *Sleeping Beauty* releases its story of sexual maturation only when the reader challenges the textual cause for the "curse" on the heroine. The reader must construct the story of Sleeping Beauty's loss of innocence in order to understand why she could not, and now can, live happily ever after. In *L'Ecumoire,* on the contrary, we must construct Tanzaï's life as husband and king on the basis of his imperfect loss of innocence.

Crébillon affirms in *L'Ecumoire* that the passage to psychosexual maturity is a life-giving event, and in so doing the author anticipates a question that Meilcour will ask Versac in *Les Egarements du coeur et de l'esprit:* "Pourquoi avons-nous besoin qu'une femme nous mette dans le monde?" The question is a startling play on words; and Versac breaks off, leaving the question unanswered. Just as Sturm suggests that Crébillon became aware of the limits of the fairy tale and thus turned to rework the same themes in *Les Egarements,* might not one suggest that Versac's failure to answer indicates Crébillon's awareness of the limits of realism? Some questions are better addressed through the potent symbols of fantasy. Fairy tales speak clearly and have much to say about the ways of love and the ways of the world.

Thomas M. Kavanagh (essay date 1993)

SOURCE: "The Moment's Notice: Crébillon's Game of Libertinage," in *Enlightenment and the Shadows of Chance: The Novel and the Culture of Gambling in Eighteenth-Century France,* The Johns Hopkins University Press, 1993, pp. 198-228.

[*In the following excerpt, Kavanagh examines the role of fate in Crébillon's writings, observing that his novels "acknowledge a limit to human power as it confronts the reality of chance."*]

There is little the characters in Crébillon *fils*'s novels would rather do than gamble. Most of their bets turn, of course, on the feminine virtue and masculine honor staked or bluffed as they maneuver each other toward an alcove, a sofa, or "one of those large armchairs as favorable to temerity as they are suited to indulgence [aussi favorables à la témérité que propres à la complaisance]." With surprising regularity, however, key events in Crébillon's novels play themselves out around the less lubricious but equally risky perimeter of the card table—an emblem of the socialized yet threatening *hasard* at the core of Crébillon's esthetic.

Crébillon's dialogue-novel *Le Hasard du coin du feu* takes place entirely in Célie's bedroom, where, on a cold winter day, she and the duc de Clerval spend a long afternoon trying to seduce each other. Célie will yield only if Clerval first tells her he loves her. Clerval, however, insists that at least at the level of *le coeur,* his fidelity to his current mistress precludes any such statement. Early on in their conversation Clerval asks Célie if she herself was ever young and naive enough to have actually believed that the "love" she so insists on hearing about could ever deliver the eternities it promises. His question prompts Célie to tell the story of her first lover. Norsan, Célie is forced to admit, had carefully calculated every stage of her seduction. And it was the social ritual of the card game that allowed him to force from her, at the level of gesture, the same declaration she would now withhold from Clerval: "We decided to play a game of brelan, and he all too easily forced me to accord to each of his actions that anxious and concerned attention which I have never known to be without danger for us, and which is itself perhaps the first symptom of love." . . .

Crébillon's best-known work, the memoir-novel *Les Egarements du coeur et de l'esprit,* likewise tells a story punctuated by card games where everything is staked and won, staked and lost. It is during a card game in her home that Madame de Lursay, secretly worshiped by the young Meilcour, overcomes her scruples at taking the first step with a younger man and reveals the affection Meilcour feels he must be certain of before he can overcome his timidity. "We sat down to cards. During the entire game Madame de Lursay, doubtless more susceptible than she believed and carried away by her love, gave all the strongest signs of it [her love]. It seemed prudence had abandoned her, that nothing now existed for her other than the pleasure of loving me and telling me so, and that she foresaw how much, if she were to beguile me, I needed to be reassured."

Later in the novel, after a chance meeting at the Opera has led Meilcour to fall in love with the young Hortense de Théville and abandon his suit of Madame de Lursay, it is around the same card table that, in no more time than it takes to turn a card, the whole of Meilcour's stake on the *belle inconnue* is swept away by her rival: "Our eyes met. The languor I saw in hers fixed in my heart the effect her charms had initiated and whose force seemed to grow with each instant. The few sighs she seemed to only half utter completed my overthrow, and at that dangerous moment, she benefited from all the love I felt for that unknown woman."

The novel's final scene is also built around a game of cards, a game recapitulating in miniature the back and forth, beckoning and repelling, understanding and mistrusting movement of the entire novel. Now completely smitten with Hortense and duped by the jaded Versac's lies about Madame de Lursay's past, Meilcour returns to her home only because he hopes to find Hortense there. While many guests are present, Hortense is not, and Madame de Lursay is engaged in a card game. Seeing Meilcour, she plays her cards in such a way that the new arrival receives exactly the message she wishes to communicate: "I was seated next to her, and from time to time she commented on the strange hands she was being dealt, but in a detached way. There was so much gaiety in her eyes, and her wit seemed so free, that I had no doubt she had forgotten me."

The finesse with which Madame de Lursay masks her true feelings generates for Meilcour a moment of self-discovery within chance that captures the very essence of the Crébillonesque scenario. Suspecting that Lursay may be feigning her lack of interest in him, Meilcour decides to study her closely as she plays. It is precisely as he is taken in and becomes certain he is not being fooled by any feigned indifference on Madame de Lursay's part that he becomes the dupe of his own unsuspected feelings: "To get to the bottom of the matter I studied her carefully. The more surely my scrutiny convinced me her change was real, the more I felt diminish the joy that thought had first brought me." Madame de Lursay invites Meilcour to join the game, to take a hand alongside the marquis de———, to whom she has been paying particular attention. Once the game resumes, she leaves little doubt who is the desired partner and who the dummy: "Each time I glanced at her I found her eyes fixed on the marquis, and she no sooner noticed my attention in observing her than she quickly brought them back to her cards, as though I were the person from whom she most wanted to hide her feelings [comme si c'eût été à moi surtout qu'elle eût voulu cacher ses sentiments]." As the stakes rise, Meilcour's own play becomes an index of the success of Madame de Lursay's stratagem: "I could not help showing signs of an impatience she knew very well was not my usual reaction to gambling and which I could thus hardly blame on it." Thanks to Lursay's consummate feints, all the pieces are now in place for the game's and the novel's final confrontation, one that will be played out alone by Meilcour and Madame de Lursay after the other guests have left.
. . . . .
Gambling is a privileged activity in Crébillon's novels not only because as social ritual it allows for the communication of nonverbal messages but also because as a

conflict of the momentary and the continuous, of what diverts and what obsesses, it is a literal twin to sexual desire as Crébillon's thematics of choice. As a dialectic of the momentary and the continuous, desire provides the organizing polarities of his most popular dialogue-novel, *La Nuit et le moment*. Late one evening, after all her guests have retired, Cidalise is surprised by the arrival in her bedroom of Clitandre. The entire novel consists of the conversation and other activities carried on by these two characters until first light the next morning. At every stage they demonstrate, in the direct present of speech and action, how desire is born, declares itself, and is consummated only to the extent that it disguises itself as what it is not.

Cidalise has chosen her guests carefully: all four of the other women visiting the chateau are former mistresses of Clitandre's. When she expresses her surprise that Clitandre should choose her bedroom as the object of his nocturnal stroll, he replies that those other women are only dim memories from a forgotten past: "Why should anyone imagine that in the midst of everything social life imposes on us, those whom chance, caprice, and circumstance once brought together for a few moments [des gens que le hasard, le caprice, des circonstances ont unis quelques moments] should recall what in fact interested them so little [se souviennent de ce qui les a intéressés si peu]?" Using an *on* that simultaneously depersonalizes his statement and establishes it as a general rule governing society, Clitandre enunciates a philosophy of desire and chance summarizing all the world-weary wisdom of the legions of dissolute ducs, marquis, and chevaliers populating so many novels and plays of early eighteenth-century France:

> We are happy together, we sleep together [On se plaît, on se prend]. And if we grow bored with each other [S'ennuie-t-on l'un avec l'autre]? We separate with no more ceremony than we took each other. Are we happy with each other again? We sleep together again with just as much pleasure as the first time we met. We separate again and never get upset about it. It is true that love has nothing to do with all this; but love— what is it other than a desire we were pleased to exaggerate, a movement of the senses our vanity enjoyed taking as a virtue?

Life and desire are presented as a succession of disjointed moments following one another with no more coherence or continuity than one might expect between cards dealt from a well-shuffled deck.

Speaking in a more personal voice, Clitandre goes on to insist that his own experience eminently confirms this law. As concerns Julie, for instance, "After all, I only had her one time after a dinner. Can you really call that having a woman?" Had it not been for the heat wave that summer, Julie's state of undress when he arrived, and most of all her blind devotion to the revered physicist Pagny, whose latest lecture she repeated to the effect that— in obvious contradiction to Clitandre's visibly rising excitement—such heat inevitably produces "an annihilation [un anéantissement] . . . caused by an excessive dissipation of the mind and a relaxing of the vital fibers," nothing would have happened between them. If Clitandre provided Julie with "the most furious refutation imaginable of her opinion," it was purely the result of *le hasard* governing this series of chance events over which he exercised no control and for which he bears no responsibility. Speaking of his affair with another of the guests, Araminte, the woman for whom Eraste, Cidalise's former lover, left her, Clitandre repeats that important term: "In returning from our walk, chance [le hasard] led us to pass by a small and dark grove. Equally by chance [Par le même hasard], we had unknowingly separated ourselves from the others."

Clitandre underlines everything that was accidental and ephemeral about his relations with these other women not so much because he would align himself with the promiscuity preached by the societal *on* of the libertine voice but to underline how different is his present with Cidalise from all those past moments. Clitandre's whole seduction of Cidalise turns on his careful manipulation of the period's distinction between desire and love. Characterized by distinct temporalities, desire exists only in the present, lasts only for the moment, and implies nothing about a future it leaves entirely free. Love, on the other hand, redefines the present as the promise of a future assured by the continuity of the lover's passion. Desire celebrates and limits itself to the present moment. Love may begin within the present, but only because that present is the single point of access to an unlimited future giving the present its real meaning.

Within the scenarios of libertinage, love is associated with virtuous women and naive young men; desire with jaded libertines of either sex. The entire plot of *La Nuit et le moment* turns on Cidalise's self-deceiving attempts to convince herself that in yielding to Clitandre, she is responding not to his desire but to his love. Clitandre's stories of his former affairs are reassuring, not because he seems forever ready to blunder into any arms that open before him, but because he insists that none of those moments of past desire imply any interest continuing into the present he now shares with Cidalise. Clitandre's strategy is to raise the payoff on the clear longshot that he is actually in love to such a level that Cidalise's narcissism can no longer resist betting on the possibility that he is not lying. His portrayal of his sexual past as a random concatenation of meaningless desires generates for Cidalise the flattering image of herself as the one woman who, unlike all those who came before, has been able to inspire true love and true passion. These maneuvers constitute Clitandre's response to Cidalise's insistence that she will surrender herself in the present only if she is convinced that their present is the beginning of a shared future.

Love and desire differ not only in their relation to the future but in the way they relate to the past. Listening to Clitandre's declaration of love, Cidalise raises what, since they have known each other for many years, is a logical objection: "Either you do not love me today or, and I have strong reasons not to believe it, you have loved me for a long time." Since Clitandre has already consigned

his earlier adventures to the insignificance of random desire, he can reply, "Yes, Madame, I have been in love with you since that happy moment I first saw you." If he did not act on his love earlier, it was because Cidalise was herself involved first with Damis and later with Eraste. Women, especially the woman to whom one is declaring one's love, are assumed to love, and as a supposedly virtuous woman, Cidalise cannot, like Clitandre, blithely dismiss her own past with those other men as nothing more than a series of passing desires. Love requires a reshaping of the past, its renunciation as a lie at last recognized as such thanks to the new light of passion's truth. Cidalise declares to Clitandre: "You cannot know how much I love you! How much I abhor having belonged to anyone else! How I hate you for waiting so long to love me [Combien même je vous hais de m'avoir aimée si tard]!" To portray herself as hating the now beloved Clitandre for not having loved her sooner is symbolic of the heavy paradox and self-deception within which Crébillon's characters continually navigate.

Clitandre may seduce Cidalise, but he must do so on her terms. Those terms, however, never remain entirely her own. Clitandre's final words to Cidalise, spoken as he leaves her bedroom the next morning, capture all the ambiguity of their enterprise: "Adieu, may you, if it is possible, love me as much as you yourself are loved!"

. . . . .

Crébillon's novels all tell different versions of a single story: that of how desire, born of a chance moment, transforms itself into, attempts to transform itself into, or disguises itself as something else—as a love capable of redefining both past and future. In telling this story, in underlining the contrasting temporalities of desire and love, Crébillon's characters ultimately speak not only of the sexual mores of the Regency but of the novel itself and its role within the society it addressed. Understanding what Crébillon's thematics of seduction tells us about the novel as a form might best begin by juxtaposing his treatment of the contrastive temporalities of desire and love with the surprisingly similar version of that opposition offered two centuries later by Jean-Paul Sartre in *La Nausée* and its critique of the illusions of storytelling. Sartre's Roquentin explains his growing disgust with what he calls "the sublime" through an analysis of how storytelling perverts and misrepresents the most fundamental reality of everything it claims to represent. His critique is developed through an extended contrast between living life and telling a story, between the event and the adventure, between a vision of the self as simply a person and the mythologizing of the self as hero.

In the same way that Clitandre presents his past seductions of Cidalise's houseguests as disconnected chance moments bearing no relation to what came before or after, Roquentin comes to accept the arid truth that life is a series of moments during which "the scenery changes, people come in and go out, that's all. There are never any beginnings. Days are tacked onto days without rhyme or reason in an interminable and monotonous addition." In the same way that Crébillon's illusion of love depends on an imaginary future inflecting every moment of the present, the bad faith Sartre denounces at the core of every "story" implies that "we forget that the future was not there yet, that the guy was walking in a night without signs which offered him its monotonous riches in a jumble and that he made no choices." Life becomes story, its events our adventures, and ourselves its hero only when, as with love's promised future, "it all began with the end. It's there, invisible and present, giving these words all the pomp and value of a beginning." Abstracted from existence as a concatenation of chance-driven moments, life-as-story begins from what it is destined to become rather than from what it happens to be: "The story goes on in reverse, its moments no longer pile up haphazardly [s'empiler au petit bonheur les uns sur les autres], they are drawn along by the end of the story [happés par la fin de l'histoire] as it conjures up each of them as well as the ones preceding it."

Crébillon's novels center on seduction, on how those who see life as a series of chance desires are able to manipulate others whose belief in a (love) story promising continuity, purpose, and meaning marks them as the perfect prey. Crébillon's demystification of love through the opposition of a self-enclosed present to an illusory future parallels Sartre's indictment of narrative through the oppositions of life to story, event to adventure, and person to hero. To be seduced is, quite literally, to listen to and believe a story. Crébillon's reflections on seduction through story thus speak of a danger that extends far beyond the tragicomic, self-deceptive scenarios of sexual conquest wherein would-be seducers are always on the prowl for victims sufficiently naive to accept the pledge of a fictitious future in return for their present surrender.

Les Egarements du coeur et de l'esprit is perhaps the best illustration of this danger. Often described as a novel of initiation, a *Bildungsroman* like Flaubert's *L'Education sentimentale* or Joyce's *A Portrait of the Artist, Les Egarements* tells the story of its principal character's worldly education. And the lesson Meilcour ultimately learns is that of the failure of all stories. The novel opens with its main character in full possession of a firm and unquestioned sense of self: "I made my entry into society at the age of seventeen, with all the advantages that can make a man be noticed there." If Meilcour knows exactly who and where he is, it is because his identity is defined by a series of mutually sustaining stories. Since like all the characters in Crébillon's novels, he is a noble, his story is in one sense another chapter continuing the already illustrious story of his ancestors. In Meilcour's case, his dead father has bequeathed him not only a name but—because he was killed fighting in the king's service—"a noble name whose renown he himself had increased." The dead father functions as the biological foundation of two complementary stories: the long-term, generational history of the family dynasty Meilcour continues and the short-term but more glorious story of the feats through which the father distinguished himself as hero. On the other side of the family, Meilcour's mother is a source of both material security—"I had expectations of considerable

wealth from my mother"—and the ongoing story of an unswerving devotion compensating for what has been lost through the death of the father: "Beautiful, young, and rich, her tenderness for me led her to imagine no other pleasure than that of educating me and making up for all I had lost in losing my father."

The ensuing 250 pages of this novel, describing a period of roughly two weeks, chip away the certainty and sense of identity with which the work begins. The novel may end with Meilcour and Madame de Lursay understanding each other, but the encounter with Hortense as well as Versac's lies about Lursay deprive that ending of the sense of closure and completed quest so ardently desired by Meilcour in the work's opening pages.

Les Egarements is a memoir-novel, a novel written in the first person by the main character long after the events he narrates. This first-person form allows Meilcour to offer a double perspective on everything he relates. At every point in his narration he retains the option of describing events either as he experienced them at the time of their actual occurrence or, using a retrospective past conditional, as he has since come to understand them from the vantage point of age and wisdom. *Les Egarements* ends with a veritable crescendo of this second perspective, and in order for the readers to understand what actually happened during its final evening, they must deduce it, not from what is actually narrated, but from the abstracted lesson Meilcour draws from his experience. The novel ends with the bankruptcy of what Meilcour had until then accepted as the sum of worldly wisdom: Versac's secret doctrine of society as a locus of universal hypocrisy demanding absolute self-control. As Meilcour first listened to Versac's revelations, he was awed by their unveiling of a previously unsuspected intellectual dimension within this older and worldly-wise man he had so long admired. Versac's extended exposition of how the world really works represents the one "true" story that, along with the earlier stories of paternal distinction and maternal devotion, might be seen as defining Meilcour's future. But the experiences of the two-week period narrated in the novel teach Meilcour something quite different. Looking back on the evening with Madame de Lursay and how her "extreme connaissance du coeur" allowed her, to his astonishment, to render him "enchanted" with the very woman he had hated only a few moments earlier, Meilcour realizes that a continued adherence to Versac's doctrine, "l'usage du monde," would only have rendered him more corrupt and more vulnerable to manipulation: "The conclusion I draw today is that had I been more experienced, she would only have seduced me more quickly, since what we call knowledge of the world only makes us wiser by making us more corrupt."

With Versac's lesson dismissed as "cette commode métaphysique," Meilcour finds himself cut off from the assurance that would have allowed him to control himself and others. Having lost faith in Versac, he has lost the ability to live life as a story whose assumed ending will provide the significance of each of its episodes. Instead, Meilcour's experiences leave him caught up in an immobilizing oscillation of antithetical feelings: "Exiled from pleasure by remorse, and from remorse by pleasure, I could not for a moment be sure of myself."

The key word in Crébillon's title, *égarement,* is all but impossible to translate into English. 'Distraction' is the term to which most dictionaries resign themselves, usually following it with examples demonstrating the English word's inability to capture the more diverse and serious connotations of the French term. Barbara Bray tried, none too felicitously, to finesse the problem by choosing as the title for her 1967 translation of Crébillon's novel *The Wayward Head and Heart.* Jean Sgard makes the point [in "La Notion d'égarement chez Crébillon," *Dix-huitième siècle,* 1 (1969)] in speaking of Crébillon's text that "the concept of *égarement* is doubly interesting: it expresses an ambiguous and disconcerting state, a 'trouble,' a 'delirium' defying analysis; and it implies at the same time a norm, as an *égarement* can only exist in relation to a straight path." While Sgard claims that *égarement* implies the existence of an abandoned norm, it is significant that Crébillon modifies his own usage of the word with two adjectival phrases—*du coeur* and *de l'esprit*—which themselves, because they represent opposing principles of human conduct, substantially compromise the possibility of any such single "correct path." *Egarement* is, according to *Le Robert,* derived from the Frankish *warôn,* meaning 'to care for, to safeguard, to secure in a sure place.' *E-garer* thus implies a lost security, a setting off into an uncertainty compromising any defined rectitude.

Les Egarements ends with Meilcour unable to continue as the admiring acolyte of a supposedly all-knowing Versac. He finds himself instead in a state where "I could not *for a moment* be sure of myself" (emphasis mine). The concept of *le moment* here alluded to functions throughout Crébillon's work as an emblem of life lived as a sequence of fortuitous events determined only by chance. Earlier, in Clitandre's explanation of his past to Cidalise, we saw its role in the libertine's ever-playful dismissal of personal responsibility. At the close of *Les Egarements,* the term appears again, but now as providing the temporality of the character's far more somber inability to know or master his fate once he is deprived of the security of stories and forced instead onto the uncertain seas of experience and contradiction.

. . . . .

[In the development of probability theory] the most important figures within that science emphasized its power to dismiss chance as an illusion. Presenting their finite permutations of the possible, of what *might* happen next, as perfectly adequate responses to the quite different question of what *will* happen next, the probabilists substituted their mathematical models for the reality they claimed to explain. I rehearse this basic strategy of probability theory because it parallels in important ways what are the distinctive characteristics of Crébillon's novelistic style. His plots usually limit themselves to the simplest situations: in *La Nuit et le moment,* Clitandre has arrived in Cidalise's room and sets out to seduce her; in *Le Hasard du coin du feu,* Célie would insist that Clerval declare he loves her before she yields; in *Les Egarements,* Madame de Lursay wants the timid Meilcour to take the first step before she reveals her own feelings. The actual texture of Crébillon's novels could be described as an infinitely extensible dialectic between two conflicting views as to what should happen next. One character argues the case for one course of action, while the other parries with a contrasting array of reasons for the alternate course.

Crébillon's narrative technique and the protocols of probability theory share a tendency to postpone indefinitely the actual occurrence of the event by opening up what becomes a potentially infinite space devoted to the analysis of its possible implications. It is precisely for this "overly analytical" or "overly psychological" style that Crébillon has been most consistently criticized. It is his style, far more than his undeserved reputation as a pornographer, that explains why, even today, his importance to the history of the novel remains unacknowledged.

There can be little doubt that Crébillon's style frustrated the reader of his time. Accustomed to the more or less realistic or more or less romanesque representation of a rapidly moving sequence of events, the eighteenth-century reader could only be perplexed by Crébillon's insistence on structuring his novels around the analysis of a static situation whose potential implications were then considered in seemingly infinite detail. This deferral of the novel's forward progress, of any easy movement from event to event, has a number of important effects. At one level, it forces the reader to realize that the standard novelistic diction of an untroubled and expeditious representation of events is an *option* rather than a rule of the genre. At another level, Crébillon's concentration on the interval between events, on the intricacies of his characters' feelings as to whether and why something should or should not be done, emphasizes the potential infinity of interpretation each character brings to a given situation. Crébillon's characters are masters of argument capable of initiating an endless dialectic around almost any question. The pleasure of reading Crébillon lies in admiring how his characters find new ways to surprise, parry, and elude the rhetorical traps they continually set for one another. By forcing his reader to recognize the difference between the event and its analysis, Crébillon emphasizes a disjunction between the two. We may speak, reason, cajole, threaten, and plead all we wish; those acts can never of themselves determine what actually happens next. The event occurs in a realm set off from the endless words spoken by its protagonists. And it is chance and the moment, far more than the characters' words, that determine what actually happens.

In writing his novels as he did, in emphasizing a diction all but antithetical to their form, Crébillon undercut what we saw to be the period's justification of the genre through a claim to didactic realism. The most frequent defense of the novel in the prefaces of the eighteenth century grounded the genre's utility in its power to represent people and events as they actually were within the real world. The novel, as Prévost argued, was a less dangerous and more accessible supplement to experience. Furthermore, the novel's ability to portray evil as punished and virtue as rewarded qualified it as teacher and reformer. Novels set in the real world of their readers could teach men and women how they should act not only morally but in accordance with the secular norms of polite society.

Crébillon subverts any such justification of the novel not so much because his characters are hardly paragons of conventional virtue as because his entire portrayal of how things happen between individuals subverts the effortless and purposeful progression from event to event at the core of the didactic novel. Crébillon's style is particularly intriguing because while it borrows probability theory's analytical bent, it works against the implicit belief in determinism that science shared with the emerging ideology of the novel. In ***Les Egarements du coeur et de l'esprit,*** all the truly decisive events in those two weeks of Meilcour's life occur by chance: one evening he is smitten with an unknown woman who happens to be seated in the box next to his at the Opera; a few days later he happens to hear that same woman's voice through the labyrinth of the Tuileries. Hurrying along its twisting paths, he positions himself so as to cross her path. Hoping to manipulate that chance encounter to his own ends, he learns instead the sad lesson of the novel's inefficacy as a Prévostian supplement to experience: "I then recalled all the episodes from novels I had read that treated of speaking to one's mistress and was surprised that there was not a single one that was of any use to me." Like probability theory, novels may teach us many things—but their lessons are never quite appropriate to the specific situation at hand.

Even Crébillon's seducers, those characters who are masters at concocting the mini-novels of love's promised future, can be stymied by the specificity of the moment. In ***La Nuit et le moment,*** Clitandre tells how his affair with Luscinde began the evening he took her home from a dinner at which her lover, Oronte, had not only insulted her but left early and taken her carriage. Clitandre's strategy is based on an excellent analysis of where, given the evening's events, Luscinde is sure to be most vulnerable. What better way to avenge herself on Oronte than a brief affair with Clitandre? The abstract appropriateness of his approach, Clitandre knows, is beyond question. The problem, as always with what is only probable, comes in applying that abstract principle to the specific here and now of the actual situation: "I had no problem convincing her she should avenge herself. But as angry as she was, I could not persuade her so easily as I liked to think I could that she should avenge herself at that very moment [dans le moment même]."

All the lessons the novel of experience might teach, like those of probability theory, are circumscribed by an inability to address the *hic et nunc* of this situation at this moment. Toward the end of ***Le Hasard du coin du feu,*** Clerval reacts to Célie's pouting remorse over her surrender with an explicit and brutal parody of all the supposed reassurance to be found in novelistic and probabilistic representations of reality. Anticipating by a century what

would become the dominant discourse of statistics, Clerval cavalierly suggests that the best way for Célie to soothe her conscience would be to situate her indiscretion within the context of the large number: "Do you really find your conduct with me so extraordinary? Alas, what has just happened between us is happening in front of more than a hundred Paris fireplaces at this very moment, and between people who, I assure you, have not nearly as good reasons for it as we." It would be difficult to imagine a strategy more alien to Crébillon's esthetics of the moment's singularity than this offhand dismissal of the couple's specificity in favor of the quantifiable aggregate. What is lost in any such referral to the average is the essence of Crébillon's limitless attention to the delicately comic yet ultimately pathetic interaction of individual desires declaring themselves within a universe ruled by chance.

. . . . .

Anchored in the complexities of the present, Clerval—like Clitandre, Versac, and so many of Crébillon's characters—enacts a scenario of libertinage. It is, however, a *libertinage du moment* whose focus on the fleeting opportunities of the passing instant is distinctly different from that portrayed a half century later by Laclos in *Les Liaisons dangereuses.* While Laclos was certainly influenced by Crébillon—*Le Sopha* was part of Merteuil's warmup reading as she prepared herself to be the hundred women in one for her lover, and many critics have chosen to read Merteuil as a feminine version of Versac—his scenarios of libertinage are always part of projects far larger and more ambitious than those found in Crébillon. When Merteuil and Valmont set out to seduce, sexuality is never an end in itself. A means for achieving something else, sexual conquest in *Les Liaisons* is only one among a number of ploys for controlling another person. And that control of the seduced other is itself more often than not an instrument whose real purpose is a more effective aggression against a third party. One tactic within a larger strategy of domination preceding and completing it, Laclos's libertinage is, in every sense of the word, *un libertinage conséquent.* Crébillon's *libertins,* on the contrary, do not act in terms of a long-range plan but are confined to an acute awareness of everything happening around them as they stand ready to seize every unexpected opportunity. Crébillon's seducers rely, not on a carefully planned strategy, but on the unpredictable luck of the hunter. His Clitandres, Clervals, and Versacs move through their world like stalkers in search of game. Never knowing when or where their quarry will appear, they are always at the ready. The success of their hunt depends on chance, on whether stalker and quarry happen to intersect at the same place at the same moment. Versac goes to Madame de Lursay's only so he can bring with him Monsieur de Pranzi, Lursay's former lover, and thus consolidate her humiliation in Meilcour's eyes. Once there, however, he comes upon a woman he has never seen before: the young and beautiful Hortense de Théville. After only a moment's surprise, he begins a stalk of which no one is more perfectly the master than he: "Surprised that so rare a beauty had so long remained hidden from him, he stared at her in astonishment and admiration. . . . He displayed his charms: he had a good leg and showed it off. He laughed as often as he could so as to show his teeth and assumed the most imposing postures to set his figure off to best advantage and demonstrate its graces." In this case his almost comic stalk is unsuccessful, but like the veteran hunter, he is always ready to try.

Crébillon often uses the term *le moment* in its more restricted sense of a specifically feminine susceptibility, often unsuspected by the woman herself, to the maneuvers of seduction. "No one is answerable for the moment; it is a realm where nature acts unhampered [il en est où la nature agit seule]," we read in *L'Ecumoire ou Tanzaï et Néardarné*. Answering Célie's query as to what he means by *le moment*, Clerval responds: "A certain movement of the senses as unexpected as it is involuntary. A woman may hide it, but if it is noticed or sensed by someone interested in taking advantage of it, it puts her in the gravest danger of being more compliant than she believed she should or could be [un peu plus complaisante qu'elle ne croyait ni devoir ni pouvoir l'être]." The element of chance inherent in *le moment* concerns, in other words, not only the objective coordinates of time and space inflecting a given *rencontre* but an aspect of our own psyches as repositories of intentions that, whatever our resolve, remain open to the possibility that we will surprise ourselves, that an unexpected event will lead us to act in ways we could never have anticipated. If Crébillon sees this aspect of *le moment* as particularly characteristic of women, it is because most of his male characters, the *libertins*, have constructed their entire persona through obsessive protocols of self-control and deception adopted as frantic attempts to extirpate all susceptibility to the tug of *le moment*.

Le moment as a force disrupting the continuity of the present with past and future inflects not only Crébillon's thematics of seduction but the very form of his novels. Listening to Clitandre's story of his brief affair with Julie, Cidalise exclaims: "That certainly worked out well for both of you, and the episode could not have ended more nobly." "Ended!" Clitandre immediately corrects her. "Ah, but we are not there yet." In fact, finishing the story is always a problem in Crébillon's novels. None of them ends on a note of real closure leaving the reader with the sense that earlier expectations have been satisfied and all remaining questions answered. *La Nuit et le moment* ends, as we saw, with Clitandre's ambiguous wish that Cidalise love him "as much as you yourself are loved." *Le Hasard du coin du feu* ends only because Clerval must leave and not because any question has been resolved. In his preface to *Les Egarements*, Crébillon promises at least six parts to a novel that in fact has only three: the first and second, showing Meilcour's innocence and first loves; *les suivantes*, of which we have only one, showing the sad influence of others on his life; and the never written *dernières*, promising his salvation by an unspecified *femme estimable*.

Crébillon's desire to preserve the openness of the present moment likewise manifests itself in his abiding preference for the epistolary form. Three of his novels are collections of letters—the *Letters de la Marquise de M——— au Comte de R———* (1732), the *Letters de la Duchesse de ——— au Duc de ———* (1768), and the *Lettres Athéniennes* (1771)—while another—*Les Heureux Orphelins* (1754)—although it begins as a translation of Haywood's *Fortunate Foundlings*, ends as an original series of letters written by the character Lord Chester to a friend in France. Crébillon's tendency toward the epistolary is a sign of his reluctance to adopt toward the events his novels recount anything like the distance and control implied by the alternative of a third-person narration. The epistolary form privileges each sentence as a statement open to whatever disruptions the present may bring.

As though even the writing present of the epistolary implied a form too determined by the remembered past of a time before pen touches paper, Crébillon's most profound stylistic tendency is toward reproduced speech, toward dialogues representing the characters' voices as they speak within a shared present. Even in a memoir-novel like *Les Egarements*, Meilcour's properly narrative voice does little more than stitch together confrontations between characters that consist for the most part of directly quoted conversations. Like an unsettlingly gallicized Ivy Compton-Burnett, Crébillon seems most himself when his writing retains the openness of actual speech to whatever might happen within an unpredictable present. His characters speak, not in complete, fully articulated sentences summarizing themselves and their positions, but in broken, interrupted fragments generated by the continual clash of all who would have their say. Speech in Crébillon's novels is speech as dialogue. Just as his narrative interest centers not on the sequence of events but on the intervals between those events, his dialogues portray not the substance of the isolated character in monologue but the interaction between characters, their repartee, the way they respond to and are redefined by what the other happens to say. Crébillon's characters continually interrupt, clash with, and rebound off one another in directions none could ever have anticipated before the actual exchange.

Novels such as *La Nuit et le moment* and *Le Hasard du coin du feu* read far more like plays or film scripts than novels. In each there is an unnamed narrative voice telling us (or winkingly hinting at) the movements and amorous activities not explicitly referred to in the dialogue. Rather, however, than consolidating any illusion of the carefully structured tale, these anonymous narrative voices satirize the conventions of the genre by alluding to the work's existence in yet another dimension of the present: that of the reader reading and imagining. In response to Cidalise's "Is it really true that you still love me?" the narrator breaks in with "Clitandre tries to banish Cidalise's fears by smothering her with the most ardent caresses. But as everyone may not prefer his method of responding to doubts, those of our readers to whom it seems appropriate may adopt another method, such as having Clitandre recite the most touching words or whatever they feel is most effective for reassuring a woman in such a case." Then, as though no break in the dialogue had occurred, Clitandre replies: "So! ungrateful one [ingrate]! are you reassured?"

Crébillon's refusal of narrative closure, his preference for dialogue, and his delight in interruptions of all kinds contribute to the strong sense throughout his work of an always changing and unpredictable present, of life lived *sur le moment*. These choices are, of course, directly contrary to the canons of the novel of experience. Writing in 1754, Fréron [in *L'Année litteraire,* 3 (1754), cited by Clifton Cherpack in *An Essay on Crébillon fils* (1962)] excoriated Crébillon's recently published **Les Heureux Orphelins** as, to his eyes, an endless and disorganized conglomeration of dialogues, enclosed stories, moralizing, epigrams, and digressions. However highly some might rate Crébillon's prose style, Fréron insisted, his works clearly lack the indispensable hallmark of the true novel: "facts which are new, necessary, and believable [des faits neufs, nécessaires et vraisemblables]." For Fréron, the true novel was one whose narrative achieved believability because its events followed each other with absolute necessity. Once the initial situation has been established, the novel's episodes should appear to take place as though they could not have happened otherwise. Fréron's rejection of Crébillon is important because it brings into focus the extent to which his novelistic practices differed from the period's mainstream expectations of the genre. It shows how his refusal of sequential determination stamped his work with the marks of the haphaz-ard and the scandalous. . . .

FURTHER READING

Free, Lloyd Raymond. "Crébillon fils, Laclos, and the Code of the Libertine." *Eighteenth Century Life* 1, No. 2 (December 1974): 36-40.

Details the influence of Versac's principles of libertinage on Crébillon's *Les Egarements* and Laclos' *Les Liaisons dangereuses.*

Smith, Peter Lester. "Duplicity and Narrative Technique in the *Roman Libertin.*" *Kentucky Romance Quarterly* XXV, No. 1 (1978): 69-79.

Explores the theme of appearance versus reality in works by Diderot, Crébillon, and Laclos.

Stewart, Philip. *Imitation and Illusion in the French Memoir-Novel, 1700-1750: The Art of Make Believe.* New Haven: Yale University Press, 1969, 350 p.

Assesses the development of the memoir-novel and the "contribution to the technique of the genre made by the serious and realistic novelists of the first half of the eighteenth century."

French Drama in the Age of Louis XIV

INTRODUCTION

The reign of Louis XIV in France from 1643 to 1715 marked a period that is often described as the "Golden Age" of French drama. Producing such dramatists as Jean Racine, Pierre and Thomas Corneille, and Molière, the theater of the period is noted for classicism, social commentary, and a growing audience outside the royal court. Tragedy and comedy, the most prominent dramatic genres of the seventeenth century, were governed by the rules of classicism, which emphasized reason over emotion, and universal, rather than personal, experience. As proponents of classicism, French theorists of the time also advocated that dramatists provide a moral lesson, avoid mixing tragic and comic aspects, and maintain dramatic unity of action, time, and place in their works. Tragicomedy, a third genre, combined components of comedy and tragedy. Although popular during the early years of the century, the genre's failure to conform to the strict guidelines of classicism contributed to its increasing disfavor. Although governed by the rules of classicism, tragedy and comedy also became vehicles for addressing social and political tensions. The most prominent of such issues was the relationship between the monarchy, the nobility, and an emerging middle class, composed primarily of merchants, traders, and non-agrarian craftsmen, which was growing in wealth and size as a result of trade and industry development. The efforts of members of this class to improve their status challenged the traditional hierarchy of aristocrats and peasants which had existed prior to Louis XIV's reign. Racine's tragedies, such as *Britannicus* (1669), encourage intellectual and emotional resistance to the monarchy among members of the middle class. In contrast, Corneille's tragedies, such as *Horace* (1640), emphasize the acceptance of the social, economic, and political conditions of monarchal rule. Molière's comedies also address the social behavior and attitudes of the newly emerging middle class. In *L'Ecole des Femmes* (1662), for example, Molière deals with the education of women, criticizing men who believed that marital security could be achieved by raising female children in an environment devoid of temptation. Seventeenth-century theater audiences expanded to include the middle class as well as the aristocracy. Despite the King's own fluctuating interest in the theater, dramas of all genres were presented to Louis and his courtiers at the French court. Additionally, nobles viewed performances alongside members of the middle class at local theaters. Enthusiasm for the theater was barely dampened by the Roman Catholic Church's indictments against actors, playwrights, and spectators. The Church's harshest criticisms involved actors and playwrights of comedy, on the basis that the genre served no moral purpose; rather, it offered lessons in the vices it purported to denounce. Proponents of comedy responded that it served as a means of moral instruction by displaying as the object of ridicule characters who embodied vice. The success of comedies such as Molière's *Le Misanthrope* (1666), *Les Chinois* (1692) by Jean Regnard and Charles Dufresny, and Florent Dancourt's *Les Bourgeoises de qualité* (1700), and tragedies such as *Horace*, Thomas Corneille's *Timocrate* (1656), and *Britannicus* deflated the public's interest in tragicomedy. Tragicomedy, commonly understood as tragedy with a happy ending, involved complicated plots filled with action and aristocratic characters. The genre began to dwindle in popularity from the mid-1600s to the end of the seventeenth century, with audiences showing less interest in the contrivances and exaggerations often typical of the genre. Theorists also displayed increasingly vehement disapproval of a genre which was not recognized by Aristotle or Horace (the main sources of the rules of classicism). As public and critical disfavor grew, some dramatists reclassified their tragicomedies as either tragedies or comedies. Pierre Corneille, for example, originally labeled *Le Cid* (1637) as tragicomedy, but the 1648 edition was published as tragedy. While seventeenth-century critics, most notably Abbé d'Aubignac, scrutinized dramatic performances primarily to gauge dramatists' adherence to classic ideals, later scholars have examined the same works with a view to understanding such issues as politics and society in the age of Louis XIV. Many critics agree that the age witnessed the advancement of drama to a new plateau in which it played an increasingly important role in society. Geoffrey Brereton claims that tragedy is recognized "as one of the outstanding achievements of [Louis XIV's] reign," and John Lough has argued that "drama saw its most brilliant period at the French court in the seventeenth century."

REPRESENTATIVE WORKS

Bouscal, Guérin de
  Le Gouvernement de Sanche Pansa (comedy) 1642
Boyer, Claude
  Clotilde (tragedy) 1659
Campistron, Jean Galbert de
  Andronic (tragedy) 1685
Corneille, Pierre
  Le Cid (tragicomedy) 1637
  Horace (tragedy) 1640
  Don Sanche d'Aragon (tragicomedy) 1650
Corneille, Thomas
  Timocrate (tragedy) 1656
  Le Comte d'Essex (tragedy) 1678
Dancourt, Florent
  Les Bourgeoises de qualité (comedy) 1700
Du Ryer, Pierre

Scevole (tragicomedy) 1647

Lesage, Alain-René
 Tucaret (comedy) 1709

Molière
 L'Ecole des Femmes (comedy) 1662
 Le Tartuffe (comedy) 1664
 Le Misanthrope (comedy) 1666
 Le Bourgeois Gentilhomme (comedy) 1670
 *Psyché (comedy) 1671

Racine, Jean
 Andromaque (tragedy) 1667
 Britannicus (tragedy) 1669

Regnard, Jean François
 †*Les Chinois* (comedy) 1692

Rotrou, Jean de
 Venceslas (tragicomedy) 1648

*In collaboration with Thomas Corneille and Philippe Quinault.

†In collaboration with Charles Rivière Dufresny.

OVERVIEW

Moses Barras

SOURCE: "The Introduction of a Regular Stage Censorship," in *The Stage Controversy from Corneille to Rousseau,* Publications of the Institute of French Studies, Inc., 1933, pp. 130-55.

[In the excerpt that follows, Barras describes the opposition of the Roman Catholic Church to seventeenth-century theatre.]

Led by [Jacques-Bénigne] Bossuet the Church presented, officially at least, a united front against plays [during the seventeenth century]. In the *Jubilee* of 1694 the condemnation of the pariah comedians was solemnly confirmed. On December 9, 1695, Guy de Sève de Rochechouart, Bishop of Arras, in accordance with the explicit policy of the Church, issued a severe *Mandement,* proscribing the stage in general with all its satellites—actors, playwrights and spectators. The French clergy soon became so intolerant that in 1696 a number of Parisian actors decided to carry an appeal to Rome. They accused the clergy specifically of refusing to grant them the sacraments. But the Papal authorities evidently considered their quarrel as of not enough importance to risk a conflict of opinion with French churchmen. The actors were notified that they should bring their case to the Archbishop of Paris, since the Papal court did not consider it weighty enough for a special decision. As was to be expected, the Archbishop fully upheld the action of the French clergy and again excluded comedians from the fold of the faithful. And yet a note of Monsignor Nuzzi, which accompanied the reply from Rome, stressed very clearly that the Papal authorities considered "infamous" only those comedians who acted indecently on the stage. The Archbishop apparently

believed that all plays were evil and therefore that all acting was unavoidably immoral. As an example of actual persecution we may cite the case of the famous actor Rosimont, [Claude la Rose, Sieur de Rosimont], who died suddenly in 1691 and was refused regular church burial. "Rosimond . . . fut enterré sans Clergé, sans luminaire, et sans aucune prière, dans un endroit du Cimetière de Saint-Sulpice où l'on enterre les enfans morts sans Baptême." And in 1697 the Cardinal de Noailles refused to allow comedians to marry, since marriage was a sacrament forbidden to outcasts of the Church. Communion was constantly denied them—and this situation lasted, in a stage-mad France that adored plays, until the eve of the French Revolution!

Yet the incessant attacks of the clergy upon the stage and actors seems to have had little effect upon the patrons of the theatre. Notwithstanding these thundering anathemas, or indeed, largely perhaps because of them, and of the attraction of forbidden fruit, they flocked in ever-increasing numbers to all kinds of spectacles. At this period the *Comédie-Italienne* was more popular—and far more immoral—than the *Comédie-Française.* In another respect also the Italian actors in Paris were more fortunate than their French *confères*—they were *not* excommunicated, and they suffered none of the undeserved penalties that hailed down upon their colleagues engaged in public amusement. In 1697 they were expelled, not because of the immorality of their acting, but because they had offended Mme de Maintenon.

But their exile did not in the least improve the decency of the Parisian stage. The *acteurs forains,* who had been drawing the crowds at the annual fairs of Saint-Germain and Saint-Laurent, did not hesitate to grasp the opportunity that offered itself through the forced withdrawal of their competitors. They promptly appropriated the Italian repertory and drew an ever-growing public to their stalls. Their productions were fully as crude,—from the moral point of view,—as those of any of their predecessors.

The last decade of the seventeenth and the early years of the eighteenth century witnessed an enormous increase in popular affluence to the theatre. Among literary men, playwrights were the only ones to get any considerable monetary recompense for their labors, although they did not receive any honoraria that could be at all compared to those of the dramatists of the end of the century. The increase in material reward for the production of popular plays acted, no doubt, as a stimulus in favor of the theatre and the dramatist, especially after 1740. Yet, even before that date Le Sage, Dancourt, Regnard and Dufresny were relatively well paid for their labors, whereas lyric or epic poets had to find a patron if they wanted their work printed at all. The stage at least had an assured public and furnished an income that, although modest and uncertain, compared favorably with the absolute non-productiveness of other literary endeavors, however highly praised.

Although censorship of plays was introduced into France during this period, the theatre enjoyed greater freedom than ever before. Strangely enough, a number of daring plays like Legrand's *Amour du diable,* which was performed in 1708, were permitted. In 1701 the lieutenant of police of Paris was given control over all plays performed in the capital. His consent had to be obtained before they could be staged. This was the beginning of the formal and organized stage censorship which was going to become so important a factor during the entire eighteenth century. A letter of Pontchartrain to d'Argenson, who was then Lieutenant of Police, brings proof that this step was taken because the King had been informed that the Parisian comedians were acting on the stage in an indecent and revolting way. This action of the civil authorities seemed to approve fully of the stand taken by the Church.

However, division of opinion was manifest even in the ranks of the clergy, and this notwithstanding the authority of Bossuet. The magnificent tradition of Richelieu lingered on and instigated many a churchman to open mutiny against the intolerance of his colleagues. Some of the most noteworthy paladins of the stage arose from among the secular abbés, whom one would expect to have been cowed by Bossuet's overbearing influence.

In 1695 Claude Boyer, an abbé and in addition a member of the French Academy, published a tragedy, *Judith.* In his preface the author defended Biblical dramas. He claimed that it was fully possible to reconcile these plays with the views of the Church on the theatre, provided that one had the ability to produce a truly Christian play. Boyer asserts that if others have failed, it was because of their lack of talent, their ignorance of art, their sterility of invention—and above all, because of their lack of feeling for matters pertaining to religion. This explains the genesis of *Judith,* for Boyer felt that he was the exception to the rule and had succeeded. His play was quite successful in its day, although entirely forgotten now. He attempts to defend comedians, and urges them to produce Biblical plays and thus prove their own worth; in fact, his preface shows that he was willing to permit all plays, provided they were decent. Soon, however, there appeared an anonymous *Réponse à la préface de la tragédie de Judith,* which tried to refute Boyer with the usual arguments against the theatre.

Pierre Le Brun, the official spokesman for the Archbishop of Paris, delivered a sermon at the Church of Saint-Magloire toward the end of 1695, taking as his text Boyer's *Judith.* The title of his sermon, which was first published in 1731, was: "S'il y a lieu d'approuver que les Pièces de Théâtre soient tirées de l'Ecriture Sainte." His thesis is that one cannot display upon the stage holy scenes without corrupting them. In spirit the two are irreconcilable.

Another clerical defender of the stage issued a volume during the same year, 1695. The Abbé Pierre de Villiers, who later evolved into one of the most liberal churchmen in the stage controversy, published an interesting work: *Traité de la satire, où l'on examine comment on doit reprendre son prochain et comment la satire peut servir à cet usage.* He claimed that the comedy owes its origin to the zeal which has always existed in attacks against evils. Although the author blames the contemporaneous theatre for its pernicious spirit, he sanctions the use of the comedy to correct certain vices.

A still more liberal-minded clergyman, the Abbé Morvan de Bellegarde, favored the stage in his *Lettres curieuses de Littérature et de Morale.* His volume appeared in 1702 at The Hague, and in 1707 at Amsterdam. This writer admitted the imperfections of the stage of his day, but claimed that they were remediable. . . .

Etienne Souciet, a Jesuit, published an article in the *Mémoires de Trévoux* for July and August, 1709, in which he gives his opinion of the moral effect of the tragedy. His basic thought is that "the Tragedy must serve morality." It must try to correct in the spectator whatever vices he may have, by causing him to be horrified at the results of the same vices on the stage, and by making him fear for himself the same punishment which he has witnessed in the play. The spectator must be made to realize that the vice which has just been chastised is the very one of which he himself is guilty. Souciet also discusses the theoretical and technical aspects of the tragedy, reducing the number of good subjects to five or six, all of which have been treated by the Greeks. His general attitude is evidently favorable to the theatre.

In 1711 the abbé Pierre de Villiers published a poem lauding the opera and other spectacles. He had himself recently composed a musical comedy, so that it is only natural that he favored this species of entertainment. The Abbé Jean Terrasson, in a discussion of the drama, contained in his *Dissertation critique sur l'Iliade,* which was published in Paris in 1715, lauds the theatre in no uncertain terms. His defense of the stage is based upon the theory that most people can be made better morally by attending plays, and not through hearing sermons. He admits that the priest performs a higher type of service for humanity than the comedian, but claims that the latter fits into a certain niche which the former cannot reach. Terrasson calls morality "the very Soul and Genius" of the drama. He views love in the same light as that in which partisans of the theatre considered plays in general, that is, he claims that in itself it is indifferent, but may become good or bad, depending upon the use which is made of it.

The protests of this minority of dissidents among the clergy prove that the anathema of the stage was not generally accepted, even among churchmen. Conclusive testimony that ecclesiastics attended the theatre is found in the decree issued in 1704 by the Bishop of Toulon, Monsignor de Chalucet, who threatened the priests of his diocese with excommunication if they further patronized the stage:

> Et nous défendons à tous Prêtres, Bénéficiers et Ecclésiastiques de ce Diocèse ou y résidant, d'assister aux Bals, Opéras ou Comédies, à peine d'excommunication encourue *ipso facto.*

On the other hand, there can be no doubt that the vast majority of the French clergy followed Bossuet's lead against the stage and against his victim Father Caffaro. The famous quarrel of 1694 awakened echoes for several years to come, and even the mere enumeration of the pamphlets, satires, and controversial writings which carried on the debate, would soon become tiresome. Yet their very number indicates how living an issue the theatre problem remained, and with what tragic earnestness it was approached by both attackers and defenders.

Among the clergymen who fully sympathized with Bossuet one may cite Pierre Bardou, Prior of La Voux, who toward the end of 1694 issued an *Epître sur la Condamnation du Théâtre*. He was an ardent admirer of Racine, but nevertheless he condemned the theatre. His epistle, which is addressed to this great author of tragedies, consists of about 150 lines of verse. Although Bardou praises *Athalie* and *Esther* and approves of Biblical dramas in general, he inveighs against the love-themes and pagan pomp which characterize plays. In his opinion, since Racine has renounced the theatre, it is really dead. He compares Racine's Biblical dramas to the sermons of Bourdaloue:

> Des poèmes si beaux, chaque fois qu'on les
> joue,
> Exercent sur nos coeurs les droits de
> Bourdaloüe.

A comparison with Bourdaloue seemed to him the highest praise he could give to Racine.

A curious document was penned in Latin by an obscure priest, L. Soucanye, in 1694, as a eulogy of Bossuet's answer to Caffaro. The title of his poem is very interesting. It is as follows: *Illustrissimo Ecclesiae Principi Jacobo Benigno Bossuet, Meldensium episcopo, artis comicae aequissimo nuper Judici. In Pestem Theatralem Carmen.* The author acclaims Bossuet as the heavenly-appointed avenger through whose labors the theatre will be destroyed. A maze of classic mythology, which must have been distasteful to Bossuet personally, adorns his rhetoric. Needless to say, this poem influenced very few people.

Ambroise Lalouette, a French priest, published anonymously at Orléans in 1697 a book entitled: *Histoire et Abrégé des ouvrages latins, italiens et françois, pour et contre la comédie et l'opéra*. His volume, which was printed with the approbation of the authorities, also appeared in the same year with the following caption: *Histoire de la comédie et de l'opéra où l'on prouve qu'on ne peut y aller sans péché*. The latter title clearly indicates the views of the author on the stage. Lalouette summarizes the church doctrine regarding the theatre, basing it upon Scripture, the Church Councils, and the Fathers. Among the limited number of works which he discusses are those of del Monaco and Ottonelli,—both of whom were Italian priests,—Nicole, the Prince de Conti, d'Aubignac and Caffaro. He also summarizes several of the replies which the famous letter of the Theatin priest evoked. Concerning Caffaro, he asserts that this author quotes only the passages of the Church Fathers which denounce plays on account of their idolatry. Like the Archbishop of Paris, he

misinterprets the answer received in Rome by the deputation of French comedians in 1696 concerning the attitude of the Church towards actors. His conclusion is, of course, that attending a play is a mortal sin.

The end of the seventeenth century witnessed many sermons which attacked the theatre. Among the priests who denounced the stage from the pulpit were Colombière, LeJeune, Girouet, Cheminais, Soanen, Le Brun and Bourdaloue. They were echoing the official severity of the Church toward plays. To defend the theatre openly at this period was attended with great risks, for not only was the clergy opposed to plays, but the king had also withdrawn his favor. People admitted that the Church was right in condemning the stage, but nevertheless they continued attending plays in great numbers. The partisans of the drama had to be content with a discreet voicing of their opinions. Thus, La Bruyère, in his famous *Caractères*, says that plays could be useful if their bad features were eliminated, for one can see on the stage such striking examples of virtue that they must have a good effect upon the individuals who compose the audience.

The Ritual of Auch, printed in Paris in the year 1701, presents an interesting commentary upon the attitude of local church authorities toward the theatre. It expressly refuses ecclesiastical burial "to those who, known as public sinners, die without giving proofs of real repentance; among these are Comedians, Farce-players and others of this category." Chalucet, Bishop of Toulon, was even more severe the next year, for his *Ordonnance* of March 5, 1702 "commands Confessors, under penalty of suspense, to refuse absolution to the Faithful who scorning his 'Mandement,' shall have attended these plays."

Esprit Fléchier, the famous Archbishop of Nîmes, issued a *Mandement* against plays on September 8, 1708. He had found some merit in Caffaro's letter of 1694, although he had not been quite sure that it was right to spread such doctrines among the masses. However, as he grew older, he must have become more severe, for his *Mandement* of 1708 shows that he thinks plays are opposed to the spirit of Christianity and morality, and that he has previously warned his flock against the dangers of the theatre.

The opinion of the Jesuits about the stage seems to have been divided. One of them, Etienne Souciet, had shown great toleration for the theatre in the *Mémoires de Trévoux* of 1709; but another, Father Courbeville, issued in 1713 a French translation of Jeremy Collier's violent attack against the English stage. The original title, which had been *A Short View of the Immorality and Profaneness of the English Stage, Together with the Sense of Antiquity upon this Argument*, was now transformed by Father Courbeville into *La Critique du Théâtre Anglois, comparé au Théâtre d'Athènes, de Rome et de France et l'Opinion des auteurs tant profanes que sacrez, touchant les Spectacles*. In his preface the translator gives the correct title of the English work. He admits that the French theatre is not as bad as the English, but nevertheless he desires its total suppression, which explains why he has translated Collier's book. What he especially objects to in plays is the ever-present love theme. What the English clergyman had objected to in the stage of his own country was the obscenity of its language, its impiety, the attacks upon the clergy, and the immorality of contemporaneous plays. Courbeville had hoped to demonstrate to the French public how immoral plays in general are; but the net result of his volume was that everyone saw clearly that the English stage, as described by Collier, was much more immoral than the French. In spite of which, the English author had tacitly admitted that he believed in the utility of plays, while Courbeville condemned them completely. The number of people attending the French theatre was not lessened by this book.

Jean Frain du Tremblay, a little-known priest who in 1685, in his *Conversations morales sur les Jeux et les Divertissements,* had denounced amusements in general, continued the attack in 1713 when his *Discours sur l'origine de la poésie* appeared in Paris. He believed that both the theatre and actors were incorrigibly wicked and that therefore nothing could be done about the matter except to abstain from attending plays.

Fénelon, Bossuet's opponent in many a theological debate, agreed with him on the condemnation of the stage. He treats the theatre very harshly in his *Lettre à M. Dacier, secrétaire perpétuel de l'Académie Française, sur les Occupations de l'Académie,* written in 1714. Fénelon protests especially against love in tragedies, although granting that it is possible to perfect them. He finds many defects in Molière, while admitting him to be a great writer of comedies. Among the great comedian's faults, one of the most unpardonable, in the opinion of Fénelon, is that Molière has made vice attractive and virtue odious. Surely the Archbishop of Cambrai has judged the great master of comedy too severely!

. . . . .

Among the laymen there was one group, that of the playwrights themselves, which, of course, staunchly defended the stage. In 1697, three years after the beginning of the Bossuet-Caffaro conflict, Boursault carried on his pro-theatre warfare by publishing an open letter to Monseigneur Harlay de Champvallon, Archbishop of Paris, "touchant une Lettre ou Dissertation en faveur de la Comédie." The author expresses his regret at not being well enough acquainted with the Archbishop to pay him a personal visit in order to expound his cause and to provide him with an explanation of the Caffaro incident. He assumes full blame for the printing of Caffaro's letter in the 1694 edition of his own plays, although he does not mention the Theatin priest by name. Strange as it may seem, while Caffaro had been punished quite severely, the real culprit did not suffer in the least.

Boursault claims that while composing a comedy in one of the French provinces, he obtained absolution from a country priest, but only upon condition that he consult someone more learned who would be able to decide whether or not he could have his plays performed without compromising the future of his soul. As a result, the dra-

matist applied to his regular confessor as soon as he reached Paris, sending him several of his plays and begging him to examine them carefully, as it was a question of his peace of mind and perhaps of the salvation of his soul. He admits that he committed a serious mistake in publishing Caffaro's answer without his knowledge or consent. His excuse, which is very weak, is that he wanted to influence the public by showing his readers that the Church Fathers and Councils forbade only indecent plays.

Among the reasons which, according to Boursault, justify the theatre are: (I) the stage is necessary in order to amuse the public, (II) the Fathers blamed only the pagan elements in plays and (III) even Popes have attended performances of plays. He praises Corneille, Racine and especially Molière. Boursault stresses the utility of the stage as an effective weapon for correcting vices and asserts that it is a moral institution. He further points out that as a result of the weak arguments alleged against plays during the commotion caused by the publication of Caffaro's letter, theatres are more crowded than ever. The reasons for which the Church Fathers and Councils condemned the stage no longer exist. As proof of the innocence of the contemporaneous theatre, he sends to the Archbishop one of his own comedies for examination. The dramatist closes his letter with an explanation of how he himself is preaching morality in all his plays.

Caffaro's letter, in the meanwhile, had become internationally known. It was utilized in London, in an English translation, as a kind of preface to a play written in English in 1698 by Motteux, a French refugee. The title of this work was as follows: *Beauty in distress. A tragedy . . . with a discourse of lawfulness and unlawfulness of plays, lately written in French by the learned Father Caffaro, Divinity professor at Paris.* England was at this time in the throes of a great struggle over the theatre, induced to a great extent by the preacher Jeremy Collier, who with great vigor had justly denounced the iniquity of the contemporaneous English stage. Curiously enough, Motteux claims to have had the same conscientious scruples as Boursault, and to have requested advice of an English clergyman, who sent him Caffaro's letter.

On the other hand, to further his campaign of propaganda against the stage in England, Jeremy Collier translated into English and published in London in 1699 the volume which Bossuet had written against plays and actors. The English title was *Maxims and Reflections on Plays.*

In France also, literary men had given their support to Boursault and Caffaro. A very compromising defender of their cause was François Gacon, the "Poète sans Fard," whose satiric rapier was wielded too frequently and against too many different persons and causes, to remain at all effective. In 1694 he published anonymously a reply in verse, an *Epître,* to Bossuet. It was inserted two years later in his volume of satires, *Le Poète sans Fard, ou discours satiriques en vers,* with a new title, *Satire à Mgr. Jacques Bénigne Bossuet, Evêque de Meaux, sur son livre touchant la Comédie.* Gacon claims that invincible obstacles block the church's desire to abolish plays. The idleness of the court will always maintain the theatre, and if people were deprived of this innocent pleasure they would perhaps find another which would be worse. Besides, as long as great prelates live in ostentatious luxury and vie in feasts with princes, in vain will they urge penitence and declaim against plays, for the public will scoff at them. Before the church can successfully do away with the theatre, the higher clergy must mend its ways. Gacon is probably attacking the renowned Archbishop of Paris. This onslaught, of course, begs the question entirely, for it merely answers one attack with another. The author's satirical style is well exemplified in the last four lines of his poem:

> C'est ainsi, Grand Prélat, que le peuple raisonne
> Et fait une leçon aux docteurs de Sorbonne:
> Pour imposer silence, il faudroit réformer
> Nombre d'autres abus que je n'ose rimer.

Gacon also mercilessly attacked Pégurier and Lelevel in 1694 in short poems, which were republished in 1696.

An anonymous volume, that may possibly have been the work of a priest, Noël Varet, appeared in 1698: *Caractères tirés de l'Ecriture Sainte et appliqués aux moeurs de ce siècle*. The author turns the tables on the censors and preachers by proclaiming his gratitude to the comedians for their effective help in combating the evils of the day, which they expose to ridicule on the boards. He remarks seriously,—or perhaps ironically,—that actors are powerful helpers and aids for weak and powerless preachers.

Beside this defense by a Catholic, we may place one by a Protestant. Under the name of Theodore Parrhase, J. Le Clerc, one of Bayle's friends, published in 1699 a work in two volumes called *Parrhasiana ou Pensées diverses sur des Matières de Critique, d'Histoire, de Morale et de Politique*. He seems to approve of plays in a rather lukewarm fashion; he quotes Aristotle's definition of the tragedy and claims that although moral plays are possible, dramatists write only in order to please. Le Clerc asserts that when morality is found in a tragedy, its purpose, from the viewpoint of the dramatist, appears usually to be an embellishment of the subject and a means of winning the favor of the audience rather than of calming the passions. For comedies the author has nothing good to say, being of the opinion that their originators seek only "to amuse the public and to gain a reputation and money by amusing it."

Baudot de Juilly, an employee of the department of finance, dared to condemn the current practice of denouncing all pleasures without exception. In his *Dialogues entre MM. Patru et d'Ablancourt sur les plaisirs,* published in Paris in 1700, he approves the theatre as an institution. His volume was suppressed by the authorities soon after it appeared in print.

A decided stand in favor of the stage was taken in 1706 by Chavigni de Saint-Martin, who published his encomium in Brussels, where he could not be so easily reached by irate French prelates: *Le Triomphe de la Comédie, ou*

Réponse à la critique des Prélats de France. He dedicated his work to the Duke of Bavaria, whom he acclaims as a patron of plays. The author tells us that he has written this volume "in order to enlighten the public concerning the injustices which are being disseminated against the theatre." He claims that it is manifestly unfair to condemn the stage of today upon the pretext of its origin. Likewise, it is not right to bring into the limelight the personal affairs of actors, for their lives are not more immoral than those of merchants. He stresses the fact that comedians have never been excommunicated by any ecumenical council. The contemporaneous stage is moral, for it blames vice and always punishes it. As for the arousing of passions, the theatre is no worse than the Bible, for passages like the description of Cain's fury against Abel abound in Scripture. Finally, he asserts that on account of their utility, plays are performed in institutions of learning. His general thesis is that the theatre is a necessary and useful relaxation in civilized countries.

A more weighty defense, though not a very long one, was furnished by Nicolas Boileau, then at the height of his European reputation as a legislator in Parnassus. In 1707 he engaged in polemics over the stage with Massillon and Jacques Losme de Monchesnay, who had been a playwright, but who, like Racine, had become "converted." Monchesnay had written for the Théâtre Italien of Gherardi several plays, such as *La Cause des Femmes,* 1687; *Mezetin, grand Sophi de Perse,* 1689; *Le Phénix, ou la Femme fidèle,* 1691, which obtained great success; *Les Souhaits,* 1693. Soon after, he recognized the essential frivolity and sinfulness of his literary occupations and "burned what he had adored." He called his plays the aberrations of his youth, and his devotional scruples incited him to decry any form of acting or singing as infected with diabolical propensities. At this time he became one of Boileau's admirers and visited him frequently, though the satirist is said not to have had any particular friendship for him. "Il semble que cet homme-là soit embarrassé de son mérite et du mien," he is reputed to have remarked. Monchesnay sent him a fiery dissertation wherein he announced a paradox which later was to be developed by J.-J. Rousseau, namely, that Molière and his plays had been the principal factor in "la corruption des moeurs."

Against him Boileau made the same point which Chavigni de Saint-Martin had brought out the preceding year. In discussing the morality of the stage, one should disassociate the question of the private lives and personal affairs of comedians from the question of the inherent morality of the plays they perform. Boileau admits that certain plays are immoral, but he does not concede that, for that reason, all performances should be indiscriminately banned. . . .

. . . . .

It has been pointed out previously that the detractors of the stage were found among Protestants as well as among Catholics. One of the principal Protestant theologians, Jean de la Placette, sometimes called "le Nicole protestant," attacked plays in a section of his *Réflexions chrétiennes sur divers sujets* (1707), entitled *De l'Usage que nous devons faire de notre temps*. He sets forth the entire group of the known religious and moral objections to prove that the stage is not a justified pastime for the Christian.

At this point it seems appropriate to take stock of the progress of the theatre quarrel and to summarize briefly the period that terminates about 1715, for the death of Louis XIV is really the historical line of demarcation between the seventeenth and eighteenth centuries in the realm of French thought. During the course of the seventeenth century the opponents and partisans of the stage based their arguments chiefly upon theological grounds—Scripture, the opinions of the Church Fathers and the decisions of the early Church Councils. Each party interprets specific utterances of the Fathers from its own point of view. Tertullian is the principal ecclesiastical authority cited against plays, and St. Thomas is quoted most frequently for the opposite side.

Those who favored the theatre claimed that Scripture does not specifically condemn plays, and that the Church Fathers and early Councils denounced only the contemporaneous stage, chiefly on account of its obscenity and idolatry, and that neither of these factors could be found in the French drama of the seventeenth century. The opponents of the theatre cited numerous local Rituals which condemned plays, but the friends of the stage countered by asserting that neither the Pope nor any ecumenical Council had ever forbidden plays in general. Toward the end of the period which we have been discussing, the partisans of the theatre begin to urge more strongly the utility of plays. This clearly foreshadows the reasoning of the eighteenth century.

Erich Auerbach on seventeenth-century audiences:

In seventeenth-century sources two new designations for those to whom literary and above all dramatic works are addressed, take their place side by side with such general terms as *lecteurs, spectateurs, auditeurs, assemblée*. These new terms are *le public* and *la cour et la ville*. . . . *La cour et la ville* were a unit which took form in the course of the century and which may already be termed a "public" in the modern sense. The two parts of this unit were to be sure distinct in formal rank, but the dividing line between them was repeatedly crossed, and above all each part had lost its authentic foundations. The nobility as such had lost its function and had ceased to be anything more than the King's entourage; the bourgeoisie, or at least the part of it that may be termed *ville*, was also alienated from its original function as an economic class. With their parasitic absence of function and common cultural ideal, *la cour et la ville* merged into a self-contained, homogeneous society.

Erich Auerbach, in Scenes from the Drama of European Literature, *Meridian Books, Inc., 1959.*

John Lough

SOURCE: "Audiences," in *Seventeenth-Century French Drama: The Background,* Oxford at the Clarendon Press, 1979, pp. 76-98.

[*In the following excerpt, Lough discusses the changing social status of the theatre during the seventeenth century and the composition of theatre audiences, observing that the middle classes were strongly represented.*]

Even if the seventeenth-century playwright probably gave no thought to the spectators in the despised provinces, he had to bear in mind that he was writing for two rather different, if overlapping audiences—that of the court and that of the public theatres of Paris. From one end of the century to the other, the king and court took an interest in drama either by having plays performed in the royal palaces in Paris or Versailles or even occasionally in the provinces or else by attending the public theatres.

It is true that the interest shown by the king and court in drama was greater in some periods of the century than in others, it is also better documented in certain reigns. We know very little about the interest shown by Henry IV in the theatre at a period when, it must be remembered, it was not yet the fashionable entertainment it was later to become. Yet we do know that he and his Italian queen, Marie de Médicis, went to great trouble to persuade companies from Italy to come to Paris and entertain them and their court. Moreover, in those days when French companies from the provinces could not long hold out at the Hôtel de Bourgogne, we find at least one reference to a visit paid to that theatre by Henry and his court. In January 1607 a contemporary noted in his Journal: 'Le vendredi 26e de ce mois fut jouée, à l'Hôtel de Bourgogne, à Paris, une plaisante farce, à laquelle assistèrent le roi, la reine, et la plupart des princes, seigneurs et dames de la cour.' In 1609 and again in 1611, first as dauphin and then as king, the young Louis XIII was taken on several occasions to see plays at the Hôtel de Bourgogne.

If we know little of Louis XIII's visits to this theatre after his early youth, it is an interesting fact that Louis XIV did not disdain to frequent the public theatres of the capital, either before he took over the reins of power in 1661 or for some time afterwards. In 1656, for instance, when he was eighteen, he went to the Théâtre du Marais for a performance of Thomas Corneille's highly successful tragedy, *Timocrate*. Two years later Louis and his court went to the rival theatre of the Hôtel de Bourgogne for a performance of a lost tragedy and shortly afterwards saw a performance given by the Italian actors. At the beginning of 1659 they went to see Pierre Corneille's latest tragedy, *Œdipe*, again at the Hôtel de Bourgogne. Molière's theatre was not left out of these visits; in 1663, for instance, La Grange recorded the king's presence at a performance of *L'École des femmes* and *La Critique*: 'Le Roi nous honora de sa présence en public'; and six months later, in January 1664, we find the following entry: 'Joué dans notre salle au Palais Royal pour le Roi la *Bradamante ridicule*'. In 1666 Louis attended a performance of Boyer's *pièce à machines, Jupiter et Sémélé,* at the Marais

Charles Robert Leslie's depiction of Molière's Le bourgeois gentilhomme.

theatre which specialized in this type of production. However, it was much more usual for plays to be performed in the royal palaces. Although our information about such performances in the first half of the century is decidedly scrappy, we catch occasional glimpses of both French and Italian actors performing at court during the reign of Henry IV. Such court performances continued during the reign of Louis XIII. We know of one particular period of intensive dramatic activity at court during his minority; in the space of fifteen months, between November 1612 and Febrary 1614, over 130 performances were given at court by professional actors, both French and Italian. Our information about theatrical performances at court during the rest of Louis XIII's reign and the regency which followed his death in 1643 is decidedly meagre, but there is no doubt that they took place fairly frequently.

It was, however, during the period between Louis XIV's assumption of power in 1661 and his estrangement from the theatre in his years of piety that the drama saw its most brilliant period at the French court in the seventeenth-century. After the death of his queen in 1683 and his attachment to Mme de Maintenon Louis gradually began to lose interest in the drama; in November 1691 the Marquis de Dangeau noted in his journal: 'Le soir il y eut comédie; le roi n'y va plus du tout.' Theatrical performances still continued at court in the latter part of the reign; even if they no longer took place with all the

splendour of of the sumptuous fêtes of the 1660s and 1670s, they had become a regular part of the routine of life at court and were to remain so right down to the Revolution. At the high point of the reign most of the performances took place in Paris or later at Versailles when the court was permanently established there; in addition, they were sometimes given at Fontainebleau or other royal palaces in the provinces.

Not only did the king and court see performed new plays or older ones which had first been put on in the public theatres; quite a number of the plays of the time were given their first performance at court. Racine's first great success in tragedy, *Andromaque,* received its first performance not at the Hôtel de Bourgogne, but at the Louvre. The *Gazette de France* carried the following item on 19 November 1667: 'Leurs Majestés eurent le divertissement d'une fort belle tragédie, par la Troupe Royale, en l'appartement de la Reine, où étaient quantité de seigneurs et de dames de la cour.' Seven years later the *Gazette* announced another court première for a Racine play, *Iphigénie* (even managing to give the author's name on this occasion):

De Versailles, le 24 août 1674,
. . . Le soir, Leurs Majestés, avec lesquelles étaient Monseigneur le Dauphin, Monsieur, et un grand nombre de seigneurs et de dames, prirent ici, dans l'Orangerie, le divertissement d'une pièce nouvelle de

théâtre intitulée *Iphigénie*, composée par le sieur Racine, laquelle fut admirablement bien représentée par la Troupe Royale et très applaudie de toute la Cour. Ensuite elles eurent aussi le divertissement d'un grand feu d'artifice sur le Canal.

When Molière and his company—known after their patron, Louis XIV's brother, as 'la Troupe de Monsieur'—made their return to Paris in 1658, the first performance which they gave in the capital was at the Louvre, as La Grange records in his register: 'La Troupe de Monsieur, frère unique du Roi, commença au Louvre devant sa Majesté le 24e octobre 1658 par *Nicomède* et *Le Docteur amoureux*.'

Indeed in the fifteen years which followed down to his death Molière became very much a court entertainer. If most of the plays—*Le Misanthrope* is a notable exception—which he put on first in the Petit Bourbon and Palais Royal theatres were given subsequently at court during his lifetime, quite a number received their first performance before the king, mostly as part of a more or less elaborate court entertainment.

It was . . . during the period between Louis XIV's assumption of power in 1661 and his estrangement from the theatre in his years of piety that the drama saw its most brilliant period at the French court in the seventeenth-century.

—*John Lough*

The long and complicated history of the most successful of all his comedies, *Tartuffe*, began in 1664 when his company took part in the fêtes held at Versailles under the title of *Les Plaisirs de l'Ile enchantée*. His company's contribution consisted of performances of a new 'comédie galante mêlée de musique et d'entrées de ballet', *La Princesse d'Élide*, specially written for the occasion; a comedy, *Les Fâcheux*, first performed three years earlier at Vaux-le-Vicomte at a fête offered by Foucquet to Louis XIV; then, according to La Grange's register, 'trois actes du *Tartuffe* qui étaient les trois premiers'; and finally a *comédie-ballet*, *Le Mariage forcé*, in which the king had danced when it was performed in the Louvre a few months earlier. Some of these court performances were given in royal palaces at quite a distance from Paris. Thus in 1670 the well-known *comédie-ballet*, *Le Bourgeois Gentilhomme*, received its first performance at Chambord, one of the royal palaces in the Loire valley, as La Grange records: 'La troupe est partie pour Chambord par ordre du Roi. On y a joué entre plusieurs comédies *Le Bourgeois gentilhomme*, pièce nouvelle de M. de Molière.' La première took place on 14 October, and it was not until 23 November that the first public performance of this new play was given at the Palais Royal theatre.

Thanks to La Grange's register we are fairly well informed about the performances given at court by Molière's company and from this and other contemporary sources we know what they performed there, whether completely new plays or others which had had their first performance in Paris. From 1680 onwards we know from the registers of the Comédie Française exactly what court performances the new company gave. Unfortunately for the period before 1680 we have only rather scrappy information about the court performances given by companies like the Hôtel de Bourgogne. We must not, however, imagine that Molière's company had anything like a monopoly of court performances between 1658 and 1673. We have seen, for instance, that *Andromaque* and *Iphigénie* were given their première at court by the rival company of the Hôtel de Bourgogne.

While it would no doubt be a mistake to imagine that all the spectators at these court performances were required to furnish written proof of their noble birth before being allowed in to enjoy the spectacle, it is pretty clear that such court audiences must have been markedly more aristocratic than those in the public theatres. Indeed for the opening decades of the century—a period of scarcely relieved darkness so far as the history of the theatre is concerned—it has often been argued that the spectators who frequented the Hôtel de Bourgogne and various improvised theatres were the very opposite of aristocratic. The striking thing about the plays of the opening part of the century—be they comedies, tragedies, tragicomedies, or pastoral plays—is their aesthetic and moral crudity. It is perhaps too easy to conclude that theatre audiences must therefore have been decidely plebeian, lacking the refining influence of the upper classes of society and especially that of respectable women. Tempting as this conclusion may be, it is not altogether borne out by the facts. The theatre was undoubtedly a much less fashionable entertainment than it was to become by about 1630; the plays produced were of little literary worth and were often extremely crude, even obscene, in their subject-matter and language. Yet though the theatre was a much cheaper form of entertainment than it was to become later in the century, there are fragments of evidence which indicate that audiences were much more mixed than is often suggested.

There is, for instance, some evidence that no only some young bloods of the aristocracy, but even some solid bourgeois attended the theatre in these decades. What is more, the documents on which historians of the theatre rely in order to exclude respectable women from audiences of the time are no more conclusive than those produced by scholars who attempt to do the same for the London theatres of Shakespeare's day. Thus the apparently categorical statement of Abbé d'Aubignac, writing in the 1660s, that 'il y a cinquante ans qu'une honnête femme n'osait aller au théâtre' is considerably modified by the rest of the sentence: 'ou bien il fallait qu'elle fût voilée et tout à fait invisible, et ce plaisir était comme réservé aux débauchées qui se donnaient la liberté de regarder à visage découvert.' In other words d'Aubignac does admit that some 'honnêtes femmes' did go to the theatre in the opening decades of the century, even if they went veiled. Charles Sorel, writing a few years later, is even further from denying that respectable women were present in the theatre at that period in the century. 'A trefois', he declares, 'toutes les femmes se retiraient quand on allait jouer la farce.' Even if information about the composition of theatre audiences at the beginning of this period is extremely hard to come by, it would certainly seem rash to conclude that neither men of the upper classes of society nor respectable women frequented the theatre in these years.

We have seen that the attitude of the court of Henry IV and the young Louis XIII to drama was not as negative as has often been imagined. Meagre as our information undoubtedly is, it suffices to prove that in these years the court did not regard theatrical performances as entirely beneath contempt, as an entertainment suited only for the plebs, for a horde of ruffians, and dissolute women. Whether the king along with other members of the royal family and his courtiers, male and female, attended theatrical performances given in the various royal palaces or (this seems to have happened much less frequently) at that alleged place of perdition, the Hôtel de Bourgogne, there is no doubt that they saw exactly the same plays—French or Italian—as were presented to the ordinary spectators in the public theatre. Clearly we do not possess, for the opening decades of the seventeenth century, one set of crude plays written for the plebeian audiences of the Hôtel de Bourgogne and another set of refined plays written to please the more sophisticated taste of the court.

It is characteristic that the only two anecdotes in Tallement's *Historiettes* relating to Henry IV's interest in drama concern encounters with actors who were particularly distinguished for their roles in farce—Arlequin and Gros-Guillaume. His Italian queen, Marie de Médicis, naturally took a keen interest in actors from her own country, but she seems also to have enjoyed performances by French actors, particularly in farce. After the murder of her favourite, Concini, she endeavoured to while away the time in her exile at Blois with visits from two well-known farce actors. The accounts of her household show that in May 1618 the sum of 90 livres was paid to 'Robert Guérin, dit La Fleur', better known as Gros-Guillaume, and in December of the same year she gave 600 livres to 'Phillipe Mondor, médecin' and to 'ceux qui l'ont assisté pour jouer les comédies qu'ils ont représentées diverses fois devant nous pour notre plaisir et service'. Philippe Mondor (his real name was Philippe Girard) was the brother of a more illustrious personage, the famous farce actor, Tabarin, of whom Boileau was to write with such contempt in the *Art poétique* where he laments the fact that in his comedies Molière should too often have

> Quitté, pour le bouffon, l'agréable et le fin
> Et sans honte à Térence allié Tabarin.

Both brothers are mentioned in another item in these accounts, dated February 1619; Marie de Médicis orders her treasurer to pay 'Philippe de Mondor, docteur en médecine, et Antoine Girard, dit Tabarin, la somme de trois cents livres de laquelle nous leur avons fait don tant en considération de ce qu'ils ont représenté plusieurs comédies devant nous pour notre plaisir et service que pour leur faire sentir notre libéralité. It is obvious that in the opening decades of the seventeenth century there was not an unbridgeable gulf between the taste of the court and that of the low-born spectators who applauded farce actors like Gros-Guillaume and Tabarin, and that the public performances given at the Hôtel de Bourgogne and at other places in Paris did not provide an exclusively plebeian entertainment.

Fortunately we do not need to get involved in the controversies concerning the social composition of theatre audiences in the opening decades of the century for which, as for other questions concerning the theatrical life of the period, solid information is sadly lacking. In contrast, for the decades of the century which concern us, the period from roughly 1630 to 1680 which saw the production of all but one of the masterpieces of Corneille, Molière, and Racine, our knowledge is much less scrappy and is sufficient to give us a fairly clear idea of what sort of people frequented the public theatres of the capital.

It may well be that with the changes which took place in the theatrical world of Paris, roughly in the period 1625-35, audiences became rather less mixed than they had previously been. With two companies permanently installed in the capital and a new generation of playwrights supported by the patronage of great noblemen and above all Richelieu, the theatre became much more fashionable. For a time one continues to find references to the presence of plebeian spectators in the different Paris theatres. As late as 1663, in Molière's little play, *La Critique de l'École des femmes,* there is the famous reference to the presence of lackeys among the audience in his theatre. In making fun of the prudish reactions of some women spectators to *L'École des femmes,* one of the characters declares: 'Quelqu'un même des laquais cria tout haut qu'elles étaient plus chastes des oreilles que de tout le reste du corps.' Indeed it seems that it was not until rather later that lackeys were banned by royal edict from attending the theatre.

It is true that the word *peuple* when applied to seventeenth-century theatre audiences can be highly ambiguous as in certain contexts it can mean simply 'audience, public', and sometimes, as in 'la cour et le peuple', it is used in a sense which obviously includes people who were very far from plebeian in the modern sense of the term.

None the less in the 1630s and 1640s there are clearly some occasions when the term *peuple* applied to part of the audience had a definitely plebeian meaning. In 1639 in his *Apologie du théâtre* Georges de Scudéry makes some extremely rude references to plebeian spectators in the *parterre* such as 'cette multitude ignorante que la farce attire à la comédie'. At about the same time (although not published until 1657, his *Pratique du théâtre* was written much earlier) Abbé d'Aubignac speaks scathingly of the low tastes of the plebeian section of the audience. . . .

Then there is the much quoted passage from Sorel's *La Maison des jeux,* published in 1642, in which he denounces the noisy *racaille* to be found among the spectators in the *parterre:*

Le parterre est fort incommode pour la presse qui s'y trouve de mille marauds mêlés parmi les honnêtes gens, auxquels ils veulent quelquefois faire des affronts, et ayant fait des querelles pour un rien, mettent la main à l'épée et interrompent toute la comédie. Dans leur plus parfait repos ils ne cessent aussi de parler, de siffler et de crier, et pource qu'ils n'ont rien payé à l'entrée et qu'ils ne viennent là qu'à faute d'autre occupation, ils ne se soucient guère d'entendre ce que disent les comédiens. C'est une preuve que la comédie est infâme, de ce qu'elle est fréquentée par de telles gens, et l'on montre que ceux qui ont la puissance dans le monde en font bien peu de cas, puisqu'ils n'empêchent point que toute cette racaille y entre sans payer, pour y faire du désordre.

If we are to believe such witnesses, the audiences for which Corneille and his contemporaries catered in the 1630s still contained a noticeable plebeian element.

It is, however, significant that from the middle of the seventeenth century until the closing decades of the Ancien Régime one finds scarcely any references to the presence of such spectators. It is only from the 1760s onwards that writers begin to refer, naturally with scorn, to the gradual infiltration of plebeian spectators into theatres like the Comédie Française and the Théâtre Italien. In the hundred years or so before that date it would seem as if the cheapest part of the various Paris theatres, the *parterre,* was largely a middle-class preserve. Among the spectators in this part of the house about whose presence we have ample evidence were budding playwrights. Naturally once they had established themselves, they enjoyed the privilege of free admission and could choose a more comfortable way of seeing a play. We are told that Pierre Corneille—the 'vieux poète malintentionné' whom Racine refers to in his savage first preface to the play—sat in a box at the first performance of his younger rival's *Britannicus,* but he himself refers in *La Suite du Menteur* to the presence of writers in the *parterre* applying the famous rules to other people's plays. In this comedy he makes the main character, Dorante, and his servant, Cliton, discuss putting their new adventures on the stage as in *Le Menteur:*

Cliton: Mais peut-on l'ajuster dans les vingt et quatre heures?

Dorante: Qu'importe?

Cliton: A mon avis, ce sont bien les meilleures;

Car, grâces au bon Dieu, nous nous y connaissons;

Les poètes au parterre en font tant de leçons,

Et là cette science est si bien éclaircie

Que nous savons que c'est que de péripétie,

Catastase, épisode, unité, dénoûment,

Et quand nous en parlons, nous parlons congrûment.

Again one of the characters in Sorel's *Maison des jeux* replies to the criticisms of the spectators in the *parterre* which we have just quoted, pointing out that 'la plupart de nos poètes qui sont les plus capables de juger des pièces, n'y vont point ailleurs.'

It may be objected that this period saw too much poverty among writers, too many 'poètes crottés' to use the language of the time, for the presence of writers in the *parterre* to throw much light on its social composition and in particular to prove that it contained many solid bourgeois. Yet there is plenty of evidence that this was the case, so much so that it would take several pages to quote all of it; only a few examples can be given here. The expression 'le noble et le bourgeois' is frequently used in writings of the time as shorthand for the theatre audiences, as when Jean Loret in his rhymed news-sheet speaks of a tragedy being performed at Molière's theatre 'pour le noble et le bourgeois'. 'Le bourgeois' is often mentioned in his own right as one of the pillars of the Paris theatres as in Loret's references to Molière's *Dom Juan* with its 'changements de théâtre/Dont le bourgeois est idolâtre', or in Chappuzeau's statement that, since the royal edict of 1673 has put an end to disorders there, 'le bourgeois peut venir avec plus de plaisir à la comédie.' That the bourgeois mainly frequented the *parterre* is made clear in official documents such as that provided by d'Argenson, the *Lieutenant de police,* who speaks of the greater part of the large number of spectators in the *parterre* of the Comédie Française one day in 1700 when disorders broke out there, as being 'gens de collège, de palais ou de commerce', that is teachers, lawyers, and merchants. A vivid picture of the spectators on the stage contrasted with the bourgeois spectators in the *parterre* of the Théâtre Italien towards the end of the century is to be found in the final scene of Regnard and Dufresny's comedy, *Les Chinois,* performed in 1692:

Les Italiens donnent un champ libre sur la scène à tout le monde. L'officier vient jusques au bord du théâtre étaler impunément aux yeux du marchand la dorure qu'il lui doit encore. L'enfant de famille, sur les frontières de l'orchestre, fait la moue à l'usurier qui ne saurait lui demander ni le principal, ni les intérêts. Le fils, mêlé avec les acteurs, rit de voir son père avaricieux faire le pied de grue dans le parterre pour lui laisser quinze sols de plus après sa mort.

There is also in the literature of the time an extraordinary number of references to the presence in the *parterre* of groups of 'marchands de la rue Saint-Denis'; these were not small shopkeepers, but prosperous retailers of luxury goods.

English travellers of the time who were men of some social position made no difficulty about standing in the cheapest part of the Paris theatres which they frequented. In 1664 Edward Browne, the son of Sir Thomas Browne, the author of *Religio Medici,* visited Paris as part of his grand tour. At this time he was only twenty-two; he was in due course to follow in his father's footsteps and become a doctor. When he went to the Palais Royal to see a performance by Molière's company, he felt no compunction about buying a ticket to stand in the *parterre:* 'In the afternoon I heard a Comedy at Palais-Royal. They were Monseir's Comedians; they had a farce after it. I gave Quinze Solz to stand upon the grounde. The name of it was *Coeur de Mari.* They were not to be compared with the Londoners.' Two years later Philip Skippon, the son of Cromwell's Major-General, a young Cambridge graduate who not long afterwards was to become an M.P. and a knight, saw both the Italian actors and Molière's company perform at the Palais Royal, and once again neither he nor his companion (or companions) made any difficulty about standing in the *parterre:*

> Palais Cardinal is a fair palace with handsome walks. Here Madame Henrietta, the duchess of Orleans, lives. At one side of this house is a public stage where the Italian and French comedians act by turns. I saw here *Il marîtaggion d'una Statua,* a merry play where the famous buffoon Scaramuccio, acted. Three antick dances pleased the spectators. The *Quatre Scaramuccie* was another pleasant Italian comedy. We stood in the parterre, or pit, and paid 30 sols apiece for seeing the first, and but 15 sols for the last.

> We saw a French comedy entitled *L'estourdye* which was better acted than we expected. We paid for seeing this, and standing in the pit, 15 sols a man.

Nor did a French nobleman disdain to stand in the *parterre* if he went to the theatre on his own or in male company. It is true that we chiefly learn of the presence of such spectators in that part of the house when they were drunk and created a disturbance, but presumably they also frequented it when they were sober.

The spectators in the *parterre* were certainly not always well behaved. We know from unimpeachable documents that twice during the last few months of Molière's life there were disorders in his theatre. On Sunday, 9 October 1672, during a performance of *La Comtesse d'Escarbagnas* and *L'Amour médecin* 'plusieurs gens de livrée et autres firent insulte à un homme d'épée auquel ils donnèrent quantité de coups de bâton desquels il est grièvement blessé, et même jetèrent plusieurs pierres aux acteurs qui jouaient la comédie.' While Molière himself was on the stage, 'il fut jeté du parterre le gros bout d'une pipe à fumer sur le théâtre'. Witnesses who gave evidence about the incident all agreed that the culprits were pages; their victim, described as 'un homme d'épée', might or might not have been an officer.

On 13 January 1673, just over a month before Molière's death, further disorders took place at the Palais Royal during a performance of the highly successful *tragédie-ballet, Psyché,* which he had composed with the assistance of Pierre Corneille and Quinault. A *commissaire au Châtelet* was fetched to the theatre by the news that 'dans le parterre il y avait quantité de gens d'épée entrés sous prétexte d'entendre la comédie . . . lesquels composaient entre eux, contre la volonté de sadite Majesté, . . . un désordre et une sédition comme il a été ci-devant fait à

l'Hôtel de Bourgogne'. The *commissaire* went on to the stage,

> d'où aussitôt que la première entrée s'est faite, avons aperçu dans ledit parterre, à la faveur de la clarté des chandelles, quelques gens d'épée à nous inconnus qui se seraient approchés dudit théâtre, lesquels murmuraient et frappaient du pied à terre, et quand la machine de Vénus est descendue, le choeur des chanteurs de cette entrée récitant tous ensemble *Descendez, mère des Amours!* lesdits gens d'épée, autant que nous avons pu remarquer être au nombre de vingt-cinq ou trente, de complot, auraient troublé lesdits chanteurs par des hurlements, chansons dérisionnaires et frappements de pied dans le parterre et contre les ais de l'enclos où sont les joueurs d'instruments.

The uproar caused by these rowdies finally brought the performance to an end; they were offered their money back, but they refused and demanded instead that the play should start all over again. When this was done, they apparently behaved themselves; at least the *commissaire's* report breaks off at this point.

Once again we have no means of telling what was the rank of these 'gens d'épée', but if this was conduct unworthy of an officer and a gentleman, we cannot necessarily conclude that they were 'other ranks'. At the Comédie Française in 1691 a performance of *La Devineresse,* the *pièce à machines* of De Visé and Thomas Corneille, was brought to an end by the disorders created by a gang of rowdies, led by a drunken officer with the delightful name of Sallo. This officer, 'capitaine au régiment de Champagne', the documents in the case relate, 'força la garde et entra dans le parterre', followed by other members of his company. Sallo then climbed up on to the stage from the *parterre* and shouted: 'Connais-tu ce bougre qui est à la porte de la Comédie? Je lui viens de foutre un bon coup d'épée dans le ventre. Je suis un capitaine qui ai vingt amis dans le parterre.'

Despite successive royal edicts trouble continued from this quarter to the end of the century. . . .

[I]f the *parterre* appears to have been largely the preserve of the middle classes, of merchants and professional men, including writers and aspiring writers, it also contained at least a sprinkling of noblemen, drunk or sober.

There is no question but that the all male spectators in this part of the theatre had a considerable influence. Thanks to the register kept by Hubert for the last year of the existence of Molière's theatre, we know that at 113 out of 131 performances more than half the spectators stood in the *parterre.* It is true that both in Molière's theatre and at the Comédie Française from 1680 the custom of doubling prices in the *parterre* during the opening performances of a new play tended to reduce the number of tickets sold for that part of the house, but under ordinary conditions these spectators formed a majority among the audience whenever older plays were revived and during the first run of new plays as soon as prices for the *parterre* had been reduced to normal. Clearly such spectators were extremely important from the numerical point of view, and even though the proportion of the audience which they represented generally fell during the opening performances of new plays, these were mostly well attended and on such occasions there could be at least three or four hundred spectators in the *parterre*. This mass of men, packed together like sardines, was obviously in a position to express its reactions in a way which could have a considerable effect on the fate of the play.

At any rate from the 1660s onwards, we continually find most flattering references to the good taste of the *parterre*. Molière's *Critique de l'École des femmes* (1663) furnishes the first example of such praise; here we see the actor-manager who knew on which side his bread was buttered and was very conscious of the fact that the spectators who bought tickets for the *parterre* generally represented more than half his audience. His spokesman, Dorante, makes a vigorous defence of the taste of the spectators in this part of the theatre when he rebukes the Marquis for his contemptuous attitude towards them:

> Apprends, Marquis, je te prie, et les autres aussi, que le bon sens n'a point de place déterminée à la comédie; que la différence du demi-louis d'or et de la pièce de quinze sols ne fait rien du tout au bon goût; que debout ou assis, on peut donner un mauvais jugement; et qu'enfin, à le prendre en général, je me fierais assez à l'approbation du parterre, par la raison qu'entre ceux qui le composent, il y en a plusieurs qui sont capables de juger d'une pièce selon les règles, et que les autres en jugent par la bonne façon d'en juger, qui est de se laisser prendre aux choses, et de n'avoir ni prévention aveugle, ni complaisance affectée, ni délicatesse ridicule.

Flattery of the *parterre* is carried much further in *Les Chinois*, the comedy written by Regnard and Dufresny for the Théâtre Italien. In the last scene the *Parterre* enters to act as judge in the debate between Colombine, representing the Théâtre Italien, and Arlequin, who represents the Comédie Française. Arlequin is made to greet the arrival of the *Parterre* with the words: 'Malepeste! il faut ouvrir la porte à deux battants, c'est notre père nourricier. Qu'il entre, en payant, s'entend.' The *Parterre* puts forward sweeping claims as to its function in the theatre: 'Ne savez-vous pas que je suis seul juge naturel, et en dernier ressort, des comédiens et des comédies? Voilà avec quoi je prononce mes arrêts (*Il donne un coup de sifflet*).' When Colombine speaks of 'son Excellence, Monseigneur le Parterre', Arlequin protests at such flattery, but she retorts with comic enthusiasm:

> Non, ce n'est point la flatterie qui me dénoue la langue; je rends simplement les hommages dus à ce souverain plénipotentiaire. C'est l'éperon des auteurs, le frein des comédiens, l'inspecteur et curieux examinateur des hautes et basses loges, et de tout ce qui se passe en icelles; en un mot, c'est un juge incorruptible, qui, bien loin de prendre de l'argent pour juger, commence par en donner à la porte de l'audience.

When the *Parterre* finally gives its judgement, Arlequin

exclaims in horror: 'O tempora! O mores! J'appelle de ce jugement-là aux loges', to which the former replies: 'Mon jugement est sans appel.'

No doubt it would be very unwise to take all this literally; one must bear in mind the effect which such paradoxes must have had on theatre audiences drawn from the profoundly aristocratic society which existed in France in the reign of Louis XIV. Given the prevailing worship of rank and social position, it was inevitable that the outlook and ideals of the aristocracy should exercise a considerable influence on the drama of the age. The section of the nobility which gravitated around the king in Paris and later at Versailles was powerfully represented in the different theatres which served Paris in the course of the seventeenth century. There was clearly a considerable overlap between the audiences present at court performances and those to be found in the public theatres.

It is obvious that the more expensive seats in these theatres were occupied by persons of rank or wealth. Theatre prices rose fairly steeply in the course of the century for all sorts of reasons, including taxes; a ticket to the *parterre* at the Hôtel de Bourgogne cost a mere 5 sous at the beginning of the century compared with 18 at the Comédie Française at the end of the reign of Louis XIV. Although numerically the *parterre* might be extremely important, its contribution to the total box-office receipts was much smaller than its numbers might at first suggest. This is particularly striking in Molière's theatre as there the best seats, those in the first row of boxes and on the stage, were very expensive. The result was that, to take the example of the first performance of *Le Malade imaginaire* in 1673, while 394 out of the 682 spectators stood in the *parterre,* tickets for that part of the theatre, even with prices doubled, accounted for less than a third of the total receipts—591 livres out of 1,892. In contrast seats on the stage and in the *premières loges* contributed more to the total—682 livres.

At the Comédie Française the charges made for the best seats in the theatre were proportionately less heavy in relation to the cost of tickets to the *parterre* than they had been in Molière's theatre. Even so, despite the large numbers of spectators present in the *parterre* on most occasions, their contribution to the total receipts of the performance fell well below 50 per cent, and could even fall as low as a quarter. Thus even if the society of the time had not accorded the respect which it did to birth and money, the men and women of blue blood and wealth who sat in the first row of boxes or on the stage had an importance, from the financial point of view, which far outweighed their numbers, and, of course, both actors and actresses did bestow upon the upper classes of the society of their age the respect which the prevailing social outlook demanded.

If the ladies of the aristocracy, with their male escorts, chiefly frequented the *premières loges,* another part of the theatre which sometimes counted among its spectators illustrious personages of both sexes was the *amphithéâtre,* the rows of seats facing the stage at the far end of the *parterre*. Thus in December 1672 Louis XIV's brother, Monsieur, accompanied on one occasion by his second wife, the German princess Charlotte Elizabeth, was twice present at performances of *Psyché* at Molière's theatre and occupied with his suit 'deux bancs de l'amphithéâtre'. The other part of the theatre which contained a high proportion of aristocrats—this time men only—was the stage. While on occasion the number of these spectators could be quite small, there were times when they were so numerous that it is difficult to imagine how both they and the actors were accommodated on the stage. On one occasion in the last year of the life of Molière's company there were as many as thirty-six, while the registers of the Comédie Française record for its first performance in 1680 as many as 150. Writers—Corneille and Molière among others—are shown by contemporary documents to have gone on occasion to this part of the house, but it seems mainly to have been frequented by the young bloods of the aristocracy. . . .

There is certainly no evidence that Louis XIV and his courtiers showed any particular discernment in their choice of plays to be performed in the various royal palaces. During Molière's lifetime *Les Fâcheux* appears to have been the play of his most often given at court, and there is no evidence that he ever performed *Le Misanthrope* there. However, to conclude that in its dealings with the theatre the aristocracy did not exhibit any particular refinement of taste is not to deny that it exercised an influence on drama commensurate with its exalted place in the society of the day. The ladies and their male escorts in the more expensive boxes and the noblemen sitting or standing on the stage did play an important part in moulding the taste of the day in the theatre as in other forms of literature. Although middle-class and even for a time plebeian spectators were undoubtedly present among the audiences of the capital, given the social structure of seventeenth-century France, the upper classes, from the princes of the blood and the *grands seigneurs* and their womenfolk downwards, exercised an influence on drama which was out of proportion to the fairly considerable numbers which they furnished to the theatre audiences of the time.

Mixed as the audiences in the public theatre undoubtedly were, from the point of view of social composition, in sheer numbers they none the less represented a small élite. It is true that it is only for the last year of Molière's career in Paris that, thanks to the *Registre d'Hubert*, we can calculate for the first time how many spectators paid to see his company perform in the course of the theatrical year. In considering these figures, we have to bear in mind that Paris probably had a population of some half a million, one which was temporarily swollen by visitors from the provinces and from further afield, some of whom, as we know from their letters and diaries, frequented the theatres of the capital. In the theatrical year 1672/73 Molière's company performed 131 times and attracted some 52,000 spectators—an average daily attendance of 400.

Thanks to the summary of the registers of the Comédie Française produced by the late Carrington Lancaster, we

can work out how many spectators paid for admission to this theatre from 1680 onwards. In attempting to interpret these figures we have to bear in mind that whereas Molière's company had to compete with several others, the Comédie Française had as its only rivals the Opéra and the Théâtre Italien, and that after the expulsion of the Italian actors in 1697, it was the only Paris theatre putting on straight plays. The total number of spectators fluctuated fairly violently from year to year, reaching in 1698/99 193,000, an exceptionally high figure, and falling as low as 109,000 in 1683/84. The average—nearly 140,000—looks at first sight very impressive until one does a little arithmetic. There is evidence that a small number of people went very frequently to the theatre, seeing a successful new play more than once and also being assiduous in their attendance at revivals. Thus a thousand people attending the Comédie Française fifty times in a year could account for over a third of this total, and two thousand more going twenty times a year could account for another 40,000 attendances; these three thousand people could leave only some 50,000 attendances for those spectators who went only once in the year or else very infrequently.

All this is, of course, only playing with figures in an orgy of guesswork. Where we are on firmer ground in trying to assess the size of theatre audiences in the Paris of our period is by finding out how large was the number of spectators which the average successful play attracted during its first run; this gives us a rough idea of how many people were in the habit of attending the Comédie Française. In the period from 1680 to 1700 Boursault's five-act comedy, *Les Fables d'Ésope,* with the quite exceptional number of 43 performances attracted over 25,000 paying spectators, while a one-act play of Dancourt, *Les Vendages de Suresnes,* had 49 performances with over 33,000 spectators paying for admission. Clearly both these plays had such a vogue as to draw in people who did not normally go to the Comédie Française. If we examine the fate of other new plays put on in the same period we find that 10,000-12,000 people represented the largest number of spectators who could be expected to support a new play unless it enjoyed a great vogue, when the total attendance would reach from 15,000 to 17,000. In other words at the end of the seventeenth-century the number of regular patrons of the Comédie Française lay somewhere between a minimum of 10,000 and a maximum of 17,000.

We may conclude then that the theatre-going public of Paris in the Classical age of French drama was numerically a severely restricted one, given the population of the capital and its attractions for provincials and foreigners. The short run enjoyed by even the most successful plays of the period makes this point clear enough. Socially that audience appears to have been much more mixed than has sometimes been suggested. Certainly the middle classes were strongly represented there, and as late as the 1630s and 1640s there was probably a sprinkling of plebeian spectators. On the other hand the more aristocratic sections of society—so important in the France of Louis XIII and Louis XIV—also formed a considerable section of the audiences in the public theatres of the time, and it is their outlook rather than that of the middle layers of society which is most clearly reflected in the drama of the age. Lip-service is paid by many play-wrights of the period to the importance of pleasing the *savants* and conforming to their rules, but in their franker moments they recognize that, in order to be successful, a play must appeal to a wider circle, to 'les honnêtes gens', few of whom (especially the ladies) could claim to be learned. Thus the drama of the age was strongly influenced by the aristocratic outlook of the society in which it was produced. It was certainly not a learned drama, written to please a tiny group of scholars and critics; indeed, especially in comedy and farce, it contains a down-to-earth element which, though attributed by Boileau amongst others to the influence of the lower and middle sections of society, suited equally well the not too squeamish or refined taste of the aristocratic spectators, both male and female.

Elliott Forsyth

SOURCE: "The Tensions of Classicism in the French Theatre of the Seventeenth Century," in *The Classical Temper in Western Europe,* edited by John Hardy and Andrew McCredie, Oxford University Press, Melbourne, 1983, pp. 47-61.

[*In the essay that follows, Forsyth describes the principles of classical doctrine and how these rules were upheld by seventeenth-century French dramatists.*]

There is a common belief in English-speaking countries that French classicism was essentially preoccupied with matters of artistic form, which it sought to regulate by means of rules derived from the Ancients, who were seen as having attained the ultimate in the search for beauty and the portrayal of human nature. This view is summed up, with a characteristic touch of irony, by Alexander Pope in his *Essay on Criticism* (ll. 713-18):

> The *Rules,* a Nation born to serve, obeys,
> And *Boileau* still in Right of *Horace* sways.
> But *we,* brave *Britons, Foreign Laws* despis'd,
> And kept *unconquer'd,* and *unciviliz'd,*
> Fierce for the *Liberties of Wit,* and bold,
> We still defy'd the *Romans,* as *of old.*

It is true that much literary debate of the classical age in France focused on questions of form and compliance with rules, and it is true that Boileau, summing them up in his *Art poétique* (to which Pope owed much), makes considerable use of Horace; but it is difficult to imagine that the major literary works of the classical period could have been held in such high esteem in many parts of Europe for a hundred years or more solely on the basis of criteria of this kind. We are thus led to ask whether the content of the great works pushes these formal requirements into the background or whether the great writers make some more constructive use of the rules. Since so many of the literary debates of the time were centred on the theatre, I propose to examine certain aspects of the relationship between form and content in the French theatre of the seventeenth century; and especially the tensions that exist

between them in the works of the major dramatists, in an attempt to show something of the nature of the classical temper in France.

But first of all, let us be clear about our terms. In France, the words 'classical' and 'classicism' are used primarily to designate the literature and other arts of a type dominant in the seventeenth century, particularly during the reign of Louis XIV. While some critics limit the strictly classical period in literature to the central part of Louis's reign (1660-1685), it seems more appropriate to place the starting-point some twenty years earlier, in about 1640, at the end of the reign of Louis XIII, when Corneille was writing his most important plays against a background of classical theory and evolving dramatic forms which had been taking shape well before this.

During this central part of the seventeenth century, we are told, the classical rules had a special place. In fact the so-called 'rules' were only elements in a structured theory, whose nature and requirements are set out, with varying emphases, in a considerable number of works written between the sixteenth and eighteenth centuries.

The main sources of these ideas were the ancient writers Aristotle and Horace. But the main sources were not necessarily tapped directly: in France, in the first half of the seventeenth century, when the knowledge of Greek acquired during the Renaissance had largely been lost, the writings of Aristotle were known mainly through Latin translations (generally glossed) and the commentaries of Italian scholars, channels which produced an interesting variety of interpretations. At the practical level, the doctrine was interpreted to a large extent through the Latin models inherited from Antiquity.

From this body of ideas and models, the French theorists derived four main principles. Firstly, following Horace, they declared that all art should have a *moral purpose* made more acceptable by an entertaining presentation. The sixteenth-century Italian theorist Scaligero, whose influence in France was considerable, had summed up the double aim of aesthetic pleasure and moral instruction in the phrase *docere cum delectatione.* There were dissenting voices, but this principle ran deep in the stream of classical theory. Secondly, the work of art must be based on *reason* (as opposed to fantasy and imagination), which guides the poet's genius and dictates his precepts. Thirdly, art must essentially be the *imitation of nature,* but we need to be aware that, for the classical writers, the term 'nature' meant primarily human nature. Finally, the finest art mingled the personal element with the imitation of the Ancients.

It's within the context of these general principles that we must see the classical rules. Of these, the ones most relevant to the theatre are *la vraisemblance,* the rule of verisimilitude; *les bienséances,* the rule of decorum, which called for internal harmony and proprieties; the rule of the *distinction of genres,* which forbade, for example, the mixing of tragic and comic elements in the same work; and lastly, the celebrated rule of the *three unities:* the unities of action, time and place. There were also rules about the main dramatic genres, and the seventeenth-century theorists, moving away from the concept of tragedy as an elegiac form, as it had tended to be during the Renaissance, saw increasingly the importance of the concentration of the action, and urged that the play begin near the climax of the drama (*in medias res*), interest being maintained by the use of suspense. Comedy was governed by few specific rules, except that its characters were to be ordinary people rather than people of noble condition, and its subject-matter was to be about everyday life and invented rather than of historical importance. Otherwise, the general rules of tragedy applied.

How then were these principles and rules applied by the major French dramatists? Is there evidence of conflict between theory and practice? Did the demands of the theorists hinder the work of the artists?

In attempting to answer these questions, we need to be aware, first of all, that the theory was not a single, monolithic block, for there was much debate about interpretation. Then too, we must be aware that the dramatists themselves were to some extent theorists and thus contributed, on the basis of their practical experience, to the development and interpretation of the theory. Finally, we should note that the more acrimonious debates between writers and critics were often stirred up by non-literary factors.

This latter point is especially true of the great comic writer and actor of the French classical theatre, Molière. The last fifteen years of Molière's life, during which he produced all his major comedies and performed frequently at the court of Louis XIV, were spent in an atmosphere of unrelenting controversy through the attacks of critics, rivals and pietists as well as those who saw themselves as victims of his satire.

The first of Molière's major comedies, *L'Ecole des Femmes,* was initially performed in 1662 with immense success, but it touched off immediately a series of virulent attacks. The play is concerned with the question of the education of women and ridicules those men who seek to promote marital security by bringing up girls in a sequestered environment, ignorant of the temptations of this world. Molière was accused by the devout and prudish alike of impiety, immorality and even obscenity (the word *obscénité* being a neologism at the time) on account of scenes which were deemed to mock religion or in which the comic effect turned on verbal ambiguity. Such features were considered to be infringements of the rule of the proprieties, and he was accused by critics and rivals of poor techniques of construction, incoherent characterization and vulgarity. But the play continued to attract an audience, and Molière wrote a short comic piece to accompany it, *La Critique de L'Ecole des Femmes,* in which he answers his detractors.

We might be tempted to think, from some of the comments made in the *Critique* and in other polemical writings, that Molière rejected the classical rules, which by this time were well established: in fact, he considers them

as simple observations prompted by good sense and wholly dependent on the ultimate rule, which is to please the public:

> DORANTE: Il semble, à vous ouïr parler, que ces règles de l'art soient les plus grands mystères du monde; et cependant ce ne sont que quelques observations aisées, que le bon sens a faites sur ce qui peut ôter le plaisir que l'on prend à ces sortes de poèmes; et le même bon sens qui a fait autrefois ces observations les fait aisément tous les jours sans le secours d'Horace et d'Aristote. Je voudrais bien savoir si la grande règle de toutes les règles n'est pas de plaire, et si une pièce de théâtre qui a attrapé son but n'a pas suivi un bon chemin.

In other words, the rules are seen as a means of achieving successful drama rather than as a criterion for judgement.

But the principle of pleasing the public is not merely a pretext for pandering to a crude popular taste. In various places, Molière proclaims that comedy has a moral purpose, thus following the fundamental principle of classical art derived by the theorists from Horace. In a letter to the King about his highly controversial comedy *Tartuffe*, he begins:

> Le devoir de la comédie étant de corriger les hommes en les divertissant, j'ai cru que, dans l'emploi où je me trouve, je n'avais rien de mieux à faire que d'attaquer par des peintures ridicules les vices de mon siècle.

Molière's claim of a moral purpose has been contested during the last thirty years or so by critics who take the view that he was primarily concerned to exploit subjects that make good theatre. This is a question which calls for more extensive debate than is possible here. Suffice it to say, in the words of one of these critics, the late Will Moore, that, implicit in Molière's pictures of misanthrope, miser and hypochondriac is at least 'a critique of the modern world'.

But what other classical elements do we find in his plays? If we look at the structure of his major comedies, particularly the *comédies de caractère,* we see that, even though the basic plot follows the pattern of a traditional comedy of intrigue, Molière builds his play according to classical principles of progression, using, for example a unified action within a limited time span in such a way as to produce a more powerful effect through concentration than would be possible with a complicated comic imbroglio. An analysis of individual scenes shows within them a masterly concern with form in matters of symmetry and dramatic progression as well as language. While the principle of verisimilitude (*vraisemblance*) may, to our modern minds, be strained by unlikely *dé ouements* dictated to a large extent by theatrical tradition, he manages to create central characters in whom there is a judicious balance of caricature and authenticity. And whatever his critics and enemies may have said about verbal ambiguities and his views on religion, there is much more respect for the proprieties in Molière's comedies than in the ancient theatre and the traditional French and Italian farce which were his main sources.

But the greatness of Molière does not, of course, merely depend on his mastery of the rules; it lies rather in his capacity to observe human behaviour with all its frailties, and to use traditions, literary sources, rules and stage techniques acquired over many years of theatrical experience to achieve a rich and critical portrayal of human nature.

This creative tension evident in the comedies of Molière is perhaps more apparent in the field of tragedy, which in many ways epitomizes the classical ideal.

When Pierre Corneille, in 1640, presented the first French tragedy generally recognized as classical, *Horace,* he was already responding to bitter criticism of his earlier work proffered in the name of classical doctrine. At this time, twenty years before Molière produced his first major comedies, tragedy modelled on the works of antiquity had been written and produced in France for nearly ninety years. A significant professional theatre had however been active for only about thirty years of that time. In the early part of the century, alongside humanist tragedies in the Renaissance style, the French theatre had seen some of the excesses of baroque tragedy, a kind of tragedy of blood reminiscent of the Elizabethan stage, often crude in style and construction but characterised by dynamic action. But tragedy had virtually died in France in the 1620s, being supplanted in the theatre by tragi-comedy, and its rebirth had taken place quite suddenly in 1634 when two dramatists, Jean de Rotrou and Jean Mairet, wrote tragedies in the style of the Ancients in response to the humanist aspirations of their protectors. Now Mairet, through his study of the theory and practice of the Italian dramatists more particularly, had become convinced of the practical value of the codified rules derived by the theorists from the Ancients. In 1634, he set out to apply the rules in a tragedy about the African queen Sophonisba, which he derived in part from the Italian playwright Trissino. In terms of the rules, *La Sophonisbe* is a rather loosely constructed play: the unities of action and place are in fact interpreted rather freely, some elements of the plot would seem more appropriate to tragi-comedy than to tragedy, the situation of the central characters is pathetic rather than dramatic, and the psychology and motivation are sometimes ambiguous and unconvincing. What stands out is the speed with which the action moves, a quality very largely due to the strict application of the unity of time, which is emphasized in the detail of the dialogue. (Sophonisba sees her husband off to battle, learns of his death, meets and marries her conqueror, consummates the marriage and commits suicide to avoid becoming a prisoner of the Romans all in the space of twenty-four hours!) It is clear that Mairet had seen the importance of the idea of concentration which underlies the three unities.

We should not conclude, however, that Mairet was a complete innovator in respect of the application of the unities or the idea of concentration. Insofar as they followed ancient models, usually the plays of Seneca, the dramatists of the sixteenth and early seventeenth centuries had implicitly adopted into the tradition of the theatre some of the principles and techniques later to be proclaimed as rules. If we look at a subject drawn from antiquity for which there was no Senecan model, such as the Coriolanus story, and compare the treatment it receives on the two sides of the Channel, we may have a clearer idea of what is happening in France. You will recall that Shakespeare offers us a kind of fresco retracing all the main events of the life of his hero as presented in Plutarch's *Lives of Famous Men.* The two French playwrights who wrote tragedies on Coriolanus at that time, Pierre Thierry (1600) and Alexandre Hardy (whose play was published in 1625 but written and performed long before this) both limit the action to the latter part of the story, and Hardy, a professional playwright of long experience, begins his drama only at the moment when Coriolanus is accused of treason by the Roman mob and decides to offer his services to the enemy—that is, at the moment when the real tragic conflict begins. We are thus plunged into an already tense situation, which shows Coriolanus as a man of iron will and intense feeling. These dramatists, especially Hardy, thus adopt the principle of beginning the action *in medias res,* as close to the climax as possible, a procedure to be advocated by the theorists of the classical period in order to strengthen the concentration of the drama and make of tragedy essentially a crisis.

In the two and a half years following the production of

Scene from a 1945 performance of Corneille's Horace *(1640).*

Mairet's *Sophonisbe,* there appeared two remarkable plays which were to have an immense impact on the development of tragedy in France: *La Mariane* by Francois Tristan L'Hermite (performed in 1636) and *Le Cid* by Pierre Corneille (performed in January 1637). (*Le Cid* was originally presented as a tragi-comedy, but in many ways its action is essentially tragic, and some time later, after revision of the text, Corneille styled it a tragedy.)

Both these plays are marked by dynamic action, powerful verse and keen psychological insight. In both cases, the dynamic action is based on a dilemma, a deep conflict which takes place within the soul of the protagonist. King Herod, in *La Mariane,* is torn between his passionate love for his reluctant wife Mariane, whose family he has murdered, and his seething desire to take revenge on her for the infidelity and treason of which he suspects she is guilty. Rodrigue, in *Le Cid,* is torn between the duty to honour and protect the woman he loves and the duty to avenge the honour of his own family by killing his mistress's father. In the first case, the inner struggle is at the level of conflicting passions; in the second, it is at the level of conflicting duties in a society in which honour is the supreme value. In both plays, the pathos is centred initially on the anguish of the dilemma, and in both, the attempt to resolve the dilemma generates dynamic action.

To my mind, this use of the dilemma or inner conflict as a tragic motif is the essential starting-point of classical tragedy, although neither of these plays is yet more than pre-classical. But we must not imagine that Tristan L'Hermite or Pierre Corneille were the inventors of the dilemma as a dramatic device: in tragedy, it first appears in France in a horror play of the baroque theatre (*Rosemonde,* by N. Chrestien des Croix, 1603), and was developed at about the same time with more dramatic skill in an earlier version of the drama of Herod and Mariane by Alexandre Hardy, whose work served as a starting-point for Tristan L'Hermite and was certainly known to Corneille.

In his preface to *La Mariane,* Tristan says nothing explicitly about the rules beyond remarking that he has no intention of filling his work with Italian imitations and studied conceits (which is no doubt a shot at Mairet); his purpose, he declares, is to study the characters of his protagonists. In fact, he observes most of the rules, at any rate as they were interpreted at the time. If we compare his play with that of Hardy, which is clearly his main source, we see that he has concentrated especially on developing the psychological motivation of his characters, which in Hardy's play is rather sketchy. Every significant action is prepared and motivated, and when Herod, wrestling with conflicting passions, tries to resolve his dilemma, which in Hardy's play he does by a rather arbitrary decision, Tristan gives a crucial role to Salomé, the sister of Herod, a sinister character not fully developed by Hardy, who, because of her hatred of Mariane, feeds Herod's anger with suspicion and anxiety to a point where, losing control of himself, he orders Mariane's execution. But once Mariane is dead, Herod's anger and desire for revenge evaporate, leaving only the enduring passion of love, with the result that Herod is plunged into the agonies of remorse and madness. By developing the psychological motivation in this way and at the same time tightening its dramatic structure, Tristan enhances greatly the verisimilitude of the action and raises the play to the level of great drama.

La Mariane achieved enormous success in the theatre and its essential dramatic structure was imitated by others. In various ways, this play marks the definitive orientation of French tragedy towards the dramatic study of character and moral dilemma, which was to reach its highest point a generation later in the tragedy of Racine. Although Tristan seems to brush the rules aside, there is no doubt that, in giving such importance to motivation in character study, he is concerned essentially with the principles of reason, verisimilitude, and the imitation of nature. Tristan's is an early example of the classical tempering of human experience, the apprehension of the universal in the individual.

Pierre Corneille, in composing *Le Cid,* did not set out to conform to the rules of the theorists, but insofar as he did in fact observe them, he seems rather to have been following the tradition of tragicomedy, which was also moving towards a more 'regular' pattern: he manages to pack the action into a period of twenty-four hours, observes the unity of place as it was understood at the time, and achieves a fairly unified action as far as the main characters are concerned; but he does show violence on the stage, introduces a secondary theme which has little effect on the main one, pays little attention to the linking of scenes and often lets verisimilitude be strained. Yet if we compare *Le Cid* with its Spanish source, we see a deliberate movement by the French dramatist towards the unity of action: he simplifies the intrigue by eliminating many secondary episodes and elements of a primarily macabre, religious or spectacular nature, tightens the action and concentrates interest on the moral crisis and the anguish of its resolution. This, more than a preoccupation with minor questions of form, is in the spirit of classicism.

However, Corneille's play touched off a long and bitter literary debate. His critics were mostly theorists, but they included Mairet, who was also a rival dramatist. Richelieu used the quarrel to enhance the authority and prestige of his newly-formed Académie française, which was called upon to arbitrate. The main criticisms made by the theorists were that the basic moral purpose of art was not respected, for the conduct of the protagonists offered a bad example, and the *dénouement* did nothing to punish them for their misdeeds; the rule of the unity of action was undermined by the introduction of a secondary plot, and the action was not true to life, for the subject, although historical, lacked verisimilitude.

In spite of these alleged weaknesses, the play had enormous success and still draws packed houses. To the modern reader, especially one more familiar with the traditions of the Elizabethan theatre, such criticisms may seem to have little weight, especially those concerned with the moral lesson. But we have seen that, for many theorists, the didactic purpose of art overrode most other considerations, and the technical requirements, based on the principle of verisimilitude, were devised to give the moral lesson greater force. Corneille was one of the few writers who took the view that the purpose of dramatic poetry is to give pleasure to the spectators, an idea which he claims to derive from Aristotle. . . .

This does not mean, then, that he rejects the idea of moral utility: it is a question of priorities. Nor does it mean that he rejects the rules; for Corneille the rules are only a means to an end. . . .

But the fact that Corneille did not reject the rules outright is shown quite clearly in his next tragedy, *Horace,* with which we began this part of our discussion and which many critics see as the first French tragedy which can be considered authentically classical. After *Le Cid,* Corneille, still smarting from the quarrel over the play, produced no new dramatic work for three years and spent much time observing plays and meditating on the dramatic art. The tragedy which emerged in 1640 is carefully constructed according to the rules.

The subject is the story taken from Livy of the inhuman combat fought by three Roman brothers, the Horatii, against three brothers of an Alban family closely related to them by marriage, the Curiatii, to determine whether Rome or Alba would rule in Latium. In the combat, all perish except one of the Horatii, who, when he returns expecting acclaim from Rome, finds himself confronted and challenged by his distraught sister, who had been betrothed to one of the dead Curiatii. In his anger, Horace kills his sister and it is only by special decree of the King in recognition of his great service to Rome that he is exempted from punishment. The action of the play begins just before the point of crisis and moves dynamically through peripateia to its climax at the end of the fourth act, when Horace kills Camille: once we have accepted the basic extraordinary but historical situation, the unity of time serves to tighten the action without any strain on our credibility. We observe the action from one room in the house of Horace, where the protagonists and secondary characters meet and where the news of the battle is reported; the unity of place thus ensures a logical perspective, for the audience has the same limited view of the action as the afflicted families who wait for news, and the tension of the drama is maintained by the fragmentary nature of our knowledge of the events. The action is centred on a confrontation of values which underlies the military confrontation, so ensuring the essential unity of the play, though if we are to believe Corneille himself, because of the 'double peril' to which Horace is subjected (the battle followed by the trial), the unity of action is not complete. And it is precisely this confrontation between patriotic values based on the demands of absolutism and human values based on love and family ties, which gives the play its tragic grandeur. To achieve this result, Corneille has centred his character study on the dilemma between the demands of patriotism and the demands of love which each of the protagonists has to face

and has let the major confrontation emerge from the attempts of each one to resolve this inner conflict. This approach goes well beyond the demands of the rules, but the rules provide a sub-structure of unity and concentration without which dramatic force would be lacking.

Here, then, we see tension between the demands of form, as exemplified in the principles and rules of classical theory, and the insight and imagination of a dramatist of genius. But the dramatist does not reject the theory: he interprets it freely according to his practical needs and uses it to discipline and concentrate his material in order to give it greater force.

Corneille undoubtedly had some difficulty at times in coming to terms with the rules, as he himself shows in the examinations of the individual plays published in the later part of his career, where he makes some pungent self-criticism. But in his four most celebrated plays at least, the rules lead him towards careful, disciplined selection of material and the concentration of dramatic elements that we see in *Horace.*

Corneille's younger rival Jean Racine moved significantly further in this direction. At a time when, many years after the composition of *Horace,* Corneille was using more elaborate plots, Racine saw that the essential core of the tragic experience lies in the crisis of inner conflict and the attempt to resolve it. He therefore focused attention on this element and thus moved towards greater simplicity and tightness of structure.

In the first of his major tragedies, *Andromaque* (1667), Racine presents a situation which he seems to have derived from an unsuccessful tragedy of Corneille entitled *Pertharite* (1653): a chain of unreciprocated love relationships in which a captive is threatened with the death of her child if she does not yield to the advances of her captor and a jealous woman seeks revenge on the lover who has abandoned her. In the Greek setting found for the situation by Racine, Orestes loves Hermione, who however loves Pyrrhus, king of Epirus, to whom she is betrothed; but Pyrrhus loves his Trojan captive Andromache, who however loves only the memory of her dead husband Hector and her child, whose life Pyrrhus threatens. Of this chain of unreciprocated love relationships, which Corneille had not really developed in *Pertharite,* Racine makes a chain of unresolved dilemmas, each dependent for its solution on the outcome of the next and finally on the decision of Andromache. The drama culminates in the dilemma of Hermione, who is torn between her passionate love for the unfaithful Pyrrhus and her intense anger and jealousy at his love for Andromache; when finally Pyrrhus persuades Andromache to marry him, Hermione's anger and jealousy gain the upper hand and she orders Orestes, as the price of her love, to avenge her by murdering Pyrrhus. But when Pyrrhus is dead, her anger, like that of Tristan's Herod, evaporates, and her frustrated love rebounds to plunge her into desperate remorse.

Throughout the play, Racine uses the principles of classical doctrine to concentrate the action and focus it on the study of human character and feeling. In spite of this, he did not escape the attacks of the critics, this time the admirers of the elderly Corneille, who failed to see the power of the drama. It is these critics whom he answers in the first preface to his next tragedy, *Britannicus* (1670), with which they had also found fault. . . .

[Within this preface is a] justification based on the classical principles of unity, reason and verisimilitude and the portrayal of human nature.

The extreme point of simplicity in action is reached by Racine in the play he produced at the end of 1670, *Bérénice*. In his preface, Racine sums up the action in two lines of his Latin source, Suetonius:

> *Titus reginam Berenicen, cui etiam nuptias pollicitus ferebatur, statim ab Urbe dimisit invitus invitam.*

> C'est-a-dire que Titus, qui aimait passionnément Bérénice, et qui même, à ce qu'on croyait, lui avait promis de l'épouser, la renvoya de Rome, malgré lui et malgré elle, dès les premiers jours de son empire.

The whole play is centred on the dilemma of Titus and the anguish of Bérénice as Titus decides that, for reasons of state, he must not marry the foreign queen whom he loves. Could any action be simpler? Racine justifies his approach in these terms:

> Il n'y a que le vraisemblable qui touche dans la tragédie. Et quelle vraisemblance y a-t-il qu'il arrive en un jour une multitude de choses qui pourraient à peine arriver en plusieurs semaines? Il y en a qui pensent que cette simplicité est une marque de peu d'invention. Ils ne songent pas qu'au contraire toute l'invention consiste à faire quelque chose de rien.

'Toute l'invention consiste à faire quelque chose de rien.' Again, an appeal for verisimilitude through simplicity. A little later in the same preface, Racine refers to critics who declared that such simple action could not conform to the rules of the theatre. Having asked them if they were bored, and learned that, on the contrary, they had been moved and would gladly see the play again, he asks:

> Que veulent-ils davantage? Je les conjure d'avoir assez bonne opinion d'eux-mêmes pour ne pas croire qu'une pièce qui les touche et qui leur donne du plaisir puisse être absolument contre les règles. La principale règle est de plaire et de toucher. Toutes les autres ne sont faites que pour parvenir a cette première.

Here, Racine joins Molière and Corneille in giving overriding importance to the pleasure of the audience. This is not a rejection of the rules, of which all three made use in greater or less degree, but rather an ordering of priorities and an acknowledgement that principles formulated on the basis of experience and reflection are a means to an end not a set of criteria for aesthetic or moral judgement. And in spite of the rivalry and controversy which

embittered relations between Corneille and Racine, we observe that, in the field of tragedy, Racine was in fact moving in the same direction as the young Corneille had done, though with an emphasis on greater simplicity. For Racine has perceived, as the young Corneille had done, that true tragedy emerges from the presentation of moral dilemmas and the anguish of their resolution, which are given dynamic force by the concentration of elements and the unification of action imposed by the disciplined classical form.

In the hands of mediocre poets and critics (and they were legion), the classical rules were commonly a formula for sterility. But the great dramatists of the age, while often disputing the priority and interpretation given to the rules by theorists and critics, found in the principles of classical doctrine a means of disciplining and shaping their artistic material, thus exploiting the demands of form to achieve a higher realization of that classical ideal, the portrayal of human nature. It is through this tension between inherited form and creative innovation that the classical temper, in their hands, lifts French drama to the level of great art.

Leo Lowenthal

SOURCE: "The Classical French Theater," in *Literature and the Image of Man: Communication in Society, Vol. 2,* Transaction Books, 1986, pp. 99-129.

[*In the following excerpt, Lowenthal discusses the writings of three French dramatists within the context of the emergence of the middle class during the seventeenth century.*]

...In Cervantes and Shakespeare, organized society is present only as a conditioning background; the human being who emerges sees himself as the responsible creator, willingly or unwillingly, of important segments of his own reality. He seeks to overcome the vacuum left by the disappearance of the feudal order not so much by relating himself to the new society as by searching his own nature. Society as an experience is an almost accidental meeting with other individuals, and the literature records the successes and failures of these meetings. Man is limited, of course, by his experiences and contacts with others, but these do not jell for him into an image of society.

The relation of the individual to the world at large began to take on a new character. The seventeenth century in Europe saw the gradual emergence of a struggle of a new type. The victory over feudalism became final, and the new middle class started on its path of conquest with the spread of industry and trade and the growth of new urban cultural institutions. The political framework in which this class appeared, however, was still that of an absolute monarchy which continued to surround itself with an aristocratic coterie.

Against this background of politico-economic stabilization and struggle a new social consciousness arose. We find that the tensions displayed in literature are no longer merely those within the person; they are increasingly those of the self-conscious relation of man to his society. The long process of middle-class socialization had begun. The French theater in the seventeenth century admirably illustrates the various facets of this process. In Corneille's drama, man adapts himself by subordinating his personal desires and claims to the exigencies of the state; the subordination resolves his tensions and conflicts and becomes the true path of his self-realization. Racine's drama portrays, on the other hand, an irreconcilable conflict between the individual and the power apparatus, and his characters find no home in the absolute state. In Molière, the middle class emerges as a force in its own right; his characters feel their way into the new institutions and learn, although with reservations, to conform to the shared modes and values of middle-class life.

The theatre of Corneille is an exercise in political behavior accepting conditions of absolute monarchy. The tragedies of Racine are an exercise in middle-class behavior expressing intellectual and emotional resistance to the same social institution—the monarchy. The comedies of Molière are an exercise in behavior under conditions that demand conformity to a new social order. In Corneille the individual finds self-realization only after having adjusted to the state; in Racine, he finds it in resistance to the state; in Molière, he is again adjusted, this time into a pattern of conformism to the values of an emergent bourgeoisie. These characterizations are simplified and stand in need of qualification, but they can serve here to emphasize briefly three divergent approaches of European man to his social situation in the period of the rise of the middle class and before its final political victory.

In his studies of the final decades of the seventeenth century, Paul Hazard declared that "never was there a greater contrast, never a more sudden transition" than that from what people "held dear" in the seventeenth to what they believed in the eighteenth century [Paul Hazard, *The European Mind: The Critical Years,* 1953]. This statement is largely true for philosophy, religious beliefs and political theory. If, however, we examine closely the great trio of French playwrights, we shall find this period of transition reflected in a decidedly less sudden way. We see not only the progressive shift of psychological views but also the gradual broadening of the social space within which the dramatic action takes place. In Corneille, the upper class is by itself, in Racine it is joined by the intellectuals—the professionals and educators—and in Molière we are faced for the first time with an almost homogeneous middle-class world.

Corneille, 1606-1684

"If he were alive once more, I would make him a prince." With these words Napoleon made Corneille a contemporary of a period when the political, legal, and economic institutions of middle-class society had achieved a definitive character. The words attest to basic social traits that had persisted over a time span of almost two hundred years. In both Corneille's and Napoleon's time, central government had to combat well-organized resistance. Strictly speaking, the similarity ends here; the government of Louis XIII set out to destroy the traditional prerogatives of the old nobility, whereas the Director and Empire of Napoleon, by dissolving the Committee of Public Safety, wrote *finis* to the tendencies toward political and economic radicalism of the French Revolution.

However, while the historical situations differ, they harbor sociological similarities. When Corneille wrote *Cinna,* a play dealing with the suppression of a political conspiracy against Augustus, he was rewarded, if not with the post-hoc generosity of Napoleon, at least with Richelieu's permission to marry a titled lady. It thus would appear that ruling groups more than 150 years apart identified Corneille with something more than mere poetical whims; the question of the social relevance of his work has been answered by persons of far-reaching influence. And if Richelieu and Napoleon did not find that the *dramatis personae* of Corneille realistically typified the actions of their contemporaries, they at least wished this were the case.

Public Power and the Individual

At first sight the major works of Corneille appear to contain motivations and conflicts similar to those found in Shakespeare. The story of *Horace* reminds us of *Romeo and Juliet;* the story of *Cinna* is thematically and even chronologically very close to *Julius Caesar;* in *The Cid,* lovers whose fathers compete for honors from the crown remind us of *The Tempest's* Ferdinand and Miranda, whose fathers also were engaged in a struggle for political supremacy. However, all these similarities are more apparent than real. Shakespeare's people stand or fall with the development of their own essential being. It is not by chance that the monologue is an indispensable dramatic vehicle in almost all his plays; the actions of his characters are the outer manifestation of internal processes. Tragic endings neither condemn nor justify the social agencies that shatter the lives of Anthony or Romeo, but are the result of individually applied creative reason or its opposite: Verona stands for the foolishness of a Montague and a Capulet; Rome for the enlightened intellectuality and morality of Octavius Caesar. Even the dramatic histories of British kings make events contingent upon the individualities of the rulers, whose interactions with other individualities seem almost accidentally to create the social word. Unity, cohesion, or disorder in society proves to be nothing but unity, cohesion, or disorder in individuals, turned outward. Every event, every institution in Shakespearean drama is translatable into a psychic process of a particular individual.

But if in Shakespeare's work society reflects the individual, in Corneille's it is a reified individual who reflects society. The dynamic processes are reversed. Corneille's figures achieve stature only in institutional roles. The state gives them distinguishable contours and provides them with principles for organizing and structuring otherwise chaotic modes of reaction and behavior. Individuation is experienced—as it will tend to be in literature from now on—as socialization.

In Corneille's time, middle-class life had gained tremendous momentum, mainly as a result of the state's mercantilist policy supporting the development of industry and trade. For despite its aristocratic look, the prosperity of the absolute state depended upon the very economic gains which were bringing the middle class with its way of life and its ethos to the fore. Prior to Corneille, the problem facing the individual had been survival within an environment disrupted by the disintegration of the old order as well as by the appearance of the new. Now the problem changed radically; it was no longer one of self-orientation midway between a twilight of chaos and a dawning reconstruction, but of accommodation in one way or another to a flourishing absolute state with its rind of regal pomp and core of stable industriousness. Corneille's dramas are full of special pleading and rhetorical persuasions designed to demonstrate that acceptance of public power is both expedient and moral.

The unity and harmony of individual existence now emanates from social agencies. The process may be described in this way: the social agencies, specifically the state, force the individual to subordinate self-interest to public interest, and this public interest is ultimately experienced by him as eminently suited to his self-interest. The subtitle to *Cinna* is *The Mercy of Augustus*. The mercy of God transplanted into the psyche—an extreme consequence of Renaissance secularization—is now replanted into the state, for there is no doubt that in the play Augustus represents the state. Mercy is taken from the sphere of individual frailty and given to a trans-individual social agency with executive strength. The *raison d'état* begets its own acts of mercy whenever they serve its purpose; the individual is thus the recipient but not the source of mercy. He must learn how to internalize and reenforce these acts of the state, but the possibility of his initiating them is removed.

The State and Interpersonal Relations

Love—like mercy—is no longer in itself an ultimate creative act. Only insofar as it is compatible with and subordinate to the claims of the state, can love by a legitimate expression of the individual. The *raison d'état* must determine the consummation, or even the destruction, of intimate relationships; personal catastrophes or satisfactions amount to little as compared to the necessities of state. Thus in *Horace,* brothers, sisters, husbands, and wives, forfeit their happiness, and even life, when the state demands it. Corneille has Horace declaim:

> To die for the Fatherland is such a pleasant fate,
>   that everyone yearns for it;
> But to sacrifice what one loves for the state, to
>   enter into lists against one's other self,
> To fight the brother of one's wife, the betrothed
>   of one's sister,
> To arm oneself for the fatherland against one for
>   whose blood I'd give my life,

That is a fate worthy of a Roman.

At the end of the wars between the Albans and Romans, the only surviving protagonist is Horace, who has killed not only his brothers-in-law but also his wife; still the play does not become a tragedy of aloneness. On the contrary, he receives from the head of state these instructions:

> Live, Horace, live, great-hearted warrior.
> Your virtue will pale your fame about your
>   deed.
> Your high-spirited ardor caused your monstrous
>   crime.
> With so beautiful a cause one must take
>   whatever result follows.
> Live to love your state.

Don Roderick, the Cid, who has slain the father of his beloved Chimène, will be united in marriage with her after the bereaved daughter has observed a suitable period of mourning. While waiting, he will engage in patriotic deeds. The king addresses first Chimène and then Roderick:

> (*To Chimène:*)
> Take, if you will, a year to dry your tears.
> Meanwhile, let Roderick win new victories.
> (*To the Cid:*)
> You have destroyed the Moors upon our shores,
> Shattered their hopes, repulsed their wild
>   assaults,
> Go now and bear the war to their own land,
> Command my army, pillage their domain.
> At the very name of Cid they quake with fear;
> They call you lord and they would make you
>   king.
> But through all mighty deeds keep faith with
>   her:
> Return if possible more worthy of her;
> And make yourself so prized for your exploits
> That pride will join with love to make her yours.

There is no conflict, in the end, between duty to the state and one's own private happiness; the latter will be immensely increased, guaranteed and glorified if one behaves as a noble soldier.

The same system of values is displayed in *Cinna*. Augustus forgives Cinna, offers the former conspirator a responsible position and reunites him with his beloved Amelia—all for reasons of state. Amelia had forsworn her passion for Cinna because of his leaving the conspiracy of which she was a part; now when Augustus proposes to make Cinna her husband at the same time he nominates Cinna as Consul, Amelia responds to the offer and thus to the system of social values in these words:

> My hate is dying, that I believed immortal;
> Is dead, and in its place, a loyal heart.
> Henceforward, in stark horror of this hate,
> Ardor of service shall replace its fury.

Her hatred had been directed against Augustus for exiling her father as a political enemy; it has also included Cinna when he withdrew from the anti-Augustan conspiracy. Prior to the denouement, Amelia is torn between loyalty to her father and love. Shakespeare's Miranda, finding herself in a similar situation, resolves her conflict through her own unique and unaided decision; there is no reference to any other moving force. Corneille's Amelia has her problem solved for her by the head of the state; her decision is simply to accept the imperial decree. By her submission, the general or social rationality represented by the decree brings order and meaning into her inconsistent and mutually exclusive desires. The superior *raison d'état* becomes her *raison d'être;* she "finds herself" by obedient identification with the political system, not by self-identification.

Prospero educates Miranda in order to make his educational efforts dispensable, and to help her achieve personal autonomy. The educational impact of organized society makes Amelia its pawn forever.

Honor and the State

The Renaissance image of mankind as a community of discrete individualities has given way to the concept of a social structure that is more than the sum total of individuals within it. The reality of the state replaces the individual dream. In Corneille's drama, the acceptance of governmental coercion is internalized and becomes a voluntary act which is glorified by the name "honor." However, it would be a sociological mistake to confuse Corneille's concept of honor with that of Calderon. For the Spanish dramatist, honor is the expression of the rigid value system of feudalism, of a society that has become obsolete; Calderon would dignify an outworn pattern as a defense against the present, but the France of Corneille is a progressive nation and his work reflects the distinction quite clearly. He is thus much closer to Calderon's predecessor Lope; both were poets of the new nationalism. But Corneille places the dynamics of secular power within the individual. Its acceptance becomes a purposive act through voluntary identification of the self with the state. His idea of honor points to the need for man to adopt the morality of the state. This becomes clear in the words of Augustus to Cinna:

> My favor makes your glory, out of that
> Your power grows; that only raised you up,
> And held you there, 'tis that the Romans honor,
> Not yourself. You have no rank or power
> Except I give it you, and for your fall
> There needs but the withdrawal of my hand,
> Which is your sole support.

The words are echoed by Cinna to whom they are directed;

> Let but my duty, reborn in my heart,
> Pledge you a faith already basely broken,
> But now so firm, so far from wavering,

The very fall of heaven could not shake it.

The Cid is a particularly good example of the conflict between the new concept of honor and the old, offering a portrayal of the process of socialization called for by the absolutistic state. The first significant action of the play is a jealous outburst between the Cid's father, to whom the education of the crown prince is entrusted, and Chimène's father, who feels that he himself should have been given this distinguished task. The result is a duel between the Cid and Chimène's father; the latter is killed. The Cid has avenged his father's honor but has also embittered Chimène who now feels obliged to avenge the honor of her house. Honor at this stage reverts to the old feudal forms. It commands Chimène to avenge her father's death even in the choice of a husband, and the Cid to alienate the woman he loves. For three acts the Cid suffers this condition until he finally breaks out and declares to his father:

> Let me at least give voice to my despair;
> Which has too long been stifled by your words.
> I feel no mean regret for having served you;
> But give me back the joy this blow has cost me.
> My arm for you was raised against my love
> And by that stroke I lost my heart's desire.
> Tell me no more; I have lost all for you;
> That which I owed you, I have paid too well.

Whereupon the father retorts:

> We have one honor only. Mistresses
> Are plentiful! Love is a pleasant toy,
> But honor is a master to be served.

An impasse has been reached: Chimène cannot marry her beloved, the killer of her father; the son has to subordinate his personal wishes to the honor code of the feudal gentleman, and the father takes no interest whatsoever in the personal desires of his son. In the end, however, the play arrives at a complete reconciliation. When the principals are faced with the symbols, tasks and proclamations of the state represented by the king, a scaling down of personal interests satisfactory to all is achieved. Love, honor, and personal initiative are acceptable values—if subordinated to the state and "your king." These are the closing words of the play, directed to the Cid:

> *King:*   Rest hope upon your courage and
>   my word,
>
>   And since already you possess her
> heart,
>
>   To still that honor which cries out
> against you
>
>   Leave all to time, your valor, and
> your king.

The State as the Ego

Corneille's moral beliefs might be likened to Cartesian metaphysics. For Descartes, the process of reason meant a cognitive progress by the individual toward ever more clear and distinct perceptions of himself; for Corneille, it meant the ever more clear and distinct perceptions by the individual of the state. *The Cid,* for example, starts with a confused semi-private, semi-official situation arising from the necessity to find a tutor for the crown prince; it ends with the problems of foreign politics and military might. So long as the *raison d'état* is perceived only in terms of private interests, rationality will fail and individuals will behave erratically in their official as well as in their private undertakings; once the superiority of the state is fully acknowledged, individuals and state act in unison, and reason triumphs. It is not without significance that the initial dramatic motif of *The Cid* is the education of a future ruler.

The location of Corneille's dramatic themes in the past, particularly in Roman antiquity, also reflects a Cartesian-like concern for safety, security, and reliability. When the data of history have been sifted again and again, the residuum assumes the qualities of unquestioned fact. Past events have become established knowledge: everyone is familiar with the early Roman wars, the conspiracy of Cinna and the fights of the Spaniards against the Moors. In addition, Roman and early Spanish history contain well-known examples of governmental practice; Corneille's models were safe and acceptable for presenting exemplary lessons on the socialization of the individual in a powerful state. Everything is accessible and articulate; nothing remains doubtful.

Thus while in Shakespeare there remains an eternal doubt as to whether Utopia will ever come about or even whether Prospero, once he has returned to Milan, will put his lessons into practice, the issue in Corneille is settled once and for all. We do not know whether the next generation of Montagues and Capulets will be more enlightened or be as big fools as their fathers, but we are certain that the Cid and Chimène will pass on to their offspring what they have learned and that the conflict of the play will be forever resolved. To the extent that Corneille's individual reconciles his private life with his social duties, he has fulfilled his potentialities; the rest is not silence, as in *Hamlet,* but articulate business in the service of an hierarchized "we" that endows the "I" with meaning.

Corneille's formula for a static harmony of the individual and society is, in its way, perfect. If the actualities of the state lived up to his idealization, all would be well, and we should no doubt have arrived at the end of drama. The individual, however, came to experience his position in the absolute monarchy as a kind of moral and social restraint that could not be resolved in the abstractions of pride and honor. Corneille's solutions came to exist only for a moment in time; history added the question mark he tried so hard to eradicate from his ideal representation on the stage.

Racine, 1639-1699

Racine, too, wrote 'classical' plays. They are worlds apart, however, from those of Corneille. If one changed the costumes of Corneille's characters to the contemporary garb of his time, most of them would be indistinguishable from French royalty and high military and civilian officials. Racine, too, wrote about kings and high persons, but they had no counterparts in the France of his day. There are no similarities between Louis XIV and the Nero of *Britannicus,* the Theseus of *Phaedra* or the Pyrrhus of *Andromache.*

A most significant change Racine effected in the *dramatis personae* is the introduction of a new type of man, the tutor; he is the unofficial intellectual, a person Corneille would not have tolerated. There are other differences. Although Racine, like Corneille, goes to antiquity for his themes, he avoids imperial Rome in favor of Greek times, and the legends he draws upon do not celebrate state power but individual passion. In addition, the titles of Racine's plays are significant, being almost invariably the names of women; and women certainly did not serve as spokesmen in the male-dominated society of seventeenth-century France. Each of these differences serves to stake out the broad gulf between the two French dramatists. Racine's plays do not point to the state as the *raison d'être* of human existence. Kings rule over states that are close to unrest, sometimes even to chaos; educators moralize from a position detached from the state machinery; wom-

Portrait of Jean Racine by his son, Jean-Baptiste Racine.

en, who have no political power, become the major spokes-men for ethical viewpoints; and the Greek locales under-line the individualistic focus of the themes.

The State and Individual Self-Expression

In Corneille's drama the relations of the individual to society are shown as a successful reciprocity in a secular-ized world. In Racine, the relation breaks down; the state loses its sacred quality and becomes merely a worldly power. Moreover, it is often an obstacle to the self-real-ization of the individual who no longer accepts the state's hierarchy of values, and who can no longer reconcile his personal aspirations with those of the preordained system.

Both Corneille and Racine show us persons who rise in stature as a result of heightened self-awareness. In Cor-neille, however, the criterion for this awareness consists of deeds in the service of the state; his heroes become administrators or military leaders. In Racine, the touch-stone is language. The heroes and heroines are encour-aged by their tutors to speak out, to say what they feel. The tutors are spokesmen for freedom of expression. Social implications become apparent once the individual realizes that such free self-expression runs counter to the demands of the prevailing institutions. Racine's heroes and hero-ines do not live according to a superimposed morality—personal aspirations are acknowledged, and there is no ready solution to the conflict between individual and so-ciety. Phaedra, for example (as Racine himself says in a preface to the play), is neither entirely guilty nor entirely innocent, and individual passion is not *per se* a sin against God or man. In short, Racine's characters appear more sinned against by the social and political order, than sin-ning.

The Tutor as Intermediary

The role of the tutor serves a specific function in this reemergence of individual claims. Rarely do any of Ra-cine's *dramatis personae* make such long speeches as does Burrus, Nero's tutor, or Theramenes, the tutor of Hip-polytus, and what they have to say are not contributions to individual introspection as in the case of Shakespeare's Gonzalo. They are, directly or indirectly, bitter attacks on a social order that permits a ruler to destroy personal happiness.

Although political stratification at Racine's time closely resembles that at the time of Corneille, the moral perspec-tive has shifted radically. This shift has the effect of re-vealing the instability of the social pyramid: the tutors (to whom we may add Phaedra's nurse, Oenone) help their wards to become aware of the moral inadequacy of the state and teach them to look to themselves for their true fulfillment.

The function of the tutors is not to try to impose their own values and motives upon those they advise, but to help them break their inner silence and put their wishes into words. (Leo Spitzer has aptly characterized them as "humanistic historiographers") [Leo Spitzer, "The Récit

de Thermanène," in *Linguistics and Literary History*, 1948]. When Phaedra tries to hide from herself her in-fatuation for Hippolytus, her nurse, Oenone, warns her:

> If you must blush,
> Blush at the silence that inflames your grief.

Similarly, when Hippolytus tries to ignore his deep affec-tion for Aricia, the royal prisoner of his father, his tutor Theramenes encourages him to speak his real feelings:

> What good to act a pride you do not feel?
> If you are changed, confess it!

The numerous confessions that appear in Racine's plays reveal an important change in the image of the self from the images in Cervantes and Shakespeare. Racine's peo-ple find out for themselves that they are tremendously complicated and that a person cannot be adequately de-scribed merely in terms of reason or the lack of it. If the Renaissance (to use Jacob Burckhardt's formulation) is the age of discovery of the individual, the seventeenth century in France witnessed the birth of his psychology. Racine's people begin to learn that the individual's en-counters with his environment may activate the develop-ment of terrifying inner conflicts, but that the outer world will not in turn offer any solution for such tensions. The serene value system that posits a rational individual, whether he is autonomous as in Shakespeare or an obedi-ent citizen as in Corneille, is now breaking down under the impact of heightened social pressures. This process leads to a great increase in knowledge of the self. The noblest of all men in Racine's dramas, the guiltless and loyal Hippolytus, pronounces the breakdown of an opti-mistic image of the rational individual when he confesses his love to Aricia. He tries to "find himself," as Shakes-peare would have said, by introspection into his own nature, but the result is a negative one:

> The fruit
> Of all my sighs is only that I cannot
> Find my own self again.

He can no longer find the naive calmness on which he relied before Theramnenes helped him to be true to him-self, and he rejects his once optimistic belief that

> Reason did approve
> What Nature planted in me.

Secularization and Love

Many writers have already dealt with the influence of Jansenism and Calvinism on Racine. They have pointed out that his people are, ultimately, helpless; the heroes and heroines are exposed to sinful passions and, presum-ably, dependent on divine grace. These critics may be correct in their estimate of the religious undercurrents in Racine's work, although it remains open to what extent his late biblical dramas were an intentional concession to the hostility of the clergy. Our interest here, however, lies in the extent to which the roots of Racine's drama emerge from the subsoil of the society of his time. From this standpoint, his characters are truly individuals who are unable or unwilling to control their passions through reason, but who nevertheless are precise observers of their inner states. Whatever the validity of religious interpretations of Racine's work, it remains possible to examine these self-observations against the social background in which they take place. The process of self-articulation becomes the basic content of the drama. The characters look in vain for a way of life that would free them from their misery, and during the genesis and the interplay of the symptoms of their condition they become increasingly aware of their inner conflicts.

Love is the most important theme in Racine's drama. It appears as the great libidinal motor force of the human being, and its range extends from mere instinctual infatuation to steadfast dedication beyond death. *Andromache* could almost stand as a textbook on the subject, including the intertwinement of love and hate. Racine uses the Greek legend to display the psychological effects of a series of unrequited loves. Orestes is in love with Hermione, daughter of the beautiful Helen of Troy. Hermione, however, is engaged to and in love with Pyrrhus, the king of Epirus, who is in love with Andromache, a prisoner from the late Trojan war and the widow of Hector. Orestes is being sent by the Greek states to Pyrrhus to ask for Andromache and her young son, who are the prisoners of Pyrrhus, in order to make sure that the survivors of the Trojan royal house will not become the core of a new Troy and therefore a danger to Greece. Before the journey, Orestes thought that his "passion had been turned to hatred" but discovers when he sees Hermione that he had "never ceased to love her." Pyrrhus, who loves Andromache but is spurned by her, says of his condition:

> I tell you that the heart that can no longer
> Love passionately, must with fury hate.

Hermione, in her love for Pyrrhus, goes through a similar experience. When the nurse Cleone asks her:

> Have you not told me that you hated him?

Hermione answers:

> Hate him, Cleone? Could my pride do less,
> When he neglects my favor, given freely?
> The heart I learned to love was treacherous.
> He was too dear not to be hated now.

Orestes, bent on winning Hermione, is even willing to accept hate as a messenger of love. When he berates Hermione for wasting her affection on Pyrrhus, she answers that there is no "need" to "envy him," "unless you crave that I should hate you." But Orestes replies:

> Yes,—
> For love might spring from such a strange
> beginning.

> I whom you wish to love,—I cannot please you,
> But if you wished to hate me, only love
> Would be obeyed, and I should have your heart.

Hermione interprets him, correctly, as meaning that her hate for Pyrrhus is prompted by her love. Her concentration on this theme through five acts of the play finally brings her to the psychological state of the *crime passionel* that culminates in the words:

> I will find
> Some way to bring me close beside my foe,
> To stab the heart I could not reach with love.

The sentiment is remarkably similar to that of Phaedra when she is thwarted in her passion for Hippolytus:

> My hands are ripe for murder,
> To spill the guiltless blood of innocence.

Pyrrhus, Orestes, Hermione (and Phaedra) are all in love with those who do not love them and experience the counterforce of hate which the situation awakens in them. The only unambivalent lover is Andromache who is lost in the memory of Hector, a dead man.

Racine's people are aware of the relaxing of rational control that passion brings about. The tutor of Britannicus comments: "Love never waits for reason"; Orestes says at one point: "The voice of reason only wearies me"; and Phaedra declares: "Now you must serve my madness, not my reason." Such examples—and they could be multiplied—do not represent a revival of the old Stoic view of the opposition of reason and passion; these qualities, rather than adding up to a formula, give rise to personal insight: psychic conflicts are raised to the level of awareness. Racine's people are shown making the kinds of discoveries about themselves which become increasingly typical in middle-class literature. When Phaedra is reminded by Hippolytus, who has spurned her love for him,

> That Theseus is my father and your husband, . .

she answers:

> Why should you fancy I have lost remembrance
> And that I am regardless of my honor?

then adds almost immediately:

> I am not half so hateful to your sight
> As to myself.

The same self-awareness is as true for guilt as for love. Phaedra tells Hippolytus that he should not think:

> That in those moments when I love you most
> I do not feel my guilt.

Later she reasserts, "I know my madness well," in much the same way as Aricia experiences her affection for

Hippolytus, her political enemy, as "the maddening draught of love." The very fact that madness and guilt become almost synonymous signifies the ascension of personal insight over a schematized system of absolute values. (Corneille would have had a neat solution to the love of Hippolytus for Aricia.) Theramenes, Hippolytus' tutor, asks him "Why should you fear a guiltless passion?" and Hippolytus himself reflects that "surely innocence need never fear," and that "the gods are just." But, in the end, his mental turmoil gives the lie to these comforting and reasonable words.

In his character portrayals Racine emerges as a depth psychologist. Besides the hate-love involvement, he shows us a number of more subtle effects which sadism and cruelty may have on love relationships. Nero, who is in love with Junia, the bride of his enemy Britannicus, makes her a prisoner in order to separate her from her lover and be close to her himself. He finds he loves

> The very tears that I had caused to flow.
> And sometimes, yet too late, I asked forgiveness,
> And often found my sighs would end in threats.
> And thus I have been nursing this new passion.

Nero takes pleasure in observing the suffering Britannicus and tells his old tutor:

> I know quite well my rival has her heart.
> I'll have my joy in making him despair!
> How pleasant is his anguish to my fancy,—
> And I have seen him doubting if she loves him!
> I'll follow her. My rival waits for you,
> And he will vent his fury. Go, torment him
> With new suspicions. Make him pay most dearly
> For boons that he despises. I will witness
> The tears she sheds for him!

Theramenes helps Hippolytus to understand that his love for Aricia is prodded by the very fact of his father's hate for the young princess. The tutor says to his master:

> His hatred kindles you to burn, rebellious,
> And only lends his enemy new charms.

In *Britannicus* again, Racine, in another surprisingly modern touch, notes the extremes of ambivalence in the mother-son relationship when Nero's mother anticipates his latent murderous intent:

> Deep in our secret heart I know you hate me.
> You would be free from gratitude's hard yoke.

Poet of Personal Rebellion

Racine is the poet of personal rebellion. His people begin to question the relationship between the *raison d'état* and their own legitimate concerns. The mood of their resistance to their social world is not such a far cry from the revolutionary temper of the eighteenth century as might at first appear. Even the theology, of the secular plays at least, is mainly negative. In passage after passage the gods

are cursed; without them and their human counterparts in the state apparatus the individual might, we are made to feel, have a chance. While seventeenth-century man is of course not yet aware of a potential revolutionary situation, Racine's people herald this awareness in their efforts to arrive at a new understanding of themselves.

Public affairs mean little to Racine's characters. Pyrrhus is primarily interested in his own passion; his responsibility for the security of the state or toward his allies in Greece is comparactively irrelevant. He threatens to kill Andromache's son unless she reciprocates his love; if she yields, he will allow the boy, who is also the son of the old archenemy Hector, to live. Similarly, when Phaedra is made to believe that her husband has died and that the Athenians want her to reign in the name of her infant son, she uses this political event for personal ends, as a lure to win the love of Hippolytus (who had also been a candidate for the succession). She instructs Oenone:

> Go, and on my behalf, touch his ambition,—
> Dazzle his eyes with prospects of the crown. . . .
> He shall control both son and mother;—try
>   him,—
> Try every means to move him, for your words
> Should meet more favor than my own could
>   find.
> Urge him with groans and tears,—say Phaedra's
>   dying,
> Nor blush to speak in pleading terms with him.
> My last hope is in you,—do what you will,
> I'll sanction it,—the issue is my fate!

All psychological tactics and all political means are permissible to reach a goal dictated by personal passion. Pyrrhus and Phaedra are extreme examples, but it seems equally clear that the goal for Britannicus is not Rome but Junia, for Hippolytus not Athens but Aricia, and for Orestes it is not the peace of Greek citizens but Hermione. Orestes, when he tries to forget his love for Hermione by taking on political missions, tells his friend Pylades:

>   I hoped
>   to find
> Freedom from other cares, in this new work,
> I hoped that, if my strength came back to me
> My heart would lose remembrance of its love.

But this act of submission to the state does no good, and he adds:

>   But soon enough
> I found my lovely persecutor taking
> Her old place in my heart.

In Corneille's dramas, when political responsibility falls on the shoulders of one of the heroes he rises to the occasion and eventually frees himself from his individual desires. But in Racine the morality of the state has ceased to be internalized. Phaedra says:

> I reign?—And shall I hold the rod of empire,

When reason can no longer reign in me?
When I have lost control of mine own senses?

Another woman, Junia, in *Britannicus,* pronounces the estrangement of the state from genuine human morality in these words:

Perhaps my frankness may not be discreet,
But never have my lips belied my heart.
Since I was not at courts, I had not thought
That I had need to learn dissimulation!

Speaking to Britannicus she proclaims the need for finding a human home—a home for lovers outside organized society as it exists:

Judge not his heart by yours, for you and he
Pursue two different courses. I have known
Nero and his court but one short day,
Yet I have learned, if I dare speak of it,
How different are their words from what they
　think;
How little mouth and heart agree in them;
How lightly they betray their promises.
How strange a dwelling, this, for me and you.

The Concept of Fate and the Indictment of the Gods

In the beginning of *Andromache,* Orestes, coming unexpectedly upon his friend Pylades, thanks his "fortune" for this good turn; but, soon after, he asks himself, "Who knows what fate is guiding me?" Later he says, "I can never now what fate has ordered." And, again, when giving a report of his adventures since he returned from Troy, he speaks of his "persecuting fates." When Pyrrhus confesses his love to Andromache, he says of her and Hermione: "Fate brought you both alike into Epirus." This idea of fate is quite different from that in Shakespeare, where fate dissolves into the actions of people and becomes human history. For Shakespeare the world is man's home, sometimes his hell, but "fate" is always a consequence of individual actions, moral or immoral, rational or irrational.

Racine's introduction of the idea of fate is not just a relapse into mythology, but reflects a comparatively open society in which people meet by chance and are brought into unpredictable situations by political, social, and economic mobility. Usually, fate appears in a context of governmental affairs; state business is full of traps that can spring on the individual; even the leaders sometimes become victims of these traps or at least react ambivalently to a social order that appears to impose insensible restraints. The person can only see himself as a victim of the blind chances of a system he did not create. When Pyrrhus, a ruling king, explains to Hermione his love for Andromache, he, paradoxically, becomes the spokesman for the individual caught between his own needs and the demands of the state:

My heart accuses me. Its voice is strong.
I cannot make a plea I know is false.

I wed a Trojan woman. Yes, I own
The faith I promise her was given you.
I could remind you that our father made
These ties at Troy; that we were never asked,
Nor were we ever bound by any choice
Or love, that was our own. But I submitted.
It is enough for me.
　　　　　　　　　　　　　　Until
　　this day
I thought my oath would hold in place of love.
Yet love has won, and by a fatal turn,
Andromache has gained a heart she hates.

The gods as well as the exigencies of the state are blamed for such conflicts. When Phaedra reveals her love to Hippolytus she says:

　　　　　　　　　　The gods will bear me
　　witness,—
They who have lit this fire within my veins,—
The gods who take their barbarous delight
In leading some poor mortal heart astray!

When Theseus finds that both his wife and son have killed themselves, he cries out:

The gods are ruthless. They have served me
　well,
And I am left to live a life of anguish
And of great remorse.

The dying words of Hippolytus to his tutor are: "The gods have robbed me of a guiltless life." Similarly, Phaedra tells her husband with her last breath:

The gods had lit a baleful fire in me,
And vile Oenone's cunning did the rest.

These unhappy people, having lived all their lives within what seemed to be a well-ordered external and spiritual world, are finally driven to realize that this world and its deities are not reliable. The cursing of the gods is, to be sure, ambiguous and does not differentiate between a rejection of social forces and the incapacity to solve one's own internal difficulties. This ambiguity suggests the intimate struggles of Racine and other intellectuals of his time, beset as they were by doubts about the stability of both their inner and outer worlds. This doubt is patently present when the gods are blamed for one's own passions, and it emerges unequivocally when they are held accountable not only for personal tragedy but for a bad state of society as such. In a most telling passage, Orestes sums up the state of the world in these words:

When have the gods been so perverse before,
Hunting the guiltless down, with crime
　unpunished?
I turn my eyes, and everywhere I see
Troubles and sorrows that condemn their justice.

Corneille's positive theology of the state has given way

to Racine's negation of theology by the individual. In the future man must look for other and newer forms of society. If the struggle of Racine's protagonists against power lacks the rationale of a planned campaign, it is nonetheless a declaration of war. Who remains alive when the drama comes to an end? Lonely kings whose wives, fiancées and children have died, and lonely innocent youths near insanity; on the one hand, the brutal Nero, the duped Theseus, the frustrated Pyrrhus—on the other, the heartbroken Aricia and Orestes. The glory of Corneille's empire does not find continuation in Racine, and only broken idols remain to take its place. The sadness of this dramatic configuration is the sadness of separation; historically it sets the tone of the prologue to the drama of emotional emancipation from an aging political structure. Racine gives us our first insight into the dynamics of the men who are about to write those enlightened treatises of the eighteenth century which will denounce the value system of the absolutistic monarchy.

Molière, 1622-1673

Dominant Motifs and Philosophical Assumptions

"Experience teaches me," Molière has one of his protagonists say with pride in *L'Avare,* and we soon discover that the familiar adage has a very precise meaning. It is the advice often given to the young man to learn to adapt to the world for his own good; it is as well the motto of the tradesman learning how to get along with his customers. "Experience," we find, definitely means the outside world and particularly the social world; we are taught only by closely observing it, by keeping a watchful eye on its mores and demands. Inner experience appears to be excluded. In fact, Molière intends this exclusion; one who listens too well to his own reason or his own passion is precisely one who does not learn from "experience." The statement also implies a special definition of the world itself. The world one learns about from experience is an evolving structure; it is no longer a ready-made idea as in Corneille, and we can find out about it only by attending to its changing qualities. The expression, we begin to see, sums up an entire morality and way of life: in three words it gives us the rationale of conformism.

Earlier we related Corneille's moral beliefs to the rationalism of Descartes by equating the state with the Cartesian ego. According to Corneille, the individual proceeds step by step to a position of secure knowledge by overcoming any uncertainties he may harbor about the rational essence of an absolutist society; the self-evidence of the rationality of the state is in effect a social extension of the self-evident rationality of Descartes' individual. For the philosophical counterpart of Molière we should have to look to empiricism, to a philosophy that found its ultimate certainty, not in innate ideas, but in sensation or the perception of discrete qualities, which have no guaranteed organization. The progress from Corneille to Molière indeed parallels closely the progress from rationalist metaphysics to empiricism then taking place. Corneille's protagonists take the state and the traditions of absolute monarchy for granted; a society thus grounded

assumes an *a priori* and secure rationality. Molière's people, on the other hand, take nothing for granted but what they can observe and test. Experience is the teacher.

Molière for a time was a student of the philosopher Gassendi, an early forerunner of empiricism. In a famous philosophic exchange, Descartes sent to Gassendi, among others, his *Meditations* with a request for critical comments. Gassendi replied in a long letter that concludes with the following remarks:

> These, my good Sir, are the observations that occurred to me in connection with your *Meditations.* I repeat that you ought not to give yourself any thought about them, since my judgment is not of such moment as to deserve to have any weight with you. For as, when some food is pleasant to my palate, I do not defend my taste, which I see is offensive to others, as being more perfect than anyone else's; so, when my mind welcomes an opinion which does not please others, I am far from holding that I have hit upon the truer theory. I think that the truth is rather this—that each enjoys his own opinion; and I hold that it is almost as unjust to wish everyone to have the same belief, as to want all people to be alike in the sense of taste; I say so, in order that you may hold yourself free to dismiss everything that I have said as not worth a straw, and to omit it altogether. It will be enough if you acknowledge my strong affection for you, and do not esteem as nought my admiration for your personal worth. Perhaps some matter has been advanced somewhat inconsiderately, as is only too likely to happen when one is expressing dissent. Any such passage which may occur, I wholly disavow and sacrifice; pray blot it out, and be assured, that I have desired nothing more than to deserve well of you and to keep my friendship with you quite intact.

The passage is quoted at length because it is in many ways a very remarkable document. The philosophic exchanges of the time tended toward extraordinary bitterness; among them this letter is an astounding and exceptional example of tolerance. No adherent of Descartes, Spinoza, or Leibnitz could have written it. The remarks anticipate the concepts of common sense and of compromise in the era of liberalism, and they highlight an attitude that Molière was to take up and develop in his plays.

In his ethics, Gassendi considered the end of human existence to be a state of beatitude that results from a maximum of pleasure and a minimum of misery. Virtue consists of moderation, the absence of extremes, and is fostered by prudence, temperance, fortitude, and justice. Anyone familiar with Molière's plays will feel that these doctrines sound like abstracts of his work. The plays announce no absolute truth. Except for the Misanthrope, no one fights to the bitter end for principles. The dynamics consist of efforts to arrive at an equilibrium in human affairs. The pervading atmosphere is one of optimism and the equilibrium is usually achieved; some people get what they want most, and those who do not (omitting outright scoundrels and the Misanthrope) still are not left in misery at the end of the fifth act.

The analysis of Molière meets with a peculiar difficulty. In the works previously analyzed, it was relatively simple to categorize the value systems of the persons portrayed. But rigid yardsticks are lacking in Molière's people, who are remarkably mundane and who regulate their lives in an experimental, almost pragmatic way. Their orientation shifts as the situation demands it, and they have a multiplicity of motives generic to a pluralist society. What we see is a small aspect of individual behavior—a glimpse of the reality of a highly mobile society—observed through the artist's eyes for the one or two hours the action of the play requires.

The Comedy of Social Tensions

With the exception of the Misanthrope, there is not a single person in Molière's plays who claims the right and the responsibility to create the world in the image of his reason as did the figures of Shakespeare and Cervantes. A completely new tone is evident. Except for a light touch of ritualized deference, no major figure in Molière feels in any way motivated by affairs and ideologies of the state, and except for the Misanthrope no person goes into mourning and despair as a result of alienation from the established mores of society. The characters refer to their concrete experience with the world as a justification for their actions; they even play games that create a laboratory for empirical observation for those who need it. There are no longer such coercive or violent forces as in the literature we have previously discussed. Middle-class society is entering a period of common sense and adjustment.

But the adjustment is not easy. The middle-class individual learns his lessons painfully. Molière's protagonists find themselves in far more difficult social situations than do the heroes and heroines of Shakespeare, Corneille, and Racine. Since they lack any final principle of justification in themselves, they must learn the lessons their society has to offer and for which they have little prior guidance. Tragedy, we begin to see, is only possible if there is at least a potential choice between the ways of the world and the self. If adaptation is shown as difficult but necessary—its manner of achievement perhaps unknown but at the same time the only possible solution—we are in the realm of comedy. We are also in the realm of anxiety, wherein even suicide, as in Racine's *Phaedra*, would be no resolvement and would most often be merely ridiculous. For Molière's people even a noble defeat is out of the question.

The Intermediaries

The tutors and other intermediary persons in Molière's plays differ radically from their counterparts in Racine. In the latter, they serve as spokesmen who mediate between the protagonists and their own inner natures; they have no importance in their own right. In Molière's plays, the intermediaries are themselves protagonists and are the friends or close relatives of the persons they advise. Chrysalde is the friend of Arnolphe; Cléante is the brother-in-law and adviser of Orgon; Philinte is the friend of

Alceste. The advisers are never simply catalysts as in Racine; they give outright information and even interfere by direct action where they believe it is needed.

The intermediaries all talk like disciples of Gassendi. They preach moderation and a measured degree of hedonism; they are spokesmen of a reasonably regulated middle-class life, giving duty and pleasure each its due. These advisers are on good terms both with social reality and with the individuals to whom they are close, and by their good offices they bring their friends to similarly good terms. If they reject absolutes of virtue or vice, it is not because they have anything against these positions per se; they reject them merely as impediments to good-natured understanding and to the harmonious conformity of the social group. The intermediary figures might well be looked on as model personalities for Molière's time and as prototypes of the era he anticipates. They symbolize the Middle Way, mediation, and compromise, and they pronounce and practice social adaptation and adjustment as the highest virtues.

These mediating figures are central to Molière's work, and the manner in which they are portrayed is of considerable importance. They are never mere colorless bystanders and their behavior is never immoral. Their key motif is the avoidance of any extreme action. They are, in short, *bourgeois* in more than one sense of the world. Cléante warns Orgon, who is victimized by Tartuffe almost to the point of complete ruin:

> You exaggerate again! You never preserve moderation
> in anything. You never keep within reason's bounds;
> and always rush from one extreme to another!

Chrysalde warns the aging Arnolphe, who is making a fool of himself by trying to wed a young girl:

> To behave well under these difficulties, as in all else,
> a man must shun extremes.

Philinte, the friend of the Misanthrope, tries to impress upon him that:

> Good sense avoids all extremes, and requires us to be
> soberly rational.

These interventions sound, of course, like philistine righteousness, but to interpret their function as humourous would be to misconstrue the dramatic intent; it is not the interveners but the people they are trying to help who become objects of ridicule.

Individual Possibilities and Social Limitations

Molière's protagonists illustrate very specifically the social change that has taken place—the transition from a tradition-bound to an open society which does not prevent its members from engaging in the relatively free development of their idiosyncrasies. True, Molière's highly eccentric types emerge as caricatures and are ridiculed; nevertheless, these extreme cases of behavior are not suppressed by an absolute and universally accepted moral code. If he wants to make an interest in his own health the center of his life, no social agency prevents the Malade Imaginaire from doing so. The Miser can if he wishes focus his whole life on the accumulation of money. The Bourgeois Gentilhomme can spend his money aping the aristocratic style of life without interference from any authority. Finally, Tartuffe, the materialist hypocrite who cloaks his appetites with ascetic virtue, and Alceste, the obsessional moralist who tries to force his precepts on everyone in his environment, are headed for opposite poles of the individualist franchise.

But such apparent liberty is deceptive: if there is less institutionalized coercion, there is certainly no less social pressure. If these people are odd, it is because society sees them as odd or because they fail to understand social reality, and not because there is any individual principle that may be worthy or entirely natural in its own right. Alceste is a Don Quixote who tends to become ridiculous. Man is no longer alone; at the very moment he challenges the reality and reasonableness of the world around him, he condemns himself to passivity, to comic ineffectuality. The more the protagonists maximize their individuality and the farther they remove themselves from the common sense represented by the intermediaries, the farther removed they find themselves from the productive center of human affairs. The intermediaries, on the other hand, accept the normal vicissitudes of social life as the boundaries of a space within which they can develop themselves and fulfill their desires. The pseudoindividualists (since they are caricatures, it is hard to think of them as true individuals) do not meet with heroic failure, which was the fate of Don Quixote and which almost befell Prospero; they are not destroyed but are ignominiously cast aside, left to their own absurdities. Molière's "radicals" are not tragic heroes whose memory is kept alive as a symbol of an ideal or a never-ending task; they are simply consigned to oblivion while the main stream of society goes on about its business. (The Misanthrope remains the special case.)

Moral Experimentalism

Certain basic trends in the relations of the individual to society remain constant: the world is not something given as in the Middle Ages but requires from man an act of continual production; the way in which man should behave is not prescribed by a set of inherited traditions but must be tried out by men themselves. However, these acts of creation and experiment are no longer conceived as the prerogative and responsibility of an unique individual, but as the efforts of socialized persons who act within a framework of consensus and whose behavior is intimately geared to the mechanism of social approval or disapproval.

When Molière uses the word *decorous* he is not referring simply to politeness and good manners; what he has in mind is, broadly, the individual's capacity for right conduct within the sphere of collective conduct. The decorous individual conforms sympathetically and successfully within the social pattern. This is not to say that the display of good form is not in itself of importance as the outward flourish of culture and breeding; but, more essentially, *décor* may be interpreted as the symptom and symbol for a new order in human affairs conceived of as the result of continuous consensus in behavior.

The world has become social practice. Orgon, the victim of Tartuffe, stops being his victim once he has decided to "judge by appearances." True, as he speaks these words he is mistaken, since he believes his son and not Tartuffe to be the real villain; but, when his family helps him to witness a considerably larger piece of reality in observing his own wife's attempted seduction by Tartuffe, he is cured. We see the would-be gentleman of *Le Bourgeois Gentilhomme* being cheated by the worthless nobleman; if he were in the position of the audience to see it (or could be made to), he would be cured of his folly. There are no inner turmoils; everything is clear as day. We the audience have the answers the people on the stage would have if they knew as much as we, or if they looked at what was happening as realistically as we do. Molière gives *us* the reality, and whenever the protagonists appear ridiculous it is because they do not or cannot see it.

If they cannot see it for themselves, they are often made to see it in experimental situations. There is a considerable difference between the experiments of Shakespeare and Molière. In Shakespeare they are an arrangement for proving the individual and his responsibility to himself; interaction with others does not deny or weaken this autonomy. The truly important phenomena reside in the inner life, and outer events serve only to confirm them.

In Molière, experiment has a radically different connotation. As the reality of middle-class society is acted out in his plays, the experiments force this reality to the attention of his deluded protagonists. The world is seen as consisting of a rapid series of happenings that are as empirical as the middle-class world is in its daily practice, and the quick give-and-take of his people have made his comedies a pleasure for three hundred years. The extremist protagonists obtrude themselves from this background by their lack of ambience, and the experiments serve to show them their place. Perhaps rather than "experiments" one should say "tricks," since they are in the nature of jokes with, however, the serious purpose of helping the extremists to gain insight into the median reality of things. (The tricks are, in fact, often arranged by the intermediaries, who see more of the real from their central vantage point than the off-center, half-blinded protagonist can.) In every case, the trick tells us that if there is no absolute truth, there is always some pragmatic truth that can be found out empirically.

In *The High Brow Ladies* socially ambitious girls swoon at lackeys when the latter are dressed as aristocrats. Orgon is made to hide under the table and watch the scoundrel Tartuffe flirt with his wife. The faked theft of the Miser's cashbox proves that Harpagon is only too glad to trade the pleasures of love for the rewards of monetary possessions. All the tricks demonstrate that moral reality is pragmatic and observable and that the values of men are realized truly and exclusively by their actions. At the same time, the tricks have a very specific societal connotation: they are the result of joint decisions. In none of them do we find a Prospero or a Don Quixote who keep to themselves or find in themselves the reasons for their experimentation. In *The Miser* it is a plot of the children-in-law and their lovers; in *Tartuffe* the trick is the combined effort of Orgon's brother-in-law, the children, the wife, and the maid; in *The High-Brow Ladies* there is an agreement between the two lovers, with La Grange expressing the moral thus:

> We will play them such a trick as shall show them their folly and teach them to distinguish a little better the people they have to deal with.

While the individual seems now to have a multitude of possible ways of behaving, society restrains and limits these possibilities. Molière's plays define these limits by asserting the virtues of discrimination, self-restraint, moderation, and common sense within a social structure that does not impose, so to speak, built-in limitations of its own. In marriage, for example, all combinations of persons seem to be possible. In *The Miser,* Harpagon, the tightwad, wants to marry Mariane who is in love with Cléante, Harpagon's son; Valère's father Anselme wants to marry Elise, the daughter of Harpagon, who is in love with Valère. Similar combinations occur in *Tartuffe* and to an almost absurd degree in *The Misanthrope.* But the resolution always sharply delimits these ambitions and is never absurd. The extremists are shown up as unrealists, the young people are united, and the intermediaries emerge as the true heroes who sometimes, as in *The Misanthrope,* gain personal advantage from their common sense.

The ability to adopt different social roles is also shown to be considerable; the people are able to change roles with astounding ease. The scoundrel Tartuffe appears as a preaching moralist; the upper-class Valère poses as a steward; the woodcutter Sganarelle in *The Physician in Spite of Himself (Le Médecin Malgré Lui)* pretends to be a physician; the bourgeois merchant Jourdan trains to become a gentleman of parts. Yet in the end everyone finds himself limited to the role which is appropriate for him in the context of social reality.

The King and the Bourgeois at Home

The comedies obviously presuppose an urban society. Role-playing, trick-playing, a diversity of social contacts, the interplay of the various strata of society—all these characteristics are possible only in cities. The miser, the hypochondriac, the hypocrite would have no field of action if it were not for the wide possibility of anonymous contacts. Scapin, in *Les Fourberies de Scapin,* can only hope to escape from the consequences of his frauds by fleeing to an anonymous crowd. The very possibility of translating the Misanthrope's moral programs into social action ends at the moment Alceste turns his back on the city and retires to the country.

The comedies show very specifically the exigencies of life in an open and mobile society. The aristocrats who come on the scene are shown in a realistic setting, and have hardly any social intercourse with the middle classes. The middle classes furnish the bulk of the protagonists and it is always their ethos that is by far the most influential. The servants, who are accepted partners in the tricks and games, display an astounding amount of middle-class knowledge. While the servants have no real life of their own, they bolster up the atmosphere of the plays and form part of the urban collectivity.

In none of the comedies does the monarch enter the scene. By and large, the people are left to their own affairs. Only when some business seems to get completely out of hand, as in *Tartuffe,* does a representative of high authority appear, but his intervention has no political meaning: Tartuffe turns out to be a criminal and it can be assumed that any high tribunal in France would have prevented his actually carrying out his fraud—while an executive act solves the dilemma of the play, still the king himself remains invisible. The absolute power of the state is no longer the dispenser of moral values as in Corneille, nor the stumbling block to individual development as in Racine. In Molière the image of the state is reduced to a mere means of keeping the affairs of men in manageable shape. In his comedies the bourgeois individual lives, emotionally if not institutionally, under a political order whose prime articles are the virtues of human interaction and the necessity of a middle course. The greatest praise the King's officer can bestow on the monarch is to endow him with middle-class qualities:

> Blessed with great discernment, his lofty soul looks clearly at things; it is never betrayed by exaggeration, and his sound reason falls into no excess.

Molière's plays do not exalt the virtues of family life as the sermonizing novels of eighteenth-century England will in a succeeding generation, but they nonetheless contain the family morality in essence. There are many instances of marital upsets in the plays: Elmire has trouble with Orgon when he seems to be forsaking his family for Tartuffe; the wife of the would-be gentleman who is eager to acquire a titled mistress does not have an easy time of it; and, on a lower level, Sganarelle, the woodcutter, has spats with his wife Martine, and Jacqueline, the nurse, has trouble with her husband Lucas, the servant. But husband and wife are never locked in a tragic struggle, and the defects that do arise in marriages are remedied before the plays end. In fact, the last act usually brings the young couples together as the final happy solution to the troubles that have been depicted—in short, the happy ending, modern middle-class style, according to which the consummation of marriage leads to unqualified bliss.

Middle-Class Optimism

In the framework of Molière's comedies, death has no place. Such a solution, when it is ventured at all, becomes material only for a joke. As Mariane threatens suicide after her father announces his intention to force her into

LE MISANTROPE

Engraving by Brissart for an edition of Molière's works (1682).

marriage with Tartuffe, her maid Dorine answers ironically:

> Very well. That is a resource I did not think of; you have only to die to get out of trouble. The remedy is doubtless admirable. It drives me mad to hear this sort of talk.

The fool Orgon, in his devotion to Tartuffe, engages in such absurdities as saying to his brother-in-law:

> I could see brother, children, mother, and wife die, without troubling myself in the least about it.

Not even the Misanthrope seriously considers suicide even though he is the only figure in all the plays who could come to a tragic end without appearing absurd.

We are at the height of middle-class optimism. Two hundred years later, an audience will feel self-conscious at the depiction of the sacrifices an individual must make on the alter of conformity, and will force Ibsen to change the ending of *A Doll's House* that had Nora close the door on her conformist husband. In the age of Molière, the Mis anthrope's friends felt they should go after him and bring

him back to his senses, bring him back from his "savage," "philosophical spleen" into the life of "ordinary customs" where we "torment ourselves a little less about the vices of our age" and are "a little more lenient to human nature."

But even this attitude of optimism is not without its implications of difficulty and instability. The values of conformity contain their own limitations and are precariously dependent upon the social climate. Only in *The Misanthrope* did Molière come close to an explicit rendering of the less optimistic side of the relation of his individuals to the society around them. The issue of Alceste's struggle must have been pitifully ambiguous for Molière. At bottom, Alceste is made to appear quite right in laying bare social hypocrisy; on the other hand, he shows himself as something of a fool for trying so hard. To his creator as well as to the spectator, Alceste is the comic underdog who awakens sympathy. Molière seems to express the concern of the intellectual that as society tends toward the stabilization of its mores and institutions, it becomes increasingly difficult for the creative individual to express himself and defend his individual claims. Molière's problem can easily become, and without much shifting of the terms, one not of adaptation but of alienation.

It may seem odd that Molière should emerge as the poet of middle-class life when, after all, he was part of a flourishing absolutistic state. French monarchy had perhaps never seemed to secure, and European aristocracy still had a long history of political and social privileges ahead of it. Nonetheless the assumption that underlies the plays is the desirability of an integrated society of the middle-class type; more than that, Molière takes for granted that the value system of such a society is already an achieved reality. He takes us beneath the surface facts of political history and shows us the everyday ethos of his time, a reality that is not just an official pronouncement or an extraordinary event. Long before the middle class could think of asking for political power, it had laid a firm hold on the everyday reality of life. It might even be said that this class could more thoroughly go about the business of making everyday reality its own by not worrying about political power. Molière was the reporter of this time of "settling in." He stands at a social crossroad: he sprang from a past of Renaissance individualism; he saw this individualism sharply curtailed in his own time by new social controls; and he sounded a note of prediction for the time when the middle class was to make the world its own on all socially relevant levels.

TRAGEDY

Maurice Baudin

SOURCE: "The People in Seventeenth Century French Tragedy," in *Modern Language Notes,* Vol. LII, No. 11, November, 1937, pp 475-81.

[*In the essay that follows, Baudin discusses the depiction of popular sentiment in seventeenth century French tragedy in relation to the changing political atmosphere of the time.*]

[Cardinal] Richelieu and Louis XIV established an order in which the people had no voice; accordingly, in the theater, public opinion, a counterpart to tyranny, was no more than a relic of another age that had become a cliché. Like obsolete tyranny, emancipation may tempt the skill of a du Ryer or a Corneille, but does not engage his convictions. Such, I believe, is the consensus of modern criticism. With due regard to the history of popular assertiveness, the temper of the government, and the persuasion of the dramatists, I submit that the tragedy of the XVIIth century embodies a new notion of the people.

Its appraisal of the people's significance is not uniform with all authors, or consistent in every play. It contains, for example, "Il faut pour être aimé régner trop mollement," "pour quiconque arrive au (trône) l'opinion publique est toujours une preuve," a speech praising Rome's sense of gratitude and deriding Roman popularity . . . with words and actions to justify all verdicts. Varied as they are, and confounding usurpers and tyrants with rightful kings, maxims and episodes invest the alien cliché with suggestions shocking to French audiences, which, says d'Aubignac, "ne *veulent* point croire que les Roys puissent estre mechans, ni souffrir que leurs Sujets, quoy qu'en apparence maltraittez, touchent leurs Personnes sacrées, ny se rebellent contre leur Puissance" [*La Pratique du Théâtre,* (1657)].

Popular clamors are not actually represented on the stage, and when voiced are not reported by a spokesman of the people. The absence of the people does not, however, annul its rôle, and can hardly be said, as Faguet has it, to have made the French historical drama inferior to its Greek models. *Athalie,* in which "cette absence du peuple est . . . bien sensible," is not the repertory of the XVIIth century; and in *Athalie* the inertness of the people helps Racine portray a fanatical Joad. But Faguet also remarked that the Greek people "s'agite autour du drame plutôt qu'il n'y agit." I propose to show that the people of French tragedy participates in the action—is reported as participating, which, for my purpose, is sufficient.

Greek drama had limited the scope of public opinion. A reprimand for Œdipus, a warning to Agamemnon reveal no serious intrusion; a show of bitterness toward Orestes is kept within bounds by an administrative routine,

> . . . if one gently yield him to their stress . . .
> Their storm might spend its force. When lulls
> the blast,
> Lightly thou mightest win thy will of them.

The Latin play *Octavia* marks a departure in political drama with an outbreak provoked by an emperor's private life. Wondering why he may not change wife as other men do, Nero learns that "the people's grief could scarce endure such marriage" on the part of one who,

being the greatest, owes the highest example. The revolt, however, is short-lived and futile.

The French Renaissance dramatized power as an enigma which baffles initiative; witness the discomfiture of the crowd whose enthusiasm is a maneuver of Satan. Seventeenth-century tragedy professes a political faith based on reason and experience (Lanson). Seneca's "Regi tuenda maxime regum est salus" is its motto. But interpretations differ. If safeguarding kingship is a king's prerogative, popular respect, it is argued, measures the accomplishment, and subjects are not bound beyond their respect. The mystery of the throne has given place to a mystery of the state, that is, in de Retz's words, a silence "dans lequel on ensevelit, en obéïssant presque toujours aveuglement aux Rois, le droit que l'on ne veut croire avoir de s'en dispenser que dans les occasions où il ne seroit pas même de leur service de leur plaire." When certain circumstances command disobedience, kings become "sujets aux lois des hommes" (Rotrou). History, as Colbert noted, tells of such circumstances, and dramatists, d'Aubignac protested, are too prone to display their erudition.

Likewise, the wisdom of conciliating opinion has ample antiquity. The policy may be attributed to the kings of a Sparta "qui ne donne à ses rois qu'un pouvoir limité," to Greek kings "dont le peuple est le suprême arbitre." But no foreign passport is needed when domestic credentials are available. Henri IV relinquishing his religion and Louis XIII publishing accounts of his affairs and explanations of his acts have naturalized the allegiance "qui se conservant sans la crainte des Lois, est le plus fort appuy de la grandeur des Rois." The procedure of Agésilas in outwitting a rival politician,

> J'ai fait, à votre exemple, ici des créatures . . .
> Comme ils étoient à vous, les peuples sont à
> moi,

claims modern precedents. The tragedy does not fail, however, to support the contention of absolutism: if, on the one hand,

> En dédisant son roy, quelque juste apparence
> Que puisse prendre un peuple, il commet une
> offense,

on the other hand,

> Un Roi qui peut céder n'est point digne de
> l'être.

On the contrary, the dramatists may be said to protest too much. They denounce the people's inconstancy,

> Sa voix tumultueuse assez souvent fait bruit:
> Mais un moment l'élève, un moment le détruit;

its buoyancy, "jamais

> Un souverain n'agit au gré de ses sujets . . .
> Et ces soins d'un pouvoir qu'il cherche à

maintenir
Sont des crimes secrets qu'ils ont droit de
   punir."

This condemnation of the people would be out of proportion if the fact that it usually comes from a lawful monarch did not attest the enormity of the menace. But the
offense is palliated, and resentment made ineffectual, by
the monarch's shortcomings. A king does not qualify as
a champion of royalty by evading a pledge. If the expos-
tulation "Est-ce de mes sujets que je dois prendre avis?"
is true to Bossuet's doctrine, Orode's predicament undermines the protest. Another rebukes his people's judgment,
then demonstrates his own by a blunder.

But opinion is not merely interested in exposing a sovereign's deficiencies. It seeks to insure the safety of the
throne and thus to protect the ruler himself. In advocating
a leadership "par où se maintient le respect des couronnes,"
it recalls to the king "qui veut de son Empire enseuelir
l'honneur," the lesson of kings "qui s'estans mal con-
duicts . . . ont esté degradez." Rarely free from excesses,
opinion is generally based upon knowledge and its fring-
es of radicalism do not mask the validity of its remon-
strances. The charge of instability which Corneille, for
example, brought up, Corneille himself refuted by showing that the people "suit toujours son but jusqu'à ce qu'il
l'emporte." In matters requiring discrimination the people
is not to be outdone; indeed, its insight suggests that
Heaven inspires its voice and "fait que ce qu'elle a dit se
trouve véritable."

Its respect for hereditary sovereignty does not exclude
opposition to an incompetent sovereign and the demand
that he be replaced, regardless of title, by an able leader.
Certain forms are observed. It is agreed that retribution,
soon or late, will overtake the usurper, although monarchs incapacitated by age, character, or sex are not superseded without the coöperation of the people. Nor am
I neglecting the possibility that state interest may move
the people to displace an appointed usurper in favor of a
prince who is legitimate and suitable.

Rebellion is not the only token of the people's power.
There is the apprehension that stirs the monarch reflecting on a subject's popularity,

   Ils vous ont jusqu'ici suivi comme fidèle;
   Et quand vous le voudrez, ils vous suivront
      rebelle.

There is the influence of the distressed subjects "qui font
parler une douleur muete." And there is the opinion that
is surmised rather than stated; the testimony, for instance,
which Suréna evokes in his quarrel with Orode, "le peuple s'attend à me voir arrêter."

If domestic intrigues and foreign alliances are matters of
interest to the people, its particular concern is with the
fate of the warrior whose renown makes him a victim of
political discipline. The abused hero is found throughout
the repertory under the names of Alcionée, Bellérophon

(Quinault), Théodat, Suréna. . . . He is an idealist who
courts exclusively "la gloire et le bruit d'une immuable
foi," and, in his chosen field, claims for the warrior a
rank second to none. The people is quick to second the
claim and eager to turn it to practical ends. Lanson overlooked the popular bent when he represented Corneille's
Nicomède alone against his enemies. The support of the
people is emphasized by friend and foe: "Le peuple ici
vous aime . . . et c'est être bien fort que régner sur tant
d'âmes" (I, 1); "Il est le dieu du peuple" (II, 1; cf. I, 5);
"Tout le peuple à grands cris demande Nicomède" (V, 4);
and Nicomède himself knows wherein lies the defeat of
his opponents,

   . . . vos peuples alors, ayant besoin d'un roi,
   Voudront choisir peut-être entre ce prince et
      moi.

                                             (IV, 3)

Nor is it without significance that the tour de force of the
perfect Cornelian hero is his refusal of the triumph which
the people would thrust upon him.

The people's enthusiasm in rewarding valor is equalled
by its instinct in rooting out mischief. The victims of its
wrath often are some Métrobate or Zénon (*Nicomède*),
the tools of mischief; but it strikes also promoters more or
less accredited by the sovereign. In a few cases resentment attains the sovereign himself. Here again, with apol-
ogies to "un grand peuple irrité" (*Nicomède*), the dramatist furnishes safeguards. *Lèse-majesté* in the form of
personal assault is avoided. It is difficult, even when (Th.
Corneille's *Mort d'Annibal*) a king perishes in a clash, to
say whether he was intentionally killed. Removal of the
king (by suicide or murder at the hands of his wife) forestalls, intervention of the hero mollifies, the people. The
quarrel may be brought to an end by the removal of the
hero. Conversion of the king affords the best solution of
all, whether it is accredited to the sovereign's magnanimity or to the realization that the popular outcry is the
voice of Heaven which "est toujours pour les Rois."

The palliatives do not conceal the intrusion of the people.
In its off-stage position, with its views construed mostly
by adversaries, the people is made manifest and—a novelty in its classical tradition—victorious. It does more than
fight tyranny. It points beyond the interest of an individual monarch to the prestige of a throne as the true warrant
of authority. The drama's awareness of the people is not
altogether alien to the French order. The reason of the
drama is not, however, the reason of Richelieu and Bossuet, who postulate the king's divine privilege of reason,
nor does it treat kingship according to principles advocated by d'Aubignac and Colbert. Tragedy concedes the help-
fulness of public opinion and demonstrates the quick consciousness and the indomitable vigilance of the people.

Henry Carrington Lancaster

SOURCE: "Tragedies by Women: Mlle. Barbier and Mme.
Gomez," in *Sunset: A History of Parisian Drama in the
Last Years of Louis XIV, 1701-1715*, The Johns Hopkins

Press, 1945, pp. 69-81.

[In the following excerpt, Lancaster provides an analysis of the works of two women who were among the most prominent female French tragedians of the late seventeenth and early eighteenth centuries.]

The seventeenth century produced eleven women dramatists. None of them attained high rank in her profession or wrote more than a modest number of plays, but they at least made it possible for women to have their productions accepted for performance at the Comédie Française. The most successful tragedy written by a woman in the seventeenth century, Mlle Bernard's *Brutus,* was given for the last time in 1699. The eighteenth century was not slow in finding for her a successor in Mlle Barbier, whose first play appeared in 1702. Her four tragedies and one by Mme Gomez, granddaughter of Raymond Poisson, constitute women's contribution to the tragedy of 1701-15. They make up almost one-sixth of the Parisian tragedies now extant, a larger proportion than women had previously supplied.

Marie-Anne Barbier, who was born at Orléans in the latter part of the seventeenth century, lived in Paris and seems to have been well read in dramatic theory and in French tragedy. She claims to have been a friend of Boursault and refers to Corneille and Racine. It was the latter's seductive style, she holds, that kept alive the controversy as to the relative merits of the two dramatists, a statement that would lead one to suppose that Corneille was the author she especially desired to imitate. Her critique of La Grange-Chancel shows that she accepted fully the doctrines of French classicists. She was a feminist who sought to emphasize in her plays the accomplishments of her sex. When an attempt was made to deprive her of the credit of writing her tragedies and the argument was used that an unaided woman could not have done so well, she listed in reply the names of such literary women as Mlle de Scudéry, the comtesse de La Suze, Mme Deshoulières and her daughter, and, as an author of tragedies, Catherine Bernard. Moreover, she selected as heroines for three of her own tragedies Cornelia, mother of the Gracchi; Arria, who had to show her husband how to die; and Tomyris, who conquered Cyrus. And when she published her tragedies, she dedicated three of them to women, to "Madame," Louis XIV's sister-in-law, to the duchesse du Maine, and to the duchesse de Bouillon.

Besides her tragedies, she wrote a comedy, three operas, a collection of tales entitled *Théâtre de l'amour et de la fortune,* and two volumes entitled *Saisons littéraires,* which contain literary criticism, fiction, and occasional verse. She died in 1742.

Her first play was *Arrie et Pétus.* Its title had already been employed by Gabriel Gilbert, but the events of his tragedy take place in the reign of Nero, those of Mlle Barbier's in that of his predecessor, Claudius. She states that Boursault suggested the subject to her and advised her to present the hero and heroine as husband and wife in accordance with history. She preferred at first not to take this advice, but she finally decided to let them marry between Acts III and IV. Though she mentions Martial, Suetonius, and Tacitus, her chief sources seem to have been the Younger Pliny and Zonaras. From them she learned of Vinicianus, of Scribonianus, prefect of Dalmatia, of their revolt in which Petus was implicated, of the latter's hesitation at the thought of death, and of Arria's heroic suicide. She added the heroine's effort to avenge her father, Claudius's love for her, Agrippina's jealousy, the flight from Rome, and the heroine's refusal to marry

---

Maurice Baudin on the political role of women in seventeenth-century tragedy:

With seventeenth-century tragedy women enter the political arena. Most of them are unworthy. Happily, their goal is generally a title, "rien n'étant plus doux que le titre de Reine," and their activities are innocuous. When they demand the reality of power it is soon apparent that perspective and discrimination are not among their talents. In short, they are no better than the men, and the average queen is not above the usual king.

*Maurice Baudin, "The Stateswoman in
Seventeenth Century French Tragedy,"*
Modern Language Notes, *May, 1938.*

---

the emperor. She kept Narcissus because, as he had urged Claudius to kill Arria's father, Silanus, he would naturally support Agrippina in her effort to keep Arria from reigning.

The emperor is represented as weak, easily deceived, influenced by flattery, love, and jealousy. Pétus, who is a consul, becomes weak only through love, fearing for Arrie, who remains as heroic as she is in the ancient accounts. She cannot live without Pétus (V, 6):

> Banni, done, cher époux, la frayeur de ton
>   ame:
>   Et ne refuse pas l'exemple d'une femme.
>   *Elle tire un poignard, & se frappe.*
> P.: Que faites-vous, Madame? O desespoir fatal!
>   O malheur!
> A. *retirant le poignard & lui le presentant:*
>   Tien, Petus, il ne fait pas
> de mal.

She is moved to avenge her father, takes an active part in the conspiracy, renounces the opportunity to become empress, and kills herself in order to impress his duty upon her wavering husband. She belongs to Corneille's school rather than to Racine's, except in the simplicity of her last words, borrowed from Pliny.

Agrippina is an ambitious woman, endeavoring to gain power, rather than, as in *Britannicus,* seeking to recover what is slipping from her grasp. She is a hypocrite and an intriguer, sure of dominating the emperor if she can get Arrie out of the way. In representing her superstitious nature and her devotion to Nero, Mlle Barbier follows Tacitus. When she learns from the "Ciel" that Nero is to reign and to kill his mother, she cries (IV, 5):

> Si mon fils doit regner, qu'il me tue, & qu'il
>   regne.

The fact that this is the first reference to Nero in the play shows that the author had not yet completely mastered her art. Moreover, both her Agrippina and her Narcisse, who is little more than a confidant, suffer by comparison with Racine's celebrated portrayal of these characters.

The plot is as simple as Mlle Barbier claims it to be, but the late mention of Nero and the fact that we are not told what happens to Sribonien prevent the unity of action from being altogether achieved. She makes no use of recognition and introduces no scene of horror, but she has elements of the *merveilleux* in the prediction regarding Nero and in Arrie's concluding words to the Emperor Claudius:

> Je vois déja le sort que le Ciel te prepare.
> Il destine une main à cet illustre emploi,
> Trop indigne de nous, mais trop digne de toi.
> Tu ne meritois pas une mort éclatante.
> Agrippine . . . à ce nom, Tyran, je meurs
>   contente.

In making her début as a dramatist Mlle Barbier had exalted her sex in its power for good and for evil by the emphasis she placed upon Arrie and Agrippina. She had prepared herself for her task by studying her sources and the methods of Corneille and Racine. Unfortunately she did not have sufficient talent to create many striking situations or phrases. Yet her tragedy was well received. Though first acted in the summer, an unusual season for new tragedies, it was given at the Comédie Française sixteen times, from June 3 to July 8, 1702, and once at Fontainebleau, on Sept. 21. Revived in 1711, it was acted six times. Its initial success may have been helped by the fact that the actors had voted on April 24, 1702, to give a "petite comédie" after it, beginning with the first performance, though this usage was not to serve as a precedent for tragedies first acted in the winter season. The *Gazette de Rotterdam* declared in 1703 that this tragedy and her *Cornélie* were "de la force de celles de Corneille et de Racine."

The complete title of her second tragedy was *Cornélie, Mère des Gracques*. It was first read before the actors on Oct. 31, 1702. They insisted that the last act must be rewritten. When this was done, it was read to them again, on Nov. 14, and was accepted, but it was acted only eight times. Like its predecessor, the tragedy has a theme drawn from Roman history that emphasizes the heroism of a woman. Mlle Barbier states that she followed Plutarch closely except that she introduced an oracle and Opimius's daughter Licinie in order to contrive a conflict between love and duty that would cause "cette suspension qui ne laisse respirer les Spectateurs qu'après la catastrophe."

She admitted that she made Gauls of certain foreigners. She also took from Plutarch details that she does not mention, but she brought into her play so many extraneous elements that its effect is quite different from that of its source.

Though Cornelia is known to have been the mother of the Gracchi, ancient accounts of her do not state that she took an active part in Caius's enterprises except to bring some strangers into Rome. Mlle Barbier increased her importance by having her win her son back to the popular cause, bring into Rome a large number of Gauls, and inspire the people to attack the senate. She is unwavering in her support of popular principles, in her demand that Tiberius be avenged, and in choosing death for her son rather than compromise. She is an imposing figure, but Caius is more dramatic, for, contrary to Plutarch, he has to struggle against his love. He is represented as highly daring and emotional, but his special political views are not explained in detail. He contrasts with Drusus, a traitor to the people's interests, and with Opimius, whose aristocratic pride and contempt for the rabble recall the character of the Roman senator in La Fosse's *Manlius*. He goes even farther, for he wishes to rule Rome himself, so that he is a predecessor of Sylla and other dictators. In the end, however, he weakens, for the fact that his life is saved by Caius wins him over completely. His daughter has inherited some of her father's prejudices, but she appears chiefly as a woman in love with an enemy of her house.

The subject is one that required a masculine pen. The personal element is made more important than the political. Questions of state lead to no rapid give and take in the Cornelian manner, though there seems to be imitation of Corneille both in Caius's argument (III, 3) that he must resist Licinie in order to be worthy of her and in his echo (III, 4) of *Horace:*

> . . . je renonce au grand nom de Romain,
> Si pour le meriter il faut être inhumain.

Some verses do, however, depict the eternal conflict between the convinced democrat and the Fascist. When Caius is wavering, he speaks to his mother verses to which she retorts sharply:

> Caius: Mais si le peuple enfin au gré de
>   son caprice
>   Rejette cette paix, & veut que tout
>   perisse;
>   Il faut qu'à sa fureur je m'oppose
>   aujourd'hui,
>   Et je dois le forcer d'être heureux
>   malgré lui.
> Cor.:   Le forcer d'être heureux, quel
>   nouvel esclavage!
>   Quoi! déja du Senat vous parlez le
>   langage,
>   Tribun. Eh! depuis quand tout ce
>   peuple à vos yeux
>   N'est-il qu'un frenetique, & qu'un
>   capricieux?

Mlle Barbier showed considerable skill in constructing a plot that would cause all the minor interests to influence the dénouement. For this purpose she made Licinie the daughter of Opimius, invented the senator's ambition to be a dictator, the rivalry of Caius and Drusus, the presence of Caius and his mother in the senate house, the capture of this building by the people. She added a touch of the *merveilleux* by her use of the oracle. It is probable that in its original form the fifth act was simpler, for we know that she altered it and that, according to her preface, it was criticized, after she had made the changes, for containing too many incidents. In reply to this charge she asks if it is not realized that nothing moves spectators more than "les *peripeties,* quand elles naissent du fond du sujet."

The sudden changes of fortune experienced in Act V by Caius, Licinie, and Opimius did not, however, keep the tragedy long in the repertory. Though the play was not censored, Cornelia and her son could hardly be expected to rouse much enthusiasm while France was being ruled by a royal dictator. It was only in Holland that it was said to recall Corneille and Racine. That it was not revived late in the century, when the French popular party had triumphed, must have been due to the fact that the plays of Mlle Barbier were by that time forgotten.

Her next tragedy, *Tomyris,* is greatly inferior to her preceding plays. It marks the substitution of romance for history as the material on which she worked. Her inspiration came only to a slight degree from Herodotus, but amply from the *Grand Cyrus.* Perhaps it was her feminism that led her to select, not only a triumphant queen as her principal character, but a novel by a distinguished woman as her source. The facts that Herodotus supplied are that Cyrus attacked Tomyris, Queen of the Massagetes; that, after some success, including the death of the queen's son, Cyrus was defeated and killed; and that the queen dipped in blood his severed head and bade it drink its fill. The characters of Mandane, Aryante, Aripithe, and Gélonide are Mlle Scudéry's creations, as are Tomyris's love of Cyrus, begun when he came to see her as an ambassador, her failure to win his affections, his devotion to Mandane, the captivity of this princess, the queen's jealousy, the final victory of the Persians, and Mandane's rescue. Unlike Mlle de Scudéry, Mlle Barbier had Cyrus perish and his own head, not that of his double, soaked in blood. She made Aryante the son, not the brother of Tomyris. She reduced the action to events that take place in a day and within the queen's tent after the death of Spargapise.

Tomyris is violent, deeply in love, jealous, domineering, and guileful, but the author fails to give her characteristics that would prepare us for the element of horror that is introduced when Cyrus's head is dipped in blood (V, 10):

> Une troupe barbare entoure Tomyris,
> Tandis que par trois fois, sans qu'aucun cri
>   l'arrête,
> Dans un vase de sang elle plonge une tête,

> Et dit, à chaque fois, d'un ton mal-assûré,
> Saoule toi de ce sang dont tu fus altéré.

Cyrus is not the great conqueror we should expect to find, but the amorous adventurer that Mlle de Scudéry had described and Boileau had held up to ridicule. Mandane is the well-behaved and devoted heroine and captive that she is in the *Grand Cyrus.* Aryante is a somewhat bewildered warrior, bullied by his mother, rebuffed by Mandane, and finally overcome despite his threats. Though the tone of the tragedy is somber, its situations are at times close to comedy, especially when Tomyris seeks to rationalize her love and when Cyrus and Mandane quarrel, then renew their expressions of affection. Cyrus even makes one think of the *Fourberies de Scapin* when he exclaims (II, 5), "Que venois-je chercher dans ce climat barbare." In short, the tragedy is a curious combination of sentimentality, violence, and horror, presented in accordance with classical regulations. It was acted only six times, Nov. 23 to Dec. 3, 1706.

The dedicatory poem published with her fourth tragedy indicates that Mlle Barbier gave up literary composition after the failure of *Tomyris,* but returned to it through the encouragement of d'Argenson. Moreover, he gratified her by weeping when she read to him *La Mort de Jules César.* Women are still important, but they do not have the two leading rôles. The source is Plutarch's *Life of Caesar,* from which most of the characters, the main facts, and some of the details are derived. The principal additions are Calpurnia's consulting an oracle, Caesar's matrimonial scheme, his being warned about the conspiracy by Brutus, his suspecting both Antony and Brutus, and his receiving a crown just before he is murdered. Much emphasis is placed upon Octavia and Portia, especially upon the part these ladies, as well as their lovers, play in the efforts made to save Caesar or to bring about his murder.

The tragedy is thoroughly classical in form. The action requires only a few hours and takes place in a room of Caesar's palace. The various themes lead up to the main event, Caesar's murder, which is reported almost at the end of the tragedy. The play must have been criticized chiefly for the delineation of character, as the author makes a special effort in her preface to defend her characterization of Caesar, Brutus, and Octavia. Accused of making Caesar fear death too much and of keeping him in a state of continual agitation, she explained that her protagonist dreaded, not ordinary death, but the death of a tyrant, that he feared to lose in a day the labor of years, and that he was moved by omens and influenced by Calpurnia, who was no ordinary woman. She added that she could not have roused pity and terror if she had made Caesar "insensible à ses propres malheurs." She insists that she did not subordinate him to Brutus, who is moved to remorse by Caesar's generosity, and that Brutus will be considered the greater of the two only by those who put devotion to liberty above other considerations. As for Octavia, since history represents her as obeying her sense of duty rather than her feelings, Mlle Barbier did not feel that it was proper to make her, in imitation of Racine, "une

Hermione ou une Roxane."

According to this apology, she violated history in order to make Caesar more dramatic than he was, but she did not dare to do so in the case of Octavia. This is the reverse of the familiar classical doctrine that an author must not alter the character of a well-known person, for Caesar is certainly far better known than Octavia. One is led to suspect that Mlle Bernard's real reason was that she preferred to attribute weakness to a man rather than to a woman. The result is that it is hard to understand how a wavering and superstitious politician could have mastered Rome, or how an audience could take much interest in Octavia, who allows herself without protest to be transferred from one prospective husband to another.

Mlle Barbier was far from writing a political pamphlet. There is no discussion of autocratic or of democratic rule. Even Brutus does not object to Caesar's power. The only point is that at Rome prejudice against kings existed and that, when a dictator attempted to make himself king, certain people, like Antony and Octavia, approved, while others, like Brutus and Portia, disapproved strongly enough to condemn him to death.

Portia is more bitterly opposed to Caesar than Brutus is. She has inherited her father's hatred of the dictator and refuses any sort of compromise, while Brutus goes so far as to warn Caesar of the conspiracy and decides to help murder him only when he hears that he has put on a crown. Octavia and Antony are similarly contrasted, she obeying Caesar blindly, he having a special reason for making Caesar king, as an oracle has predicted that only under the leadership of a king will Rome conquer Persia.

The play is unlike earlier tragedies on the subject, but it seems to have been influenced by *Cinna* in the scenes in which Caesar consults Antony and Brutus. The author's feminism is shown in the fact that each of the three principal men is deeply influenced by a woman: Caesar by Calpurnia's dream and her consulting an oracle; Brutus, by Portia's uncompromising attitude; Antony, by the loss of Octavia and by the permission he ultimately receives to marry her. The *merveilleux* has a larger part than in the author's earlier tragedies. She claims that her last three acts won more applause than she had expected, an admission that the first two were less successful. The fourth and fifth are, indeed, more dramatic than the earlier acts, which are largely devoted to plans for marriages in which we take little interest. Where matters of large political consequence are involved, Caesar's schemes for getting support by arranging marriages seem absurdly out of place.

Like *Tomyris*, the tragedy had only six performances, but, as the author received from them over 400 francs, some of them must have been well attended. A lengthy criticism by "D. E.," written not long after the play was acted, was published by Mlle Barbier in the second volume of her *Saisons littéraires*. The critic praises the author for her constructive imagination, for verses that he considers worthy of Corneille, and for the historically accurate characters of Brutus, Portia, and Antony, but he has no kind words for the portrayal of Caesar and Octavia, as the former is easily frightened, his niece cold and tiresome. He holds that the oracle should be mentioned in the second act rather than the fourth and objects to the fact that the spectators have to wait for this fourth act before their interest is aroused. He also points out anachronisms and violations of the proprieties.

It is with this play that ends the career of Mlle Barbier as an author of tragedies. She had composed a larger number of them than any French woman who had preceded her. She suffered from her admiration for Corneille and Mlle de Scudéry, as the novelist led her into the absurd romanticism of *Tomyris* and the dramatist lured her into attempting political themes that she was unable to develop. In her most successful tragedy, *Arrie et Pétus*, these influences are less apparent than elsewhere. Her creative ability, her taste, and her gift of expression are less striking than her knowledge of classical technique and her ingenuity in plot construction. But she must be remembered for the brave fight she made in behalf of her sex. Her Tomyris puts her Cyrus to death. Her Arrie, Cornélie, and Portia proclaim to hesitant males their duty. Her leading women never compromise their ideals. But the presentation of their strength, though gratifying to feminists, does not compensate for poverty of imagination or mediocrity of expression.

The only other woman who wrote tragedies for the Parisian stage at this time was Madeleine-Angélique Poisson (1684-1770), daughter of Paul Poisson and wife of a Spaniard, de Gomez. She was the author of many *contes* and turned quite naturally to dramatic composition as her grandfather had written plays and her parents and grandparents, as well as her brother Philippe, were or had been professional actors. The first of her four plays was *Habis*, derived, according to the frères Parfaict, from a tale by Mlle de La Roche-Guilhem. They declare that she took from it her subject, the "marche" of her action, her chief persons, and the dénouement, which they consider the most successful part of the play. They reproach her for asserting that she wrote it "seule, sans aucun secours," but, as French tragedies regularly had sources, she must have meant, not that her play had no source, but that she had no collaborator. She was probably replying to the charge that she had one. As similar accusations had been made against Catherine Bernard and Mlle Barbier, it seems that there was considerable support in France for the belief that a woman, unaided by a man, was incapable of dramatic composition.

Except for the correctness of the form, which strictly fulfills classical requirements, the play resembles a romantic tragi-comedy. An oracle constitutes an important motif. The hero, condemned to death when a child and rescued from the sea, arouses his relatives' emotions before they know who he is and is recognized with the help of a birthmark. The happy ending is brought about by a sentimental change in the attitude of the principal villain. The tale from which the play was derived was probably inspired by Herodotus's account of Cyrus's youth, a subject dramatized by Danchet eight years before Mme Go-

A portrait of Louis XIV by Hyacinthe Rigaud.

mez's tragedy appeared, but, if this is true, geographical and historical names have been completely altered.

The only preparation for the king's final change of heart is found in a slight feeling of remorse that is assigned to him and in his growing affection for his grandson, but this is hardly consistent with his continued cruelty towards his daughter, kept in confinement for twenty years. During this period her maternal instinct has remained fresh,

---

R. C. Knight on the definition of tragedy:

[Tragedy is a] dramatic action in which personages above the common have to react to a situation above the common, in that it involves a danger usually of death. This is a *minimal* definition [of tragedy], a highest common factor. The results can be minimal—can be trivial, in fact; all depends on the use made of the latitude given; and latitude is vital for any genre which is to be popular and long-lived. A strict formula admits of only a restricted number of solutions; the formula I have proposed is a good deal narrower than that of the novel in our day.

I do not seek to deny that the finest Tragedy—or the only Tragedy really great—occurs when the situation seems to be an inspired commentary on, or a revelation of, the facts of our nature and our universe as we recognize it—leading (sometimes with Corneille) to imagined ideal sublimities of achievement or aspiration, or (with Racine) to equally imaginative profundities of pity and fear at the spectacle of impotence and defeat. Nor do I deny that the second solution is the more truly tragic—is alone tragic in the eyes of the aesthetic critic, who focuses his definition on these supreme realizations.

But the scholar may legitimately call attention to the lower basis common to . . . valuable and significant works; to the natural habitat whence the loftier shoots could rise during that not very long period when this Form, or Kind, of tragedy was alive in France.

R. C. Knight, "A Minimal Definition of Seventeenth-Century Tragedy," French Studies, *October, 1956.*

---

but she has not learned prudence and is almost tricked by her father into revealing her son's identity. This noble son and his beloved Erixène are but superficially characterized. A more interesting character is Phesrès, the wily statesman, who works in the interests of Habis while retaining the confidence of the king. He is foiled only by Habis himself. His is a type found in *Amasis* and in several other tragedies of the period. The only thing worth noting about the minor characters is that one of them, Erixène's confidant, is given nothing to say.

The author preserves the unities, maintains suspense almost to the end of the play, introduces elements of the *merveilleux,* and shows on the stage three scenes of recognition. Perhaps these last and the striking, if sentimental ending are what brought the tragedy remarkable success. It was acted twenty-five times between April 17 and

June 19, 1714, continued to be performed in the two years that followed, and was revived in 1732-4. As there were in all forty-eight performances, it was acted more frequently than any other tragedy of the period except two by Crébillon and two by La Grange-Chancel. Mme Gomez was encouraged to write other tragedies, but they were most unsuccessful. Her original good fortune must have been due to the acting, or to some fancy of her audiences, weary, perhaps, of more somber tragedies and enjoying romance and scenes of recognition.

However this may be, the part played by women in French dramatic history has now become less negligible than ever. There had been great actresses in the seventeenth century. Their traditions were carried over into the eighteenth by la Beauval, la Duclos, and la Desmares. There had been influential women who showed interest in the theater. Mme de Maintenon, the duchesse de Bourgogne, the duchesse du Maine, and the princesse de Conti were active patrons of drama in the last years of Louis XIV. It remained for Mlle Barbier and Mme Gomez to replace Mlle Desjardins, Mme Deshoulières, and Mlle Bernard as dramatists. It may be said of them that Mlle Barbier composed a larger number of tragedies than any of her feminine predecessors, and that Mme Gomez produced the tragedy that was the most frequently acted of all written by women before the end of 1715.

Lacy Lockert

SOURCE: An introduction to *Studies in French-Classical Tragedy,* The Vanderbilt University Press, 1958, pp. 9-26.

[*In the following excerpt, Lockert discusses the weaknesses of several critics' assessments of French neo-classical tragedies and argues that greater consideration should be given to the works of minor dramatists of the time.*]

Though seventeenth-century France, like the England of Elizabeth and the first two Stuarts, was notable for one of the four or five really great flourishings of dramatic literature that have ever occurred, critical and historical investigation of this French "classical" drama—more properly called "neo-classical"—was long confined to its major figures. To speak of tragedy alone, . . . not until the latter part of the nineteenth century were any serious efforts made to rescue from oblivion the almost forgotten contemporaries of Corneille and Racine—efforts comparable to those of Lamb, Hazlitt, Gifford, and others in renewing interest in the contemporaries of Shakespeare, more than two generations earlier. And whereas the study of Elizabethan drama begun by these pioneers has progressed steadily ever since their day, the monographs of Gustave Reynier on Thomas Corneille and N. M. Bernardin on Tristan l'Hermite, inadequate though they were, have been followed and superseded by no others on either of these dramatists or any of their fellow-writers of tragedy, with the sole exception of the huge, exhaustive volume on Quinault by Etienne Gros—not, that is, in France itself. There, except for that single book and for a few pages in histories of literature and in books about the major dramatists, there seems to have been no critical discussion of the minor ones for many decades—until the tercentenary of Rotrou's death evoked some small interest in him, which subsided immediately afterwards. Only in the monumental work of the eminent American scholar Henry Carrington Lancaster have we been given a detailed history of the entire period, in which the development of its several dramatic types has been traced and every author and extant play received attention.

Yet some acquaintance with the lesser dramatists of a great period of drama is necessary if anyone is to see its great men with proper perspective and appreciation. This has long been recognized by British and American students of Shakespeare. Since the appearance of Lancaster's volumes, there has been a greater realization of it by French critics—notably Mornet and J. Scherer. But some of the lesser French dramatists are worth knowing for their own sake also, just as the Elizabethans are. Critics generally have held them in slight esteem, and—perhaps on that account—have too often been strangely careless even as to facts.

Let us take, for instance, the treatment accorded to Thomas Corneille, one of the most prolific and important of them.

Jules Lemaître begins a discussion of *Andromaque*—his brilliant though idolatrous *Jean Racine* is the publication of a course of lectures—by stating that to realize the originality of this play one must know what sort of tragedies had been written in the years immediately preceding its appearance.

> Between 1660 and 1667 were produced Pierre Corneille's *Othon, Sophonisbe, Agésilas,* and *Attila;* Quinault's *Astrate, Bellérophon,* and *Pausanias;* and Thomas Corneille's *Camma, Pyrrhus, Maximian, Persée et Démétrius,* and *Antiochus.*

Lemaître says that he has read, "of course," the ones by Pierre Corneille, and has either read or "glanced through" (*parcouru*) those by Thomas Corneille and Quinault. He then says, however, that he will speak of none of these, but of Thomas Corneille's *Timocrate,* dated 1656.

It might be supposed that he would at least have read *Timocrate,* and not merely have glanced through it. He makes merry over the absurdities of this fantastic "romanesque" drama, in which the hero fights alternately on his own side and on the enemy's, now as Timocrates and now under the name of "Cleomenes." "He has won, as the perfect lover," says Lemaître, "the heart of the princess Eriphyle; she is his for the taking. But he wants also to deserve her as a hero and a great commander; and that is why, as soon as his father's death sets him on the throne, he comes, without a word to her, and besieges the city of the woman whom he adores. And in truth, 'such gallantry is unusual.'"

It is much more than unusual; it simply does not exist in the play *Timocrate.* There, a far greater barrier of hate stood between the hero and his beloved than that which separated Romeo and Juliet. Eriphyle's father, the king of Argos, had been captured in war by Demochares, king of Crete, and had died a prisoner; his queen believed his death foully encompassed and, though she had to make peace at that time, was determined to avenge him. Soon afterwards, the Messenians attacked Argos, and the unknown soldier of fortune, "Cleomenes," came to its defense, defeated them, and then disappeared. Now the Queen launched her blow against Crete, sweeping all before her; Demochares was besieged in his last city, and triumph seemed within her grasp, when the prince Timocrates, long absent and supposed to be dead, arrived in the nick of time and routed her forces. Demochares died; Timocrates became king of Crete. he could not reasonably aspire to her daughter's hand as the adventurer "Cleomenes." As Timocrates, the son of her hated foe and the thwarter of her vengeance, he was doubly hated. The story of his twin roles, in which he drew his sword now on one side and now on the other that he might win his heart's love, is of course sheer stuff of romance. Yet how else could he have won her?

It may be objected that this is only an instance of the carelessness in details that is individually characteristic of the brilliant Lemaître. But the mistakes are not his alone—nor even primarily his. He must have prepared himself for his lecture, not by "glancing through" *Timocrate,* but by reading about it in Gustave Reynier's *Thomas Corneille,* a book which he recommends and from which he quotes the phrase "*la galanterie est rare.*" A perusal of Reynier's discussion of *Timocrate* (too long to reproduce here) discloses the fact that Lemaître has only followed him in the misstatements which I have cited above, though adding later at least one of his own.

Lemaître, as we have seen, had selected this drama for contrast with the one which was the subject of his lecture. But Reynier's mistakes were made in a monograph on the author of *Timocrate* itself, an entire book on Thomas Corneille, the only book ever devoted to him. And the errors in it regarding *Timocrate* are by no means its only flagrant ones. If that was Thomas Corneille's most influential play and the one which had the greatest immediate success, his *Ariane* has been the most habitually praised. Let us turn to Reynier's treatment of this tragedy, which deals with the desertion of Ariadne by Theseus.

According to *Ariane,* the heroine's younger sister, Phaedra, has fled with them from Crete after the killing of the Minotaur; and Theseus and Phaedra fall in love and abandon Ariadne in Naxos. The King of that island loves Ariadne; but Reynier has no warrant whatever to call his pity for her, when she is forsaken, "hypocritical"—nor to say of Pirithoüs that by his "base inaction" he "made himself an accomplice in the treachery of his friend", for Pirithoüs is unmistakably represented as convinced that nothing could be done to rectify the situation. Reynier proceeds:

> And Phaedra? Can this vicious little person inspire the slightest interest? She was not impelled by affection to follow her sister, but rather by a craving for adventure;

she has stolen her sister's lover in the most nonchalant manner. She at first resists Theseus, but only from coquetry, in order to inflame his passion the more; she presently goes off with him, well satisfied and light-hearted, as if she recked nothing of her crime—but she is practical, too, taking care to exact solemn promises from him before yielding:

And who will assure me that thou wilt be
   faithful?
THESEUS.
My troth, which neither time nor angry heaven .
  . .
PHAEDRA.
My sister had that, when she fled with thee. . . .
Thou leavest her in Naxos, bowed with grief;
Thy fickleness might leave me somewhere else. .
  . .

Et qui me répondra que vous serez fidèle?
THÉSÉE.
Ma foi, que ni le temps ni le ciel en courroux . .
 .
PHÈDRE.
Ma sœur l'avait reçue en fuyant avec vous. . . .
Vous la laissez dans Naxe en proie à ses
  douleurs,
Votre légèreté peut me laisser ailleurs. . . .

Who would recognize in her the Phaedra of Euripides and Racine—the destined victim of Venus? It seems that she has no heart, nor even any sense. She does not love Theseus, no matter what she may say about it. But she enjoys having made a 'conquest' of an already famous hero, a king's son who will soon be king himself, and a man whom her sister adores.

There is nothing in the play which supports any of the statements derogatory to Phaedra in that paragraph. Some of them—those in the last two sentences, for instance—are indeed not positively contradicted by the text; others, however, are demonstrably untrue. Ariadne says it was only with great difficulty that she persuaded her sister, reluctant and in tears, to flee with her:

Je vous fis malgré vous accompagner ma fuite.
   . . . Phèdre, elle de qui le pleurs
Semblaient en s'embarquant présager nos
  malheurs!
Avant que la résoudre à seconder ma fuite,
A quoi, pour la gagner, ne fus-je pas réduite!
Combien de résistance et d'obstinés refus!

Despite thyself, I made thee share my flight.
   . . . Phaedra, her whose tears
Seemed, when we sailed, a presage of
  misfortune!
Before I could persuade her to accompany
My flight, what was I not obliged to do!
How loath she was! how stubbornly she refused!

On Phaedra's first appearance in the play, she tells The-

seus that they must renounce each other and part, for though she loves him she cannot forget Ariadne's tremendous claims on him. Later, she proves too weak for her suggested self-sacrifice and accepts his plan of trying to persuade her sister to be reconciled to his inconstancy and marry King Oenarus; but when the forsaken woman begs her to plead with Theseus for her, she does this, against her own interests, so eloquently that Pirithoüs is convinced that her lack of success makes plain the uselessness of any further efforts to persuade the recreant lover to fulfil his obligations—yet still she wishes to try once more. Only when she learns of Ariadne's determination to discover the object of Theseus' affections and kill her, does she consent, in terrified dismay, to fly with him; and even then she remains keenly conscious of the piteousness of her sister's position.

How she will suffer! Gods! What woe! what
  tears!
I feel born in my heart the ghastliest fears.
I see with horror what must come to pass.

Dieux! qu'elle en souffrira! que d'ennuis! que de
  larmes!
Je sens naître en mon coeur les plus rudes
  alarmes:
Il voit avec horreur ce qui doit arriver.

There is here, surely, no nonchalance observable in her attitude, no complacency or light-heartedness or callousness, no ground for charging her with coquetry or with not loving Theseus or with finding a piquancy in taking her sister's lover from her.

Nor have French critics become very much more careful, in their statements about these lesser dramas and dramatists of the seventeenth century, since the days of Reynier and Lemaître. The late Daniel Mornet is scarcely more successful than they were in his attempt to sketch the plot of *Timocrate*, [*Jean Racine,* 1944] and he, like them, appears to be more interested in being facetious than in being accurate about it. According to him, the hero was already king of Crete when he went to Argos as "Cleomenes"; and Mornet says that it would seem as though kingdoms in those days could somehow dispense with a ruler, and represents Crete as being without one in its final expedition against Argos while Timocrates-Cleomenes is still in that city. But according to the play itself, Timocrates' lengthy absence from Crete occurred during his father's lifetime and reign; he returned to Crete to repel the Argive invasion of the island, and was there at the time of—and after—his father's *subsequent* death; and he led the final Cretan expedition against Argos, absenting himself from his newly acquired royal duties for only a few hours to reappear briefly in Argos as "Cleomenes" when the play opens. Robert Brasillach in his interesting *Pierre Corneille* [1938] repeats some of Lemaître's and Reynier's misrepresentations of *Timocrate*.

Criticism of Thomas Corneille—to continue to use him as our example—has been no less inadequate than inaccurate. Neither in Reynier's monograph nor in the brief treatment him by others has anyone before me, I believe, stressed his "ability to invent striking if melodramatic situations, of immense effectiveness on the stage, which was his greatest gift as a dramatist." Nor has anyone pointed out that the principal defect of his dramaturgy is a tendency to relegate crucial plot-details to the intervals between the acts instead of having them occur before the eyes of the audience, or off-stage while the act is playing. In other words, there has been no study of him at all as a manipulator of dramatic effects, which is what he largely was.

The work of the minor playwrights of this great period of drama should be more carefully examined and appraised, as that of the Elizabethans has been, not by one critic or by a few critics but by many with diverse views. . . .

Every important type of drama has its distinctive merits, and to demand that it should have those of some other dramatic type results in such unintelligent and unappreciative criticism as Rymer's and Voltaire's of Shakespeare by neo-classical canons, Saintsbury's of Corneille and Racine by those of Shakespearean tragedy, and William Archer's of the Elizabethans by those of the school of Ibsen. But on the other hand there are certain features of good drama which will be found in the best plays of every period, and certain things which are to be condemned wherever they occur. The perception of these latter—or at least the full force of them—may sometimes escape the specialist who is familiar only or chiefly with his own field; the widest possible acquaintance with drama is desirable for the best dramatic criticism. Jules Jusserand's pages treating of Elizabethan drama in his history of English literature showed how its faults in their worst extremes, often little censured by English enthusiasts, appeared to a French critic who had not grown callous to them through long specialization in it.

There is one point which seems to me of primary importance in appraising drama of any sort or period whatsoever, but which traditional French dramatic criticism has not sufficiently taken into account. I therefore have been obliged to stress it in my own criticism of French-classical tragedies.

For a play to be effective, some, at least, of its characters must be able to elicit sympathy. Almost every critic of these plays, in considering the characters for whom one's sympathy is necessary if the proper dramatic effect is to be secured, thinks any conduct or feelings of theirs acceptable which would have been approved by that public for which the plays were first produced. But their conduct or mental attitude is usually what was prescribed or sanctioned by the frequenters of the salons of that period, whose highly artificial code of behavior is generally observed in the tragedies written then. Students of those dramas become so habituated to such behavior of the dramatis personae as to lose all natural reactions to it, both of the intellect and of the moral sense, and cease to realize how abhorrent it often is to those who encounter it without the familiarity that breeds acceptance. Yet unless the intendedly "sympathetic" characters in a play can

win the sympathy of people in subsequent times as well as in its own, that play will fail to produce a satisfactory dramatic effect in subsequent times and therefore—to the extent that such sympathy is important—should be recognized as of somewhat ephemeral value.

We do not, of course, have to see absolutely eye to eye, on moral issues, with a dramatist and his intendedly sympathetic characters; but the behavior of these characters must be such that we can, while the play in which they appear is before us, at least view them with imaginative sympathy. This we can do, for example, in plays dealing sympathetically with revenge, whatever our own ethical ideas, professed or sincere, about that—as the success of such plays, from the *Coëphoroe* down through *Hamlet* and the *Cid* to *Monte Cristo* and still later, abundantly testifies. Calderon's *The Devotion of the Cross,* on the other hand, depicts a bandit who has many crimes on his head but who is miraculously saved from hell and admitted to heaven because in all his nefarious career he has never said or done anything disrespectful to the Cross! That drama may have been acceptable to a Spanish audience of the seventeenth century, but it certainly has no abiding appeal. As a matter of fact, in regard to all plays—be they Elizabethan, Greek, or whatever else—except those of the French-classical period, critics have not failed to judge the attractiveness or unattractiveness, the acceptableness or unacceptableness, of the characters by permanent standards of behavior rather than by eccentric notions prevalent when the plays were written, and have appraised accordingly the effect and merit of each play for all time, and not for its own brief age.

George Bernard Daniel

SOURCE: "The *Tragédie Nationale* in the Seventeenth Century," in *The Development of the "Tragédie Nationale" in France from 1552-1800,* The University of North Carolina Press, 1964, pp. 36-67.

[*In the following excerpt, Daniel analyzes the treatment of history and the use of classical form in historical tragedies, arguing that while French history offered the potential for theatrical exploitation, the public did not approve of dramatists' departures from classical ideas.*]

François Hédelin, abbé d'Aubignac (1604-1676), known primarily for the *Pratique du théâtre* (1657), wrote three prose tragedies. All were turned into verse by other dramatists. Neither *Zénobie* (1645) nor *Cyminde* (1642) concern us here. *La Pucelle d'Orléans,* acted in 1641 and published in 1642, was exceptional in its choice of subject and development of plot.

D'Aubignac's saccharine treatment of Jeanne d'Arc was an indication why, during the century, national historical tragedy never became important. The dramatists who endeavored to tap the rich sources of French history were inferior and unsure. They twisted history to such a degree that little or no element of historical fact remained. The result unfortunately was a melodramatic slush that revolted even the least sensitive spectator.

When d'Aubignac wrote *La Pucelle,* he did not sign his name. François Targa, who published the first edition from a manuscript surrendered to him by some actor, told how he would have run into difficulties with the authorities if d'Aubignac had not identified himself as the author and in turn authorized publication of the play, already completely printed. Targa also had much to say about the subject of the play, the actors who interpreted it, and the scenery which was used:

> L'histoire de la Pucelle d'Orléans est un grand et magnifique sujet pour un poème héroïque, . . . mais pour un poème dramatique, c'est, à mon avis, un sujet bien difficile et peu capable du théâtre; car ce poème ne pouvant représenter aux yeux des spectateurs que ce qui c'est faict en huit heures ou pour le plus en un demy jour, ou n'en peut fonder le dessein, que sur un des plus signalez accidents.

Continuing, he complained of the ignorance among the actors who presented his play. According to him they were even too stupid to read the rôles even with a copy in their hands. . . .

D'Aubignac allowed himself complete freedom in the treatment of his subject. The most striking derivation from history is in the circumstance of having Jeanne d'Arc in love with the Count of Warwick. The Countess, his wife, is indeed jealous of this peasant maiden who seeks to steal her husband.

The extreme which the author allowed himself was explained away in the *Pratique du théâtre:*

> Ils (les poètes) prennent de l'histoire ce que leur est propre, et y changent le reste pour en faire leurs poems, et c'est une pensée bien ridicule d'aller au théâtre pour apprendre l'Histoire.

Appearing in 1642, the verse translation of d'Aubignac's tragedy was attributed to both Benserade and La Mesnardière. Nevertheless, it was first included in the dramatic works of Benserade. The Benserade-La Mesnardière version is almost a phrase by phrase translation of the original.

Claude Boyer (1618-1698), one of the contemporaries of Corneille and Racine, wrote one historical tragedy, *Clotilde* (1659). The tragedy, containing five acts and in verse, was performed on May 18, 1659, at Bernay and destined to "augmenter la munificence d'une fête que M. le comte de Lyonne donna au Roy (Louis XIV)". The action of the play takes place in the royal palace one month after the arrival of Deuthère and her daughter Clotilde at the court of Théodebert, King of Metz. Elements of a romanesque love triangle are introduced in act one. Clotilde is in love with Clidaman, a favorite of Théodebert and benefactor of Deuthère; Clidamant loves Deuthère, who is ambitious to be crowned queen; Théodebert grows fonder of Clotilde with the passing of time; Deuthère is very jealous of

the attentions to her daughter; Clodomire, Théodebert's son, is also in love with Clotilde but has not revealed his feelings.

As the play opens Clotilde admits her affection for Clidamant:

> Clidamant seul peut estre avoüé de mon coeur
> Ses yeux ont pour les miens ie ne sçay
> quoy d'aimables
>
> (Act I, Scene I)

She is even jealous of her mother, and although Clidamant has said nothing about it, Clotilde believes he loves her. Deuthère also reveals her love for Clidamant and is reminded her duty should lie in being faithful to Théodebert. Angered to learn of Deuthère's intention of marrying the King, Clidamant accuses his friend of treason. Deuthère haughtily replies that she desires the crown upon her head. Clidamant warns of his power with the King. This outburst warrants a word of precaution from Lucinde. Deuthère retorts that she is capable of handling any enemy. Trying the scheme of diplomacy, Théodebert suggests to Deuthère that she marry Clidamant, and relinquish her daughter to him. Filled with rage that Théodebert, a man her own age, would advance such a weird proposal, Deuthère storms at her suitor who meekly replies: "J'adore en vostre sang vostre vivant portrait." (Act I, Scene V). Moved to the need of confession by Deuthère's fit of anger, Théodebert confides in Sigile. The latter cautions the King of the extravagance of his thoughts. To this, the King answers cavalierly:

> Qu'importe à mon repos celuy de mon Empire?
> Mon amour n'est plus cher que l'Empire et le
> jour.
>
> (Act I, Scene VI)

Having met with little sympathy, Théodebert tells Clodomire of his love for Clotilde, and commissions his son to bear the message of his love to her.

In act two Deuthère, whose increasing jealousy has left her dazed, promises her daughter first to Clidamant and then to the King. Deuthère believes Clotilde's aspirations for the throne have usurped the power of her own charms over Théodebert. Seeing the scepter rapidly disappearing from her grasp, Deuthère exclaims:

> Qu'un peu plus de beauté que ma Fille à sur
> moy
> Qu'un peu plus de jeunesse a fait manquer de
> foy.
>
> Je meurs de jalousie et de haine et d'amour.
>
> (Act II, Scene II)

When confronted by her mother, Clotilde declares nothing could persuade her to become Théodebert's wife. Deuthère accuses her daughter of lying. Clotilde then confesses her love for Clidamant. Deuthère immediately promises to support her daughter in this affair. Clidamant arrives at a propitious moment, and when informed that Clotilde is his for the taking, he accuses Deuthère of using her daughter as a pawn. . . .

In her confusion Deuthère offers Clotilde to Théodebert. Clidamant realizes Deuthère's sudden change of heart is not sincere. Nevertheless, the King, having heard the news he has been longing for, dispatches Clodomire on the happy mission to tell Clotilde she will soon be queen. With no quarter Clodomire blurts out his passion for Clotilde. Finding himself suddenly the rival of his own son, Théodebert pleads for understanding! "Si tu pourrois, mon Fils, te vaincre en ma faveur." (Act II, Scene IX).

In act three Théodebert almost concedes defeat in the struggle between himself and Clodomire for Clotilde's love. In order to seek vengeance upon Clidamant Deuthère decides to permit the marriage between Clodomire and Clotilde. On the point of recanting his love for Clotilde, Théodebert's passion boils anew upon seeing her. Clotilde primly accuses her suitor of infidelity. This increases the King's esteem for her all the more. Clidamant claims Clotilde is acting so coyly only out of obedience to her mother. He admonishes Théodebert to ignore Clodomire with the assurance Clotilde will be the new queen.

Clidamant's determination to have Deuthère or murder someone in the process is the main theme of act four. Deuthère reassures a hopeless Clodomire. Clotilde calmly notifies her mother she will obey as a dutiful daughter, but after all Deuthère has freed her to pursue Clidamant. In her blind fury Deuthère presumes Clidamant must be exterminated. Clodomire threatens Clidamant who scarcely pays any attention. The act ends with Clidamant's appraisal of his fate:

> J'estois né pour aimer, et le ciel à mon âme
> Avoit fait en naissant un destin tout de flâme.
> (Act IV, Scene VI)

Having found his destiny impeded, Clidamant's attitude has changed to hate: "Je me perdray moy-même afin de me venger" (Act IV, Scene VI).

The puzzle is resolved in act five with the suicide of Deuthère and Clidamant. Clodomire will marry Clotilde and Théodebert will bury his chagrin in busying himself with affairs of state. Clotilde expresses her independence in refusing to marry Clodomire. In the only interview with Clidamant, she discovers his obstinacy. Although she denies any desire to be queen, Clidamant claims she is at the mercy of her mother's diabolical schemes. She defends her position eloquently while telling Clidamant openly that he is more important to her than her mother and the throne. Clidamant answers: "Si vous m'aimez, scachez que je n'en veux rien croire." (Act V, Scene II). Clotilde is naturally offended by Clidamant's manner. In the meanwhile, Deuthère has decided her daughter can love whom she pleases. Disgusted with the intrigue surrounding her, Clotilde chooses to love no one. Deuthère misunderstands her daughter's sincerity and interprets it

as another of her ruses to deceive Théodebert. The King wants to force Clotilde to marry him. He meets his son, sword in hand mistakingly thinks Clodomire has come to kill him. The sword is for Clidamant whom Clodomire intends to murder. Théodebert has a change of heart which involves punishing Clidamant and marrying Deuthère.

Clidamant recounts a fantastic adventure he has just experienced with Deuthère and Clotilde. He surprised Deuthère on the point of killing her daughter with a sword, and, to prevent the catastrophe, he jumped between the two. Clotilde fainted, and Deuthère, full of remorse and thinking her daughter dead, committed suicide by thrusting the blade of the sword in her heart. Before dying, she pronounced a curse upon Clidamant. Immeasurably happy, Clidamant wants to die because Deuthère is dead. Théodebert summons him to choose the manner in which he wishes to die. Full of self-reproach because of the unhappy turn of events, Théodebert is assured by Clotilde that she is responsible; Clodomire blames everything on Clidamant. Presently Sigile reports Clidamant's suicide. The king benevolently offers Clotilde to Clodomire.

This is a tragedy written according to the classical rules. The plot, involving four separate intrigues, is somewhat diffuse, but the development is so well handled the reader is unaware of this shortcoming. Although there is no mention of the unity of time, the events could have taken place within the twenty-four hour period. The unities of place and action are closely followed.

Although the name of the play is *Clotilde,* the leading character is Deuthère. Major emphasis is placed on the outcome of her ambition to become queen. Placed by the author as the scheming competitor of her daughter, Deuthère's blinding ambition evolves into a jealous passion that drives her to attempt murder and then suicide. The analysis of Deuthère's emotions anticipates the tragedies of Jean Racine. Clotilde's gentle and predisposing character is in striking contrast to that of her impetuous and frenzied mother. Clotilde would emerge as a meek and nondescript daughter if it had not been for a surprising development in the fifth act. In her refusal to follow the wishes of Deuthère and marry Clodomire, Clotilde expresses an independence of spirit that makes her a real personality. However, her usual equilibrium is cast awry by the unprovoked charge, in the third act, against Théodebert for infidelity. Although Boyer was evidently attempting to project woman's coquettish nature, it is incongruous to believe Clotilde ever had the faintest romantic inclination toward Théodebert.

Cast in the roles of anguished competitors for the same woman's love, Théodebert and his son Clodomire are ludicrous. Instead of being concerned with affairs of state as is natural to a man of Théodebert's age, the King subjects himself to the romantic sufferings of a stripling. His occasional flashes of reality only serve to heighten the burlesque character of the situation.

Clodomire's timid nature is accentuated by his hesitation in admitting his love to Clotilde, and, instead of creating interest, his state is made all the more ridiculous. The prince's harried maneuvers enter the realm of the burlesque when, in the fifth act, he brandishes his sword, intended for the murder of Clidamant, and it is mistaken by Théodebert as his own death weapon.

Although the past relationship between Deuthère and Clidamant is referred to only vaguely, it plays an important part in their present status. Depicted as a fatal man born only to love, Clidamant has had time to fall deeply in love with Deuthère and become insanely jealous of her. When she dies by her own hand, he can triumph only by committing the same act. Although Boyer inadvertently created a comic character in Théodebert and introduced a needless complication of plot with intrigues of love, his mastery of the alexandrine and the analysis of Deuthère's overpowering obsession to be queen are indeed noteworthy.

According to Loret, reporting in *La Muze historique* of May 24, 1659, *Clotilde* was favorably received at the Comte de Lyonne's festival. . . .

Louis Ferrier wrote one historical tragedy, *Anne de Bretagne*. In five acts and in verse, the play was presented in 1678 and published a year later. The work contains an important preface in which the author defends his choice of subject and discusses the unfavorable attitude of the enlightened public toward the use of French history as a source for tragedy. . . .

Anne de Bretagne (1477—1514) had a very interesting career. She was the daughter of François II, Duc de Bretagne, and Marguerite de Foix. She succeeded her father as Duchesse de Bretagne in 1488. Charles VIII, King of France, wished to establish his authority over her; Alain d'Albret wished to marry her; Jean de Rohan claimed the duchy; and her guardian, the Maréchal de Rieux, was soon in open revolt against Charles VIII. In 1489 the French army invaded Brittany.

Anne formed an alliance with Maximilien of Austria and married him by proxy in 1490. Affairs in Austria kept Maximilien too busy to consider helping his bride. With no help from her husband, Anne, besieged at Rennes, was compelled to seek negotiations with Charles. The terms of the treaty stipulated that Anne should marry the French king. This, of course, meant that France would have jurisdiction over Brittany. Anne concurred in the terms of the treaty, broke her marriage with Maximilien, and became queen of France.

After the death of Charles VIII in 1498 Anne returned to Brittany, and in 1499 she married Louis XII, thus again becoming queen of France. In 1504 she made an agreement for the marriage of her daughter, Claude de France to Charles of Austria, the future Emperor Charles V. This agreement was broken and Anne arranged for her daughter to marry François d'Angoulême, who became, in 1515, Fran ois Premier, King of France.

The theme of Ferrier's play is concentrated on the efforts

of Anne to select a husband. As the play opens it is revealed that Anne is sought by three men: the Maréchal d'Albret, Maximilien of Austria and Charles VIII of France. None of these intrepid warriors is to her liking. She loves the Duc d'Orléans (Louis XII), and would marry the latter except for a fit of ill-conceived jealousy which makes her choose Charles VIII.

The so-called tragedy was praised by the *Mercure galant* of November, 1678. . . .

The *Mercure* mentioned the pleasure of the King and Queen with a performance they attended. Even though characterization in the work is acceptable to us today, there is little unity of action and practically no interest. Ferrier distorts history to such a degree that the queenly Anne becomes a soap opera heroine. Fortunately Ferrier had no influence on his contemporaries. It is lamentable, however, that no great tragedy writer in France opened successfully the rich field of French history.

Another national historical tragedy presented in 1678 was the unpublished *Princesse de Clèves* based on the novel by the same name of Madame de La Fayette. The only two performances took place at the *théâtre de Guénégaud* in December, 1678. This play, by Edne Boursault (1638—1701), was allegedly later known under the title of *Germanicus*. . . .

Because of the comparatively recent date (sixteenth century) of its events, Boursault knew that an audience would not appreciate his work. With this in mind he had written a prologue in defense of subject matter for tragedy being drawn from French national history. The prologue was in the form of an allegory with Fame and Melopene discussing the problem under consideration. Melopene, surfeited with subjects taken from ancient history, seeks new outlets for tragedy. Fame suggests: "Et depuis si longtemps que la France a des Rois, ne s'en trouve-t-il point que meritent ton choix? Choisis quelque grand nom sur les bords de la Seine."

One other *tragédie nationale* written in the century was *Le jugement équitable de Charles le Hardy, dernier duc de Bourgogne*. The Frères Parfaict have a long analysis. The essential action centers around Rodolfe, governor of Mastric, and admirer of Mathilde, the wife of Albert. In order to fulfill his desire to have Mathilde, Rodolfe accuses Albert of treason and has him executed forthwith. Once Albert is dispatched, Rodolfe's passion becomes a frenzied desire, and he attempts to violate Mathilde. She faints at the propitious moment. After the spell has passed, Mathilde seeks out Charles, Duc de Bourgogne, who has been spending a few days in Mastric. The Duc orders that Rodolfe marry Mathilde. The marriage is performed, and Rodolfe is hastily imprisoned to await death. A lady, Frédégonde, appears to plead Rodolfe's case. He is really the son of Charles and a dead sister of Frédégonde. It is too late to retract the sentence, since, at the very moment Charles commanded a messenger to relay his order sparing Rodolfe, another messenger brings the unhappy news that he is dead.

The play is extremely melodramatic and rhetorical. Too much of the plot is left up to chance. The Frères Parfaict commenting on the work admired the author's mastery at

---

Geoffrey Brereton on the characteristics of romanesque tragedy:

[Thomas Corneille and Quinault] were writing plays styled tragedies or, more rarely, tragicomedies, in the later 1650s and throughout the 1660s. These plays were contemporary with most of the productions of Pierre Corneille. . . . They also overlapped Racine's work. In a sense they formed a bridge between the work of the two major dramatists, though that statement in itself does not fully represent the true position in a drama in which cross-influences were of such importance. But it can at least be said that they reflected the majority taste of theatre audiences in the fifteen years beginning towards 1655. This taste was for romanesque tragedy, whose principal features were that it derived from contemporary or near-contemporary novels or, when ostensibly based on other sources, as it frequently was, observed the ethos and attitudes found in the novels. The treatment of love was similar. The plots, full of misunderstandings between characters and surprising vicissitudes, depended excessively on cases of disguised or mistaken identity.

By no means all the plays written by Thomas Corneille in the period under review exhibit these characteristics, and Quinault also produced some exceptions. Nor can either author—and this applies particularly to Thomas—be judged only on his work written during these particular fifteen years. . . . From the 1650s on there was no serious competition, except dubiously from the now less fashionable Pierre Corneille, for the romanesque play to face. It assumed the name of 'tragedy', came at times to deserve it, and for a time dominated the stage under that description. In this period of its greatest success and most extreme development Thomas Corneille and Quinault provided the best examples of it.

Geoffrey Brereton, in French Tragic Drama in the Sixteenth and Seventeenth Centuries, *Methuen & Co., Ltd., 1973.*

---

development, but considered the theme unsuitable for French tragedy.

. . . [T]he main source of tragedy throughout the seventeenth century was ancient history and mythology. Histories of other nations were of much less importance. Although there was some criticism in favor of using French national history, novelty in the choice of subject matter was not sanctioned by the public. The only successful play derived from modern history was *Le Comte d'Essex* (1678) of Thomas Corneille. Modern subjects, however, were frequently disguised in order to give them an ancient or Byzantine setting. Notable among these was *Andronic* (1685) of Campistron in which is recounted the tragic story of Prince Don Carlos, son of Philip II of Spain.

As in the sixteenth century much of the political satire of

the seventeenth was written in dramatic form and belongs to political rather than dramatic history. Brief mention is made of such plays in this study only because they were classified as tragedy. They were actually nothing more than pamphlets in dialogue form. Many were published outside of France and circulated surreptitiously in the country. Among famous people, the Maréchal d'Ancre and his wife, Richelieu, Mazarin, Louvois, and Mme. de Maintenon were the object of bitter satire. Of course, the old animosities between Protestants and Catholics were kept alive.

Due to a predilection for the classical ideal of *imitation, règle* and *goût* innovation in tragedy was discouraged. Infrequent references to the use of French history as a source for tragedy drew little attention or passed completely ignored. Of the more than two hundred tragedies that appeared during the century, less than thirty were drawn from French history. Only four of these works were inspired by events from the national history occurring before the fifteenth century. The entire production of national historical tragedy was highly propagandistic, prolix, periphrastic and stripped of interest.

Geoffrey Brereton

SOURCE: "After Racine and Conclusion," in *French Tragic Drama in the Sixteenth and Seventeenth Centuries,* Methuen & Co Ltd, 1973, pp. 282-93.

[*Brereton is an English scholar who has written extensively on French literature of the sixteenth, seventeenth, and eighteenth centuries. In the following excerpt, Brereton analyzes the lack of development within the genre of tragedy during the end of Louis XIV's reign.*]

After Racine until the end of Louis XIV's reign there were no significant developments in French tragedy. The most successful of the older dramatists, Thomas Corneille and Quinault, had already abandoned it in the 1670s. The Abbé Claude Boyer (1618-98), a good journeyman who had been writing tragedies since the forties in search of a success which never came conclusively, had nothing new to offer. Having followed fashion conscientiously, he came nearest to a theatrical triumph with the biblical play of *Judith* which, with his earlier *Jephté,* was written for Saint-Cyr in the wake of Racine's *Athalie.* Produced professionally at the Comédie-Française in 1695, *Judith* met with considerable applause—largely due, according to Boileau, to the performance of la Champmeslé in the title-part. Boyer's career ended in 1697 with the libretto of an unsuccessful opera.

Jacques Pradon (1644-98) wrote ten tragedies in all, seven of which followed his notorious *Phèdre et Hippolyte.* This near-contemporary of Racine had begun in 1673 with *Pirame et Thisbé,* an attempted renewal of Théophile's fifty-year-old play. After *Phèdre* he wrote two tragedies on Greek subjects which had been treated by Seneca and Euripides, then turned to Roman history. This gave him his only real success, the tragedy of *Regulus* (1688). These later plays showed the influence of both Pierre and Tho-

J. Le Pautre sketch depicting spectators on stage during a performance.

mas Corneille, with the romanesque tendencies associated particularly with the latter. The acid remark attributed to Racine, that 'the difference between M. Pradon and myself is that I know how to write', provides an acceptable explanation of Pradon's mediocrity.

Of a younger generation born in the 1650s, easily the most prolific was Jean-Galbert Campistron (1656-1723). Between 1683 and 1693 he produced nine tragedies in addition to a comedy and three opera libretti. Only three of his tragedies enjoyed any considerable contemporary success. The others were complete or relative failures and two of them were never printed. The seven that survive were competent exercises in drama, Racinian in their regularity of construction if in no other respect, and generally derivative in their situations and characters. In *Alcibiade,* Campistron went back as far as Du Ryer's *Thémistocle* for the plot and other suggestions.

None of Campistron's contemporaries came near to equalling his output. Antoine de La Fosse (1653-1708) and Longepierre (1659-1721) are both remembered for one play among the three or four tragedies each wrote. The *Manlius Capitolinus* (1698) of the first had a complicated

political plot, with the usual love element, based on Roman history. This play, a contemporary success when first produced, acquired an additional interest for critics and scholars as a partial imitation of the *Venice Preserved* (1682) of Thomas Otway, and so as a first faint sign of French awareness of English drama, though certainly not significant of a trend. Longepierre's *Médée* (1694) was a renewal of the theme treated by Euripides, Seneca and Pierre Corneille. Described by the author in his Preface as 'une pièce à peu près dans le goût des Anciens' and a return (echoing d'Aubignac and Racine) to 'simplicity', this *Médée* failed on first production but became popular throughout the eighteenth century, after which it virtually disappeared.

Like these two, other writers composed occasional tragedies, but failed to establish themselves as regular tragic dramatists. The only men who might be said to have done so belonged to a still younger generation which appeared round the turn of the century. Joseph La Grange-Chancel (1676-1758) produced eight tragedies between 1694 and 1716 and after a long interruption, due to his political opinions which earned him imprisonment and exile, two further tragedies acted in the 1730s. Claiming, no doubt with some justification, to have been advised by Racine, he failed, more markedly than even Campistron had done, to take over the succession. His main group of tragedies were based for the most part on nominally Greek themes but were more influenced by the French novel and treated in a romanesque way. The original story of his *Méléagre* (1699) is in Ovid, but had been dramatized long before by Benserade, whom he may have read, and by Hardy, whom he is unlikely to have known.

In the seven tragedies of Prosper-Jolyot Crébillon (1674-1762), produced between 1705 and 1726, there are some signs of innovation, consisting principally in his cultivation of horror, which has often been stressed as his characteristic feature. He owed this reputation to his third tragedy, *Atrée Thyeste* (1707), of which the story is certainly horrible, requiring a father to be deceived by his vengeful brother into eating a meal composed of the flesh of his own murdered sons. Crébillon educed this grisly feast (described with ghoulish relish in the original *Thyestes* of Seneca) to a cup of blood, and even that was not actually drunk. In his last plays there are one or two severed heads, but the audience does not see them. Crébillon's horrors were rhetorical rather than visual. In their day they represented a mild challenge to the old *bienséances*, which were to be more flagrantly violated in the *drame* than in tragedy itself.

If Crébillon's work can be found to contain certain intimations of the eighteenth-century taste for the macabre (the 'Gothic' sensibility), none of the other dramatists so far mentioned can be described as anything but backward-looking. They pillaged earlier dramatists for themes, only rarely going beyond the Roman, Greek and romanesque sources already drawn on. In their treatment of these themes they occasionally attempted new approaches but were incapable of establishing a new drama, or even the basis of one. Their timid innovations were generally melodramatic, better suited to tragicomedy if that class of play had still been current. But it had long ceased to be so and for the *fin de siècle* playwrights the only alternatives to tragedy were comedy, which was still flourishing, and various kinds of spectacle, principally opera. It is apparent that after Racine tragedy lost its drive, together with any clear sense of future direction. The causes were perhaps less in the writers than in the moment, an unusual one in the history of French literature.

The last three decades of Louis XIV's reign were a period of pause in French culture. New ideas were beginning to germinate in the social and political fields, though very tentatively. In art, the Quarrel of the Ancients and the Moderns, which occupied literary minds in the 1680s and 1690s, typified the situation. Against the Ancients and their champions, who argued that the Greeks and Latins had set up well-proved standards of excellence and that imitation of them in a broad sense was the only sure foundation for modern literature, the opponents of this classical tradition pointed to the brilliant talents which their own age had produced. But they were still looking back, though not so far as to Greece and Rome. Charles Perrault's poem, *Le Siècle de Louis le Grand* (1687), which

was the immediate cause of this polemic, mentioned not a single French writer who was still alive at that date and the majority of the examples given had flourished before 1650. The Quarrel reflected a certain pride, not to say self-satisfaction, felt by elderly Academicians in the achievements of the *Grand Siècle,* but contained nothing at all, beyond a vague theory of progress, which concerned future prospects. Anything less revolutionary, or even dynamic, it would be hard to conceive.

The period of 1680-1715 was thus one of stocktaking in the arts, of a disinclination to innovate, of a certain lassitude such as is perceptible in La Bruyère's *Caractères,* but particularly of a tendency to cling to acquired values. This was the predominant temper both of the ageing court and of educated society as a whole.

In the circumstances it was natural that tragedy, a genre recognized as one of the outstanding achievements of the reign, should stagnate. The foundation of the Comédie-Française in 1680 had left only one theatre in which it could be performed. Though the number of new tragedies produced in Paris did not decrease perceptibly, the theatre in its monopolistic position was disinclined to experiment. It could also be contented with shorter runs. If these were unprofitable for the authors, it made little difference to the actors who had plenty of other material in hand. Lancaster has calculated that during 1689-1700 about fifty per cent of the performances of tragedy at the Comédie-Française were of Corneille and Racine, twenty-five per cent of other plays previously produced (going back as far as Du Ryer and Tristan), and only twenty-five per cent of new tragedies. For these last the authors were paid their share of the takings but the others, in modern terms, were out of copyright. A company which could draw on this rich repertory costing it nothing, using scenery and costumes so largely stylized that they were often interchangeable from play to play, naturally became conservative. Corneille and Racine still drew the necessary audiences and long continued to do so. Tragedy as a serious entertainment was not dead, it simply ceased to develop. The principal new interest, such as it was, centred on the actors and actresses and their art, on interpretation rather than on creation. . . .

· · · · ·

The sixteenth-century academics and their pupils introduced to France an idea of tragedy derived ostensibly, and sometimes actually, from the ancient Greek dramatists, but in practice more frequently from Seneca. From the experiments of the Boncourt-Coqueret group, beginning with Jodelle's, a form of play emerged which was consciously intended to replace, at least for cultivated audiences, the chaotic and spectacular medieval drama. It had five acts with choruses, a comparatively small number of actors, a limited playing-time, and was normally concerned with a single major event and the effect of this event on the principal character or characters. To interest its audiences it relied almost exclusively on words in preference to scenic effects, and, after a few early hesitations, these words were cast in the form of alexandrine couplets with alternate masculine and feminine rhymes. Verbal elaboration was of the first importance for the dramatists and the spectators alike and can convincingly be shown to be based on the principles of rhetoric as then taught in the schools. The result, as seen in the work of Garnier and later of Montchrestien, was often a display of splendid or florid eloquence—according to the point of view—and an overall impression of static speech-making which minimized the elements of continuity and surprise.

The lack of what were later to be considered as essential dramatic qualities in sixteenth-century tragedy is easy to point out, and in comparing it with seventeenth-century drama the contrast is too visible not to be remarked. Modern scholars have objected, however, that to apply such criteria to Renaissance tragedy is to ignore its true nature. It should be approached as a different art-form, entirely deserving of study in its own right. While the argument, put in those terms, is a strong one, and a necessary corrective to the tendency to consider Garnier and his contemporaries merely as inept forerunners of Corneille and Racine, some comparisons are nevertheless illuminating and inevitable. The *form* established by humanist learned drama persisted, minus the choruses, in seventeenth-century tragedy, as did the virtual elimination of physical action. The rhetorical principles on which the first was largely based recurred in the second in such features as the *tirade,* the *récit,* stichomythia and the *sentence,* though the effects obtained from them might often be different, precisely because of the development of a 'dramatic' sense. More general features, such as the final speech of lamentations and the dream of foreboding, also persisted in the later drama.

It is true that the seventeenth century could have drawn all this from alternative sources, going back as the sixteenth century had done, but independently, to Seneca or the Greeks or to Italian models and theory and readapting them to a new conception of drama. If insisted on, this interpretation would mean drawing a line after Renaissance tragedy and so segregating it in its period and implying an entirely fresh start towards 1630. But even if such an extreme position were adopted, it would still not exclude humanist tragedy from any general account of the emergency of tragic drama in France. Humanist tragedy would still be of interest as a first if ultimately sterile attempt to find a substitute for the dying drama of the Middle Ages.

But it was certainly more than that. Although there is little concrete evidence of any precise textual imitation of Garnier or Montchrestien by the dramatists of the 1630s (and this is natural, since the latter were consciously innovating in some contempt of the past, and particularly of its poetic diction), there are abundant traces of what can fairly be called a transition.

This should be placed in the period 1590-1620, a time of confusion and mediocrity in French drama, though not of sterility. The fact that Montchrestien's plays were written around 1600 and at least some of them were certainly performed, indicates that as late as this pure humanist

tragedy could coexist with the cruder and apparently more popular types. The nature of some of these was mixed, proving again the persistence of the humanist influence, however debased, upon other writers. There was potential development here, unrealized for lack of talent and opportunity, but fortunately the example of the only considerable dramatist of the period proves beyond doubt that a transition of some kind was possible.

Alexandre Hardy apparently intended to write in the tradition of Garnier, who, with Seneca and Ronsard, was the only model he mentioned. He used the apparatus of Renaissance tragedy, the warning ghosts, the over-ornamented speeches, the long rhetorical discussions, but he used it dynamically. While one or two of his tragedies are as deficient in movement and point as the sixteenth-century precedents, without the compensation of a convincing pathos, in the great majority there is a preoccupation with movement, often in the form of violent action on stage. His plays seem primitive because the action is episodic and badly co-ordinated with the story-line. In short, he was weak in plotting, so that in place of a steadily gathering interest he offers a series of shocks and surprises. It is hardly necessary to repeat that a more skilful playwright would have organized the material better. What is relevant here is that he achieved a kind of union between the static humanist tragedy and the tragic drama of his own century. His work can profitably be analysed from either point of view: both for what it preserves from the earlier age and for what it foreshadows in his successors. If his surviving plays could be dated with any accuracy, it might be possible to trace a development within Hardy himself, but as things are this can only be conjectural. Whether or not his tragicomedies were the more recent part of his work, they certainly pointed forward to a type of play that flourished for several decades after him. Often derived from recent prose fiction, they contained in their totality all the principal features of the melodramatic tragicomedies of the 1630s and 1640s and even - making full allowance for the triumph of the *bienséances* and greatly improved techniques of plot construction—some of the features of the romanesque drama of the fifties and sixties.

. . . . .

No history of drama is entirely separable from the history of the theatre. The actors and audiences from whom the plays were written must influence their nature. Reciprocally, the standing and function of the theatre in a society is reflected, even if unconsciously, in the plays.

The learned tragedies of the Renaissance were originally acted by students and continued to be for a long time: not only in schools and universities but occasionally at court or in aristocratic houses when a special performance was called for to entertain the guests. Local fraternities not necessarily composed of students also combined in various towns to mount plays which were at least nominally tragedies and which seem to represent a communal effort similar to that shown in the medieval drama but on a more modest scale. Finally there were the travelling companies whose sole profession was to entertain and whose repertories evidently included both learned tragedies and other less regular types. There was thus considerable theatrical activity, both amateur and professional, of various kinds. But it had no focal point, no geographical centre which could have given it some social and cultural cohesion. Paris might have provided this, but even after 1600, . . . it failed for some time to do so. The Hôtel de Bourgogne was used only intermittently by French companies, and then with dubious success. If Hardy, working for a manager who enjoyed security of tenure, had been able to write long enough for a public with known and constant tastes, his production might well have been less disjointed. As it was, he was obliged, like his lesser contemporaries, to improvise for various audiences whose responses must often have been unpredictable.

It was nevertheless the professional companies that eventually established a serious theatre in the capital and in the 1620s prepared the way for a new drama which could definitely equal the medieval drama in social importance and had sufficient prestige to attract and form writers of the first rank. In the 1630s the theatre became respectable (except for those who condemned it on religious grounds), it was securing influential patrons, and it could offer substantial rewards in money and status. Above all, it could now reflect, more immediately than any other art-form, the tastes and aspirations of the community as a whole. This position was maintained, with only minor variations, throughout most of the century.

The growing importance of the theatre attracted not only new dramatists but critics. There was interaction between them, making it impossible to define the share of each in the development of French classical tragedy, as it has come to be called. What can be said is that the dramatic theorists, as nearly always, were rarely the same men who wrote the plays. By far the greatest of these, Corneille, discussed, though for the most part at a later date, the underlying principles of his work. But both then, in the *Examens* and *Discours* of 1660, as in his earlier prefaces, the general tone of his writing is justificatory. If not necessarily on the defensive, he is seeking to reinterpret critical theory in the light of the proved effectiveness of his own plays. For him, the successful practitioner, the two things are not identical, however genuine his desire to reconcile them may have been. Other prominent dramatists—Rotrou, Du Ryer, Tristan L'Hermite—published their plays with fulsome dedications to aristocratic patrons, but without a sentence that could be construed as critical comment. Only Mairet in his preface to *Silvanire* and Scudéry in his *Observations sur le Cid* attempted anything approximating to dramatic theory. With Mairet this led to the actual composition of regular plays, though he departed from regularity in his later work, Scudéry applied some general criteria, which he attempted to observe in some of his own tragicomedies, to his examination of Corneille's play. But his *Observations* was primarily an opportunist work, brought into being by the desire to join in a contemporary polemic rather than to expound his own artistic creed. A polemical impulse can, of course, be ascribed to most, if not all, significant criticism, and

this does not invalidate it, but when it is as occasional as Scudéry's it loses something in weight.

The critics who were not practising dramatists were polemists also. They attacked and defended plays and their authors for personal motives, including the building-up of their own literary reputations. Yet their writings had a foundation of doctrine, expressed in somewhat fragmentary from in the 1630s and given its most complete expression in the Abbé d'Aubignac's *Pratique du théâtre* of 1657. It must be remarked in passing that d'Aubignac had composed towards 1640 three tragedies in strict accordance with his theories, though written exceptionally in prose since he had no talent for verse. They enjoyed only slight or very temporary success. It is also noteworthy that his *Pratique du théâtre,* though it originated in the Quarrel of *Le Cid* and expanded certain critical ideas which he had expressed at that period, was published much too late to have exerted any formative influence on classical tragedy. It was a statement resuming what the theorists had desired or intended and its principal interest lies in that. It did not spring from the heart of a new movement and any influence which it had was on the generation of Racine.

All this may appear to lead towards the conclusion that French classical regular tragedy was an idea in the minds of theorists which was realized rarely in practice and, when it was, mainly in secondary works. This would be too extreme a view. It could only be based on conceptions of purity and conformity which may well be put forward as critical absolutes but are unattainable in the actual theatre. One has only to compare French tragic drama of the mid-century with earlier French drama, or with English Jacobean drama, or with Spanish drama up to and including Calderón, the contemporary of Corneille and Rotrou, to see the concrete results of the movement towards regularity. Linguistic and scenic proprieties were generally observed, with relatively minor exceptions in the latter. There was an awareness of moral *bienséance,* at least on a superficial level, though on the deeper level of moral utility it posed impossible conditions for writers of tragedy. *Vraisemblance* was aimed at conscientiously, though sometimes at the expense of twisting it into some very curious shapes. Play-construction, embracing structure, was immensely improved. It digested the more mechanical unities of time and place until they could go virtually unnoticed. It achieved in a fair number of plays the much more important unity of interest which is the characteristic feature of French classical tragedy and the ultimate justification of all its other conditions. Much of value had to be discarded in the process, but for a long time it was accepted as a desideratum and inspired works which were not only typical, but major by any standards.

Plays which fell short of the 'classical' requirements on one or more points were nevertheless numerous—in fact very much more numerous than those that can strictly be said to have satisfied them all. They begin with the plays of the thirties that can clearly be seen to be irregular because they were so in a technical sense. They continue with plays that may appear conventionally regular, but which in their conception and often their structure are considerably removed from the classical norm. For the most part these are the plays classed under tragicomedy, but the distinction between this and tragedy is not absolute and can only be used as a rough working-guide. Tragedy also retained a strong element of melodrama, theoretically incompatible with the classical ideal, but generally present in practice. The single decade of the forties produced Corneille's *Rodogune, Théodore* and *Héraclius,* the major tragedies of Rotrou, and Tristan's *Mort de Sénèque* and *Mort de Chrispe,* in all of which the melodramatic element is perceptible, particularly in the violent and sometimes arbitrary nature of the dénouments. This may be concealed but is not removed by the fact that the worst violence occurs offstage.

It has become usual to describe this drama as baroque, a classification depending on analysis from several different angles, including the approach through language and prosody. One of the generally agreed features of the baroque is ambiguity, whether traced down to the deeper levels of consciousness and personality or seen merely as a display of distorting mirror-images. On that more superficial level the identity plays of the fifties and sixties can also be included in the baroque, which is thus extended to the time of Racine. But Racine himself, though he made some use of ambiguity, cannot be fairly classed as baroque. In his case the term ceases to be significant and it is more profitable to trace in his work the discreet persistence of the romanesque and the melodramatic. . . .

On that basis he constructed plays which remain as the finest examples of French classical tragedy, a genre which without him would lose enormously in interest and standing. By his reaffirmation in practice of the principles first laid down in the thirties, he saved it for some time from the sterility into which it afterwards fell and which, to judge by the work of his own contemporaries, was already threatening it when he began to write. He provides a striking example of an exceptional talent working within an accepted formula which, whatever its merits, can have no virtue in itself to create outstanding work. Ultimately, even in the theatre, the individual talent is everything, while the method or the 'school' is at best an aid, at worst a hindrance. With Racine conformism paid. With others it was a handicap, even if unrealized at first.

In the course of the eighteenth century this began to be seen more clearly, and the history of that drama is characterized by attempts at modification or escape. They were still, however, not radical enough to inspire a genuinely new drama. It was left to the Romantics to reject openly what they saw as an intolerably restrictive tradition, narrowed by then by several generations of mediocre tragic dramatists, and to return to a vein which Pierre Corneille, among others, had already opened up. The romanced historical dramas of Hugo and Dumas *père* bore resemblances to seventeenth-century tragicomedy, and particularly to the *comédie héroïque* as Corneille conceived it in writing *Don Sanche d'Aragon.* For this play Corneille invoked the example of Hardy to justify his introduction of Plebeian characters (Dedication). He acknowledged his

debt to the Spanish *comedia* in his *Examen.* Rotrou might much more often have done the same.

COMEDY

Eleanor F. Jourdain

SOURCE: "Comedy," in *Dramatic Theory and Practice in France: 1690-1808,* 1921. Reprint by Benjamin Blom, 1968, pp. 6-43.

[In the following excerpt, Jourdain discusses the development of comedy by Molière's successors.]

It would have been difficult for any successors of Molière to avoid the dangerous homage of imitation of his methods. Molière had succeeded in making the theatre national in France, and in popularising the painting of manners in the middle classes of society. Now the whole tendency of the drama in the eighteenth century was to throw more light on the middle classes, and it is important to notice that from the days of Corneille onwards they had become regular playgoers in Paris. The early efforts of eighteenth-century comedy were therefore on Molière's lines, though at first of the nature of caricature of his methods. When writers of comedy began to reflect their own time more exactly, the relation with the spirit of Molière became greater, while the direct imitation of the master was slighter. Then appeared the more original dramatists of the comic stage of the eighteenth century, Marivaux and Beaumarchais; and definite homage was paid to Molière by writers of the new *genre,* the *drame sérieux,* who did not yield to the writers for the comic stage in their appreciation of Molière's general aim.

In the transition from the works of Molière to those of the writers who are characteristic of the eighteenth century, the most important comedies are those of Regnard, Dancourt, and Le Sage. Le Sage marks the transition from the imitators of Molière to the writers of comedy with a political and social bias, the greatest of whom was Beaumarchais. Marivaux (1688-1763), though historically earlier than Beaumarchais (1732-1799), is not in the same line of development, and his original treatment of a limited dramatic field must be considered separately.

Of these writers, J. F. Regnard (1656-1710) was the closest to Molière both in time and in the character of his work. Like Molière he worked at first on the lines of Italian comedy, an early journey to Italy having interested him in the art of that country. His strange adventures gave him experience but did not damp his ardour. He was captured together with a Provençal lady by an Algerian corsair, and spent some years of slavery in Constantinople, from which condition he was finally ransomed. He travelled in Flanders, Holland, Denmark and Sweden, Lapland, Poland, Hungary, and Germany. Love and cards shared his interest with travelling, but at last he settled down to a quiet life in his country house at Grillon, and wrote most of his comedies there. He attempted at one time a tragedy, *Sapor*; he worked sometimes alone and sometimes with Dufresny. But after making many conventional experiments, he took Molière as his pattern, and his best comedies are formed on his master. As Molière had drawn upon the humours of the provinces, Regnard imitated him, and in *Le Joueur* made fun of the Auvergnat, Toutalas, and in *Le Bal* of the Gascon, Le Baron, but he had also come across many other types in his travels of which he made full use.

The form of his plays is very varied, their length may be one, or three, or five acts. For in Regnard the length of the play really depends on the size of the subject and thus his form is not conventional. A modern audience sometimes, and somewhat unfairly, finds him long-winded in the longer plays. This is partly no doubt because his imitation of Molière leads Regnard to employ Molière's plan of catch-words or catch-phrases (like Orgon's 'Le pauvre homme'). Regnard, like Molière, repeats a comic effect when he once has achieved it, but Regnard sometimes trusts to an earlier comic association to make the second or third allusion seem amusing. So, in *Le Légataire universel*, he uses the catch-phrase of '*léthargie.*'

The names given to the characters are the conventional ones. Lisette is a *suivante*, sometimes supplanted by Nérine: the heroine is Léonor, or Isabelle, the regular names of Italian comedy, or sometimes Angélique. The lover is Valère, or Dorante, or Éraste. Géronte is a name for an old man. The valet has many names: he is sometimes Crispin, or Merlin (who really produces wonders on the scene). Valets and soubrettes play a large part in this drama, so do masques and music. Lawyers and usurers are a butt for Regnard's sarcasm as doctors were for Molière's, but the attack on lawyers is one common to the whole of the eighteenth century, as is the insistence on the comic characteristics of the provinces of Normandy, Brittany, Gascony, Burgundy, Auvergne. Madame Bertrand and Madame Argante (both usual comedy names) jostle one another in the drama of Regnard.

One important difference between Molière and the writers of comedy in the eighteenth century is that Molière at his best does without accessories for his characters. Their calling and their views so far as they are external to the plot are neglected; the necessary setting and no more is given to the personages of his drama. We are aware that the households in *L'Avare* and *Le Bourgeois Gentilhomme* are the ordinary middle-class households of the time: we can see the stratum of cultivated society in which the characters in *Le Misanthrope* and *Les Femmes savantes* move. But we are given no previous history and practically no present details of their circumstances, except where, as in the case of *Le Bourgeois Gentilhomme*, it is important to know that M. Jourdain has prospered. But in eighteenth-century drama (and in this respect nineteenth-century drama has followed closely on its antecedents) opinions and social conditions are insisted on, even when these are quite external to the plot. Now Regnard is not himself exempt from this habit; he shows, in fact, the first symptom of the change, in *Le Joueur*, and *Le Legataire univer-*

sel: though he has less of what, from the point of view of drama, we may call a defect, than the writers of the *drame bourgeois*. A good deal of time is however taken up in his plays by the description of circumstances that do not develop character. We are told at length in *Le Légataire universel* about Géronte's will, about his relations and the different plans for the disposal of his money: but Géronte is left by the dramatist in the last scene of the last act exactly where he was at first. In *L'Avare* we are aware of a conflict in the mind of the miser, but while Géronte's opinion in *Le Légataire universel* is puzzled and changeable, he goes through no crisis of feeling or thought. Regnard, however, possesses a power of psychological description in detail which shows that he can observe human nature even though he cannot concentrate motives and action into the plot of his play. For example, he treats the subject of jealousy with great ability. In the scene in *Le Joueur* between La Comtesse and Angélique, the subtle change from the well-mannered woman of the world to the jealous primitive woman is excellently indicated. Again, in the same play Angélique, softening to Valère, is heard to say harder and harder things to him in a gentler and gentler voice: while the soubrette approves less and less as the scene goes on. Here is an opportunity for a good actress to express the psychology of the real emotion of Angélique. But these character-studies do not control the plot. In *Le Joueur*, which had its English origin, and had been already treated by Dufresny, Regnard desired to make the character of Valère consistent all through the play. Valère goes off the stage saying to his valet:

Va, va, consolons-nous, Hector: et quelque jour
Le jeu m'acquittera des pertes de l'amour.

This trait certainly gives the play a unity of meaning, but the extreme consistency of the hero's behaviour removes the action from life to mechanism and destroys our interest. Regnard's plays thus are precursors of the 'well-constructed plays' of Scribe in the nineteenth century; the pleasure of the audience lies in an admiration of the author, who unravels a subtle mystery, or works out a problem set just one step in advance of the public which follows his moves. Besides exciting this interest in the plot as in a game to be guessed, Regnard produces amusement by insisting on laughable traits. This he does all through his *théâtre*, from the scene in *Le Bal* where the lover is hidden in the 'cello case, to the farcical scenes of plot and counterplot in *Le Légataire universel*. The sermon and the moral are to his mind of minor importance.

Regnard was followed by Dufresny (1648-1724), a slighter writer, with whom he often worked, but the *Esprit de contradiction* and *Reconcilation normande* are both amusing and vivacious though long drawn out. In *Le Mariage fait et rompu* the last words show Dufresny's inheritance of Molière's hatred of hypocrisy:

Tout bien considéré, franche coquetterie
Est un vice moins grand que fausse pruderie.
Les femmes ont banni ces hypocrites soins;
Le siècle y gagne au fond, c'est un vice de moins.

The titles of Dufresny's plays always take the form of the paradox which suggests the type of plot treated in them; besides those already mentioned we might instance *Le Double Veuvage* and *Les Mal-assortis,* and *La Malade sans maladie.* They are written in prose, and are so witty that they repay reading, even though what Dufresny calls 'l'architecture de la pièce' is sometimes hurried and imperfect. In some of his plays Dufresny has introduced 'vaudevilles' and songs, obeying the taste of the time for bringing in music to vary the monotony of a play. Like Regnard, Dufresny works on quite conventional lines, trusting to the brilliance of his dialogue to carry off his pieces. He enhances this effect by constantly bringing on to the stage some character who is acutely aware of the motives and absurdities of the others. Frosine acts this part in *Le Double Veuvage.*

Dancourt (1661-1725) was attracted, like Molière, by the desire to paint the manners of the middle classes. At the end of the seventeenth century and beginning of the eighteenth there was a great deal to observe, for the love of money and the love of pleasure dominated all classes, and produced a kind of confusion of values in which we find the strongest possible contrast to the century in which Corneille had reigned. Self-interest in every department was the motive of a society that lived under a corrupt government and had the example of a corrupt court before its eyes. Hopeless of being able to apply a remedy, the French at that time consoled themselves by getting all the material pleasure they could out of life. The drama of Dancourt reflects this condition, which he has finely observed. No character stands out in heroic contrast to the rest, but a whole bevy succeed one another in an eternal race for advantage. Dancourt had the qualities necessary for getting sharp impressions of this society upon paper. He got his effect by putting down a great deal of detail without feeling any fear of boring his audience. Take a little one-act play like *Le Tuteur.* The mystification of persons by night foreshadows a more famous scene in Beaumarchais' *Mariage de Figaro,* but there is very little comparatively at stake in *Le Tuteur.* Bernard and his accomplice, Lucas, are too evidently intended to be fooled by the rest. The moral is that only the person with wits can pursue an advantage and keep it. In the series of plays beginning with *Le Chevalier à la mode* we have better characterisation. Madame Patin has her ambitions, which are like those of Monsieur Jourdain in *Le Bourgeois Gentilhomme,* but the idea of the play is carried out more farcically than was the case in Molière's, and it is without the witty back-handed attacks by which the dupe, M. Jourdain, expresses his criticism of the society in which he attempts to move. There is, in the process, an immense amount of talking done on the stage, and this is in itself a satire on a class of society that engineered results by words instead of by wholesome labour.

In *Le Chevalier à la mode* Migaud, who is courting Madame Patin, says that he has always been afraid of her disposition, but is willing to marry her on account of family interests, while Le Chevalier, who also is courting her, says to Crispin, the valet, in the plainest words, that he is in love with her money. He is in the meantime accepting presents of horses and a carriage from a baroness to whose hand he is also a pretender. In these circumstances Migaud's plan is successful and the Chevalier, who is excluded, says that he only regrets Madame Patin's money and is intending to pay further attentions to the baroness. Dancourt has lifted the veil that obscures low motives, and thus his drama is an account not so much of what people were accustomed to say, but of what they actually thought. The truth of the painting was undeniable, and the fidelity of his dialogue to unavowed reasons for conduct makes for a psychological realism that is at the same time strangely lacking in bitterness. While the attack on the vices of the time is as sharp as Balzac's on those of the age of Louis Philippe, there is no trace of resentment in Dancourt. He writes in a detached and good-humoured way that at first hides from the reader the selfishness and brutality of the human nature he exposes to view.

Dancourt works out his ideas further in *Les Bourgeoises à la mode* (1697) and *Les Bourgeoises de qualité* (1700). In the last-named play the characters only gradually detach themselves from their background, and this is one of the effects of Dancourt's very real art. They appear first of all to show some fixed idea, some clear tendency of the mind, and then touch after touch reveals them as persons. For example Naquart the *procureur* in the first scene says:

> Il ne s'agit point de conscience lâ-dedans; et entre personnes du métier. . . .

while Le Tabellion answers:

> . . . Pourvu que je sois bien payé, et que vous accommodiais vous-même toute cette manigance-là, je ne dirai mot, et je vous lairai faire, il ne vous en faudra pas davantage.

In the next scene with the Procureur du Châtelet Naquart shows his extreme indifference to the evil of luxury, while Blandineau regrets the better old times.

His wife has the gaming habit of the age:

> J'ai joué, j'ai perdu, j'ai payé, je n'ai plus rien, je vais rejouer, il m'en faut d'autre en cas que je perde.

and explains to her husband that it is by 'complaisance' that she lives in a cottage in the country with him and his tiresome family, 'J'aime à paraître, moi; c'est là ma folie.'

It is the waiting-maid, Lisette, who presently makes the situation clear. While Blandineau considers that his wife must be out of her mind, Lisette remarks that Madame is very wise, she takes her pleasure, and gives her husband all the trouble. 'Qui est le plus fou de vous deux?' Blandineau can make no real impression on the conditions round him. As one person after another comes on to the scene, all are moved by some spring of selfishness, but their selfishness reveals itself as different in different characters. Blandineau will not face the new standard of life, his wife will not give up her ambition, nor her sister her desire to be a great lady and to be worshipped as young and beautiful. Angélique is less unsympathetic because her faults are the faults of youth, and she is puzzled by life, while Lisette is clear-sighted; but the scheme by which Angélique gains her lover and M. Nacquart marries Blandineau's sister-in-law is a stage trick which would only be tiresome were it not that the result shows up the shallowness of La Greffière, who is to become Madame Nacquart, and of the other characters in the compact. Every one has been ready to take the easy path, and to give up love and honour for an income. It is thus a decadent society which Dancourt paints: the nobility has lost its glory, the bourgeoisie is losing its simplicity in imitating the decadent. As the chorus of peasants sing at the end of the play:

> Chacun ressent la vérité
> Du ridicule ici traité:
> Tout est orgueil et vanité
> Dans la plus simple bourgeoisie.
> Du ridicule ici traité
> Paris fournit mainte copie.

Geoffrey Brereton on comedy's reflection of society during the reign of Louis XIV:

Louis XIV was a long time dying. Literally six days, but as an effective and successful ruler at least twenty-five years. Two lengthy wars, the War of the League of Augsburg (1688-97) and the still more exhausting War of the Spanish Succession (1701-13), rallied all Western Europe against France and milked the country's wealth, still based primarily on agriculture, into notoriously leaky buckets. Ostentation, financial corruption in both the public and private sectors (though the two were so interlocked that no clear distinction could be drawn) and the abdication of responsibility by potential sub-leaders traceable back to the policy of concentration of power in the crown begun long before by Richelieu, combined to erode the national economy. The confident times in which Molière wrote, when most Frenchmen knew their social place or thought they did, were succeeded by a free-for-all in which class distinctions were increasingly blurred and money, diminishing in real value year by year, was openly seen as the key to eminence.

Comedy came to reflect an acquisitive society, nakedly materialistic and an excellent field for adventurers of several kinds and both sexes. It did not analyse the deeper long-term issues—that was hardly its function—but it mirrored their effects in plays of a lively realism more pointed and witty than the comedies of Pierre Corneille. Romance, requiring some idealization of love and woman, was completely out.

Geoffrey Brereton, in French Comic Drama from the Sixteenth to the Eighteenth Century, *Methuen & Co., Ltd., 1977.*

Even as early as 1700, when this play was first acted, there were many allusions to revolutionary feeling in the air. The high prices and expense of living are mentioned, together with an assurance that the world was in an epoch of revolution, while offices are bought by Madame Carmin and Madame Blandineau for their husbands.

The names Dancourt gives his characters show very little change from Molière. The *suivante* is generally Lisette, the *ingénue* Angélique, the farmer Lucas, the valets La Fleur, L'Olive, L'Epine, La Montagne, or sometimes Crispin or Jasmin. Many peasants come in, whose names are those of the peasants of light opera, and the dialect is (as in Molière) that of the surburbs of Paris, or the country closely adjoining the capital. There is then the traditional frame in Dancourt, but a realism of treatment which prepares us for the more bitter realism of the plays which come later in the century, and the type of which is the *Turcaret* of Le Sage. Piron and Gresset, Boissy and Fagan were writing comedies of society during this time of transition.

Le Sage, in *Turcaret* (1709), which is his most remarkable play, uses the method of realism which we have found in Dancourt, but succeeds in creating a type that is a worse satire on the *bourgeois* than Dancourt's characters had been. Turcaret has risen in the world, but brings up to the surface all the vices of the different strata of society with which he has mixed. And it is made clear that each section of society claims to rise in turn until the very lowest moves up. At the end of the play Frontin, the *valet trompeur,* rejoices at Turcaret's defeat, and believes that his own reign has begun. In the *critique* of the play Le Sage makes one character in the dialogue ask if Frontin's reign would not end, as Turcaret's did, in disaster. Asmodée, the demon, answers: 'Vous êtes trop pénétrant.' In the same dialogue one of the two interlocutors says that the picture of the times is too true to life: while a Spaniard is made to complain of the lack of intrigue in the play, for intrigue was still demanded in Spain at the time, though the French comedy of character did without it. From the point of view of public success, says the demon Asmodée, the piece is not interesting. It is realistic, and makes vice hateful, but it does not excite sympathy for the characters: 'faire aimer les personnages.'

Le Sage's criticism of his own play, then, shows that public opinion has swung round, partly through the influence of the *drame,* to demanding in comedy some characters with which the audience would be in sympathy. On the whole, however, Le Sage's plays take little part in this new development.

Le Sage (1667-1748), in his desire to live by the results of his literary work, expressed one change that was rapidly taking place in the eighteenth century. The literary patron who ensured the freedom of the artist from all the anxieties of life, and left him to exercise the highest and most delicate art in the most comfortable conditions, was already a thing of the past. In the future, art must appeal to the populace, and the artist must live upon the sale of his work. Not only then in the drama, but in other forms

Scene from a 1961 performance of Lesage's Tucaret *(1709).*

Sage, but he had also the native French sense of form, and reduced the play *No ay Amigo para Amigo* from five acts to three before its representation in Paris in 1702. His first original play, *La Tontine,* was written in 1708, but was withdrawn by the author, and then produced again in 1732. It is extremely slight and imitative. *Crispin rival de son maître,* acted in 1707, marks a considerable advance on the earlier plays. The characters all bear the conventional names of comedy; but Crispin, in this play as in *La Tontine,* is the person of invention and skill, the valet upon whom his master wholly depends, and who takes a tone of equality with him from the first moment of the action. The satire on a society in which the valet could be taken for a gentleman is sufficiently marked, and the dishonesty of Crispin is equalled by the dishonesty of his young master, who does not pay him his wages and lets him live by his wits. The selfish hunting for money is expressed here as in Dancourt's plays, but instead of bare realism, Le Sage uses satire, and the whole treatment is more light and witty than in Dancourt. Valère is speaking of his attraction to Angélique, and the riches of her father:

> VALÉRE:　Oui, il a trois grandes maisons dans les plus beaux　quartiers de Paris.
> CRISPIN:　L'adorable personne qu'Angélique!
> VALÉRE:　De plus, il passe pour avoir de l'argent comptant.
> CRISPIN:　Je connais tout l'excès de votre amour . . .

Madame Oronte, the mother of Angélique, with her weak heedlessness, is well depicted. Though she is only moved by the emotion of the moment, and is subject to flattery, she believes herself to be guided by reason.

> Effectivement, Lisette, je ne ressemble guère aux autres femmes: c'est toujours la raison qui me détermine.

Le Sage treated vice like folly by making it ridiculous, but as there were few good traits in the play (except perhaps the honesty of Monsieur Orgon) upon which to dwell, the whole play had the effect of satire, and it was not under the prevailing influence of the *drame. Turcaret* (1709) was written at a bitter moment, when the war of the Spanish Succession was at its height. It is possible that the unconscientious juggling with money to serve private ends, which was one of the consequences of the condition of public finance, urged Le Sage to greater harshness in his attitude to all forms of making profit or pleasure out of money. Allusions to play occur all through the piece: and in the third act occurs the conversation with M. Rafle in which the latter details to Turcaret the cases of honest men who have been swindled and beggared. The tone of the whole play would suggest a later date in the eighteenth century, but in reality it comes early, though the note of bitterness forestalls the attitude of the people under Louis XVI, when they revolted again, and with effect, against the pressure of money exactions on the part of the government. Le Sage then reflects satirically in his plays the elements of danger in contemporary manners.

of literature, the writer had henceforth the public in his mind. He had gained his liberty from a sometimes oppressive aristocratic patronage, but he had bartered it for the favour of the crowd. Le Sage felt the difficulty of the position. 'Je cherche à satisfaire le public,' he said, when reproached for his bitter attacks against actors in *Gil Blas,* 'mais le public doit permettre que je me satisfasse moi-même.'

The country from which Le Sage drew his inspiration was Spain; both his prose-writing and his drama bear the marks of this influence. As a dramatist Le Sage used several *genres.* He wrote for the Théâtre de la Foire, and contributed largely to its temporary revival. He also wrote for the Opéra-comique, and did a great deal for this new *genre* of drama.

Even in the translations from the Spanish, which formed the material for all his earlier plays, Le Sage showed that he had the gift of style; and a style that could accommodate itself to the delineation of many different types of characters. Spanish liveliness seems to have communicated itself to him; he had the gift of beginning his scenes with appropriate and easy dialogue, and ending them on a note of expectation which linked the different scenes and acts together. The facts that the Spanish play included a well-marked intrigue, and also that the characters were individual, were not without their influence on Le

Bonamy Dobrée

SOURCE: An introduction to in *Restoration Comedy, 1660-1720,* 1924. Reprint by Greenwood Press, 1981, pp. 9-16.

[*An English historian and critic, Dobrée distinguished himself both as a leading authority on Restoration drama and as a biographer who sought, through vivid depiction and style, to establish biography as a legitimate creative form. In the following excerpt, Dobrée comments on the relationship between comedy and political change, and describes what he considers to be the three distinct types of comedy.*]

Drama and Values

In the history of dramatic literature there are some periods that can be labelled as definitely 'tragic', others as no less preponderatingly 'comic', though of course both forms exist side by side throughout the ages. Taking the period of Aeschylus, Shakespeare, and Corneille as markedly 'tragic', we find that these writers throve in a period of great national expansion and power, during which values were fixed and positive. At such times there is a general acceptance of what is good and what is evil. Out of this, as a kind of trial of strength, there arises tragedy, the positive drama; there is, as Nietzsche suggested, 'an intellectual predilection for what is hard, awful, evil, problematical in existence owing to . . . fulness of life'.

In the great 'comic' periods, however, those of Menander, of the Restoration writers, and at the end of Louis XIV's reign and during the Regency, we find that values are changing with alarming speed. The times are those of rapid social readjustment and general instability, when policy is insecure, religion doubted and being revised, and morality in a state of chaos.

Yet the greatest names in comedy, Aristophanes, Jonson, Molière, do not belong here: these men flourished in intermediate periods, in which the finest comedy seems to be written. In form it still preserves some of the broad sweep of tragedy, and is sometimes hardly to be distinguished from the latter in its philosophy, its implications, and its emotional appeal. Think of *The Silent Woman* or *Le Festin de Pierre.* In this period we find that tragedy has lost its positive character, and begins to doubt if the old values are, after all, the best. It begins to have a sceptical or a plaintive note, as in Euripides, Ford, and Racine. Values are beginning to change; they are not yet tottering.

Keeping this in mind, let us cast a cursory glance at the nature of comedy.

Comedy

Everybody will agree that *Othello* is not a comedy, and that *The School for Scandal* is not a tragedy. But on the other hand *Volpone* is at least as different from Sheridan's play as the latter is from Shakespeare's. Similarly, in the period under consideration, Etherege's *The Man of Mode* is not at all the same kind of thing as Wycherley's *Plain Dealer,* though both are called comedies. Again, if we are certain of the mood we get from *Lear* or *The Importance of Being Earnest,* what are we to say of *Measure for Measure, Le Tartufe,* or *Le Cid?*

It is not surprising, then, that no theory of comedy yet developed, from Aristotle to Meredith or M. Bergson, seems to cover all the ground; . . . [therefore] it will be useful to distinguish three kinds of comedy, or at least three elements in comedy. . . .

1. *Critical Comedy.* The vast bulk of comedy is of the 'critical' variety. What, for instance, was Aristophanes doing but 'to laugh back into their senses "revolting" sons and wives, to defend the orthodox faith against philosophers and men of science'? Menander, to judge from Terence, was doing the same kind of thing, as was Terence himself. This is the classical comedy from which much modern comedy is derived. It sets out definitely to correct manners by laughter; it strives to 'cure excess'.

This comedy, then, tends to repress eccentricity, exaggeration, any deviation from the normal: it wields the Meredithian 'sword of common sense'. It expresses the general feeling of the community, for which another name is morality; it is, to quote Meredith again, the 'guardian of our civil fort', and it is significant that when comedy has been attacked, it had always been defended not on aesthetic but on moral grounds. But the defence has never been very successful, for the morality preached by comedy is not that of fierce ardour, of the passionate search after the utmost good, that in itself is excess, and subject for comedy (e.g. *Le Misanthrope*); but, as we continually find from Terence to the present day, it supports the happy mean, the comfortable life, the ideal of the *honnête homme.* Its lesson is to be righteous, but not to be righteous overmuch, which in the mouths of those who hold the doctrine becomes

> J'aime mieux un vice commode
> Qu'une fatigante vertu.

Its object is to damp enthusiasm, to prick illusions. It is in a sense prig-drama; it flatters the vanity of the spectator, for whose amusement the weaknesses of his friends are held up.

One might imagine that confronted with comedy clothed in the garb of conscious virtue, the writers of comedy themselves would cry 'Fudge'. But these, in the seventeenth century at least, always fell back upon the moral argument, as though they lacked the defiance of their raillery. Jonson declared that comedy was 'a thing throughout pleasant and ridiculous, and accommodated to the correction of manners', saying in the preface to *Epicene:*

> The ends of all, who for the scene do write,
> Are, or should be, to profit and delight!

a charming alternative, of which, fortunately, he sometimes took advantage. Molière, in his preface to *Le Tartufe,* implicitly accepted the position when he wrote, 'If the use of comedy is to correct the vices of men . . . ', as though merely restating an unquestionable axiom. 'One can easily put up with a rebuke,' he said, 'but one cannot bear chaff. One may have no objection to being wicked, but one hates to be ridiculous.' Corneille, however, declared that 'Dramatic poesy has for object only the delight of the spectators', but he was forced to add that Horace was right, and that everybody would not be pleased if some useful precept were not at the same time slipped in, 'et que les gens graves et sérieux, les vieillards, et les amateurs de la vertu, s'y ennuieront s'ils n'y trouvent rien à profiter'.

In the period [from 1660-1720], the same ground was taken up. Shadwell, in attempting to continue the tradition of the Comedy of Humours, wrote of Jonson:

> He to correct, and to inform, did write.
> If poets aim at nought but to delight,
> Fiddlers have to the bays an equal right,

a statement which reveals Shadwell's limitations as clearly as his point of view. Congreve and Vanbrugh—Wycherley's moral purpose is overwhelmingly evident in three of his plays—stimulated by Collier's declaration that 'The business of plays is to recommend virtue and discountenance vice', were loud in their protestations. Congreve even forestalled the frenzied divine in his preface to *The Double Dealer,* where he said 'it is the business of the comic poet to paint the vices and follies of humankind'. Vanbrugh in his heart thought that the object of plays was to divert, and to get full houses, but he accepted the moral standpoint in his *Short Vindication,* saying, 'the business of comedy is to show people what they should do, by representing them on the stage doing what they should not'. Who would refuse to be moralist on those terms? Farquhar, modifying the claims of comedy, declared in his preface to *The Twin Rivals,* 'that the business of comedy is chiefly to ridicule folly; and that the punishment of vice falls rather into the province of tragedy', thus curiously forestalling Coleridge, who thought wickedness no subject for comedy.

Indeed the description of the morality as 'a play enforcing a moral truth or lesson' might almost be taken as a definition of any comedy that deals with types, or 'humours'. For comedy, in so far as it is a generalization, can scarcely avoid type, and once this form has been accepted, the pontifical robes of the moralist descend almost inevitably upon it.

The foregoing may throw a light upon why it is that comedy appears when it does. Comedy of this type is not a phosphorescent gleam upon the surface of a decaying society, but a conservative reaction against change. It is, in short, a social corrective.

2. *'Free' Comedy.* There are, however, some comedies which seem to produce quite a different effect in us, comedies in which we feel no superiority, and which inculcate no moral, but in which we seem to gain a release, not only from what Lamb called the burden of our perpetual moral questioning, but from all things that appear to limit our powers. Of this kind of comedy, the plays of Etherege and Regnard are perhaps the best examples, though much of the laughter of Aristophanes is evoked in the same way. Here we feel that no values count, that there are no rules of conduct, hardly laws of nature. Certainly no appeal, however indirect, is made to our critical or moral faculties. We can disport ourselves freely in a realm where nothing is accountable; all we need to exact is that the touch shall be light enough. We take the same delight in the vagaries of Sir Fopling Flutter as we do at the sight of an absurdly gambolling calf. Judgement, except the aesthetic, is out of place here. We are permitted to play with life, which becomes a charming harlequinade without being farce. It is all spontaneous and free, rapid and exhilarating; the least emotion, an appeal to common sense, and the joyous illusion is gone.

I have named this comedy 'free' because it depends upon there being no valuations whatever; it is possible only in a world where nothing matters, either because one has everything, or because one has nothing. Since it can afford to be careless, it can be completely unmoral. Etherege wrote in the first exuberance of the return from exile of a court to which no moral argument could appeal. In the *Chanson Faite à Grillon* Regnard wrote:

> Il sera gravé sur la porte:
> Ici l'on fait ce que l'on veut,

a motto that might be prefixed to each of his comedies. And if the above are examples of free comedy written by those who had everything, the Commedia dell' Arte may stand as an example of that performed by those who had nothing, and which flourished most when the spectators and actors had least; for when there is nothing more to be lost, there can be no further responsibility. Life and its appropriate comedy can be perfectly free.

3. *Great Comedy.* There is, however, a third comedy, perilously near tragedy, in which the balance is so fine that it seems sometimes as though it would topple over into the other form, as in *Volpone* or *Le Misanthrope.* And here to leave the instances definitely recognized as comedy, are not *Troilus and Cressida* (Shakespeare's), *Measure for Measure,* and *All's Well that Ends Well* also of this kind? Is not Mr. Shaw right in regarding *Coriolanus* as the greatest of Shakespeare's comedies? Indeed the really great figures of comic literature can hardly be thought of apart from their tragedy: who can regard the melancholy knight of La Mancha without pity, or disentangle the elements of the tales that beguiled the road to Canterbury?

The greatest comedy seems inevitably to deal with the disillusion of mankind, the bitterness of a Troilus or an Alceste, the failure of men to realize their most passionate desires. And does not this enable us to come to some conclusion as to what comedy really is? Cannot we see from the very periods in which it arises in its greatest forms with what aspect of humanity it needs must deal? It comes when the positive attitude has failed, when doubt is creeping in to undermine values, and men are turning for comfort to the very ruggedness of life, and laughing in the face of it all. 'Je suis le rire en personne,' says Maurice Sand's Polichinelle, 'le rire triomphant, le rire du mal.' There he represents 'great' comedy.

For comedy does not give us anything in exchange for our loss. Tragedy moves us in such a way that life becomes rich and glowing, in spite of pain and all imaginable horror, perhaps because of them. In tragedy we are left in admiration of the grandiose spectacle of humanity stronger than its chains, and we are reconciled when a Cleopatra, hugging the asp, whispers:

> Peace, peace!
> Dost thou not see my baby at my breast
> That sucks the nurse asleep?

In tragedy we are made free by being taken outside the life of the senses into that of imaginative reality.

Comedy makes daily life livable in spite of folly and disillusion, but its vision, though as universal, is not that of tragedy, for it laughs at the spirit as much as at the flesh, and will not take sides. Tragedy is all that is commonly said of it, in depth, revelation, and grandeur; but comedy is not its opposite. The latter is not necessarily more distant from life, nor is it life apprehended through the mind rather than through the emotions. Neither is it the triumph of the angel in man over our body of the beast, as one has said, nor, to quote another, the triumph of the beast in man over the divine. It is nothing so fleeting as a triumph. It is 'a recordation in man's soul' of his dual nature.

Goethe sought in art courage to face the battle of life. But it is doubtful if life is a battle, or a game, or a chaos through which we walk with slippery feet. And comedy gives us courage to face life without any standpoint; we need not regard it as a magnificent struggle nor as a puppet play; we need not view it critically nor feel heroically. We need only to feel humanly, for comedy shows us life, not at such a distance that we cannot but regard it coldly, but only so far as we may bring to it a ready sympathy freed from terror or too overwhelming a measure of pity. . . .

Henry Phillips

SOURCE: "Moral Instruction and Comedy," in *The Theatre and Its Critics in Seventeenth-Century France,* Oxford University Press, Oxford, 1980, pp. 131-50.

[*In the following excerpt, Phillips examines the debate between the religious moralists and the dramatic theorists concerning the morality of seventeenth-century comic drama.*]

Against the religious moralists' conception of drama as morally and socially harmful the dramatic theorists held that drama fulfilled a didactic function and that man was led thereby to moral improvement. Not surprisingly, the moralists were highly sceptical of this claim. This was particularly so in the case of comedy where, according to dramatic theorists, the source of instruction lies in the correction of vice by its exposure to public ridicule. The moralists utterly reject comedy with its particular concern for ridicule and laughter as a means of moral improvement, especially when they consider *Le Tartuffe* which, in its portrayal of the hypocrite, is alleged to have a positively harmful effect on the spectator. The *Lettre sur la comédie de l'Imposteur,* in upholding the play as an important contribution to our protection against hypocrites, will therefore serve as an interesting contrast to the religious moralists' views. First of all, however, how do they regard the notion of moral instruction in general?

An important feature of moral instruction was the punishment of vice and the reward of virtue. Pégurier contests the very basis of this principle; 'le châtiment ou la recompense d'une action ou d'une parole n'en change pas la nature, et n'est pas une preuve de sa bonté ou de sa malignité'. In other words, the punishment or reward of an act is not necessarily a moral guide to the value of that act. Moreover, Lamy believes that the poet's deference to his audience rules out the effectiveness of punishment and reward; since poets do all in their power to make us love and esteem a character it then becomes necessary to fulfil the spectators' expectations for that character, 'et qu'enfin il luy arrive le bien qu'ils luy souhaittent'. Equally poets never fail to bring the vengeance of heaven upon their hero's enemies 'et de leur faire souffrir quelque peine extraordinaire'; they cannot allow the audience to leave without such consolation because they would then leave the theatre dissatisfied. Here punishment has no moral foundation and is determined by the likes and dislikes of the spectator. One wonders to what extent Lamy was familiar with the theoretical writings of Corneille.

But for Lamy the very portrayal of vice is not conducive to moral improvement, especially when hatred and ambition are depicted so as to make them attractive. Although some vices in drama may inspire our horror this is owing rather to their nature than to their portrayal; as far as Oedipus' parricide and incest are concerned 'La seule crainte des supplices rigoureux ordonnez par les Loix retient assez de ce côté-là.' Poets can claim no virtue in such cases. Finally, the hero . . . embodies the false values propagated by drama in such a way that they call for emulation not rejection; although poets do not openly praise vice itself they praise the characters in whom it is found.

The fact that punishment comes only at the end of a play is a further cause of concern to the religious moralists, who contend that by this time the spectators have already been corrupted. Gerbais remarks that even if crimes such as parricide and incest are finally punished on stage 'c'est aprés avoir laissé la liberté à des impies de blasphêmer, et d'insulter au Ciel et à ses foudres'. Similarly, Coustel observes that although in *Dom Juan* the central character

becomes in the end an example of divine justice his punishment makes much less impression on the heart of an
evil spectator than 'les maximes detestables qu'on luy
entend debiter, n'en font sur les esprits'. What is more,
punishment of this sort is ineffectual because men have
made an amusement of heaven's wrath and even of hell;
how can a man be moved by the truth of religion when
he finds all this agreeable and can even laugh at it? The
comic context in itself is sufficient to render the effect of
punishment null and void.

Besides the element of punishment dramatic theorists also
recommended the use of moral sententiae, although these
were subject to many restrictions. They advised that if
vice remains unpunished it must at least be condemned
by one of the characters in the play. For Conti this is
clearly insufficient: after spreading his poison throughout
the play 'd'une maniere agreable, delicate et conforme à
la nature et au temperament', the poet 'croit en estre quitte
pour faire quelque discours moral par un vieux Roy rep-
resenté, pour l'ordinaire par un fort méchant Comedien,
dont le roole est desagreable, dont les vers sont secs et
languissans, quelques fois mesme mauvais: mais tout du
moins negligés, parce que c'est dans ces endroits que [le
poète] se deslasse des efforts d'esprit qu'il vient de faire
en traittant les passions'. Moral instruction is thus far
from being the main object of the poet and moral maxims
are seen as a form of relaxation after the effort exerted in
portraying passion. Moral instruction is an afterthought.

Bossuet's opinion of moral teaching in the theatre is that
'la touche en est trop legere' and 'il n'y a rien de moins
sérieux, puisque l'homme y fait à la fois un jeu de ses
vices et un amusement de la vertu'. The fact that drama
is an entertainment precludes the dramatist from any serious attempt to improve man's conduct in society. For
Vincent the problem is more fundamental in that stories
which are scripturally or historically authenticated are far
more suited to teach than plays 'qu'on sçait estre de nuës
fictions, et des contes forgés à plaisir'. It is because drama is fiction that it cannot be used for moral instruction.

There are, however, certain attitudes among the spectators which in themselves render the moral instruction in
drama useless. Yves de Paris is concerned about the audience's realization of the difference between the social
status of the characters and their own: he explains that
compared with the great crimes of political usurpers the
sins of ordinary life appear to spectators as inconsequential; 'leur conscience s'y tient asseurée, et sans en concevoir des remords, elle se croyt assez juste de n'estre
point si meschante'. For Héliodore too the comparisons
made by the spectators with the characters have the opposite of a moral effect; the weaknesses we recognize in
ourselves seem more excusable 'dans la multitude des
complices' and slight alongside those which make such
an impression on the stage. The spectator, confronted with
crimes beyond his capacity and with weaknesses shared
by many others, sinks into a sort of moral self-satisfaction.

But it is the concupiscent nature of man that is seen as the

major obstacle to the success of moral instruction. As
Lamy comments, evil makes a stronger impression than
good on a man's mind; for one person who imitates a
hero's virtue there are a thousand who imitate his vices.
Rivet refuses to believe that the presentation of 'les sin-
istres evenemens des amours mal entrepris' or other reprehensible acts are useful when men are 'bien plus sus-
ceptibles du mal qui est enseigné, qu'émeus par la peine
qui le suit; se promettant tousjours qu'ils seront plus fins
et plus advisés, et [ils] se garderont bien de l'evenement,
contre lequel ils semblent estre premunis'. Again the
opposite of a moral effect is achieved because we learn to
be more cunning in committing sinful acts rather than
learning never to commit them.

One point arising from this discussion is that, if man is
more receptive to evil than to good, it follows that to give
moral instruction by portraying evil is a contradiction in
terms. Yves de Paris writes that: 'Quand le dessein principal seroit de condamner la tyrannie, en faisant voir ses
progres tousjours orageux, et sa fin ordinairement miserable, ces noires pratiques salissent tousjours l'esprit des
assistances: elles y laissent les idées d'un mal, dont la
passion se peut servir en mille rencontres, et qu'il estoit
meilleur d'ignorer.' Héliodore sees the inclusion of evil
characters in certain plays as not necessarily leading to
evil but as none the less obstructing the efforts of virtue;
the spectator feels movements of virtue and vice according to the different roles; he hesitates between the two
when actors recite something morally indifferent and is
moved to neither virtue nor vice. Vincent states quite
simply: 'Il ne faut pas faire une plaie sous esperance de
la guerir.'

An important aspect of man's concupiscent nature is his
inclination for pleasure; moral instruction in drama runs
directly counter to this inclination and is therefore greatly
attenuated in its effect. In the words of Godeau 'Le remede
y plaist moins que ne fait le poison.' Voisin seems in no
doubt that pleasure and amusement rather than moral profit
are what the spectator seeks in the theatre. Lamy suggests
that, far from being dissuaded from vice, the corrupt indulge in the pleasure of seeing and hearing what they are
particularly inclined towards: furthermore, we are not able
to suffer those who are of the opposite opinion to ourselves and we look upon them as censors. Moral instruction is repugnant to the very people who need it because
it interrupts their pleasure.

Some writers refuse to believe that there is any intention
of instructing in the first place. The poet in fact models
his characters on the corrupt nature of his audience precisely in order that they should derive the maximum pleasure from their own corruption. Voisin says that the sole
aim of drama is to 'plaire au peuple, dont le plus grand
nombre estant vitieux, il faut necessairement que la Comedie ait quelque chose de vitieux pour luy estre agreable';
this must be so, he adds, because one of the greatest playwrights of the century is obliged to admit that the aim of
drama is not to 'avoir égard aux bonnes mœurs'. Nicole
refers to the way a poet defers to his audience when he
mentions that since the poet's aim is pleasure, he flatters

the inclinations of his audience, which tend towards the most harmful passions. Consequently, he adds, there is nothing more pernicious than 'La Morale Poëtique et Romanesque' which is but a mass of false opinion derived from man's concupiscent nature and pleasurable only in so far as it flatters the spectator's corrupt instinct. Senault points out that poets are men like any others and subject to the moral disorder which spares no man; moreover, they are able to express violent and unjust passions better than their opposites, so well in fact that they unintentionally encourage the sin they wish to destroy and help the fight against the virtue they wish to defend. Corrupt playwrights cannot improve corrupt spectators with corrupt maxims.

In the earlier discussion of the dramatic theorists it was observed that despite their admission that man was reluctant to be taught, they were none the less optimistic regarding the possibility of man's correction through the dramatic experience. It is, however, clear that the religious moralists considered such optimism to be totally unfounded. Theory does not coincide with practice; as Conti remarks, it is only in books of poetics that moral instruction is the aim of drama: this aim exists 'ny dans l'intention du Poëte, ny dans celle du spectateur. Le desir de plaire est ce qui conduit le premier, et le second est conduit par le plaisir d'y voir peintes des passions semblables aux siennes: car nôtre amour-propre est si delicat, que nous aimons à voir les portraits de nos passions aussi bien de ceux de nos personnes'. The vanity produced by our own corruption encourages us to admire rather than to eradicate it.

From the religious moralists' rejection of the general claim of drama to instruct, the more specific question of comedy which is alleged to correct vice by exposing it to public ridicule can be considered. Dramatic theorists regarded comedy as much less worthy of attention than tragedy and as a result tended to dismiss it in a few brief sentences. Scudéry's manner is certainly condescending when he writes that 'quelque facetieuse que soit la Comedie pure, elle ne laisse pas de servir aux mœurs et d'enseigner en divertissant', although evidently he does not deny its usefulness. Similarly, La Mesnardière says that comedy 'n'est pas tellement inutile à l'institution du peuple, bien qu'elle semble estre formée pour son divertissement, qu'elle ne corrige ses mœurs, lors mesme qu'elle les expose'. But Rapin is more explicit: the purpose of comedy is to 'corriger le peuple par la crainte d'estre moqué', and he defines comedy as 'une image de la vie commune' which corrects 'les defauts publics, en faisant voir le ridicule des défauts particuliers'. Furthermore, comedy is worthless 'dés qu'on ne s'y reconnoist point, et dés qu'on n'y voit pas ses manieres et celles des personnes avec qui l'on vit'. We must therefore be able to recognize ourselves in the stage character or we shall not be in a position to correct the faults which expose us to public ridicule. The claim for comedy as a useful moral corrective is made by Molière in his preface to *Le Tartuffe* where he holds that 'rien ne reprend mieux la plupart des hommes que la peinture de leurs défauts'; he goes on: 'C'est une grande atteinte aux vices que de les exposer à

la risée de tout le monde. On souffre aisément des répréhensions, mais on ne souffre point la raillerie. On veut bien être méchant; mais on ne veut point être ridicule.'

D'Aubignac, however, is not at all sure that comedy is a suitable vehicle for moral instruction, although admittedly he is writing about pre-Molière comedy where the emphasis on intrigue reduced the possibilities of instruction in any case. But, d'Aubignac explains, if the playwright does introduce moral maxims or 'les nobles mouvements de la Vertu' he runs the great risk of boring the spectator 'parce qu'on sort du genre Comique pour passer dans un autre plus élevé'. Moral instruction has no place in comedy because it is not appropriate to the lowly rank and station of the characters. Indeed 'méme il faut souvent y corrompre les beaux sentimens de la Morale, et les traiter en burlesque, c'est-à-dire, Comiquement'. Instruction is undesirable in comedy because, in order to maintain the tone of the genre, moral sententiae would have to be burlesqued.

The *Lettre sur la comédie de l'Imposteur* is the only work of any length which does full justice to comedy in the seventeenth century as a serious dramatic form. This document (which, if we accept René Robert's arguments, was written either by Molière himself or by someone directly inspired by him) was provoked by the adverse reactions to the 1667 version of *Le Tartuffe*, which had as title *L'Imposteur*, and in which the principal character was not Tartuffe but Panulphe. The *Lettre* offers not only an extended and intelligent analysis of the play itself but also contains a detailed argument regarding the moral function the play serves in striking a blow against would-be seducers. The author particularly stresses the positive effect the play has on the spectator which derives from the experience of seeing the ridicule of vice in action. The most important feature of the *Lettre*, however, is a theory of comedy which, while based on a single play, has far-reaching general implications, particularly as regards the concept of the ridiculous, and the manner in which the spectator responds to its presentation in a play.

The author begins his argument with the general proposition that we are all possessed of Reason and hence able to follow it. But in addition Nature has provided Reason with 'quelque sorte de forme extérieure et de dehors reconnoissable'. When we see this we experience 'une joie mêlée d'estime'; equally, when we see something that departs from the reasonable we experience 'une joie mêlée de mépris'. The latter is none other than the means we use to recognize *le ridicule*. The author's precise definition of *le ridicule* is the 'forme extérieure et sensible' which Nature in her providence has attached to 'tout ce qui est déraisonnable'.

But in order to appreciate fully what is ridiculous we must, the author considers, first understand the reasonable. The latter has as its 'marque sensible' the *quod decet* of the Ancients, which he translates as *bienséance;* this in turn is a concrete manifestation of *convenance*, i.e. that which is congruous. Thus 'ce qui sied bien' is always founded on 'quelque raison de convenance'. The ridiculous is thus a matter of *disconvenance*. Panulphe's attempted seduction of Elmire is, according to the author, incongruous for two reasons: firstly, because his public image of piety does not conform with his *galanterie* in private; secondly, because the means he chooses do not succeed—in other words, they are inappropriate to his design.

There now follow more precise indications as to the value of our experience of Panulphe for our future conduct. The spectator cannot fail to recognize what is ridiculous in Panulphe because of the playwright's exaggeration of Panulphe's technique of seduction and his failure to succeed. The author of the *Lettre,* however, foresees the possible objection that what is made to look 'extremely' ridiculous in Panulphe will not appear so to the same degree in other such persons we may encounter elsewhere. His reply is that on any other occasion that a man like Panulphe attempts to seduce a woman she will be warned because she will experience the same pleasure (i.e. 'une joie mêlée de mépris') as when she saw the play. Moreover, this experience of pleasure will prevent her, in her initial reaction at least, from distinguishing between Panulphe and her would-be seducer. The existence of pleasure in her reaction derives only from the features shared by the two persons. The author makes the general (and unwittingly controversial) point that since we are reluctant to change our attitude towards things we have considered ridiculous, we can never treat them seriously again. This remark assumes great importance when considering the religious moralists' objections to the way true and false piety are allegedly confused in *Le Tartuffe.*

But while the experience of the ridiculous is pleasurable for the woman who is the object of an attempted seduction, it is certainly not so for the person who is the object of ridicule. The author of the *Lettre* explains that the 'sentiment du ridicule' is the coldest of all responses for a person making amorous advances. In this sense the feeling that one has been found ridiculous, especially by the woman one is trying to seduce, is enough to make anyone stop in their tracks. And indeed it is not merely by reference to *L'Imposteur* that such would-be seducers are ridiculous; they are so absolutely speaking, since any *galant* who adopts this kind of approach must, given that he could not honourably avow his motives publicly, be in some degree 'dissimulé et hypocrite', and 'tout mensonge, déguisement, fourberie, dissimulation, toute apparence différente du fond, enfin toute contrariéte entre actions qui procèdent d'un même principe, est essentiellement ridicule'.

The 'joie mêlée de mépris' we experience before the ridiculous thus serves to warn us of certain types of behaviour. But there is another feature of our response to *le ridicule:* 'la providence de la nature a voulu que tout ce qui est méchant eût quelque degré de ridicule, pour redresser nos voies par cette apparence de défaut de raison, et pour piquer notre orgueil naturel, par le mépris qu'excite nécessairement ce défaut, quand il est apparent comme il est par le ridicule'. Pride, then, is an additional factor in

our response and is an integral part of 'une joie mêlée de mépris'. Indeed our scorn for the person who is ridiculed derives from the conviction that we are his moral superiors, since we do not share the fault which leads to his exposure as ridiculous.

But there is a little more to it than this. Comedy is seen as a means of actively persuading ourselves and others of our moral superiority; the author explains that the soul 'se défiant, à bon droit, de sa propre excellence depuis le péché d'origine, cherche de tous côtés avec avidité de quoi la persuader aux autres et à soi-même par des comparaisons qui lui soient avantageuses, c'est-à-dire par la considération des défauts d'autrui'. Comedy is a monument to our vanity, a fact which will not be overlooked by the religious moralists.

The author of the *Lettre* is in no doubt that the notion of *le ridicule,* as he outlines it, is 'une des plus sublimes matières de la véritable morale'. But it is clear from our analysis that the author of the *Lettre* does not envisage the moral value of comedy in the same way as Scudéry, La Mesnardière, or even Molière in the preface to *Le Tartuffe.* There is in the *Lettre* not one word about the value of comedy as a corrective of vice; at the very most the suggestion is that the Panulphes of this world will, because they find being ridiculed disagreeable, desist from their immediate efforts at seduction. The spectator is not corrected in any way because he is from the start convinced of his own moral perfection. Comedy in the *Lettre* is seen rather as a means of arming us against certain types of conduct which we may encounter on future occasions. The person instructed is not the person who practises vice but the person who might otherwise become its victim.

Those writers who believe that comedy may correct faults talk in very general terms without at the same time specifying the limitations of the genre. Certain religious moralists, however, are firm in the belief that comedy's powers are limited and that ridicule is an inadequate weapon for its supposed task. Lamy points to the restricted nature of the faults comedy may correct when he remarks that poets effectively condemn by ridicule only minor defects such as the moodiness of old men, their meanness, their harsh treatment of young people, and the ease with which they allow themselves to be deceived. On the other hand, 'l'impudicité regne dans leurs Ouvrages, quoy qu'elle y paroisse sous les habits de la vertu', for the idol of comedy is still a young man 'brûlé d'un feu criminel'. Bossuet too considers that the most important vices are left untouched; Molière has shown how little advantage is to be gained from moral teaching in the theatre which attacks only 'le ridicule du monde, en lui laissant cependant toute sa corruption'.

Lamy too denies the usefulness of ridicule in the war against vice: he comments that certainly avarice is ridiculed, and the debauchery and love life of young men condemned; but it is not 'par des railleries que l'on détruit le vice, particulierement celuy de l'impureté'; such a vice is too important to be cured by such a feeble remedy, 'et même souvent on prend plaisir à s'en voir raillé'. Ridicule is too weak to combat vice, especially when combined with the pleasure of the experience, for, as remarked on earlier, the vanity of man leads him to derive pleasure from his own corruption. It is Lamy's contention that our inclination for pleasure is too strong for restraint by shame alone and in any case 'on espere toûjours la pouvoir eviter par le secret, dont on tâche de couvrir ses desordres aux yeux des hommes'. Comedy is thus considered to have the opposite effect of that desired by Rapin and others in that public exposure of our vices leads us to be more secretive.

There are some writers who attack comedy not on the grounds that it is inadequate to instruct but on the grounds that it provides lessons in the very things it is supposed to eradicate. Vincent refers to portraits of filial disobedience and seduction. Coustel considers not only that Sganarelle in *L'École des maris* is talking sense, but that many young people will learn how to act the passionate lover from Arnolphe's example! Moreover, Lamy and Lebrun believe that the values which are most often ridiculed should rather be proposed as exemplary; for the latter, quoting the author of the *République des lettres,* Molière's plays are dangerous because 'on y tourne perpetuellement en ridicule les soins que les peres et les meres prennent de s'opposer aux engagemens amoureux de leurs enfans'.

What, according to the religious moralists, is the spectator's response to comedy? An analysis of the *Lettre sur la comédie de l'Imposteur* showed that comedy was based on man's attempt to affirm his moral superiority by magnifying the ridiculous in the faults of others. Lamy attacks comedy for this very reason: comedies where man's faults are brought to our notice are a source of pleasure for us either because we are 'bien aise dans le desordre où on est, d'avoir des compagnons avec qui on partage la honte du peché', or because we derive a secret satisfaction from seeing that we are exempt from the faults of others: 'On s'élève au dessus d'eux, et on les meprise. Outre cela, on attribüe facilement les fautes qui sont exposées à la risée de tout le monde, à quelqu'un sur lequel on seroit bien-aise qu'en tombât l'infamie.' Lamy sees our response as something approaching active malice and far from the objective experience described by the author of the *Lettre.*

Lelevel views the problem in a more precisely theological context, explaining comedy in terms of the Fall, where reason was taken from man, leaving him with only ridicule. But, he continues, reason was not so totally extinguished that man could not perceive the faults of others, although nobody was able to recognize his own; consequently, feeling, on the one hand, the need for perfection, yet, on the other hand, not knowing how to find it, 'on a pris le parti de s'observer et de se critiquer les uns les autres; et non seulement on a sçû se réjoüir par cette voye, mais encore chacun a sçû tirer de là comme un témoignage de son excellence, parce qu'il ne se peut que celui qui critique ne s'imagine être plus parfait que celui qui est critiqué'. The faults of others become the yard-

Portrait of Jean François Regnard.

stick of our own perfection. The author of the *Lettre sur la comédie de l'Imposteur* could not have put it better.

There is of course the suggestion here that we do not recognize ourselves in the characters portrayed on the stage. For Lelevel this is often an unwitting act on the part of the spectator; in his reply to Caffaro he defines the audience at a comedy as 'une assemblée de railleurs où personne ne se connoît, et où chacun rit des defauts, qui les rendent tous également coupables et ridicules'. In Lelevel's *Entretiens* Théodore is made to say that according to some people Molière and Harlequin 'representoient au naturel bien des gens', but that 'personne ne s'y reconnoissoit, et ce qu'on apprenoit avec eux, c'étoit à se moquer les uns des autres'. How can we correct our faults if we fail to recognize ourselves in the characters?

Pégurier considers the rather different case where a particular individual may indeed be recognized in the character of a play: although people are not named when some vice or other is condemned portraits are often so natural that the originals are not difficult to recognize. He continues: 'Et quand une fois on a par ce moyen perdu quelqu'un de reputation, si dans la suite touché de Dieu il change de sentimens, s'il quitte le vice qu'on luy a reproché pour embrasser la vertu; tout cela n'est pas pour l'ordinaire capable de détruire la méchante idée qu'on en a donné au public.' Not surprisingly, Molière is cited as guilty in this respect.

A similar criticism is envisaged by Molière himself in the *Critique de l'École des femmes,* where in scene vi Climène complains of offensive satire of women contained in *L'École des femmes* itself, thus implying that she feels herself to be personally attacked. Uranie's reply is delicately barbed: these satires 'tombent directement sur les mœurs' and 'ne frappent les personnes que par réflexion'; she remarks that we might profit from the lesson of comedy 'sans faire semblant qu'on parle à nous'; moreover, the 'peintures ridicules' are 'miroirs publics où il ne faut jamais témoigner qu'on se voie', and 'c'est se taxer hautement d'un défaut que de se scandaliser qu'on le reprenne'. In other words, comedy aims at presenting an image of behaviour which is applicable to no one individual, but corresponds to an objective truth which is independent of the play. The similarity of this idea with that found in the *Lettre sur la comédie de l'Imposteur* is obvious. Furthermore, if the individual concerned recognizes the similarity between himself and the comic character it is better that he remain silent, for should he protest, he becomes his own accuser. One may, however, feel uneasy at such a reasoning: many vices or faults have in reality extremely recognizable features and it is possible that the audience will indeed point an accusing finger 'par réflexion'. Equally, it is possible that a person may be publicly ridiculed for a fault which is but a small part of his or her personality, whereas comedy makes the part represent the whole. Pégurier's doubts about comedy may indeed possess a measure of justification.

All this leads the reader to the problem of *Le Tartuffe* itself, where the main point of contention is the possible confusion arising from the portrayal of a hypocrite who has all the attributes of a real *dévot*. In the *Lettre* the author had written that once we had considered something ridiculous in a play it would be difficult to take it seriously in the future. This is precisely the objection made by some religious moralists regarding the portrayal of Tartuffe as a *dévot;* they argue that real piety will suffer because of the similarity of certain of its features with those exhibited by the hypocrite. In the words of Coustel, 'sous pretexte de ruiner la fausse devotion, il represente les brutalitez de son Tartuffe avec des couleurs si noires, et il luy fait avancer des maximes si detestables, que la corruption du cœur humain ne manquera pas de les faire appliquer, non à un Tartuffe de Theatre: mais à un véritable homme de bien'. It is interesting that Coustel should base his criticism on man's inability to distinguish between truth and falsehood, when this is the very thing denied in the *Lettre.*

But the controversy over *Le Tartuffe* involves many complex issues, and H. P. Salomon has provided a revealing discussion of them in his *Tartuffe devant l'opinion française.* He shows for example that at the time of the play and before it there were many moralists, including St. Vincent de Paul and le P. Lejeune, who bitterly attacked the fashion of employing a *directeur de conscience.* Professor Butler also remarks upon this phenomenon and suggests that if the Lamoignons and the Péréfixes of this world were outraged it was not because Molière had been spreading untruths but because 'il a visé trop juste et . . . toute vérité n'est pas bonne à dire'. M. Salomon's other major contribution to the problem of *Le Tartuffe* in the

seventeenth century is his demonstration that the controversy is directly linked with certain attitudes towards the immodest dress of women, parts of whose bodies were exposed for all to see. Thus Tartuffe's outburst in II, ii was seen by the predominantly Jansenist clergy of Paris as a parody of their rigorist attitudes.

The subversive nature of the play is a prominent theme in the work of the authors under consideration. Two developed criticisms of *Le Tartuffe* by Massillon and Bourdaloue deserve special attention here for they both consider in detail the play's effect on other Christians and on Christianity as a whole. Massillon, in his sermon on *Les Gens de bien,* while agreeing that the hypocrite deserves 'l'exécration de Dieu et des hommes' and that his abuse of religion is the greatest of crimes, refers to the inadequacy of ridicule in this particular case; 'les dérisions et les satires sont trop douces pour décrier un vice qui mérite l'horreur du genre humain; et qu'un théâtre profane a eu tort de ne donner que du ridicule à un caractère si abominable, si honteux et si affligeant pour l'Eglise, et qui doit plutôt exciter les larmes et l'indignation que la risée des fidèles'. In other words, ridicule and laughter have no serious connotation and as a result no effect on such a serious vice.

But, Massillon goes on, these continual outbursts against virtue, the confusion of *l'homme de bien* with a hypocrite, the spitefulness which 'en faisant des éloges pompeux de la justice, ne trouve presque aucun juste qui les mérite' (presumably a reference to Cléante's speech in I, v), all this 'anéantit la religion et tend à rendre toute vertu suspecte'; consequently the impious are offered more arguments against religion at a time when so many other scandalous occurrences 'n'autorisent que trop l'impiété'. Although Tartuffe is recognized for what he is, Massillon seems to be criticizing the play for not publicizing the ways of orthodox religious conduct; Cléante in particular would not appear to be the right person to oppose the hypocrite. But *Le Tartuffe* is attacked not so much for being a libertine play itself, but for giving *libertins* an excuse for attacking religion. Massillon adds to the above statement that when we think we are laughing at false virtue we are in fact blaspheming against religion: 'en vous défiant de la sincérité des justes que vous voyez, l'impie conclut que ceux qui les ont precédés et que nous ne voyons pas leur étaient semblables'. Even martyrs would not be exempt from such treatment.

Massillon is, however, particularly concerned that Molière should have dealt with a subject pertaining to religion at all: these scandalous things should not be exposed in public with an air of triumph, but effaced from the memory of man; the Law condemned 'celui qui découvrait la honte et la turpitude de ceux qui lui avaient donné la vie' but 'c'est la honte et le déshonneur de l'Église votre mère, que vous exposez avec plaisir à la dérision publique'. This is no doubt a reference to the notion of sexual taboo found in Leviticus 18: 7, where the Law forbids one to uncover the nakedness of one's mother; here the latter is the Church and the act of introducing religion into comedy is seen as an act of defilement.

Bourdaloue devoted some time to the question of *Le Tartuffe* in his sermon on hypocrisy and he too sees it in terms of the *libertin:* if the latter is forced to admit that not all piety is false he will at least maintain that it is suspect, and as a result all piety will be weakened in its effect. Indeed this is what the *libertin* hopes to gain 'en faisant de ses entretiens et de ses discours autant de satyres de l'hypocrisie et de la fausse dévotion'. Bourdaloue continues by saying that since real and false piety have much in common it is more or less inevitable that 'la mesme raillerie qui attaque l'une, interesse l'autre', and that 'les traits dont on peint celle-cy defigurent celle-là', unless, of course, one takes 'toutes les precautions d'une charité prudente, exacte, et bien intentionnée, ce que le libertinage n'est pas en disposition de faire'. Such, according to Bourdaloue, is not the aim of the 'esprits prophanes' when they undertake the censure of hypocrisy, for they in no way have the interests of God at heart; they do not wish to reform the abuse of religion, which they cannot do in any case, but to 'faire une espece de diversion dont le libertinage pust profiter, en concevant, et en faisant concevoir d'injustes soupçons de la vraye pieté par de malignes representations de la fausse'. Molière is therefore condemned for spreading impiety just as he is for providing lessons in vice. But, as M. Salomon points out, Bourdaloue's argument marks a new phase in the debate. He does not dispute the fact of Tartuffe's hypocrisy; as Bourdaloue says, the comedy exposes 'à la risée publique un hypocrite imaginaire, ou mesmes, si vous voulez, un hypocrite réel'. Bourdaloue's reproach is not that Tartuffe is not hypocritical enough but, in the words of M. Salomon, '[il] ne veut pas d'un hypocrite sur la scène'.

For Bourdaloue, however, the *libertins* revel in an already established impiety: his great concern is the effect of such a play as *Le Tartuffe* on weak-minded Christians: firstly, they become afraid to pass for hypocrites, this fear arising from the similarity of conduct in real and false devotion, and they are prevented from performing their Christian duties; secondly, they conceive 'un degoust de la pieté' for, although piety is 'solide en elle-mesme, et estimable devant Dieu', it is subject to men's censure and to the spitefulness of their judgements; thirdly, 'ils tombent par là dans un abattement du cœur, qui va souvent, jusqu'à leur faire abandonner le parti de Dieu, plutost que de s'engager à soutenir la persecution, c'est-à-dire, à essuyer la raillerie, qu'ils se persuadent que ce reproche odieux, ou mesmes que le simple soupçon d'hypocrisie leur attireroit'. Molière is accused of turning people away from religion by his exposure of those who ill use it.

Thus, while *Le Tartuffe,* an isolated example, is considered an anti-Christian play it is clear that laughter in itself achieves the opposite of a moral effect. Some religious moralists go so far as to suggest that laughter is an un-Christian act, thereby attacking comedy in its fundamental aim. Bossuet relies mainly on the authority of the Fathers for his views on the subject. He reports St. Thomas as putting *bouffonneries* among the vices: 'la plaisanterie', he says, is forbidden to Christians because it is 'une action légère, indécente, en tout cas oisive . . . , et

indigne de la gravité des mœurs chrétiennes'. Another of his sources is St. Basil, who is reported to have said that men may '"égayer un peu le visage par un modeste souris"; mais pour ce qui est de "ces grands éclats et de ces secousses du corps", qui tiennent de la convulsion, selon lui elles ne sont pas d'un homme "vertueux et qui se possède lui-même", ce qu'il inculque souvent, comme une des obligations du christianisme'. As in the experience of passion, so laughter leads to the spectator's losing control. A modern scholar, however, assures us that, contrary to what Bossuet says, the Fathers were moderate in their condemnation of laughter; it was rather the excess with which they found fault.

But comedy in its use of ridicule and sometimes in its choice of targets, sins against charity; this is indeed implicit in the statement of Pégurier quoted earlier, where a man ridiculed in a comedy later changes his ways but remains the object of ridicule because people remember only his portrayal in the play. Bourdaloue's argument that by including religious elements in comedy one exposed the whole Church to public ridicule has also been mentioned before. Lejeune implies that the ridicule of individuals is no less a sin against the very founder of Christianity; 'quel est le Chrestien . . . qui se moque de Jesus-Christ? il faudroit estre barbare et athée. Saint Paul vous répond, quand vous pechez contre votre frère Chrestien vous pechez contre Jesus-Christ'. Comedy, given this definition of relationships between men, is the ultimate act of profanity.

C. E. J. Caldicott

SOURCE: "Baroque or Burlesque? Aspects of French Comic Theatre in the Early Seventeenth Century," in *The Modern Language Review,* Vol. 79, No. 4, October, 1984, pp. 797-809.

[In the essay that follows, Caldicott examines several common "burlesque" features of seventeenth-century comedy.]

It is, of course, quite paradoxical that the term 'baroque' should still be widely used in literary criticism when nobody is entirely sure what it means. Following in the footsteps of Wölfflin and romantic criticism (which found an affinity with the baroque), Eugenio d'Ors took it to be an eternal element in the cycle of alternation in art between the regular and the irregular—an unending diastole and systole; in other words, there would always be a baroque and always a classical mode of creation. The existence of the one notion always implied the presence of the other. Jean Rousset, on the other hand, explored a more strictly defined period in *La Littérature de l'Âge baroque en France* (1954), citing the 'année climatérique 1629—1630' and giving a thematic description of the literature of the period which vindicated the subtitle of his book, *Circé et le paon,* by highlighting qualities of transformation and display. It would be self-defeating to attempt to summarize all that has been written on the baroque in literature since then, particularly after the syntheses of Claude-Gilbert Dubois. But there remain some specific points to be made.

Rousset's original book on the baroque should not be read without its sequel, *L'Intérieur et l'extérieur* (1968), with its rather sad last section entitled 'Le Baroque en question': there he bravely contemplates his work of fourteen years earlier and concedes that it was only 'un premier temps de l'investigation', which had to be followed by the 'méthodes éprouvées de la recherche érudite et de la philologie'. As if in confirmation of this, the philologist Kurt Baldinger, a companion of von Wartburg, comments helpfully on my own work with a reminder of the importance of the *Französisches Etymologisches Wörterbuch* in any appraisal of the qualities of French language in the early seventeenth century. Rousset's lucid second book was published only shortly after Gérard Genette's important *Figures I* (1966) and undoubtedly benefits from it; in his final evaluation of the work done on the baroque, Rousset quotes Genette: 'La pensée moderne s'est peut-être inventé le baroque comme on s'offre un miroir'. In the meantime, the *Journées Internationales d'Étude du Baroque* soldier on into their twentieth year at Montauban; in a recent review of the work accomplished there, no less a person than Henri Lafay writes:

> Alors que l'epithète et le substantif 'baroque' sont désormais passés dans l'usage du langage critique courant et qu'on se réfère tranquillement à la notion correspondante, les réflexions des plus grands spécialistes: littéraires, historiens des civilisations, historiens de l'art, philosophes ne sont parvenues à un accord ni sur une définition du concept de baroque, ni sur une périodisation reconnue par tous.

And that after twenty years of discussion.

All labels are misleading: it is clear that none could be more so than the term 'baroque' in literature; it really tells us more about its antonym—classical literature—than about itself. It retroactively presupposes that classical literature is a goal in itself, a point at which everything reaches a proper maturity. It must presumably be a judgement of a later period on the earlier one: unlike the term 'burlesque', 'baroque' was not used in critical language in the seventeenth century. The term 'burlesque' can be found in all standard dictionaries of the time: Cotgrave (1660), Ménage's *Les Origines de la langue française* (1650), Richelet (1685), *Le Grand Dictionnaire de l'Académie Françoise* (1687), and Furetière (1690). The term 'baroque' on the other hand, is found only in the two last-named works, and then only with the following restricted meaning:

> Le Grand Dictionnaire: *baroque:* adj. se dit seulement des perles qui sont d'une rondeur fort imparfaite: Un collier de perles baroques.

> Furetière: *baroque:* terme de joaillier: qui ne se dit que des perles qui ne sont pas parfaitement rondes.

One might have been able to buy a necklace of irregular baroque pearls before 1690, but certainly not a baroque play: nobody would have understood that particular application of the word. The judgement of the later period is, of course, the enduring one, stifling and obscuring from us any form of pre-classical self-perception. As a critical, often pejorative, construct of a later period the term is profoundly dissatisfying. The definition of the 'baroque' by the *Shorter Oxford English Dictionary* says it all: 'a florid style of late Renaissance architecture prevalent in the 18th c[entury].' One essential difference between the 'baroque' and terms such as 'classique' and 'romantique' is that the latter were born of their own times. Worse still, the favour accorded to the term 'baroque' in critical language during the last twenty years has greatly complicated the difficulties entailed in trying to reach an understanding and a contemporary self-appraisal of the early seventeenth century in France. The evidence that something like a 'dissociation of sensibility' occurred under the reign of Louis XIV, to be institutionalized by Voltaire in *Le Siècle de Louis XIV,* leads one, in a paraphrase of T. S. Eliot, to look for 'something which had happened to the mind of France between the time of Thèophile or Scarron and the time of Hugo and Gautier'. The persistence of eighteenth-century perceptions and misapprehensions obscures the real seventeenth century, the first half of which could legitimately be defined as a late Renaissance period.

The urgency of the need to return to the texts of the period is best demonstrated with a few figures: of the thousand or more plays printed in France in the seventeenth century there are, at most, thirty preserved and performed regularly in the modern French theatre. Of these 1,000 plays, approximately 300 are comedies, of which nearly eighty date from before 1650. These numbers would be considerably increased if one-act comedies, farces, and comedies not printed in Paris were to be included. Although almost no comedies were published in the period 1600-1619, nearly seventy appeared in the years 1620-1650; in the wake of that, following the success of Scarron, thirty comedies were printed in the year 1650-1659. In other words, approximately one-third of the total number of comedies written in the seventeenth century were printed in the period 1620-1660. With the exception of some of Corneille's work, all the seventeenth-century comedies retained in the modern French repertoire date from the second half of the century, the classical period. It could perhaps be objected that as we advance in time the selection of older plays retained in the repertoire of modern theatres is bound to diminish. If one could feel confident in the criteria of selection and in the availability of printed versions of these early plays, this argument would seem more palatable and the wall of indifference constructed in the reign of Louis XIV less harmful. Corneille is the only dramatist of the first half of the century to get past that wall; perhaps this is because he remained ready to adapt his early work to the tastes of the second half of the century. The *Examens* of 1660 are remarkable for the readiness shown by the author to criticize his own work. Rotrou, Mairet, Thomas Corneille, and Scarron are sometimes performed, but it could hardly be said that they command a safe, unchallenged place on *this* side of the wall. Others excluded from cisalpine recognition include Scudéry, Gougenot, Rayssiguier, Charles Beys, André Mareschal, Pierre du Ryer, Le Metel d'Ouville, Guérin de Bouscal, Boisrobert, and Claude de l'Estoille. These are all dramatists who, to the best of my knowledge, have never been performed since the seventeenth century, unless, of course, one takes into account the plagiarism of Dancourt. The ostracism of these dramatists was so complete, yet their work was so good, that in the early eighteenth century Dancourt was able, with impunity and profit, to present plays by Du Ryer (*Les Vendanges de Suresnes*) and Guérin de Bouscal (*Le Gouvernement de Sanche Pansa*) as his own. Molière's own favourite comic *reprises*—that is comedies not written by himself (because, of course, he continued to perform plays by other dramatists throughout his career)—were *Dom Japhet d'Arménie* (1650) by Scarron and *Le Gouvernement de Sanche Pansa* (1642) by Guérin de Bouscal. He presented and performed each of them thirty times or more. If they were good enough for him, we are tempted to ask. . . . He certainly borrowed material from these dramatists (and from Le Metel d'Ouville, Cyrano and others) and seems to have learned from them.

A final example of the virtual exclusion of the first half of the century from the literary (if not the philosophical) life of the *Grand Siècle* can be found in the error-ridden histories of the French theatre which appeared early in the eighteenth century. These, it should be added, may often be manifestations of an attempt to correct the record and to put things right. The earliest history of this kind is that of Beauchamps, *Recherches sur les théâtres de France,* published in three volumes in 1735. All honour to Beauchamps for having produced such a work and for having tried to delve into the history of the theatre in that remote and barbaric age which preceded the reign of Louis XIV. That there should be so many errors in his work, all concentrated in the first half of the century, is perhaps just a measure of the impermeability of Louis XIV's France to the artistic life of Louis XIII's kingdom; after a hundred years of neglect, the historic records would have been difficult for Beauchamps to reconstitute. In an unjustly forgotten article, Carrington Lancaster drafted an inventory of the number of mistakes known to him in Beauchamps's work: he found an error rate of 16% sixty years ago. The number of identifiable mistakes has, of course, increased considerably since then with the amount of research completed. One example of consequence is that of Guérin de Bouscal: baptized 'Guyon' by Beauchamps, with his death dated in 1645, this most interesting dramatist was in fact called Daniel and he lived till 1675. Archival and textual research shows that Molière knew his work and probably met him in 1653, eight years after his supposed date of death. That information could not have been established by relying on Beauchamps and the names and dates he gives. The significance of Beauchamps is that he is the *first* theatre historian in the field, and that most subsequent historians copy his errors (the *frères* Parfaict, de Léris, the chevalier de Mouhy, for example) thereby enshrining them in a seriously flawed history of French theatre. Such errors of detail have contributed to, and derived from, the misrepresentation of the

first half of the seventeenth century: the belittling of Descartes by Voltaire and the inclusion by him of Pascal's *Lettres Provinciales* in the reign of Louis XIV set the seal on the process. By a curious coincidence, Lancaster's searching little article appeared only one year after Eliot's influential essay on the metaphysical poets. If only the two Americans had pursued their ideas together!

In using the term 'burlesque' instead of 'baroque' one is at least taking a few steps nearer an intact contemporary view. The term 'burlesque' has, it is true, unfortunate connotations. Like the term 'metaphysical' at the time of Eliot's essay, it has 'long done duty as a term of abuse, or as the label of a quaint and pleasant taste' but there are definitions on which to build. The term was known to the scholars, creative writers, and critics of the period in question, it is found in every dictionary of the time, and it constitutes a precise literary term. The term is, however, used to define the use of language in *all* contexts— poetry and the novel as well as the theatre: my concern here, of course, is the theatre.

The first full dictionary definition I have discovered is that of Ménage in *Les Origines de la langue française:*

> Burlesque—*De l'italien burlesco qui a esté fait du verbe burlar* qui signifie *railler* . . . Il n'y a pas si longtemps que ce mot burlesque est en usage parmi nous; et c'est M. Sarasin qui le premier s'en est servi. Mais c'est M. Scarron qui le premier a pratiqué avec réputation ce genre d'escrire.

Ménage maintains a modest silence about his own excursion into the burlesque with *La Requête des dictionnaires* (1637). The 1660 edition of Cotgrave offers as translation/definition of burlesque: 'jeasting; or in jest, not serious; also mocking, flouting'.

Boileau scoffs at the burlesque, 'que ce stile jamais ne souille votre ouvrage', he advises. To understand how the author of *Le Lutrin* can, in all honesty, say such things, one must turn to a more dispassionate view, that of Charles Perrault in his *Parallèle* for example:

> Le Burlesque, qui est une espèce de ridicule, consiste dans la disconvenance de l'idée qu'on donne d'une chose avec son idée véritable . . . or cette disconvenance se fait en deux manières, l'une en parlant bassement des choses les plus relevées, et l'autre en parlant magnifiquement des choses basses.

This, of course, introduces the distinction between burlesque and mock-heroic. The stance of ironic distance is the same in each, but the effect differs: a poltroon playing the part of a hero can be vulgar, but a Boileau, talking in elevated style about a mere lectern, may be trivial, but is not, in fact, using base language. This is the 'new' burlesque. Brunot makes much of this distinction in his *Histoire de la langue française,* but it will be seen that in the theatre only the principle of distance matters.

Robert Garapon offers confirmation of this, even if his definition of the baroque leaves us groping: 'L'auteur baroque', he informs us, 'ne peut refuser à chaque mot, à chaque phrase qu'il écrit, la plénitude de son autonomie expressive', while the burlesque 's'amuse à employer le langage comme un instrument malicieusement faussé, emphatique pour les sujets triviaux, trivial pour les sujets sublimes'.

There is thus a development of incongruity between style and subject in the French burlesque theatre. This works both on horizontal and on vertical planes, as a contrast in styles between the characters in any given play, and as a contrast between a given character and what is normally expected of him (a poltroon acting the part of a hero). One therefore finds a keen sense of linguistic self-awareness in the play. In addition, there is frequently a sense of complicity established with the audience on the vertical plane—in the understanding that is created of the extent to which the poltroon (for example) misrepresents the norms of behaviour expected. There is a gap which is knowingly opened and exploited between the character on stage and the rôle he/she so comically *mis*-represents, between the text and the meta-text. This frequently leads to pastiche (*Le Cid* was a contemporary play which lent itself to endless pastiche), and to an aspect of the burlesque noted by Charles Sorel in his *La Bibliothèque française* (1664): 'Le burlesque est un style particulier à l'auteur, qui est de faire raillerie de tout, même dans les narrations où il parle luimême'. The complicity created in the shared understanding of a comic role subverting a widely-known model leads, then, to explicit authorial intervention: as a novelist, Sorel would offer Cervantes's *Don Quixote* as an example, or perhaps his own *Le Berger extravagant*. The consequence, or perhaps the cause, of this authorial intervention in the theatre is that one finds, in Garapon's words, 'une relative indifférence à l'égard de la psychologie chez les auteurs'. Character is still essentially language, and more particularly the comic contrast of language; as such, it should more frequently be regarded as a playful *exercice de style* than as parody.

It is perhaps time for a few examples. Corneille's comedies set off a number of contrasts in style: none more so than *Mélite* (1629), his first work. In the first scene of the play we are offered a dialogue between Tircis and Eraste: Eraste the soulful lover of the pastoral tradition declaims his adoration of his loved one thus:

> Le jour qu'elle naquit, Venus, bien
> qu'immortelle
> Pensa mourir de honte en la voyant si belle.
>
> (I.i. 73-74)

After Eraste has continued at some length, the dry Tircis comments:

> Tu le prends d'un haut ton, et je crois qu'au
> besoin
> Le discours emphatique irait encore bien loin.
>
> (I. i. 79-80)

The contrast in their styles, a frequent device in Corneille's comedy, is typical of the linguistic self-awareness which has been alluded to. These aspects are even more evident in Mareschal's *Le Railleur* (1636), one of the finest comedies of the period. The *railleur* Clarimand is out of the same stable as the Tircis of *Mélite* (they both derive from the Hylas of *L'Astrée*) and he mocks the *style boursouflé* of the lovers in similar fashion:

> Que de cérémonie et de sourds compliments!
> Voyons-les, écoutons leurs discours de romans!
>
> (I. ii)

or, in even more caustic alexandrines, 'Ce stile est de haut prix, et pour les mieux chaussés' (I.ii). The world *style* recurs often and its explicit use is significant. There is, for example, a *poète à gages* named Lyzante who boasts of having found the *juste milieu* in his verse: 'passé le bas stile et fuy le pédant!', he exclaims (II. iii). But then the contrast of styles on the horizontal plane continues. There is the *miles gloriosus*, the Capitan Taillebras 'L'Alcide occidental et l'honneur des Pyrénées'. He is as florid in his style as the *filou* Beaurocher is subtle and insinuating. This is how the *railleur* expresses his admiration of Beaurocher's epistolary skill:

> J'apprends qu'également un double feu t'alume,
> Et celuy de l'épée et celuy de la plume,
> Que tu scais doucement sur un stile flatteur
> Escrire en cavallier en non pas en auteur.
>
> (V. i)

The lovers, the *railleur,* Lyzante the poet, Taillebras, and Beaurocher offer us five different styles, but there is a sixth, that of the elegant but cynical courtesan la Dupré. Cold and calculating, well informed of what is happening at court, she strikes a different note of realism when talking of the lesbians in the retinue of Anne of Austria:

> Et se faignant par jeu ce qu'en effet nous
> sommes,
> Elles se font l'amour ne l'osant faire aux
> hommes.
>
> (IV. iii)

There are few characters in seventeenth-century theatre who go as far in realistic social commentary as she does.

The contrast in styles to be found in *Le Railleur* is taken to extreme lengths by Desmarets in *Les Visionnaires* (1637). A few examples will suffice to illustrate the self-conscious differentiation of levels of language. The conceited but attractive Hespérie interprets so *literally* the high-flown compliments of her many suitors, her *mourants,* that she announces: 'Le monde va périr si on me laisse vivre' (I. vi), and then:

> On compterait plutôt les feuilles des forêts,
> Les sablons de la mer, . . .
> Que le nombre d'amants que j'ai mis au
> tombeau.
>
> (I. vi)

In a literary discussion with her theatre-mad sister Sestiane, Amidor the poet comments: 'Cette pièce est sçavante et d'un stile fort haut.'

The contrast across a horizontal plane in these plays also includes a development of well-known models on a vertical plane. The ironic commentary of the Clarimands and Tircis develops the position of Hylas, the well-known cynic of d'Urfé's *L'Astrée,* while the new, realistic urban setting of Paris in these plays invites comic contrast with the idyllic sylvan background of the pastoral. In *Les Visionnaires,* the metatexts are numerous and alluded to explicitly, creating pastiche. In tuning his voice, Amidor the pretentious poet resorts to a pastiche of Ronsard:

> Desja de toutes parts j'entrevoy les brigades
> De ces Dieux chevre-pieds et des folles Menades
> Qui s'en vont célébrer le mystère Orgien
> En l'honneur immortel du père Bromien.
>
> (I. iii)

One of the most brilliant examples of pastiche in the theatre of the time is to be found in *Le Gouvernement de Sanche Pansa* of Guérin de Bouscal. After an extraordinary take-off of the récit of Rodrigue's battle against the Moor by a *filou* talking about a trivial street fight, with the same cadences, the same historic present and sometimes the same rhyme as *Le Cid,* concluding:

> Il appelle ses gens, je ramasse les nôtres
> Il anime les uns, j'encourage les autres.
>
> (III iv. 1013-14)

the author gives us echoes of *Horace, Polyeucte,* and then Rabelais. Sancho then intervenes: 'Mais parlons par escot: que vouliez-vous qu'il fît?' That *parlons par escot* [*écot*] is taken from Frère Jean in Rabelais's *Cinquième Livre.* The original line is: 'Mais parlons un peu par escot, docteur subtil.' But at the same time as he has Sancho quoting Rabelais, the dramatist is intervening playfully in the text with a resounding pun: the *écho* = É-C-H-O = of the original *escot* = E-S-C-O-T = constitutes a statement in itself of the comic device being employed, *before your very eyes,* by the dramatist. This sort of echo reverberates, if sometimes less self-consciously, throughout the comic theatre of the time. The sense of complicity, playfulness, and authorial intervention are all here. The pastiche, even parody of Corneille later became such a feature of the performance of Scarron's comic hero Jodelet that he became known as *l'anti-Rodrigue.* The best-known feature of burlesque language is, however, the neologism, the creation of entirely new comic language; examples are too numerous to list, but it is important to remember that the linguistic virtuosity of Scarron and his contemporaries does extend beyond the repeated imitation of contemporary masterpieces.

The comic verve and invention so often expressed in neologism have often been held to be the only positive qualities of burlesque writing, the first manifestation of preciosity. The recognition of verve and linguistic flair then often leads in a rather facile way to an assumption

Portrait of Florent Carton Dancourt.

of carelessness and lack of control. As Dufresny's reflection on the burlesque in the *Parallèle d'Homère et de Rabelais* (1710) was later to show, verve and invention are not necessarily incompatible with careful writing. The skill with which the techniques of comic writing were inserted into the theatre and into the traditional canons of rhetoric will be examined shortly, but it is important to counter the all-too prevalent charge of carelessness with the early observation that there are, in fact, very few comedies of the first half of the century which do not show considerable skill and balance in the grouping of characters, the reversing and virtual *doubling* of roles. Rotrou's *La Bague de l'oubli* (1635) is remarkable in this respect, as are du Ryer's *Les Vendanges de Suresnes* (1635) and Mairet's *Les Galanteries du duc d'Ossonne* (1636). The delicate choreography of Rotrou, the finely-observed distinctions between *le bourg* and *la ville* of du Ryer, and the innovative use of scenic space by Mairet all create a sense of fresh, lively, but *controlled* experiment. There is an identifiable early group of dramatists, including Mareschal, du Ryer, Guérin de Bouscal, Gougenot, Rayssiguier, and Claude de l'Estoille, who have much in common, and who probably even worked together; like Corneille and Rotrou, they were all trained in law and were thus sensitive to conventions of language. As will be seen, work at the bar imposed rigorous criteria of rhetorical decorum.

The work of these writers constitutes a particularly bold and innovative change of direction in French comedy. They were modernists, appreciative of Malherbe's proposals and ready to experiment with language. The subsequent 'Spanish' generation of burlesque dramatists, led by the extraordinary Le Metel d'Ouville and including Scarron, Boisrobert, and Thomas Corneille, benefited considerably from the earlier experiments in theatre. Their adaptations of Calderón and Lope de Vega sometimes even run the risk of appearing repetitive in their systematic application of the *trouvailles* of 1633-1643; this should not, however, be a hindrance to recognition of their ability and the merit of their formula. The liveliness of their language matches that of their predecessors, and their contemporary success is testimony to the importance of the earlier experiments in burlesque writing. Their sudden eclipse in the second half of the century probably stems less from literary considerations than from the matrimonial and political accidents of Louis XIV's liaison with Mme de Maintenon ('la veuve Scarron') and his desire to obliterate all associations with the humiliating period of the Fronde. Mention of the name of Scarron was prohibited in his presence, while the political imagery of Latona and her lonely protection of her child Apollo, which is incorporated in the gardens of Versailles, confirms his *mauvais souvenir* of the years of his minority.

Kibédi Varga has suggested that the burlesque is a manifestation of the *monde à l'envers* of the Carnival: he quotes Marmontel's *Eléments de littérature* in support of this view: 'Le but de ce genre d'écrits [le burlesque] est de faire voir que tous les objects ont deux faces; de déconcerter la vanité humaine.' This may sometimes be the case, and Marmontel's contribution to the subject is a useful reminder that the burlesque is not an isolated, ephemeral phenomenon; it is important to note the survival of a medieval *théâtre de participation,* as distinct from the *théâtre du regard* of the later neo-classical period. Since its terms of reference do not go beyond the world of literary creation, the burlesque theatre cannot as a rule, however, be said to be as committed as Varga suggests. It is more purely playful in its spirit.

There is the sense of realism which sometimes comes from the ironic contrasts with the world of the pastoral, and there is another realism of a more subtle nature which emerges from the burlesque theatre. It is of the kind that Anne Righter has traced in her *Shakespeare and the Idea of the Play:* she shows how the tradition of audience participation in the *soties* and *sermons joyeux* of the Middle Ages ultimately gave way to the metaphor of theatre—'All the world's a stage . . . '. An early example of this audience participation is the thirteenth-century play *Le Garçon et l'aveugle,* in which the audience, solicited by the blind beggar for money, become participants in the play: the onlookers really do become the crowd from whom he begs alms and 'in whose sight he is gulled by the boy Jehannet'. There is a pretence that the actors share a common reality with their audience. This is constantly to be found in burlesque comedy: the conspiratorial wink in the direction of the audience when an obviously exaggerated send-up of a recognized, illustrious source is introduced explains the success of the many literary pastiches used in the plays of the period. Furthermore, the linguistic self-awareness and the multiplicity of *styles* which are so evident in the burlesque can often find sophisticated theatrical expression in a multiplicity of *masks,* creating a *jeu de rôles* and *le théâtre dans le théâtre.* There, the illusion of reality, if rather particular, is complete.

The deliberate confusion of the notions of illusion and reality constitutes one of the most recurrent and successful paradoxes of the burlesque theatre. *L'Illusion comique* (1635-36) of Corneille is perhaps the most familiar example with which to illustrate the point, although the same device is used more successfully in several other plays of the time. It is also the device used by Molière in *Les Précieuses ridicules.* In these plays we are candidly shown a play within a play and invited to watch the inner play as a play, alongside Alcandre and Pridamant (or La Grange and du Croisy) for example, sharing a bench with them in the framing outer scenes as if we were one of them. The exposure of the play as a play and of the actor as an actor makes the distinction between illusion and 'reality' very difficult to make, impossible in fact. In exposing the inner workings of the work of art the dramatist assumes an air of realism; pretending to have abandoned illusion, he in fact extends it. This is what happens in the two plays entitled *La Comédie des comédiens,* one by Gougenot (1633), the other by Scudéry (1635). It is also found in *Le Gouvernement de Sanche Pansa* (1642), *L'Illusion comique* as we have seen, and in all the plays of Scarron where a particularly well-known actor, Jodelet, with identifiable traits known to the audience, pretends to adopt a disguise required by the plot, and where he is simply seen as Jodelet playing a part and being *himself* in an uncongenial role. When he comes on in Molière's *Les Précieuses ridicules* he does not fool anyone, and his deliberately ill-adjusted 'performance' as a *vicomte* is enjoyed by all. The device is an essential part of the *commedia dell'arte* and, in fact, in Scudéry's *La Comédie des comédiens,* where a troupe of actors engagingly discusses its problems, there *is* a role for Harlequin. It is historically the case, then, that the devices of role-playing and the play within the play are given new life by play and experiment with contrasting levels of language; indeed, it would seem to be the case that role-playing is a natural theatrical consequence and expression of experiment with language. It is thus all the more extraordinary that, having noted the proliferation of *le théâtre dans le théâtre* in the seventeenth century in his *Le Théâtre dans le théâtre sur la scène française du XVIIe siècle,* Georges Forestier should fail to comment on this evolution from burlesque language to *jeux de rôle,* from language to character.

To recapitulate, it does not seem possible to divide, as some critics have, the *adequatio* and *aletheia* of burlesque theatre, saying for example that at such and such a date *adequatio* disappears in favour of *aletheia.* . . . The elements of illusion and reality are systematically confused with each other in many plays of the time, creating one of the most appreciated paradoxes in this theatre of paradox. In addition, there is a rising tide of official approval for the theatre, as confirmed by: (a) the creation of a royal troupe of actors (1630), (b) the creation of the company of *les cinq auteurs* (1635), (c) Rotrou's dedication of *La Bague de l'oubli* to Louis XIII (1635), and (d) Louis XIII's own edict of 16 April 1641, affirming the dignity of the actor's profession. This would seem to offer some encouragement to dramatists to promote the theatre as a metaphor for life, as did Corneille, for example, in *L'Illusion comique*. The energy, confidence, and progress of the burgeoning comic theatre of the time command attention: it is astonishing that it should have been neglected for so long by publishers, theatre directors, and critics.

The ingenuity deployed in reorganizing the scenic space to contain the play within the play also created considerable freedom for the dramatists. If one is offered a play within a play, freely presented as such, then one is inclined to admit the 'reality' of the performance and suspend criteria of *vraisemblance*—because, after all, it is only a play. Similarly, the illusion of reality is enhanced by the coincidence of stage time with real time, an important consideration for theorists such as l'Abbé d'Aubignac who later recommended it in his *Pratique du théâtre* (1657).

The play within a play is, of course, a universal device which goes back to *Pathelin* and reaches to the present, but it is important to observe how it develops in the seventeenth century from the burlesque juxtaposition of contrasting styles of language: language having eventually become character, the burlesque use of contrasting styles inevitably creates *jeux de rôle,* with the consequent effect of *le théâtre dans le théâtre*. The initial impetus for this so-called 'baroque' device is thus linguistic rather than visual. It is also important to remember that, although apparently swept aside in the second half of the century in the name of *bienséance* and *vraisemblance,* these lively, inventive comedies of the first half of the century created for themselves their own theoretical justification for roaming free in time and space; the play within which the often eccentric inner performance takes place has, as its precise location and confines, the here and now of the theatre within which you currently find yourself. This is an essentially theatrical experience which has been created universally by too many dramatists to be confined to the outhouse of the 'baroque'. The answer is perhaps to say that the theatre of the time was so lively that other art forms became theatrical.

'Je ne sçay qui t'ameine icy, toy qui es la plus inutile pièce d'un poème', says the Prologue to the Argument in Scudéry's *La Comédie des comédiens.* 'Et je ne sçay qui t'y peut conduire, toi qui est la moins nécessaire', replies the Argument. Iconoclastic, playful too, Scudéry is above all resolutely modern in his approach, as are most of his contemporaries; he does, however, take the precaution of staging his inconoclastic excesses in the *inner* play, *L'Amour caché par l'amour,* of his production. The sense of care and responsibility shown in their work by the

earlier generation of dramatists is best understood, perhaps, in the case of Pierre du Ryer. A lawyer and one of the most active translators of the classics of his day, he translated the works of Cicero and brought his specialized legal rhetorical training to this quite particular interest in language; he was probably the leading figure of a circle of writers and wrote a number of encouraging liminary pieces for his contemporaries. The homage he wrote for Rayssiguier's pastoral tragi-comedy *L'Aminte du Tasse* (1632), the first dramatic adaptation of *Aminta* in French, is revealing:

> Amy, par ta seule industrie
> Qui nous a charmés tant de fois
> Aminte a quitté sa Patrie,
> Et se vient rendre bon François:
> Si les habiles de la France
> Admirent la persévérance
> Qui le porta dans le danger
> Ils s'estonnent bien davantage
> D'apprendre auiourd'hui leur langage
> D'un simple pasteur estranger.

Rayssiguier, too, was a lawyer; he also adapted *L'Astrée* and in 1633 wrote the burlesque comedy *La Bourgeoise ou la promenade de St Cloud*. The translation and adaptation of the chivalric romances seem frequently to have been part of a cycle of experiment, vulgarization, and then original comic creation. It is particularly interesting that this work should also have been the work of lawyers. Marc Fumaroli has called attention to this in his recent work on seventeenth-century rhetoric, referring to a 'véritable ruée de jeunes avocats vers le théâtre' in the 1630s. Why should this be?

The manual and model of parliamentary and legal style—the *Stilus Curie Parlamenti* by Guillaume du Breuil—had been established since the fourteenth century; re-edited in the sixteenth century by the Parisian *jurisconsulte* Charles du Moulin, it was quoted as an authority by Loisel in 1604. Urging gravity of gesture and bearing, and smiling only in moderation, the chapter entitled *De modo et gestu quem debet habere advocatus* seems a long way away from the verve, gaiety, and apparent improvisation of the burlesque. Fumaroli suggests that the burlesque is a manifestation of the *basoche* at play, but even at play the *basoche* can be careful and scholarly. . . .

Incitement to clever linguistic experiment was bound to follow in the wake of the Reformation and the Erasmian reformulation of rhetorical canons; the impact of his *copia verborum* has been carefully studied by Terence Cave. Rhetoric was also, of course, an essential part of the Jesuit *Ratio Studiorum,* established by the edict of 8 January 1599: quite how much experiment there was in the vernacular in their colleges falls outside the domain of this study, but François de Dainville, himself a Jesuit, has underlined the regrettable tendency in seventeenth-century France to complete one's studies under the Jesuits with rhetoric without going on to the final year of philosophy. Knowledge and science were sacrificed to the study of rhetoric, giving to literary studies based on rhetoric a 'primauté abusive'.

In this context, plays which deliberately insert an eccentric register of language into the theatre (as is evident in such titles as the *Comédie de proverbes* (1618), *Comédie des académistes* (1637), *Comédie des chansons* (1639), and *L'Intrigue des filous* (1648)) can be seen as a modern, educated, playful response to old precepts and to the antiquated *commedia sostenuta*. As we have seen, they evolve gradually and naturally towards the presentation of eccentric *characters*—the *visionnaires, imaginaires,* or inappropriately disguised main characters who are so much a stock-in-trade of later seventeenth-century comedy. Updated versions of the pastoral romances, whether it be Tasso according to Rayssiguier or *L'Astrée* according to Corneille, also offer opportunity for experiment. Fumaroli has even gone so far as to show how Alcandre follows formal phases of rhetorical deliberation to plead for and save Clindor in Corneille's *L'Illusion comique:* 'Organisant un jeu savamment ambigu où rhétorique et dramaturgie s'entrelacent et se soutiennent.' In an exchange in Gougenot's *La Comédie des comédiens,* Turlupin and Mlle Boniface claim that the famous Roman actor Roscius was really a French citizen and 'c'est luy qui enseigna Cicéron l'art de bien réciter un discours'. Cicero and Roscius, rhetoric and theatre, the associations in the seventeenth century are constant, leading, appropriately enough, to the final paradox enunciated by Genette:

> L'esprit de la rhétorique est tout entier dans cette conscience d'un hiatus possible entre le langage réel . . . et un langage virtuel . . . qu'il suffit de rétablir par la pensée pour délimiter un espace de figure. . . . La figure est un écart par rapport à l'usage, lequel écart est pourtant dans l'usage
>
> . . . , le signe est défini par l'absence de signe.

In this sense every burlesque speech assumes the status of a performance, overlaid with several strata of virtual and actual, veiled and explicit, meanings. The discovery (or rediscovery) of this tremendous potential of language to share a moment of conspiracy with an audience, and then to progress beyond the intellectual game towards portrayal of a diversity of characters is obviously an important specific moment in the history of comic theatre: it is the achievement of a much-neglected body of writers and yet it provides the basis for contemplation of the function of the actor by Molière. It also confirms a substantive difference in dramatic language between comedy and tragedy: comic dialogue offers a rich diversification of language in Molière (e.g., Horace in *L'École des femmes,* Don Juan, the *marquis* in *Le Misanthrope,* not to mention the numerous peasant dialects)—the mould having already been broken by the burlesque writers. As Beaumarchais said of his own comic characters, 'Chacun y parle son langage; eh! que le dieu du naturel les préserve d'en parler d'autre.' But the dramatic language of tragedy remains, in essence, unchanged: tragic characters thus continue to be positions for study, vehicles for argument, drawing their means of expression from the same seam of elevated, universal language as each other. Bearing in mind the essential difference between the *substance* of a speech and its *means*

of expression, it can be said that heroes and villains, men and women, all use the same codified means of expression in seventeenth-century tragedy. If the characters of French tragedy sometimes appear less complete on stage than those of comedy it is because they rarely express themselves in their own individually diversified language; this is perhaps another way of measuring the special contribution made to French comedy by comic writers in the first half of the century. Garapon contends that the burlesque disappeared with the arrival of Molière and the development of the comedy of character; it should be remembered that, far from putting an end to the burlesque, Molière harnessed and maintained its main devices. He frequently performed the work of its talented exponents who, although relegated to the obscure realms of the 'baroque', still provide refreshing distraction from the admirable but unending heroic statuary of the reign of Louis XIV.

TRAGICOMEDY

Henry Carrington Lancaster

SOURCE: "Subsequent History of the Tragi-Comedy," in *The French Tragi-Comedy: Its Origin and Development from 1552 to 1628,* 1907. Reprinted by Gordian Press, Inc., 1966, pp.148-54.

[*In the following excerpt, Lancaster explains the decline of French tragicomedy in the late seventeenth century.*]

Toward 1650, . . . the number of tragi-comedies that appeared each year was decreasing and by 1660 had become very small, if one may judge by those of which the names have been preserved. With the *Psyché* of Corneille, Molière, and Quinault (1671) and the *Parfaits Amis* of Chappuzeau (1672) the *genre* practically ceases to exist, although sporadic examples of the use of its name recur during the following centuries. The causes of this decay are not far to seek.

In the first place the popular taste had reacted from the spirit of the early seventeenth century, which had found expression in the *romanesque* tragi-comedy, as well as in the *précieux* Hôtel de Rambouillet and in the romances of Honoré d'Urfé and Madeleine de Scudéry. The Parisian public, grown weary of the multiplicity of incident and exaggerated portrayal of character, found in the tragi-comedy, turned from that *genre* to the truer representations of life that they found on the classical stage. It is after the appearance of *Horace* and *Polyeucte* that the tragi-comedy begins to decline, not long after the successes of Molière and Racine that it ceases to exist.

But in addition to the change in the taste of the Parisian public and the increasing popularity of the classical stage, the tragi-comedy suffered from certain changes in its own composition and in the use of the terms, tragedy and comedy, which brought about its confusion with these *genres*. As early as Mairet's *Chriseide et Arimand* (1625) tendencies toward unity of plot existed in tragi-comedies. In his *Silvanire,* a *tragi-comédie pastorale,* and his *Virginie,* a tragi-comedy, Mairet continued these tendencies, which were carried further by Desmarests in *Mirame,* a tragi-comedy which preserves the classical unities. At the same time psychological struggles, which had formerly held a distinctly subordinate place in tragi-comedies, became important in the *dénouements* of *La Fidelle Tromperie* and *Agésilan de Colchos* and formed the essence of the plot of Rayssiguier's *Celidee.* Thus it is that the unity and psychology of the *Cid* did not prevent its being called a tragi-comedy, a title that fitted well its *romanesque* plot and happy *dénouement.*

While the tragi-comedy was thus approaching the tragedy by a greater unity of plot and a more careful study of the emotions, another barrier that had separated the two *genres* in France, the nature of the *dénouement,* was removed by Corneille, when, following the example of Euripides, he showed in *Cinna,* and partially in *Horace,* that a tragedy could have a happy *dénouement,* a usage approved by d'Aubignac. . . . Thus, the more serious tragi-comedies, which showed an approach to classical unity and psychology, came to be called tragedies, in spite of their happy *dénouement.* The *Cid,* first known as a tragi-comedy, was called a tragedy along with *Polyeucte* and *Rodogune.*

On the other hand, certain tragi-comedies, as *L'Ospital des Fous,* approached the comedy by an increase in the comic element, as did others by a *bourgeois* spirit that enters more especially into *La Bourgeoise* and *L'Esperance Glorieuse.* The term *comédie,* moreover, was now applied to translations of the Spanish *comedia* and related plays, which differed little in their essential qualities from the lighter forms of the tragi-comedy. Thus some tragi-comedies were confused with comedies, as others were with tragedies. The two terms that had the sanction of Greek and Latin usage were gradually extended to occupy the intermediate ground formerly held by the tragi-comedy. Thus French dramatists, answering the demands of their age, either ceased to write tragi-comedies, or called them by another name. As an independent *genre,* the tragi-comedy ceased to exist.

Such is the history of the French tragi-comedy. Drawing its substance from the medieval drama and its form from the Greek and Roman stage, it united these elements after the example of the *genre* in other European countries and came into existence in 1552. During the sixteenth century it represented a number of medieval *genres,* connected by their partially classical form and happy *dénouement.* One variety, the *romanesque,* showed its superior qualities, becoming with Hardy in the seventeenth century the only active form of the tragi-comedy. Before the establishment of the classical tragedy this *romanesque* tragi-comedy became the most popular and extensively written dramatic *genre* in France. But its preëminence was brief, for, encroached upon by the closely related tragedy and comedy, and out of harmony with the classical spirit of the time, it fell into disuse and, toward 1672, ceased to have

a more than sporadic existence.

Unless the *Cid* be considered a tragi-comedy, the *genre* left behind no great literary monument, since it neglected the study of character and passion for the *romanesque* and the melodramatic, thus attaining a large popularity, but making no permanent or universal appeal. But the tragi-comedy holds an important position in the history of the French stage, serving as a connecting link between the theater of the middle ages and that of the classical period, and by its influence making it possible for Corneille's tragedy to succeed where Jodelle's had failed. It preserved the popular qualities of the medieval drama, modernized them, and passed them to the classicists, thus establishing itself as an integral part of the most continuously excellent of national theaters.

Marvin T. Herrick

SOURCE: "French Tragicomedy from Garnier to Corneille," in *Tragicomedy: Its Origin and Development in Italy, France, and England,* University of Illinois Press, 1955, pp. 172-214.

[In the following excerpt, Herrick examines several tragicomedies by mid-seventeenth-century dramatists Pierre Du Ryer and Jean de Rotrou.]

[Pierre Du Ryer's] best tragedy, and the most famous of all his plays, is *Scevole* (1647), which is actually a tragedy with a happy ending.

Du Ryer found the plot of *Scevole* in Roman history (Livy) and added a love intrigue. The Etruscan king Porsenne (Lars Porsinna), an ally of the deposed Tarquin, has defeated the Romans and begun the siege of Rome. A captive Roman maiden, Junie (Cloelia), is brought before Porsenne for questioning. Du Ryer made Junie the heroine of the play and the lover of the Roman hero Scevole (Gaius Mucius, called Scaevola or "Left-Handed"). Junie has given up Scevole as dead, but now hears that he is also in the Etruscan camp, either as a prisoner or a traitor. Her doubts are resolved early in Act 2 by the appearance of Scevole himself, who informs her that he has come to assassinate Porsenne. Junie, who admires the Etruscan king, argues with her lover to spare him. Thereupon Scevole's jealousy is aroused, and the complication of a lovers' quarrel animates the action. There is a further complication as well, a triangle, for Arons (Arruns), the son of Porsenne, is also in love with Junie. Tarquin, who is growing impatient, accuses Porsenne of allowing his fondness for the Roman girl to delay his prosecution of the siege. In Act 3, Junie urges Porsenne to raise the siege and to repudiate his alliance with the tyrant Tarquin. When Porsenne fails to make up his mind one way or the other, Junie reluctantly decides that Scevole is right, that the Etruscan king must be assassinated. And so the action reaches a crucial turning point at the close of the third act.

Act 4 . . . is very dramatic, full of suspense and discoveries. Junie's confidante reports a camp rumor that Porsenne has been assassinated. Scevole is suspected, of course, and apprehended. But Porsenne has not been killed, nor was Scevole his attacker, though the Roman hero openly laments the failure when he learns that the Etruscan king is still alive. Arons, who has been friendly to Scevole, now learns that his friend not only seeks to kill his father but is also his rival in love. Thereupon Arons is placed in a tragic dilemma, unable to decide how he should act: "Whatsoever I can do, if I do my duty, I shall injure myself." When Scevole is brought before Porsenne and Tarquin he boldly admits that he came to the Etruscan camp to kill Porsenne, the enemy of Roman liberty.

> *Porsenne:*   Did ever an assassin show more audacity? It is he who   ought to tremble, and it is he who threatens.
>
> *Scevole:*   It is for tyrants to fear and tremble; it is for   Romans to conquer and destroy them.
>
> *Porsenne:*   Good gods, what madness!
>
> *Scevole:*   It is not madness that urges my hand and heart . . .   I am like the ministers of the gods.
>
> (4.6)

When Tarquin asks why he was not attacked instead of Porsenne, Scevole scornfully replies that his tyrant's blood is not worthy of a Roman sword. Since Scevole refuses to name any accomplices, he is led away to torture by fire.

At the opening of Act 5, Arons is still debating with himself as to what he should do. Junie pleads with him, and finally offers to give up Scevole if Arons will save him. A captain brings word that the fires have been lighted for the torture. Before Arons can act Porsenne enters exclaiming at the prodigious courage and fortitude of the Roman prisoner, who has already held his right hand in the flames until it burned off. Now Porsenne cannot bring himself to order more torture for so brave an enemy. When Junie quarrels with him, however, he resolves to continue the torture, until Arons persuades him to be more merciful. Then Tarquin and Scevole enter. Tarquin demands the death of Scevole, but Porsenne, who has never liked Tarquin, sets the Roman hero free and tells him to return to his people.

> *Scevole:*   Truly, noble Porsenne, you could never subdue me by the fear of pain; but I must admit that you have vanquished me by this notable act of generosity.
>
> (5.5)

Not to be outdone in generosity by his father, Arons resigns all claim to Junie. Porsenne gives the young couple his blessing: "Burn, then, with an immortal flame. I shall never break the love-knot which so nobly joins such generous hearts; and since they have both gained the victory, let each one be the prize and the glory of the other. Rome owes this marriage to your just desires, and to celebrate it I give her peace." And so the outcome is a happy one for both hero and heroine. Only the villain, Tarquin, is discomfited.

Scevole, which appeared ten years after the *Cid,* is a good example of tragedy with a happy ending. The unities are carefully preserved save for the unity of action, which wavers somewhat between the story of Scevole and the story of Porsenne. There are no deaths on stage; in fact, there are no deaths. All deeds of violence, e.g., the attempted assassination of Porsenne and the burning of Scevole's hand, take place off-stage. All the characters are of noble blood and all save Tarquin are highminded and virtuous. The style is consistently elevated, and there are no comic passages. Like [Pierre-Sylvain] Mareschal, Du Ryer followed the various stages that French tragicomedy passed through between 1630 and 1640, from *drame libre* to neoclassical tragedy with a happy ending, from *Clitophon* to *Scevole.*

. . . . .

Jean de Rotrou was Corneille's chief rival and himself a fairly prolific writer who drew upon a variety of sources, Latin, Greek, Italian, and Spanish, borrowing from Seneca, Plautus, Euripides, Italian *novelle,* Cervantes, Lope de Vega, and others. Lancaster calls him the "first French adapter of Spanish plays." His 35 plays have been divided into 7 tragedies, 12 comedies, and 16 tragicomedies; but this classification is not very satisfactory since his tragicomedies overlap with both his comedies and tragedies. His first play, for example, *L'Hypocondriaque ou le mort amoureux* (c. 1628), was a tragicomedy resembling the pastoral as well as comedy. In it two pairs of lovers undergo a series of intrigues and misadventures which drive the hero temporarily insane. The heroine disguises herself for a time in male attire. There is a happy ending, nevertheless, and the lovers are properly matched. Rotrou's best known play, *Venceslas* (1648), was called indifferently tragedy or tragicomedy, and the majority of his plays were tragicomic.

Laure Persécutée (1638), adapted from a play by Lope de Vega, is, I think, the best of his tragicomedies, and one of the best French tragicomedies of the time. This play has an admirably dramatic beginning. There is no prologue, no long-winded soliloquy, but a swift plunge *in medias res.* A count, accompanied by guards, accosts the hero, Orantée, Prince of Hungary.

> *Count:*   Seigneur, I arrest your Highness in the name of the   king.
>
> *Orantée:*   You're joking?
>
> *Count:*   I am obeying, and my duty is clear.
>
> *Orantée:*   Count!
>
> *Count:*   Seigneur!

There is no joke; the king has had his son arrested in order to break up his love affair with a young woman of unknown birth called Laure. The king has already arranged a match for the prince with a Polish princess.

Laure, the heroine, is introduced in the next scene, talking to her confidante Lydie. Octave, a courtier supposedly friendly to the prince, tells Laure about the arrest of Orantée. This news places Laure in a very unhappy and dangerous position.

> *Laure:*   Very well! If this is the decree of fate, I must die.   No one avoids death though many have wished to. After all,   this is the fruit of Orantée's love.
>
> *Octave:*   Happily enough, one remedy presents itself.
>
> *Laure:*   What?
>
> *Octave:*   Disguising yourself.
>
> *Laure:*   And in what attire?
>
> *Octave:*   As one of the prince's pages, and in this attire to   occupy a place near him as mistress and as page. One of those   who waited on him died three days ago. But you must hurry.
>
> *Laure:*   Gods, be my refuge!

Before the first act is over, Laure, now disguised as Celio the page, comes face to face with the king, who questions her about herself. Then she meets Orantée, who easily sees through her disguise. The two lovers discuss the impending marriage of Orantée with the Polish princess, and the prince tries to reassure Laure that he will never desert her. They are interrupted by the re-entry of the king, who demands an explanation for his son's escape from prison. This scene (1.11) is especially good theater; the disguised Laure has to stand by while the king abuses her and the prince defends her. The count, who carries the traditional role of counselor, tries to calm the angry king. Finally Orantée tells his father that he will obey him, but he soon demonstrates, after the king and his suite have left, that he has no intention of abandoning Laure.

This first act, containing twelve short scenes, is lively theater throughout. It is conventional exposition, to be sure, but so skillfully presented that the audience is caught up in what seems to be straightforward action. It would be difficult for any playwright to maintain such a pace, and Rotrou did not; the action slows down in the next act and the speeches grow longer.

The first scene of Act 2 is a soliloquy by the prince, a traditional complaint of the frustrated lover in tragicomedy. The language, however, though hardly devoid of conceits, is relatively simple and direct: "I know, Love, your everlasting power; my soul is your temple and my heart your altar. But do not demand this shameful sacrifice; rather make both altar and temple perish. Gods, but I love Laure!" In the next scene, the treacherous Octave informs the king that he can break up the affair between the prince and Laure for a price.

> *King:*   But what will pay for this very great favor?
>
> *Octave:*   You will pay it, Sire, with Laure herself. If I   render this service to your majesty, that is the price I want for my fidelity.
>
> *King:*   Done. Steal Laure, and Laure will be yours.

The king has only contempt for a sycophant like Octave, but is willing to use him.

In 2.4, the count, who is an honorable man, introduces a beautiful stranger to the king. This ravishing young lady gives the name of Eliante and relates a sad tale of disappointed love. Now she demands punishment for her betrayer. The king is so charmed by her that he orders the count to track down the villain who deceived her, and meanwhile to court the lady as well. The king has fallen in love with her, and the count arranges an assignation for him. The lady, of course, is Laure. But Orantée soon enters to disclose her true identity and thereby to confound his father.

Villainous complications begin to appear in Act 3. Octave conspires with Laure's confidante, Lydie; he persuades her to disguise herself as her mistress. Octave shows himself a pretty accomplished villain, though not of the strictly tragic kind; he is closer akin to Marston's Mendoza than to Shakespeare's Iago.

> *Octave:* With these various detours, the path is difficult; but in this labyrinth one must be a Theseus; one must promise all and do all for himself. In order to cheat the prince, one must cheat the king. We shall use Laure herself in this comedy; the one will mistake Lydie for Laure, the other Laure for Lydie. . . . Love, subtle boy, support my project.
>
> (3.2)

It is a comic project, or at all events a tragicomic project, because it is *ex amore;* but Octave realizes that he is playing a dangerous game.

In 3.7, the king, the prince, and the count eavesdrop on a love scene between Octave and Lydie (disguised as Laure). The passionate young prince, like Beaumont and Fletcher's Philaster, is quickly convinced that his mistress is faithless; he seethes with anger while his father triumphs. Orantée then confronts Octave with his treachery, but the villain maintains that it was Laure who pursued him. Now Orantée's temple and altar of love are actually shattered. Now he seeks vengeance on the wicked traitress. When she appears he savagely upbraids Laure, who is bewildered by this sudden change in her lover.

> *Laure:*   Alas! what have I done?
>
> *Orantée:*   (*aside to Octave*): She dissembles well.
>
> *Octave:*   Very well.
>
> *Laure:*   What is this secret talk between you? In what, my   dear Octave, have I offended him?
>
> *Orantée:*   "My dear Octave"! Infamous!

Laure protests her innocence, but Orantée orders her to leave him.

Thus, as is proper in a regular play, the action reaches a crisis at the close of the third act.

Although the prince has ordered Laure to leave him, he cannot leave her, and Act 4 discloses him standing with drawn sword at her door. He declaims a rather extravagant lament: "Beautiful heaven of my sun, house so longed for, street where my freedom has been so led astray, fair portal of Laure, where that star of love, opening or closing you, rejects or offers daylight, window hereafter forbidden to my eyes, why, caitiff, did I ever see you?" Octave joins the prince and rebukes him for his weakness. Orantée admits that his love for Laure endures together with his jealousy. After some discussion Orantée commands Octave to knock on the door. When Octave protests, Orantée draws his dagger.

> *Orantée:* Do it quickly, or I plunge this dagger in your breast.
> *Octave:* Very well, I'm going to knock.
> *Orantée:* No, don't do it, stop! My honor holds me back when my love is ready, and the one blinds me while the other opens my eyes.
> *Octave:* Honor surely counsels you better. Let us withdraw.
> *Orantée:* Wait until this transport subsides.

The prince asks Octave to tell him a love story, but pays no attention to it. Then Octave offers to call Laure, and he does call her as Orantée hides himself near the doorway. Like Cyrano, Octave disguises his voice to sound like Orantée's. Rotrou, in this scene (4.2), which became celebrated, was closely imitating Lope de Vega. Finally the prince himself knocks at the door, and disguises his voice to sound like Octave's. Laure talks with "Octave" a while, giving every indication of innocence; but the prince has made up his mind that she still dissembles. Then Laure, accompanied by Lydie (holding a torch), comes down to the street. And then the truth about the imposture comes out, for both Lydie and Octave confess.

Thus the fourth act, which contains the most theatrical scene in the whole play, comes to a close with a promise of better times to come for hero and heroine. The struggle between love and honor seems to be over, with love the victor.

The opening of Act 5 shows Orantée and Laure happily reconciled. But this play has a *catastasis;* a servant brings word that the Polish princess is arriving in Hungary. At the same time, one Clidamas, like Crito in the *Andrian* of Terence, like Carino in Guarini's *Pastor fido,* like many another last-act character in comedy and tragicomedy, appears on the scene. This Clidamas, Laure's guardian and supposedly her father, obviously holds the key to important information, in this instance information about the heroine's obscure birth: "My daughter, bless this happy day; she [the princess] will teach you from whom you are descended. With the arrival of the princess the moment has come when your illustrious station must be revealed to you, when you must shake off the yoke of my distress, and when you will lose and recover a father." (5.3)

The Polish princess enters with the king, the prince, and the royal suite. Laure appeals directly to the princess; she frankly confesses her love for a young man whose father has refused to sanction the match. The princess very gra-

ciously acknowledges the justice of Laure's plea: "Love is not bound to a parent's consideration; he relies upon himself alone; that willful boy, in order not to comply with a father, was willing to be born without one. Immortal, he holds absolute power, and pays no heed to the law of duty." (5.8) Laure thanks her, and then reveals that Orantée is her lover. The princess is taken aback at this disclosure, but, after eloquent pleadings from both Laure and the prince—Orantée now waxes almost as wordy as the heroes of Italian tragedy—finally yields to her own advice.

At this propitious moment, old Clidamas steps forward with a letter to the princess from her mother, the queen of Poland. Not altogether to the surprise of the reader, the letter reveals that Laure is herself the sister of the Polish princess. Clidamas explains that the Polish king, fearing dissension between two rival heirs, had ordered the queen to get rid of one. The queen, unable to destroy her child, had entrusted the infant to Clidamas, who brought her up. When the king of Hungary learns that Laure is of royal blood, his objections to her marrying Orantée vanish, and he offers himself as a consolation to the disappointed princess. Stretching a double knot to a triple one, Laure persuades Octave to marry Lydie. As Guarini had recommended for tragicomedy, the villain and villainess repent and reform, the good people are rewarded, and all ends with a comic catastrophe.

The best French tragicomedy, excepting Corneille's *Cid,* Rotrou's *Laure Persécutée* is similar to tragedy with a happy ending. Nevertheless, despite its lack of comic passages—the only flurry of humor is in Orantée's servant, who makes a brief appearance in 5.2—the emphasis on romantic love, the disguises, the mistaken identities, the machinery of transforming an obscure heroine into a princess put the play into the now traditional class of tragicomedy. *Laure Persécutée* resembles the lighter kind of Cinthian *tragedia di lieto fin,* the *Antivalomeni;* but Rotrou had a lighter and surer dramatic touch than did Cinthio. Rotrou had a better understanding of action; his action is sustained throughout every act. His strokes at characterization, while not profound, are sharper than Cinthio's. His dialogue for the most part is excellent, lively and natural, admirably fitted to the stage. How far Rotrou's excellencies in *Laure Persecutée* were owing to Lope de Vega I shall not presume to estimate.

Rotrou's *Venceslas* (1648) was definitely closer to tragedy than was *Laure.* The romantic, rather violent argument was taken from another Spanish play, one by Francesco de Rojas. Venceslas, the king of Poland, has two sons, Alexandre and Ladislas, both of whom are in love with the duchess Cassandre. The hot-tempered Ladislas does not suspect his brother of being a rival, but does suspect Frédéric, a duke, who is actually carrying on a love affair with Théodore, sister to Alexandre and Ladislas. In the dark of the night Ladislas goes to Cassandre's bedroom and stabs her bedfellow, who turns out to be his brother Alexandre, secretly married to the duchess.

Such in outline is the melodramatic action up to the denouement in the last act. In a very moving scene (5.4), King Venceslas condemns his own son, Ladislas, to death. As the prince is led away to execution, Venceslas speaks in soliloquy: "O inhuman justice and hostile duties! To save my scepter I must destroy my son! But let them act, importunate fondness, and you, my eyes, hide your tears and my weakness. I can do nothing for him; blood yields to the law, and I cannot be a good father to him and a good king." (5.8)

The situation here is genuinely tragic; the good king must suffer, whatever he does. The people, however, rescue Ladislas from the executioner, and the king, bowing to the will of the mob, places his own crown upon the head of the prince, saying, "Be king, Ladislas, and I, I shall be a father." (5.13) To complete the happy catastrophe, Frédéric is matched with the princess Théodore, and Cassandre, like the heroine of the *Cid,* will in time accept a murderer for husband.

Venceslas is a tragedy with a happy ending, which could be called, as it sometimes was, a tragicomedy. Unlike his great rival, Corneille, the author did not excel in both tragicomedy and tragedy, for Rotrou's dramatic gifts were essentially tragi-comic.

Perry Gethner

SOURCE: "Providence by Indirection in Seventeenth-Century Tragicomedy," in *Themes in Drama,* Vol. 5, 1983, pp. 39-51.

[*In the following excerpt, Gethner discusses the use of moral and religious conventions in seventeenth-century tragicomedy.*]

The seventeenth century, called the golden age of French drama, was not conducive to the development of religious theatre. Except for two brief periods of interest in the 1640s and 1690s, plays on religious themes virtually disappeared, and the handful of acknowledged masterpieces produced during those few years failed to initiate a national tradition. At the same time, France produced some of her most brilliant religious writers, and general interest in spiritual matters is known to have been intense. This astonishing development had, to be sure, quite a number of causes, such as the Church's hostility to all forms of theatre, increasing sophistication of the audiences with a marked effect on popular taste, and the proscription in classical theory of the *merveilleux chrétien.* Yet all these factors seem somehow inadequate to explain the radical secularization of the art form that tapped so much of the country's creative genius.

A possible answer to this problem emerges from a close study of a minor genre that flourished in much of Europe in the early decades of the seventeenth century. Tragicomedy, having evolved from diverse sources and in various countries during the Renaissance, was becoming recognizable, if not uniform, as an independent genre, characterized by its action-filled plot, aristocratic charac-

ters and happy ending. Less noted, but no less frequent, are the references to divine providence in these plays. Almost invariably, the happy ending of the play, displaying the rewarding of the virtuous and the disgrace or destruction of the evildoers, is perceived by the characters as the work of heaven.

These references to the justice and direct intervention of the gods, too numerous to be considered accidental, are often dismissed as meaningless clichés. Such an interpretation is hardly satisfactory, however, since the clichés call attention to the structural inadequacies and the sheer implausibility of the plots. It is as if the playwrights were reveling in their careless plot construction and the blatant artificiality of their dénouements.

If, on the other hand, one takes the theological references seriously, they appear to serve a useful function by providing a moral and religious framework for the action. The characters use their belief (or disbelief) as a guide to their conduct and as a source of hope during their many vicissitudes. The convention of poetic justice vindicates both the heroes and their gods, whose primary aims seem to be enforcing ethical rules and promoting human happiness.

The phenomena just described hardly suffice to make the tragicomedies genuinely religious plays. In fact, with very few exceptions, these works limit themselves to secular subjects with only occasional references to sacred matters. It must be remembered, however, that in this period, following the definitive break (especially in France and England) between liturgical drama and the secular stage, God could no longer be represented directly. As biblical and other sacred subjects became less popular, writers interested in conveying the idea of transcendence had to find new techniques. What I shall call indirection (hinting at the existence of the sacred from within a purely human world) could be accomplished in at least three ways in drama. The first and most obvious of these is through the dénouement, by means of the convention of poetic justice. The fortunate outcome, insuring that all the characters get their just deserts, is called miraculous, although explainable in terms of ordinary cause and effect. The miracle is at bottom the contrivance of the playwright, for the dizzying succession of adventures culminating in poetic justice is a time-honoured convention of romance, which in turn provided the plot for many a tragicomedy. Providence may also be evoked through language . . . and through the décor.

It should be stated at the outset that the doctrine of providence found in these plays does not coincide with discussions of the same subject in writings of Reformation or Counter-Reformation theologians. In attempting to combat materialist theories that eliminated God and attributed the governance of the universe to blind chance, the theologians focused on the bestowal of grace that made salvation or conversion possible for the righteous and also on the punishment of tyrants, notably those who persecuted Christians. Especially appropriate for their view of retribution were the biblical concept of the 'scourge of

God' (an evil man chosen to execute divine wrath upon others but who eventually will receive his own punishment) and the Stoic doctrine that divine justice, however, delayed, is inevitable. That God shows concern for the plight of the virtuous and ultimately rewards them is never disputed by these writers, but the rewards are usually reserved for the next world. This view of providence did in fact inspire a number of secular tragedies, especially in England, but it simply would not do for tragicomedy, where heaven is expected to arrange events in such a way that everything will turn out right in this life and that the young lovers (the normal protagonists of such plays) will still be young when they are finally united. Since discussions of poetic justice, often found in the concluding scene of a tragicomedy, tend to follow the same general pattern, a single example should suffice:

> Our bark at length has found a quiet harbour,
> And the unspotted progress of our loves
> Ends not alone in safety, but reward;
> To instruct others, by our fair example,
> That, though good purposes are long withstood,
> The hand of Heaven still guides such as are
>   good.

The closing lines of an English tragicomedy, Fletcher and Massinger's *The Custom of the Country,* exhibit all the standard features: 'the hand of Heaven' has been contin-

uously at work in the preceding action, although the characters were previously unable to understand the hidden plan; the love, always respectful and chaste, between the hero and heroine has received divine sanction, culminating in their marriage at the end of the play; and there is the didactic technique of casting the protagonists and their adventures in an exemplary role.

Although the gods sometimes intervene directly in the action in the form of oracles, dreams or warning signs (such devices occurring mostly in pastoral plays), their role is normally limited to that of silent spectators and protectors, invoked or discussed by the human characters. In moments of grave danger, a helpless innocent may appeal to heaven for aid or warn the villain that the gods will not let him act with impunity. Here, for example, is the cry of a prince surrounded by assassins hired by a king:

> Le Roy peut commander; mais le Ciel plus
>   puissant
> Peut contre vous, & luy sauver un innocent,
> Ses favorables soins à vos destins sinistres
> Puniront d'un tyran les infames ministres. . . .
> Et le visible effect d'un secours invisible,
> Te fera voir le Ciel à mon affront sensible.
>   (Rotrou, *Les Occasions perdues,* I, ii)

(The King may command, but stronger Heaven can save an innocent man despite you and him. Its favoring care, fatal to your designs, shall punish a tyrant's infamous henchmen. . . . And the visible outcome of an invisible aid will show you that Heaven is sensitive to my wrongs.)

As is usual in such cases, the hero is rescued just in the nick of time, thus vindicating his faith in providence. The very thought of heaven may suffice, in the case of a male hero, to restore his confidence and spur him on to act:

> Dieux! qui voyez ce crime enorme comme il est,
> Par sa punition montrez qu'il vous déplaist.
> Mais sans chercher au Ciel le secours du
>   tonnerre,
> Ayde toy des moyens que tu trouves en terre.
>   (Mairet, *Sidonie,* IV, iii)

(Gods, who see the enormity of this crime, show by its punishment that it displeases you. But without seeking the aid of the thunderbolt in Heaven, help yourself with the means that you find on earth).

Faith in divine justice may also serve to sustain morale even in the most difficult circumstances. One of the most eloquent of such declarations occurs in Du Ryer's *Alcimédon:*

> Daphné, le mesme Dieu qui nous veut faire
>   naistre,
> Est curieux aussi de conserver nostre estre.
> Si comme les plus hauts, les plus bas des
>   humains,

Portrait of Alain-René Lesage.

Táchent à proteger l'ouvrage de leurs mains,
Si mesme par l'instinct dont l'animal abonde
Il conserve & deffend ce qu'il a mis au monde.
Penses-tu que ce Dieu qu'on implore au besoin,
Ayt formé les mortels pour en perdre le soin?
Non, non, sa providence est tousjours sans
    pareille.

                (V, i)

(Daphne, the same God who wills our being born is also concerned with preserving our life. If the highest and lowest of humans try alike to protect the work of their hands—if even the animals operating by instinct preserve and defend their young, do you think that this God whom one implores in time of need has formed mortals only to lose his care for them? No, no, his providence is always peerless.)

Since the heroes of tragicomedy are not presented as totally flawless, they may momentarily yield to frustration and despair. On such occasions they ask heaven why it has failed to intervene and redress earthly wrongs. Such anguished questioning always stops short of blasphemy and rejection of faith.

Il semble que les Dieux ont changé de nature,
Ou que tout icy bas n'aille qu'à l'adventure,
Puis qu'on void l'injustice en ce degré qu'elle
    est,
Et la vertu soumise à tout ce qui luy plaist.
(Scudéry, *L'Amour tyrannique,* I, iii, 213-16)

(It seems that the gods have changed their nature, or that everything in this lower world moves only by chance, since we see injustice at its pinnacle, and virtue subjected to whatever pleases vice.)

The obvious complement to such a passage is the statement of gratitude and admiration when the character realizes that all's well that ends well.

Qu'en tous lieux ce miracle eternise vos faits,
Dieux! de qui la justice a de si beaux effaits;
Que la place, & le jour soyent à jamais celebres,
Où vous avez tiré la clarté des tenebres,
Et fait voir clairement aux yeux de l'Univers,
Que vos mains tost ou tard punissent les pervers.
        (Mairet, *Virginie,* V, vi)

(May this miracle everywhere give eternal fame to your deeds, gods, whose justice has effected such splendid things! Forever famous be the day and place where you brought forth light from darkness and showed clearly to all the universe that your hands sooner or later punish the wicked.)

While most references to the gods are provoked by specific events, several plays feature lengthier discussions of providence which bear no immediate relevance to the plot. Rotrou's tragicomedy, *La Pèlerine amoureuse,* opens with a debate between two rivals on the question of whether the gods take any interest in human affairs. This atypical

introduction can hardly be the result of inadvertence; it has no parallel in the Italian play which was almost certainly Rotrou's source, and the French poet was by no means a careless craftsman. The opening debate serves to justify the manifold surprises of the dénouement, in which the two debaters are supplanted by a third suitor, who turns out to be the long-lost brother of one of his rivals and to bear the same first name as the other. Lucidor, the unbeliever who had declared that the gods are too busy with the management of natural phenomena to intervene in human affairs, is refuted by the arrival of his beloved Angélique, whom he had thought dead. Angélique, the amorous pilgrim of the title, lives up to her name by devoting herself to the quest of the man whom heaven had destined for her and to the service of any person who requests her assistance. Her religious convictions are sincere enough to cause her uneasiness about using a religious guise to cover her search for an earthly lover:

Je ne visite point les temples de nos Dieux,
Vers eux, nostre priere arrive de tous lieux
Je suy d'aveugles feux dont mon ame est
    atteinte,
Une profane ardeur prend le nom d'une saincte.

           (III, ii)

(I do not visit the temples of our gods; our prayer arrives to them from all places. I am following a blind passion with which my soul is smitten; a profane love takes the name of a holy one.)

Nonetheless, Angélique believes, and the dénouement confirms, that her quest enjoys the sanction of heaven and is not really a sacrilege. The play could properly be subtitled 'Faith Rewarded'.

I have mentioned décor as the third method of indirection in tragicomedy. In the period before the unity of place was officially recognized as a key element in French dramaturgy, the unhampered use of scene changes permitted a visual, as well as symbolic, representation of the difference between sacred and profane space. It also allowed for neutral space, in which divine intervention could be clearly manifested. Tragicomedies of the preclassical era abound in episodes, usually set in a forest or on a seacoast, in which a hero or heroine is assailed by assassins, robbers or pirates. In every instance the virtuous protagonist escapes with his life, while the villains often meet their death, confessing with their last breath that the gods are just and vigilant, after all.

Sacred space may enter the world of tragicomedy in a concrete and visible form through the use of temples and sacred groves as stage settings. Besides providing a conducive setting for prayer and meditation, such scenes may introduce religious ceremonies (especially weddings and funerals) and priests or seers. The *Mémoire de Mahelot,* the notes of one of the earliest professional Parisian stage designers, list no fewer than eight tragicomedies, most of them pastoral tragicomedies which featured temple scenes, as well as a sizable number of plays utilizing cemeteries, magician's grottos and prisons—all of which could sometimes, though not invariably, serve as places for prayer or religious rites.

The effect which such décor can exercise upon the characters should not be underestimated. The most rebellious souls cannot help feeling awed in the presence of the sacred world. One particularly striking example is the sudden transformation of the blaspheming tyrant Gondebaut in Jean de Mairet's *Chryséide et Arimand.* Upon learning that his captives have escaped, the King rails at the gods for thwarting his plans, denies that their power is greater than his own, vows to overthrow their altars and them, and finally proclaims that they are nought but inert marble (IV, i). Yet in his next appearance, Gondebaut is persuaded to appease the gods and seek their aid. In the sacred grove, the 'sacrificateur' delivers a solemn lecture, warning the King that what the gods require of men, far more than sacrifice, is purity of heart and upright conduct. The special aura of this grove, coupled with the nobility of soul exhibited by the protagonists, makes the tyrant relent and liberate the lovers. His change of heart is also a religious conversion, since he finally comes to admit the justice and superior might of the gods. When the officiant declares that the hand of providence is manifest in these events, Gondebaut agrees without hesitation:

> *Sacrificateur.* Sire, je croy pour moy, qu'on ne peut sans offense,
> Haïr ceux dont le Ciel entreprend la deffence;
> Il me semble vrayment que cette affaire icy
> Tient plus que de l'humain.
> *Roy.* Il me le semble aussi;
> Je croy que tous ces flots si divers en leurs courses
> N'ont d'ailleurs que du Ciel leurs invisibles sources.
> (V, iii, 1671-6)

(*Celebrant.* Sir, I for one believe that we cannot without offense hate those whom Heaven undertakes to defend. It truly seems to me that this affair shows a power more than human.

King. I have the same impression. I believe that all these events, so different in their courses, have their invisible source not elsewhere than in Heaven.)

There is one special case where an evil character is not cowed by his entry into a sacred space. When armed with a device furnished by black magic, the character has the impression that the powers of darkness have definitively prevailed. In Rotrou's *L'Innocente infidélité,* the villainous Hermante disrupts a royal wedding ceremony by entering the temple with a magic ring that instantly casts a spell over the King and rekindles his lustful passion for his former mistress. The speed of her triumph leads Hermante to gloat:

> Enfers, dessus les Cieux, vostre pouvoir l'emporte,
> Superbes habitants de ces champs azurés
> Qui par nostre ignorance estiés seuls reverés,
> Cedés à d'autres Dieux cet orgueilleux Empire. .
> . .
> Et qu'au lieu de monter descendent nos encens!
> (II, ii, 326-32)

(Hades, your power wins out over Heaven. Haughty denizens of the azure fields, who through our ignorance are alone revered, yield this proud dominion to other gods. . . . And let our incense descend rather than rise!)

L'Innocente infidélité is a particularly remarkable tragicomedy, because in addition to exploiting to the fullest all of the techniques of indirection discussed above, it shows the forces of good and evil becoming progressively incarnated by the main characters. Hermante, in fact, begins as a distraught but not wicked woman who had been seduced by the King of Epire under promise of marriage. With the magic ring on her finger, she willingly assumes the personification of lust, and in the final act she seems to believe that she really is what the other characters have already called her: a witch. When the ring is finally snatched away and the spell is broken, Hermante becomes hysterical, calling for the total destruction of the universe to accompany her execution. Her final appeal to chaos reveals the extent to which she has merged herself with her role as the champion of evil:

> Que l'Enfer pour le moins, s'ouvre aux voeux que je faicts,
> Qu'il engloutisse tour, Roy, sorciere, & Palais,
> Pour reparer un crime au Ciel épouvantable
> Confondés l'innocent avecque la coupable,
> Faictes pour mes forfaicts souffrir tous les mortels,
> Renversés les Cités, les throsnes, les autels. . . .
> Que le cahos renaisse, et que tout soit confus
> Dieux! tonnés, Cieux, tombés, Astres, ne luysés plus.
> (V, v, 1331-6, 1351-2)

(May Hell at least open at my wish; may it swallow up tower, king, witch and palace! To expiate a crime abhorrent to Heaven, confound the innocent with the guilty; make all mortals suffer for my villainy! Overthrow cities, thrones, altars! . . . May chaos be reborn, and may all things be jumbled! Gods, sound your thunder; skies, fall; stars, shine no more!)

At the same time, Parthénie, the fair young Queen, appears more and more like the exemplary figure of a saint. Her total submission to the King's orders, however cruel and unjust, her trust that heaven will one day restore her husband's affection, and her unhesitating acceptance of her death sentence seem to go beyond the ordinary dimensions of the virtuous heroine. She goes so far as to implore the gods to tolerate her husband's philandering and to inflict any suffering he might merit upon *her* (III,

iii). But because this is a tragicomedy, the heroine, despite her desire for martyrdom, cannot be allowed to die. The good counselor Evandre, who represents prudence and loyalty, pretends to carry out the King's sentence of execution on Parthénie and spreads the false report of her death. Once the monarch has repented, Evandre produces her in a highly theatrical fashion: he brings her into the temple while a funeral service is being performed upon her empty tomb. All present believe that she has come back from the grave, which indeed she has in terms of the play's symbolism. Hermante's profanation of the temple earlier in the play, leading to the King's fall into lust and criminality, is fittingly undone by a new interruption in the same temple and with the same characters present. The King, who had earlier flaunted his double personality, apropos of his taste in women:

> J'ayme au temple leur crainte, et leur honnesteté,
> Au lict leur belle humeur, et leur facilité
>
> (II, iv, 459-60)

(In temple I like their reverence and honesty; in bed, their docile humor and facility.)

moves, quite symbolically, in act V from the spatial representation of lust (the bedroom, where he has just spent the night with Hermante) to the sacred precincts of the temple, where he remains in prayer at the conclusion of the play.

As the preceding remarks have suggested, Rotrou has evoked, behind the suspenseful and sensational plot, an allegorical battle of abstractions, reminiscent of the medieval morality play. The names of the characters were almost certainly chosen for their symbolic value: Parthénie suggests virginity, Evandre means good man, Félismond would seem to indicate that the King has been predestined for happiness. The name Hermante may be derived from the Spanish *hermana,* or sister, suggesting a forbidden sexual relationship. Likewise, despite the supposedly pagan setting, Christian rites and symbols are very much in evidence in this play. Marriage is described as an inviolable sacrament, and the royal marriage ceremony, performed on stage by a priest, is first profaned by Hermante and her magic ring and later restored by the penitence of Félismond and the 'resurrection' of Parthénie. Since this is not an explicitly Christian play, the Queen's rescue is effected, not by a supernatural event, but by the courageous acts of her faithful friends. Nevertheless, the happy ending is ascribed to the gods, even by those active characters who are, on the human level, responsible for it. It is not surprising that Evandre's triumphant proclamation of poetic justice, constituting a direct reply to Hermante's earlier gloating monologues, is unusually explicit:

> L'Enfer n'a plus de droict, son pouvoir abatu
> Laisse du vice enfin triompher la vertu,
> Le Ciel marche à pas [lents] au chastiment des
>   crimes
> Sa Justice irritee ouvre tard ses abysmes,
> Mais quand son bras enfin s'applique au

chastiment
> Il repare le temps, par l'excés du tourment.
>
> (V, iv, 1315-20)

(Hell's sway is no more; its power overthrown lets virtue triumph over vice at last. Heaven moves with slow steps towards the punishment of crimes; its angered justice opens its abysses late; but when its arm finally applies itself to chastisement, it compensates for the delay by the excess of the torture.)

In total contrast to the Christian symbolism and the neutral references to 'the gods' are the allusions to specific figures in Greco-Roman mythology, which occur almost exclusively in the speeches of the sinful characters. These focus on the sexual permissiveness and criminality of the gods; in short, the types of story used by the early Church to discredit paganism as a religious doctrine. To cite the most striking example, Félismond, in his ecstasy at obtaining a kiss from Hermante, exclaims that their delights surpass those enjoyed by other adulterous lovers of classical fame:

> Tels ne furent jamais les baisers de l'Aurore
> Treuvant son favory sur le rivage More,
> Ny tels ceux de Venus, embrassant ce chasseur
> Qui nasquit d'un inceste, & fut fils de sa soeur.
>
> (III, i, 589-92)

(The kisses of Aurora, finding her beloved on the Moorish shore, were never so sweet, nor were those of Venus, embracing the hunter born of an incest, who was his sister's son.)

Rotrou does not fail to profit from the sensuality and the poetic power of his mythological references, while at the same time exploiting them to suggest the forbidden world of evil. The subtle but pervasive use of Christian and pagan themes contributes to the suggestion of a spiritual dimension that is not shown in direct form.

Since the use of religious motifs in tragicomedy was by no means limited to France, I would like to conclude with an example from England, even though virtually no contact existed between dramatists of the two countries in this period. I have selected John Fletcher, a writer whose interest in religious questions and dramatic didacticism was hardly extensive or profound, the better to show that the idea of providence had become a fixed component of the genre. The explicit use of religious vocabulary is rare in Fletcher's works, but spiritual themes are present, however indirectly, in the majority of his tragicomedies.

The Loyal Subject, subtitled *Honour's Martyr,* portrays a world sharply polarized between good and evil characters, and focuses on the heroic defense of an ideal under the most adverse conditions. Nothing—not even disgrace, poverty, imprisonment and torture—can make the fanatically loyal general, Archas, break faith with his King. Further enhancing the hero's sublimity is the shocking ingratitude and immoral behavior of that King, which eventually drive most of the other honorable characters

---

Herrick on tragicomedy's contribution to modern drama:

What has tragicomedy actually contributed to the modern drama since the Renaissance? Tragicomedy, whether actually so called or not, has always been the backbone of the modern drama, which has always been a compromise between classical tradition and the modern way of life, and a compromise between classical tragedy and classical comedy. Even the term was once significant and important, for the Roman *tragicocomoedia* provided an authoritative label for many Renaissance plays, in Latin and in the vernaculars, that could not be made to fit the molds of either ancient tragedy or ancient comedy. Ther term tragicomedy gave some assurance to poets who were willing, som of them even anxious, to follow classical tradition, but at the same time were compelled to satisfy the modern demand for a freer form. The term is now antiquated, for traditional labels have lost their importance, but most of the significant modern dramas still occupy a middle ground between tragedy and comedy.

Marvin T. Herrick, in *Tragicomedy: Its Origin
and Development in Italy, France, and England,*
The University of Illinois Press, 1955.

---

into open rebellion against him. Archas's shining example and simple eloquence shame the rebels into submission and help convert the young monarch to the ways of goodness. The term 'martyr' is fully appropriate, for the general unhesitatingly undergoes every test of his loyalty and comes close to dying for it.

There are at the same time features which serve, perhaps deliberately, to detract from the play's didactic force. For one thing, Archas's ordeal is presented as gratuitous. The King is not fundamentally depraved, and on several occasions he appears to have reformed, only to fall back into his old ways under the prompting of the wicked counselor, Boroskie. The decision to subject Archas to the ultimate ordeal of wrongful imprisonment, which leads to the mutiny of the army, occurs after the King is converted, this time permanently (we are to assume), through the efforts of Archas's fair daughter. We never learn why the King deems this additional test necessary, but Fletcher clearly had a tendency to sacrifice motivation to emotional effect. The other surprise from the didactic point of view is the sudden deflation of the evil characters in the final scene, making the audience wonder whether evil truly has an independent existence or is simply a bad dream that is easily dispelled. Fletcher was certainly not the only playwright to allow his villains to repent hastily as soon as they see the finality of their defeat, but it is rare for a conquering hero to be as trusting as Archas, who after recommending that the punishment of his enemy, Boroskie, be suspended predicts that, if given another chance, this erstwhile villain will be found a perfect man!

Fletcher's most explicit use of religious themes occurs in *The Island Princess.* Even here the religious conflict is introduced fairly late in the play and without any warning. The first half of the tragicomedy shows how a valiant young Portuguese adventurer named Armusia succeeds against all odds in liberating the imprisoned King of Tidore and in winning the affection of his lovely sister, Quisara. The swashbuckling but totally secular world of the play is suddenly transformed when the princess demands, upon orders from a fanatical hermit, that Armusia, as final proof of his love, renounce his faith and become a pagan. Hitherto unconcerned with the religious differences between him and his beloved, the hero must now confront his experiences in the spiritual categories of temptation, lust and damnation. When Armusia is arrested and threatened with death, his role begins to resemble that of the Christian martyr: steadfast, fearless of death and contemptuous of all things worldly. This saintly heroism, as in the *Acta Sanctorum,* does not fail to have an effect on the pagan onlookers. Quisara, enthralled by Armusia's perfect virtue, embraces Christianity and demands to die with him. At the end of the play the King indicates that he may convert, as well. Thus, the events in the play may be interpreted retroactively as a salvific tale in which Armusia's earlier adventures serve to produce the combination of circumstances leading to the conversion of the Moluccan rulers to Christianity.

The differences between Armusia and the usual pattern of saints' lives indicate a second type of providential scheme within the play; namely, the divine dispensation of rewards and punishments in this life, known as poetic justice. This is, as we have seen, a standard feature of tragicomedy, and, even in this play, does not require a Christian formulation. In the final lines of *The Island Princess,* the King proclaims:

> An universal gladness fly about us;
> And know, however subtle men dare cast,
> And promise wrack, the gods give peace at last.
>
> (V, v, 90-2)

Since this is not a tragedy but a tragicomedy, the hero and heroine must be delivered by their loyal friends. As in other plays in his corpus, Fletcher surrounds the protagonists with virtuous sympathizers who need but a sufficient pretext to mount a full-scale rescue mission, often comprising a general insurrection. For the same reason, the miraculous deeds of the martyr, which would ordinarily accompany and follow his death, here *precede* his death and obviate the necessity for actual martyrdom.

The Island Princess fails as religious drama for a number of reasons. Armusia's transformation from chivalrous lover to Christian martyr in the space of one scene is unconvincing, and Fletcher, who uses such metamorphoses with some frequency in his plays, seems to have gone out of his way to make this one implausible. Armusia's extravagant protestations of love at the beginning of the scene culminate with the equation of courtly love and paradise:

> 'Tis equity that man aspires to heaven
> Should win it by his worth, and not sleep to it.
>
> (IV, v, 19-20)

Moments later the same love is placed at the furthest possible distance from paradise:

> Love alone then—
> And mine another way, I'll love diseases first, .
> . .
> Have mercy, heaven! how have I been
>   wand'ring!
> Wand'ring the way of lust, and left my Maker! .
> . .
> Trod the blind paths of death! forsook assurance,
> Eternity of blessedness, for a woman!
>   (IV, v, 52-61)

Part of the problem is the fundamental lack of opposition in the play between East and West. Since, as the technique of indirection requires, Moluccans and Portuguese share the same code of honor and virtue, which is quite independent of Christianity, there is never any genuine incompatibility between them. The pagan characters are just as outraged by the hermit's bloodthirsty counsels as the friends of Armusia, and the reason which the princess gives for her own conversion is the hero's accomplishments according to the secular code:

> I have touch'd ye every way, tried ye most
>   honest,
> Perfect, and good, chaste, blushing-chaste, and
>   temperate,
> Valiant without vain-glory, modest, staid,
> No rage, or light affection ruling in you;
> Indeed, the perfect school of worth I find ye,
> The temple of true honour.
>   (V, ii, III-16)

In fact, as Eugene Waith has accurately stated, 'The whole pagan attack upon Christianity has masked the fundamental attack upon honor and chastity. . . . Armusia's noble defiance of heathendom is merely the culminating proof of his heroic individuality.' Finally, as the audience knows all along, the play's religious crisis is precipitated by fraud, since the sinister hermit is actually the villain in disguise. Having relied primarily on the rhetorical technique of *ethos* (proof of the speaker's good moral character) to persuade the Moluccan rulers, his unmasking in the final scene is deemed a full refutation of all his religious views. It is as if the truth-value of a religious sect depended solely on the moral integrity of its adherents and not at all on its tenets.

If Fletcher's use of sacred themes seems, in the word of one recent critic, 'meretricious', one may legitimately wonder why he returned so often to poetic justice and to the spectacle of honor persecuted. I should like to suggest that Fletcher and some of his colleagues found the religious elements accidentally rather than by design within the conventions of tragicomedy and were capable of reacting to religious motifs latent in the plots they chose, while never bothering to make those motifs central to the plays. In Fletcher's theatre, the glimpses of a sacred world are mere epiphenomena, appearing briefly and sporadically, with no inevitable link to the play's main theme.

This excursion into English dramatic history seems to confirm what we have found in France: playwrights were sensitive to the religious motifs latent in the tragicomic vision and were capable of appreciating both the exciting, action-filled plots on one level and the spiritual world which could on occasion emerge from those plots. Writers with a profound interest in religious subjects, such as Rotrou, could devise methods of integrating these more fully into the secular plot, but the presence of what I have called indirection in a preponderance of tragicomedies indicates that the age desired a theatrical outlet for its abiding interest in sacred subjects and that indirection, whatever its inadequacies on this score, helped meet a very real need.

Perry Gethner

SOURCE: "Affairs of State and French Tragicomedy in the Seventeenth Century," in *Renaissance Tragicomedy: Explorations in Genre and Politics,* edited by Nancy Klein Maguire, AMS Press, 1987, pp. 177-95.

[In the following excerpt, Gethner contends that a political dimension is typically present in seventeenth-century French tragicomedies and is often closely related to other elements of the plot.]

The difficulty of providing a comprehensive definition of tragicomedy in the sixteenth and seventeenth centuries has long been recognized. The corpus is so amazingly diverse that one is entitled to wonder whether the authors themselves maintained a consistent view of the genre and whether the audiences, as a new tragicomedy was announced, could accurately predict what they were about to see. Further complicating the process of definition is the fact that the genre underwent evolution in several key respects over the course of its slightly more than one hundred years of existence in France. Even the theorists, who generated a sizable body of writings about poetics and dramatic theory, provide little assistance. Most fail to discuss the intermediate genre at all, while those who do are often vague and superficial.

The present [essay] will not attempt to arrive at a new, all-encompassing definition of French tragicomedy, nor to summarize the results of previous scholarship. Its aim is rather to explore a significant aspect of the genre that has generally been overlooked. Political considerations, although never a *sine qua non* of the genre, are found in over half of the plays, and indeed in the overwhelming majority of tragicomedies composed after 1650. They are sometimes tangential, but in many cases they play a crucial role in the plot. Roger Guichemerre, in the best comprehensive study of French tragicomedy to date, notes that certain political themes recur in a number of the plays: reflections on tyranny and the legitimate exercise of royal power, on the nefarious effect of bad advisors, on the benefits of peace and the misfortunes produced by war. Discussions of these political topics are sometimes well integrated into the action but at other times appear to be superfluous. However, Guichemerre considers such faults minor because, in his view, it is always love, rather than politics, that constitutes the central motivation of the protagonists, thus dominating the plots. He adds that the minimal role accorded to affairs of state is one of the major features that distinguish tragicomedy from tragedy:

> Certaines tragi-comédies s'inspireront tout de même de l'histoire, mais, à la différence des tragiques qui analysent les desseins des princes et des grands ambitieux, ou qui exposent longuement les problèmes politiques de l'époque qu'ils évoquent dans leurs pièces, les auteurs de tragi-comédies ne s'intéressent guère qu'aux passions et aux problèmes sentimentaux de leurs personnages, c'est-à-dire à ce qui a le moins retenu l'attention des historiens et qui laisse donc toute liberté à leur imagination romanesque. [Guichemerre, *Tragi-comédie*]

> [Certain tragicomedies will be based on history all the same, but, as opposed to writers of tragedies who analyze the projects of princes and men of great ambition, or who expound at length the political problems of the period which they evoke in their plays, the authors of tragicomedies show minimal interest in matters other than the passions and sentimental problems of their characters; in other words, the aspect that has least engaged the attention of historians and which, therefore, leaves complete freedom to their fictional imagination.]

This statement contains a certain amount of truth, but needs careful reexamination. Leaving aside the suggestion that French authors took more liberties with history when they called their plays tragicomedies, I shall turn to the corpus of tragicomedies as a whole, looking for trends in regard to two main features: the presence and function of kings and queens in the *dramatis personae,* and the impact of political or patriotic considerations on the protagonists' internal conflicts and on their resolution. We shall see that, although politics never fully displaces romantic love and divine providence as the dominant themes, it may share the spotlight with them and become an indispensable component of the plot.

If one looks at the development of French tragicomedy in a purely chronological fashion, the period preceding the emergence of Pierre Corneille, roughly from 1550 to 1630, offers little of interest to our discussion. In the heterogeneous works written in the period, few of which have any literary merit, the political dimension is frequently nonexistent. Even in tragicomedies of the next generation that feature romanesque plots, affairs of state are not necessarily a major factor. To the extent that the lovers are constantly moving from place to place and battling diverse obstacles to their union, the plots leave little room for the conventional representatives of law and order. The world that the characters experience in their travels is unstable and often chaotic. Kings, when they appear, are frequently lustful, tyrannical, and blasphemous; robbers and pirates abound unchecked; judges and priests (unwittingly, for the most part) condemn innocent victims. To compensate for the lawlessness within or between human societies, the gods emerge as the genuine policemen of the universe, rescuing the good characters and punishing the villains. In some cases, the dénouement includes the restoration or selection of a legitimate and just ruler, but the political stabilization is overshadowed by the reuniting of lovers and of families. Likewise, the texts of the plays rarely feature detailed critiques of lawless societies and unjust rulers, even when such discussions would be directly relevant.

It was Corneille who most clearly perceived the need to achieve a fusion of political issues and adventure-filled plots in tragicomedies. As he would later admit, his first serious play, *Clitandre* (like many other tragicomedies of that period), failed to integrate these components successfully, but the proper role of the sovereign and the conflict between justice and tyranny are two of the principal themes. Most of the action is set in two contrasting locales: the king's palace and a nearby forest, each representing a different type of order and justice. The palace is the seat of government and law. King Alcandre sincerely believes in justice, although he acts improperly by con-

Elizabeth White Hartley as the title character in Racine's 1667 production of Andromaque.

demning to death the innocent Clitandre on a charge of murder. Even though the evidence against him is purely circumstantial and though both the intended murder victim and the members of the royal council request a regular trial, the king orders Clitandre's immediate execution. Of course, since the play's original subtitle is *L'Innocence délivrée,* Clitandre's best friend must arrive in the nick of time, having found the real felon.

In contrast to the depiction of flawed human justice within the palace, reinforced by several prison scenes, the forest episodes reveal a world of total anarchy and unbridled sensuality and criminality, restrained only by divine providence. It is only through a series of fortunate coincidences, which the virtuous characters attribute to the gods, that the schemes which the criminals attempt to perpetrate in the forest are thwarted and their intended victims saved. The gods' benevolent influence then spreads to the palace, making the final restoration of order and justice possible. The melodramatic plot of *Clitandre* inspires little faith in the efficacy of human political and judicial systems, but, unlike the practice of Corneille in his mature masterpieces, there is not much sustained discussion of these issues.

Looking back at the play in 1660, Corneille found the king's role unsatisfactory because Alcandre acts not as a king or as a man, but strictly as a judge. Such a peripheral role is beneath his dignity as a monarch: "il est introduit sans aucun intérêt pour son Etat ni pour sa personne, ni pour ses affections, mais seulement pour régler celui des autres. . . ." ["He is introduced with no interest for his state, nor for his person and affections, but solely to settle the interests of others," Corneille, *Théâtre complet,* ed. Georges Couton, 1971]. *Clitandre* is totally unconcerned with affairs of state; in fact, Corneille does not deign in the original edition to specify the country where the action—admittedly fictional—is set. The second edition (1644) places it in Scotland, but no further reference to geography occurs in the text. The plot deals with the love affairs of the king's two daughters, but they could just as well have been any young noblewomen, and the king could have been replaced by a non-royal father with minimal impact upon the dénouement.

Le Cid (1637) marks a radical departure from earlier French tragicomedy. It features genuine heroes, rather than a group of victims and aggressors, and the most significant conflicts are internal. For the most part, it is reason, as opposed to unruly passions, that guides the protagonists' actions and helps them establish their priorities when faced with conflicting obligations. Moreover, the characters find that they can to a large extent control their own destinies, and there is no need for the playwright to rely for his happy ending on the intervention of divine providence (which receives only a few passing references in the play).

Among Corneille's innovations in *Le Cid* is the fusion of the love story with a political drama. So tightly are they linked that neither strand of the plot can be resolved without the other. Don Fernand, King of Castille, aiming

to transform his country into a nation-state in which centralized royal authority takes absolute precedence over that of the feudal lords, is frustrated by his dependence on Don Gomès, Count de Gormas, an obstinate representative of the feudal mentality who places self-interest and self-affirmation (values belonging to the traditional Spanish conception of honor) above obedience to the king. The obstacle that will come between the two lovers, Rodrigue and Chimène, arises from the refusal of the heroine's father, Don Gomès, to ratify the king's choice of Don Diègue, Rodrigue's father, for a special honor he desired for himself. The ensuing quarrel between the fathers leads to a duel, but one in which Don Diègue, too aged and feeble to fight, is replaced by his son. The young man wins, but in the process loses all hope of marrying Chimène.

It is Don Fernand's incalculable good fortune that Rodrigue proves to be, not merely the equal in prowess of Don Gomès, and a brilliantly effective general in the battle against the Moors, but also a partisan of the new view of kingship, accepting the principle of absolute loyalty to the monarch. (That all of this is anachronistic for eleventh-century Spain need hardly be stated.) At the end of the play Don Fernand adopts, or annexes, Rodrigue as an instrument of the crown, who will henceforth owe sole loyalty to the king, rather than to his clan. The young hero's amorous misadventures have a direct bearing on the destiny of the state, since they lead immediately to Rodrigue's whirlwind campaign against the Moors and to the promulgation of a new political order. At the same time, Rodrigue, a newly-made knight who has never fought prior to the start of the play and whose first duel is against one of the most powerful men in Spain, needs a royal protector, and the king cements the alliance between them by ordering Chimène to wed the hero (whom she has never ceased to love).

In addition to giving special prominence to the political aspect of the story, Corneille effects a remarkable transformation of the concept of love. No longer a given, love is now something to be earned and justified—a rational goal fully compatible with the heroic code. Such a view of love leads to the paradoxical, and potentially tragic, situation of Rodrigue and Chimène: if either shirks his or her duty to safeguard the family honor, he or she becomes unworthy of the other's esteem. This means that Rodrigue must fight a duel with Chimène's father, while she must do all she can to bring her father's slayer to justice. In addition, the lovers believe they have a moral obligation to one another: Chimène promises to commit suicide if she causes Rodrigue's death, and he declares that he will not even try to defend himself against any champion she sends against him. The only way to overcome this seemingly hopeless situation is for the king to intervene, changing Rodrigue's name and status. Thus, a third type of obligation, loyalty to the sovereign, both supersedes and protects the allegiance to one's family and to one's beloved. It can hardly be an accident that the king has the final say and that the very last word in the play is "roi."

Despite the triumphant success of *Le Cid,* Corneille abandoned tragicomedy for tragedy, largely due to pressure exerted by the French Academy and by Cardinal Richelieu. The theorists, although not the theatregoing public, were showing growing hostility to tragicomedy—a genre not acknowledged by Aristotle and Horace. Corneille must also have recognized his extraordinary talent for political drama and grasped the possibilities that Roman history provided for the type of heroic tragedy that suited his temperament.

When Corneille returned to tragicomedy with *Don Sanche d'Aragon,* he produced a play that differed markedly from his earlier works in the genre although it does retain several of the main themes of *Le Cid* (the relationship between weak sovereign and invincible general, the dilemma of a princess who loves a man of inferior rank but superior merit, the happy ending effected by the hero's change of name). He chose the label "comédie héroïque" when he first published *Don Sanche* in 1650 and would use it for two subsequent plays. The term had actually been coined by Desmarets de Saint-Sorlin for a political allegory play, *Europe,* performed privately in 1642 for Cardinal Richelieu, who may well have been its real author, but neither the play nor the term made much impact at the time. Moreover, Corneille, presumably as a concession to his critics, expunged the term "tragicomedy" from his collected works, relabeling *Le Cid* a tragedy in the edition of 1648. He would accord the same honor to *Clitandre* in the edition of 1660.

The question at once arises whether Corneille thought of *comédie héroïque* as a brand new genre or rather as a somewhat modified form of tragicomedy. The dedicatory epistle of *Don Sanche* indicates that he was not fully certain on this point. He begins by declaring that a playwright's paramount consideration must be to please his public, even at the expense of fidelity to the ancients:

> Voici un poème d'une espèce nouvelle, et qui n'a point d'exemple chez les anciens. Vous connaissez l'humeur de nos Français; ils aiment la nouveauté; et je hasarde *non tam meliora quam nova,* sur l'espérance de les mieux divertir. . . . Je vous avouerai toutefois qu'après l'avoir faite je me suis trouvé fort embarrassé à lui choisir un nom. [Corneille, *Théâtre complet,* ed. Maurice Rat, 1960]

> [Here is a poem of a new type, which has no example among the ancients. You know the temperament of our Frenchmen; they like novelty; and I am hazarding something not so much better as new, in the hope of better entertaining them. I will admit, though, that after writing it I found myself quite embarrassed as to the choice of name for it.]

Obviously, Corneille was undisturbed by generic impurity, provided that the play was well received. In 1650 he seemed more willing to engage in serious dialogue with the theorists, even though some of his ideas about dramatic genres were strikingly original and unorthodox. The *Don Sanche* dedication contains a number of significant observations about genre: the hero of tragedy does not have to be of noble birth; if tragedy is to produce pity and fear in the spectator, it ought to do so more successfully if the hero's condition resembles the spectator's (a justification for bourgeois tragedy); a play cannot be a tragedy unless the hero faces genuine, life-threatening peril; a comedy is not required to make us laugh. The first two observations, however much they anticipate developments in later centuries, were to have no effect on Corneille's own production, and the latter two fail to clarify the existence of an intermediate genre between tragedy and comedy.

An analysis of *Don Sanche* suggests that *comédie héroïque* is not a totally new departure, but rather a type, or subgenre, of tragicomedy. Its main characteristics may be summarized as follows: 1) the plot centers around the marriage of young kings and queens, involving a conflict between love and reasons of state; 2) the latter term refers to the sovereign's power and prestige, but no real danger faces the state as a result of the choice of spouse; 3) the guaranteed happy ending involves no deaths, no villains to be punished and no risk of death for the protagonists; 4) serious ethical and political issues can be debated without great risk, since the dénouement obviates the need to take the arguments to their logical conclusion. At the same time, certain elements of the older romanesque tragicomedy could be retained.

In *Don Sanche* there are several potentially explosive issues: namely, a commoner's love for two queens (reciprocated by both ladies), and the possibility of his rise into the aristocracy, even to the throne, solely on the basis of his heroic exploits. Carlos, a dashing and invincible young adventurer, utters ringing declarations that deeds, not birth, are the sole genuine criterion for nobility (I. 2; V. 5), and his example makes the ladies incline to that view. Thanks to the traditional devices of *deus ex machina* and the switching of children in infancy, Corneille can skirt these intriguing questions in his last act. Carlos is revealed to be the long-lost heir to the throne of Aragon; his feeling for Elvire, discovered to be his sister, is attributed to the conventional "call of blood"; and all the obstacles to the marriage of the lovers abruptly disappear. Yet, although the play's happy ending restores peace and stability to Spain, the hero's change of name, unlike that of Rodrigue in *Le Cid,* does not lead to the formation of a new political order. In fact, Carlos, who seems constantly bent on teaching the arrogant grandees a lesson, ultimately makes his peace with the feudal system. With the revelation that he is indeed Don Sanche, his unsettling theory is exorcised: heredity and heroism are synonymous, after all, and the traditional view receives a striking new confirmation. Of course, given the label of the play and the way the plot is constructed, it would be hard to imagine Corneille writing any other ending.

In the final scenes the characters refer with increasing frequency to divine justice, which is expected to arrange human affairs properly and which is ultimately credited for the happy ending. The play's last words are "digne récompense" (fitting reward). Nevertheless, the concept of reward clashes with that of genetic determinism or predestination, already rejected by Carlos in his theory of merit divorced from heredity. If the hero *must* act in a certain way because of his birth, to what extent does he *deserve* a reward? The play suggests this dilemma but makes no attempt to resolve it; a decade later Corneille would face up to it squarely in his *Oedipe* and conclude in favor of free will.

The preceding discussion suggests a possible definition of *comédie héroïque:* it is a type of political tragicomedy with a nonhistorical plot that raises serious issues within a potentially tragic situation, only to avert the tragedy and dispel any disturbing hypotheses. André Stegmann is in basic agreement when he suggests that *Don Sanche* unveils not a new genre, but a new technique in which irony comes to supersede the tragic and produces an ambiguous emotion in the spectator. Although his characterization of that emotion as "un pathétique issu de la dissonance du sublime et du dérisoire" seems excessive, he is perfectly right to note that the play creates doubt about the basic assumptions of the heroic code, such as the primacy of honor and merit, and the importance of self-sacrifice as the outward sign of moral nobility. *Comédie héroïque,* more than other types of tragicomedy, is a play that makes the audience wonder "what if."

It should be noted that Corneille never composed any further plays in the manner of *Don Sanche.* The two late plays to which he also gave the label of *comédie héroïque, Tite et Bérénice* and *Pulchérie,* are not tragicomedies at all, but rather historical tragedies dealing with the matrimonial problems of kings and queens and involving no loss of life. Both plays end with the royal lovers sacrificing their happiness for reasons of state and parting forever. Presumably, Corneille felt obliged to deny the label of tragedy to these works since he had earlier listed as one of that genre's prerequisites that the protagonist must be put in a life-threatening situation. In any event, the label *comédie héroïque,* although used by a number of subsequent playwrights, did not displace that of tragicomedy. Both virtually disappeared by the 1670s.

Having followed the career of the genre's most illustrious practitioner in France, we have been able to observe some of the ways that tragicomedy changed over time. In order to gain a fuller understanding of the genre's relation to political themes, however, historical and chronological considerations need to be supplemented by a more synchronic perspective. Perhaps the most practical manner of gauging the importance of these themes is to examine the role of characters who care profoundly about affairs of state: kings, ministers, generals, and would-be kings. I have decided, for reasons of space, to restrict consideration primarily to reigning monarchs. In analyzing the role of these characters we need to pinpoint those factors which 1) make the monarch a prominent figure in the play and 2) give weight to the political discussions which may occur in the course of the play. Table I, though hardly exhaustive, is at least a useful point of and without warning, may evaporate just as suddenly at

---

TABLE I

Principal Aspects of the Monarch's Role Within any Type of Play

a. Age
  Young
  Old (usually father or father-figure)
b. Amorous status
  In love, requited
  In love, unrequited
  Indifferent (often father or judge)
c. Moral status
  Good, just
  Tyrannical
  Switches from one to the other
d. Position within state
  Strong
  Weak (often dependent on young hero)
e. Concern with affairs of the state
  Conscientious
  Indifferent to the common weal
f. Centrality to plot
  Is protagonist
  Is friend of protagonist
  Is enemy of protagonist
  (The friend/enemy either has important decision-making power, or has no impact on dénouement.)
g. Status at end of play
  Gets married to proper partner, makes peace
  Relents or abdicates or yields beloved to
  rightful partner
  Killed or deposed

TABLE II

Most Common Scenarios of Monarch's Role in Tragicomedies

A. Young, falls in love with the wrong person (or becomes estranged from the right person), turns from a good ruler into a tyrant (or at least commits a series of unjust and irrational actions), is forgetful about affairs of state.

B. Young, falls in love with the right person and is loved in return, just, strong, concerned about affairs of state (and it is here that the obstacles to the marriage tend to occur).

C. Old, father, either indifferent to love or rival of his own son, tyrannical, opposed to the lovers' union (concerned about making a politically expedient marriage, against misalliance).

D. Old, father, indifferent to love, just, friend to the lovers, powerless to help them, dependent on the hero's aid.

departure.

Since it is obvious that the possibilities listed here may be found in other dramatic genres besides tragicomedy, we must try to find the combinations that occur most often in tragicomedy, limiting the examples to seventeenth-century France. The next step will be to determine whether there is an inherently tragicomic quality to such scenarios. Leaving aside those plays where the role of the king is marginal, the most frequent combinations seem to be those listed in Table II.

Pattern A might well be labeled "reason lost and regained." The sovereign is a basically just and conscientious ruler whose misconduct is but a passing episode, quickly corrected and forgotten. Since the dénouement restores the order found at the beginning of the play, it allows for a straightforward ternary (A-B-A) structure. The royal misbehavior normally arises from a violent and unrequited passion or from a serious misunderstanding, frequently due to disguise and/or deception on the part of those surrounding the sovereign. The latter is thus a kind of victim, whose temporary loss of control does not cause the audience to hate him. Moreover, there is no sense of tragic inevitability since 1) the love that erupts suddenly the end of the play, thanks to a) the birth of a new love for a more appropriate partner, or b) the reemergence of the king's nobility of character; alternatively, 2) the misunderstanding or disguise or deception is revealed and cleared up in time to avert catastrophe.

One of the crucial components in Pattern A is the monarch's metamorphosis. Although such drastic changes of personality may be induced by black magic, as in Rotrou's *L'Innocente infidélité,* they usually do not receive adequate explanation. The playwrights, more often than not, sacrifice verisimilitude and psychological coherence in order to maximize the impact of the surprising situation. No preparation need be given during the play's exposition for the character's later outbursts of jealousy or vindictiveness, but likewise, none is required at the dénouement when the transformation is undone. It is clear that the monarch in this scenario cannot appear as a melodramatic villain devoid of all redeeming qualities. Even in an extreme case, such as Tiridate in Scudéry's *L'Amour tyrannique,* who is already wicked at the start of the play and who undertakes a bloody expedition to destroy his father's kingdom and to take possession of his sister-in-law, with whom he has become infatuated, the audience is repeatedly told that the character is not dead to virtue and is capable of reform. In some cases the king has a monologue in the course of which his will and reason prevail over his illicit passion (notably in Tristan L'Hermite's *La Folie du sage*). What counts in all plays of this group is that the misconduct is to be viewed as something separable from the essence of the king, so that the happy ending remains an ever-present possibility.

The monarch's temporary insanity or injustice obviously has a profound effect upon the other characters. Persecuted heroines display heroic defiance, rejected fiancées feel confusion and anguish, rejected wives demonstrate saint-ly patience and humility. The most fascinating response is the shattering of an innocent and virtuous character's metaphysical beliefs, raising the specter of "what if." In Rotrou's *Don Bernard de Cabrère* the title character optimistically maintains his belief in divine justice, while his friend, Don Lope de Lune, loses all trust in a rational power governing human affairs. Don Lope's endless series of disappointments raises an unsettling possibility: what if a hedonistic king and court fail to recognize and honor their greatest warrior, driving him into despair and exile? Rotrou avoids tackling a solution by arranging a belated happy ending. Perhaps the most extraordinary loss of faith is that of the sage Ariste in *La Folie du sage,* who, faced with the suicide of his virtuous daughter who has preferred death to the lustful advances of the king, denounces the philosophers who taught him the existence of a rational order guiding the universe and who confidently proclaimed man's ability to control his emotions and remain firm amid life's vicissitudes. Ariste's two full-length "mad scenes" call into question the nature of man and the role of the gods with an intensity reminiscent of *King Lear.* As always, the nightmare vision (the "what if") must be fully dispelled in the last act.

Pattern A does not exist, to my knowledge, in any French tragedy of the classical period, although an analogy might be made with certain plays, especially in the eighteenth century, in which an odious villain unexpectedly repents on his deathbed, usually under the influence of divine grace, as in Voltaire's *Alzire.* It is, therefore, a basically tragicomic scenario, and it counts among its prerequisites such features as the ultimate restoration of sanity and justice and sudden transformations of character. There may be a diabolical villain, such as Amalfrède in Quinault's *Amalasonte* or Hermante in *L'Innocente infidélité,* who is eventually destroyed, but this villain can never be the king. Villainous usurpers who require elimination—a not uncommon element in tragedy—are understandably rare in tragicomedy, and even then they are normally kept completely offstage, as in such plays as *Don Sanche,* Molière's *Don Garcie de Navarre* and Quinault's *Agrippa.* Montfleury's *Trasibule,* a play once thought to have been based on *Hamlet,* is an atypical work in that it features the usurper as one of the major characters.

Pattern B is mostly confined to tragicomedy, although there are occasional examples in tragedy, either ending happily with one or more royal marriages, as in Racine's *Alexandre,* or unhappily with the sovereign's heroic death, as in Thomas Corneille's *Camma.* This scenario, like the preceding, is inherently tragicomic in that the audience strongly sympathizes with the virtuous young couple and hopes for a marriage at the dénouement. In theory there need be no insurmountable obstacle to their union, for at least one member of the couple is a head of state. Thus, the playwright must select a problem of sufficient gravity to make the happy ending appear truly jeopardized; at the same time, he must be able to dispose of the problem by the end of the play. One of the most unsatisfactory and least common obstacles is religion. Convincing a character to abjure a false religion, especially if that character is a paragon of virtue, does not suffice to fill up an entire tragicomedy. In Mairet's *Athénaïs,* in fact, the pagan heroine's conversion to Christianity only occupies one act, and the other acts introduce other delays and complications in violation of the unity of action. When a religious conversion involves more serious psychological or political complications, the play tends to end in martyrdom and is labeled a tragedy. Likewise, if the adherent of the true religion fails to convert his or her beloved, there can be no marriage, and the play will probably end tragically.

More frequent is the danger of incest. Real incest has been a standard theme of tragedy ever since the time of Sophocles, but in a tragicomedy the taboo must be avoided and the final revelation of the protagonist's real identity must enable him or her to marry the beloved. In cases where there has been a double substitution of infants, the protagonist receives two staggering revelations: the first leads him/her to believe that the adored fiancé(e) is a brother/sister, while the second, either by confirming the protagonist's original identity or by granting him/her yet another one, eliminates all obstacles to the desired marriage. Such plays necessarily feature confusing and convoluted plots (for example, Boisrobert's *Cassandre,* or Quinault's *Le Mariage de Cambyse* where the threat of incest hangs over two couples).

In other plays affairs of state may be the force separating the lovers. Magnon's *Tite* combines several redoubtable challenges: the traditional hostility of Rome to foreign-born queens, Tite's obligation to his most valuable friend and supporter, Mucian (dictating a marriage to the friend's daughter, Mucie), and the queen mother's strong endorsement of that match. Ultimately, everyone relents, moved by Bérénice's beauty and nobility of character, so that the marriage between the Roman emperor and the Judean queen may take place, contrary to history. The most common obstacle is that of war. A number of tragicomedies show a queen in love with the most valiant of her generals. Unless he is not of noble birth, as in the case of *Don Sanche* (an obstacle easily removed by the traditional device of a last-minute revelation of the hero's true parentage), the match is contingent upon winning the battle in progress or about to begin. Defeating the enemy is required to preserve the queen's throne and to confirm the hero's worthiness, but a further complication may arise if the leader of the opposing army is also in love with the queen and aims to get possession of her by force. The unwanted suitor is never successful, and in some cases he finds the strength of character to conquer his passion and make peace, as in Scudéry's *Eudoxe* and *Andromire.*

The most complex obstacle arises when the hero and heroine come from warring kingdoms. The young prince or king must disguise himself in order to gain access to the beloved, and if she has been sequestered in an all-female retreat, the hero must pass for a woman, as in Du Ryer's *Argénis et Poliarque* or Rotrou's *Agésilan de Colchos.* Meeting the lady and gaining her love is, of course, only the first step. Obtaining parental consent depends on the hero's performing service in battle for the heroine's country or on his fulfilling certain conditions set by the parent. An especially paradoxical situation is the following: the heroine's mother, bent on avenging her late husband's death in a war, has vowed that the princess shall wed none other than the man who presents her with the head of the enemy ruler. If that enemy ruler happens to be the young hero, he may, after arriving in disguise, reveal his true identity to the queen and demand to wed the princess before being executed, at which point the mother either relents or abdicates (for example, Scudéry's *Le Prince déguisé,* Thomas Corneille's *Timocrate,* billed as a tragedy but very much in the style of romanesque tragicomedy). Plays where war and peace are central issues sometimes feature extended political discussions, although such passages are not as common as one might expect. It seems that the public was keenly interested in such topics, so that the choice of including them or not may have depended on the skill or preference of the individual playwright.

The third and fourth patterns feature older monarchs, who are usually parents of the young lovers. It should be stated at once that these patterns may overlap with the first two whenever one of the young people is also a head of state. Pattern C, which tends to show the king as unjust and heartless, is potentially the closest to tragedy. In fact, since the king does not have to relent unless reasons of state are satisfied, this pattern does occur in tragedies, especially those of Corneille (*Rodogune, Nicomède, Oedipe, Suréna*). The fathers are not only insensitive to the feelings of their offspring; they are not above using devious, even criminal methods to carry out their plans. Furthermore, they tend to act in a more sternly authoritarian manner than the circumstances warrant. Thus, the king in Rotrou's *Laure persécutée,* who has a legitimate reason to block his son's marriage to the beautiful but poor heroine (he has already arranged a match between the prince and the Infanta of Poland), expresses his indignation in terms most suited to an evil tyrant: he solemnly swears that if his son dares to disobey him, the punishment will be so exemplary

> Que tout langage humain, tout âge et toute histoire
> En gardera l'horreur avecque la mémoire;
> Sans rendre ni raison ni compte de mes voeux,
> Je veux ce que je veux, parce que je le veux.
>   (I. 10. 336-339)

[That every human language, every age, every history will preserve the horror of it along with the memory. Without giving any reason or accounting for my wishes, I want what I want because I want it.]

On occasion the father may become the rival of his own son, for whom his feelings alternate between love and hatred or jealousy (Quinault's *Stratonice,* Mlle. Desjardins's *Manlius*), although ultimately his better nature prevails. If the motives for the king's refusal include genuine reasons of state, the happy ending requires a last-minute revelation, normally of a character's true identity, occasionally of a character's guilt or innocence.

The fourth pattern, by showing the monarch as a benevolent but basically impotent figure, tends to spotlight the vulnerability of the institution of monarchy. The king or queen may be victimized by evil plotters or by a set of bizarre circumstances beyond his or her control. In Mairet's *Virginie,* for example, the impeccably virtuous Queen Euridice, already engaged in a protracted war, is threatened from within by ambitious enemies who seek to depose her by accusing her of adultery with a handsome young stranger. The good-hearted monarch may be faced with an anguishing dilemma when a child (nephew, protégé, etc.) has, either in fact or in supposition, committed a capital crime. Unwilling to appear capricious and unjust, the king must do violence to his paternal affection and sentence the criminal to death. In Rotrou's *Venceslas,* called a tragicomedy in the first edition of 1648, the title character, realizing that he cannot save his beloved son from the scaffold so long as he retains power, decides to abdicate in his favor. In plays like *Célie* and *Don Lope de Cardone,* by the same author, the ruler learns in the nick of time that a character believed to have been killed has in fact survived, thus allowing the offenders to be pardoned. Billard's *Genevre* uses a *deus ex machina* figure to unmask the villain and rescue the innocent heroine, whose royal father is powerless to intervene on her behalf. Plays dealing with the sacrifice of Iphigenia, although labeled as tragedies, use Diana as a literal *dea ex machina* to save the heroine, after the efforts of her irresolute father Agamemnon and her impetuous lover Achilles have failed.

Pattern D is perhaps the least conducive to sustained political discussions since in most instances the monarch is a secondary figure whose dilemmas are rarely explored in depth. *Venceslas,* a play dominated by the imposing and moving royal father, is the most notable exception. One might also mention *Le Cid* here, since the king functions as a surrogate father for the young lovers. In the majority of cases, though, the monarch is passive and must rely on prayer in moments of supreme peril. The queen in *Virginie,* like so many ladies in medieval romance, must hope that a champion will arrive to undertake her defense (V. 5). Following the providential deliverance, the rescued rulers can do little more than express their gratitude and astonishment.

The search for patterns in the function of rulers in tragicomedy has confirmed our original hypothesis: since the massive disruption and final restoration of order constitutes one of the basic elements of the genre, it is natural to find the destiny of states interwoven with that of heroic individuals. At the same time, however, human effort does not suffice to solve the complex obstacles that arise: despite the undeniably heroic qualities of the protagonists, the dénouement is usually miraculous. Even the characters may find the fantastically implausible resolution of events a bit hard to believe. This imbalance between the efficacy of human activity and divine providence helps to explain why references to the latter are ubiquitous in tragicomedy, whereas sustained political discussions are found only sporadically. As for the gods, ever vigilant over the lives of individuals, their intervention may preserve or restore the fortunes of whole states, as well. The happy ending suggests the ideal of cooperation between just heaven and an enlightened ruler, even though in the course of the tragicomedies this ideal is never realized.

> Or puisqu'il plaît aux Dieux de sauver cette terre,
> Eteignons pour jamais le flambeau de la guerre.
> (V. 7. 1905-06)

[Now, since it pleases the gods to save this land, let us extinguish forever the torch of war, Scudéry, *L'Amour tyrannique.*]

The difficulty in trying to reduce all the French tragicomedies to a coherent pattern stems largely from the fact that the relation between heaven, romantic love, and affairs of state is never mandatory in these plays. Providence consistently pays attention more to individuals than to states; the reuniting of heroic lovers may cement the prosperity of a kingdom by providing it with a virtuous monarch or an invincible general, but this additional benefit does not always occur. Likewise, the protagonists may or may not view loyalty to the state as one of their personal obligations. The political dimension, as Guichemerre correctly pointed out, is not an indispensable prerequisite. But it is often closely linked with the other main elements of the plot, and that link provides much of the richness in the finest tragicomedies.

FURTHER READING

Baudin, Maurice. *The Profession of King in Seventeenth Century French Drama.* The Johns Hopkins Studies in Romance Literatures and Languages, vol. XXXVIII. Baltimore: Johns Hopkins Press, 1941, 111 p.

> Provides a detailed analysis of several topics related to the role of the king in seventeenth-century French drama, including the king as conqueror, and the role of the people in the drama of this time period.

Fuller, Edmund. "The Theatre of France," in *A Pageant of the Theatre,* pp. 137-160. New York: Thomas Y. Crowell Co., 1965.

> Discusses the work of several seventeenth-century French dramatists including Jean Racine and Molière.

Howarth, William D.; McFarlane, Ian; and McGowan, Margaret, eds. *Form and Meaning: Aesthetic Coherence in Seventeenth-Century French Drama.* Amersham, England: Avebury Publishing Co., 1982, 203 p.

> Includes fifteen essays, each dealing with the topic of aesthetic coherence, with some essays focusing on individual dramatists or plays of the time period.

Lancaster, Henry Carrington. *The Period of Corneille: 1635-1651. A History of French Dramatic Literature in the Seventeenth Century,* Part II, vols. I and II, 1932, 804 p.

> Exhaustive study of tragedy, comedy, and tragicomedy

during this time period.

―――. *The Period of Molière: 1652-1672.* A History of French Dramatic Literature in the Seventeenth Century, Part III, vols. I and II, 1936, 896 p.

Comprehensive discussion of the tragedy, comedy, and tragicomedy of this time period.

Lawrenson, T. E. *The French Stage in the XVIIth Century: A Study in the Advent of the Italian Order.* Manchester, England: The University Press, 1957, 209 p.

Discusses the influence of Italian theatre on French drama during the seventeenth century.

Lough, John. "From Corneille to Lesage," in *Paris Theatre Audiences in the Seventeenth & Eighteenth Centuries,* pp. 45-162. London: Oxford University Press, 1957.

Analyzes middle-class and aristocratic theatre audiences and the role of these audiences in dramatic performances.

Alain-René Lesage

1668-1747

(Also Le Sage) French novelist, dramatist, and translator. The following entry provides criticism of Lesage's works published from 1942 through 1988. For further information on Lesage's life and career, see *LC*, Volume 2.

INTRODUCTION

Lesage has been called the creator of the French picaresque novel and the first writer of his country to produce the popular *roman de moeurs* (or "novel of manners") which later influenced such English novelists as Henry Fielding and Tobias Smollett. His most famous novel, *Histoire de Gil Blas de Santillane* (1715-35; *The Adventures of Gil Blas*), has become a classic of European literature and contributed significantly to the growth and popularity of the picaresque narrative in eighteenth-century Europe. As a dramatist, Lesage had less of an impact on world literature, but his finest plays—*Crispin, rival de son maître* (1707; *Crispin, Rival of His Master*) and *Turcaret* (1709)—have led many critics and scholars to compare his wit and satire with Molière's and to praise his comedic insight into human nature. Besides his own works, Lesage's translations and adaptations of important Spanish writers, including Francisco de Rojas Zorrilla and Pedro Calderón de la Barca, helped expose both France and all of Europe to Spanish literature, particularly the many great novels and dramas of the seventeenth century that either had gone untranslated or had been forgotten.

Biographical Information

Lesage was born in Sarzeau, a small coastal village in Brittany. His father was a counselor, notary, and registrar at the Royal Court of Rhuys who provided his family with a relatively comfortable existence. Beyond this, little is known of Lesage's early life until the death of his parents, after which he was placed under the guardianship of two uncles. Unconcerned with the child's welfare, his guardians squandered his sizable inheritance. Almost penniless, Lesage entered the Jesuit College at Vannes, concentrating on rhetoric and the humanities until he reached the age of eighteen. He then pursued law studies in Paris, where he was called to the bar in 1692. While in Paris, Lesage met Antoine Danchet, a literature student who later became a poet and librettist, who encouraged Lesage to translate foreign works into French. After his marriage to Marie-Elisabeth Huyard, and the birth of his first son, Lesage began translating Greek poetry, and in 1695 was introduced to the literature of Spain through his friendship with the Abbé de Lyonne, who provided him with an annual stipend, which he received for the next twenty years. At the Abbe's suggestion, Lesage began translating and adapting the works of Rojas Zorrilla, Calderón, and Lope de Vega, and by 1707, he had turned

to writing his own material. The farce *Crispin,* performed at the Comédie-Française, was an immediate success, and in the same year Lesage published his first significant prose work, the novel *Le diable boiteux* (1707; *The Devil upon Two Sticks*), which sold through numerous printings. Two years later, Lesage completed *Turcaret*—a drama satirizing the powerful French financiers who controlled the country's economy through their management of tax revenues, which he submitted to the Comédie-Française for production. Because of the play's sensitive material, the company refused to perform the work until ordered to do so by the government. *Turcaret* enjoyed but seven successful performances before the Comédie-Française withdrew the piece from its schedule, possibly because financiers succeeded in bribing the actors. After this incident, Lesage abandoned the Comédie-Française and devoted his energies to writing fiction and composing both short farces and comedies of manners for the Théâtre de la Foire. *Gil Blas,* published in four volumes over twenty years, was Lesage's greatest popular success, though many of his contemporaries, including Voltaire, argued that the novel was a translation from an unpublished Spanish manuscript and not an original creation. In addition to this immense achievement, Lesage produced a number of adaptations from Spanish sources, including *Histoire de Guzman d'Alfarache* (1732; *The Pleasant Adventures of Guzman of Alfarache*), *Histoire d'Estevanille Gonzales* (1734; *The Comical History of Estevanille Gonzales*), and *Le bachelier de Salamanque* (1736; *The Bachelor of Salamanca*), all of which demonstrated his skills as a translator and adaptor but evidenced a decline in his imaginative powers. Toward the end of his life, Lesage became almost totally deaf and was forced, because of poverty and ill-health, into the care of one of his sons at Boulogne-sur-Mer, after which he became extremely reclusive. He died at the age of seventy-nine.

Major Works

Lesage's work can be divided into three major categories: his short farces for the Théâtre de la Foire; his Molièresque comedies *Crispin* and *Turcaret*; and his prose fiction, including his translations and adaptations. Though the majority of his canon consists of the nearly one hundred one-act plays he wrote alone or in collaboration for the Paris fairs, these reveal formulaic writing and little artistic refinement. They remain historically important, however—through Lesage's involvement with the Paris Fairs, he helped unite the numerous small companies into the Opéra Comique, which remains a thriving aspect of the French theater. *Crispin* and *Turcaret* comprise Lesage's best work as a dramatist. Both social satires, the former depicts the quest for advancement by the title character, a resourceful and unscrupulous valet. Although Lesage's aim was to satirize the weakening of traditional class barriers, in the process he created a unique character in Crispin, a self-serving individual superior to his master in both intellect and resourcefulness. This element of social and moral satire is more harshly repeated in *Turcaret,* Lesage's only full-length drama. The play traces the downfall of a wealthy financier at the hands of a group of schemers. Critics consider *Turcaret* comparable to the best works of Molière for its wit, topical satire, vivid characterization, and ruthless portrayal of human vices. Lesage's fiction includes his Spanish adaptations, of which critics generally consider *The Bachelor of Salamanca* the most artistically satisfying; as well as his semihistorical novel *Les aventures de Monsieur Robert Chevalier* (1732; *The Adventures of M. Robert Chevalier*), which demonstrates his ability to write an accomplished story outside the Spanish picaresque tradition; and his satire *The Devil upon Two Sticks,* which established its author as a satirical novelist. Although the latter narrative began as an adaptation, Lesage quickly abandoned his Spanish model and developed a line of wit and caustic commentary entirely his own. The story depicts the chance encounter between the devil and a young gentleman, and the evening they spend atop a tower spying into the private lives of Madrid's inhabitants. Blending supernatural elements with realism, and satire with melodrama, the author created an original work with universal appeal. Lesage's picaresque epic, *Gil Blas,* is by far his most satisfying and imaginative novel. Critics have variously interpreted it as a picaresque biography, a study in moral and spiritual education, a satirical

allegory of French society under Louis XIV, or a combination of all three. Neither hero nor martyr, the title character personifies the common man in a corrupt world, the individual who is willing to accept things as they are and adapt to changing conditions. As in the German *bildungsroman* (or "novel of development"), he begins as an innocent and ends, after initiation into the evils of the world, as a reformed sinner. Because of the development of Gil Blas's character, most critics view the novel as more complex than the traditional rogue biography, which characteristically focused on incidents rather than characterization. Others, however, have argued that Lesage merely adapted the picaresque story to his specific needs and created his own literary form, into which he incorporated both middle-class and aristocratic values.

Critical Reception

Modern discussions of Lesage's work have focused on style and literary techniques, comedic aspects, the significance of Lesage's works in relation to literary and historical developments of his age. Analyzing the artistic intent of *Gil Blas,* Malcolm Cook has proposed that Lesage used the novel to express his satiric vision of humanity and his personal dislike of institutions such as the medical profession, which levied enormous fees for highly questionable, and often deadly, treatments. Studying the structure of *Gil Blas,* V. S. Pritchett and Vivienne Mylne have discussed the narrative's placement in the picaresque tradition. Contending that the protagonist possesses qualities of both the rogue and the puritan, Pritchett proposed that *Gil Blas* was composed during a period of literary transition, when the rogue was losing some of his knavish traits and assuming an increasingly naive persona. Mylne has argued that the narrative is a blend of the picaresque novel and the *roman comique* (or the satirical novel). Critics have also expounded on the significance of Lesage's theatrical canon. Roseann Runte, for example, has explored his dramas as counterparts to his novels, surveying the plots, themes, language, characters, and style of both genres, and observing that each of these elements points to Lesage's overall comedic vision. Focusing on the theatrical aspects of *Crispin,* Walter E. Rex has investigated the concept of *vraisemblance*—or the appearance of truth—in the play, documenting how the dramatist followed eighteenth-century literary conventions by relying on contrivances and formulae, including crafty language and the staging of illusions, to achieve plausibility. Perhaps the most significant issue among contemporary scholars centers on the influence of eighteenth-century cultural events on Lesage's works, particularly *Crispin* and *Turcaret.* Citing the increased importance of monetary wealth over aristocratic birth in the social hierarchy, several critics have viewed *Crispin*'s master-servant relationship as representative of the social turmoil of the period. Several scholars, for instance, have equated the rise of Crispin, a servant whose personal ambition takes precedence over the needs of his master, with the rising bourgeoisie of eighteenth-century France. Tracing the increasing power of the *financier* (or tax collector) during the era, other critics have examined the pointed satire of the world of finance in *Turcaret,* whose vain, pretentious title character suffers a humiliating downfall prompted by his quick-witted valet.

PRINCIPAL WORKS

Le point d'honneur [translator and adaptor; from the drama *No hay amigo para amigo* by Rojas Zorrilla] (drama) 1702

Crispin, rival de son maître [*Crispin, Rival of His Master*; adapted from a play by Hurtado de Mendoza] (drama) 1707

Le diable boiteux [*The Devil upon Two Sticks*] (novel) 1707; also published as *Le diable boiteux* [enlarged edition], 1726; also published as *Asmodeus; or, The Devil on Two Sticks*, 1841

Don César des Ursins [translator and adaptor; from the drama *Peor está que estaba*, by Pedro Calderón de la Barca] (drama) 1707

La tontine (drama) 1708

Turcaret, ou Les Etrennes (drama) 1709

Histoire de Gil Blas de Santillane [*The Adventures of Gil Blas*] 4 vols. (novel) 1715-35

Roland amoureux 2 vols. (verse novel) 1717-21

Les aventures de Monsieur Robert Chevalier, dit de Beauchêne, capitaine de flibustiers dans la nouvelle France [*The Adventures of M. Robert Chevalier, Called de Beauchêne, Captain of Privateers in New-France*; translator and adaptor; from a novel by Vicentio Espinella] (novel), 1732

Histoire de Guzman d'Alfarache [*Pleasant Adventures of Guzman of Alfarache*; translator and adaptor; from the novel *Guzmán de Alfarache*, by Mateo Alemán] (novel) 1732

Histoire d'Estevanille Gonzalès, surnommé le garçon de bonne humeur [*The Comical History of Estevanille Gonzales, Surnamed the Merry Bachelor*; translator and adaptor; from a novel by Louis Vález de Guevara y Dueñas] (novel) 1734

Le bachelier de Salamanque; ou, Les memoires de D. Chérubin de la Ronda [*The Bachelor of Salamanca; or, Memoirs of Don Cherubin de la Ronda*; translator and adaptor] (novel) 1736

Mélange amusant de saillies d'esprit et de traits historiques des plus frappants (novel) 1743

Le théâtre de la foire (librettos), 1783

Oeuvres. 12 vols. (dramas, novels, and journal) 1821

CRITICISM

V. S. Pritchett (essay date 1942)

SOURCE: "Sofa and Cheroot," in *A Man of Letters: Selected Essays*, Random House, 1985, pp. 193-96.

[*Pritchett, a modern British writer, is respected for his*

mastery of the short story, and for what critics describe as his judicious, reliable, and insightful literary criticism. In the following essay, originally published in 1942, he discusses how Gil Blas *has positively influenced English writers and helped shape the growth of the picaresque narrative. Pointing out that Lesage served as an "intermediary between ourselves and that raw, farcical, sour, bitter picaresque literature of Spain," the critic suggests that the novel's appeal arises from its "clear, exact, flowing style which assimilates the sordid, the worldly, or the fantastic romance with easy precision, unstrained and unperturbed."*]

When we ask ourselves what the heroes of novels did with themselves in their spare time, a hundred to a hundred and fifty years ago, there can be no hesitation in the answer. Novel after novel confirms it, from *Tom Brown at Oxford* back to Fielding and Smollett: they stretched themselves on a sofa, lit a cheroot and picked up again ***The Adventures of Gil Blas***. Once more they were on the road with that hopeful young valet from the Asturias as he went from town to town in Old Castile in the reign of Philip IV, always involved in the love affairs and the money secrets of his employers, until, a model of Self-Help, he enters the valet-keeping classes himself and becomes secretary to the Prime Minister. Say your prayers (his loving parents advised him when he set out for the University of Salamanca which he never reached, at least not to become a student), avoid bad company, and above all keep your fingers out of other people's property. Gil Blas ignored this good advice from the beginning and returned home at last to a benign retirement as a rich man and a noble. Not exactly a sinner, not exactly virtuous, Gil Blas is a kind of public statute to what we would call the main chance and to what the Spaniards call *conformidad* or accepting the world for what it is and being no better than your neighbour.

English taste has always been responsive to Le Sage; his influence on English writers and his vogue were far greater among us than they were in France. Defoe probably read him; Smollett translated and copied him. Le Sage became the intermediary between ourselves and that raw, farcical, sour, bitter picaresque literature of Spain which, for some reason, has always taken the English fancy. Gil Blas took the strong meat of the rogues' tales and made it palatable for us. He put a few clothes on the awful, goose-fleshed and pimpled carnality of Spanish realism, disguised starvation as commercial anxiety, filled the coarse vacuum, which the blatant passions of the Spaniards create around them, with the rustle and crackle of intrigue. We who live in the north feel that no man has the right to be so utterly stripped of illusion as the Spaniard seems to be; Gil Blas covered that blank and too virile nakedness, not indeed with illusions, but with a degree of elegance. It was necessary. For though the picaresque novel appealed to that practical, empirical, rule-of-thumb strain in the English mind, to that strong instinct of sympathy we have for an ingenious success story—and all picaresque novels are really unholy success stories—we have not the nervous system to stand some of the things the Spaniards can stand. What is *Lazarillo de Tormes*, the most famous of the picaresque novels, but the subject of starvation treated as farce? We could never make jokes about starvation.

Compared to the real Spanish thing, **Gil Blas** is a concoction which lacks the native vividness. It belongs to the middle period of picaresque literature when the rogue has become a good deal of the puritan. Historically this transition is extraordinarily interesting. One could not have a clearer example of the way in which the form and matter of literature are gradually fashioned by economic change in society. The literature of roguery which Le Sage burgled for the compilation of **Gil Blas** is the fruit of that economic anarchy which early capitalism introduced into Spanish life. In England the typical character of the period is the puritan; in Spain his opposite number is the man who has to live by his wits. A system has broken down, amid imperialist war and civil revolt, poverty has become general among those who rely on honest labour. There is only one way for the energetic to get their living. They can rush to the cities and especially to the Court and help themselves to the conquered wealth of the New World, to that wealth or new money which has brought poverty to the rest of the population by destroying the value of the old money. I am not sure how far economists would confirm the generalisation, but it seems that Spain used foreign conquest and the gold of the New World to stave off the introduction of private capitalism, and the parallel with Nazi policy is close. At any rate, instead of the successful trader, Spain produces the trader frustrated, in other words, the rogue.

> When we ask ourselves what the heroes of novels did with themselves in their spare time, a hundred to a hundred and fifty years ago, there can be no hesitation in the answer. They stretched themselves on a sofa, lit a cheroot and picked up again The Adventures of Gil Blas.
> —*V. S. Pritchett*

They are, of course, both aspects of the same kind of man, and that is one of the reasons why Defoe and English literature got so much out of the picaresque novel, so that it is hard to distinguish between Defoe's diligent nonconformists and his ingenious cheats and gold-diggers. Gil Blas himself represents the mingling of the types. He is not many hours on the road before he is adroitly flattered and cheated. It is the first lesson of the young and trusting go-getter in the ways of the world. Until he gets to Madrid his career is one long list of disasters. He is captured by robbers, robbed by cocottes in the jewel racket. The hopeful young man on the road to an estimable career at the university is soon nothing but a beggar and is well on the way to becoming a knave by the time he sets up in partnership with a provincial quack doctor. Madrid really saves him from the louder kinds of crime. Intrigue is, he learns, far more remunerative. He goes from one household to another as a valet, filling his pockets as he goes. The knave has given place to the young man with an eye for a good situation and whose chief

social ambition is to become a *señorito* or *petit maître*, extravagantly dressed and practising the gaudy manners of the innumerable imitators of the aristocracy. No one is more the new bourgeois than Gil Blas—especially in his great scorn for the bourgeois. And there is something very oily about him. How careful he is to worm his way into his master's confident so that he may become a secretary and rake off small commissions or in the hope that he will be left something in the old man's will! Much later, by his attention to duty, he becomes a secretary to a Minister, and sells offices and pockets bribes. What of it?—he is no worse, he says, than the Minister himself, or the heir to the throne who has dirty money dealings all round, or those old ladies who pose as aristocrats in order to palm off their daughters on wealthy lovers. There is a sentence describing an old actress which puts Gil Blas's ambition in a nutshell. She was 'Une de ces héroïnes de galanterie qui savent plaire jusque dans leur vieillesse et qui meurent chargées des depouilles de deux ou trois générations'.

'To be loaded with the spoils'—that is very different from the fate of the real *picaro* of the earlier dispensation, and Gil Blas is not entirely cynical about it. 'After all' (he seems to say, his eyes sharp with that frantic anxiety which still exercises Spaniards when there is a question of money), 'after all, I worked for it, didn't I? I served my master's interest? I'm a *sort* of honest man.' And when he decides to keep a valet of his own and interviews the applicants, there is a charm in the way he rejects the one who has a pious face and picks out one who has been a bit of a twister too.

The character of Gil Blas himself could hardly be the attraction of Le Sage's book, and indeed he is little more than a lay figure. The pleasures of picaresque literature are like the pleasures of travel. There is continuous movement, variety of people, change of scene. The assumption that secret self-interest, secret passions, are the main motives in human conduct does not enlarge the sensibility—Le Sage came before the sensibility of the eighteenth century awakened—but it sharpens the wits, fertilises invention and enlarges gaiety. But again, the book is poor in individual characters. One must get out of one's head all expectation of a gallery of living portraits. Le Sage belonged to the earlier tradition of Molière and Jonson and foreshadowed creations like Jonathan Wild: his people are types, endeared to us because they are familiar and perennial. You get the quack, the quarrelling doctors fighting over the body of the patient, the efficient robber, the impotent old man and his young mistress, the bluestocking, the elderly virgin on the verge of wantonness, the man of honour, the jealous man, the poet, the actress, the courtier. Each is presented vivaciously, with an eye for self-deception and the bizarre. The story of the Bishop of Granada has become the proverbial fable of the vanity of authors. And that scene in the Escorial when the Prime Minister, in order to impress the King and the Court, takes his secretary and papers out into the garden and pretends to be dictating though he is really gossiping, is delicious debunking of that rising type—the big business man.

The pleasure of *Gil Blas* is that it just goes on and on in that clear, exact, flowing style which assimilates the sordid, the worldly, or the fantastic romance with easy precision, unstrained and unperturbed. It is the pleasure of the perfect echo, the echo of a whole literature and of a period. You are usually smiling, sometimes you even laugh out loud; then boredom comes as one incident clutches the heels of another and drags it down. No one can read the novel of adventure for adventure's sake to the end; and yet, put *Gil Blas* down for a while, and you take it up again. It is like a drug. Self-interest, the dry eye, the low opinion, the changing scene, the ingenuity of success, the hard grin of the man of the world—those touch something in our natures which, for all our romanticism and our idealism, have a weakness for the *modus vivendi*. The puritan and the rogue join hands.

Vivienne Mylne (essay date 1965)

SOURCE: "Lesage and Conventions," in *The Eighteenth-Century French Novel: Techniques of Illusion,* second edition, Cambridge University Press, 1981, pp. 49-72.

[*In the following essay, Mylne focuses on Lesage's literary technique and method in* Gil Blas, *particularly his character development, narrative style, and use of language. The critic also speculates on the reasons for the stylistic inconsistencies between the early and later volumes of the novel.*]

Lesage states that in *Gil Blas* he intends to portray 'la vie des hommes telle qu'elle est' (I, I). To the reader of the period this announcement would indicate clearly enough that the book was of the kind known as a *roman comique* or *roman satirique,* that it would present a humorously critical view of various social types, and had no pretensions as to being 'historical'. The further admission, 'J'avoue que je n'ai pas toujours exactement suivi les mœurs espagnoles', would provide a hint, if any were needed, that Lesage had drawn his material from French society: for 'Madrid', read 'Paris'. Many of his readers would in any case be familiar with his previous book, *Le Diable boiteux* (1707), which had proved extremely popular. This work contains a number of satirical sketches set in a pseudo-Spanish milieu. The 'local colour' is however limited to superficial details with which most French readers would be familiar: duennas, guitar-playing and the like. In some cases the supposedly 'Spanish' personages are palpably modelled on French originals; the *inquisiteur malade* whose anxious female penitents compete to supply him with remedies is plainly less an Inquisitor than the kind of *Directeur* we shall meet again in *Le Paysan parvenu*. For Frenchmen, Lesage's 'Spain' was therefore no unfamiliar territory, and the reader of 1715, as he began *Gil Blas de Santillane,* might well expect to be offered the same kind of entertainment as he had already enjoyed.

The first pages of the novel itself would however show that Lesage was now following a different convention. In *Le Diable boiteux* he had borrowed, as a framework for his sketches, the fairy-tale device of a djinn or demon who has been imprisoned in a bottle. When this Devil is released he entertains his liberator, Don Cléophas, by showing him the secret life which goes on beneath the roofs of 'Madrid'. In contrast to this fantasy-framework, the opening paragraphs of *Gil Blas,* where the hero describes his upbringing and sets out on his travels, indicate that the book is cast in the mould of the picaresque novel. Even within the limits of the first chapter, however, the story has become picaresque-with-a-difference. Gil Blas's parents, though poor, are respectable; he has an uncle who is a canon of the Church; and the boy is given as good an education as the town of his birth can provide. This is already in contrast to the opening pages of most Spanish picaresque novels: these 'heroes' start their stories as ragged foundlings or as the children of rogues and swindlers, and are left to fend for themselves at an early age. (The life-story of Scipion, in *Gil Blas,* is typical in this respect.) For Gil Blas himself, Lesage has adapted the convention and lifted his narrator above the squalor and poverty, the brutality and coarseness of the traditional *picaro*:

> Ce n'est plus le même monde, ce ne sont plus ces gueux pouilleux, cette vermine repoussante, ces va-nu-pieds sans feu ni loi, ces ventres creux et affamés, ces aigrefins sans vergogne ni conscience. Si Gil Blas se souvient de son origine picaresque, le picaro du moins a été sérieusement décrassé.

[quoted in *Essai Sur Lesage romancier* by Léo Claretie, 1890]

The same kind of conclusion emerges if, because of Lesage's opening promises, we compare *Gil Blas* with earlier French satirical novels. These too laid much emphasis on the sordid, on grotesque physical details and crude or scabrous incidents. (Such an approach was often part of a deliberate protest against the ridiculously over-refined attitudes of heroic novels.) By its general tone, therefore, *Gil Blas* marks a shift away from both the picaresque novel and the *roman comique,* towards a world which, without being idealized, does observe certain standards of polite society. This does not entirely preclude vulgar episodes and scatalogical details, but in the overall effect coarseness has become the exception rather than the rule.

If we look for precedents in the urbane presentation of a first-person story, then memoirs and memoir-novels are the obvious comparable form. These works, generally written—or supposedly written—by persons of birth and breeding, usually kept within those limits of discretion and decency which a gentleman might be expected to observe.

Gil Blas can therefore be described as a fusion of at least three kinds of work: while covering much the same subject-matter as previous satiric novels, its plot begins along the lines of the traditional Spanish picaresque novel, and it has the tone of the more recent French development, fictional memoirs. Lesage's originality lies in his combination of these different elements.

The aspect of *Gil Blas* which readers remember most clearly is probably the general tone or 'feel' of the book, and we shall consider this first. The most important factor in this urbane atmosphere is the prose style which Lesage attributes to Gil Blas, as narrator. This style would have been inappropriate for a rough-and-tumble *pícaro,* since it is the mode of expression of an educated man with a neat turn of verbal wit. Gil Blas was eventually to owe his political power to a gift for clear, effective writing; the Duc de Lerme gave him a job largely on the strength of a written report which Gil Blas had prepared. It may not be safe to assume that Lesage foresaw this turn of the plot when he began writing, but whether by accident or design he made Gil Blas narrate his adventures in a style which is happily consistent with his education and his capabilities.

In vocabulary and grammar this style is 'neutral'. It avoids the pretentious inflated effects of some heroic novels, and also eschews low or vulgar terms. A more original and idiosyncratic aspect of Gil Blas's narrative manner is its peculiarly witty and astringent quality. This can be called 'ironic' in the general sense that many statements do not mean what they appear to say, but it is not always the simple irony of suggesting the opposite of the surface meaning. For instance, when the cook and the negro servant try to persuade Gil Blas that he is well off in the robbers' den, they use the very terms and arguments which could be used—and doubtless often were—to convince some reluctant postulant of the advantages of the monastic life:

> Vous êtes jeune, et vous paraissez facile; vous vous seriez bientôt perdu dans le monde. Vous y auriez indubitablement rencontré des libertins qui vous auraient engagé dans toutes sortes de débauches, au lieu que votre innocence se trouve ici dans un port assuré. La dame Léonarde a raison, dit gravement à son tour le vieux nègre, et l'on peut ajouter a cela qu'il n'y a dans le monde que des peines, Rendez grâce au ciel, mon ami, d'être tout d'un coup délivré des périls, des embarras, et des afflictions de la vie (I, 23).

This kind of wit-by-implication and various other forms of irony, usually employed for criticism, are frequent in Gil Blas's narrative, and one consequence of this trait is that the reader is, or should be, continually on the alert.

Such wit and irony are appropriate to the general attitude of Gil Blas towards his own adventures and the foibles of other people. Lesage has thus given an added piquancy to the cheerful if disillusioned outlook of the traditional *pícaro.* But a consistently ironic style has its disadvantages. The coolness and detachment which generally characterize this manner may be out of place in sad or pathetic situations, and can become an obstacle to the adequate treatment of serious feeling.

Admittedly it is not often that Gil Blas is deeply touched, since his ebullient nature makes light of incidents which would be catastrophic for more impressionable characters. However, on the rare occasions when Lesage does deal with some moving experience in Gil Blas's life, the limitations of the ironic approach become evident. One may take as an instance the death of Gil Blas's first wife, Antonia. He refers to this as 'un événement que plus de vingt années n'ont pu me faire oublier, et qui sera toujours présente à ma pensée' (II, 269). He then describes his immediate reaction to Antonia's death:

> Je tombai dans un accablement stupide; à force de sentir la perte que je faisais, j'y paraissais comme insensible. Je fus cinq ou six jours dans cet état; je ne voulais prendre aucune nourriture; et je crois que, sans Scipion, je me serais laissé mourir de faim, ou que la tête m'aurait tourné: mais cet adroit secrétaire sut tromper ma douleur en s'y conformant; il trouvait le secret de me faire avaler des bouillons en me les présentant d'un air si mortifié, qu'il semblait me les donner moins pour conserver ma vie que pour nourrir mon affliction.

There is surely something slightly comic about the mortified air of Scipion bringing in the soup; and the neat play on words in 'conserver ma vie' and 'nourrir mon affliction' is not particularly suggestive of a man still feeling the full bitterness of his loss. Furthermore, this and other emotional crises of Gil Blas's life are dealt with so briefly that such passages may make little impression on the reader. Thus the moments of stress lack the emphasis which can come from ample development as well as from stylistic differentiation.

We must not however be led into concluding that Lesage was, in general, unwilling to portray the deeper emotions. He certainly tried to do so in *Gil Blas,* and he can even be said to have cultivated a different style for such subject-matter. The novel contains two tragic love-stories, *L'Histoire de doña Mencia* and *Le Mariage de vengeance,* as well as several other tales in which feelings run high. And it is obvious that Lesage adapts his manner to suit these narratives. The style in such episodes tends to be more elevated, and there is clearly some attempt to achieve effects of deep emotional stress and pathos. This attempt, we may feel, is not wholly successful. Lesage relies too much upon simple predictable reactions in his characters and a conventional expression of their feelings. For instance, the dialogue between Blanche and the young King in *Le Mariage de vengeance* (I, 224-5) is built on emotional as well as verbal clichés. As M. Bardon justifiably points out, when she protests that both her marriage-vows and her *gloire* forbid her listening to the King's pleas, 'Blanche parle ici comme une héroïne de Corneille' (I, 387, n.756). But Lesage has not established either the dramatic tension or the poetic context which could support such language.

One might also criticize Lesage for failing to differentiate between the speaking voices of the various aristocratic characters in their misfortunes. Doña Mencia's first husband says, as he resigns himself to leaving her, 'Je vous aime plus que moi-même; je respecte votre repos, et je vais, après cet entretien, achever loin de vous de tristes jours que je vous sacrifie' (I, 42). Don Alphonse, forced to leave Séraphine because he has killed her brother in a

duel, strikes the same note: 'Je vais attendre avec impatience à Tolède le destin que vous me préparez; et, me
livrant à vos poursuites, j'avancerai moi-même la fin de
mes malheurs' (I, 272). One reason for these similarities
is that the noble characters in Lesage's serious stories
rarely if ever go beyond the limits of their strict code of
ethics and behaviour; they conform to type.

Not all the interpolated stories, however, are attributed to
the nobility. We hear the adventures, as told by themselves, of the *garçon-barbier* and Don Raphaël, of Laure
and Scipion. And here again one's verdict must surely be
that these characters share a common style rather than
possessing any distinctive tone which might mark them
off as individuals. It is, in essentials, the manner of Gil
Blas himself, and a number of verbal echoes accentuate
the family ressemblance. Gil Blas, arriving in the robbers' den, is told that he is to work under Léonarde. He
says, 'La cuisinière (il faut que j'en fasse le portrait) était
une personne de soixante et quelques années' (I, 14). Don
Raphaël, taken prisoner by corsairs, becomes the servant
of a Pacha, and observes, 'Ce pacha (il faut que j'en fasse
le portrait) était un homme de quarante ans . . . ' (I, 299).
Apart from such repetitions, these lower-class narrators
have the same turns of speech, the same bent for irony,
and a general homogeneity of expression which tends to
make the narrative manner of any one of them indistinguishable from that of the others, or indeed from that of
Gil Blas himself. Once again we are dealing with types
rather than with unique individuals, and this is an aspect
of Lesage's characterization we shall need to consider
more fully at a later stage. Here we can conclude that at
a purely linguistic level, Lesage has two distinct narrative
styles: the neutral manner of Gil Blas and his compeers,
frequently spiced with irony and wit; and the rather more
elevated mode of expression of the aristocracy, generally
serious, and often verging on bombast when it aims at a
high and tragic tone.

The doctrine of stylistic levels was of course a commonplace of literary theory in the seventeenth and eighteenth
centuries. (Auerbach, in *Mimesis,* sees the breakdown of
this hierarchy of styles as a crucial factor in the development of realism.) In practice, it was based on three inter-
dependent factors: the social status of the characters involved; the nature of the subject-matter—tragic, serious
or gay; and on the established hierarchy of literary genres.
In *Gil Blas* the element of class would seem to predom-
inate, for, as we have seen, Gil Blas and his equals are
not made noticeably to change their normal style when
they suffer some serious misfortune. Unlike the aristocrats, they have no heights of language which may help
to express their feelings in moments of stress. Against
this, however, one must set the contemporary notion that,
by the very nature of things, the sufferings of kings and
nobles are inherently more important, more deserving of
our interest and sympathy, than any misfortunes of a
person of lower social status. Beresford Cotton, for instance, suggests that de Pontis's *Mémoires*

> may suffer in some people's esteem because the person
> whose life is described attained to no higher a post

than that of a Captain in the Guards and Commissary-
General of the Swiss troops [quoted in *Memoirs of the
Sieur de Pontis,* translated by Charles Cotton (1694)].

He then explicitly formulates, and accepts, the idea on
which such criticisms were based:

> I own that persons of the first quality are more
> entertaining subjects, as their virtues and their vices
> commonly bear proportion to their higher station. They
> have it most in their power to be eminently good or
> bad; and consequently such relations fill our minds
> with greater and more surprising ideas.

The unhappy incidents in the aristocratic stories in *Gil
Blas* are therefore automatically more serious than any
mishaps undergone by lesser men, and the language of
the noble episodes is thus geared to the true gravity of
events, as well as to the class of the narrator.

The third factor, the correlation between various levels of
style and their appropriate literary genres, seems to break
down in *Gil Blas,* since in this work the different styles
are juxtaposed in successive chapters. Here, however, we
are dealing with a consequence of the freedom which the
comic novel enjoyed, largely because it was outside the
dictates of serious literary theory. Writers of comic novels paid no allegiance to the concept of unity of style.
They could and did bring passages of lofty rhetoric into
their more colloquial and vulgar narrative, for purposes
of burlesque. Another procedure utilized in the comic
novel, and apparently at odds with its general aims, was
the use of an elevated style for episodes which were clearly
meant to be taken seriously. Such episodes were often
inserted stories of the type known as *nouvelles,* and were
supposedly related by someone other than the principle
narrator.

This device raises two problems of technique: a question
of realism concerning the style of the secondary narrator;
and the larger issue of plot-structure and interpolated stories.

In the picaresque novel and the memoir-novel we have, in
theory, only one narrator. When other characters 'tell us'
their stories, these tales are, in the fictional situation,
merely passed on to us by the chief narrator himself. But
supposing such stories are couched in a different and
distinctive style? If we apply real-life standards, the question then arises whether anyone is likely to be able to
repeat a whole story faithfully, in the exact terms of the
original narration, without altering it according to his own
habits of speech and thought. An author who shows some
awareness of this problem is already utilizing, to however
slight a degree, a criterion of realism: he is conscious of
possible disparities between the postulated fictional situation and the corresponding situation in real life. As early
as 1599, Aleman noticed the problem and attempted a
solution. In *Guzman de Alfarache,* about one-third of Book
I is taken up by the tale of Daraja and Osmin, related by
one of the group of people with whom Guzman is travelling. After the story, Guzman makes an appreciative

comment on how it had held their interest, and adds: 'Howbeit, it was somewhat more enlarged by the author, flourished over with finer phrases and a different soul to that which I have delivered unto you.' But remarks on this subject are exceptional among the early writers of first-person novels. They tend to follow implicitly the literary convention that their narrator has a memory like a tape-recorder, and can play back a story exactly as it was told to him. Lesage took this line, and it is by this criterion that we can blame his failure to convey individual differences within his two main narrative styles. Later novelists, more alive to questions of realism and plausibility, were to give the problem more attention. Reported stories and reported conversations, as we shall see, became the subject of comments and explanations by writers who were concerned with creating an effect of authenticity.

As for the larger question of how and why novelists made such a generous use of inserted stories, we are dealing here with the combined effects of several literary models and traditions.

On the one hand we have the *nouvelle,* a genre whose development in France was linked to its growth in Italy and Spain. The early examples of such stories were usually grouped in collections, with a framework which described the occasion on which the tales were supposedly narrated. The *Decameron* and Marguerite de Navarre's *Heptameron* illustrate this pattern. The stories thus grouped together often had no connection with each other or with the framework situation. It was therefore a simple matter to lift them from their context and 'borrow' them for use in other settings or in another language. This ease of transfer probably contributed to the development of the *nouvelle* as an independent form. Thus a story from *Don Quixote, Novela del Curioso impertinente,* was translated into French and published separately in 1608, before the whole novel had appeared in French. As this example indicates, Spanish writers of comic or burlesque novels had begun to insert *novelas* into the body of their works. (The tale of Daraja and Osmin, in *Guzman de Alfarache,* shows the same process in the picaresque novel.) French authors, too, soon made a habit of introducing *nouvelles* in comic novels.

The method of presenting the interpolated *nouvelle* is simple, and somewhat reminiscent of the framework situation devised for collections of tales. In the novel, some reason is provided for a principal character to have a few hours on his hands, and at this juncture someone happens to be present who happens to know an interesting story, and proceeds to tell it. The story does not, as a rule, involve the person who recounts it. Occasionally this secondary narrator reappears at a later stage in the novel, but more often he or she drops out after telling the *nouvelle,* and is never seen again.

The narrator of an *histoire,* on the other hand, is generally a character who plays some part in the main action of the novel. Moreover, the *histoire* itself is often concerned with the narrator's own adventures. Theoretically, there-

fore, the *histoire* should be more closely linked to the whole work than is an interpolated *nouvelle.* The link may nevertheless be slight or almost nonexistent. When the barber has told his life-story to Gil Blas, the latter does go on to share in the festivities provided by the barber's uncle, and he even begins the next chapter: 'Je fis quelque séjour chez le jeune barbier' (I, 130). But this is the last we hear of the barber, and the whole episode could be deleted from the book without in any way affecting the course of Gil Blas's career. An *histoire* which is brought in like this has scarcely any more connection with the novel as a whole than the average *nouvelle.*

In contrast to this example, Doña Mencia's *histoire* does have some bearing on the main plot. It is to save her that Gil Blas devises his stratagem to escape from the robbers' den, and she later gives him some money which sets off his next adventure. Her story also explains how she came to be making the journey on which the robbers killed her husband and captured her. This kind of *histoire,* one might agree, has a legitimate function in the structure of the whole novel, while this particular example also possesses the merit, to our eyes, of being fairly short. More debatable are the *histoires* related by Don Raphaël, Laure and Scipion. Apparently Lesage himself realized that Don Raphaël's account had exceeded the appropriate limits: Gil Blas comments that 'le récit me parut un peu long' (I, 334). The *Histoire de Scipion* also takes up a good deal of space. As for their bearing on the plot, these three characters do all exert some influence, in their varying ways, upon the course of Gil Blas's life. But one might still be tempted to query the relevance of much of the information they supply about their past lives.

A further refinement or complication of technique is the *histoire* which is split into two or more instalments. In the Tower of Segovia, Don Gaston de Cogollos relates the misfortunes which attended his love for Doña Helena (II, 151-65). Several years later, when he meets Gil Blas again, he is in a position to describe the incident which has brought his love-affair to a happy conclusion (II, 306-8). The trouble here is that as Don Gaston plays no appreciable rôle in the main plot, the reader has heard nothing of him for nearly thirty chapters, and may well have some difficulty in remembering the first part of his story when the sequel is presented.

All these types of interpolated *histoires,* and yet more complicated variants, had been current in the seventeenth century, not only in comic and satiric novels, but in serious fiction such as *L'Astrée* and the heroic novels of the mid-century. (In the more ambitious works, the *histoires* were of course of a prevalently refined tone.) It was this practice of inserting minor narratives into the main story-line which earned such novels the label of *romans à tiroir.* Since the use of interpolated stories like these is now quite foreign to our ideas of plot-structure and coherence, we shall understand it only if we discover the reasons which led to its adoption.

The most obvious reason is the existence of an early and respected model. The *Aethiopica,* a novel written in the third century A.D. by Heliodorus, was as near as the genre could get to a truly 'classical' precedent. A copy of this work was discovered after the sack of Budapest, and was published at Basle, in Greek, in 1534. Amyot's translation appeared in 1547, and Magendie lists seven re-impressions up to 1626, as well as other versions and adaptations of the novel. More than any other single work, this story of the adventures of Theagenes and Charicleia helped to shape the seventeenth-century serious novel. Huet says of the work:

> Tel qu'il est, il a servi de modèle à tous les faiseurs de Romans, qui l'ont suivi, et on peut dire aussi veritablement qu'ils ont tous puisé à sa source que l'on dit que tous Poètes ont puisé à celle d'Homere.
>
> [quoted in *Traité des romans*]

This model consists of a main story, episodic in structure, which acts as a framework for other intercalated stories.

Some writers also defended *histoires* on the basis of supposed similarities between serious novels and the epic. The episodes of epic poems and the 'histories' in novels were classed together and described as 'plutôt des beautés que des défauts' [quoted in Scudéry's *Ibrahim, Préface*].

Apart from such appeals to respected literary antecedents, there were even some claims that the use of interpolated *histoires* presented positive literary advantages. Stories told by minor characters could add variety to the main plot by introducing new points of view. They could provide moments of respite and repose in the flow of the central narrative. They could create suspense by intervening to delay the outcome of some crucial incident. They could even contribute to *vraisemblance,* since it is 'natural' for two people meeting for the first time to tell each other something about their past life.

These arguments would not, I imagine, carry much weight with most modern critics. And already in the seventeenth century there were some writers who were prepared to attack the procedure:

> Outre que l'auteur en déduit lui-même l'histoire principale, il introduit plusieurs personnages qui en récitent d'autres, avec un langage qui est souvent trop affecté pour le temps et le lieu. . . . Et même pour embrouiller davantage le roman, ayant introduit un homme qui raconte quelque histoire, celui-là rapporte aussi celle qu'un autre a raconté, avec ses propres termes, faisant une histoire dans une autre histoire, ou le roman d'un roman; de sorte qu'on a peine à se ressouvenir qui c'est qui parle, de l'auteur, et du premier personnage, ou du second; et quelque attention qu'y donne le lecteur, il ne sait plus enfin où il est.
>
> [quoted in *De la Connoissance* by Sorel]

Some sixty years later Lenglet du Fresnoy, looking back on the history of the genre, saw these complications as a cause of the decline of the long heroic novel:

> Les aventures des grands romans . . . étaient si coupées et si embarrassées les unes avec les autres, que l'attention se partageait trop . . . .
>
> On s'est rebuté de tant d'embarras dans une lecture qui doit instruire sans fatiguer. Les petits romans ont suppléé à ce désagrément.
>
> [quoted in *De l'Usage des romans,* 1734]

Even if this diagnosis is true as regards the *grands romans,* the practice of inserting subsidiary stories lingered on until well into the eighteenth century. The last volume of **Gil Blas,** containing the *Histoire de Scipion,* came out in 1735. It was in 1742 that Marivaux published Parts IX, X, and XI of *La Vie de Marianne,* devoted to the life-story of Marianne's friend, the nun. And Prévost's unfinished *Le Monde moral* (1760) likewise shifts its centre of interest from the narrator's adventures to those of the Abbé Brenner.

Were there, perhaps, unavowed or unrecognized reasons for this widespread and persistent habit? One mundane practical consideration not likely to be mentioned by the novelists themselves, is that such intercalated stories helped to spin out the work. The ease with which they could be inserted spared the writer the effort of extending or elaborating his main plot, or of creating sub-plots. For an author like Lesage, not skilled in the structure of long stories, such a method was extremely useful in padding out his successive volumes.

A further and more specifically literary reason for the practice is that the chief interest of novels, at this time, lay in their story-line, in the adventures, in the element of what-happens-next. At this level, any story with lively events is a good thing; and the more stories a novel contains, the better it will be. This attitude would account for the apparently gratuitous inclusion of *nouvelles,* which seem to have even less artistic justification than *histoires.* And the relative importance attached to interpolated stories as such is shown, for instance, by the fact that the eighty or so *histoires* in *L'Astrée* are separately indexed in each volume, as though they were attractions to which the reader might want to return. Indeed, when the intercalations are on this scale, the novel seems to be moving towards the form of the collection of *nouvelles,* where the framework is no more than a pretext for assembling the stories.

There is not much explicit evidence to support this suggestion that actions and events took pride of place in the novel. Indeed, the occasional plea for greater subtlety and verisimilitude in characterization would seem to imply that some novelists were aware of other potential sources of interest in the genre. Nevertheless, the multiplicity of separate tales, the speed of events, the way that novelists press on to the next adventure, all seem to bear out the notion that the story-line was the prime object of interest for writer and reader alike.

This approach to the novel is a simple one, indeed it is little more than the child's love of a 'good story'. But we

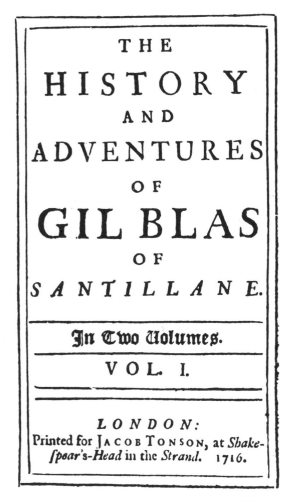

THE

HISTORY

AND

ADVENTURES

O F

GIL BLAS

O F

SANTILLANE.

In Two Volumes.

VOL. I.

LONDON:
Printed for JACOB TONSON, at *Shake-spear's-Head* in the *Strand.* 1716.

Title page of the first English translation of Gil Blas.

should not on that account adopt a condescending or dismissive attitude towards it. A 'good story' has never ceased to be a merit in the novel. However, it is obvious that the seventeenth-century taste for a wealth of interwoven stories produced works which are, by modern standards, confused as to structure and artistically unsatisfying. We can scarcely recover the approach of those early readers, who had learnt to suspend their interest in the hero so as to follow up the adventures of some other character. But at least we can realize that for such readers these interpolations were not unexpected distractions, but an accepted element of the novel as they knew it.

Apart from the stories, there is in **Gil Blas** another element which can be seen as digression. This is the portrayal of people who cross Gil Blas's path without affecting his career. A case in point is the former actor, Carlos Alonso de la Ventoleria. When he calls on the actress Arsénie, Gil Blas provides a brief description of his appearance (I, 184). Curious as to the character of this *Señor cavallero,* he then turns for information to Laure, who says: 'Je vais te le peindre au naturel', and proceeds to sketch in the actor's past life and present habits. Gil Blas rounds off the description with: 'Tel fut le portrait que

ma soubrette me fit de cet histrion honoraire.' The portrait is thus made to stand out as something of a set-piece. A page or two later comes another vignette, this time a playwright who is forced to accept the actresses' haughty treatment in order to get his play a reading. Here it is the situation, and especially the behaviour of the actresses, which is the point of the picture, and Lesage obtains his effect by showing the personages in action.

On other occasions we are given a whole group of portraits together. In the *salon* of the Marquise de Chaves, an obliging colleague sums up for Gil Blas the characters of the various *habitués* as they appear, providing illustrative anecdotes, and ending up with a sketch of the Marquise herself (I, 253-5).

In the mind of Lesage and his first readers, there was a distinction to be made among these portraits. Some were drawn from specific models, and readers in the know would recognize the actor Baron or a distinguished *salonnière* like Mme de Tencin. (It was to cover cases of this kind that Lesage included his assurance that he had *not* portrayed any particular person.) Others were based on familiar Parisian types like the *petit-maître,* and such descriptions would have been qualified at the time as *caractères.* Generally speaking, the *caractère* stresses some specific trait or tendency in its subject, such as the frivolity and fatuity of the *petits-maîtres.*

The individual *portrait,* after being a pastime in seventeenth-century *salons,* found its way into novels such as Mlle de Scudéry's *Clélie,* which were *romans à clef.* These portraits tended to be isolated set-pieces. We have seen how Lesage draws attention to his portrait of La Ventoleria-Baron, and we shall find Marivaux following the same method in *La Vie de Marianne.* The literary *salons* had also fostered the writing of *caractères,* a minor genre which might have faded into oblivion had it not found a master-hand in La Bruyère.

In **Gil Blas** the modern reader cannot always distinguish between these two kinds of character-sketch, unless there are editorial notes to supply the requisite information. However, the difference in origin is obviously of minimal importance nowadays. It is rather the literary merit of these sketches, whether specific or typical, which deserves our attention. Lesage would seem to have enjoyed creating them; they are usually well and wittily executed, with a neat and vivid touch; and they exhibit his special flair for highlighting motives of vanity.

Since the character-sketches in **Gil Blas** possess these real merits, it is perhaps thankless to ask whether they should be there at all. Yet the fact remains that they are, from a structural point of view, a defect rather than an asset. During the *histoires,* Gil Blas is reduced to the rôle of a listener; for the kind of portrait we have been discussing, he has become a passive spectator. And in either case, his own story is temporarily shelved. To be fair, one should notice that just as he *can* integrate an *histoire* into the main plot, Lesage can also work his social portraits into the stuff of Gil Blas's life. The group of *petits-maîtres* and their valets who give Gil Blas his first notions of the life of fashionable young aristocrats are just as much types as the guests in the Marquise's *salon*. But Gil Blas learns from the valets, so that the episode affects him and is a stage in his development. The actor, the playwright, the guests of Mme de Chaves, merely pass before his eyes, exert no influence on him, and disappear after having halted the action yet once more.

The justification for these supernumerary portraits lies of course in Lesage's undertaking to show us life as it is. And their presence reveals his interest, an interest which overrides considerations of plot, in the various kinds of foolishness and self-importance which flourished in the society of his day. We see people not only as participants in unusual actions and adventures, but carrying out their everyday rôle in society, as flatterers or would-be intellectuals or quarrelsome men of letters. The whole purpose of passages like these is to capture the essence of certain social types.

This fondness of Lesage for the typical personage goes even deeper, and underlies his whole approach to the portrayal of character. The majority of his characters in *Gil Blas* are types: we can fit them into categories, and their behaviour is always predictable within the limits of that category. Among the remaining characters, many could be termed eccentrics, but even those eccentrics whom Lesage chooses to portray follow a clear pattern. The character simply carries to extremes one of the traits which is in any case associated with his class or type. Spaniards are by reputation dilatory and fond of idleness; Don Bernard de Castil Blazo takes this to the point of arranging his whole life so that he can avoid even the trouble of managing an income. Many Church dignitaries are vain of their talents as preachers, and the Archbishop of Grenada shows how far such vanity can go. Doctors are ignorant, but each of them swears by his own system; Dr Sangrado's excesses are only an extension of this habit. What is lacking, in such cases, is the unexpected touch which lifts a character out of the rut and gives him individuality.

Since some critics have expressed doubts as to whether Gil Blas himself is a complete and convincing character, it is clear that even he, the hero of the book, may not convey to every reader that vivid sense of a unique personality which is created by masters of characterization. Gil Blas, it may be claimed, has no trait, no quirk of feeling or behaviour, which makes him absolutely distinct from other characters of his kind and class. On this particular and crucial case, opinions may differ; Gil Blas's own adventures do after all dominate the novel, and his reactions may seem variable enough, within their limited range, to evoke for some readers the image of a complete and credible personality. The fact remains, however, that Lesage's talents lie more in the portrayal of types and recurrent traits than of unique individuals.

From all this it would seem that Lesage, whatever his failings, did at least fulfil his initial promise to provide a general portrait of society. But as the novel progresses,

we move from a timeless scene, with a transparent veneer of Spanish local colour, to a specific period, with Spanish historical events and personages dominating the action. From the middle of Book VIII onwards, *Gil Blas* becomes as much an 'historical novel' as some of the seventeenth-century works with their inflated claims to historicity. Since this development is scarcely foreshadowed in the earlier part of the novel, we need to consider how the historical element makes its appearance, what effects it produces on the work as a whole, and the possible reasons for its introduction.

The first chapters of Gil Blas's story are timeless. They are set in a vague past which is Gil Blas's youth, but have no precision as to a date or even a decade. If any reader were interested in pinning the story down to a definite period, he could find his first clue in the course of the barber's story. In the discussion of contemporary playwrights which the barber overhears (I, 104), two living authors are mentioned. The elder of these, Luis Velez de Guevara, died in 1644. Therefore, even allowing for the lapse of time in the barber's life since this incident, we might safely suppose this stage of Gil Blas's story to be happening before 1650. Actually, of course, it seems highly unlikely that the average reader of *Gil Blas* would have either the interest or the requisite factual knowledge to date the episode in this way. Nor can I believe that Lesage had any intention of fixing his story in time by a reference of this kind. The names of the two writers are thrown in partly as local colour, and partly to confirm the prestige of the barber's uncle, who is mentioned as having more talent than either of them.

The same approach is evident at a later stage, when Fabrice speaks of three contemporary writers, Lope de Vega, Cervantes and Gongora (II, 61). The point here is that Fabrice has chosen Gongora as his model in matters of style.

However, by this stage in the novel (Book VII), Lesage had at least become aware of the problem of period. In the first edition of Volume I, Gil Blas listened to Don Pompeyo telling the story of some recent events which were supposed to have taken place in Portugal before Philip II's conquest of that country in 1580. Unfortunately, this episode turned out to be an anachronism in relation to the events of Gil Blas's career in Volume III. It is here, only six or seven years after hearing Don Pompeyo's story, that Gil Blas begins to work for the Duc de Lerme, a minister of Philip III—and de Lerme's period in power ran from 1598 to 1618.

Having thus fixed the novel in time by references to the Duc de Lerme and Philip III, Lesage realized the discrepancy between this dating and that of the Don Pompeyo episode. In the preface of 1724 he offered the reader his excuses:

> On a marqué dans ce troisième tome une époque qui ne s'accorde pas avec l'histoire de Pompeyo de Castro qu'on lit dans le premier volume. Il paraît là que Philippe II n'a pas encore fait la conquête du Portugal

et l'on voit ici tout d'un coup ce royaume sous la domination de Philippe III sans que Gil Blas en soit beaucoup plus vieux. C'est une faute de chronologie dont l'auteur s'est aperçu trop tard, mais qu'il promet de corriger dans la suite avec quantité d'autres.

Lesage corrected this mistake by the simple expedient of transferring the story to a Polish setting, though without bothering to alter the references to things Portuguese, such as bull-fights. As for the other mistakes, he did not succeed in eradicating them all, and a score or so of chronological inconsistencies remain in his final text.

We shall discuss more fully, in a later chapter, the whole problem of the novelist's accuracy in factual and practical details. For the moment it is enough to say that eighteenth-century authors attached far less importance to such details than do most modern writers. And in the case of *Gil Blas,* the chronological slips are not serious enough to distract the reader or be considered as major flaws in the work.

It is, then, by the introduction of the Duc de Lerme that Lesage takes the decisive step into history. Most of his early readers must have recognized de Lerme as a real person; he had, after all, been a famous statesman of a major European power, and had lived not much more than a century earlier. Much the same effect might be produced nowadays, for English readers, by bringing a person such as Talleyrand into a novel set in France. A majority of readers, though not possessing much detailed knowledge about him, would still be aware that this was an historical personage. This particular effect of the Duc de Lerme's appearance has now faded; unless there are editorial notes to help them, most readers will not appreciate the 'reality' of this character. And how many readers, when they come across mentions of two successive Kings of Spain, pay any heed to the authenticity of the events in which Gil Blas is involved? It seems likely that time, shifts of political power, and increasing literary sophistication have largely destroyed for us the effect of Lesage's incursion into history.

On the other hand, the move into real time produced an effect upon the plot of *Gil Blas* which is still perceptible. Having chosen to link his hero's career with the successive 'reigns' of the Duc de Lerme and the Comte d'Olivarès, Lesage found himself tied down to a precise chronology instead of a vague slipping past of the years.

In the first part of the novel there is little attempt to convey a realistic impression of the passing of time. We move from one event to the next, and the periods between events are briefly dismissed, often with a mere phrase such as, 'Après six mois', or 'Quelques semaines plus tard'. One might say that this is a picaresque handling of time. Just as the traditional *picaro* wanders freely from town to town, not bound by any ties of place, so his actions follow on each other's heels without any apparent relation to objective standards of time. This rambling method is quite suitable for Gil Blas's early days, but breaks down when his life has to obey the exigencies of history. In particu-

lar, Lesage does not manage to suggest the length of the period when the Comte d'Olivarès is in power. It comes as a distinct shock when, after a brief sequence of episodes taking up some sixty pages, the Count talks of his twenty years of service (II, 337), or when Gil Blas mentions the lapse of twenty-two years since Antonia's death (II, 348).

It would seem, from all this, that Lesage increased his own difficulties by choosing to combine Gil Blas's life with the events of a given historical period. Why did he make the choice?

One likely reason depends on his persistently derivative method of writing. Apart from the translations and adaptations which he published as such, Lesage always drew largely on other authors for anecdotes and situations, and Claretie has shown that he also plagiarized himself. In 1734 Lesage published *Estebanille Gonzalès,* his adaptation of a quasi-picaresque work which purported to be the memoirs of a clown in the service of the Duke of Amalfi. Volume IV of *Gil Blas* appeared in 1735, and it is clear from the similarities between the two that much of the historical matter in this last part of *Gil Blas* was adapted from the 'Life' of Gonzalès. Since the historical episodes of Volume IV follow coherently and smoothly from those of Volume III, it seems more than likely that Lesage had already studied the Spanish 'memoirs' when he was writing the chapters which introduce the Duc de Lerme and the historical background. The shift into history may therefore be a development suggested merely by Lesage's other current occupations.

Apart from this external stimulus, it may be argued that there were artistic reasons for this development, since it fulfils certain logical requirements of the plot. One should not, I think, accept too easily the assertions of some critics that the novel has no coherent plot. We have already noticed the various digressions and distractions which may blur the outlines of the central story, but there *is* a main thread to be discerned: Gil Blas's gradual rise from helplessness and poverty to power and wealth. This rise is conducted on three levels. Gil Blas works in households of successively higher social status (the few weeks with Arsénie are the only backward step in this otherwise steady progress). Within these households he occupies positions of increasing trust and responsibility, from valet to steward to confidential secretary. And finally there is a parallel increase of self-assurance and sophistication in his own character and behaviour. This progress may be the simplest of linear plots, but it does provide a story which is more than a sequence of casually juxtaposed episodes.

In relation to this plot, Gil Blas's move into the realm of history can be seen as an artistic necessity. By the end of Book VI he is not merely the trusted employee of a rich noble, Don Alphonse, but even his friend. In Book VII he has a position of trust with the Comte Galiano which involves overseeing the whole household, including the *intendant*. After this, if he is to continue his gradual rise in status, the inevitable step is from service with a 'private' aristocrat to working for a grandee who is involved in public affairs, and who is thus known and 'historic'. This development can therefore be seen as logically consonant with the preceding stages of the plot of the novel, and even as a necessity.

In a sense, once Gil Blas has become confidential secretary to the Duc de Lerme, there are no more worlds for him to conquer. Lesage has given the story a new lease of life, however, by making him become corrupted by power, so that a fresh field for improvement is in fact open to him—the reform and mastery of his own vices. This conquest of character is adroitly fitted into the pattern of historical events. Gil Blas is disgraced for his part in the Prince's *affaire* with Catalina. This has the effect of separating his career from the Duc de Lerme's, and when the Prince comes to the throne and de Lerme falls from power, the way is open for Gil Blas to return to court. The interval in Gil Blas's life between his release from prison and his service with the Comte d'Olivarès is chiefly taken up with the idyllic interlude of his love-match with Antonia, which shows him in a new light. And when, after Antonia's death, he comes back to Madrid and regains his previous heights of influence, he shows that his change of heart in prison has taught him to resist the temptations of power. The period serving the Comte d'Olivarès is therefore a contrast to, and not a mere repetition of, the years with the Duc de Lerme. So it seems fair to say that Lesage has shown considerable skill in his dovetailing of Gil Blas's moral development into the successive 'reigns' of de Lerme and d'Olivarès.

It can safely be assumed that Lesage never had in mind any 'master-plan' of *Gil Blas*. With its linear plot, the story could grow indefinitely by the mere addition of fresh episodes showing the continuance of Gil Blas's progress. And Volume III carries on this trend, established in the first two volumes. Nevertheless, once he began drawing on his sources of Spanish history, Lesage must surely have realized that the novel was taking a fresh turn. His prefatory remarks, and especially the assurance that he had portrayed no particular persons, were clearly contradicted by the introduction of historic Kings and courtiers. Why, then, did Lesage not alter his *Déclaration* when he revised his first two volumes?

Various reasons, alone or in combination, may account for his letting this inconsistency remain. There is, first, the general insouciance about accuracy which has already been mentioned. Secondly, Lesage may have considered that the comic or satiric aspect of the novel was more important than the historic element, which did not merit any special mention. Thirdly, he may not even have fully appreciated the fact that his utilization of specific historic 'truths' might be inconsistent with the aim of offering general truths about society.

Lesage was indeed, as far as one can gather or deduce, the very reverse of a conscious artist. Steadily occupied with all kinds of writing, some of which amounted to little more than hack-work, he seems to have given little or no thought to the theory of his craft. What he did, in practice, was to draw freely on all the resources of prose fiction which were familiar to him, and to make his novels follow any convention of form or subject-matter that seemed to him convenient or likely to please the public. Where he accepted the conventions without query or modification, he is generally, by modern standards, at his weakest. This is most obvious in the *nouvelles* and *histoires,* the *portraits* and *caractères* with their effect of cumbering and confusing the plot. Where he adapts the traditional elements to his own ends, the change tends to be advantageous. His alterations to the picaresque convention, making the hero rise through society instead of remaining in the gutter, meant that he covered a far wider range of social strata and callings than any previous writer of satiric novels. *Roman de mœurs* is a phrase often used rather loosely; if it implies a work which provides an overall impression of a given society, then there is much to be said for calling *Gil Blas* the first true *roman de mœurs* in French. At the same time, Lesage's avoidance of the coarser elements hither-to associated with comic and satiric novels, showed that this type of work could be respectable by both social and literary standards.

On these two counts alone, it is clear that *Gil Blas* is important, a landmark in the development of the novel which cannot be neglected by anyone who is studying the history of the genre. This is not however to affirm that it can necessarily claim a place among world masterpieces, or even among French ones. Apart from its unsatisfactory structure, a defect one may learn to ignore, this novel seems, by comparison with the works of comic masters such as Cervantès or Molière, both superficial and obvious. Lesage's penetration of emotions and motives is rarely more than skin-deep, and is totally lacking in subtlety. In successive episodes he illuminates the surface of his world, but throws scarcely any light into the depths of more complex feeling and behaviour. The human reactions he can effectively convey are limited both as to range and as to intensity.

What merits remain when we have made these reservations? Even if the work is episodic, many of the episodes are brilliantly handled. Gil Blas's first experience of being a valet—and a legatee—in the household of the cosseted canon; his sad lesson concerning the penalties of honesty with the Archbishop of Grenada; these and many another incident are concisely, wittily and vividly narrated, and linger in the memory. Even if we complain that the characters are types rather than individuals, and broadly sketched in rather than delineated with subtle detail, we still remember Laure and the rogue Don Raphaël, Dr Sangrado and the grandee whose life revolved round his pet monkey. We remember, that is, those characters and those episodes which are fully in harmony with the novelist's most distinctive trait: that lucid, ironic style which is the voice not only of Gil Blas, but of Lesage himself.

Robert Niklaus (essay date 1970)

SOURCE: "Lesage—Marivaux—Prévost," in *A Literary History of France: The Eighteenth Century, 1715-1789,*

Ernest Benn Limited, 1970, pp. 78-119.

[In the following excerpt, Niklaus analyzes the evolution of Lesage's writings in relation to events in his life, contending that the author "recorded faithfully and in a straightforward, incisive manner his own . . . experience; the picture of his times which he gives us may be over-dramatised, yet it strikes one as exceptionally vivid, illuminating, basically accurate, and often penetrating."]

Alain-René Lesage was born on 8 May 1668 at Sarzeau, near Vannes, in Brittany, and he retained many Breton characteristics, including a love of independence that led him to accept poverty rather than to forfeit his freedom of action and his integrity. He was the only son of Claude Lesage, barrister, solicitor, and recorder of the royal court of Rhuis, who died in 1682; since his mother, Damoiselle Jeanne Brenugat, had died in 1677, he was made the ward of two uncles, Gabriel Lesage and Blaise Brenugat. His mother was of an old Breton family, and his early childhood, unlike his later life, was spent in reasonable affluence. About 1686 he was sent to the Jesuit college of Vannes, where he received a good education, and developed his taste for the theatre. In 1690 he was sent to complete his education in Paris, where he studied first philosophy, then law, and was ultimately called to the Bar. He made the acquaintance of the poet and librettist Danchet, and the friendship which followed was to last sixty years.

In order to earn his living he became a notary's clerk and clerk to a financier and led a free and easy existence; he was well liked in the salons and frequented the Société du Temple, the home of the Vendôme family, and that of the duchesse de Bouillon. He met Dancourt, who befriended him and urged him to become a dramatist; it is believed that he had a liaison with a lady of quality, but soon became interested in a poor and beautiful girl, Marie-Elisabeth Huyard, the daughter of a carpenter, whom he married in 1694. He had three sons and one daughter, and is known to have enjoyed a happy family life. By 1695 Lesage lost interest in his legal career, and turned to writing. On Danchet's advice, he translated the *Lettres galantes d'Aristénète* (probably from a Latin version of the Greek original), from which he derived no financial profit. The abbé de Lyonne took him under his protection in 1698, securing for him an income of 600 livres. He advised Lesage to learn Spanish, and to seek inspiration in the picaresque novels, suggesting that he translate the plays of Calderón and Lope de Vega. In 1700 he published two five-act comedies under the title *Théâtre espagnol, Le Traître puni* (imitated from Rojas) and *Don Felix de Mendoce* (imitated from Lope de Vega). In February 1702, Lesage presented on the stage of the Théâtre Français *Le Point d'honneur,* a three-act play adapted from Rojas. This skit on duelling was not well received, and ran for only two nights. Lesage then published a free translation of Fernández de Avellaneda's continuation of Cervantes' work under the title *Nouvelles Aventures de l'admirable Don Quichotte de la Manche* (1704, 2 vols.). In 1707 he met at last with literary success. The Théâtre Français performed a five-act comedy,

Don César des Ursins, an adaptation of a Calderón play, which proved a failure; but the performance included a one-act play, inspired by Hurtado de Mendoza's *Los Empeños del mentir,* with the title *Crispin rival de son maître,* which proved extremely popular outside court circles (15 March). In the same year he published his first great prose work, *Le Diable boiteux,* which he was subsequently to expand. This work is once more drawn from Spanish sources (Guevara's *El Diavolo coivelo*), but is in fact a satire aimed at Parisian society, only the framework being truly Spanish. We find in it anecdotes about Ninon de Lenclos, Dufresny, Baron, and other contemporaries. The character of the devil Asmodée has been transformed. In 1708-9, Lesage offered a one-act play, *La Tontine,* to the Théâtre Français, which declined to put it on, probably for political reasons, and it was only much later that it was performed at the Théâtre de la Foire, under the title *Arlequin colonel,* and later still, in 1732, on the stage of the Comédie Française. *La Tontine* was a public loan to which individuals subscribed according to their age group, in order to qualify for an annuity which increased as their numbers in the same age group died off. The second of these loans had been raised in 1696 and the whole scheme became the object of heated discussion in 1708. This accounts for Lesage's interest in the subject, and also for the criticism he evoked. With characteristic persistence, Lesage then offered a new one-act comedy, *Les Etrennes,* in 1708, which was again turned down by the *Comédiens français.* He expanded this play into five acts, but *Turcaret ou Les Etrennes,* as it was now called, did not fare any better. The *traitants,* a group of vulgar, newly rich financiers whom Lesage had satirised in his play, were successful in getting the play suppressed, largely through their connections with the actresses of the Théâtre Français.

Lesage read his play in the salons to rouse interest in it, and the circulation of a story that financiers had offered him 10,000 francs to keep the play off the stage proved to be excellent publicity. *Turcaret* was eventually put on at the Théâtre Français, thanks to the intervention of Monsieur, but it was withdrawn after seven performances (14 February 1709), as a result of which Lesage became involved in a quarrel with the *Comédiens.*

His abortive experience with *La Tontine* and *Les Etrennes* led him to turn away from the Théâtre Français and towards the more popular, if less exalted, Théâtre de la Foire. The winter fair of Saint-Germain and the summer fair of Saint-Laurent attracted mountebanks and strolling players, supplemented after the expulsion of the Italian players from Paris in 1697 by companies performing so-called *commedia dell'arte* scenarii in the Italian manner and others containing lesser players from the expelled company who fled to the fair booths rather than return to Italy or tour the provinces. From these bastardised forms of Italian comedy a genre including acrobatics and dancing, to fit the requirements of players and audience, evolved with great rapidity and popular success. These *forains* were further stimulated by a lively and continued struggle waged with the Théâtre Français, which continued until the Revolution broke out. Throughout the century the *Comédiens du Roi* strove to exert their own monopoly and to deprive the *forains* of their right to perform, by any means which came to hand, fearing a rivalry that might, and did, rob them of their audiences. Throughout the century, the *forains* evaded every edict, and avoided destruction; they continued to evolve a form of theatre based upon Italian comedy, and which developed despite all the stresses imposed upon it by the *Comédiens*. They enjoyed an increasing popularity, drawing their patrons from among the workers, the bourgeoisie, and the aristocracy. Their struggle for survival made them alert and adaptable, revolutionised stage technique, and as time went on offered the possibility of satiric drama of a direct, ebullient, and often virulent kind.

From 1712 until 1734 Lesage wrote for this theatre, which offered better financial reward as well as greater artistic freedom. Eighty-eight of his plays are to be found in the *Théâtre de la Foire* (10 vols., 1737).

Twenty-nine of the plays appear under the name of Lesage alone, twenty-three in collaboration with d'Orneval, thirty-two with d'Orneval and Fuzelier, one with d'Orneval and Autreau, one with d'Orneval and Piron, and one with Lafont and Fromaget. His first are: *Arlequin empereur dans la lune* and *Arlequin baron allemand, ou Le Triomphe de la folie* (in three acts with *vaudevilles* and *écriteaux*), in collaboration with Fuzelier and Dominique. . . .

[Lesage's] considerable [dramatic] output is in addition to the ill-fated *La Tontine* (one act), given without success at the Théâtre Français in February 1732, and the following novels: *Le Diable boiteux* (1707); *Gil Blas de Santillane* (Books I-VI of which appeared in 1715, Books VII-IX in 1724, and Books X-XII in 1736); *Roland amoureux,* a novel in verse, taken from the Italian Boïardo (1717-1721, two vols.); *Entretiens des cheminées de Madrid,* added to the third edition of *Le Diable boiteux* (1726); *Histoire d'Estevanille Gonzalès* and a dialogue entitled *Une Journée des Pargues* (1734); and *La Valise trouvée* (1740). Finally there is the *Mélange amusant de saillies d'esprit et de traits historiques des plus frappants* (1743).

Lesage is one of the most prolific writers of *comédies-vaudevilles* or *comédies mêlées d'ariettes,* genres considered to be the forerunners of comic opera. The form of these plays resulted from the prohibition of dialogue and singing on all stages except that of the Théâtre Français and that of the Opéra, imposed by the *Comédiens* and circumvented by the *forains.*

Even this long list of works is incomplete, for in the year in which he brought out the first part of *Gil Blas,* Lesage also wrote the adventures of Marie Petit, who kept a Paris gaming-house in the early years of the century, and in 1703 *M. Fabre, 'envoyé extraordinaire de Louis XIV en Perse',* a work which he later abandoned. He also undertook adaptations and translations. His *Histoire de Guzman d'Alfarache nouvelement traduite et purgée des moralités superflues* (1732) is an abridged version of

Mateo Alemán's romance, which had also inspired Chapelain (1621), Gabriel de Brémon (1696), and others. *Les Aventures de Monsieur Robert Chevalier, dit de Beauchêne,* which has been held to be an authentic autobiographical document, is from the work of Vicentio Espinella. *Le Bachelier de Salamanque ou Les Mémoires de don Chérubin de la Ronda* (1736-38), is also based on a Spanish manuscript. Lesage in the course of his work in the theatre developed a strong dislike of all actors, and bitterly resented his own sons' desire to go on the stage. His eldest son, René-André, became an actor of repute under the name of Montménil, and on 28 May 1726 he played Mascarille in Molière's *L'Etourdi* with great success; he then toured the provinces, returning two years later to Paris, acting the part of Hector in Regnard's *Le Foueur,* of Davos in Terence's *Andria,* and of La Branche in *Crispin rival de son maître,* and finally Turcaret. But his father remained unreconciled and the news that his third son was to take up a stage career in Germany, under the name of Pittence (1730), only added to his grief and anger. This third son eventually returned to Paris, where he put on two comic operas, *Le Testament de la Foire* and *Le Miroir véridique,* at the Foire Saint-Germain. The second son, the Abbé Julien-François Lesage, who lived at Boulogne-sur-Mer, was successful in arranging a temporary *rapprochement* between his father and his brothers, but only after Lesage had been induced to see Montménil's performance in the role of Turcaret; and his last years were saddened by the death of his eldest son in 1743. Too old to work, extremely deaf, and quite poor in spite of his prodigious output, he went to Boulogne with his wife and daughter, Marie-Elisabeth, to live in the home of the abbé, his second son. He dined almost every day with the Abbé Voisenon, who wrote of his kindly wit. He had quiet obstinacy and the independence of the Breton. His deafness at the age of forty obliged him to use an ear trumpet, which he referred to as his 'bienfaiteur'.

Two plays and two novels stand out from this vast output. *Crispin rival de son maître* is generally considered to be one of the best-constructed one-act plays ever to be staged. The plot is unoriginal, borrowed from a Spanish play by Hurtado de Mendoza, in which an adventurer tries to marry the sister of a man whose life he has saved by posing as her fiancé. Professor T. E. Lawrenson has reminded us that there is in fact a close resemblance between Mendoza's play and the adventure of Jérôme de Moyadas in *Gil Blas.* The play provides a social document of interest. It heralds the regency and the new social confusion, underlined by the language spoken by both servants and masters, and also the rise of men of intrigue. The milieu is bourgeois; M. Oronte, father of Angélique, is a tax-farmer, and Valère a *chevalier d'industrie* (an adventurer or card-sharp). Lesage gives to his valets exuberance of temperament and speech and the ability to cope with situations, before Beaumarchais ever created Figaro. He has what Lintilhac called *le mot qui ramasse,* an ability to use telling short-cuts. His style of writing owes nothing to the preciosity of the salons. Lawrenson rightly speaks of its drama of the outspoken, as opposed to the drama of half-statements which characterises the theatre of Marivaux. Minor scenes lead naturally and logically into major ones.

There is great dramatic economy, and the structure of the play allows for rapid movement, which creates a sense of speed and suspense, and the possibilities of discovery are piled on at an increasing rate as the play reaches its finale.

Crispin is a brilliant comedy of intrigue, to be compared in this respect with the plays of Regnard. Lesage developed his technical skill by learning how to modify the action of Spanish dramas to suit French taste. By cutting out monologues and tirades, he speeded up the action and promoted a new liveliness on the stage. Crispin himself is interesting from another point of view, for he belongs to a long line of *valets de comédie* bearing that name (1654-1853). Lawrenson has traced him from Scarron's *L'Escolier de Salamanque* through plays by Poisson, Hauteroche, Champmeslé, Montfleury *fils,* La Thuillerie, Lesage's own Crispin in *Le Point d'honneur* (1702), Lafont, Regnard, Delon, Mayet, Pessey, and Leclercq. He was incarnated by three generations of actors belonging to the same family, the Poissons, which partly accounts for the surprising degree of consistency in playing the part of this cunning and very self-confident valet. Lesage changed a popular stock character into a Crispin unique in that he becomes his master's rival, and in this he is clearly differentiated from the valets who preceded him, the Mascarilles, the Jodelets, the Scapins, the Frontins, and from his Italian counterpart Arlequin, who was dominating the Théâtre de la Foire at that time. The full story of the *valet de comédie* is as long as that of comedy itself. Comedy was born in a society based on slavery, and the *servus* of Plautus and Terence (whose *Andria* Lesage had translated) survived the passing of time, albeit in a new guise. The servant-master relationship changed with evolving social patterns, but ultimately became conventional in the theatre, the servant always concerned with his freedom or his wages first and the interest of his master second. With Lesage he is for the first time solely concerned with his self-advancement and usurps the function of the master. The bold title of this short and often acted play was to resound throughout the century, for the spectators were able to witness the rise of a servant in a society now primarily concerned with money, and no longer with aristocracy of birth. *Crispin rival de son maître* is essentially a comedy of intrigue, with a character title, a plot, and some repartees that were to gain in significance with the passing years. Certain slogans taken out of their context, such as 'La justice est une si belle chose qu'on ne saurait trop l'acheter', and individual expressions of opinion, such as Crispin's 'Que je suis las d'être valet! . . . je devrais présentement briller dans la finance', presage Beaumarchais, but Crispin himself belongs to a world that still hopes for reform and does not foresee revolution. Crispin is less dangerous than Frontin in *Turcaret.*

Turcaret is the second play under review, and the social background it reflects needs to be borne in mind if the work is to be properly understood.

France was enduring military defeat from all quarters. In 1708 the British and their allies took Lille and in 1709 the French were seriously defeated at Malplaquet. Court life had long since lost its golden glitter. The ageing Louis XIV and Mme de Maintenon had turned to religion, the cost of living had gone up, and the nobility were in a changed position, one in which it was increasingly difficult to cut a figure in Paris and at the same time maintain their estates in the provinces. At Versailles and in Paris fortunes were lost by the nobles at the gaming tables. The bourgeoisie, on the other hand, was growing in power; the prevailing mood was a desire to enjoy life to the full. Tragedy had become unpopular and comedy, especially farce, was welcome, provided that it had vitality and movement. Perhaps the most peculiar social change at that date was the rise of the *financier,* also called *commis, agent de change, sous-fermier, fermier, traitant, partisan,* and *maltôtier.* These were in fact tax-collectors, and went back to the time of Colbert who, in 1681, had established a *Compagnie de quarante financiers,* required collectively to pay the government 670,000 livres per annum, but entitled to recoup themselves by levying customs, *traites, aides* (on drink), and *gabelle* (on salt). The lease or *traite* (hence the word *traitant*) to collect certain taxes in specified areas was ceded for six years to a financier embodied by Lesage in *Turcaret,* who received 4,000 livres per annum for his services. A whole world of *directeurs, inspecteurs, contrôleurs, ambulants, vérificateurs,* and *commis buralistes* gravitated around them, exempt from paying taxes and hoping for preferment to the nobility. Around them flocked *agioteurs,* or speculators, and usurers. All these men were disliked by the nobility, for they amassed enormous fortunes as the aristocracy were losing them. Some set themselves up as patrons of the arts, as did Crozat, who helped Watteau, and others later became publishers, who favoured the *philosophes.* The peasants, like the aristocrats, hated them and generally held them to be responsible for the bad state of the country. In his play *Turcaret* Lesage drew on contemporary conditions and on *libelles,* or satirical pamphlets, as also on varied works such as *Les Agioteurs* by Dancourt, and *Factum de la France* (1707) by Boisguillebert; on Giton in La Bruyère's *Les Caractères,* Harpagon in Molière's *L'Avare,* Dorante in his *Le Bourgeois Gentilhomme,* and La Rapinière in Jacques Robbe's play of that name (1682), in which there is a scene similar to that between Rafle and Turcaret; on *Le Mercure galant* by Boursault (1683) and *Esope à la cour, Esope à la ville, and La Coquette,* by Baron; and on *L'Eté des coquettes* by Dancourt, *Le Banqueroutier* by N. de Fatouville (1687), to be found in Gherardi's collection of Italian plays, *La Foire de Besons* (1695), and *La Foire Saint-Germain* (1696). The name Turcaret has been linked with that of the lackey Cascaret, to be found in the *commedia dell'arte* and in Dancourt. In Gherardi's collection, Lesage could find Regnard's *Arlequin, homme à bonne fortune,* and could also draw on his *Le Foueur* and his *Critique du 'Légataire universel'* (1708). Lesage borrowed from Dancourt's *Le Chevalier à la mode, La Folle Enchère* (1690), *Les Fonds perdus* (1686); also from Dufresny's *Les Bourgeoises à la mode* (1692); and finally from his own *Diable boiteux* and *Crispin rival de son maître.* But these varied and general sources merely add to the contemporary relevance of the play. Turcaret himself stands out as a character and his name has become a byword.

The play is often said to be gloomy. It is not realistic in the modern sense, for the décor is virtually non-existent. It is not as well constructed as *Crispin rival de son maître*. The tempo is fast, especially in the last two acts, and owes something to the movement of *commedia dell'arte*. This prevents the mood from becoming too serious. The technique has much in common with the narrative technique utilised in *Gil Blas,* which is essentially a picaresque novel. We find a similar discontinuity in the episodes of the play, and we move from comic scene to comic scene. 'Le jeu de l'argent et de la surprise' has been suggested as a sub-title.

The plot revolves around the question of whether the financier will succeed in marrying the young widow, but the fifth act vindicates arbitrary justice, rather than providing a solution. The return of Mme Turcaret, and the intervention of the king's justice, which bring the play to an end, are external factors; and the demise of Turcaret is a kind of *dénouement postiche,* or contrived ending, which has been likened to that of *Tartuffe*. The final triumph of the servant Frontin is full of irony. Frontin summed up very adequately the subject of the play in the following words: 'Nous plumons une coquette; la coquette mange un homme d'affaires; l'homme d'affaires en pille d'autres: cela fait un ricochet de fourberies le plus plaisant du monde.' Over the years we see that critics have questioned the comic element in the play. Today, however, through a better understanding of *commedia dell'arte,* and a close examination of other plays of the time, it has been possible to present a gayer interpretation of a comedy which has *lazzi,* or gags, and fantasy as well as realism, though the characters should be taken seriously; even when highly stylised they belong to professions which have determined their nature and their actions. The Chevalier is a melancholic yet passionate gamester, full of vanity; Turcaret is bold, careless, libidinous; the Baronne, a widow and a coquette, is clearly a stock character; Frontin is in the tradition of Arlequin, Scapin, or Crispin; and Lisette is a variant of Colombine. Lesage extends sympathy to none of them. His cold detachment, his quick wit, and his feeling for sharp repartees and well-timed ripostes, coupled with his unfailing ability to construct a scene, would have sufficed to establish his claim to distinction among French dramatists. It is, however, his satire of the world of finance and money, and his presentation of a vast and corrupt society unredeemed by a single example of a good man, which have won him a special place in the history of the theatre. If Turcaret was not the first financier to be put on the stage, he was the first character of the kind to be studied in depth against his social background, in his relations with others, and especially as he had evolved through the exercise of his profession. There are therefore serious undertones to this comedy which leave a sour taste in the mouth—a fact which enhances Lesage's moral condemnation of the characters. *Turcaret,* although now judged more comic than has hitherto been thought, does nevertheless serve as a pointer to the *drames* of the latter half of the eighteenth century, and contains many biting remarks that are worthy of Voltaire's pen in their sophisticated wit.

Frontin now belongs to the same social class as his master; he has grown in power since Crispin, who had merely confined himself to hopes of a great financial future. Frontin has a better technique, an abler assistant, and more real power, and the triumph of this *valet de comédie* heralds that of Figaro. The closing lines of the play show

---

An anonymous nineteenth-century critic on Lesage:

He had, even in youth, been affected with symptoms of deafness, which increased with his years, but his natural gaiety was not lessened. His conversation abounding with wit, anecdote, and shrewd observations, and shown to the best advantage by a manly and various elocution, was heard always with delight. The picture of the author of *Gil Blas,* advanced in life, surrounded by a throng of youthful admirers, the more distant mounted on chairs and tables, in order to catch every word of his discourse, recals what we may have heard of our own glorious John Dryden at the Coffeehouse.

"The Author of Gil Blas," *in* Household Words,
Vol. X, No. 250, 1854-55, pp. 488-93.

---

a mastery of nuance and a felicity of language which all alert spectators will relish, and which has only been equalled by Voltaire:

Lisette: Et nous, Frontin, quel parti prendrons-nous?

Frontin: J'en ai un à te proposer. Vive l'esprit, mon enfant! Je viens de payer d'audace: je n'ai point été fouillé.

Lisette: Tu as les billets?

Frontin: J'en ai déjà touché l'argent; il est en sûreté; j'ai quarante mille francs. Si ton ambition veut se borner à cette petite fortune, nous allons faire souche d'honnêtes gens.

Lisette: J'y consens.

Frontin: Voilà le règne de M. Turcaret fini; le mien va commencer.

The proposal of marriage is unusual in its form and the real implications are clear. Love for the likes of Frontin and Lisette is a very special thing, as their choice of words and form of persuasion reveal. Lesage can say all in a few words, and with crystal clarity, by compression and implication. A rascally financier as the essential theme of a play will be found in Balzac's *Mercadet* (1851), O. Mirbeau's *Les Affaires sont les affaires* (1903), E. Fabre's *Les Ventres dorés* (1905), and especially H. Becque's *Les Corbeaux* (1882).

The same qualities of style are to be found in Lesage's *Histoire de Gil Blas de Santillane,* which is a long comdy of manners presented in the form of a picaresque novel. Voltaire thought that Lesage had borrowed his episodes from Vicente Martìnez Espinel, whose partly autobiographical novel *Relacions de la vida del escudero Marcos de Obregón* was published in 1618 and soon translated into French, under the title *Relation de la vie de l'écuyer Marcos Obregon;* in fact Lesage did borrow ten passages from this work. The Jesuit priest P. Isla thought that Lesage had translated a Spanish manuscript since lost, so he retranslated **Gil Blas** into Castilian with some success. An academic controversy over Lesage's originality ensued. It must be obvious that Lesage, like Molière, borrowed from all sundry, but that the essence of **Gil Blas,** its style and tone, its realism and fantasy and satire, is original. The Spanish setting mainly lends piquancy to an unmistakably French scene, and contemporaries of Lesage had the added pleasure of experiencing a slight if somewhat bogus sense of *dépaysement,* such as was exploited, among others, by Montesquieu in the *Lettres persanes,* and Beaumarchais in the *Barbier de Séville.* In **Gil Blas** Lesage shows his ability to portray characters which seem to have the authenticity of the theatre rather than that of ordinary life, and offers a wealth of realistic details which lead us to accept inconsistencies in the plot. The work abounds in brilliant scenes and stylised dialogue which call for production on the stage. The same rapid movement carries all before it and the structure of each episode—but not of the work as a whole—is as taut as in his plays.

We witness a series of *tableaux* owing something to the literary technique of La Bruyère, conjuring up haphazardly a whole world of people of all ranks and characters, with their peculiar manners, tastes, and foibles. There are petty thieves and canons, doctors and writers, prelates and actors; there are old men in love with young girls of dubious morals laying snares for the old and rich; there are Ministers, dukes, and servants. Dr Sangrado with his hopeless remedies, Fabrice the poet, Raphaël and Laméla, who, weary of their role of penitents, abscond with the monastery funds, and many other characters stand out in one's memory. They come and go and reappear in very different moods. Both Smollett (who translated **Gil Blas**) and Walter Scott were filled with admiration at the richness and vitality of Lesage's *comédie humaine.*

The hero, Gil Blas, is on the high road at the age of seventeen. He is gay and full of illusions, and is bent on social advancement, financial success, and, above all, personal happiness. He moves through life without any strong moral principle, concerned mainly with personal advancement and survival in the jungle of society. He is an *arriviste* who only succeeds late in penetrating into high society. He becomes *intendant* of Don Alphonse, and then secretary to the duc de Lerme. But his success leads to his corruption. A further twist of fortune leads him to end his days at home, in the role of the good father. Gil Blas is Everyman, neither more nor less moral than most ordinary men, whose behaviour and standards are determined by events. He is neither vicious nor moral,

but natural, somewhat naïve, and disarming. He is without prejudice and humorously self-centred. He grows in maturity with the author himself who worked on the novel over a period of more than twenty years. He may be likened to Candide; Lesage's rapier thrusts, anti-clerical wit, and use of irony bring home the similarity.

Lesage, like all the novelists of the period, who were constantly being attacked for immorality or uselessness, is at pains to stress the moral benefit to be derived from his tale, as well as the enjoyment. He can be placed in the moralist tradition of La Bruyére. In fact it is his restraint in the use of moral lectures that commends the book to us today; and nineteenth-century criticism, centred on an attempt at moral justification for the novel, leaves present-day readers indifferent. His fictional technique is of greater consequence. Lesage lacked the creative power and the penetration of Cervantes, who incarnated in Don Quixote and Sancho Panza two opposite yet complementary aspects of mankind. We have to wait for the dialogue between Jacques le Fataliste and his master in Diderot's last novel to rediscover, in a very different setting and intellectual climate, something of the dichotomy of man and his mind. But Lesage recorded faithfully and in a straightforward, incisive manner his own more limited experience; the picture of his times which he gives us may be over-dramatised, yet it strikes one as exceptionally vivid, illuminating, basically accurate, and often penetrating.

Roseann Runte (essay date 1979)

SOURCE: "Parallels Between Lesage's Theatre and His Novels," in *Enlightenment Studies in Honour of Lester G. Crocker,* edited by Alfred J. Bingham and Virgil W. Topazio, The Voltaire Foundation, 1979, pp. 283-99.

[*In the following essay, Runte evaluates Lesage's dramatic works as complements and reflections of his novels, with a focus on structure, characterization, language, and plot patterns.*]

In Turcaret's shadow an eloquent troupe of Arlequins, Scaramouches, Clitandres and Alis has long been eclipsed. Lesage's theatre has, like many of his translations and novels (**Don Quichotte, Don Guzman d'Alfarache, Les Aventures de M. Robert Chevalier, dit de Beauchêne, Estevanille Gonzales, Le Bachelier de Salamanque**), been classed as secondary literature despite appeals such as that made by Eugène Lintilhac [in *Lesage* (1893)]: "Pourtant elles [ces œuvres secondaires] ont un titre général à l'indulgence de la postérité, celui d'avoir nourri leur auteur en lui permettant de polir son **Gil Blas** vingt ans durant. Elles en ont d'autres d'ailleurs, et l'une, au moins de ces œuvres alimentaires, le Théâtre de la Foire, mérite d'etre lue."

It is not the purpose of this essay to justify a reading of Lesage's theatre by attributing extraordinary literary merits, hitherto undiscovered, to the plays. Rather, it is to consider the plays as alimentary works contributing to and reflecting the conception of those novels for which we remember Lesage. Some of the plays preceded the novels, as in the case of the **Aventures de Robert Chevalier,** while others succeeded the novel as in the case of **Le Diable boiteux** and **Arlequin invisible**. We will seek parallels and common themes. Rather than individual cases of influence, we will note general exchanges between the genres and will consider the importance of the dramatist's art in the composition of the novels. Charles Dédéyan says [in *Lesage et Gil Blas* (1965)]: "Du Théâtre de la Foire, à la Foire sur la Place, sinon à la Foire aux Idées, la distance ne sera pas grande." Dédéyan goes on to remind us that according to Palissot Lesage's novels "semblent avoir été brochés au sortir du spectacle", and traces a comparison between Molière and Lesage. Other critics have also noticed that 'the novelist is everywhere reinforced by the dramatist, a rare and excellent combination' [quoted in *Minuet* by F. C. Green (1935)]. Some theatre specialists, including Maurice Albert [in *Les Théâtres de la foire (1660-1789)* (1900)], have suggested that Lesage, "ce malicieux et pénétrant observateur [,] voulut que son théâtre nouveau fût une sorte de second **Gil Blas,** un **Gil Blas** dramatique et populaire". At least two critics have noted that a study of the theatre might lead to a better understanding of the novels. Lintilhac teases the imagination with his remark on the theatre: "on y trouve d'utiles renseignements sur la conception de la vie et la meilleure des clefs de **Gil Blas**" [quoted in *Lesage et Gil Blas*]. More explicitly, Agueda Pizarro indicated that 'the plays may be thought of as prototypes of the novels, particularly where the elaboration of character is concerned' [quoted in the unpublished dissertation *Lesage, Picaresque Paradox and the French Eighteenth-Century Novel*, 1974].

The first similarity between the two genres, as executed by Lesage, lies in their structure. His novels are *romans à tiroirs* and his theatre, a ricochet of *fourberies,* presents strings of cameo sketches which may be called a *théâtre à tiroirs*. In his article, 'Récit et "histoires" dans les romans de Lesage', Jean Oudart notes that the novelistic *tiroirs* are of two varieties: homodiegetical (linked to the hero or the plot) and heterodiegetical (totally independent). Similarly, the *tiroirs* of the plays are homodiegetical as in **Les Trois commères** in which the tales of the three wives are tied together by the competition which inspires them or in **Roger de Sicile, surnommé le roi sans chagrin** in which the characters are linked by the relationship between Roger, Lizette and Arlequin and by their universal quest for happiness. The *tiroirs* are heterodiegetical in plays which are like reviews: **La Foire des fées, Le Temple de mémoire, Les Amours déguisés**. In these plays, each scene may be viewed and understood without reference to the others. They are loosely joined by an exposition and by the stage presence of a single character or characters. In **La Foire des fées,** for example, the fairies hold court and are presented with a number of demands by a series of unrelated characters such as the naïve Nicette who desires the gift of coquettishness. Although the plays hardly follow the three unities, both the number of subplots and their development are limited. It might be more appropriate in this context therefore, to consider the theatre as a picaresque whole through which

Arlequin travels in various disguises and assumes different ranks and roles. Each of the plays represents another chapter.

Jean Oudart finds that the heterodiegetical stories are of such similar conception that 'à vue de titres, elles pourraient même permuter entre elles: "L'histoire de Belflor et Léonor" (**Le Diable boiteux**) prendre la place de celle de "Dom Alphonse et la belle Séraphine" (**Gil Blas**) ou de "Dom André d'Alvarade et de Dona Cinthia de la Carrera" (**Le Bachelier de Salamanque**)' [quoted in *Bulletin de recherches et travaux de l'Université de Grenoble* (1976)]. The case of the independent scenes in the theatre, and indeed, of the theatre considered as a picaresque whole, is similar. This interchangeability is the result of the repetition of ideas, themes, situations and characters. Lesage's work resembles an abstract mosaic or puzzle with interlocking pieces which may be replaced at will. The multiplicity of similar *tiroirs* may be one of the contributory factors to the neglect of such a large part of Lesage's work. The scenes tend to become blurred in one's memory and give the impression of *déjà vu*. In another context, F. C. Green calls *Turcaret* Lesage's only memorable comedy. It may well be that the **Théâtre de la foire** as a whole followed the way of its parts, few of which are strikingly different in conception. On the other hand, this similarity observed among the *tiroirs* of the two genres individually, may be generally recognised among the parts of Lesage's work as a whole. As stories may be exchanged with each other, so may they be replaced by scenes from the theatre.

Lesage seems to have been conscious of creating dramatic scenes in his novels. In **Gil Blas,** for example, when Laure has just deceived the marquis de Marialva, she says 'Avoue, Gil Blas, [. . .] que nous venons de jouer une plaisante comédie! Mais je ne m'attendais pas au dénouement.' Not only do the characters act and speak as if they were on the stage, but their intrinsic theatricality is proved by the transposition of Asmodée and Don Cléofas to the stage in the prologue to **Turcaret** and Asmodée's presence in plays such as **Arlequin invisible** and the preface and the **Critique de Turcaret**. In both novel and theatre, the episodes are linked by the personality of a Gil Blas, a Don Cléofas and an Asmodée or an Arlequin. The exposition and denouement of the play introduce and explain the action to the spectator. The narrative passages linking the independent tales in the novel perform the same function.

The characters who give unity to the two genres have certain similarities as well. They are alternatively spectator and participant in the action. Both Gil Blas and Arlequin visit nearly all levels of society. **Arlequin, roi de Serendib, Arlequin Mahomet, Arlequin Hulla, Arlequin Colombine, Arlequin Endymion** and **Arlequin, roi des Ogres** are a theatrical parallel for Gil Blas student, rogue and minister. The people whom they observe and with whom these picaresque protagonists interact are, as Lester Crocker has said, animals. The menagerie includes cocks, chickens, nightingales, pigeons, larks, leeches, doves, barbary apes, tigresses, kittens, dogs, wolves, mackerel, lambs, doves, kites, werewolves, suckling pigs, etc. In both the novel and the theatre the human race is divided into two classes: the hunters and the hunted. However, the classification, like the society, is never stable. At one moment in *Gil Blas* the prosecutor is a kite who is clutching a dove in his claws (*GB*,i.445). At another, he is the quarry sought after when a loan is needed (*GB*.ii.147). Similarly a woman may be perceived to be a lamb yet may actually be a tiger (*GB*.ii.14-15). In the theatre she will treat her unwanted lovers 'comme chiens dans un jeu de quilles' [in *Le Théâtre de la foire ou l'opéra comique* (1721)]. The prosecutor can be a disagreeable person, a nasty pigeon (*F*.ii.285), or a fish which those seeking financial assistance must trap: 'Nous n'avons pas fait une heureuse pêche. Le poisson a vu l'hameçon, il n'a point voulu mordre à l'appât' [in *Recueil des pièces mises au théâtre français* (1739)]. In like manner a woman, once a dragon, becomes a sheep after only a few years in the convent (*F*.vii.29). The choice of animal representing the human is linked to sex (women are chickens, doves, nightingales, sheep and tigresses while men are cocks, dogs, pigeons, owls, fish and mackerel) and to occupation (financiers are either suckling pigs or wolves; clerics are suckling pigs as well; lawyers are kites or other birds of prey), and to role (the hunter versus the hunted). The animal representation varies as well depending on the situation of the perceiver and his relationship to the other human 'animal'. At times no specific animal is mentioned but the human assumes animal characteristics which tend to debase him. For example, in *Le Monde renversé*, Arlequin describes philosophers: "Et quand ils disputent, on dirait qu'ils vont se manger le blanc des yeux" (*F*.iii.223). In *Gil Blas* the philosophers in discussion foam at the mouth (*GB*.i.34). The emphasis on the ignoble animal traits (foaming at the mouth suggests mad dogs, and eating the eyes the pecking of carrion birds) is employed here for a satirical effect obtained through the contrast of supposedly rational humans and irrational beasts. Robert Chevalier excuses his use of violence for the same satiric reason: 'Si j'eusse eu affaire à des gens raisonnables, j'aurais employé les prières et les politesses' [in *Les Aventures de Monsieur Robert Chevalier, dit de Beauchêne, capitaine de flibustiers dans la Nouvelle-France* (1780)].

When characters are not compared to animals in simile or assigned their traits in metonyms, they dream symbolic dreams of animals. In *Le Diable boiteux* we see two women,

> l'une rêve qu'elle prend des oiseaux à la pipée, qu'elle les plume à mesure qu'elle les prend; mais qu'elle les donne à un beau matou dont elle est folle et qui en a tout le profit. L'autre songe qu'elle chasse de sa maison des lévriers et des chiens danois dont elle a fait longtemps ses délices, et qu'elle ne veut plus avoir qu'un petit roquet des plus gentils, qu'elle a pris en amitié.

In dream the first woman resembles both Robert Chevalier's first mistress and the Baronne in *Turcaret,* in action. In *Le Tableau du mariage* Diamantine refuses to

marry at the last minute because she dreamt that 'j'ai vu deux pigeons qui sortaient d'un colombier'. The female caressed the male who responded by pecking her and flying away (*F*.ii.280). The characters have claws and animal snouts; they nest and graze. They extend hooks and nets and set traps to ensnare each other. They are characterised by their appetites which are shockingly violent. When they are not pursuing a suckling pig or turtle dove to consume—'La faim fait sortir le loup hors du bois' (*F*.iii.451)—they are endeavouring to escape someone else's cooking pot. The metaphor is substantiated in *Arlequin, roi des ogres ou les bottes de sept lieux* where Arlequin narrowly escapes being cooked and eaten by the ogres and is, in turn, offered his choice of dish by nationality (French, Spanish, Dutch) and by sex and profession (*petit-maître,* etc.). A similar evocation of cannibalism is present in *Les Aventures de Robert Chevalier* in a satirical passage which imagines that if the Indians had discovered Europe they would have been greeted by people with very strange habits, not the least of which was to disdain eating those killed in battle. The justification in both scenes is worth noting as it demonstrates a similar concern:

ARLEQUIN: Que vous êtes barbares!

ADARIO: Moins que les autres hommes.

ARLEQUIN: Manger son semblable! Quelle cruauté!

ADARIO: Hé, n'en faites-vous pas paraître davantage, vous autres, lorsque vous égorgez d'innocentes bêtes pour vous nourrir de leur chair, après qu'elles ont labouré vos champs, après qu'elles vous ont donné leurs toisons pour vous couvrir? Nous, en mangeant des hommes, nous croyons en même temps purger la terre de mauvais animaux, de monstres pleins de malice qui ne songent qu'à nous nuire. Vous, qui pensez avoir en partage toute l'humanité, comment en usez-vous les uns avec les autres? Vous vous querellez, vous vous chicanez, vous vous pillez, chez vous le plus fort ôte au plus faible la subsistance, cela ne s'appelle-t-il pas se manger?

(*F*,iv.155-56)

Il est naturel qu'ils [les sauvages] tuent leurs ennemis [. . .] pour quelle raison voulez-vous qu'ils ne les mangent pas? Trouverions-nous bien raisonnable, un chasseur qui n'ayant jamais vu que des perdrix rouges, n'en tuerait pas une grise qui viendrait dans son canton, ou qui l'ayant tuée, et la voyant grosse et grasse, l'enfouirait plutôt que de la manger?

(*B*,iii.53)

The final sentence of the play is practically a summary of Lesage's view of society and the manner in which he portrays it in his works. The passage in the novel is followed by a critique of the violence, inhospitality and religious intolerance of Europeans in the style of *Les Letters persanes*.

Not only do people seek to devour each other, but they are devoured by their passions. Lust is a metaphoric dog which bites his victim who, in *Les Enragés,* suffers 'distemper' or 'rabies'. In *Gil Blas* passion is 'une maladie qui vous vient comme la rage aux animaux' (*GB*.i. 178). When pushed to excess, even noble sentiments like justice become bestial and grow claws (*T*.ii.56). In *Gil Blas,* vanity causes Séphora to become enraged 'à un point que, si vous [Gil Blas] ne sortez au plus vite de ce château, sa mort, dit-elle, est certaine' (*GB*.ii. 16). In *Les Enragés* a poet is put in a cage, so poisoned is he by his own venom. 'Morbleu!' cries he, 'si je les tenais ces beaux Messieurs les Quarante! Morbleu! si je les tenais, comme je les croquerais!' (*F*.vi.94).

The animality stresses man's consuming passions, his brutality, violence and cruelty. Yet at the same time, the constant reference to man as animal adds an element of realism to a novel replete with mythological references and to a theatre whose stage is crowded with gods, fairies, demons and other exotic personages. Lesage stresses repeatedly the fact that man must have some passions. He cannot live on water, but must have meat and wine. In *La Tontine* (*T,* ii.373):

> AMBROISE: [. . .] faites-moi mettre à la broche une bonne oie.
>
> M. TROUSSE-GALANT: Rien n'est plus indigeste.
>
> AMBROISE: Donnez-moi donc des saucisses de cochon.
>
> M. TROUSSE-GALANT: Cela sera trop salé.
>
> AMBROISE: Trop salé, trop doux, trop cru, trop cuit; que diable voulez-vous que je mange?
>
> M. TROUSSE-GALANT: Une once de fromage mou [. . .] avec deux ou trois verres de tisane hépatique.
>
> AMBROISE: Je suis mort. Je suis enterré.

And in *Gil Blas* (*GB,* i.138-39):

> Mais s'il [le docteur Sangrado] nous défendait, à la servante et à moi, de manger beaucoup, en récompense, il nous permettait de boire de l'eau à discrétion [. . .] après avoir été huit jours dans cette maison, il me prit un cours de ventre, et je commençai à sentir de grands maux d'estomac, que j'eus la témérité d'attribuer au dissolvant universel et à la mauvaise nourriture que je prenais.

In *Les Aventures de Robert Chevalier* the hero nearly dies twice from lack of meat and wine. He attempts to subsist on grass and leaves and water and becomes ill. As we learn in the 'hermit's' dissertation on food in *Gil Blas,* delicate meats and exquisite stews inspire sensuality and corrupt natural, pure taste. On the other hand, a crust of bread and water are not sufficient to sustain life. Gil Blas has to learn to balance his diet. He goes from extremes,

enforced hunger (due to poverty) to over-consumption (due to greed) to a desire to return to absolute simplicity (due to disgust). This last desire is in the end moderated by Scipion's advice that they sufficiently arm themselves against hunger in order to render their retreat pleasant. This change in diet parallels Gil Blas's development from deceived to deceiver to one aware of deception but able to accept it—he has two children 'dont je *crois* religieusement être le père' (*GB*.ii.486). Gil Blas is at first victim of the strong, then one of the victors. At the conclusion he withdraws from the world of the consumer with a large enough supply of experience and nourishment for his now reasonable desires.

In concluding this section, let us examine a few favourite expressions repeated in both theatre and novel to demonstrate the remarkable similarity between the two genres. In the theatre Lesage says that a painter who lodges in a cabaret is 'comme un poisson à l'eau' (*F*.ix.451). Arlequin amorously sighs in *La Queue de la vérité* to Zaïde, 'Hélas! éloigné de vos yeux j'étais comme un maquereau hors de la mer' (*F*.iv.194). Gil Blas thinks to himself when he has found a comfortable position: 'à juger sur les apparences, tu seras dans sa maison comme le poisson dans l'eau' (*GB*.ii.99). Copies or mimics are repeatedly classed as monkeys as we note for example in *Le Diable boiteux* (*DB*.ii.262) and in *Le Traître puni* where Don Garcie says to Don André, in an enthusiastic outburst on their friendship: 'Enfin, vous êtes le singe de mes actions et je crois que si je me perçais le sein de mon épée, vous seriez tenté d'en faire autant.' Don André's valet, in an ironic aside, replies, 'Oh! pour cela non. Voilà ce que le singe ne feroit pas sur ma parole' (*T*.i.13). Don André is both too reasonable and too vicious to be a *singe*. Don Garcie, in his naïve ardour, fails to recognise the serpent behind his mask. In speaking of the Baron's advice about women, Beauchêne says, 'il me semble que le Baron est comme ce rat, lequel ayant perdu sa queue, voulait persuader aux autres animaux de son espèce que les queues ne faisaient que les embarrasser, et qu'ils devaient tous s'en délivrer' (*B*.ii.121). However, in *La Queue de la vérité* we find the same animal appendage serving a much nobler purpose in a rather ignoble, mixed metaphor: 'Ah! si tous les souverains avaient une semblable queue, ils manieraient bien le gouvernail de leur empire! Qu'ils éviteraient d'écueils avec une pareille boussole!' (*F*.iv.217). It is the equivalent of Diderot's speculation on the state of a world where all philosophers would be kings and kings philosophers. In this second example, the monkey's tail is a symbol of truth and the king did not wear it but used it in the same manner as the magic ring in *Les Bijoux indiscrets*. Another recurrent image is that of the turtle doves symbolising the happy marriage. In both theatre and novel the image is employed satirically, for, in Lesage's world, there are few virtuous people and consequently, few happy couples. In *Les Aventures de Robert Chevalier* Dame Bourdon marries a giant, devil of a woman with one eye to a mere slip of a man, a petulant tailor, because she is sure that he 'n'osera souffler devant sa femme, quand une fois il aura connu de quel bois elle chauffe'. This way she is sure they will not fight and gives her blessing to these two *tourterelles* (*B*.ii.12-13).

Prior to their violent argument over the number of years they have been married, M. and Mme Pépin ironically swear, in *Le Tableau du mariage,* that they have always lived together in peace (*F*.ii.310):

> M. PEPIN: Mme Pepin est une franche brebis.
> MME PEPIN: M. Pepin est un vrai petit mouton. Il y a trente-huit ans que nous vivons ensemble comme deux tourterelles.

In *La Pénélope moderne* Olivette swears her loving fidelity to her absent husband: 'Je veux toujours, dans ce château / Gémir en chaste tourterelle, / En attendant mon tourtereau.' The valet, Pierrot, informs us, 'Je ne suis point la dupe de cette Tourterelle-là. Je la vois un peu trop souvent prendre son vol du côté du jardin où Groscolas notre jardinier [. . .]' (*F*.vii.8).

The list of repetitions could be endless but even this brief example reaffirms the correspondence between the two genres and it signals the fact that Lesage's menagerie is both limited and domestic. The list of dramatic *personae* in the theatre and of characters in the novels does not include exotic beasts. The use of common animals to represent people brings them close to home even when they wander abroad. The same animals represent people of every class and profession making their appetites and failings universal. Lesage was obviously not seeking new and brilliant metaphors. He was attempting to be realistic and easily comprehensible. The theatre audience had to capture the essence of the character in a brief time on a single verbal cue. The animal metaphors and metonyms are for Lesage a kind of shorthand he employs to describe in one word the distinguishing traits of the character. Like the masks and costumes in the theatre, these zoological sallies provide an instantly recognisable caricature of the personage. Finally, they lead us to note that most frequently caricature is a substitute for character in Lesage's works.

The references to mankind as a menagerie of rapacious animals echoes a similar usage to be found in the works of three authors of the preceding century. On the one hand, these images are reminiscent of La Bruyère who speaks of 'des loups ravissants, des lions furieux, malicieux comme un singe' [quoted in *Les Caractères* (1956)]. Lowering man to an animal level, removing his rationality and making him prey to his passions is a typical device of the satirist. Lesage's humanity is well armed with tooth, claw and horns: 'Un cocu, Monsieur, est tout le contraire du coq. Le coq a plus d'un coq' (*F*.iii.241). However, we must agree with both Charles Lenient who states: 'les loups, les singes et les vautours tiennent une assez large place dans le monde qu'il [Lesage] nous décrit, sans leur en garder trop de rancune' [quoted in *La Comédie en France au XVIIIe siècle* (1888)], and with Lester Crocker who sums up the question in the following sentence: 'In *Gil Blas* as in *Le Diable boiteux,* Lesage portrays men and women as a compound of good and evil, animals in the main, but having truly human potentialities that are sometimes realised' [quoted in *An Age of Crisis*]. The satirist's vision is black and white, Lesage's is chequered,

more droll than bitter. He invites us to laugh with him at his characters in their motley garb, not at ourselves.

We turn thus from satire to comedy and find another forerunner of Lesage in Molière who also used these images in his theatre. For example, Philinte exclaims in *Le Misanthrope:*

> Oui, je vois ces défauts dont votre âme murmure
> Comme vices unis à l'humaine nature;
> Et mon esprit enfin n'est pas plus offensé
> De voir un homme fourbe, injuste, intéressé,
> Que de voir des vautours affamés de carnage,
> Des singes malfaisants, et des loups pleins de rage.
>
>   [quoted in *Oeuvres complètes*, 1971]

Molière is usually less cynical and simply states in *Tartuffe,* for example: 'L'homme est, je vous l'avoue, un méchant animal' [quoted in *Oeuvres complètes*]. It is nearly an understatement when the situation in which it was uttered is considered. Lesage's novels are more closely related to comedy than to satire. While satirical elements are present, the overall effect is comic. As F. C. Green has noted in his comparison of Lesage and Smollett, Lesage's observations, unlike those of Smollett, are made from a certain distance. Lesage shows us life as a comedy of errors, full of faults. He was neither an optimist nor a pessimist: he was a realist. He realised that society could not be changed. In that sense he is neither reformer nor revolutionary. When Gil Blas develops a conscience, he does not become a crusader; he withdraws from society. Although Lesage was cynical, he did admit the possibility for improving human nature by controlling (moderating) the passions. We might recall that Don Cléofas has seen all of three cases of happy love and at least one virtuous woman: 'Elle se débarrassa de ses mains, et ce qui jusqu'alors n'était arrivé à aucune fille; elle sortit de ce cabinet comme elle y était entrée' (*DB*.i.170). This sentiment is echoed in the preface to *Turcaret:*

> il y a de fort honnêtes gens dans les affaires; j'avoue qu'il n'y en a pas eu trés grand nombre, mais il y en a qui, sans écarter les principes de l'honneur et de la probité, ont fait actuellement leur chemin et dont la Robe et l'Epée ne dédaignent pas l'alliance. L'auteur respecte ceux-là. Effectivement il aurait tort de les confondre avec les autres. Enfin il y a d'honnêtes gens dans toutes les professions. Je connais même des commissaires et des greffiers qui ont de la conscience.
>
>   [quoted in Pizarro's *Lesage*]

Likewise in *Roger de Sicile* and in *La Statue merveilleuse* a virtuous, faithful woman is found (albeit after a long search). In *Le Traître puni* the exception to the rule is again applauded: 'Je sais bien qu'il y en [des femmes] a dont le coeur et la tête tournent à tout vent comme une girouette; mais il en est aussi de moins changeantes et de vertueuses' (*T*.i.8). Mercure appears on stage just before Pandore opens her famous box in *La Boîte de Pandore* and tells us that we are about to witness what may be the last example of innocent love on earth. Lesage takes care to document these exceptions.

The inhabitants of Lesage's menagerie are a mixture of caricatures of contemporary figures (Voltaire, Law, Lecouvreur) and characters from 'le monde bariolé de la Régence: traitants, gens de robe, abbés, valets, joueurs, agioteurs, Normands, Picards, robins' [quoted in Chaponnière's 'Les comédiens de moeurs du théâtre de la foire']. What is remarkable is that Molière's types such as Tartuffe, representing a vice, have been replaced by a social class represented by an occupation. Turcaret became a type, but a social type, by definition anchored in an occupational category. He is greedy and cruel but so are all of the other characters. Their passions (animal appetites) are fed by their desire for social mobility. In *Le Diable boiteux* the *intendant* dreams happily that he is getting rich while his master is ruining himself. In *Turcaret* Frontin does not dream, he acts. Few characters wish to remain in their present condition. The financier (*le cochon*) in *Les Animaux raisonnables* is an exception: 'Je veux rester cochon toute ma vie, c'est ma première vocation, [quoted in Chaponnière's 'Les comédiens de moeurs du theatre de la foire']. The more common case is given expression by Crispin who says, 'Que je suis las d'etre valet! Ah, Crispin, c'est ta faute, tu as toujours donné dans la bagatelle, tu devrais présentement briller dans la Finance. Avec l'esprit que j'ai, morbleu, j'aurais déjà fait plus d'une banqueroute' (*T*.ii.105). Even in jail Robert Chevalier struggles to be 'le coq des prisonniers' (*B*.i.129-30). In the *Théâtre forain,* Arlequin would be a *vrai petit-maître* if he had more money (the key to social mobility) (*F*.i.296). Likewise, Gil Blas, when serving a *petit-maître,* apes his airs and is told by a friend 'que pour être illustre, il ne me manquait plus que d'avoir de bonnes fortunes' (*GB*.i.238). Since this meant an affair with a lady of quality, it involved acting the part of a wealthy noble, his master. However the deceiver in this case is also deceived and his wealthy beauty turns out to be an actress (he was so occupied playing his role that he did not perceive her mask) who informs him that 'tu es en homme ce que je suis en femme' (*GB*.i.245). The society painted is extremely mobile. Not only do valets replace their masters, but in *Zermine et Almanzor,* the supposed shepherd is king while the princess turns out to be a shepherdess. In the constant struggle for upward movement, characters risk imprisonment. The images of cages, cells and caves oppose those of freedom which is expressed in terms of motion. Gil Blas travels when he is his own master. In *Le Théâtre de la foire* the trip is often the pretext to seek freedom. For example, in *Le Jeune vieillard* Arlequin is obliged to set sail to liberate himself from the spell of an enchanter. In numerous plays, and in *Le Diable-boiteux* as well, the lover is obliged to travel to foreign lands to free his mistress who was kidnapped. In both genres the protagonists voyage to free themselves of the effects of their passions (usually the morose effects of a love scorned or lost).

Since the animals are rational, strength in the contest for power and position in society is measured not only in terms of physical prowess but also of intelligence or wiliness. Characters must perceive what animal is actually their opponent. The kite may hide his talons and appear to be a dove when attempting to obtain his prey.

La Fontaine is the third seventeenth-century author with whom Lesage's vision of society as jungle is comparable. Beaumarchais's observation could be conceived of as referring to Lesage: 'Dans la fable les animaux ont de l'esprit et [. . .] dans notre comédie les hommes ne sont souvent que des bêtes, et qui pis est, des bêtes méchantes,' [quoted in *Oeuvres complètes*].

When Lesage invites Momus on stage to speak to the *Gent ratier* (*F*.v.16), the reference is overt. Similarly in *Le Diable boiteux* we see a reference to actors as the *Gent comique.* (*DB*.ii.199). Lesage obviously sees some of his illustrations as fables in prose. For example in *Gil Blas* he refers to a previously recounted tale as 'la fable du cochon' (*GB*.i.270). In scenes of flattery, the parallel with the fable of the Fox and the Crow is evident. Crispin calls M. Oronte 'le phénix des beaux pères' (*T*.ii.158). Gil Blas, prey to a flatterer, relives the fable in its entirety. The fable begins 'Maître corbeau', a title already indicating the flattery intended. The parasite in *Gil Blas* commences his address in a similar fashion: 'Seigneur écolier' (*GB*.i.40). His use of *savantissime* reflects the superlative in the fable. Gil Blas, 'la huitième merveille du monde', ['le phénix des hôtes de ces bois'] is given the same lesson by his admirer as the crow in the fable: 'Soyez désormais en garde contre les louanges' ['Tout flatteur / Vit aux dépens de celui qui l'écoute']. However, unlike the crow who 'Jura, mais un peu tard, qu'on ne l'y prendrait plus', Lesage's hero pays the bill for his dinner 'dont j'avais fait si désagréablement la digestion' and continues on his way 'en donnant à tous les diables le parasite, l'hôte et l'hôtellerie' (*GB*.i.44). Unfortunately, Gil Blas does not learn his lesson that easily. He repeatedly falls victim to the same trap, learns to use the art of flattery himself, and finally recognises the dangers of playing the role of either the fox or the crow. While Lesage does not appear to attempt to preach the moral of the fable, he does not forget its existence. The continual reference to the animal world recalls the world of the fable. If Lesage is not a moralist, the world he describes is not a world without moral. Lesage read La Fontaine's *contes* as well as his fables. We note that entire plays like *La Matrone d'Ephèse* and *Les Trois commères* rely on La Fontaine for inspiration. His interest in the comic vision far outweighed his concern for moral predication.

A trait which Lesage shares with all three seventeenth-century authors is his portrayal of professional characters. While Dédéyan supposes Sangrado to be inspired by Molière, Green thinks that he is considerably modified by the influence of the Regency. The images of doctor, *fausse-dévote*, Tartuffe, lawyer, and author are common to all four authors. The variations are slight. However, it should be noted that Lesage's Sangrado also has his parallel in the theatre. For example, M. Trousse-Galant who appears in both *L'Obstacle favorable* and in *La Tontine,* expresses the same faith in bleeding and purging as Sangrado. M.

Galbanon in **Les Enragés** demonstrates a similar confidence in the marvellous qualities of water. All lose cases in strikingly similar circumstances. All are unreasonably stubborn in following their precepts despite the disastrous results. The obvious ridicule of a M. Trousse-Galant, diagnosing the malady of a young man as pregnancy, demonstrates the satire to which this profession is exposed through these caricatures. Examples of the similar attitudes of these characters may be easily found:

> *Sangrado*: Gil Blas, under the influence of this doctor, says, 'Le désagrément que j'avais eu chez l'épicier ne m'emêpcha pas d'ordonner dès le lendemain, des saignées et de l'eau chaude.'
>
> (***GB***.i.149)

> *La Tontine*: The apothecary says to the doctor: 'Je n'ai pas bonne opinion de cette tisane rafraîchissante que vous me faites faire pour les Pleurétiques.' The Doctor replies: 'Effectivement, en voilà douze qu'elle emporte, sans compter M. Bonnegriffe [. . .] Un bon médecin va toujours son train sans se rendre à des épreuves qui blessent des principes établis et reçus dans l'Ecole.'
>
> (***T***.i.359)

> *L'Obstacle favorable*: When informed that 'M. le Bailli empire à vûë d'oeil, depis la chienne de drogue qu'ous li avez fait prendre [it is the servant who speaks] (***F***.vi.281), the doctor increases the dosage.

The main characters have more in common than their travels and appetites. Both are comic heroes. For example, Crispin refuses to fight just as did Gil Blas. They are both cowards. Crispin says to his opponent: 'Me prenez-vous pour un Cid?' and accepts whatever insults his opponent wishes to offer him (***T***.i.323). Similarly Gil Blas reveals that 'je me sentis tout à coup siasir, comme un héros d'Homère, d'un mouvement de crainte qui m'arrêta. Je demeurai aussi troublé que Pâris, quand il se présenta pour combattre Ménélas' (***GB***.ii.13). He replaces his sword and decides to talk rather than fight. Here, the reference to great heroes in both cases makes the protagonist smaller and more humble.

The portraits of actors are again similar. The actresses possess the universal talent of pleasing men in public and ruining them in private. Their mores are questionable and their relationship to authors remains far from satisfactory. In novels and plays the opinion expressed about curés is the same. However, the references to them in the theatre are all indirect. There is not one who actually appears on stage. Other characters speak of them. In **Crispin, rival de son maître,** for example, Crispin has a letter in his pocket which was addressed to 'M. Gourmandin, Chanoine' (***T***.ii.13). This reminds us of the Chanoine Sedillo who left Gil Blas two books: a cookbook and a treatise on indigestion (***GB***.i.136). All priests like good food in copious quantities, in Lesage's universe. Like professions some nationalities have a specific character. Germans (***DB***.i.23) become Swiss on stage. They are drunkards, described in a word by their appetites for liquid nourish-

ment.

Lesage paints a picture of the society of his day. It is no wonder that the characters in both genres which describe the same world would be similar. The characters exercise the same professions; their motivation is universal and their unscrupulous means of obtaining their ends are common coin.

The plays and the novels are further related by similarity in situation and incident. In both, disguises (male as female, female as male), serenades under balconies, kidnappings abound. The plot of **La Princesse de Chine** is the same as that of the story of the Prince Farrukrouz and Princesse Farrukhnaz (the hero becomes deranged on viewing the princess). The plot of **Les Mariages de Canada** recalls the intercalated tale in **Les Aventures de Robert Chevalier** in which those who arrive in Québec have marriages arranged for them by a lady who distributes her stock of 'merchandise' (women) according to her whim.

Similar situations arise too frequently to take note of them all. However, in **Le Diable boiteux** we observe a youth who is described as follows: 'C'est un nouveau marié. Il

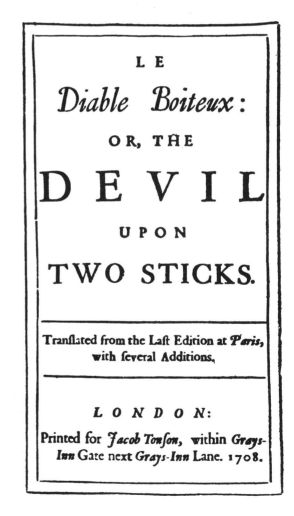

LE

Diable Boiteux :

OR, THE

DEVIL

UPON

TWO STICKS.

Tranflated from the Laft Edition at *Paris*, with feveral Additions,

LONDON:

Printed for *Jacob Tonfon*, within *Grays-Inn* Gate next *Grays-Inn* Lane. 1708.

Title page of the first English translation of The Devil upon Two Sticks.

y a huit jours que sur le rapport qu'on lui fit des coquetteries d'une aventurière qu'il aimait, il alla chez elle plein de fureur, brisa une partie de ses meubles, jeta les autres par les fenêtres, et le lendemain il l'épousa' (*DB*.i.299). This certainly recalls Turcaret who goes to great expense to redeem himself for his fit of anger during which he broke the Baronne's dishes because he believed Marine's report. *Le Traître puni* features two friends as rivals as in *Le Diable boiteux*. In the same play we see a scene involving a nocturnal entrance into the bedchamber of a sleeping damsel which is similar to that in *Gil Blas* (*GB*.i.382). The woman ruining the rich financier to enrich a young lover is repeated in *Le Diable boiteux, Turcaret, Gil Blas* and the *Aventures de Robert Chevalier*. The noble who becomes jealous of a citizen who appears richer than he is common to *Achmet et Almanzine,* the *Contes persans* and *Gil Blas*. The liberated captive who returns to discover some changes in his domestic situation is found both in *Le Diable boiteux* and *La Pénélope moderne*. The presence of so many similar and repeated incidents and characters may stem from the fact that Lesage often used the same sources for his inspiration in both the theatre and the novel.

The transfer of Lesage's dramatic style to his novels has often been noted. Green signals the absence of many descriptive or digressive passages and the preponderance of verbs—'doing words' [quoted in *Minuet*]. Dédéyan remarks: 'Enlevons les dit-il, les répond-il, les j'expliquai, les je répondis, et nous aurons constamment dans Gil Blas de remarquables monologues ou dialogues de théâtre' [quoted in *Lesage et Gil Blas*]. As the theatre presents a rapid succession of portraits in review, so in the novel do we find the same technique. An example is the series of portraits sketched at the home of the Marquise de Chanves. In both genres, they are satiric and rely on the exaggeration of a single trait, often an animal appetite, to achieve their effect in a swift movement.

This brief survey tends to bear out the initial premise that the theatre shares a great number of similarities with the novels. The question which remains is, does the theatre shed any further light on the novels? Is it a key to understanding their meaning and composition?

On the level of composition, a reading of the theatre brings out in a more striking fashion the dramatic nature of the novels. The technique of the author who speaks in *Le Diable boiteux* recalls the stage director and the dramatist conscious of the requirements of his audience. Lesage sets the stage rapidly and focuses on the dialogue. Portraits are painted through dialogue or action and the action in the novel repeats that of the theatre. The slapstick chamberpot which lands on Gil Blas's head is reminiscent of that worn by Arlequin in *Arlequin, roi de Serendib*. Gil Blas's stealthy and comic exit from the home of Dona Mergelina, for example, reads like a scenario for a stage presentation. The juxtaposition of gross appetites and literary and mythological metaphors creates humour in both genres. The animality of man is rendered in each case by simile and a sustained metonymical system. The use of proverb and fable renders the works more familiar and personal.

On the level of ideas, the theatre does offer, in a sense, a key to the novel. The key lies in the preponderance of references to man as a voracious animal. He is seen as a rational animal prey to appetites of lust, interest and vanity. Carried away by these, he loses his capacity to reason and vies for power, money and social status like an animal without a conscience. Lester Crocker says correctly that the majority of the inhabitants of the world of Lesage bear out Hobbes's phrase: *homo homini lupus*. However, happiness lies in overcoming the passions and living under the discipline of virtue. For Lesage this discipline is attained in a state of voluptuous repose like that advocated by the proponents of *la philosophie naturelle*. It is the median between indifference (boredom) and passion. It lies in moderation which brings physical health and spiritual tranquillity. Pleasure is good while ambition for glory and money are rejected. The reduction of man's mental processes to elements of simple sensations reflects the philosophy of Hume. However, Lesage separates reason and passion. In his view, man must satisfy the physical desires. Gil Blas is neither a hermit nor an ascetic. The pleasures of the table and his chosen society allow him to exist in a state of repose and control his passions. Thus we see that while Lesage does reduce man to an animal, he also retains the possibility of man's transcending this nature. Like La Fontaine, he saw man engaged in a power struggle in which the strongest would rule. Both authors, nonetheless, retained an ideal. They each saw true friendship, true love and noble, faithful sentiments as a possibility. They retained an essentially comic vision of the world. If La Fontaine saw his fables as an 'ample comédie à cent actes divers', the same could be said of Lesage's novels. La Fontaine was criticised by eighteenth-century fabulists for placing the value of amusement before that of instruction. La Motte even speculated that the fabulist had gotten so carried away with the joy of narration that he neglected the moral. La Fontaine, he suggested, wrote the fable and later attempted to find a moral to suit it. Lesage's compositions might follow a similar pattern. At times the author seems to be so intrigued with his adventure story that he neglects to stop for reflection. Like his heroes whose peregrinations lead them across vast and often imaginary spaces, the author becomes occupied with providing food and lodging, necessary to sustain them. Yet the moral of moderation (virtue) is visible throughout the several volumes of *Gil Blas* and in the individual plays in microcosm. Two patterns repeat themselves with only slight variations. Arlequin finds himself in the lap of luxury, his life is subsequently imperilled, and finally he accepts an intermediate, reasonable level at which to find happiness. The second pattern involves a true lover, separated from his mistress by a series of obstacles which, once overcome, will allow them to live happily. The two patterns in the theatre reflect the two poles of Lesage's writing: realism and a kind of romantic escapism. Like the fairy tales then in vogue, Lesage's works blend fantasy and reality producing a release for the reader/spectator which allows him to view the real world from a new perspective and appreciate the satirical elements inherent in the works. Within the pattern, the encounter of a bumbling and lusty Pierrot and the omniscient enchanter, Merlin, carries on the clash of opposites, providing dramatic tension. The reader is at once invited to enter a fantasy world and to return to a supremely real world where man's faults are magnified. The effect is like looking through a pair of bifocals or through both ends of the telescope at once. Lesage continues the use of contrast in juxtaposing utopia and reality. In *Le Monde renversé* every aspect of the perfect society is juxtaposed with its counterpart in the real world. The same technique is used in the *Aventures de Robert Chevalier* where the ideal society is created by the Indians and is contrasted to a very satirical vision of European civilisation. The juxtaposition of contrasting elements and ideas: domination/submission, male/female, freedom/incarceration, vice/virtue, deceit/disclosure, illusion/reality are typical of Lesage's Spanish predecessors in the picaresque novel. They are also effective tools for satire. Man is caught between these poles. When he gives in to his appetites, he becomes consumed by them and is their victim. He is like the young girl in *Les Routes du Monde*. She must choose her path in life: *le chemin de la vertu* (a rocky path), *le chemin de la fortune,* or *le chemin de la volupté.* She is completely free to make the decision by herself, just as Pandore in *La Boîte de Pandore* is at complete liberty to open the box or to leave it closed. In both cases the temptations are stronger than the influence of the parents. Indeed, they are so inviting that it would be the rare human who could resist. However, once the step is taken, it is difficult to return to the path of virtue. Once initial innocence is lost, it can never be recaptured. However, serenity can be found as we see with Gil Blas in his second marriage and with Mezzetin in *Les Mariages de Canada*. Mezzetin is accorded his first wife in a second marriage and left to learn love: 'Dans un dé ert, où la Nature ne fournirait pour nourriture / Que de l'eau claire et du pain, / Un amant avec sa Maîtresse / Oublierait le genre humain. / Contentement passe richesse' (*F*.ix.360). This idea is frequently repeated. Love and friendship are pure emotions and do not require the excessive alimentation necessitated by passions which lead men to lose their rationality and become carnivores without conscience.

The separation between rationality and animality is pointed out in *Le Diable boiteux* where we learn that 'c'est vers la pointe du jour que les songes sont plus vrais, parce que dans ce temps-là l'âme est dégagée des vapeurs des aliments' (*DB*.i.185). We see Gil Blas looking for pure, simple nourishment. This reflects his desire to remove himself from the temptations of society which he has begun to recognise as the false road to happiness. Yet, separating himself from this way of life does not necessarily lead man to happiness. He can be haunted, like the comte-duc d'Olivarès. When the passions have been fed beyond a certain extent, they in turn devour man. Gil Blas is never corrupted so thoroughly that he cannot return to virtue and honesty. He is proud of the

fact (*GB*, ii.9):

> Je pouvais faire ce coup [voler de l'argent] impunément, je n'avais qu'à voyager cinq ou six jours, et m'em retourner ensuite comme si je me fusse acquitté de ma commission. Don Alphonse et son père n'auraient pas soupçonné ma fidélité. Je ne succombai pourtant point à la tentation; je puis même dire que je la surmontai en garcon d'honneur. Ce qui n'était pas peu louable dans un jeune homme qui avait fréquenté de grands fripons.

The iron grip of habit, the power of vice, is evidenced as well in *Crispin, rival de son maître* where Crispin and La Branche fall on their knees to implore their masters' leniency and compassion. 'Franchement la dot nous a tentés. Nous sommes accoûtumés à faire des fourberies, pardonnez-nous celle-ci à cause de l'habitude' (*T,*ii. 189). The guilty parties are rewarded with wives and a fortune. Like the ridiculous Venus in disguise, Mme Turcaret, the vicious are rendered foolish but they are not overly punished. The audience is invited to forget Turcaret's problems with the law and to laugh with the marquis: 'Ah, ma foi, chevalier, tu me fais rire, ta consternation me divertit, allons souper chez le traiteur, et passer la nuit à boire' (*T*.ii.374). A certain distance is always maintained. The spectator is ever to laugh at the foibles of the stage personalities. The finger of condemnation is never pointed specifically at the spectator. In this respect Lesage is like La Fontaine. Neither accuses his reader of having the faults criticised. Like La Fontaine, if La Motte's accusation has even an element of truth, Lesage is more conscious of entertaining than educating. Gil Blas is not a *Bildungsroman* and there is no development in character throughout the many volumes of the theatre. Arlequin and Gil Blas may learn to modify their behaviour but they remain human animals. The only difference between them is that, with each play, Arlequin begins with a clean slate. Gil Blas, on the other hand, retains the lessons of his experiences (albeit often ill learned) from one chapter to the next. Virtue is a discipline, like regulating one's diet. It is a difficult task to accomplish when one is a hungry animal in a world of tempting dishes. In both theatre and novel when the hero strays from the path of virtue and is caught with his face besmeared with cream, we laugh with Lesage.

If the theatre is a key to the ideas contained in the novels, it is perhaps first of all because it reminds us that Lesage's vision is essentially comic. The key is universal and it unlocks a stage door which carefully distinguishes the space between spectator and scene. In both genres the structure is linear and the social movement is vertical (the rise of Frontin and the fall of Turcaret). The plot patterns, situations, characters and even bits of dialogue found repeated in both genres give emphasis to the theme of man as beast whose appetites, sex and interest, cause him to vie for a position of dominance in a society which values power, money and sexual gratification. In turn man is prey to his bestial passions. If he succeeds in dominating them, he will be rewarded with repose and happiness and the feat will undoubtedly be recorded in Asmodée's memory.

George Evans (essay date 1987)

SOURCE: "Impact," in *Crispin rival de son maître and Turcaret,* Grant & Cutler Ltd., 1987, pp. 76-84.

[*In the following essay, Evans explores the comic impacts of* Crispin, Rival of His Master, *and* Turcaret, *finding the former primarily a farcical piece, and the latter an ironic social commentary.*]

If in previous chapters we may have seemed to stress similarities of method in ***Crispin rival de son maître*** and ***Turcaret,*** this should not lead us to forget that even plays using broadly similar structures and techniques can have quite different overall impacts. In general terms, the nature of the comic impact will initially depend on whether the laughter is felt to be more or less an end in itself or whether it is harnessed to other purposes, whether we simply delight in watching the comic sparks fly or whether, as in satire, we are called upon through the laughter to make a judgement of sorts on what we are shown. Our reaction to the classic comic incident involving someone slipping on a banana skin will depend on who falls, in what circumstances the fall takes place and whether the result is bruised buttocks and hurt dignity or a broken spine and total paralysis. In other words, the nature of the comic impact will depend on the nature of the characters involved and on the context, consequences and outcome of the comic action.

In ***Crispin rival de son maître*** there are some lines which assume the character of social satirical sallies of a rather general kind. This is the case when Crispin says to himself, 'Ah, Crispin . . . tu devrais présentement briller dans la finance. Avec l'esprit que j'ai, morbleu, j'aurais déjà fait plus d'une banqueroute' (2,1-5), when La Branche says of Damis, 'S'il est sage, Madame! Il a été élevé avec la plus brillante jeunesse de Paris' (8,18-19), or when he comments on Orgon's lawsuit with the remark that 'la justice est une si belle chose qu'on ne saurait trop l'acheter' (10,20-21). Such lines, which are fairly rare, are nevertheless for the most part incidental, and any attempt to give social satirical force to the play as a whole is certainly to distort its effect. ***Crispin rival de son maître*** is a relatively unalloyed comic piece, a version of farce even if the comic agilities are more intellectual than physical, more verbal than knockabout. This appears to have been the view of the contemporary audience, if we accept the (not always reliable) evidence provided by the Frères Parfaict's commentary on the play's reception in their *Histoire du Théâtre Francais*: 'la comédie de ***Crispin rival*** fut regardée comme une farce . . . ***Crispin rival*** ne présente qu'un petit évé ement, et qui ne peut intéresser que par la force du comique, qui règne dans cette pièce du commencement à la fin.' But its particular character can be judged if it is compared with another, more recent description of one of the fundamental forms taken by farce: 'The simplest kind of farce requires little more than a suitable victim, a practical joker and a good idea for a prank . . . one clown says to another, "Let's do the old man" or "Let's do the old man again" and the farce moves forward. At this level, farce is very little removed from

ordinary circus clowning . . . without any particular purpose being served by his (i.e. the victim's) humiliation.'

Of course, Crispin and La Branche are more than mere pranksters, even if the former does have a bright idea and the latter's willingness to get involved stems in part from a kind of aesthetic appreciation of the 'beau coup à faire'. They are more *pícaros* than practical jokers; they hope to get more than fun out of their trickery. And yet they do not represent any real threat or danger to the social fabric. The title of the play may be arresting; in genuine social terms its content is a good deal less daring. The two rogues, we might remember, have only re-entered service because they have come to grief in their criminal ventures, and Crispin's real complaint—one not shared by La Branche, notice—is that he happens to be serving a master whose lack of funds prevents him from enjoying the style of life to which he (and, no doubt, his master also) would like to become accustomed. So, in their scheming, these servants seek merely to profit, not to usurp. If they had succeeded in obtaining some ill-gotten gains from their schemes, they would have been content to skip the country, and they are more than happy when a 'legitimate' outlet can be found to satisfy their ambitions. There is nothing subversive in any of this.

Furthermore, neither the rogues' self-seeking nor the victim's potential loss have the stature and substance to warrant the kind of highly aggressive treatment which sets out to provoke outrage or indignation. The stakes are neither high enough nor made real enough for that. Combined with this is the fact that the outcome of the play is not disaster and the humiliation of persons, but an ironic happy ending which depends on the schemers' integration into society being viewed with wry worldly amusement, and certainly not with real concern or bitterness. Such an ending is merely the splendid, theatrically appropriate final twist given to this self-contained comic tale: it *exploits* the generally accepted view of the world of finance without constituting any serious or significant comment. For Lesage and his audience, if not for the rogues, fun is the major objective in ***Crispin rival de son maître***.

If ***Crispin rival de son maître*** has been widely appreciated for the deftness of its comic structure and the slickness and humour of its dialogue, the range of critical opinion regarding the impact of ***Turcaret*** is broader and more varied, as the review of reactions given in Lawrenson's edition reveals. Opinions differ as to the overall character of the play and to the relative emphasis to be placed on the non-satiric and the satiric aspects. There is also disagreement about the scope and the tone of the satire. More recent descriptions of the play have tended, rightly in my view, to highlight the more frankly entertaining aspects, that is, the wit and irony of the dialogue, the essentially comic nature of the characterisation and the structural fun provided by the action. Nevertheless, many critics would still wish to stress the boldness and bitterness of Lesage's attack on the financier, or to point to the absence of sympathetic characters—a feature of the play which has clearly disturbed a lot of people from the period of its first performances onwards—in order to underline the somewhat grim, even pessimistic view of social life which, it is claimed, underpins the play and gives it a rather unattractive atmosphere.

There can be no doubting the particular pointedness of *Turcaret* in its own day. The play's power to offend financial circles has been cited as the cause of the difficulties Lesage had getting it performed and, if we are to believe the *Critique,* led to the presence of cabals at its first performances. No wonder then that the author felt obliged to defend his play against charges that it discredited all financiers. The arguments he used to do so are deliberately related to what Lesage clearly regarded as the respectable and successful precedent set by Molière when he was called upon to defend one of his 'dangerous' plays, *Le Tartuffe:*

> ASMODEE. . . . c'est aujourd'hui la première représentation d'une comédie où l'on joue un homme d'affaires. Le public aime à rire aux dépens de ceux qui le font pleurer.
>
> DON CLEOFAS. C'est-à-dire que les gens d'affaires sont tous des . . .
>
> ASMODEE. C'est ce qui vous trompe; il y a de fort honnêtes gens dans les affaires; j'avoue qu'il n'y en a pas un très grand nombre; mais il y en a qui, sans s'écarter des principes de l'honneur et de la probité, ont fait ou font actuellement leur chemin, et dont la Robe et l'Epée ne dédaignent pas l'alliance. L'Auteur respecte ceux-là. Effectivement il aurait tort de les confondre avec les autres. Je connais même des commissaires et des greffiers qui ont de la conscience.
>
> DON CLEOFAS. Sur ce pied-là, cette comédie n'offense point les honnêtes gens qui sont dans les affaires.
>
> ASMODEE. Comme *Le Tartufe* [sic] que vous avez lu, n'offense point les vrais dévots. Eh! pourquoi les gens d'affaires s'offenseraient-ils de voir sur la scène un sot, un fripon de leur corps? Cela ne tombe pas sur le général. Ils seraient donc plus délicats que les courtisans et les gens de robes, qui voient tous les jours avec plaisir représenter des marquis fats et des juges ignorants et corruptibles. (29-51)

In such a defence, depending as it does on claiming that only the offensive could feel offended, there is, to be sure, a healthy measure of the tongue-in-cheek, as is shown by the ironic touches (e.g. 'j'avoue qu'il n'y en a pas un très grand nombre', je connais même des commissaires et des greffiers qui ont de la conscience'). It was no doubt true that financiers were in reality as mixed a bunch as the merchants, who, as Niklaus has shown, would in a few decades' time become mythologised as figures embodying all the finest qualities of the 'enlightened' hero. Nevertheless, the vulgar, the crooked and the heartless had sufficient reality to make them serious targets, especially in times of economic hardship, even if one might

suspect that Lesage's initial conception did not owe too much to the spirit of daring originality and downright denunciation.

Be that as it may, *Turcaret* does, of course, involve the exposure and downfall of a financier; for him the outcome is but the culmination of the whole series of humiliations and embarrassing revelations to which he is subjected throughout the play, and there is for him a real disaster to cap it all. Moreover, unlike Crispin and La Branche, Turcaret is a worthy subject for such an attack because he has no redeeming features and, more important, he has the power to affect people's lives for good or ill. His wealth gives him an authority and influence which are respected even by those who otherwise despise him: he remains *Monsieur* Turcaret until the end. Although we do not see anyone suffering at his hands on stage, we learn enough about his treatment of others not to treat him as an inconsequential figure. He is indeed knavish enough to warrant being made a fool of. But because the principal methods used against him by Lesage are ridicule and discomfiture, it is natural that Turcaret is made to appear more emphatically a fool than a knave in his behaviour. Indeed, . . . the attack is carried out by giving Turcaret a number of those general characteristics (vanity, self-importance, pretentiousness, gullibility, etc.) which comic characters often have. Yet a number of critics have been unhappy with what they see as an unsatisfactory contradiction between his success as a financier and his obvious foolishness. While this criticism is perhaps based on rather dubious 'realistic' grounds, it must also be said that within the play Turcaret himself admits, not without a touch of typical boastfulness, that, in financial circles,

> un bel esprit n'est pas nécessaire pour faire son chemin. Hors moi et deux ou trois autres, il n'y a parmi nous que des génies assez communs. Il suffit d'un certain usage, d'une routine que l'on ne manque guère d'attraper. Nous voyons tant de gens! Nous nous étudions à prendre ce que le monde a de meilleur; voilà toute notre science.
>
> (II,4,29-35)

Moreover, it is very much part and parcel of the irony involved in the attack that the failings and limitations of his own character should help to ensure his disgrace. As we are constantly reminded during the course of the play, his use of power and influence is strictly related to his own personal needs and desires, that is, to his need to appear to be what he is not (well-bred, cultured, tasteful, perceptive, etc.), but most especially to satisfying his sexual desires. As Flamand reveals to the Baronne,

> le commis que l'on révoque aujourd'hui pour me mettre à sa place, a eu cet emploi-là par le moyen d'une certaine dame que M. Turcaret a aimée et qu'il n'aime plus.
>
> (V,3,42-45)

Rather than the emphasis being put on the grim unpleasantness of such self-centredness, this is shown to be the source of the character's foolishness, as his own sister points out,

> c'est un vieux fou qui a toujours aimé toutes les femmes, hors la sienne. Il jette tout par les fenêtres dès qu'il est amoureux: c'est un panier percé . . . il a toujours quelque demoiselle qui le plume, qui l'attrape.

(IV,10,95-102)

This kind of concentration on the inherent comedy of Turcaret's character clearly focuses the attack on the personal nature of the corruption and abuse. There is no radical political edge to it. Even if some of the social consequences of the economic system in force in the France of the day (including an impoverished nobility and a good deal of social mobility due to the importance given to money) are present as part of the general atmosphere of the play, the targets are not tax-farming as such, or the wider economic system which could allow such a figure as Turcaret to prosper. It is for this reason, indeed, that *Turcaret* is not so tied to contemporary issues that it remains fixed in its own time. Turcaret's foolishness and its consequences survive and retain their comic form as does the whole pattern of the action in which the satirical elements are integrated.

For it would be wrong to reduce the whole play to being an attack on Turcaret alone. It if were, his downfall alone would be enough to complete the pattern. But his exposure is largely conducted by people whose own behaviour does not leave them immune from attack or, like Madame Turcaret, are his match when it comes to foolishness. The other principal characters may show some degree of intelligence and certain verbal skills lacking in Turcaret, but they too are (comically) hampered by their own passions and over-confidence. Indeed, they form with Turcaret a continuous chain of intertwined knavery and foolishness, thereby giving the play its particular consistency. This is also helped by the concentrated setting admitting no intrusions from, or excursions to, a wider outside world. There are no truly innocent victims in *Turcaret,* but neither are there completely unblinkered rogues. All the characters inhabit the same comic world where lack of total awareness and a greater or lesser degree of credulity lightens the unpleasantness. Here too the structure and outcome of the play are informative. As we saw, characters other than Turcaret are exposed and their purposes frustrated, even if the collapse of their schemes does not take the conclusive form that Turcaret's downfall does. The complete failure of the Baronne and the Chevalier depends not only on Turcaret's fate, but upon Frontin's seeming success. But by getting the money and seeing himself as a replacement for Turcaret, Frontin hints at a continuity, even a recurrent cycle of events, with all that that implies for his future in turn.

It is for such reasons also that it would be unwise to jump too readily to the conclusion that the absence of 'good' characters reflected a pessimistic view of life or even a cynical acceptance of the way of the world. Although the ending of the play may not point to any major correction of the world which is represented, it does not mean that the writer endorses, or even tolerates, the rogues' view

which dominates the action. It is not Frontin who has the last laugh, it is Lesage, if we respect the final irony. And if Frontin believes that cheating and being cheated adds up to a complete picture of 'le train de la vie humaine' and that you can only 'beat them by joining them', we do not have to share that opinion. Indeed, only those who do not share it can appreciate the full ridiculousness of a world based on such views. Here again, the absence of moral characters within the play does not mean the absence of values and countervailing assumptions about the necessary basis of true social behaviour. If the cynical viewpoint is the one which underlies the conduct of the characters, the writer nevertheless relies on the audience being aware of other values and assumptions. Even if they have no clear spokesman or spokeswoman in the play, these values and assumptions are indirectly, and sometimes comically, alluded to. For instance, in her complaints about her brother's fraternal and marital behaviour, Madame Jacob refers us to a quite different emotional world of human relationships. Indeed, Turcaret's callousness can only be properly registered by the implied allusion to other, opposite qualities.

However, it is perhaps the Marquis who, in his own frivolous way, is the most interesting figure in this context. He has a certain attractiveness which the others do not have. This is in part due to the fact that he does not stand to benefit from the financier's ruin, in part from the detached amusement with which he seems to view himself and others. To this extent he offers a standpoint from which to judge the other characters. Of course, the detachment is still only partial in his case. His cruel treatment of the Turcarets, for example, is clearly inspired by a need to avenge himself. Nevertheless, when, in a parody of the strong-willed hero of Corneille's tragedies, he encourages the Chevalier to give up all claims on Madame Turcaret by commenting that 'il est beau de se vaincre soi-même' (V,11,15), he unwittingly points to what is indeed the only real possibility of salvation or reform for all the characters in this grasping, hedonistic world.

What leads the characters to 'defeat themselves' in the comic sense is the fact that they cannot overcome their own desires. Their failure to do so is the source of both their perversity and their absurdity. In *Turcaret* we are shown how self-centred materialism and pleasure-seeking lead people to prey upon one another and turn them into victims of each other. In such a world 'fourberies' will inevitably ricochet. Abusers attract abusers, and thus viciousness becomes a sort of self-defeating folly. It is a farcical form of social life which has no true social relationships, no social cement. It is the ironic concentration on the ludicrous consequences of such an unstable world which prevents the excesses of selfishness and hedonism from being merely disgusting or dispiriting.

This is not to claim that in *Turcaret* Lesage is necessarily saying that the whole of his contemporary society is like that, or that the play's value lies in its 'presentation of a vast and corrupt society': the range of characters and the scope of their activities would seem to be rather too narrow for that. What the play does show, in its unmoralistic way, is that if and when social behaviour follows such lines, it becomes ridiculous. This comic insight will remind us that the play is informed by a set of humane values, based partly on the classical virtue of lucidity, about oneself and others, of which irony is the natural expression, partly on the bourgeois certainty of the need for selflessness in private relationships and probity in public ones. If these values remain outside the world represented in *Turcaret,* their absence highlights the unsavoury follies which result. In the end, this is what takes *Turcaret* beyond the entertainment of *Crispin rival de son maître* and beyond dated topical attacks on tax-farmers and a section of early eighteenth-century society, so that it becomes an ironic comedy about social life which can still speak to us.

Walter E. Rex (essay date 1987)

SOURCE: "Crispin's Inventions," in *The Attraction of the Contrary: Essays on the Literature of the French Enlightenment,* Cambridge University Press, 1987, pp. 73-82.

[*In the following essay, Rex investigates the role of vraisemblance—or the appearance of truth—in* Crispin, Rival of His Master, *proposing that "the whole text is a forgery to make us believe in ersatz imitations."*]

Even before Hegel had given the theme such a grandiose philosophical setting in his *Phenomenology,* numerous individuals in the late eighteenth and early nineteenth centuries had been aware of the special importance of the master-slave (valet) relationship for the literature of Enlightenment, and today it has become a commonplace of theatrical criticism to cite the developing drama one observes in the social oppositions, as one goes from Molière to Beaumarchais, that is, from the fascinating complexities in the tensions between master and valet as depicted by the greatest writer of the seventeenth century, to the end of the trail, which is the revolutionary impudence that explodes in *Le Mariage de Figaro* (1784). Unfortunately for literary historians, however, in between these poles the course is anything but steady, and "progress" toward the emancipation of the valet at the master's expense is anything but regular. In Marivaux there is positive backsliding, while the author dallies and toys with the possibility of raising the valets out of their menial positions, only to lock them finally into a social machinery whose functioning assumes they will be content to stay in their place as inferiors. In a playwright such as Le Sage we find a different sort of muddying of the waters: this author, fully aware of the social potentialities of the situations he creates, nevertheless appears to be taking perverse enjoyment in deliberately refusing to let his master-valet relationship produce the kind of contrary tension these elements would develop later—despite a grandly deceptive hint in the title that they would do just that. To be sure, with this clever and calculating author one must ever be on one's guard against being taken in. But before entering into the details of the matter, the discussion must move just a bit further upstream.

Playwrights seeking to subvert or enliven life's banalities in eighteenth-century France could draw on a whole battery of clown characters for their comedies—most of them Italian, and deriving specifically from the *commedia dell'arte* traditions. But two very famous clowns were French: Pierrot, who was so popular he has survived until today, albeit now endowed with romantic traits he did not originally possess. And then, Crispin, who originated in the seventeenth century, maintained a respectable following in the eighteenth, and is still remembered, chiefly because Alain René Le Sage immortalized him in one of his most accomplished creations at the Comédie Française (before his famous move to the *foire*): *Crispin rival de son maître.* This play, staged while Louis XIV was still alive (1707), is an amazingly bold work of social criticism, as scholars have already noted. In terms of theatricality it is also extraordinarily interesting, as I hope to suggest.

What a sordid plot! Valère, the handsome, young, aristocratic suitor, is apparently motivated solely by money as he goes after the rich man's daughter, Angélique. At least this is what his valet, Crispin, says to him, and he doesn't protest in the slightest. For the rest, hounded by his creditors, Valère has already resorted to the most tawdry devices to get cash: using a wealthy Marquise's affection (lust?) for him to pay an alleged debt to his tailor, when actually he and the tailor are in league to bilk her for all they can; dishonest manoeuvers to borrow money against dubious collateral. . . . Morally, he is no better than his own quite unscrupulous valet, so that it is hard to feel indignant when we find Crispin scheming with another servant-friend, La Branche, to betray Valère, and get rich themselves.

At this point the plot gets a little complicated, by modern standards. No doubt we should have been raised on the knotty tangles of the pretenders to the Spanish throne, *c.* 1701, as Le Sage's generation had been, or, at least, have spent our childhoods watching the fantastic complications of the comedies at the *foire.* To enjoy Le Sage's play, one has to be ready to swallow anything, and fortunately, as the play proceeds, the impudent buoyancy of the author's style lifts us effortlessly over all the plot involvements.

Thus far we have encountered only one pair of lovers: aristocratic, debt-ridden Valère, and rich, bourgeois Angélique; meanwhile the two valets, Crispin and La Branche, are busily scheming to get the money for themselves. Actually, they intend to capitalize on a situation so perfectly suited to their talent for creative improvisations one would think fate had deliberately placed it in their path: Angélique has had another suitor, in fact a fiancé, named Damis, who lived in Chartres. This pair had been as good as married: contracts had been drawn up; all that remained was the paying of the dowry. But then, suddenly, the fiancé reneged: Damis found himself forced into a shot-gun wedding with a noble lady from Chartres whom he had gotten pregnant (an occurrence that is repeatedly brought to our attention during the course of the comedy). In fact, La Branche had been sent from Chartres to bring the urgent message that the wedding with Damis had been called off because the groom was already married to someone else. The contracts were to be annulled, and the obviously large dowry would not be coming out of the coffers.

This was what set Crispin's fertile imagination to work: suppose he, Crispin, were to impersonate the erstwhile fiancé and pretend he had just arrived from Chartres to marry Angélique? The wedding was scheduled for that very day; La Branche even had the groom's wedding attire with him. It was merely a question of putting on the clothes and getting through the few hours before the dowry was counted out, at which point he (perhaps accompanied by his accomplice, though this is not so sure) would slip out of town and head for the border.

It is clear that this extravagant scheme—in the play's own terms—could never have succeeded, and Crispin's clownish make-up and costume constantly showing through the groom's clothing are reminders of the fact that the impersonation can't work. Obviously, Valère will recognize Crispin and tell everyone that he is not Damis; furthermore, Valère is a close friend of Damis who had informed him by letter of his marriage to the other girl in Chartres; besides, Damis' father is about to arrive in town to convey the news of the annulment in person; we note too, that Angélique didn't even want to marry the real Damis (whom she had never seen), and her objections are likely to grow far stronger when confronted with this vulgar clown who spends most of his time flirting with her mother. In addition . . . But why go on? The humor and dramatic interest of the comedy lie in watching the doomed, but sometimes inspired, efforts of the two valets to stave off the mountainous evidence pressing more and more weightily on the fragile surface of their unlikely bubble that by all the laws of reason should have popped long ago and exposed them for what they were: fakes.

What saves them time and again in the various crises that dot the action of the play turns out to be the laws, written and not written, of *vraisemblance*, a notion that, like so many literary phenomena in the eighteenth century, was turning unexpectedly problematic. The word itself meant literally, of course, *giving the appearance, or illusion, of truth*, and everyone agreed that it was essential to any idea of theatricality. According to the grand classical tradition, it was assumed that *vraisemblance* reflected the truths of nature at the same time as it followed the rules of art, each having equal importance in the production of the whole. This combination of nature and art was thought to explain the extraordinary integrity we experience in the greatest dramatic poems of Racine and Corneille. In the eighteenth century, the concept was becoming unbalanced, shifting generally in the direction of all the rules, contrivances, and formulae that were thought to compose an "art." (Critics find these easier to talk about than the elusive qualities of nature; minor authors like to cling to them.) In extreme cases, playwrights seemed to feel that, natural or not, anything could be made believable (*vraisemblable*) provided the right rules were being observed.

No doubt the "doctrine" of *vraisemblance* had numerous

components and definitions, and it might be approached from several different points of view, but judging by the *practice* of eighteenth-century playwrights, one of the ingredients thought to be most essential in producing *vraisemblance* was consistency. Put bluntly, it was their conviction that if each line spoken by each *personnage* was entirely consistent with the character he or she was supposed to be, and also with the given dramatic situation (no easy task), this would infallibly produce the illusion of truth, i.e., *vraisemblance,* and at the same time the audience would be bound to believe in it. There is a real shift in emphasis here, if one looks back to the preceding century. Certainly, in Corneille and Racine consistency in this sense was assumed to be necessary, and classical authors were ready to justify their characters' behavior according to this criterion. But in the age of Voltaire the rules of consistency became to a greater degree the *means* by which the illusion was attained.

Today we are not always so impressed with the results: consistency spreads like some awful pall over Piron's empty tragedy, *Gustave-Wasa,* whereas in its day this work was highly respected, perhaps actually enjoyed, and certainly thought to be a well-sustained dramatic illusion. Even if one takes the most successful eighteenth-century tragedy, Voltaire's *Zaïre,* one senses how much the author is banking not merely on the powerful set of characters he has created, and on the pathos of his heroine's plight, but on the seamless consistency of every line spoken: perhaps if the consistency is totally airtight, sheer lack of oxygen will keep the audience from rising in rebellion against the unlikelihoods of the basic plot.

> O rage! O désespoir! O vieillesse ennemie!

moans the helpless father of Corneille's most famous hero, in a scene everyone who went to the theatre in the eighteenth century knew by heart.

> . . . ô trahison! ô rage! / O comble des forfaits!

moans the equally helpless hero of *Alzire* (II, 6) by Voltaire. As readers of Voltaire's tragedies had long been aware, examples of such much-too-close-to-be-coincidental imitations of Corneille or Racine are legion, and one of the many reasons Voltaire was so eager to fit these hemistichs from famous classical plays into his own dramatic system was that, provided he could have the lines spoken in dramatic contexts resembling those created by the original authors, their efficacy was proven. Though their power might have dimmed slightly with the passing of time, these lines were magic formulae that could invariably be counted on to light up and sustain his own dramatic illusions with tested *vraisemblance*. Needless to say, Voltaire saw to it that they were so exactly, so marvelously suited to the theatrical situation he was creating, the audience had no choice but to go along.

Actually we have not wandered so far away from the topic at hand as it might appear, for in our comedy by Le Sage, the valets, Crispin and La Branche, are playwrights, too, of a sort, staging their own—very unlikely—illusion for the other characters. Just as in a tragedy, the fiction on which these two "authors" rely is that if only they can present their deceit in a way that has internal consistency (thus producing *vraisemblance*) the other characters have no choice but to believe in it; their "audience" will automatically be hoodwinked. The trick is to find just the right words at the right time. If they can, the valets will have total control over the illusions they are creating, no matter how objectively absurd the whole contraption may appear to us—the very real, sophisticated spectators who see behind everything, of course.

Surrounded by so many sharp pins of reality ready to prick the bubble of their deception, their task is not easy. Let us consider, for example, Crispin, appearing for the first time in the groom's finery, nervously engaged in finding suitably flowery compliments with which to greet his pretended parents-in-law-to-be, just as the real groom would have done:

> Ma joie est extrême de pouvoir vous témoigner l'extrême joie que j'ai de vous embrasser.
>
> (scene 9)

he declares to the father of the bride, barely making it to the end of the sentence, coming close to bogging down permanently in his compliment. One more "extrême joie" or "joie extrême" and he would have looked like a fool. Of course his mistake was in throwing all the logs on the fire at once: "joie" already goes pretty far, and "extrême" is by definition perched on the outer edge and leaves no room for further advance. Perhaps he will be doomed to spend the rest of the scene revolving round and round with the same immutable adjective welded, bonded, cemented to the noun that says it all. But fortunately for him, no one ever notices his near blunder, first, because he diverts attention by flirting with the mother of the bride, and second, for the very good reason that, even though he almost gets stuck with them, he has found two words that were just exactly right for the situation, so that no one has any choice but to believe they emanate from the person for whom they are so well suited: a real groom.

Also helping him through this difficult moment was another critical element working in his favor, namely, the fact that he knew quite precisely the kind of words he was expected to say, the kind of syllables he was to pronounce. This was an advantage he sorely missed, a moment later, after La Branche had left him alone with the bridal party, in order to arrange for the horses to assure their getaway (it always tempts fate, to count the chickens before they are hatched). Suddenly the father of the bride inquires about the lawsuit the real groom's father has been deeply involved in. Lawsuit? Crispin finds himself obliged to manufacture syllables relating to a complicated situation he never heard of. Since La Branche is not there to help, he has to brazen it out, and wisely realizes that the best way to get rid of this uncomfortable topic, and put it behind him, is to pretend the suit is over. He simply announces that the suit has been won—and the strategy works like a charm. Not only the father of the bride, but

the mother, too, declares herself most satisfied to hear the good news. Crispin is just in the clear when unfortunately he makes the mistake of not leaving it at that. Perhaps he feels it is a little early to drop this obviously consequential topic, or perhaps he suffers a spell of overconfidence. Whatever the reason, he finds himself improvising further reflections on how much it meant to his father to win, how much money it had cost, but then (fatal garrulousness, that, given the crook saying the words, is just asking heaven for trouble), justice is such an excellent thing, it's worth any price. . . . Whereupon, he utters one syllable that looks so innocent it couldn't hurt anyone, but which suddenly rears up and throws his whole feigned identity into jeopardy: he refers to the alleged opponent in the lawsuit as "[le] plus grand chicaneur [. . .] de tous les hommes." "Men???" But the real opponent in the real lawsuit was a *woman*. The real father made that very clear, so what is he talking about? Suddenly all is crisis.

Actually the situation is not hopeless, if only because Crispin has learned, albeit through a dangerous blunder, a magic syllable—*femme*—that he can attach to his phrases, and that will brighten everything with *vraisemblance*. All he needs is a verbal extension cord; even "homme" will light up, too, as we see:

> Oui, sa partie était une femme, d'accord, mais cette femme avait dans ses intérêts un certain vieux Normand qui lui donnait conseils. C'est cet homme-là qui a fait bien de la peine à mon père [. . .]
>
> (scene 10)

The point is that, provided one observes the main law of *vraisemblance,* "homme" is just as serviceable as "femme." In fact, since both of them are the merest illusions anyway, they are actually interchangeable. Any word would do: even "chien" might have been used instead, if only Crispin had known enough about the "real" lawsuit to make it fit. The play's verbal surface is so thin, meaning is so lacking in depth and weight as to skim off into meaninglessness.

In this connection, if one wanted to pick out the single most important trait of this comedy, perhaps one might choose slipperiness, for, even in the language of the play, the syllables are constantly sliding in and out of place, just as "homme" slides in for "femme," and then Damis, the suitor from Chartres, slips in and out of the wedding (and into bed with another girl at the last moment), while Crispin tries to slip into his place, and into Valère's place, alternating giddily between fake suitor and valet. Aristocratic Valère slides far down the social scale in his sordid conduct, as we saw (his name almost rhymes with "valet"), while the real valet, La Branche, sliding up the scale, describes his recent *fourberies* using a *précieux* language that makes him sound positively upper class. And frictionless substitutions are everywhere in this well-oiled comedy: naturally the two valets can change places whenever they wish, one taking over for the other, but even the mother of the bride—whose youth obviously belongs to a distant past—can stand in for her daughter, blushing prettily at the fake groom's compliments, and acting positively nubile when he assures her he would have preferred her instead.

In the supple manipulations of *vraisemblance,* one of the most daring strategies is invented by La Branche to get himself out of an especially tight corner (scene 14)—a problem, incidentally, that the audience could see coming for some time. We had already learned that Valère was supposed to be personally acquainted with Damis, who had informed him by letter of his sudden marriage to the other woman in Chartres. Naturally we expect that Valère will tell Angélique that Damis is already married—so she is free to marry him, Valère. Naturally, too, the father of the bride will be informed of the other wedding, and will confront La Branche with the facts and denounce him as the deceiver he is. This is the tight corner mentioned above.

Faced with the father's accusation, La Branche first pretends that, far from admitting guilt, he cannot even understand what the father is talking about. This rather weak ploy fails; indeed the father threatens to summon the police commissioner, a clear and present danger that inspires La Branche to reach new heights of invention: just who was it, he asks the father, told him about Damis' marriage to the girl in Chartres? Valère? But of course, that explains everything: Valère is himself in love with Angélique and wants to marry her. He dreamed up the false story and forged a letter to make it seem plausible. Enter Crispin, who plays along, adding that Valère did it all to get the dowry. Everyone knows about Valère's debt; the creditors are pounding on the door. Meanwhile, there are roars of laughter from La Branche (What a devil, that Valère!), grand hilarity from the father (Imagine that young fellow thinking he could put something over on a clever person like me!); and rather nervous spasms of laughter from Crispin (Ha! Ha! Ha! But it was a close call, and the news about Damis' wedding may cause trouble yet!).

La Branche's strategy flawlessly conforms to the laws of *vraisemblance.* First, his story all hangs together because there is so much allegedly certifiable "truth" in it. Most of the events "really" happened that way: indeed there is supposed to be a suitor; in fact, there are supposed to be two suitors pursuing Angélique. There is a forged document making it all seem possible, too (just like the text of the play by Le Sage). The father is being hoodwinked into a false belief (not unlike the audience in the theatre), just as La Branche stated, and Valère is depicted as being in debt, and hence very interested in the dowry. Of course, much of the "truth" of the story applies to themselves, the valets, rather than to Valère; it is essentially the tale of their own *fourberie,* "falsely" attributed to Valère, that La Blanche is relating. But actually it doesn't matter to whom, if anyone, the events "happened." It suffices that they have the ring of truth. Since the *vraisemblance* is flawless, the success is assured: the indignant father on the spot wants to advance the hour of the wedding, so as to thwart Valère and his creditors all the sooner. But the supreme masterstroke comes from Crispin, who even manages to convince Valère that the letter from Damis doesn't actually say what in fact it actually says. Illu-

sion is so rampant, no one can know any more where the "real" truth lies.

To give another example: in a later scene (18), the two valets are discussing their getaway plans (a fateful topic that has already brought on one mishap, as we saw). Has La Branche procured the horses? He has. Crispin suggests that the Flanders road is the one they should take. Meanwhile La Branche stares off distractedly into the distance. No doubt he is looking in the very direction of their escape, imagining Crispin and himself on those galloping horses, money bags clanking with coinage, going so fast they're already just a speck in the distance . . . When suddenly the dream of their departure reverses itself and comes back toward them, walking on two rather elderly feet, coming right onstage. The speck in the distance La Branche has been staring at has turned into M. Orgon, La Branche's employer from Chartres, Damis' father, who has come to Paris expressly to break off his son's marriage in person. Obviously if the father of the ex-groom meets the father of the bride, the game will be up, and the two valets perform prodigies of ingenuity to keep each out of sight of the other. But their efforts are useless; they are beaten before they start: the two fathers' names are Orgon and Oronte, no one can keep that straight, or apart. They belong together, in fact they are virtually identical, so that it's the most natural thing in the world when, at the end of the play, Orgon slips into Oronte's place and takes the other man's wife off to the dance.

But the most curious illustration of slipperiness comes in scene eight, where La Branche tries to hand over to the father of the bride a forged letter supposedly written by Orgon in Chartres. This bit of *écriture* is a key piece in the construction of the illusion the valets are creating because it allegedly identifies and authenticates Crispin as the groom to be and gives a plausible explanation for Orgon's absence from the wedding of his own son. (He allegedly has the gout, which also is supposed to explain why the letter is written in an *écriture* so trembly it can hardly be deciphered, much less compared with any other specimen of his handwriting.) But oddly, at this critical moment, La Branche, three times in a row, either hands over, or almost starts to hand over, to the father wrong letters—letters addressed to other persons, for other purposes. It's a droll scene, to be sure, when the father, expecting an envelope addressed to himself, bearing his identity, is suddenly brought up short by:

A Monsieur Craquet, médecin dans la rue du Sépulcre

which brings on the inevitable joke about a doctor making his residence in the same quarter as his patients.

Again, La Branche pulls out a wrong envelope:

A Monsieur Bredouillet, avocat au Parlement, rue des Mauvaises Paroles

And there is still a third:

A Monsieur Gourmandin, Chanoine de . . .

Critics have been somewhat embarrassed by this part of the scene. The jokes on the envelopes are rather low comedy—one-liners; they interrupt the action, and they are certainly gratuitous.

But perhaps that is just the point, for these letters don't belong in this comedy at all. They suggest, in fact, other fictional possibilities, other plot situations, other texts, *écritures,* that, had the envelopes been opened and the letters actually read, might well replace the fictions at hand. Again there's a slightly uneasy feeling about the momentary slippage, about a play whose main plot is so loosely tied into place, whose characters are so inherently light-weight—wobbly and inconsequential, like the weak-headed mother of the bride—it wouldn't matter very much if they sailed off into other situations and other identities. It begins to seem as if everything in this play, from the syllables, words, and sentences, to the characters, the exposition, and the outcome, might change places with something else, and this implies a curious system of values working throughout the comedy in which everything is equal.

Perhaps not quite everything. For one factor at least seems to be standing against the leveling forces in this brilliantly conceived comedy: after all, the valets have deliberately created false roles for themselves. Crispin is not the fiancé he claims, and La Branche, too, knows who is lying. Surely the one element that cannot be abolished or interchanged is the basic opposition between the "real" characters supposed to be concerned with real weddings and real sons and daughters, and these mystifying clowns who knowingly put on masks and hoodwink for purposes that are quite different from the motives they feign.

This may seem like solid ground, yet even here the distinctions break down (ultimately there are no distinctions in this play, even the one between male and female is in jeopardy): for when the bubble finally bursts and both valets' *vraisemblance*-producing syllables run out, when the jig really is up and the culprits are forced to admit their guilt and tell the truth about themselves, we suddenly find that, on the flimsiest of pretexts (it's all supposed to be a gesture of gallantry toward the giddy, vain mother of the bride) the valets have been not only pardoned by those they have deceived, but instantly welcomed into the fold as business *partners,* friends, allies, virtual members of the family. So that, at the end, the deceivers collapse into the deceived, and from the celerity and ease with which it happens one can only conclude that there never had been any real differences between them in the first place. Indeed nothing remains standing, the whole play has deconstructed—not that we have any time to think about it. For already the characters are going off to the wedding festivities, the curtain at the Comédie Française is falling, and the applause of the (at last) real audience reminds us that it was all fakery, anyway, fraudulence, clowning. The whole text is a forgery to make us believe in ersatz imitations, a pack of cards.

If one were still writing amid the critical modes of the 1960s or 1970s it might make a fitting conclusion to this discussion to observe that Le Sage's consciousness of the void beneath the words, constructing and deconstructing the scenes, makes his art seem astonishingly modern. But now that we are in an era more sympathetic to history, the emphasis naturally shifts: we move beyond the problematic confinements of language to note how many of the play's most ingratiating qualities depend on its origins in a time quite unlike our own, and also, how well this playful approach to illusion and theatricality at the Comédie Française was preparing Le Sage for his starring role as impudent librettist at the *foire.*

Malcolm Cook (essay date 1988)

SOURCE: "A Comic Novel," in *Gil Blas,* Grant & Cutler Ltd., 1988, pp. 45-58.

[*In the following essay, Cook examines the comic elements in* Gil Blas *by concentrating on several targets of the novel's satire—including the judicial system, the medical profession, and the theatrical world—and the title character's encounters with their intrinsic hypocrisy and artificiality.*]

If Lesage's novel can still be read with pleasure today it is essentially because of the author's comic vision. Lesage managed to produce a work which is both general and specific in its comedy, treating both types and individuals, dealing with what is comic in reality and producing imagined scenes of wit and insight. The ironical position of the narrator is one obvious source of comedy: we laugh at Gil when he expects us to, but we also laugh when he expects it least. Lesage sees that the world is intrinsically comic: people take themselves too seriously and appear not to understand that others see them as part of the human comedy. Lesage's vision of humanity leads, naturally, to satire—of types, institutions and of real characters. At the same time the narrator's perception of reality will introduce comedy which is part of the observation of the real world. Comedy represents the unifying tone of the novel; it is not surprising that, in a comic novel, even the serious and tragic tend towards comedy, since the reader is expecting a sudden surprise or trick on every occasion. It is hard to take the serious seriously.

SATIRE:

(i) *Medicine*

The most obvious element of comedy in the novel is that which satirises the medical profession. There is a clear debt to Molière in the presentation of characters who ask fortunes to kill off their patients. Sangrado plays the largest part in this satire; the language Gil uses to describe his activities is extravagant and indicative: 'Ce savant médecin avait l'extérieur grave. Il pesait ses discours et donnait de la noblesse à ses expressions. Ses raisonnements paraissaient géométriques, et ses opinions fort singulières' (p. 82). The reader smells a rat! We sense hypocrisy, deceit and trickery, but Gil, at the moment of the experience, appeared less aware of the reality than he does now, in retrospect. Clearly we laugh at Sangrado but we also laugh at Gil.

Sangrado's pompous pronouncements on the nature of the human being make us, as readers, immediately suspicious: 'C'est une erreur de penser que le sang soit nécessaire à la conservation de la vie. On ne peut trop saigner un malade' (p. 82). His medical philosophy is to drain the body of all its blood and to replace the blood by water. Not surprisingly, his success rate is low, and Gil soon realises the nature of the universal panacea and appreciates that with such a simple philosophy he too can become a doctor and, eventually, earn a fortune. Which is what he intends to do, at least until his life is threatened and he abandons his promising medical career. Now, later, Gil appreciates the inefficacy of Sangrado's cures. At the time, however, he was not able to perceive the reality which is only too clear to us: 'Comme je n'étais qu'un jeune médecin qui n'avait pas encore eu le temps de s'endurcir au meurtre, je m'affligeais des événements funestes qu'on pouvait m'imputer' (p. 99). The double perspective of Gil then/Gil now heightens the comedy for the reader. We care little for the unfortunate patients who are expedited to an early grave. They are purely functional beings who have no place in our range of sentiments. But Gil, to his credit, expresses some concern.

If Sangrado were the only doctor involved in this satire we might conclude that Lesage is simply trying to introduce a scene which is intrinsically comic. But he goes one stage further. When Gil, much later, retraces his footsteps, he returns via Valladolid and finds Sangrado drinking wine, something which he had expressly forbidden. Sangrado knows he is caught out, but manages a comic response; he has found the perfect compromise: he dilutes his wine with water ('mon vin est bien trempé', p. 469).

On practically every occasion in the novel when Gil or anyone has recourse to a doctor we find a brief, critical remark decrying the 'profession'. So, for example, when don Alphonse is struck down by a fever which threatens his life, he survives because there were no doctors available (p. 308). When Gil is unconscious and treated, at great expense, by doctors he remarks, on recovery: 'je maudissais jusqu'aux universités où ces messieurs reçoivent le pouvoir de tuer les hommes impunément' (p. 377). There are similar, critical, remarks throughout the novel: pp. 180, 186, 224, 379-80, 455-56, 528, 534, and finally p. 601, when three doctors combine to kill off d'Olivarès and bring the novel to a conclusion. On one occasion only, in the story of don Gaston, can the medical profession be praised for its efficiency: 'Tout dangereusement blessé que j'étais, l'habileté des chirurgiens me tira bientôt d'affaire' (p. 443). Surgeons are not doctors, however, and cannot redress the balance of the novel as a whole. Lesage's repetition of the theme is, eventually, as comic as the theme itself. The reader comes to expect a critical remark in every appearance of a doctor, and he is seldom disappointed.

(ii) *The Church*

Such comedy can be described as traditional: it is not simply comic because of the nature of the profession but because behind the façade of a doctor we see a hypocrite. Much the same kind of analysis can be made for the clergy and the judiciary as they appear in the novel. Gil's uncle, a cleric, learns to read his breviary correctly for the first time while he is teaching Gil to read. The archbishopric of Grenada houses both 'vrais' and 'faux dévots', as Melchior de la Ronda points out to Gil (p. 324). And in Laure's story, in her description of Pedro Zendono, the steward of the hôpital de la Pitié, she remarks to Gil: 'Tu n'as jamais vu de face si hypocrite, quoique tu aies demeuré à l'archevêché' (p. 339). But the clergy are not important figures of satire. Lesage, like Marivaux in *Le Paysan parvenu,* was more interested in highlighting recognisable 'faux dévots' than in attacking the church or its beliefs.

(iii) *Justice*

The criticism of the judiciary in the novel is levelled more at the agents of the law than at the laws themselves or the judges who interpret them. Indeed, the satire here is comic only in that we see Gil becoming an innocent victim of forces greater than himself on occasions when he felt he had escaped. He is searched after his wrongful arrest when accompanying doña Mencia: 'ils vidèrent tout doucement mes poches et me prirent ce que les voleurs même avaient respecté, je veux dire les quarante ducats de mon oncle' (p. 57). When he is released from prison he remarks: 'Je ne me plains pas de la justice [. . .] Elle est très équitable. Je voudrais seulement que tous ses officiers fussent d'honnêtes gens' (p. 60). This satire of justice and the references we find elsewhere (pp. 94, 98-99, 286) tell us more about Gil's perception of human nature than justice itself. As Gil ages, so he realises that men are basically very similar: they wear different disguises but these appearances do not mask their real characters. The comedy of this form of satire is directed as much at Gil himself as it is at the apparent object of satire.

Gil's *naïveté* means that he is unaware of the corruption of the world and can fully understand it only when he is part of it. His changing status broadens his vision and introduces a vast range of satire.

(iv) *The State*

As secretary to the duc de Lerme, and, to a lesser extent, when he is secretary to d'Olivarès, Gil realises the power he can exert. He sells favours and soon amasses great wealth. Such rises to fortune were not unknown in the Regency. What Gil does not appear to understand, however, is that he is attempting, in his rise to power, to resemble those people he has served and despised. In satirising others, he is also satirising himself. Only after his imprisonment and disgrace is Gil lucid enough to state the lesson he has learnt: 'Les biens ne sont propres qu'à corrompre mes moeurs. [. . .] Les richesses sont un fardeau dans une retraite où l'on ne cherche que la tranquillité' (p. 461). Of course the state is not excluded from the satirical intentions of the author. But his real skill lies in his ability to satirise both hero and others simultaneously.

(v) *'Littérateurs'*

Lesage is at his best and most critical when satirising those elements of society he knew best: the world of literature and the world of the theatre. It is mainly through the character of Fabrice that Lesage introduces his presentation of the literary scene which allows a clear statement of his own prejudices and beliefs. There appears to be a constant, unifying theme that there is no reliable guide to literary quality: fashion, taste, self-interest and conceit all play a part in defining success, but, according to Lesage, quality and success should not necessarily be equated.

In the description of the salon of the marquise de Chaves (assumed to be the real-life marquise de Lambert (1647-1733) who was well known for her twice-weekly salon) Gil notices a disparity between the taste of the *habitués* and the general public. Comedy was generally despised:

> On n'y regardait la meilleure comédie ou le roman le plus ingénieux et le plus égayé que comme une faible production qui ne méritait aucune louange; au lieu que le moindre ouvrage sérieux, une ode, une églogue, un sonnet y passait pour le plus grand effort de l'esprit humain. Il arrivait souvent que le public ne confirmait pas les jugements du bureau, et que même il sifflait quelquefois impoliment les pièces qu'on y avait fort applaudies. (p. 228)

One gets a very clear impression of satire here, of people, readers and critics, whose taste is based on prejudice rather than quality, to the detriment of comic authors like Lesage himself. The adverb 'impoliment' is crucial in this remark, suggesting, ironically, impudence on the part of the general public which has the cheek to disagree with the opinion of the few.
The consistent belief which Lesage appears to be putting forward is that good works will be harshly criticised while mediocrity will slip through unnoticed. So, for example, in don Raphaël's story, he explains how he became a poet: 'Je m'érigeai même en poète et je consacrai ma muse aux louanges du prince. Je demeure d'accord de bonne foi que mes vers n'étaient pas bons. Aussi ne furent-ils pas critiqués' (p. 281). Lesage is trying to state what appears to be a paradox which works to the detriment of quality and to the advantage of mediocrity. We can see that *Gil Blas* represents not only a comic vision of the world but a specific attack on certain prejudices and beliefs. It becomes a mouthpiece for Lesage himself. We are a far cry from the picaresque novel and much closer to a comic *roman de mœurs*.

When Gil meets Fabrice at court having lost sight of him after leaving Valladolid in a hurry, he is not told immediately of the important change which has taken place. Fabrice's new lot in life appears to be a happy one. His 'appartement' is, in fact, a room divided into four, reached by a dark and narrow staircase and decorated with maps and old theses. The bed is old and worn and the rest of the furniture is showing clear signs of age. We are kept in the same suspense as Gil. Fabrice appears to be happy, apparently unaware of the reality which surrounds him, yet which is perceived by Gil and which represents the only indicative descriptive reality of the novel. Finally, Fabrice announces his new occupation: he is an author! Moreover, he says, modestly(!), he is a good author. Gil is, not unnaturally, surprised at Fabrice's new condition. Fabrice soon explains how he came to write: he wrote a play which, on his own admission, was worth nothing but which was a great success. He concluded: 'Je jugeai par là que le public était une bonne vache à lait qui se laissait aisément traire' (p. 364). And so begins an important literary debate. Fabrice, like other authors, has an elevated view of himself. Gil is detached and ironic in his remarks and is allowed to comment on one of Fabrice's sonnets (one remembers Alceste's remarks on Oronte in Molière's *Le Misanthrope*). Gil finds the poem obscure and incomprehensible, to which Fabrice responds: 'tant mieux! Les sonnets, les odes et les autres ouvrages qui veulent du sublime ne s'accommodent pas du simple et du naturel. C'est l'obscurité qui en fait tout le mérite' (p. 365). Gil disagrees, of course, but Lesage has made his point. If the public is unable to distinguish between quality and worthlessness, it deserves all the bad authors who supply its needs. As we read the novel we get an ever growing impression that what Lesage is saying is that literary success is not a guarantee of literary quality. Other factors are at play: the literary world is a refined version of the real world where hypocrisy and pomposity are constant features.

When Gil dines with a number of poets brought by Fabrice he is led to the conclusion that 'la nation des auteurs est un peu vaine et glorieuse' (p. 412). Fabrice is no exception to this general rule, nor indeed are other writers as they are presented in the novel: the archevêque de Grenade (pp. 321-31), Gabriel Triaquero (pp. 483-85), don Ignacio de Ipigna (p. 533) and, of course, Gil himself, who is quite conscious of the excellent quality of his prose! ('J'étais devenu une espèce d'auteur', p. 358, and on page 550, his style is remarked upon by d'Olivarès.)

The world of literature is a world of hypocrisy and petty jealousy, a world of rivalry and antagonisms where literary quality appears unimportant. One senses an expression of Lesage's own views of the unjust treatment he felt he had received at the hands of critics. Fabrice, from this point of view, is an ideal character. He plays the part of a poet to perfection—perhaps he plays it too well since he takes himself seriously. But eventually his own opinion of himself is deflated. He finishes in the poorhouse: 'cette maison sert souvent de retraite aux beaux esprits' (p. 553). He has decided to give up writing poetry and to abandon the muses. He states, apparently unaware of the comic contradiction, 'quand tu es entré dans cette salle, je composais des vers pour leur dire un éternel adieu' (p. 554). As Laufer points out, Fabrice, at the end of the novel, has become the mouthpiece for Lesage himself: 'j'ai pris le public en aversion. Il ne mérite pas qu'il y ait des auteurs qui veuillent lui consacrer leurs travaux' (p. 554). The view expressed is one of bitterness and resentment. What Lesage appears to be saying is that contemporary popularity is worth little: it serves to bolster the pride of authors. But the only real guide to quality is that which is long-lasting, and this is something which contemporaries are ill-equipped to predict. It is also, of course, the perfect defence of an unsuccessful writer. The same idea is stated more pointedly, as we shall see, in the portrait of Gabriel Triaquero, normally considered to be Voltaire.

Fabrice makes a come-back, however. Don Bertrand Gomez del Ribero needed a poet to write his 'billets galants'. Fabrice got the job and is now prostituting his 'art' with considerable success. Moreover, his play, written on an idea inspired by his rich patron, was such a dreadful flop that don Bertrand, staggered at the bad taste of the public, had decided to reward the unfortunate author with a pension for life. As Fabrice now realises only too well, quality and success do not always go hand in hand. He is lucid enough at the end to conclude: 'les sifflets m'ont mis tout d'un coup à mon aise pour le reste de mes jours' (p. 562).

Scipion too remarks on the nature of fate which rewards mediocrity and is harsh towards quality (p. 562). The point has been made clearly enough and the personal nature of Lesage's novel is apparent through the character of Fabrice. His financial stability is short-lived, through no fault of his own, and he finishes his life in mediocrity, happy with his lot, living a life of independence and without ambitious pretentions. Fabrice's conclusions are not dissimilar to those of Gil himself. Chance and fate determine one's life, not merit and quality. In such a world ambition plays little part.

(vi) *The Theatre*

The novel is full of allusions and references to the world of the theatre, and there can be no doubt that there must be a relationship between this emphasis and the meaning of the text as a whole. It is apparent, throughout the novel, that Lesage is saying that the theatre is not simply to be found on the stage. Critics have disagreed about the significance of the theatrical elements.

Whatever meaning such episodes may have, one cannot escape the conclusion that the world of the theatre is, of all the worlds described by Gil, the one which appears to be most authentic and most personally motivated. It is, I think, the satire of the theatre and of actors generally which is the most effective. We see actors constantly criticising the authors who supply them with their conditions of livelihood. Book III, Chapter XI (pp. 171-74) is devoted almost entirely to an analysis of the relationship between actors and authors. At the end of the meal an author arrives: the company of actors treats him with scorn and obvious superiority. His reaction is one of fear and embarrassment. When he leaves, the conversation turns to more general comments about authors: 'Les auteurs sont-ils dignes de notre attention? [. . .] Traitons-les toujours en esclaves, et ne craignons point de lasser leur patience'

(p. 174). Gil concludes the chapter with apparent objectivity: 'Ces histrions les mettaient au-dessous d'eux, et certes ils ne pouvaient les mépriser davantage' (p. 174).

It is apparent, throughout the novel, that Lesage bears a grudge against the 'official' theatre. The Théâtre du Prince (du Roi?) contains actors who deserve to be on the road but who have entered the troupe out of favour, as Melchior Zapata points out (p. 122). Don Pompeyo de Castro, an objective observer from Portugal, is asked to comment on the acting performance he has seen at the Théâtre du Prince. Fashion plays no part in his ambitions as he enumerates the actors and actresses he has seen, stressing particularly their inability to appear natural on stage. The audience, he maintains, is not always the best judge of quality ('Il applaudit même plus rarement au vrai mérite qu'au faux', p. 155), and he introduces the comic anecdote about the peasant and the pig (pp. 155-66).

In his presentation of the theatre Lesage is making the same general statement as the one he made about literature: There is no guarantee that merit will bring success. Actors and actresses have inflated views of their own importance; they are unable to see the true nature of the roles they are playing in society. . . . [It] is the theatrical

Lesage

metaphor which points to the essential meaning of the novel.

(vii) *'Real' Figures*

As I have already remarked, the illusion of Spain is constantly contradicted by allusions to French reality. The comic satire of *littérateurs* and *comédiens* is both of a general and a personal nature. The fictional characters introduced by Lesage have clear 'real' counterparts. . . . It is essentially, but not entirely, the world of literature, taken in its broadest sense, which provides these characters. The most obvious one, and the one which did most to harm Lesage's reputation, is Gabriel Triaquero, otherwise known as Voltaire. Voltaire, offended by his portrait in *Gil Blas,* accused Lesage of having taken the novel entirely from *La vida del escudero don Marcos de Obregón* and the accusation was not fully dismissed until some one hundred years later, in the edition of the novel by the comte de Neufchâteau. It is not surprising that Voltaire took exception to his portrait. Gil goes to see the first performance of a play by this 'poète à la mode' (p. 483). The theatre is fully booked in advance, such is the reputation of Gabriel, and the play is, of course, a resounding success. The author goes 'modestement' from box to box to receive his praise (p. 487). After the performance Gil returns to dine at don Alphonse's palace. There is one dissenting voice from the praise heaped on the new play: a 'gentilhomme de Madrid, qui avait de l'esprit et du goût' (p. 484). Clearly his opinion is going to be significant: he wishes to reserve his judgement. Quality is *not* apparent simply from one performance of the play, he claims. The play must be read if its full value is to be appreciated. The implication is, very clearly, that Gabriel is praised too readily out of pure fashion. Another *cavalier* disagrees: 'Il suffit que nous sachions que c'est une production de don Gabriel pour être persuadés qu'elle est sans défaut' (p. 484). The gentilhomme de Madrid, prompted by the ridiculous statement of the *cavalier,* starts to criticise the play with severity: 'C'est un poème farci de traits plus brillants que solides. Les trois quarts des vers sont mauvais ou mal rimés, les caractères mal formés ou mal soutenus, et les pensées souvent très obscures' (pp. 484-85). Lesage is careful to assert that his critic is both intelligent and of good taste. His remarks are damning indeed, and Voltaire would have felt peeved with reason. The most successful tragedian of the period was being humbled by a writer of novels and comedies, and called, no doubt much to his distaste, 'ce nouveau nourrisson des Muses' (p. 485). Lesage's short chapter no doubt expresses his own jealousy of Voltaire's success, and at the same time he underlines the view that while fashion may define success, literary merit will lie with posterity. One might conclude that Lesage was at least partly justified: Voltaire's tragedies are rarely performed or read today.

Lesage uses *Gil Blas* to express a satirical view of his own dislikes and antagonisms. The characters we can now identify would have been immediately recognisable to a contemporary readership, but the novel can still be enjoyed even if the 'real' characters remain purely fictional.

One of the most striking portraits in the novel is the one of Carlos Alonso de la Ventoleria (pp. 171-72), given by Laure, who is said to represent the actor-author Baron, a rival and enemy of Lesage. He is old, dyes his hair, and claims to be twenty years younger than he is. He is conceited and self-satisfied, vain and affected. The character is described in such detail that the reader has no trouble in imagining him in real life. Contemporary readers would have picked up the one obvious clue to his identity: he had left the stage and returned much later. The satire is comic in its exaggeration, yet colourful and effective. It is clearly double-edged.

Such is the case for the other characters in the novel who are said to represent real figures. They add variety and colour to the novel: they are precisely described in a way that obviously fictional characters are not. And the illusion benefits consequentially. Boindin, the critic, is introduced as 'un petit homme' (p. 215). In Scipion's story Scipion works for don Ignacio de Ipigna (Bouhours) an author who has a unique method of composition: he writes down on cards the apophthegms he reads in classical authors, and when they are full he threads them on to metal wire, makes a garland of them, and each garland constitutes a volume: 'Que nous faisions de mauvais livres! Il ne se passait guère de mois que nous ne fissions pour le moins deux volumes, et aussitôt la presse en gémissait' (p. 533).

Gil Blas is not, I think, a *livre à clef,* but Lesage introduces 'real' figures when they can appear naturally in the text and enhance the comedy. I suspect that a number of characters have not been identified who may well, originally, have been contemporary figures of satire. The transposition of reality into fiction allows the author to increase the range of his comic vision.

COMIC SCENES

It has been said that Lesage the novelist is never far removed from Lesage the playwright. Lesage's great skill in *Gil Blas* is in imagining a number of highly dramatic scenes whose main function is to make us laugh, normally at the expense of Gil himself. This is the crucial element of comedy and one which defines humour in the novel. We laugh at Gil and find him sympathetic because he is now, retrospectively, able to laugh at himself. We laugh at others and reject them because they take themselves too seriously.

A number of scenes remain vividly in the mind: Gil responding to the archevêque de Grenade's appeal to be warned when his age adversely affects his capacity to write (he does so and is promptly sacked (pp. 321-31), but the lesson in human nature is worth the loss of occupation); Gil's completely wrong assessment of Camille and her advances towards him, which we pick up very early on (pp. 67-71); the meeting with don Annibal de Chinchilla and the comic description of him ('Outre qu'il lui manquait un bras et une jambe, il avait la place d'un oeil couverte d'une large emplâtre de taffetas vert, et son visage en plusieurs endroits paraissait balafré. A cela près, il était fait comme un autre', pp. 356-57); Gil's wrong assessment of his mistress Aurore, whom he assumes to be in love with him (pp. 179-85). He spends all his money on creams, perfume and clothes, arrives for the rendezvous covered in lotion two hours too early and imagines, with obvious anticipation, the delightful scenes which are to follow. He tries to recall the plays he has seen which might include a scene he could make use of in the present circumstances, but when he arrives his mistress laughs at his antics—she wants him simply as a go-between. The hero is suitably deflated and proved to be quite wrong in his appreciation of the true situation. He invites laughter and gets his due.

It is when Gil shows himself to be less than heroic that we are most amused at him: he leaves Valladolid in a hurry to avoid a possible fight; in the showdown with his rival for the hand of Lorenza Séphora, whom he cares little about, we see Gil Blas mechanically responding to expectation: he is supposed to be angry and seeking revenge. He confronts his rival: 'Je me mis à considérer mon homme, qui me sembla fort vigoureux; et je trouvai son épée d'une longueur excessive' (p. 317), and is only too pleased to find a good reason not to fight. Gil is not the dashing hero of the adventure story: he is the ordinary, normal human being who is seeking to improve his lot. He remains in our affection because of his fallibility and this capacity to laugh at himself.

Lesage does not miss a trick in this comic novel: the irony of the narrator looking back and describing himself with detachment but in the knowledge of ultimate contentment lends itself to comedy; the use of certain forms of language and the witty phrase are constant comic factors: Gil Blas goes to sleep 'en bâtissant des châteaux en Espagne' (p. 352); the proverb 'Tu es du bois dont on fait les flûtes' becomes, in the language of Manuel Ordoñez, 'Tu es du bois dont on fait les économes' (p. 364). But it is Gil's ability to laugh at himself which provides the essence of comedy in the novel. At the end, his future assured, he spends three hours getting ready for his wedding: 'Pour un adolescent que se prépare à voir sa maîtresse, ce n'est qu'un plaisir; mais pour un homme qui commence à vieillir, c'est une occupation' (p. 608). The final phrase in the novel as he refers to his two children 'dont je crois pieusement être le père' (p. 609) alerts us to the fact that even in this sentimental ending Gil cannot avoid a slanted remark about himself. It is clearly time to analyse in more detail the character of Gil. He is the dynamic force of the novel. The comedy revolves around his account of the world and his confrontation with it. Gil, unlike the figures of satire, is mobile and free. He moves through different social echelons providing us with a seemingly detached view of the reality he observes. The comic element is stronger when the distance between Gil and his current reality is greatest; as he starts to mature and to become part of the social world he had previously mocked, so the comedy of the novel diminishes. Gil, to the end, is unaware of the assessment we are likely to make of him. He conveniently forgets his past when he observes his present reality, but we, as readers, view Gil with a detachment which may well be more critical than he, through his account, would have desired.

FURTHER READING

Biography

"The Author of *Gil Blas*." *Household Words* X, No. 250 (1854-55): 488-93.
    Descriptive and anecdotal biography of Lesage, including a concise history of the French stage during the playwright's era and a synopsis of contemporary reaction to *Gil Blas.*

"Claretie's Life of Le Sage." *The Nation* 53, No. 1381 (17 December 1891): 464-65.
    Brief and generally favorable assessment of M. Léo Claretie's biography *Essai sur Le Sage,* which the unnamed critic calls "a very readable volume."

Criticism

Grieder, Josephine. Introduction to *The History and Adventures of Gil Blas of Santillane,* Vol. I, by Alain René Le Sage, pp. 5-11. New York: Garland Publishing, 1972.
    Examines the complexities present in *Gil Blas,* including the psychological and moral development of the title character and the novel's significant incidence of social satire.

Laden, Marie-Paule. "*Gil Blas* and *Moll Flanders:* Imitation, Disguise, and Mask." In her *Self-Imitation in the Eighteenth-Century Novel,* pp. 23-68. Princeton: Princeton University Press, 1987.
    Detailed comparison of the first-person narrative styles of *Gil Blas* and Daniel Defoe's *Moll Flanders,* in which the critic examines the relationship between the inner character of the protagonist and the discourse of the narrator.

Reish, Joseph G. "Lesage's Dramatization of a Social Cycle: The Ups and Downs of the Likes of Turcaret." *French Literature Series* XV (1988): 31-40.
    Analyzes the development of the drama's valet-master dichotomy, in which the critic concludes that the "emerging character configuration" of Turcaret-Frontin reflects "successive stages of a single extended persona."

Molière

1622-1673

(Pseudonym of Jean Baptiste Poquelin) French dramatist.

The following entry provides critical discussion of Molière's works from the last four decades. For further information on Molière's life and works, see *LC,* Volume 10.

INTRODUCTION

Molière is widely recognized as one of the greatest comic writers of seventeenth-century France and one of the foremost dramatists in world literature. In such masterpieces as *Le Tartuffe* (1664; *Tartuffe*), *Dom Juan* (1665; *Don Juan*), and *Le misanthrope* (1666; *The Misanthrope*), he succeeded in elevating the traditional status of French comedy from farcical buffoonery to that of an influential forum for social criticism. While Molière's daring parodies of the pretentiousness of the Parisian upper classes and the hypocrisy of many religious leaders became extremely popular with audiences, they were also the source of heated controversy throughout his life.

Biographical Information

Born in Paris and christened Jean Baptiste Poquelin, Molière was the eldest of six children. His father held a prestigious appointment as *valet de chambre* and *tapissier,* or upholsterer, to Louis XIII. Molière was apprenticed in his father's trade, but was little interested in the family business. He instead became fascinated with the theater while attending one of the best secondary schools in Paris, the Jesuit Collège de Clermont, where he studied classical dramas by such authors as Terence and Plautus. After leaving Clermont, Molière studied law briefly before inheriting his father's position at court. In 1642, possibly while traveling as *valet de chambre* to Louis XIII, he became romantically involved with an actress named Madeleine Béjart, who strongly influenced his decision in 1643 to renounce his royal appointment in order to pursue a more precarious theatrical career. He adopted the stage name of Molière and established the troupe L'Illustre Théâtre with Madeleine Béjart and her family. Numerous expenses, general inexperience, and Molière's dubious abilities as a tragic actor, however, caused the troupe's collapse in July, 1645. Following a brief imprisonment for the theater's debt, Molière continued to pursue his dramatic career, touring the provinces with the Béjarts for the next thirteen years and writing his first plays—*La jalousie de Barbouillé* (1645; *The Jealousy of Le Barbouillé*), *Le mèdecin volant* (1645?; *The Flying Doctor*), and *L'étourdi* (1653; *The Blunderer*)—all short adaptations of Italian farces in the tradition of the commedia dell'arte. Upon returning to Paris in 1658, the troupe performed Molière's farce *Le dépit amoureux* (1656; *The Amorous Quarrel*), which was greeted with overwhelm-

ing enthusiasm, and earned the favor of Louis XIV. While Molière's next work, *Les Précieuses ridicules* (1659; *The Affected Ladies*), was also a popular success, the comedy's mockery of the pretentiousness of the Parisian upper class insulted many aristocrats who believed themselves to be the targets of the parody. Molière thus earned the first of many socially prominent enemies, and thereafter, his life and plays continued to generate controversy. In 1662, Molière married Armande Béjart, a twenty-year-old woman who was thought to be either the sister or the daughter of Molière's former mistress, Madeleine Béjart. The union was marked by periodic separations, and Armande's uncertain parentage and rumored infidelities became the subject of hostile pamphlets and malicious gossip by Molière's enemies. Molière was also frequently plagued with charges of impiety, which culminated in the censorship battle surrounding his most renowned work, *Tartuffe,* which presents a daring criticism of the Catholic church. Although *Tartuffe* was extremely popular with audiences and was acclaimed by Louis XIV, the Archbishop of Paris issued a decree threatening to excommunicate anyone who performed, attended, or even read the play. In the midst of the controversy, Molière produced *Don Juan,* which provoked further censorship from outraged church officials, who managed to suppress the play after only fifteen performances. Louis XIV, who had previously protected Molière from censorship, became reluctant to oppose powerful religious interests. It was not until 1669 that Molière was permitted to perform *Tartuffe*. Plagued with recurrent illnesses due primarily to exhaustion, Molière was diagnosed a hypochondriac by doctors who were offended by his parody of the medical profession. Ironically, he died of a lung disorder in 1673 following the fourth performance of his final comedy, *Le malade imaginaire* (1673; *The Imaginary Invalid*), in which he played the role of the hypochondriac. Denied both the ministrations of a priest and interment in consecrated ground because of his profession, Molière was granted only a serviceless funeral, and that only after Louis XIV intervened on his behalf.

Major Works

While Molière's early plays may be divided into full-length *comédies littéraires* in verse, such as *Dom Garcie de Navarre* (1661; *The Jealous Prince*), and one-act farces, such as *Les Précieuses ridicules*; from *L'École des femmes* (1662; *The School for Wives*) onwards these two forms became fused. W.D. Howarth commented: "Molière's originality is thus to have created a formula which combined the 'classical' structure, the linguistic refinement and the portrayal of manners belonging to the accepted conventions of 'comedy,' with the heightened, even caricatural, characterization proper to farce." Commentators have consistently emphasized the vivid personalities of Molière's characters, often deeming characterization the central element of interest and unity in his plays. His works typically focus on ordinary people in recognizable societal roles who are perverted or corrupted by a particular obsession or character flaw—for example, the obsessive avarice of Harpagon in *L'avare* (1668; *The Miser*). Relationships between the sexes, particularly between older men and much younger women, were also the focus of several plays. Written within a few months following his marriage, for example, *The School for Wives* concerns a middle-aged man's attempt to create a wife who is incapable of betraying him by raising her from her childhood in complete isolation from the outside world. While Molière sought above all to entertain, his view of comedy gradually evolved to embrace the belief that "the business of comedy is to present, in general, all the defects of man and principally of our country." Thus, social criticism played a prominent role in his satirical works such as *Tartuffe*, which portrays a hypocritical priest who ingratiates himself into a household by posing as his host's spiritual director, and then usurps control of his property.

Critical Reception

Variously considered a blasphemer, a social satirist, and a writer of pure comedy, Molière has, as Alvin Eustis notes, "borne a different message for each successive generation since his own." His introduction of realism to the seventeenth-century French stage brought to the fore a longstanding debate over the role of comedy in literature in a society in which most writers and critics deemed comic drama intrinsically inferior to tragedy. Although Molière remained highly popular during this time, he battled many attempts to discredit his plays as the works of a mediocre farceur. During the eighteenth century in France, both the popularity and critical reception of Molière's works declined sharply, as his natural style was rejected in favor of the more elegant comedies of Pierre Marivaux and Nivelle de la Chaussée. The French Restoration of the nineteenth century, however, witnessed a tremendous resurgence of Molière's works; his plays were by far the most frequently performed of the era, and, except for the detractions of the influential German critic August Wilhelm von Schlegel, he was widely considered the purest representative of the classical theater of the age of Louis XIV. Twentieth-century assessments of Molière's works have been predominantly concerned with characterization and comic technique. While critics during the first half of the century frequently focused on the emotions and motivations of Molière's characters, much criticism since the 1960s has focused on the playwright's use of language, and the unifying structural elements of his works. Alvin Eustis, for example, proposed that each of Molière's works are constructed around an ironic situation or paradox. Recent criticism has also addressed the plays in the context of seventeenth-century social history, exploring the influence of social hierarchy on Molière's writing process, the possible moral and cathartic functions of the productions, and the psychology that may have motivated the fearful reaction surrounding many of his works.

PRINCIPAL WORKS

La jalousie de Barbouillé [*The Jealousy of Le Barbouillé*] (drama) 1645?
Le médecin volant [*The Flying Doctor*] (drama) 1645?
L'estourdy; ou, Le contre-temps [*The Blunderer*] (drama) 1653; also published as *L'étourdi*, 1888
Le dépit amoureux [*The Amorous Quarrel*] (drama) 1656
Les précieuses ridicules [*The Affected Ladies*] (drama) 1659
Sganarelle; ou, Le cocu imaginaire [*The Imaginary Cuckold*] (drama) 1660
Dom Garcie de Navarre; ou, Le prince jaloux [*Don Garcia of Navarre; or, The Jealous Prince*] (drama) 1661
L'école des maris [*A School for Husbands*] (drama) 1661
Les fâcheux [*The Impertinents*; also translated as *The Bores*] (drama) 1661
L'école des femmes [*A School for Women*; also translated as *The School for Wives*] (drama) 1662
La critique de "L'école des femmes" [*"The School for Women" Criticised*; also translated as *"The School for Wives" Criticised*] (drama) 1662
L'impromptu de Versailles [*The Impromptu of Versailles*] (drama) 1663
Le mariage forcé [*The Forced Marriage*] (drama) 1664
La Princesse d'Élide [*The Princess of Elis, being the Second Day of the Pleasures of the Inchanted Island*] (drama) 1664
Le Tartuffe [*Tartuffe: or, The Hypocrite*; also translated

as *Tartuffe: or, The Imposter*] (drama) 1664; revised versions also performed as *L'imposteur,* 1667 and *Le Tartuffe; ou, L'imposteur,* 1669

Dom Juan; ou, Le festin de pierre [*Don John; or, The Libertine*; also translated as *Don Juan; or, The Feast with the Statue*] (drama) 1665

Le médecin malgré lui [*The Forced Physician*; also translated as *The Doctor in Spite of Himself*] (drama) 1666

Le misantrope [*The Misantrope; or, Man-Hater*; also translated as *The Misanthrope*] (drama) 1666; also published as *Le misanthrope,* 1851

Amphitryon [*Amphitryon; or, The Two Sosias*] (drama) 1668

L'avare [*The Miser*] (drama) 1668

George Dandin; ou, Le mary confondu [*George Dandin; or, The Wanton Wife*] (drama) 1668

Monsieur de Pourceaugnac [*Monsieur de Pourceaugnac; or, Squire Trelooby*] (drama) 1669

Le bourgeois gentilhomme [*The Bourgeois Gentleman*] (drama) 1670

Les fourberies de Scapin [*The Cheats of Scapin*; also translated as *The Rogueries of Scapin*] (drama) 1671

Psiché [with Pierre Corneille] [*Psiché*; also translated as *Psyche*] (drama) 1671

Les femmes savantes [*The Learned Ladies*] (drama) 1672

Le malade imaginaire [*The Hypocondriac*; also translated as *The Imaginary Invalid*] (drama) 1673

The Works of Mr. de Molière. 6 vols. (dramas) 1714

The Dramatic Works of Molière. 6 vols. (dramas) 1875-76

The Plays of Molière in French with an English Translation. 8 vols. (dramas) 1902-07

CRITICISM

Robert J. Nelson (essay date 1960)

SOURCE: "The Unreconstructed Heroes of Molière," in *The Tulane Drama Review,* Vol. IV, No. 3, March, 1960, pp. 14-37.

[*Nelson is an American critic and educator whose works on French literature include* Play Within a Play: The Dramatist's Conception of His Art *(1958), and* Corneille: His Heroes and Their Worlds *(1963). In the following essay, he discusses Molière's treatment of the relationship between appearance and reality in* Le Tartuffe, Dom Juan, *and* Le Misanthrope, *"in order to assess [the meaning of this theme] for Molière's art in particular and for comic theory in general."*]

There are, as Bailly has said [in *L'Ecole classique frangλaise*], no conversions in Molière. To the end, Arnolphe remains a bigot, Harpagon a miser, Jourdain a parvenu, Argan a hypochondriac. Thus Molière remains true to a rule of comedy far more important than the conventions of time, place, and unity considered the hallmarks of classical dramaturgy: the rule of the unity of character. For, conversion would take the spectator into affective and moral regions where the satiric purpose—laughter—might

be compromised. A repentant Arnolphe, a disabused Jourdain, an enlightened Argan might satisfy our sense of the pathetic or the propitious, but only at the expense of our pleasure. In fact, to make us feel sorry for such characters at the end of the play or to make them share our superior view of their previous conduct would come dangerously close to identifying us with them in that previous conduct as well. In leaving these characters "unreconstructed" Molière earns our gratitude as well as our applause.

Yet, this "non-conversion" disturbs us in three of his greatest comedies: *Le Tartuffe,* in which the hypocrite remains a hypocrite; *Dom Juan,* in which the "sinner" refuses to repent; *Le Misanthrope,* in which the hater of men hates them more at the end of the play than at the beginning. Holding a similar place in the Molière canon to *All's Well, Troilus and Cressida,* and *Measure for Measure* in the Shakespeare canon, these plays might be described as Molière's "bitter comedies." In them, as Borgerhoff has observed [in *The Freedom of French Classicism*], Molière has reversed his usual dramaturgy, unsettling the categories into which we have cast his work: triumph of the golden mean, the importance of common sense, the essentially bourgeois outlook, etc. Usually, the "hero" (in the purely structural sense of the major role) is a monomaniac, a person lacking what Ramon Fernandez has called "la vision double" [in *La vie de Molière*] or the capacity for what I have described in an earlier essay [in *Play Within a Play*] as "the deliberate multiplication of the self." In a Molière play, the "others" have this capacity: the Agnès, the Toinettes, the Scapins who use it to check the effects of the principal character's monomania. "The true hero of a comedy," I wrote in that essay, "is, in fact, the 'others' and their view ought more appropriately be compared with that of the tragic hero in any discussion of the tragic and the comic. . . . The comic 'others' are ready to assume a mask, they are willing to play a double game. The central figure (an Argan, an Harpagon) simply cannot play such a game, for he does not know of its possibility. Ironically, the tragic hero yearns for the singleness of vision of the comic figure, for whom appearance and reality coincide. However, if the tragic figure and the comic 'others' are alike in their doubleness of vision, they differ in the very essence of that vision: where the tragic hero sees discrepancy and even duplicity, the comic 'others' see combination and complementarity: of the social and the natural, of the logical and the illogical, of the conditioned and the instinctive, of the material and the spiritual." Through the use of mask or ruse the "others" usually get the upper hand over the monomaniacal figure. However, in *Le Tartuffe* the unscrupulous Tartuffe also possesses the usually commendable "double vision." Indeed, short of the King's intervention, his wiles prove more effective than those of the "others" (Elmire, Dorine). In *Dom Juan,* throughout much of the play, the relationship between the "hero" and the "others" is turned completely inside out: aware of the doubleness of vision of the "others," Dom Juan asserts the moral superiority of his single vision and, in spite of a complex departure from it himself, succeeds in imposing it upon the spectator if not upon the "others." Finally, in *Le Misanthrope* as in *Dom Juan,* the monomaniac, though fully aware of doubleness, tries to impose his single vision upon the double vision of the "others." However, unlike Dom Juan, Alceste does not find ultimate victory in the very face of defeat.

These three plays are marked by a questioning and at times aggressive outlook and their dates suggest that the outlook was an enduring one: *Le Tartuffe* (in its first version during the festivities at Versailles) dates from May 1664; *Dom Juan* from February 1665; *Le Misanthrope* from June 1666. Only *L'Amour médecin* (September 1665) interrupts this mood, a fact to which I shall return. Whatever causes account for this mood (professional bitterness at the prudish criticism of *L'Ecole des femmes;* personal unhappiness because of marriage difficulties, etc.) the outlook itself, the patent reversal of dramaturgy and the chronology of the plays suggest that at this stage of his career Molière sees in a different light the relationship between appearance and reality, the theme which Lionel Trilling has described [in *The Liberal Imagination*] as the essential theme of all literature. I should now like to look at Molière's "review" of this theme in some detail, in order to assess its meaning for Molière's art in particular and for comic theory in general.

1. *Le Tartuffe*

Though Molière has divided the limelight between the Impostor and his victim, the play can still be inserted into the typical formula of Molière dramaturgy: the monomaniac (Orgon) is the butt of the satire and the entire action is organized around the effort to break down his fanatical devotion to Tartuffe. The play thus resembles the very last, *Le Malade imaginaire,* with Tartuffe corresponding to the doctors (and possibly Beline), Orgon to Argan, Elmire to Béralde, Dorine to Toinette, etc. Yet, certain aspects of *Le Tartuffe* make it very untypical: the monomaniac is finally disabused—Organ sees the light about Tartuffe as Argan does not about the doctors; the "others" are saved not by their own wit but by "chance." At first glance, of course, the "chance intervention" of the king need not be seen as untypical: chance also frustrates Arnolphe on the verge of triumph in *L'Ecole des femmes.* Yet, the nature of "chance" in the two plays is profoundly different. In *L'Ecole,* though Enrique's return has been "dramatically" prepared for in Horace's (casual!) reference to his father's expected return (I.iv), the timing of the return could not be more fortuitous. It is conceivable within the terms of the situation that the return be too late—with Agnès wed to Arnolphe. But in *Le Tartuffe,* the king's intervention is not really a matter of chance. However dramatically surprising it may appear at this time, it was bound to occur in time to frustrate Tartuffe's ultimate designs. For, the king has been wise to Tartuffe for a long time:

> Ce monarque, en un mot, a vers vous détesté
> Sa lâche ingratitude et sa déloyauté:
> Et ne m'a jusqu'ici soumis à sa conduite
> Que pour voir l'impudence aller jusques au bout
> Et vous faire par lui faire raison de tout.
>
> (V.vii)

Like God in the work of Flaubert, the king has been "partout dans l'oeuvre, mais nulle part visible." The appearance of the *exempt* "just in time" is not the mere convention (a *deux ex machina*) it appears to be; the king—through the *exempt*—is a key character and his intervention is not a "convenient" way out of the dilemma but the only way out of it.

Now, this interpretation of the king's role would seem to support those Molière scholars who have maintained against Michaut that a supposed three-act version of the play without the king's saving role did not exist—at most, the three acts of May 1664 were either only the first three acts of the five-act version or simply a compression of the present five acts. Yet, as Michaut has insisted almost in vain, [in *Les Luttes de Molière*], there is nothing incompatible between a three-act version without the king's saving role and the play as we now have it. We need not be shocked that Molière might have written *Le Tartuffe* first of all without a "happy ending," with Tartuffe in full command of the situation, master of Orgon and his possessions. In this case one is not so much shocked by the hypocrisy of Tartuffe as by the gullibility of Orgon. Michaut's brilliant thesis has been rejected by leading Molière scholars for reasons which tell more about the prevailing climate of Molière criticism than they do about the climate in which the play was written. Thus, seventy-five years ago, Mesnard and Despois in their monumental edition of Molière [*Oeuvres*] summarized and fixed that didactic approach to the play which characterizes most of the criticism surrounding it. They believed that Molière had envisaged the king's intervention from the very beginning of the play, holding it to the very end in order to show "la fausse dévotion en train de devenir maîtresse de la société avec une entière sécurité d'insolence, si la plus haute des puissances tutélaires ne l'arrêtait pas." The plural "puissances tutélaires" is revealing, casting as it does the absolute power of the king in the anonymous functions of modern theories of government, robbing the act of its personal providential character and of its status as a tribute to Molière's patron, Louis XIV. Again, Lancaster, [in *History: Part Three*], while accepting the possible existence of a completed three-act version, includes the intervention of the king in both versions on the grounds that comedy demands a "happy ending"—a requirement called for also by Mornet (who differs from Lancaster, however, in rejecting the existence of a completed three-act version on purely historical grounds). Finally, the most recent and the most scrupulous of those scholars who have studied the problem, John Cairncross, [in *New Light on Molière*] has rejected Michaut's thesis of a triumphant Tartuffe, although he has reconstructed his own three-act version terminating with the exposure of Tartuffe at the end of the present Act IV. "The *Urtartuffe,* was, it will be remembered, described as a 'comédie fort divertissante.' It could not therefore conceivably have terminated . . . on such a sombre note as the ruin of an entire family owing to the donation or even (if it is admitted that the donation was only added in 1667) on the expulsion of Damis from home and the seduction of Elmire. It is worth stressing the consistency with which in seventeenth century France virtue is always rewarded and vice punished on the stage.

Nor is it likely that Molière should have gone out of his way to weaken his hand in dealing with the dévots by so obviously running counter to the accepted convention." One senses behind these and similar objections the didactic view of Molière as a judge handing out rewards and punishments in his "lecture plays." (There is, too, perhaps an unconscious fear of facing up to the fundamentally tragic bases of satire, a notion to which I shall return here.) Evidently, if we accept the widespread view of Molière as a social satirist with a bourgeois outlook, it is difficult to conceive of him writing such a "vicious" play as a *Le Tartuffe,* without the rescue of Orgon by "tutelary" intervention of some kind.

However, certain critics have discovered in the great comedian not a bourgeois but an aristocratic poet in whom cruelty toward the Prud'-hommes is a marked trait. Such a poet could write a *Tartuffe* showing the impostor triumphant at the end; such a *Tartuffe* would make negatively the same point that the present version makes positively: the king is as powerful in the moral realm as in the physical. In laughing at Orgon, helpless at the hands of Tartuffe, the king in no way approves of the unscrupulous Tartuffe. On such an occasion the king can enjoy undiluted the pleasure of laughing at that figure who almost everywhere in the work of Molière, according to Bénichou, [in *Les Morales du grand siècle*] "est médiocre ou ridicule": the bourgeois. Louis XIV did not want to laugh at false devotion (Tartuffe) but at blind devotion (Orgon). Neither Molière nor the king had any doubts about the evil of false devotion, but in a version destined expressly for the king's pleasure there was no need to spell out the obvious. Thus, as Michaut has conjectured, in the first version Tartuffe probably remained in the margin and the ridiculous Orgon held the spotlight. A dangerous procedure undoubtedly, for there was no protagonist on-stage—a fact which provoked the wrath of Molière's enemies, the *dévots,* and a fact which might have led Molière to take the royal protagonist out of the audience and to put him into the play itself when he decided to rewrite it.

Nevertheless, until the "ur-*Tartuffe*" is found (or another reliable document on the contents of the 1664 performance), Michaut's thesis must be treated for what it is: a brilliant but debatable conjecture. Yet, whether we regard the scene of the *exempt* as tacked on to an earlier version or as part of the play in all of its versions, we must acknowledge that it strikes an unusual, though not necessarily unpleasant, note in the play. In contrast to the satirical realism of the preceding scenes, it is lyrical in effect. The speech of the *exempt* is less a reproach to Tartuffe than a eulogy of the Roi Soleil. The king is a "Prince . . . dont les yeux se font jour dans les coeurs"; the king "donne aux gens de bien une gloire immortelle"; with this king "le mérite . . . ne perd rien, / Et que mieux que du mal il se souvient du bien" (V.vii). The tone of the speech is affirmative, expansive, exultant; if this king is a *deus ex machina* the emphasis is upon the divinity and not the vehicle. And it is upon the divinity of the king himself: nowhere in this speech of forty verses do we hear the king speak in that role traditionally associated with the Catholic Monarchs of the *ancien régime:* Defender of the

Faith. Nor is the divinity of the god-king Christian in any sense: Louis's divine faculties of omniscience (the emphasis in the speech on metaphors of vision-intelligence) and Justice (his reward to Orgon for services rendered and his judgment upon Tartuffe) are not tempered by the specifically Christian attribute of the godhead: Mercy. The king rescues Orgon not out of merciful understanding of his weakness in supporting the Fronde, but on balance: his service outweighs his misdeeds. In short, the king who appears in these verses looks less to the royal saint whose name Louis continued than to the splendid figure of the pagan divinity who was to be the hero of Molière's most emphatic tribute to his royal patron, the Jupiter of *Amphitryon*. However briefly, the dénouement of *Le Tartuffe* is marked by the euphoria which pervades the whole of *Amphitryon* and the so-called court plays in general.

Given the essentially lyrical character of the intervention, then, is it surprising that for a number of critics the dénouement destroys the realistic focus of the rest of the play? Even if we maintain that the intervention is the only solution for the moral anarchy of "Tartuffism," we cannot help but note that the tone of the dénouement does not fuse with the rest of the play. Molière has used a dramatic form inappropriate to his inattention to flatter the king. To recall Baudelaire's division of the Molière canon, the dramatist has used the mode of the "comique significatif" to create an example of the "comique grotesque." Or, more precisely, he has juxtaposed the two modes. One cannot sing the praises of anyone with mordant satire; satire is by definition negative and to sing of glories some other form is required. Earlier in 1664 Molière had begun to work in such a form with *Le Mariage forcé,* his first *comédie-ballet.* Possibly, with the first version of *Le Tartuffe,* he counted on the context of *Les Plaisirs de l'Ile Enchantée,* which included his second *comédie-ballet* as well (*La Princesse d'Elide*), to dilute the negativism of the satire (just as he counted on the "dilution" of the bitterly satirical *George Dandin* in the context of *Le Grand Divertissement royal de Versailles* in 1668). Be that as it may, in the final version of *Le Tartuffe* he has tried with the scene of the *exempt* to "take back" the negativism of the satire—and failed. The "significatif" and the "grotesque" did not fuse and would not until much later with *Le Bourgeois gentilhomme* and *Le Malade imaginaire.*

2. *Dom Juan, ou le Festin de Pierre*

As the quarrel of *L'Ecole des femmes* has already taught us, Molière is not one to back down in a close fight. So, in *Dom Juan,* he gives a fuller, more affirmative expression of the ideals only negatively implied in most of *Le Tartuffe* and brought out briefly in the final scenes of that play. The statement is astonishing only if we persist with generations of unsympathetic critics in taking the Dom Juan of the first part of the fifth act as the same character we see earlier in the play or if we see in the dénouement Molière's own punishment of the legendary lover. For Dom Juan adopts hypocrisy in the fifth act only temporarily and in clear contrast with his open behavior in the first four acts, where he gives himself only for what he is. In fact, as James Doolittle has shown in a character-by-character analysis of the play ["The Humanity of Molière's *Dom Juan*," PMLA, LXVIII], it is just this honesty which sets Dom Juan in such violent conflict with the "others" of this play. But, one objects, perhaps Dom Juan is honest with Sganarelle and Dimanche and Dom Luis—but what about his behavior with Elvire and the peasant girls? Yet, can we really judge these "deceptions" on the same ethical grounds as the deceptions of Tartuffe? We have only to compare Dom Juan's courtship of the peasant girls with the nervous, sly courtship of Elmire by Tartuffe to sense immediately a profound difference between the two "hypocrites." With Dom Juan, "hypocrisy" is not a matter of ethics but of esthetics: he is a hypocrite only in the etymological sense of the word: an actor. The lies of courtship are only conventions of his role in the game of love. The Charlottes and even the Elvires are well aware of this. However, like many an actor in this game, they forget or want to forget that the first and most important rule of the game is that it must not be taken seriously. Unlike Tartuffe, Dom Juan seeks no victims in his "conquests"—only fellow-actors. Thus, if the other "actors" take the game too seriously, they have only themselves to blame. That Charlotte and Mathurine should get burned in this games does not affect us too deeply, for, as even the most antipathetic critics have admitted, we identify with the appealing Dom Juan even in disapproving of him. However, the nobility of Elvire's worldly station and her dignified airs make her defeat in the game of love seem especially pathetic. Yet, this "grande dame" is less honest with herself than the relatively simple peasant girls and so deserves our sympathy even less. In reproaching Dom Juan she blames him not for infidelity—she knows the rules of the game too well for that—but, as Doolittle says, "for his seeming inability to hide it . . . for his silence . . . for his failure to cloak his action in a set of conventional phrases." For, the game being over, Dom Juan in all honesty makes the clear distinction between appearance and reality which the occasion calls for. Indeed, if his conduct in the courtship of the peasant girls is any clue, even in courtship Dom Juan makes the more subtle but no less clear distinction between appearance and reality which the occasion calls for; we assume, then, that he acted in the same way in his courtship of Elvire which we do not actually see in the play. Being pure conventions, the deceptions of courtship do not really obscure the courtier's objective of sensual satisfaction; rather, they "sublimate" animal drives, translate them into human terms. Not that I would minimize the importance of physical possession for this "grand seigneur." Dom Juan is no Marivaux prince wryly delighting in the playing of the game of love for its own sake; his sense of reality is too great to allow that. Nevertheless, Dom Juan is not Lady Chatterly's lover either and to miss the conventionality of his courtships is to miss his humanity.

No matter how much we may ultimately justify the amorous aspects of Dom Juan's behavior in terms of the rest of the action and whatever the emphasis in the legend, criticism of the play has made too much of Dom Juan's "attachments." Actually, much of the action is concerned not with Dom Juan's supposedly unscrupulous wooing but with the shortcomings of the "others" of this play: Sganarelle, who blandly justifies selling phony medicine to gullible peasants on the sole authority of appearances, the doctor's robes the buys (III.i); Dom Louis, who presumptuously identifies his own with God's purposes; Alonse, whose brutish loyalty to the code of honor makes a mockery of that code as it is more sympathetically represented in his brother, Carlos; etc. These self-deceivers remind us by contrast of Dom Juan's chief virtue: his refusal to deceive himself, his intention to give himself on every occasion only for what he is. Nor is this virtue simply moral in character—*vertu;* it is also *virtu,* the manliness of a brave man as is clearly evident in Dom Juan's rescue of Carlos and in his courage before threats made by the highest as well as the lowliest of powers: the Statue and Pierrot (who are, by the way, linked etymologically as well in the very sub-title of the play: *Le Festin de Pierre*):

Thus Dom Juan is the most authentic of Molière's heroes, a *généreux* in the Cornelian mold who refuses to accept any compromise of his ideal of self-assertion. This affiliation with Corneille inevitably calls to mind Poulaille's thesis, [in *Corneille sous le marque de Molière*], so let me say immediately that I am in no way subscribing to the preposterous notion that Corneille really wrote Molière's plays in whole or in part. Nevertheless, Poulaille, like Bénichou more responsibly, has sensed a kinship between the two writers, one that I feel I should explore in some detail before going on with my assessment of **Dom Juan's** place in the entire Molière canon.

Remembering the parodistic rehearsal of various Cornelian dramas in *L'Impromptu de Versailles,* we tend to read Molière comedy as the very evacuation of "Cornelianism"—nothing, we feel, could be further from its supposed posturings. Yet, both as producer and dramatist, Molière had quite sincerely turned at an earlier stage of his career to the Cornelian mold. Fernandez reminds us that Molière had been formed intellectually and artistically in the "age of Corneille" and that a tragedy of Corneille accompanied each of the new comedies Molière presented upon arriving in Paris. And most critics agree that this preoccupation with Corneille gives a decidedly Cornelian stamp to Molière's only attempt at a "serious" play: **Dom Garcie de Navarre, ou le Prince jaloux** (first presented in February 1661, although generally believed to have been written much earlier). It should be said, however, that most of these critics feel that the Cornelianism is incomplete or misdirected: the heroine, Elvire, is Cornelian; the hero, Dom Garcie, is not. Fixing an interpretation of the hero which has obtained throughout the history of the play's criticism, Rigal, writing fifty years ago, objected that Dom Garcie's jealousy, unlike that of Othello and Alceste, is unmotivated. Lancaster, following Michaut, regards Dom Garcie as "un maniaque de jalousie," while Fernandez, in the most pointed criticism of the play to date, regards him as an "intrus dans un monde dont il est indigne, ou comme un enfant gâté pour lequel on est trop bon." Dom Garcie doesn't belong in the same world as Elvire because "d'après les canons cornéliens la jalousie est un crime contre l'amour: elle ravale l'objet aimé et l'amant lui-même, elle donne le pas à l'animal sur l'homme; surtout elle rompt tout rapport entre l'amour et les hauts principes de l'idéal humain." The subject, indeed, seems more Racinian than Cornelian, so that Rigal and others perhaps do a disservice to Molière in asking him to justify the hero's behavior: in Dom Garcie, ever ready to accuse his mistress of infidelity, we could read an instance of the Racinian character's tendency to find in reality the confirmation of his own inmost desires—whether it is there or not. In short, intelligence at the service of will or desire. Thus, Léon Emery has been led [in *Molière: du metier à la pensée*] to describe Dom Garcie as "un document à illustrer le passage du style cornélian au style racinien de la tragédie. Plus de complications romanesques en dehors des postulates conventionnels que tout le monde connaît; plus de tirades qui se déroulent avec pompe ou qui jaillissent comme des épées nues."

Yet, in Dom Garcie himself, we are with neither Corneille nor Racine; Molière's attitude toward his hero is very much his own. Though nowhere so subtle as in the great plays, Molière's dramaturgy is familiar enough here. Following W. G. Moore's brilliant analysis of *Le Misanthrope* [in *Molière: A New Criticism*], we might say that in *Dom Garcie de Navarre*, too, "the successive scenes do not so much narrate events as expose an attitude and a relationship." However, the early play lacks the poetic subtlety and the dramatic complexity (the "suffusion" as Moore speaks of it) of the later one: Molière concentrates too exclusively on a single dramatic device for "illuminating" the central aspect of character (jealousy) which is his subject in the play. Each act is like a little play in itself, but we get the same little play over and over: Elvire assures Dom Garcie that she loves him; he comes upon something (a letter [used twice]; the presence of a "rival", etc.) which feeds his jealousy; she finally disabuses him. There is some forward motion at the ending of certain acts as a secondary character (the Iago-like Dom Lope) or the report of some new circumstance feeds the hero's jealousy, but instead of carrying us along in an ascending dramatic movement, the successive acts remain at the same expository level of dramatic interest. The "surprise ending" is a happy enough one, but rather than being a dénouement (in the strictest sense) to the problem of the play, it seems more designed simply to bring the repetitive action to an abrupt halt. Dom Garcie's jealousy never issues in a tragic insight into himself, a recognition of his "tragic flaw." Indeed, his "flaw" is without such universal significance; rather, like the obsessions of Molière's other monomaniacs, it is peculiar, beyond the human as it were. The mechanical, repetitive dramaturgy of the play suggests a quizzical, tentative attitude on the part of Molière in the face of this peculiarity, as if his desire to remain "serious" prevented him from taking the obvious comic attitude which the hero's obsession calls for. Circumstance, not the wiles of the "others" of this play, provides the temporary resolution of the conflict of the play: Dom Sylvie, the supposed triumphant rival for Elvire's love, turns out to be her brother, Dom Alphonse. I say "temporary," for here as well, Bailly's "rule of non-conversion"

holds true: even this latest circumstance, Dom Garcie admits, finds him "tombé de nouveau dans ces traitres soupçons" and Elvire accepts him "jaloux ou non jaloux."

Given Dom Garcie's character, then, we might see in the play the proof of Molière's "international" criticism of Corneille in *L'Impromptu*. Yet, this would be to forget the presence of a truly Cornelian character in the play: his mistress. "Elvire," writes Fernandez, "est une hèroîne de Corneille, une cousine de Pauline, un peu à la mode de Bretagne. Toujours, dit-elle, notre coeur est en notre pouvoir, et s'il montre parfois quelque faiblesse, la raison doit être maîtresse de tous nos sens." It is true that even Elvire's *générosité* is inevitably compromised in the love she bears Dom Garcie, for, unlike her Cornelian counterparts, she cannot really be said to find in her lover a perfect reflection of herself. Nevertheless, as Baumal has argued [in *Molière: auteur prècieux*], her pity is dictated to her by her reason—she recognizes that Dom Garcie's vice is "incurable et fatal"—and her reason thereby teaches her that she cannot deny her lover the "estime" she otherwise owes him. Her love as seen in this gesture is not of the heedless, self-destructive kind in Racine's *Andromagne,* for example, but recalls rather Auguste's patronizing and self-congratulatory clemency in Corneille's *Cinna.* Though she is indeed touched by her lover's incurable malady, Elvire accepts him because "on doit quelque indulgence / Aux défauts oú le Ciel fait pencher l'influence" (V.vi). One owes such indulgence to the victim himself, of course, but, more fundamentally, one owes it to oneself. Elvire's love is narcissistic.

Molière's serious imitation of Corneille in the character of Elvire should make us wary of that tradition which pits Molière against Corneille almost as automatically as it does Racine. To link Molière and Racine in this way against Corneille is to misconstrue both Molière comedy and Corneille "tragedy." Actually, with his unlimited confidence in man Corneille is the least tragic of writers. As for Molière, once we begin to see that not the limiting motions of satire but the expansive notions of what we can only call the "pure comic" are the real essence of his work, then we can begin to see his true relation to Corneille. Both the comedian and the so-called tragedian have an optimistic view of "man's fate." There is, to be sure, a crucial difference between the two: Corneille's optimism is cerebral and is expressed as an unrestrained voluntarism; Molière's is visceral and is grounded in a confident naturalism. In Cartesian terms, if the will follows the intelligence (*entendement*) so closely as to be identified with it in Corneille, in Molière the will follows the appetitive so closely as to be identified with it. (I am speaking of this relationship in "others," of course. Also just as the will is passional in Corneille, so the appetitive is intelligent in Molière—witness the naturally wily Agnès and the numerous shrewd peasant-types.) There is, in sum, in the two writers a difference in both the psychical functions and in the ends to which man should direct those functions, but in each there is no doubt that man has it within his power to direct those functions to whatever ends he chooses. The difference from the truly tragic sense of human limitation in Racine could not be greater.

And so the failure of **Dom Garcie** is not due to a contradiction between two radically different views of the human condition. True, the play is fractured in conception, but it is fractured in terms familiar to us already in **Le Tartuffe**: Molière has tried to fuse not the tragic and the comic but two modes of the comic—the heroic and the satiric. As with all Molière plays, the hero's obsession (here, jealousy) is not symbolic of irrational, destructive forces which really govern "la condition humaine." Rather, that obsession is peculiar and special—fantastical, as Béralde might put it—and we can accommodate ourselves to it. What makes Dom Garcie exceptional in the Molière canon is that the means of accommodation are not the familiar ones of ruse and wile and justified duplicity, carefully articulated throughout the entire play. Accommodation is possible, rather, because of a frankly "noble" conception of the heroine's character. And, most significantly for my purposes here, that "nobility" is undoubtedly Cornelian.

In light of Molière's demonstrated sympathy for Corneille then, we might take a very different view of the parodistic rehearsals from Corneille's plays in **L'Impromptu**: it is more the director aiming his satire at the acting style of his rivals than it is the dramatist aiming his barbs at the writer whom he had so frankly imitated in his own career. Further, in light of that imitation, Bénichou's interpretation of **Dom Juan** [in *Les Morales*] is given an especially Cornelian force: that play the critic believes, is based "sur la conception d'un héros souverain, dont les désirs se prétendent au-dessus du blâme et de la contrainte." Of course, *générosité* in **Dom Juan** is far more concrete in its expression than it was in Elvire and certainly more so than in any Cornelian hero (although, even in the case of the latter, the tendency to abstraction and introversion has been vastly exaggerated). Nevertheless, the *données* of characterization are the same: self-assertion and self-definition in action.

Yet, this authentic Cornelian hero becomes a hypocrite. Dom Juan is a Molière character who, at a certain point, undergoes a conversion. Bailly's term becomes richly ironic in this play: from an anti-religious outlook Dom Juan pretends to convert to a religious one. Now, from a strictly religious point of view, Bailly's "rule of non-conversion" is sustained, of course: Dom Juan only pretends to be converted. Nevertheless, the rule of Molière comedy is broken: in the very act of pretending to be converted to religion Dom Juan no longer gives himself for what he is; he converts to hypocrisy not in the etymological sense of "play-acting" but in the acquired moral sense of "lying." He ceases to be *généreux*.

Now, it is for this derogation from the purely human ideal of *générosité* and not from the Christian ideal of sincere self-abnegation that Dom Juan is to be reproached as a hypocrite. Christian doctrine has too readily regarded hypocrisy as a vice having particular reference to its system of values. This is understandable: of all vices, hypocrisy is the most fundamentally destructive of any system of sanctions, but especially one of invisible sanctions. The sinner who admits to wrong-doing acknowledges the validity of the moral code according to which he is reprimanded. But a hypocrite rejects radically the whole system of values and sanctions which pretends to reprimand him. Doctrinally speaking, what we might call the true hypocrite does not believe in an ultimate day of judgment and he is incapable of feeling remorse based on a fear of hell, the threat of damnation which is the Christian moralist's ultimate weapon. At most, this weapon can hope to reach only those sinners who might be described as unsystematic or half-hearted hypocrites: the gamblers of the Christian faith who count on weekly confession or deathbed repentance or God's inscrutable mercy to "insure" the risks they run. Such "hypocrites" are unworthy of the name, for, in the very act of hoping to get by the sanctions, they admit their existence. But the only sanctions which a true hypocrite recognizes are of a more practical nature: threats to his physical safety or of an exposure which will make it impossible to continue to practice of his duplicity. Since, theoretically, the final proof of exposure depends on the hypocrite himself, on his decision to drop his pose, it is impossible to "catch" a true hypocrite. Indeed, the true hypocrite will turn every attempt at exposure by others to his own advantage. Thus, Tartuffe's attempt to pass himself off as the self-sacrificing instrument of the very power which arrests him reveals the frightening moral anarchy to which a thoroughgoing hypocrisy leads.

"N'aurons-nous donc pas de règle?" The poignancy of Pascal's question is felt even by that thinker whom we usually pit against him: Descartes. The very founder of modern rationalism required a Guarantor of the truth of his first principles. Like Pascal, though by a different route, he found his Guarantor of moral as well as epistemological truth in God. And Molière, does he too find his Guarantor of Truth in God? One wonders. We may speculate endlessly about the extent to which his conventional deferences to religion (for example, the baptism of his children or the remarks of the first and second Placets to **Le Tartuffe**) reflect a genuine piety. As for the plays, at most they suggest a secularist separation of the things of this world from those of the next and, at worst, from the religious viewpoint, an exclusively human solution to the moral dilemmas they pose. Thus, in **Le Tartuffe,** the king is Molière's answer to the poignant question of Pascal: he and not God is the Guarantor of Truth. Lest it be objected that, in good monarchial theory, the king is only God's surrogate on earth, I would point once again to the decidedly non-Christian tone of the *exempt's* speech. In the resplendent image of the king, who restores order and truth to the anarchical situation created by Tartuffe, man, Molière tells us, is his own Guarantor of Truth.

This anthropocentrism, which emerges only in the dénouement of **Le Tartuffe,** is the guiding theme of **Dom Juan**. Dom Juan's humanism harks back to the ancient pagan and aristocratic ideal of man as self-sufficient and self-determining. This ideal, which Christianity tried in vain to assimilate, persisted in the ideals of feudalism which were still felt in the seventeenth century. For practical reasons it was unnecessary and for moral reasons unthinkable to the holders of this ideal to use hypocrisy to achieve their ends: practically, their power was subject to almost no checks, since, being aristocrats, they were to be found at the top of the social and political structure; morally, they could not tolerate the thought that any situation could require the *concealed* expression of their power. Obviously, the dynamics of such an outlook are ultimately destructive of the outlook itself: at some point, one aristocrat's self-assertion will run counter to another's. Both theoretically and practically, only one aristocrat can hope to attain to the purest embodiment of the ideal: absolute monarchy. Even this expression of the ideal has proved historically untenable: the self-assertion of the absolute monarch has run counter to the combined assertions of the other elements of society and been frustrated by revolution. But the historical and the political ramifications of the ideal need not concern us here. More to the present point is the moral basis of the ideal: the injunction to an absolute identification between appearance and reality, between intention and deed. In pretending to convert to religion, Dom Juan breaks this injunction. This constitutes his real hypocrisy and his real conversion.

Why does Molière have Dom Juan convert to hypocrisy? Did he wish to appease his religious enemies by "exposing" the legendary scourge of Christian morality? In the Dom Juan who scolds Sganarelle at the beginning of the fourth act, Michaut sees the signs of a bad conscience—as if Dom Juan were anxiously trying to deny to himself the truth of the Christian view. Yet, these transports might as easily be explained as revealing the impatience and exasperation which finally attains a Dom Juan forced to live in the world of the Sganarelles and the Dimanches. It is difficult to be—or to remain—Dom Juan in such a world. In Dom Juan's irritability we get a glimmering of that other Molière hero who finds himself in a world too confining for his noble ideals: Alceste, the *généreux* become *atrabilaire*. In fact, one lesson of Dom Juan's hypocrisy seems to be that the only way in which he can fulfill the law of his being—the overriding drive to self-definition in action—is through hypocrisy. Yet, the context of his hypocrisy suggests that there is a higher lesson to be learned from it. For it is a curious hypocrisy which exposes itself even before it is practiced: Dom Juan announces his intention to be a hypocrite to Sganarelle. His servant (and we the audience) thus becomes his witness that the hypocrisy is not "for real." Rather, we learn that it is only a tool to show the "others" the futility and inhumanity of their reliance upon a system of invisible sanctions. In attacking the "dévots" against whom it was presumably aimed, **Dom Juan** attacks the very idea of religion and the social ideas which flow from the Christian religion in particular: the notion of man's nature as fallen from a "state of grace" and the reliance upon sanctions outside of man to regulate his "fallen" nature. Dom Juan's adoption of hypocrisy is a frightening pendent to the king's crushing of it in *Le Tartuffe*. In the latter, the highest example of humanity guaranteed truth and restored order; in Dom Juan, the highest example of humanity abandons truth and disrupts the true order which he has represented in the play to this point. And Dom Juan is *obviously* the highest example of humanity: in him appearance and reality coincide not only with respect to

moral intention and deed, but in moral nature and physical appearance. Dom Juan's handsomeness not only explains his appeal to the ladies—it defines his inner reality: truth and beauty are one. Thus, if the highest example of humanity shall adopt hypocrisy, who shall be the guarantor of truth? If Dom Juan, the enemy of illusion and self-deception in the first four acts, shall hypocritically claim to speak in God's name, who can really be said to speak in God's name? If we cannot trust to the natural appearances of integrity, how can we trust to *artificial* evidences: a priest's robes, for example? Sganarelle's donning of doctor's robes to sell patent medicines gives special point to this question. This is the lesson of Dom Juan's hypocrisy in the larger context in which it occurs.

Nevertheless, we cannot deny that this larger context is itself compromised by Dom Juan's hypocrisy. "I hope you have not been leading a double life," Cecily says to Algernon in Oscar Wilde's *The Importance of Being Earnest,* "pretending to be wicked and being really good all the time. That would be hypocrisy" (Act II). In Dom Juan's compromised *générosité* we see that the only way in which humanity can affirm its self-sufficiency is in an act of pretended dependence; the only way in which man can affirm himself is through an act of pretended self-denial. Dom Juan's good intentions in some larger context notwithstanding, the appearance which Dom Juan gives to the world belies the reality; unlike the Dom Juan of the first part of the play, the one who speaks as a Christian convert to Dom Carlos in V.iii does not give himself for what he is. At least in the Christian world, Dom Juan's hypocrisy tells us, there are limits to the power of *générosité,* cases in which it can express itself only by denying itself. This cruel perception borders on the tragic. Yet, the dénouement of the play robs this tragic paradox of its force. In refusing to repent for his false conversion both before the specter and the statue, Dom Juan actually repents or "re-converts" to the ideals we saw him uphold in the first part of the play. In "testing" the specter, which Michaut sees as a symbol of Divine Grace, Dom Juan clearly resists God in his most mysterious and supposedly irresistible form. As for the statue, there is a sublime simplicity in Dom Juan's "La voilà" as he gives it his hand. In light of this gesture it is difficult to accept W. G. Moore's view of Dom Juan as "a man who despises humanity, who sets himself apart and above the rest and is thus bound, being human, to fail." Suicide and damnation are the means by which Dom Juan defines the superiority of his purely human ideals over the Christian ideals represented by the specter in their most appealing forms and by the statue in their most terrifying forms. In best Cornelian fashion, Dom Juan uses death as an instrument of self-assertion. In this test with the highest power, the *généreux* proves himself without limits, transcending tragedy not through resignation but through affirmation.

But what of Dom Juan's last words before falling into the abyss?—"O Ciel! que sens-je? Un feu invisible me brûle, je n'en puis plus, et tout mon corps devient un brasier ardent. Ah" (V.vi)! Do they not acknowledge a "tragic illumination" of his "failure?" Possibly, although they do no more than acknowledge the failure and express no particular attitude toward it. Merely recording a physical event, this "illumination" contains no repentance: at most, Dom Juan admits a limitation ("je n'en puis plus") without in any way disowning what he has been able to do up to this point. Indeed, in this purely objective recognition of the supernatural we can see a reproach directed not at Dom Juan, but at the supernatural for using brute force to overwhelm an adversary who has proved its equal in the spiritual realm.

We can understand, then, that in spite of the orthodoxy of the dénouement, the *dévots* did not like *Dom Juan* any more than they did *Le Tartuffe*. The manner of Dom Juan's death belies the orthodoxy of the damnation itself. In the language of one of its Jansenist critics, the play offended "ce qu'il y a de plus saint et de plus sacré dans la religion." It reaffirmed the "orgueil des grands" against which Bossuet and the Jansenists in particular directed their anathemas: it depicted man as self-sufficient, able to get along without God in order to achieve his fullest dignity as a man. Nevertheless, this heroism is defended with a disturbing aggressiveness. In spite of the good intentions behind it, Dom Juan's hypocrisy strikes a jarring, unpleasant note in the play. Furthermore, the satiric butts of Dom Juan's aggressive *générosité* share the limelight as much as he: like Alceste in the next play, Molière uses this hero as a dramatic lever to force the "others" in all their ridiculousness into our view. Thus, *Dom Juan* shows a lack of fusion similar to that in *Le Tartuffe,* though obviously not so pronounced as in that play. Here Molière has done more than juxtapose two modes of comedy, but, to borrow a metaphor from chemistry, the combination is as yet only a mixture. It will not be a compound until he suffuses it with the poetry of his *comédies-ballets*.

3. *Le Misanthrope*

If Tartuffe is the only hypocrite in a world of innocents, Alceste is the only innocent in a world of hypocrites. In describing the most controversial of Molière's characters as "innocent" I am not implying that he is naïve nor in stressing his uniqueness do I mean to forget Philinte and Eliante. Like Dom Juan, Alceste knows only too well the duplicity of human behavior. He himself compromises his integrity in his behavior with the writer of the sonnet and with Célimène. Nevertheless, to the contrary of the "others" of this play, at the moment of ultimate decisions he upholds the ideal of absolute integrity; his deeds then match his intentions. In his readiness to pay the supreme price "selon les lois constitutives de l'univers de la pièce" Alceste differs from Philinte and Eliante. The latter are but relatively innocent, set apart by the "virtue" of their tolerance from the rigid Alceste, cast very much in their relationship to him as Le Pauvre to Dom Juan.

Isolated from the "others" of this play, Alceste is a kind of Dom Juan *raté,* one seen in the distorting mirror of "la vie mondaine," one who salvages nothing from his defeat at the end of the play. The implicit lessons of *Le Tartuffe* and *Dom Juan,* obscured in the triumphant accents of the final scenes, become explicit in the final scenes of *Le Misanthrope*. The absence of a Guarantor has been re-

marked and Alceste does not banish himself to his "désert" with the *éclat* of Dom Juan sublimely proferring his hand to his destroyer. The anarchy of hypocrisy has reached man not in his relations with the invisible but in his relations with his fellow-man. In *Le Misanthrope* Molière questions the root idea of society: the good faith of its members upon which the social contract is based. The dénouement offers us two symbols of the most sombre significance: Célimène telling us that society is committed to doubleness, to a discrepancy between appearance and reality, between intention and deed; Alceste telling us that the correspondence of intention and deed is possible only in a social void.

Alceste's *désert* is, of course, only metaphorical. "On le dit . . . d'un homme qui, aimant la solitude, a fait bâtir quelque jolie maison hors des grands chemins et éloignée du commerce du monde, pour s'y retirer." Yet, given Alceste's quasi-religious fervor, the term re-acquires some of its literal meaning, evoking for us those early Christian saints who monastically retreated to the desert in their search for purity. In announcing his intention Alceste is only making explicit what we assume about the other great monomaniacs of Molière comedy: they too go to a desert at the end of the play. Not that the dénouement of *Le Misanthrope* simply repeats the lessons of the other plays. We should remember that Alceste willingly banishes himself to his desert; the Harpagons and the Arnolphes are banished unwillingly. Or more precisely, unwittingly. In fact, they have been living psychologically in a desert from the very beginning of the play: the desert of their particular obsessions. Monomania prevents them from effectively participating in society, the arena of compromise, self-criticism and, to a certain degree, self-sacrifice. What makes Alceste unique among these monomaniacs is his awareness of the compromise upon which society is based. Thus, his self-exile constitutes a powerful doubt as to the value of self-sacrifice for the sake of society. For the first time the self is posited as an equal and possibly superior value to society. Alceste represents that bifurcation of the personality into public and private selves which characterizes man in society and which creates the tensions of "civilization and its discontents." As the demands of society become greater, moulding the self to acceptable "norms," the self is forced into its own recesses, into its own "désert."

Of course, in the ideal world of the *généreux,* Alceste would have no problems—were he not so single-minded, paradoxically enough, in his *générosité*. For, in spite of a basic similarity, Alceste differs from Dom Juan in one essential aspect: he is incapable of that esthetic hypocrisy which justifies, from a moral point of view, Dom Juan's behavior towards women. If Alceste is right in his condemnation of many of the forms of society, he is wrong in his failure to recognize the value of the esthetic in the domain of love. There, his integrity dehumanizes him and renders him ridiculous. Does this mean that Célimène's behavior is implicitly justified? Hardly, for her estheticism is only an opposite extreme to Alceste's integrity. She is an artificial character: Half Dom Juan, half Tartuffe. Like the former she plays a role, but like the latter she plays the role everywhere. In Dom Juan, the esthetics of courtship led to sensual satisfaction; in Célimème they are subverted to the purely social: satisfaction is frustrated in order that the game might go on. Her sociability exacts as high a price as Alceste's sincerity. Her "tartuffism" is not thoroughgoing, of course: she accepts exposure, admits to wrongdoing. But in the very admission she remains unconverted: looking forward to the spirit of Marivaux comedy, she believes that everything can be arranged after the damage is done in the simple admission that her intentions were not after all vicious, that it was all only a kind of game—a cruel one, to be sure, but a game.

Le Misanthrope ends in a moral stalemate. It is a comedy without a happy ending, a tragedy without a tragic illumination. Both Célimène and Alceste are presented to us with strong reservations; each is the object of Molière's satire. The play is, in fact, Molière's supreme achievement in the satiric mode. In this mode he invites us to laugh at man's foibles, to delight in the depiction of man's obsessions and pretentions and so to rise above such "vices" in ourselves. Now, it is in this self-protective laughter that we usually locate the essence of Molière's "comic view of life." Yet, it is debatable whether the definition of comedy as self-protective or dissociative laughter is a valid one—at least in contradistinction to tragedy. Satire points up the discrepancy between ideals and performance, between reality and appearance; it emphasizes man's limitations. Indeed, to the extent that in the "non-conversion" of the comic figure a given limitation is shown to be ineradicable, Molière satirical comedy repeats the lesson of tragedy without offering the paradoxical victory of tragedy: in the very act of perceiving the limitation which is inherent in the scheme of things (fate) man transcends his limitation.

Seen in this perspective, the happy endings of the satiric plays are "smoke screens" to cover up the negative, depressing view of the unreconstructed comic figure who has just been taught a lesson whose point he cannot see. In the euphoria of Horace's union with Agnès, for example, we lose sight of the fact that Arnolphe has been left "holding the bag," we are spared the uncomfortable reminder of his humanity. Traditionally, criticism has tried to escape this bitter lesson by locating the real lesson of the play somewhere in between convention and obsession—in the moderateness of the Chrysaldes and the Philintes. Thus, with Philinte's marriage to Eliante, *Le Misanthrope* seems a typical Molière play, one teaching a familiar lesson: society, the marriage of different wills and temperaments, depends on a spirit of compromise. But is it not indeed a watered-down euphoria which this marriage creates? Eliante, we remember, takes Philinte as a sort of consolation prize. Moreover, far from seeing Molière's position in Philinte's moderation, we might see in it only a dramatic foil which casts the extremes on either side of it in a stronger light. Even so, whether dramatic principle or lesson of the play, this moderation accepts the basically tragic notion of man as a limited creature, ultimately frustrated in his fondest ambitions and his highest aspirations.

Indeed, a professional psychiatrist, Ludwig Jekels, has seen in the climate of comedy the same preoccupation with Oedipal guilt which we have become accustomed to find in tragedy. He reads the ascension of the young in comedy as a "doing away with the father" so that the son can fulfill his wish to take the father's place sexually. In such a reading, the son is the true monomaniac, but he transfers his monomaniacal love rivalry and its attendant guilt feeling onto the father figure. "This withdrawal of the super-ego and its meaning in the ego are all in complete conformity with the phenomenon of mania . . . In each we find the ego, which has liberated itself from the tyrant, uninhibitedly venturing its humor, wit and every sort of comic manifestation in a very ecstasy of freedom." ["On the Psychology of Comedy," *Tulane Drama Review*, II, No. 3, May, 1958.] Frankly admitting the Bergsonian echoes of his theory, Jekels says that "comedy represents an esthetic correlate of mania." Yet, such a theory of comedy fails to account for those comedies in which the father figure remains dominant, or in which the pattern of relationships cannot be fitted into the Oedipal scheme. By its very premises, of course, the psychoanalytical interpretation must regard the former types as tragedies and the latter type as nonexistent. Thus, Jekels reads into *Le Tartuffe* a disguised Oedipal relationship: Tartuffe is the son who displaces his guilt onto Orgon. Yet, what would Jekels make of *Dom Juan,* where the "mania" is not displaced but is steadily defended by the son-figure? Indeed, the whole point of *Dom Juan* in Freudian terms is that the son refuses to accept as blameworthy his desire to replace the father and, as I have shown, successfully defies both father figures of the play (his biological father and the statue). Or to take a Molière play in which the father figure remains dominant, in *Amphitryon* we might read the pattern of relationships between father and son figures in two ways, but in each the father-figure remains dominant: (1) Jupiter, without being a clear rival of his "son" Mercure, keeps the latter in his place—a pattern repeated in the Amphitryon-Sosie relationship; or in a truer Freudian parallel (2) Jupiter and Mercure play father figures to Amphitryon and Sosie respectively displacing their "sons" in the love intrigues of the play. Yet these plays, like the "Oedipal comedies" Jekel cites, also end in a "very ecstasy of freedom." Obviously, comedy in which this is true is an "esthetic correlate" of something different from mania.

Thus, we can define Molière's "comic view of life" in the Jekelian sense only by dismissing that part of his work in which a different sense of the comic prevails. This is in the so-called "court work," the series of *comédies-ballets* which makes up nearly one-half the canon, but which has been treated as "minor" by the main current of Molière criticism since the early nineteenth century. Essentially liberal-bourgeois in ethos, this criticism has found it difficult to assimilate these poetic plays, created to please Molière's royal patron, into its portrait of the "scourge" of the *ancien régime,* the unmasker of social hypocrisy in a class-structured society, the enemy of all absolutisms in the very hey day of absolutism. Yet, however convenient, the division of the canon into major and minor, satire and poetry, is ill-founded. The entire canon expresses a single, consistent "comic view of life." Like the first *Le Tartuffe,* the satiric plays reflect an aristocratic bias negatively. This negative bias reached its peak in *Le Tartuffe, Dom Juan* and *Le Misanthrope,* in the period of approximately one year between the first version of *Le Tartuffe* (May 1664) and the completion of *Dom Juan* (February 1665). For, as Jasinski has shown [in *Molière et le Misanthrope*] in conception *Le Misanthrope* belongs between those two plays, Molière having completed the first act before writing *Dom Juan.* All three bitter comedies are enclosed between two *comedies-ballets: La Princesse d'Elide* of May 1664 and *L'Amour médecin* of September 1665. *Le Misanthrope,* with its unhappy ending, is "negative" only in the sense that the positive faith on which it is based is implicit. The absence of a Guarantor of truth in the play does not mean that one does not exist: he is in the audience in the person of Molière's royal patron. Or was to have been, the play having been first shown to the "town" due to the unforeseen departure of the king and much of the court just before the scheduled premiere. Like the plays which immediately surround it, the play was written with the court in mind, Molière actually having read it before its production to members of the court and accepting minor revisions. Rousseau notwithstanding, the stalemate with which the play ends is thus no more of a tragic defeat for man than was the triumph of the hypocrite at the end of the three-act *Le Tartuffe.* In the negativism of this great satiric play we see only the underside of Molière's "comic view of life."

However, the dates show that even while bringing the mode of "le significatif" to perfection, Molière has been experimenting with "le grotesque." The revision of *Le Tartuffe* actually dates from the period of the *comédies-ballets,* a fact reflected in the imperfect fusion of the two modes in the play. You cannot move towards the "grotesque," you must start from it; it must inform—literally: give form—to the entire work. Of the fifteen plays written after *Le Misanthrope* (including *Psyché*) ten are *comédies-ballets* as against three out of fifteen in the period preceding. The first *Le Tartuffe* and *Le Misanthrope* are the only directly satirical plays between *L'Impromptu de Versailles* (October 1663) and *George Dandin* (July 1668), itself contained in a festival atmosphere like the first *Le Tartuffe.* Remembering that the very combination of modes makes *Dom Juan* problematic, only *Le Médecin malgré lui* (August 1666) in this period comes close to *Le Misanthrope* in the directness of its satire. Yet, like the later *Fourberies de Scapin,* the satire of this comedy is edulcorated by the emphasis upon the instrument of comedy, the wily Sganarelle, rather than the butt, Géronte, and by its ballet-like treatment of physical action as the rhythmic vehicle of meaning. The comedy in these plays is not satire, a species of tragedy; it is pure.

"Pure comedy" shows man not as a creature of limitations but of possibilities. In the "naturalism" of plays like *L'Amour médecin* and *Le Malade imaginaire* we find the moral bases for this confident outlook. In a play like *Amphitryon* the physiological bases of this naturalism become explicit. In celebrating the sexual conquests of Jupiter, Molière is doing more than justifying the love affairs of his royal patron. Such a subject provides the perfect symbolism for affirming a comic belief in life's possibilities, even as death provides a perfect symbolism for recognizing life's limitations. Comic belief rather than comic relief lies behind the laughter of such a play. For all its value, Bergson's theory of laughter cannot explain the comedy of *Amphitryon,* where laughter expresses not a release from forces which threaten to mechanize life but a release of forces which give life. In sexual release there is undoubtedly a sense of physiological relief, but we should be wary of reading into it an analogue of the superior laughter which is the essence of satiric comedy. In the latter, the "life" which is in danger of being mechanized is the artificial, man-made life of society, just as the threats to its functioning are artificial: hypocrisy, pretense, obsession, etc. "Society," to paraphrase the Marxists, "contains the roots of its own destruction." So it is not surprising that Jekels should find that the true psychological climate of satiric comedy is anxiety. However, to the very contrary of the man-made tensions on which satiric comedy is based, true comedy is based on the natural tensions of the sexual act, those from which we can always expect a happy release. For orgasmic release is predictable and inevitable and, most importantly, fruitful. It will go on and because of it life will go on. The psychological climate of true comedy is thus the very opposite of that of satiric comedy: confident rather than anxious, optimistic rather than pessimistic. This is the real meaning of Molière's naturalism, an affirmation of rather than an accommodation to the "facts of life."

This affirmation of nature in its most basic function—self-perpetuation—is heard even in the satiric comedies. Significantly, it is usually a marriage between young people which the socially derived obsession of the central figure threatens: Arnolphe's fear of cuckoldry leads him to raise Agnès in a "social hothouse" where she will be unable to succumb to the court of "jeunes galants" like Horace; the "femmes savantes" would put the library in the bedroom; etc. But nature inevitably overcomes obsession and, seen in this light, the "conventional marriage" at the end is not a smoke screen to conceal the monomaniac's defeat but itself expresses the "pure comic." Our very sympathy for the "others" of satiric comedy lies in their desire to restore the "law of nature," as they abet the young people in their wiles against the monomaniac. The "happy ending" of these comedies is possible only because the natural has been "given its head." Agnès in *L'Ecole des femmes* is a wonderful example of this naturalism: her wiles are defensible because they serve natural purpose, while Arnolphe's are blameworthy because they would frustrate nature. Nevertheless, naturalism is less important in the satiric plays than its opposite: the over-socialization of the central figure. And in certain "oversocialized" figures we see that even the comic instrument of natural wile can be subverted to unnatural ends: Tartuffe and Célimène are the real anti-heroes of Molière comedy, not Dom Juan and Alceste. The subversion of natural wile must be undone and truth or "natural law" guaranteed by a more worthy exemplar of humanity.

Molière's naturalism need not be construed as a classical

anticipation of the Lawrentian mystique of sex. Sensualism is not an end in itself. Even in Dom Juan, the legendary lover, Molière stresses the ethical significance of the hero's behavior: the drive toward self-satisfaction, the exaltation of self-reliance, the autonomy of the human. In *Amphitryon* the emphasis upon the ethical becomes even more pronounced. Jupiter's "treacherous love affair" is justified on the grounds that from it will be born humanity's greatest hero, Hercules. This legendary exemplar of man at his best is a worthy son of the Olympian creature in whom Molière is said to have portrayed the noblest man of his age, Louis XIV. In the blinding image of this Roi Soleil of classical mythology we are reminded of a Pascalian truth without a Pascalian pathos: the order of the "grands" is distinct from the other social orders and the laws of the latter cannot be made to apply to the former. Inevitably, Jupiter's "intervention" into the inferior social order of Amphitryon and Alcmène must be condemned by the laws of that order. But, the king's "self-exposure as a 'hypocrite'" reveals that a higher ethical purpose has been at work. Jupiter's sensual self-indulgence has really been more than that. Amphitryon's body, the physical sign of his humanity, has not been a mere plaything of the gods; it has been their instrument. In the divine purpose (the half-man, half-god Hercules) appearance (Amphitryon) and reality (Jupiter) coincide. Hercules, man at his best, thus stands in stark contrast to Tartuffe, man at his worst; the eulogy of man which we hear only at the end of *Le Tartuffe* informs the entire conception of *Amphitryon*. Against the unconverted monomania of the Arnolphes and the Harpagons, against the throughgoing hypocrisy of the Tartuffes of Molière's world we must place the unconverted integrity of the king-figures, who guarantee the truth of the natural order. In its most glorious exemplars, mankind knows no limitations.

We cannot dismiss *Amphitryon* as an opportunistic compliment to Louis XIV nor discount the role of the King in *Le Tartuffe* as a meaningless convention. Molière's king-figures (including Dom Juan) remind us that in both the "significatif" and in the "grotesque" his comedy is pivoted on an axis of faith in man. In its very lack of fusion the definitive version of *Le Tartuffe* arrests the "development" of that faith like a film suddenly brought out of the "dark room" in the midst of processing. For in the truly comic *comédies-ballets* which make up the bulk of his work after *Le Tartuffe* of 1664 Molière is not reversing himself; he is only printing the "positives" from the "negatives" he took earlier in his career. This relation of the "court" to the "town" plays, of pure comedy to satiric comedy, gives special meaning to Bailly's observation that there are no conversions in Molière.

J. D. Hubert (essay date 1962)

SOURCE: "The Seducer as Catalyst," in *Molière and the Comedy of Intellect,* University of California Press, 1962, pp. 113-29.

[*Hubert is an American essayist and critic. In the following essay, he discusses characterization, setting, and language in* Dom Juan, *which he considers to be one of Molière's most controversial and unique works.*]

Dom Juan stands out as Molière's most controversial play. Like *Tartuffe,* it struck the *parti dévot* as an abominably irreligious work. Unlike *L'Imposteur,* it has appeared to many critics, irrespective of their religious convictions, as an artistic failure in spite of a certain number of redeeming scenes. A few admirers of Molière, however, regard this comedy his masterpiece, superior even to *Tartuffe* and *Le Misanthrope.* This controversy probably arose from the fact that *Le Festin de Pierre* differs so greatly from any other play by Molière or his contemporaries. Instead of providing his usual neatly contrived dramatic machine, Molière appears to have strung together a certain number of tableaux. Even the central character, Don Juan, who, by his mere presence, gives a semblance of unity and continuity to the play, behaves at times inconsistently, if not incoherently. But perhaps we should not judge this strange comedy according to so-called classical standards, for it may, after all, possess its own peculiar unity, comparable to the poetic coherence of some of Shakespeare's plays. Professor Doolittle, in an important article ["The Humanity of Molière's *Dom Juan,*" PMLA, June, 1953], has shown that *Dom Juan* by no means lacks this unity and coherence. We agree with his interpretation according to which the exposure of convention is a central theme. We feel, however, that it is the Don himself, and not only his victims, who behaves in a conventional manner.

Critics have generally placed too much emphasis on Don Juan's belief or disbelief in the same manner that they have overemphasized the psychological aspects of Tartuffe's hypocrisy. And they assume that Molière intended only to create a convincing hypocrite and an equally convincing seducer with atheistic leanings, and therefore that character study preoccupied him more than any other aspect of dramaturgy. Recently however, M. Simon has stressed the importance of Sganarelle [in his *Molière par lui-même*], who serves as an intermediary between the isolated seducer and the audience. His theory corroborates, in some respects, that of Professor Doolittle's, for it transforms the Don into a different sort of creature, set apart from the general or conventional run of humanity. Still, this isolation—a feature of many of Molière's characters—does not make Don Juan any the less conventional, as we shall presently see. Rather, his separation from the rest of the world puts him at times in the same category as Tartuffe himself, or Arnolphe, or even Alceste.

Enough has been said about Don Juan as a realistic portrait of a seventeenth century libertine and aristocrat, but perhaps too little about the effect he produces on others. After all, his very existence as a legend, and even as a dramatic figure, depends primarily upon the reactions of his victims—and in Molière's version, upon the behavior of Sganarelle. If, in *Tartuffe,* the gullibility of Orgon and Madame Pernelle matters at least as much as the artifices of the impostor, why then should not susceptibility to temptation count as much as the personality of the seducer? To Orgon's eagerness to play the part of dupe corresponds the enthusiasm with which Don Juan's victims succumb to the first temptation that happens to come their way. After all, Faust did invite the devil; and, as readers, we pay less attention to Mephistopheles than to Faust himself. In *Le Festin de Pierre,* Don Juan plays on occasion the part of devil, which does not mean that we can consider him as evil incarnate or as the spirit of deprivation. Only on one occasion does the truly diabolical side of his nature come to the fore—in his jealousy of an obviously happy couple:

> La tendresse visible de leurs mutuelles ardeurs me donna de l'émotion; j'en fus frappé au cœur et mon amour commença par la jalousie. Oui, je ne pus souffrir d'abord de les voir si bien ensemble; le dépit alarma mes désirs, et je me figurai un plaisir extrême à pouvoir troubler leur intelligence, et rompre cet attachement, dont la délicatesse de mon cœur se tenoit offensée (I, 2).

In most instances, however, he acts as a catalyst of evil as well as of good, and his attempts at seduction serve mainly to test the mettle of others. In short, we may regard Don Juan's role as primarily functional and as analogous in this respect to that of Tartuffe. Nonetheless, we consider both the seducer and the repulsive hypocrite as convincing, lifelike characters, even though this aspect of dramaturgy need not concern us in these pages. The Don, however, is much more complex than Tartuffe, perhaps because we can see in him not only the portrait of a courtier, but because he combines within himself the traits of two quite different characters: that of the Spanish Don Juan Tenorio and that of Hylas. Indeed, this composite nature of Molière's seducer might explain an apparent lack of coherence in his behavior.

Movement

Molière has neglected at least one of the three classical unities in *Le Festin de Pierre:* that of place, which changes more frequently than in almost any other play of the period. In this respect, Molière was merely following tradition, for the original version by Tirso de Molina as well as the various Italian and French imitations, contained a wealth of entertaining incidents. But in Molière's play, the perpetual agitation of the hero happens to be merely one aspect of a conflict between motion and immobility. The key word in this antithesis is *demeurer.* Don Juan succeeds in exerting a strong attraction on people who remain confined to a village or to a convent, but who would love to escape and go to an imagined paradise. He seduces all those who show discontent with their lot, such as Elvire, a nun imprisoned in a convent, or Charlotte, a peasant girl engaged to a rustic whom she does not even like. Characteristically, Don Juan tells Charlotte: "... vous n'êtes pas née pour demeurer dans un village," (II, 2) whereas Sganarelle, upon his master's departure, gives the two peasant girls a piece of advice diametrically opposed to his: "... demeurez dans votre village." (II, 4). Previously, the seducer had confessed to Done Elvire: ". . . je vous ai dérobée à la clôture d'un couvent," before telling her to return "à vos premières chaînes," or, in other words, to her previous immobility and *engagement*

(I, 3). And the Don, whom Sganarelle describes as "le plus grand coureur du monde," refuses to stay in one place and limit his endeavors to the chains of a single love. His eloquent and lengthy speech about his amorous conquests opens with a question worthy of Honoré d'Urfé's Hylas: "Quoi? tu veux qu'on se lie à demeurer au premier objet qui nous prend?" Concerned only with pursuit and conquest, he speaks in the name of all seducers when he exclaims: ". . . nous nous endormons dans la tranquillité d'un tel amour, si quelque objet nouveau ne vient réveiller nos désirs." Refusing all limitations in time, space, or numbers, he seeks, like Alexander the Great, new worlds ". . . pour y pouvoir étendre mes conquêtes amoureuses" (I, 2).

In his conquests, Don Juan sees himself as moving from one seduction to another with so much speed that none of his victims will ever manage to catch up with him; but, unfortunately for him, he no longer moves quite as rapidly as he imagines. We first realize that the Don has slowed down when Elvire "en habit de campagne" unexpectedly catches up with him—an event which greatly annoys him. Worse still, in his pursuit of the young couple whose love had so offended him, he is badly outdistanced and very nearly drowned for his pains, after having miserably failed to separate the lovers by his seductive words. Thus, in his first two encounters, he moves too slowly to maintain his reputation as a *coureur,* in spite of the fact that his heart, according to Sganarelle, is "le plus grand coureur du monde" (I, 2). Moreover, his enemies (the brothers of Done Elvire) do not give him enough time to damage the reputations of the two peasant girls who have so readily succumbed to his charm and to his promises. In spite of these failures, he maintains throughout the first half of the comedy, a high degree of mobility and the dashing pace of a seducer. While fleeing his pursuers, he encounters the beggar, frustrates the bandits in their attempt to kill Don Carlos, and finally wanders into the cemetery where he finds the statue of an erstwhile victim: the Commander. [In a footnote, the critic adds: "Movement is also a sign of affection, e.g., 'la grosse Thomasse' is always pushing her friend Robin around, whereas Charlotte has no more life to her, according to Pierrot, than a log."] And he attributes to chance almost everything that happens to him.

During the second half of the play, the situation is reversed: everybody seems to wander into Don Juan's house, from Monsieur Dimanche to the marmorean statue of the Commander. In a sense, the hero finds himself besieged and reduced to a state of immobility. He impertinently invites his father to sit down; he orders a chair for the statue; to Elvire he says: "demeurez ici" and "Madame, vous me ferez plaisir de demeurer." But nobody will heed him except the stupid Monsieur Dimanche who accepts his offer of an armchair. Against the ceaseless motion around him, where even a marble monument, "une statue mouvante et parlante," easily catches up with him, he has recourse to hypocrisy (where outward tranquillity hides the agitation going on within) and, as a last resort, to a more intense form of immobility: he strives to make himself *inébranlable.* As he has made himself motionless and unmovable, he cannot avoid being crushed, for the essence of Don Juan consists in his mobility, in his changeability: he is a *coureur* both in the literal and figurative sense. In inaction lies his own negation. Conversely, he cannot resist the call to action, a tendency which goes far towards explaining his heroic and spontaneous decision to rush to the help of Don Carlos. We should add, however, that as Don Carlos, in facing a very real peril, does his utmost to defend himself, he is bound to enlist the help of Don Juan whose existence depends to a large degree on the actions of others. Similarly, the strong convictions of the Poor Man practically force Don Juan to give him the Louis d'or. The hero cannot help but render tribute to all those who demonstrate their worth. On the other hand, he shows no pity to those who give evidence of weakness. Thus he plays the part of tempter and devil on a purely secular level, testing everyone he encounters until his destruction by convention—by a convention which he had had himself formally invited. And he cannot survive once he has switched from movement and action to immobility and hypocrisy.

Words

Words, which we may regard in many instances as a form of gesture, appear in all of Molière's comedies as the greatest enemies of action and the staunchest upholders of convention. As such, they fare scarcely better than reasoning. One of the axioms in these comedies is that no amount of *raisonnement* can ever persuade a person to change the impertinence of his conduct. These *raisonneurs* are frequently the most frustrated of characters who, though rarely ridiculous in themselves, provoke laughter by the inextricable situations in which they find themselves—and by the inevitability of their failure.

One of the key terms in **Dom Juan** is the unobtrusive word *dire,* with related expression such as *parler, parole, mot, discours, redites, expliquer*—in the sense of putting into words—*faire*—in the sense of *dire—bouche, entendre, ouïr, répondre, disputer.* . . . The verb *dire* recurs nearly one hundred times in the course of the comedy. By adding the ten or so *faire,* the thirty-odd *parler,* and such related verbs as *réitérer, sarmonner, répondre, faire signe* . . . , we discover that the idea of communication intrudes some one hundred and fifty times. Moreover, the term *parole* appears no less than fifteen times. Usually, in Molière's comedies, a key word may reappear six or seven times: just enough to establish a theme, to drive home an idea, to clarify an issue; but this deluge of *dire* and *parler* must have a special function, for it does more than establish a theme. Indeed, it appears to express a way of life, a mode of existence. Whereas in previous plays the author had created characters who tend to substitute words and concepts for action and existence, in **Dom Juan,** he makes speech itself a substitute for action.

Sganarelle does more talking than any other character in the play with the exception of his master. But he constantly acts at cross-purposes: his thoughts and his pronouncements contrast with his behavior. Sganarelle frequently attempts to convert his master by argumentation,

in which endeavor he of course fails miserably. As M. Simon has pointed out, the servant represents a *reductio ad absurdum* of a character typical in Molière's previous comedies: the *raisonneur* who never convinces even though Molière sometimes rewards him, as in **L'Ecole des femmes,** with the last laugh. But in Sganarelle, Molière has created a *raisonneur* who cannot reason and who finally utters a veritable tidal wave of clichés in order to persuade his master of some deep religious truth. Not that we can accuse Sganarelle's arguments of being meaningless. As Professor Doolittle has shown, they do signify even though they sound very much like nonsense.

The conversations between Sganarelle and Don Juan often take the form of an argument or, as the valet calls it, a *dispute.* The servant, after his master's lengthy speech about the pleasures of seduction, praises him for talking just like a book. Unable to find an answer, he asserts that he will write down his *raisonnements* in order to convince Don Juan that he, Sganarelle, has truth on his side. Previously, the valet had compared a sequence of events in his master's existence to a chapter in a book. The omnipresence of *dire* and *parler,* together with the comparison between Don Juan and a literary work, that is with words in their most finished form, suggests that Molière, for reasons which we intend to discuss later, was gleefully trying to reduce existence to so many words— to its verbalizations. Indeed, in many of the speeches, we notice that characters recount not only actions and events but even conversations. For instance, Pierrot tells his reluctant fiancée not only about his rescue of Don Juan but repeats the dialogue between himself and Lucas which preceded it. Elvire's first speech to Don Juan reveals her inner dialogue or debate: "Mes justes soupçons chaque jour avoient beau me parler: j'en rejetois la voix qui vous rendoit criminel à mes yeux, et j'écoutois avec plaisir mille chimères ridicules qui vous peignoient innocent à mon cœur." If she has thus put herself *en campagne* to find Don Juan, it is merely to hear more words: "Je serai bien aise pourtant d'ouïr de votre bouche les raisons de votre départ. Parlez, Don Juan, je vous prie, et voyons de quel air vous saurez vous justifier." Her suffering consists mainly in hearing cruel words: "Il suffit. Je n'en veux pas ouïr davantage, et je m'accuse même d'en avoir trop entendu." She finally renounces, at least to a certain extent, the use of words, a domain where she has met with total defeat: "N'attends pas que j'éclate ici en reproches et en injures: non, non, je n'ai point un courroux à exhaler en paroles vaines" (I, 3).

It is thus mainly through words, those Trojan horses of temptation, that Don Juan gains access to the minds of his victims. In **Le Misanthrope,** words will represent a form of bargaining. But for Don Juan, traditionally a liar, they must serve as weapons with which he will conquer his intended victims. They help him to seek out some inveterate weakness in a human being. He thus derives his power mainly from words and appearances, from empty gestures which cannot prevail against a person like the Poor Man, who has strong convictions and who refuses to compromise. For that reason, words, in this and in many other of Molière's comedies, are frequently equated with money. Don Juan does not hesitate to use flattering words and gestures in order to avoid paying Monsieur Dimanche:

> DON JUAN: Je suis votre serviteur et de plus votre débiteur.
>
> DIMANCHE: Ah! Monsieur . . .
>
> DON JUAN: C'est une chose que je ne cache pas, et je le dis à tout le monde (IV, 3).

Thus, Don Juan clearly pays his debts in words. The Poor Man, on the contrary, receives real money in the name of humanity, not so much because Don Juan happens to take pity on him, but because, as Professor Doolittle has shown, he recognizes in this beggar a man worthy of the name. Characteristically, the seducer asks him to curse—to commit a sin in words. Sganarelle, who thinks nothing of blaspheming from here to tomorrow, encourages him to comply with his master's command. But if the Poor Man had obeyed, the tempter would probably have hypocritically refused to give him a farthing. Such, indeed, was his reaction to Elvire's demand of an excuse. His hypocritical answer, which as he well knows neither Elvire nor anyone else will take seriously, merely corresponds to his

Engraved handbill produced for early performances of L'ecole des maris.

victim's own moral and religious anguish: "Il m'est venu des scrupules, Madame, et j'ai ouvert les yeux de l'âme sur ce que je faisois. J'ai fait réflexion que pour vous épouser, je vous ai dérobée à la clôture d'un couvent, que vous avez rompu des vœux qui vous engageoient autre part, et que le Ciel est fort jaloux de ces sortes de choses" (I, 3). Don Juan ironically and cruelly echoes the sort of reflections that must have passed through Elvire's tormented mind just before she decided to elope with her dashing young lover. In short, he leaves her with her sin and does not even bother to renew his false promises, for he really has no further use for her. Experience will be her sole reward. Still, her seduction may, from a religious standpoint, have served a worthy purpose. Her love for the unattainable tempter has perhaps enabled her to discover her true vocation: she will return to the convent out of choice after having sublimated her earthly passion into spiritual love. Needless to say, both her passion and the resulting vocation come from within her, and Don Juan has acted mainly as a catalyst. We cannot claim, however, on the basis of Elvire's self-discovery, that *Le Festin* is a religious as opposed to an irreligious play. Indeed, we can derive a secular meaning even from Elvire's conversion: each person must reward himself, in the sense that he has an obligation to seek out his own values and live in accordance with them. Sganarelle, who takes clichés for moral values, superstitions for religion, and who never practices what he preaches, will not even receive his wages at the end of the play. In trying to protect Pierrot, he receives a punch from his master for his pains: "Te voilà payé de ta charité" (II, 3). Thus, the absence of reward stands out as a major theme in this play. Every single character, including the Poor Man, meets, at one time or another, with frustration. The beggar does receive a reward in the form of a gold coin, but most of the time he lives in a state of misery and his prayers go unheeded, at least in this world. Ironically, the only time when he has a reward thrust upon him occurs upon his refusal to utter a word! In this respect, we can regard *Dom Juan* as a comedy of frustration and paradox, as a play about the absurdity of the human predicament. When Sganarelle asks his master what he thinks about the Commander's tomb, he receives an answer which reveals the absurdity of human values or rather of conventional values: "Qu'on ne peut voir aller plus loin l'ambition d'un homme mort; et ce que je trouve admirable, c'est qu'un homme qui s'est passé, durant sa vie, d'une assez simple demeure, en veuille avoir une si magnifique pour quand il n'en a plus que faire" (III, 5). Don Juan ironically stresses man's tendency to take gestures for values. And the Commander has truly attained the height of absurdity in this respect: "Parbleu! le voilà bon, avec son habit d'empereur romain!" It would seem that the worthy Commander has geared his entire existence to the perpetuation of a magnificent funeral, to the petrification of a commanding gesture. In a sense, the Commander has immortalized himself, or rather that public image of himself which very nearly coincides with status. When Don Juan invites this vain image to supper, Sganarelle raises a very sensible objection: "Ce seroit être for que d'aller parler à une statue," thereby establishing a connection between the absurdity of words and this ridiculous marble monument which we may consider as absurdity in its most spectacular and most concrete form.

The Fallacy of Misplaced Concreteness

The idea of discernment plays an important part in practically every scene of the play. Like words, it maintains the closest connections with rewards and money. The most impressive scene from the standpoint of discernment is Pierrot's description of the rescue. Pierrot prides himself on his ability to see two men swimming in the sea, as opposed to the blindness of his friend Lucas who accuses him of double vision. Moreover, Pierrot has the wisdom to wager money on his splendid eyesight, and he thus reaps the rewards for his discernment. On the other side of the ledger, Pierrot does not exactly benefit from his rescue of the seducer, a fact which shows once again the discrepancy between service and reward. Indeed, Don Juan tries to seduce his fiancée and then beats him. And the unfortunate Pierrot exclaims: ". . . ce n'est pas là la récompense de v's avoir sauvé d'estre nayé" (II, 3).

Elvire's speech in Act I, Scene 3 reveals in a more subtle manner the struggle between discernment and imagination, which she defines as "mille chimères ridicules." And she admits: "J'ai été assez bonne . . . ou plutôt assez sotte pour me vouloir tromper moi-même, et travailler à démentir mes yeux et mon jugement." The eyes appear to be less susceptible to illusion than the ears or the imagination. Actually, Elvire has deluded herself. Paradoxically, she has been Don Juan's chief accomplice in her own seduction.

The idea of discernment reappears in relationship with the marble statute. Don Juan tries at first to deny the testimony of his senses: ". . . nous pouvons avoir été trompés par un faux jour, ou surpris de quelque vapeur qui nous ait troublé la vue" (IV, 1). He thus finds himself in the same situation as Gros Lucas, who had been indulging in horseplay with his friend Pierrot. Sganarelle, like Pierrot, refuses to deny his senses: "Eh! Monsieur, ne cherchez point à démentir ce que nous avons vu des yeux que voilà." He thus establishes a further connection between discernment in the sense of physical perception, and proof or argumentation. Later in the scene, Don Juan, revolted by his servant's "sottes moralités," threatens to whip him with a bull's pizzle. The valet quickly changes his tone, because his master says things "avec une netteté admirable." Don Juan's "words," which like Hart Crane's gringo canons in "Imperator Victus," "No speakee well / But plain," appear even clearer to Sganarelle than the Commander's nod of acceptance.

What then can be the connection between discernment and proof, between argumentation and words, for these various themes intermingle in various ways throughout the play? Discernment inevitably leads to knowledge; in one instance, it leads, as we have seen, to a reward in the form of a fruitful wager. Pierrot, as a matter of fact, has bet on a sure thing; but Don Juan, who refuses to find any real significance in the signs and warnings which he perceives, will be chastized. Does this mean that we should take his destruction by a preposterous statue seriously? Of course not. But however we interpret this mysterious ending, we still would have to take into account the close connection that both words and perceptions maintain with reasoning.

From the beginning of the comedy until its theatrical *dénouement,* Molière creates a deliberately false air of philosophical discussion. The play opens with a pseudo-philosophical discourse on the virtues of tobacco. In his praise of tobacco, Sganarelle takes the apparently friendly gestures and generosity of smokers or takers of snuff for moral worth: the smoker, by virtue of his favorite drug, becomes an "honnête homme." And the play starts off ludicrously with a sweeping statement: "Quoi que puisse dire Aristote et toute la Philosophie, il n'est rien d'égal au tabac." We encounter in this opening sentence our key word: *dire,* as well as the idea of value: "il n'est rien d'égal." Professor Doolittle rightly interprets Sganarelle's speech about smoking as a criticism of gesture. We may also regard it as a *reductio ad absurdum* of reasoning, as a subtle way of connecting Aristotle with smoke and gestures, for tobacco smoke was used by seventeenth century writers as a symbol for meaningless ideas and dreams, or even lies and illusions, as in the current word: *fumisterie.* In fact, this opening gambit is reminiscent of Saint-Amant's well known sonnet: "La Pipe": "Car l'une n'est que fumée / Et l'autre n'est que vent," showing that the poet equates his dreams of success with the smoke spiralling upwards from his pipe.

Sganarelle's ludicrous equation between tobacco and human worth would imply that Molière never intended that his public take at face value the servant's subsequent pronouncements on religion. Rather, we should regard them as farcical variations on the opening statement. Moreover, Sganarelle exhibits here for the first but certainly not the last time his strange tendency to materialize thought. Referring to tobacco, he claims: "Nonseulement il réjouit et purge les cerveaux humains, mais encore il instruit les âmes à la vertu, et l'on apprend avec lui à devenir honnête homme." Absurdity, in this passage, results not only from the confusion between gesture and moral behavior, but from the still more fruitful identification of material objects such as tobacco or smoke with abstract thought and moral virtue. Later, while discussing with his master the proof of God's existence by proximate causes, he gets carried away by the movement of his own cogitations, much like La Fontaine's Perette, and he falls flat on his face. Don Juan comments, laconically: "Bon! voilà ton raisonnement qui a le nez cassé" (III, 1). The comic effect of this remark depends on the ludicrous confusion between the abstract and the concrete. Similar in nature was Sganarelle's previous statement about the doctor's robe he uses as a disguise: "... cet habit me donne de l'esprit." And the final argument with which the valet hopes to convince his master brings about a total confusion of verbal clichés and concrete examples, all under the guise of thought and reasoning.

An analogous mixture of abstract thought and spiritual values with concrete reality appears in the various signs that obsess the tempter towards the end of the play: the specter, which changes into the conventional symbol of Time the Reaper, and, of course, the marble statue, Previously, Don Juan had discoursed ironically about the discrepancy between spiritual values and material rewards, for instance in his conversation with the Poor Man, whose function in life consists precisely in praying Heaven every day for the prosperity "des gens de bien qui me donnent quelque chose" (III, 2). The beggar probably gave a spiritual meaning to "gens de bien" and even to "prospérité," but this does not prevent his words from suggesting rather subtly the ideas of wealth and material success. Don Juan, on the strength of this equivocation, can remark: "Il ne se peut donc pas que tu ne sois bien à ton aise?" Upon the beggar's negative reply, he exclaims in mock disbelief: "Tu te moques: un homme qui prie le Ciel tout le jour, ne peut pas manquer d'être bien dans ses affaires," as though there must be a direct relationship between material and spiritual values. Under these circumstances, and granting the importance of the confusion between the abstract and the concrete, we can expect that the Heaven which the Poor Man invokes in his prayers should avenge itself on the impious seducer by taking the most preposterously concrete form imaginable: that of the marble statue of a general attired like a Roman emperor. Spiritual values and the supernatural finally materialize themselves in so crude a manner that it almost seems as if poor Sganarelle had planned or imagined the whole spectacle all by himself! Could this strange catastrophe imply that virtue will be rewarded and evil punished when Hell freezes over? Well then, the tempter's unlikely destruction would merely add a final touch to the utter confusion of all values, intellectual as well as moral, which so characterizes the play.

We have to admit, however, that Don Juan, who constantly uses false values and plays the part of a counterfeiter in words, is fully paid back in kind, defeated by an incredible illusion, by a gesture, as empty as his own playful invitation to supper, or his marriage promises, or his indebtedness to Monsieur Dimanche, or Sganarelle's hope of finally receiving his wages. Thus, this creator of illusions is finally crushed by an illusion and a convention. In fact, Don Juan not only creates illusions, but he bases his success on a skilful manipulation of conventions to which he himself subscribes. When he sees Elvire "en habit de campagne," he exclaims in shocked surprise: "Est-elle folle, de n'avoir pas changé d'habit, et de venir en ce lieu-ci avec son équipage de campagne?" (I, 2). According to the Don, one should at least keep up appearances and wear appropriate clothing in a palace. When he flees Done Elvire's brothers, he wears country as opposed to courtly clothes, for he can be recognizable only when fashionably attired. Pierrot's minute description of Don Juan's clothes not only makes the peasant ridiculous because of his ignorance of aristocratic dress, but transforms the seducer himself into a figure of fun; and we suddenly have the feeling that he owes his success with women partly to his costume, and partly to his rank, but precious little to his innate charms. Thus our dangerous seducer, who frightens poor Sganarelle into serving him against his will, has some of the silly faults of those *petits*

marquis whom Molière will satirize in *Le Misanthrope*.

The confusion between abstractions and concrete reality pervades also the realm of morality. Don Juan refuses to be tied down, and he regards the laws of the land as well as those of the Church as so many chains which he has so far succeeded in eluding. However, various other characters complain about these chains and obligations. Don Carlos, for instance, sees the aristocratic concept of honor as a form of enslavement. In a sense, the analogy of chains emerges here and there in the course of the comedy; and practically all of Sganarelle's arguments refer to a chain of causes which bind man morally and physically to his Creator. With the exception of Don Juan, everyone tends to sacrifice existence itself to these imprisoning moral bonds and conventions, everyone including of course the Commander whom the protagonist had killed, honorably, in a duel. His ornate tomb, complete with marble statue, represents the triumph of "moral" essence over life, freedom, and common sense. At the *dénouement,* all these immaterial obligations, all these social essences which man has created in his own image, but which he attributes to God, finally materialize in order to destroy Don Juan, who had done his utmost either to flout them or to turn them to his advantage. Everything in the play seems to lead up to this apocalyptic materialization.

Stage Props

Although Molière consistently plays with ideas throughout *Dom Juan,* stressing such intellectual niceties as perception, discernment, moral obligation, the efficacy of good, the goodness of knowledge, one must not attempt to transform the play into an ordered set of philosophical beliefs or moral tenets. That Molière should poke fun at various types of reasoning, both on the religious and the *libertin* side, does not necessarily mean that he has written a philosophical treatise or a thesis-play. Actually he has used philosophy as grist for his comic mill. And why should we be surprised that an author of the age of rationalism should have written an intellectual farce? In previous plays, Molière had made fun of intellectuals—of people who try to substitute a ready-made system for the vagaries of existence. But in *Dom Juan,* he has written a comedy not so much about would-be intellectuals as about man's intellectual and moral predicament to which he has given as absurd a solution as the most dogmatic irrationalist could wish. Still, all this intellectualism is no more than the subject matter and the pretext of the comedy. As such, it can tell us very little about Molière's artistic intent.

We might plausibly describe *Le Festin* as a play about words. Don Juan uses words to great advantage, even the liturgical words pronounced by a priest at a wedding. He also becomes the victim of the word he has given the Commander—the only word for which he will have to pay. But this theory concerning the comedy will not lead very far unless we explain why such a subject appealed to his theatrical talents in the first place. We know that the Italian comedians and other dramatic companies had performed various versions of *Dom Juan,* a "pièce à machines" that made the public flock to the theater. Indeed, *Le Festin de Pierre* has a most theatrical plot—so theatrical that even Molière's intellectual version offended many men of classical tastes. (The destruction of Don Juan by a moving statue might appeal to Spaniards.) But Molière may have seen in this strange subject with its tawdry and offensive *dénouement* the theater incarnate, the theater in all its marvelous absurdity as make-believe. And the sheer scandal of this walking and talking statue crushing an aristocratic and mercurial seducer must have had an irresistible appeal for him. A dramatist, an actor, a theater director could not help seeing in this marble general a stage prop to end all stage props—a stage prop all dressed up in one of Molière's favorite costumes, that of a Roman emperor, that of Julius Caesar! After all, he let Mignard paint him in such a garb. At the end of the play, we have a vision of the very essence of the theatrical crushing the protagonist. In fact, the play seems to put an end to itself by the shere impetus of its own movement, by the final materialization of all its words and concepts. The hero himself, according to Sganarelle, talks like a book and lives by chapters instead of years. Moreover, he needs servants to dress him for the part of seducer. In ordinary clothes, he behaves rather differently, just like Brecht's pope in *Galileo Galilei*. Finally, like the author himself, he spends much of his time in testing his fellow men, in bringing out their shabbiness or conversely in precipitating their worth. He is the active ingredient,

---

Robert Bechtold Heilman on Molière's characters:

Molière had a lasting interest in neurotic characters, witness the title of an early play, *Sganarelle, ou le cocu imaginaire* (1660), and of his last play, *Le Malade imaginaire* (1673). The troubled personalities that invent their own miseries are of course easy to laugh at, for they permit us to think our own difficulties more genuine (a lesser neurotic personality appears in Faulkland, the fearful and suspicious lover in Sheridan's *The Rivals* [1775]). Their illnesses lack the deep roots or the irreversibility that begets true sick comedy. Yet Molière finds moral significance in the self-troubled character by showing that he uses his disability for self-service or power. . . . But the chief element that helps preserve a comic tone against the satirical tendency—this is true of various Molière plays—is the role of the common-sense characters frequently present. They finally prevent the operations of the neurotic and self-deluded characters from getting out of hand and doing real damage. By such dramatic means these characters are accepted as a part, if not a very lovable part, of the world rather than set up as simple objects of condemnation.

Robert Bechtold Heilman in his The ways of the world: Comedy and Society, *University of Washington Press, 1978.*

---

the energumen of the comedy, who sets everything in motion, at least during the first-half of the work. In short, his function resembles that of Mascarille the intriguer, of Scapin, or of the evil Iago. Like them, he seems to create plots as he moves along. This does not mean that the

resourceful Don Juan expresses any of Molière's ideas. One may even claim that he does not have any ideas whatever. Nonetheless, the author has entrusted his creative functions to him without forgetting a single artifice. And thus the destruction of this tester and catalyst of all values, of this inventor of stratagems, in short, of the Artist himself, by the strangest and unlikeliest of stage props is perhaps one of Molière's most original dramatic achievements. It strikes us as no less theatrical than the ballets which end *Le Bourgeois gentilhomme* and *Le Malade imaginaire*. We witness not so much the victory of absurdity as the triumph of the artistic imagination, which is the supreme and only valid illusion.

Lionel Gossman (essay date 1963)

SOURCE: "Molière in His Own Time," in *Men and Masks: A Study of Molière,* The Johns Hopkins Press, 1963, pp. 164-251.

[*Gossman is Scottish essayist and educator. In the following excerpt, he discusses "the comic hero's relation to the world" in Molière's plays, focusing on the themes of social class and the rejection of society.*]

We tend, occasionally, to think that some of Molière's comedies are gay and light-hearted, whereas others are more somber and ambiguous. A Jourdain or a Magdelon presents audiences with no problems, but an Alceste leaves them perplexed and uncertain. Jourdain and Magdelon are figures of unalloyed fun, according to this view, pure fools as anyone can easily discern; Alceste, on the other hand, does not seem very funny and to some he even seems almost tragic. Oddly enough, Molière's contemporaries do not seem to have entertained these uncertainties. We hear, of course, of opposition to *Dom Juan* and to *Tartuffe,* but we know that there was also opposition to *Les Précieuses ridicules* and to *L'Ecole des femmes*. Most people appear to have laughed at *all* the comedies. As for ambiguity, there is, as we shall see, a good deal of it in *Le Bourgeois Gentilhomme*. A very sentimental reader might find Monsieur Jourdain almost as pathetic and as misunderstood as Alceste. Romantic interpretations of *Le Misanthrope* can easily be extended to all the plays. While it must be recognized that there is a difference between two types of comedy in Molière, between the comedies of the *Bourgeois Gentilhomme* type and the comedies of the *Misanthrope* type, if we may make a loose initial distinction, this difference cannot be perfunctorily attributed to the fact that one group is funnier than the other or less mysterious and ambiguous. We should rather try to elucidate it by examining the more or less complex form of the comic hero's relation to the world.

The final judge and the transcendence to which the tragic hero of Racine looks for the ground of his being and the value of his existence is God. The comic hero, on the other hand, looks to others to give him his value and his being. The sign of recognition that Phèdre expects from God, the Jourdains, the Cathoses, and the Alcestes expect from the world. Whereas one group of Molière's characters make no attempt to conceal their idolatry, however, another group of characters affect to despise the idols whose recognition they desire, postulating instead their own superiority and setting themselves up as idols for others to worship.

With the notable exceptions of Dom Juan and Jupiter, the majority of Molière's best known characters are bourgeois of one degree or another. Within this bourgeoisie it is nevertheless possible to distinguish an upper and a lower range. While Alceste obviously belongs to a social class very close to the nobility, perhaps even to a long established family of *noblesse de robe,* Jourdain is a very ordinary, if rather well-off, merchant, the son of a draper. Corresponding to this hierarchy of ranks, there is the hierarchy of Paris and the provinces. While it is not possible, as it would doubtless be in the work of later writers like Balzac or Stendhal, to identify absolutely attitudes and modes of being in Molière with social class, it is broadly speaking true to say that the "open" comic heroes, those who recognize their models and superiors without shame, are characters of the lower bourgeoisie and the provinces. The "closed" comic heroes, those whose resentment of their idols, precisely for being idols, leads them to deny their recognition of them, belong rather to the upper bourgeoisie and the aristocracy, to those groups that are close to social equality or who have social equality with their idols. The vanities and illusions of the first group, being openly avowed, have a quality of naïvety that makes comedies like *Le Bourgeois Gentilhomme* or *Les Précieuses ridicules* hilariously funny. It is not hard for us to discern and transcend the folly of Jourdain. The vanities and illusions of the second group are less easily discerned as comic, for they resemble those we ourselves conceal, those of "in-groups," courtiers, artists, professional people—"tous ces métiers dont le principal instrument est l'opinion que l'on a de soi-même, et dont la matière première est l'opinion que les autres out de vous," as Valéry describes them.

In the first case the desire to *be distinguished* is a desire to be distinguished from one group by being recognized as a member of a superior group, the superiority of which the aspirant himself necessarily recognizes. "Mon Dieu! ma chère," exclaims Cathos, "que ton père a la forme enfoncée dans la matière! que son intelligence est épaisse, et qu'il fait sombre dans son âme!" "Que veux-tu, machère," Cathos answers contritely. "J'en suis en confusion pour lui. J'ai peine à me persuader que je puisse véritablement être sa fille, et je crois que quelque illustre aventure, un jour, me viendra développer une naissance plus illustre" (*Précieuses,* sc. 5). "Lorsque je hante la noblesse, je fais paroître mon jugement," says Jourdain to his wife, "et cela est plus beau que de hanter votre bourgeoisie" (*Le Bourgeois Gentilhomme,* III, 3). A little later he accuses his good wife of having "les sentiments d'un petit esprit, de vouloir demeurer toujours dans la bassesse" (*Le Bourgeois Gentilhomme,* III, 12). There is nothing secret about the reverence these characters have for their idols, and they seek quite openly to elicit from their silent or masked or absent divinity the sign of recognition that for them is a sign of salvation. "Pour moi," says

Mascarille ironically, "je tiens que hors de Paris, il n'y a point de salut pour les honnêtes gens." "C'est une vérité incontestable," answers Cathos (*Précieuses,* sc. 9). "Est-ce que les gens de qualité apprennent aussi la musique?" asks Jourdain. "Oui, Monsieur," says the Maître de Musique. "Je l'apprendrai donc," Jourdain rejoins without hesitation (*Bourgeoise Gentilhomme,* I, 2).

More complex and less immediately comic in their desire to achieve distinction are those who will not share it with anybody, who refuse the models that everyone else accepts and who, far from recognizing their idols, go to great lengths to conceal their mediation by others. They make a point of loudly scorning the ways of the world, those very ways that a Jourdain and a Cathos revere so unquestioningly. Madame Pernelle in *Tartuffe* refuses the courtesies of her daughter-in-law: "Ce sont (. . .) façons dont je n'ai pas besoin" (I, 1, 4). Harpagon likewise condemns the manners of the world. He reproaches his son with the very imitation that is the butt of Molière's satire in *Le Bourgeois Gentilhomme:* "Je vous l'ai dit cent fois, mon fils, toutes vos manières me déplaisent fort: vous donnez furieusement dans le marquis (. . .) Je voudrois bien savoir, sans parler du reste, à quoi servent tous ces rubans dont vous voilà lardé depuis les pieds jusqu'à la tête, et si une demi-douzaine d'aiguillettes ne suffit pas pour attacher un haut-de-chausses? Il est bien nécessaire d'employer de l'argent à des perruques, lorsque l'on peut porter des cheveux de son cru, qui ne coûtent rien" (*L'Avare,* I, 4). Arnolphe has his own taste in women and it is not that of everyone else:

> Moi, j'irois me charger d'une spirituelle
> Qui ne parleroit rien que cercle et que ruelle,
> Qui de prose et de vers feroit de doux écrits,
> Et que visiteroient marquis et beaux esprits!
> (*L'Ecole des femmes,* I, 1, 87-90)

Sganarelle, like Harpagon, refuses the fashions of his contemporaries. His brother, he complains, would have him ape the manners of the "jeunes muguets." But he will have none of

> (. . .) ces petits chapeaux
> Qui laissent éventer leurs débiles cerveaux,
> Et de ces blonds cheveux, de qui la vaste enflure
> Des visages humains offusque la figure.
> De ces petits pourpoints sous les bras se
>   perdants,
> Et de ces grands collets, jusqu'au nombril
>   pendants.
> De ces manches qu'à table on voit tâter les
>   sauces,
> Et de ces cotillons appelés hauts-de-chausses.
> De ces souliers mignons, de rubans revêtus,
> Qui vous font ressembler à des pigeons pattus . . .
>   etc., etc.
> (*L'Ecole des maris* I, 1, 25-34)

No, Sganarelle will follow his own fashion in complete indifference to everyone else—"Et qui me trouve mal, n'a qu'à fermer les yeux" (*ibid.,* 74).

The rejection of society is not, clearly, confined to articles of clothing and a few superficial customs. It is the entire way of life of everybody else that these characters ostensibly reject. People enjoy company, entertainment, balls, receptions, conversations? Madame Pernelle will have none of them. On the contrary she will make a virtue of solitude, abstention, and even brusqueness. Money is spent on carriages, fine clothes, amusements? Harpagon will not spend it at all. Instead he will treasure and revere it for itself. Everybody wants an entertaining, witty, and sociable wife? Arnolphe and Sganarelle will choose a "bête," and they will value precisely that in her which nobody else seems to admire, her ignorance and simplicity. The world is full of flattery and soft with compromise? Alceste will be brusque, frank, and scrupulously uncompromising. Society observes certain codes of behavior, of decency, and of propriety? Dom Juan will flout them and will be blatantly indecent and immoral. These characters—Harpagon, Arnolphe, Sganarelle, Alceste, Dom Juan, Madame Pernelle, Orgon—refuse to recognize that they are mediated by others; the almost childlike guilelessness of Jourdain's fascination with the nobility gives way in them to a subtle concealment by the character of his true desires, and of their source. Far from recognizing their mediators, these characters pretend they have none. Several of them appear to be in thrall to idols; Orgon and Madame Pernelle to Tartuffe, Philaminte and her daughter to their Trissotin, Harpagon to his *"cassette."* The last example reveals these idolatries for what they are, however. As we pointed out in our chapter on **Tartuffe,** Orgon is bent on using Tartuffe as much as Tartuffe is bent on using him. The *femmes savantes,* like the *dévot,* see in their idols an instrument for asserting their superiority to the world around them, and it is on this world that their eyes are really turned. "Nul n'aura de l'esprit hors nous et nos amis" declares Armande: "Nous chercherons partout à trouver à redire, / Et ne verrons que nous qui sache bien écrire". Likewise Orgon sets himself up *against* society as the only true Christian in it. The function of Tartuffe is to guarantee Orgon's superiority to *everybody* else. In the case of Harpagon the idolatry of the instrument has reached its climax in total alienation and fetishism. In all three plays the idol is used to assert an opposition to society, a distinction from it and a superiority to it. Philaminte and her daughters do not really care about science, Orgon and his mother do not really care about religion (both texts illustrate this amply), and Harpagon does not really care about wealth—on the contrary, his wealth is used to keep him poor. What these characters want above all is *to be distinguished,* but they refuse to adopt the usual method of social advancement and privilege, since this method offers only a *relative* superiority to others, whereas the superiority they desire is *absolute.* They are comic not only because there is a constant contradiction between what they are and what they affect to be, but because their attempt to transcend all social superiorities and to reach an absolute superiority misfires. *La Cour et la ville* will not be convinced that stringent devoutness or erudition are more desirable than social advantage and worldly success. They are no more envious of the spiritual insights of Orgon and the telescopes of Philaminte than they are of Harpagon's beloved

"cassette." Philaminte, Orgon, and Harpagon do not see this of course. Harpagon imagines that everyone is after his *cassette,* that there is a vast plot to deprive him of this mark of his superiority. Likewise Orgon imagines that his whole family is plotting to remove Tartuffe out of jealousy. Arnolphe and Sganarelle, convinced that the eyes of the entire universe are upon them and that everybody desires to corrupt the virtuous young persons, in the possession of whom they find the mark of their superiority, shut them up and guard them as jealously as Harpagon guards his *cassette.* While choosing to be *different* from everybody else, while turning away from what they castigate as the vain ambitions of the world in order to devote themselves to "authentic" values, these characters nevertheless have to believe that they are envied by everybody else. Thus while Orgon raves that the world in its corruption does not appreciate the saintliness of his Tartuffe, he also imagines that everyone is jealous of his special relation with Tartuffe; while Arnolphe prefers *une bête,* who will interest no one, to an elegant society girl who would be the object of everybody's attention, he still imagines that the entire universe is pursuing his Agnès.

Underlying the apparent indifference of the Arnolphes and the Orgons there is in reality the same fascination with others that we find among the Jourdains or the Cathoses. Orgon could after all practice his devotions quietly, without ostentation. Arnolphe and Sganarelle could avoid being made cuckold by remaining bachelors. But they never entertain this notion. The true object of their craving is not a faithful wife—or in Orgon's case salvation through Christ—but the recognition by others of their superiority. The goals which they choose to pursue are not after all pursued for themselves, nor do they themselves select them as they imagine they do. They are determined for them by their very opposition to society. Arnolphe and Sganarelle are not content to do without a wife; on the contrary; but she must be the opposite of all other wives. Orgon is not content to withdraw inwardly from public life; on the contrary, he continues to live a remarkably public life, but one which is the opposite of the life everyone else leads. Harpagon is not content to renounce material riches; he continues to pursue them but he gives them a meaning and a value absolutely opposed to the meaning and value they have for everyone else. All the posing of the Orgons and the Arnolphes and the Harpagons—though in this last instance it must be admitted that the pose has become truly the only reality of the man; Harpagon has so completely alienated himself that he can even run after his own body (cf. **L'Avare,** IV, 7)—cannot conceal that they are as dependent on others and as mediated by them, whatever claims to independence they may make, as simple fools like Jourdain and Cathos or Magdelon. Their basic folly is the same and all their cleverness is used not to eradicate it, but to disguise it from themselves and others. This becomes particularly clear in **La Comtesse d'Escarbagnas.** At the end of this play the Countess, having failed to distinguish herself in her little provincial society by aping the noble ladies of the Court, decides to distinguish herself by inverting this imitation, by seeming to reject it in favor of a superiority all her own. She marries Monsieur Tibaudier just to prove her absolute superiority to everyone. "Oui, Monsieur Tibaudier," she says, "Je vous épouse pour faire enrager tout le monde" (sc. 9). Unable to attract the gaze of the world by acting *with* it, the Countess resolves in desperation to attract the attention she craves by acting *against* it. The world and not Monsieur Tibaudier remains, however, the object of her fascination.

In fact, of course, the world is not the least bit *enragé.* The play closes with the Viscount's ironical: "Souffrez, Madame, qu'en enrageant, nous puissions voir ici le *reste du spectacle*" (italics added). The countess has failed absolutely to fix the world's attention on herself in the way she wanted. On the contrary, it has watched her as it would watch a comedy—which the Countess' behavior *in fact* is—and it is now off to watch another comedy, another stage play. The truth is that it is not the comic heroes who are indifferent to the world, it is the world that is indifferent to them. It is not they who fascinate the world; they are fascinated by it.

The world, indeed, has to be forced by the hero to give him its attention. It is only when Harpagon tries to impose the rules of his crazy universe on others that they begin to be seriously concerned with him. It is only because Philaminte, Armande, and Bélise are not content to be "blue-stockings" quietly on their own, but insist on organizing the lives of Chrysale and Henriette around their own obsessions that father and daughter find themselves forced to take note of them. If Arnolphe had not forcibly embroiled Agnès in his plans, Horace and everyone else would simply have regarded him as an eccentric misogynist and would not have given him a second thought. This seemingly inevitably imposition of themselves on others is a revealing characteristic of the comic heroes of Molière. It confirms that their professed indifference to others is a sham. Far from seeking to live the good life himself, Alceste is concerned only to impress on others that they are not living it and that they do not have his superior moral vision. . . . [The] hero's withdrawal to his desert at the end of the play is itself a *spectacular* gesture, and it is for this reason one that will constantly have to be renewed and revived. It is by no means final. Dom Juan is not simply indifferent to the world: he has to arouse its wrath—and thereby its attention—by perpetually flouting its rules, seducing its virgins and wives, blaspheming against its God. The sadism of Orgon has already been alluded to; it is in no way exceptional in the work of Molière. Orgon's relation to Mariane has its counterpart in the relation of Harpagon to Elise or Cléante, of Argan to Angélique or little Louison, of Monsieur Jourdain to Lucile.

In the comedies of Molière the hero's transcendence is the world of others. The silence of this world is intolerable to him, but he is obliged to *force* it to speak and recognize his existence. In the early tragedies of Racine, as we have already suggested, the hero's transcendence is also the world of others and he too has to resort to violence in order to have himself recognized. It is not surprising, therefore, that sadism is a characteristic shared by comic and tragic heroes alike. This parallel of the early Racinian heroes and of the comic heroes of Molière can be pursued in some detail.

Almost all Molière's comedies oppose ruse to ruse, hypocrisy to hypocrisy, violence to violence: how are we to choose between Jupiter and Amphitryon, Alceste and the two *marquis.* Orgon and Tartuffe, Dandin and Angélique, Argan and Béline? Likewise how are we to choose between Pyrrhus and Hermione or between Hermione and Oreste or between Nero and Agrippine? That salvation and purity are impossible in the world forms part of the tragic vision of Racine. In Molière also participation involves compromise. In a world in which fathers brutalize their children, mothers are jealous of their sons, guardians stultify their wards, no one who participates can be innocent. The only weapon against violence and blackmail is ruse and hypocrisy. "La sincérité souffre un peu au métier que je fais," Valère admits; "mais quand on a besoin des hommes il faut bien s'ajuster à eux; et puisqu'on ne sauroit les gagner que par là, ce n'est pas la faute de ceux qui flattent mais de ceux qui veulent être flattés" (*L'Avare,* I, 1). Lamenting the fact that sons have to get into debt on account of "la maudite avarice des pères," Cléante protests: "et on s'étonne après cela que les fils souhaitent qu'ils meurent" (*L'Avare,* II, 1). Covielle in **Le Bourgeois Gentilhomme** mocks his master for the naïve honesty of his dealings with Jourdain: "Ne voyez-vous pas qu'il est fou? et vous coûtoit-il quelque chose de vous accommoder à ses chimères?". In a world in which the only law is willfulness and the only authority is tyranny, no one can remain pure without becoming a victim. Elmire, Horace, and Valère do not seek out ruse and hypocrisy, but they cannot escape them either, for these are the instruments of survival. Even little Louison in **Le Malade Imaginaire** has to learn how to deal with her father's tyranny and violence by cunning and deceit. Those who remain pure and innocent risk becoming victims, like Mariane in **Tartuffe** or Angélique in **Le Malade Imaginaire,** and if they escape this fate it is only because someone more energetic and less scrupulous has intervened in their behalf. Sometimes they do indeed become victims, as Alcmène does, and sometimes they preserve their innocence through an enigmatic absence or abnegation of desire which places them outside the world, like Eliante in **Le Misanthrope** or Elvire in **Dom Juan,** after her conversion. These characters are as peripheral in Molière's comedies as Racine's Junie, whom Goldmann adjudges the sole tragic character in *Britannicus.* Goldmann saw—rightly it seems to me—that the *innocent stratagème* by which Andromaque hoped to foil Pyrrhus' attempt at blackmail seriously compromises her tragic stature. A similar problem was encountered by Molière in *L'Ecole des femmes,* where Agnès has to be at the same time desiring, active, and innocent. If we look closely at the text, we find that Agnès never *consciously* disobeys Arnolphe. Both her desire for Horace and her active participation in the plot against Arnolphe are conceived entirely on the level of instinct. Only in this way could Molière preserve the innocence of his heroine, while at the same time allowing her to act in pursuit of her own desires.

In both Molière's comedies and Racine's early tragedies the main characters are moved primarily by their desire to force the world to recognize them. In both, the instruments of this desire are imposture and sadism. In both, the heroes fail to make the world break its silence. Racine's characters find themselves refused in the very suffering they inflict on those whose recognition they demand. The comic hero's victims defend themselves against his tyranny by ruse and hypocrisy, and he thereby becomes for them not the transcendent subject of his intention but an object to be tricked and manipulated. The mock-recognition of Jourdain at the end of *Le Bourgeois Gentilhomme* or of Argan at the end of *Le Malade Imaginaire* has its counterpart in the mock recognition of Oreste by Hermione in *Andromaque* or in the scenes between Nero and Agrippine in *Britannicus*. If we look up the scale in *Andromaque* from Oreste to Andromaque herself we find that for every character the character above is a transcendent subject who is adored and yet at the same time resented precisely on account of this transcendence, which negates the transcendence that the idolator desires and claims for himself. If we look down the scale, we discover that for every character the character below is an object to be manipulated and used. The refusal of the "upper" character to recognize the "lower" one confirms the "lower" character in his adoration and at the same time intensifies his desire to reverse the positions. The same pattern is found in the comedies of Molière, though in less schematic form. The verbal battles that make up almost the whole of *Andromaque* have their counterpart in innumerable scenes in Molière's comedies.

If we examine some of the structural elements of *Andromaque* and *Britannicus* in particular, it is impossible not to see in them the ingredients of comedy. The celebrated ladder structure of *Andromaque,* to which we have already alluded, is in fact a characteristically and traditionally comic one from Shakespeare to Marivaux. In *As You Like It,* the folly and illusion of love-vanity is emphasized by the travesties: Silvius loves Phebe who loves Rosalind—Ganymede who loves "no woman," but Orlando. In *A Midsummer Night's Dream,* the illusory prestige of the beloved idol is delightfully exposed by means of the spell which inverts all the previous relations while maintaining and even intensifying the passions that inform them. Helena loves Demetrius who loves Hermia who loves and is loved by Lysander. Under the spell the situation alters: Hermia loves Lysander who loves Helena who loves and is loved by Demetrius. The meaning of the comedy is revealed by the infatuation of Titania, the Queen of the Fairies, for Bottom, the weaver, in his ass's costume. The same structure appears again, much later, in Proust: Saint-Loup loves Rachel who loves the polo player who loves André. (Note how they travesty element in Shakespeare is taken up again by Proust in the last of these relations. The meaning of all the infatuations is revealed by the homosexual relation that crowns them just as the key to all the infatuations in *A Midsummer Night's Dream* lies in Titania's love for an ass, and not even a real one at that!) Without making his situation blatantly comic, Proust does emphasize the sameness of these enslavements. They constitute a tiresome *ronde* of futility and illusion. If we

do not laugh, we can at least smile at the stupidity and blindness of these characters as they pursue the will o' the wisps that they have themselves invested with reality. Oreste loves Hermione, who ignores him and loves Pyrrhus, who ignores her and loves Andromaque, who ignores him and remains faithful to her dead husband. The situation is strikingly similar to those we find in Shakespeare or Proust, and Goldmann has rightly underlined the utter futility and inauthenticity of all these characters:

> Avec Hermione, Oreste, Pyrrhus, nous sommes dans le monde de la fausse conscience, du bavardage. Les paroles ne signifient jamais ce qu'elles disent; ce ne sont pas des moyens d'exprimer l'essence intérieure et authentique de celui qui les prononce, mais des instruments qu'il emploie pour tromper les autres et se tromper lui même. C'est le monde faux et sauvage de la non-essentialité, de la différence entre l'essence et l'apparence.

Now this world is precisely the world of the comedies of Molière, a world of vain words and names and appearances, a world in which the characters pursue empty titles and hollow forms.

J. Cameron Wilson (essay date 1973)

SOURCE: "Expansion and Brevity in Molière's Style," in *Molière: Stage and Study,* edited by W. D. Howarth and Merlin Thomas, Oxford at the Clarendon Press, 1973, pp. 93-113.

[*Wilson is an English educator and critic. In the following essay, he discusses the characteristic comic techniques of Molière's dialogue.*]

Molière's style, long praised for its naturalness and truth to life, possesses a degree of artifice which suggests that its intention is quite different from this. It is the unobtrusive nature of this artifice, however, which both guarantees its success in achieving its aim and explains the fact that critics have been so slow to recognize it. Unlike that of many of his predecessors in seventeenth-century French comedy, the stylistic artifice of Molière is so integrated into the dramatic dialogue that it rarely draws attention to itself.

Although no play can be an exact transcription of real life in dialogue or in any other respect, we must admit that in many ways Molière seems to be attempting in his use of language precisely what so many have praised him for: truth to life. For one thing, his style shows variety. His language adapts itself to the individual character or type; his use of technical jargon and of dialects is wide as well as remarkably accurate; his style is suited to the occasion and to the kind of conversation entailed. Nor do we have the impression of a cerebral, wooden, and unconvincing language deriving not from real life but from the author's mind. Life is very much of the essence of the impression this language makes, for it is animated, fast-moving, and vigorous. In Molière's own day, too, it was for the naturalness of its style of acting that his theatre, unlike the rival Hôtel de Bourgogne, was noted.

There have nevertheless been critics, even as far back as Molière's own time, who have sensed that Molière's comedies offer something different from the simple observation and imitation of human behaviour. The more apparent cases of exaggeration in his plays have not been overlooked, nor has the stylization of the so-called *grandes scènes,* like that between Célimène and Arsinoé in *Le Misanthrope,* been ignored. Devices such as repetition and stichomythia have been noted, and the merits and demerits of Molière's versification have been debated. Few critics have begun to realize, however, that a characteristic stylization informs Molière's dramatic style as a whole, that the basic essentials of this stylization are common to the great majority of Molière's works, and that it is the simplicity and appropriateness of the techniques he employs that hide their artificial nature. Molière's style possesses a form and a discipline, and I believe a purposefulness, which are expressed in its thoroughly functional nature; but the style is functional, not in terms of a depiction of real life, but in terms of the interpretation of human experience which the plays present. This form and discipline are expressive of the essential factors in a situation, and the precision and acuteness of their presentation of these factors is of the comic kind.

One way in which control is unobtrusively, but decisively, exercised over this dialogue, at first sight so natural, is in the regulation of the length of individual speeches. This may seem an obvious or unimportant point, but we realize on closer investigation the extent to which this simple factor contributes to the effectiveness of entire scenes and even plays. It is, furthermore, a central way in which Molière's comic style may be distinguished from that of his predecessors. With them verbosity was a stock device, exploited with zest, and usually associated with a certain type of character. In Molière it is hardly ever found as a comic technique in its own right, nor does it often serve to characterize an individual. Indeed, it is only rarely found at all, and certain speeches which show traces of it, and which in some ways hark back to the types of verbose utterance in earlier comedies, derive their effectiveness primarily from other sources. Molière's longer speeches are not detachable pieces of virtuosity, boldly exceeding all limits of credibility in their uncontrolled expansiveness. They are effective, rather, by virtue of the context in which they stand, the way in which they arise in the dialogue, and the form and polish which they exhibit within themselves. Orgon's expansive speech describing the development of Tartuffe's hold over him in Act I, scene v of *Le Tartuffe* derives much of its comic effectiveness from the rounded regularity of its structure; while the lengthy definition of physics by the Maître de Philosophie in Act II, scene iv of *Le Bourgeois gentilhomme* occurs at a point of carefully prepared comic climax in the dialogue and is effective chiefly for that reason.

It has been said that Molière's stylistic skill lies in his 'breaking up' of the dialogue of comedy, which makes

for greater dramatic movement, and it is true that what may be called verbosity frequently occurs in Molière over a series of shorter speeches rather than in the form of a tirade. This is the case in both Act II, scene ix and Act V, scene ii of *Les Femmes savantes,* where Chrysale's reiteration of his intention to act like a man is the more comic for being spread over a whole series of speeches with interpolated responses from Ariste or Henriette. The art of brevity is another manifestation of the precise control which Molière possesses over his language.

Fundamentally, however, neither the avoidance of verbose developments for their own sake nor the skill Molière shows in the art of brevity represents his major achievement in the handling of dramatic dialogue. Molière recognizes that the nature of an utterance is of greater significance than its mere length, and he also recognizes that expansion and brevity are qualities of language rather than mere quantities of it. He thus achieves some-thing subtler and more flexible than simple verbosity, as he succeeds in conveying an expansive quality or tone which is more comically incisive than mere numbers of words; while similarly he uses brevity of utterance, not because of any desire to reach the ultimate in succinct pithiness, but only where the tone afforded by such utterances is appropriate to the comic context.

The contrast between expansive and brief verbal elements in this sense is one of the most frequently employed and decisively comic techniques in Molière's dialogue, and is a major source of that animation and variety of which we have spoken. The contrast occurs, however, not in order exactly to represent real life, but in order to convey a comic point and simultaneously to forward the dramatic movement. The artifice of the contrast is effective in relation to the embodying and illuminating of the essential comic clash or conflict which underlies the particular incident or scene. The variety of ways in which expansive and brief elements are thus brought together guards against excessive artifice, however, and prevents the monotonous recurrence of a standard verbal procedure.

The primary comic effect of such contrast between expansive and brief verbal elements, normally exploited in the reply of one speaker to another, is often found in the reciprocal emphasis achieved. This may take the form of a single contrast, as when Cléonte's long tirade on feminine ingratitude in Act III, scene ix of *Le Bourgeois gentilhomme* ('Je fais voir pour une personne . . . ') provokes Covielle's terse reply: 'Je dis les mêmes choses que vous'; or of a multiple series, such as that in which Martine's eloquent comments on the relationship between Chrysale and Philaminte in Act V, scene iii of *Les Femmes savantes* are punctuated by Chrysale's 'Sans doute. . . . Il est vrai. . . . C'est parler comme il faut. . . . Oui. . . . Fort bien.' The comic stress may, however, fall more appropriately upon one or other of the elements. Anticlimax is thus frequently the basis of the single contrast of expansion and brevity, the stress here falling decisively upon the brief component. It is in this way that illusion and reality, fantasy and truth, theory and practice are often comically opposed; and in the last-mentioned case we find that on occasion it is the theory which is reasonable while the practice appears ridiculous, whereas at other times the theory is the ridiculous term and the practice represents what is reasonable. We recall Sganarelle's brief rejoinder to his master's words on the departure of Done Elvire:

> DOM JUAN: Sais-tu bien que j'ai encore senti quelque peu d'émotion pour elle, que j'ai trouvé de l'agrément dans cette nouveauté bizarre, et que son habit négligé, son air languissant et ses larmes ont réveillé en moi quelques petits restes d'un feu éteint?

> SGANARELLE: C'est-à-dire que ses paroles n'ont fait aucun effet sur vous.

Henriette's incredulous 'Moi, ma mere?' [in *Les Femmes savantes*] as the only response to Philaminte's expansive, emphatic, and carefully constructed speech in which she proposes Trissotin as her daughter's husband, provides us with a parallel verse example.

As well as in the relationship of consecutive speeches, effects of the same kind are also to be found within single speeches of individual characters, for instance when Vadius's twelve-line condemnation of authors who seek praise for their works is comically rounded off by the couplet:

> Voici de petits vers pour de jeunes amants,
> Sur quoi je voudrais bien avoir vos sentiments.

In other cases the same contrast occurs between an entire dialogue and a single remark, as when Monsieur Jourdain finally requests [in *Les Bourgeouis gentilhomme*], after his investigation of the erudite fields of study successively proposed by the Maître de Philosophie: 'Apprenez-moi l'orthographe.' Elsewhere again, a contrast may be effected between the cumulative expansiveness of the speeches of one character in a scene, and the brevity of some following remark from the same speaker. In Act V, scene ii of *Les Femmes savantes,* for example, it is only Chrysale's brief imperative 'Secondez-moi bien tous', uttered at the approach of Philaminte, which lends full comic force and significance to the accumulation of his outraged questions and absolute declarations throughout the scene.

It may be mentioned here that the fact that Molière, despite his art of brevity, is not at all a 'quotable' dramatist is attributable to the way in which his memorable individual lines are integrated into, or rather appear to arise naturally from, the surrounding dialogue. In this connection it is often from their contrast with the expansive build-up from which they emerge that the occasional single lines which seem to sum up whole aspects of the comic situation gain much of their force and effectiveness. This is the case, for example, with Alceste's pregnant line in Act V, scene i of *Le Misanthrope*: 'J'ai pour moi la justice, et je perds mon proces'; with Chrysale's paradoxical complaints concerning his household in *Les Femmes savantes* (II. vii): 'Et le raisonnement en bannit la raison'

and 'Et j'ai des serviteurs, et ne suis point servi'; and with Argan's revealing declaration, which emerges at the climax of a whole expansive dialogue in *Le Malade imaginaire* (I. V): 'Je ne suis point bon, et je suis méchant quand je veux.'

Particularly within single speeches the contrast of expansion and brevity can well convey an effect of surprise, as when the final line of a speech suddenly contradicts the lines leading up to it. Philaminte's words to the valet Julien show this:

> Reportez tout cela sur l'heure à votre maître,
> Et lui dites qu'afin de lui faire connaître
> Quel grand état je fais de ses nobles avis
> Et comme je les crois dignes d'être suivis,
> Dès ce soir à Monsieur je marierai ma fille.

Contrasts of expansion and brevity occurring in a multiple series, although clearly not appropriate to the conveying of surprise or to achieving the once-for-all effect of anticlimax, are valuable means of providing added dramatic impetus for a scene, as we see from Act I, scene iv of *Le Malade imaginaire,* where the insertion of a brief reply from Toinette after each question of Angélique not only comically stresses the degree of Angélique's expansiveness by isolating each individual question, but also contributes to the dramatic animation and speed through the repeated contrast in length and by keeping us constantly in touch with both speakers. There are, finally, multiple contrasts of expansion and brevity where the primary comic effect derives not from the simple emphasis of one element by the other, but from the repetition itself and from the way in which this expresses the total situation of the moment. The pattern of the dialogue is here directly expressive of a basic relationship or conflict which underlies the scene. The pattern in *Le Tartuffe* (I. V), *Dom Juan* (III. i), and *Le Misanthrope* (III. i), for example, is that of verbal pursuit and withdrawal. Orgon will make no definite answer to Cléante's inquiries regarding his plans for Mariane's marriage; Dom Juan responds with meaningless brevity to Sganarelle's questions about his beliefs; and Acaste replies to Clitandre's series of questions with brief ironical declarations. In Dom Juan's interview with Monsieur Dimanche (*Dom Juan,* IV. iii) and Argan's with Monsieur Purgon (*Le Malade imaginaire,* III. V), on the other hand, the comic pattern formed by the contrast of expansion and brevity is that of one character's loquacity and the other's inability to speak.

Wherever we look at this technique of contrast between expansive and brief verbal elements in Molière's style, we find a combination of comic purposefulness and formal stylization. Let us now consider in greater detail, however, two special uses of the contrast to which we have not so far referred: verbal expansion following restraint, and the interruption of expansive language.

By the regulated use of verbal expansion following restraint Molière can succeed in conveying a comic situation and in ensuring constant movement. This restraint on the part of a character, although expressing itself occasionally in complete silence, consists normally of brief utterances, which lead at a particular point to an expansive outburst. This is a technique used to advantage in the opening scenes of both *Le Tartuffe* and *Le Misanthrope*. Madame Pernelle and Alceste are each brought, after the first few lines of the play in question, to an expansive outburst which develops into a chief comic resource of the whole opening scene. It is Elmire's insistence on pursuing the departing Madame Pernelle and on requesting an explanation of her departure which causes the old woman to delay leaving and to express in full the reasons for her dissatisfaction. It is, likewise, Philinte's insistence in addressing the uncommunicative Alceste and, in particular, his incidental use of the word *amis* [in *Le Misanthrope*] which prompt the flood of exaggerated language from Alceste. If an opening scene is to be based on the expansive expression of strong feelings, it is clearly much more dramatically engaging that this expansion should emerge before us, as the direct consequence of a situation and a dialogue with which we are made acquainted, than that it should begin with an unprepared tirade immediately the curtain rises. Both by virtue of its fragmentation and integration in the dialogue and by its emergence from the initial brief exchange in each case, the expansiveness escapes any likeness to a static recitation. Comically, it is the one who at first had to be persuaded into speaking whose subsequent expansiveness predominates in the scene. The example from *Le Misanthrope* is perhaps the more striking of the two, as it is also the more directly related to the presentation of the central character; and here the outburst of Alceste is reinforced by means of interruption and of seizure upon a word quite incidentally uttered:

> PHILINTE: Dans vos brusques chagrins je ne puis vous comprendre,
> Et quoique amis, enfin, je suis tout des premiers . . .
> ALCESTE: Moi, votre ami? Rayez cela de vos papiers.
> J'ai fait jusques ici profession de l'être;
> Mais après ce qu'en vous je viens de voir paraître,
> Je vous déclare net que je ne le suis plus,
> Et ne veux nulle place en des cœurs corrompus.

As long as Philinte's questions and remarks were brief and direct, Alceste's responses remained curt and uninformative; but once Philinte seems to have given up trying to elicit an answer and seems about to launch into a full-length speech, he is made to say something which causes Alceste actually to cut him short. Molière's simple technique here prepares us for what will be a recurring source of comedy in the presentation of Alceste: the alternation of restraint, be it surly or polite, and exaggerated outburst.

Expansion following restraint is often employed to convey the comic effect of indirect expression giving way to more direct utterance. In *Les Femmes savantes* (II. iii)

the main source of comedy in the first part of the scene is the suspense in which Bélise keeps Chrysale and Ariste by asserting that it is not Henriette whom Clitandre loves, without, however, revealing straight away her belief that it is really she herself. Despite Ariste's repeated objections Bélise refuses either to withdraw or to substantiate her assertion. Her responses are brief and lack content, and even when she speaks for five consecutive lines she still reveals nothing new. Indeed, her greater fullness here is comic in that it simply restates at greater length what she has already said, whereas what is wanted is an explanation. The techniques of delay and of seizure upon an insignificant word (in this case the exclamation 'Hay!') are again used here in order to prompt the expansive flood of direct language.

> ARISTE: Mais, puisque vous savez tant de choses, ma sœur,
> Dites-nous, s'il vous plaît, cet autre objet qu'il aime.
> BÉLISE: Vous le voulez savoir?
> ARISTE: Oui. Quoi?
> BÉLISE: Moi.
> ARISTE: Vous?
> BÉLISE: Moi-même.
> ARISTE: Hay, ma sœur!
> BÉLISE: Qu'est-ce donc que veut dire ce 'hay',
> Et qu'a de surprenant le discours que je fai?
> On est faite d'un air, je pense, à pouvoir dire
> Qu'on n'a pas pour un cœur soumis à son empire;
> Et Dorante, Damis, Cléonte et Lycidas
> Peuvent bien faire voir qu'on a quelques appas.

It is especially clear in this instance that the essential comic contrast is not so much between brevity and length as between restraint and outburst, the former affording a build-up to the latter: it is the nature of the language rather than its mere quantity which is significant. A further point to be made on the basis of this example is that the switch from indirect to direct language marks, as it frequently does, the turning-point of the whole scene. Not only is Bélise's direct outburst the culmination of the sustained indirect build-up and, more immediately, a response to Ariste's expression of surprise; but her speech also contains within it the elements of which the rest of the scene is composed, in that the names of her supposed lovers are used individually by Molière later in the scene as the basis for a rising sequence of single-line exchanges which prompts Chrysale's use of the word *chimères* and the end of the scene.

Indirect language gives way to direct, again with similar technique and effect, in two well-known scenes: Alceste's outburst concerning Oronte's sonnet, and the point in the same play at which Célimène finally turns to a direct attack upon Arsinoé. In both cases we sense that the moment for direct expression has come: either Alceste's indirect responses to Oronte's questions have come as close to directness as they can without crossing the borderline, or the insinuations of Célimène and Arsinoé have become as patent as may be conceived while still retaining the verbal overlay of objective politeness. There may be greater apparent form in the words with which Célimène scornfully attacks her rival, but in fact the outburst of Alceste (beginning at line 376: 'Franchement, il est bon à mettre au cabinet'), for all its comparative lack of poise, is just as skilfully formed—in this case to translate the comedy of the man who, having previously refused to make any statement, now speaks in such a way that the normal gaps and pauses left for others to reply simply do not appear. Not until some forty lines later, when Alceste has said all he has to say, does Oronte make any reaction at all, and then his brief rejoinder 'Et moi, je vous soutiens que mes vers sont fort bons' only re-emphasizes the expansiveness of Alceste. In this scene and in that referred to between Célimène and Arsinoé (III. iv) we again see how the turn from indirect to direct expression marks a kind of watershed in the scene and hastens on its conclusion. Alceste's outburst of direct criticism of Oronte is both the culmination of the indirect speeches which precede and the basis for the increasingly insulting sequence of brief *répliques* which forces the interview to a close. Célimène's direct attack on Arsinoé, beginning 'Et moi, je ne sais pas, Madame, aussi pourquoi', gains in effectiveness by virtue of her foregoing ironical restraint, but it also serves to prompt, particularly by its stinging final couplet, the long speech of Arsinoé which leads by a persuasive logic, which is of the language only, to the ridiculous concluding assertion: 'Que l'on a des amants quand on en veut avoir.' Célimène's rejoinder to this claim ('Ayez-en donc, Madame, et voyons cette affaire') forces Arsinoé to capitulate, thus bringing the scene to an end.

Not infrequently Molière draws our attention to verbal expansion by an explicit reference to it, as we see in Philaminte's line, referring to Trissotin [in *Les Femmes savantes*]: 'Si nous parlons toujours, il ne pourra rien dire', or in Sganarelle's words to Gusman in Act I, scene i of *Dom Juan*: 'Écoute, au moins: je t'ai fait cette confidence avec franchise, et cela m'est sorti un peu bien vite de la bouche.' It is not that we need to have the expansiveness pointed out to us, but rather that these comments are themselves comic in the mouths of their respective speakers. In the first case Philaminte's recognition and stating of the obvious is a form of the comedy of the over-explicit, at which Molière excels; and in the case of Sganarelle realization of the frankness and spontaneity of his own outburst concerning his master comically underlines the forced duality of his own character and language.

In this last speech of *Dom Juan* (I. i) we see again verbal expansion following upon restraint for comic ends. All Sganarelle's previous speeches concerning the reasons for Dom Juan's departure from Done Elvire have been either brief and undeveloped or expressed in indirect or guarded terms. Again it is a turn of phrase from his interlocutor which prompts Sganarelle to abandon his indirect language: Gusman's 'je ne comprends pas' prompts Sga-

narelle's 'Je n'ai pas grande peine à le comprendre, moi.' Yet even now the full outburst is withheld until Sganarelle has safeguarded himself by a series of attenuating clauses and phrases ('Je ne dis pas que . . . tu sais que . . . par précaution . . . *inter nos* . . . '), although rather than attenuate, they comically stress by delay the outburst when it occurs (' . . . que tu vois en Dom Juan, mon maître, le plus grand scélérat que la terre ait jamais porté . . . '). The length of Sganarelle's preamble only adds to the comedy of the contrast with what follows, for instead of the preamble foreshadowing an equally restrained description of Dom Juan's failings, all caution is left behind in the preamble, in order to allow full verbal indulgence in the body of the speech. As elsewhere in Sganarelle's role, the extremes of reticence and frankness are boldly juxtaposed. Even within the expansive speech once launched, however, there is a form and clear use of certain characteristic devices. Accumulation is regulated, as usual, to achieve but not to overshoot the comic point in view, and thus we find here the technique, frequent in Molière, of pursuing a line of thought just a little further than it would be pursued in reality. Dom Juan 'ne croit ni Ciel, ni Enfer, ni loupgarou'; together with Done Elvire 'il aurait encore épousé toi [Gusman], son chien et son chat'; he treats marriage lightly 'et c'est un épouseur à toutes mains'. We note too how the accumulated form of the three clauses in the sentence beginning 'Suffit qu'il faut . . . ' gives them a comic lack of emphasis, considering the extreme nature of their contents:

> Suffit qu'il faut que le courroux du Ciel l'accable quelque jour; qu'il me vaudrait bien mieux d'être au diable que d'être à lui, et qu'il me fait voir tant d'horreurs, que je souhaiterais qu'il fût déjà je ne sais où.

The construction of this sentence also fulfils a formal purpose with regard to the speech as a whole, for its summarizing and concluding tone, especially when taken within the context of the sentences immediately preceding and following, makes for the greatest comic effectiveness in the prompt appearance of Dom Juan himself, who has just been so decisively summed up. It is most satisfying that Dom Juan should appear, thus, at the very moment when Sganarelle's expansive speech seems to have reached a definitive conclusion. We see by this, as we have seen in the other instances discussed, how Molière does not lose dramatic impetus by overplaying his effects, any more than he seeks to maintain it at the cost of stylistic form. He does not indulge in a situation which has been, so to speak, 'achieved': once these expansive outbursts have been released, Molière, while deriving comic effect within them from expansive verbal means, uses such expansion only in order to precipitate a further stage in the dramatic development.

The interruption of expansive language is a second characteristic form which Molière's exploitation of the contrast between expansion and brevity assumes. A more striking impression of a character's expansive tendency may often be conveyed by cutting short an expansion which we might have expected to continue, than by allowing it to proceed to a conclusion. The dramatist's control of his characters' expansiveness by this means serves a well-defined comic purpose and, indeed, enhances the effect of the expansive language which is suppressed.

It is often the expansiveness of convention which is interrupted. Thomas Diafoirus is introduced in Act II, scene V of *Le Malade imaginaire* by means of the long set speeches, over-flowing with conceit and metaphor, which he addresses to Argan and Angélique. Their length and superficial erudition contrast with the obvious empty-headed stupidity of the speaker, and their lack of spontaneity contrasts with the supposed feelings they are intended to convey. Thomas's repeated questions aside to his father make this lack of spontaneity ridiculously obvious. But we also recall the false start made by Thomas to Angélique and his interruption by Argan:

THOMAS DIAFOIRUS *à Angélique*: Madame, c'est avec justice que le Ciel vous a concédé le nom de belle-mère, puisque l'on . . .

ARGAN: Ce n'est pas ma femme, c'est ma fille à qui vous parlez.

The false start is interpolated between two fully developed expansive addresses, and as well as providing variety in the dialogue, it sheds comic light on the nature of the completed compliments. We note, first, how the interruption serves to emphasize the superficial and conventional nature of the speeches: they bear no relation to the actual person addressed. Secondly, the interruption gives comic expression to the complete lack of adaptability of the speaker, stopped unexpectedly and unable to proceed in any way other than that which he has learned. Thirdly, the speech thus curtailed foreshadows the situation in II. 6, when Thomas, finally confronted with Béline, is still unable, as a result of the latter's untimely interruption, to conclude the same ill-starred compliment. The interruption of Thomas's incipient expansiveness thus both comically stresses the conventional nature of that expansiveness and assists the dramatic construction and impetus of the scene and the play.

When such interruption is employed in the verse plays, the verse form can give added force through the rhyme. High-flown expansive developments are halted before they have got under way, and the direct rejoinder, reducing the situation once more to the terms of reality, gains in force by the way in which it is made to rhyme with the last full line of the interrupted speech. Two examples from *Les Femmes savantes* show how the element of surprise is particularly strong in verse interruptions:

TRISSOTIN: Je ne sais que vous dire en mon ravissement,

Madame, et cet hymen dont je vois qu'on m'honore

Me met . . .

HENRIETTE: Tout beau, Monsieur, il n'est pas fait encore

and:

ARMANDE: On voit briller pour vous les soins de notre mère,

Et son choix ne pouvait d'un plus illustre époux . . .

HENRIETTE: Si le choix est si beau, que ne le prenez-vous?

The close combination of often insincere expansiveness and trenchant brevity within one rhyming couplet stresses the true situation and destroys the apparent finality of tone of the interrupted utterance. Once again, also, such interruption is used to speed the scene onward, sometimes by means of provoking a highly stylized verbal exchange as in the second example quoted, and sometimes, as with the first example, by precipitating the rapid conclusion of the scene as a whole.

Interruption is also appropriately employed in relation to the expansive language of enthusiasm. Eagerness to convey some vital piece of information can result, as with Nicole at the beginning of *Le Bourgeois gentilhomme* (III. viii), in an enthusiastic expansiveness which is interrupted, comically, before the actual information is conveyed, and thus misunderstanding is credibly introduced. Enthusiasm for one's own merits also expresses itself in verbal facility. In both individual speeches and patterned sequences a constant ready flow of words characterizes, for instance, Trissotin and Vadius in *Les Femmes savantes*. A single word may serve as the basis for the interruption of the one by the other, as does the noun *vers* in Act III, scene iii. Vadius's speech which ends with the offer of a recitation of love poetry provokes a response from Trissotin, arising from the word *vers,* which is comic as an interruption of Vadius's intention. The interruption occurs, however, at precisely the point where the stark comic contrast—already referred to—between Vadius's theory and practice is clearest. It also has the function of deflecting any reading of Vadius's poetry (we have already heard Trissotin's), and of combining comic delay in this connection with an increase of tempo in the to and fro of brief replies thus unleashed. It is in the interest of the comic structure of the scene that here and twice more (at lines 988 and 1006) the incipient expansiveness of Vadius is curtailed, but its curtailment on three successive occasions increases rather than reduces the impression one receives of his expansiveness. The suggestion of the latter may be much more effective, dramatically and comically, than its full development.

What is commonly referred to as comedy of character arises at times from the incipient expansive utterance which is interrupted. The irascible aspect of Orgon is shown up in this way when, after attempting to silence Dorine during his conversation with Mariane, he finally breaks forth in expansive exasperation:

ORGON: Te tairas-tu, serpent, dont les traits effrontés . . .

DORINE: Ah! vous êtes dévot, et vous vous emportez!

The effectiveness of breaking off Orgon's metaphor, rather than allowing it to develop unhindered, is apparent, for Dorine's unanswerable interruption at the point of climax of Orgon's anger gives the most pointed comic expression to the situation. Again here rhyme assists the effect, and the speed of the scene is maintained.

It is not by any means always the case that expansive language is interrupted by Molière shortly after it has begun: the dramatist's discipline and skill are also seen in his choosing the best moment at which to interrupt a speech which he has seen fit to develop at some length. Not infrequently self-interruption, having an intrinsic comic potential, is how this manifests itself. This self-interruption often derives its comic power from the absolute contradiction between what precedes and what follows; and this comic contrast would be impossible, were there not a considerable degree of expansion before the interruption takes place. It is the fact that Lucile in *Le Bourgeois gentilhomme* (V. v) gets as far as she does in her declaration to her father that she is unwilling to marry anyone but Cléonte which makes her sudden and complete swing to obedient submission (and her father's acceptance of this) so pointedly comic. The same comic effect of stark juxtaposition is produced by Sganarelle's self-interruption on catching sight of Dom Juan while talking to the peasant girls at the end of Act II, scene iv of *Dom Juan*. The effectiveness of the contradiction here again depends upon the amount Molière has allowed Sganarelle to say before he notices Dom Juan, as the second part of Sganarelle's speech beginning 'Mon maître est un fourbe' consists of an exact and explicit negation of the four declarations of the first part. Whether or not Sganarelle is in control of his verbal flow, Molière certainly is.

It is not always some outward cause such as sudden recognition or the appearance of another character that prompts self-interruption in Molière. It can also arise from inability, real or feigned, to say more on a certain subject. It is fitting, in the well-known line of Orgon in Act I, scene v of *Le Tartuffe*: 'C'est un homme . . . qui . . . ha! un homme . . . un homme enfin', that Orgon should be unable to proceed beyond the very first element in his attempt to give a full and adequate description of Tartuffe. However, in the case of Toinette, ironically and calculatedly extolling Béline in Act III, scene xi of *Le Malade imaginaire,* the best effect is to be derived from allowing a fuller expansive description first. The comic impact increases with each patently untrue declaration of Toinette's, and the same effect could not have been obtained had Argan himself replied to Béralde's accusation concerning Béline; but Toinette's pretended inability to express to the full Béline's devotion to Argan emphasizes her ironical words better than any further attempt at description could have done.

Frequently, advanced expansiveness in a speaker is interrupted by another speaker. Dorine and Mariane both interrupt each other in the midst of expansive speeches in Act II, scene iii of *Le Tartuffe,* and in both cases it is at a crucial point for the comic progress of the scene. The first occasion is at the point where Dorine assumes an ironical attitude towards Mariane, in order to spur her to positive opposition to her father's plans; the second is thirty lines later, at the point where Mariane can stand no more of Dorine's ironical expansiveness. In the first instance the degree of expansion which Molière has allowed to Mariane in the speech which is interrupted and which forms a climax to all she has said before makes the impact of the interruption more comically effective. The pattern established in the interrupted speech itself leads us to expect and anticipate the completion of at least her third rhetorical question.

> MARIANE: Mais par un haut refus et d'éclatants mépris
> Ferai-je dans mon choix voir un cœur trop épris?
> Sortirai-je pour lui, quelque éclat dont il brille,
> De la pudeur du sexe et du devoir de fille?
> Et veux-tu que mes feux par le monde étalés . . .

Dorine's interruption, however, gives a new turn to the dialogue, thus guarding against monotony and sluggishness. The same device of interruption is used, on the second occasion mentioned, in order to curb the excessive development of Dorine's ironical words. Each of the accumulated strokes in Dorine's picture of provincial life with Tartuffe overcomes Mariane with greater horror, and Dorine's picturesque speech clearly seems capable of expanding still further. The 'Si pourtant votre époux . . . ' at the close would lead us to expect a further development of several lines, presenting a full alternative to the pastimes described in the previous lines. Again Molière chooses the most appropriate moment at which to curtail Dorine: she is interrupted in mid-line, suggesting that her inventiveness is inexhaustible, and at just that point where we feel that Mariane can contain herself no longer. The interruption also allows a switch to shorter speeches which both affords variety and hastens on the climax of the exchange in Dorine's resolute 'Non, vous serez, ma foi! tartuffiée.'

Tartuffe's bold approaches to Elmire in Act III, scene iii of the same play are rendered comic by a repeated use of this interruption of partially developed expansive language. Three times Elmire interrupts the expansive Tartuffe, and all three interrupted speeches are cut short half a line after an expansive use of the conjunction *et*. Elmire's interruptions have the effect not only of breaking up the speech of Tartuffe into briefer elements, thus assisting the dramatic movement, but also of comically deflating each of Tartuffe's attempts to express his lustful feelings. The structure of the dialogue thus renders comic, rather than distasteful or crude, Tartuffe's first advances towards Elmire; and the emphasis is placed, through the judicious use of interruption, on the quickness of Elmire in rebuffing Tartuffe rather than on Tartuffe's action itself.

We should note lastly, in connection with the interruption of expansive language, that Molière exploits the possibilities of combining verbal with active interruption. The entry of a character frequently serves to interrupt the dialogue to comic effect, as when Arsinoé appears during Célimène's denunciation of her in *Le Misanthrope* (III. iii-iv). The carefully patterned expansion of Célimène's speech beginning 'Oui, oui, franche grimace' is used to prepare effectively for Arsinoé's appearance. The speech is long enough to establish a verbal pattern which we

---

Erich Auerbach on Molière's portrayal of seventeenth-century French society:

One can see in Molière's art the greatest measure of realism which could still please in the fully developed classical literature of the France of Louis XIV. Molière staked out the limits of what was possible at the time. He did not conform completely to the prevailing trend toward psychological types; yet with him too the peculiar and characteristic is always ridiculous and extravagant. He did not avoid the farcical and the grotesque, yet with him too any real representation of the life of the popular classes, even in such a spirit of aristocratic contempt as Shakespeare's, is as completely out of the question as it is with Boileau. All his chambermaids and servingmen, his peasants and peasants' wives, even his merchants, lawyers, physicians, and apothecaries, are merely comic adjuncts; and it is only within the frame of an upper bourgeois or aristocratic household that servants—especially women—at times represent the voice of down-to-earth common sense. But their functions are always concerned with their masters problems, never with those of their own lives. Not the slightest trace of politics, of social or economic criticism, or of an analysis of the political, social, and economic bases of life is to be found. Molière's criticism is entirely moralistic; that is to say, it accepts the prevailing structure of society, takes for granted its justification, permanence, and general validity, and castigates the excesses occurring within its limits as ridiculous.

Erich Auerbach, in his Mimesis: The Representation of Reality in Western Literature, *1946. Reprint by Princeton University Press, 1953.*

---

expect to continue, but the pattern also suggests that Célimène's diatribe is approaching its emphatic completion: interruption occurs at exactly the point where it produces the strongest impact and the most comically pointed effect.

Physical action other than the entry of a character sometimes causes the comic interruption of expansive language, and one last example may suffice. Sganarelle's speech in *Dom Juan* (III. i) beginning 'Mon raisonnement est qu'il y a quelque chose d'admirable dans l'homme' strikes us and remains in our memory principally because it is comically interrupted by his falling to the ground. This interruption stresses with comic intensity the recurring succession in Sganarelle of expansive indignation and resigned brevity before his master's conduct and beliefs. Had the speech been a completed whole, such a comically pointed contrast would not have been achieved. Further, the whole

expansive build-up of Sganarelle's argument is instantly deflated and emptied of all power to convince by the abruptly physical nature of the interruption. Sganarelle thus, comically, destroys his own argument; and since the nature of the interruption is intimately related to the content of the argument, our attention is drawn not simply to a farcical incident which makes us forget whatever serious content the foregoing speech might have possessed, but to a practical negation of the words so persuasively built up. Had the speech not been as expansive as it is, the deflating effect could not have been so pointed.

The interruption, at an early or advanced stage, of expansive language reveals especially clearly Molière's attitude to the degree of verbal fullness in comedy. It may be true, as we said at the outset, that the mere number of words used is less significant than the quality or tone of the utterance; but it is equally true that Molière's regulation of the length of his speeches is a vital means towards the conveying of the tone intended and the obtaining of the comic effect. The great marks of Molière's style are, it seems to me, its correspondence to the underlying situation of the scene or play, and its constant movement. Verbal expansion is only the outward expression of an element in a situation—if we may use the term, the 'conservative' element, that which tends towards continuance and unhindered development on the basis of the foregoing. It is in the opposition it meets that this verbal expansion betrays its comedy, and the opposition which combines brevity with interruption is especially pointed and vivid. The precision evident in Molière's use of the technique demonstrates that his object is not to indulge in verbosity, but to give fitting expression to a comic situation. It is to be noted, however, that it is a comic situation in the dramatic sense of the word, for the opposition or conflict which Molière's language embodies originates not in the real world, but in the mind and imagination of the artist, which is capable of perceiving *le ridicule*.

Alvin Eustis (essay date 1973)

SOURCE: "Paradox, Plot, and Outcome," in *Molière as Ironic Contemplator,* Mouton & Co., N. V., Publishers, 1973, pp. 61-99.

[*Eustis is an American critic, translator, and educator. In the following excerpt, he discusses the structure of Molière's plays and suggests that an ironic situation or paradox is at the center of each of the comedies.*]

Twentieth-century criticism has contributed to a better comprehension of Molière's theater by minimizing the importance of plot construction in drama. As long as the concept of the well-made play reigned, his dénouements were considered arbitrary, many of his acts padded or short of action, and his plotting defective. The result had been until fairly recent times to attempt to reduce his plays to the linear development of an action, whereas more fundamental structural elements had been ignored. For example, critics have shaken their heads at the *Bourgeois Gentilhomme's* loose construction, not seeing that it represents a stage of perfection in Molière's ironic comedy, thanks to the greater variety of incident and superb handling of ironic repercussions. Or take *Dom Juan's* extremely subtle structure, which has not yet been completely adumbrated. The highflown diction in the last scene of Act I, for example, is obviously placed in ironic juxtaposition to the peasants' thick jargon in the first scene of Act II.

W. G. Moore, it is true, feels that it is pointless to inquire into Molière's structure, since the plays were written with too much haste. [Will G. Moore, *Molière: A New Criticism*] However, Molière spent two or three years writing several of them, and for a dramatist there is no direct ratio between speed of composition and complexity of structure. The best feature of Dr. Moore's book is furthermore its pioneer discussion of structural elements, which he seems led to treat in spite of his assertion. Dr. Moore sees at work in Molière's theater not intellectual processes of deduction and motivation, but rather a "principle of suffusion" whereby scenes are grouped around a master concept and serve to illustrate it. On the other hand, it will be shown that Dr. Moore goes too far in maintaining that there is no progression based on cause and effect or on development in time, whether the latter concept is taken to mean the action's span or the tempo of individual and grouped situations. It is precisely the large number of action words, short sentences, and agile gestures that make Molière's scenes seem to move forward with great rapidity. The fact remains, as René Bray, too, has pointed out [in *Molière homme de théâtre*], that we now conceive of Molière's plays in terms of series or clusters of situations bearing a certain relationship, congruous or incongruous, to one another. In a cluster structure ironic possibilities already abound, but clusters in any given play are also fused together in a fundamental unity of irony.

At the core of most of Molière's comedies therefore lies something quite different from the apparent plot: an ironic paradox, that is, an ironic situation encompassing, permeating, giving form to all the actions and episodes that constitute the play. A young master who is convinced of his own ability is not only constantly obliged to beg his valet's help but through his blundering ruins all the valet's schemes (*L'Etourdi*). An unfavored suitor is certain that he has married the girl who spurns his advances (*Le Dépit amoureux*). Two silly girls from the provinces prefer a couple of lackeys to two eligible Parisian gentlemen (*Les Précieuses Ridicules*). Two couples reproach their respective partners for infidelities that have no basis in fact (*Sganarelle ou le Cocu imaginaire*). A jealous lover persists in accusing his sweetheart of betraying him in the face of overwhelming evidence to the contrary (*Dom Garcie de Navarre*). A younger brother who in ideas, speech, deportment, and costume belongs to a generation older than his own loses his intended bride because of his selfish tyranny; an older brother who at sixty dresses like a coxcomb in the height of fashion and keeps his bride because of his modern permissiveness is destined to wear horns (*L'Ecole des Maris*). However much we may curse importunates, we ourselves are importunate in other eyes (*Les Fâcheux*). The holding of every trump card will not prevent young love from finding a way: "Coup sur coup je verrai par leur intelligence [i.e., connivence] / De mes soins vigilants confondre la prudence? / Et je serai la dupe, en ma maturité, / D'une jeune innocente et d'un jeune éventé?" (Arnolphe in *L'Ecole des Femmes*, IV, 7, 1184-87). A group of self-infatuated individuals persist in attacking a play whose excellence has been proven by its success with the public (*La Critique de l'Ecole des Femmes*). A play can be made out of nothing in no time at all (*L'Impromptu de Versailles*). A vain and selfish man who considers only the advantages of marriage is gradually forced into wedding a spendthrift who counts on being a widow and marrying her lover within six months (*Le Mariage forcé*). A princess spurns her devoted suitors and falls in love with one whom she thinks is indifferent to her charms (*La Princesse d'Elide*). A boor from the provinces succeeds in hoodwinking a Parisian and his mother, making love to his wife, and obtaining all his property (*Le Tartuffe*). A nobleman is convinced that he can retain all the privileges of his caste without assuming any of the responsibilities; a pursuer of innocent women, he himself is in flight during the whole play and fails to accomplish a single seduction (*Dom Juan*). For love of life men put themselves in the hands of charlatans who kill them (*L'Amour médecin*). A jealous lover thinks that he can command absolute fidelity in a flirt, who in turn, though profiting by society's advantages, is sure that she can defy its conventions with impunity (*Le Misanthrope*). With respect to the intimate ironic relationship among Molière's three greatest plays it may be observed that in one a character (Tartuffe) conceals what he thinks, in *Dom Juan* a character (Sganarelle) is not allowed to say what he thinks, and in the third a character (Alceste) is determined on saying exactly what he thinks. Clothes make the monk (*Le Médecin malgré lui*). No citadel however well guarded is proof against Love's arrows (*Le Sicilien*). If fate and the gods have decided that you are to be a cuckold, there is nothing that you can do; but conversely a god must assume man's guise in order to have his way with mortal woman (*Amphitryon*). A peasant thinks that he has acquired the nobility's perquisites, particularly the right to avenge his honor, in acquiring a noble wife (*George Dandin*). A bourgeois is determined to retain all the trappings of his rank and the respect of his neighbors even while taking a young wife, pinching pennies, and practicing usury (*L'Avare*). An impostor meets his defeat at the hands of impostors (*Monsieur de Pourceaugnac*). A suitor without rank or riches is preferred to those possessing both (*Les Amants Magnifiques*). A bourgeois is acquiring, he thinks, with money the kind of nobility that only birth can give; but an impoverished aristocrat demeans himself by defrauding the bourgeois (*Le Bourgeois Gentilhomme*). The wisdom of settled elders is no match for a wily servant's inventive genius (*Les Fourberies de Scapin*). A provincial aristocrat is certain that her manners can impress members of Parisian high society (*La Comtesse d'Escarbagnas*). In a time when a husband has all the legal rights, a wife succeeds in wearing the trousers; but the husband, plagued by an excessively modern household, would prefer an excessively archaic one (*Les Femmes Savantes*). A perfectly healthy man enjoys his conviction that he is seriously ill

(*Le Malade Imaginaire*).

Nearly every situation in the play exists in function of the central paradox, at times driving it home to the audience by illustration, at others introducing implications, corollaries, or consequences. Some plays where plot is slender or traditional farcical elements are preponderant contain many comic situations that are ironic only through their identification with the central paradox. That is to say, plays like *Les Précieuses Ridicules, L'Amour médecin, Le Médecin malgré lui, Le Sicilien,* or *Monsieur de Pourceaugnac* are insufficiently developed for their situations to generate their own irony in addition to that of the central paradox. *La Princesse d'Elide* on the other hand is exceptional in that the only striking secondary ironies are found in situations concerning cowardly Moron, where connection with the basic paradox is tenuous. In the special type of play that Molière conceived for his polemics, *La Critique de l'Ecole des Femmes,* where plot is practically non-existent, the same tactic is visible throughout a number of barely differentiated episodes: to create for his adversaries a series of false situations from which they cannot extricate themselves and whereby their arguments are reduced to the absurd.

Le Dépit amoureux is also a special type of play; the first act contains three distinct ironic situations (the rivals' certainty that each has Lucile's favor, Mascarille's lying when he believes that he is telling the truth, the lovers' quarrel over a trifle). However, much of the ironic flavor of those situations is lost for the audience since they come too early in the play and the exposition is not complete until the first scene of Act II, when a new, quadruple ironic situation unfolds: Albert has a guilty secret, but does not know that he is a biter bit; Ascagne also has a guilty secret, and she knows a little more about Albert's secret than he, but is still partly in the dark; Valère is certain that he has married Lucile in a secret ceremony; Eraste is just as certain that Lucile is faithful to him. In the rest of the play the relationship between a complicated plot and the central paradox is so clumsily handled that scarcely a single ironic situation impresses itself upon the spectator.

At the beginning of *Les Fourberies de Scapin* Octave assures his Hyacinthe that he already feels a "terrible aversion" for the girl whom his father wishes him to marry, little realizing that a romantic plot will make the two girls coincide in Hyacinthe (I, 3). However, it is only on reseeing or rereading the play that this dramatic irony becomes apparent.

These exceptions should not conceal the typical pattern, which is for a situation to develop a double irony, that of the central paradox and its own.

An ironic situation may occur only once, as when Mascarille is obliged to refuse a tip because he does not wish Anselme to realize that his purse, whose contents are indispensable to Mascarille's schemes, has dropped to the ground or when he has Pandolfe persuade Anselme to purchase the slave girl who will thwart Anselme's plans

to have Lélie marry his own daughter (*L'Etourdi,* I, 5, 7). Similarly in *L'Avare* the audience knows that Elise and Valère are secret lovers, whence the irony of the brother's telling her that she cannot know what it is to be in love (I, 2) or of Harpagon's giving absolute power over his daughter to Valère (I, 5), which is a variant of Orgon's having placed his wife under the protection of her would-be seducer Tartuffe (III, 7). Clitandre is able to tell Lucinde under her father's nose that he has disguised himself as a doctor in order to pay her court, since the father is convinced that she is mad and that Clitandre is a real doctor come to cure her (*L'Amour médecin,* III, 6). In III, 4 of *Le Misanthrope* the two consummate hypocrites, Célimène and Arsinoé, suddenly reveal a blunt frankness to each other that could hardly be surpassed by the protagonist, Alceste. George Dandin by his complaint and his parents-in-law by their bungling bring the future guilty lovers together for the first time; go-betweens without knowing it, they thus further the affair (I, 6). And when the wily pair outwit George Dandin in the same scene, placing him in the wrong, he cries out: "J'enrage de bon cœur d'avoir tort lorsque j'ai raison." At the close of Act II of *Le Bourgeois Gentilhomme,* as the ballet begins, M. Jourdain accomplishes the symbolic gesture of buying title after title as the tailor's apprentice throws them to him in ascending order of importance (II, 5).

More important structurally is the recurrent situation, which not only binds the play together but gives the audience a feeling of identity in difference by bringing back several times in new garb the same fundamental situation. Four times Don Garcie appears before Done Elvire and swears that he trusts her; then he allows his suspicions to become inflamed by appearances and forces her to prove her innocence; four times he is finally confounded and expresses his repentance (I, 3; II, 5-6; IV, 8-9; V, 3 and 6). Three times in the second act Sganarelle takes an ambiguous message from Isabelle to Valère and brings back an answer; the last time he brings back Valère as well; in the third and last act the structure shifts slightly and Isabelle becomes her own messenger (*L'Ecole des Maris*). Four times Arnolphe encounters Horace and learns that his well-laid plans for Agnès have been flouted; the more he tries to hinder the lovers, the more he furthers their affair (I, 4; III, 4; IV, 6; V, 2).

> *Horace*:   Euh! n'admirez-vous point cette adresse d'esprit?
>   Trouvez-vous pas plaisant de voir quel personnage
>   A joué mon jaloux dans tout ce badinage?
>   Dites.
> *Arnolphe*:   Oui, fort plaisant.
> *Horace*:   Riez-en donc un peu.

Sganarelle consults his friend Geronimo, the two philosophers Pancrace and Marphurius, and finally two gypsy girls to learn whether his contemplated marriage will make him a cuckold. It is obvious from the very start that the marriage will lead to horns, but at the end of each interview he is furious because he has not received an un-equivocal answer. Three times George Dandin complains to his parents-in-law of his wife's conduct, and three times he is outwitted; the first two times they show up by themselves, the third time he sends a messenger to rout them out of bed. In *Les Amants Magnifiques* the function of arbiter passes from the mother, Aristione, to Eriphile, who is also the prize, and finally to Sostrate who is also the lover.

In several of Molière's plays the technique of the recurrent situation embodies the theme of the *contretemps,* or sudden interruption that snatches victory away. Ten times Mascarille builds up a scheme in *L'Etourdi* and ten times L'élie knocks it down by his blundering: "Et trois: / Quand nous serons à dix, nous ferons une croix. / C'était par mon adresse, ô cervelle incurable!" Mascarille announces at the end of the first act (9, 440-443). Eraste plans to see his sweetheart in a public garden; each time that they are about to meet, an incident occurs to prevent it, usually an importunate acquaintance's arrival but also the blunders of Eraste's valet and two misunderstandings of the lovers (*Les Fâcheux*). H. Gaston Hall has pointed out [in his essay "A Comic Don Juan"] that the amorphous *Dom Juan's* fourth act is constructed in the same manner: each time that Don Juan is about to sit down to supper, he is interrupted by a visitor. And Molière's masterpiece, *Le Misanthrope,* is akin to *Les Fâcheux:* Alceste comes to Célimène's house determined to have out with her the reason why she encourages so many men to pay her suit. Célimène is not at home. While awaiting her return, Alceste has to put up with Oronte's flattery and insolence. At the beginning of the second act a first interview with Célimène is fruitless because it is interrupted by a couple of suitors. Alceste not only is obliged to listen to their vapid conversation but cannot outstay them, since at the end of the act he is haled before the Tribunal des Maréchaux to settle his dispute with Oronte. All of Act III is designed to fill the time elapsed during his absence. Coming back at the end of the act, he ironically creates an obstacle for himself by rushing off with Arsinoé to obtain proof of Célimène's infidelity. Before he can return it is the middle of Act IV and time for the climactic showdown between the lovers; but the scene is interrupted by the arrival of Alceste's valet bringing the news that Alceste must flee. Thus obstacles keep arising to the very end of the play. When in the last scene Alceste is finally able to reach an understanding with Célimène, the other suitors have taken themselves off and his efforts have become pointless.

In order to knit his plays even more closely together Molière frequently combines the recurrent situation with two other devices, ironic links between scenes and ironic buildup and reversal. The ironic link may be the frequent repetition from scene to scene of key words that reinforce the ironic paradox: *étourdi* and *contretemps* in *L'Etourdi, fâcheux* in *Les Fâcheux* (usually pronounced by one *fâcheux* concerning another *fâcheux*), *honneur* and *vengeance* in *George Dandin;* or the link may be synonymous repetitions of an idea, like the constant warnings of divine wrath, invariably scoffed at by the hero, in *Dom*

Juan. III, 2 of *Les Femmes Savantes* develops the ironic results, when women deny their natural functions, of the extravagant metaphors of a baby and a repast that are applied to Trissotin's poem in III, 1.

The ironic link may also be built into the plot, as in *Le Bourgeois Gentilhomme* where a number of later episodes express the ironic implications of M. Jourdain's various lessons and clothes-fitting in the first two acts: his costume's effect on his servant Nicole (III, 2), the duel in which he is worsted by Nicole (III, 3), or the elaborate bow with which he greets Dorimène in III, 16. In III, 15 Dorante in his private conversation with Dorimène has taken all the credit for M. Jourdain's banquet; when Mme Jourdain surprises the diners in IV, 2, Dorante staves off her attack by stating that he is paying for everything and M. Jourdain, thinking it merely a stratagem, hastens to agree. In I, 4 Mme de Sotenville rebukes George Dandin for addressing her as "ma belle-mère"; in II, 7 he carefully calls her "Madame". This is a refinement of *La Jalousie du Barbouillé,* where in the second scene the pedant objects to being called "vous", with the result that in scene 6 Barbouillé takes care to say "Mon-

Engraved handbill produced for early performances of
Le misanthrope.

sieur le Docteur". If in *L'Avare* Harpagon comes to greet Mariane wearing his glasses and pointedly refers to them in III, 5, it is because Frosine has told him that the girl prefers older men who have to wear glasses (II, 5). Philaminte's assertion in III, 2 that she is a great admirer of ethics is an ironic link with IV, 4 when over Henriette's protests and out of spite at Vadius's message she decides that her daughter shall marry Trissotin that very evening (*Les Femmes Savantes*). The rapid pacing of the action in *Les Fourberies de Scapin* is accompanied by just as rapid an ironic linkage: in II, 1 Argante tells Géronte of his son's misconduct; in II, 2 Géronte upbraids his son; in II, 3 the son beats Scapin for having informed on him; in II, 4 the son is obliged to get on his knees, beg Scapin's pardon, and plead with Scapin to help him out of his predicament; in II, 5-6 Scapin takes his revenge on Argante by cheating him and on Géronte by getting money out of him "for the Turk" in II, 7 and beating him in III, 2. With the same rapidity but on a more verbal plane befitting a contemporary drawing room, Uranie states in scene 1 of *La Critique de l'Ecole des Femmes* that her door is open to all callers, rebukes her lackey in scene 2 for letting in the *précieuse* Climène, and in scene 4, the lackey having taken her at her word and attempted to shut out the foppish marquis, she has to scold him for barring her door in order to assuage the marquis's ruffled feelings.

Not only are scenes and acts thus ironically joined but also outcomes are foreshadowed in a parody of tragic irony. In I, 2 Lélie remarks dreamily about his slave girl: "Pour moi, dans ses discours comme dans son visage / Je vois pour sa naissance un noble témoignage / Et je crois que le ciel dedans un rang si bas / Cache son origine et ne l'en tire pas." Mascarille retorts: "Vous êtes romanesque avecque vos chimères" (***L'Etourdi***, I, 2, 27-31). The irony is that Lélie's musing will be right and Mascarille's common sense wrong. In IV, 1 the ironic joke is intensified when Mascarille expresses disbelief through verbal irony in his own cock-and-bull story:

> Si j'ai plutôt qu'aucun un tel moyen trouvé
> Pour les ressusciter sur ce qu'i a rêvé,
> C'est qu'en fait d'aventure il est *très ordinaire*
> De voir gens pris sur mer par quelque Turc corsaire,
> / Puis être à leur famille *à point nommé* rendus
> Après quinze ou vingt ans qu'on les a crus perdus.
> Pour moi, j'ai déjà vu *cent contes* de la sorte.
> Sans nous alambiquer, servons-nous-en; qu'importe?
>   (1332-40)

Here the irony is that the cock-and-bull story will come true at the end of the play. Feeling absolutely certain of his dupe, Tartuffe adjures Orgon to believe Damis's accusation: "Et comme un criminel chassez-moi de chez vous", accurately but unknowingly forecasting his own fate (III, 6, 1084). M. Loyal also adds to the dramatic irony by insisting to Orgon in V, 4: "Le ciel perde qui veut vous nuire / Et vous soit favorable autant que je désire" (1733-34).

Ironic buildup and reversal are even more effective than

the ironic link; after the first reinforces the comic character's hubris, the second lets him down with a jolt. Although the two are usually associated in comedy, there are numerous examples in Molière of sudden ironic reversal without buildup that have as point of reference an overweening character that has already been depicted in words and gestures. Functionally this type of ironic reversal is usually a sudden, wry twist of the situation against the schemer and resultant respite for the dupe; it also serves as a means of heightening tension within the scene. Thus triumphant Sganarelle in *Le Médecin Volant* undergoes three reversals, each increasing his danger of exposure: (1) the meeting with the lawyer (sc. 8), (2) the coming upon Gorgibus when not disguised (sc. 10), (3) the unmasking by Gros-René (sc. 15). Mascarille has just succeeded in unfastening Anselme's purse and dropping it to the ground when suddenly Anselme reaches for it in order to give him a tip (*L'Etourdi*, I, 5). When pert Marinette leaves Eraste and Gros-René in I, 2, all is sweetness and light; when she rejoins them in I, 5, they both turn on her and upbraid her without in their anger troubling to tell her why (*Le Dépit amoureux*). Isabelle succeeds so well in her wiles that Sganarelle, delighted with her seeming modesty and professed love for him, tells her that instead of making her wait a week he will marry her tomorrow; as in the previous reversal of *Le Dépit amoureux* Molière places this scene last in the act (*L'Ecole des Maris*, II, 10). In a scene of the accuser accused, headstrong Damis, who has failed to convince Orgon of Tartuffe's guilt, is forced to his knees and made to beg Tartuffe's pardon: "Allons, qu'on se rétracte et qu'à l'instant, fripon, / On se jette à ses pieds pour demander pardon" (III, 6, 1131-32). In *Amphitryon* Jupiter uses all his skill to persuade Alcmène to place the blame for the quarrel on the husband and disculpate the lover; by her adamant refusal she inflicts a serious setback on the master of the gods (II, 6). Toinette receives her just deserts from her master when he abruptly decides to listen to the music lesson, thus unintentionally thwarting her plans for the lovers to steal away together (*Le Malade Imaginaire*, II, 2). And in the same play clever Angélique is suddenly worsted in a spirited argument with toadish Thomas Diafoirus; that she is definitely worsted Molière underlines by having Toinette intervene immediately with verbal irony and Béline change the situation by baiting Angélique (who has been baiting Thomas—II, 6).

Much more frequent and effective is the combination of ironic buildup and reversal, which allows the dramatist to give internal coherence to larger areas, sometimes within a scene, more often on the scale of several scenes or an entire play. In scene 13 of *Le Médecin Volant* Valère is just exclaiming delightedly that he had not thought it possible for Sganarelle to do so well when Sganarelle rushes in and confesses that he has bungled the job. In the last scene of *Le Tartuffe* the protagonist gloats over Orgon's predicament and waxes more and more vindictive until suddenly the king's officer takes *him* into custody. Lisette rushes in shrieking to inform Sganarelle that a misfortune has befallen his daughter; tension increases as he learns that in despair over the way he has treated her she has gone up to her room, opened the window overlooking the river, and declared that rather than live with her father's anger she prefers to die:

> *Sganarelle*:   Elle s'est jetée.
> *Lisette*:   Non, Monsieur: elle a fermé tout
>   doucement la fenêtre et s'est
>   allée mettre sur son lit.
>   (*L'Amour médecin*, I, 6)

In the prologue to *Amphitryon* Night protests against the service that Jupiter requires of her, declaring sarcastically that the name applied to one who renders such a service is indeed an honorable one. Mercure scoffingly lords it over her: "Pour une jeune déesse, / Vous êtes bien du bon temps! / Un tel emploi n'est bassesse / Que chez les petites gens. / Lorsque dans un haut rang on a l'heur de paraître, / Tout ce qu'on fait est toujours bel et bon, / Et suivant ce qu'on peut être, / Les choses changent de nom." / But Night's reply puts him in his place: / Sur de pareilles matières / Vous en savez plus que moi, / Et pour accepter l'emploi / J'en veux croire vos lumières." (124-135). Throughout II, 5 of *L'Avare* Frosine flatters Harpagon outrageously, stressing his youthful appearance and how delighted Mariane will be to marry him; at the end of the scene when she asks for money, Harpagon dashes off without giving her a cent. In II, 3 of *Le Bourgeois Gentilhomme* the philosophy teacher in the name of wisdom rebukes the other teachers for losing their temper and preaches moderation and patience; he ends up quarreling more violently than they. Géronte takes pleasure in disclosing to Argante his son's turpitudes and blames them on his faulty upbringing; Argante then proceeds, according to the motif of the biter bit, to narrate to Géronte the even less edifying deeds of *his* son (*Les Fourberies de Scapin*, II, 1). La Flèche's "quelques petites conditions" at the beginning of II, 1 in *L'Avare* turn out to be the long series of almost intolerable stipulations of the as yet unknown Shylock. In *Les Femmes Savantes* Philaminte grows increasingly indignant over her servant's heinous crime; it transpires that she has made a mistake in grammar (II, 6). In III, 3 of the same play when Vadius and Trissotin meet, the hyperbolic compliments grow more and more exaggerated until the question arises of whose work will be praised first; then the flattery changes to name calling. At the beginning of III, 3 of *Le Malade Imaginaire* Argan promises Béralde, rather impatiently it is true, that he will have no trouble keeping his temper; as the scene progresses he grows angrier and angrier.

Contiguous scenes are often joined by the same technique. The just quoted scene of *L'Avare* is itself an ironic buildup for the next scene, when the usurer is revealed as Cléante's own father (II, 1-2). Once the misunderstandings have been cleared up at the end of *Sganarelle ou le Cocu imaginaire,* Lélie airily says that now they can be married, since Celie's father has already given his agreement; in the next scene the father refuses to keep his word (sc. 27-28). The first scene of *Amphitryon* in which Sosie grows jauntier and jauntier as he rehearses his triumphant entry into the town is a skillful buildup for the following one in which he is soundly drubbed and even refused his identity by Mercure. II, 3 in which Sbrigani

misinforms Oronte of M. de Pourceaugnac's intentions and II, 4 in which he misinforms M. de Pourceaugnac of Oronte's intentions explode in the brilliant quarrel of II, 5. Orgon's conviction that he alone is right and his extreme vindictiveness towards his family expressed in IV, 3 lead directly to the following scenes in which he is forced to admit that Tartuffe is an impostor. At the end of III, 3 Mme Jourdain tells her husband that Dorante will never repay the money that he has borrowed, and M. Jourdain insists that he will. The buildup continues in the following scene when Dorante asks how much he owes, so that he can settle up. M. Jourdain mentions the various amounts that he has lent him, triumphs over his wife, only to hear Dorante finally say: "Mettez encore deux cents pistoles que vous m'allez donner, cela fera justement dix-huit mille francs que je vous payerai au premier jour." In *Les Femmes Savantes,* II, 4-5 in which Chrysale suddenly asserts his domination over the household by approving of Henriette's marriage to Clitandre and taking the servant under his protection prepare II, 6-8 in which he collapses like a deflated dummy when faced with his wife's determination. IV, 1 of the same play in which Armande turns her mother against Clitandre in order to spoil her sister's marriage leads to her discomfiture in the next scene when she throws herself at Clitandre's head and is rebuffed. When in IV, 1 Don Juan cries, "Allons, qu'on me fasse souper le plus tôt que l'on pourra", he prepares by his impatience the following series of *contretemps* that will prevent him from dining at all. Alceste declares in I, 1 of *Le Misanthrope* that he likes friends who can discern his intrinsic worth. Oronte arrives in the next scene and satisfies that requirement: but Alceste is the opposite of happy, since Oronte is his rival and requests approval of a sonnet that he has prepared for Célimène.

More striking is the reversal separated from the buildup by intervening scenes or acts. In II, 4 of *Le Tartuffe* Dorine promises Mariane's sweetheart: "Nous allons réveiller les efforts de son frère" in order to avert a marriage with Tartuffe. Then in III, 1 the brother himself tempestuously promises: "Que la foudre sur l'heure achève mes destins, / Qu'on me traite partout du plus grand des faquins / S'il est aucun respect ni pouvoir qui m'arrête / Et si je ne fais pas quelque coup de ma tête!" The author's ironic pun on "coup de ma tête" (i.e., [1] coup de mon invention, [2] coup de tête) in the last line makes III, 4 appear inevitable, when Damis bursts in on Tartuffe and Elmire, declaring triumphantly that he now has proof that will convince his father of Tartuffe's duplicity; not only does he thus ruin Elmire's carefully laid plan but in the next scenes his father will refuse to be convinced and will disinherit him. The ironic buildup for Orgon's having to admit that Tartuffe is a blackguard (IV, 6) begins as early as III, 7:

> *Tartuffe*:   On ne manquera pas de poursuivre
> sans doute,
>   Et ces mêmes rapports qu'ici vous
>   rejetez
>   Peut-être une autre fois seront-ils
> écoutés.

Orgon: Non, mon frère, jamais.

(1158-61)

Then, in the same scene Orgon insists on throwing Elmire and Tartuffe together: "Et je veux qu'à toute heure avec elle on vous voie" (1174).

In III, 2 Mercure under the guise of Sosie is extremely insolent with Amphitryon; the next time that the real Sosie meets his master, he receives a beating for his insolence (III, 4). II, 5 of *L'Avare* in which Frosine lies to Harpagon about Mariane's sentiments and III, 4 in which she lies to Mariane about Harpagon's life expectancy culminate in their meeting for the first time in III, 5 with embarrassing results for Frosine. The scene in which Chrysale finally stands up to his wife (V, 3) comes as a comic surprise to the audience; but at the same time the author has been at pains to prepare this ironic reversal at Philaminte's expense since the second act: II, 9; III, 6; IV, 5; and V, 2 all contain episodes that are intended to warn us that the worm will finally turn. To this structure of *Les Femmes Savantes* may be compared that of *Le Bourgeois Gentilhomme* in which both Acts I and II are an ironic buildup for the deflation of M. Jourdain by his wife and servant in Act III. Also, III, 16 in which M. Jourdain makes Dorimène back up, so that he will have room for his third bow, is the ironic reversal of II, 1, where the dancing master has impressed upon him the necessity of making three bows to flatter a lady of quality. And so fundamental is this particular structure to *Le Tartuffe* that it could be argued that the play is constructed on two major ironic buildups, followed by their reversals: (1) Orgon's infatuation with Tartuffe which culminates in the deeding of his property to the rascal and (2) Tartuffe's overweening arrogance once his rascality is exposed to Orgon. If this hypothesis is correct, then the pivotal scene of the play is IV, 7, containing in one speech by Tartuffe (1557-64) both the reversal for Orgon's situation which has been building up since the opening scene ("C'est à vous d'en sortir, vous qui parlez en maître: / La maison m'appartient, je le ferai connaître") and the beginning of the buildup that will culminate in Tartuffe's downfall at the end of the play: "Et [je] vous montrerai bien qu'en vain on a recours / Pour me chercher querelle à ces lâches détours, / Qu'on n'est pas là où l'on pense en me faisant injure, / Que j'ai de quoi confondre et punir l'imposture, / Venger le ciel qu'on blesse et faire repentir / Ceux qui parlent ici de me faire sortir." The heights of technical virtuosity are reached in those plays where recurrent situations furnish a framework upon which Molière may drape his buildups and reversals. The rudimentary form is contained in *Le Tartuffe,* where a situation recurs only once, but with an ironic reversal of roles. In IV, 3 Orgon refuses to believe his family and prefers to place his trust in appearances (1317); when in V, 3 he tries in turn to convince his mother of Tartuffe's villainy, she refuses to believe *him:* "Mon Dieu, le plus souvent l'apparence déçoit" (1679). And Dorine drives the point home with: "Juste retour, Monsieur, des choses d'ici-bas: / Vous ne vouliez point croire, et l'on ne vous croit pas" (1695-96).

The eleventh scene of *La Jalousie du Barbouillé* gives Molière the idea for the structure of *George Dandin,* each of whose three acts constitutes an ironic buildup, with the protagonist increasingly sure of his triumph until the ironic reversal at the end of the act. The ten *contretemps* of *L'Etourdi* are preceded by ironic buildups of which they are the reversals; each time that Lélie or Mascarille exults the audience knows that a new reversal is in the offing. Scenes 6 through 12 of *Les Précieuses Ridicules* show the girls compromising themselves increasingly with the pseudo-aristocrats and prepare the spectator for the sudden unmasking in scene 13. Each of the recurrent situations in *Dom Garcie de Navarre* is constructed on the same principle, with the protagonist more and more convinced each time that his suspicions are finally grounded in fact - and each time they redound to his discredit. The entire last act of *L'Ecole des Maris* is devoted to Sganarelle's preparation of the trap that is to catch his brother's ward and cover the brother with confusion; he carries out his task with increasing glee and attentiveness up to the moment when the prisoner in the trap turns out to be his own ward.

In *L'Ecole des Femmes* an identical structure is present throughout: after the first three scenes have revealed Arnolphe's mockery of others' conjugal misfortunes, delight in his foolproof system, and immense self-satisfaction, I, 4 shows him rejoicing over Horace's conquests at the expense of his neighbors until he discovers that the young man's present conquest lives in his own house; in III, 4 he ironically expresses his sympathy for Horace, whose plans seem to have fared badly, until he learns that he himself has been outwitted by Agnès; in IV, 5 he voices his satisfaction with his arrangements only to find in the next scene that he has lost once again; in V, 1 he thinks that he has succeeded too well, since his servants appear to have killed Horace, but in the following scene he realizes that Horace not only is alive but has spirited Agnès out of the house; in V, 6 he agrees ironically to support Horace's refusal to marry the girl of his father's choice, does just the opposite, backs up Horace's father, triumphs in having separated Horace and Agnès, and then is apprised that the father's choice is Agnès. Thus the whole play reposes on a series of ironic buildups and reversals culminating in the protagonist's final discomfiture.

La Princesse d'Elide has a different structure that might explain why it is not among Molière's better plays. The ironic buildup covers the first three acts and part of the fourth: in II, 1 the princess declares that she will never fall in love; in II, 4 she expresses her conviction that in trying to ensnare Euryale, whose indifference has piqued her, she runs no danger of falling in love herself; in III, 1 her servant assures her that upon seeing her sing and dance Euryale is certain to succumb to her charms. Not until III, 4 do the reversals start when Euryale first rebuffs her advances; then, when the princess pretends to love another in order to lead him on, he declares that he is in love with the princess's cousin (IV, 1); and her cup brims over when she is obliged to give herself away in trying to prevent a match between Euryale and the cousin (V, 2). To judge by this example, it would seem that the device must present a regular alternance of buildups and reversals in order to structure properly a play of any length.

In Molière's theater *quid pro quo,* or deliberately prolonged misunderstanding, is not only a powerful auxiliary of ironic buildup and reversal but also an important structural element in its own right. The ironic implications of situations in which one or several characters are in the dark, but not the audience, have already been made obvious. In Trufaldin's presence Mascarille tells Célie that his master has fallen in love with a young beauty; since he is ostensibly consulting Célie as a fortune teller, Trufaldin thinks that the beauty is someone else, whereas Mascarille and Célie understand each other perfectly (*L'Etourdi,* I, 4). Anselme, whom Mascarille has convinced of Pandolfe's demise, persists in addressing him as a ghost (*L'Etourdi,* II, 4). When the two old men, Albert and Polydore, meet, each with a guilty conscience and fearing the other's wrath for a different reason, they are overwhelmed by each other's forbearance, fall to their knees, and remain there until the situation's ambiguity is gradually cleared up (*Le Dépit amoureux,* III, 4). Agnès and Arnolphe are both delighted that Agnès wishes to be married; each grows more and more enchanted with the idea until it transpires that Agnès expects Arnolphe to give her to Horace (*L'Ecole des Femmes,* II, 5). The same situation reappears in *L'Avare,* I, 4 where Harpagon raises his son's hopes concerning Mariane only to tell him that he is planning to marry her himself, and again in *Le Malade Imaginaire,* I, 5 when Argan announces to his daughter after some ambiguity that she is about to be married not to the young man of her choice, but to a doctor's son. In his two interviews with Elmire Tartuffe thinks each time that she has summoned him to give in to him (her language is ambiguous), whereas the first time it is to ask him to support Mariane's marriage to Valère and the second to betray him to her husband (III, 3 and IV, 5). In one of the most ingenious situations in Molière's theater Don Juan manages to make each of two peasant girls believe that she is his chosen one and the other an impostor:

> Que voulez-vous que je dise? Vous soutenez également toutes deux que je vous ai promis de vous prendre pour femmes. Est-ce que chacune de vous ne sait pas *ce qui en est sans qu'il soit nécessaire que je m'explique davantage?* Pourquoi m'obliger là-dessus à des redites? Celle à qui j'ai promis effectivement *n'a-t-elle pas en elle-même de quoi* se moquer des discours de l'autre et doit-elle se mettre en peine, pourvu que j'accomplisse ma promesse? Tous les discours n'avancent point les choses; *il faut faire et non pas dire, et les effets décident mieux que les paroles.* Aussi n'est-ce rien que par là que je vous veux mettre d'accord, et *l'on verra, quand je me marierai, laquelle des deux a mon cœur. (Bas, à Mathurine)* Laissez-lui croire ce qu'elle voudra. *(Bas, à Charlotte)* Laissez-la *se flatter dans son imagination. (Bas, à Mathurine)* Je vous adore. *(Bas, à Charlotte)* Je suis tout à vous. *(Bas, à Mathurine)* Tous les visages sont laids auprès du vôtre. *(Bas, à Charlotte)* On ne peut plus souffrir les autres quand on vous a vue (II, 4).

Relying on traditional material, Molière introduces into *Le Sicilien* a lover disguised as an artist, into *Le Bourgeois Gentilhomme* a lover disguised as the Grand Turk's son, and into *Le Malade Imaginaire* a lover disguised as a music master, then a maid disguised as a doctor; on each occasion, thanks to the resultant ambiguities, much fun is had at the expense of a guardian or father. Maître Jacques having falsely accused Valère of the theft of Harpagon's cash box, Valère is haled before the miser; since his conscience is troubling him over his relations with Harpagon's daughter, he admits to one kind of theft and Harpagon takes it for admission of another kind until the ambiguity is resolved:

> *Harpagon*:   Hé! dis-moi donc un peu: tu n'y as point touché?
> *Valère*:   Moi, y toucher? Ah! vous lui faites tort aussi bien qu'à moi,   et c'est d'une ardeur toute pure et respectueuse que j'ai brûlé pour elle.
> *Harpagon*:   Brûlé pour ma cassette!
> *Valère*:   J'aimerais mieux mourir que de lui avoir fait paraître aucune   pensée offensante: elle est trop sage et trop honnête pour cela.
> *Harpagon*:   Ma cassette trop honnête!
> *Valère*:   Tous mes désirs se sont bornés à jouir de sa vue, et rien de   criminel n'a profané la passion que ses beaux yeux m'ont inspirée.
> *Harpagon*:   Les beaux yeux de ma cassette! Il parle d'elle comme un amant   d ' u n e maîtresse (V, 3).

Harpagon's last remark is meant to be self-applied, and the misunderstanding is extremely important in that Molière thus establishes an identification with the Bible's "treasure in the heart" (Matt. 6: 21) that will reinforce the play's ironic outcome.

When M. de Pourceaugnac meets Oronte and quarrels with him in II, 5, thanks to Sbrigani's machinations he thinks that Oronte wishes to unload on him a daughter who plays fast and loose, whereas Oronte thinks that Pourceaugnac is a fortune hunter who wants to use her dowry to pay off his creditors. Believing that it is Dorante who has given her a diamond and banquet with music, Dorimène finds M. Jourdain uncivil when he belittles them (*Le Bourgeois Gentilhomme,* IV, 1). Zerbinette, not knowing who Géronte is, describes to him at great length how he has been duped by Scapin (*Les Fourberies de Scapin,* III, 3). Early in *Les Femmes Savantes* Clitandre comes to ask Bélise's help in his attempt to marry Henriette. The lady is convinced that all men are in love with her; she takes his request as a concealed proposal and refuses to be convinced of the contrary (I, 4); in the following act she continues in the same vein when her brothers also come to enlist her aid (II, 3). In the same play Vadius, asked by Trissotin what he thinks of a new sonnet that is going the rounds of polite society, replies that it is bad; he has not realized, contrary to the audience, that Trissotin is its author (III, 3).

Four of Molière's plays utilize the device of the prolonged misunderstanding for their fundamental structure. The plot of *Le Dépit amoureux* requires that characters be kept in varying degrees of ignorance all the way to the outcome; the trouble is that the audience, prepared for ironic comedy, is at times also kept in the dark and given romantic comedy instead. *Sganarelle ou le Cocu imaginaire* is constructed entirely on a series of ironic misunderstandings: Sganarelle thinks that his wife is Lélie's mistress, and his wife, that he is Célie's lover; Célie thinks the same as Sganarelle, and Lélie, that Célie has married Sganarelle. To cap the resultant series of misunderstandings Molière places the two characters who think the same in a situation where they talk at cross-purposes: Célie, misled by Sganarelle, heaps coals of wrath on Lélie's absent head; Sganarelle, not realizing that he has before him a woman spurned, coyly misinterprets her words as an expression of solicitude for his own affliction (sc. 16). Unaware of Arnolphe's odd preference for the name of M. de la Souche, or 'blockhead' (Arnolphe being cuckolds' patron saint), Horace, from one end to the other of *L'Ecole des Femmes,* takes Arnolphe for his confidant and keeps him apprised of the progress of his love affair with Agnès. *Amphitryon* contains the most inextricable series of misunderstandings of any of the plays, with Alcmène taking Jupiter for Amphitryon, Cléanthis taking Mercure for Sosie, Amphitryon taking Mercure for Sosie, and Sosie in an ironic variant taking Mercure as his *alter ego.*

Critics have long recognized the presence in Molière's theater of delightful scenes embodying a lovers' quarrel, or *dépit amoureux.* Based on a misunderstanding and consisting of a tempest in a teapot, the situation is rich in ironic possibilities. It has been traced back as far as Horace's ode, *Donec gratus eram* (III, 9), and was used in Italian and French comedy before Molière. Molière himself has stressed its importance as an ironic theme in his theater with a chorus of *Les Amants Magnifiques*: "Amants, que vos querelles / Sont aimables et belles! / Qu'on y voit succéder / De plaisirs, de tendresse! / Querellez-vous sans cesse / Pour vous raccommoder. / Amants, que vos querelles / Sont aimables et belles." (third intermezzo, sc. 5).

Critics have however done Molière a disservice in limiting *dépit amoureux* to the play of that name, *Le Tartuffe,* and *Le Bourgeois Gentilhomme* and viewing its presence in the two latter plays as padding utilized to fill out acts in which plot material was deficient. Such an argument cannot hold water when applied, for example, to *Le Bourgeois Gentilhomme,* where Act III would be unusually long even without the three scenes devoted to the theme. On the contrary, *dépit amoureux* is a structural element in a round dozen of Molière's plays and constitutes a fundamental theme on which he rings all the changes. Instead of being a stock situation thrown into a play to round out the action, it is usually so carefully woven in that it is preceded by ironic buildup and sometimes given an ironic aftermath.

In order to appreciate the full sweep of *dépit amoureux* and its many variants our point of departure should be the famous third and fourth scenes of Act IV in the play that gives the situation its name and general pattern. Those scenes are prepared from the beginning. In I, 1 Eraste admits that he is of jealous temperament and finds his rival Valère too sure of his place in Lucile's affections; Gros-René on the other hand is content to leave matters be and even close his eyes to certain of Marinette's actions as long as she tells him that she loves him. In I, 2 Marinette reassures Eraste and brings him a note from Lucile authorizing him to ask her father for her hand; Marinette approves of Gros-René's easygoing attitude and warns Eraste that lack of trust could advance a rival's cause and bring Lucile to rescind the note. Despite the warning Eraste is in high spirits as Valère approaches and Gros-René remarks: "Je plains le pauvre hère, / Sachant ce qui se passe" (193-194). But to Eraste's astonishment Valère remains confident even when shown the note (I, 3). In order to ascertain the truth Eraste pretends to Valère's valet Mascarille that he has withdrawn his suit; Mascarille then lets the cat out of the bag: Lucile and Valère are secretly married and meet every night (I, 4). When Marinette comes back quite unsuspecting to tell Eraste that Lucile will see him that evening in the garden, he turns on her in a rage and sends back Lucile's note with a message that all is over between them; the invective that Gros-René flings at Marinette is a parody of his master's towering passion and a foretaste of the approaching showdown (I, 5). Before it, however, the audience is let in on the secret while the actors are still kept in the dark: Lucile's sister Ascagne, whom everybody believes to be a boy, has tricked Valère into marrying her under the impression that she is Lucile (II, 1). In II, 4 Lucile and Marinette express their indignation over their lovers' conduct and work themselves into the proper mood for a first-rate quarrel. Lucile declares that nothing can make her forgive Eraste and forbids Marinette ever to intercede for him, declaring her 'firmness' of intention in such a way as to impress on the audience the ambivalence of her sentiments: "Et *même* si mon cœur était pour lui tenté / De descendre *jamais* à quelque lâcheté, / Que ton affection me soit *alors* sévère / Et tienne comme il faut la main à ma colère" (641-644). In a burlesque of her mistress's language and sentiments Marinette tells her not to worry, since she is just as angry with Gros-René and would rather be an old maid than marry him.

Owing to a complicated plot, the counterpart of this scene between the girls in which the two men prepare for combat does not take place until IV, 2 immediately before the quarrel, which it ushers in. Eraste has several times sent Gros-René to beg in vain for an appointment with Lucile. Eraste is furious: her rejection of his offer to beg her pardon, to believe in her when appearances are against her, and her refusing to make allowances for his justifiable suspicions have convinced him that she cannot be worthy of so great a love as his; he would do well to look elsewhere. Gros-René goes him one better by swearing off women altogether. Then the moment of battle is upon them; as the girls approach, Gros-René cautions Eraste not to weaken and Eraste reassures him, a warning that is echoed on the other side of the stage by Marinette to Lucile just before the struggle is joined.

Eraste starts out by disabusing Lucile of thinking that he wishes to discuss his love for her, since on the contrary he wishes to get over it and realizes by her anger over so trifling a matter that he never has had much hold over her affections; besides, he owes it to himself to react to her scorn. Of course, he must admit that he can never hope to find so great a love again and that his heart will take a long time to mend; there is no question of his ever loving another woman. But all that, he continues, obviously does not matter to her, and this is the last time that he will annoy her by placing his love at her feet. Lucile curtly replies that that will suit her perfectly. Stung to retort, Eraste answers that he will carry out her wishes to the letter and swears on his life that he never will speak to her again.

> *Lucile*: Fine, that's just what I have requested.

Eraste, perhaps insisting too much, repeats that he will not break his word; even if he should be so weak as to fail to erase her from his heart, she need not think that he would give her an undue advantage by coming back to her.

> *Lucile*: There would be no point in doing so.

Eraste would rather die a thousand deaths after the vile way she has treated him.

> *Lucile*: All right. Let's drop the subject.

Agreed, replies Eraste. And in order to prove how irrevocable his decision is he returns her portrait. Not to be outdone, she returns a diamond that he has given her. Other gifts follow, then letters which with bitter comments they tear up before each other's eyes.

> *Gros-René to Eraste*: Keep up the good work.
> *Marinette to Lucile*: Hold firm.

Then both call on Heaven to strike them down if they fail to keep their word.

All that is left is to say goodby; yet in spite of their servants' exhortations they are strangely reluctant to withdraw. Eraste points out that she will never find another love like his, and Lucile finally gets to the cause of the quarrel, his lack of trust. The quarrel flares up again; but Lucile goes so far in defending her point of view as to admit in an unguarded moment that she is angry because she still loves him, then tries to cover up her slip by remarking, what can that matter if they are breaking up?

> *Eraste*: Are we breaking up?
> *Lucile*: Of course; isn't it over and done with?
> *Eraste*: And you are satisfied with such an arrangement?
> *Lucile*: Oh, I feel as you do about it.
> *Eraste*: As I do?
> *Lucile*: Of course. It's a sign of weakness for a girl to let a man see that she is affected by losing him.
> *Eraste*: How cruel you are! You are the one who

insisted on breaking up.
> *Lucile*: I? Of course not; it was *you*.
> *Eraste*: I? But I thought that that was what you wanted.
> *Lucile*: Not at all. You were interested only in doing as you pleased.
> *Eraste*: However that may be, suppose, just suppose that my heart longed to be forgiven . . .

Lucile can hold out no longer and confessing to her weakness, she allows him to see her home (IV, 3). How deliberately pointless these quarrels are is borne out by the fact that Lucile and Eraste have made up without settling their difference over Lucile's rumored marriage to Valère.

The two servants remain alone on the stage, thoroughly disgusted by their master's and mistress's lack of firmness. They then go through the quarrel's motions themselves, returning presents and making a series of coarse remarks that are a parody of their betters' highflown language. At the climax of their quarrel they are standing back to back in the middle of the stage; suddenly peering around, they get the giggles and make up without ceremony (IV, 4).

Between *Le Dépit amoureux* and *Le Tartuffe* lie five plays in which the theme is either touched upon or fully exploited. In *Sganarelle ou le Cocu imaginaire* it is as carefully woven into the structure as in the previous play and is given a new dimension by being placed in counterpoint to two scenes of quarrels between an older married couple whose ardor has long since cooled, but who are fiercely jealous all the same. Inextricably linked, the lovers' quarrel and the married couple's quarrel build up together.

Célie's tyrannical father has broken her engagement to Lélie, who is absent on a journey. While showing his portrait to her maid, Célie is overcome with emotion. Sganarelle happens along and supports her while the maid goes for help; his wife sees him from their house and is immediately convinced that he is deceiving her (sc. 2-5). Sganarelle comes back after carrying Célie home and finds his wife sniffing Lélie's perfumed portrait, which Célie has let drop; each accuses the other in a scene whose language comes from farce (sc. 6) and which anticipates by ironic contrast the young lovers' approaching quarrel.

Lélie comes rushing back from his journey, alarmed by a rumor that Célie's father has forced her into another marriage; he thinks the worst when Sganarelle designates the portrait, declaring that he has received it from his wife (sc. 7-10). Left alone, Lélie nearly faints with grief and Sganarelle's wife offers him shelter in her house; Sganarelle sees him coming back out and *he* thinks the worst when Lélie, believing him to be Célie's husband, says to him bitterly: "Oh! trop heureux d'avoir une si belle femme" (sc. 11-15). Célie then comes up to Sganarelle who, pointing to Lélie in the distance, tells her that there goes his wife's lover; she departs swearing vengeance (sc. 16).

In scene 20 the two lovers finally meet and upbraid each

other; Lélie sarcastically wishes Célie happiness with her new husband (meaning Sganarelle) and she replies that she intends to be very happy with him (meaning the man whom her father has chosen for her). Lélie asks her what right *she* has to be angry with him, whereupon she accuses him of being a hypocrite. The quarrel continues in the next scene, but now against the background of Sganarelle who, in a variant of the braggart soldier motif, arrives armed to the teeth and seeking a terrible vengeance on Lélie who has broken up his home and robbed him of his honor. While the lovers pursue their quarrel, he tries to steel himself to attack; but each time that Lélie looks his way he collapses in conformity with the literary type:

Lélie:	Ah! je vois . . .
Célie:	Cet objet suffit pour te confondre.
Lélie:	Mais pour vous obliger bien plutôt à rougir.
Sganarelle:	Ma colère à présent est en état d'agir;
	Dessus ses grands chevaux est monté mon courage,
	Et si je le rencontre, on verra du carnage.
	Oui, j'ai juré sa mort: rien ne peut l'empêcher;
	Où je le trouverai, je le veux dépêcher.
	Au beau milieu du cœur il faut que je lui donne . . .
Lélie:	A qui donc en veut-on?
Sganarelle:	Je n'en veux à personne.
Lélie:	Pourquoi ces armes-là?
Sganarelle:	C'est un habillement
	Que j'ai pris pour la pluie.
	(A part.)
	Ah! quel contentement
	J'aurais à le tuer! Prenons-en le courage.
Lélie:	Hay?
	Sganarelle, *se donnant des coups de poing sur l'estomac [i.e., poitrine] et des soufflets pour s'exciter.*
	Je ne parle pas.
	(A part.)
	Ah! poltron dont j'enrage!
	Lâche! vrai cœur de poule!

(510-523)

Célie points to Sganarelle as proof of Lélie's crime towards her (that is, Lélie as Sganarelle's wife's lover), Lélie points to Sganarelle as proof of Célie's crime towards him (that is, Sganarelle as Célie's new husband), and Sganarelle finally screws up his courage to accuse him of stealing his wife; thereupon Lélie defends himself and Célie taxes him once again with hypocrisy. The madness reaches a climax in the third and final scene devoted to the lovers' quarrel when the fourth partner, Sganarelle's wife, arrives and accuses Célie of robbing her of her husband; Célie rejects the accusation as a feint of the wife's to conceal her guilty affair with Lélie. Confusion reaches such a pitch that the maid, in a role antic-

ipating Dorine's in **Le Tartuffe,** steps in and forces each of the four contestants to explain himself clearly. The lovers are finally reconciled and the married couple mollified, if not reconciled (sc. 22).

William A. Mould (essay date 1975)

SOURCE: "Illusion and Reality: A New Resolution of an Old Paradox," in *Molière and the Commonwealth of Letters: Patrimony and Posterity,* Roger Johnson, Jr., Editha S. Neumann, Guy T. Trail, eds., University Press of Mississippi, 1975, pp. 521-26.

[*Mould is an American educator and critic who specializes in seventeenth-century French theater. In the following essay, he examines Molière's treatment of the paradoxical relationship between illusion and reality in his plays.*]

Molière is the first French dramatist to use the paradox of illusion and reality to express a sophisticated world view. His work transformed a dramatic device into a powerful statement of belief in man's ability to create his own universe. The distinction between illusion and reality forms the basis of theatrical experience, implicit in all drama, and explicit at certain moments in dramatic history. The earliest Greek plays used masks and other visible exaggerations partially to emphasize the nonreality of the spectacle; Plautus and Terence often had one character disguise himself to deceive another. Early French drama and the *commedia dell'arte* also offered on occasion primitive plays within plays, and the baroque theater of Rotrou's *Saint Genest* (1646) and Corneille's *Illusion comique* (1636) shows a renewed interest in the device. Although Rotrou had employed the play within a play to blur the distinction between tragic reality and the illusion of tragedy on stage, and although Corneille had used the device to excellent comic effect while enhancing the aesthetic impact of his comedy, it was Molière who used the play within a play to create a new perception of reality. "Corneille's subject [wrote Robert J. Nelson in his *Play within a Play* (1958)] is not the theatricality of life but the theatricality of the theater. . . . Sure of his values, the artist does not confuse appearance and reality except to the extent that he deliberately does so in order to please."

The seventeenth century had a real passion for the theater, perhaps because everyday life was itself so theatrical. The tribunes of Gothic and Renaissance cathedrals became the theater loges of the Jesuit-style church of Saint Paul-Saint Louis. Extraordinary etiquette and polite circumlocutions veiled genuine feelings. High titles and great offices were costly, empty charges. Versailles was a gigantic theater, the monarch its chief actor, the Hall of Mirrors its symbolic deception. People from all walks of life went often to the theater, and in real life frequently acted as if they were playing roles. The reality of this theatrical illusion was prevalent in human activities and is mirrored in Molière's theater. His audience liked to recognize on stage representations of characters and situations familiar to their daily life, yet they wished the theater to be far enough removed from the reality they knew to be comic. Molière's theater created a link between the reality of illusion in life and the illusion of reality in the theater. His plays are often very realistic in their portrayal of characters and social mores; the illusion closely resembles the reality of daily existence. It was, of course, precisely this realism which so delighted and infuriated Molière's contemporaries.

The comic universe is based in part on the ironic disparity between illusion and reality. Molière invents doctors who do not cure, a sick man who is not ill, a misanthrope in love with a coquette, and, for *Tartuffe,* a Monsieur Loyal who "porte un air bien déloyal." Eventually, the comic spectacle created through interaction among the characters will be generally superseded by the comedy of illusion resulting from self-deception. The Mascarille of *L'Etourdi* is the prototype for Scapin, adding ruse to plot, but always maintaining a clear distinction between the real and the imaginary world. The Mascarille of *Les Précieuses ridicules* refuses to leave his fantasy world where he is a cultivated marquis, just as Monsieur Jourdain remains convinced at the end of *Le Bourgeois gentilhomme* that he is a true "mamamouchi." The hypocrisy practised by Tartuffe, with its creation of sinister illusions, is another form of Molière's investigation of the problem of illusion and reality. Finally, the process finds its culmination in *Le Misanthrope* where Alceste, the iconoclast, is so self-deceived that his concept of reality is itself an illusion.

Molière has several approaches to the paradox of illusion and reality, and these approaches become more sophisticated as he matures. At first, like his predecessors, Molière uses it principally as a theatrical device to amuse, with only accidental deeper import. The play within a play is the principal manifestation of this early approach, and it first appears in *L'Etourdi* (1658). Mascarille (his name means, appropriately, "little mask") is a valet serving the love of his master Lélie for the beautiful Célie. The servant piles playlet upon playlet, creating illusions almost more quickly than they can be dispelled. Like a medieval *meneur du jeu,* Mascarille tries to induce others to play roles, but he is continually foiled by the honest naiveté of his master. Lélie, like Pridamant in *L'Illusion comique,* is always the spectator, so the audience is never completely deluded by Mascarille's playlets. Lélie tries time after time to join in his valet's illusions, but he is incapable of it; he has an indirect role, and rather than acting in Mascarille's spectacles, he reacts to them from outside. This helps the spectator to remain very certain as to the line between illusion and reality. That clarity occurs frequently in Molière's theater: Toinette in *Le Malade imaginaire* (III. 8 and 10) is obviously in disguise as a doctor; the same is true of Clitandre in *L'Amour médecin.* Only the fools Argan and Géronte are deceived in the latter play, just as only old Argante and Géronte are fooled by the *fourberies* of Scapin. In the end, Lélie wins Célie, not through any of the increasingly theatrical machinations of Mascarille, but by virtue of his honesty and inability to feign. All of Mascarille's schemes are pointless: the goal is reached

without him. Lélie, completely open and truly incapable of deception, cannot function in a world of illusion, but triumphs with the weapon of truth. If the later Scapin wins out through trickery more malicious than Mascarille's, it is perhaps due to the progressive darkening of Molière's attitudes. Despite the possible significance of the victory of naiveté in *L'Etourdi,* the real function of these playlets is dramatic and not ethical. A play within a play renders the main drama more "real," because the spectator's awareness of illusion is transferred to the second play. In later comedies such as *Tartuffe* and *Le Malade imaginaire,* the play within a play presents an illusion which leads to the truth. Elmire, pretending affection for Tartuffe, convinces her husband of the hypocrite's treacherous nature. Argan, feigning death, learns the true sentiments his wife and his daughter hold for him. In both cases, an illusion has been constructed in order to clarify reality.

When Molière approaches illusion on a more significant level, his attitude is often highly critical. In *Tartuffe* we are no longer dealing with light-hearted machinations designed to serve young love but with vicious hypocrisy whose goal is self-advancement and universal destruction. In the hands of Tartuffe, truth is twisted into lies; he convinces Orgon that his own son, Damis, has falsely accused the hypocrite:

> Vous fiez-vous, mon frère, à mon extérieur?
> Et, pour tout ce qu'on voit, me croyez-vous meilleur?
> Non, non, vous vous laissez tromper à l'apparence,
> . . . . .
> Mais la vérité pure est que je ne vaux rien. (III. 6)

Only Tartuffe is dishonest; the other characters could say, with Mme Pernelle, "Je vous parle un peu franc, mais c'est là mon humeur" (I. 1). Gradually, the construction of appearances which forms Tartuffe's existence leads even the honest Orgon to equivocate. The casuistry of Tartuffe causes Orgon first to lie to his brother-in-law Cléante about Mariane's marriage, and then to "faire des serments contre la vérité" (V. 1), swearing that he does not have papers which, for all practical purposes, he does possess. Tartuffe's world of deception leads others, especially Orgon, to be incapable of distinguishing appearance from reality. Orgon believes that he, too, can create a world by the sheer effort of his will: "Mais je veux que cela soit une vérité" (II. 1). His attempt to fuse illusion and reality is doomed, for the fusion would be based on transforming his daughter's affection for Valère into distaste, and her loathing for Tartuffe into love. Mythopoesis can function only when the new universe corresponds to the desires of its participants; that is, the illusion created by Tartuffe for Orgon and Mme Pernelle is acceptable to them because they wish to find a person of his sort of piety. It matters little that Cléante is able "du faux avec le vrai faire la différence" (I. 5); the world built by Tartuffe can be destroyed only by the suspension of belief on the part of Orgon.

The dénouement of *Tartuffe,* like the endings of so many of Molière's plays, has often been attacked for its lack of verisimilitude. It is, indeed, fantastic that the King's justice should descend on all, condemning Tartuffe and pardoning Orgon. Such extravagant scenes, which mark the endings not only of *Tartuffe,* but of *L'Ecole des femmes, L'Avare, Les Fourberies de Scapin* and *L'Etourdi,* are sometimes thought to be due to the impoverished imagination of their author. Mascarille may well say:

> C'est qu'en fait d'aventure il est très-ordinaire
> De voir gens pris sur mer par quelque Turc
>   consaire,
> Puis être à leur famille à point nommé rendus,
> Après quinze ou vingt ans qu'on les a crus
>   perdus.
>
> (*L'Etourdi,* IV. 1)

There is nothing at all ordinary about such adventures. In each of these dénouements Molière has created a new illusion. Such extravagance underlines with heavy irony the very impossibility of happiness and balance in a universe dominated by monomania and hypocrisy; a huge and improbable illusion is constructed in the final scene, so that the comedy may end happily. These dénouements, springing from recognition scenes, are dependent on events beyond the control of the characters, but the final scenes of *Le Bourgeois gentilhomme* and *Le Malade imaginaire* rise out of the obsessions of the major characters. Monsieur Jourdain will live forever in the belief that he has attained the noble rank of "mamamouchi"; Argan is convinced of the validity of his farcical initiation into the medical fraternity. In both cases, happiness for the other characters, especially the young lovers, can be attained only by acceding to the illusions of the monomaniac and by constructing a final, everlasting illusion around him. Illusion becomes the only way to bear the horror of a reality which would dictate that Jourdain's daughter marry an unknown nobleman she cannot love, and that Argan's Angélique be wedded to the atrocious Thomas Diafoirus. The men who give themselves over to these illusions have departed from a reality which rejects their foibles. Fortunately for them, both Monsieur Jourdain and Argan are in a position to create their own reality; it suffices that each believe his obsession to be satisfied, for all of the results to occur as if that illusion were true. Such, of course, is not the case with the valet Mascarille of *Les Précieuses ridicules,* described by his master as "un extravagant qui s'est mis dans la tete de vouloir faire l'homme de condition" (I. 1). In this first play (1659) where Molière shows a fusion between illusion and reality, the servant enters so well into his role of foppish marquis, that the blows and insults heaped on him at the end of the play do not really seem to disabuse him. He is so taken with his role that he confuses illusion and reality, and refuses to abandon his assumed identity: "Je vois bien qu'on n'aime ici que la vaine apparence, et qu'on ne considère point la vertu toute nue" (sc. 16). Nonetheless, valet or master, mamamouchi or doctor, Molière's men will often insist on living in a world where they have fused their illusions with reality in order to create a bearable existence.

In some of his most sophisticated plays, the dramatist Molière joins his characters in operating a fusion between illusion and reality. Now, there is no one left on stage who does not deal with nonreality to considerable extent. *Amphitryon* (1668) is the story of a complicated illusion created by Jupiter to seduce the faithful Alcmène. Jupiter disguised as Amphitryon, and Mercure as the valet Sosie, play their roles perfectly. Until the very end, neither god does anything to break the illusion they have created; unlike Tartuffe, Mascarille (*Les Précieuses ridicules*), or Sganarelle (badly disguised as a doctor in *Le Médecin malgre lui*), they remain quite in character. The gods have created a new reality, accepted by all the characters save Amphitryon. The general's inability to accept the new reality leads to his ridiculous posture in the scenes forming the second half of Act III. It is Jupiter himself, the master illusion maker, who tries to re-establish the boundaries between the old reality and the new. In his attempt to appropriate some of Alcmène's love, he tries to force her to distinguish between her husband (Amphitryon) and her lover (Jupiter). But Jupiter's illusion is perfect, and Alcmène refuses to make a distinction which seems to her unrelated to any needs her husband might have. Jupiter, in the unusual role of both magician and iconoclast, is unable to re-establish a reality which he has definitively altered by the injection of imperceptible illusion.

It is, unsurprisingly, in *Le Misanthrope* that the fusion between illusion and reality is most complete. Like Amphitryon, Alceste is ridiculous because he refuses to accept illusion as reality. Here, the illusion is much more universal, for it includes the very foundations of human society. As Philinte says: "Tout marche par cabale et par pur intérêt; / Ce n'est plus que la ruse aujourd'hui qui l'emporte" (V. 2). Philinte also suggests the necessity of accepting illusion and hypocrisy as a reality forming the basis for social existence:

> Lorsqu'un homme vous vient embrasser avec
>   joie,
> Il faut bien le payer de la même monnoie,
> Répondre, comme on peut, à ses empressements,
> Et rendre offre pour offre et serments pour
>   serments.
>
> (I. 1)

W. D. Howarth (essay date 1982)

SOURCE: "Molière's Comic Vision," in *Molière: A Playwright and His Audience,* Cambridge University Press, 1982, pp. 244-57.

[*Howarth is an English educator and critic whose works on French literature include* Life and Letters in France: The Seventeenth Century *(1965), and* Sublime and Grotesque: A Study of French Romantic Drama *(1975). In the following essay, he discusses Molière's view of human nature, the problems of contemporary production of Molière's plays, and the moral function of Molière's drama. Howarth concludes that "the cathartic function" of the Molière's comedies was "to preserve a healthy view of the relationship between the individual and society."*]

Before Molière's day, as we have seen, French comedy was lacking anything that could be called 'comic vision'. The world of the farces, and of Scarron's Jodelet plays, was a world of two-dimensional theatrical characters, a world of fantasy whose only relationship with reality was that of parody or burlesque. In Corneille's comedies, on the other hand, the characters, though more rounded and lifelike, were colourless, and the plots remained tied to the complex artificiality inherited from the pastorals; so that although his plays can be accepted as portraying reality after a fashion, we should look in vain here too (except perhaps to some extent in *Mélite* and *L'Illusion comique*) for an authentic comic vision on the playwright's part.

It must have seemed to contemporaries at the beginning of Molière's career that whatever promise this new arrival showed, there were few signs of his departing from traditional patterns of comedy established by predecessors. *L'Étourdi, Dépit amoureux, Les Fâcheux* are all recognisably in the comic idiom of 1640-58; and the comedies based on the Mascarille type of character (the same will also be true of *Les Fourberies de Scapin*) offer no more of a comic vision—that is, an identifiable philosophy of life than *Le Menteur* or *Dom Japhet d'Arménie*. But with the creation of the Sganarelle figure; the evolution of the formula 'ridicule en de certaines choses et honnête homme en d'autres'; the transfer of the comic scene indoors; and the treating of contemporary topics such as preciosity, *honnêteté, dévotion* or social climbing: with such highly individual innovations, Molière fashioned a totally new type of comedy that demanded to be related to the real world outside the theatre.

How are we to define Molière's comic vision? More than any other writer of comedies has ever done, he offers us a valid and consistent view of human nature. His major plays are of course rich enough for commentators to be able to argue about this or that detail of their interpretation; but there is general agreement about the broad lines of a coherent philosophy. This is in the first place critical, or negative, in that it holds up to ridicule certain tendencies that are unsociable, or anti-social, in character there is a common denominator of egoism and self-interest in all the Sganarelle figures but it is also possible to deduce from the plays a constructive social ideal: an ideal very close to that of the *honnêtes gens*. It is not put forward didactically as a programme to be followed; rather it is to be inferred as a more or less implicit social norm against which the Sganarelle figures offend.

In conveying to the spectator this positive recommendation of a social norm, one group of characters has a particular importance, namely the so-called 'raisonneurs': the Chrysaldes, Cléantes and Béraldes of Molière's theatre. From having been looked on by earlier critics as lay figures playing a role as mouthpieces of the author in an essentially didactic form of comedy, this group of characters has recently come to be seen in a more theatrical light, as taking one side in a dialectical confrontation which Molière puts before us objectively, without himself tak-

ing sides: what Moore calls 'a dialogue on humanity' [in *Molière: A New Criticism*]. Bray, who also considers these characters to be satisfactorily integrated into the dramatic scheme of the plays, goes so far as to declare: 'Il n'y a pas de raisonneurs dans le théâtre de Molière. Chaque personnage est exigé par sa fonction dramatique, non par une prétendue morale inventée par la critique' [in *Molière, homme de théâtre*].

What is the true role of the *raisonneurs,* and what do they stand for? There is a distinct family likeness between the two Aristes (in *L'École des maris* and *Les Femmes savantes*), Chrysalde (*L'École des femmes*), Cléante (*Tartuffe*) and Béralde (*Le Malade imaginaire*): all of these are mature characters 'd'un certain âge', standing somewhat to one side of the dramatic action, but showing a sympathetic interest in the fortunes of the central figure, with whom they are connected by family ties or by long-standing friendship. Philinte, the other character who is often labelled a 'raisonneur', corresponds in the main to this description; and although he clearly belongs, like Alceste, to a younger age-group, his phlegmatic temperament seems to be that of the *raisonneur* type in general. To say that their function is merely to express the viewpoint he wants his audience to adopt, is to ascribe to Molière a very limiting and simplistic view of the comic process. On the other hand, to claim that the opening dialogue between Arnolphe and Chrysalde on cuckoldry, or that between Alceste and Philinte on sincerity, is presented in a completely neutral manner, and to maintain that the spectator is not expected to find one of the characters much more reasonable than the other, seems to fly in the face of all one's experience in the theatre; moreover, even Bray seems to concede that Cléante, at least, is an episodic character whose presence is hardly essential to the plot of *Tartuffe*. But is it not possible that there is another way to justify the existence of the *raisonneur*? If we consider Molière's comedy as having evolved as the result of a two-way process, in response to the demands of a cultivated audience who were in turn being invited to approve a new form of comic drama which went beyond these demands, then would it not be legitimate to see this group of characters, who make their appearance in the most original, and most provocative, of the plays those that belong to the category of 'comedy of ideas' as a sort of 'objective correlative' of the *honnêtes gens* in the audience: recognisable, sympathetic figures expressing a point of view with which they could identify? Only Philinte, it is true, is fully representative of the *honnête homme* in the exclusive, aristocratic sense of the term: he is an enlightened courtier, whereas Chrysalde, Cléante and the others are bourgeois exponents of *honnêteté*. But they all represent the virtues of moderation, tolerance, and charity; they are all good listeners, wise counsellors, not doctrinaire theorists but practical men, thoroughly integrated into the society to which they belong; and all of them are good friends who can be depended on in an emergency. It would surely not be unreasonable to see their urbane, civilised manner, and the way of life they practise, as an illustration, if not of the aristocratic social ideal formulated by the Chevalier de Méré, at any rate of the code of *honnêteté* as it was accepted by some of his less exacting contemporaries.

In one important sense, the term *raisonneur* is a misnomer; and Littré's definition: 'Personnage grave de la comédie, dont le langage est celui du raisonnement, de la morale' hardly does justice to this group of characters in Molière's theatre. For Molière's *raisonneurs,* though they certainly stand for *la raison* in the sense of reasonableness or common sense, should not be identified with *le raisonnement* or *la raison raisonnante.* On the contrary: it is the doctrinaire characters, the *imaginaires* who inhabit a world of their own, who constantly make dogmatic use of their reasoning faculty in an attempt to coerce others into accepting their opinions. This can be seen particularly clearly in the opening scenes of *L'École des femmes* and *Le Misanthrope,* where in each case it is Arnolphe or Alceste who takes the initiative, arguing aggressively, while the so-called 'raisonneur' adopts a defensive posture, speaking in the name of ordinary human experience in a reasonable but by no means a rationalistic manner:

> *Arnolphe:* Mon Dieu, notre ami, ne vous
>   tourmentez point:
> Bien huppé qui pourra m'attraper sur ce point.
> Je sais les tours rusés et les subtiles trames
> Dont pour nous en planter savent user les
>   femmes,
> Et comme on est dupé par leurs dextérités.
> Contre cet incident j'ai pris mes sûretés;
> Et celle que j'épouse a toute l'innocence
> Qui peut sauver mon front de maligne influence.
> *Chrysalde:* Et que prétendez-vous qu'une sotte,
>   en un mot . . .
> *Arnolphe:* Épouser une sotte est pour n'être
>   point sot.
>
>   (*L'École des femmes* lines 73-82)

> *Philinte:* Tous les pauvres mortels, sans nulle
>   exception,
> Seront enveloppés dans cette aversion?
> Encore en est-il bien, dans le siècle où nous
>   sommes . . .
> *Alceste:* Non: elle est générale, et je hais tous les
>   hommes:
> Les uns, parce qu'ils sont méchants et
>   malfaisants,
> Et les autres, pour être aux méchants
>   complaisants,
> Et n'avoir pas pour, eux ces haines vigoureuses
> Que doit donner le vice aux âmes vertueuses . . .
>   (*Le Misanthrope,* lines 115-21)

The relationship between the *raisonneur* and the central comic character presents few problems of interpretation in most of the plays; though the reason why Chrysalde should defend, as he does, the 'douceurs' and the 'plaisirs' of cuckoldry (*L'École des femmes,* lines 1244ff., 1302-5) has given rise to a certain amount of theorising by the critics - as has, much more importantly, the enigmatic question of Cléante's religious standpoint. But generally speaking, there seems to be no reason why an au-

dience of *honnêtes gens* should not have been able to identify with the point of view expressed by Cléante, Chrysalde or Béralde, since that coincided with the attitudes they acknowledged themselves, or the social ideal to which they aspired; and by the same token, they presumably found no difficulty in accepting Orgon, Arnolphe or Argan as ridiculous inasmuch as their behaviour obviously departed from these accepted norms. But the relationship between Alceste and Philinte is another matter. In Alceste, contemporary spectators found a character who seemed to be one of themselves: a courtier, a would-be *honnête homme,* and a man with a highly developed sense of honour and personal integrity; and it must be acknowledged, to judge from such comment as has been preserved, that some of them found it easier to admire Alceste than to laugh at him. That the critical debate over the interpretation of Alceste's character should still be a live issue after three centuries shows that it was not just a problem of communication between Molière and contemporary audiences; though twentieth-century spectators should be better able than their seventeenth-century counterparts to situate Alceste in the context of Molière's whole comic *oeuvre,* to perceive the filiation that links him to the early Sganarelles, and to recognise the shaky foundations of self-importance and self-interest on which his crusade for sincerity is based. But Alceste will always have his champions; and Philinte, the embodiment of moderation and common sense, the *honnête homme par excellence,* will always seem to some playgoers less attractive than his headstrong, opinionated friend. And a degree of ambiguity is inevitable: ambiguity is, indeed, inherent in the formula 'ridicule en de certaines choses et honnête homme en d'autres'; and however convinced some of us may be that Alceste remains 'ridicule', we must agree that he is by far the most rounded, the most interesting, and the most sympathetic of Molière's comic characters. As Jean Emelina puts it in a most perceptive passage: [from *Les Valets et les servantes dans le théâtre comique en France de 1610 à 1700*]:

> La simplification psychologique, dans un genre plus populaire que la tragédie, est une nécessité pour le rire et pour la satire . . . La comédie ne peut, sans risquer de se détruire, prétendre sérieusement à une authentique lucidité. Elle est l'univers rassurant et clair du manichéen. Elle est l'univers de l'invraisemblable et de l'imaginaire tant pour les êtres que pour les situations, parce que le rire se nourrit de l'irréel. L'inévitable ambiguïté des personnages d'après nature, 'ni tout à fait bons ni tout à fait mauvais', ne peut pas être son lot, car de l'ambiguïté naît le malaise. Térence, Molière ou Marivaux, par les étranges résonances que font parfois lever en nous certaines de leurs créations, montrent assez que tout réalisme psychologique, que toute finesse d'analyse au sein de la comédie risquent, fatalement, de frôler le pathétique.

On the one hand, we know that Molière's plays were written for a company who were the favourite entertainers of Paris and the Court in the 1660s, and were the product of an intimate relationship with the audiences of his day. On the other hand, they are more frequently, and more widely, played in the twentieth century than ever before. What problems of understanding or interpretation arise for today's spectators from the fact that these comedies were created in response to the demands of a society so different from ours?

First of all, there is a group of comedies depending on fantasy and virtuosity, whose seventeenth-century reference is almost nonexistent; this group includes plays which are conspicuously successful with modern audiences, such as *Le Médecin malgré lui* or *Les Fourberies de Scapin*, and there is no reason to believe that their appeal for us today differs essentially from the appeal they had for their first audiences three hundred years ago. A second group does, it is true, present certain problems of comprehension because of the seventeenth-century setting; but all that is required of us, really, is a minimum of factual knowledge about, say, *préciosité* or the *salons,* so that *Les Précieuses ridicules* or *Les Femmes savantes* should be at least as easy of access for twentieth-century spectators as *The Recruiting Officer* or *The Rivals.* On the other hand, plays like *Dom Juan, Tartuffe* and *Le Misanthrope* (and one could add *L'École des femmes* and *George Dandin*) pose genuine problems of interpretation, which largely derive from changes in the intellectual and moral climate between Molière's day and our own; and in such cases a great deal must obviously depend on the way in which a director views his role in guiding the response of an audience.

There seem to be two temptations for a modern director producing Molière. One is the temptation to update, to impose on the seventeenth-century play an arbitrary link with a selected period of modern history. Veteran theatregoers will no doubt have had a chance to experience *Le Misanthrope* in Edwardian dress, *Les Femmes savantes* in the costumes of the 1920s, *Tartuffe* in the dress and decor of *la belle époque,* or other productions based on similar historical analogies. One problem with such an approach is of course the very specific nature of the contemporary references in Molière's text: to take obvious examples, what does one make of the detailed evocation of seventeenth-century fashions in Alceste's scathing portrait of Clitandre (*Misanthrope,* lines 475-88) if the actors are all wearing Savile Row suits, or of the references to Descartes and other thinkers in *Les Femmes savantes* which become quite meaningless in a twentieth-century context? Perhaps the most distinguished of such productions was Jean Anouilh's *Tartuffe* at the Comédie des Champs-Élysées in 1960: set in the period around 1900, it evidently succeeded in saying something important about the continuity of certain moral and social attitudes across the centuries. But to point an analogy so clearly must result in a very limiting interpretation of Molière's play: striking as such links may be, it is surely too restricting to insist on a single modern analogue to the exclusion of others that are possibly just as valid; and this kind of updating is best left to the alert spectator's imagination as he watches the play. The second temptation, irresistible to many modern directors, is to leave the play in the seventeenth century, but to subject it to a highly subjective, often political or sociological, interpretation. This has been above all the manner of Roger Pl-

anchon's productions at the Théâtre National Populaire; and both his *George Dandin* of the late 1960s and his *Tartuffe* of the mid-seventies took the form of explicit commentaries on the class-structure of the Grand Siècle. Not only does such a tendentious approach leave far too little to the imagination of the audience, but it leads to a solemn interpretation of Molière's plays which risks turning them into humourless *drames bourgeois.* The 1979 production of *Dom Juan* at the Comédie-Française by Jean-Luc Boutté illustrated a similar approach, dictated not so much by political conviction or sociological doctrine as by a personal resolve to be different at all costs, added to a damaging lack of confidence in Molière's text.

For this is the inescapable conclusion: one reason why directors find it necessary to treat Molière thus is the desire to divert the audience's attention from a text that they presumably judge to be hackneyed, out of date, or lacking in theatrical qualities. Louis Jouvet gave a clear warning to his fellow-producers in the following passage from his *Témoignages sur le théâtre:*

> Dans cet art de métamorphoses qu'est le théâtre, seules comptent les pensées du poète; elles sont la vertu du théâtre. Ce que nous appelons pensées n'est qu'un vêtement de sentiments et de sensations. Généreusement le poète nous l'offre, et chacun s'approprie ce manteau, et chacun s'en revêt à son tour, pour vouloir penser à sa manière. Ce n'est là qu'une usurpation. L'usage véritable d'une pièce de théâtre est d'y réchauffer son corps et son coeur.

The text is sacred: this is Jouvet's message. It must never become a *pretext* for a priori sociological doctrine, for flashy theatricality, or for gratuitous embellishments in the name of 'relevance'. There will always be difficulties, ambiguities, possibilities of various layers of meaning, in certain of Molière's plays that is partly what gives them their special quality but the way to arrive at a meaningful reading of the text, on stage as well as in the study, is, as Jouvet says, to 'subir l'oeuvre avant de la comprendre et de l'apprécier': patiently to elucidate and interpret the original, not to substitute for it a subjective, anachronistic version of our own invention.

It is not difficult to create a convincing decor for the indoor comedies, whose text surely demands a firm link with a certain historical reality; and that can be done without indulging in the obsessive and obtrusive realism of Planchon and other directors. The seventeenth-century setting, which helps to establish the social context that is so necessary to a proper understanding of *Tartuffe, Le Misanthrope, L'Avare* or *Les Femmes savantes,* is not in any way exclusive: like all comic masterpieces, Molière's great plays combine the local and the topical with the universal, the individual with the general. It is a commonplace of literary theory that tragedy deals with individuals, comedy with general types. As Diderot puts it [in *Writings on the Theatre*]:

> Le genre comique est des espèces, et le genre tragique est des individus . . . Le héros d'une tragédie est tel

ou tel homme: c'est ou Régulus, ou Brutus, ou Caton; et ce n'est point un autre. Le principal personnage d'une comédie doit au contraire représenter un grand nombre d'hommes. Si, par hasard, on lui donnait une physionomie si particulière, qu'il n'y eût dans la société qu'un seul individu qui lui ressemblât, la comédie retournerait à son enfance, et dégénérerait en satire.

Diderot is quite right in his conclusion; but perhaps the terms he uses need looking at more closely: the notions of 'type' and 'individual' tend to be accepted too uncritically. For the pure stage *types* the braggart soldier of Renaissance comedy, the stereotyped 'characters' of the eighteenth century remain two-dimensional, and what gives a comic character that third dimension which brings him dramatic life is the successful blend of the general type to which he belongs with the individual features that distinguish him from that type.

Almost without exception, the comedy of Molière's contemporaries fails to achieve such a synthesis. Orgon, Alceste or Harpagon, on the other hand, although they are rooted unmistakably in the world that Molière and his audience knew, have the same universal reference as characters like Volpone and Falstaff. As with the most memorable creations of other comic dramatists, we can put this universality to the test in the case of Molière's characters when, as sometimes happens to us all, we draw on our experience as playgoers to help us to characterise acquaintances in the real world. It is not so very unusual for us to think of people we know as 'a Falstaff' or 'a Harpagon': convincing proof that these characters possess some quality or other that transcends the boundaries of time and place.

If we recognise our neighbours, then, or at any rate traits of character that we associate with our neighbours, in figures like Harpagon or Argan, what does that tell us about the moral function of comedy? Do we recognise ourselves as well? If not, it is difficult to see how comedy could fulfil the corrective role traditionally ascribed to it, even if one were to accept the sternly moralistic approach of some nineteenth-century commentators, enshrined in Meredith's well-known description of Molière [in *An Essay on Comedy and the Uses of the Comic Spirit*]: 'Never did man wield such a shrieking scourge upon vice. But the more nearly one approaches to the notion of satire in one's definition of comedy, the more difficult it surely is to believe that the moral effect attributed to Molière's comedy works in such a way. There have been periods when dramatists have proclaimed a fervent belief in the corrective power of the theatre, and have matched that belief in practice by writing a heavily didactic kind of play; but in Molière's case we are entitled to discount the sort of claim he puts forward in the Preface to *Tartuffe,* where he is conducting a defensive campaign against those, precisely, who had accused his play of immorality. Emile Augier, for all his faith that 'de tous les engins de la pensée humaine, le théâtre est le plus puissant, voilà tout', was realist enough to concede that it is asking too much of the dramatist to demand the conversion of individuals: 'd'ailleurs le but n'est pas de corriger quelqu'un, c'est de

corriger tout le monde'. [Preface to *Les Lionnes pauvres*]

In any case, even if we assume that there were real-life counterparts of Molière's characters in the society for which he wrote, are we also to assume that they went to the theatre? Can we really imagine a real-life Tartuffe (or even a real-life Orgon), a Harpagon or an Argan among the audience for whom the plays were performed? Such moral correction was never the business of comedy; this is certainly not the way in which the moral effect of Molière's comedy operates, and Alain is surely nearer the mark when he writes [in *Propos*]:

> Ce n'est point ton semblable, cet Avare qui dit son secret, car de ton semblable tu ne connais jamais que le dehors; toutefois ce qui est mis sur cette scène, c'est ce que chaque homme connaît de lui-même. Chacun est Harpagon, chacun a pensé le 'Sans dot', mais personne ne l'a jamais
>
> dit . . .
>
> Qui n'a jamais été ridicule ne sait point rire. Au reste un tel homme n'est pas né. Si l'avarice était une sorte de maladie rare, qui donc en rirait? Et si l'on me fait un portrait d'avare, d'après l'anecdote, j'éprouverai le faible plaisir de mépriser. Mais chacun est avare, de vraie avarice, et jaloux, de ridicule jalousie; chacun est Purgon et Jourdain en importance, cent fois par jour.

'We are all of us miserly, jealous, and self-important, every day of our lives . . . ': this shows a similar insight to Augier's 'le but n'est pas de corriger quelqu'un, c'est de corriger tout le monde'. We are all of us implicated in the comic process: not because as individuals we are the counterparts of either the *malade imaginaire* or the pompous doctors who attend on him, but because of the common humanity we share with the rest of the theatre audience. Some of us may imagine it is easy to preserve a comfortable detachment as we watch the follies of Orgon or Monsieur Jourdain; but can we say the same thing about Alceste? Here is a very different case, for we all have moods in which we think we are better, nobler, purer than the world we live in; in which we imagine that our merits are unrecognised or unrewarded. There is something of Alceste in all of us, in our most intimate relationships with those we love as well as in the broader context of our social behaviour. How many of us have not at times thought, even if we have not given expression to the thought:

> . . . Je verrai, dans cette plaiderie,
> Si les hommes auront assez d'effronterie,
> Seront assez méchants, scélérats et pervers,
> Pour me faire injustice aux yeux de l'univers?
>   (*Le Misanthrope*, lines 197-200)

How many of us, by the same token, have not often felt, even if we have never voiced the feeling:

> . . . C'est pour mes péchés que je vous aime
>   ainsi . . .

Mon amour ne se peut concevoir, et jamais
Personne n'a, Madame, aimé comme je fais?

(*ibid.*, lines 520-4)

And how many of us, if we were honest, would not have to admit to occasional fantasies such as the following:

Oui, je voudrais qu'aucun ne vous trouvât
   aimable,
Que vous fussiez réduite en un sort misérable,
Que le Ciel, en naissant, ne vous eût donné rien,
Que vous n'eussiez ni rang, ni naissance, ni
   bien,
Afin que de mon coeur l'éclatant sacrifice
Vous pût d'un pareil sort réparer l'injustice,
Et que j'eusse la joie et la gloire, en ce jour,
De vous voir tenir tout des mains de mon
   amour?

(*ibid.*, lines 1525-32)

We can all see something of ourselves in Alceste. And we may be quite sure that in confronting us with the truth about ourselves in this way, Molière never intended either to reinforce our self-esteem or to justify our anti-social impulses. For the mirror he holds up to us is the distorting mirror of comedy, and the 'truth' is exaggerated and caricatured by the comic process; so that if we can recognise the absurdity of Alceste's behaviour, we may be led to acknowledge the absurdity of any similar tendencies in ourselves. We laugh at the critical portrait of the *honnête homme imaginaire,* and thereby express our solidarity with the civilised way of life his behaviour so constantly flouts. The confrontation with a comic exaggeration of faults latent within ourselves acts as a painless corrective: this therapeutic effect is common to all Molière's great comedies, and **Le Misanthrope** is no exception. Experience teaches us, however, that there are spectators who are resistant to this process; and Alain might have been thinking of Rousseau's reaction to **Le Misanthrope** when he wrote [in *Les Arts et les dieux*]: 'Heureux celui qui ne sait pas être important sans être ridicule; mais ces bonnes chances ne vont pas sans un peu d'humeur. La comédie nous guérit mieux, sans la honte; car la force du spectacle fait que personne ne pense au voisin.'

Are we perhaps now in a position to offer an interpretation of the comic process, to which it might not seem too inappropriate to attach the label 'a comic catharsis'? Is it possible to discern an analogue for the spectator of comedy to the purging of the passions which, from Aristotle's day onwards, has been recognised by most theorists as a valid formulation of what we experience as spectators of tragedy? The fact that Aristotle did not include his projected section on comedy in the *Poetics* has not prevented commentators from constructing the theory of comedy to which he might have given expression; and W. Lane Cooper went so far as to produce a full-scale adaptation of the *Poetics* [in *An Aristotelian Theory of Comedy, with an Adaptation of the Poetics*], substituting concepts appropriate to comedy for those referring to tragedy. The essence of Lane Cooper's 'Aristotelian' definition is as follows:

A comedy is the artistic imitation of an action which is ludicrous (or mirthful), organically complete, and of a proper length ... As for the end or function resulting from the imitation of such an object ... it is to arouse, and by arousing to relieve, the emotions proper to comedy.

And his amplification of the last phrase provides a most interesting commentary on one of the central notions of the *Letter sur l'Imposteur,* namely 'la disconvenance':

Here we shall assume that, as men in daily life are accustomed to suffer from a sense of disproportion, it is this that is relieved or purged away by the laughter of comedy; for comedy (witness the comic mask) distorts proportions; its essence is the imitation of things seen out of proportion. By contemplating the disproportions of comedy, we are freed from the sense of disproportion in life, and regain our perspective, settling as it were into our proper selves.

As with the tragic catharsis, such a process can be interpreted in two very different ways: one, as a direct, exemplary or corrective function, and the other, as an uplifting aesthetic experience of a much less specific nature. There is a world of difference between the interpretation advanced by Corneille in his *Discours de la tragédie:*

La pitié d'un malheur où nous voyons tomber nos semblables nous porte à la crainte d'un pareil pour nous; cette crainte, au désir de l'éviter; et ce désir, à purger, modérer, rectifier et même déraciner en nous la passion qui plonge à nos yeux dans ce malheur les personnes que nous plaignons

and Racine's version of the cathartic process, surely more consistent with the mature classical spirit, according to which what is 'purged' or 'tempered' is not the specific passion portrayed on stage, but any harmful excess of the very emotions of pity and fear that have been aroused by that portrayal. By the same token, what we have called the comic catharsis has been seen by many as a moralistic or didactic process, but it too can be interpreted as something much less direct and specific and again, I have no doubt that this subtler interpretation is more in keeping with the fully-developed classical aesthetic. Molière's purpose in his comedies was not to 'scourge' a particular vice; it is noteworthy that when he did set out to do something like that, in **Dom Juan,** he was forced to resort to a corrective process other than that of laughter. The punishment of a *grand seigneur méchant homme* lies outside the scope of the comic catharsis, and the playwright had to use dramatic, not comic, means to achieve that end. But elsewhere, Molière's aim to 'corriger les hommes en les divertissant' was to amuse all his audience, and to instruct all his audience, not merely such misers, misanthropists or learned ladies as might happen to be present. The heroes of classical comedy are not annihilated, like Dom Juan, but neither are they cured. They remain the intransigent outsiders, the impenitent egoists that they have been shown to be throughout the five acts of the play. They are in a sense the imaginary scapegoats of society, and by laughing at them in the social microcosm of the theatre the individuals composing the audience are enabled, as Lane Cooper puts it, to regain their proper perspective: that is, to preserve a healthy view of the relationship between the individual and society. This, then, is the cathartic function of Molière's comedy: to send us all away from the play purged and regenerated, as social beings, by the restorative process of laughter.

'Molière n'eût pas été classique', writes Charles Lalo [in *Esthétique du rite*], 's'il n'avait défendu la bonne société établie en son temps contre les excentriques et les snobs, comme Alceste, les femmes savantes ou les précieuses ridicules; les parasites, comme Tartuffe, Harpagon ou Même Dom Juan; les usurpateurs de dignités consacrées, comme le Bourgeois gentilhomme ou George Dandin.' To see Molière as exemplifying this kind of *rire conformiste* would be to take a very restrictive view both of the relationship between the individual and society in his theatre, and of the nature of classical art. As L. J. Potts has written [in *Comedy*]:

> Society, in the sense in which the word defines the setting of a comedy, stands for an idea rather than for a particular set of persons. It stands for coherence; for a common body of opinions and standards and a disposition to cooperate. It can be contracted to a very small class living together in a small area; it can be extended to the whole of humanity . . .

It would no doubt have been easy for Molière, once he was firmly established in the King's favour, to write comedies appealing to a narrowly-defined, self-contained Court audience, playing on that superficial sense of the proprieties which, as Stendhal says somewhere, is always the source of the courtier's notion of the comic. If he had done no more than this, his plays would long ago have become trivial museum-pieces. Instead, his comedy reflects a larger, more generous concept of society, neither exclusively aristocratic nor exclusively bourgeois; one that owed a good deal to the civilising force of Renaissance thought that had been handed down to Frenchmen of his age by the humanist tradition of previous generations. Biographers have often sought to emphasise the significance, as a guide to Molière's fundamental philosophy of life, of his translation of Lucretius and his friendship with free-thinking disciples of Gassendi. Such factors will probably always remain speculative; but the influence of the *social* ideas of the Renaissance humanists is much more tangible, and the society reflected in his theatre has considerable affinities with the ideal envisaged by thinkers like Erasmus and Montaigne. We know that in practice the France of Louis XIV's reign had its fair share of privilege and corruption, but the selective picture given by the artists and the writers of the age was not a complete misrepresentation of reality: French classical literature emphasises the values of an ordered, civilised way of life in which men and women of culture did genuinely believe, and which many of them honestly tried to practise. This aspect of the classical ideal, as a reflection of the highest aspirations of the civilisation of an age, is one that applies as fully to comedy as to any other art form;

and when we speak of 'classical comedy' in this context, we think almost exclusively of Molière.

Harold C. Knutson (essay date 1986)

SOURCE: "Molière's Reactionary Theater," in *Proceedings of the Annual Meeting of the Western Society for French History,* Vol. 13, 1986, pp. 115-22.

[*Knutson is an American educator and critic whose writings on French literature include* Molière: An Archetypal Approach *(1976). In the following essay, he examines Molière's portrayal of social hierarchy and asserts that his theater may be considered "reactionary."*]

Tragedy conveys its political message through the prism of exemplary history and its royal protagonists. The comic dramatist usually mirrors the affairs of lesser mortals, normally in their own time setting. To grasp the political significance of comedy, then, we must perforce look at the social fabric which it purports to replicate. We are thus led to social history and the uses that a literary scholar—in this case the Molière specialist—can make of it.

Our view of seventeenth-century social history in France has changed dramatically in recent years. The cut-and-dried picture of a society polarized between a stratified aristocracy and a rising bourgeoisie has yielded to the image of a complex, evolving hierarchy composed of loosely allied segments within the nominal orders, and with much more assimilation than was hitherto thought.

This new insight into seventeenth-century French social organization has had a considerable impact on literary scholars concerned with the relationship between cultural products and the society which produces and consumes them. It became readily apparent that many generalities about seventeenth-century French literature were founded on a simplistic interpretation of social background. Indeed, literary scholars were all too prone to study literature as a direct mimesis of social history. We now realize that literature, or comedy at least, offers an image of reality subject to an intricate process of idealization, caricature, amplification, and deletion.

It is natural that Molière, more than any of his contemporaries, should be at the focal point of these trends. Traditionally, comedy has been seen as a mimesis of mores, as in Cicero's famous definition "imitatio vitae, speculum consuetudinis, imago veritatis." And of all the comic dramatists of the period, Molière reproduced most persistently an image of his own life and times. Indeed, he was the first great practitioner in world drama of the comedy of manners.

A complex social reality whose intricacies are still being unravelled, a master of comedy who used that reality as his raw material, such are the given elements which I try to address in the following remarks. What picture of his times, however distorted, does Molière convey to us? How faithful is he to reigning values? To answer that question fully we would need to review the totality of that society itself—a task which obviously exceeds the scope of this paper. But perhaps if we limit ourself to one far-reaching aspect of that reality—the social hierarchy and the most problematic level in it, the nobility—and concentrate on Molière's picture of that particular order, we should be able to reach some tentative conclusions, or at the least invite a deeper study of the issue.

A final *précaution oratoire* before we get under way in a brief review of hierarchy in seventeenth-century France: my use of the word *reactionary* may seem unpardonably anachronistic; after all, the term dates only from the early nineteenth century. But one definition of the word seems quite timeless for me, and I would do well—if only for self-protection—to quote it from *Webster's New Collegiate Dictionary*: *reactionary*: "relating to, marked by, or favoring reaction." Now, *reaction*: "resistance or opposition to a force, influence, or movement, esp. tendency toward a former and usually outmoded political or social order or policy."

If the feudal tags still adhere to the various levels of society in seventeenth-century France, it is because the period itself viewed its image through the feudal prism and its three-fold divisions: Clergy, Nobility, and Commoner. To a degree, of course, it is proper to speak of these three estates, as they still existed as a political concept and occasionally as a reality. But under this nomenclature, momentous changes had occurred. The nobility in particular was in a state of crisis. Its feudal cohesion had already been eroded under the pressures of social and political developments. There was, of course, the surviving traditional caste which traced its ancestry far back in time and which took pride in the long-standing authenticity of its titles. But the growth, in the sixteenth century especially, of offices or *charges,* and the custom of awarding noble title with them, notably in the magistrature, led to a new nobility. We know it of course as the *noblesse de robe.*

The matter became further complicated at the beginning of the seventeenth century, when titles held by the *robins* became hereditary. Thus by Louis XIV's reign, three generations later, a second hereditary caste had come into existence. At the same time, a yet newer nobility was being created as a consequence of the centralizing thrust of a growing absolutism. The *noblesse de robe* had become entrenched and protective of its prerogatives and titles, however recently acquired. Richelieu, and later Louis XIV himself, slowly and relentlessly undermined its position and its institutional locus, the *parlement,* by fashioning an administration directly responsible to the crown and rewarded with instant noble rank, sometimes instantly hereditary. La Bruyère was scathing in his denunciation of these "premiers nobles de leur race," to paraphrase his scornful comment. Among the beneficiaries of this kind of accession was the commoner Colbert who became a *marquis,* and Le Tellier who had received the title of duke in 1650. An even more spectacular promotion had taken place in England, where James I made George Villiers first a knight, then a viscount, then an earl, then a *marquis.*

Thus new offices with their concomitant claim to rank and privilege multiplied in the seventeenth century as the crown sought to drain away the assets accumulated by financiers, speculators and the like, in return for a title and respectability together with the opportunity to amass yet more through fresh means of extortion. One thinks of the tax-farmer bitterly caricatured by La Bruyère who began his career as a valet and, after various shady deals, "devenu noble par une charge," goes on to social distinction.

Thus an instant moneyed nobility penetrated more and more insistently the ranks of the Second Order, not only by the purchase of *charges* but by the acquisition of land, a distinctive sign of status, and a hypergamy reluctantly accepted by impoverished ancient families forced to exchange daughters for cash. There was consequently a fair amount of upward mobility—what Méthivier terms [in *La Fronde*] an "osmose fréquente des familles d'épée et de robe"—so much so that there was no longer any real line of demarcation between the Second Order and the Third Estate. To suggest, however, that there was a massive invasion of the nobility is to discount various inhibiting forces which made sure that no great dislocation of the social order took place. One had to work at advancement over generations sometimes and go patiently through the various steps of the process—"se décrasser par degrés," to quote Mousnier's vivid image.

A dynamic, shifting social scene, then, where noble values dominated, to be sure—why else would a taxfarmer spend vast sums to buy a bubble title?—but where great families, the more recent *noblesse de robe* and a cluster of freshly ennobled nouveaux-riches took their place under the same umbrella, eyeing each other warily and with a fair amount of hostility and contempt. For while the new nobility enjoyed its status de jure, it still had to seek social validation from a contemptuous *gentilhommerie,* while the latter was often scorned by the recently ennobled who felt that rank should be a matter of merit, not of birth. We have already seen how La Bruyère views the crass beneficiaries of sudden wealth—"les biens de fortune"—although, in a characteristic ambivalence, he showers contempt as well on truly titled grandees who fail to live up to their prerogatives. Does Molière share the same negative attitude toward social contamination, the same yearning for an ancient and perhaps mythical order where walls were impenetrable, where status symbols had only one meaning, and where rank and merit always dwelt together?

To address these questions, we shall have to examine Molière's portrayal of social hierarchy, the degree to which he idealizes, simplifies, caricatures, and ignores what he sees around him. For comedy, as was suggested earlier, holds only a distorting mirror up to nature. It is also unable, because of its very identity, to present the whole gamut of the various strata. We should not expect to find there the high prelates of the First Order, nor lofty kings and queens, properly at home in what Racine called the majestic sadness of tragedy. Comedy, as tradition would have it, is the purview of the commoner and his trivial pursuits.

L'AVARE

Engraved handbill produced for early performances of L'avare.

Yet Molière did depict a princely caste on occasion. His only attempt at truly serious drama, the early **Don Garcie de Navarre,** presents that lower level of royalty; and even in the full momentum of his comic career, he wrote court-ly entertainments like **La Princesse d'Elide** and **Les Amants magnifiques** where princes and princesses go about their amorous pursuits in a mood of refined idle-ness. But generally speaking, and certainly in Molière's renowned masterpieces, the highest nobility of the court, while lauded for its consummate taste (as in **La Critique de l'Ecole des femmes** and **Les Femmes savantes**), is kept respectfully at a distance.

Even so, Molière frequently added upper-class characters to the conventional social spectrum of his down-to-earth comedies. We must ask then how Molière situates them in the social hierarchy and what value judgments he at-tributes to their position. In the first instance, Molière's aristocrats can be classified geographically: those who belong to the minor provincial nobility, and those who live in Paris or who display metropolitan manners. The dramatist's picture of nobility beyond Paris and Versailles is invariably derisive: George Dandin's hide-bound fa-

ther-in-law, "le baron de Sotenville"; Monsieur de Pourceaugnac, the self-styled "gentilhomme limousin . . . qui a étudié en droit" (thus a kind of hybrid *seigneur de robe*); and the ludicrous country countess of **La Comt-esse d'Escarbagnas**. We may dismiss these characters as examples of a backward, dull and uncouth provincial life—except that in reality the provinces were the eco-nomic base of the entire country and boasted their own political and cultural centers. There was a much stronger regionalism in France than an essentially metropolitan high literature would suggest. In dismissing the positive side of life in the provinces, Molière simply echoes the smugness of his audience in its idolatry of Paris.

The remaining nobility may be conveniently divided into two broad categories: those carrying specific titles (for example, viscount, *marquis*), and those bearing unspeci-fied rank but with stated or implied noble status. The latter group polarizes into members of the traditional warrior caste and characters to whom a "qualité" is attrib-uted, but obviously not a high dignity.

Only two characters in Molière are true "gentilshommes": Dom Juan (by implication, as Done Elvire's brothers, who refer to themselves as "gentilshommes," place Don Juan in the same caste); and Adraste, the "gentilhomme français" of **Le Sicilien**. At the opposite end of noble dignity we find lower-ranking members of the gentry, people of "quality" but not carrying named rank. Thus the mincing Climène in **La Critique de l'Ecole des femmes,** and the poetaster Oronte from **Le Misanthrope**.

In between we find the largest category, characters with noble title: One count, the cultivated D'orante of **Le Bour-geois gentilhomme** (also described as a "grand seigneur"—an indication of the status we are to attribute to him); two viscounts (we may dismiss of course the "Vicomte de Jodelet" in **Les Précieuses ridicules**); Angélique's courtly suitor Clitandre in **George Dandin,** and the well-bred Cléante of **La Comtesse d'Escarbagnas**. There is one *chevalier,* Molière's spokesman Dorante in **La Critique de l'Ecole des femmes**. No fewer than four *marquis* pop-ulate Molière's theater (not counting the fraudulent "Mar-quis de Mascarille" in **Les Précieuses ridicules**): Acaste and Clitandre from **Le Misanthrope,** the anonymous *marquis* from **La Critique de l'Ecole des femmes,** and the same character as he reappears in **L'Impromptu de Ver-sailles,** together with yet another *marquis*. (Monsieur de Sotenville, it will be recalled, is a baron, the only one in Molière's theater.) Among female characters, we find two *marquises* (Dorimène, the lady courted by Monsieur Jour-dain) and the prolongation of Climène in **L'Impromptu de Versailles** where a specific rank is added to her "qual-ité." (We remember that the heroine of **La Comtesse d'Escarbagnas** is a Countess.)

To round out this inventory of rank in Molière, we should note that there is only one reference to office-holding. Cléonte in **Le Bourgeois gentilhomme** disclaims being a "gentilhomme" and scorns those who pretend to such rank, but he insists that his parents held "charges" Cléonte could thus belong, say, to the *noblesse de robe,* but, significantly, no title is indicated. There are as well four memorable examples of "double identity" whereby a low-born person claims a fraudulent title: Arnolphe/Monsieur de la Souche in *L'Ecole des femmes,* as well as the allusion to Thomas Corneille/Monsieur de l'Isle in the same play; George Dandin/Monsieur de la Dandinière in *George Dandin,* and Monsieur Jourdain/Mamamouchi (in the latter case the bourgeois is the victim and the beneficiary of a deception). A fifth, more marginal example could be added: Tartuffe's pretention to "gentilhomme" status (vv. 494-5).

So far we have confined ourselves to precise references to rank, merited, undeserved, or fraudulent as the title may be according to the various cases. But external attributes, life-style could denote a high position in society as well. Several families depicted by Molière could well belong to the gentry or the recently ennobled; such householders as Orgon (*Tartuffe*) or Chrysale (*Les Femmes savantes*) obviously "live nobly"—they enjoy an opulent existence as *rentiers* which absolves them from all demeaning "work." Indeed, only one character from that stratum is shown as economically active: Harpagon, the miser, whose usury is clearly seen as a betrayal of status. A final complication may be noted from the engravings which accompany the 1682 edition of Molière's works. Even in a bourgeois milieu like that of *L'Avare,* Valère, Harpagon's *intendant,* is shown wearing a sword, a status symbol which, in theory at least, only a nobleman could carry.

The picture of rank in Molière admits therefore of some ambiguity; we are after all in the realm of comedy where inconsistencies and fanciful elements are bound to occur. But in the interests of clarity, I will confine my qualitative remarks to the empirically evident, the specific references to dignities.

It is obvious, first of all, that Molière does not idealize all bearers of rank. The *marquis* in particular—a high order in the actual *gentilhommerie*—is subject to extreme caricature, although his rank is never considered fraudulent. He has simply become a clown figure, just as in English Restoration comedy, the knight recurs as a ludicrous stock-type.

Even at the top of the scale, with Don Juan, we must speak of a portrait with many nuances: clear-sighted lucidity, bravery where lack of it would be *dérogeance* blends in Molière's hero with bluster, unfeeling egocentrism and disrespect. In his depiction of the marquise, Molière shows neat even-handedness: one (in *Le Bourgeois gentilhomme*) is a cultivated, well-bred lady, the other (*L'Impromptu de Versailles*) is a posturing *précieuse.* The most consistently favorable picture emerges from the counts, viscounts, and the *chevalier,* all seen as people of taste and discrimination, whatever their moral blemishes—one, the Clitandre of *George Dandin,* is endeavouring to seduce the peasant's wife, while the Dorante of *Le Bourgeois gentilhomme* shamelessly gulls his middle-class friend.

Like La Bruyère, then, Molière shows us a broad gallery of noblemen, some deserving their station and preroga-

tives, some farcically inept. But nowhere does the dramatist suggest that a character should be stripped of rank; nowhere does he challenge the right to hereditary title. But what of that other social reality, the large group of commoners ennobled in the past or the present by royal decree? We have seen that Molière makes only one passing reference to office-holding without suggesting any noble rank attached to it. Men of wealth who aspire to the Second Order he invariably derides as frauds guilty of absurd social pretensions—Arnolphe (and Thomas Corneille), Monsieur Jourdain, George Dandin. As Chrysalde exclaims to Arnolphe: "Quel abus de quitter le vrai nom de ses pères / Pour en vouloir prendre un bâti sur des chimères" (*L'Ecole des femmes,* vv. 175-6)—expensive "chimères" at that. The dramatist implies that one must be to the manner born, that the code of gentility cannot be learned (although rank alone does not guarantee genteel conduct!). Only one instance of extensive economic activity—Harpagon's money-lending in *L'Avare*—occurs in all of Molière. It is in this respect particularly that the dramatist blurs the realities of his time. Loans, especially to the crown, were made by the wealthy at all levels of the hierarchy, and Louis XIV was forced by his grandiose projects and costly wars to resort more and more to deficit financing. We have already noted the proliferation of functions and titles by which commoners acquired instant de jure presence in the Second Order. It is this shift which Molière all but ignores in his theater. In short, he seems to reflect the prejudices of the old nobility and their refusal to grant respectability to a new title, however firm its legal foundation.

It is beyond the scope of this paper to discuss the Third Estate in any detail. But when Molière represents it, the perspective is always that of this aristocracy. Servants may be perceptive and well-intentioned, but their speech and manners mark them as social inferiors. Peasants, such as those portrayed in *Dom Juan,* are uncouth and infantile creatures. Representatives of the middle class are labelled patronizingly as "bons bourgeois," ignorant, tyrannical and mean-spirited, incapable of the refined life-style of the happy few. Even fully-fleshed burgher characters like Arnolphe and Monsieur Jourdain are portrayed as inextricably enmeshed in their own inborn mediocrity.

When one adds to the picture of the Second Order these features of the Third Estate, it becomes evident that Molière presents society as largely fixed and immutable. The bourgeois belong forever to the Third Estate, and all attempts to escape upward are doomed to ridicule and failure. The nobility is insulated and protected by its long-standing titles, even if some of its members do not live up to aristocratic expectations. Such is Molière's theatrical image, then, so at variance with a fluid and ambiguous reality, a dynamic, shifting amalgam of orders and interests, characterized especially by a moneyed middle class on the rise and anxious to obtain status and privilege. While social climbing was hedged in by all sorts of strictures, the eroding boundary between the Second and Third Orders made it possible.

Given this distortion of social realities, it is quite proper,

I think, to label Molière's theater as basically reactionary; the vision of society depicted is stratified, with each class in its eternal place, and with an uncontaminated nobility on top. Molière, like La Bruyère, seems to express a conservative reaction against forces pressing upward upon the Second Order and threatening to transform it.

Yet Molière's plays were successful with an audience which reflected almost the full gamut of his society—royalty, *les grands,* the gentry, the ennobled parvenu, as well as various sub-groups of the despised Third Estate. How could middle-class merchants, speculators, nouveaux-riches, and instant nobles derive mirth from a theater which dismissed their claim to status, which relegated them implicitly to mockery and oblivion? Here we leave the empirical for the speculative. It seems to me, first of all, that the human race has a great capacity for detachment when it comes to the depiction of its faults. As Sartre said somewhere, in tragedy we see ourselves, in comedy we see others. No doubt the garishly attired social climber of Molière's time, fresh from the purchase of an expensive title, took great mirth in the portrait of a Monsieur Jourdain.

Yet something else comes to mind. Supposing Molière had portrayed an open society, where the Arnolphes and the Jourdains could acquire discretion and taste by proper schooling and penetrate with full juridical *and* social credentials an upper class ready to accept them? What if everyone in our profession received Guggenheim fellowships and honorary degrees? The value of an honor is directly proportional to its rarity, or, to paraphrase a quip from Gilbert and Sullivan, "when everyone is somebody, then no one's anybody."

Viewed then from another angle, Molière's theater could well present a balanced picture of his time. While leaving the true nobility secure in its traditional ranks, he collaborates in a sense with the newly titled by endowing their status with a mystique of non-accessibility. The more difficult the jump may be seen to be and the rarer the success it betokens, the more value it will have. If a bourgeois who tries to become a gentlemen fails in comedy, the one who makes it in real life can only congratulate himself on a singular and well-deserved success.

A reactionary theater? An accommodating one? If we recall the dictionary definitions quoted earlier, reaction means resistance to social change, an allegiance to "a former and usually outmoded political or social order or policy." The order presented by Molière was surely out-of-date, an apparent reaction to strong forces shaping a new social reality. But in times of change we need perhaps a reassuring image of stability and permanence to help us digest threatening innovations. Thus the ideological content of Molière's theater could be less a political stance than a comforting statement that all is well offered to a society poised on the threshold of momentous changes.

Mitchell Greenberg (essay date 1992)

SOURCE: "Molière's *Tartuffe* and the Scandal of Insight," in *Subjectivity and Subjugation in Seventeenth-Century Drama and Prose: The Family Romance of French Classicism,* Cambridge University Press, 1992, pp. 113-40.

[*In the following excerpt, Greenberg offers a psychoanalytic explanation for the fearful reaction against* Le Tartuffe *during the seventeenth-century.*]

Unquestionably **Le Tartuffe** is Molière's most scandalous comedy. From its creation at Versailles as part of the royal festivities known as the "Plaisirs de l'Ile Enchantée" in May of 1664 to its withdrawal from the stage and the royal government's refusal to allow its public performance for a period of several years, the play, in its different versions, ignited a debate rarely paralleled in the annals of the French stage. During the period of its prohibition, Molière, his supporters and enemies engaged in heated controversy over the real or imagined attack on piety and "dévots," and over the social, moral and ethical role of the theater in society. Until its rehabilitation in 1669, the play, perhaps more than any other of the seventeenth century, generated a dizzying whirlwind of charges and countercharges that clearly situates it as the focal point of an entire epistemological dilemma, of a sensitive, overly charged threat to all social order, to, even (if we listen to the ravings of Pierre Roullé) the invasion of the well-ordered world of ecclesiastical and monarchal order by the "satanic": Molière was accused of being "un démon vêtu de chair et habillé en homme."

The nature of this scandal, the way it polarized opinion in the small but acutely politicized world of the court and of the Parisian intelligentsia, may strike modern readers (as surely as it appears to have struck Molière and his supporters) as exaggerated, but queasily disturbing. What was really at stake in this uproar? Was it merely a cabal of religious and political fanatics bent on destroying a playwright who catered too intimately to the whims of a young, undocile king? Or, on the other hand, is it possible that such men as Lamoignon and Péréfixe, the archbishop of Paris, actually saw through the "appearances" of religious scandal to a more profound, more unsettling, less containable disruption that the comedy sets in motion?

Molière claims in his preface that it is not possible to confuse the truly pious with his hypocrite, since, as he states, he has taken all necessary precautions lest this confusion occur:

> j'ai mis tout l'art et tous les soins qu'il m'a été possible pour distinguer le personnage de l'Hypocrite d'avec celui du vrai Dévot. J'ai employé pour cela deux actes entiers, à préparer la venue de mon scélérat. Il ne tient pas un seul moment l'auditeur en balance; on le connaît aux marques que je lui donne et, d'un bout à l'autre, il ne dit pas un mot, il ne fait pas une action, qui ne peigne aux spectateurs le caractère d'un méchant, et ne fasse éclater celui du véritable homme de bien que je lui oppose.
>
> (*Préface,* ed. Rat, p.682)

Nevertheless, despite this and similar denegations, the confusion occurs, occurs with a vengeance and a fury that betray more than just bad faith. The real nature of the confusion seems, and of course this is not novel, to be less a matter of intention less, that is, the scandal of the author's avowed purpose in composing his play—than a scandal of interpretation, of subjectivity, of the subjectivity that inheres in all representation, and the representation that constitutes subjectivity.

This, of course, is what the more subtle censors of the play knew. It would be an act of extraordinary hubris on our part to think that Bourdaloue, for instance, was less perspicacious than we. It was simply that he saw the threat of the play as a real danger to an entire epistemological system, in which not only his religion but his being (as if one could separate the two) were invested. And in this he and his allies were, after all, right. They did see what Molière and the others didn't: that when a work questions the foundations of knowledge, those signifying systems that define certain supposedly "natural" institutions the monarchy, the church, the family—and shows their predicates to be vulnerable, the entire edifice of the social life they subtend is shaken to the point that its eventual collapse becomes inevitable.

Tartuffe's scandal, therefore, is the scandal of literature, of representation. What the uproar over the play reveals is perhaps the first modern (even though unthought-of as such)'battle waged between a totalitarian impulse towards domination and mastery—towards the reification of the Law of the Father that at the beginning of Louis's personal reign was too shakily in place not to resort to overt displays of its own insecurity and a signifying system, a semiosis, that by its very nature cannot be contained in an univocal way. In this, then, Molière's play is symptomatic of a much greater threat, of a far more compelling scandal than the ostensible attack on religion. Religion is only a symptom, a particularly acute and sensitive symptom, of one of the ideological apparatuses the play invades. It would, however, be a mistake only to look at the individual symptom and ignore that symptom's insertion in the greater whole. The scandal of *Tartuffe* is its attack on the totalizing ideology that underlies the world of the "ancien régime," an attack waged by the indeterminacy of its own psycho-semiotic structures.

In order to understand the complex nature of the play's scandal, of the scandal of literature, we would do well to turn to the text and see how it inscribes within itself, and comments upon, its own scandalous plot. The word "scandal" appears twice in the play, twice in one of the most important scenes (IV, i) and both times in the mouth of Tartuffe. In response to Cléante's plea that he reestablish peace between Orgon and his son, Tartuffe responds:

> Après son action, qui n'eut jamais d'égale,
> Le commerce entre nous porterait du scandale . .
>
> (IV, i, 1209-1210)

and:

> Mais après le scandale et l'affront d'aujourd'hui,
> Le Ciel n'ordonne pas que je vive avec lui.
>
> (IV, i, 1231-1232)

For Tartuffe, Damis's abortive attempt to reveal to his father Tartuffe's lust, the sexuality that threatens the stability of Orgon's marriage and that usurps his own sexual position as master of his wife and head of his household, is the scandal in the play. The outburst has, as we know, a contrary effect: Orgon, taken in by Tartuffe, banishes Damis from his presence, from his house (we shall return to this important act later on). The scandal of the play is the revelation from Tartuffe's own mouth although he uses it as a deflection of his attack on Orgon as husband, and his manipulation of him as father. The scandal which Tartuffe's self-defense underlines is, therefore, not just a supposed attack on piety (although it is that too) but his undermining of the family, that unit upon which all social, political and religious cohesion is based.

Le Tartuffe is central to Molière's production, not only in time but more importantly in the way it concentrates all the concerns of both the farces and the "serious" comedies on the dilemma of the family. Of all Molière's plays, and one might look even more far afield into the familial world of Cornelian or Racinian tragedy, we have no more complete an example of family (grandmother, mother, father, sister/daughter, brother/son, uncle) on the seventeenth-century stage. The play begins and ends with all the members of the Orgon household family either on stage or invoked on stage. The comedy thus repeats, in its structural integrity and in its narrative circularity, the very closure of the family as a fixed immutable unit that the machinations of hypocrisy would attack and subvert.

As the curtain rises this attack is already underway. What the crisis of Mme Pernelle's visit and her verbal onslaught serve to reveal is that an invasion of the family, its decomposition, has begun and that the very center of the familial fortress, the place of the father, is vacant. Although the banter between Mme Pernelle, a figure of both comic and terrifying proportions, and the members of her son's household constantly undercuts the initial impact of this absence, an absence that is articulated either as an abdication or an usurpation, this ambivalent state of familial affairs has far-reaching consequences for the social order as a whole.

Borrowing the term *oïkodespotès* from J. Habermas who uses it to describe familial-economic organization in Greek society [in *L'Espace public*], I would suggest that the word fits admirably into our own purposes as a way of introducing the socio-sexual dimension of the role of the Father in Molière's comedy. It combines both the etymological connotations of house, home (and by extension husbandry, "household-economy") with the term for controller, ruler. This latter term echoes with the proleptic resonance of "despot." It is precisely the absence of both these things that Mme Pernelle laments. What she finds most distressing in Orgon's household is the lack of any economy; all of her criticism points to disorder ("la cour du roi Pétaud"), excess, and spending, be it the excess of language ("Vous êtes, ma mie, une fille suivante / Un peu trop forte en gueule"), the lack of being properly "rangé" ("Vous êtes un sot en trois lettres, mon fils . . . Vous preniez tout l'air d'un méchant garnement, / Et ne lui donneriez jamais que du tourment") or simply financial irresponsibility ("Vous êtes dépensière; et cet état me blesse, / Que vous alliez vêtue ainsi qu'une princesse."). What Mme Pernelle notices, and is frightened by, is that this family is no longer the bourgeois unit she desires. Orgon's family has fallen out of order and into a chaos that frightens and threatens her. It has left the realm of hoarding, enclosure and economy for the more threatening world of "dépense." Confronted with this disorder, a disorder where she no longer has a place, which excludes her, it is not surprising that she, alone among the different members of the family, shares her son's infatuation with Tartuffe. Rather than an usurpation of her son, she (mistakenly) sees Tartuffe as an extension of him, as his surrogate who will aid in the restoration of order in the tumult that surrounds her. In a sense, therefore, but in a very overdetermined sense, Mme Pernelle is placed in the position of appealing to the mistaken unity of Orgon/Tartuffe, which she sees as the Father, that is, the ruler of the house (the *oïkodespotès*). The desire to be tyrannized, to be subjected to the "despot" in order to find one's place and have one's being ratified, is only the first of a series of sexual/political poles that the comedy of *Tartuffe* sets in motion as the play begins. Mme Pernelle ardently desires her own subjection to the Law of the Father and his representative as the only salvation both for the family and for herself.

In a perverse reversal, which nevertheless retains its comic thrust, the members of the household also see Tartuffe as a despot. The words used to describe his invasion of the family are clearly charged with political overtones bringing into the center of the domestic realm those searing debates about just and unjust monarchy that so actively engaged political thinkers and writers during the premiership of Richelieu and the troubles of the Fronde. "Un pouvoir tyrannique," "contrôler tout," "s'impatronniser," and "faire le maître" point to him as having taken the place of the rightful head of the household. In this sense we are, or rather the text is, drawing a fine line of distinction in the world of patriarchy between the rights and rewards of a legal, benevolent monarchical/familial power, and the perversion of that power, its usurpation and corruption as "tyranny."

Clearly, then, the play begins as a debate, a debate between the "Mother" who represents a bourgeois order of economy and the concomitant desire for containment (one might even say confinement), setting off one of the poles, the masochistic, around which the whirlwind of scandal will revolve; and the other, the order of the family as "dépense," but *dépense* that is coded as freedom (perhaps the intrusion, the comic intrusion into this bourgeois household of nobiliary pretensions?). And, at the beginning, as we've seen, the center of the family is already absent. Both physically and metaphysically, the role and place of the Father, the pivotal structure around which the family

and thus the State are organized, is empty. It is this absence of the father and the usurpation of his place that sets the play in motion, aspirating into its center, in ever more complex levels of sexual and political disarray, those signifying systems the family both anchors and naturalizes. At the same time the disarray in this family signals a general threat to society. We must not forget that in the tightly structured world of patriarchal monarchy, one can never attack the father without in some way committing a crime of "lèse-majesté," Every father in his household is the mirror of the King, the "father of the Nation," in his kingdom.

The *Tartuffe,* then, as comedy, situates itself within the same anxiety as the major tragedies of the period, the anxiety of patricide, the desire/fear of the father, of the Father as object both of love and of aggression, and the greater fear, the unthinkable of seventeenth-century French political musings, of a society unhinged from the father's Law, a society which abandons the father and kills its King. It would seem hasty, therefore, to define comedy, in its opposition to tragedy, as "the triumph of the son over the father" [as stated by Mavron in *Psychocritique du genre comique*] . . . that opposition may work (or be made to work) only in some abstract psychoanalytic framework which ignores the mutual imbrication of ideology and the unconscious and where, more to the point, in that psycho-ideology, the son is always also the father and vice-versa.

The political role of the father in this play is inseparable from his sexual role, and both are necessary for the grounding of his relation to his world, and to that world's ability to define itself. It will not surprise us, therefore, to learn that the political disarray into which Orgon's family has been thrown immediately takes on sexual overtones is immediately sexualized by the comic rhetoric of Dorine:

> Mais il est devenu comme un homme hébété
> Depuis que de Tartuffe on le voit entêté;
> Il l'appelle son frère, et l'aime dans son âme
> Cent fois plus qu'il ne fait mère, fils, fille, et femme.
> C'est de tous ses secrets l'unique confident,
> Et de ses actions le directeur prudent;
> Il le choie, il l'embrasse, et pour une maîtresse
> On ne saurait, je pense, avoir plus de tendresse;
> . . .
> Enfin il en est fou; c'est son tout, son héros. . .

> (I, ii, 183-190; 195)

Although Dorine's explanation of the new state of affairs of the Orgon household is meant to appear funny, the connotations underlying her speech betray a sexual malaise that the comedy can only hesitantly keep at bay. All the words that Dorine uses to describe the indescribable, to indicate what has suddenly gone wrong with Orgon, point to a sexual attraction that cannot be normalized. What we learn about the relation between the two men is that, from Orgon's side at least, it is a desire for totalization. Tartuffe has taken the place of all his other affections. Orgon treats him with more respect, attention and fondness than if he were a "mistress," and finally, for Orgon, Tartuffe is his "tout" (everything, but more resonantly, his "all," his plenitude).

The relation between Tartuffe and Orgon has been analyzed and commented upon by all those critics who have attempted to explain the play; L. Gossman comes closest [in his *Merand Masks*] to unraveling the complexity and the danger of this liaison by pointing to its dialectical nature:

> Orgon . . . must believe in his idol himself; he too must feel himself seduced, captivated, carried away, not indeed by any deliberate effort on the part of Tartuffe, but by the very nature of Tartuffe's superior being. At the same time, however, since he wants to have this idol for himself, to enjoy through him the absolute superiority that he recognized in him, he must attach him to himself, win him over, make him into an inalienable part of himself. He must in short seduce Tartuffe.

While Gossman's own discussion is based on a finely tuned analysis of the subject-object dialectic that Tartuffe and Orgon refigure, a dialectic that, as we see in the above quotation, his own vocabulary sexualizes, his analysis does not explore the theoretical implications of its own insights. It will appear obvious that the dialectic that is established between the two men enters into the dynamics of mastery and submission, as that dynamic functions as a sexual, that is a homoerotic, attraction. I would not want to reduce the complexity of this textual nexus to a banal discussion of what was obviously unthinkable for the characters and audience of the play: Orgon is not (just), as a character, a representation of repressed homosexuality (to Cléante's question what can he possibly see in Tartuffe, the only answer Orgon can come up with, is the erratic, ejaculative "C'est un homme . . . qui, . . . ha! un homme . . . un homme enfin"). Rather, it seems to me that in the constellation of sexual and political forces the play, as representation of patriarchal society, sets in motion, we must see this homoerotic element as meshing into a larger circle of ideological forces: forces of representation, forces of normalization and of verisimilitude, that constitute the essential parameters of power, and therefore meaning, in the comedy.

Obviously, the very definition of ideology implies its invisibility: ideology is what cannot be directly seen or perceived by the members of any given society, but which nevertheless controls and directs what they apprehend as the limits and possibilities of their own subjective insertion into the "real" that surrounds and eludes them. It should come as no surprise, therefore, were I to suggest that the unraveling of the text's inner network reveals the blind spot of its ideological investments. I would like to suggest that at the very center of the complex textual network there exists a "master code" that permits the functioning of all the signifying systems in the play, that includes in itself the indeterminability of both the sexual and the political investments of the comedy, that accounts

largely for the comedy itself of the play, and finally that engages the characters in the ambiguous dialectics of seeming and being, of truth and hypocrisy, that the theater (as a particularly overdetermined instance of representation) both affirms and denies in its own dialectical seduction of the spectators by the spectacle. The single most insistent linguistic sign in the comedy of *Tartuffe* is the polysemous indeterminacy of the verb "voir" with all the echoes, literal and metaphoric, attached to it. Lest this affirmation seem hasty, I would like to remind us that Molière himself, in the several prefaces and "placets au roi" that he placed before the published version of *Tartuffe,* engages our interpretation in a network of visual metaphors by his own rhetorical figures:

> Voici une comédie dont on a fait beaucoup de bruit . . . Les marquis, les précieuses, les cocus et les médecins ont souffert doucement qu'on les ait représentés, et ils ont fait semblant de se divertir, avec tout le monde, des peintures que l'on a faites d'eux. . . .
>
> (*Préface,* p. 681)

> Le devoir de la comédie étant de corriger les hommes en les divertissant, j'ai cru que, dans l'emploi où je me trouve, je n'avais rien de mieux à faire que d'attaquer par des peintures ridicules les vices de mon siècle. . . .
>
> (*Premier placet,* p. 686)

From the beginning, then, Molière describes his play as a "painting" in the metaphorical sense that word carries as a (visual) form of representation. At the same time, in these same defenses of his text, the play is of course called a "poem":

> il ne faut qu'ôter le voile de l'équivoque, et regarder ce qu'est la comédie en soi, pour voir si elle est condamnable. On connaîtra, sans doute, que n'étant autre chose qu'un poème ingénieux, qui, par des leçons agréables, reprend les défauts des hommes. . . .
>
> (*Préface,* p. 683)

There is a slippage in Molière's own rhetoric between words and paintings, between the lexical and the visual, whose difference is erased in their communality as representation. This effacement is interesting, if only when we remember to what degree the study of "optics" invaded seventeenth-century thought, philosophy and representation. The most celebrated example is, of course, the *Discours de la Méthode,* which was originally a preface to Descartes's own work on optics. It is precisely this slippage between the lexical and the visual that coheres in *Tartuffe* around the paradigmatic chain of the verb "voir," which in its several and ambivalent meanings engages the very heart of the debate raging around the *Tartuffe* as a form of representation: it is this ambivalence that engages the seduction of theater, in its collapsing "truth and illusion" into representation that allows for the impossible battle of interpretation that the *Tartuffe* spawned and which has not ceased to the present day.

The verb "voir," because of its constant oscillation between literal and metaphorical connotations, because of the easy slippage between "seeing" and "knowing," is essential for understanding the way diverse textual networks of the comedy slide into each other creating an homogeneous representation of the "real" of the text. The dynamics of vision, where vision is evoked as an appeal to some available "truth," engages the heart of the play's dilemma between being and seeming that is central to the controversy over religious piety and hypocrisy. It is also imperative for understanding the relation between sexuality and subjectivity as they are revealed and determined by the characters' relation to the scopic drive as it meanders through and across the text, joining and separating the main characters first in a dialectics of voyeurism and exhibitionism, then in this dialectics' imbrication in a thematics of narcissism. Finally, the verb serves as a pivot in the comedy of the play, uniting the spectators to the characters, thus engaging the very dynamics of theater as they are enmeshed in the ideology of patriarchy. In a world of appearances, in a world that exists in order to know and constantly reaffirm the "truth" - that is, in a world that needs constantly to be able to confirm its own sexual and political a-prioris, that needs to dissect reality down to its most indivisible particles, down to the most unassailable grounds, in order thereupon to anchor the subject of this world - seeing is invoked in all its supposed transparency, in all its supposed ability to discern reality from mere appearance. In this supposed visual anchoring of the world, the characters of the *Tartuffe* are set adrift, unhinged by the very ambivalence of the word, of the act, that they invoke for their own salvation,

As Jacqueline Rose reminds us in *Sexuality in the Field of Vision,* from the very beginnings of Freud's explorations of the unconscious, of his discovery of the role that sexuality, both repressed and conscious, plays in determining the way the human being comes to situate him/herself in the symbolic gendering of the body, visual representation plays a key role:

> Freud often related the question of sexuality to that of visual representation . . . He would take as his model little scenarios, or the staging of events, which demonstrated the complexity of an essentially visual space, moments in which perception founders . . . or in which the pleasure in looking tips over into the register of excess . . . The sexuality lies less in the content of what is seen than in the subjectivity of the viewer, in the relationship between what is looked at and the developing sexual knowledge of the child. The relationship between viewer and scene is always one of fracture, partial identification, pleasure and distrust. As if Freud found the aptest analogy for the problem of our identity as human subjects in failures of vision or in the violence which can be done to an image as it offers itself to view.

Vision is always excessive, always a too-much of pleasure that threatens the subject with dispersion, fragmentation. It is both constitutive of the suture of the imaginary and symbolic registers that situate the subject along the axes of gendering and disruptive of any stable fixing of this gandering. It is always what attempts to "elude"

castration and what finally lures the subject into the Law of sexual difference. Paradoxically, the force of the visual, the desire of the scopic drive, is part of the very forging of sexual identity which nevertheless remains insecure, unstable, exposed to the excessive thrust of the drive.

The odd couple that Tartuffe and Orgon present to the incomprehension of their entourage can be read as but two poles of the visual dialectic. On the one hand Orgon seems most radically marked as a desire to see, as a *Schaulust,* with all the connotations that term has as a particularly coded "masculine," drive: it is a desire to possess, to know, to penetrate; a desire to cut off, divide and make order. It is also (and this will not surprise us), on a metaphysical level, the desire to find an integrity of being, an apprehension of the self as entire that is, in diverse ways, essential to all of Molière's (male) protagonists. It is the desire for integrity that situates Molière's protagonists firmly within a patriarchal economy based precisely on the dichotomization of a "full," "self-sufficient" masculinity, always threatened by the menace of castration, and the "lacking" (because already castrated), excessive economy imputed to "femininity."

In this economy, Tartuffe, in relation to Orgon, exists not so much to see as to be seen, and more to the point, to see himself being seen. He is pure projection, constantly offering himself to the vision of the other(s), either actually, or metaphorically in his rhetoric (and it is here that the slippage between seeing and saying, between the visual and the lexical, that we have already noticed in the *préfaces* returns in the dynamics of the comedy. I will return to this presently.) He is, in his constant self-positioning, in the way that he is always aware of how he is being seen, in the way he sees himself seeing himself, a perfect example of the "feminine" as J. Lacan would define it.

This feminine, based as it is on the illusion of vision, on the vision of an illusion, is incorporated by Lacan into what he calls (following J. Rivière) the dialectics of the "masquerade." This masquerade is the feminine holding up to the masculine what it wants to see, the masculine participating in this same masquerade by pretending to give the feminine what it wants to have. Together they form the illusory vision of sexual complementarity. In this masquerade of sexual illusions the feminine serves as a form of *trompe-l'œil* for the masculine.

None of the members of Orgon's household can understand, any more than we, the hold Tartuffe has over their father. From the valiant bourgeois he was during the troubles of the Fronde, doing his duty, defending his king, he has undergone a radical change that has left him "hébété." His stubborn refusal to see what all the members of his household see is, for them, inexplicable. They can only articulate his new state as a bewitchment, a spell. His relation to Tartuffe is described as a "caprice," an "enchantement," a "charme," all words that point to something that escapes the reality of their world, that conjures up a vocabulary of magic, of sorcery, in its attempt at explaining the inexplicable. At the same time these words come from and share the traditional Petrarchan vocabulary of *innamoramento,* thus carrying with them the shudder of a love that is not natural, that has strayed from its proper object and come, inverted, into the space of domestic intimacy. How can we understand Orgon's passionate attachment to Tartuffe, his "blindness" ("votre aveuglement fait que je vous admire. . . ") except in the terms in which it is presented to us, except as a visual dysfunction? Orgon, we are told, is "ébloui par un faux éclat," seduced by "cent dehors fardés."

Orgon is the prisoner of a vision, of an image, but at the same time he is primarily trapped within this vision as it focuses on his own desire. In his conversation with Cléante (I, v), Orgon narrates to him his first encounter with Tartuffe, a narration that is entirely inscribed within a visual framework:

> Ha! si vous aviez vu comme j'en fis rencontre,
> . . .
> Chaque jour à l'église il venait, d'un air doux,
> Tout vis-à-vis de moi se mettre à deux genoux.
> Il attirait les yeux de l'assemblée entière
> Par l'ardeur dont au Ciel il poussait sa prière;
> Il faisait des soupirs, de grands élancements,
> Et baisait humblement la terre à tous moments.
>
> (I, v, 281, 283-288)

The most remarkable revelation in this narration of his originary *innamoramento* is its obsessive, repetitive nature it is an image that occurred "chaque jour" so that in a sense, each sighting is a re-sighting, a recapture of the gaze that is not allowed to wander but always comes back to its own point of departure, and that point inscribes itself in this dialectic as a desire for mirroring, a desire in which what the subject is "looking for" is somehow its own projection reflected in the returned glance of the object. What seduces Orgon is the reflection of himself which Tartuffe presents to him by creating himself as his mirror "Tout vis-à-vis de moi se mettre à deux genoux." In another context, N. Gross tells us [in *From Gesture to Idea*] why this positioning, in a church, is particularly remarkable: "Tartuffe seems to face Orgon, while his gestures of mortification and worship seem addressed to Orgon, drawing attention to both of them and distracting from the service at the altar." In fact, Tartuffe, by making a spectacle of himself, that is by positioning himself as Orgon's reflection, his mirror, positions this reflection as a vision of unity, of integrity, as the lure of the subject who is complete. He does become Orgon's god. He becomes his double/other, the image of completeness, of wholeness, that ensnares and traps Orgon, a creature of desire and therefore of lack (that this lack be interpreted in spiritual terms, or not, is not the point). Tartuffe entraps his prey, in such a way as to pleasure him: Orgon claims that in his subjugation to Tartuffe ("qui suit ses leçons") he both becomes another and "savors" a profound tranquility ("goûte une paix profonde"). It is this unfathomable repose that most notably marks the aphanisis of the wounded subject we must suppose Orgon to be, his volatilization into a nirvana-esque (re-)union with his own desire. Paradoxically, this "quietude" may be com-

pared in religious terms to a "ravissement," to a dispossession of the self and to its integration in an image in which it exults. In this way, we may compare the ecstatic reaction of Orgon to the famous "infant" described by Lacan jubilating at his captured image in the mirror:

> Il y suffit de comprendre le stade du miroir comme une identification au sens plein que l'analyse donne à ce terme: à savoir la transformation produite chez le sujet quand il assume une image. . . .
>
> L'assomption jubilatoire de son image spéculaire par l'être encore plongé dans l'impuissance motrice . . . nous paraîtra dès lors manifester en une situation exemplaire la matrice symbolique où le "je" se précipite en une forme primordiale. . . .

What, of course, is significant in this jubilation, in this capture of an image of wholeness, is that it precipitates an illusory apprehension of subjectivity as integrity. For any reader of Molière it will come as no surprise that Orgon is just one in a declension of "partial" characters who are problematic precisely because they desire integrity, as does perhaps the whole of the Molierian corpus, while that integrity constantly eludes them. It would not be too much of an exaggeration to suggest that this is perhaps the underlying dynamic of all of Molière's great creations, all those plays that supposedly represent the Classical ideal. Think of Arnolphe, Argan, Dom Juan, Alceste, all men, all undone by a flaw that sunders them, renders them "childlike" and therefore comic. This flaw is exaggerated by the very laughter they spawn, which is the laughter of the other to whose place they aspire, though it is forever denied them. We must, therefore see this jubilation as complicitous with the defeat of the integral subject they would be, because it is both jubilatory and mortiferous. The reflection of the mirror stage condemns the subject, the core of whose "ego" is herein constituted, to its own alienation as a necessarily fractured subjectivity. Before Lacan, Freud had warned us of both the jubilatory and the nefarious attraction of doubling. On the one hand the double can represent an enhancing of the ego. On the other, it also signals the ego's destruction:

> This invention of doubling as a preservation against extinction has its counterpart in the language of dreams. . . . Such ideas, however, have sprung from the soil of unbounded self-love, from the primary narcissism which holds sway in the mind of the child as in that of primitive man, and when this stage has been left behind the double takes on a different aspect. From having been an assurance of immortality, he becomes the ghastly harbinger of death.

Tartuffe serves as Orgon's mirror, serves as his double, his completion. He lures him into the seduction of the imaginary, and there traps him, clasps him to himself in an erotic embrace, which like all eroticism has a double valency: both and at the same time exalting and deathly. It is in this visual embrace that Orgon's subjectivity is produced, whole, illusory, as subjugation. Orgon is subjugated to the illusion of Tartuffe as masquerade. There is a mise-en-abyme of subjectivity that only starts here. But it is one way for us to understand the desperate (funny?) attachment Orgon demonstrates towards Tartuffe, to understand the pathos in his cry, "Non, vous demeurerez: il y va de ma vie," when Tartuffe pretends he will leave the household. For in this "cri de cœur" we hear the fear and anxiety of a subject who knows that without his mirror he no longer exists, no longer knows the sweetness of "une paix profonde" that he can only find, not with his family, not with his wife, but with his "semblable," his "frère."

Only when we understand the totalizing, death-dealing capture of Orgon by Tartuffe can we begin to understand the enormous threat Tartuffe, as masquerade, as hypocrite, and as supreme narcissist, presents for the safety and stability of Orgon's, and the King's, family. Narcissism, from its very inception as myth, is intimately related to, cannot be separated from, death, and that death is itself carried along, supported, by the fascination of the visual/image.

Orgon believes what he sees: "Je suis votre valet, et crois les apparences," he tells his wife. Orgon's blustering betrays one of the valences of narcissism the childish belief in the power of one's own ego to dominate the world, to create reality ("Mais je veux que cela soit une vérité," he tells his daughter, "Et c'est assez pour vous que je l'aie arrêté") that in its violent, imperialistic form meshes perfectly with the greater, more perverse narcissism of Tartuffe. Tartuffe's narcissism, his ability to project an image of himself that is totally enclosed on itself, an image that exists without a discernible desire that would betray its lack, its point of fracture, is best realized in his production of himself as a work of art, as an artifice, and finally, as far as Orgon is concerned, as a perfect "trompe-l'œil," in the sense that J. Baudrillard has given that term:

> On sent que ces objets se rapprochent du trou noir d'où vient la réalité, le monde réel, le temps ordinaire. Cet effet de décentrement en avant, cette avancée d'un miroir d'objets à la rencontre d'un sujet, c'est, sous l'espèce d'objets anodins, l'apparition du double qui crée cet effet de séduction, de saisissement caractéristique du trompe-l'œil: vertige tactile qui retrace le vœu fou du sujet d'étreindre sa propre image, et par là même de s'évanouir. Car la réalité n'est saisissante que lorsque notre identité s'y perd, ou lorsqu'elle ressurgit comme notre propre mort hallucinée.

Tartuffe's entire being exists as a work for the eyes. For him, to be is to be seen. He exists only insofar as he can enter into and colonize the visual field of the other, draw that other into his artifice, and there kill him.

Certainly his entrance on to the stage, an entrance that has been, as Molière reminds us ("J'ai employé pour cela deux actes entiers à préparer la venue de mon scélérat," *Préface,* p.682), minutely prepared, is only the most obvious indication that Tartuffe exists to satisfy the appetite of the eye. Molière inscribes one of his very few didascalia "Tartuffe, apercevant Dorine" to tell us how Tartuffe is to make his entrance. Tartuffe enters the world of the play not only with all eyes fixed upon him, but knowing that those eyes are there, knowing that they are waiting for him, knowing that he is there to satisfy the appetite of those eyes. Tartuffe enters the universe of the play, and the world of the playgoers, seeing himself being seen. He is there to draw the eye's attention to himself, and by so doing, to trick it, to betray it: he offers himself as an image that passes itself off as real, as substantial, but which in reality is only a mirror, the eye caught in the game of seeming/being. Tartuffe's role, his enormous narcissistic production of himself, is precisely to situate himself in the field of vision of that (those) eye(s) and to hide/reveal by that visual seduction the artificiality (that is, the essence, as "art" artifact production) of the "world."

I have been attempting to describe the dialectics of mastery and subjugation that links Orgon to Tartuffe as a form of homosexuality subtended by the dynamics of seeing/being seen that is polarized in the couple they form. I would like to carry this dynamic one step further. I have intimated that Tartuffe is narcissistic in a way that would, in the ideology of patriarchy that informs this comedy, associate him with a perversely passive femininity. Even in his first "tête-à-tête" with Elmire even, that is, when he is alone for the first time with the object of his desire Tartuffe articulates his satisfaction through a strangely visual construction:

> J'en suis ravi de même, et sans doute il m'est doux,
> Madame, de me voir seul à seul avec vous.
> (III, iii, 899-900)

The self-enclosed reflexivity of the construction "me voir" points, it seems to me, to the essential feature of Tartuffe's self-perception, as a closed off, self-contained wholeness. It is this state that appears as a non-desirous being that works to entrap Orgon. This self-enclosure, which we have already noted in the didascalia, the way he enfolds the visual world on himself, creating himself, one could say, as the "visible spot (*tache*)" that ensnares the eye, reflects a narcissistic hold on the world that Freud associates primarily with "beautiful women, noble felines, and great criminals." This type of character has, we are told, "great attraction for those who have renounced part of their own narcissism and are in search of object-love" ("Narcissism," p. 89). Tartuffe's presentation of himself, his production of himself as image/lure, is therefore particularly attractive for Orgon. First because of the way this illusion of self-enclosure seduces him, but more importantly when we look behind the image to see (as A. Green reminds us), beyond the appearance, the invisible object whose lure exerts such seduction on the beholder.

I would like to suggest that behind the appearance of Tartuffe, behind Tartuffe as image, hides a more dangerous, more threatening fantasy, the fantasy of union. This fantasy is hinted at not only in Orgon's own words, "paix profonde," but also in Dorine's derision, "son tout," "son héros." This "hero" is, of course a mistress, and hides, I would suggest, the "image" of the One, towards which all narcissism tends as the pre-Oedipal unit of the child and mother. I am hinting at Tartuffe's seduction of Orgon being essentially the play of a certain desire for the Mother. (Let us remember that the words that describe Tartuffe, "gros," "gras," "le teint vermeil," as well as the scene in which these words occur a scene that associates Tartuffe with nourishment, the pleasure of ingestion lurk in the memory of the text as one more possible association to the maternal as both attractive and repulsive.) What this particular illusion of unity reminds us of is, paradoxically, the floating image of a stage of pre-sexuality, of an amorphous composite body that exists before the scission, before the imposition of the Law of the Father, and the child's entrance into sexual difference and into language that traduces that difference. Orgon is seduced by Tartuffe as image and this, I suggest, is the real danger of Tartuffe: the danger of the "imaginary" instance that coexists in a tenuous dialectic with the institution of the symbolic as the Law of the Father, and that represents for that law a destabilizing drive.

The character who is meant to represent Tartuffe's moral opposite, Cléante, is also, in terms of the visual imagery that dominates the rhetoric of the play, the most interesting for his completely opposite visual valency in the economy of the text. Whereas Tartuffe, as hypocrite, is characterized by his imaging of himself, his production of himself as artifact that forces its recognition in the play's field of vision, Cléante is characterized, ethically, by his invisibility. He is, he tells us, in his use of words, transparent:

> Et je vous ai trouvé.
> Pour vous en dire net ma pensée en deux mots.
>
> Je vous le dis encore, et parle avec franchise.

Cléante is clear and frank. In this he seems to be different from the other characters, who all exist in a universe of unclear signs, or at least in a world in which they are suspicious of their ability to interpret signs correctly. They would seem to represent a lingering malaise that signals us that for them, for the world of the play, for the world of Molière, the revolution in epistemology that (according to Foucault) was occurring at this time, carrying the world out of the order of resemblances and into the order of transparency, has not as yet taken place. Or rather, it is taking place for some but not for others. For the other characters who are constantly interpreting Tartuffe's actions, who suspect him of being a hypocrite, there still remains, attached to the relation of words and things, an obscurity, an apotropaic talismanic quality that pushes them to interpretation without that interpretation being articulable as anything other than a "suspicion," a wary mistrust in which the possibility of their own error, their own inability to interpret correctly, floats just below the surface of their discourse.

Cléante, on the other hand, does not seem to have these problems, these doubts ("Je sais, pour toute ma science / Du faux avec le vrai faire la différence"). His identifying mark in the comedy is precisely a stance in the world that does not need interpretation. He is what he says. This,

however, is neither as easy nor as unproblematic as it first appears. On the contrary, in a sense Cléante, the "honnête homme" of the play, is in perhaps the most ideologically overdetermined subject-position. If by "Classicism" we mean that epistemic moment when the difference between words and things is reduced to the merest hair's breadth, where words are the transparent signifier of reality, Cléante's definition of himself as "transparent" makes of him Classicism incarnate. With the transparency of Classicism coded as progress, we must ask ourselves what does it mean, in an Absolutist state, for a subject to be invisible to himself, to others, to power?

"Honnêteté" is what exists in society by not being seen. It is the position of the subject who is so entirely subjugated to the gaze of the Other (Monarch) that he has become one with this gaze. He has internalized it to such a degree as to become one with it. An "honnête homme ne se pique de rien" means that in the world of "honnêteté" one is "honnête" in one's inability to react in any way that would make one visible, call attention to one's presence, that would separate one from the total, symmetrical reflection of the Sovereign's gaze, or if we wish, of the gaze of society (an accepted set of social/value judgments) and be particularized. To the degree that Cléante is "frank" ("net") he is precisely not visible, cannot and will not exist as an "attrape-l'œil," as a spot that can stop, fix, the gaze of the world. It seems, therefore, that when a critic like G. Defaux states that Cléante is the center of the play, that Cléante is Molière's representative, he is correct, but perhaps not for those reasons he offers, for Defaux does not seem aware of the terrible price of invisibility, its terrible collusion with a power it apes, and that has already vampirized it (Cléante), and its (his) position in the world.

The dynamics of the play, as we have been discussing them up to this point, all swirl around the visual, around the production and seduction of images and subject-positions. Tartuffe, as I have suggested, is the most coded visual presence in the play: his hypocrisy is dangerous precisely because it is essentially a false image, but one so intimately camouflaged that it confuses the essence of "true" meaning with only a superficial appearance of devotion. It is precisely this confusion, this invasion of "the true" of, that is, an entire system by which a culture renders its productions verisimilous, "natural" that is effaced by its colonization by the imaginary, by the seduction of the image. In a further twist of our own interpretation, it now appears that what is really at stake in *Tartuffe,* what is the cause of its "scandal," is that the Law of the Father upon which the entire ideology of patriarchy is grounded, the symbolic order based on castration and difference, is being invaded and undermined by the Imaginary. Released from its subordination to order by Tartuffe's seduction of the Father, the Imaginary now threatens to overwhelm the entire domain of patriarchal authority.

If Tartuffe were only a "visual" image he would be much less effectively threatening. From the visual field Tartuffe parasitizes the symbolic itself by his mastery of devotional rhetoric (and from this rhetoric the entire semiotic order of Christianity). Not only does Tartuffe exist as a visual reflection for Orgon: more importantly, his narcissistically invested homilies and recriminations serve as a linguistic mirror that reflects back a troubling, troubled subjectivity to those who share the metaphysical premises of a language grounded in a severely dichotomous opposition between good and evil, sacrifice and redemption, heaven and hell. It is a discourse whose predicates suppose and uphold a universe of Law, of order, of God.

The slippage we have noted in Molière's own rhetoric between visual and lexical representations is encoded in the text of the play, where Tartuffe uses words to reflect back to his interlocutors his and their own bad faith:

> Dès que j'en vis briller la splendeur plus
>   qu'humaine,
> De mon intérieur vous fûtes souveraine;
> De vos regards divins l'ineffable douceur
> Força la résistance où s'obstinait mon cœur.
> Elle surmonta tout, jeûnes, prières, larmes,
> Et tourna tous mes vœux du côté de vos
>   charmes.
> Mes yeux et mes soupirs vous l'ont dit mille
>   fois,
> Et pour mieux m'expliquer j'emploie ici la voix.
>   (III, iii, 973-980)

Clearly in his mouth words serve as both offensive and defensive weapons. The seduction takes place in the moment of slippage, in the abandonment where one rhetorical trope evolves into the other. It is at this moment of aphanisis of language, its apparent vaporization as vision, that Tartuffe seduces Orgon, and hopes to seduce Elmire.

It is in this dangerous passage from the visual to the lexical that Tartuffe is most pernicious. Tartuffe's use of language brings out the inherent ambivalence of words, their status of sign rather than reality. Language is not a crystalline mediation between words and things but a turbulent, beckoning, ever-changing reflection of the person to whom the speaker addresses himself. Tartuffe uses words in such a manipulative way as to make them into self-conscious reflections not of some exterior reality but of their own unreality, of their own status as "social productions." Tartuffe's rhetoric, as seduction, infuses words with desire, unhinging them from any anchoring in a "reality," and sets them adrift as pure illusion. The effect of this seduction by rhetoric is to point out not the "truth" of a world grounded in language, but its vanity, its hollowness: what this language points to is itself. This is not a small accomplishment, for in the fervent religious climate of the seventeenth century (but also in ours as well, where perhaps not religion, but certainly other equally invested ideological systems, continually try to disguise their own predicates), when the medium of the message is shown to be free-floating it undermines any attempt at fixing a meaning that would be immutable, absolute.

In Tartuffe's mouth words are dangerously seductive, for they never point to any reality that is not him. His speech is an artificial, narcissistic mirror that Tartuffe turns to the world to capture in his person/discourse not its presence, not its material weight, but its metaphysical assumptions, its "invisibility": that is, those beliefs—religious, metaphysical, philosophical that structure the world, that legislate the parameters inside of which individuals are subjected to Law. By his manipulation of the words governing that legislation Tartuffe points to their artificiality, their status as "artifact," rather than to their status as fact, and thereby undoes not only the illusion of "truth," and of religion, but also that of the family and of the State. Once these institutions have been set adrift as in the mirror of words, the subject formed at their interstice, as well as the very possibility of subjectivity, is shown to be impossible.

The full implications of this threat to the patriarchal family are staged for us in the scene that pits Damis against Tartuffe and which ends with Orgon's committing the most "unnatural" act on the seventeenth-century stage. This scene is particularly perverse in its demonstration that there is no truth (for Orgon) other than the truth of Tartuffe's image (verbal and visual). What strikes us about the scene is the representation of contrition, Tartuffe's miming the pose of supplication he is on his knees and how this image is used to counter the veracity of his confession, a confession that, although using words to say the "truth," reflects to Orgon not guilt but spiritual superiority. The dovetailing of word and image authorizes Orgon to hear, to interpret, those words in a sense that is directly contrary to their literal meaning, but perfectly consonant with their cosmetic function. All these words do is to use a rhetoric of Christian contrition to seduce Orgon, who does not hear the "truth", but sees an image:

> ORGON: (A son fils) Ingrat!
> TARTUFFE: Laissez-le en paix. S'il faut, à
>   deux genoux,
>
>   Vous demander sa grâce. . .
> ORGON: (à Tartuffe) Hélas, vous moquez-
>   vous?
>
>   (à son fils) Coquin! vois sa
>   bonté.
>   (III, vi, 1114-1116)

The scene which starts out with the exultation of the son who has finally, he believes, the proof of Tartuffe's perfidy in hand ends not with the conversion of the father to truth, but with the banishment of Damis. Damis is chased, cursed, from his father's house:

> Vite, quittons la place.
> Je te prive, pendard, de ma succession,
> Et te donne de plus ma malédiction.
>   (III, vi, 1138-1140)

In his stead, Tartuffe is enthroned as his replacement:

> Je ne veux point avoir d'autre héritier que vous,
> Et je vais de ce pas, en fort bonne manière,
> Vous faire de mon bien donation entière.
>   (III, vii, 1177-1179)

This scene can only be read as the final triumph of Tartuffe over the Law of the Father, if we understand Damis's banishment as a metaphorical castration of the son. In the ideology of patriarchy this must be also and coterminously a castration of the Father. By depriving himself of his "legal" progeny (in social, economic, and political terms) he is effectively and retroactively denying his own position in the realm of patrilineal descent and undoing his role as familial centre. It is for this reason that the father's "cutting off" of his son is the most heavily invested act in the play. It is here that the greatest threat to the family occurs. It is no longer in the realm of the repressed, but passes into the domain of the real with potentially fatal consequences.

This act, the direct consequence of Orgon's perverted seduction by Tartuffe, is an "unnatural" act in several resonant senses. First, as I have mentioned, the castration of the son is also a self-mutilation—the deprivation of one's future as a man in a male-ordered economy of descent. By "castrating" the son the father effectively destroys the ties, the ties of sublimation, that bind him both to his past (his father) and his future (his son) along a well-ordered progression of male prerogative, based precisely on the repression of castration and its sublimation in an universal obedience that binds all men together in a masculine essentiality under the Law. When Orgon refuses this sublimation, he not only threatens his own subjugation to the genealogical order of descent that defines him, gives him a place and an identity: he also threatens the "order" as such. He is effectively denying family as a system of male privilege.

Even more, it is clear that this destitution is intimately connected with a homosexual desire to be united to Tartuffe through the latter's union with his own daughter. When we consider the conflicted, unconscious sexual attractions between parents and offspring, Orgon's imposition of Tartuffe on Mariane, his insistence on their marriage, can only be seen as a sexual ploy whereby Mariane is being used to mediate Orgon's own unavowable ambivalence. She serves as the mediating object not only of Tartuffe's lust, but of Orgon's, and even more perversely, of Orgon's lust for Tartuffe. It is only through her that Orgon can ever achieve the unthinkable, but no less desired, union with Tartuffe. Only by eliminating the son, the symbol of his own investment in heterosexual masculinity, and by substituting, through a marriage to his daughter, a new lover/son, can Orgon, in one more avatar of exchange, be placed in his daughter's bed and there be united with the Father/son of his own desire. Thus by threatening the family as its very heart, by substituting for an economy of masculine descent and prerogative a descent through the female (the prospective marriage of Mariane to Tartuffe), by the intrusion of an homoerotic passion (produced, as we've seen, by the lure of the imaginary) into the world of heterosexual ordering (the symbolic ordering of sexuality) there results a strange crossing-over of familial/sexual lines that effectively condemns first the family, and then the State that it reflects, to its ruin.

By the end of Act III, therefore, the family seems to be mortally wounded. Sexually and politically it has been undone. It needs only the economic "coup de grâce" of Act IV to be effectively eliminated. It is at this juncture, when all seems lost, when Orgon seems to have abandoned all contact with (familial) reality, all contact with himself, that the family regroups around Elmire, that strangely ambivalent figure of femininity (mother/wife/ mistress), to save itself from its own demise.

By all reckoning Act IV is one of the most "hilarious" in Molière's comic production. While up to this point it may appear that I have left aside, forgotten, that the *Tartuffe* is a comedy I have only been waiting to arrive at the high point of the comic to demonstrate what I stated at the beginning of this essay: that the visual is integral to the comic aspect of the play, that it is the pivotal link between the internal world of the spectacle and the exterior reality of the parterre, and that rather than undermining my own argument it the comedy is essential for understanding the imbrication of laughter and ideology in the formation of the Classical subject.

When things are at their most desperate Elmire steps in to take the matter in hand. Although presented as a rather shallow character, Elmire has insight enough to know that the only way to re-establish flagging familial order an order in which, we note, she, like the other women, is but an object of exchange among men is to engage Orgon where he is most vulnerable, most desirous, in his scoptophilia:

> J'admire, encore un coup, cette faiblesse étrange.
> Mais que me répondrait votre incrédulité
> Si je vous faisais voir qu'on vous dit vérité?
> (IV, iv, 1338-1340)

> Quel homme! Au moins répondez-moi.
> Je ne vous parle pas de nous ajouter foi;
> Mais supposons ici que, d'un lieu qu'on peut prendre,
> On vous fît clairement tout voir et tout entendre,
> Que diriez-vous alors de votre homme de bien?
> (IV, iv, 1343-1347)

The comedy of this scene that Elmire stages for the pleasure of her husband and ours is, I suggest, intimately connected to the scopic drive as it orchestrates what is, finally, a "dirty joke" in the sense Freud gives to this term:

> Generally speaking, a tendentious joke calls for three people: in addition to the one who makes the joke there must be a second who is taken as the object of the hostile or sexual aggressiveness, and a third in whom the joke's aim of producing pleasure is fulfilled.

I am less interested in the particulars of this scene than in its dynamics. What finally is funny? What makes us laugh? Clearly, it seems to me, the cause of our mirth is Elmire's discomfiture, her vulnerability to Tartuffe's lust from which she expected to be protected by her husband, while her expectations are deceived. Our laughter is produced precisely because Orgon does *not* burst forth from his hiding place to save his wife from the sexual advances of Tartuffe. We laugh because he constantly delays appearing, constantly waits for something else. His waiting, which increases Elmire's anxiety, makes us laugh. What exactly, we might ask, is he waiting *for?* What, in other words, does he want to see? The answer to this enigma, the punch line of the joke, is given us by him in response to his own mother's refusal to believe Tartuffe's duplicity (a reversal, a comic come-uppance that repeats Orgon's own "blindness" at the beginning of the play) in Act V. To her incredulity, to her refusal to believe, what now he knows to be true knows it because he has "visual proof" he sputters out the truth of his own desire, the cause of our laughter in Act IV:

> ORGON: Vous me feriez damner,
> ma mère. Je vous di
>   Que j'a vu de mes yeux un crime
> si hardi.
> MME PERNELLE: Les langues ont toujours
> du venin à répandre,
>   Et rien n'est ici-bas qui s'en puisse
> défendre.
> ORGON: C'est tenir un propos de sens bien
> dépourvu.
>   Je l'ai vu, dis-je, vu, de mes
> propres yeux vu,
>   Ce qu'on appelle vu . . .
> MME PERNELLE: Il est besoin
>   Pour accuser les gens, d'avoir de
> justes causes;
>   Et vous deviez attendre à vous voir
> sûr des choses.
> ORGON: Hé! diantre! le moyen de m'en
> assurer mieux?
>   Je devais donc, ma mère, attendre
> qu'à mes yeux
>   Il eût . . . Vous me feriez dire
> quelque sottise.
>   (V, iii, 1670-1676, 1684-1689)

In the ellipses of the three dots ("Would you have wanted me to wait until he had . . . her in front of my very eyes?") is the punch line of our visual joke. The answer is, of course, "yes" (and "no"). What Orgon was waiting for, what kept him in his hiding place and kept us laughing, was, I would suggest, his desire to see the "primal scene" of adult sexuality. He wanted (we wanted) to "see" Tartuffe reveal his desire, unveil the "phallus" that had masqueraded as "indifference" (that is, not there, not visible, "no-thing") and by so doing recreate an Oedipal scenario that would "correctly" sort out the confused sexual roles, that would establish the primacy of the symbolic over the imaginary and re-insert, into confusion, order. In other words, we were all waiting to see Tartuffe rape Elmire.

What this scene also underlines for us is the sadistically aggressive side of the scopic drive that pleasures in the suffering sacrifice of Elmire, thus pointing to the collu-

sion between the laughter evoked by Molière's comedy with an entire patriarchal order that is based on the sacrifice, destruction, of women. This "destruction" is not, however, a simple exploitation. Elmire situates herself in this scene; she in fact orchestrates this scene, which places her in the center of everyone's gaze as a sexual object. It is as if the only choice left to women in an Absolutist, patriarchal monarchy was the pleasure in the masochistic sacrifice of their subjectivity. In order to exist, they must opt for the negative empowerment of their own alienation. Women must assume the alienating position of object (object of exchange) in the sexual attraction/rivalry of men. Elmire places herself squarely in the visual field of Orgon (and, by extension, of the spectators, whose own gaze is relayed by Orgon's) as the mediating object, the sexual object of exchange between the men. This object "exchanges" a male homoerotic binding for the sadistic consumption of the female, who exists in this scene as the symbol of sexual difference. She is the "difference" that assures men of their difference, as power, as superiority. In this scene of sado-masochistic aggression and laughter, Elmire assumes the non-identity that is hers in a patriarchal society, sacrifices her subjectivity in order to save

Engraved handbill produced for early performances of
Le malade imaginaire.

that society from its own self-destruction in a homoerotic embrace that would effectively signal the disappearance of all those signifying systems based on the initial, essential imposition of sexual scission, of the entire semiotic order based on phallocentric symbolization which is generated around the fear/fantasy of castration.

The importance of Elmire's self-sacrifice cannot be underestimated for the dynamics of subjectivity that subtend the production of the comedy in the play. As I've suggested, what she stage for the pleasure/appetite of Orgon's eye is the origin of his "I," that is the origin of his subjectivity as that subjectivity comes into being through the imposition of difference, through the imposition on the imaginary of the Law of scission, which is, as Lacan has claimed, coterminously the entrance into language/sexuality. What the primal scene orchestrates, what it fantasizes, is the "origin of the individual who always sees him/herself figured in the scene," [as stated in *Fantasme Originaire, Fantasmes des origines, Origines du Fantasme*] as the product of sexual difference. We can thus also understand why structurally Orgon cannot come to his wife's rescue, for in this scene, caught up as he is in his/its fantasmatic power, he exists not as husband, but as child. He has effectively been placed in such a way that his *Schaulust,* that has held him in its sway, is here brought back to its/his originary moment, where it is directed at what it always wanted: to see sex, to see sexual splitting (as difference) and in that splitting to found Orgon's subjectivity as gendered. The trauma of the scene, as Freud reminds us in his analysis of the Wolfman [in "A Case of Infantile Neurosis"] is precisely

> the wish for the sexual satisfaction which he was at that time longing to obtain from his father. The strength of this wish made it possible to revive a long-forgotten trace in his memory of a scene which was able to show him what sexual satisfaction from his father was like; and the result was terror, horror of the fulfilment of the wish. . . .

Freud theorizes, in another essay ["Some Psychological Consequences of the Anatomical Distinction of the Sexes"] that the fear of this castration is inseparable from the "narcissistic interest" young boys have in their genital organ. By following this hypothetical line of reasoning, we are thus able to see the coming together in this scene of all the visual/psychic elements that have structured the play all along their coming together and their sorting out, through Orgon's "shock" (trauma) of seeing what all along has been denied him. This shock shatters the utopic plenitude of Orgon's vision of Tartuffe. In a sense it is the shock of visual excess that imposes on the subject held in the sway of the imaginary the cutting weight of the symbolic, of sexuality as difference. The vision is a sexual one in that it reveals the sex of the Father/Mother. By revealing (uncovering, showing) their truth, it does away with Tartuffe's "illusion," his masquerade, and its projection of non-difference. This flashing, blinding vision of sexuality re-situates Orgon into the order of masculine, sexual economy, returns him to the center of his *oikos* as "Father" (that is, no longer sexual mate of Tartuffe, but

sexual rival), and reinstates the integrity of the family:

> Comme aux tentations s'abandonne votre âme!
> Vous épousiez ma fille, et convoitiez ma femme!
> J'ai douté fort longtemps que ce fût tout de bon,
> Et je croyais toujours qu'on changerait de ton;
> Mais c'est assez avant pousser le témoignage:
> Je m'y tiens, et n'en veux, pour moi, pas
>   davantage.
>   (IV, vii, 1545-1550)

Orgon's re-inscription in his "place" comes, alas, too late. He no longer is master of his household. In fact, there is no longer any household. Tartuffe is now in legal possession of Orgon's house, and in a scathing reversal orders Orgon and his family out:

> C'est à vous d'en sortir, vous qui parlez en
>   maître:
> La maison m'appartient, je le ferai connaître.
>   (IV, vii, 1557-1558)

So the comedy that began with the absence of an *oikodespotès* ends (almost) in the very real absence of *oikos*. The family, defined most radically by its situation as that unit that lives together under one roof, is now roofless, no longer "domesticated" but cast out on to the street, with (as we soon learn) its head under the threat of death. The family is symbolically, but also legally and very physically, at the point of its dispersion, its ruin, its extinction.

It is, of course, at this juncture, when all seems lost, when Tartuffe as pure lust has reduced the family to nothingness, that some exterior force must intervene to save the family and thus the state from its demise. When we understand the intimate connection that the sexual/political economy of the family has for the regime of Absolute monarchy, how it is the basic and most heavily invested of all those "apparatuses" by which the state defines itself, maintains itself and its subjects in the proper relation to their own sexuality, to that sexuality as "proper" and "natural," the ending of the play no longer seems quite so contrived, the *deus ex machina* no longer so unmotivated. Rather, this *deus ex machina,* which in this instance is a *rex-(s)ex-machina* is so totally imbricated in the ideology of family, patriarchy and sexuality that has been threatened by Tartuffe's image-ing of himself that it/he cannot enter on to the scene of comedy. He enters it as the "invisible" (the prince is not seen, he is represented), as the "real" veiled phallus the sign of power/desire that functions as the Law of the symbolic who, through the very visual imagery that has disoriented the subject/father of the play, restores it/him to its and his rightful place.

The entire metaphoric structure of the last speech, the speech of truth and resolution, describes the Prince, his power, in visual terms. What distinguishes the Prince is that his vision, as opposed to the unreliable father's, is infallible:

> Nous vivons sous un prince ennemi de la fraude,
> Un prince dont les yeux se font jour dans les

cœurs,
Et que ne peut tromper tout l'art des imposteurs.
(V, scène dernière, 1906-1908)

The prince sees through artifice. He alone sees what is true and is capable of separating out truth from falsehood. His vision is piercing, penetrating; it sees beyond appearance into the "soul" of his subjects, into their true nature: "D'abord, il a percé, par ses vives clartés / Des replis de son cœur toutes les lâchetés" It is also an irresistible force ("de pièges plus fins on le voit se défendre"). His vision is "straight" ("droite vue") and upholds a rigid understanding ("ferme raison") of the workings of human nature. What these obvious references bolster is the phallic presence of the prince, the prince as phallus, who, precisely, controls and directs the "excessive" drive of *Schaulust* into culturally acceptable channels of desire. In a strange, paradoxical way, this sovereign who is described as an "Omniscient eye/I," as the invisible but all-present, all-knowing model who watches over all his subjects, who sees into their innermost recesses, who knows who's been bad or good:

Et c'est le prix qu'il donne au zèle qu'autrefois
On vous vit témoigner en appuyant ses droits,
Pour montrer que son cœur sait, quand moins on
     y pense,
D'une bonne action verser la récompense,
Que jamais le mérite avec lui ne perd rien,
Et que mieux que du mal il se souvient du bien
(V, scène dernière, 1939-1944)

and who deals out fit punishments or rewards - is never there. He is not localizable except in a discourse of invisibility, a discourse of his vision/power that cannot be seen but is everywhere. In a sense, what this panoptic power of the prince represents is his power to be part of every one of his subjects. They are part of his gaze (the best example, again is Cléante). This vision is an internalized sense of one's being watched, of living under an omnipotent eye. What this sense of being contained in the eye of some never-present beholder represents is the coming into being of a subjugation and subjectivization that, although repressive, is felt as salutary: it saves the family (that is, us) from its own demise. It is only under the eye of this just Monarch/father, in his adoration by his subjects, in their subjugation to him, that the play can end. The anxiety caused by Tartuffe's near-destruction of the family, his playing too freely with all those systems that his manipulation of images shows to be too vulnerable to ground subjectivity in any way that is not already undermined, is itself overcome by and through the "incorporation" of the Absolutist gaze. At the end of the play the family, newly situated at the very center of its invisible Lord's field of vision, significantly reestablishes its preeminent situation at the center of the represented universe. Sure of its newly bolstered foundations, the family, as the mediating locus of an Absolutist imperative of the sexual and economic organization of society, can safely propel itself into a future of perpetual continuation, and this "comedy" that almost fell into the tragic can at last end, as all comedies do, with the promise of marriage.

FURTHER READING

Bibliography

Edelman, Nathan, ed. "Molière." In *A Critical Bibliography of French Literature: The Seventeenth Century, Vol. III*, pp. 226-43. Syracuse, N.Y.: Syracuse University Press, 1961.
     Bibliography of criticism on Molière's works.

Criticism

Cholakian, Patricia Francis. "The 'Woman Question' in Molière's *Misanthrope.*" *French Review: Journal of the American Association of Teachers of French* LVIII, No. 4 (March 1985): 524-32.
     Focuses on the portrayal of women and communication between the sexes in *Le misanthrope.*

Cruickshank, John, ed. *French Literature and Its Background.* 6 vols. London: Oxford University Press, 1969.
     Includes an analysis of Molière's major works. Also provides essays on such relevant topics as "Religion and Society," "Social Structure and Social Change," and "Louis XIV and the Arts."

Ekstein, Nina. "The Portrait on Stage in Molière's Theater." *Romance Quarterly* 36, No. 1 (February 1989): 3-14.
     Discusses "literary portraiture" in Molière's plays in relation to stagecraft and characterization.

Gaines, James F. "The Burlesque *Récit* in Molière's Greek Plays." *The French Review* LII, No. 3 (February 1979): 393-400.
     Discusses the role of the clownish servant in a group of Molière's plays with Greek settings: *La Princesse d'Elide, Mélicerte, Amphitryon,* and *Les Amants magnifiques.*

Gossman, Lionel. *Men and Masks: A Study of Molière.* Baltimore, Md.: Johns Hopkins Press, 1963, 310 p.
     Offers critical analysis of the following works: *Amphitryon, Dom Juan, Le Misanthrope, Le Tartuffe,* and *George Dandin.*

Howarth, W.D. "Classicism: the Creative Years 1660-1680." In *French Literature from 1600 to the Present,* rev. ed., pp. 17-26. London: Methuen & Co., 1974.

     Discusses the cultural values of *honnêteté* and *préciosité* that influenced seventeenth-century dramatists.

Jones, Dorothy F. "Love and Friendship in *Le Misanthrope.*" *Romance Notes* XXIII, No. 2 (Winter 1982): 164-69.
     Argues that "a proper acknowledgment of the relationship between Philinte and Alceste is crucial to our understanding of *Le Misanthrope.*"

————. "The Treasure in the Garden: Biblical Imagery in *L'Avare.*" *Papers on French Seventeenth Century Literature* XV, No. 29 (1988): 5167-28.
     Examines the symbolism of Harpagon's "chère cassette" in *L'Avare.*

Lawrence, Francis L. *Molière: The Comedy of Unreason.* Tulane Studies in Romance Languages and Literature, No. 2. New Orleans, La.: Tulane University, 1968, 119 p.

Presents "a treatment in chronological order of the early plays, the work before the great controversial pieces, *Tartuffe, Dom Juan* and *Le Misanthrope.*"

McBride, Robert. *The Sceptical Vision of Molière: A Study in Paradox.* New York: Barnes & Noble Books, 1977, 250 p.

In-depth analysis of Molière's dramas, examining autobiographical and literary influences.

Peacock, N.A. "The Comic Role of the 'Raisonneur' in Molière's Theatre." *The Modern Language Review* 76, No. 2 (April 1981): 298-310.

Discusses the ambiguity and paradox surrounding the role of the *raisonneur* in Molière's plays.

——. "Lessons Unheeded: The Dénouement of *Le Misanthrope.*" *Nottingham French Studies* 29, No. 1 (Spring 1990): 10-20.

Examines the ambiguous ending of *The Misanthrope*, which has frequently been interpreted as tragic, attempting to "reaffirm the comic status of the dénouement."

Phillips, Henry. "Molière and *Tartuffe*: Recrimination and Reconciliation." *The French Review* 62, No. 5 (April 1989): 749-63.

Discusses the debate surrounding Molière's alleged anti-clericalism in relation to *Tartuffe.*

Riggs, Larry W. "Ethics, Debts, and Identity in *Dom Juan.*" In *Romance Quarterly* 34, No. 2 (May 1987): 141-46.

Discusses the theme of the relationship between individual identity and society in *Dom Juan.*

Shaw, David. "Harpagon's Monologue." *Nottingham French Studies* 23, No. 1 (May 1984): 1-11.

Suggests that the "scene of Harpagon's monologue [in *L'Avare*] both reflects and concentrates the complexity of the play as a whole."

——. "Molière's Temporary Happy Endings." *French Studies: A Quarterly Review* XLV, No. 2 (April 1991): 129-42.

Examines unconventional aspects of the denouements of Molière's plays.

Spingler, Michael. "The Actor and the Statue: Space, Time, and Court Performance in Molière's *Dom Juan.*" *Comparative Drama* 25, No. 4 (Winter 1991/92): 351-68.

Focuses on Molière's handling of scenic structure in relation to the codes of social "performance" which governed seventeenth-century life at court.

Sylvester, Joy. "Molière's *Dom Juan*: Charity's Prodigal Son." *Romance Notes* XXXII, No. 1 (Fall 1991): 23-27.

Offers an analysis of act III, scene 2 of *Dom Juan,* which is considered an important and controversial episode in French drama.

Wagner, Monique. *Studies on Voltaire and the Eighteenth Century: Molière and the Age of Enlightenment, vol. CXII.* Banbury, Oxfordshire: Voltaire Foundation, 1973.

Includes discussion of the popular and critical reception of Molière's works during the eighteenth century.

Zwillenberg, Myrna Kogan. "Dramatic Justice in *Tartuffe.*" *Modern Language Notes* 90, No. 4 (1975): 583-90.

Considers the effectiveness of Molière's use of a *deus ex machina* in Act V of *Tartuffe.*

Jean Racine

1639-1699

French dramatist and poet.

INTRODUCTION

With Pierre Corneille, Racine was one of the premier authors of French dramatic tragedy during the reign of Louis XIV. His more renowned plays, all of them written in verse, include *Bajazet* (1672), *Mithridate* (1673; *Mithridates*), *Iphigénie* (1674; *Iphigenia*), and *Phèdre* (1677; *Phaedra*), tragedies which rework themes from classical Greek models. As in Greek tragedy and Corneille's works, Racine's plays emphasize the exposition of character and spiritual conflict, eliminating nearly everything not central to each drama's theme. His accomplishment was summarized in glowing terms by Anatole France, who wrote that Racine's "period, his education, and his nature, conspired together to make of him the most perfect of French poets, and the greatest by reason of the sustained nobility of his work."

Biographical Information

Born the son of an attorney in La Ferté-Milon near Soissons, Racine was orphaned as an infant. He was raised by his paternal grandparents in the fervently Jansenist city of Port-Royal, where his education afforded him a wide knowledge of Greek and Latin literature as well as Jansenist doctrine. (The Jansenists, named after Bishop Cornelius Jansen of Ypres, were a sect within the Roman Catholic Church which emphasized the complete perversity of the natural human will and the belief that sin is overcome only in the lives of individuals predestined for such by divine grace.) Having written several odes to country scenes near Port-Royal by his late teens, Racine was admitted to the College d'Harcourt in the University of Paris. Several years later, having entered into friendships with Molière, Jean de La Fontaine, and Nicolas Boileau, he began writing for the Parisian stage, with the neoclassical theorist Boileau being an especially strong influence upon him. In 1664 Racine's *La Thébaïde* (*The Thebans*) was produced by Molière, who also mounted the young dramatist's second play, *Alexandre le Grande* (*Alexander the Great*), the next year; these works brought their author much acclaim. But when *Alexander* opened, Racine acted upon the first of several key decisions that brought him strained relations with friends—if not influential enemies—throughout his career. Immediately dissatisfied by Molière's production of *Alexander* at the Palais-Royal, he mounted a rival production at the Hôtel de Bourgogne, deeply offending Molière and ending their friendship. At about the same time, due to a misunderstanding, Racine publicly broke with the Jansenist Catholics of Port-Royal by publishing an open letter—which he later regretted—filled with ill-spirited caricatures of

and anecdotes about key Jansenist figures. Having split with the Jansenists and now considered a rising rival of Corneille, Racine embraced the worldliness of the Parisian dramatic world, taking actresses for mistresses and actively competing in dramatic popularity with the older writer. In the drama *Britannicus* he not only ventured into political drama, at the time considered Corneille's exclusive domain, but he also attacked Corneille himself (though not by name) in his introduction, having come to believe that a cabal led by Corneille had sought to undermine his drama's success. He also answered Corneille's *El Cid* with his own *Andromaque* (1667; *Andromache*) and pitted his superior *Bérénice* (1670; *Berenice*) against Corneille's *Tite et Bérénice*, which appeared almost simultaneously. The other plays by which Racine is most distinguished appeared during the next few years, and in 1674 he was elected to the Académie Française, becoming its youngest member. But by the mid 1670s, the ill will he had engendered among his peers and their admirers affected his own career. One of his more powerful enemies, the Duchesse de Bouillon—a niece of Cardinal Mazarin and sister of the Duc de Nevers—learned of Racine's *Phaedra* during its composition and persuaded a minor dramatist, Jacques Pradon, to write a rival version of the play, which opened two days after Racine's production. Further, it is said that she reserved many of the main seats for the earliest performances of Racine's play, leaving these seats empty on the crucial opening nights. Although *Phaedra* was eventually seen as superior to Pradon's tragedy, Racine was badly shaken by this episode and its aftermath, which included having his personal safety threatened by the Duc de Nevers. Thus, at the height of his career, he retired from the professional theatre; he married, became the devoted father of seven children, and accepted the post of Royal Historiographer, a position he shared with Boileau. For two decades Racine enjoyed access to the most influential political and literary circles; he and Boileau also travelled with Louis XIV on military campaigns, recording the Sun King's exploits. In 1689, at the request of the king's wife, Madame de Maintenon, Racine produced a new play, *Esther*, based on the biblical story, which was performed at a religious school in Saint-Cyr. Praised by the king himself, this play was so well received that Racine wrote another biblical drama, *Athalie* (*Athaliah*), which was performed at Saint-Cyr two years later. During his remaining years, he wrote four spiritual hymns (*Cantiques spirituelles*) and a history of Port-Royal (*Abrégé de l'histoire de Port-Royal*). Racine died in 1699 after a long illness.

Major Works

Several scholars have written that in Racine, the world of Jansenist Port-Royal and the neoclassical world were in constant warfare. But they were arguably complementary, in style and in form. The influence of Jansenist teaching, which stressed human depravity and predestined salvation, is evident in Racine's dramatic characters, who—like their forerunners in classical Greek drama—are undone by their passions, driven to ruin by ungovernable impulses. The simple neoclassical tragic form was well fitted to Racine's themes and poetic style, which has been praised for its simplicity, harmony, and rhythmic flow; of all his contemporaries, Racine was the first to achieve success within a framework which had been deemed too difficult to master since its inception during the Italian Renaissance. His style has been described as simple yet polished, smooth yet natural. Robert Lowell has praised Racine's dramatic verse for its "diamond edge" and "hard, electric rage," calling Racine "perhaps the greatest poet in the French language." In most of his plays, Racine employed a basic plot structure in which a monarch demands something of a particular underling, often a prince or princess, who denies this demand. The monarch then attempts to force his subject's obedience, with tragic results. Launched upon a course of impending doom, Racine's characters know what must be done to avert disaster but are unable to subdue their desires to take prudent action. This is readily discernable in *Phaedra*, the tragedy often considered Racine's finest. Based upon Euripides's *Hippolytus*, this play concerns a woman who wrestles unsuccessfully with her unlawful love for her stepson, Hippolytus, and is struck down by him or her husband, Theseus, each time she moves toward redemption. Kenneth Rexroth went so far as to say that the protagonist of *Phaedra* "is damned, and predestined to damnation."

Racine's only comedy, *Les plaideurs* (1668; *The Litigants*), is the single exception to this general pattern.

Critical Reception

During their author's lifetime, Racine's dramas, though popular, were attacked for what some critics considered their crude realism and their focus upon passion. Jean de La Bruyère wrote of Corneille and Racine that "the former paints men as they should be, the latter paints men as they are." Like La Bruyère, many critics compare the intents and accomplishments of Racine with those of Corneille, often to Racine's advantage. "Unlike Corneille," wrote Irving Babbitt, "Racine moved with perfect ease among all the rules that the neo-classic disciplinarians had imposed upon the stage. Indeed, it is in Racine, if anywhere, that all this regulating of the drama must find its justification," here speaking of the unities of time, space, and action prescribed by neoclassical theorists. Over time, Racine's work grew in critical stature and popularity. In one of the seminal discourses upon Racine's achievement, *Racine et Shakespeare* (1823-25), Stendhal wrote of Racine—in his preoccupation with passion—as an artist of *romantisicme*, the literary element which satisfies an ever-changing standard of beauty. Several scholars have compared the theatricality of Shakespeare and Racine, with David Maskell observing that they "provide examples of a common visual vocabulary which is the peculiar feature of theatrical language, and which unites dramatists who can exploit its rich potential." Other major French critics of Racine's work have included Jules Lemaître, Ferdinand Brunetière, Jean Giraudoux, François Mauriac, and Roland Barthes, while English-language criticism and translation of Racine's works has been dominated by Martin Turnell, Geoffrey Brereton, and Kenneth Muir, among others. Many scholars concur in spirit with the judgment of George Saintsbury, who wrote of Racine, "Of the whole world which is subject to the poet he took only a narrow artificial and conventional fraction. Within these narrow bounds he did work which no admirer of literary craftsmanship can regard without satisfaction."

PRINCIPAL WORKS

La Thébaïde, ou Les frères ennemis [*The Thebans, or The Enemy Brothers*] (drama) 1664
Alexandre le Grand [*Alexander the Great*] (drama) 1665
Andromaque [*Andromache*] (drama) 1667
Les plaideurs [*The Litigants*] (drama) 1668
Britannicus (drama) 1669
Bérénice [*Berenice*] (drama) 1670
Bajazet (drama) 1672
Mithridate [*Mithridates*] (drama) 1673
Iphigénie [*Iphigenia*] (drama) 1674
Phèdre [*Phaedra*] (drama) 1677
Esther (drama) 1689
Athalie [*Athaliah*] (drama) 1691
Oeuvres complètes (dramas) 1962

CRITICISM

Elizabeth Inchbald (essay date 1808)

SOURCE: "Remarks: *The Distressed Mother*," in *The British Theatre; or, A Collection of Plays, Vol. XVIII*, translated by Ambrose Philips, Longman, Hurst, Rees, Orme, and Brown, 1808, pp. 3-5.

[*Inchbald was an English dramatist of the late eighteenth and early nineteenth centuries. In the excerpt below, she remarks upon the dramatic effect of* The Distressed Mother, *Ambrose Philips's translation of* Andromaque.]

The French and the English stages differ so essentially, that every French drama requires great alteration, before it can please a London audience, although it has previously charmed the audience of Paris.

The gloomy mind of a British auditor demands a bolder and more varied species of theatrical amusement than the lively spirits of his neighbours in France. The former has no attention, no curiosity, till roused by some powerful fable, intricate occurrences, and all the interest which variety creates—whilst the latter will quietly sit, absorbed in their own glowing fancy, to hear speeches after speeches, of long narration, nor wish to see any thing performed, so they are but told, that something has been done.

The Distressed Mother [a translation of *Andromaque*] partakes of the common quality of French dramas in this respect—much more is described to the audience than they see executed: but every recital is here in the highest degree interesting; and the dignity of the persons introduced on the stage seems to forbid all violence of action, which might endanger their respective grandeur.

The mere falling on the knee, by Andromache, when she exclaims to her victor—

Behold how low you have reduced a queen!

is perhaps more affecting, more admirable, in the character of a mother, haughty, like the queen of the Trojans, than any event which could have occurred in the play, than any heroic deed, which, either in grief or in rage, she could have performed.

The love of Hermione for Pyrrhus, founded on ambition, is, again, as natural a representation of that love, which but too often governs the heart of woman, as could be given: and Orestes, doting with fondness, the more he finds she, whom he loves, loves another, is equally as true a picture of this well-known passion, as it rules over the heart of man.

Frequently as this tragedy has been acted, and much as it has been approved by an English audience, it will still gain more favour with a reader than a spectator. Imagination can give graces, charms, and majesty, to Hector's widow, and all the royal natives of Troy and Greece,

which their representatives cannot always so completely bestow; and, as the work is chiefly narrative, reading answers the same purpose as to listen.

C. A. Sainte-Beuve (essay date 1855)

SOURCE: "Racine," in *Portraits of the Seventeenth Century, Historic and Literary*, translated by Katharine P. Wormeley, G. P. Putnam's Sons, 1904, pp. 283-314.

[*Sainte-Beuve is considered the foremost French literary critic of the nineteenth century. Of his extensive body of critical writings, the best known are his "lundis"—weekly newspaper articles which appeared over a period of several decades, in which he displayed his knowledge of literature and history. While Sainte-Beuve began his career as a champion of Romanticism, he eventually formulated a psychological method of criticism. Asserting that the critic cannot separate a work of literature from the artist and from the artist's historical milieu, Sainte-Beuve considered an author's life and character integral to the comprehension of his work. In the following excerpt from an essay originally published in 1855, he surveys the career of Racine, offering high praise for his overall accomplishment, especially the religious dramas* Esther *and* Athalie.]

The great poets, the poets of genius, independently of their class, and without regard to their nature, lyric, epic, or dramatic, may be divided into two glorious families which, for many centuries, have alternately intermingled and dethroned one another, contending for pre-eminence in fame: between them, according to periods, the admiration of men has been unequally awarded. The primitive poets, the founders, the unmixed originals, born of themselves and sons of their own works,—Homer, Pindar, Æschylus, Dante, and Shakespeare,—are sometimes neglected, often preferred, but are always contrary to the studious, polished, docile geniuses of the middle epochs, essentially capable of being educated and perfected. Horace, Virgil, and Tasso are the most brilliant heads of this secondary family, reputed, and with reason, inferior to its elder, but, as a usual thing, better understood by all, more accessible, more cherished. In France, Corneille and Molière are detached from it on more sides than one; Boileau and Racine belong to it wholly and adorn it, especially Racine, the most accomplished of the class, the most venerated of our poets. . . .

Racinian poesy is so constructed that at every height are stepping-stones, and places of support for weaklings. Shakespeare's work is rougher of approach; the eye cannot take it in on all sides; I know very worthy persons who toil and sweat to climb it, and after striking against crag or bush, come back swearing in good faith that there was nothing higher up; but, no sooner are they down upon the plain than that cursed enchantment tower appears to them once more in the distance, a thousand times more imperatively than those of Montlhéry to Boileau. But let us leave Shakespeare and such comparisons and try to mount, after many worshippers, a few of the steps, slippery from long usage, that lead to Racine's marble temple. . . .

We find him, in 1660, in communication with the actors of the Marais about a play the name of which has not come down to us. His ode on the *Nymphes de la Seine,* written for the marriage of the king, was sent to Chapelain, who "received it with all the kindness in the world, and, ill as he was, kept it three days to make remarks upon it in writing." The most important of these remarks related to the Tritons, who never lived in rivers, only in the sea. This poem won for Racine the protection of Chapelain, and a gift in money from Colbert. . . .

[His] ode on *La Renommée aux Muses* won him another gift of money, an entrance at Court, and the acquaintance of Boileau and Molière. The *Thébaïde* followed rapidly.

Until then, Racine had found on his path none but protectors and friends. But his first dramatic success awakened envy, and from that moment his career was full of perplexities and vexations which his irritable susceptibility more than once embittered. The tragedy of *Alexandre* estranged him from Molière and Corneille; from Molière, because he withdrew the play from him and gave it to the actors of the Hôtel de Bourgogne; with Corneille, because the illustrious old man declared to the young man, after listening to the reading of the piece, that it showed great talent for poesy in general, but not for the stage. When it was performed, the partisans of Corneille endeavoured to hinder its success. Some said that Taxile was not an honourable man; others that he did not deserve his fate; some that Alexandre was not lover-like enough; others that he never came upon the scene except to talk of love. When *Andromaque* appeared, Pyrrhus was reproached for a lingering of ferocity; they wanted him more polished, more gallant, more uniform in character. This was a consequence of Corneille's system, which made all his personages of one piece, wholly good or wholly bad from head to foot; to which Racine replied, with good judgment:

> Aristotle, far from asking us for perfect heroes, wishes, on the contrary, that the tragic personages, that is to say, those whose misfortune makes the catastrophe of the tragedy, shall be neither very good nor very bad. He does not wish them to be extremely good, because the punishment of a good man would excite more indignation than pity in the spectators; nor that they be bad to excess, because no one can feel pity for a scoundrel. They should therefore have a mediocre goodness, that is to say, a virtue capable of weakness, so that they fall into misfortune through some fault that causes them to be pitied and not detested.

I dwell on this point, because the great innovation of Racine, and his incontestable dramatic originality, consist precisely in this reduction of heroic personages to proportions more human, more natural, and in a delicate analysis of the secret shades of sentiment and passion. That which, above all, distinguishes Racine, in the composition of style as in that of the drama, is logical sequence, the uninterrupted connection of ideas and sentiments; in

him all is filled up, leaving no void, argued without reply; never is there any chance to be surprised by those abrupt changes, those sudden *volte-faces* of which Corneille made frequent abuse in the play of his characters and the progression of his drama.

I am, nevertheless, far from asserting that, even in this, all the advantage of the stage was on the side of Racine; but when he appeared, novelty was in his favour, a novelty admirably adapted to the taste of a Court in which were many weaknesses, where nothing shone that had not its shadow, and the amorous chronicle of which, opened by a La Vallière, was to end in a Maintenon. It will always remain a question whether Racine's observing, inquiring method, employed to the exclusion of every other, is dramatic in the absolute sense of the world; for my part, I think it is not; but it satisfied, we must allow, the society of those days which, in its polished idleness, did not demand a drama more agitating, more tempestuous, more "transporting"—to use Mme. de Sévigné's language; a society which willingly accepted *Bérénice,* while awaiting *Phèdre,* the masterpiece of Racine's manner.

Bérénice was written by command of Madame [Henriette], Duchesse d'Orléans, who encouraged all the new poets, and who, on this occasion, did Corneille the ill-turn of bringing him into the lists in contest with his young rival. On the other hand, Boileau, a sincere and faithful friend, defended Racine against the clamouring mob of writers, upheld him in his momentary discouragements, and excited him by wise severity to a progress without intermission. This daily supervision of Boileau would assuredly have been fatal to an author of freer genius, of impetuous warmth or careless grace, like Molière, like La Fontaine, for instance; it could not be otherwise than profitable to Racine, who, before he knew Boileau, was already following (save for a few Italian whimsicalities) that path of correctness and sustained elegance in which the latter maintained and confirmed him. I think, therefore, that Boileau was right when he applauded himself for having taught Racine "to write with difficulty easy verses"; but he went too far if he gave him, as it was asserted that he did, "the precept of writing the second line before the first."

After *Andromaque,* which appeared in 1667, ten years elapsed before *Phèdre,* the triumph of which came in 1677. . . .

For some time past, since the first fire of youth, the first fervours of mind and senses were spent, the memory of . . . [Port-Royal] had again laid hold upon Racine's heart; and the involuntary comparison forced upon him between his peaceful satisfaction in other days, and his present fame, so troubled and embitered, brought him to regret a life that once was regular. This secret feeling, working within him, can be seen in the preface to *Phèdre,* and must have sustained him, more than we know, in the profound analysis he makes in that play of the "virtuous sorrow" of a soul that sees evil and yet pursues it. His own heart explained to him that of Phèdre; and if we suppose, what is very probable, that he was detained in spite of himself at the theatre by some amorous attachment he could not shake off, the resemblance becomes closer, and helps us to understand all that he has put into *Phèdre* of anguish actually felt, and more personal than usual in the struggles of passion.

However that may be, the moral aim of *Phèdre* is beyond a doubt; the great Arnauld himself could not refrain from recognising it, and thus almost verifying the words of the author, who "hoped, by means of this play to reconcile a quantity of celebrated persons to tragedy, through their pity and their doctrine." Nevertheless, going deeper still in his reflections on reform, Racine judged it more prudent and more consistent to quit the theatre, and he did so with courage, but without too much effort. He married, reconciled himself with Port-Royal, prepared himself in domestic life for the duties of a father, and when Louis XIV appointed him, at the same time as Boileau, historiographer, he neglected none of his new duties: with these in view, he began by making excerpts from the treatise of Lucian on **"The Manner of Writing History,"** and he applied himself to the reading of Mézeray, Vittorio Siri, and others.

From the little that we have now read of the character, the morals, and the habits of mind of Racine, it is easy to foretell the essential fine qualities and defects of his work, to perceive to what he might have attained and, at the same time, in what he was likely to be lacking. Great art in constructing a plot; exact calculation in its arrangement; slow and successive development rather than force of conception, simple and fertile; which acts simultaneously as if by process of crystallisation around several centres in brains that are naturally dramatic; presence of mind in the smallest details; remarkable skill in winding only one thread at a time; skill also in pruning and cutting down rather than power to be concise; ingenious knowledge of how to introduce and how to dismiss his personages; sometimes a crucial situation eluded, either by a magniloquent speech or by the necessary absence of an embarrassing witness; in the characters nothing divergent or eccentric; all inconvenient accessory parts and antecedents suppressed; nothing, however, too bare or too monotonous, but only two or three harmonising tints on a simple background; then, in the midst of all this, passion that we have not seen born, the flood of which comes swelling on, softly foaming, and bearing you away, as it were, upon the whitened current of a beauteous river: that is Racine's drama. And if we come down to his style and to the harmony of his versification, we shall follow beauties of the same order, restrained within the same limits; variations of melodious tones, no doubt, but all within the scale of a single octave.

A few remarks on *Britannicus* will state my thought precisely, and justify it, if, given in such general terms, it may seem bold. The topic of the drama is Nero's crime, the one by which he first escapes the authority of his mother and his governors. In Tacitus, Britannicus is shown to be a young lad fourteen or fifteen years of age, gentle, intelligent, and sad. One day, in the midst of a feast, Nero, who is drunk, compels him to sing in order to make him ridiculous. Britannicus sings a song in which he makes allusion to his own precarious fate, and to the patrimony of which he has been defrauded; instead of laughing and ridiculing him, the guests, much affected and less dissimulating than usual because they were drunk, compassionated him loudly. As for Nero, though still pure of shedding blood, his natural ferocity has long been muttering in his soul and watching for an occasion to break loose. He tries slow poison on Britannicus. Debauchery gets the better of him; he neglects his wife Octavia for the courtesan Actea. Seneca lends his ministry to this shameful intrigue. Agrippina is at first shocked, but she ends by embracing her son and lending him her house for the rendezvous. Agrippina, mother, granddaughter, sister, niece, and widow of emperors, a murderess, incestuous, and a prostitute, has no other fear than to see her son escape her with the imperial power.

Such is the mental situation of the personages at the moment when Racine begins his play. What does he do? He quotes in his preface the savage words of Tacitus on Agrippina: *Quæ, cunctis malæ dominationis cupidinibus flagrans, habebat in partibus Pallantem*, and adds: "I merely quote this one sentence on Agrippina, for there are too many things to say of her. It is she whom I have taken the most pains to express properly, and my tragedy is not less the downfall of Agrippina than the death of Britannicus." But in spite of this stated intention of the author, the character of Agrippina is inadequately expressed; as an interest had to be created in her downfall, her most odious vices are thrown into the shade; she becomes a personage of little real presence, vague, unexplained, a sort of tender and jealous mother; there is no question of her adulteries and her murders beyond an allusion for the benefit of those who have read her history in Tacitus. In place of Actea we have the romantic Junia. Nero in love is nothing more than the impassioned rival of Britannicus, and the hideous aspects of the tiger disappear, or are delicately touched when they must be encountered. What shall be said of the *dénouement?* of Junia taking refuge with the Vestals, and placed under the protection of the people?—as if the people protected any one under Nero! But what, above all, we have a right to blame in Racine, is the suppression of the scene at the feast. Britannicus is seated at the table; wine is poured out for him; one of his servants tastes the beverage, according to the custom of the day, so necessary was it to guard against crime. But Nero has foreseen all; the wine is too hot, cold water must be added, and it is that cold water which must be poisoned. The effect is sudden; the poison kills at once; Locuste was charged to prepare it under pain of death. Whether it were disdain for these circumstances, or the difficulty of expressing them in verse, Racine evades them; he confines himself to presenting the moral effect of the poisoning on the spectators, and in that he succeeds. But it must be owned that even on that point he falls below the incisive brevity, the splendid conciseness of Tacitus. Too often, when he translates Tacitus, as he translated the Bible, Racine opens a path for himself between the extreme qualities of the originals and carefully keeps to the middle of the road, never approaching the sides where the precipice lies.

Britannicus, Phèdre, Athalie, Roman, Greek, and Biblical tragedy, those are the three great dramatic claims of Racine, below which all his other masterpieces range themselves. I have already expressed my admiration for *Phèdre,* and yet one cannot conceal from one's self that the play is even less Greek in manners and morals than *Britannicus* is Roman. Hippolytus, the lover, resembles Hippolytus, the hunter, the favourite of Diana, even less than Nero, the lover, resembles the Nero of Tacitus. Phèdre, queen-mother and regent for her son, on the supposed death of her husband amply counterbalances Junia, protected by the people and consigned to the Vestals. Euripides himself leaves much to be desired as to truth; he has lost the higher meaning of the mythological traditions that Æschylus and Sophocles entered into so deeply; but in him we find, at any rate, a whole order of things—landscape, religion, rites, family recollections, all these constitute a depth of reality which fixes the mind and rests it. With Racine all that is not Phèdre and her passion escapes and disappears. The sad Aricia, the Pallantides, the divers adventures of Theseus, leave scarcely a trace in our memory.

This might lead us to conclude with Corneille, if we dared, that Racine had a far greater talent for poesy in general than for the drama in particular. Racine was dramatic, no doubt, but he was so in a style that was little so. In other times, in times like ours, when the proportions of the drama are necessarily so different from what they were then, what would he have done? Would he have attempted it? His genius, naturally meditative and placid, would it have sufficed for that intensity of action that our *blasée* curiosity demands? for that absolute truth in ethics and characters that becomes indispensable after a period of mighty revolution? for that higher philosophy that gives to all things a meaning, that makes action something else than mere imbroglio, and historical colour something better than whitewash? Had he the force and the character to lead all these parts of the work abreast; to maintain them in presence and in harmony, to blend, to link them into an indissoluble and living form, to fuse them one into the other in the fire of passion? Would he not have found it more simple, more conformable to his nature, to withdraw passion from the midst of these intricacies in which it might be lost as if poured into sand? to keep it within his own channel and follow singly the harmonious course of grand and noble elegy, of which *Esther* and *Bérénice* are the limpid and transparent reservoirs? Those are delicate questions, to which we can only reply by conjectures. I have hazarded mine, in which there is nothing irreverent towards the genius of Racine. Is it irreverent to declare that we prefer in him pure poesy to drama, and that we are tempted to ally him to the race of lyric geniuses, of religious and elegiac singers, whose mission here below is to celebrate Love—love as Dante and Plato saw it?

The life of retirement, of household cares, and study, which Racine led during the twelve years of his fullest maturity, seem to confirm these conjectures. Corneille also tried for some years to renounce the theatre; but, though already in declining years, he could not continue the attempt and

soon returned to the arena. Nothing of this impatience or this difficulty of controlling himself appears to have troubled the long silence of Racine. His affections went elsewhere; he thought of Port-Royal, then so persecuted, and took delightful pleasure in memories of his childhood. . .

He woke with a start, at forty-eight years of age, to a new and wonderful career, taken in two steps: *Esther* for his first attempt, *Athalie* for his masterpiece. Those two works, so sudden, so unexpected, so different to the others, do they not confute our opinion of Racine, and escape all the general criticisms I have ventured to make upon his work?

Racine on Hebrew subjects is far otherwise at ease than on Greek and Roman subjects. Nurtured from childhood on sacred books, sharing the beliefs of the people of God, he keeps strictly to the Scripture narrative; he does not think himself obliged to mingle the authority of Aristotle in the action of the play, nor, above all, to place at the heart of his drama an amorous intrigue (and love is of all human things the one which, resting on an eternal basis, varies most in its forms according to the ages, and consequently leads the poet more surely into error). Nevertheless, in spite of the relationship of religions, and the communion of certain beliefs, there is in Judaism an element apart, inward, primitive, oriental, which it is important to grasp and put forward prominently, under pain of being tame and unfaithful; and this fundamental element, so well understood by Bossuet in his *Politique Sacrée,* by M. de Maistre in all his writings, and by the English painter, Martin, in his art, was not accessible to the sweet and tender poet who saw the Old Testament solely through the New, and had no other guide to Samuel than Saint Paul.

Let us begin with the architecture of *Athalie;* with the Hebrews all was figurative, symbolical; the importance of forms was part of the spirit of the law. Vainly do I look in Racine for that temple wondrously built by Solomon, in marble, in cedar, overlaid with pure gold, the walls gleaming with golden cherubim and palm-trees. I am in the vestibule, but I see not the two famous columns of bronze, eighteen cubits high, one named Jachin, the other Boaz; nor the sea of brass, nor the brazen oxen, nor the lions; neither can I imagine within the tabernacle the cherubim of olive-wood, ten cubits high, their wings stretched out and touching one another until they encircled the arch of the dome. The scene in Racine takes place under a Greek peristyle, rather bare, and I am much less disposed to accept the "sacrifice of blood" and "immolation by the sacred knife" than if the poet had taken me to the colossal temple, where King Solomon offered unto Jehovah, for a peace-offering, two-and-twenty thousand oxen and one hundred and twenty thousand sheep. Analogous criticism may be made upon the characters and speeches of the personages.

In short, *Athalie* is an imposing work as a whole, and in many parts magnificent, but not so complete nor so unapproachable as many have chosen to consider it. In it Racine does not penetrate into the very essence of Hebraic oriental poesy; he steps cautiously between its naïve sublimity on the one hand, and its naïve grace on the other, carefully denying himself both.

Shall I own it? **Esther,** with its charming gentleness and its lovely pictures, less dramatic than **Athalie,** and with lower aims, seems to me more complete in itself and leaving nothing to be desired. It is true that this graceful Bible episode is flanked by two strange events, about which Racine says not a single word: I mean the sumptuous feast of Ahasuerus, that lasted one hundred and eighty days, and the massacre of their enemies by the Jews, that lasted two whole days, at the formal request of the Jewess Esther. With that exception, and perhaps by reason of that omission, this delightful poem, so perfect as a whole, so filled with chastity, with sighs, with religious unction, seems to me the most natural fruit that Racine's genius has borne. It is the purest effusion, the most winning plaint of his tender soul, which could not be present where a nun took the veil without being melted to tears—an incident of which Mme. de Maintenon wrote: "Racine, who likes to weep, is coming to the profession of Sister Lalie."

About this time, he composed for Saint-Cyr four spiritual canticles, which should be numbered among his finest works. Two are after Saint Paul, whom Racine treats as he has already treated Tacitus and the Bible; that is to say, by encircling him with suavity and harmony, but sometimes enfeebling him. It is to be regretted that he did not carry this species of religious composition farther, and that in the eight years that followed **Athalie** he did not cast forth with originality some of the personal, tender, passionate, fervent sentiments that lay hidden in his breast. Certain passages in his letters to his eldest son, then attached to the embassy in Holland, make us conscious of an inward and deep-lying poesy which he has nowhere communicated, which he restrained within himself for long years; inward delights incessantly ready to overflow, but which he never poured out except in prayer at the feet of God, and with tears that filled his eyes. . .

From his own time until ours, and through all variations of taste, Racine's renown continues, without attack and constantly receiving universal homage, fundamentally just, and deserved as homage, though often unintelligent in its motives. Critics of little compass have abused the right of citing him as a model; they have too often proposed for imitation his most inferior qualities; but, for whoso comprehends him truly, there is enough, in his work and in his life, to make him for ever admired as a great poet and cherished as a heart-friend.

Paul Verlaine (essay date 1894)

SOURCE: "Shakespeare and Racine," in *The Fortnightly Review,* Vol. LVI, No. CCCXXXIII, September, 1894, pp. 440-47.

[*A nineteenth-century French poet, Verlaine captured the musicality of the French language perhaps more than did any other poet. By using rhyme structures and meters that had previously been rare in French poetry, he is said to have liberated French poetics from the strictures of classicism and the rhetoric of Romanticism, and helped define the Symbolist theory of poetics. In the following excerpt, Verlaine compares the accomplishment of Racine with that of Shakespeare, finding the former in some ways superior.*]

Some young men, who keep guard over what they are pleased to term my reputation, have, in all good faith, rashly asserted that, in the familiar chat of a *café,* I said, in opposition to my master and friend Auguste Vacquerie, that Racine was to be preferred to Shakespeare.

Every one is free to have an opinion, but I do not prefer one man to another in point of art, when those in question are "in the realm of equals," as Victor Hugo expresses it in his fine work on "William Shakespeare."

Being myself French, perhaps, I love and admire Racine enormously, above all as a man more distinguished by passion than by anything else, and I love Shakespeare (how can I express my admiration for him?) as a man rather more intellectual than passionate. For unquestionably Racine has surpassed Shakespeare in the delineation of woman, in throwing a strong light upon her and revealing some of the innermost recesses of her nature. The divine imagination of Shakespeare has chiefly depicted her in an idealised form, impersonal, like Lady Macbeth, who represents Ambition; Desdemona, the passive creature, the modest woman; Ophelia, the young girl, a pure dream: all are *types.* How different from Racine's women! Phèdre and Bérénice are Love in its two extremes; Monime is the calm heroine; Athalie, the queen who was beautiful and remembers it; Esther, the woman who is beautiful and knows it: all are *characters.* Racine holds woman in his hand, Shakespeare in his mind: what poets and malicious wits they both are! Both held her in their hearts, but there is no doubt that Racine cherished her the more deeply, and in all literature there is only Molière, that I am aware of, who perhaps knows, detests, adores, and raves about her, more than he does. . . .

[Shakespeare's] inexhaustible eloquence, whatever forms it may borrow, the most vulgar or sublime, never repeats itself and never rants wildly. It is a beautiful, at times, a terrible torrent, a majestic stream or a river winding among grass and flowers, a dreamily murmuring if not a babbling merry brook.

This is so; yet since the course of this article logically takes me back to the "divine Racine," as Victor Hugo describes him, in the precocious but sweeping "Preface to Cromwell"—is Racine, who is the most fluent of talkers, as well as a great poet, wearisome at all? *Bon dieu, non!* but a certain regularity, a beauty, perhaps, that rather lacks variety, in his pure, easy language, might, though very unjustly, be considered monotonous in some passages, and I shall now endeavour to prove my deep conviction that such an accusation is quite unfounded. It is evident that the despotic metre created by Ronsard and Malherbe, and subjected to the severe test of Corneille's handling which Racine was forced to use for his tragedies, contributed to the appearance of excessive regularity, inasmuch as the author of the **Plaideurs** had already evolved the most wonderful instruments of rhythm and rhymes which the cleverest, most skilful modern versifiers, like Banville, have chiefly adopted from the "master" and reverentially ascribe to him. But all this more strongly confirms me in my assertion that Shakespeare, in spite of his prolixity which is never tedious, or even of his few rare insipidities, which come upon us as pure surprises—one would think they were put there on purpose—is always and under all circumstances amusing: amusing in the sense in which Baudelaire applied the word to the *Iliad* and to Edgar Poe's stories—always interesting as legend, as

---

Leigh Hunt on an 1818 production of *The Distressed Mother* (*Andromaque*) :

[*The Distressed Mother,* translated by Ambrose Philips from Racine] is French all over, that is to say, dramatically speaking—pompous, frigid, and ranting. Instead of the grand elemental feelings of the Greeks, who half in sublimity and half in superstition talk like the creatures of a newly created and passionate world, sincere and awful, all things, with the usual modesty of the old French system, are brought down to the pitch of the Court of Louis the 14th. The French were too much occupied to go to Nature, and so Nature must come to them; and all the "vasty spirits" of poetry and passion shrink themselves into coals and bag-wigs, as the devils in Milton's Pandaemonium did into pigmies. The persons "Madam" it away, like the ladies in the *Beggar's Opera.*

Leigh Hunt, in Leigh Hunt's Dramatic Criticism: 1808-1831, *edited by Lawrence Huston Houtchens and Carolyn Washburn Houtchens, Columbia University Press, 1949.*

---

philosophy, almost as theology (for instance, in passages of *Hamlet* and of several other plays, the titles of which have escaped my memory), and also as fairy and ghost lore! It is this quality of being a *story,* tragic, grotesque, philosophical, or fantastic, the special attribute of the Shakespearean drama, which renders it perpetually amusing, since, be it understood, the master's touch is always present. Racine's tragedy, on the other hand, to quote the words of Napoleon I. in speaking of French tragedy in general, is a *crisis:* in it passion reaches its culminating point; it has nothing to do with anecdotes, it is Venus, it is Mars, always some keen feeling,

A leur proie attachés.

Hence the tension of the style is adequate to the tension of the action, and it is obvious that the poetry itself, divested of all parasitic ornament and entirely directed to the immediate end, contracts a stiffness and a certain inevitable dryness from its very precision. Still Racine

knew how to cover and mitigate these necessary sacrifices with his harmonious language, the most harmonious of all French language, without ever weakening their effect. We must therefore give more credit and feel more grateful to Racine than to all other French dramatists worthy of the name (I allude to Corneille, Rotrou, sometimes Crébillon the elder, and even Voltaire), for the literary interest, for the literary amusement even, if I dare so to speak, attaching to the famous and severely-modelled French drama of more than one or two centuries ago.

From all that I have said in Racine's praise do I mean to infer that Shakespeare, when the situation requires it, is lacking in the necessary gravity and sobriety? Not by any means! Do Macbeth and his worthy spouse declaim so many metaphors and inflame their passions in such interminable speeches as that would imply? Does not Othello, when he once makes up his mind, fall into a superb fury that is quite natural and direct? Does not even the hesitating, troubled Prince Hamlet rush at last, almost without a word, upon Polonius, after dismissing his mother with a quiet gesture? But there it is! the texture of the Shakespearean drama would not, until the very end, permit the use of this sober language, perhaps too much so for the taste of many people, which is the supreme honour of the, in other respects, and even in spite of this quality, truly, intensely, essentially, *poetic* Racine, who can also justly claim the lyric crown, for he and Victor Hugo are certainly the greatest French lyrists. Read his canticles, his translation of some of the Psalms of David and, above all, the sublime choruses of the **Esther** and the **Athalie**:

D'un cœur qui t'aime,

Mon Dieu, qui peut troubler la paix? . . .

Quelle Jérusalem nouvelle
Sort du sein des déserts, brillante de clarté?

Au delà des temps et des âges,
Au delà de l'Eternité.

If we now speak of wit, who had more of it than Shakespeare? No one. And how it sparkles upon a dazzlingly luminous background! White upon white, as in Whistler and a few other painters, who are so modern as to be existing almost in the future! His dialogue is inexhaustibly diverting in the noblest sense of the word: witty both in the French and English meaning of the word *spirituel* and full of the English *high spirits* and *animal spirits,* expressions which can scarcely be translated into French, for the words *belle humeur* and *bonne humeur* convey no adequate idea of their meaning.

Well, Racine is supremely gifted with this *belle humeur, this bonne humeur;* it is first seen in the **Plaideurs,** which is a rolling fire of wit, also in his epigrams, which are at times so cruel, in most of his prefaces, and lastly in his youthful letter to the "Messieurs" of Port Royal, in which he lashes their crass pedantry and odious *dévocieuseté,* if I may risk the ungainly word.

The nature of the mind of these two great men, though essentially the same, was evidently modified in each case by their early education and the life that ensued.

Racine, the son of a state functionary, had the advantages of a thorough education and a pecuniary competence. He was brought up in habits of sincere piety, but still a little too much in the fashion of his age to be deeply influenced by the fanatical or the enthusiastic in religious matters; he was brought up, moreover, in Paris, and was precociously clever; soon he became a courtier (indeed, a very worthy one) of dignified and most respectable behaviour, and although amongst the most brilliant of his rank, he was even then greatly honoured as a man of letters; a courtier, in short, whom death broke sooner than bent—what a contrast to the poacher, the theatre callboy, etc., etc., the son of a butcher, who in the prime of his youth, already precocious at fifteen, "killed his oxen with some pomp," as a biographer says.

Shakespeare was quite an unpolished youngster, able only to read with fair ease, to write badly, and to count in a way. He completed this most elementary instruction by desultory reading of fables, Mother Goose's stories, chronicles, songs, more often learnt through the ears than from books; he possessed the classics, Plutarch, etc., only in translations, most frequently from the French; Racine, on the other hand, to annoy his masters, once learnt by heart and copied from memory a Greek novel, *Theagenes and Chariclea!*

So Shakespeare borrows his jests from all sources, and invests them with a charm peculiarly his own, free, fantastic, reminiscent of the artisan, the peasant, even the courtesan, if needful, and always entirely original, genuine and genial, cleverly graceful, or extremely grotesque, like Cellini's figurines, like architectural masks, heraldic serpents and *tarasques*. Racine's gaiety, light and smart as it is, slightly savours of the student and the gentleman. The Attic salt often (though not too often) seasons his Gallic humour—very Gallic when necessary.

> Tirez, tirez, tirez . . . . —*Les Plaideurs*.

There exists therefore between these two geniuses, so apparently dissimilar, not a little through the fault of curiously special conditions in each case, a similitude on the whole which seems to me the result of the kind of parallel which I have dared, dwarf as I am, to venture upon in regard to the work and a little in regard to the life of these giants. It is true, that so many stupidities and platitudes respecting them have been vomited forth in French, English, German, and every other European language that this modest and only too justly timid study of mine might in some sort make me proud. For what has been left unsaid, if we start from Voltaire, who damned Racine with faint praise, blasphemously attacked Corneille and lost all his intelligence when it came to Shakespeare, down to fat Dr. Johnson, that malicious pedant, and even to the literary myrmidons of every land, of both sexes, I was about to say, of every. . . gender?

Brander Matthews (essay date 1903)

SOURCE: "The Development of the French Drama," in *The International Quarterly*, Vol. VII, No. 3, March, 1903, pp. 14-31.

[*An American critic, playwright, and novelist, Matthews wrote extensively on world drama and served for a quarter century at Columbia University as professor of dramatic literature; he was the first to hold that title at an American University. Matthews was also a founding member and president of the National Institute of Arts and Letters. Because his criticism is deemed both witty and informative, he has been called "perhaps the last of the gentlemanly school of critics and essayists" in America. In the following excerpt, Matthews presents an overview of Racine's significance and the nature of his accomplishment, comparing Racine to Corneille in many areas.*]

Racine, who followed Corneille, as Euripides followed Sophocles, took over the form of tragedy which the elder poet had marked with his own image and superscription, altho the younger poet modified it in some slight measure to suit his own powers and his own preferences. Corneille had been over-lyric at times, altho he had been far less epic than many of his predecessors as a playwright; Racine was more rigorously dramatic. Accepting the limitation imposed by the rules of the Three Unities, which were in accord with his temperament, Racine condensed still further the themes he treated. He focussed the attention upon fewer figures; and he simplified again the action until English critics are wont to deem his plays bare and cold, altho in fact a fire of passion is ever glowing within them. He was an adept in construction; and his plots, narrow as they may be, are exquisitely proportioned, revealing the most consummate art in the conduct of the story. Always does he avoid scrupulously all digressions and underplots and parasitic episodes.

The extraordinary situations that Corneille had been delighted to discover in history, Racine rejected altogether, choosing rather to deal with what was normal and natural, the growth of a man's love for a woman who loved another or the consequences of a woman's mad passion for a youth who cared nothing for her. He handled like a master this common stuff of life, which is ever tragic enough in the sight of those who can understand it. In his plays, as indeed often in Corneille's also, the action is internal rather than external; and the moral debate within the heart of man is not always accompanied by mere physical action, visible to the heedless spectator. Racine did not seek to interest the audience in, what his characters were doing before its eyes but rather in what these characters were in themselves and in what they were feeling and suffering. He was an expert playwright as well as a master of psychologic analysis, and this is why he was able to accomplish the difficult feat of making his study of the inner secrets of the human soul effective on the stage. His story might be slight, but in his hands it was always sufficient to express a tensity of emotion and to command abundant sympathy.

In the tragedy of *Andromaque* the spectator is made to see how Pyrrhus, son of Achilles, is about to abandon his promised bride, Hermione, daughter of Helen, because he is desperately enamoured of Andromache, widow of Hector. On behalf of the Grecian chiefs, Orestes, son of Agamemnon, comes to demand of Pyrrhus the sacrifice of the son of Hector and Andromache. Orestes loves Hermione, who loves the faithless Pyrrhus, who longs for Andromache, who is devoted to her husband's memory. To save her son Andromache weds Pyrrhus, resolved to slay herself as soon as the boy's safety is assured. In the agony of her jealousy, Hermione hints to Orestes that she will be his, if he will slay Pyrrhus before the wedding with Andromache. But when Pyrrhus is killed and Orestes comes to claim his reward, Hermione recoils with horror and reproaches him for his evil deed; and then she rushes forth to put an end to her own life upon the bier of the man she had loved in vain. The death-dealing blows are never given before the eyes of the spectators; and yet this artistic reticence results in no loss of interest, since the attention of the audience is directed, not to the mere doings of the characters but to the effect of these doings, first upon Hermione and then on Orestes.

His conscious possession of the power of arousing and retaining the interest of the playgoers of his own language in his minute discrimination between motive and emotions, may be one of the reasons why Racine was prone to choose a woman as the central figure in most of his plays; and here again is a point of resemblance to Euripides. He was led also to make use of love as the mainspring of his action, partly, perhaps, because the passion of man for woman had not often been considered by Corneille, and partly because this was of all the passions the one Racine himself best understood. A loving woman Racine would ever delineate with delicate appreciation and with illuminating insight. His touch was caressingly feminine; whereas the tone of Corneille was not only manly but even stalwartly masculine. Corneille, argumentative as he was at times and even declamatory, was forever striving to fortify the soul of man, while Racine with a softer suavity was seeking rather to reveal the heart of woman,—to lay it bare before us, palpitating at the very crisis of passion. As we gaze along the gallery of Racine's fascinating heroines, we observe that desire often conquers duty; but when we call the roll of Corneille's heroes, we behold men curbing their inclinations and strong to do what they ought.

Thus it may be that Racine was the nearer to nature, since it is often a strain upon the spectator to lift himself up to the level of Corneille's exaltation. Racine's language also was more familiar than Corneille's, easier, homelier, and therefore less open to the accusation of being stilted. Not only had Corneille a lyric fervor, but he was also a minter of maxims, an incomparable phrase-maker; Racine sought rather to be simple and never strove for sententiousness, which is not a feminine characteristic. On the other hand, the younger poet had a gift of pictorial evocation; and his verse had often an insinuating and serpentine grace. It was admirably adjusted to the organs of speech; it lent itself to delivery on the stage; and yet there were few purple patches in Racine's plays and scarcely a bravura passage existing for its own sake. The poetry was not something applied from the outside; it was the result rather of a perfect harmony between the sentiment and its expression. Racine's melodious verse is evidence that French is not so unpoetical a language as those have said who cannot feel its music or who dislike its nasal tone.

But even in Racine's hands the rhymed Alexandrine seems to us distended and monotonous. As a dramatic meter it is inferior to the dignified iambic of the Greeks and to our own varied blank verse; and even if rhyme is really needed in a language as unrhythmic as French, it cannot but appear artificial to those who happen to be unaccustomed to it. This impression of artificiality is deepened by Racine's enforced employment of the conventional vocabulary of gallantry to express sincere and genuine emotion. It was the misfortune of Corneille also, that he had to deal with the universal in terms of the particular; and that his plays, like Racine's, were conditioned by the sophisticated taste of the playgoers before whom they were performed. If we contrast the courtly audiences of Racine with the gathering of Athenian citizens to judge a drama of Sophocles, and with the spectators of all sorts thronging to applaud the plays of Shakespeare, we can see one reason why French tragedy lacks the depth and the sweep of the Greek, and why it has not the force and the variety of the English. French tragedy appeared, as Taine has told us, "when a noble and well-regulated monarchy, under Louis XIV., established the empire of decorum, the life of the court, the pomp and circumstance of society, and the elegant domestic phases of aristocracy"; and French tragedy could not but disappear "when the social rule of nobles and the manners of the antechamber were abolished by the Revolution."

Lytton Strachey (essay date 1908)

SOURCE: "Racine," in *Books and Characters: French & English,* Chatto and Windus, 1922, pp. 3-24.

[*Strachey was an early twentieth-century English biographer, critic, essayist, and short story writer. He is best known for his biographies* Eminent Victorians *(1918),* Queen Victoria *(1921), and* Elizabeth and Essex: A Tragic History *(1928). According to P. Mansell Jones, translator of Eugène Vinaver's* Racine and Poetic Tragedy *(1955), "Curiosity about Racine was considerably stimulated in Anglo-Saxon countries by the publication of Lytton Strachey's essay [in* Books and Characters] *in 1922." In the following excerpt from that essay, originally published in the* New Quarterly *in 1908, Strachey summarizes the difficulty of fixing Racine's place among the world's poets, and comments upon the great emotional power of his dramas.*]

It is difficult to 'place' Racine among the poets. He has affinities with many; but likenesses to few. To balance him rigorously against any other—to ask whether he is better or worse than Shelley or than Virgil—is to attempt impossibilities; but there is one fact which is too often forgotten in comparing his work with that of other poets—with Virgil's for instance—Racine wrote for the stage. Virgil's poetry is intended to be read, Racine's to be declaimed; and it is only in the theatre that one can experience to the full the potency of his art. In a sense we can know him in our library, just as we can hear the music of Mozart with silent eyes. But, when the strings begin, when the whole volume of that divine harmony engulfs us, how differently then we understand and feel! And so, at the theatre, before one of those high tragedies, whose interpretation has taxed to the utmost ten generations of the greatest actresses of France, we realise, with the shock of a new emotion, what we had but half-felt before. To hear the words of Phèdre spoken by the mouth of Bernhardt, to watch, in the culminating horror of crime and of remorse, of jealousy, of rage, of desire, and of despair, all the dark forces of destiny crowd down upon that great spirit, when the heavens and the earth reject her, and Hell opens, and the terrific urn of Minos thunders and crashes to the ground—that indeed is to come close to immortality, to plunge shuddering through infinite abysses, and to look, if only for a moment, upon eternal light.

Irving Babbitt (essay date 1909)

SOURCE: "Racine and the Anti-Romantic Reaction," in *Spanish Character, and Other Essays,* Frederick Manchester, Rachel Giese, William F. Giese, eds., Houghton Mifflin Company, 1940, pp. 89-104.

[*With Paul Elmer More, Babbitt was one of the founder of the New Humanism (or neo-humanism) movement which arose during the twentieth century's second decade. The New Humanists were moralists who adhered to traditional conservative values in reaction to an age of scientific and artistic self-expression. In regard to literature, they believed that the aesthetic qualities of a work of art should be subordinate to its moral and ethical purpose. They were particularly opposed to Naturalism, which they believed accentuated the animal nature of humans, and to any literature, such as Romanticism, that broke with established classical tradition. In the following excerpt from a review which originally appeared in the* Nation *in 1909, Babbitt explores Racine's accomplishment as an heir of the neoclassical tradition in drama.*]

If we are to arrive, then, at an intelligent estimate of Racine, it should seem necessary, above all, to determine in what respects he is genuinely classic and in what respects neo-classic or pseudo-classic, not failing to note at the same time certain other respects in which he is inspired rather by the spirit of romance.

The neo-classic element in French tragedy goes back, of course, to the Aristotelian commentators and literary casuists of the Italian Renaissance. Perhaps the most striking feature of this neo-classical regulation of the drama from the very start is its tendency to apply rational rather than imaginative standards, even to the point of abolishing the distinction between the world of poetry and the

world of logic and everyday fact. Any play that overstepped the bounds of ordinary reality or failed to develop with a strict logical sequence was condemned as 'improbable.' This somewhat narrow and mechanical conception of dramatic verisimilitude is mainly responsible for the most famous of all the rules, the unities of time, place, and action, of which the second is not in Aristotle at all, and only the third can be said to be truly Aristotelian. The three unities, along with the *liaison des scènes* (the 'scenes unbroken'), another expression of the demand for logicality, have been summed up in the lapidary verses of Boileau:

> Qu'en un lieu, qu'en un jour un seul fait accompli
> Tienne jusqu'à la fin le théâtre rempli.

Unlike Corneille, Racine moved with perfect ease among all the rules that the neo-classic disciplinarians had imposed upon the stage. Indeed, it is in Racine, if anywhere, that all this regulating of the drama must find its justification. From a minute study of treatises like that of Heinsius (*De Tragoediae Constitutione*, 1611), he absorbed the quintessence of the Aristotelian lore of the Renaissance. As a result, he has attained in several of his plays, not simply a strictness of structure, but an actual perfection of dramatic technique that is unsurpassed in ancient or modern literature; and this is no mean merit, even though it does not in itself take the place of the divine spontaneity of Greek art at its best.

The neo-classic rules fell in with Racine's own tendency to concentrate—to portray only one passion and to take that passion itself in its very crisis and culmination. Racine is more interested in the psychological drama than in the outer action in which this drama finds expression. A recent writer (G. Michaut in *La Bérénice de Racine*, 1907) has maintained that the most Racinian of Racine's plays—the play toward which his whole conception of dramatic art tended—is *Bérénice,* which comes near realizing the popular notion of French tragedy as a five-act conversation. Yet the psychological drama in *Bérénice* is intense, and it is a better acting play than many a romantic melodrama crowded from beginning to end with tumultuous incident. It is also to Racine's concentration that we must ascribe in part his lack of 'local color,' all the concrete and picturesque details that diversify human beings in time and space, a lack for which he has been reproached by critics from his contemporary Saint-Évremond to the present day. Like all the classicists, Racine aimed to represent human nature in its essence rather than as locally modified, but was often too prone to identify this essential human nature with forms of human nature peculiar to his own time. 'The French poets,' says Dryden, 'are generally accused that wheresoever they lay the scene, or in whatsoever age, the manners of their heroes are wholly French. Racine's Bajazet is bred at Constantinople; but his civilities are conveyed to him by some secret passage from Versailles into the Seraglio.' At all events, Racine had the virtues of his limitations and did not allow himself to be diverted from the real business of the drama to the pursuit of the local color that was the fetish of the romanticists of 1830. . . .

One of the ways in which the neo-classic writer becomes pseudo-classic is by failing to distinguish between the permanent laws of good taste and what Lowell calls the parochial by-laws of etiquette. The ancients, says Lessing, knew nothing about politeness. Seventeenth-century French tragedy, on the contrary, is permeated by a refined social convention; and Racine, who was at once an accomplished humanist and a perfect courtier, was peculiarly fitted to achieve this fusion of the standards of the classicist and the standards of Versailles. The distinction between the polite and the vulgar is all-pervasive in his plays, from the chief characters who must be of a certain rank to the language which must be free from all plebeian taint. It has been said that Plato and the fishwives of Athens used the same vocabulary. At all events, words were not officially classified at Athens as 'noble' or 'low,' and the same is, of course, true of Elizabethan England. In commenting on the first scene of *Hamlet,* Voltaire is especially shocked that a mouse should dare to stir in tragedy. Exact comparison is not easy, but we may estimate that the ideas of dignity and decorum of his time restricted Racine to a vocabulary less than one half the size of Shakespeare's. From the charmed circle of convention in which French tragedy moves, everything harshly realistic is banished. Its personages seem to feed on nectar and ambrosia. Little is said about the mind's action on the body, virtually nothing of the action of the body on the mind.

Racine was, of course, too good a classical scholar not to be aware of the difference in this respect between his own art and that of the ancients. He knew that if the art of the ancients was fastidious and selective, it was not squeamish. 'In our French poetry and even in our novels,' he writes, 'there is no more talk of eating than if the heroes were gods who were not subject to the need of nourishment, whereas Homer sets his heroes to eating on every occasion.' The *Odyssey* especially, we may add, is remarkable for the amount of eating and drinking it contains (the 'eating poem of the *Odyssey,* ' as Fielding called it); so much so that when Odysseus would raise the spirits of the departed, he offers them the ghostly equivalent of a good dinner.

'This overdelicacy of the French,' Racine concludes, 'is a genuine weakness.' To understand how French society and literature came to move in this world of refined convention, we must, of course, go back to the beginning of the seventeenth century and the growing influence of women and the drawing-rooms at that time. We should note especially that the men and women who gathered about Madame de Rambouillet deliberately patterned themselves upon the heroes and heroines of the great literary success of the period, Honoré d'Urfé's interminable pastoral romance, *L'Astrée.* The *grand monde,* as conceived by Madame de Rambouillet and her group, is a curious transformation of the pastoral dream that, in some form or other, has always haunted the human heart. 'So understood,' says Amiel, 'society is a form of poetry; the cultivated classes deliberately recompose the idyll of the past

and the buried world of Astraea.' In entering a seventeenth-century drawing-room one entered an intensely artificial Arcadia, but an Arcadia none the less, from which the cares and concerns of ordinary life were banished and where one was free to discourse of love. This discourse of love, it is true, often ran into mere *préciosité,* into what has been termed wire-drawn and super-subtilized gallantry; but at the same time a great deal of real insight into the passions resulted from all this anatomizing of the heart.

Now the tragedies of Racine have been influenced in a marked degree by this love-making of high society. The young lovers of his plays—his Alexander and even his Pyrrhus—are first cousins to the pastoral youth (who are at the same time fine ladies and gentlemen) that sigh and languish through the numerous volumes of d'Urfé and his imitators. Racine, as we have said, was familiar with the Greek pastoral romances and had even met in one of them the very situation he afterward developed in *Phèdre.* But love in the Greek pastoral is something very different from that of the French drawing-room. If the ancients knew nothing about politeness, they likewise knew very little about gallantry. Love as understood by the *précieux* and *précieuses* goes back to the refinements of the Italian Renaissance, which can, in turn, be traced to Petrarch, and ultimately to the cult of the 'lady' and the courts of love of the Middle Ages. The strenuously classical Rymer complains that the French will still be off on 'the wild-goose chase of romance,' and it is true that Racine's preoccupation with love as the supreme motive is romantic, rather than classical. At times, his presentation of love is not only romantic, but chivalric and medieval. The sole object of his Alexander in conquering the world is that he may lay his conquest at his lady's feet. Pyrrhus tells Andromache that as a result of her fair glances, he is burned by more flames than he ever lit in Troy. In *Phèdre,* Racine has altered the whole sense of the ancient legend, by making Hippolytus sigh for the charms of Aricia. 'Where the poet ought,' says Dryden, 'to have preserved the character as it was delivered to us by antiquity, when he should have given us the picture of a rough young man, of the Amazonian strain, a jolly huntsman, and, both by his profession and his early rising, a mortal enemy to love, he has chosen to give him the turn of gallantry, sent him to travel from Athens to Paris, and transformed the Hippolytus of Euripides into Monsieur Hippolyte.'

We must not, however, dwell too long on the element of artificiality and convention in Racine. It is, after all, more or less superficial. What we most often find when we get beneath the somewhat overdecorous surface of his Alexandrines is the keenest psychology and the severest realism. There is less that is farfetched and fantastic, less of *préciosité* in his treatment of love than in Corneille's. At his best he utterly transcends the Arcadian affectations of the drawing-rooms. So much so that to these drawing-rooms themselves he seemed violent and even ferocious. There is more truth in this opinion than in the opposite charge of tameness which is often brought against him by foreigners. Racine is pre-eminent among the dramatists of the world for the mingled power and delicacy with which he has portrayed nearly all the aspects of love, from the mere refinements of gallantry to the ground-swell of elemental passion—passion that in **Phèdre** especially is heightened and intensified by Christian remorse:

> Hélas! du crime affreux dont la honte me suit
> Jamais mon triste coeur n'a recueilli le fruit.

We may learn from Racine what we have tended too much to forget since the romantic triumph, that the expression of emotion may be intense and at the same time restrained.

We may conclude, then, that foreign indifference to Racine arises in part from legitimate dislike of the pseudo-classic element in his work, but even more perhaps from failure to do justice to his genuinely classical virtues. For example, the attitude of seventeenth-century England toward Racine was due not so much to a loftier and less conventional view of the drama as to a crude romanticism. The very public that was indifferent to Racine applauded 'heroic plays' inspired by the bombast and preposterous gallantries of inferior French writers like La Calprenède and Scudéry; just as many persons today may be counted on to prefer the rant and fustian of Hugo's *Hernani* to the exquisite art of plays like **Athalie** and **Phèdre**. The average Englishman or American is apt to see proof of his imaginative superiority in a failure to appreciate Racine; in nine cases out of ten it is proof rather of a limitation.

George Saintsbury (essay date 1911)

SOURCE: "Racine," in *French Literature and Its Masters,* edited by Huntington Cairns, Alfred A. Knopf, 1946, pp. 68-83.

[*Saintsbury was a late-nineteenth and early-twentieth-century English literary historian and critic. Hugely prolific, he composed histories of English and European literature as well as numerous critical works on individual authors, styles, and periods. In the following excerpt from an article which originally appeared in the 1911 Encyclopædia Britannica, Saintsbury offers a summary appraisal of Racine's significance, noting his accomplishment as both a dramatist and poet.*]

Racine may be considered from two very different points of view,—(1) as a playwright and poetical artificer, and (2) as a dramatist and a poet. From the first point of view there is hardly any praise too high for him. He did not invent the form he practised, and those who, from want of attention to the historical facts, assume that he did are unskilful as well as ignorant. When he came upon the scene the form of French plays was settled, partly by the energetic efforts of the Pléiade and their successors, partly by the reluctant acquiescence of Corneille. It is barely possible that the latter might, if he had chosen, have altered the course of French tragedy; it is nearly certain that Racine could not. But Corneille, though he was himself more responsible than any one else for the acceptance of the single-situation tragedy, never frankly gave himself

up to it, and the inequality of his work is due to this. His heart was, though not to his knowledge, elsewhere, and with Shakespeare. Racine, in whom the craftsman dominated the man of genius, worked with a will and without any misgivings. Every advantage of which the Senecan tragedy adapted to modern times was capable he gave it. He perfected its versification; he subordinated its scheme entirely to the one motive which could have free play in it,—the display of a conventionally intense passion, hampered by this or that obstacle; he set himself to produce in verse a kind of Ciceronian correctness. The grammar-criticisms of Vaugelas and the taste-criticisms of Boileau produced in him no feeling of revolt, but only a determination to play the game according to these new rules with triumphant accuracy. And he did so play it. He had supremely the same faculty which enabled the rhétoriqueurs of the 15th century to execute apparently impossible *tours de force* in ballades couronnées, and similar tricks. He had besides a real and saving vein of truth to nature, which preserved him from tricks pure and simple. He would be, and he was, as much a poet as prevalent taste would let him be. The result is that such plays as **Phèdre** and **Andromaque** are supreme in their own way. If the critic will only abstain from thrusting in tierce, when according to the particular rules he ought to thrust in quart, Racine is sure to beat him.

But there is a higher game of criticism than this, and this game Racine does not attempt to play. He does not even attempt the highest poetry at all. His greatest achievements in pure passion—the foiled desires of Hermione and the jealous frenzy of Phèdre—are cold, not merely beside the crossed love of Ophelia and the remorse of Lady Macbeth, but beside the sincerer if less perfectly expressed passion of Corneille's Cléopâtre and Camille. In men's parts he fails still more completely. As the decency of his stage would not allow him to make his heroes frankly heroic, so it would not allow him to make them utterly passionate. He had, moreover, cut away from himself, by the adoption of the Senecan model, all the opportunities which would have been offered to his remarkably varied talent on a freer stage. It is indeed tolerably certain that he never could have achieved the purely poetical comedy of *As You Like It* or the *Vida es Sueño,* but the admirable success of **Les Plaideurs** makes it at least probable that he might have done something in a lower and a more conventional style. From all this, however, he deliberately cut himself off. Of the whole world which is subject to the poet he took only a narrow artificial and conventional fraction. Within these narrow bounds he did work which no admirer of literary craftsmanship can regard without admiration. It would be unnecessary to contrast his performances with his limitations so sharply if those limitations had not been denied. But they have been and are still denied by persons whose sentence carries weight, and therefore it is still necessary to point out the fact of their existence.

Malcolm Cowley (essay date 1923)

SOURCE: "Racine," in *The Freeman,* New York, Vol.

VIII, Nos. 187 and 188, October 10 and October 17, 1923, pp. 104-06; 132-33.

[An American critic, editor, poet, translator, and historian, Cowley made valuable contributions to contemporary letters with his editions of the works of such American authors as Nathaniel Hawthorne, Walt Whitman, and Ernest Hemingway, his writings as a literary critic, and his chronicles and criticism of modern American literature. In the following excerpt, Cowley places Racine's technical, stylistic, and thematic accomplishment within the context of his era.]

Versailles is one of two perfect expressions of the seventeenth century in France. The other is the tragedies of Jean Racine.

He expressed a definite society and therefore could not exist without it. One can imagine him, with effort, against the background of another age, but rather as politician or general: a man of action, in any case, with a terrible or proud career. It was the conditions of his own century which led him to verse and the stage. His work depends on the thousand anonymous collaborators with which it supplied him: anonymous in the sense that their names are printed on the titlepage of none of his editions, and collaborators because they made his work possible. They are such men as Vaugelas, of the earliest French grammar; Chapelain, who first enforced the rule of the three unities; Lancelot and his Garden of Greek Roots; all the humble malignant critics and all the literary salons of the day, to omit great names like Malesherbes and Corneille and Boileau. They formed a tradition which suited his genius better than theirs. A tragedy like *Phèdre* is the summary of all their achievements, the inscription on all their monuments.

No century was more articulate or more critical than the seventeenth, and this in spite of its lacking what we understand as the machinery of criticism. There was, in Racine's day, exactly one review which took an interest in the theatre; with this exception there were few periodicals of any sort. The great mass of criticism was oral. It was broadcasted not through weekly journals but rather by means of a dozen literary salons, among which the French Academy was dullest and supreme. Printing was a later resort. In general it was regarded only as a method of recording and reduplicating the spoken word, and the pamphlet often retained the form of dialogue. The age forced everybody to hold literary opinions. Review, pamphlet, salon: if all these means of vulgarizing literature are justified, it is only to form an intelligent public, which in turn exists to make an intelligent literature possible, or more specifically an audience for the highest form of literature, which is the poetic play.

His audience was ready for Racine; in all ways it seemed that his age had conspired to make him great. It educated him in its best school, gave him an important prize before his majority, and after his second tragedy—undoubtedly his worst—wished to compare him already with the grand Corneille. One might almost be led to say that the seventeenth century produced Racine as a sort of natural fruit, but to reach this extreme would be a profound mistake. What it produced was a milieu in which he could exist as a dramatist. It produced a society, which can be studied elsewhere, and this society evolved a set of conventions by which the tragedies of Racine are governed. . . .

The Racinian tragedy resembled his in the sole respect of containing five acts, but the scene never changed and during the course of no act could the stage be emptied. Rhyme was demanded and a metre which was not left to the caprice of the author: lines of twelve syllables with a cæsura after the sixth and couplets whose rhymes were alternately masculine and feminine. The tragic vocabulary was limited to a couple of thousand words; none of them could name too definite objects; to be vulgar was the last of crimes.

In the creation of a tragedy, every circumstance was contrived to suppress trivialities and detail, but none more skilfully than the arrangement of the stage itself. Imagine for setting a temple, a palace or some other abstraction of the carpenter, without properties, without a single attempt for local colour. Were any such attempt to be made, the presence of spectators on the stage would defeat it surely. The actors are magnificently dressed as the Romans, Turks or Spaniards of convention. They advance; they speak, pompously, in the full understanding that it is not prose but verse which they declaim; they announce Theseus returning from the dead or lament the dead Britannicus; their gestures are measured to the dignity of an assumed rank. People often speak of a tragedy by Racine as being realistic, but when used in his connexion the term needs definition. To actors who deliver rhyming couplets on a stage empty of properties and crowded with spectators; to an author who writes for production on such a stage, any illusion of everyday reality is impossible. It becomes necessary to create another reality instead; a reality which is an affair of the emotions purely, which is produced by a sort of lyrical technique, and which condenses into a single cry of pity or guilty love or terror at some astonishing moment before the curtain falls.

Of all forms of literature it is the drama which most depends on its audience. One can imagine a lyric poem whose manuscript is lost for several centuries; it is discovered finally, and printed, and is great. The fortunes of a play are different: it exists to be played; the audience is one of its vital organs, just as the drama itself is one of the functions of each particular civilization. To be universal is the privilege of other arts. As for the classical tragedy, French or Greek, it can be translated into foreign civilizations, praised with violence, but it must be altered out of recognition or else, by the change of dramatic and moral values, cease to be tragedy. There is no other moral to be drawn from the attempts to naturalize Racine in England. The translators could supply a text which would retain one or more of the qualities of the original, but the Racinian public was impossible to supply.

It was an element in all his dramas: a collaborator and critic that determined the sole conditions under which the playwright was allowed to work. It determined them even with a tyrannous attention to detail that would seem to make any sort of writing difficult and original writing almost impossible. However, in Racine's case, the conventions it dictated and which he followed produced an opposite effect: by regulating the details of composition they made writing easy. Such questions as the number of acts, the style, the choice of subject hardly existed, and as a result he could devote his attention to expressing emotions and unfamiliar characters in the most polished verse of which he was capable; or better, as he phrased it himself, to creating "a simple action, sustained by the violence of the passions, by the beauty of the sentiments and by the elegance of the expression."

If the conventions simplified writing for the stage by emphasizing important problems, their effect went considerably farther, and notably they were useful by suppressing the accidents of plot or setting. A Racinian tragedy can depend on no mechanical details to take the place of thought or feeling; such details are regulated in advance by the conventions, or else ignored. I can remember one of Mr. Belasco's productions which succeeded because of a cat which yawned nightly when it crossed the stage. From *Phèdre* or *Andromaque* one carries a different sort of memory: that of a single clear emotion like the love of Andromaque for her dead husband or Phèdre's incestuous love. Everything else is subordinated. To use the jargon or the studios, a tragedy by Racine is stylized to such an extent that it becomes a sort of abstract painting of an emotion.

The curtain rises; an emotion takes form. During a little more than four acts it follows an ascending curve of intensity. The curve is broken by minor climaxes, little emotional peaks, till it reaches a final summit and descends abruptly into disaster. Or, to use another comparison, a tragedy by Racine is not a series of events but rather a situation which opens like a flower. The first act is the perfect bud of the catastrophe, containing all its elements. The progress of the play is the revelation, to one character after another, of a secret which affects their fortunes and their resolves. When the situation has been revealed to the last of them, when it has poisoned the last of them, the curtain falls. The whole action could be diagrammed into one or more abstract figures.

The elements of literature are not words but emotions and ideas. To be abstract a literature need not be unintelligible; on the contrary. An abstract literature is one in which ideas or emotions, expressed with the greatest possible exactness, are combined into a unity which possesses a formal value, and which is something more than a copy of experience. Evidently Racine comes nearer this ideal than Gertrude Stein, and immensely nearer than our contemporary neoclassicists, most of whom have never even conceived it. The Racinians of to-day are not writers but painters: men like Picasso or Braque whose attitude toward the exterior world is much the same as his, and who, by utilizing conventions almost in his fashion, arrive at a fantastically similar result.

They invent most of their own conventions; Racine was more fortunately born to observe those which existed already. His originality, and nobody ever questioned it, was an affair not of vocabulary but syntax, not of the subject but his fashion of conceiving it. His interest in a situation began two minutes before the crisis, when emotions had already reached the heat of explosion. Their violence is too painful, too great; they require to be softened by distance and dignified by the importance of the characters. For all these reasons the conventions embarrassed him not at all: neither those of language, nor of history, nor the three famous unities. If they had not existed, he might have wasted most of his career to create them and to force them on an untrained audience. He demanded a discipline. Left to himself he would have evolved another set of rules, but he would have followed them as faithfully and it is doubtful whether they would have served his purpose better. . . .

In France the classical theatre has persisted with so few changes that you feel actors and scenery and even the audience to have survived from an age more heroic and slightly ridiculous. When somebody taps a little bell three times, when the curtain rises on a velvet hanging and four pillars, when a young man in a white peplum reaches out his arms to a young man in a purple peplum, surely your first instinct is to laugh. Who designed these pillars, so painfully Corinthian, so shaky that the least touch makes them hesitate on their crazy pedestals? Who copied these two androgynes from a vase? Listen! they are reciting verses; their posture announces a splendid phrase; eyes are raised toward the fourth gallery and arms drape forward. What archæological interest stifles your guffaw? Somebody applauds instead. The play continues.

As it proceeds you suddenly discover yourself to be taking an interest in these people. You have known them a long time, and thoroughly. They have created their own background in your mind: a background not physical but emotional, being composed of passions and memories. They are people living so near that you could almost touch them, and yet there is more than the wall of the footlights holding you back; there is a sort of glass before your eyes that magnifies their actions into heroisms. To place them three thousand years in the past was a purely mechanical device with little more than a mechanical value. Racine went further: he made the action depend on their personal memories to the extent that it is really not Andromaque or Pyrrhus who is chief actor in his tragedy, but the buried Achilles and the dead unburied Hector. Before your eyes he is creating a poetry of distance. The first act ends with scattering applause.

The play continues, suggesting definitions which you can frame only a long time afterwards. The characters of Racine have the dignity of cats. They purr in alexandrines till passion or terror startles them; suddenly they hiss, claw, scream, forsaking their social dignity for a dignity of another kind, which is that of natural forces in action. The action is hidden from your eyes; words are the symbol of it and acquire tremendous meanings; you have the feeling that every speech is the pressing of an electric button which produces upheavals and catastrophes. The characters are only the foci of their passions. The stage itself is a focus. Love and death are events without dignity, but Racine invests them with an importance so terrible that you feel tears to be a vulgar tribute. He has made language the instrument of death. "Who told you?" asks Hermione, and Oreste goes mad, first thanking the gods for bearing him to the absolute summit of human misfortunes. And Hermione herself, dead, sacrificed where the corpse of Pyrrhus lies. Or is it Phèdre that fails of a slow poison, under our stare, to a music out of the past or from undersea?

It is difficult to analyse the impression that persists after a tragedy by Racine, especially because it has always been outside my powers to decide whether a given emotion was moral or æsthetic. I admire the facility with which the disciples of Croce settle such questions, but in the case of Racine æsthetics and morality are mingled to such a degree that it requires nothing less than a Crocean act of faith to disentangle them. Racine himself made no such attempt. In the preface to **Phèdre** he explains how the least faults of his characters are severely punished, and how the mere thought of crime is regarded with as much horror as crime itself; he might be writing a pageant for Holy Week; and yet, in the preface to **Bérénice,** where he gives a general definition of his art, he mentions only the "beauty of the sentiments," as if he disregarded their moral value. One has a choice of interpretations. However, even Croce might be surprised to find that it is the tragedies written with a definite moral purpose which are most satisfying from the standpoint of pure æsthetics. Can a pure æsthetic exist? To deny that literature has moral significance leaves the conception of morality intact, but it subtracts an important element from literature.

As a matter of fact, the Racinian tragedy, for all its plastic value, is moral to a supreme degree. It is moral for reasons which neither Croce nor Racine himself has mentioned: because it reasserts, in the face of doubts which assail us constantly, the importance of man's destiny, the reality of his passions, the dignity of the human animal. We are apt to lose interest in these qualities. Our actions have no more meaning than is conferred on them by art or religion. To write about fashions, travels, books, is a trade which any intelligence can perform; judge an author rather by his manner of describing death and maternity and love, or by his courage to assail these commonplace subjects. After Racine the mass of contemporary literature seems tangential and petty. He takes our attention violently, and it is precisely the violence of his tragedies that makes them a moral spectacle.

The statement holds good for Webster or John Ford; there are more bonds than a common subject between **Phèdre** and *'Tis Pity She's a Whore.* But the tragedies of Racine have another quality, foreign to the Jacobean drama. After a performance of **Phèdre,** of **Athalie,** even of **Andromaque,** the impression which persists is one of absolute perfection. These verses you have heard can not be considered as more or less successful; they are right: in all this audience, in all this city there is nobody who could change

them for the better. The action pleases you or displeases; you have no power to improve it; the characters have a life independent of your own. The tragedy as a whole is perfect, not in the sense of something excavated from a former civilization and pronounced more elegant than the Venus de Milo, but perfect as a living organism to which nothing can be added and which any amputation leaves grotesque. It is the attainment of the classical ideal. There is no English translator, from Otway to John Masefield, who has not tried to improve on Racine.

Since the beginning of our century, a return to classical standards has been agitated, but nobody has succeeded in explaining what these standards are. To define romanticism is considerably easier; it is a historical phenomenon which can be limited in time; by describing the characters of the era which began in England with the close of the eighteenth century, in Germany somewhat earlier and in France more exactly in 1830, one can arrive with sufficient precision at the meaning of the word. Classicism also is a historical phenomenon. However, it can not be confined to a single epoch; it belongs to the age of Pericles and that of Augustus; it is the atmosphere of the reigns of Anne and Ming Huang and Louis XIV: periods which differed widely one from another and still more widely from the fourth-hand classicism of to-day. When demanding classical standards, to which of these periods, or to which qualities of all the periods, do theoreticians refer? Are they not falling into a sentimental reverence for the past, a vague ecstasy which is the opposite of every classicism? Who comes nearest their ideal: Pope or Chaucer or the Greek odists?

It would be wiser to agree on Racine as the classical type. In this case classicism becomes possible of definition: it is an approach, through arbitrary conventions, to a form which is perfect and abstract. It remains intelligible at the same time, and human. It is concerned with people instead of with nature or the supernatural; it considers the moral rather than the picturesque value of their actions; it does not avoid their most rigorous ideas or their most violent emotions. It is a discipline and the spirit of discipline. Such an ideal is tenable in any age, to-day more than ever, for by following its principles one can create a literature which is fresh and unimitative, which is contemporary, and which avoids the excesses of contemporary sentiment.

Maurice Baring (essay date 1924)

SOURCE: "Racine," in *Punch and Judy & Other Essays,* Doubleday, Page & Company, 1924, pp. 145-73.

[During the early twentieth century, Baring—along with G. K. Chesterton and Hilaire Belloc—was considered one of the most important Catholic apologists in England. He was proficient in a number of different genres, but is remembered mainly as a novelist. He also wrote several acclaimed books on Russian and French literature and introduced English readers to the works of Anton Chekhov, Ivan Turgenev, Leo Tolstoy, and other prominent

Russian authors. In the following excerpt, Baring discursively examines several of Racine's dramas, particularly Bérénice, *while addressing the question of Racine's stature as a dramatic poet.*]

Is Racine the greatest of French poets? I will not be so bold as to answer. There is Molière, and there is La Fontaine. Molière as a dramatist is more universal, and La Fontaine as a poet is more peculiar—by more peculiar I mean more exceptional. He is a product of France and of France only, and is *hors concours* in his line, whereas Racine competes with all the poets of the world. It is unnecessary to draw up a list, to place him here or there, above this one or below that one. It is enough to say that he is a great poet, and I think one could safely add that his work constitutes the purest gem of French dramatic literature. There is no drama in French literature which is at the same time so passionate, so strong (as far as the matter is concerned), so disciplined as to the form, so truthful, and so poetical. Let us take him first as a dramatist. As a playwright, he is a writer of human plays—of plays which, although they are about kings and queens, ancient Greeks, Roman emperors, Jews, Turks, and Sultanas—are in reality French men and French women of the epoch of Louis XIV. That is to say, they are men and women, and that is enough. The style in which they talk matters no more than their wigs, or their broad brocaded hoops. All that is a question of externals; it is the frame, the vehicle, the cup; if the cup is exquisite, the wine is none the less exhilarating. Mozart's music is none the less divine because it is written for an eighteenth-century harpsichord.

Under the trappings of the eighteenth century, Racine discerned and portrayed the eternal passions of the human heart, and although his verse has the accent of his epoch it has also, since it is sincere, noble, and beautiful, an underlying note which belongs to all time. There is nothing tedious about his drama in itself; actors can make it tedious by acting it badly; but when it is well acted, it is not considered tedious by the crowd, by the holiday-makers in Paris: it fills a large theatre; it is popular; it pays. Badly acted it disgusts—to see *Phèdre* badly acted is an excruciating experience—that is another question. It is not of any age, but for all time; the theme, and the manner in which the theme is dealt with, appeals just as much to an audience of the present day as it did to audiences in the days of Louis XIV. Take, for instance, the play of *Bérénice*. It is built out of a sentence of Suetonius. *Titus reginam Beronicen, cui etiam nuptias pollicitus ferebatur . . . statim ab urbe dimisit invitus invitam;* or, as Racine translates it, "Titus qui aimoit passionnément Bérénice, et qui même, à ce qu'on croyait, lui avait promis de l'épouser, la renvoya de Rome, malgré lui, et malgré elle, dès les premiers jours de son empire." That is the whole subject of the play. There are no incidents and no action. . . .

There is no action, but out of this *rein* Racine has made a perfect work of art, which rivets our attention and touches our feelings by the passion, the beauty of what is felt and how it is said.

I wish to analyse this play; but I wish to translate it from the particular terms in which it is written into more general terms. The subject of the play, as it is written, concerns the marriage of Titus, emperor of Rome, and Bérénice, queen of Palestine: an unsuitable match. The marriage has been arranged; it is to happen—such is the latest gossip—immediately. Titus, the emperor of Rome, is desperately in love with Bérénice, queen of Palestine, and is determined to marry her whatever the drawbacks may be; but there is another person who is in love with Bérénice, and you can call him Antiochus, king of Commagene, or you can call him Mr. Jones. In the first act we learn through a conversation between Mr. Jones and a friend of his that Mr. Jones has loved Bérénice for five years, but that she has never loved him. At last he presents an ultimatum; he tells her that he has made up his mind to leave Rome for ever; and when she asks him why, he says to her: I have loved you all this time although I have said nothing about it, and I can no longer bear your "friendship," which means that you tell me every day, in detail, how and how much you love some one else. He says good-bye; and his way of expressing what he feels affords a fine example of Racine's talent; of his knowledge of the human heart, and of his power of expressing what he knows. The words might have been spoken in Rome in the days of the Cæsars, or at Versailles at the Court of Louis XIV., or in Paris or in London to-day, or anywhere. So long as unrequited passion exists, and so long as a man loves a woman who in her turn needs him merely as a friend—so long as this situation exists, the following speech will always seem poignant and new:

> J'évite, mais trop tard,
> Ces cruels entretiens où je n'ai point de part.
> Je fuis Titus; je fuis ce nom qui m'inquiète,
> Ce nom qu'à tous moments votre bouche répète:
> Que vous dirai-je enfin? Je fuis des yeux
> distraits,
> Qui, me voyant toujours, ne me voyaient jamais.
> Adieu. Je vais, le cœur trop plein de votre
> image,
> Attendre, en vous aimant, la mort pour mon
> partage.
> Surtout ne craignez point qu'une aveugle douleur
> Remplisse l'univers du bruit de mon malheur;
> Madame, le seul bruit d'une mort que j'implore
> Vous fera souvenir que je vivais encore.
> Adieu.

So much for the first act.

In the second act we see Titus, emperor of Rome, the statesman, the public man, the man of duty, talking over the question of his marriage with his private secretary. He asks his secretary what impression his marriage would make on public opinion, on the man in the street; he tells him he wishes to know the truth. The secretary tells him the truth; and the truth, as usual, is unpleasant; it is to the effect that the Emperor's marriage with the Queen of Palestine would be looked upon by the man in the street as a disgrace, an insult, a national calamity. The Emperor repeats the story of his love—it has never been stronger than it is now—he confides the hope he has entertained that his love might one day be fulfilled with the crowning end of marriage; but at the same time he confesses that he has no delusions about the effect of his marriage. He knows quite well what his subjects would think about it. He only says this so as to hear his own feelings confirmed by another. He knows quite well that he must sacrifice his own private happiness to the public welfare, and he realises what it will mean both to her whom he loves and to himself. His friend—the man we have called his private secretary—whom Racine calls Paulin—applauds his patriotism and his sense of duty, and the Emperor speaks as follows:

> Ah! que sous de beaux noms cette gloire est
>   cruelle!
> Combien mes tristes yeux la trouveraient plus
>   belle,
> S'il ne falloit encor qu'affronter le trépas!

Bérénice, he says, was the cause of his regeneration and his victories, those which he won over himself and those which he won over his enemies:

> Je lui dois tout, Paulin. Récompense cruelle!
> Tout ce que je lui dois va retomber sur elle:
> Pour prix de tant de gloire et de tant de vertus,
> Je lui dirai: Partez, et ne me voyez plus.

Nothing could be more true to life, nor more subtly expressed, than the speech . . . in which he tells his friend the truth about his relations with Bérénice. It is what we call *modern;* when in a Greek play, or in Cicero's *Letters,* or an Icelandic Saga, we feel that something hits the bull's-eye because it expresses what we ourselves have felt, we call it *modern;* it would be more correct to call it *human,* because it is neither ancient nor modern, but eternal. . . .

After this Titus tried to tell Bérénice the truth, but he breaks down; he cannot bring the words across his lips. He leaves her in bewilderment, but with a faint suspicion of the truth; she suspects it, but dismisses it from her mind.

In the third act the Emperor commands his friend to tell the whole truth to Bérénice, and, further, he commits her to his charge; he bids them both leave Rome together. But the friend in question is almost convinced that if he should break the news to Bérénice, her love for the Emperor would turn to hate. He breaks the news to her as gently as he can; at first she disbelieves it, but when, at last, she is convinced, stunned and overcome by the news, she bids the Emperor's friend, namely, Antiochus, king of Commagene, or Mr. Jones, leave her sight, and never come back no more.

In the fourth act we come to the climax. Titus and Bérénice meet when she is fully aware of the truth. Titus tells her that life to him without her will be as death; his life can but end with their separation:

> Scheiden ist der Tod!

after that, he will go on reigning, but not living. She answers him in what are, perhaps, the most beautiful lines of the play:

> Hé bien, régnez, cruel, contentez votre gloire:
> Je ne dispute plus. J'attendais, pour vous croire,
> Que cette même bouche, après mille serments
> D'un amour qui devait unir tous nos moments,
> Cette bouche, à mes yeux s'avouant infidèle,
> M'ordonnât elle-même une absence éternelle,
> Moi-même j'ai voulu vous entendre en ce lieu.
> Je n'écoute plus rien: et, pour jamais, adieu, . . .
> Pour jamais! Ah, seigneur! songez-vous en vous-
>   même
> Combien ce mot cruel est affreux quand on
>   aime?
> Dans un mois, dans un an, comment souffrirons-
>   nous,
> Seigneur, que tant de mers me séparent de vous;
> Que le jour recommence et que le jour finisse
> Sans que jamais Titus puisse voir Bérénice,
> Sans que de tout le jour je puisse voir Titus?

Here we reach the high-water mark of Racine's verse: the words are those of everyday conversation, the sentiments exactly what a woman in the situation of Bérénice would say at any time in any country, and the effect that of great poetry. Never has the immense despair of separation been contracted into so close an utterance. For the moment Titus hesitates, but, finally, he regains his self-control, and he recalls the countless examples of self-sacrifice on the part of his ancestors. Bérénice leaves him saying she means to kill herself, and the Emperor is summoned to the Senate House.

In the last act Bérénice has decided to take her life; she means to leave Rome, leaving a letter behind for the Emperor, telling him what she has done. The Emperor, being informed that she means to go, insists on seeing her once more: they meet. He tells her that this love is stronger than ever, and she upbraids him with toying with her despair. He reads the letter which she had written to him when she meant to kill herself, and he says his cup of sorrow is full, that since she is determined to die, he can no longer battle with life; but—and this is what gives nobility and dignity to his character and to his speech—he is resolved more than ever now, not to disobey the dictates of his conscience, nor to thwart the wishes of his people:

> L'Empire incompatible avec votre hyménée
> Me dit qu'après l'éclat et les pas que j'ai faits
> Je dois vous épouser encor moins que jamais.

He will not leave all and follow her, for, he says, she would merely be ashamed of him for having chosen thus.

The end is brought about by Antiochus (Mr. Jones), who reveals to the Emperor that he has loved Bérénice for so long. Now that I have brought you together, I hope that you both will live happily for ever after; as for me, I shall not live at all; I shall kill myself. Bérénice, self-disgusted, blames herself for being the cause of all this trouble, and, with serene resignation, bids a last farewell to Titus. She explains to him what she has passed through. She had feared at first that he had ceased to love her; but now that she has realised her mistake, she is willing to leave him, and ready to live. She bids Antiochus learn submission from her example, and from that of Titus. . . .

Racine shows his instinct in ending the drama softly with a sigh: the "Hélas" of Antiochus. Thus, at the end, *dimisit invitus invitam*. Coventry Patmore's "Ode" applies to the final situation:

> With all my will, but much against my heart,
> We two now part.
> My Very Dear,
> Our solace is, the sad road lies so clear.
> . . . . .
> Go thou to East, I West.

This play would be just as interesting if transposed in terms of 'Arry and 'Arriet, and if it all took place in Green Park, or on Hampstead Heath, on a Bank holiday.

I have analysed the play thus, in detail, in order to show the framework of Racine's architecture—to show how out of nothing he produces a play more rich in human interest, more poignant and passionate, than dramas crowded with incident and noisy with action; arousing our pity and our interest, simply, as he says, by the nobility of the sentiments, the conflict of the passions, and the beauty of the language: and thus attaining high ends by simple means. *Bérénice* remains, and probably will remain, the final utterance of the tragedy of lovers separated by the conventions of the world. Just as, in *Macbeth*, Shakespeare said the last word on the subject of murder, and touched every fibre of the psychological situation, so does Racine in *Bérénice* exhaust the possibilities of the subject of the seemingly causeless but inevitable separation of lovers; the conflict between love and duty which it brings with it; the various phases of hope, fear, doubt, altercation, despair, reconciliation, and submission which this twofold conflict passes through.

Even in a bald analysis such as I have made, the harmonious proportions of the construction will be apparent. But the play must be read, and still better, seen played (fortunate are those who have seen Madame Bartet—the ideal Bérénice—in the part!), for the delicate gradations to be appreciated by which the scale of passion rises, swells, and subsides, and dies away on a note of melancholy resignation. The architectural beauty of Racine's work, the reasonableness of proportion, the purity of outline, the absence of any jarring note, of anything forced, exaggerated, or unnecessary, are nowhere better displayed than in this play. The drama arises naturally and inevitably from the characters, and the circumstances in which the characters are placed—the one acting on the other—and proceeds, step by step, to its logical and inevitable close. We know from the first that, given the character of

Titus, and the circumstances in which he is placed, he cannot possibly marry Bérénice, and that however deeply she may suffer, no misunderstanding can be finally possible between the two lovers. The great merit of this kind of work is apparent when we compare it with that of lesser masters. In such plays the drama, instead of arising out of the characters of the persons, is brought about by an external and fortuitous *Deux ex machinâ*. Misunderstanding is caused in such plays not tragically, by the blundering of souls in the darkness, but in a concrete fashion, by the intercepting of letters, or the overhearing of conversation behind doors, or possibly the arras. Racine, on the other hand, knows and is able to show, that there is quite enough in the human soul to cause tragedy, without having recourse to the adventitious aid of any melodramatic trickery, accident, or coincidence. Here character is destiny and "passions spin the plot." To find a parallel to this in modern drama, we have to turn to Ibsen and Maeterlinck; or to Turgenev's novels and Tolstoy's and Tchekov's plays.

I said that in *Bérénice* Racine exhausted the subject of separation. You will realise this if you see or read one of the most successful plays of modern times: M. Donnay's *Amants,* the play which made the author's reputation. It is a modern *Bérénice,* or rather, as M. Lemaître called it, a *Bérénice;* its fundamental framework is built upon precisely the same lines as Racine's work.

Bérénice illustrates in the subtlest manner the first great fact about Racine's genius; his power of psychological analysis and presentation. The psychology of all his dramas is as true, as subtle, and as "modern" as that of any modern French or even Russian psychologist. The "classical" drama arising from the incidents of everyday life is just as strong as is the "realist" drama of Ibsen. The passion from being expressed with dignity and restraint is none the less vehement and even violent. Racine's women are as wild in their impulses, as uncontrolled in their passion, whether it be ambition or love, fear or rage, as any of the heroines of Bourget or Alexandre Dumas fils, or Bernstein. If you wish to test the quality of Racine's dramatic power at its youngest and at its freshest, you must turn to *Andromaque*. Here the quality of the passion is swifter and more fiery, more youthful, perhaps, than in any of his other plays. *Andromaque* is to Racine's work what Swinburne's *Atalanta in Calydon* is to his other plays; it has the high, pure note as of silver cymbals and celestial harps. The verses blossom like white lilies, and march past in white and shining ranks. But in order to realise Racine's full power as a dramatist and as a psychologist, his insight into the human heart, his sensibility;—his unique blend of sensitiveness and violence, it is necessary to study *Phèdre;* to read it and to re-read it, and to see it played.

Phèdre is without doubt the most important play in the French classical repertoire. It is the *Hamlet* of the French stage, and the actress who triumphs in the part must needs be a great personality. *Phèdre* is too well known to need any analysis or description; but there is one point to which I should like to call attention. It is this: the objection which is made to all Racine's plays about the discord between the remoteness of his subject-matter and the seventeenth-century accent and tone of his characters, has been more vehemently urged in the case of *Phèdre,* since, whereas the framework and central idea of the play are Greek, its spirit is Christian. But in making Phèdre herself a Christian, conscious of her guilt, and horrified at herself, Racine has merely heightened the tragedy of her plight. Again, what I have already said about the eternal fundamental essence of Racine's characters and the superficial and external nature of their manner and accent, applies especially to this case. For the important fact about *Phèdre* is that, just as in *Bérénice,* Racine wrote the eternal tragedy of separation, so in *Phèdre* he gives us the eternal tragedy of the woman who is the prey of an involuntary criminal passion; and nowhere has this passion been more faithfully portrayed, nor the gradation of the martyrdom more subtly traced. Here are two instances of Racine's delicacy of treatment. The first occurs in the initial scene between Phèdre and Œnone, before she has confessed her guilty secret; she lets the first hint of it be perceptible when suddenly, in a moment of distraction—and unconsciously giving way to her dominating preoccupation; the thought of Hippolyte—she says:

> Dieux, que ne suis je assise à l'ombre des
>   forêts?
> Quand pourrai-je, au travers d'une noble
>   poussière,
> Suivre de l'œil un char fuyant dans la carrière?

Could any indication be more subtly introduced?

The second passage occurs when Phèdre, after having confessed her passion to Hippolyte, learns that her husband Theseus is still alive.

> Mourons. De tant d'horreurs qu'un trépas me
>   délivre;
> Est-ce un malheur si grand que de cesser de
>   vivre?
> La mort aux malheureux ne cause point d'effroi.
> Je ne crains que le nom que je laisse après moi.
> Pour mes tristes enfants quel affreux héritage!
> Le sang de Jupiter doit enfler leur courage:
> Mais quelque juste orgueil qu'inspire un sang si
>   beau,
> Le crime d'une mère est un pesant fardeau,
> Je tremble qu'un discours, hélas! trop véritable
> Un jour ne leur reproche une mère coupable!
> Je tremble qu'opprimés de ce poids odieux
> L'un ni l'autre jamais n'osent lever les yeux.

Nothing could be more exquisitely delicate and tender; nothing more true: no utterance more dignified. It is especially in his women that Racine is psychologically most successful. Women in his work play a more important part than men, although the studies of Mithridates, and of Nero in *Britannicus* rival those of Hermione and Phèdre in subtlety. Certainly among his women-characters the most subtle and striking of all is Phèdre.

One more word about *Phèdre.* It is sometimes said that Racine's drama, fine as it is, is vastly inferior to the *Hippolytus* of Euripides; that in Racine's drama the character of Hippolyte himself, with his trumpery love affair for Aricie, is a poor creature compared with the fatal victim and unblemished devotee of Artemis. But this simply means that Euripides was a Greek and Racine a Frenchman, and it would have been altogether wrong and untrue to nature for Racine to have portrayed an Hippolytus after the manner of Euripides in the setting and atmosphere and among the other personages he chose for his play. His play is a reflection of his period, just as Euripides' drama is a picture of his time; but if you wish, from the purely technical point of view, to study how extraordinarily skilful a dramatist Racine is, you have only to read the opening dialogue in the Greek play between Phèdre and the nurse, and then turn to the French play and see what Racine has made of the same situation. . . .

And yet *Phèdre,* although it is the most subtle, the most theatrically effective, the most arresting, the most rich in human interest, is not generally reckoned Racine's masterpiece. Racine himself preferred it to all his plays. But I think it is universally recognised among French critics that his crowning masterpiece is *Athalie.* Other poets have written plays as fully charged with passion and subtlety as *Phèdre;* no one has written just such a work as *Athalie;* it is in its way unique, unique as *Lycidas* and *The Tempest* are unique. Nobody in the world could have written it save Racine. *Phèdre* may be said to suffer from the comparison with the *Hippolytus* of Euripides; no such damaging comparison can be made in the case of *Athalie,* although the influence of Euripides is felt in *Athalie,* and contributes to its beauty. Voltaire, writing about *Athalie,* called it "l'ouvrage le plus approchant de la perfection qui soit jamais sorti de la main des hommes." Sainte-Beuve said the final word on the subject: "*Athalie,* comme art, égale tout." The work is the fruit of the maturity of the poet's genius; the fruit of twelve silent years of meditation. It is as if Shakespeare had written a play after his six years of retirement at Stratford. All Racine's qualities are seen here in their highest development: his nobility, his religious fervour, his passion for the Scriptures, and for antiquity.

But what makes Racine's plays so great is not only that the human passions in them are dealt with by a master hand, and that the psychology is subtle, interesting, and true, but also that the background, the historical and mythological background, is poetical. There is no local colour in Racine's plays, and yet he suggests a mythological, legendary, or historical setting, as the case may be, by the subtlest means. He has atmosphere; and here again he proves that he is a great poet. So much for Racine as a dramatist. To sum up: he is not only a dramatist, but a psychologist—the first Frenchman to introduce psychology into drama—and one of the greatest, most subtle analysts of woman's heart. Even in a translation, even in the baldest prose translation, any student of human nature would admit this to be true, should he read of the doings and follow the utterances and actions of Racine's heroines: Phèdre, Hermione, Roxane, Bérénice, and Athalie.

There is another great fact about Racine: he is a truthful writer; he does not shun the truth even although it may hurt and shock his principles or his beliefs. He depicts human nature as it is; he faces facts as fearlessly as a surgeon.

Last of all, his diction, his verse is poetic, and he is, perhaps, the greatest of all French verse-writers. It surprises and even shocks intellectual Englishmen if you say that Racine is a greater poet than Victor Hugo, or Musset, or Leconte de Lisle; but there is nothing more surprising or shocking in such a statement than there is in saying that Milton is a greater poet than Byron, Shelley, or Keats. You may maintain the contrary—I do not say that one theory is more right than the other—but I do say that, just as you can make out a case for considering Milton a greater poet than any of the later English poets, so, and in exactly the same way, you can prove that Racine is a greater poet than Victor Hugo or any of the French poets of the nineteenth century.

To compare him with Victor Hugo may be said to be unfair; because Victor Hugo is a lyrical poet and Racine is a dramatic poet. But Victor Hugo has also written plays—plays in which he sought to shatter the tradition established by the plays of Racine; plays which are still acted with triumphant success. Some critics indeed, and among them one of the most scholarly and delicate of judges (William Cory, for instance), say that Victor Hugo's plays are the finest that have been written since those of Shakespeare. But the French put the qualities of Racine still higher. At first sight the range of Victor Hugo's work, the elemental quality of the passions with which it deals, the lyrical heights to which it rises, the depths of feeling into which it dives, the variety and multiplicity of the strings of his lyre, would seem to form a more portentous achievement; compared with this multitudinous orchestration the work of Racine seems like the thin utterance of four stringed instruments delicately played in an eighteenth-century drawing-room. This, however, is exactly the point. Let us say that in an eighteenth-century drawing-room four fiddles or a fiddle and a clavier are interpreting the music of Mozart or of Beethoven. What actually takes place? Bach or Beethoven or Purcell—let alone Mozart and Schubert—can write a melody, perhaps one of three bars only, or even of one single bar, and review it in all its architectural possibilities; and this review, which may entail the marriage of the tune with another tune (thence permutation and commutation), will need for its interpretation perhaps only four stringed instruments, perhaps only a fiddle and clavier, harpsichord, or pianoforte; perhaps only a little portable clavichord—the instruments were played possibly in an eighteenth-century drawing-room by people in cities, or on a London concert platform by spectacled Teutons, and yet . . . from this simple conception and with these limited means of execution things are said and suggested, doors are opened, temples and pyramids are built, unearthly fabrics, whose building the educated and cultivated musician will enjoy *consciously,* and the uneducated and uncultivated listener will (if he hears it often

enough) enjoy *unconsciously,* and whose architecture and proportion will not escape him; and these unassuming methods, this seemingly modest and limited means and vehicle of expression, may and do lead the listener up to a catastrophe, when he feels as if he were standing on the edge of his own planet, and enjoying the sense of being caught up in the wheels of unchangeable harmonious laws, or of being borne on a stream that

> Broadens for ever to infinity,
> And varies with unvariable law,

and of being whirled into eternity.

This effect will seem greater to the musician than the catastrophe achieved by terrific engines, by hypnotic persuasion, complex machinery, and accessories in the music dramas of Wagner, in which the factor of literary inspiration is almost always present.

To some, Wagner's catastrophe will seem in comparison with that of Bach or Beethoven or Mozart like a railway accident.

Now, in the opinion of the French, Racine is to Victor Hugo much like what Beethoven or Bach is to Wagner in the opinion of the trained musician. Of course the comparison must not be pushed too far, but the principle of Racine's greatness, and the reason of his superiority over Victor Hugo (in the eyes of those who think he is superior), resembles the principle of the greatness of the music of Purcell; say, for instance, "When I am laid in Earth" in *Dido and Æneas,* or any of Beethoven's or Mozart's great phrases and melodies that seem to open out their arms and embrace the universe; and the *reason* of their superiority over Wagner (in the eyes, that is to say, of those who think they *are* superior).

This was written before any one had discovered that Beethoven had no sense of "musical form." Perhaps some one will discover that in Racine's verse there is no scansion, no order, no shape, and no sense.

One of the secrets of the greatness of Racine's verse is, as in the case of Milton, his nobility of purpose and design, and his loftiness of utterance. Since in Racine's poetry the form is inseparable from the subject-matter, by illustrating the one it is possible to indicate the other; for his diction, at its finest, is accompanied generally by a majestic and magnificent gesture, which appertains alone to great souls.

The following passage from **Andromaque** represents his diction at its finest:

> Non, non, je te défends, Céphise, de me suivre;
> Je confie à tes soins mon unique trésor:
> Si tu vivais pour moi, vis pour le fils d'Hector.
> De l'espoir des Troyens seule dépositaire,
> Songe à combien de Rois tu deviens nécessaire.

Veille auprès de Pyrrhus. Fais-lui garder sa foi:
S'il le faut, je consens qu'on lui parle de moi.
Fais-lui garder l'hymen où je me suis rangée;
Dis-lui, qu'avant ma mort je lui fus engagée;
Que ses ressentiments doivent être effacés;
Qu'en lui laissant mon fils, c'est l'estimer assez.
Fais connaître à mon fils les héros de sa race;
Autant que tu pourras, conduis-le sur leur trace.
Dis-lui par quels exploits leurs noms ont éclaté,
Plutôt ce qu'ils ont fait, que ce qu'ils ont été.
Parle-lui tous les jours des vertus de son père,
Et quelquefois aussi parle-lui de sa mère. . . .

Here is an instance of his simplicity. The words are spoken by the child Joas in *Athalie:*

Dieu laissa-t-il jamais ses enfants au besoin?
Aux petits des oiseaux il donne leur pâture.

The passages which I have quoted, although few, are sufficient to illustrate the qualities of Racine as a poet; in order to appreciate his merits as a playwright, you must see his plays well acted, and acted by the players of the Comédie française, who are trained in the ancient traditions of declamation. If an Englishman is able to perceive beauty in these quotations, he is able to appreciate the genius of Racine; if not, he is tone-deaf to the language, and there is an end of the matter. He should admit it, and pass on; as a rule, he is not content with such a course. Unable to apprehend these beauties, he denies their existence, just as one denies the likeness of a portrait which, perceived by others, does not strike one's own eye. Yet the beauties are there; to the French they are an object of reverent adoration; the richest jewel of their national inheritance. They are perceptible, too, to all continental artists and critics who know French well. It is only the proud and insular Briton who has the arrogance to deny their existence. Matthew Arnold maintained that French poetry was not poetry; but Matthew Arnold's criticism of French poetry has the same value as would have had Dr. Johnson's criticism of German music. Charles XII. and Prince Eugene, Schiller and Dostoyevski, bore witness to the beauties of Racine. Napoleon said that Racine was *son favori.* I have tried to indicate the nature of his qualities, to illustrate his peculiar charm and excellence. But when all is said and done, when we have pointed out the harmony of proportion, the absence of effort and emphasis, the delicate tact and talent of selection, the suppleness, the grace, and the distinction which mark the works of Racine, there is still something left—an indefinable suavity, an intangible sense of perfect balance, an elusive play of light and shade, a delicacy and charm of texture, a tenderness, a sensitiveness, which cannot be defined by any stereotyped formula. All we can say is, that Racine is among the noble few of whom in reality it deserves to be said that they "built the lofty rhyme"—and he built it after the serene and noble fashion of Sophocles. He ranks with the radiant children of Apollo, whose notes of music are like fountains of pure water. He may not be with Homer, Shakespeare, and Dante; but he is with Praxiteles, with Virgil, and Mozart. . . .

Anatole France on the converging factors that made for Racine's genius:

Jean Racine lived at the moment when the French genius was at its full, when the language had taken final shape, but was yet in its youth, at its golden age. The old poets were his study and his delight, and he bound himself as with cords in that Greek and Latin tradition, all of reason and of beauty which made and gave us the forms of poetry, the ode, epopee, tragedy, and comedy. The poet's tenderness, his joy in the senses, his ardours, his desire for knowledge, his very weaknesses brought him acquainted with the passions that furnish matter for tragedy, and gave it him to express pity and terror.

And so his period, his education, and his nature, conspired together to make of him the most perfect of French poets, and the greatest by reason of the sustained nobility of his work.

Anatole France, in The Latin Genius, *translated by Wilfrid S. Jackson, Dodd, Mead & Company, 1924.*

Benedetto Croce (essay date 1928)

SOURCE: "The Poetry of Racine," translated by Raffaello Piccoli, in *The Dial*, Chicago, Vol. LXXXIV, No. 6, June, 1928, pp. 483-88.

[*An Italian educator, philosopher, and author, Croce developed a highly influential theory of literary creation and a concomitant critical method. In defining the impetus and execution of poetry, Croce conceives of the mind as capable of two distinct modes of thought, which he terms cognition and volition. Cognition mental activity is theoretical and speculative, while volition is the mind's practical application of ideas originating in the cognitive realm. For Croce, a poem, as an intuitive creation, belongs to the cognitive sphere, and exists within a poet's mind as a complete, independent, and unified image. In his view, the original conception of a poem must be motivated by a dominant emotion, and this emotion must be clearly and effectively translated into the actual poem if the work is to succeed as art. From these theories, Croce derives his definition of the proper role of criticism: to determine a poem's original, intuitive image, to ascertain the emotion that both prompted it and is an integral part of it, and, finally, to judge the relationship between these two factors. In the following excerpt from a review of Karl Vossler's German-language study* Jean Racine *(1926), Croce focuses upon the high poetic achievement of Racine's dramas, notably* Athaliah.]

There is good reason to-day for reverting to the poetry of Racine; not as poetry merely, founded upon an incomparable purifying power, but because qualities in it uniquely provide an antidote to loose, noisy tendencies in contemporary pseudo-poetry. . . .

Looking for a "point of view" from which Racine's poetry should be considered in order to determine its constitution, the law peculiar to it, and its motive, Vossler first makes it clear to us that it is essentially an interior force—an active principle or will, but not of the kind that exhausts itself in external action, for then it would shine in its successes as in epic poetry or in history, where deeds and works are more important than individuals. It would be broken, driven back or withdrawn, hindered, curbed, repentant. Instead of achieving its aim and dying, it rebounds to its author and kindles a consuming flame in his breast. It is, in a way, always failure that is celebrated in these tragedies; not failure in the abstract, however, as we know it in pessimistic lyric or satire; and its virtue lies in that self-evaluation, that getting hold of self, which it induces in the characters. This is Racine's true inspiration. Thus Vossler examines and interprets the tragedies, from the **Thébaïde** to **Athalie,** not omitting the comedy of the **Plaideurs,** in which the same fundamental situation reappears. Only in the two last plays, the two religious plays, **Esther** and **Athalie,** do the characters achieve success, and in them not through the exercise of the personal and particular will, but by submitting to one which is higher and is universal; and these two plays are also the only ones in which unity of place is not observed—exceptions which confirm the rule.

This is subtle and ingenious although slightly artificial and perhaps too subtle, too ingenious since still bound up with the concepts of "drama," "epos," and "lyric," as things that can be rigorously distinguished; and it cannot be applied to the whole of Racine's work, for there are various exceptions, notably in the instance of the last tragedies; especially the last and greatest one. It seems to me that critical interpretation might proceed more simply and satisfactorily by considering again the common verdict which makes Racine—in opposition to Corneille—the "poet of the passions": a verdict which is rather vague but deserving of attention because, like all popular verdicts on poetry, it conveys the impression which the poetry made for the most part, and is still making. To be more explicit we might say that Racine's inspiration is the mysterious and rapacious character of passion—delighting itself or tormenting itself. Passion in a pure or impure, in a mild or fierce, in a noble or evil heart; passion relapsing in ruin and death, or issuing triumphant; passion aided or crushed: by powers human; by powers divine: by the principle of good, leading to salvation; by the power of evil oppressing and destroying: such are the protagonists of Racine's plays; but the constant centre of each is always passion, and it is passion transfused into poetry that invests them with charm. It is passion in Andromaque who, loyal to the memory of Troy and Hector, eager for solitude and oblivion for herself and her surviving son, is ready to find peace in death, but determined to preserve untainted that fidelity to the past which is her secret source of strength; it is passion in Bérénice who struggles persistently for the possession of the man she loves, and who—unwilling to surrender—finally, in the very strength of her passion, finds strength to overcome it and make it subordinate in the complexity of human interests. She becomes aware that Bérénice *"ne*

vaut pas tant d'alarmes," that personal affection must not overthrow the social order and make *"l'univers malheureux."* In Eriphile, the lonely, furtive child of guilt, it is burning passion—a turbid, unwholesome mania, irremediable till destroyed in the ill-born creature's self-destruction; and the passion of Phèdre is in origin and growth a little similar to, and a little different from Eriphile's, accompanied as it is by consciousness of sin and feelings of self-abhorrence. But it is also Acomat's wholly political and ambitious passion for power and revenge, undeviating, careful, and deliberate but instantaneous in action, contemptuous of love except as the tool of strategy, and annoyed by it only as it interferes with higher game; it is passion in Mithridate, an illimitable dream of empire, of beneficent salvage, and of the conquest of Rome; and by way of conclusion, it is passion in Joad and in **Athalie**—a manifestation in the former from the depths of traditional Jewish priestly dominance; aroused in the latter by the shedding of her kindred's blood, in avenging which with blood, she founds on bloodshed a tyrannic power which intoxicates yet frightens her. Critics who have interpreted passion in these plays as purely erotic, delimit Racine's soul, unless eroticism be synecdoche for passion in general; on the other hand I should say that Vossler also narrows the concept by emphasis on renunciation, which is but a single aspect or transmutation of passion. Nor can I entirely disagree with those critics who deny religious feeling to Racine, even in his religious plays; not that he is not earnestly religious, or that the religious accent in his plays seems false, but because the impact predominately is that of passion as such, not that of religious exaltation. One remembers what Madame de Sévigné said of those plays: *"Il aime Dieu comme il aimait ses maîtresses; il est pour les choses saintes comme il était pour les prophanes."*

If we keep in mind this poetic centre in Racine's work, we can understand why the tragedies seem rich poetically, in proportion as they become the song of passion, and why those passages which speak most directly to our souls, which become part of our souls, are the situations and moments of passion, the passionate and emotional characters—the greater ones which we have cited and lesser ones like Junie in **Britannicus,** and Monime in **Mithridate.** But almost invariably in the tragedies there is also something else: there is the dramatic tissue, with the characters and actions that weave it and stretch it; and such actions and characters are often from the point of view of poetry merely decorative, though dramatically essential. Which characters and actions, one may ask? And I should say, the ones that do not speak, or that speak not so directly to our souls—that we do not cherish in memory equally with the rest. Racine studies them always with very great care and with a fine power of psychological analysis; but they spring rather from intellect than from imagination; from requirements of plot, not at the voice of the emotions. Such elements are to be found in all the tragedies, in differing proportions and degree: Oreste and Pylade, even Pyrrhus, and Oenone in **Andromaque,** have this aspect of the made character if we may call it such. This may also be said of Hippolyte and Thésée in **Phèdre,** and of one or other character in each play. Their language tends to be madrigalesque, flowery, polite, and courtly, while Andromaque knows how to speak the simple words: *"Quel charme ont pour vous des yeux infortunés!"* and thus Bérénice: *"Mais parliez-vous de moi quand je vous ai surpris?"* and Acomat: *"Moi, jaloux! Plût au ciel qu'en me manquant de foi, L'imprudent Bajazet n'eût offensé que moi!"* A critical examination of single tragedies cannot but establish this varying relationship between personal-fantastic creation on the one hand, and construction on the other; the naïve reader is conscious of it and it constitutes indeed the critical problem in Racine as in other poets. This relationship must be dealt with delicately for the two things often pass into each other, and Racine is always the exquisite artist, permitting himself no unconsidered separation of the poetic from the non-poetic; but it is a thing we must take into account. . . .

There are two plays, however, in which the critical problem no longer consists in that relationship since its terms are not found in them, or at any rate are not distinct and contrasting: namely, those two plays of religious argument composed by Racine after his twelve years' silence, **Esther** and **Athalie**. In the former the contrast is lost in the fairy-tale intonation, that something of *lächelnder Märchenzauber* which is so well perceived by Vossler, whose analysis I accept entirely; in the latter it is submerged in the wholly passionate, wholly mysterious intonation, full of *horror sacer,* which gives life to that admirable play and creates its characters, its plot, its scenes. Vossler, like all critics, feels the greatness of this work, the greatness of the masterpiece; but in consequence of his definition of Racine's dramatic sentiment—as of the relationship between *Misserfolg* and *Selbstbesinnung*—he remains bewildered in its presence; so much so that, in order to elude his perplexity, he adopts Imbriani's definition of Faust: a mistaken masterpiece, with the emphasis on the second word. For him, *Athalie* "transcends dramatic form," and the action loses itself "in epic grandeur and in prophetic distance"; "the style of Racine's times was not prepared for, and fortified against, the vigour of that poetry." To tell the truth *Athalie* transcends the preestablished criterion, the somewhat scholastic concept of dramatic action, but does not transcend poetry—the only thing that matters. *Athalie* does not belong to a Racine attempting the impossible, but rather to a Racine who has reached the perfection of his passionate expressive tendency. The hero of the play, the priest Joad, is not "a hero after Racine's heart," says Vossler, "but Racine need not on this account belittle him, suspect him, or disapprove of him: it is impossible to speak either of inclination or of repulsion in the presence of a mere *phenomenon* such as this is." And it is true that this *phenomenon,* the phenomenon of passion, the "phenomenal passion," dark, religious, sanguinary, all will and all obedience to the will of God, which attracts Racine—attracts him to Joad as, somewhat differently coloured, it attracts him to Athalie, impious and tyrannical, to Mathan, corrupt and sacrilegious, and to the predestined child Eliacin-Joas: we do not know what he will be in the future, after taking power in his hands; so respectful and pious and so perfectly educated by the priest, concentrating in himself the heritage of so much blood and of so many evil deeds, having, as Vossler observes with great penetration, a Janus head. In the light of prophetic hints, against the background of his preceptor's preoccupations the lovely child's face presents to us *das abgewandte Verbrechergesicht,* the averted profile of a criminal.

Jean Giraudoux (essay date 1930)

SOURCE: "The World and the Theatre, in *Theatre Arts Monthly,* Vol. XIV, No. 9, September, 1930, pp. 727-30.

[*A French dramatist and novelist, Giraudoux is recognized primarily for his highly stylized works centering around the elemental themes of love, death, and war. In the following excerpt from an essay originally published in a longer form in* La Nouvelle Revue Française, *he discusses Racine's method, emphasizing the dramatist's exemplary accomplishment while working within an established context: his own, distinctly literary age.*]

Those who believe in genius have the opportunity, when contemplating Racine, to verify the fact that a civilization which has reached its pinnacle . . . is itself a genius—the genius of Pericles or of Louis XIV. . . . One of its virtues is that, instead of the smaller means by which writers in less complete epochs acquire their experience—misfortune, observations of men in daily life, affairs of the heart or conjugal crises—there is substituted in these happier periods, an instinctive knowledge of great spirits and great moments. Racine is the most perfect illustration of this. No childhood was further removed than his from the laws of childhood. . . . His adolescence was not less theoretical. . . . Studying and the joys of studying were to him the substitutes for all contact with life, all happiness, all catastrophes, up to the day when he entered a world even more devoid of steadiness: the theatre. He knew people and actions only in fancy-dress. Yet, from the contact of this young man without youth and this artificial society, was suddenly born the most direct and most realistic work of the century.

Aesthetic laws are, no doubt, as rigid as mathematical laws: Racine evolves his discoveries about human beings with an abstraction, a detachment from humanity as lofty as the indifference of the geometrician for the family life of figures. There is not one sentiment in Racine that is not a literary sentiment. . . . Nothing in him is visionary or real, frantic or discouraged. His bitterness, when he is bitter, does not come from his being lame or imposed upon; his mellowness from being at peace; his power from being athletic—but from his being a writer.

His method, his only method, consists in taking from the outside, through style and poetics, as through a fish-net, a catch of truths of which he himself only suspects the presence. . . . The yeast of his talent is purely literary. Not only did Racine never take his inspiration from the questions that the intellectual currents . . . urged upon his time . . . but he did not let even one of them touch his inner life. . . .

There was no "question of the theatre" at the time Racine began to write. . . . It would have irritated him, moreover, to waste time in reforms and innovations. The theatre is a microcosm where the poetical, moral and material preferences and tastes of an age should shine forth in their greatest splendor and passions, but the theatre cannot create perceptions in the spectator; it takes them for granted. A literary generation, a literary age, can end with a theatrical era but never starts with one. Good drama is an accumulation of perfections; although the reader may look for new discoveries in the course of his reading, the spectator wants only enjoyment from his spectacle. This excludes from the theatre every manifestation which is only a quest or a lesson; which does not instinctively embrace dramatic life such as actuality has created it. . . . Great drama is the drama which convinces minds already convinced, moves souls already shaken, dazzles eyes already enlightened. It is as a student submitting to the customs and the laws of its genre that Racine came to the theatre.

M. Joubert (essay date 1939)

SOURCE: "Racine," in *Contemporary Review,* Vol. 156, December 1939, pp. 729-36.

[*Below, Joubert offers a general essay on the accomplishment and significance of Racine, noting his artistic statements against governmental tyranny.*]

In a broadcast for French schools dealing with Racine's place in the history of dramatic literature, the lecturer pronounced the significant words: "In spite of Racine's unquestionable superiority as poet and psychologist, the French nation will, during the time of a national crisis, always turn to Corneille." This statement seems to me to represent in a nutshell the historical and æsthetic valuation of the two greatest dramatists of French literature, and at the same time to emphasise the necessity of a comparison between them, without which an appreciation of the younger poet's position as innovator of French dramatic technique would be futile.

Corneille represents artistically and morally—the two terms are inseparable in French drama—the definite end of a period, Racine the beginning of a new era which has not yet reached its end. Corneille, the grand old man of French drama, wrote for an audience whose chief interest was politics, taking part as actors or spectators in the vicissitudes of the Fronde, a struggle in which unbending willpower turned ordinary mortals into heroes, but also their speech, as the *Mémoires* of the *Cardinal of Retz* show us, often into heroics. Corneille's art was in full accordance with his political background and with the moral spokesman of his time, Descartes, whose *Traité des Passions* had become the breviary of his contemporaries: "By the outcome of those struggles we can gauge the power or weakness of our soul." This strength of character can, of course, prove its mettle only in situations of great moment demanding weighty resolutions, patriotism, renunciation, uncompromising faith, etc. Corneille thus relegates love into the background, replacing the wavering, storm-

driven impulses of sexual passion by the sublime and heroic, painting, according to La Bruyère's famous comparison between Corneille and Racine, "men as they ought to be." His characters, therefore, are often the outcome, not the creators, of the dramatic situation, ready-made moral abstractions, suffering from a hieratic hardness and rigidity, obsessed by an all-absorbing ethical *idée fixe,* looking in one direction only with the metallic stare of a Russian icon.

Compare with this attitude Racine's self-portrait in one of his Canticles:

> Mon Dieu, quelle guerre cruelle!
> Fe trouve deux hommes en moi:
> L'un veut que, plein d'amour pour toi,
> Mon cœur te soit toujours fidèle,
> L'autre, à tes volontés rebelle,
> Me révolte contre ta loi!

With Mazarin's death a new generation enters upon the political and social horizon. The young, temperamental and politically autocratic Louis XIV surrounds himself with a coterie vastly different from a La Rochefoucauld or a Madame de Longueville of the time of the stiff-necked Fronde. Madame Henriette d'Angleterre, Mademoiselle de La Vallière, Madame de Montespan now give rhythm and colour to the voluptuous symphonic poem composed and conducted by the Roi-Soleil. Politics has become too dangerous to be mentioned and is replaced by the multi-coloured carnival of pomp and circumstance and amorous intrigues before which Corneille's supermen are paling into oblivion. The stage clamours now for heroes less heroic, for heroines more human than Polyeucte or Chimène, briefly for the dramatic analysis of the tender passion. For a short time Quinault supplies this want, thus becoming the link between Racine and Corneille, who bitterly complains that now *"la seule tendresse est toujours à la mode."*

With *Andromaque* (1667) this *"tendresse"* became changed into *"sentiment."*

Quinault's delineation of love as a modish, somewhat affected descriptive programme to the lavender-scented *clavecin* music of his day (he was a really charming librettist), developed under Racine's magic wand into the powerful portrayal of a universal instinct. This new dramatic motive, evolving out of a mere safety-valve for the political passions of the day, no longer to be indulged in, became since Racine the corner-stone of French drama, conveniently labelled as *"amour-passion."* As such it forms the basic element of Racine's art and deserves therefore a closer study. The idea of love was, as most things in France, from the earliest times subject to fashion. The *chevaleresque* woman-worship of the medieval *trouvères,* the reckless passion of the learned ladies of the Renaissance, the metaphysical sentimentality of the *Précieuses* in the seventeenth century, tinged according to clerical influence at Court with religious fanaticism, the dissolute life of actors and actresses, all this forms a kaleidoscopic picture which might well tempt an artist of Racine's strong sensuous temperament.

But multiform and complex as his excursions into the Bluebeard chamber of erotic sensations were, he felt prevented from giving free play to his innate naturalist tendencies by three weighty considerations. First: by the ever-present religious background of the seventeenth-century society, second by his stern moral upbringing at Port-Royal, third by the philosophical training of French thought constantly directed towards the dissection and diagnosis of emotions. The first acted as a kind of invisible but rigorous censor, the second deeply coloured Racine's psychological and ethical treatment of human passions, the third provided him with the scientific insight into the last causes of the impulses and inhibitions of his heroines and heroes. But the most powerful influence in his artistic complex was his Jansenist education, an influence often apparently counteracted and even obliterated, owing to the worldly surroundings of his career as dramatic poet. In an age fettered by tradition and the double autocracy of an all-powerful Church and King, Racine represents youth in art and outlook on life. In the eyes of his teachers of Port-Royal he even became a heretic, owing to his unequivocal stand for separation of religious discipline from the dramatic expression of psychological facts. This becomes evident in Racine's virulent attack upon his old master Nicole, who had dared to rank dramatic poets amongst public poisoners of the soul. And yet the very characters in Racine's plays which most interest the modern reader, audience, actor and actress, are those in which the poet endeavours—and how subtly and successfully!—to apply the Jansenist tenets to the study of the human soul. Phèdre, Eriphile (*Iphigénie*), Athalie, Bérénice, Agrippine, Néron, they all are tormented, recalcitrant pupils of Port-Royal, analysing their own *état d'âme,* accepting reluctantly the fatality of their sinful passions, condemning them, and yet following their lure to the bitter end, for how can they resist, free will being denied to them?

And there Corneille's and Racine's ways part; the older poet rigidly establishing the moral law as legislator in his dramas, the younger, and this makes him almost our contemporary, letting our ethical conclusions arise out of the swaying, passion-ridden souls of his *dramatis personæ*. It is this monastic trait in Racine's character, which neither the sirens of the theatre nor the intoxicating splendour of the Court of Versailles could eradicate, that gives us the clue to the generally misunderstood reasons for his retirement from the theatre at the age of 38.

With the adaptability of his fluid nature, he followed the trend of events at Court. Military disasters, the growing misery of the people and the prevailing influence of the Jesuits upon Madame de Maintenon, who had become more and more the King's spiritual director, had plunged the Court into an atmosphere of gloom and depression, a veritable Ash Wednesday following the frenetic carnival of *joie de vivre,* unfavourable for the appreciation of Racine's dramatic genius, as displayed in his **Phèdre,** whose Jansenist spirit had reconciled him with Arnauld of Port-Royal, but had alienated the King's favour. To all

that must be added the failure of his **Phèdre** (the *affaire Pradon*), the desertion of his mistress and best actress, La Champmeslé, the threat of assassination, owing to a brilliant but tactless sonnet written by the poet against the Duc de Nevers, brother of his arch-enemy, the Duchesse de Bouillon, and the general feeling of frustrated hopes and ideals. In a fit of Pascalian despair he intended becoming a monk, *"un Amen continuel au fond du cœur"* (Fénelon). Racine had started his spiritual education at Port-Royal, had flagrantly denied its teaching through the worldliness of his life, whilst subconsciously applying it to his dramatic work, and was finally rediscovering its soothing balm in the afterglow of a retrospective existence and in the statuesque grandeur of his swan-song, *Athalie.*

Racine foreshadowed with an almost prophetic power some problems which beset the spiritual life of our day: the instability of sexual relations, the craving for domination, the brittleness of moral and religious convictions, though all eventually corrected and settled by a theodicy whose high priest has received his training in Port-Royal. The fearless advocate of justice does not shun his sovereign's displeasure by scarcely veiled political allusions. Already in his second play, *Alexandre le Grand,* we find an outbreak of indignation against autocracy which could only have passed unnoticed in this early drama of the still little-known poet and which even to-day might give food for thought to present-day fascist demi-gods:

> Porus: "Quelle étrange valeur qui, ne cherchant
>   qu'd nuire,
> Embrase tout sitôt qu'elle commence à luire:
> Qui n'a que son orgueil pour règle et pour
>   raison;
> Qui veut que l'univers ne soit qu'une prison,
> Et que, maître absolu de tous tant que nous
>   sommes,
> Ses esclaves en nombre égalent tous les
>   hommes.
> Plus d'états, plus de rois; ses sacrilèges mains
> Dessous un même joug rangent tous les
>   humains."
>
> (*Alexandre,* ii, 2.)

In **Bérénice,** that moving dramatisation of Suetonius' *"Invitus invitam dimisit,"* Racine's contemporaries were invited to draw a parallel between Titus-Bérénice and the young Louis XIV and Maria Mancini whom he too had to renounce: *"invitus invitam"*!

And **Esther,** Racine's first play in which *la grande passion* is replaced by racial patriotism and religious ecstasy, which made Madame de Sévigné exclaim: "Racine has surpassed himself! He loves God as he used to love his mistresses." **Esther** must have appealed to the elect audience of Saint-Cyr as an undisguised plea for the official recognition of Madame de Maintenon as Queen of France: Ahasuerus' command: *"Soyez Reine"* (i, I) sounded like a trumpet-call to King and nation.

But the poet's most courageous attack upon the King's

autocratic indifference to justice is the High Priest's warning to Joas (*Athalie*, iv, 3), symbolising Fénelon's pupil, the little Duc de Bourgogne, heir-apparent to the thorne:

> Loin du trône nourri, de ce fatal honneur,
> Hélas! Vous ignorez le charme empoisonneur.
> De l'absolu pouvoir vous ignorez l'ivresse,
> Et des lâches flatteurs la voix enchanteresse.
> Bientôt ils vous diront
> Qu'un roi n'a d'autre frein que sa volonté
>   même;
> Qu'aux larmes, au travail le peuple est
>   condamné.
> Que, s'il n'est opprimé, tôt ou tard il opprime.

We need not be surprised that neither King nor Court savoured such home-truths and that *Athalie* was not granted a public performance. Nor is Schiller's *Don Carlos* performed in Hitler's Germany!

I believe that our current text-books emphasise too much Racine's insistence upon the sexual problems presented in his dramas. In two plays, *Bérénice* and *Mithridate,* he proved that he was able successfully to steal the thunder from his elder rival. "Renunciation and will-power," Corneille's slogans for his whole dramatic work, are acting also as levers in *Bérénice,* with the sole difference that in Racine's play the clash between duty and desire is never lost sight of. The most Corneillean of his tragedies is *Mithridate,* in which the poet's art makes the Pontian King's imposing personality, like Wotan in *Gotterdämmerung,* seem ever-present, even when bodily off the stage. The Racine, however, who claims the interest of the modern reader is the feminist whose field of psychological research is almost exclusively the emotional life of woman. His heroes, with the exception of Oreste (*Andromaque*), Néron, Mithridate and Joas (*Athalie*), occupy a second, or even third place in his gallery of character portraits. I single out Oreste as a curious study in Freudian inhibition, and as a romantic anachronism in the seventeenth century, a René (Chateaubriand) with a touch of Hamlet.

> Fe ne sais de tout temps quelle injuste puissance
> Laisse le crime en paix et poursuit Pinnocence.
>   (*Andromaque*, iii, I.)

and in the same scene:

> Excuse un malheureux qui perd tout ce qu'il
>   aime,
> Que tout le monde hait, et qui se hait lui-même!

Racine's most sombre study in depravation is Néron. A sadist by nature,

> Fe me fais de sa peine une image charmante
>   (ii, 8.)

he is the dramatic counterpart of Tacitus' verdict: "He was made by nature to hide his hatred under the cover of treacherous gentleness":

> F'embrasse mon rival, mais c'est pour l'étouffer.
>   (iv, 3.)

But Racine's most complex characters will always remain his heroines. From the touching simplicity of unselfish love:

> F'aimais, Seigneur, j'aimais, je voulais être
>   aimée
>
>   (*Bérénice,* v, 7.)

to the outbursts of primitive passion, goaded on by the infuriated goddess, a terrifying picture of prehistoric, ritualist Greek life:

> C'est Vénus tout entière à sa proie attachée
>   (*Phèdre,* i, 3.)

Racine has gone through the whole gamut of passions ravaging a woman's soul. Andromaque's self-sacrificing love for her child and mystic devotion to Hector's memory, Agrippine's thwarted craving for domination over Rome and her son:

> Britannicus le gêne, Albine, et chaque jour
> Fe sens que je deviens opportune à mon tour

culminating in Athalie's lurid personality, oriental in thought and speech, treacherous, despairing before the doom awaiting her, and, autocrat that she is to the end, tormented by feminine hysteria:

> La peur d'un vain remords trouble cette grande
>   âme;
> Elle flotte, elle hésite, en un mot, elle est femme
>   (iii, 3.)

and at last, breaking down with the heart-rending confession of defeat, but still as equal to equal:

> Dieu des Fuifs, tu l'emportes!
>
>   (v, 6.)

These three instances of heroic types chosen from the poet's plays show us that the *"tendre"* Racine knew very well when the situation arose, how to create heroines which could rival Shakespeare's greatest achievements. When drawing the sum-total of Racine's portraits of tragic women, Phèdre, "the incestuous queen, a Christian to whom divine grace is denied" (Arnauld), the sinner whom confession and penance lead out of the wilds of demon-haunted Greece into the precincts of Port-Royal, and Athalie, who, more than any of Racine's heroines, can claim to produce in the listener the Aristotelian reaction of cleansing terror and pity, these two figures will stand out as the poet's sublimest dramatic creations. With Racine woman has come into her own in French drama.

No appreciation of Racine's work can be adequate without an analysis of his technique; his language is based on the French of the seventeenth century, clipped, polished, but, also, impoverished and almost drained of all poetical possibilities by that *"gratteur des syllabes"* Malherbe. Words which may seem to us affected and stereotyped have to be understood in their original sense, e.g. *Madame, Seigneur, ennui, aimant, gêner* and that terrible word *"tendre,"* which contributed so much to the misunderstanding of the poet's artistic personality. But once familiar with this aspect of Racine's idiom, we can only admire the supreme art with which he wielded the weapon handed on to him. Though writing verse, he was no versifier. His chief aim was the psychological development of his plot, and for that reason he sketched his plays first in prose; then he could safely say: "Now I have only to transcribe it in metre." In the use of the antithesis he went farther than Corneille, but with the difference that he always treated it as a vehicle of psychological significance. Two instances will show what I mean:

Hippolyte est sensible et ne sent rien pour moi.
                                  (***Phèdre,*** iv, 5.)

F'entendrai des regards que vous croirez muets.
                                  (***Britannicus,*** ii, 4.)

Racine developed his æsthetic views in his *Préfaces,* analytical studies of the poet's technique compared with that of Corneille and the Ancients. He was also an innovator in the treatment of the *confidant(e),* whom Corneille still accepts as a necessary evil. In Racine's plays they act the part of the modern *raisonneur,* frequently, as in the case of Oenone (***Phèdre***), rising to superb dramatic heights.

With regard to his metrical skill and infinite variety of musical shades, he is beyond praise or cavil. Jules Lemaître's words on his prose can be literally applied to the poet's verse: "Racine's prose is delicious. It is the most winged, most ethereal of the seventeenth century." But, I may add, for this very reason untranslatable. Racine is the only representative of French classical tragedy who has survived all the vicissitudes of schools and fashions. Inimitable craftsmanship, dramatic genius of the highest order, all crowned by lofty idealism and understanding for human frailties: these qualities alone will secure to Racine his place amongst the Immortals.

A. F. B. Clark (essay date 1939)

SOURCE: "The 'Profane' Plays, 1664-1677," in *Jean Racine,* Cambridge, Mass.: Harvard University Press, 1939, pp. 99-221.

[*In the following excerpt, Clark examines* Andromache *and* Brittanicus *in depth, noting the close thematic relationships between the plays.*]

When one has said the best one can of Racine's first two tragedies, the fact remains that they are mediocre works and give no intimation of the genius that suddenly unveiled its full radiance with the performance of ***Andromaque*** at the Hôtel de Bourgogne or at court some time in November 1667. It is no exaggeration to say "its full radiance," for though personal taste may place this or that play of Racine ahead of ***Andromaque*** for one reason or another, though the extreme greatness of the title role may give ***Phèdre*** precedence, though the dramatist may be deemed to have achieved a firmer and chaster style in ***Britannicus*** and his religious plays, yet he never wrote again a play so instinct with life and passion in every nook and cranny of its being, so completely an emanation of his own genius and so independent of extraneous influence, nor one with so many equally interesting characters and written in such a successful blend of colloquial and poetic speech. In ***Andromaque*** Racine emerges completely from the shadow of Corneille which had clouded his natural gifts before, and which is to dog him again in the tragedies that follow; the influence of Quinault, though present in greater measure, is of a superficial kind. No more "great souls" plotting schemes of ambition, no more political debates on the rights of kings and conquerors; on the other hand, no more dallyings of languorous world-conquerors with coquettish queens. Racine's own particular contribution to drama and literature, the revelation of *amour-passion* in all its tragic splendor, its exaltations and despairs, its self-sacrifice and its criminality, bursts forth in a perfect carnival of love and hate which engulfs three of the four leading characters and leaves only the serene figure of Andromache above the storm.

Such a sudden passage from the literary exercises of a clever sophomore to the searing truth of life itself seems to suggest the intervention of a personal experience on the part of the dramatist. . . .

Andromaque is often counted among the tragedies imitated from the Greek. But, as Racine points out, the subject of Euripides' *Andromache* is quite different from his own play, and he borrowed little from it except some suggestions for the portrait of Hermione. Some similarities between situations in Racine's play and those of French predecessors, like Rotrou's *Hercule Mourant* and Corneille's *Pertharite,* have been pointed out, but their importance is slight. The main source of ***Andromaque*** is the passage of eighteen lines from Virgil's Aeneid, Book III, which Racine quotes in his Preface. The framework of the play recalls that type of the old pastoral drama which presented a chain of lovers (Orestes loves Hermione, who loves Pyrrhus, who loves Andromache). The influence of Quinault is perhaps to be seen in the extent to which the dialogue is studded with the jargon of gallantry—one of the few serious blemishes in an otherwise almost perfect work of art.

The situation at the opening of the play may be summarized as follows: The scene is the palace of Pyrrhus, son of Achilles, and now king of Epirus. Pyrrhus is in love with his Trojan captive, Andromache, who, however, in her fidelity to her dead husband, Hector, refuses to yield to his advances. Also at the court of Pyrrhus is Herimone, daughter of Menelaus and Helen, waiting for Pyrrhus to carry out his promise of marriage to her. When the play opens, Orestes, an old lover of Hermione's, has just arrived, ostensibly as ambassador of the Greeks to persuade Pyrrhus to hand over to them Astyanax, the son of Hector

Scene from a Comédie-Française production of Andromaque.

and Andromache, but with the secret hope of winning Hermione away from Pyrrhus. Obviously, the less he succeeds in his ambassadorial mission, the more likely he is to accomplish his own hopes; for, if Pyrrhus refuses to give up Astyanax, Andromache in gratitude may accept his love, and Hermione in despair may return to Orestes. Such is the ideal crisis-situation with which we are presented when the curtain goes up, and which must be settled within twenty-four hours. The interest will consist in watching how, out of this situation, Racine spins his web of psychological action and reaction.

The four characters mentioned in this summary—Pyrrhus, Orestes, Andromache, and Hermione—obviously will mark the limits of the magnetic field over which the electric current of the action is to play. There are some minor characters of the *confident* variety, whom we can deal with as we meet them. But the four protagonists are among the most remarkable of Racine's or, indeed, of any dramatist's creations. They all have the three-dimensional qualities of Shakespeare's people, which can hardly be said of so many of the characters in any other one play of Racine. They all attain a universal quality through blending the traditional Greek figure with the traits of Racine's own contemporaries; they even seem to take on a surprisingly modern coloring at times. Andromache adds to her prestige as the widow of Hector the charm of a Christian tenderness and resignation (as Chateaubriand pointed out), and one cannot help fancying that some memory of the

pious, serene women of Port-Royal went into her composition; it has even been suggested that that great political exile, Henriette de France, widow of Charles I and mother of Racine's patroness, the Duchesse d'Orléans, may have sat for the portrait in part. Hermione is not only the daughter of Helen; she is also a *grande dame,* full of sensitive *orgueil* like the Duchesse de Bouillon, and ready, like her, to dabble in crime when her sensibilities are hurt. Pyrrhus is a barbarian king, but he is also an amorous monarch like Louis XIV. He is more of a mixture even than that; in his interviews with Hermione, he shows himself something of a psychological bully, not to say a sadist; he is something we do not associate with French classicism, "a problematic nature," as the Germans used to say. As for Orestes, he is, under the guise of a man pursued by the Furies, an extraordinary portrayal of the neurotic, suffering from an inferiority complex, trying desperately to keep his hysteria down, but bursting out in accesses of fatalistic bitterness until finally he goes down in defeat and madness.

The structure of the play illustrates perfectly Racine's art of bringing an apparent simplicity into a rather complicated action. There are really two separate themes, the attempt of Pyrrhus to gain the love of Andromache, and Orestes' plan to carry off Hermione. But, by making Hermione's attitude to Orestes depend on Andromache's attitude to Pyrrhus, Racine has made Andromache and her decision the pivot of the play, thereby giving the latter perfect unity and fully justifying Andromache's place in the title.

With this preamble let us attempt the task of analyzing (with the aid of quotations) that most representative of all Racine's tragedies, **Andromaque**. This attempt, if it has any measure of success, should carry us straight into the heart of Racine's dramaturgy.

Act I

The first scene is an admirable example of the *scène d'exposition* which the crisis-character of French tragedy necessitates at the beginning in order to put the hearer in possession of the situation. The art is to combine this with dramatic naturalness. When the curtain goes up we find Orestes in conversation with his old friend Pylades, whom he is surprised to meet at the court of Pyrrhus. Explanations are naturally called for on both sides, and in the course of the dialogue we learn of Orestes' "mélancolie." Then in a long speech, which is a perfect model of well-composed exposition but at the same time a passionate self-revelation, Pylades and we are informed both of the ostensible and the underlying reasons for Orestes' appearance at Pyrrhus' court. The speech reaches its culmination in these closing lines, which reveal Orestes' desperate fatalism and his ultimate purpose, and which illustrate well Racine's flexible use of the Alexandrine line for expressing the quick succession of various emotions, resignation, passionate resolve, and urgent curiosity:

Je me livre en aveugle au destin qui m'entraîne.

J'aime: je viens chercher Hermione en ces lieux,
La fléchir, l'enlever, ou mourir à ses yeux.
Toi qui connais Pyrrhus, que penses-tu qu'il
    fasse?
Dans sa cour, dans son cœur, dis-moi ce qui se
    passe.
Mon Hermione encor le tient-elle asservi?
Me rendra-t-il, Pylade, un bien qu'il m'a ravi?

Pylades sends the neurotic suddenly into ecstasy by the artfully dropped remark about Hermione, when he is relating her humiliation at Pyrrhus' hands:

Quelquefois elle appelle Oreste à son secours,

then urges him to concentrate on his actual mission and deliver his message to Pyrrhus in such a way as to anger him against the Greeks and thus bring him and Andromache closer together.

Pressez: demandez tout, pour ne rien obtenir.

This line of Pylades is the clue to the policy Orestes pursues in the next fine scene, which is the interview between Pyrrhus and the ambassador. The courtly dignity of Orestes' opening address to the monarch might be a model for one of Louis XIV's own ambassadors appearing at a foreign court. Nor does he make in this speech any overt threats; he simply sets forth the displeasure of the Greeks at the protection offered the Trojan child by Pyrrhus. Pyrrhus answers without anger at first, but with that ironical impatience we shall see is characteristic of him. The tone of lordly contempt at once characterizes him:

La Grèce en ma faveur est trop inquiétée.
De soins plus importants je l'ai crue agitée,
Seigneur; et, sur le nom de son ambassadeur,
J'avais dans ses projets conçu plus de grandeur.

But, as his speech continues, his rising anger is registered with great delicacy, until the final words,

L'Epire sauvera ce que Troie a sauvé.

Now, Orestes, seeing his scheme working out as he hoped, decides to clinch the matter by introducing threats. At once the action warms up. To the preceding long speeches succeed fragments of dialogue. Pyrrhus blazes out at the Greek threats. Let them come and attack him!

Qu'ils cherchent dans l'Epire une seconde Troie.

At Orestes' mention of Hermione, who will, he
    says, intervene on behalf of the Greeks,
    Pyrrhus relapses into bored irony:

Hermione, Seigneur, peut m'être toujours chère;
. . . . .
Vous pouvez cependant voir la fille d'Hélène
. . . . .
Après cela, Seigneur, je ne vous retiens plus,

Et vous pourrez aux Grecs annoncer mon refus.

Now the action is started! Pyrrhus has made a decision—the decision Orestes hoped he would make.

After Orestes departs to see Hermione, Phoenix, the confidant of Pyrrhus, expresses surprise that the latter should send Orestes to Hermione, his old love. At this Pyrrhus' irritation bursts out and he reveals his true attitude to Hermione in this realistically expressive speech:

Ah! qu'ils s'aiment, Phoenix, j'y consens.
    Qu'elle parte.
Que, charmés l'un de l'autre, ils retournent à
    Sparte:
Tous nos ports sont ouverts et pour elle et pour
    lui.
Qu'elle m'épargnerait de contrainte et d'ennui

He is about to make further explanations when Andromache appears; at once he is all eyes for her.

Andromache is wafted onto the stage on the wings of lines as soft as swan's-down. These exquisite verses not only sing to us all of Andromache's subdued sorrow and resignation, but they paint for us all the refinement and delicacy of her character. Their effect seems only attainable in a language having the peculiar evenness of accent of French:

Je passais jusqu'aux lieux où l'on garde mon
    fils.
Puisqu'une fois le jour vous souffrez que je voie
Le seul bien qui me reste et d'Hector et de
    Troie,
J'allais, Seigneur, pleurer un moment avec lui:
Je ne l'ai point encore embrassé d'aujourd'hui.

But Pyrrhus is determined to utilize his decision to protect Astyanax in order to wrest an acceptance of his love from Andromache. He begins to allude darkly to Greek threats. Andromache shows alarm, whereat Pyrrhus allays her fears but at the same time pleads for some reward for his protection of her son. Andromache upbraids him for being generous only for the sake of a reward. This nettles Pyrrhus somewhat, but he restrains himself and offers, in return for Andromache's love, to restore her son to the throne of Troy. Andromache's answer is admirable for its mingled pathos and pride:

Seigneur, tant de grandeurs ne nous touchent
    plus guère.
Je les lui promettais tant qu'a vécu son père.
Non, vous n'espérez plus de nous revoir encor,
Sacrés murs, que n'a pu conserver mon Hector!
A de moindres faveurs des malheureux
    prétendent,
Seigneur; c'est un exil que mes pleurs vous
    demandent.
Souffrez que loin des Grecs, et même loin de
    vous,
J'aille cacher mon fils, et pleurer mon époux.

Votre amour contre nous allume trop de haine;
Retournez, retournez à la fille d'Hélène.

Pyrrhus replies that he cannot, and remarks how much joy the love he shows Andromache would cause Hermione if he showed it toward her. At that, all Andromache's suppressed memories of Pyrrhus and his father's wrongs to her and her race well up, and she bursts out:

Et pourquoi vos soupirs seraient-ils repoussés?
Aurait-elle oublié vos services passés?
Troie, Hector, contre vous révoltent-ils son âme?
Aux cendres d'un époux doit-elle enfin sa
    flamme?
Et quel époux encor! Ah! Souvenir cruel!
Sa mort seule a rendu votre père immortel,
Il doit au sang d'Hector tout l'éclat de ses
    armes,
Et vous n'êtes tous deux connus que par mes
    larmes.

Stung by these defiant words, Pyrrhus, in his turn, fires up. He threatens to revoke his decision not to hand over Astyanax to the Greeks.

La Grèce le demande, et je ne prétends pas
Mettre toujours ma gloire à sauver des ingrats.

Mollified somewhat by Andromache's sorrow at this threat, he dismisses her with the following words, which close the act and leave once more the great decision in suspense, after we thought it had been settled:

      Allez, Madame, allez voir votre fils.
Peut-être, en le voyant, votre amour plus timide
Ne prendra pas toujours sa colère pour guide.
Pour savoir nos destins j'irai vous retrouver.
Madame, en l'embrassant, songer à le sauver.

Act II

The second act is Hermione's, as the first was Andromache's. That makes our task of analysis more difficult, for, settledness of purpose being Andromache's dominant trait, a scene in which she appears lends itself fairly well to summary, whereas there is no way of representing in abbreviated form the infinite variety, the constant twistings and veerings of Hermione's impetuous, impulsive temperament under the pressure of her humiliating situation. Nowhere in literature has an agitated spirit been represented with more minute fidelity than in the amazing portrait of Hermione in this and the following acts. But we must renounce the hope of giving here even an approximate idea of that portrait and concentrate on following the main line of the action.

At the rise of the curtain we find Hermione awaiting Orestes' visit. She has consented to see him, but is already regretting having given that consent. She tells her confidante, Cléone, that she shrinks from meeting the man whose love she had once slighted and who now will be in a position to triumph over her. Cléone tells her not to

fear; Orestes loves her too madly to think of triumphing over her. Why not leave with Orestes, since she says she hates Pyrrhus anyway? To which Hermione replies, deceiving herself, that she wants to break with Pyrrhus violently, not just slip away; then she says, brokenheartedly:

Il n'y travaillera que trop bien, l'infidèle.

Cléone is horrified to think that Hermione is waiting for some greater insult and suggests that, if Pyrrhus could ever offend her, he has done enough to offend her already. Hermione replies with a speech which is very typical of her agitation; it passes from pathos and self-pity to anger, which leads to the decision to leave; then she is pulled up by the thought of Pyrrhus' possible repentance after she left; then her anger wells up again; then she decides to stay in order to torture the lovers. I quote this whole speech as a fine example of Racine's subtle analysis:

Pourquoi veux-tu, cruelle, irriter mes ennuis?
Je crains de me connaître en l'état où je suis.
De tout ce que tu vois, tâche de ne rien croire;
Crois que je n'aime plus, vante-moi ma victoire;
Crois que dans son dépit mon cœur est endurci;
Hélas! Et s'il se peut, fais-le moi croire aussi.
Tu veux que je le fuie. Hé bien! Rien ne
    m'arrête:
Allons. N'envions plus son indigne conquête:
Que sur lui sa captive étende son pouvoir.
Fuyons. . . . Mais si l'ingrat rentrait dans son
    devoir!
Si la foi dans son cœur retrouvait quelque place!
S'il venait à mes pieds me demander sa grâce!
Si sous mes lois, Amour, tu pouvais l'engager!
S'il voulait . . . ! Mais l'ingrat ne veut que
    m'outrager.
Demeurons toutefois pour troubler leur fortune;
Prenons quelque plaisir à leur être importune;
Ou, le forçant de rompre un nœud si solennel,
Aux yeux de tous les Grecs rendons-le criminel.
J'ai déjà sur le fils attiré leur colère:
Je veux qu'on vienne encor lui demander la
    mère.
Rendons-lui les tourments qu'elle me fait
    souffrir;
Qu'elle le perde, ou bien qu'il la fasse périr.

Then Cléone objects: If Andromache had any complicity in the affair, why should she show so much coldness to Pyrrhus? This brings a very human retort from Hermione. In her jealousy she suspects Andromache's apparent coldness of being a form of coquettishness, and she contrasts this supposed subtlety with her own straightforwardness; *she* has not "led" Pyrrhus "on" enough. . . .

Then, in a striking passage, she recalls the romantic circumstances (the return of the heroes from Troy) in which she fell in love with Pyrrhus, ending with the absurdly natural reproach to Cléone that she and all the others, who shared her enthusiasm for Pyrrhus, were responsible for her betrayal, even before Pyrrhus betrayed her. After all, Orestes has his points.

> Il sait aimer du moins, et même sans qu'on
> l'aime.
> Et peut-être il saura se faire aimer lui-même.
> Allons, qu'il vienne enfin.

But when Cléone says, "Here he is!" out comes this exquisite *cri du cœur:*

> Ah! Je ne croyais pas qu'il fût si près d'ici.

The scene between Hermione and Orestes is an extraordinary duet in which each tries to be diplomatic and at the same time unconsciously wounds and exasperates the other. Hermione wants to keep Orestes for possible use and yet cannot help showing him that all her love is for Pyrrhus; Orestes wants to persuade her to leave with him but keeps offending her by reminding her that Pyrrhus is neglecting her. Here is a fragment of this fencing-match:

> *Oreste.*   Je vous entends. Tel est mon
> partage funeste:
>   Le cœur est pour Pyrrhus, et les
> vœux pour Oreste.
> *Hermione.* Ah! Ne souhaitez pas le destin de
> Pyrrhus:
>   Je vous haïrais trop.
> *Oreste.*   Vous
> m'en aimeriez plus.

But when he says incidentally,

> Car enfin il [Pyrrhus] vous hait; son âme ailleurs
> éprise
> N'a plus . . . ,

her pride stiffens up and she interrupts,

> Qui vous l'a dit, Seigneur, qu'il me méprise?
> · · · · ·
> Jugez-vous que ma vue inspire des mépris?
> Peut-être d'autres yeux me sont plus favorables.

Then Orestes in his turn stiffens:

> Poursuivez: il est beau de m'insulter ainsi.
> Cruelle, c'est donc moi qui vous méprise ici?

Finally she bids him go to Pyrrhus and tell him he must choose between Astyanax and her. If he chooses Astyanax, then she will leave with Orestes. Another decision has been made, and Orestes, already knowing, as he supposes, Pyrrhus' decision, goes into a characteristic rhapsody of triumph after Hermione has left.

Then comes the first great *coup de théâtre* or *péripétie* of the play. While Orestes is exulting with that *hybris* which, according to the Greeks, always invites divine Nemesis, Pyrrhus enters and with a few hammer-strokes annihilates Orestes' happiness. He apologizes for rejecting so abruptly Orestes' overtures in the name of the Greeks, and announces his final decision to hand over Astyanax to him. While Orestes is trying to recover from this blow, Pyrrhus staggers him with the further announcement that he will marry Hermione the next day, and then delivers the knockout blow with the ironic command to Orestes to carry this news to Hermione and to prepare to give her in marriage the next day to him (Pyrrhus).

Then we remember that the first act closed with Andromache going off to make her final decision, and we realize that this decision, an unfavorable one, has been communicated to Pyrrhus and has motivated his change of heart, but that Racine, with cunning art, so as to provide a tremendous surprise at this point, has not put this scene between Pyrrhus and Andromache on the stage.

The current of the play now sets in a contrary direction. Yet so careful is Racine to prepare his most distant effects, and so *nuancé* is his psychology, that in the last scene of this act, after Orestes has staggered off the stage, he suggests that that current might easily resume its first course again. This is the scene where Pyrrhus, after thumping himself, so to speak, on the chest and boasting to Phoenix that he has mastered his love instincts, begins to slip back immediately toward Andromache, and ends with proposing to have another interview with her, deceiving himself with the idea that his purpose is to show her more completely his scorn for her. Phoenix, however, holds up the mirror to his true backsliding, and the scene ends with Pyrrhus reluctantly consenting to carry out his resolve to marry Hermione. It is really a scene of the most exquisite high comedy, worthy of Molière, and shows that Racine could have excelled in that genre as well as in the farce-comedy of *Les Plaideurs*. This caused great heart-searchings among contemporary critics like Boileau who appreciated the truth to nature of the scene but knew they should not approve of such mingling of comedy with tragedy. For the modern reader, exempt from such qualms, it adds to the fascination of the play.

Act III

The effect of Pyrrhus' announcement on the neurotic Orestes is to drive him into a state of desperation, which appears in his dialogue with Pylades in scene 1. He will carry Hermione off by violence. Pyrrhus' cruel irony has particularly got under his skin:

> Il veut pour m'honorer la tenir de ma main.
> Ah! Plutôt cette main dans le sang du barbare. . . .

The last line prepares us for the denouement. Racine then gives a remarkable picture of a man suffering under the delusion of persecution. Pyrrhus is marrying Hermione only to make him (Orestes) desperate:

> Le cruel ne la prend que pour me l'arracher.

And just at the moment when Hermione was turning to him!

> Ses yeux s'ouvraient, Pylade; elle écoutait
>   Oreste,
> Lui parlait, le plaignait. Un mot eût fait le reste.

But Pylades does not believe that.

> Jamais il ne fut plus aimé.

Orestes would be well-advised to forget her. If he married her, she would hate him all her life.

Orestes makes a remarkable answer:

> C'est pour cela que je veux l'enlever.
>   . . . . .
> Non, non, à mes tourments je veux l'associer.

His bitterness reaches great heights, and in lines of power and metallic resonance Racine practically draws the picture of the *homme fatal* of Romanticism:

> Mon innocence enfin commence à me peser.
> Je ne sais de tout temps quelle injuste puissance
> Laisse le crime en paix et poursuit l'innocence.
> De quelque part sur moi que je tourne les yeux,
> Je ne vois que malheurs qui condamnent les
>   Dieux.
> Méritons leur courroux, justifions leur haine,
> Et que le fruit du crime en précède la peine.

Pylades abandons the hope of dissuading him from his plans to carry off Hermione, and promises to aid him; only let him conceal his purposes. He sees Hermione approaching and leaves.

The situations of Hermione and Orestes in this interview are reversed. Now it is Hermione who must restrain her temptation to triumph. Her new embarrassment is as skillfully portrayed as her previous one. Through her deprecating utterances one feels (and Orestes feels) her joy bursting forth:

> Qui l'eût cru, que Pyrrhus ne fût pas infidèle?
>   . . . . .
> Je veux croire avec vous qu'il redoute la Grèce.
>   . . . . .
> Mais que puis-je, Seigneur? On a promis ma foi.
>   . . . . .
> L'amour ne règle pas le sort d'une princesse.

But this make-believe only irritates Orestes. However, he restrains his anger, and takes leave of Hermione with bitter dignity:

> Tel est votre devoir, je l'avoue; et le mien
> Est de vous épargner un si triste entretien.

After his departure Hermione expresses to Cléone her surprise at his moderation, but Cléone opines that there is something ominous about it. When Cléone suggests that there may be a connection between the ultimatum of the Greeks and Pyrrhus' decision, Hermione bursts out in indignation, then in triumph:

> Tu crois que Pyrrhus craint? Et que craint-il
>   encor?
>   . . . . .
> Non, Cléone, il n'est point ennemi de lui-même.
> Il veut tout ce qu'il fait; et, s'il m'épouse, il
>   m'aime.
> Mais qu'Oreste à son gré m'impute ses douleurs;
> N'avons-nous d'entretien que celui de ses pleurs?
> Pyrrhus revient à nous. Hé bien, chère Cléone,
> Conçois-tu les transports de l'heureuse
>   Hermione?
> Sais-tu quel est Pyrrhus? T'es-tu fait raconter
> Le nombre des exploits. . . . Mais qui les peut
>   compter?
> Intrépide, et partout suivi de la victoire,
> Charmant, fidèle enfin, rien ne manque à sa
>   gloire.
> Songe. . . .

Here Hermione has her great moment, as Orestes had had his in the previous act. And her exultation, her *hybris,* is rising, as did his. Will it bring Nemesis, as his had done? We are in the middle of Act III, where the final decisions of Fate are made. Hermione must beware.

At this critical climax of the tragedy, Andromache enters in tears. The scene which follows is short, but it is the keystone of the play. We spoke above of the *galbe* of French tragedy, its symmetry as of a shapely vase. Here it is beautifully illustrated. This clinching scene is in the precise mathematical center of the play; it is the only one in which the two main protagonists meet; and it settles everything. It is at the apex of the dramatic pyramid, which rises to it on one side and falls away on the other.

It is Andromache who is in despair now over the fate of her son. In lines of exquisite pathos and eloquence she pleads with Hermione to use her influence with Pyrrhus to save him:

> Mais il me reste un fils. Vous saurez quelque
>   jour,
> Madame, pour un fils jusqu'où va notre amour;
> Mais vous ne saurez pas, du moins je le
>   souhaite,
> En quel trouble mortel son intérêt nous jette,
> Lorsque, de tant de biens qui pouvaient nous
>   flatter,
> C'est le seul qui nous reste, et qu'on veut nous
>   l'ôter.

This alone was lacking to Hermione's triumph. Will she be able to keep her head and answer with wisdom and magnanimity? No. She answers with cold scorn, and thereby decides her own fate and that of all the other people in the play:

S'il faut fléchir Pyrrhus, qui le peut mieux que
    vous?
Vos yeux assez longtemps ont régné sur son
    âme.
Faites-le prononcer; j'y souscrirai, Madame.

As Hermione sweeps from the stage, Andromache is at
first overwhelmed. It is Céphise, the humble confidante
(as I pointed out above), who, at this very apex of the
drama, suggests that Andromache take Hermione's ironically proffered advice literally:

Je croirais ses conseils, et je verrais Pyrrhus.
Un regard confondrait Hermione et la Grèce.

At this moment Pyrrhus appears. He pretends to be seeking Hermione and not to notice Andromache, who points
out to Céphise how little influence she can have on him.
But Pyrrhus' asides to Phoenix tell us that he is only
waiting for Andromache to show that she notices him.
When Pyrrhus utters ostentatiously the words,

Allons aux Grecs livrer le fils d'Hector,

Andromache throws herself at his feet and implores his
pity. He is unresponsive at first, but when, in her desperation, she has appealed to him by some harmless flattery
which has caused her to be accused of "coquetterie ver-
tueuse," he says briefly to his confidant,

Va m'attendre, Phoenix,

and we know that again he is in Andromache's power if
she decides to make the slightest concession. It is his turn
to make an eloquent plea to her to accept his love for her
son's sake as well as for her own. But at the close his plea
takes on a very firm and menacing tone, and we know
that this time Andromache's decision will be final for
both of them. . . .

When he leaves the stage, Andromache remains with
Céphise. The closing scene is an expression of the most
heart-rending anguish, as Andromache wrestles with her
contending passions of fidelity to Hector and love for her
son. She comes to no decision, but undertakes to arrive at
one after consultation with the dead.

Allons sur son tombeau consulter mon époux.

It is in the course of this scene that there occurs one of
those few passages of set rhetoric that can be quoted (and
this one often is quoted) apart from their context. It is the
famous picture of the sack of Troy, the vision which
Andromache calls up of that dreadful night when Pyrrhus
first burst upon her view. How, she says to Céphise, can
she accept the hand of the man whom she first saw in
those circumstances?

Songe, songe, Céphise, à cette nuit cruelle,
Qui fut pour tout un peuple une nuit éternelle,
Figure-toi Pyrrhus, les yeux étincelants,
Entrant à la lueur de nos palais brûlants,

Sur tous mes frères morts se faisant un passage,
Et de sang tout couvert échauffant le carnage.
Songe aux cris des vainqueurs, songe aux cris
    des mourants,
Dans la flamme étouffés, sous le fer expirants,
Peins-toi dans ces horreurs Andromaque éperdue:
Voilà comme Pyrrhus vint s'offrir à ma vue;
Voilà par quels exploits il sut se couronner;
Enfin, voilà l'époux que tu me veux donner.

This is often quoted as an example of the "rhetoric" of
French tragedy, but in its context the heightened style
corresponds to the climactic moment of Andromache's
desperation. The reader of the preceding pages will not
think it typical of Racine's normal style, though quite
suitable in the place where it occurs.

Act IV

At the close of Act III the issues of the play were in
suspense again, as they were at the end of Act I. But in
Act IV the irrevocable decisions are finally arrived at. It
is an act heavy with fate and contains some of the most
powerful scenes a dramatist has ever composed.

In scene 1 we find Andromache and Céphise together,
and learn from Céphise's first speech that Andromache
has decided to accept Pyrrhus' hand. But Céphise does
not know all of Andromache's decision, and when Andromache says, "Allons voir mon fils," Céphise wonders
why there is any hurry about that, as she is free to see
him any time now. She is horrified at Andromache's reply:

Céphise, allons le voir pour la dernière fois.

It then appears that Andromache has decided to marry
Pyrrhus, thereby binding him (for she has no doubt of his
honor) to protect her son, but then to slay herself after the
ceremony and thus preserve her fidelity to Hector. She
then bids Céphise promise to bring up her son, and her
instructions to her regarding his education are couched in
verse of incomparable beauty, bearing the same authentic
stamp of Andromache as the verse which first introduced
her:

Fais connaître à mon fils les héros de sa race;
Autant que tu pourras, conduis-le sur leur trace.
Dis-lui par quels exploits leurs noms ont éclaté,
Plutôt ce qu'ils ont fait que ce qu'ils ont été.
Parle-lui tous les jours des vertus de son père,
Et quelquefois aussi parle-lui de sa mère.
Mais qu'il ne songe plus, Céphise, à nous
    venger:
Nous lui laissons un maître, il le doit ménager.
Qu'il ait de ses aïeux un souvenir modeste:
Il est du sang d'Hector, mais il en est le reste:
Et pour ce reste enfin j'ai moi-même en un jour
Sacrifié mon sang, ma haine et mon amour.

These smooth legato measures make a dramatic contrast
with the shrill staccato outbursts of Hermione in the rest

of the act; for all the remainder of it belongs to her, and it is one of the most remarkable feats in sustained and intense passion drama has ever seen. On the departure of Andromache and Céphise, Hermione and Cléone come on the stage, and Cléone's first words suggest the dangerous mood Hermione is in. She is consumed by deep and silent fury, having learned of Pyrrhus' new betrayal. On Cléone's expressing alarmed astonishment at her continued silence regarding this insult, she snaps out these words:

> Fais-tu venir Oreste?

At this moment Orestes arrives and launches out in a rapturous expression of gratitude for being summoned by Hermione. But she cuts him short with:

> Je veux savoir, Seigneur, si vous m'aimez.

Orestes starts protesting his devotion, to be cut short again with:

> Vengez-moi, je crois tout.

Orestes misunderstands; he thinks she means he should stir up the Greeks to attack Pyrrhus. She soon sets him right:

> Je veux qu'à mon départ toute l'Epire pleure.
> Mais si vous me vengez, vengez-moi dans une
>   heure.
> Tous vos retardements sont pour moi des refus.
> Courez au temple. Il faut immoler. . . .
> *Oreste.*   Qui?
> *Hermione.*
>   Pyrrhus.

Orestes is aghast, but his hesitation infuriates Hermione. In her mad impatience she pours out in a furious tirade her hatred and her love for Pyrrhus all mixed together, logic and consideration for Orestes' feelings all thrown to the winds:

> Ne vous suffit-il pas que je l'ai condamné?
> Ne vous suffit-il pas que ma gloire offensée
> Demande une victime à moi seule adressée;
> Qu'Hermione est le prix d'un tyran opprimé;
> Que je le hais; enfin, Seigneur, que je l'aimai?
> Je ne m'en cache pas; l'ingrat m'avait su plaire,
> Soit qu'ainsi l'ordonnât mon amour ou mon
>   père,
> N'importe: mais enfin réglez-vous là-dessus.
> Malgré mes vœux, Seigneur, honteusement
>   déçus,
> Malgré la juste horreur que son crime me donne,
> Tant qu'il vivra, craignez que je ne lui pardonne.
> Doutez jusqu'à sa mort d'un courroux incertain:
> S'il ne meurt aujourd'hui, je puis l'aimer
>   demain.

To Orestes' further pleading for postponement of the murder until that night, at least, comes the dreadful cry:

> Mais, cependant, ce jour il épouse Andromaque.
>   . . . . .
> Revenez tout couvert du sang de l'infidèle;
> Allez, en cet état soyez sur de mon cœur.

At Orestes' further protests, her fury rises to the pitch of madness:

> C'est trop en un jour essuyer de refus.
> Je m'en vais seule au temple, où leur hymen
>   s'apprête,
> Où vous n'osez aller mériter ma conquête.
> Là, de mon ennemi je saurai m'approcher:
> Je percerai le cœur que je n'ai pu toucher;
> Et mes sanglantes mains, sur moi-même
>   tournées,
> Aussitôt, malgré moi, joindront nos destinées:
> Et, tout ingrat qu'il est, il me sera plus doux
> De mourir avec lui, que de vivre avec vous.

When Orestes gives his desperate consent to do the deed and rushes out, Hermione is left a prey to doubts as to whether she can trust him to really do it. She thinks for a moment of doing the deed herself. Then she wonders whether Orestes, if he does slay Pyrrhus, will make him realize he is dying Hermione's victim. And, above all, Andromache must be kept away from his dying gaze! Last comes the savage cry:

> Chère Cléone, cours! Ma vengeance est perdue,
> S'il ignore en mourant que c'est moi qui le tue.

Just at the height of this deafening fortissimo, Pyrrhus is seen approaching. A terrific revulsion occurs in Hermione. Perhaps at the last moment Pyrrhus is coming back to her:

> Ah! Cours après Oreste; et dis-lui, ma Cléone,
> Qu'il n'entreprenne rien sans revoir Hermione.

A last terrible disillusionment is in store for poor Hermione. The scene which now begins (the last of Act IV) is perhaps the most original in the play. It anticipates the modern fondness for morbid moods and piquant psychological situations, and shows astonishing accuracy in the notation of them. It is also instinct with pathos and tragedy of the profoundest kind. It is the last chance both for Pyrrhus and Hermione—his last chance to escape death, her last chance to recover her lover. I wish I could quote this whole great scene. It consists of four fairly lengthy speeches, two by each of the characters. Pyrrhus' first words reveal his curious mood of frank apology mingled with what I called above "psychological cruelty." There is something still stranger; there is the confession that Andromache is marrying him without loving him, and even out of this he seems to get a grim and morbid satisfaction:

> L'un par l'autre entraînés, nous courons à l'autel
> Nous jurer, malgré nous, un amour immortel.
> Après cela, Madame, éclatez contre un traître,
> Qui l'est avec douleur, et qui pourtant veut

l'être.
Pour moi, loin de contraindre un si juste
  courroux,
Il me soulagera peut-être autant que vous.

Hermione, who sees by these words that her last hope, which had flickered up once more at Pyrrhus' approach, is gone, utters slowly and heavily a speech charged with all the hatred into which her love has been temporarily transformed. With withering scorn she sneers at Pyrrhus' pretended frankness and his real inconstancy:

Non, non, la perfidie a de quoi vous tenter;
Et vous ne me cherchez que pour vous en
  vanter.
    . . . . .
Me quitter, me reprendre, et retourner encor
De la fille d'Hélène à la veuve d'Hector?
    . . . . .
Tout cela part d'un cœur toujours maître de soi,
D'un héros qui n'est point esclave de sa foi,

then, in two terrible lines, she seems to correctly diagnose his attitude,

Vous veniez de mon front observer la pâleur,
Pour aller dans ses bras rire de ma douleur.

(Notice how the throwing-back of the accent to "rire" makes the word almost scream out Hermione's indignation at Pyrrhus' cruelty.)

If a man could say anything fitted to raise Hermione's cold fury to a still higher pitch, Pyrrhus replies by saying that thing. He takes her hatred at its face value, not as love turned inside out:

Je rends grâces au ciel que votre indifférence
De mes heureux soupirs m'apprenne l'innocence.
    . . . . .
Mes remords vous faisaient une injure mortelle;
Il faut se croire aimé pour se croire infidèle.
    . . . . .
J'ai craint de vous trahir, peut-être je vous sers.
    . . . . .
Rien ne vous engageait à m'aimer en effet.

The poison of these words reaches the depths of Hermione's heart, and she reacts in one of the most passionate speeches that Racine ever wrote. I shall quote most of it. Notice the way in which the meter, the accenting of the syllables, infallibly brings out the emotional emphasis; notice the ebb and flow of passion, now headlong and menacing, now subdued and pleading; and observe particularly the subtle shift during several lines from the *tu* to the *vous* form of address, where for the moment the fierceness of her love-hatred which justifies the familiar second singular gives way to a restrained, courteous form of final appeal made in the formal second plural; and finally note how, as she scrutinizes Pyrrhus' face and sees no sign of sympathy or coöperation, her passion surges up again and she reverts to the brutal-tender *tu:*

Je ne t'ai point aimé, cruel! Qu'ai-je donc fait?
    . . . . .
Je t'aimais inconstant, qu'aurais-je fait fidèle?
Et même en ce moment où ta bouche cruelle
Vient si tranquillement m'annoncer le trépas,
Ingrat, je doute encor si je ne t'aime pas.
Mais, Seigneur, s'il le faut, si le ciel en colère
Réserve à d'autres yeux la gloire de vous plaire,
Achevez votre hymen, j'y consens. Mais du
  moins
Ne forcez pas mes yeux d'en être les témoins.
Pour la dernière fois je vous parle peut-être:
Différez-le d'un jour; demain vous serez maître.
Vous ne répondez point. Perfide, je le voi,
Tu comptes les moments que tu perds avec moi!
Ton cœur, impatient de revoir ta Troyenne,
Ne souffre qu'à regret qu'un autre t'entretienne.
Tu lui parles du cœur, tu la cherches des yeux.
Je ne te retiens plus, sauve-toi de ces lieux:
Va lui jurer la foi que tu m'avais jurée,
Va profaner des Dieux la majesté sacrée.
Ces Dieux, ces justes Dieux n'auront pas oublié
Que les mêmes serments avec moi t'ont lié.
Porte aux pieds des autels ce cœur qui
  m'abandonne;
Va, cours. Mais crains encor d'y trouver
  Hermione.

As Hermione rushes with this last warning from the stage, Phoenix expresses fear as to her purpose. But Pyrrhus turns coolly to him, saying:

Andromaque m'attend. Phoenix, garde son fils.

Act V

The last act begins with a long distracted monologue by Hermione, more or less in the tradition of French tragedy. Even at this more than eleventh hour she wavers between her love and her hatred of Pyrrhus. At the end of the speech she is inclining toward saving him at the last moment:

L'assassiner, le perdre? Ah! devant qu'il expire. . . .

At this juncture Cléone enters and informs Hermione of Pyrrhus' radiant happiness as he leads his bride to the altar. In a line that paints vividly the bridegroom's bliss, she tells how she saw him

S'enivrer en marchant du plaisir de la voir.

At once Hermione is again all hate. But she longs to know if Pyrrhus did not give some sign of worrying about what she might do.

Mais as-tu bien, Cléone, observé son visage?
Goûte-t-il des plaisirs tranquilles et parfaits?
N'a-t-il point détourné ses yeux vers le palais?

Cléone replies,

Madame, il ne voit rien. Son salut et sa gloire
Semblent être avec vous sortis de sa mémoire.

Here let us give a full section of the dialogue:

Hermione. Le perfide! Il mourra. Mais que t'a
dit Oreste?
Cléone. Oreste avec ses Grecs dans le temple est
entré.
Hermione. Eh bien! A me venger n'est-il pas
préparé?
Cléone. Je ne sais.
Hermione.   Tu ne sais? Quoi donc?
    Oreste encore,
        Oreste me trahit?

Cléone says that Orestes had entered the temple, still
hesitant. Then Hermione flies into another fury, where
the humiliation and despair of the proud woman whom
both suitors have gone back upon are rendered once more
with great power. Her outburst ends with wild and whirl-
ing words, announcing she will do the deed herself:

Je ne choisirai point dans ce désordre extrême:
Tout me sera Pyrrhus, fût-ce Oreste lui-même.
Je mourrai; mais au moins ma mort me vengera:
Je ne mourrai pas seule, et quelqu'un me suivra.

As she utters this shriek, Orestes, pale and haggard,
suddenly appears in the doorway, and she hears these
words:

Madame, c'en est fait, et vous êtes servie:
Pyrrhus rend à l'autel son infidèle vie.

From Hermione comes nothing but three stunned words,

Il est mort?

Orestes, oblivious to the transformation that is taking place
in Hermione, gives a detailed account of the scene in the
temple where Pyrrhus, just as he was putting the crown
on Andromache's head, was attacked by such a crowd of
Greeks that Orestes himself could not find a place to strike.
He himself saw Pyrrhus fall at the altar; and then he hurried
out to come and carry off his beloved Hermione. Hermione has yet only half realized what has taken place. She
gasps out,

Qu'ont-ils fait?

Orestes thinks she is disappointed that he did not slay
Pyrrhus with his own hand as her envoy.

        Pardonnez à leur impatience.
            . . . . .
Mais c'est moi dont l'ardeur leur a servi
    d'exemple;

            . . . . .
Madame, et vous pouvez justement vous flatter
D'une mort que leurs bras n'ont fait qu'exécuter.
Vous seule avez poussé les coups. . . .

These words, intended to appease her, have the effect of
arousing her at last to full consciousness of what has
happened; all her hatred for the dead Pyrrhus vanishes
and her love comes rushing back in a tide. She springs
at Orestes like a tigress, and overwhelms him with a
tirade which ends with that famous cry, the masterpiece
of irony and unreason, "Qui te l'a dit?"

                                Tais-
    toi, perfide,
Et n'impute qu'à toi seul ton lâche parricide.
Va faire chez tes Grecs admirer ta fureur:
Va, je la désavoue et tu me fais horreur.
Barbare, qu'as-tu fait? Avec quelle furie
As-tu tranché le cours d'une si belle vie?
    . . . . .
Mais parle: de son sort qui t'a rendu l'arbitre?
Pourquoi l'assassiner? Qu'a-t-il fait? A quel
    titre?
Qui te l'a dit?
Oreste.   O Dieux! Quoi? Ne m'avez-
    vous pas
        Vous-même, ici, tantôt, ordonné son
    trépas?
Hermione. Ah! Fallait-il en croire une amante
    insensée?
        Ne devais-tu pas lire au fond de ma
    pensée?
        Et ne voyais-tu pas, dans mes
    emportements,
        Que mon cœur démentait ma bouche à
    tous moments?
        Quand je l'aurais voulu, fallait-il y
    souscrire?
        N'as-tu pas dû cent fois te le faire redire?
        Toi-même avant le coup me venir
    consulter?
        Y revenir encore, ou plutôt m'éviter?
        Que ne me laissais-tu le soin de ma
    vengeance?
        Qui t'amène en des lieux où l'on fuit ta
    présence?
        Voilà de ton amour le détestable fruit:
        Tu m'apportais, cruel, le malheur qui te
    suit.
        C'est toi dont l'ambassade, à tous les
    deux fatale
        L'a fait pour son malheur pencher vers
    ma rivale.
        Nous le verrions encor nous partager ses
    soins;
        Il m'aimerait peut-être, il le feindrait du
    moins.
        Adieu. Tu peux partir. Je demeure en
    Epire:
        Je renonce à la Grèce, à Sparte, à son
    empire,
        A toute ma famille; et c'est assez pour moi,
        Tratre, qu'elle ait produit un monstre
    comme toi.

Here the play, as psychological action, virtually ends. The

rest is the clearing-up of "unfinished business" which the tradition of tragedy, as Racine states in one of his prefaces, requires. We have Orestes' consternation, then the news of Hermione's suicide and Andromache's succession to control of the state, and finally the onset of Orestes' madness.

I trust that my analytical summary of this play will have made clear to the reader Racine's methods in the conduct of plot, the nature of his characterization, and the main features of his style. No play of his could represent all of these so fully as *Andromaque*. It is to be hoped that some tenacious misconceptions about French tragedy have been dispelled and that its passionateness, the continuity of its psychological action, its elimination of every irrelevance, its vivid portraiture of real life, and the forceful simplicity and directness of its style have impressed themselves on the reader.

Andromaque had a sensational success, equaling that of *Le Cid* thirty years before. Madame de Sévigné, who saw it played by a country troupe at Vitré near her country residence of Les Rochers in Brittany, had to admit its effectiveness: "I went to the play; it was *Andromaque,* which made me weep more than six tears; that's enough for a country troupe." However, the Corneille clique, on the whole, gave it grudging admiration. Saint-Evremond, in a *Lettre à M. de Lionne,* said, "All in all, it is a fine play, much above the average but a little below greatness," and in a second *Lettre* made the curious remark that "one might go further in the passions." From the stinging epigrams of Racine against the Marquis de Créqui and the Comte d'Olonne we infer what their conversational criticisms against *Andromaque* were. But the sharpest attack on the play was the parody by Subligny, *La Folle Querelle ou la Critique d'Andromaque,* played by Molière's troupe in 1668 and suspected by some at the time of being from Molière's own hand.

The criticisms against *Andromaque* were mainly of the niggling sort, such as were characteristic of seventeenth-century criticism and such as Corneille had had to put up with a generation before. Racine had failed to observe some of the minute laws of the theater; he had altered history more than a dramatist is permitted to do; he had not observed verisimilitude in making a gentleman like Pyrrhus go back on his engagement, etc., etc. Often the criticisms destroy each other: to some Pyrrhus is too brutal, to others he is too refined and *galant* for a barbaric king. But there were just two lines of criticism that got under Racine's skin. One was Subligny's objections to certain of his expressions as insufficiently correct and pure. The style of *Britannicus* will be noticeably more carefully worked over, chaster than that of *Andromaque*. Above all, the critics, while praising the moving character of his play, seemed to question his ability to rise to the "beautés pleines" of Corneille and write a great historical and political tragedy. Racine's reply will be to write *Britannicus*. . . .

Britannicus was first performed at the Hôtel de Bourgogne on December 13, 1669. In the "Second Preface" (written for the 1676 edition of his plays) Racine said: "This is the one of all my tragedies on which I may say that I have bestowed the most pains . . . if I have done anything solid and deserving of praise, most *connaisseurs* agree that it is this same *Britannicus*." From this passage of Racine himself comes the common designation of this play as the "pièce des connaisseurs." This phrase, taken along with Racine's remarks, suggests very neatly both the stronger and the weaker points of *Britannicus*. Racine has put into the making of this play all his talent and artistic conscience, but, I think, a somewhat less full measure of spontaneity than he put into *Andromaque*. As a matter of fact, *Britannicus* is what the French call a *gageure;* it originated in the deliberate desire to beat Corneille at his own game, the great Roman play of political ambition and plots. This inevitably put a certain constraint on Racine, and it is a great tribute to the flexibility of his talent that he came off with such honors as he did.

The central theme of the play is the emergence of Nero the monster from Nero the benevolent monarch of the early years of his reign; and the immediate provocation of this vicious development is the sudden sensual passion he conceives for Junia, the fiancée of Britannicus, and his resulting jealousy and criminal intents regarding the latter. This is the real Racinian core of the play and of all that is most typical of the dramatist in its characterization and situation. But this inner plot is enmeshed in a grandiose fabric of Agrippina's machinations to recover her influence over Nero out of the hands of his adviser Burrhus and of the tug of war between Burrhus, the virtuous counsellor and Narcissus the evil one, for the soul of Nero. The play ends with the poisoning of Britannicus by Nero.

Racine found his material mainly in Tacitus, to whom his debt extends far beyond the limits of the historic facts. In his second Preface, indeed, he is rather overmodest about his own originality: "I had copied my characters from the greatest painter of antiquity, I mean from Tacitus. And I was then so filled with my reading of this excellent historian that there is hardly a striking touch in my tragedy that did not come from his suggestion." It may be added that many of the speeches are veritable centos of Tacitus. But Racine's deepest debt to Tacitus, probably, is the atmosphere which pervades the play, and this is perhaps its most striking feature. *Andromaque* seems to take place outside of time and space, so complete is the interpenetration of ancient and modern traits in its characters. *Britannicus* is definitely localized in Nero's Rome. The spell of imperial Rome—and of just that moment of imperial Rome—is upon us from the first line to the last, its grandeur and its corruption, its sense of world-responsibility and its criminality; and this is subtly conveyed without any recourse to the Romantic methods of calling up local color, without any descriptions of Lucullan banquets or visions of the Circus Maximus. To a large extent this atmosphere is summoned up simply by the style itself, which is of Tacitean terseness, like the inscriptions hammered out on a Roman coin. Here, instead of the passionate expansiveness of *Andromaque,* we have a menacing reticence and concentration. The music is not that of the high notes of the violin and the woodwinds; it is the diapason of the double-basses and the tubas. This is, no doubt, what Boileau meant when he said that Racine had never written more "sententious verses." Ever since the seventeenth century, critics have been agreed that the style of **Britannicus** has a sustained purity and firmness unequaled by any of his other "profane" tragedies, and is freer from the abuses of the jargon of gallantry.

The center of interest, of course, is Nero himself, one of the greatest portraits of a historic figure in dramatic literature. From the moment the young voluptuary enters the stage, saying to Narcissus:

> Narcisse, c'en est fait, Néron est amoureux

to the last terrible line—surely one of the most remarkable that ever ended a play—in which the horrified Burrhus leaves us, as the curtain falls, looking down a perspective of the criminal future,

> Plût aux Dieux que ce fût le dernier de ses
>   crimes!

we sit spellbound before this remorseless unfolding of a vicious nature. For that is what it is—an unfolding, not a development. There would be no time within the twenty-four-hour scheme of French tragedy for the development of a virtuous nature into a criminal one. Racine says: "I am not representing him as a virtuous man, for he never was one. In a word, he is a *monstre naissant*." The rapid unfolding of the monster is explained by the sudden concourse of his violent passion for Junia with Agrippina's insistent nagging and Narcissus' wily temptings. The psychological action of the play is made up of the alternating advances of Nero toward villainy and his relapses into virtue according as he lends an ear to Narcissus or to Agrippina and Burrhus.

And just there we put our finger on what seems to me a relative weakness in the play as compared with **Andromaque**. The sparks which the current of the plot—or the dialogue—is constantly emitting in the latter play come from the fact that all the characters between whom the current passes carry an equal charge of emotion. Now in **Britannicus** Nero himself is heavily charged, but the other personages who converse with him—though we know theoretically that they too are feeling intensely—too often use an oratorical style, full of moral and political argument rather than of direct passion. This does not apply to the superb duel between Nero and Britannicus in Act III, nor, in general, to the interviews between Nero and Narcissus, especially the masterly decisive interview in Act IV. In the latter Racine manages to make us feel, under the reasonings of Narcissus—surely worthy of rank with Iago as one of the two arch-insinuators of literature—the throbbing of his evil and self-seeking heart. I must confess that I do not feel these throbbings under the well-marshaled arguments of Burrhus nor even under those of Agrippina, grand as this latter figure is in its statuesque

way. As for Britannicus and Junia, though they come to life occasionally they are admitted to be, on the whole, rather conventional figures. Corresponding to this lower tension of the psychological action is the relatively archaic character of the dialogue. In **Andromaque** Racine had developed a wonderfully flexible scheme of broken and semi-colloquial dialogue within the framework of the Alexandrine *couplets*. In **Britannicus** he reverts, again under the shadow of Corneille, to the older forms of the long harangue—Agrippina's speech to Nero in Act IV has over one hundred lines—and of stichomythia (the modeling of the retort in a dialogue on the same lines as the speech of the first interlocutor).

I should be very sorry, however, if, by using several times the expression "the shadow of Corneille," I left the impression that the net result of Racine's *gageure* was the production of an imitation of Corneille. I am speaking of a cause, not of an effect. The general effect of the play is not Cornelian, but thoroughly Racinian. Even Agrippina, the nearest of all Racine's characters, except Mithridates, to the heroic types of the older dramatist, is a study in nuances that Corneille would have been either incapable or contemptuous of. She is shown not merely as the ambitious plotter but as the mother who resents the loss of her influence over her son, not merely as the clever dialectician but as the woman liable to imprudent fits of temper. Similarly Burrhus and Narcissus are much more complex, much less *tout d'une pièce,* than such types would be in Corneille. Burrhus' virtue is mitigated by certain prudential considerations; Narcissus is a villain of a subtlety and psychological insight never before seen in drama outside of Shakespeare.

After these general considerations on **Britannicus,** I shall refer to or quote some of the more striking passages of the play, without, however, attempting a continuous analysis of the action after the manner of our dissection of **Andromaque**.

The first act is Agrippina's. In two long discussions, one with her confidante Albine, and one with Burrhus, she complains of the way in which Nero and his advisers are treating her; she is particularly alarmed by the news of the abduction by Nero of Junia, Britannicus' fiancée. Britannicus had been jockeyed out of the succession to the imperial throne on the death of his father, Claudius, by Agrippina's machinations in behalf of Nero, her son by Domitius Ahenobarbus. But now Agrippina, in order to preserve a sort of balance of power, is supporting the marriage of Britannicus and Junia against Nero's wishes. Agrippina's speeches are imposing in their metallic Roman gravity and show the "sententious" quality of the style at its most striking. . . .

The second act begins with the fine scene between Nero and Narcissus containing the justly celebrated speech in which the former describes the circumstances under which his sudden passion for Junia flamed up. The description is not only marvelously picturesque in itself (it has been compared to a Delacroix painting)—thereby dispelling the idea that Racine's style is always abstract—but the importance attached to the influence of romantic accessories in the genesis of a love affair is surely very modern. Further, the whole aesthetic coloring of the passage suggests the Nero who died exclaiming, "Qualis artifex pereo"; certain lines even suggest discreetly the decadent and the sadist in him. The piece is striking also for the musical beauty of the verse. . . .

Later in the act comes the almost equally fine scene between Nero and Junia in which he declares his intention to make her his wife. The dissimulation, the steel hand under the velvet glove, and the cruel irony of Nero are painted in masterly strokes. Did the pride of the Roman emperors ever blaze forth in such terrifying splendor as in the short dialogue where Nero declares his plans to the astounded Junia? Junia has just said that, in paying court to her, Britannicus is but following Agrippina's, and therefore, she supposes, Nero's own wishes.

> *Néron.* Ma mère a ses desseins, Madame, et j'ai
> les miens.
>   Ne parlons plus ici de Claude et
> d'Agrippine;
>   Ce n'est point par leur choix que je me
> détermine.
>   C'est à moi seul, Madame, à repondre de
> vous;
>   Et je veux de ma main vous choisir un
> époux.
> *Junie.* Ah! Seigneur, songez-vous que toute autre
> alliance
>   Fera honte aux Césars, auteur de ma
> naissance?
> *Néron.* Non, Madame, l'époux dont je vous
> entretiens
>   Peut sans honte assembler vos aïeux et les
> siens:
>   Vous pouvez, sans rougir, consentir à sa
> flamme.
> *Junie.* Et quel est donc, Seigneur, cet époux?
> *Néron.*   Moi,
> Madame.
> *Junie.* Vous?
> *Néron.*   Je vous nommerais, Madame, un
> autre nom,
>   Si j'en savais quelque autre au-dessus de
> Néron.

Toward the end of this scene Nero adds horror to her amazement by announcing a cruel stratagem. He has told Narcissus to admit Britannicus to Junia's presence and to leave him under the impression that this interview has been procured for him without Nero's knowledge. He now announces to Junia that Britannicus is about to appear before her. Her joy at this announcement is quelled by Nero's further explanation:

> Je pouvais de ces lieux lui défendre l'entrée;
> Mais, Madame, je veux prévenir le danger
> Où son ressentiment le pourrait engager.
> Je ne veux point le perdre. Il vaut mieux que
> lui-même

Entende son arrêt de la bouche qu'il aime.
> Si ses jours vous sont chers, élognez-le de
> vous,
> Sans qu'il ait aucum lieu de me croire jaloux.
> De son bannissement prenez sur vous l'offense;
> Et soit par vos discours, soit par votre silence,
> Du moins par vos froideurs, faites-lui concevoir
> Qu'il doit porter ailleurs ses vœux et son espoir.

When Junia objects that, even if she could obey Nero in her words, her eyes would betray her real feelings to Britannicus, Nero replies,

> Caché près de ces lieux, je vous verrai, Madame.
> Renfermez votre amour dans le fond de votre
> âme.
> Vous n'aurez point pour moi de languages
> secrets:
> J'entendrai des regards que vous croyez muets:
> Et sa perte sera l'infaillible salaire
> D'un geste ou d'un soupir échappé pour lui
> plaire.

(Note the boldness of expression of the fourth line in the above.)

This scene is not only very dramatic in itself, but it ushers in another scene (the interview announced) the peculiar intensity of which can be imagined from the very way in which it is announced. Junia carries out Nero's cruel instructions with great skill. She warns Britannicus in these significant, yet noncommittal words:

> Vous êtes en des lieux tout pleins de sa
> puissance.
> Ces murs même, Seigneur, peuvent avoir des
> yeux;
> Et jamais l'Empereur n'est absent de ces lieux.

Britannicus, naturally, misunderstands her attitude and goes out heartbroken.

The high-spot of Act III is the superb encounter between Nero and Britannicus. While Agrippina and Nero are in consultation, Junia escapes to seek Britannicus and, finding him, reveals the secret of her strange behavior during the recent interview. As Britannicus throws himself at her feet in remorse for his misunderstanding of her intentions, Nero enters. The spirited passage at arms which follows, in which Racine manages to convey the majesty of a Roman emperor as well as the jealousy, the controlled fury, and the arrogance of Nero, is largely composed in the archaic form of stichomythia mentioned above, which gives it a flavor of the encounter between Don Diègue and Don Gomez in *Le Cid.* . . .

The famous scene between Agrippina and Nero in Act IV, which begins with the mother's homely and patronizing,

> Approchez-vous, Néron, et prenez votre place,

to the son who has just put her under virtual arrest, and which ends with Nero's apparent yielding to her wishes, is utterly incapable of illustration by extracts. But some idea of the snakelike Narcissus at his best (or worst) in the last scene of Act IV where he neutralizes the effect of Burrhus' pleadings in the preceding scene may be gained from the following fragment. Narcissus arrives with the news that preparations are complete for the poisoning of Britannicus. Note the cool cynicism of his first speech, his quick utilization of Nero's revised decision to enforce still more strongly his own point of view, and the short, sharp struggle with Nero's conscience which he brings to triumphant issue by his poisonous allusion to Agrippina's boastings.

It is impossible to quote the lengthy closing speech of the scene; but the psychological subtlety of Narcissus is well illustrated by this fragment:

> *Narcisse.* Seigneur, j'ai tout prévu pour une mort si juste.
>> Le poison est tout prêt. La fameuse Locuste
>> A redoublé pour moi ses soins officieux:
>> Elle a fait expirer un esclave à mes yeux;
>> Et le fer est moins prompt, pour trancher une vie,
>> Que le nouveau poison que sa main me confie.
> *Néron.* Narcisse, c'est assez; je reconnais ce soin,
>> Et ne souhaite pas que vous alliez plus loin.
> *Narcisse.* Quoi? pour Britannicus votre haine affaiblie
>> Me défend . . .
> *Néron.*   Oui, Narcisse, on nous réconcilie.
> *Narcisse.* Je me garderai bien de vous en détourner,
>> Seigneur; mais il s'est vu tantôt emprisonner:
>> Cette offense en son cœur sera longtemps nouvelle.
>> Il n'est point de secrets que le temps ne révèle:
>> Il saura que ma main lui devait présenter
>> Un poison que votre ordre avait fait apprêter.
>> Les Dieux de ce dessein puissent-ils le distraire,
>> Mais peut-être il fera ce que vous n'osez faire.
> *Néron.* On répond de son cœur; et je vaincrai le mien.
> *Narcisse.* Et l'hymen de Junie en est-il le lien?
>> Seigneur, lui faites-vous encor ce sacrifice?
> *Néron.* C'est prendre trop de soin. Quoi qu'il en soit, Narcisse,
>> Je ne le compte plus parmi mes ennemis.
> *Narcisse.* Agrippine, Seigneur, se l'était bien promis.
>> Elle a repris sur vous son souverain empire.
> *Néron.* Quoi donc? Qu'a-t-elle dit? Et que

voulez-vous dire?
> *Narcisse.* Elle s'en est vantée assez publiquement.
> *Néron.* De quoi?
> *Narcisse.*   Qu'elle n'avait qu'à vous voir un moment:
>> Qu'à tout ce grand éclat, à ce courroux funeste
>> On verrait succéder un silence modeste;
>> Que vous même à la paix souscririez le premier,
>> Heureux que sa bonté diagnât tout oublier.

It is unnecessary to dwell on Act V. Except for the effective final line (quoted above), the denouement has been usually admitted to be lacking in power and to be too long drawn-out. It has nothing of the sharp dramatic impact that is so striking in the close of *Andromaque.*

Britannicus was not a success at first. This was a great chagrin to Racine, for he considered it, as we have seen, one of his most painstaking efforts. Yet in his second Preface he admits "that its success did not at first come up to my hopes." This is confirmed by the testimony of Boursault, who in the opening pages of his novel *Artémise et Poliante* (1670) has left us a vivid account of the play's first performance. We see old Corneille "alone in a box" and the members of the authors' *cabale* scattered about, "for fear of being recognized." Boursault reports that all admitted the beauty of the verse but criticized severely the action and the characters. From pointed and bitter references in Racine's first Preface we gather that Corneille had put himself at the head and front of this critical offending. One of the objections that Racine takes up concerns his alteration of the ages of Britannicus and Narcissus. "I should not have spoken of this objection," he adds, "if it had not been made with some heat by a man who has taken the liberty to make an emperor reign twenty years who reigned only eight." This is an unmistakable reference to Corneille's *Héraclius.* Later on he asks, "What would one have to do to satisfy such finicky judges? It would be easy, if one were willing to betray good sense. All that would be necessary would be to depart from nature in order to plunge into the fantastic . . . for example, represent some drunk hero who would fain make his mistress hate him out of pure gayety of heart, a Lacedæmonian who is a great talker, a conqueror who did nothing but utter love-maxims, a woman who gave lessons in pride to conquerors." These last are definite allusions to Corneille's plays *Attila, Agésilas,* and *Pompée.* ***Britannicus*** had the effect therefore of exacerbating the quarrel between Racine and Corneille's party.

It is probable that from the reception of his ***Britannicus*** Racine concluded that the taste for great political discussions was passing away and that he would do better to confine himself to the passion of love, which, after all, was his forte and which had served him so well in ***Andromaque.*** In ***Bérénice*** he was to find a way of doing this and at the same time of preserving a Cornelian element.

Paul Valéry (essay date 1942)

SOURCE: "On Phèdre as a Woman," in *The Collected Works of Paul Valéry: Occasions,* translated by Roger Shattuck and Frederick Brown, Bollingen Series XLV, Princeton University Press, 1970, pp. 185-95.

[*A prominent French poet and critic, Valéry is one of the leading practitioners of nineteenth-century Symbolist aestheticism. His work reflects his desire for total control of his creation; his absorption with the creative process also forms the method of his criticism. In his prose, Valéry displays what is perhaps his most fundamental talent: the ability to apply a well-disciplined mind to a diversity of subjects including art, politics, science, dance, and aesthetics. His critical writings are collected in the five volumes of* Variéte *(1924-44;* Variety) *and his personal notebooks, the* Cahiers *(1894-1945). In the following excerpt from an essay originally published in 1942, Valéry ruminates upon the psychological inferences of Phèdre's character.*]

After reading *Phèdre,* or seeing the theater curtain fall, I am left with the idea of a certain woman, a sense of the beauty of the verse; a future reserve resides in me in these durable effects and values.

The mind resumes its normal course, which is a riotous stream of sensations and thoughts, but unknowingly it has selected from the work the elements that it will henceforth treasure among its supply of ultimate standards and criteria of beauty. It never fails to single out, unconsciously, these elements from the pretexts and combination of happenings which had to be contrived so that the play might exist. The plot, the intrigue, the incidents soon fade, and whatever interest may have attached to the dramatic apparatus as such vanishes. It was merely a crime: wished-for incest, murder committed by proxy, with of course a god to carry out the act. But what can be made of a crime once the horror of it has subsided, once justice has been done, and death has claimed the innocent and the guilty alike, for death like the sea closes over every temporary scheme of events and acts. The emotion born of the presence and condensation of the drama disappears along with the decor, while the gripped heart and eyes, which had so long remained fixed, find relief from the constraint exerted upon the whole being by the speaking, luminous stage.

Everyone disappears, save the queen: poor, pitiable Hippolyte, the moment he lies shattered on the resounding shore; Théramène, his message just declaimed; Thésée, Aricie, Œnone, and Invisible Neptune himself—all melt into absence. They have stopped pretending to be, having *been* only to serve the author's essential design. They were not made of lasting substance; their roles have used them up. They live only long enough to incite the ardor and wrath, the remorse and terrors typical of a woman *insane* with desire; they are used to bring forth from her Racinian depths the noblest expressions of concupiscence and remorse ever inspired by passion. They do not survive, but she does. Memory reduces the work to a monologue; within me it changes from its originally dramatic form into a purely lyric one—for lyricism is precisely that, the transfiguration of a monologue.

Love, provoked beyond measure in the person of Phèdre, has none of the tenderness it assumes in Bérénice. She is ruled by the flesh whose sovereign voice calls, unanswerably, for the possession of the beloved's body and has one single goal: the perfect attunement of concordant ecstasies. Life thus falls prey to images so intense that its days and nights, its duties and its falsehoods are torn apart. The power of physical passion, forever thirsting because it is never slaked, may be compared to an open wound which keeps aggravating itself: it is an inexhaustible source of pain, for the pain can only increase while the wound remains open. That is its law. By definition, one cannot get used to it for it insists on its hideous presence as though it were always new. It is the same with an incurable love lodged in its victim.

With Phèdre, nothing veils, mitigates, ennobles, adorns, or elevates her sexual frenzy. The mind, with its profound, subtle, shifting play, its outlets, its intuitions, its inquisitiveness, its refinements, can do nothing to embellish this consummately simple passion or divert it from itself. Phèdre has read nothing. Hippolyte is, for all we know, a fool. What does that matter? This incandescent queen needs only enough mind to serve her vengeance, invent stratagems, and enslave itself to instinct. As for the soul, it becomes nothing more than its obsessive power, the ruthless and unwavering will to clasp its prey, draw him under, to moan and die of pleasure at his side.

This love, devoid of metaphysics, is love as described or presupposed in the literature of an age which rarely mentioned the soul except in philosophical speculations, an age when lovers were never seen invoking the universe between embraces and fretting over "the World as Will and Idea" by their bedside. . . .

Racine knew better than to sweeten that desire in the raw which Phèdre radiates and sings. She could scarcely have inherited from her makers, Minos and Pasiphaë, what was not in their nature. It was not given them to feel as we do, when we yield unreservedly to the weakness of cherishing another person, a surge of tenderness that deliciously calms and eases all the forces of the soul. They were a callous pair of beings. Primitive love, as it appears in most myths, shows nothing but its implacably instinctive essence. It is, at this stage, simply a "force of nature," borne and acknowledged as such. It does not yearn for the exaltation that comes of One and One uniting beyond, through, above their keenest mutual spasm: it is satisfied to be this visceral lurch, for nature requires nothing more enduring than a flash. In simple love, anything that distracts from the consummation of pleasure runs contrary to nature. This necessary and sufficient love is too intent on seizing the body of its prey to spare its sensibilities; it will get what it wants by hook or by crook. It is not at all above fraud, rape, abduction. The gods of that age, whose sole function it was to enact the designs vainly suggested to us by our desire, accomplish effortlessly what we can only dream of doing: they make sport of feelings as well as of natural laws and, by force, by guile, or even by corrupting if need be, they satisfy their cravings. Mythology is essentially bestial. Zeus turns into a swan, an eagle, a bull, a shower of gold, a cloud, thus refusing to take advantage of his identity. The conquest itself is all that matters to him: he does not care to figure in dreams. But perhaps these metamorphoses are only symbols of the various tricks and ploys men use to achieve their sensual goals, replying, as the occasion and their wits dictate, on one advantage or another, on a repertory of grimaces, exploiting their visible manliness, their fortune, their fame, their brilliance—or the opposite of all these, for there are unfortunates whose misfortune, whose ugliness, even to deformity, will excite a feeling of pity verging on love, and move some heart to give its all; nothing is impossible where human taste is concerned, and I have observed the oddest conquests.

Though his Phèdre is largely ruled by instinct, Racine presents her feral nature in the most elegant terms, revealing its depths as the drama unfolds. The particular case that his tragedy lays bare would, moreover, appear to be less anomalous than deplorable. Unrequited love cries for vengeance. God Himself says to us, "Love me, love me or I shall deal you eternal death." And in the Bible we read that "Joseph, being well-made and comely, it came to pass that the wife of his master cast her eyes upon him, and said, 'Lie with me.'" Courteously rebuffed, Potiphar's wife denounced him, charging him with seeking to take her by force, just as Thésée's wife accused Hippolyte and so brought down upon him the paternal curse, executed by Neptune. I fear, then, that in our mind's eye we must see Phèdre in the same pitiless light as Rembrandt saw Potiphar's wife. In his engraving he showed her furiously twisting and stretching toward Joseph, who is straining to get away. The etching is remarkable for its powerful lewdness. In it, the biblical female, her belly naked, fleshy, dazzling white, exposed, clings to Joseph's robe, while he strives to tear himself from the clutches of this stark madwoman whose transport drags not only her ponderous flesh, but the whole soft bulk of her devastated bed, spilling a tangle of sheets to the floor. Everything focuses on this delirious belly, which sustains, concentrates, and radiates the painting's luminous power. Never has desire unleashed been portrayed so brutally, with a keener sense of the ignoble force that compels flesh to offer itself like the yawning of a monster's jaws. The Egyptian woman is not beautiful, but there is no reason why she need be. Through her plainness she shows how confident she is that her aroused and desperate sex will prevail unaided. This is not an uncommon error; it is not always an error. Yet I cannot imagine Phèdre otherwise than very beautiful, in the full flower of beauty, of her beauty, which I shall come to presently.

The passion of love secretes a fatal poison that is, at first, only faintly active, easily eliminated, and passes unnoticed. But a few trifles can quicken it so that, suddenly, it can overwhelm all our powers of reason, and our fear of men and gods.

By this I mean that, in becoming strongly enamored of

Sarah Berhhardt in the title role in Phèdre.

someone, we unconsciously invest the object of our love with a power to make us suffer which far surpasses the power we grant him or her (and look for) to make us rapturously happy. And if the need to possess some one person takes such complete hold of us as to form the condition of life itself (which is the way absolute love works), this now-vital affection, once it is torn by despair, sets little store by life. It familiarly entertains the idea of murder. This soon mingles with the idea of suicide; which is absurd, thus natural.

Having lost hope, Phèdre kills. Having killed, she kills herself.

Phèdre cannot be a very young woman. She is at the age when women who are truly, one might even say expressly, born for love, come into possession of their powers. She has reached that moment when life recognizes its fullness and its unfulfillment. In the offing are physical decay, rebuffs, and her own ashes. But here and now, bursting with life, she can experience feeling to its uttermost degree. What she is worth dictates, in the recesses of her mind, what she desires, so that her burdensome resources very gradually devote themselves to some potential but unknown plunderer who will take them by surprise, exalt and then exhaust them; whoever he is, for he has not even appeared yet, he is already gifted with all the charms conferred on him by impatient suspense, by a thirst every moment more searing. The internal processes of our living substance lose their normal function, which is to assure the survival of the organism. The body comes to anticipate the self, and to see farther ahead. It floods with a superabundant sense of being, and the mysterious anxiety arising from this excess riots in dreams, in temptations, in risks, in feverish attention alternating with lapses of mind. The flesh itself becomes a proposal. Like a plant overwhelmed by the weight of its own fruit, and bent forward as though begging to be plucked, woman offers herself.

Perhaps this has to do with some dark conflict being waged between the forces that so strangely coexist in our beings—and ones which continually produce us, that is, which keep us living, and the others which tend only to reproduce us. The individual succumbs to the species, which insidiously promotes itself throughout the whole person whose sensibility and general economy are invaded by the energies of a minute egg as it ripens, becoming at once the product, the disturbing component, the enemy, and finally dominating the whole living body. The injunction to outlive struggles and pits itself against the importance of living. The indefinable sensations provoked by an unmated seed influence, *by remote control,* the whole mental disposition, which has been so primed for the coming adventure that it will see in it, when it does unfold, an event of infinite magnitude. *Venus* calls the tune and *Psyche* plays.

Phèdre is in the midst of her second puberty, and embodies all the alienation, the anxiety of that age.

What I have said up to now was by way of preparation for that eminently noteworthy adjective set in the famous line:

C'est Vénus tout entière. . . .

So Venus is the culprit, and Venus "tout entière." How can this name Venus be translated into nonallegorical language, and what is the precise meaning of "tout entière," an expression so admirable and felicitous that I hesitate to belabor it? Racine could take such perfection in his stride, without lingering over it, but today these words have connotations which his age did not as yet clearly recognize. We are able to uncover treasures the author did not suspect he had buried and see in his words evidence of a prescient mind. This prescience refers to the physiological aspect which, for lack of knowledge, I shall not explore, but I believe I have suggested the lines that someone more expert might follow, and I shall confine myself to what little I can say, offhand.

With Phèdre having come to the unstable pass I have described, her life has all the makings of an emotional tempest. Suddenly the event takes place. Someone appears and is at once recognized as the very one who was destined to appear. Why not someone else? We are always free to wonder if any other captain of handsome presence might have brought matters to a head. But no, it was Hippolyte, who draws down upon himself the burden of desire that weighed so heavily on her uneasy soul.

Instantly, everything is transformed, within her—and around her. The days change color. Even the passage of time becomes irregular. The body's organic routines are upset. The heart is caught, and the breath as well: a glance, a hesitation, a hint, a footfall, a shadow will quicken or suspend them. The basic functions of life have found their master . . . in a phantom, in a troubling figment. Incredible superstitions gain credence. Her mind has astonishing lapses, or pays obsessed attention; it gives birth to the maddest inventions, or falls into a stupor lasting for hours, for days during which it shows no palpable signs of thought, as if it were arrested, like the body of a wounded man who expects intolerable pain to come of his least movement. All those vain ornaments, those veils, would not seem so heavy to the queen were she not a woman already overwhelmed by love. Her entire life is reorganized around a fundamental anxiety, all values are at the mercy of a whim that is not hers, subordinated to the infinite Value she attaches to Another, to the promise he seemed to embody. And when, having offered him her entire being (a gesture that in itself compromises her organic, psychic, and social equilibrium), this all-embracing gift is answered with resistance and refusal, then all the honey of prospective ecstasies, all the sap of hoped-for love, whose influence had overcharged her inmost vitality, all this turns into a poison of the rarest virulence. There is nothing which that distillation of hatred and fury does not attack, corrode, and eat away. The vital exchanges, the natural functions, the habits, the ethical and civil laws that firmly establish a person within his life, fall apart. *C'est Vénus tout entière à sa proie attachée.* When Venus first grew fast to her, the woman in love appeared transfigured by a relish for life, by a will to ascend the highest heights of ecstasy, her desire exerting such influence that her very flesh grew increasingly desirable as her desire grew increasingly ardent. Phèdre, beautiful in her own right but, like all beautiful women, beautiful even before love, attains the full splendor of her beauty when she declares her passion. I say *splendor* because the fire of a decisive act illumines her face, makes her eyes glow and animates her entire person. But afterward, that sublime brow falters; it is overwhelmed by pathos; it sags beneath its burden, and the eyes grow dim. Pain, the lesion of the soul, contrives a new and frightful beauty—a mask whose pinched features alter to those of a Fury. Venus is at last abandoning her prey. The venom of love has done its work. A woman has passed through the successive stages of passion; there is nothing left for her to do on earth. One draught of a different poison, the product of ordinary chemistry, will spirit her to Hades for a final reckoning.

As for the language of this play, I shall not importune the reader by saying the obvious, or what has been said before, very often and very well. I shall not sing the praises of a form that achieves the consummate synthesis of art and the natural, that carries its prosodic chains so lightly as to make of them an ornament, a kind of garment draping the nakedness of thought. In *Phèdre,* the strict discipline of our Alexandrine retains and fosters a higher form of freedom; it makes eloquence sound so easy that one does not at first realize what craft and labors of transmutation that ease must have entailed. I shall take the liberty of relating an experience I had once, for in my mind it is inseparably bound to what I have just written. I hope that this personal anecdote will not be seen as an intrusion of vanity. Not many years ago, I composed the libretto of a cantata, and had to do it rather quickly, in Alexandrines. One day, I laid this work aside to go to the Academy and, my mind still absorbed in working out the cadence of a period, I found myself gazing absent-mindedly through a shopwindow on the quai, where a lovely page of verse stood on display, beautifully printed in large typeface. A remarkable interchange sprang up between myself and this fragment of noble architecture. As though still at work on my draft, unconsciously, for the better part of a minute I began to try out word conversions on the exhibited text. I felt like a sculptor who had seized a chunk of marble, while dreaming that he was molding soft and still moist clay.

But the text would not allow itself to be rehandled. *Phèdre* resisted me. I thus learned, through direct experience and immediate sensation, what is meant by perfection in a work. It was a rude awakening.

Wallace Fowlie (essay date 1948)

SOURCE: "Second Cycle: Racine, the Sun in *Phèdre*," in *Love in Literature: Studies in Symbolic Expression*, 1965. Reprint by Books for Libraries Press, 1972, pp. 51-7.

[*Fowlie is among the most respected and comprehensive scholars of French literature. His work includes translations of major poets and dramatists of France (Molière, Charles Baudelaire, Arthur Rimbaud, Paul Claudel, Saint-John Perse) and critical studies of the major figures and movements of modern French letters (Stephane Mallarmé, Marcel Proust, Andre Gidé, the Surrealists, among many others). Broad intellectual and artistic sympathies, along with an acute sensitivity for French writing and a first-hand understanding of literary creativity (he is the author of a novel and poetry collections in both French and English), are among the qualities that make Fowlie an indispensable guide for the student of French literature. In the following excerpt from an essay originally published in 1948, he explicates* Phèdre *as a play representative of Racine's vision of "the human heart finding its pleasure in suffering, jealous of every unknown agony and form of sadism."*]

Each age is comprehensible and distinct according to its doctrine on human suffering. In the seventeenth century the evolution of this doctrine forms a unified and complete lesson. The hero of Corneille seeks his happiness and safeguards it in life and in death. Pascal, a tragic hero like Horace and Polyeucte, sought for his salvation and safeguarded it in the suffering of his body and in his spirit tormented by the agony of his God. The heroine of Racine completes this evolution because she seeks not only to destroy herself but to destroy all those who exist around her. If Corneille seeks to avoid suffering and Pascal to embrace it, Racine represents the triumph over suffer-

ing and the immeasurable widening of its domain. He represents the human heart finding its pleasure in suffering, jealous of every unknown agony and form of sadism.

After the image of man always accompanied by woman which Corneille gives us, and after the solitary humanity of Pascal, Racine offers us the image of solitary woman. Hermione, Bérénice, Phèdre are alone with themselves, but they keep the memory of the species and preserve the meaning of continuity. Each one of his heroines appears on the stage bearing over her features the mask of eternal woman, eternally alone, eternally necessary to man who turns his back on her and escapes from her. At each entrance of Phèdre, the stage becomes empty and she remains alone with her memory peopled by its own species, alone before all the elements of nature, alone as if she were some bewildered victim who had wandered away from her executioner.

The first words which Racine has Phèdre say, her first apostrophe which never ceases resounding throughout the tragedy, her

soleil, je te viens voir pour la dernière fois,

announces everything. The radiation of the sun is the permanent symbol of tragedy in *Phèdre.* The triumph of the sun—it is at the zenith when Phèdre comes to contemplate it for the last time—first marks the tragedy. The sun is not only the ascendency of Phèdre, since her mother, Pasiphaé, was daughter of the Sun—it is also the triumph of man in his phallic symbolism, the piercing power of the male which Phèdre in her woman's flesh cannot extinguish or embrace. The sun, at first a god for Phèdre to whom she is bound by close consanguinity, is above all for her the image of young Hippolyte who mounts with the day like a corporeal star and descends into the night to fill it with his presence and his memory.

At the beginning of the play, Phèdre appears under the full light of the sun, and it is impossible for her during all the unfolding of the tragedy to retire within the shade, to sit down, as she longs to, 'à l'ombre des forêts'. Rather than diminishing, the force of the sun grows in each act. The soul of Phèdre grows more and more shining under the solar rigour, and at the end of the work, the intensity of suffering, which is intensity of light, reaches the moment of conflagration. Phèdre perishes in her own flames. The tragedy ends in a chemical and supernatural fire.

Phèdre herself never becomes, even for an instant, the sun. She never leaves the purity of her own drama. She is always the victim of love, of the sun, and of man. She is the victim who receives, if not the fecundating and real force of love, at least its imagined and cruel force. She receives, during this one day of the tragedy, all the superabundant energy of the sun, as if the energy of the cosmos was being spent for her in some effort of nature to perfect divine creation by destroying her. Racine created in his work a solemn and terrible cult. The sun-ravisher strips Phèdre of her clothes and leaves her nude before the eyes of the spectators. Each line she recites, as in some propitiatory sacrifice, translates an act of the sun perpetrated on her flesh and on her soul. Before our eyes she is slowly consumed by the love which strikes her in the heat and the light of the sun. The force which Phèdre would like to have felt in Hippolyte, she feels in all of nature which rushes through her in flames of poison. Love is not for her a man, it is the sun incapable of appearing in a human and desirable form. The supernatural surrounds Phèdre and wards off the natural.

When she learns, in the fourth act, of the love of Hippolyte for Aricie, and when jealousy, the new and final suffering, is added to her passion, Phèdre, in her most poignant line, evokes the innocency of that other love by means of a familiar image:

> Tous les jours se levaient clairs et sereins pour
> eux.

The passion of Hippolyte and Aricie unites them in a love comparable to the light and the justification of the day. The world of men welcomes this kind of love, as the universe welcomes the return of the sun, but Phèdre, who seeks to flee the light, cannot escape from the sun before falling inert and consumed by its force. Alone before the sun, Phèdre presents to it the flesh of her body and suffers even in the memory of all her race. The sun captures all the agitations in the being of this woman who, during the moment of her race when it was permitted her to live, dared oppose the celestial fires and arrest their burning menaces. This was Phèdre's struggle against the natural cosmos and against the divine order of the cosmos. Her disorder, which is felt, imperceptibly at least, by all beings, is suppressed by them and relegated to the secret parts of the subconscious. Most men prefer to forget or destroy such a passion rather than to live in the vast solitude it exacts, with nature itself, the sun and all the stars, as the eternally vigilant enemy destined to triumph.

Phèdre is never separated from her heart, as most men and women are daily. Her tender and terrible faith is reminiscent of the solemn perfection of Jansenism, that philosophy of man in which Racine as a boy had learned to touch the most intimate secrets of the heart. Phèdre is not a criminal because her love for Hippolyte is not literally incestuous, but she foresees the crime for the future and at the same time she dreams of the past. She dreams of her mother and thereby suffers for all the maternal sins. This is the way in which horror and monstrosity stifle Phèdre. She deceives us, and we believe, in listening to her, that passion is incorruptible. We learn to believe that this daughter of Pasiphaé has warded off all the angels of the resurrection and that she will always remain faithful to her flesh, accomplishing her mission of fidelity to the earth, eternally remembering the rocks and the trees, dissimulating nothing of what is in her nature and no part of the sun's dark action on her.

But this drama of the flesh ends in the drama of purity. After the first scene when Phèdre remains alone with the sun composed of her ancestors, of her heart, and of the terrible future, and after the central scene when jealousy heightens her passion and transforms her soul into a site of paroxysm, comes the final scene when Phèdre, in the presence of the spectators, and her ancestors, and all of nature, enters death while experiencing for the first time in her body an unknown coldness, and while converting her heart into a purity worthy of rivalling the purity of daylight. The last speech of Phèdre resembles the poison which is flowing through her veins and diminishing all the signs of life in her body. Her very words denude and transform the meaning of life. Only material substance counts, and the words are lost in the new conversion where flames triumph over the body and where Phèdre fails for the first time to see the sun because she is entering it in the midst of her ancestors. This final drama of purity is the congenital catastrophe where Phèdre, after struggling against the cosmos, is assimilated by the cosmos into its most immaterialized sphere.

The principal action of Phèdre is therefore not so much her attack against modesty as her struggle against the sun which she is forced to look at and which is destined to destroy her. Racine understood above all in the character of Phèdre the maternal and primitive trait of woman who struggles for the preservation of the race and whose tragedy is the loss of self before the re-creation and justification of self. Every woman is tragic who is unable to become, in her racial and solemn rôle, mother of all men and history. The absolutism of passion, manifested in Racine's Phèdre and in Shakespeare's Cleopatra is the absolutism of the void and of ashes, that absolutism which crowns both works in the implacable resolution of the final purity. Purity absolves the passion of Phèdre and Cleopatra by destroying it, even in its memory.

Woman is with the race and creation, but man is alone, more tragically alone. That is why the tragedy of a woman, alone with her passion and incapable of converting it or appeasing it in accordance with the simple and practical law of reproduction, appears more monstrous than all the tragedies of men. Phèdre and Cleopatra both have in their speech a sequence of words which describe the evolution of their passion: its unfolding and its death in the cosmic fire:

Phèdre: acte I: soleil—forêts—horreur—crime—fureur—
      Vé us—proie.
    acte II: fureur—abhorrer—feux—monstre.
    acte IV: douleur—rebut—crime—inceste—soleil—
      enfers—bourreau.
    acte V: incestueux—funeste—poison—jour—pureté.
Cleopatra: act I, scene 5: mangragora—treason—eunuch—
      poison—unpeople.
    act II, scene 5: eunuch—barren ears—melt gold—
      serpents.
    act III, scene II: blown rose—cold heart—poison—stone—pelleted storm—graveless.
    act IV, scene 13: sun—knife—drugs—serpents—
      heaviness—melt—withered garland.
    act V, scene 2: ruin—ditch—naked—abhorring—
      cinders—ashes—marble—fire and air.

The two tragedies of passion contain a similar evolution

in their imagery. In *Antony and Cleopatra,* it is progress from fertility to dissolution, and in **Phèdre,** it is progress from desire to dissolution. For Cleopatra, love is at first symbolized by the earth and the mud of the Nile, and at the end of the tragedy, it is vaporized into flames and into the air. The transformation which Phèdre undergoes is similar, because the transports of love she feels at the beginning of the tragedy are metamorphosed into the purity of day. The love of Phèdre and Cleopatra was always death, but it is called by its real name for the first time at the end of the tragedies in the purgation of all the terrestrial elements. Born from passion, Phèdre and Cleopatra expire in passion.

Both tragedies describe a cycle of overpowering and total passion. Phèdre, goddess and lover, personifies the terrible unity in love and death exacted by the gods and the psychology of woman. Cleopatra, actress and lover, personifies the diversity in this unity. For Phèdre, the sun is lover and executioner, beginning and end of an experience which wilfully destroys her in agreement with the orders of the gods and of men. For Cleopatra, the Nile and the fertile lands periodically covered by the waters of the Nile symbolize the love of abundance she claims, but this same soil, when it is used and worn out symbolizes the exhaustion of love. The language of Phèdre mounts toward the sun until the moment it catches fire and is extinguished in the flames. The language of Cleopatra descends toward the Nile and the over-rich lands of the Nile until the moment it loses its form in the viscous slime.

Phèdre is a profoundly religious work. An eschatalogical work. As the heroine's language mounts toward the sun, the meaning of sacrifice becomes increasingly clear. At the conclusion of the work, Phèdre appears as a victim suspended between heaven and earth. The victim and the target of the sun.

> Thy face
> From charred and riven stakes, O
> Dionysus, Thy
> Unmangled target smile.
> (Hart Crane, *Lachrymae Christi*)

The stake of Dionysus, god of vegetation, of wine, recalls the Cross of Jesus, God of men. But in the last scene of Racine's tragedy, the body itself of Phèdre is a stake and a cross while it becomes for an instant the target of men and of the gods. Dionysus, in expiating passion, is the target of the world's concupiscence; Christ, in expiating sadism, is the target of the world's sin; and Phèdre, who will be replaced in the nineteenth and twentieth centuries by the artist, in expiating pride, is the target of the world's cruelty.

The fury of Phèdre is impossible to conceive without the dogma of grace. Grace exists by its absence in the tragedy of **Phèdre.** It is grace which, absent or present, places on the face of a woman her tragic mask. Without grace, Phèdre would be purely a woman and would not be that creature we know solicited by all the demons and all the

angels. Without the concept of grace, Phèdre would resemble Molly Bloom who, in the long soliloquy at the end of *Ulysses,* sings solely of the carnal and cosmic principle of women, and reproduces the circular movement of the earth, the natural history of the cosmos, the woman waiting in her bed for her husband and who is going to say yes to him in adherence to the instinctive law of the species.

In the heroes of Corneille, carnal passion is subordinated to the passion of order: it becomes in Rodrigue, and to a certain degree in Chimène also, philosophic passion. In the thought of Pascal, love reproduces the order of charity in which man surpasses himself, after he had been made greater, purely as man, in the universe of Corneille. In Racine, love seems always to equate self-annihilating passion. Phèdre incarnates tragic passion which is dissolved. Thus Corneille, finding what is noblest in man, announces Pascal who, finding outside of man what is divine, yields his place to Racine who finds in man what is most corrupt.

As if what is corrupt in man hasn't the right to exist, Racine prepares for the final scene a conflagration in which the whole being of Phèdre, contaminated by evil, burns and loses its form. And this woman, who had never renounced the spirit during her dream of the flesh, rediscovers in death that purity of spirit which the saints rediscover in life through their denial of the flesh.

Eugène Vinaver (essay date 1951)

SOURCE: "Discords and Resolutions," in *Racine and Poetic Tragedy,* translated by P. Mansell Jones, 1955. Reprint by Manchester University Press, 1962, pp. 27-46.

[*In the following excerpt from an English-language edition of a volume originally published in French in 1951, Vinaver examines Racine's tragic poetry, particularly its employment in* Andromaque, Brittanicus, Bajazet, Bérénice, *and* Mithridate.]

It would be unjust to reproach the contemporaries of Racine with the small account they made of his originality. Belonging to an epoch which believed less in genius than in talent, they could not pay him greater homage than to place him by common accord in the rank of the worthiest craftsmen of the regular theatre. In the funeral oration which he pronounced at the Academy on the 27th of June 1699, Valincour with his fine sagacity did indeed recognize in the author of **Andromaque** and **Phèdre** the merit of having opened 'new roads'; he praised him even for having 'filled his audience with that terror and that pity which, according to Aristotle, are the veritable passions which tragedy should produce'. But twelve years before, La Bruyère had said of these passions that they constituted the common ground of all tragedy, that of Corneille as well as Racine's. And as for those privileged witnesses who on the 17th of November 1667 had applauded in the Queen's apartments the first presentation of *Andromaque,* all we know is that they judged its author capable 'one day of equalling and perhaps surpassing' the great Corneille. Those for whom feeling came first naturally honoured *Andromaque* with their tears; this was the case with the Duchess of Orléans, to whom Racine had read the piece, and with Madame de Sévigné who, a few years later, saw it played by a provincial company. But the accredited critics, those whose mission it was to judge the first great tragedy of the young poet, gave it their approval just in so far as it exemplified the purest and most esteemed type of play.

The astonishing thing is that we have advanced so little beyond that point: not through literary conformity, but out of obedience to a method which willingly sacrifices the text to the 'movement'. A cruel sacrifice when one thinks that still today Racine's tragedies serve to consummate it. From the eighteenth century there has been no lack of commentators to 'place' his work. Nearly all however have refused to discern the least conflict between the Racinian conception of tragedy and the framework within which it moves. It is in vain that the author of a celebrated work on Philippe Quinault affirms that 'the tragedy of Racine is, in the history of the theatre, a happy exception', and that another critic says that in Racine's century his tragedy 'represents an exception of the most extraordinary kind'. His tragedy fits so well into the contours of the type of theatre called classical, and brings it to such a degree of stability, that it has no defence to offer against the efforts ceaselessly renewed to reconcile it with the spirit of its time. What more 'regular' indeed than the structure of *Andromaque?* What a masterstroke in favour of the unity of purpose and of interest is this simplification of an action which passes between four characters and offers at first glance a double plot! 'Notice', says Paul Janet in his study of *Les Passions et les Caractères dans la Littérature du XVIIe Siècle,* 'what is the subject and the nucleus of his tragedy: three pairings of four persons who repel and attract one another at the same time. You could almost give this quadrille the form of an arithmetical proposition and say: Hermione and Pyrrhus are the two means of which Oreste and Andromaque are the two extremes. Oreste is to Hermione what Pyrrhus is to Andromaque. And what is the action of the drama? It is entirely in the coming and going of the two middle terms, now approaching, now withdrawing from the two extremes. Sometimes Pyrrhus in desperation turns from Andromaque and comes back to Hermione who then hastens to abandon Oreste; and thus the two extremes remain alone, Andromaque in her joy, Oreste in his fury. 'Sometimes, on the contrary, hope brings Pyrrhus back to Andromaque; and Hermione, in her turn desperate and exacerbated, returns to Oreste, full of scorn and rancour at first, then of rage and vengeance.' What Paul Janet does not say is that this skilful construction is Racinian only in the perfection of its balance. It is inspired by a banal procedure, that of the dramatic utilization of a chain of passions. Brought into fashion by the *Diana* of Montemayor these 'elusive' passions had been a great success at first in the non-tragic genres: the novel, the pastoral play and tragi-comedy. In the *Alphée* of Alexandre Hardy they had served to relate one to another

seven characters, each enamoured of the person who had no love for him or her. Mélanie desires Euryale who has promised his heart to a dryad; the latter covets a satyr who pursues Corinne; Corinne is promised to Daphnis who adores Alphée. Similarly in the *Délie* of Donneau de Visé, played by the troupe of the Palais Royal some weeks before *Andromaque,* a shepherdess loved by two shepherds, Licidas and Cléante, is obliged to make a choice; she ends by declaring for Licidas to the joy of Orphise who is in love with Cléante. This pattern is no less frequent in the regular theatre: it recurs in the *Mort de Commode* and the *Camma* of Thomas Corneille as well as in the two pieces which Racine had in mind when writing *Andromaque:* the *Pertharite* of Pierre Corneille and the *Hercule Mourant* of Rotrou. To animate a type of subject-matter so polymorphous as Greek legend, Racine had only to apply a formula consecrated by usage and capable of resolving the dramatic problem it presented—a formula which of itself set all the springs to work, thus assuring perfect unity of action.

And it is precisely with reference to the structure of this play that an attentive reader would be tempted to wonder how Racine succeeded in preventing it from destroying the tragic nature of the subject. If it is necessary that to each movement of the dramatic springs there should correspond a new pattern of feelings and that these feelings should be conceived in view of a simple concordance with the rhythm of the action, the moral life of the character is bound to present itself as a regular alternation of happy and unhappy states. Now tragedy in the authentic sense of the term, that 'song of despair' of which, according to the words of Pierre-Aimé Touchard, one must not demand either solutions or vain illusions, supposes an ever-deepening vision of the misery of man, an understanding ever more complete of the ineluctable in life. It is this that the Greeks felt to be the divine malediction, confounding and crushing human beings and leaving them only capable of feeling its terrible effects. For this ironic game of the divine powers a world freed from Olympus must substitute an act of tragic consciousness which reveals in the misfortune overwhelming man the faithful image of his condition. What will become of such an act when man allows himself to be enticed by the movement of a plot, the object of which is to procure him moments of relaxation and respite?—when a Pyrrhus, a Britannicus, a Bajazet, caught in the wheels of drama, believe they can weight their chances of safety? Is it not to be feared that at such moments their triumph will appear possible? Pyrrhus thinks, and the spectator agrees, that he will succeed against the scruples of Andromaque and the rages of Hermione. He rushes to the temple, sure of seeing 'this storm dissipate in tears'. Hence in the spectator the absence of all dismay, of all feeling of terror, as if he beheld an indifferent event arising outside the tragic zone of life. As much could be said of the adventure of Britannicus and Junie. These young persons, strangers to the tragic, traverse sunlit regions where faith is reborn in a happiness fully deserved, and only the resurgence of the 'monstre naissant' deprives them of all hope. How can we prevent ourselves, on seeing the snare into which they slip, from thinking that things could have happened otherwise and that the stratagem of Narcisse which at the decisive moment forces the determination of Nero, could have been countered or postponed? Britannicus and Junie, just like Pyrrhus, play a game of equal chances with fate. This is what is required by the *facture* of a 'regular' drama with its vaunted alternations of hope and fear.

If despite the presence of this pattern **Andromaque** impresses us as a genuine tragedy, it is because a more profound action, entirely inward, rules the fate of Oreste, Hermione and Andromaque herself. Horace thought that Orestes should be always a sad character, *tristis Orestes,* and Louis Racine is right in saying that this precept is 'well carried out' in the French **Andromaque:** 'Oreste's every word bears witness to a man plunged in melancholy.' On two occasions Pyrrhus's conduct has repercussions along the whole length of the chain of passions, propelling Oreste towards the illusion of happiness. Not once however does he indulge in it as the spectator does at times, and as a hero would who was submissive to the discipline of reversals. In vain Hermione shares his alarms and desires to see him; in vain she tells him

> Vous que j'ai plaint, enfin que je voudrais aimer;

Oreste never forgets what his share really is:

> Le cœur est pour Pyrrhus, et les vœux pour Oreste.

And even when Hermione summons him a second time and charges him with the task of avenging her, no hope slips into his bruised heart, unless it be that of preventing the death of Hermione and Pyrrhus in each other's arms. It is not the possibility of a recompense which urges him on: he knows beforehand that to make him expiate the murder, Hermione's eyes will tell him what they have always told him. He acts under the impetus of a destiny similar to that of his Greek prototype, the murderer of Clytemnestra: knowing like him his victim, he also knows before acting the full horror of his deed. Like the celebrated scene in the *Electra* of Euripides, the dialogue with Hermione fixes for ever his fate and his torment. For Electra's rending appeal is substituted the cry of vengeance of the insensate lover, for the parricide's gesture of despair the voluptuous enjoyment of a blind submission. Indifferent to the changing scene which displays happiness and misfortune, joy and suffering, the Oreste of Racine remains faithful to the tonality of immutable legends. A tragic hero, he frees himself from the bonds of the plot.

Less resigned to destiny, Hermione yields at first to the lure of varying situations. In the happy moments which the arrangement of episodes reserves for her, she thinks she can recover Pyrrhus and triumph over her rival: *Pyrrhus revient à nous!* But immediately terror seizes her:

> Dieux! ne puis-je à ma joie abandonner mon âme?

Andromaque appears and, advancing towards her, in the humblest words touches the most painful spot:

> N'est-ce point à vos yeux un spectacle assez doux?

The irony is doubtless involuntary; involuntary too but pitiless this reminder of a truth which Hermione had almost succeeded in concealing from herself:

> Je ne viens point ici, par de jalouses larmes,
> Vous envier un cœur qui se rend à vos charmes.

That is enough: long before the 'treason' of Pyrrhus, before the fatal change of mood which must provoke the vengeance of Hermione, her happiness proves to be illusory. More distraught even than Andromaque, she flings this reply at her, as cruel for herself as for her rival:

> S'il faut fléchir Pyrrhus, qui le peut mieux que vous?

She need hardly wait to learn the misfortune which she announces almost unwittingly: she guesses it already; she knows that the gleam on the horizon is only a mirage which will vanish as soon as perceived. She knows Pyrrhus has but one thought: when he seems to listen to her, his looks are elsewhere, his mind is lost in a dream she fears to know as she fears 'to know herself in the state in which she is'. As Racine reveals her to us at the beginning of the second act, so she remains until the end of her torment, now seeking to believe that 'her offended pride has hardened her heart', now shuddering at the single name of Andromaque, without her voice ever leaving the tragic mode.

To the ample themes of Oreste and Hermione is added the more constrained theme of Andromaque. Whoever seeks to subordinate it to the oscillations of a pendulum is obliged like Paul Janet to assume an Andromaque who, once abandoned by Pyrrhus, 'remains in her joy'; an assumption so unreal as to condemn the theory which requires it. When does Andromaque know joy? Certainly not at the moment when Pyrrhus exclaims:

> Que de pleurs vont couler!
> De quel nom sa douleur me va-t-elle appeler?

Nor in that scene in which, a prey to mortal anxiety, she weeps at the feet of Hermione. From the moment she goes to find her son, her words reveal an ever-increasing distress, a pain which becomes the very principle of her life. It cannot even be said that she behaves like a character involved in a drama of the conscience. From the end of the first act, she sees herself thrown back upon her fate: to save her dearest possession, the memory of Hector, she must lose her son. Like the Andromache of the *Trojan Women* of Euripides, she strives in spite of all to snatch him from the vengeance of the Greeks. But faced by the menace which weighs on this beloved being, she keeps clearly in sight her one duty, her one passion. Ready for all renunciations, she sees only the image of a lost hero and seems to aim in the great scenes of the third act simply at understanding better the sense of her loss. Would it not be to mistake the bearing of these scenes of horror and pity—an almost colourless fresco of a woman whose eyes are 'always veiled in tears'—to examine them for velleities of compromise or for the promise of a change from bad to good? It is certain that these are *scenes of action;* for the suffering that has gone to the depth of a pure and inviolable soul reveals a latent energy, that of a consciousness which itself traces the curve of its misfortune. But instead of dividing her thoughts between hope and fear, Andromaque, the least violent of Racine's heroines and whose pain alone confers beauty on her acts, advances with her head high towards her chosen destiny. And when three years later Racine declares in the Preface to *Bérénice* that only an action which is 'simple and great' is tragic, he will recall without naming it this first encounter with the tragic in a human situation which had enabled him to represent, under the features of a character drawn from drama and placed in a cadre skilfully contrived, the purest and most simple of the themes of tragedy. One thinks of that transposition of *Antigone* in which three centuries later Anouilh makes the chorus say:

> It's clean, is tragedy. It's restful, it's safe. . . . In drama with its traitors, its desperate villains, its persecuted innocence, those avengers, those Newfoundland dogs, those gleams of hope, it becomes dreadful to die, like an accident. You might perhaps have been able to save yourself, the good young man could perhaps have arrived in time with the police. In tragedy there is nothing to worry about. For one thing we are all in it. And every one of us is innocent! And then above all it's restful because you know there is no more hope, filthy hope; you know you are caught, caught at last like a rat, with the whole sky on your back.

Need we then be surprised that this form of the tragic, safe, restful, ineluctable, free from all accident, 'with the whole sky on your back', should be so rare in the theatre, and that Racine himself did not always light upon it? The cult of curiosity in French tragedy of the seventeenth century and the indifference it showed to the pathetic were such that if Racine had been content to obey the taste of his time, no really tragic work could have come from his hands. As a beginner, he had not been able to avoid the temptation of tragicomedy and of heroic tragedy. 'He had conceived in his childhood', Louis Racine tells us, 'an extraordinary passion for Heliodorus: he admired his style and the marvelous art with which he tells his story.' It was during his sojourn at Uzès that he had begun *Théagène et Chariclée,* a play drawn from the novel of Heliodorus, which he abandoned subsequently, 'no doubt because he felt that romantic adventures were not worthy of the tragic stage'. Then he sought to confront on their own ground the masters whose fame embarrassed him. The announcement of a *Thébaïde* by Boyer made him think of this subject consecrated by antiquity and he took the plunge with *La Thébaïde ou les Frères ennemis,* a play in which Rotrou and Corneille had greater shares than Racine and Euripides. Then came *Alexandre le Grand.* Still more than *La Thébaïde* this second essay in tragedy was the work of a disciple, and it was

necessary to wait for *Andromaque* to see him set out on 'new roads'. But before long, with *Britannicus,* he returned to the genre consecrated by his elders, not to go beyond it but to perfect it. Anxious above all to conduct the action to its close with a perfect economy of means, he gripped and mastered it from the start as it gushed forth. What craftsmanship in the sketching of characters, in the adjustment of scenes, in the conduct of the dialogue! Two violent characters who dispute absolute power, two 'genii' who symbolize one good, the other evil, and two innocent victims; each act divided into symmetrical sections which now retard, now precipitate the catastrophe; each reversal arriving at a definite point following a series of speeches skilfully disposed. It is only when the plot is unfolded and Burrhus comes 'to weep over Britannicus, Caesar and the whole state' that one sees appearing the pathetic theme, the importance of which Racine emphasizes in his first preface: the last monologues of Agrippine (*Poursuis, Néron . . .*) and of Albine (*Pour accabler César d'un éternel ennui . . .*) are, he says, listened to 'with as much attention as the close of any tragedy'. Beyond the peripeteia of the drama the pathetic, he seems to say, attains a higher plane, that on which is played the fate of Rome. And the fate of Rome, we know, is the destiny of entire humanity, of man victim of the violence he bears in himself, of the blind fury which 'enflames itself in its course'. A new world rises in this final scene, a world unknown to pity, implacable as the look in the tyrant's eyes, and like him constant in its indifference: the world created by man to abolish what is human. But confronted by the symbolical vision of the banquet at which Britannicus dies—a vision more dramatic than moving in its impact—one does not think of Junie or Agrippine or even of Britannicus. Instead of becoming incarnate in the characters, terror spreads over a stage which is henceforth empty save only for the witnesses of the action, while that powerful poetry which works in the abstract lights up the problems and situations in which people are involved rather than the depths of their existence, thereby cutting itself off from access to what is tragic in man. Hence the perfect coherence of this 'play for connoisseurs', in which Corneille recognized himself better than in any other work of his young rival; it made him indignant at an intrusion in a domain where he thought himself destined to reign alone. For *Britannicus* represented the apogee of the genre that owed its fame to him: high political tragedy which, when once circumscribed in its facts and ideas, refuses to quit its luminous area for the vague horizons of the individual conscience. A fair and rich tradition to which all that had been lacking so far was naturalness in handling the action and the spell of poetry.

As if the better to yield to this spell Racine passes immediately to another Roman subject, the least dramatic that could be: *Titus reginam Berenicen dimisit invitus invitam.* 'That is,' he says at the beginning of his Preface, 'Titus who loved Bérénice passionately . . . sent her away from Rome in spite of himself and of her, in the first days of his rule.' 'A subject quite as simple', he says again, 'and at the same time quite as rich as that of the separation of Aeneas and Dido.' What does he mean by that? How does he conceive a subject at once simple and rich, which is enough 'for a whole canto of heroic poetry' and which, according to him, constitutes in itself alone the subject of a tragedy? He explains this by saying, 'it suffices that the action should be great', that is, 'appropriate to the theatre by the force of the passions it is able to excite'. Instead of compressing into the limits of five acts submitted to the discipline of the unities a vast ensemble of facts, why not allow a subject infinitely reduced in extent to develop freely in depth—a development 'intensive' in essence, the value of which would be in inverse ratio to the duration it required? The form of art to which it would accommodate itself best would be precisely that which deprives the event of all efficacy and suppresses with 'blood and dead men' all vain expectation. 'Idyll', 'eclogue', 'charming and melodious fancy', say the critics who despair of being able to place ***Bérénice*** in the dramaturgy of the period.

The reason is that this tragedy of sacrifice and of sacrificed souls, the truest 'tragedy' of all those which Racine wrote, seeks its references beyond the tragedy of his time, beyond Seneca even and Euripides, in the canon of tragic beauty fixed by Sophocles. At the level at which is abolished all constraint external to man, it is no longer Rome which rules the behaviour of the characters, but their knowledge of the will of Rome. *All is silent:* only the tormented soul of Titus is unfolded before us, preparing the sacrifice. What can the speeches of Paulin teach him that he does not already know?

> Si je t'ai fait parler, si j'ai voulu t'entendre,
>
> Je voulais que ton zèle achevât en secret
>
> De confondre un amour qui se tait à regret.

T. S. Eliot on *Bérénice*:

To my mind, Racine's ***Bérénice*** represents about the summit of civilisation in tragedy; and it is, in a way, a Christian tragedy, with devotion to the State substituted for devotion to divine law. The dramatic poet who can engross the reader's or the author's attention during the space of a ***Bérénice*** is the most civilised dramatist—though not necessarily the greatest, for there are other qualities to consider.

T. S. Eliot, in The Use of Poetry and the Use of Criticism: Studies in the Relation of Criticism to Poetry in England, *Faber and Faber Limited, 1933.*

No messenger comes to confirm him in the idea that Rome will remain implacable: the piece is played *en vase clos,* in an infinitely reduced space, sustained to the end by the 'cruel constancy' of souls worthy of their fate and capable of measuring its significance. Where Titus thought he was going to find a solution, he perceives he has done nothing but turn in a circle; his monologue of act IV, punctuated by exclamations which contradict one another: *Tes adieux sont-ils prêts. . . . Rome sera pour nous. . . . Rome jugea ta reine,* is split into two sections which represent the one the apogee, the other the collapse of the illusion. Titus discovers in himself a power more cruel still than the laws of Rome: one which puts him into a state of lucidity before an ill without remedy. Bérénice reaches lucidity at the same moment, after having traversed all the distance which separates 'a heart content with its lover' from the sacrifice of its dearest possession: for this it is necessary that she should not know her fate, that she should learn it, refuse to admit it, then that she should attain martyrdom without ever knowing any other reason for doing so than her constancy, nor other pain than her passion. Never was human speech more autonomous or more decided. The characters advance towards the crisis as Andromaque had done, without the help of a tragic deed, driven to the very end by the sheer intensity of their misfortune. But while Oreste and Hermione substitute themselves for Andromaque to carry the play to its conclusion, in ***Bérénice*** only the pure souls are called to bring the action to its close. A bold conception, too bold doubtless for Racine to dare resort to it again. The attraction of purity had led him to the extreme limit of the genre, to the point at which tragic art by dint of decanting itself risked losing all substance. The heroic experience obliged him to seek another way.

And now this first Racine 'who abandons himself' or, according to the happy expression of Sainte-Beuve, 'who forgets Boileau', is superseded by the playwright who in ***Bajazet*** seems to forget Racine. The poet who declared 'blood and dead men' useless and sought to abolish the plot to the advantage of the pathetic presents two years later a play with a conspiracy which ends in a frightful massacre. 'One cannot perceive the reasons for this great butchery,' said the judicious and, as we should say today, the impressionistic Madame de Sévigné. After three centuries of exegesis, the reasons escape us still. Atalide and Bajazet, caught in a snare, act each of them with so much ingenuity that their safety appears, if not assured, at least probable: one ruse more in their game of skill and nothing could spoil their happiness. Only a theatrical trick ruins them—the letter that Zatime steals from Atalide—and the same letter decides the fate of Roxane. 'Frightful like an accident,' Anouilh would say. For Roxane who up to that point 'wants to know nothing', also does not know those depths of the soul in which Hermione and Phèdre recover each instant their terrible lucidity. She belongs to another spiritual family, that which never feels itself menaced from within, the line of ferocious souls who obey only the laws of fighting to the death. Among her ancestors she counts the Roxelane of Mairet, the Amalfrède of Quinault and the Arsinoë of Boyer—fierce princesses who had taught the French public the taste for their bloody adventures and the sweetness of their cold vengeances. Amalfrède consents 'with joy and without trouble' to make Théodat perish to prevent him from marrying Amalasonte, just as Roxane quietly assumes the role of arbiter over the life of Bajazet and sends him to his death as soon as she learns that he loves someone else. The tragic colour it is customary to lend to the *Sortez!* of act V is belied by the sangfroid of Roxane herself who thinks henceforth only of multiplying murders. The final accident alone prevents her from enjoying her triumph, an accident which no inner motive calls for and which comes from the level of mere *faits divers*. We recognize its penalty in the amorphous lines with which the piece is decked out:

Mon malheur n'est-il pas écrit sur son visage? . .

Ah! de la trahison me voilà donc instruite.

Not a tone of Racine's voice is heard and even the few *trouvailles* which one picks out—such as the *tranquil fury* of Roxane—remain, in the general atonality, too much dispersed to restore the poetic current.

This silence of the tragic muse is due also to the nature of the subject, to the falsely exotic climate of those 'grandes tueries' which delighted the public of the period. The great obstacle in subjects of this kind is the lack of *crystallization,* that active force which, as archaeology is well aware, only a fertilizing *tradition,* a beneficent *influence* and a regenerative *experience* can bring to the imagination of an author. These conditions are indispensable to prevent the work falling into the snare of local colour and to save it, at moments when the historical matter is exhausted, from the terrible *mundus senescit* which so often frustrates the effort of the poet. The tradition is originally a vital urge which, coming from a remote time, is quickly displaced by the fable which deforms it. Once transmitted from one generation to another, it represents the collaboration of fiction with the teaching of history. Before the story reaches the author innumerable infiltrations gradually help to establish a reasonable basis of agreement which commentators honour with the name of influence. In this lies the secret of the consensus of human interest in the ancestral images of the biblical and homeric epics. Lastly without experience guided by the instinct of recreation the exotic subject-matter dries up: it becomes no more than an expressionless exchange between the author and the public, as it had been between the author and the event. It is because he had not found in the subject of *Bajazet* any of these conditions of renewal that Racine attempted in his second Preface to reassure the reader by an argument *ad hoc:* 'The remoteness of the countries compensates to some extent for the too great proximity of time.' He knew that this too great proximity was irremediable and that even by modifying the psychological data he could not purify the theme: it gained nothing in feeling because the feelings had not been reinforced. The rawness of the facts, undeformed because traditionally undeformable, had veiled the fatalism of the motives and at one blow suppressed the mystery through which are disclosed the will of the gods and the all-powerfulness of destiny.

It is only with *Mithridate* that Racine begins a new period of experiments in the realm of the tragic; and it is to the liberty he enjoys when confronted by a subject already deformed by history that the stuff of this piece, cast in the same mould as *Bajazet* and originating in the same climate, owes not only a certain grandeur but its fitness for rejuvenation. The ancients themselves had related the facts a long time after they had happened. The characters in the story and their contemporaries had long disappeared when Plutarch produced the portrait of Mithridates and his family. After him, to judge by their contradictions, Appian, Dion Cassius, Justin and Sallust contributed to the development of the written traditions. This marked the progress towards crystallization. From that point to a certain degree of legendary truth there was but a step: the diversity of judgments and the exaggerated combination of oriental and late-hellenistic *mœurs* made it possible to work in a fluid subject-matter, and to develop characters and events in depth. The centuries had created more distance than space itself had done and it was above all on distance that depended the success of the effort. As in *Bajazet,* Racine attaches exaggerated value in *Mithridate* to the plot and its potentialities. Recurrences of fear and hope correspond here again to real chances of ruin and escape. Each of the principal characters knows that a ruse can lose or save him. The relation of Xipharès and Monime to Mithridate is in all points analogous to that of Bajazet and Atalide to Roxane: their fate is in the hands of a jealous tyrant. But it is precisely this resemblance which brings out the development. For the oriental prince, a contemporary of the author and of the spectators in the stalls, is substituted a princess 'snatched from the soft bosom of Greece', heroic without gestures and condemned by the very purity of her sentiments to suffer in her heart the most inhuman of tortures:

En quelle extrémité, Seigneur, suis-je réduite?

That extremity, we are told, is the risk she runs of betraying herself, but it is also the fact that her whole being rises against a state of things she has accepted, against a bitter and humiliating constraint which she takes as legitimate and which leaves her scarcely a few moments' respite. It is in flashes and almost without believing in it that, with her 'soul rent in secret', she glimpses the day when she will contrive to liberate herself. The very resonance of the verse warns us that the fires of the tragic spectacle, extinguished, it would seem, since *Bérénice,* are ready to flare up again:

Les dieux me sont témoins qu'à vous plaire bornée,
Mon âme à tout son sort s'était abandonnée.

That resonance is prolonged when, at Monime's side, appears the tyrant 'nourished on blood and athirst for war', who while confronting her in the very situation of Roxane before Bajazet, yet attains true greatness. 'The piece', says La Harpe, 'has the movement and tone of a tragedy only from the moment when Mithridate is announced.' Not that this proud warrior forgets to play the role which is allotted to him in the strategy of the piece: he too, like Roxane, is an oriental tyrant, habituated to blood and treason; skilled in replying to crime with more crime, he lacks nothing to reinforce the plot in which he is involved. But over this cruel face marked by the flight of time, gleams pass now and then which confer upon it a rare dignity. And at the moment when Mithridate prepares to drag from Monime the avowal of her love for Xipharès, unexpected accents escape him:

> Enfin, j'ouvre les yeux et je me fais justice.
> C'est faire à vos beautés un triste sacrifice
> Que de vous présenter, Madame, avec ma foi,
> Tout l'âge et le malheur que je traîne avec moi.
>
> . . .
>
> Et mon front, dépouillé d'un si noble avantage,
> Du temps qui l'a flétri, laisse voir tout l'outrage.

This greatness which condemns itself, this majestic denunciation of a glory declining with age—is not this something other than a skilful manœuvre? And can we be sure that Monime, before being disarmed by the 'adroit falsehood' of Mithridate, has not allowed herself to be convinced by the emotion betrayed by his words and his tortured heart? To the torment of suspicion which Roxane experienced is added that of a terrible certitude:

> Ah! qu'il eût mieux valu, plus sage et plus
>   heureux,
> Et repoussant les traits d'un amour dangereux,
> Ne pas laisser remplir d'ardeurs empoisonnées
> Un cœur déjà glacé par le froid des années!
> De ce trouble fatal par où dois-je sortir?

Scattered gleams, it is true, gleams which the 'gloire' of Mithridate never catches. His pride demands 'other sentiments than those of pity'. His barbarian lands, hardly touched by the sun of Greece, remain as ignorant as he is of the ultimate meaning of the myth created by man to unwind the skeins of destiny: only the spectator dimly feels the myth is at hand.

John Gassner (essay date 1954)

SOURCE: "Corneille and Racine: Polite Tragedy," in *Masters of the Drama,* third revised edition, Dover Publications, Inc., 1954, pp. 267-85.

[*Gassner, a Hungarian-born American scholar, was a great promoter of American theater, particularly the work of Tennessee Williams and Arthur Miller. He edited numerous collections of modern drama and wrote two important dramatic surveys,* Masters of Modern Drama *(1940) and* Theater in Our Times *(1954; 3rd ed. 1954). In the following excerpt from the former, Gassner surveys Racine's career as a dramatist and assesses his significance in the development of Western drama.*]

Racine was fortunate in possessing two indispensable qualifications for tragedy: he possessed a dramatic temperament and a strange perturbation of the spirit. His talent may be likened to a small volcano covered with a patch of flowers. His polished lines are more dramatic than a casual reading, particularly in their inadequate English translations, would reveal. Recited by a competent artist, not to speak of a Rachel or a Sarah Bernhardt, the precise phrases rise and fall with emotion. Lines like Hermione's cry in the ***Andromaque,*** after she has ordered

the assassination of the man she loves, are typical:

> Où suis-je? Qu' ai je fait? Que dois-je faire
>   encore? . . .
> Errante et sans dessein, je cours dans ce palais.
> Ah! ne puis-je savoir si j'aime ou si je hais?

Such lines are not merely plentiful in Racine's work but preponderant.

Nor are the passions he describes dammed up by victorious reason or morality, as in Corneille's plays. They are too strong to be restrained even when their danger is apparent to the individual himself, and from his characters' inability to liberate themselves from an obsession arise inner conflicts that are little short of infernal in their agony. It is, indeed, customary for English readers to condemn Racine as undramatic on very insufficient grounds. He has held the French stage for more than two and a half centuries and his heroines have been played by nearly every self-respecting French actress. . . .

His first tragedy *Amasie* was bought but not produced by the Bourgogne company. Fortune smiled on him, however, when Molière befriended him and produced his second play *Thebaide* in 1664. It proved successful and was followed by another treatment of Greek material—a study of Alexander the Great, ***Alexandre le Grand.*** Ungratefully, Racine gave the play to Molière's rivals at the Hôtel de Bourgogne shortly after it was produced by his benefactor's company. The Bourgogne players being more adept at tragedy than Molière's Comédiens du Roi, the comparison of the two productions was unfavorable to the latter. Molière, who had lent Racine money and continued the run of ***La Thebaide*** at a loss, was deeply hurt and never spoke to Racine again.

Racine, however, was pleased to find the excellent Bourgogne company at his service, and soon, in 1667, gave them his first memorable tragedy, ***Andromaque*** or ***Andromache.*** The play is a powerful study of character and passion. Andromache, Hector's widow, is loved by her conqueror Pyrrhus, the son of Achilles who had slain her husband at Troy. The memory of the hero she had loved is too great for her to bear the thought of a second love. But bear it she must because only by marrying Pyrrhus can she save her infant son from destruction by the Greeks who are eager to remove the seed of Hector. She agrees, therefore, to marry Pyrrhus after exacting from his a promise to protect her son and resolving to kill herself after the marriage ceremony. The tragedy comes to a climax when the Greek princess Hermione, whose love for Pyrrhus is a consuming obsession, has him assassinated by her lover Orestes and then stabs herself.

Although the theme is remote, Racine succeeds in giving emotional reality to the inner conflicts of a woman who is loyal to her first love but must accommodate herself to circumstance and of a girl whose passion drives her to destroy the man she loves. The subtleties of Racine's dramatic method are exemplified by such a detail as Hermione's exclamation concerning Pyrrhus,

And do not trust my anger's wavering
Till death removes this monster; for unless
He dies today, tomorrow I may love him.

Only the wooden behavior of Orestes reduces the potency of this play. Of course, too, the whole situation may easily strike us as narrow. It is never so when treated by Euripides who knew how to make his tragedies a criticism of life because he had the gift of seeing mankind in the large whereas Racine rarely rose above the immediate situation of his play. But Racine's tragedy also has its validity—as a psychological drama. It is a moving elaboration of human passion.

Racine next turned to comedy with an amusing and mordant adaptation of Aristophanes' *Wasps* entitled **Les Plaideurs** or **The Litigants**. He wrote most of the piece in a fashionable tavern as an exercise of wit, not putting much stock in the piece. But this did not prevent him from extracting considerable comic vitality out of his judge who is so enamored of his calling that he sleeps in his judicial robes and out of the overzealous lawyer who opens his plea with an account of the Creation of the World. Moreover, after this casual excursion into foreign territory, Racine returned to his own domain in **Britannicus,** a powerful representation of Nero and his court.

Racine could not write a chronicle of Nero's life within the confines of the unities of time, place, and action. He could only concentrate on one situation which ushered in this tyrant's career. Nero's ambitious mother Agrippina, who has made him king, soon has reason to regard his future course with misgivings. He is unscrupulous in his passions and allows himself to be guided by an evil counselor Narcissus. Being infatuated with Junia, who is betrothed to the legitimate heir to the throne Britannicus, he seizes her and poisons Britannicus while pledging friendship to him. Junia flees to the vestals and dedicates herself to the gods and Narcissus is killed by an outraged populace when he tries to drag her from the altar. Nero is overcome with helpless rage, and his mother and tutor can only hope that this crime will be his last. Nero is thus left at a critical point in the development of his character. What the Elizabethans would have made merely the beginning of a tragedy here becomes the complete play. Nevertheless, Racine makes the crisis which dominates the entire play exciting and fraught with psychological and dramatic portent.

Mithridate, written in rivalry with the aging Corneille, was another effective drama of a man's passion for a woman, even if it lacked the scope and depth of **Britannicus**. Its superiority over Corneille's work was patent and its success considerable. About this time, too, Racine won the signal honor of being elected to the French Academy which chose him instead of Molière when the latter refused to abandon the humble acting profession.

Racine had begun to make enemies with his sharp tongue and haughty behavior, and the friends of Corneille hated him wholeheartedly. One of those literary cabals which keep the French at boiling point was organized against

him, and the new playwright Pradon was trotted out and pushed into eminence. Racine, however, countered with his **Iphigénie,** a version of the sacrifice of Iphigenia at Aulis that was full of gratifying sensibility. Racine triumphed again, even if his new tragedy was not for the ages. Nor could there be any dispute about the distinction of his next depredation on Euripidean drama, **Phèdre.**

In Euripides' *Hippolytus,* Racine found a theme of love-passion which called forth his greatest powers. When it is compared with the Greek tragedy, Racine's drama is only a minor triumph. Gone in the French tragedy is the provocative symbolic conflict between the two human instincts respectively represented by Artemis and Aphrodite. Gone, too, is the deep psychological symbolism of a young man destroyed by the love instinct or the Aphrodite he has denied in himself. Here, instead, is a neatly composed obbligato played on the one string of a woman's consuming passion for her stepson Hippolytus. The latter is even supplied with a sweetheart, since Louis XIV's bright courtiers would have found the chaste young man of the Greek story an object of ridicule. There is consequently much "prettification" and sentimentalization in **Phèdre**. Still, within the limits of French classicism, the play could only appear as a tremendous *tour de force,* since it is remarkable for its exploration of the recesses of a passion-obsessed mind.

The growth of Phèdre's passion for her husband's son and her struggle against her infatuation, which is making her pine away, are vividly realized. She has rejected food for three days. Finally, Oenone, her nurse, discovers the source of her malady and devotedly proposes to heal it. Since, in particular, Theseus is reported to have been killed during his travels, she argues that Phèdre's passion is no longer criminal. In an anguished scene Phèdre, therefore, reveals her passion to Hippolytus. But she is rebuffed by him, and overwhelmed with shame she hurries away. Suddenly Theseus returns and fearing that Hippolytus will accuse her mistress to his father, the devoted nurse resolves to accuse him first. Hippolytus, too honorable to cast shame upon his mother by justifying himself, allows himself to be cursed by his father. The curse destroys him, and Phèdre, overwhelmed with grief, kills herself.

The elaborate and sensitive presentation of Phèdre's passion, shame, and grief requires a more extended analysis than can be given in a synopsis. No one can question its effectiveness, and the role of Phèdre is so magnificent that it became the *pièce de resistance* of every French tragedienne. The famous Rachel and Sarah Bernhardt won no laurels more honorable than their triumphs in the part.

By now, however, the cabal was up in arms against Racine and hit upon the expedient of getting another **Phèdre** by Pradon produced two days after the premiere. Buying seats for Racine's opening they left them unoccupied, casting a chill over the performance. Instead they repaired to Pradon's play and made it a signal success. The *affaire* **Phèdre** was such a conspicuous example of viciousness and Racine was so deeply wounded by it that he retired from the stage. Sick at heart he returned at the end of 1677 to Port Royal, which eagerly took its prodigal son back into the fold. Theologically, they could argue, his last play had been sound Jansenism; was it not the tragedy of a woman who possessed every quality but the grace of God without which there can be no salvation! Dominated by her *flamme funeste,* and supremely conscious of her guilt and damnation, Phèdre was a heroine decidedly acceptable to the Jansenists. Port Royal won its author back completely, and gave the erstwhile lover of popular actresses a pious wife who never read a line of his plays. Racine himself began to regard them as a crime against the true religion.

Racine, it is true, did not wholly give up the world and remained a courtier to the last. He resumed residence in Paris and continued his literary labors as historiographer to the king, a position which he owed to the favor of Louis XIV's Madame de Montespan. But he returned to playwriting only on two occasions, both sacerdotal, when the King's pietistic new love Madame de Maintenon requested him to write two biblical plays for her girls' school at St. Cyr. *Esther,* the first of them, retold the familiar story of Haman and the Jewish queen who saved her people from an early pogrom. Written in excellent verse and supplied with choruses of great beauty, the piece was received enthusiastically when it was produced in 1689 before an audience which included the King and Mme. de Maintenon. It was particularly appreciated for its allusiveness; Ahasuerus was Louis XIV, Madame de Maintenon was the pious Esther, and the discarded first queen Vashti was none other than Madame de Montespan who had recently suffered a similar débacle. The analogy between Queen Esther and Madame de Maintenon, who had belonged to the Huguenot Protestant sect which was being oppressed by Louis, who revoked the Edict of Nantes, was strained, since the new French Queen had been too discreet to intervene in behalf of her former co-religionists. But the discrepancy between Esther and de Maintenon was not regarded as a criticism of the latter. Nor was the suggestion in the play that a king could be misled in signing a decree prejudicial to religious liberty considered an allusion to Louis XIV who had signed the Edict of Nantes only four years before. That indefatigable letter-writer Madame de Sévigné echoed the opinion of the literati concerning Racine: "He now loves God as he used to love his mistresses." *Esther,* which strikes this reader as only a cut above a beautiful academic exercise, won the admiration of the court.

Although Racine refused to countenance its presentation in the public theatre, he turned to the drama again with renewed enthusiasm, and within a year he produced the second St.-Cyr tragedy *Athalie* or *Athaliah* which many consider his greatest work. The tragedy met Madame de Maintenon's request for a loveless drama to perfection and none of her tender charges had their innocence tempted by so much as a word. Nevertheless, *Athaliah* is a stirring work. Nowhere is Racine's lyric power greater and nowhere did he fill his severely limited stage with so much movement and excitement. The idol-worshiping queen Athaliah who had assumed power by murdering the royal family is troubled by a dream that warns her that an heir to the throne still lives. He does in the person of young Joash who had been rescued by the high priest and brought up in the temple. Athaliah enters the temple, interviews Joash without learning who he is, and is singularly moved by affection for him. But the time has come to enthrone the young prince, who will observe the true Hebrew religion faithfully. The high priest, therefore, arms the Levites, separates Athaliah from her guards, and has her slain. The play concludes with a rhapsodic hymn of triumph.

The powerful characterization of the guilt-laden Queen and of the sweet-tempered lad, the effective dialogue, and the magnificent lyrics of this tragedy create an impression of rare majesty. If some of us must find its labors academic, it is difficult to withhold one's admiration for Racine's virtuosity or deny this work the right to be considered the greatest of all biblical plays.

Although again withheld from the public stage, *Athaliah* was produced with resounding success in 1691 at both St. Cyr and Versailles. Nevertheless, Racine's last days were clouded by disgrace at court. . . . He worried himself into an illness and died on April 21st, 1699, in extreme pain.

Racine left a heritage in his collected works which gave expression to some of the most typical elements of French genius. Its sensibility and converse with the passion of love live splendidly in his plays, but the national talent for order, cerebration and analysis is likewise present in them. The famous critic Jules Lemaître has put this more precisely when he declared that Racine expressed *"la génie de notre race—ordre, raison, sentiment mesuré, et force sous la grâce"*—order, reason, measured sentiment and force underlying gracefulness. Racine substituted character analysis and emotionalism for the major Corneillian motives of moralization and "admiration"—that idealization of human behavior which is supposed to evoke admiration for the protagonists. Except indirectly in his biblical plays, Racine wrote drama of "admiration" only in *Berenice,* in which Titus denies his love in deference to the Roman custom which forbade an emperor to marry foreign royalty.

Passion was the proper province of the playwright of whom it has been said that his female characters were "fair women full of Attic grace but who lack the grace of God." Whereas Corneille celebrated man's strength, Racine, always a partial Calvinist, dramatized man's weakness, and the tragic failure of his characters in most of his plays represents the victory of the passions over reason. It is in this manner that Racine paid dual tribute to the "sensibility" prevalent in the courtly life of his times and to the rationalism that dominated both political theory and philosophy. And the same dualism appears in his technique, which is more orderly than Corneille's. Concentration on the crucial moment in the lives of the characters rather than on the developments that led to the crisis makes for a compact, rationally ordered dramatic form. Action, moreover, is relegated to off-stage events, reported by messengers, and becomes secondary to analysis in works of this order; "what happens is of less importance than the mental reactions of the characters . . . action is practically confined to the mind." Nevertheless, his compression of passion into one major crisis generally provided the greatest intensification of feeling.

To the Anglo-Saxon reader such compactness seems the acme of literary constipation, and the analytic approach to the emotions strikes him as a form of pernicious anemia or atrophy of emotion. There is, indeed, little doubt that Corneille and especially Racine made a contribution to the drama and humane letters that does not meet the modern demand for action. Nevertheless, their real limitation is not structural. If one can be irritated by Corneille, it is because he is so high-flown and sententious. If one can dislike Racine it is because one can become sick of the passions, the *"soupirs et flammes,"* of his heroines; one tires so easily of torrid femininity. In introducing order into playwriting, Racine, as a matter of fact, made an important advance which was to serve the realistic drama greatly. The later drama of prose and of ordinary life could not afford the diffuseness of Elizabethan or later romantic tragedies. Plays like *Ghosts* or *Hedda Gabler,* no matter how greatly they may depart from Louis Quatorze taste in other respects, possess a compactness of structure without which they would lose most of their power.

Lucien Goldmann (essay date 1956)

SOURCE: "The Structure of Racine's Tragedies," in *Racine,* translated by Alastair Hamilton, Rivers Press, 1972, pp. 3-22.

[*In the following excerpt from a work originally published in 1956, Goldmann narrowly defines dramatic tragedy and then discusses how Racine structured his dramas as tragedies.*]

The concept of tragedy and the "science" of literature

If we denote any attempt to understand reality as *science* or theoretical thought we must admit that a considerable discrepancy has appeared between what are normally known as the "exact sciences"—mathematics, physics, chemistry—and the "human sciences". This discrepancy can be seen not only in the contrast in the scope and precision of the findings achieved in each of these domains, but also as far as the terminology is concerned. The terms habitually employed in the human sciences lack both *precision* and *functional capacity,* two essential properties if investigators are to agree, if not about their theories and analyses, at least about the actual object of their study, about the nature of the truths they investigate and the ideas they advance. Besides, a similar discrepancy also exists within these human sciences—we need only compare the "science of literature" with the other branches of sociology and history—and at present the scientific study of literature is far more an aspiration than a reality.

There is nothing surprising, therefore, in my starting this study of Racine with the problem of language and defini-

tion. The collective consciousness, or the "common sense" of critics and spectators, has produced a statement which I am quite ready to accept, anyhow for the time being: *Racine is above all a tragic writer.* But in order to use this statement as my starting point it has to be given a precise meaning and this presupposes the definition of the terms *tragedy* and *tragic.*

Though most historians and critics agree to classify a certain number of writers—Aeschylus, Sophocles, Euripides, Racine, and, partially, Shakespeare—as tragedians, they also refer to the "tragedies" of Rotrou, Quinault, Corneille and even Victor Hugo. They hardly ever ask themselves whether *all* the theatrical works of writers reputed to be *tragic* are really *tragedies.*

From the vast quantity of literature devoted to tragedy there emerges one hypothesis, formulated with greater or less clarity: an essential bond exists between the idea of tragedy and the idea of *destiny* or *fatality.* And there is no doubt that this can be applied to a whole series of works by Aeschylus, Sophocles and Shakespeare, as well as to Racine's *Phèdre.* Had this hypothesis, however unsatisfactory it might be, been taken more seriously it would no longer have been possible to speak of the "tragedies" of Quinault, Garnier or Corneille. A considerable advance would have been made in the knowledge and use of words, for, though the idea of *destiny,* regarded as an incomprehensible fatality dominating the hero's existence and acts, is valid for characters like Orestes, Oedipus, Macbeth or Phèdre, it obviously cannot be applied to Antigone, Andromaque, Junie or Titus. Rather than give up this idea, therefore, we should merely regard it as the characteristic of one form of tragic literature. What we still need to do is to find a definition capable of embracing the *two* forms of tragedy.

Another idea, implicit rather than explicit, which appears together with that of *destiny* in most works on tragedy, is the idea of the "serious play". But this is far too general to have any functional value. Besides, it includes the concept of *drama,* which is just as vague but which seems to have a different significance. I therefore suggest that we adopt, temporarily and for as long as it is practicable, a distinction which might be a first step towards the development of a precise and scientific terminology. I shall call a "tragedy" *any play in which the conflicts are necessarily insoluble,* and a "drama" *any play in which the conflicts either are solved* (at least on a moral level) *or fail to be solved because of the fortuitous intervention of a factor which, according to the laws governing the universe of the play, might not have operated.*

If we bide by this definition not only plays like *Le Cid, Horace* or *Polyeucte,* but **Bajazet, Mithridate, Iphigénie, Esther** and **Athalie** are dramas and not tragedies, the term *tragedy* only being applicable to **Britannicus, Bérénice, Phèdre** and, up to a certain point which I shall examine in due course, **Andromaque.** No *intramundane* solution exists to the problems facing Junie, Titus, Phèdre and, to a certain extent, Andromaque, while Bajazet's and Athalide's scheme fails accidentally (owing to a swoon and the discovery of a letter) and might have succeeded and formed a splendid comedy in the style of Marivaux. In the other plays all the problems are solved in the end, except for those of Eriphile, a *tragic character,* but one on the outskirts of the play who has *no influence* on the coherent and closed world constituted by the leading characters.

Let us pause to consider the implications of my original hypothesis—that tragedy is defined by the necessarily insoluble nature of the conflicts which occur. To start with this means that, in every tragedy, there is an absolute primacy of morals over the actual state of affairs, of *what ought to be* over *what is.* It means that a tragedy is the representation of a universe dominated by a conflict of values and that every attempt to understand it on the basis of the characters' *psychology* is a misapprehension and is doomed to fail. Indeed, the conflicts between the various "egoisms", conflicts of interest or passion, are never *essentially* insoluble. It is always by *accident* that the passions of two particular individuals are not reciprocal, that Oreste loves Hermione, while Hermione loves Pyrrhus, who loves Andromaque. On the other hand it is an absolute *moral* duty for Andromaque to remain faithful to Hector and to do everything in her power to save the life of Astyanax. Similarly it is always by *accident* that one of the antagonists triumphs over the other in a conflict of interests or ambition, that Néron should get the better of Agrippine and not vice-versa.

So all these characters are in themselves essentially *dramatic,* and if the plays where we encounter them are tragedies it is precisely because the unity and coherence of their universe only appears from the point of view of other characters who are entirely different, characters like Andromaque, Junie, Titus and Phèdre who are dominated by an *ethical* need, and whom we can call *tragic heroes.*

Yet it is not enough to characterise tragedy solely by the primacy of morality and the conflict of values, for the universe of *drama* is also frequently based on an ethical problem: take Corneille's plays and Racine's *dramatic* works, **Mithridate, Iphigénie** or **Athalie.** The tragic universe is one where values and their corresponding moral requirements are absolute, dominated by the category of *all or nothing,* without *the slightest notion of degree or compromise.* The tragic universe knows no nuance. It only knows right and wrong, reality and unreality, and contains neither graduality nor transition.

In tragedy an insuperable gulf separates the characters lacking value and reality (either because they live a compromise or because they are so obsessed by passion or ambition that they lack any form of consciousness) from the *real* tragic characters, who are aware of both their needs and their limitations and whose every act counts, independently of all motives and psychological explanations, with the same force and intensity.

Apart from historic hope and action, inaccessible to the tragic view, everyday life consists of unawareness, selfish ambition and blind passion, approximate and partial accomplishments and half-realized hopes. Its inhabitants either resign themselves to it or seek consolation in an inner life or in dreams. This is why everyday life remains a confused and ambiguous mixture without ever becoming a clear, univocal structure. This is also why it never reaches that extremely elevated threshold of consciousness and rigour required by the tragic universe whose law Pascal expressed when he said that all that is not fully valid with relation to the infinite, all that is not true and right, is equally valueless, false and wrong. We see why tragic conflicts are insoluble from the start. The need for *absolute* values, for the totality which rules the universe of every tragedy, is radically and irremediably opposed to a world dominated by compromise, relativity and the more or less.

Here, then, are three constituent elements of every tragedy: *an essentially insoluble conflict* resulting from the clash between a *world* which knows only relativity, compromise, the more or less, and a *universe* dominated by the need for *absolute values,* for *totality,* and governed by the law of *all or nothing.*

But who is it who demonstrates this need in the eyes of the world? Sometimes, or more precisely, in the tragedies "without peripeteia or recognition", it is the tragic hero himself: Andromaque, Junie or Titus. But these characters remain aware that they are conforming to an external need which surpasses them. And what of the tragedies of fatality "with peripeteia and recognition", as in the cases of Oedipus, Orestes or Phèdre? There is only one answer, and it brings us to the third and most important figure in the tragic universe: fatality, transcendency, God.

This last term is probably the most precise provided we realize that it does not mean the God of any specific religion. Tragedy is no more connected with Christianity than with the religion of the Greeks, although the Christian God, like the Greek gods, or those of any other religion, can have a tragic aspect. Consequently, Racine had no difficulty in transposing an almost unmodified version of Port-Royal's concept of Christianity into a pagan universe.

We have thus come to a fourth *essential* element of every tragedy: the existence of a figure who demands the realization of an absolute justice alien to any compromise and who observes the unfolding of the action. *Tragedy can be defined as a spectacle under the permanent observation of a deity.*

But we still have to specify the characteristics of the tragic God or gods whose most salient trait is primarily negative. The deity who rules the universe of tragedy is the very opposite of the providential God, for he never shows the hero which path he should follow in order to realize an authentic existence. Though he is *always present* this God remains a *hidden god,* a god who is *always absent.* This is the key to tragedy. The protagonists are perfectly capable of living both away from the deity, in the absence of God (all those who form the *world* do so), and in the presence of God and under his protection. The paradox of his continual presence and absence alone obstructs the "false consciousness" of an ignorant world as much as it does the certainty of the mystic. It makes life impossible.

In the words of the greatest tragic thinker in French literature the perpetual presence of the deity prevents men from "falling asleep", while his perpetual absence turns this sleeplessness into an agony (Pascal, *Pensées*). Moreover, the absence, the hidden nature of the deity, can appear in the two different ways which constitute the two forms of tragedy. As in most Greek tragedies and in *Phèdre,* the gods can blind man; they can leave him a prey to evil, to the illusion of being able to live, although he has long entered the universe of their absolute and implacable justice, only at the last moment revealing to him his fault and its consequences. These are the avenging gods of the tragedy "with peripeteia and recognition", of the tragedy of destiny. Or they can give the hero from the outset that which, in the other type of tragedy, they only allow him at the end: the full awareness of the divine requirements and of the impossibility of satisfying them in this life. But they then become spectators. Under their observation Junie, Titus, Bérénice (at the end of the play) and (up to a point) Andromaque act as the heroes of tragedies "without peripeteia or recognition". They act as the heroes of tragedies of human greatness and *refusal.*

In both cases, however, the tragic God remains a hard and implacable God, a God whose sentence disregards any motive or explanation, a God who knows neither forgiveness nor meekness and who judges nothing but the *act* (whenever the act has touched the essence, from however great a distance and for however short a time) and not the man, his life, his intention. He is also a God who disregards the unessential world which is too unreal and transparent to detain his attention.

Racine's tragic hero

I have just enumerated the three main figures or characters of tragedy in general and of Racine's tragedies in particular: God, man and the world. I shall now proceed to analyse each of them in turn.

The first thing that characterises the tragic deity, apart from his hidden nature (his avenging and justiciary nature in the tragedies of destiny and his nature as a spectator in the tragedies of refusal), is the fact that his requirements, which constitute the very existence of the hero, *cannot be satisfied* in the world. In the language of a being who lives in the world or confronting the world, they are consequently *contradictory.*

A man, said Pascal, "does not show his greatness by being at one extreme, but by touching both extremes at once and by filling in the space between them." But he also knew that this was impossible in life and in the world because "the extremes meet and reunite precisely because they are far apart . . . in God and in God alone." This need to reunite the two extremes dominates all of Racine's tragedies, from *Andromaque* to *Phèdre.* The gods'

requirement, and the sole meaning of the heroes' existence, is totality, the union of opposites. Thus Andromaque needs to save Astyanax's life and to remain faithful to Hector, Junie to save Britannicus' life and to marry him, Titus to observe the Roman law and to marry Bérénice, Phèdre to satisfy both love and honour. Seventeenth century tragedy expresses the conflict between the pseudomorality of the world (which is a morality of choice) and the new morality of the tragic man who lives in the sight of God—a morality of *totality* and *refusal.*

For totality, the reunion of opposites, is only accessible in God. Even at the height of tragic consciousness man remains equidistant from God and from the world. Too far from the latter to renounce his need for totality and too far from the former to be able to satisfy it, suspended between a world without God and a God who has abandoned and forgotten the world, the hero is the last link between the constituent elements of the universe. It is precisely because of this that he can act in the universe by deluding himself or by rejecting existence, but it is also because of this that he cannot live in it authentically. At every moment the hero's consciousness reminds him not only that all choice is a crime against God and the truth since *all choice* is a sin against the essence, but also that every need for totality, for the reunion of opposites, is absurd, criminal and unrealizable in the world.

The tragic hero is therefore a being who lives in the sight of God, a God who, as Lukács pointed out, recognises nothing but the essence and disregards and destroys all that is accidental—a God for whom the "miracle" alone is real. Now, in a world in which *every* demand for true truth and for just justice is paradoxical and contradictory, the miracle is called *clarity and absence of ambiguity.* In the tragic universe once the conversion has taken place the hero's existence is no more than an immutable demand for clarity, for a miracle. And the miracle is never performed, the contradiction subsists, and life becomes impossible. But, by demanding a miracle, an unachievable clarity, the hero pits himself against the equivocal world for he is the only being who is clear and unambiguous either from the start (Andromaque, Junie, Titus) or by the end of the play (Bérénice, Phèdre). He thus constitutes the only real miracle in the tragic universe, the only real being for a deity who sees nothing but the essential.

As I have said, this appears in the hero's consciousness in the form of two contradictory requirements. But we should beware of critical analysis, concepts and philosophy. There are never any concepts in the universe of a work of literature: there are only individual beings, situations and things. Thus the contradictory requirements of the deity are usually expressed by a division of the deity himself. The hidden God of Racine's tragedies frequently possesses two faces: Hector and Astyanax, the Roman people and love, the Sun and Venus (we shall later see why there is no such division in *Britannicus,* in reference to the Temple of Vesta).

Observed by the deity's double, but at the same time sin-

gle, eye, and confronted by the deity's contradictory requirements, man finds himself pulled with *equal* strength
towards the two opposite extremes, and *every step* he takes,
every gesture he makes towards one of them, simply increases his sense of failure before the other extreme and
makes it all the more attractive. As Pascal said:

> Nature has placed us so delicately in the middle that
> if we alter one of the scales we inevitably disturb the
> other one too. This leads me to believe that there are
> certain mechanisms within our heads which are
> arranged in such a way that whoever touches one of
> them also affects its opposite.

For the tragic hero, enamoured of justice and purity, *every worldly action* is a conscious or unconscious fault,
and, in the tragic universe which lacks any form of degree, this is tantamount to mortal sin. So the real content
of all Racine's tragedies is the same: the hero's "conversion" and his refusal of life and the world, the only free
and valid act that he can perform.

Yet the statement that the content of all Racine's tragedies is the universe engendered by "conversion" requires
closer analysis. "Conversion" is the *sudden* and *atemporal* passage from nothingness to being, from error to truth.
It is the passage from an intramundane life without God,
dominated by selfish, criminal (because partial) pleasures,
by passion and ambition, to the clear awareness of the
new morality, dominated by the need to reunite opposites,
for totality. Finally, it is the passage to the awareness that
authentic life is life observed by a God who is real and
absent from the vanity of the world. Man's only liberty is
the choice which he must make, and which he cannot
avoid making, between nothingness and being, between
apparent life in the world and real life in eternity. Conversion is a radical break both with the present world and
with the past, with all that has existed or exists in time
and space. This can hardly be expressed better than by
Lukács:

> Too alien to be enemies, the unveiled and the unveiler,
> chance and revelation, confront each other. For whatever
> reveals itself through an encounter with chance is alien
> to chance; it is more elevated and hales from another
> world. It is with alien eyes that the soul which has
> found itself now judges its previous existence. It seems
> incomprehensible, unessential, unreal to it. At most
> the soul could have dreamed of being otherwise—for
> its present existence is existence, whereas once a chance
> occurrence used to put dreams to flight and the accidental
> chimes of a distant bell used to bring morning awakening.

This "conversion", this moment of awareness which separates men from the world, does not necessarily create an
obvious and tangible bond, a community between him
and the deity. Indeed, the same awareness of the unremitting need for absolute values which makes every bond
between him and the world inconceivable also makes him
fully aware of his own limitations and of the infinite distance still separating him from the deity.

In the *Ecrit sur la conversion du pécheur,* one of the

masterpieces of tragic thought, Pascal started by describing the position of the soul between a vain and tangible
world on the one hand and the real and hidden God on
the other:

> Pious exercises appear even more obnoxious to it than
> the vanities of the world. On the one hand the presence
> of visible objects touches it more than the hope for
> invisible ones, and on the other the solidity of the
> invisible objects affects it more than the vanity of the
> visible ones. Thus the presence of the former and the
> solidity of the latter compete for the soul's affection,
> while the vanity of the former and the absence of the
> latter stimulate its aversion, thereby leading to disorder
> and confusion within the soul.

The soul, he concluded,

> begins to know God and desires to accede to Him; but
> since it has no idea how to do this, if its desire is
> genuine and sincere, it follows the course of the man
> who, aware of having lost his way, asks people who
> know it and . . . It decides to act in accordance with
> His wishes for the rest of its life; but since its natural
> weakness, together with the fact that it has grown
> accustomed to the sins in which it has lived, have
> made it incapable of reaching this state of happiness,
> it begs Him, in His mercy, to show it the way of
> acceding to Him, of joining Him and of remaining
> eternally united with Him . . . It thus realizes that it
> must worship God as a creature, render the thanks that
> are due to Him, give satisfaction to Him as a sinner,
> and pray to Him in its need.

This is to say that the tragic hero, equidistant from God
and from the world, is *radically alone.* So alone is he that
the real problem of the tragedy is to know how a dialogue
can still exist in this *absolute solitude,* where there is no
more than a paradoxical bond between man and God—a
fundamental and unremitting bond, no doubt, but at the
same time one which is completely hidden and is bereft
of any ostensible concrete existence. For if tragedy is the
expression of a universe and a solitude, it nevertheless
remains a play containing five acts which presuppose two
or three hours dialogue between several characters.

How can the hero's *absolute solitude* and the impossibility of forming the slightest real bond between him and the
world as well as between him and the deity be expressed?
The problem is not, of course, really insoluble. In order
to solve it Racine disposed of three elements, different
combinations between which enabled him to write his
four tragedies:

(a) *Intramundane dialogues* between the characters forming the world: Pyrrhus-Oreste, Oreste-Hermione, Néron-
Agrippine, Néron-Britannicus;

(b) *Pseudo-dialogues* between the tragic character and a
character of the world: Andromaque-Pyrrhus, Junie-Néron,
Bérénice-Antiochus, and finally

(c) the essential element of tragedy, *dialogue between the hero and the deity,* a paradoxical dialogue in which only one of the interlocutors talks to the other, who never answers and may not even be listening. Speaking of *Phèdre,* the distinguished critic Thierry Maulnier used the term "incantation". I prefer the more precise term "solitary dialogue", coined by Lukács.

The solitude of the tragic hero, the abyss separating him both from God and from the world, presented Racine with a further problem of composition—the *chorus.* Like most modern tragedians Racine was constantly preoccupied with it and was always looking for a means of introducing it into his plays as the ancients had done. But this problem was, and remains, insoluble. The chorus has a specific significance. It is *the voice of the human community* and therefore the voice of the gods. Greek tragedy told of the destiny of a hero who, in a universe made harmonious by the accord between community and deity, broke the traditional order with his "hybris" and drew divine vengeance on himself by leaving the community and enraging the deity.

In Racine's tragedies—and in all great modern tragedies—the authentic community of men has long disappeared, and not even a memory of it remains. The world, which is no longer linked to the hero, is a jungle of rapacious selfishness and oblivious victims. It is this world which, according to Pascal, crushes humanity; but man is greater than the world, for he knows that he is being crushed while the world is unaware of it. This is why he can no longer be a frightened, or merely impassive, witness of events.

In Racine's tragedies God's silence, the lack of a chorus and the hero's radical solitude are three aspects of one and the same phenomenon. They therefore all disappear as soon as the only valid transcendence of tragedy which the hero can acknowledge, *the divine universe,* appears behind the scenes or—in the sacred dramas—on the stage. In this universe man is no longer alone, for he returns both to God and the authentic community, the people, to which mundane characters such as Néron and Pyrrhus can never gain admission.

When Junie seeks refuge in the Temple of Vesta the people who protect her interpose themselves between her and the world, killing Narcisse and preventing Néron from entering. The last scene of *Britannicus* clearly shows the two opposing universes, that of the gods, legitimate royalty, the people and purity, and that of ambiguity, tyranny and crime. . . .

In *Bérénice,* too, when Titus is informed of the arrival of the people and the Senate, he does not doubt for a second that it is the voice of the gods which is reminding him of their requirements:

> RUTILE
> Seigneur, tous les tribuns, les consuls, le sénat
> Viennent vous demander au nom de tout l'Etat.
> Un grand peuple les suit, qui, plein d'impatience,
> Dans votre appartement attend votre présence.

> TITUS
> Je vous entends, grands dieux! Vous voulez rassurer
> Ce coeur que vous voyez tout prêt à s'égarer.
> PAULIN
> Venez, seigneur, passons dans la chambre prochaine,
> Allons voir le sénat.
> ANTIOCHUS
> Ah! courez chez la reine.
> PAULIN
> Quoi! vous pourriez, seigneur, par cette indignité,
> De l'empire à vos pieds fouler la majesté?
> Rome . . .
> TITUS
>   Il suffit, Paulin, nous allons les entendre.
>   (To Antiochus)
> Prince, de ce devoir je ne puis me défendre,
> Voyez la reine. Allez. J'espère à mon retour
> Qu'elle ne pourra plus douter de mon amour.
>   Act IV, scene 8

(Rutile: My lord, the tribunes, the consuls, the senate are asking for you in the name of the State. A great mob is following them and impatiently awaits you in your chambers.

Titus: I hear you, great gods! You want to reassure this heart which you see on the verge of going astray.

Paulin: Come, my lord, let us go to your chambers. Let us see the senate.

Antiochus: Go to the queen!

Paulin: What, my lord! Could you trample upon the majesty of the empire by committing such an indignity? Rome . . .

Titus: Enough, Paulin. We shall hear them. (To Antiochus) Prince, I cannot avoid this duty. See the queen. Go. I hope that on my return she will no longer doubt my love.)

Finally, when Racine goes beyond tragedy, in *Esther* and *Athalie,* and presents the universe of the triumphant God on the stage, the hero is no longer solitary but finds a genuine community with the chorus.

A classical writer is primarily a realist. Racine, who was above all a classical writer, never succumbed to the illusion of being able to unite tragedy and the chorus artificially. They were incompatible elements and it was aesthetically impossible to situate them in the same universe.

The atemporal instant

In connection with the problems of composition I should also mention the problem of *unity of time,* entailing the two other unities of place and action. It has become something of a commonplace to say that the rule of the three unities, which constituted a more or less external corset for Corneille, never troubled Racine. We are still bound to explain why what, for Corneille, was a problem of reducing the events to twenty-four hours, became, for

Racine, one of filling five acts with an essentially *atemporal* action.

It seems to me that the answer has already been outlined in the preceding pages. The "time" of the tragedy is the time of the "conversion", of the refusal of the world and life, of the voluntary choice between solitude or death. Now, "conversion" is an instantaneous event, sudden and with no preparation, which is to say it has no duration. At the moment when the curtain rises in **Andromaque, Britannicus** and **Bérénice**, the conversion of the hero, or at least of one of the heroes, has already taken place. The die has been cast, the future has long been settled, and the past is an ever-present, imminent threat. The three dimensions of temporality are thus contracted into an *atemporal* present which leads only to eternity. The tragedy is set at the moment of refusal or of death, at the time when the hero's relationship with what he loved is coming to an end, when he sees the object of his love "for the last time."

> *Andromaque:* Céphise, allons le voir pour la
> dernière fois . . .
> (Act IV, scene 1)
> *Junie:* Et si je vous parlais pour la dernière fois
> . . .
> (Act V, scene 1)
> *Titus:* Et je vais lui parler pour la dernière fois.
> (Act III, scene 2)
> (*Andromaque:* Céphise, let us see him for the
> last time.
> *Junie:* And if I were speaking to you for the
> last time . . .
> *Titus:* And I shall talk to her for the last time.)

The twenty-four hours undoubtedly exist for the beings of the world, for Hermione, for Néron who will slay Britannicus, for Bérénice who will only be converted at the end of the play, thereby entering the universe of tragedy:

> *Bérénice:* Pour la dernière fois, adieu, seigneur.
> (Act V, scene 7)
> (*Bérénice:* For the last time farewell, my lord.)

But these twenty-four hours could equally well be two hours or forty-eight hours—that is of no importance. The world is *inessential,* and, in the sight of that God who creates the tragic universe, only the essence, the "miracle" (and that means the tragic character alone) really exists. There is no time, no future for Andromaque, Junie, Titus or Bérénice after her conversion: they live—it comes to the same thing—in the instant and in eternity. In relation to the world their existence is simply a *no,* an inexorable refusal, nothing else.

No doubt time appears to exist for Phèdre, but it is the time of an illusion, a paradoxical time, circular and deceptive. **Phèdre** starts with the same situation as the three other tragedies, *Soleil, je viens te voir pour la dernière fois* (Sun, I come to see you for the last time. Act I, scene 3) and ends at the moment when Phèdre again encounters

the initial situation. In the play her final conversion, which suppresses the past, removes all reality from the process whose accomplishment she obviously demanded. Thus **Phèdre** ends with the same negation of time with which the other tragedies had begun.

The tragic fault

Of the three figures between whom tragedy is played, God, man and the world, I have tried to describe the first two. We come now to the third.

The world of tragedy is a world without *God,* in which *no* real value can ever be either *realized* or *approached.* It is a world in which the pseudo-existence of the protagonists (in relation to the constituent values of tragedy) is defined by injustice and error, a world of beasts and puppets. I said earlier on that all opposition of interests, ambitions or passions, taken as the subject of a play, must necessarily be accidental and therefore *dramatic.* But when this opposition is situated within the tragic universe it is, *in as far as it is an accident,* typical or representative of a world which does not know and can never attain the essence.

I must now introduce a notion of paramount importance: the fault. In the tragic universe we must distinguish between *worldly* faults—injustice and error, which both imply complete absence of consciousness—and the *tragic* fault which is the consequence of the sharp and clear consciousness accorded to man by his entry into the tragic universe, his "conversion". In this context *to know* means to know the absolute needs which separate the hero from the world, as well as his limitations which separate him irremediably from God. . . .

In 1653, long before Pascal had written his *Pensées* or Racine his tragedies, the Church condemned what it called "the Jansenist heresy" for having asserted that the most perfect state which man could attain, the true human state, was not that of Adam or the angles, but that of St Peter who denied Jesus, the state of the *just sinner.* A long and fastidious philological discussion ensued, and still continues three centuries later, in order to establish whether Jansen did or did not really support these propositions. But barely forty years after the condemnation the little group of French Jansenists had given birth to the two masterpieces of tragic literature, Pascal's *Pensées* and Jean Racine's plays. This, it seems to me, cuts across the debate more efficiently than any theological or philological discussion. By formulating the "five propositions" Rome defined Jansenism with amazing concision, better, perhaps, than the best theoreticians of Port-Royal could have done. But, by condemning them, Rome also condemned the tragic thought and literature which constitute one of the human mind's most realistic, most powerful and most valid forms of expression.

Kenneth Muir (lecture date 1959)

SOURCE: "Racine," in *Last Periods of Shakespeare,*

Racine, Ibsen, Wayne State University Press, 1961, pp. 61-88.

[In the following excerpt from the text of a lecture deliv-
ered in 1959, Muir focuses upon the final two dramas of
Racine, Esther *and* Athaliah, *finding the latter in partic-*
ular a reflection of Racine's effort to, in effect, repudiate
the libertinism of his middle years and return to the
Christian practice of his youth.]

Between 1664 and 1676, between the ages of twenty-five
and thirty-seven, a space of twelve years, Racine wrote
ten plays. During this next twelve years, between the ages
of thirty-seven and forty-nine, he wrote nothing for the
stage. Then, in his last period, he was persuaded to write
the two Biblical plays, **Esther** and **Athalie**. Any critic of
Racine's work is confronted with the twelve years' silence following the twelve years of continuous dramatic
activity. However we explain his long retirement from the
stage we can be sure that there was more than one reason,
and it is not difficult to guess that the reasons were inter-
related. In the first place, he gave up the irregularities of
his sexual life, as many men do on the threshold of middle age, and married a pious woman who seems to have
disapproved of the stage, the more heartily because one
of Racine's discarded mistresses had taken the leading
role in his tragedies. Second, Racine became reconciled
to his former teachers at Port Royal, who objected to
most secular literature and disliked plays as violently as
the Puritans of Shakespeare's day. Nicole, who taught
Racine Latin, declared in a pamphlet that plays and novels were horrible when considered according to the principles of Christianity. A dramatist, he said,

> is a public poisoner, not of the bodies but of the souls
> of the faithful; who ought to regard himself as guilty
> of an infinity of spiritual murders. . . . The more care
> he takes to cover with a veil of respectability the
> criminal passions which he describes, the more
> dangerous he has made them, and the more capable of
> surprising and corrupting guileless and innocent souls.
> Such sins are all the more dreadful, in that these books
> do not perish, but they continue to spread their venom
> amongst those who read them.

Racine was aware of Nicole's views on the immorality
and profaneness of the stage and, it would seem, increasingly uneasy about his profession. In the preface to **Phèdre,** the last of the secular plays, Racine is careful to
point out how scrupulous he has been to depict virtue in
a favorable light, to punish severely the smallest faults, to
regard the very idea of a crime with as much horror as the
actual deed:

> The passions are presented only to show all the disorder
> of which they are the cause; and vice is everywhere
> depicted in such colors as to make people recognize it
> and hate its deformity. That, indeed, is the aim which
> every man who works for the public should propose
> for himself.

Racine had, of course, always held the view that tragedy
has a moral function; but in this preface he was particularly anxious to claim that, in spite of Phèdre's incestuous
desires, and in spite of the sympathy aroused for her, the
moral tone of the play is unexceptionable.

But Racine could not be reconciled to Port Royal so long
as he was writing for the stage, and the desire on his part
to be reconciled was one cause of his retirement from the
stage. Another factor, perhaps, was the failure of **Phèdre,**
when it was first performed, through the intrigues of his
enemies. They got to hear that he was writing a play
about Phaedra and Hippolytus and they commissioned a
second-rate poet to write a play on the same subject. They
filled the theatre of his rival with an enthusiastic audience
and boycotted Racine's play.

The last cause of Racine's retirement from the stage was
his appointment as historiographer royal, and this appointment was made on the understanding that he would sever
his connection with the theatre. He seems to have regarded the post as more respectable than that of being the
greatest poet of the century, and even in his youth he
seems to have looked on his genius as a means of social
advancement. Before we condemn Racine we should recall that Shakespeare had moods when he disliked the
theatre and that he was anxious to obtain the right to call
himself a gentleman.

The various motives I have mentioned reacted one upon
the other. Like Jason in Anouilh's play, Racine wished to
lead a more orderly life, to marry, to settle down; he
wanted to make his peace with his religious advisers and
to escape from the bitter conflicts of the theatre; and his
official appointment provided him with a suitable opportunity.

In spite of which, the twelve years of silence were not
without problems for the poet. On the one hand, he loved,
admired, almost worshipped Louis XIV; on the other, he
had become reconciled to his old teachers who were persecuted by the King: so that Racine was inevitably torn
between his love for Port Royal and his desire for advancement at court. Giraudoux, indeed, in his brilliant
essay on Racine, suggests that the two Biblical plays may
be explained by the Catholicism of the King, rather than
by that of the author, and that his

> period of dissipation had never been a period of
> impiety; he was reconciled not with God, but with his
> aunt; he had himself buried not at the feet of a saint,
> but at the feet of the man who had taught him Greek
> verbs.

This is witty; but, like most witty remarks, it is not entirely true. It is part of Giraudoux's argument that Racine's inspiration was wholly literary. In fact, his conversion, his reconciliation with Port Royal, was genuine, and
it was a landmark in his life. He had written the greatest
tragedies in the French language, but he was still profoundly dissatisfied. As Giraudoux puts it, "The purest
French that had been written was no longer the perfect
language for Racine but the dialect of a country he had

deserted." During the next twelve years Racine translated seventeen hymns from the Breviary, as Milton, during the years before he began to compose *Paradise Lost,* versified a number of Psalms. Racine's hymns are not so feeble as Milton's psalms, but no one would suspect that they were written by a great poet.

Madame de Sevigné observed that Racine loved God as he had formerly loved his mistresses. She might have added that whereas his mistresses had inspired *Andromache* and *Phèdre,* God seemed, at first, to be less fortunate in the work he inspired. In 1688, however, a way was found to reconcile poetry and piety. Racine was invited by Madame de Maintenon to write a Biblical play to be performed by pupils of a girls' school of which she was the patron. Somewhat unwillingly, Racine accepted the invitation; and the play, *Esther,* was a great success. Madame de Maintenon asked him for another religious play; but the King stipulated that there should be no dresses or scenery, and the first performance of *Athalie* was little more than a recitation in an ordinary room. It was afterwards performed at court. There was one performance before the exiled James II, who must have viewed the overthrow of Athalie with mixed feelings. There is good reason to believe that Racine chose his subject partly with the Glorious Revolution in mind; but, of course, he did not regard the revolution as glorious. Although the play shows a successful rebellion against a reigning monarch, both he and his audience would identify Athalie not with James II, but with the usurper, William III; and they would identify Joas with the infant son of James II, who had escaped from England with his mother. The restoration of this boy to the throne would not merely involve the overthrow of the usurper, it would restore the true religion in place of the worship of Baal, or Protestantism. Yet Louis did not approve of the play. Nor is this surprising: Joad, the High Priest, might reasonably be regarded as a Jansenist; and Mathan, the renegade, had gained his sovereign's ear by arts which resembled in some ways those by which the Jesuits were thought to control Louis XIV:

> My soul
> Attached itself entirely to the court,
> Till by degrees I gained the ear of kings,
> And soon became an oracle. I studied
> Their hearts and flattered their caprice. For them
> I sowed the precipice's edge with flowers.

François Mauriac suggests that Louis might have used of Arnault, the head of Port Royal, the phrase which Athalie addresses to Joad in the last act of the play: "Eternal enemy of absolute power." Indeed, the picture painted by Racine of the corruption of absolute power in the Queen's entourage was, however unconsciously, an attack on the whole principle of absolutism, absolute power corrupting absolutely. Although Racine could declare, in prose, that Louis was "the wisest and most perfect of all men," he put into the mouth of the chorus a description of Athalie's court:

> Within a court where Justice is unknown,
> And all the laws are Force and Violence,

> Where Honor's lost in base obedience,
> Who will speak up for luckless Innocence?

No intelligent tyrant could listen to such sentiments without seeing that the cap fitted. These lines were either omitted from the first edition of the play—either by accident or because Racine realised that they were dangerous—or else they were added in the second edition. But there were plenty of others on the dangers of absolute power which apply as accurately to the reign of Louis XIV. One of Joad's speeches, in the scene in which he reveals to the boy Eliacin that he is the lawful king, is a most moving account of the evils, and the dangers, of absolutism.

> My son—I still dare call you by that name—
> Suffer this tenderness; forgive the tears
> That flow from me in thinking of your peril.
> Nurtured far from the throne, you do not know
> The poisonous enchantment of that honor.
> You do not know yet the intoxication
> Of absolute power, the bewitching voice
> Of vilest flattery. Too soon they'll tell you
> That sacred laws, though rulers of the rabble,
> Must bow to kings; that a king's only bridle
> Is his own will; that he should sacrifice
> All to his greatness; that to tears and toil
> The people are condemned and must be ruled
> With an iron sceptre; that if they're not
>   oppressed,
> Sooner or later they oppress—and thus,
> From snare to snare, and from abyss to abyss,
> Soiling the lovely purity of your heart,
> They'll make you hate the truth, paint virtue for
>   you
> Under a hideous image. Alas! the wisest
> Of all our kings was led astray by them.
> Swear then upon this book, and before these
> As witnesses, that God will always be
> Your first of cares; that stern towards the
>   wicked,
> The refuge of the good, you'll always take
> Between you and the poor the Lord for judge,
> Remembering, my son, that, in these garments,
> You once were poor and orphaned, even as they.

It is significant that nearly a hundred years later, on the eve of the French Revolution, this speech was interrupted at almost every line by enthusiastic applause. It is still more significant that Fouché, the head of Napoleon's secret police, compelled the actors to omit it. Poets, as Plato realised long ago, are dangerous people in a totalitarian state; for even when they consciously desire, as Racine apparently did, to gain the favor of a tyrant by flattery, they are impelled by forces stronger than themselves to tell the truth. Racine, when he wrote *Athalie,* was certainly doing his best to please Madame de Maintenon and the King; he had no wish to intrude Jansenist and, still less, disloyal sentiments; but all great poets are George Washingtons in spite of themselves—they cannot tell a lie. Racine's conception of the good king was constant throughout his career. In *Berenice* Titus declares that he undertook the happiness of a thousand who were unhappy and later asks, "What tears have I dried? In what satisfied eyes have I savored the fruit of my good deeds?" In *Esther* the chorus distinguishes between a victorious king, who triumphs through his valor, and the wise king who hates injustice, prevents the rich from grinding the faces of the poor, who is the protector of the fatherless and the widow, and to whom the tears of the righteous suitor are precious. It must have been difficult to identify Louis XIV with such a monarch, though such is the mystique of royalty that many probably did. . . .

[We] do Racine a great injustice if we regard him as a tyrant's laureate. *Athalie* is not only a great tragedy, a great work of art, it is also a precious manifesto in the history of human freedom, and as Voltaire said, a masterpiece of the human spirit.

On the other hand, religious people have not always been judicious in their praise of the play. The Abbé Bremond, for example, says that *Athalie* should be studied in the chapel rather than in the classroom. Either fate seems to me undeserved for what is after all a great dramatic masterpiece. Just as misguided critics have argued that *King Lear* cannot be acted, so some French critics have said that to act *Athalie* is as sacriligious as to touch the Ark of the Covenant.

There is a long doctoral thesis on Racine's use of the Bible in the play. We are not likely to get much illumination from that angle. The use Shakespeare made of his sources in one possible road to an understanding of his genius; but the story of Athaliah in the Bible is so brief, and Racine takes such liberties with it, that we can learn very little about his genius from this kind of approach. But one thing does emerge from a study of the Bible which explains in part why Racine chose this particular story. Joas was in the direct line of descent between David and Jesus. That is why his preservation, both in his infancy and during the course of the play, is of cosmic importance. On his safety depends, one might almost say, the redemption of man. That is why Joad's prophecy about the Messiah is perfectly appropriate, and why Maulnier says that in *Athalie* the celebration of fate is associated with the celebration of faith. "The unity of action is established here, by divine command, the unity of place by the sanctuary, the unity of time by the sacrifice."

One of the most remarkable things about *Athalie* arises from the poet's consciousness of the significance in religious history of the action of the play. He contrives in the two hours' traffic of the stage, in incidents which take no longer than the time of representation, to show both the past and the future. Jezebel's death is described by Joad in Act I, twice by Athalie herself in Act II, and there is a reference to it in the last act. The murder of Ahaziah's children and the escape of Joas are described by Josabeth in the first act, by Athalie in the second act, by Joad in Act IV, and there are continual references to it throughout the play. The long feud between Athalie's family and the priests makes her a victim of circumstances. We have

for her something of the pity Thomas Hardy evokes for Jezebel in the poem describing the "proud Tyrian woman who painted her face":

> Faintly marked they the words "Throw her
>   down" rise from time eerily,
> Spectre-spots of the blood of her body on some
>   rotten wall,
> And the thin note of pity that came, "A King's
>   daughter is she,"
> As they passed where she trodden was once by
>   the chargers' footfall.

Racine was prevented by his artistic conscience from making Athalie merely detestable, and indeed from making Joad entirely sympathetic—Voltaire regarded the character as fanatical and superstitious. Athalie not merely gives her name to the play: she is the dominating character, and she is depicted not without sympathy. Over and over again we are reminded of the savage way in which her mother had been murdered. She tells Josabeth:

> Yes, my just fury—and I boast of it—
> Avenged my parents' deaths upon my sons.
> I saw my father and my brother butchered,
> My mother cast down from her palace window,
> And in one day (what a spectacle of horror!)
> Saw eighty princes murdered! For what reason?
> To avenge some prophets whose immoderate
>   frenzies
> My mother justly punished.

Even more striking, and more calculated to arouse sympathy for Athalie, is her famous dream, in which Jezebel appears to her and warns her that the God of the Jews will soon prevail over her also:

> In uttering these frightful words,
> Her ghost, it seemed, bent down towards my
>   bed;
> But when I stretched my hands out to embrace
>   her,
> I found instead a horrible heap of bones,
> And mangled flesh, and tatters soaked in blood
> Dragged through the mire, and limbs
>   unspeakable
> For which voracious dogs were wrangling there.

I am not, of course, suggesting that Racine was, as Blake asserted that Milton was, of the Devil's party without knowing it. It was simply that, like every good poet, Racine believed in giving the Devil his due. Shakespeare (as Keats declared) took as much delight in depicting an Iago as an Imogen; and Racine took as much delight in depicting an Athalie as a Joad. Indeed, the greatness of the play depends partly on the tension in the poet's mind between his artistic integrity and his religious feelings and, in the play itself, on the tension between the drama as a work of art and the drama as an act of worship. Racine on his knees and Racine in his study were not quite the same in their thoughts and feelings.

In her last speech Athalie prophecies that the innocent child, Joas, will do that which is evil in the sight of the Lord, profaning his alter, and so avenging Ahab, Jezebel and Athalie. Although Joas prays that the curse shall not be accomplished, we know from the Bible that he afterwards turned against the priests, thereby fulfilling the curse. Athalie was, in fact, triumphant after her own death, even though David's line—the line of descent between David and Jesus—was preserved. The knowledge of Joas' subsequent fall, which Racine could assume in his audience, makes some passages in the play unbearably poignant in their irony.

The scene in Act II where Athalie questions the boy about his life in the temple shows the haggard old queen, corrupted equally by her power and her crimes, face to face with innocence. The boy is later described by the chorus by the use of imagery which stresses this quality:

> Thus in a sheltered valley
> A crystal stream beside,
> There grows a tender lily,
> Kind Nature's love and pride.
> Secluded from the world from infancy,
> With all the gifts of heaven graced,
> The contagion of wickedness has not defaced
> His spotless innocency.

The irony of the scene depends not only on the fact that we know Joas will be corrupted, but also on the strange tenderness which Athalie feels for the boy who, in her dream, had stabbed her to the heart and who was eventually to be the cause of her death. For her love of Joas is the love of an old woman for her lost innocence, the maternal love which she had repressed at the bidding of vengeance. The weakness which blinds and destroys Athalie is the pity she thought she had conquered in herself. She is destroyed by the milk of human kindness, by the small residue of her virtue.

According to Aristotle, the most moving thing in tragedy is when a course of action intended to produce a certain result produces the reverse. So Athalie, by demanding from Joad the treasure of David and the boy Eliacin, and by threatening to destroy the temple if her demands are refused, is herself delivered into Joad's hands. What she thinks will be her final triumph over Jehovah turns out to be his final triumph over her. She asks for the child and for David's treasure, and she discovers that the child is the treasure and is the treasure precisely because he is her own successor. Her recognition of the truth is a good example of another of Aristotle's points:

> Thou hast conquered, O God of the Jews!
> Yes, it is Joas, and I seek in vain
> To deceive myself. . . .
>   I see the mien and gesture
> Of Ahaziah. Everything recalls
> The blood which I detest. . . .
>   Remorseless God,
> Thou hast brought everything to pass.

Although I have stressed the fairness with which Racine depicts Athalie, it would be quite wrong to pretend that there is nothing to choose, morally, between the two parties and the two religions. All through the play there is a contrast between the worldly glory of the court and the service of righteousness in the temple; between the time-serving, hypocritical, treacherous Mathan, who does not believe in the religion he professes, and the austere and noble Joad; between the low standards of morality accepted by the worshippers of Baal, and the righteousness demanded by the worshippers of Jehovah. Some critics, it is true, have condemned the equivocation of Joad in the last act of the play, when he pretends to Abner that he will hand over to Athalie the treasure she had demanded. He does not tell a lie, though he deceives Abner by a calculated ambiguity. Racine, in the notes he jotted down on the play, defends Joad's prevarication by Biblical and Patristic precedents. But since Athalie is being lured into the temple so that she can be assassinated, it is needless to complain of Joad's deceit which is necessary for the purpose. The art of war consists very largely in making the enemy believe something which you wish him to believe. The prevarication, moreover, is necessary if Abner's integrity is to be preserved.

It will be noticed that in spite of the significance of the plot as a means of preserving David's line, and in spite of Joad's prophecy about the Messiah and the New Jerusalem,

> What new Jerusalem rises now
> From out the desert shining bright,
> Eternity upon her brow,
> Triumphing over death and night?
>   Sing, peoples, Zion now is more
>   Lovely and glorious than before.
>
> Whence come these children manifold
> She did not carry at her breast?
> Lift up thy head, O Zion, behold
> These princes with thy fame possessed;
>   These earthly kings all prostrate bow,
>   And kiss the dust before thee now.

In spite of this passage the general spirit of the play is Hebraic rather than Christian. In this Racine was wiser than some of his critics, for the intrusion of a Christian spirit into the more primitive story of Jezebel and Athaliah would have been unhistorical. Though Racine was probably more consciously religious after his conversion than Shakespeare had ever been, and though his last two plays were written on Biblical subjects, the plays of Shakespeare's last period, with their emphasis on reconciliation and forgiveness, seem to me to be much more Christian in spirit than either *Esther* or *Athalie*.

It is significant that whereas Shakespeare was treating afresh in his last years themes which had exercised him before—jealousy, treachery, the reunion of those who had been separated, the forgiveness of sins—Racine moved away from the themes with which he had formerly been concerned. This was partly due to the fact that as the plays were being performed by school-girls, he had been asked to avoid the subject of love. They had performed *Andromache* with its murderous jealousies and suicidal loves, and Madame de Maintenon was afraid the girls might imbibe feelings of the wrong sort. Most of Racine's heroines are unsuitable models for well brought-up young ladies. Hermione incites Orestes (who loves her) to murder Pyrrhus (whom she loves but who prefers Andromache). Roxane first makes Bajazet choose between marriage to her and death; and when he wisely chooses death she gives him a final opportunity of watching the strangling of the woman he loves:

> Follow me instantly
> And see her die by the mutes' hands. Set free
> Then, from a love fatal to glory's quest,
> Plight me thy troth. Time will do all the rest.

Phèdre, on being repulsed by her stepson, allows him to be accused of having attempted to ravish her. Agrippine is a murderess. Beside these furies, the virtuous heroines appear very colorless. Aricie is unwilling to elope with a man whose life is in deadly danger until she has her marriage certificate in her pocket; Junie is merely pathetic; and Andromache derives all her interest from the tragic situation in which she is placed.

Although both Racine's Biblical plays illustrate the workings of Providence, it has been said that he found in *Athalie* a fate more pitiless than that of the ancients. Instead of the Greek destiny he had used in *Andromache* and *Phèdre* he showed a Jehovah who "with more native cruelty than Zeus ordained a precise destiny for man." Josabeth, a sympathetic figure, filled with maternal love, hails with delight the murder of the old queen. Perhaps Maulnier exaggerates when he says that there is more ferocity in *Athalie* than in the tragedies of sexual passion:

> Between the fate which orders the murder and the murder itself the body and its lover no longer serve as intermediaries; the road of crime no longer passes through the territory of desire and exaltation.

The supernatural ferocity of the play, however much we may wish to modify Maulnier's views, is dependent on Racine's deliberate restriction of the action to those scenes which God himself, as it were, had prepared. "The different moments of the action are no other than the different moments of His thought." The divine action is substituted for the human action.

> Neither does the actor suffer
> Nor the patient act. But both are fixed
> In an eternal action, an eternal patience
> To which all must consent that it may be willed
> And which all must suffer that they may will it,
> That the pattern may subsist, for the pattern is
>   the action
> And the suffering, that the wheel may turn and
>   still
> Be forever still.
>
> (T. S. Eliot)

Of course, in a sense, in Shakespeare's last plays the divine action supersedes the human action or interpenetrates it. But whereas the villains in *Esther* and *Athalie* are destroyed, in *Cymbeline* and *The Tempest* Iachimo and the three men of sin are brought to repentance, and even Caliban decides to be wise hereafter and seek for grace. The spirit of *Athalie* is nearer to the spirit of *Samson Agonistes* than to that of *The Tempest*. Milton's Old Testament tragedy, though ending avowedly with "calm of mind, all passion spent," has as its climax the destruction of the Philistines, both innocent and guilty, by the champion of the Lord, and the chorus, with Milton's approval, sings a hymn of triumph. This, like the concluding sentiments of *Athalie,* is in accordance with the spirit of the stories on which the plays are based; but, of course, it is significant that both Racine and Milton should choose such subjects out of all the possible ones in the Old Testament.

The characteristics which have been found in *Athalie* by modern critics—brutality, ferocity, frenzy, murderous rage, religious exaltation—do not suggest the marmoreal calm of classic art. The classical form serves as a dam which controls and utilises an enormous pressure of emotion. Primitive passion and violent hatreds are combined with a passion for righteousness; and all are expressed with the deceptive clarity and simplicity of great art.

There is, I suppose, some prejudice amongst English-speaking readers against French classical tragedy, just as many Frenchmen, at the bottom of their hearts, regard Shakespeare as an "erring barbarian." It is unfortunate that typical English classical tragedies have been written by scholars for scholars. Daniel's *Cleopatra* and *Philotas,* with all their delicacy and charm, seem deliberately designed to avoid arousing any excitement: they are the ideal plays for people who have already had one attack of coronary thrombosis. Even *All for Love* is a decorous affair compared with *Antony and Cleopatra*; and the Victorian lady who remarked at a performance of Shakespeare's play, "How unlike the life of our own dear queen!" would not have been upset by Dryden's. Addison's *Cato* is a by-word for laudable dullness; and no one, I suppose, has read Arnold's *Merope* more than once. But Racine's plays possess the intensity which Keats rightly demanded of a work of art, and this intensity is increased rather than diminished by the rigid classical form. Racine, unlike Corneille, obeys the rules so easily that the audience is unconscious of them. In *Athalie,* as I have mentioned, we live as much in the past as in the present; and we are made to realise that we are witnessing one episode in the continuous war between idolatry and righteousness.

The eloquence and order which the older critics found in Racine's work are, of course, to be found there. But recent critics have tended to stress the chaos and frenzy on which the order is superimposed, the terror which is never far beneath the surface. A scene in his plays has been described as "the explanation which closes for the time a series of negotiations between wild beasts." Racine's heroes "confront each other on a footing of terrible equality, of physical and moral nudity. . . . It is an equality and truth of the jungle." His plays are often terrifying. Beneath the civilised surface there is a volcano of passion. The characters, periwigged and elegant as they are, are often frenzied creatures plotting violent crimes. They address each other as "Seigneur" and "Madame," but they recall often the animal imagery of *King Lear* and *Othello*:

> If that the heavens do not their visible spirits
> Send quickly down to tame these vile offences,
> It will come—
> Humanity must perforce prey on itself
> Like monsters of the deep.

In fact the perverted passions of Racine's characters are more horrifying than the straightforward violence of the jungle, and the order which is imposed on chaos at the end of the play is more often the quiet of exhaustion than the conscious restoration of an order which has been overturned by human passion.

I have mentioned Giraudoux's theory that Racine's inspiration was entirely literary and that it dated from his reading of the classics: his true liaisons were with the heroines of Greek plays, and the experience embodied in his tragedies was derived from the literary passions he had experienced in adolescence with the complicity of his schoolmasters. This is all very well, and it is a useful corrective to the theory that the tragedies may be explained by his love of Marquise du Parc and Mlle. Champmeslé; or the recent theory of René Jasinski that Agrippine, in *Britannicus,* is a symbol of Port Royal, the devouring mother from which Racine is unable to free himself. It is unnecessary to accept either the theory that the plays were purely literary in their inspiration or that they were symbolic representations of events in the dramatist's life. There have been hundreds of writers who studied Greek drama at school without afterwards being obsessed with the passions therein displayed; and we may suppose that Racine found in Greek plays something that combined with later experience.

It is a pity that after English critics have exploded what Charles Jasper Sisson calls "the mythical sorrows of Shakespeare" French critics should now try and explain the more classical plays of Racine as the reflection of his personal experience, in any narrow autobiographical sense. But it is probably true that in a broad sense they do reflect his own experience of life. He chose to write on sexual passion and power. It is significant that he was apparently never tempted to write on Oedipus or Antigone, and that although he started a scenario of the *Iphigenia in Tauris* he never progressed beyond the first act. *Phèdre* already reveals the conflict in his mind which led to his abandonment of the theatre; and his last two plays reveal both what Mauron calls the regressive form of religion into which he relapsed in his later years and his views on the corruption of the court.

Although no one would pretend that *The Winter's Tale* and *The Tempest* are greater works of art than *King Lear* or *Macbeth,* it is arguable that they display a ripeness of wisdom and a sense of reconciliation with life which was

not present in the great tragedies. They do not repudiate the tragic sense of life: they recollect it in tranquillity. In Racine's last plays, on the other hand, partly because the subject-matter is different, he seems rather to have turned away from his former themes and obsessions. He has not subsumed them under his new religious outlook in which forgiveness plays very little part. It is significant that the converted poet should refer in contemptuous terms to a woman he had loved for years, the actress who had created Phèdre. There are, however, some positive values expressed in *Esther* and *Athalie.*

M. Raymond Picard calls *Esther* "a spiritual canticle in action," and it is, except for *Bérénice,* the most immediately attractive of Racine's plays. The choruses, however, which carry the chief burden of religious sentiment, seem to me be little more than a pleasant libretto, of small poetical importance:

> O sweet Peace!
> O eternal Light!
> Beauty ever bright!
> Happy the heart which thou dost please!
> O sweet Peace!
> O eternal Light!
> Happy the heart which loves thee without cease!

We have already touched on the positive values in *Athalie*—the stern sense of righteousness, the lofty courage of Joad, the loving-tenderness of Josabeth, the puzzled integrity of Abner, the faith and innocence of the chorus. The lyrical interludes of the chorus are excellent poetry in their own right and are the best answer to the corruption of Athalie's court and Mathan's false religion. But perhaps the scene which best expresses the unspoiled innocence of life in the temple is the scene between Eliacin and Athalie. Shakespeare when he wishes to symbolize the age of innocence usually presents two young lovers—Perdita and Florizel, Miranda and Ferdinand—or a pastoral life such as that led by Imogen's brothers. Once, at the beginning of *The Winter's Tale*—in lines I quoted in my last lecture—he speaks of the boyhood of Polixenes and Leontes and their denial of hereditary guilt, original sin. But Shakespeare, whether because of the pagan settings of *The Winter's Tale* and *Cymbeline* or for some other reason, avoids any overt religious reference. He seems to express a faith in the natural goodness of man when not corrupted by society. Racine, on the other hand, emphasizes the religious basis of Eliacin's innocence. The life Eliacin led in the temple is perhaps an indirect tribute to the atmosphere of Racine's schooldays at Port Royal.

Athalie asks Eliacin (Joas) who looked after him in his infancy. He replies:

> Has God ever left
> His children in want? He feeds the tiniest birds;
> His bounty stretches to the whole of nature.
> I pray to him daily, and with a father's care
> He feeds me with the gifts placed on his altar.

Athalie's fear and hostility gradually change to love. She

asks Joas what he does with his time:

> I worship the Lord and listen to his law.
> I have been taught to read his holy book,
> And I am learning now to copy it.

The law states

>   that God demands our love;
> That he takes vengeance, soon or late, on those
> Who take his name in vain; that he defends
> The timid orphan; that he resists the proud
> And punishes the murderer.

Athalie asks what his pleasures are; Joas answers:

> Sometimes to the High Priest at the altar
> I offer salt or incense. I hear songs
> Of the infinite greatness of Almighty God;
> I see the stately order of his rites.

She invites him to live in the palace and tells him that there are two gods; he retorts that his god is the only true god and that

> The happiness of the wicked passeth away
> Even as a torrent.

It will be noticed that there is some justification for Athalie's complaint that the boy has already been indoctrinated and taught to hate her and all she stands for. Racine's innocent already has been taught to distinguish between good and evil; but one is bound to believe that Racine would not have been able to dally with the innocence of love.

Great as *Athalie* is as a play, it represents not the natural culmination of Racine's work but rather an achievement in a totally new field of drama. The long conflict in his mind between the secular and the religious, which had begun in his schooldays, could not be resolved by compromise. At Port Royal he had defiantly read the Greek romances which his teachers had regarded as pernicious. After his initial failures as a poet, he had dallied with the idea of becoming ordained. Then he had broken with Port Royal and written plays which had shocked them more than his sexual irregularities. When he turned his back on the stage and became reconciled to Port Royal he could consecrate his poetry to his jealous God, but he could not interfuse the emotions of his past life with spiritual significance—he could only repudiate them altogether.

Robert Lowell (essay date 1961)

SOURCE: "On Translating *Phèdre*," in *Collected Prose*, edited by Robert Giroux, Farrar Straus and Giroux, 1987, pp. 230-31.

[*Winner of two Pulitzer Prizes and a National Book Award, Lowell is generally considered the premier American poet of his generation. One of the original proponents of the*

confessional school of poetry, he frequently gave voice to his personal as well as his social concerns, leading many to consider him the prototypical liberal intellectual writer of his time. Lowell was also a widely acclaimed translator and playwright as well as critic and editor. In the following excerpt from the introduction to his 1961 translation of Phèdre, *he comments upon the difficulties of translating Racine's poetry, with "the justness of its rhythms and logic, and the glory of its hard, electric rage."*]

Racine's plays are generally and correctly thought to be untranslatable. His syllabic alexandrines do not and cannot exist in English. We cannot reproduce his language, which is refined by the literary artifice of his contemporaries, and given a subtle realism and grandeur by the spoken idiom of Louis XIV's court. Behind each line is a for us lost knowledge of actors and actresses, the stage and the moment. Other qualities remain: the great conception, the tireless plotting, and perhaps the genius for rhetoric and versification that alone proves that the conception and plotting are honest. . . .

No translator has had the gifts or the luck to bring Racine into our culture. It's a pity that Pope and Dryden overlooked Racine's great body of works, close to them, in favor of the inaccessible Homer and Vergil.

Racine's verse has a diamond edge. He is perhaps the greatest poet in the French language, but he uses a smaller vocabulary than any English poet—beside him Pope and Bridges have a Shakespearean luxuriance. He has few verbally inspired lines and in this is unlike Baudelaire and even La Fontaine. His poetry is great because of the justness of its rhythm and logic, and the glory of its hard, electric rage.

Martin Turnell (essay date 1972)

SOURCE: "Approach to Racine," in *Jean Racine: Dramatist*, Hamish Hamilton, 1972, pp. 3-25.

[*Turnell has written widely on French literature and has made significant translations of the works of Jean-Paul Sartre, Guy de Maupassant, Blaise Pascal, and Paul Valèry. In the following excerpt, he quotes several critics* contra *Racine, using them as a springboard to his thesis that "when properly performed, Racine is still the greatest French tragic dramatist" and that the negative pronouncements of Racine's critics speak more to the issue of access than to that of dramatic accomplishment.*]

'Of all our authors', François Mauriac once said, 'Racine is one of the least accessible to the peoples of other countries'.

Racine presents special difficulties for foreigners. They are by no means confined to foreigners. There are at present two generally accepted approaches to the French classic dramatists. You can either wipe away the veneer which has accumulated with the passage of time and obscures the work of the master and try to think yourself back into the seventeenth century, or you can argue that no great writer belongs exclusively to a particular period and insist on the importance of the plays as dramatic *experience*. The first of these approaches is the safer, the second the more rewarding and also the more dangerous.

The dangers are illustrated by a controversy which began in France some fifteen years ago and is perhaps still not ended. In 1955 the Compagnie Madeleine Renaud-Jean-Louis Barrault decided to mount a production of *Bérénice* at the Théâtre Marigny and to mark the event by the publication of a special number of the company's *Cahiers* devoted to Racine. Henry de Montherlant was invited to write the introduction to it. He called his article 'Racine Langouste'. He drew a comparison between the conventions of seventeenth-century drama and the lobster's shell. If you scrape and prod long enough and hard enough, you may get a few tasty morsels from the animal. In the same way you may extract a few fragments of poetry from Racine—Montherlant put the aggregate at twenty-seven lines for the twelve plays—if you are prepared to spend your time 'painfully and interminably removing the shell'.

Four years later Jean Vilar, who had consistently opposed all attempts to persuade him to add Racine to the repertoire of the Théâtre National Populaire on the grounds that he was not suitable for 'popular' consumption, yielded to public pressure and produced *Phèdre* with Maria Casarès in the name part. It was Roland Barthes' turn to enter the lists. In an article published in *Théâtre Populaire,* the TNP's own journal, he declared that the production was a misfortune for Casarès who 'had risked a lot and lost a lot'. The dramatist did not escape. If we go to see *Phèdre,* said Barthes, 'it is on account of a particular actress, a certain number of felicitous lines, some famous *tirades* set against a background of obscurity and boredom. We tolerate the rest.' 'I do not know,' he concluded, 'whether it is still possible to perform Racine today. It may be that on the stage his work is three-quarters dead.' . . .

It cannot be too often repeated that the true test of a dramatist is his effectiveness, or his continuing effectiveness, on the stage. Racine's critics were not suggesting that owing to a lean period among the *sociétaires* of the Comédie Française Racine should be given a rest. They were saying that though he had undoubted merits as a poet, the plays themselves were no longer actable, that they should be removed permanently from the theatre to the study, that Racine should in fact be treated like Robert Garnier, the great sixteenth-century writer, whose works are almost certainly no longer actable because they are dramatic poems rather than plays.

The thesis I am going to defend is that when properly performed, Racine is still the greatest French tragic dramatist and that the pronouncements of the critics from Montherlant to Barthes and Dutourd are perfect examples of Mauriac's problem of *access*.

One way of tackling the problem is to take a look at Racine's imagery. The setting of eight of the tragedies is a palace. In *Athalie* it is a temple with a palace not far away; in *Alexandre* and *Iphigenie* a military camp. This means that at the start of nine of the tragedies we, the public, find ourselves metaphorically speaking outside a stately building, separated by a formidable array of masonry from a world which, as one critic put it, does seem 'far from us'. Our job is to secure 'access' to the palaces and the temple, to find out what is going on behind those walls and to merge ourselves in palace life. Racine himself provides a clue—we might almost call it a 'pass'—in the opening scenes of three of the plays.

In *Bérénice* Antiochus says to his confidant:

> Arrêtons un moment. La pompe de ces lieux,
> Je le vois bien, Arsace, est nouvelle à tes yeux.

In *Bajazet* the vizir asks his confidant to follow him into the palace and report on the mission he has just completed. The confidant replies:

> Et depuis quand, Seigneur, entre-t-on dans ces lieux
> Dont l'*accès* était même interdit à nos yeux?

Finally, in *Esther* the queen's confidant says to her mistress:

> De ce palais j'ai su trouver l'entrée.
> O spectacle! O *triomphe* admirable à mes yeux,
> Digne en effet du bras qui sauva nos aïeux!

In each of the plays a person who knows the way round introduces a confidant or servant into a palace which is totally unknown to him or her. Their reactions are different. In *Bérénice* the accent falls on novelty and grandeur; in *Bajazet* on the difficulties and dangers of 'access'; in *Esther* on the staggering sight which greets the confidant's eyes.

In every case it is an ordinary person who is admitted or finds a way into the palace and is confronted by what seems an entirely new mode of life. That is the position of the audience. It is not enough to watch a production of Racine as though it were a faintly remote spectacle and cavil at the way in which it is mounted. We have to identify ourselves with the newcomer, follow him into the palace, listen to the explanation that the guide offers, which is Racine's exposition, and then see for ourselves.

The moment we enter we are conscious of a marked change of atmosphere. We have somehow been translated to a different plane. On the surface everything looks, sounds, feels different from the world we know. Next, we have the contradictory feeling that life in the palace has a strange dualism about it. It is at once very unlike and very like our world: unlike because of the setting; like because of the human frailty of its occupants. We are aware from the first of an almost suffocating tension in the air combined with a desperate effort to maintain some sort of control which frequently breaks down. The tension is pervasive;

it is also contagious. It is the atmosphere which produces fascinating and frightening revelations about human nature—about ourselves. It is only by surrendering to it that we gain psychological as well as physical access to Racine's world and that we come to share his vision.

The palaces vary considerably in style. Three are Greek, two Roman, three oriental. They have one thing in common. There is something of the prison about them. We have the impression that the community is somehow confined within their walls, that while 'access' may be difficult, once you are in it is almost impossible to get out again. The sense of confinement is partly psychological, but in some of the palaces we shall find that one or two members of the community are literally prisoners. Some of the palaces are more disturbing than others. They are huge, dark, claustrophobic. They give the occupants the alarming impression that they are constantly being watched, that their lives are in danger and that disaster may overtake them at any moment.

The situation of the palaces is important. Four of them stand by the sea; most of the others are within reasonable distance of it. One of the palaces looks out on a sunlit sea which seems, tantalizingly, to beckon to the prisoners, inviting them to abandon their troubles, to leave the claustrophobic palace and enjoy freedom in the open air—to live instead of to languish. In another we hear the waves beating, a trifle ominously, against the walls of the building. In still another the waves merely 'lap' against the palace walls. The occupants of most of the palaces are acutely aware of the proximity of the sea. They mention it repeatedly in their conversation; their language contains what on the face of it appears to be a surprising number of nautical images. There are references to storms at sea, to shipwrecks, to people flinging themselves or being flung into the sea and drowning, and in one instance to a phenomenal calm at sea which actually determines the unfolding of the drama. At the same time their attitude is decidedly ambivalent. The sea does, indeed, offer a prospect of escape from their prison and their troubles, but in their heart of hearts they know that it is an illusion, that the hope will never be realized, or if it is their escape will turn out to be not freedom but separation from the loved one, or they themselves will be dead by the time their henchmen, who have survived a palace massacre, make a bolt by way of the sea.

If the prospect of escape is an illusion, there is nothing illusory about the threat from the sea. It is in a sense a two-way traffic. For practical purposes the outward journey is never accomplished; the inward journey from the sea invariably is. It is the sea which brings all sorts of people to the palace who have a dangerous and disrupting effect on life inside: the outsider posing as an ambassador who provokes disaster; the return of a tyrannical father, reported missing believed dead; the murderous slave who stabs nearly every occupant of the palace to death.

It is time to turn from the buildings to their inmates.

The palaces are royal in every sense. The inhabitants are for the most part kings, queens, princes, princesses, and their retainers. The structure of society is a simple one. There are strictly speaking only two classes: masters and servants, the rulers and the ruled, royalty and 'the people'. Yet the combination of the two, as we shall see, plays an important part in the development of the drama.

We are not merely inside a palace; we are at court. The court is a small one. There are two or three people belonging to the same family. They are joined on occasion by some one from outside: a prince seeking the hand of one of the royal daughters, or a princess who is betrothed to a member of the family as well as by the dangerous outsiders and unwanted relatives who arrive by sea.

The protocol plays a large and important part in the life of the court. The members know one another intimately, but their deportment strikes the visitor as curious. Parents, to be sure, address their children familiarly except when a monarch loses his temper and switches from 'enfant' to 'Prince'. So do brothers and sisters. In a moment of euphoria a young man may call his girl 'Belle Monime!' Or an angry woman may scrap all titles and simply call the man who has rebuffed her by his name. In most other cases, whether they are husband and wife, engaged couples or simply servants speaking to masters and mistresses, they use, or begin by using, the standard form of address: 'Seigneur', 'Madame', 'Prince', 'Princesse'.

This sounds at first like mere convention. In these palaces it is a good deal more. It is a sign of the occupants' status certainly; it is also a sign of their state of mind from moment to moment. It serves to some extent as a safety device. As long as the standard forms of address are in use the speakers retain some degree of control over their emotions. When they go, everything goes. They are in fact the life line. The life line snaps. This produces the tragedy.

It is obvious from the moment we enter the building that this is no ordinary day in the life of the palace, that we have arrived in the middle of a major crisis. As we watch the expressions on the faces of the occupants and listen to what they are saying, we realize that they are intelligent, civilized, sensitive, perceptive, but that they are also incredibly highly strung, 'touchy' in the extreme. They are visibly making prodigious efforts to control themselves, to maintain some sort of balance, but the artificial restraint does nothing to diminish the growing tension. It simply intensifies to an almost unheard of degree the violence of the outbursts and the final explosions when they come.

There are only two people in the room: a young prince and his father's middle-aged confidant. The prince is telling the confidant that he has just heard that the army of the king, his father, has been routed by the Romans and the king himself killed in the battle. He goes on to speak of his bad relations with his half-brother who is suspected of plotting a sell-out to Rome. It is the first news of the family feud which is characteristic of palace life. Then comes the most serious thing of all which the prince describes, significantly, as his 'secret'. He is deeply in love with his father's youthful fiancée and believes that the treacherous half-brother is after her too. The prince suddenly catches sight of the fiancée and hurriedly dismisses the confidant. She has in fact come to enlist his help against his half-brother who is 'importuning' her. This is too much for the prince who plunges into a declaration of love. The half-brother joins them. The argument begins. Then the fiancée's confidant rushes breathlessly into the room with the worst news of all. The king is not dead. He had just landed at the port—'come in from the sea'. All three are badly shaken. The fiancée and her confidant depart, leaving the half-brothers to discuss the situation. The potential traitor proposes a pact. He gets no response. They leave. The fiancée returns with her confidant and proceeds to disclose her 'secret'. She is in love with the young prince. They leave. The king makes his entry with his two sons. He sends them away and remains alone with his confidant. He explains that he is still desperately in love with his betrothed. He is suspicious of his sons' attitude and questions the confidant. The confidant ducks. The fiancée reappears. During our day at the palace we shall find that after several meetings the king very basely tricks her into revealing her 'secret'.

This sets the pattern and the pace. The word 'secret' is on everybody's lips. Nearly everyone has something to hide from some one else. The 'secrets', as we can see, are concerned with love and politics. They divide the community into factions, into pursuers and pursued, aggressors and victims.

The attempts of one party to hide and the other to discover its 'secrets' determine the pace of palace life. The palace is a hive of activity. The occupants are perpetually on the move. There are continual comings and goings: meetings, encounters, separations. Racine's casts are small. It is unusual for more than three of the principal characters to be present at the same time and this only happens occasionally. For the most part the activity consists of a rapid succession of couples, sometimes with and sometimes without their confidants: unhappy meetings of thwarted lovers; stormy encounters between pursuers and pursued; furious clashes between 'rivals'. They are interspersed with conversations between individuals and their confidants. Voices drop to a murmur as a problem is debated by a young man and a young woman, or by lovers and their confidants. Suddenly a voice rises in anguish or ends in a scream. With every meeting the crisis gathers momentum.

Although there is nothing comparable to the conferences which take place in the Cornelian palaces with most of the court assembled, some meetings are rather more formal than others. A king is receiving an ambassador or outlining plans for a military campaign. On other occasions a speaker makes highly provocative or even deeply wounding remarks, but though the people to whom they are addressed may be twitching with rage the situation is governed by the protocol. They do not interrupt; they hear him out and hold their fire until he has had his say.

These occasions bring home to the visitor one important point. There is a basic language which is common to all the inhabitants of the palaces. It is simple, measured, dignified or, to borrow an expression used by Valbuena Prat of one of the Spanish seventeenth-century dramatists, it is the 'sober, elevated palace style'. It provides a background which underlines and throws into relief the contrast between the formal meetings and those scenes in which disappointed lovers and angry rivals let their hair well and truly down. For the meetings between the couples are usually highly emotional. That is the crux of the matter. It is not only what people say that counts; it is the tone in which it is said: the voice that goes straight to the heart and does more than almost anything to involve the visitor in the life of the palace. And here one might interject that one of the most important qualifications for the Racinian actor or actress is a rich, strong, vibrant voice. The content of the speech naturally determines the tone, but speaking for myself it is the tone that finally 'gets' me.

The palaces are massive; there are long winding corridors with innumerable rooms leading off them. But we, the visitors, are only admitted to a single room. The whole of the drama is concentrated inside it. In that one room every major decision is taken or, if not, it is duly reported there. Equally, almost every word of importance is spoken in our hearing and before our eyes. The drama is an internal one. What interests us most is what is happening inside the occupants' minds and comes out in their speech. Except for an occasional suicide, there is properly speak-

A scene from a Comédie-Française production of Mithridate.

ing no action in the room: no duels or only furious verbal duels and threats; no lovemaking; simply word and gesture. At the same time, we are aware that the room, or more accurately, the palace, is a world within a world which it is trying to dominate. We hear people talking about 'the empire', 'the world' and even 'the universe'. Messengers come hurrying in and deliver terrifying reports of actions taking place in the outside world or in a distant part of the palace. A king has been assassinated; a lover has been done to death in a different room, or a mistress has committed suicide on the steps of an altar where her lover married a rival; rebellion by the army or the people is imminent. The message is nearly always: 'All is lost'.

Confinement to a single room contributes enormously to the claustrophobic atmosphere and greatly increases the tensions. There is no relaxation, or if there is it is illusory and a prelude to a vast storm. There is no escape either from pursuers who have a nasty way of turning up at precisely the wrong moment and finding a 'rival' slumped at the girl's feet. When they have discovered, or think they have discovered, the other party's 'secret' they denounce their behaviour in the most violent terms. This is the signal for an explosion.

The explosions are frequent, sudden, complete. The protocol goes by the board, producing an extraordinary contrast between past dignity and present violence. The last vestiges of civilized deportment vanish. There are no titles, only savage denunciation or agonized protest, or both. The Words 'perfide', 'infidèle', 'traître' and 'barbare' echo and re-echo all over the palace. There are switches from the polite 'vous' to the bitingly contemptuous 'tu'. The language of the courtier is replaced by the harangues of the fishwife. The ferocious denunciation turns into a verbal battle which will end in murder or suicide. The aggressors, who are not invariably male, behave like wild beasts determined to drag the victims into bed, or failing that, to tear them to pieces. The victims of the male aggressors are distraught women staggering through the rooms of the palace or falling to the ground and describing themselves as 'égarées' and 'éperdues'.

The contrast between the outward dignity of palace life and the ferocious passions unleashed is so extraordinary, the ending with reports of violent deaths pouring in and the sight of principals who have poisoned or stabbed themselves to death, intensified in one instance by the ranting of a madman, that we feel slightly dazed, wondering how it could all have happened, how people could have got themselves into quite such a mess. It is not difficult to explain. At the root of most of the trouble is the erotic instinct. A loves B who is in love with C who returns his or her love. This form of triangle is basic in palace life. We can anticipate by saying that A is usually the aggressor, B and C the victims. A father, as we have seen, returns defeated from the wars to find that not one, but both his sons are in love with his betrothed. An emperor is sick of his unexciting wife whom he was forced to marry against his will for political reasons, and is carried away by his half-brother's fiancée. He murders the half-

brother and the fiancée takes the veil. A sultana is tired of being bedded by a lecherous sultan and is madly in love with the sultan's half-brother who is in love with his childhood sweetheart. She has the man murdered, is murdered herself by the sultan's slave and the girl commits suicide. Another father returns from a womanizing expedition to discover after endless misunderstandings that his wife has tried unsuccessfully to seduce her stepson and is nearly mad with jealousy because the stepson, too, has fallen for another girl. In still another case A loves B who is in love with C, but is prevented from marrying him by Roman law. This does for the lot of them as completely as the dagger or the poison cup.

Although the origins of several of the tragedies are sexual there is a close connection between public and private interests. Royalty are never free agents. They have naturally enough a public as well as a private role and their private actions have public repercussions. Unless the individual is subordinated to the public personage, there is bound to be trouble. The union of A and B or B and C may be open to moral, political or legal objections, or to all three. When the objections are disregarded, as they usually are, the consequences are catastrophic. They create divisions in public and private life. There is a danger of uprisings by the army or the people and of the awakening of homicidal impulses in the family, producing the family feud. War is often in the air. In one case the enemy is actually advancing on the capital in order to capture the monarch and probably to burn his palace to the ground. The sexual rivalry of a father and son leads to civil war with father and son on opposite sides. In another play there is a danger of a war which was supposed to be over and done with breaking out afresh, or of a preventive civil war to put a stop to it. In still another a sultan has defeated a foreign enemy and is on his way back home in order to put down a palace revolution only to find, on arrival, that the family feud has done the job for him.

It is evident that the crisis is caused mainly by the fact that, whatever the cost and even if it means that everybody will perish in the process, A is absolutely determined to get B. That is where the confidants come in.

Racine's confidants have been sweepingly dismissed as faceless individuals only fit to run errands, deliver messages and try to comfort masters and mistresses. This might be a possible comment on Corneille for the simple reason that his protagonists are usually too tough morally to need the sort of help confidants can offer. It cannot be accepted without considerable reservations in the case of Racine. It is true that some of his confidants are nonentities, but others have an important role. Although they are all born into the same class there are sub-divisions. A number have risen from the ranks, become commanders, governors or advisers to their masters. A few are more complex than the rest and look like projections of their masters' and mistresses' good and bad impulses. The bad confidants encourage the protagonists' weaknesses and hasten the disaster. The good ones adopt a much more positive attitude. They are simple people partly no doubt because the structure of the tragedies does not leave room for the elaborate characterization of confidants even if it were desirable, but mainly because what Racine needed in these parts were simple, honest, clearsighted, down-to-earth people. The right kind of confidant is the one who is class-conscious in a wholly laudatory sense, who sees himself as the representative of 'the people' and does his best to protect their interests against the vagaries of royalty. These confidants stand for common sense; they take an objective view of the situation; they weigh the pros and cons; they know which path the master ought to take and do everything they can to convince him of it. The fact that they nearly always fail is immaterial. It is they who help to provide a balance—the balance found in a single individual in Corneille—and enable us to see the actions of the protagonists in their true perspective.

We can perhaps summarize the function of the palaces in this way. They are not simply impersonal buildings which provide a setting for the tragedy or mere status symbols of the occupants. They represent a particular order. The drama centres round the fortunes of this order. It is in control at the beginning of the play, but its fate varies from one play to another and is of critical importance. In some plays it is preserved; in others it is destroyed. In others still there is a conflict between two orders which ends in the destruction of one and its replacement by the other.

The drama centred on order naturally has an immediate impact on the inmates of the palace and is largely responsible for dividing them into parties or factions: those who are trying to maintain the existing order and those who are trying to escape from its clutches or replace it by another order. I have said that there is something of the prison about the palaces, that their effect is partly physical and partly psychological. The inmates not only suffer from a sense of confinement; the palaces often isolate, and in some cases insulate, them from everyday life, cut them off from 'the people'. That is why many of them get their values so badly wrong and why I have emphasized the importance of the confidants.

The occupants are continually using a group of words expressing their sense of confinement: 'captif', 'captive', 'esclave', 'dompter', 'fers', 'lier', 'piège', 'joug', 'noeud'. They are the 'prisoners', 'captives' or 'slaves' of an order or a régime. In many cases they are equally the 'captives' or 'slaves' of their own impulses or the impulses of other people. They get caught in 'traps', are forced to submit to a 'yoke', are bound by 'fetters' or a 'knot'. Release is impossible unless they manage to dodge the 'trap', shed the 'yoke', or cut the 'knot'.

This shapes the action which on occasion takes the form of a palace intrigue or a palace revolution. 'Secret' is also one of a recurring group of words: 'cacher', 'dissimuler', 'déguisement', 'feindre', 'tromper', 'artifice', 'stratagème'. The drama is taken up with the attempts of the aggressors to wrest their victims' 'secrets' from them and the victims' efforts to safeguard their rights by preserving their 'secrets'. In order to do so they are obliged at times to resort to the same subterfuges—the 'artifices' and 'stratagèmes'—as the aggressors. This adds up to a desperate attempt to shed the 'yoke', cut the 'knot' or simply to 'escape'. 'Fuir' and its variants are used 165 times in the plays. They usually stand for frustration and failure. And that spells death and disaster, or at best a refuge in the sanctuary of the Vestal Virgins after the aggressor has poisoned your beloved.

I want to take a closer look at what I have called the erotic instinct. I was once scolded by an academic for speaking of the references to 'bed' in Racine. The truth of the matter is that he is a sexier writer than appears on the surface. He suffered from the inhibiting effect of the *bienséances* which left French dramatists with much less freedom than their English and Spanish contemporaries or even than contemporary French authors of prose fiction. It applies particularly to Spanish dramatists who did not mind a rape or two or a stepmother actually bedding her stepson though the penalties admittedly were devastating. It would no doubt be an exaggeration to describe *Bajazet* as Racine's X Certificate play, but he came as near in it as he dared to writing a sex play. He was still a long way off as we can see by comparing it with one of his sources—the novelist Segrais' story, 'Floridon ou L'Amour imprudent'. And whatever Louis XIV's relations with Marie Mancini, I always goggle at the idea of that five years' courtship in *Bérénice* without a single go!

Discussion of the erotic instinct brings us to some of the differences between Corneille and Racine. Corneille, as we know, was a pupil of the Jesuits, Racine a pupil of the Jansenists. There is a tendency at present to play down the influence of Jansenism on Racine's work. This seems to me to be a mistake. Jansenism was much more a matter of atmosphere than of doctrine. The Jesuits laid great stress on free-will. Jansenist teaching was strongly coloured by the Lutheran teaching on original sin. The Fall had led to the complete ruin of human nature which was incapable of any good action without the direct intervention of divine grace. The Jansenists also leaned towards the doctrine of predestination. This added to the gloom, but it fitted in quite neatly with the conception of destiny in those of Racine's plays which were Greek in inspiration.

Corneille's protagonists are fighters. They use their will power to the full in withstanding the ravages of original sin. When faced with a moral dilemma they stand back, take stock and decide on the right course of action. Even if they lose their lives in the process they end up as better men than they started. They have experienced the moment of truth: the transcendental moment when they see what they must do and know that they have the moral strength to do it. In Corneille the conflict is purgatorial: in Racine it is plain hell. The drama opens with the proverbial *coup de foudre*. A man catches sight of a girl or a girl of a man. The damage is done. They are predestined to disaster from that very moment. They at once become the victims of an irresistible impulse which sends them down the dizzy slope to destruction. The dagger or the poison cup which ends their lives is no more than consummation on the *physical* plane of the total ruin which has already taken place on the *psychological* plane.

This has sometimes created the impression that the conflict in Racine is not a moral conflict, but simply a clash of personalities who are determined to batter the beloved into submission or smash a rival. The short answer is that if this were so Racine would not be the master that he is. Violence is endemic in his work; there are times when will power scarcely seems to exist and his principal characters are certainly people of extremes. It does not mean that they are unaware of what they are doing or are devoid of all moral scruples. It depends on the nature of the erotic impulse.

We can best approach it by way of Corneille's celebrated pronouncement in the dedication of *La Place Royale:*

> It was from you that I learnt that the love of a decent man (*honnête homme*) should always be voluntary; that we must never let things reach a stage at which we cannot stop loving; that if we go as far as that love becomes a tyranny whose yoke must be cast off; and that lastly, the person whom we love has much more reason to be grateful for our love when it is the result of our choice and her merit than when it comes from blind inclination (*inclination aveugle*).

Although the dedication was published two years before Racine was born, our reaction is obvious. It sounds, we say, like a commentary on Racine. It is a forthright statement of the 'rules' of love. Corneille's own greatness depends on the fact that his finest characters never fail to keep them; Racine's on the fact that his seldom fail to break them. We must, however, distinguish. I have spoken so far as though there were only one kind of love in Racine. This is not so. There is the frantic passion of the aggressors and the moderate and reasonable love of the victims. For simplicity therefore I shall call the first 'passion' and the second 'love'.

With this reservation, we may fairly describe the dedication as an intriguing account of Racinian passion. A number of phrases leap to the eye: 'voluntary', 'tyranny', 'cast off the yoke', 'blind inclination', as well as the references to 'choice' and the 'merit' of the loved one. In Racine passion is never 'voluntary'; it is always 'tyrannical'; the characters never manage to 'cast off the yoke'; it is invariably a 'blind inclination' which is never the result of reasoned 'choice' or the 'merit' of the beloved. Corneille's characters announce the victory of 'reason' over 'inclination'; Racine its total defeat. This is Corneille:

> Une femme d'honneur peut avouer sans honte
> Ces surprises des sens que la raison surmonte;
> Ce n'est qu'en ces assauts qu'éclate la vertu,
> Et l'on doute d'un coeur qui n'a point combattu.
>   (*Polyeucte*, I, 3)

> Ma raison, il est vrai, dompte mes sentiments;
> Mais quelque autorité que sur eux elle ait prise,
>   Elle n'y règne pas, elle les tyrannise;

> Et quoique le dehors soit sans émotion,
> Le dedans n'est que trouble et que sédition.
>   (*Polyeucte*, II, 2)

This is Racine:

> Puisqu'après tant d'efforts ma résistance est
>   vaine,
> Je me livre en aveugle au destin qui m'entraîne.
>   (***Andromaque,*** I, 1)

> Je me suis engagé trop avant.
> Je vois que la raison cède à la violence.
>   (***Phèdre***, II, 2)

There are people who regard the moral conflict in Corneille with a certain degree of scepticism. What I want to stress here is its power and its authenticity. There is nothing facile or mechanical about it, no conventional adulation of 'reason'. In Corneille 'reason' is the faculty which imposes order and preserves the unity of the person. For Pauline its workings are decidedly painful as we can see from the contrast between the verbs 'régner' and 'tyranniser'. She is outwardly calm, but her mind is in a state of turmoil. In the present context—she is speaking to Sévère—'trouble' has a sexual undertone, but it is widely used and is a comparatively mild word. It is followed by the strong word, 'sédition', which matches 'tyrannise'. It will be observed that Pauline sees the conflict in political terms as a conflict between public and private interest. 'Reason' has to operate 'tyrannically' and repress by force an uprush of the senses which in moral terms are trying to violate the rights of the husband in favour of a rival and are therefore 'seditious'. The accent falls finally on words signifying victory: 'surmonte' and 'dompte'. In the passages from ***Andromaque*** and ***Phèdre*** the words 'livre', emphasized by 'aveugle' and 'cède', are the sign not merely of defeat, but of a rout. Corneille's characters accept 'reason' as a necessary discipline however painful its operation: the attitude of Racine's is usually one of unqualified hostility:

> Pylade, je suis las d'écouter la raison.

> Tant de raisonnements offensent ma colère.
>   (***Andromaque***, III, 1; IV, 3)

Although Racine's characters are inclined to treat 'reason' as an exasperating obstacle which keeps them out of the beloved's bed, it will be apparent that in both Racine and Corneille the conflict is basically the same: a conflict between public and private interests or between personal inclination and the rights of another human being. The difference lies in the result and there it is absolute.

The position becomes clearer still when we look at two other sets of words. They are 'trouble', 'agité', 'inquiet', 'transport', 'désordre', 'égaré', 'éperdu' and their opposites: 'repos', 'tranquillité', 'douceur', 'clarté', 'bornes', 'ordre'. They represent the two ways of life which offer themselves to the protagonists. For Corneille once again they are a positive goal. The use of the verbs 'surmonter', 'dompter', and in another place 'vaincre', show that it is not only attainable, but has been attained. In Racine the first set of words is the reality, the second the mirage.

Two of the lines I have quoted from *Polyeucte* deserve a second look:

> Ce n'est qu'en ces assauts qu'éclate la vertu,
> Et l'on doute d'un coeur qui n'a point combattu.

In spite of its painfulness, Pauline welcomes the conflict because it puts her to the test and demonstrates her integrity. This explains the difference in the moral weight of the words 'vertu', 'honneur' and 'gloire' in the two dramatists. In Corneille the victory of 'vertu' is a sign of 'honneur' or personal integrity which leads to 'gloire' or a public reputation for moral integrity. Except when used of victory on the battlefield, Racine's 'gloire' is a much more personal and much less moral affair, really amounting to little more than self-esteem. Racine's characters are very sensitive to their reputations which means that on occasion they are prepared to sacrifice 'vertu' to something which is no more than keeping up appearances, however deceptive. So we have Oenone's advice to Phèdre:

> pour sauver notre honneur combattu,
> Il faut immoler tout, et même la vertu.

When we come to **Bérénice,** we shall find that even when reason or will power appears to triumph, the effects are destructive. We are back at the formula I once used in another place. Corneille's characters are people *qui se construisent,* Racine's people *qui se défont.* Corneille's moment of truth is matched in Racine by the moment of disintegration when the character begins to have doubts about his identity.

I have drawn a distinction between the 'passion' of the protagonists and the 'love' of the young couples who are sometimes known as the *jeunes premiers.* Although their love is doomed to disaster through the intervention of the protagonists, they stand for a virtuous and a balanced love which if satisfied would bring happiness without harming the rights of anybody. They have an obvious and a close link with the more impressive confidants. They provide perspective and contrast; they show that tragedy could have been avoided if the protagonists had possessed the same restraint, the same respect for the given word as themselves.

The reason why innocent love is only satisfied in two or the plays is explained by the word 'tyranny'. The protagonists, too, are convinced that success in love will bring them happiness, but their obsession has reached such an extreme degree that they are faced with the choice between union with the victim of their passion or death. Their peculiar helplessness in the throes of a passion which has turned into a malady is evident in one of Pyrrhus's pronouncements:

> Je meurs si je vous perds, mais je meurs si
>   j'attends.

The tyranny is twofold. The protagonists suffer from the tyranny of a passion which they are powerless to resist. It is because of their anguish that they themselves become tyrants. The word 'blackmail' has been used by more than one critic. In five of the plays A, whether a man or a woman, is a tyrant who is determined to blackmail B into breaking off relations with C and marrying him or her. The blackmailer holds the carrot, usually a crown, in one hand, and the dagger or the poison cup in the other. There is Néron's ultimatum to Junie which is disguised as an offer:

> ne préférez point, à la solide gloire
> Des honneurs dont César prétend vous revêtir,
> La gloire d'un refus, sujet au repentir.

And when the unhappy Junie does precisely that Britannicus is handed the poison cup in the guise of a 'loving cup'.

The tragedy is the outcome of impassioned individuals who break all the rules, brush aside morality, the law, the claims of State and the rights of fellow human beings certainly; it is equally the outcome of the determination of the victims to preserve their integrity, to fulfil their pledges, to remain in a literal sense 'faithful unto death'.

I must return now to the criticisms that I mentioned at the outset and attempt a more specific assessment of Racine's relevance for the present age. They amount to two main charges, neither of them particularly original. The first is that Racine's tragedies are simply a reflection of seventeenth-century life, that his metaphorically periwigged figures are anachronisms and that his psychology is out of date. The second is that the rules of classical drama were so rigorous and so artificial that even if what he said were relevant, communication, at any rate on the stage, has become impossible.

Nobody doubts any longer that like Corneille Racine was very much a man of his time. One critic has gone to extreme lengths in trying to discover 'originals' for virtually every character in the secular plays except the confidants. There have been others who sought to establish a connection between the action of some of the plays and political events such as the English Revolution. I am not convinced myself that this kind of speculation does much to increase our appreciation of Racine's art, but it helps to situate him. No writer can be indifferent to contemporary events which even in a classical period are bound to leave some impression on his work or possibly provide him with inspiration. We shall see in due course that in some of the plays there are tributes to Louis XIV, and that **Bérénice** probably contains a reference to an early love affair, but we shall also see that the importance of the age is somewhat different.

What seems to me to matter is less the events and personalities than the ethos in which Racine lived and wrote. It is a change of ethos which goes a long way towards explaining the celebrated rivalry between Corneille and Racine and the differences in their work. Corneille's first masterpieces are heroic plays in the strict sense. One of the reasons for the failure, or comparative failure, of the plays of the middle period is that the heroic age was past, and that in trying to go on writing heroic plays Corneille was writing against the grain of the new age. It was a belated recognition of the situation which led to a changed approach, to what is known as 'the eclipse of the hero', in the last plays of all which show a move in the direction of Racine. Now Racine was the product of an unheroic age which is reflected in nearly all his plays from the first one to the last. There are no heroes in them in the Cornelian sense for the simple reason that, as I have said, one of his principal themes is the frailty of human nature. The ruler is always a tyrant; the society is aristocratic; there is a contrast between the polished surface and the internal corruption; the disaster is the result of the predatory designs of the tyrant. This was no doubt an accurate picture of the periods in which the tragedies are set; it is certainly a fair picture of Racine's own age. We may as well call things by their names. Racine lived under an absolute monarchy which was the seventeenth-century equivalent of the modern dictatorship; he moved in aristocratic circles; there was the same startling contrast between the outward splendour of 'the Golden Age' and its inner weaknesses and corruption. It was the century of unhappy love, the *mariage de raison* which so often went wrong with the most unfortunate consequences. Louis XIV himself is a good example. As a young man he was compelled for political reasons to abandon his projected marriage to Marie Mancini. It is a fair inference that if he had been in a position to decide for himself he would have done nothing of the sort, but would have set out to get the girl with the same ruthless determination, the same disregard of everybody else's interests as a Racinian protagonist. This was followed by the spectacle of a neglected queen weeping alone in her room; La Vallière departing in tears to a convent; the arrival of Mme de Montespan, a woman with the mentality of a Roxane; her eventual dismissal and replacement by the prudish Mme de Maintenon. There is one other resemblance between Louis and the Racinian protagonists. The Bourbons were a notoriously highly sexed family. In his later years the king still insisted on two goes a day with his morganatic spouse. She got no comfort when she complained to her confessors about the monarch's 'excessive demand'. They told her bluntly that she was bound to perform her wifely duties in order to prevent her husband from indulging in still more adulterous associations.

The parallels between past and present draw attention to one of the more curious contradictions between the man and the writer. From the first the ambitious young man set out to cultivate the king. When he abandoned the theatre to become one of the royal historiographers, he also became one of the most obsequious of courtiers. Although it was no doubt unconscious, it can hardly have been accidental that four of the plays are attacks on the kind of regime under which he was living. In **Britannicus** a tyrannical order is strengthened; in **Bajazet** it is preserved, and in **Mithridate** it is destroyed. We shall find that in **Athalie** he goes furthest of all. With the help of religion he not only delivers his most vigorous attack on

despotism; he exposes the inherent dangers of absolute power.

One of the principal claims made by and for classical periods is *finality*. The writers are convinced that they see humanity *sub specie aeternitatis,* that it is basically unchanging and that what they see remains true for succeeding generations. There is a good deal of substance in the view that it was precisely because Racine was so much a man of his time that he was able to concentrate on aspects which are valid for all time. His contemporaries were right in arguing that his characters were not Greeks or Romans or Turks, but Frenchmen. They were wrong in holding it against him. The greatness of his work depends not only on his findings, but on the way in which they are integrated into their environment, on the matching of the inner and the outer man. Although integration is an artistic essential, we must recognize that the vision of a great writer transcends time. When we look into it, we can see that his interests and the reactions of his characters are remarkably like our own and would be the same if they found themselves in the twentieth century. What he shows bears an uncomfortable resemblance to the happenings of the present age: ruthless dictatorships; the horrors of wars in which all human standards go by the board; conflicts between public and private interests, between the desires of the individual and the rights of a fellow human being which today are consistently leading to murder and suicide; the spread of violence to every walk of life.

We have seen something of the workings of the erotic instinct in his work. Now the French theory of the *femme fatale* is not entirely moonshine. We have to admit, if we are honest with ourselves, that whatever our beliefs or principles, there exists somewhere in the world a man or a woman who would be fatal to *us,* would send us straight off the rails and make us behave in much the same fashion as Racine's protagonists if we had the misfortune to meet him or her as Racine's protagonists always do.

We must take a closer look at what might be called individual psychology. I mean by this, particular characters, the way in which they appear to us and the interpretations we put on them today. We must do so because the claim to universal validity is not restricted to Racine or to France. The criticisms I have been discussing could be, in some cases have been, applied to other dramatists in other countries; to Shakespeare in England, to Lope de Vega and Calderón in Spain.

Although she apparently supports the claim to universal validity, Annie Ubersfeld has observed in an illuminating essay on **Andromaque** that Pyrrhus is a seventeenth-century monarch and Hermione a seventeenth-century princess, and thinks that it would be difficult to envisage them in any other capacity. This was not exactly the view of the great Louis Jouvet. Here is what he said about Junie to one of the girls—her name was Viviane—attending his practical acting course at the Paris Conservatoire in 1939:

The characters of the classics are whatever one likes

to make of them. According to the period, Junie has been a young virgin martyr, a young Christian, a young republican. *A character in one of the classics is a revolving lighthouse.* It all depends where you happen to be standing in relation to the lighthouse; you are caught by certain flashes which light you up. Junie will touch you by flashes which are sensitive and human and which you will receive from the character because you are you, Viviane.

The same might be said of Shakespeare. Hamlet is a seventeenth-century prince, an intellectual, an Elizabethan melancholic whose melancholy incidentally (metaphysics apart) has affinities with Oreste's. Without going so far as the late Ernest Jones, it is not difficult to see him as a twentieth-century neurotic with a touch of the Oedipus complex which wrecks his relations with poor Ophelia. Whichever way we look at him, his soliloquies do not cease to grip. And think of the interest the French took in him in the nineteenth century. What again could be more 'modern' than Shakespeare's Achilles in *Troilus and Cressida,* or more horrifying than the 'stratagem' he uses to defeat the gallant Hector in the field—an all-time dirty trick? . . .

The conclusion I reach is that in the case of the masters the claim to universal validity is justified and that it is precisely this which distinguishes the true master from the lesser figures: Shakespeare from a Webster or a Tourneur; Pierre Corneille and Racine from a Thomas Corneille or a Quinault.

The second criticism of Racine is a matter of pure artistic judgement. If one critic can only find an aggregate of twenty-seven lines of poetry in the whole of the plays; if another thinks that 99 per cent of the verse in **Bajazet** is rhetoric and only 1 per cent poetry, we are bound to suspect that they have failed signally to secure 'access'. But since these views have been expressed by sensitive and intelligent people, they cannot be dismissed out of hand. An attempt must be made to answer them briefly in general terms.

There is one factor which cannot be too strongly emphasized. Racine displays enormous skill in placing his characters in a virtually impossible situation which is a combination of temperament and circumstance. It is impossible in the sense that none of the characters can extricate themselves from it and live happy, peaceful lives without inflicting irreparable damage on other characters. The basic situation explains the immense impact of the greatest of the tragedies when properly presented to the right audience. It can only be communicated because the other qualities of the work match the dramatist's genius in devising the basic situation.

Although it is necessary for the purpose of analysis and appreciation to discuss versification, language, structure and psychology separately, the end-product naturally depends on a very close synthesis of all these elements. Versification and language are largely responsible for the formality which is characteristic of palace life. Together

they have the effect of raising tragedy to the special plane which is proper to it. Structure, which is the method of presenting situations dramatically, is necessarily of the first importance: it makes or mars the play. Lytton Strachey once remarked that the technique of Elizabethan drama had been taken over by the novelists and that Racine's technique had been adopted by modern playwrights. Comparisons between Racine and modern dramatists must not be pushed too far, particularly as Strachey's comment was made nearly sixty years ago, but in substance it is correct. Racine's genius enabled him to turn even the rule of the three unities to his advantage. The essence of the tragedies is their intense concentration on emotional states. For this he relies on simplicity of action, tightness of structure—the way in which one scene leads to another, in which they fit into one another, contrast with or are parallel to one another, in which words and phrases from different scenes echo and answer one another—and above all the *speed* with which the drama unfolds, the couples come and go, which explains why Racine unlike Corneille is now always performed without an interval, as he should be. We are near boiling point at the start; we are carried along by the rising temperature and gathering momentum until we reach the tremendous ending.

It is hardly surprising in an age like our own that critics have tended to dwell on the psychology of his characters and to treat him primarily as a master psychologist. Their view has recently been attacked by Raymond Picard. 'The psychological depth which is commonly admired in Racine', he writes, 'is to a large extent an optical illusion.' This does not or should not mean that Racine's psychology is shallow or that the findings of a psychoanalytical critic like Charles Mauron are necessarily wrong. It simply means that the form of classic tragedy inevitably precluded a minute and leisurely examination of the characters' psychology and that the dramatist was mainly confined to the basic human emotions. Although Baudelaire once spoke of 'the power of Racinian analysis' the truth is that, as I have said in other places, there is no such thing in Racine as analysis. His characters do not brood over their feelings, argue about them, take them to pieces. Their discoveries are the result of intuition, the sudden insights into their own and other people's minds. The expression of emotion is spontaneous and immediate. It is something like 'instant' emotion: the direct presentation of the basic impulses unencumbered by the kind of detail that we find in the psychological novel. What I want to stress is that the closeness of the synthesis mentioned above depends to a large degree on this psychological simplicity of presentation.

I have discussed the importance for the final synthesis of four different but closely connected elements. It remains to add that there is one other which is difficult to define, which is something more than a combination of versification and language, something that transcends them. It is the *poetry.* For it is the poetry which provides the unifying element and transforms the play into an experience which has an immediate impact on the audience and is ultimately responsible for transmitting the dramatist's vision to them.

If there are grounds on which Racine is open to criticism, the main one is that though his insight into human nature often went deep the field is comparatively narrow and several tragedies are variations on the same theme. This takes us back to comparisons between Corneille and Racine. Corneille's supporters admired him because they found his plays uplifting. They criticized Racine's because they were not. 'Tendre' in its seventeenth-century sense was not a term of unqualified praise; it meant that Racine was sensitive, easily moved and that though his tragedies were moving, too, they were not exalting and did nothing to boost morale.

The answer is of course that their professional rivalry is a thing of the past, and that they are both 'constants' of the French genius who complete and possibly correct one another. They both give expression to something permanent in human nature. It is the sign of a master that he is irreplaceable. Corneille occupies a place that Racine could never have filled and the same is true of Racine. Their effect on us is entirely different. We love Racine because he speaks to us as man to man, exposes our weaknesses to our shocked and fascinated gaze. This should not prevent us from responding to the immense élan, the enormous 'lift', that comes from a good production or even a proper reading of Corneille. Speaking for myself, there are some moods in which I prefer Racine and others in which I prefer Corneille. But of one thing I am certain: they are both necessary to me.

Geoffrey Brereton (essay date 1973)

SOURCE: "Jean Racine," in *An Introduction to the French Poets: Villon to the Present Day,* revised edition, Methuen & Co Ltd, 1973, pp. 67-81.

[*Brereton is an English scholar who has written extensively on French literature of the sixteenth, seventeenth, and eighteenth centuries. In the following excerpt, he examines specifically the poetry of Racine's dramas.*]

Racine is considered here almost exclusively as a poet. He was, in fact, a dramatic poet and any division is necessarily artificial. But any attempt to do justice to the dramatist would lead us far beyond the bounds of our subject and we must be content with illustrating this side of his genius with a single example. To go further in that direction might obscure a truth which English readers sometimes find it difficult to accept—that, apart from the requirements of the stage, Racine was a supreme verbal artist. His verse, as verse, has been admired by poets of such radically different temperaments as Voltaire and Valéry and has influenced them profoundly.

An admirer himself of Malherbe, no rebel against the conventions of *préciosité,* an imitator of the Greeks and a respecter of contemporary good taste, his verse should have been well-mannered and slightly dull. Possibly it even appears so on a first acquaintance, but to be halted

by this surface impression is to turn back on the brink of a new world—an alien world, perhaps, but one full of power, subtlety and beauty. That such qualities should have emerged from the influences current in Racine's day, and which he did not reject but fulfilled and reconciled, is one of the perennial surprises of literature. Is there, after all, a virtue in the French classical formula, as applied to poetry, which can inspire work of the highest kind, given the artist to execute it? Or can the great artist transform any formula, however unpromising, into a recipe for excellent work?

Faced with the incompatibility between 'classical' theory (words should be tailored to fit sense) and Racinian performance (words and meaning coalesce, and are impregnated in addition with a seemingly natural poetic perfume), some critics have been driven into supposing a Racine who slipped into greatness by accident and never fully realized what he was achieving. If, as a conscious artist, he followed Boileau, how could he have written as he did? The explanation is sometimes sought in the historical moment—but a moment which somehow eluded the Malherbe-Boileau hour-hand. For Jean Giraudoux, writing of Racine's extraordinary psychological penetration, Racine was perhaps only a 'supreme talent'; the 'genius' was in the age which produced him and which gave him 'an inborn knowledge of great hearts and great moments'. For Marcel Raymond, writing more specifically of the poet,

> he had the good fortune to appear at one of the mature stages of a culture and a language; he had mastered his technique; and an infallible intuition, a feeling of continuous beauty, enabled him to create—as though just at the emergence from sleep, in the white light of the first morning—that potent instrument, that royal language which still holds us enthralled.

This second appreciation is the more acceptable. It imputes no more to the age than can be readily conceded. One would allow the debt of almost any poet to the culture and idiom of his time. Yet even Marcel Raymond, while rightly refusing to see Racine as an unconscious operator, places him as near to the unconscious as possible—at the emergence from sleep, when the dream may still be in possession of the mind.

There should be nothing remarkable about such a process. No one is surprised when a revolutionary poet like Rimbaud produces, part consciously, part unconsciously, a highly original body of work from the books read in the classroom and in the municipal library at Charleville—and from the particular nature of his lived experience. But when Racine, who was not in appearance revolutionary, follows the same road, the need for some explanation seems to be felt. Either he was moving with some cultural current different from that of which he was aware; or perhaps he was deceiving his contemporaries into accepting at its face-value work which he knew perfectly well had another significance. Either Racine misunderstood himself, or his age misunderstood him.

Much has been written on this point and more could be. But, whatever the complexity of Racine's art and psychology, this particular difficulty need never have arisen. If Racine had been studied first as an individual case, one contradiction at least would have disappeared. But instead—as with the 'baroque' writers—a picture has been built up of 'classicism' based partly on literary theory, partly on a simplification of the historical background. Racine does not entirely fit into this picture. Hence the artificial 'paradox' of a classic who transcends classicism. Much confusion could be avoided if it were recognized that it is the picture, or rather the map, which is out of scale, not the individual writer. The first is always expendable and can be redrawn if necessary. The second, whether more or less well explored, is a landmark which certainly exists. It would continue to exist if all the maps were lost. . . .

For all his apparent simplicity, Racine is a difficult poet. The best approach to him is to follow what was certainly his own approach and to begin by considering his dramatic verse in its functional aspect.

It is functional because it is always suited to the character who is speaking and renders every shade of his reactions to the situation in which he finds himself. At the same time, it explores for the audience, sometimes with a closely controlled irony, all the implications of that situation. It does this without becoming out of character, or rather without going beyond character to state some general truth. Racine is never the moralist that Shakespeare often is. When Gloucester observes:

> As flies to wanton boys, are we to the gods;
> They kill us for their sport,

or Macbeth soliloquizes

> Tomorrow and tomorrow and tomorrow . . .

they are moving outside their immediate situation, or at least enlarging it. Racine's characters do not do this. They keep strictly to the point—to the particular circumstances which bear on their dilemma. What is lost is the more strikingly 'poetic' quality of what might possibly be called Shakespeare's baroque style—the rhetorical extension which becomes, in the right hands, a link between the particular and the universal. Racine denies himself this kind of poetry. His characters are turned inward so that all their discoveries are made in the depths of their own natures and expressed in terms of themselves. Psychologically, therefore, his plays appear self-suffing and self-contained—which in theory is one of the attributes of French classicism. Poetically, an element is lost. This element may be called the impingement of the infinite on the finite, the association of the macrocosm with the microcosm, or simply the metaphysical imagination. In its absence, what remains but the small change of poetry—the minor and technical qualities? To this highly difficult question no wholly satisfactory answer has ever been given, yet it is a matter of experience that Racine's verse, whether read or heard in the theatre, is 'poetic'. It de-

lights the ear, stirs the feelings, fascinates the intellect and even—both occasionally and in its total effect—excites the imagination, though along lines deliberately traced by the poet. With no justification at all could it be described as merely rhymed prose.

This is true even when it is most 'functional'.

In the fourth act of **Britannicus,** the Dowager Empress of Rome, Agrippina, is attempting to bring to heel her son Nero. He has been made emperor by her intrigues—in plainer words, her crimes—and is now beginning to defy her. Struggling to regain her influence, the unscrupulous old woman recalls how, as a widow, she had made a second marriage with the late emperor Claudius; how she had persuaded him to set aside Britannicus, his own son by a former marriage, and to adopt her own son, Nero, as his heir; and how, when Claudius was about to die and at last realized the true position, she consummated her plan:

> Cependant Claudius penchait vers son déclin.
> Ses yeux, longtemps fermés, s'ouvrirent à la fin:
> Il connut son erreur. Occupé de sa crainte,
> Il laissa pour son fils échapper quelque plainte,
> Et voulut, mais trop tard, assembler ses amis.

The tone is factual, brisk, completely ruthless in its context. The dying Claudius, whom she had married, is envisaged purely as an instrument which must be discarded before it causes complications:

> Ses gardes, son palais, son lit m'étaient soumis.
> Je lui laissai sans fruit consumer sa tendresse;
> De ses derniers soupirs je me rendis maîtresse.

The second line—'I let him fret out his affection fruitlessly'—must be one of the cruellest ever spoken on the stage, unless it is surpassed by the third: 'I took control of his last sighs.'

Her business now was to keep the disinherited Britannicus away from his father until the latter was dead. The death is noted in two words, the rumour that she had caused it by poison is shrugged off in seven:

> Mes soins, en apparence épargnant ses douleurs,
> De son fils, en mourant, lui cachèrent les pleurs.
> Il mourut. Mille bruits en courent à ma honte.

It will be noticed that no relevant feature of the material situation or the physical scene has been blinked. Nothing is veiled or inflated. Yet, while the reader has everything necessary to reconstruct the scene realistically in his imagination, if he so wishes, the language used is largely figurative. The figures are conventional, but instead of hanging limply they are recharged with their full literal meaning and more, so that they acquire the elastic strength of the understatement. When Claudius was 'drawing towards his end', suddenly 'his eyes were opened'. 'He realized his mistake—but too late,' adds his widow laconically. He was completely in her power: 'Ses gardes, son palais, son lit m'étaient soumis.' 'Sans fruit' is almost a cliché.

So is 'derniers soupirs', but here they are completely apt expressions. 'Mes soins'—an abstract word which might be translated here as 'ministrations'—has, of course, a double edge. This colourless word, whose associations range from the *petits soins* of the salon lover to the *soins officieux* of the poisoner Locusta who a little later in Racine's play 'zealously' provides a poison after first demonstrating its efficacy on a slave, gives an effect comparable to Lady Macbeth's:

> What cannot you and I *perform*
> On the unguarded Duncan?

But Agrippina, a more hardened criminal than Lady Macbeth and certainly no sleep-walker, has not finished her recital. She had to conceal the death of Claudius until the army had taken an oath of allegiance to Nero as his successor. Meanwhile the Roman people, on her orders, had been offering prayers to the gods for the recovery of the old emperor, until the moment came when it was safe for him to be shown to them, already dead. In these narrative lines can be detected—again if one wishes—Agrippina's sardonic pleasure in the situation. On a more open level is her insistence on her own role in the affair—'conduit sous *mes* auspices'—'*mes* ordres trompeurs'—underlined now to stress Nero's present indebtedness to her:

> J'arrêtai de sa mort la nouvelle trop prompte;
> Et tandis que Burrhus allait secrètement
> De l'armée en vos mains exiger le serment,
> Que vous marchiez au camp, conduit sous mes
>   auspices,
> Dans Rome les autels fumaient de sacrifices;
> Par mes orders trompeurs tout le peuple excité
> Du prince déjà mort demandait la santé.
> Enfin des légions l'entière obéissance
> Ayant de votre empire affermi la puissance,
> On vit Claude; et le peuple, étonné de son sort,
> Apprit en même temps votre règne et sa mort.

These, concludes Agrippina (with much else previously related), were all my crimes. The tone is that of an injured lover excusing himself for having been perhaps too attentive:

> C'est le sincère aveu que je voulais vous faire:
> Voilà tous mes forfaits.

This single example must suffice to suggest the force and subtlety which lie in Racine's apparently conventional use of imagery and metre. In the same verse-form he can be ironic, vigorous, brutal, or even flat, as the situation demands:

> Est-il juste, après tout, qu'un conquérant
>   s'abaisse
> Sous la servile loi de garder sa promesse?
>
> (*Andromaque*)

or:

> Mais je m'étonne enfin que, pour reconnaissance,

> Pour prix de tant d'amour, de tant de confiance,
> Vous ayez si longtemps, par des détours si bas,
> Feint un amour pour moi que vous ne sentiez
>   pas.
>
> (*Bajazet*)

or simply—the depth of utility:

> Madame, tout est prêt pour la cérémonie.
>
> (*Iphigénie*)

In using and perfecting the alexandrine—his almost exclusive medium—Racine mastered it completely. It was his vehicle both for the 'Roman' tone of *Britannicus* and for the comic effects of *Les Plaideurs:*

> Voilà votre portier et votre secrétaire;
> Vous en ferez, je crois, d'excellents avocats:
> Ils sont fort ignorants.

On occasion he broke most of the technical rules laid down by his less gifted contemporaries and which the Romantics flung overboard so noisily a hundred and fifty years later. But his infringements were discreet and never wanton, dictated always by an impeccable ear. He observed Boileau's pedestrian prescription for the alexandrine.

> —Que toujours, dans vos vers, le sens, coupant
>   les mots,
> Suspende l'hémistiche, en marque le repos—

sufficiently often for his verse to pass as 'regular' until it is carefully probed.

While the functional kind of verse just examined is poetic in its compression, its economy and rightness in the choice of words, and its inconspicuous rhythms which lead the speaking voice to follow the most effective sound-patterns relative to the sense, it would hardly be enough to mark Racine as a great poet. The verse of *Britannicus* and of *Bajazet,* which were written roughly midway through his career, is perfectly dramatic and basically Racinian. But, using always the same basis, he could build higher.

In the earlier *Andromaque,* purely human passion is fanned (as in the character of Hermione) to white heat and the tone rises in places almost to a scream. It still does not break the finite barrier, but goes as close as is possible without doing so.

In *Bérénice,* the music of the Racinian line comes into play and produces some of those *tirades* which have been aptly compared to arias in which the voice can take wing on the subtly varied rhythm of the alexandrines:

> Le temps n'est plus, Phénice, où je pouvais
>   trembler.
> Titus m'aime; il peut tout: il n'a plus qu'à
>   parler.
> Il verra le sénat m'apporter ses hommages,

Et le peuple de fleurs couronner ses images.
    De cette nuit, Phénice, as-tu vu la splendeur?
Tes yeux ne sont-ils pas tout pleins de sa
    grandeur?
Ce flambeau, ce bûcher, cette nuit enflammée,
Ces aigles, ces faisceaux, ce peuple, cette armée,
Cette foule de rois, ces consuls, ce sénat,
Qui tous de mon amant empruntaient leur éclat . . .

Or the still more famous:

Je n'écoute plus rien; et pour jamais, adieu.
Pour jamais! Ah! Seigneur, songez-vous en vous-
    même
Combien ce mot cruel est affreux quand on
    aime?
Dans un mois, dans un an, comment souffrirons-
    nous,
Seigneur, que tant de mers me séparent de vous?
Que le jour recommence, et que le jour finisse,
Sans que jamais Titus puisse voir Bérénice,
Sans que de tout le jour je puisse voir Titus?
Mais quelle est mon erreur, et que de soins
    perdus!
L'ingrat, de mon départ consolé par avance,
Daignera-t-il compter les jours de mon absence?
Ces jours si longs pour moi lui sembleront trop
    courts.

Both these passages are also 'functional', though in a less immediate way than the scene quoted from **Britannicus**. The first renders the elation of Berenice when she feels confident that her lover will marry her; the second, the pathos of her distress when she sees that they must separate. The tone, the musical quality, correspond to her feelings at those particular points in the drama. But they can be quoted apart from the drama and still retain a certain life. This becomes truer still of the last two plays which Racine wrote before his retirement: **Iphigénie** and—to a greater degree—**Phèdre**. Both were based on the Greek mythology which had persisted in Racine's mind since his schooldays and which seems to have fired his normally disciplined imagination as no other subject did. **Phèdre** in particular furnished the critic Henri Bremond, writing in the 1920s, with examples for his theory of 'pure poetry', according to which there is an autonomous language of poetry, valid in itself, as music and some painting can be argued to be valid in themselves, without reference to external associations. Just as you cannot adequately transcribe the theme of a piece of music in words, so 'pure poetry' exists independently of rational meaning and of emotions connected with the lived experience of the reader. Such a line as

La fille de Minos et de Pasiphaé

becomes a self-contained creation, having its own beauty and originating its own overtones quite apart from its significance in the mouth of a stage-character or its evocation of Greek legend. Bremond even went further and likened the language of 'pure poetry' to the language of prayer.

This theory, with its streak of mysticism, was certainly too extreme. In view of the predominantly functional qualities of Racinian verse, it would seem astonishing that it should have been applied to this particular poet at all. But he does, as we have seen, comply with one half of the requirements. By his concentration on the matter in hand he eliminates the external associations which in 'pure' poetry are worse than irrelevant: they are a distraction. It only remains to persuade oneself that he fulfills the second condition—that his verse can be detached from its dramatic context without essential loss—and he becomes the supreme example of poetic purity.

This can be done in a limited number of instances, though it may safely be said that it was never Racine's conscious intention and that the impact of his lines is always stronger when they are left in their context. Outside it, however, there is still an incantatory quality in, for example, the opening scene of **Iphigénie,** which occurs just before dawn:

A peine un faible jour vous éclaire et me guide.
Vos yeux seuls et les miens sont ouverts dans
    l'Aulide.
Avez-vous dans les airs entendu quelque bruit?
Les vents nous auraient-ils exaucés cette nuit?
Mais tout dort, et l'armée, et les vents, et
    Neptune.

This is poetry at the opposite extreme to Hamlet's:

But look, the Morn, in russet mantle clad,
Walks o'er the dew of yon high eastward hill.

So is:

Ariane, ma sœur, de quel amour blessée,
Vous mourûtes aux bords où vous fûtes laissée!

Or Phèdre's querulous:

Que ces vains ornements, que ces voiles me
    pèsent!
Quelle importune main, en formant tous ces
    nœuds,
A pris soin sur mon front d'assembler mes
    cheveux?
Tout m'afflige et me nuit et conspire à me nuire.

Yet all these lines, perfect though they are, betray a certain conscious virtuosity on the poet's part. Just as Shakespeare, one feels, may have paused with a certain satisfaction after composing the 'russet mantle' image, so Racine must have experienced a small moment of triumph when he had written the words 'et Neptune'. No doubt he had even planned for it. The beautiful modulation of the 'Ariane' quotation, with the management of the vowels in the second line (ou-ou-u-(e)-o-o / ou-ou-u-(e)-è-é) seems hardly fortuitous. Neither does the discreet alliteration in the last passage quoted and least of all the insistent *i* sound in:

Tout m'afflige et me nuit et conspire à me nuire.

These are nearer to what Valéry termed 'calculated lines' than to 'given lines'. It is the 'given lines', simpler and apparently spontaneous, that represent Racinian poetry in its purest state.

They are so simple that they easily pass unnoticed. What is noticeable is less their presence in Racine than their absence in other poets. They seem to have been produced without effort—to occur rather than to have been composed. Such are the lines which immediately follow [a] passage from *Iphigénie*. . . :

Heureux qui, satisfait de son humble fortune,
Libre du joug superbe où je suis attaché,
Vit dans l'état obscur où les dieux l'ont caché.

Or, from *Athalie:*

Promettez sur ce livre, et devant ces témoins,
Que Dieu fera toujours le premier de vos soins;
Que, sévère aux méchants, et des bons le
    refuge,
Entre le pauvre et vous, vous prendrez Dieu
    pour juge;
Vous souvenant, mon fils, que caché sous ce lin,
Comme eux vous fûtes pauvre et comme eux
    orphelin.

Or, from *Phèdre:*

Dans le fond des forêts votre image me suit.

And, perhaps the most perfect of all:

Le jour n'est pas plus pur que le fond de mon
    cœur.

In these lines there is no ostentation of any kind. Imagery, rhetoric, and the musical effects that can be drawn from alliteration and assonance are either excluded or reduced to a minimum. Denying himself even the barest 'ornaments', the artist has come face to face with his basic materials, with less than which he cannot work at all: words and syntax. To shape them, he has allowed himself only his auditory sense, a feeling for sounds and rhythm which enables him to produce the most delicately varied effects within an apparently rigid framework. In this sense one can say—without subscribing to the whole of Bremond's, or even Valéry's, theory of 'pure poetry'—that Racine's verse sometimes becomes 'the language of poetry itself'.

Anything approaching a 'baroque' Racine is of course unthinkable. But it must be remembered that not all his verse is so perfectly distilled as that just described. His earliest known poems, odes describing the country round Port-Royal, were modelled on the 'libertine' poets Théophile de Viau and Saint-Amant, who did not conform to Malherbe's principles. They contain numerous fanciful metaphors. . . . Butterflies are 'ces vivantes fleurs'. Birds'

nests are 'ces cabinets si bien bâtis'. Oaktrees are 'ces géants de cent bras armés'. There is the pompous image of the great trees which seem to prop up the skies and 'lend their powerful backs to the thrones of the sun':

L'on dirait même que les cieux
Posent sur ces audacieux
    Leur pesante machine,
Et qu'eux, d'un orgueil nonpareil,
    Prêtent leur forte échine
A ces grands trônes du soleil.

But perhaps what Racine wrote at the age of about seventeen and never published is not evidence. Or evidence only of a strain capable of development but deliberately suppressed. Yet it crops out again in a more temperate form in *Esther* and *Athalie* and the few sacred songs of his later years. The influence of the Bible, with the bold images and picturesque idioms of Hebrew poetry, is now perceptible. The English reader will feel more at home when he comes upon some violent nightmare like the dream of Athalie, or reads such lines as

La nation entière est promise aux vautours,

or

Et de Jérusalem l'herbe cache les murs;
Sion, repaire affreux de reptiles impurs . . .

which are evocative in the last degree, and the opposite of 'pure' poetry. Or he will hear Racine—echoing the Psalmist and the Book of Job—speak with the authentic voice of Jehovah out of the whirlwind:

J'ai vu l'impie adoré sur la terre;
Pareil au cèdre, il cachait dans les cieux
    Son front audacieux;
Il semblait à son gré gouverner le tonnerre,
    Foulait aux pieds ses ennemis vaincus:
Je n'ai fait que passer, il n'était déjà plus.

(*Esther*)

This is also Racine, writing a stanza so perfectly constructed that it floats with its own lightness. . . . The technical reasons for Malherbe's greater heaviness would require a long analysis, but it is really unnecessary. It is enough to read the two poets aloud. Some of the difference is due to the greater variety of Racine's metrical scheme. In this one stanza he uses lines of 10, 10, 6, 12, 10 and 12 syllables.

Yet Racine had learnt something from Malherbe, just as he took something from Corneille (particularly in *Britannicus*). His verse as a whole, considered over the whole of his mature period, is a compound made from these two poets, from fashionable courtly speech with the slightest touch of the *précieux,* from colloquial speech and from the Greek and Latin poets whom he read and adapted so assiduously. These various elements are so perfectly synthesized that the amalgam (unlike Ronsard's) appears as one clear, consistent material and can be held up, deservedly if paradoxically, as the model of classical purity.

The factor so far omitted from the analysis—since analysis would not show it—is Racine's personal way of approaching and handling his material. This all-important personal quality cannot of course exist in a vacuum, i.e. without the material to work on. But neither can the material exist in any coherent form without it. It is the beginning and end of art: the beginning because it provides the artist with his original bias, the end because it conditions the impression which his work will make on the reader. In both aspects it can be called his idiom. Racine's idiom, with its peculiar intonations, its mannerisms, its vocabulary, and of course its defects, is less a variety of French poetry than a poetic branch of the French language, as—though with directly contrasting qualities—Abbey-Theatre Irish is a poetic branch of English. The comparison, overlooking all other differences, can be used to explain the fascination of Racinian verse for Frenchmen. It is a delightful and irresistibly flattering idealization of his ordinary speech. So he might talk in dreams, if he were perfectly eloquent and perfectly lucid. (The Englishman, on the contrary, dreams of perfect eloquence allied to perfect intoxication, that is, freedom from inhibitions.)

In this language of the lucid dream, characters endowed with a precision of feeling which assimilates them more to passionate machines than to the untidy attempts at gods of the Shakespearian tradition speak their minds with a frankness which embraces every subtlety of perception of which they and their author are capable. Hence both the clarity which immediately strikes an audience and their interest for the modern psychologist, who has to admit the deeper accuracy of their findings. Here the dramatist joins the poet and any further division along these lines becomes unprofitable.

For Racine's immediate successors, he was the poet who had demonstrated that verse could be dignified, elegant, harmonious, supple and clear, and at the same time wholly French. He had at last realized Du Bellay's old ambition of a French literary tongue as civilized and expressive as Greek and Latin. He could therefore be quoted as a proof of national excellence and a model for imitation.

It was perhaps unfortunate. Racine is no easier to imitate than to translate. In spite of his prestige in the eighteenth century, none of his disciples surpasses the second-rate. The great Racinian scholar Paul Mesnard once listed Jean-Baptiste Rousseau and Fontanes as the sole approximate successes. What a fall is here, and how dangerous it is to single out certain qualities which one finds congenial in a poet and then to believe that one holds the formula for composing similar poetry. Racine was richer than his age and, although it is unlikely that without him the poets of the next century would have followed a much different course, it is a pity that his example could be used at all to justify their mediocrity.

With time, the matter appears in better perspective. A 'classic' or not, Racine remains a great poet in his own right, to whom poets completely emancipated from the classical tradition as formulated by Boileau look back as a master. Even those Romantics who abominated it always respected him.

> Sur le Racine mort, le Campistron pullule,

wrote Hugo, conceiving the great dramatist as a dead lion infested by lice. But it is obvious today that Racine, with his lucid, wiry talent, is by no means dead. In fact, he has survived in better shape than the more massive Hugo.

Gordon Pocock (essay date 1973)

SOURCE: "The Dramatic Art of Racine," in *Corneille and Racine: Problems of Tragic Form,* Cambridge at the University Press, 1973, pp. 216-36.

[*In the following excerpt, Pocock seeks to demonstrate that "the basis of Racine's art was his concern to express those irrational and even infantile passions that are fed from the unconscious, but that he masked them as far as possible behind a perfect neo-classical façade."*]

After 1670, Racine was the reigning monarch of the stage. *Bajazet* was acclaimed not just as a success but as an improvement on his earlier plays. *Mithridate* triumphed, and was Louis XIV's favourite tragedy. Then came *Iphigénie*—Racine's greatest success, with the Court, the Town, and the critics. Until the end of the eighteenth century and beyond, it was regarded as one of his greatest plays—perhaps his greatest. I will consider for a moment these three plays by Racine at the height of his success, and try to discover from them some of the characteristics of his mastery.

Traditionally, the great strength of Racine is his portrayal of women in love. *Bajazet* may stand as an example. We may instance Act II, Scene i, with its powerful and subtle drawing of Roxane's conflicting emotions. She swings from formal elegance to a direct proposal of marriage. When Bajazet prevaricates, she first reasons with him, and then becomes indignant, though for a moment her rage is so suppressed by her effort to remain calm that it comes through only as irony. Then her brutality and rage break through, and she threatens him with death. At this, she recoils, and pleads with him with tenderness and urgency—only to rebound into threatening violence at his coldness. The dramatic power is obvious. The verse expresses every nuance of feeling, every shift in the situation. The tension builds up, the twists and the resolution are unexpected yet logical. This is one example among many, and a relatively simple one, but it justifies Racine's reputation for psychological subtlety combined with dramatic urgency.

Mithridate has the same qualities. It also shows more clearly than *Bajazet* another quality for which Racine is famous: the sweetness and elegance of his verse, especially in scenes of pathos or sentiment (as in the rôle of Monime). More relevantly for our present purpose, it also shows qualities which are often undervalued in Racine, and which we more readily associate with Corneille: a poetry of energy, heroism and politics. If we admire the discussion of Auguste with Cinna and Maxime, it is hard to withhold our approval from Mithridate's discussion with his sons. The scene lacks nothing in firmness and energy of expression, and shows a grasp of political realities: if Mithridate overrates the Italians' respect for blue blood ('If they followed Spartacus, how they will fight for a king!') we can say that this shows Racine's awareness of the psychology of a half-oriental monarch. In *Mithridate* he skilfully brings together a romantic plot and an historical background and makes them set each other off: the pathetic dilemma of the old king gains in intensity when seen as part of the situation of a man who has long made headway against the power of Rome, and in defeat plans an audacious counterstroke.

At this stage Racine seems to have reached the point where he can do what he likes with his medium. In *Iphigénie,* more than in any of his other plays, an interesting plot leads smoothly from dramatic situation to dramatic situation. As in *Bajazet,* suspense is aroused to a high degree, but here we never feel that the machinery is arbitrary. There are four, even six, interesting and well-drawn characters, subtly contrasted, each drawing our sympathy or admiration in various degrees, but none of them appearing either too evil or too good to be interesting. Their reactions are subtly observed and expressed. Each character is satisfying as an individual creation, and together they form a beautifully balanced group. But the great glory of *Iphigénie* is its verse. For the rôle of Iphigénie herself, Racine has found a perfect harmony and simplicity, but the range of tone is wide. Against Iphigénie's tenderness we can set the deeper note of Clytemnestre's rage. Nor is there lacking that strange sexual undertone that creeps into Racine's verse and gives it just a hint of perversity. . . .

Most beautiful of all—and it is on the significance I give to these that my estimate of the play must largely rest—are the lines that cluster round the rôle of Agamemnon, especially in the first scene of Act I:

> Heureux qui, satisfait de son humble fortune,
> Libre du joug superbe où je suis attaché,
> Vit dans l'état obscur où les Dieux l'ont caché!
> Nous partions; et déjà par mille cris de joie
> Nous menacions de loin les rivages de Troie.

> Un prodige étonnant fit taire ce transport:
> Le vent qui nous flattait nous laissa dans le port.
> Il fallut s'arrêter, et la rame inutile
> Fatigua vainement une mer immobile.

In *Bajazet, Mithridate* and *Iphigénie,* we seem to have all the dramatic virtues. Yet have we? These three plays are such that it is difficult to trace any weakness in them, yet do we find them really compelling? This question is so important for an understanding of Racine that we must look at them again.

Bajazet is sometimes considered the weakest of the

three. From its first appearance, critics have fastened on the *grande tuerie* at the end, which has been thought insufficiently prepared. In realistic terms, however, the deaths seem well prepared. It is likely enough that those who plot treason at the court of an Eastern despot will get killed, and virtually certain if they mix love and politics—much more probable and inevitable, for instance, than that those who drive chariots will be killed because sea-monsters frighten the horses. To try and get at the reasons for dissatisfaction with the dénouement, let us examine the verse.

The plainness of much of it is famous (Madame, j'ai reçu des lettres de l'armée'). Frequently it has also a prosaic, disenchanted realism:

> Roxane en sa fureur peut raisonner ainsi.
> Mais moi, qui vois plus loin, qui, par un long usage,
> Des maximes du trône ai fait l'apprentissage,
> Qui d'emplois en emplois vieilli sous trois sultans,
> Ai vu de mes pareils les malheurs éclatants,
> Je sais, sans me flatter, que de sa seule audace
> Un homme tel que moi doit attendre sa grâce.

The style of Act V is especially revealing. In the earlier acts, there is time to drape the bare facts in poetic conventions; but by the last act the pace is too hot ('Les moments sont trop chers pour les perdre en paroles'). Racine can here draw great dramatic effect from the simplest phrases: 'Retirez-vous'; 'Que faut-il faire?'; 'Sortez'; 'Qu'estce?'; 'Quoi! lui?' But the force comes from the context of events, not from the verse: the banal phrases are energised by the happenings around them, not by any poetic current which they themselves generate. Where the verse is less abrupt, it often has difficulty in accommodating the events it has to present, and on occasion its awkwardness recalls that of some of the verse in Corneille's later plays:

> Je puis le retenir. Mais s'il sort, il est mort.
> Vient-il?
>   —Oui, sur mes pas un esclave l'amène;
> Et loin de soupçonner sa disgrâce prochaine,
> Il m'a paru, Madame, avec empressement,
> Sortir, pour vous chercher, de son appartement.

Even the emotional statements have a bluntness that pretends to no literary grace:

> Mais je m'étonne enfin que pour reconnaissance,
> Pour prix de tant d'amour, de tant de confiance,
> Vous ayez si longtemps par des détours si bas
> Feint un amour pour moi que vous ne sentiez pas.
> —Qui? moi, Madame?
>   —Oui, toi.

Bajazet's death can be announced with the most banal fierceness:

> Bajazet est sans vie.
> L'ignoriez-vous?

Clearly, *Bajazet* is not poetic in method. The separate virtues of plot, character, and even verse are great, but the play has no pretensions to tragedy. It is because the tragic spirit is lacking that the final deaths, however probable and necessary, appear arbitrary.

If the verse of *Bajazet* is coarse in texture, that of *Mithridate* has an elegance which doubtless helped to make it Louis XIV's favourite tragedy. But since the seventeenth century it has never been regarded as one of Racine's greatest plays, whereas *Iphigénie* has. Boileau's tribute in *Epître VII* is well-known, and critics have reasonably seen the ideal of tragedy set forth in Chant III of *L'Art Poétique* as related to *Iphigénie*. Later neo-classic critics endorsed this estimate of the play. Voltaire's views are well known ('J'avoue que je regarde *Iphigénie* comme le chef-d'oeuvre de la scène') and in *L'Ingénu* he holds it up as a touchstone of true taste, apparently because of its power to play on the audience's emotions.

These judgments and the continued success of *Iphigénie* on the stage are certainly not without justification. Yet, despite all its virtues, would we really place *Iphigénie* on the same level as *Phèdre* and *Athalie*? Despite Voltaire, we clearly would not. To ask a more difficult question: do we prefer *Iphigénie* to *Andromaque,* whose standing is more equivocal? Again, the answer is clear: despite the slight awkwardness of *Andromaque* when compared with the ripeness and perfection of *Iphigénie,* in the last analysis the later play is less impressive than the earlier. Why, then, is *Iphigénie* inferior, when its evident merits are so great?

In an attempt to answer this, I look first at the one element in *Iphigénie* which has been adversely criticised: the handling of the mythological *donnée*. Obviously, this presented great difficulty to a seventeenth-century poet, committed at the same time to *le vraisemblable* and *les bienséances*. How could refined members of seventeenth-century French society be at ease with the concept of gods who would hold up the winds until a princess was sacrificed? Such ideas were unacceptable, not necessarily because the temper of the age was sceptical (though sceptical currents of thought were certainly influential in certain quarters), but because at the level of secular society they were uncouth, and at the level of orthodox religious thought they were either untrue or simply evil. Caught between these two conflicting but powerful devaluations of myth, poets were recommended to regard the individual myths as ornament—at best expressing allegorically some truth of conventional wisdom, at worst merely decorative. This is Boileau's position, and is implicit in neo-classical theory, with its pronounced tendency towards naturalism. Racine, with his earnest desire to recapture the seriousness of ancient tragedy, had little room for manoeuvre: it was unthinkable that he should treat the myth as a fairy-tale with a few allegorical trimmings—this was the operatic solution, which, in his preface he by implication repudiates. Alternatively, he could hardly adopt a whole-heartedly rationalistic interpretation, in which the whole affair was a fraud devised by wicked priests: the time was fortunately not ripe for such a solution to be popular, and Racine must surely have perceived that its crudity quite removed it from the sphere of tragedy. Faced with this dilemma, he equivocates.

The legend of Iphigenia inevitably raises one terrible question: why did the gods demand the sacrifice? Racine evades it: he accepts the demand, and the assumption that after the sacrifice the winds will blow again, as Aristotelian 'improbabilities before the drama'. The advantage of this is that he can avoid all the moral and theological difficulties the question raises. The disadvantage is that he had to direct the audience's attention away from a natural source of interest in his play, and must therefore provide sufficiently attractive alternatives. His solution, at the beginning of the play, is to focus the interest on Agamemnon. The evocative lines in the first scene mark a powerful attempt to direct us to this alternative theme: that of a proud king seeing himself as the victim of the gods because of his position, and following, though reluctantly, his destiny. Vinaver has persuasively maintained that the poetic centre of the play is to be found in this direction. Basing himself solidly on what are undoubtedly the most impressive clusters of verse in the text, he draws the conclusion that through the agency of these 'vers prestigieux' Racine assimilates his courtly drama to the more significant realm of myth:

> A tout moment, dans chacune des scènes où figure Agamemnon, le mythe tragique côtoie et explique le drame humain, et dans la crainte même d'y faire apparaître les dieux, on sent un respect qui, peu à peu, grandit, se nuançant de terreur. Malgré son pretendu souci de l'"ordinaire", Racine n'avait jamais poussé aussi loin le culte du surnaturel, ni sa poésie accompli miracle plus rare.

Yet we may doubt whether this is so. The theme is certainly present in Act I, but the ruse of the letter, and then Iphigénie's arrival, point to other and more superficial sources of interest: the surprise and suspense engendered by the plot. In Act II, Racine's hesitations between the myth and the plot are resolved: he introduces 'l'heureux personnage d'Eriphile, sans laquelle je n'aurais jamais esé entreprendre cette tragédie'. The scene between Eriphile and Doris includes those subtly sensual lines we have quoted, and which point to a deeper source of Racine's strength. But there can be little doubt that the matters of interest he is more concerned to offer us here are psychology (the nuances of Eriphile's emotions) and suspense (the mystery of Eriphile's origins and fate). From now on, the play runs securely on the 'intrigue' level. We may have a scene of pathos when Iphigénie greets Agamemnon (II.ii), a scene of jealousy between Iphigénie and Eriphile, and so on. It is difficult to believe that Racine is focussing on any of them. He is certainly not focussing on the rôle of Agamemnon. Act IV magisterially plays all the variations on Agamemnon's situation, but the interest is in the feelings of the characters and the twists and turns of the plot.

Finally, Act V raises in the most acute form questions which Racine has tried to evade: the significance of the sacrifice itself, and hence the rôle of the gods in the action. Before looking at his treatment of the sacrifice and its attendant miracles, we may glance at his handling of the gods—bearing in mind that he had to keep in play, yet avoid committing himself too completely to, two different conceptions of them: the gods as real *numinosa* (which was incredible to his audience's Christian or sceptical beliefs—'quelle apparence de dénouer ma tragédie par le secours d'une déesse . . . qui pouvait bien trouver quelque créance du temps d'Euripide, mais qui serait trop absurde et trop incroyable parmi nous?') and the gods as dignified ornaments (which was acceptable to his audience, but denatured his subject).

If we look at the text, the extent of his equivocation is obvious. 'Dieu' or its plural occurs no less than eighteen times in the act, but the mixture of tones in which it is used betrays Racine's uncertainty. Some references appear to invoke real *numinosa*:

> il faut des Dieux apaiser la colère . . .
> Leurs ordres éternels se sont trop déclarés.

But others are merely sentimental:

> Dieux plus doux, vous n'avez demandé que ma
>   vie . . .
>   vivez, digne race des Dieux.

Others again are no more than expletives:

> Dieux! Achille?
> Mais, Dieux! ne vois-je pas Ulysse?

When Iphigénie goes off to the sacrifice, there remains the prospect of tragedy: we believe she is to be killed, and there is perhaps still time for Racine to invest her death with significance. Clytemnestre denounces Agamemnon in impressive verse. Then thunder sounds, and she attributes it to the gods. Arcas also credits them with interrupting the sacrifice—'N'en doutez point, Madame, un Dieu combat pour vous'—but this interpretation is rather devalued by the line which follows: '*Achille* en ce moment exauce vos prières.' The struggle is between Achille and a demagogic priest: 'Achille est à l'autel, Calchas est éperdu.' Then Ulysse comes to relate the dénouement. Iphigénie is safe, and it is the work of the gods: but 'the gods' are little more than a figure of speech. The narration is a careful balancing act. Achille's purely secular intervention 'partageait les Dieux'. Calchas then reveals the secret of Eriphile's parentage. Racine makes him attribute this to 'Le Dieu qui maintenant vous parle par ma voix', but is careful to add that Calchas had purely human means of knowing, and to hint that he may merely be expressing his malice towards Eriphile:

> *Je vis moi-même alors* ce fruit de leurs amours.
> D'un sinistre avenir je *menaçai* ses jours.

Eriphile kills herself, but not out of deference to the sacredness of Calchas's words:

> Le sang de ces héros dont *tu me fais* descendre
> Sans tes *profanes* mains saura bien se répandre.

So Iphigénie is not *the* Iphigénie; the subject of the play is not the sacrifice of Agamemnon's daughter; and the central character is Eriphile. Now we come to the miracles. Racine starts with the more credible parts (the weather could break and the winds blow), and boldly associates them with another miracle: 'La flamme du bûcher d'ellemême s'allume.' This detail is not in Euripides: Racine is surely trying to make his miracle more credible by appealing to his Christian audience's recollection of the pyre on Mount Carmel at which Elijah confounded the priests of Baal. But immediately he equivocates again:

> Le *soldat* étonné *dit* que dans une nue
> Jusque sur le bûcher Diane est descendue,
> Et *croit* que s'élevant au travers de ses feux,
> Elle portait au ciel notre encens et nos voeux.

The final couplet of the play keeps the balance: Clytemnestre attribute[s] the happy ending to the gods and to Achille.

It is clear enough, from this brief survey of the text, that Racine is careful not to commit himself on the central issue of his play. He is not using the elements of his play to express any coherent pattern of experience: he is exploiting them for what interest they will yield in their own right. Barthes puts his finger on the play's weakness:

> *Iphigénie* est une 'grande comédie dramatique', où le Sang n'est plus un lien tribal, mais seulement familial, une simple continuité de bénéfices et d'affections. La conséquence critique est que l'on ne peut plus réduire les rôles entre eux, tenter d'atteindre le noyau singulier de la configuration; il faut les prendre les uns après les autres, définir ce que socialement, et non plus mythiquement, chacun d'eux réprésente.

The method, of course, has certain advantages. Hence the brilliance of the play, the perfectly articulated plot, the range and subtlety of the verse and characterisation: there is no central meaning to make things difficult, and Racine can display his virtuosity. Indeed, to make his play interesting at all, he must decorate it as brilliantly as he can.

If we now go back over the scenes in these middle plays which we singled out as showing Racine's mastery of his medium, we can see what they lack. In Act II, Scene i of *Bajazet,* the portrayal of Roxane's emotions and the control of dramatic tension are masterly, but they are the only two elements of interest in the scene. There is no larger significance to them, as there is in a scene like IV.v of *Bérénice,* where an equally acutely observed scene at the same time functions as part of the expression of a complex poetic theme. As with *Bajazet,* so with *Mithridate.* Its excellences are many, but what is the subject? We can only describe it in terms of the characters and plot: we cannot divine from the play any central theme, any reinterpretation of human experience. Why is the scene in which Mithridate explains his plans to his sons so inferior to Act II, Scene i of *Cinna*? Not because of any obvious weakness in Racine's verse, nor because Corneille shows a firmer grasp of political realities. It is certainly not because of any superiority in Corneille's character-drawing: in his scene he plays havoc with the characters of Cinna and Maxime. The reason for the difference in quality is that the scene in *Cinna* means something. It is part of a pattern which involves us in a particular interpretation of experience. In **Mithridate,** the political scene is just a political scene: another scene we can enjoy in a play which is full of them. **Mithridate** is close to some plays of Corneille's middle period, in method if not in content. Like so many of Corneille's plays after *Cinna,* it could very easily slide into domestic comedy: it is not for nothing that one of the most famous scenes recalls a situation in *L'Avare.* Again like Corneille's more naturalistic plays, *Mithridate* is full of that other symptom of naturalism, a complacent indulgence in contemporary jargon. Hardly anything in Corneille, even in *Oedipe,* can match the reaction of Xipharès when Monime says she has betrayed him:

Quoi! Madame, c'est vous, c'est l'amour qui
   m'expose?
Mon malheur est parti d'une si belle cause?
Trop d'amour a trahi nos secrets amoureux?
Et vous vous excusez de m'avoir fait heureux?

We may believe that **Mithridate** pleased contemporary taste.

This brings us back to the question of the reputation of these plays. It has often been remarked that all Racine's plays, except his first two, have retained their place on the stage. The situation with Corneille is very different: plays such as *Pompée* and *Rodogune* have steadily lost their reputations. But let us look more closely at the fortunes of **Bajazet, Mithridate** and **Iphigénie.** The reputations of masterpieces, or at least the reasons for which they are admired, often fluctuate: their power to arouse violent reactions and to provoke different interpretations is a sign of their greatness. The fate of **Bajazet, Mithridate** and **Iphigénie** is more depressing. Their evident merits have always been admired, but after their rapturous reception by contemporaries their reputations have suffered a slow but uninterrupted decline. The naturalist is committed to investing in the representation of contemporary behaviour: he may get quick returns, but the stock is ephemeral. **Bajazet, Mithridate** and **Iphigénie** suffer from just this weakness.

It follows from our argument that these three plays are not among Racine's best. Racine's mastery in them—of plot, character and verse—is of course as great as anyone has ever said it is. The difficulty is that this mastery is present to a higher degree in them than in his acknowledged masterpieces; and if we accept that excellence of plot, character and verse are the criteria of the value of a play we can hardly avoid calling **Iphigénie** Racine's

masterpiece, as Voltaire was logical and honest enough to do. If we are not prepared to do this, it follows that the reason for the superiority of some of Racine's other plays is more basic. I have maintained, in my [here unexcerpted] studies of **Andromaque, Britannicus** and **Bérénice,** that the reason for this superiority is that in them Racine makes use, with increasing sureness, of the poetic as distinct from the naturalistic method. This brings us face to face with another question: what type of theme does Racine use this poetic method to express? *Cinna* is poetic, but none of Racine's plays resembles it in tone or content. I have argued, and will argue, that Racine's best plays are tragic. Our central problem is this: on what basis was Racine able to found his tragedy?

The best starting-point is perhaps to look again at the most obvious strength of Racine, which has figured in every critical evaluation of his work from the appearance of **Andromaque** onwards. It has always been said that his special strength is in the portrayal of love. Whatever reservations we may make on his method of expression, Turnell is undoubtedly right to stress the importance of the erotic instinct in Racine. But I think we should emphasise that in Racine this erotic element is more all-embracing than that of a romantic love-story. We certainly do not attribute his power to the elegance with which he portrays his young lovers. The insipidity of Britannicus, Bajazet or Xipharès makes this one of the weakest features of his plays. By 'love' we really mean the elemental passion which he portrays: passions which may be profoundly sensual, as in Phèdre, but which are also often touched with sadistic and masochistic impulses, as in Néron or Titus, and may be more a lust for power than any other lust, as in Agrippine. Racine's contemporaries were very understandably shocked by the subversiveness of his plays. The way in which he wrote about love leaves no doubt of the daemonic force behind it.

It is no part of my purpose to discuss the scientific status of any psychological theory. Nevertheless, when modern critics discuss Racine, they are often drawn to speak of him in terms of modern depth psychology. This tendency seems to me a sound one, if only because it highlights some aspects of Racine which are difficult to account for in any other terms. . . .

My argument so far can be summarised as follows. The experiences to which the concept of the unconscious refers give poets a claim to seriousness in their work which enables them to evade the secondary rôles imposed on poetry by critical doctrines of the type of neo-classicism and naturalism; and these experiences are especially relevant to tragedy. My argument will now be that Racine based himself on a similar appeal to the unconscious to evade the naturalistic critical demands powerful in his environment, and that this opened his way to tragedy.

I believe that this assertion is supported by the evidence of his plays, but it may seem less odd if we link it with two other lines of thought. The first is the generally accepted view that he has affinities with the Greek tragic poets. I will come back to this in my next chapter. To anticipate, I think we must agree with Lapp that Racine's special affinity is with Euripides, and that it shows itself not by any means in sympathy with Euripidean technique ('The Greek writer's structure could only have seemed erratic to the Frenchman. And compared to the highly inventive Euripides, who added to or changed the established stories at will, Racine was extremely cautious, requiring a precedent for almost every innovation') but in a common attitude to the deep, irrational forces of the mind and their relation to the civilised, conscious order ('The lack of any specific divine cause for the tragedies of Racine's Jocaste, his Agamemnon, his Phèdre, is thus essentially Euripidean . . . for Racine as well as the Greek dramatist the natural life force is equated with the divine'). The affinity, in fact, is in a common attitude to 'the gods'. 'The gods', in Greek thought, are not theological abstractions: 'They are not merely dramatic fictions, but they personify the forces of necessity to which man must yield'. As such, they are often equivalent to powerful psychological impulses: 'A "god" is the personification of any more than human power in nature, or any force within the heart of man which is also greater than the individual because it is shared by all individuals'. As such, they come close to the modern concept of the unconscious, and to the seventeenth-century concept of *le coeur*.

This brings us to our second line of thought. There is one very significant tradition of thought in seventeenth-century France which was concerned to analyse as precisely as possible the irrational compulsions that determine human behaviour. La Rochefoucauld is sometimes presented as an author of cynical wisecracks. If we examine the *Maximes* at all carefully, we find they embody a more sombre attitude than this judgement implies:

> La durée de nos passions ne dépend pas plus de nous que la durée de notre vie.
>
> Nous n'avons pas assez de force pour suivre toute notre raison.
>
> Qui vit sans folie n'est pas si sage qu'il croit.
>
> Il y a plus de défauts dans l'humeur que dans l'esprit. Il s'en faut bien que nous ne connaissions toutes nos volontés.
>
> On ne souhaite jamais ardemment ce qu'on ne souhaite que par raison.

La Rochefoucauld's theme is one from which Euripides and Freud would not have dissented: 'L'esprit est toujours la dupe du coeur'.

As Bénichou pointed out, La Rochefoucauld's work rests on the concept of unconscious mental processes. What is striking is that he sees them as truly unconscious, not merely at the margin of consciousness. The similarity of his attitude and subject-matter to those of more recent psychologists is notable, particularly in some of the material he cancelled. The original opening 'Maxime' reads like a passage from *The Book of the It* or a Freudian paper on the instincts. Maxime XXXIII of the original edition describes the mechanism of projection. Maxime XLIV in the definitive edition insists on the biological basis of psychology. The suppressed No XII of the *Réflexions Diverses* propounds a psychosomatic theory of disease. The Maximes show a concern with the most bizarre aspects of human behaviour: La Rochefoucauld seems to have been especially fascinated by the incident of the lackey who danced on the scaffold before being broken on the wheel.

Adam links the *Maximes* with the work of Saint-Réal, who for a while was the mentor of Racine. Saint-Réal was drawn to 'l'étude du coeur humain', which soon led him to see 'que la bizarrerie ou la folie sont le plus souvent les causes des actions les plus éclatantes, que la malignité est le plus fréquent motif de nos sentiments, que surtout chez les femmes et chez les enfants il y a plaisir à faire le mal et à voir souffrir'. Adam adds a note:

> Saint-Réal n'est pas seul à s'intéresser à ces régions obscures de la vie des sentiments. Dans une de ses *Lettres,* Méré cite un mari qui 'plaisait plus à certains hommes qu'un homme ne doit souhaiter', et ce mari ne pouvait trouver son plaisir avec sa femme, qui était très belle, qu'en l'imaginant dans les bras d'un autre . . . . Il posait devant son secrétaire, sur un ami inconnu, ces étranges questions: 'Pourquoi voit-il une putaine si laide, lui qui a une si belle femme? Comment peut-il aimer les garçons?'

We need not think that in emphasising Racine's irrationalism we are merely projecting back into the seventeenth century our twentieth-century views: the student of Euripides, the contemporary of La Rochefoucauld and the friend of Saint-Réal had ample opportunity to arrive at such views for himself.

There is a strong negative argument for the hypothesis: how else can we account for the strength of Racine? As I have tried to show, we can hardly explain his compelling force if we regard him only as continuing and perfecting Corneille. Precision of plotting, subtlety and force of characterisation, sweetness and strength of verse: all these are present to a high degree in **Mithridate,** and to the point of perfection in **Iphigénie**. But neither of these plays can take us by the throat as some others can. They are much superior to *Le Comte d'Essex,* but they are not obviously different in kind. We may feel that Thomas Corneille, if only he had possessed a little more skill and sensitivity, might have risen to **Mithridate**. **Phèdre** is of a different order entirely. It is this differentness of Racine that the critic has to explain.

We can approach the question from another angle. There is one special strength of Racine which marks him out from his minor contemporaries, of which he himself was conscious, and which is obviously a major source of his power: his poetry. Poetry, far more than prose, is equipped to embody intuitions from below the level of consciousness. As Brereton has remarked, Racine's verse 'retains the slight haze always necessary to poetry'. Poetry is based directly on experience: it can afford to draw only a little material at second-hand, from the findings of external disciplines. It characteristically has a range of meanings that cannot be formulated in prose-simultaneous views, as it were, of many sides of an experience. It is this richness which produces the haze. This does not mean that poetry is less clear than prose; on the contrary, it can say with immediate clarity and force what prose cannot say at all. This is true to an especially high degree of poetic drama: the whole complex of means of expression—plot, character, situation and the rest, which are elements in the poetic substance—is removed further still from conceptual discourse than that of a non-dramatic poem, which consists of words alone. If the only elements called into play are the non-verbal ones, the work will lack the conceptual clarity which words, uniquely, combine with emotional resonance derived from the whole range of human experience. If this combination of verbal and non-verbal means is essential to the statement made by the work (and not merely sugaring of a prose pill) the meaning expressed must therefore be inexpressible by normal prose statements. Such inexpressibility is characteristic precisely of those experiences which are closest to the unconscious mental processes. It is possible for a very great artist to match the elements which express the meaning inexpressible by prose so exactly with a rational surface that the irrational part of the total statement can be missed by the insensitive. I have argued that this almost perfect matching occurs in **Bérénice**. More commonly, in responding to a work of art we feel the daemonic impulsion, and are aware that it could not be accommodated in prose terms. In all the most powerful of Racine's plays we feel this compelling presence of a meaning that is more than the plot or the characters and cannot be reduced to any prose message. We may also note in Racine's verse surface features that fit awkwardly into the conventions of rational discourse: ambiguities, unexpected collocations, recurring images and patterns, and, above all, paradox. Neoclassical poets are fond of antithesis, but in Racine the antitheses—especially in **Phèdre** and **Athalie**—are sharpened to the point of paradox.

This brings us to a further problem. We have argued that the basic tradition of neo-classicism was naturalistic, and that in the age of Louis XIV it was evolving ever towards greater reasonableness, greater formal elegance, and away from any inconvenient attempt to express a central substance. Set in this tradition we have Racine, a profound poet, struggling to express his sense of passion and violence in human experience. This poetic impulse put him in touch with those unconscious forces whose strength and immediacy gave him a firm base from which to resist the secondary rôle assigned to the arts by naturalism. At the same time, the critical code of elegant decencies forbade expression of these uncouth impulses; and Racine himself certainly subscribed to the code. What might we expect would be his technique in such a situation?

It may help us to look at two analogies: Freud's theory of dream-formation and Eliot's tactics in writing his plays.

Freud came to the conclusion that the conflict between unconscious forces and the moral and other tendencies resisting their expression is temporarily resolved (still below the level of consciousness) in a compromise: the repugnant unconscious material is disguised behind a façade which is acceptable to the repressing tendencies, but which is found, on analysis, to express the unacceptable content behind it. This façade is as far as possible given a reasonable, coherent form by a process of 'secondary revision' which takes account of the standards of rationality of the conscious mind. In a perfect dream, the façade might appear perfectly rational. In practice, there are always some incongruities which betray the fact that the dream conceals something more elemental.

Eliot's tactics, though quite conscious, involve a somewhat similar process. They are set out most starkly in a letter to Pound:

> If you can keep the bloody audience's attention engaged, then you can perform any monkey tricks you like when they ain't looking, and it's what you do behind the audience's back so to speak that makes your play IMMORTAL for a while.

> If the audience gets its strip tease it will swallow the poetry.

We can see this technique in, for instance, *The Cocktail Party*. In this case, the 'monkey tricks' are the Christian meaning which Eliot wishes to convey, and which he thinks his audience will reject as alien; the 'strip tease' is the popular West End light comedy. The problem is then to convey the meaning in this form: the Christian idea of martyrdom must be expressed through drawing-room comedy. Here again, but this time by design, a few elements which cannot be assimilated to the humdrum surface direct our attention to the meaning underneath: the Guardians pour libations. This approach is not characteristic of all poetic drama, and is unlikely to succeed if applied in cold blood. In Eliot's case it fails. This is not necessarily because the method is at fault. It seems more likely that if it fails in this case, this is because the meaning to be expressed is not a poetic meaning inexpressible in other terms than those of the play itself, but a preconceived doctrine which he wishes to insinuate in a sugared form.

These two examples are offered as models of Racine's method, which may be stated as follows. He takes a story or situation, not simply because it offers striking characters or an exciting plot, but because he feels that it can help him to embody the meaning he is struggling to express. His task, as a poet, is to bring out and articulate with the greatest possible clarity this hidden meaning. But the literary conventions of his day forbid a crude expression of some elements of this hidden meaning: what these conventions (which he shared) do demand are a clear plot, interesting characters and elegant verse, all conforming to orthodox morality and common sense (except insofar as poetry may have licence to tell agreeable lies, providing they are not to be taken seriously). His problem is then to find a naturalistic surface which will satisfy his critics (and himself) and at the same time serve as a façade which will harmonise with his underlying meaning. In Racine, this façade (the 'strip tease') is always beautifully constructed. To the careless eye, the effect of the play seems to be due to the perfection of the façade. But this is not so, as two pieces of evidence show: first, the plays with the most perfect façades (*Mithridate* and *Iphigénie*) are not the most powerful; and second, in some of the most powerful of his plays (*Andromaque, Britannicus, Phèdre* and *Athalie*) there are evident discontinuities between the façade and the meaning behind it. . . .

This view of Racine explains much in his prefaces. He defends laboriously the historical accuracy and 'vraisemblance' of every detail of his plays—that is, of their façades. But two things arouse him to fury: when the critics are not satisfied with his façade, in spite of all his trouble with it (see the first preface to *Britannicus*); and when they suggest that he has broken the 'rules' in general—that is, that although he may have meticulously observed the individual rules of the unities, the *liaison des scènes,* and so on, he has departed from the basis of neo-classical dramaturgy. The second accusation hurts because it is true. Racine's defence is the only possible one: he appeals to the powerful effect his plays make on the spectators who are not concerned with the rules. There is a fundamental discrepancy between the two imperatives of neo-classical art: 'to please' and 'to follow the rules'. In Racine the two imperatives correspond to the two levels of his plays: 'to please', he relied on the powerful appeal of the latent content to our passions; but 'to follow the rules' it is necessary to produce a façade pleasing to the rational mind. We find in his art, in fact, an ambivalence which we find also in his attitude to Jansenism and to his life at Court: an anxiety to please, shadowed by an inner defiance.

I have travelled around a good deal in an effort to illuminate Racine's tragic method. My purpose, however, has been to set off and make understandable the nature of his achievement, not to subordinate it to yet another schematic explanation. We are still left with the paradox of Racine, the perfect neo-classicist and poet of anarchic passion. In the last analysis, perhaps we can only say it was his temperament, or his genius—in either case, an insoluble mystery—which led him to intrude the archaic bull into the Dresden china shop. But even genius must have some path along which to travel, some associative link to connect his intuitions with an accepted form which can help him express them. This link lay to hand in another element in the neo-classical tradition: the use of antique subject-matter. Tradition approved the use of either ancient history or mythology. Racine, far more than Corneille or his own contemporaries (except when they were being operatic) chose myth. The great myths of Greece live because they are intimately connected with the most emotion-laden and frequent experiences of human beings. If we want to explain the differentness of Racine, we must reaffirm what has been said by many others: Racine alone, in the words of Vinaver, 'entrera dans le domaine du mythe avec la volonté d'en respecter les données és-sentielles et d'émouvoir le spectateur par les choses mêmes "qui avaient mis autrefois en larmes le plus savant peuple de la Grèce".' We may doubt whether this is true of *Iphigénie*. There is no doubt that it is true of *Phèdre*.

My view, then, is that the basis of Racine's art was his concern to express those irrational and even infantile passions that are fed from the unconscious, but that he masked them as far as possible behind a perfect neo-classical façade.

David Maskell (essay date 1993)

SOURCE: "Racine and Shakespeare: A Common Language," in *Comparative Literature Studies,* Vol. 30, No. 3, 1993, pp. 253-68.

[*Maskell is the author of* Racine: A Theatrical Reading *(1991). In the following excerpt from a later work, he compares the theatricality—specifically, the "visual language"—of Shakespeare and Racine.*]

When writers' names become symbols this can obscure what they actually wrote. Racine and Shakespeare stand in symbolic opposition. Shakespeare represents full-blooded theatricality; Racine stands for an abstract disembodied form of tragedy. This opposition deserves to be challenged. Of course there are substantial differences between Racine and Shakespeare. Racine has no witches, no gravediggers, no storms, no battles on stage. Racine's tragedies have no low-life subplots and no deliberate excursions into the comic register. Furthermore Shakespeare's exuberant poetry is far removed from Racine's laconic formality. But these differences should not overshadow the similarities. Their theatrical relationship can be better understood by considering what they have in common, in particular the visual dimension of their dramatic art. If one supposes a scale of physical action from the batting of an eyelid to the fighting of battles, one can say that Shakespeare used the whole scale whilst Racine avoided the latter extreme. However, there remains a substantial range of visual language which both dramatists shared and both exploited for significant effect. . . .

Whilst for decades an abundance of works have explored Shakespeare's theatricality, Racine has lagged far behind. Yet the studies of Shakespeare's theatricality are by no means devoted entirely to battles, crowd scenes, or large groups of characters on stage. Only two out of eight chapters deal with these topics in Styan's *Shakespeare's Stagecraft;* the rest treat matters of relevance of Racine. The bulk of Slater's *Shakespeare the Director* is made up of chapters on action and expression, position on stage, kneeling, kissing and embracing, weeping, silence and pause, costume, properties—just those elements of visual language which Shakespeare shares with Racine, and which Racine exploited more fully than most of his contemporaries who wrote French tragedy in the second half of the seventeenth century.

The study of theatricality must begin with the stage directions, explicit and implicit, which the dramatist writes into his text. Paradoxically these are often neglected in actual performances, though they are essential to the study of the dramatist's stagecraft. [In his *Acting and Action in Shakespearean Tragedy* (1985), Michael] Goldman insists on the stage direction *"Thunder and lightning"* at the start of Macbeth: "This effect, so clear and definite in the text, is strangely muted in most modern productions." A similar complaint has been voiced in connection with Racine, where excessive attention to speech leads to neglect of the theatrical situation. The final scene of Racine's *Andromaque* should be dominated by the tumult and violence resulting from the murder of King Pyrrhus. Pylade begs Oreste to flee with him: "Sortons de ce palais, . . . Nos Grecs pour un moment en défendent la porte. / Tout le peuple assemblé nous poursuit à main forte" (5.5.1583-86). In modern performances, even though the situation demands agitation and movement, Pylade usually steps dutifully aside to let the actor playing Oreste deliver his celebrated "Pour qui sont ces serpents qui sifflent sur vos têtes" speech. Pierre Henri Larthomas deplores this failure to portray the realities of the situation:

> Mais quoi! dans ce palais cerné par le peuple pas un cri? Pas de coups frappés à la porte? . . . Mais Pylade attendant presque patiemment qu'Oreste se soit évanoui? C'est inadmissible. Car dans cette scène de la folie, unique par sa violence dans notre théâtre classique, véritablement shakespearienne, oserions-nous dire que la situation a autant d'importance et plus d'importance peut-être que les mots?

The only thing to query in Larthomas's comment is the suggestion that this scene in *Andromaque* is unique in French classical drama. Racine ends *La Thébaïde* with Créon's madness, and most of his plays have scenes where there is tumult: the cries of the dying and shouts of victory in *Alexandre;* commotion engendered by the poisoning of Britannicus; shouts and rebellion in *Mithridate;* noisy crowds and thunder in *Iphigénie;* Athalie falling into an ambush on stage.

Racine's system of stage directions is similar to that of Shakespeare. They are sometimes explicit but more often written into the text. The word "thus" signals gesture or expression to the actor:

> MALVOLIO. I extend my hand to him thus, quenching my familiar smile with an austere regard of control.
> (*Twelfth Night,* 2.5.65; emphasis added)

In Racine, Monime signals in similar fashion her sudden change from submission to defiance of Mithridate:

> MONIME. Mais le dessein est pris. Rien ne peut m'ébranler.
> Jugez-en, puisqu'ainsi je vous ose parler,
> Et m'emporte au delà de cette modestie
> Dont jusqu'à ce moment je n'étais point sortie.
> (*Mithridate,* 4.4.1362-65)

More frequently "thus" (*ainsi*) in Racine refers to the gesture or expression of the interlocutor, as when Britannicus chides Junie: "Quel accueil! Quelle glace! / Est-ce *ainsi* que vos yeux consolent ma disgrace?" In like manner Lady Macbeth hisses at her husband mesmerized by the ghost: "Shame itself, / Why do you make *such* faces?"

Retrospective stage directions also play their part in both Racine and Shakespeare, when characters subsequently recall a preceding scene and give information relevant to its performance. [In her *Shakespeare the Director* (1982), Anne Pasternak] Slater shows how details of the assassination of Julius Caesar are leaked out later. Racine uses the same technique for the farewell of Axiane and Porus in *Alexandre,* for the interrogation of Monime in *Mithridate,* and for Phèdre's struggle with Hippolyte's sword in *Phèdre.* So in writing scripts which contained directions for performance on stage there is a close connection between Racine and Shakespeare—theatrical directors both.

In order to understand how the two dramatists used scenery and stage space, it is necessary to keep in mind the main features of the playhouses for which they composed their plays. Despite the many differences, there were points in common between the theatres, which permit comparisons to be made. Public playhouses in London were round or polygonal. The chief features of the acting area were a large platform stage up to 40 feet across, the façade of the player's changing room with two or more doors, a gallery above, and a trap-door. The audience surrounded the acting area on three sides. The public theatres in Paris were enclosed rectangular boxes with the stage at one end. The spectators looked down the box at the acting area which measured about 30 by 30 feet within the confines of the canvas scenery. Whilst one can demonstrate clear links between the scenic features of the plays and the staging conditions of the theatres in both Paris and London, none the less dramatists and actors had to be flexible, since plays were performed in other venues, such as at court or in private houses. The physical conditions of the theatres were not a rigid framework, but they need to be borne in mind as a guide to understanding the plays in performance.

One area where Racine and Shakespeare did differ was in the matter of scenery. In spite of the often repeated statements that Racine's tragedies unfold in a banal vestibule or antechamber, most of Racine's plays contain some element of scenery significant for the whole action. In *Andromaque* the backdrop of sea and ships represents Oreste's mission to the court of Pyrrhus. In *Iphigénie* the backdrop representing becalmed ships is a constant reminder of reasons for Agamemnon needing to sacrifice his daughter. Backdrops of this sort were possible because of the convention of unity of place in French drama. Racine differs from Shakespeare not in the use of a vague all-purpose antechamber, but because he used fully representational scenery, which was never a feature of the public theatres in London in Shakespeare's time. Yet in other respects they both exploited the staging conditions for which they composed their plays. The stage-trap was traditionally the entrance to hell. It may have been used for the ghost who "cries under the stage" in *Hamlet*

(1.5.148) or for the graves in the same play: The gallery above the tiring room façade could represent an upstairs in *Romeo and Juliet* (2.5), or more often city ramparts. The English scale the ramparts and the French jump down from them, according to the stage direction: "The French leap o'er the walls in their shirts" (*1 Henry VI*, 2.1.38). There are no parallels in Racine's tragedies, but his one comedy *Les Plaideurs* uses levels above and below the stage: an upstairs window from which Dandin jumps (1.3), and a basement out of which he pokes his head, only to have it twisted back and forth by the two litigants until they both tumble down to join him: "Ils sont, sur ma parole, / L'un et l'autre encavés" (2.11.575-76). The use of curtains for concealment or discovery occurs in several Shakespearean plays and in two of Racine's: Néron eavesdrops on the lovers in Act II of *Britannicus;* in the last act of *Athalie* the boy-king is concealed behind a curtain and then revealed, after which the backdrop opens to show the interior of the temple and the armed Levites who surround Athalie. The large open stage of the Elizabethans allowed plays to be planned in three dimensions using upstage and downstage as well as significant groupings of characters. The proscenium stage in Paris allowed less scope for this, since actors usually came to the front of the stage to speak, but Racine does suggest the three-dimensional positioning of actors by stage directions placed before speeches such as "Antigone, *en s'en allant,*" "Néron, *sans voir Burrhus,*" "Titus, *en entrant.*" Assuérus withdraws after a speech *"Le roi s'éloigne."* In spite of the major differences between the English and French stages, there are therefore some general points of similarity between Racine and Shakespeare with regard to their use of stage space. More important, however, are those cases where both use décor in conjunction with movement on stage to speak visually or "parler aux yeux," as Voltaire's phrase has it.

The doors of the Elizabethan stage could be used symbolically. On several occasions stage directions require characters to enter by separate doors emphasizing the division between opposing sides:

> *Enter at one door King Henry, Exeter . . . and the other Lords; at another Queen Isabel, the King of France . . . and other French.*
>
> (*Henry V*, 5.2)

Racine used doors in a similar fashion. In Act IV of *Bérénice* the spectator sees Antiochus enter from Bérénice's door urging Titus to prevent the queen from committing suicide. A few lines later a Roman messenger enters from the opposite door, announcing that the senators await the emperor in his apartment. Titus is caught between his love for Bérénice and the demands of state. His dilemma, the subject of the play, is represented in a theatrical tableau, as he listens to Paulin and Antiochus, representing Rome versus Love, standing by opposing doors and exhorting him to leave the stage in their respective directions.

Shakespeare highlighted differences between characters by divergent exits through separate doors. "Bertram sends his newly married Helena 'home, where I will never come' through one door, and promptly slips away through the other." Racine uses divergent exits in *Iphigénie* when Ériphile orders her confidant not to follow the royal family as they go to save Iphigénie from sacrifice: "Suis-moi. Ce n'est pas là, Doris, notre chemin" (4.9). They exit in a different direction to indicate that Ériphile intends to betray Iphigénie to the high priest.

Another element of décor which permits a precise comparison is the raised throne. In a banal sense it denoted the royal status of its occupant, but more interestingly its significance could be subverted by other occupants. Shakespeare tried it first in *3 Henry VI* when York takes the throne so that King Henry has to stand beneath him: "My lords, look where the sturdy rebel sits, / Even in the chair of state" (1.1.50-51). Then again, more subtly, Richard II's throne is occupied by Bulingbrooke, while unthroned King Richard grows in kingly stature:

> BULINGBROOKE. In God's name I'll ascend the
>   regal throne. . . .
> K. RICHARD. Alack, why am I sent for to a king
>   Before I have shook off the regal thoughts
>   Wherewith I reign'd?

Only in *Esther* does Racine use a formal throne. It denotes the terrifying kingship of Assuérus, before which Esther collapses in a faint. Yet it has the potential to protect the Jews, a development in the plot symbolically foreshadowed by Esther's command to her girls at the end of Act II:

> Et vous troupe jeune et timide,
> Sans craindre ici les yeux d'une profane cour,
> A l'abri de ce Trône attendez mon retour.
>   (*Esther*, 2.8.710-12)

Later in the play the spectators see Assuérus turn from persecutor into protector. The central theme of the play is expressed in these actions around the throne.

Entrances and exits are used by both Racine and Shakespeare for theatrical effect. In addition to obvious devices such as surprise entrances or ceremonial parades, there are more subtle ways in which the movement of characters on and off stage can have significance. Arrested movement and delayed exits abound in *Hamlet*. Characters say they are leaving but they linger. After the first ghost episode Hamlet urges his companions away with the words "Let's go together" but he pauses and hesitates before finally deciding to depart (1.5.190). After "To be, or not to be," Hamlet in conversation with Ophelia thrice utters "Farewell" and thrice stays on stage (3.1.132-40). "Thus the element of delay in *Hamlet* [wrote Robert Hapgood, in his *Shakespeare the Theatre-Poet* (1988)] is not just a debatable matter concerning the characterization of the Prince. The playwright has built delay into the plot and choreography." Choreography would be a suitable word for the movements of Hippolyte in Racine's *Phèdre*. He is constantly seeking to escape from Troezen and repeatedly sketches movements of flight during the scenes in which he appears. He is visibly impatient to leave Phèdre in Act II, Scene 5, and she remarks upon this in a retrospective stage direction: "Comme il ne respirait qu'une retraite prompte!" (*Phèdre,* 3.1.745). Yet when Hippolyte's father orders him to leave, driving him away with "Fuis, traître. . . . fuis: . . . fuis, disje," Hippolyte stays on stage (4.2). Indecision is also represented visually in other plays. Pyrrhus says he is leaving to deliver Andromaque's son to certain death but he fails to exit. Roxane swears vengeance against Bajazet, but prevents Acomat leaving the stage to carry out her order to have him killed. Arrested actions convey the dynamic quality of these tragedies of vacillation.

Shakespeare used seating arrangements to speak visually. In *Macbeth* the banquet opens in harmony: "You know your own degrees, sit down," but ends in disorder when Lady Macbeth dismisses the guests: "Stand not upon the order of your going, / But go at once." Racine breached etiquette in *Alexandre* to break up a formal embassy in muted disorder, when the ambassador Éphestion, who has been seated before the two Indian kings, rises without permission to signal Alexandre's arrogant declaration of war. Contemporary spectators would have been more sensitive to protocol than are modern audiences. The list of stage properties in the *Mémoire de Mahelot* makes it clear that Éphestion sat upon a stool ("tabouret") to signify his inferior status whilst the two Indian kings sat on chairs with arms ("fauteuils") as befitted their rank. *Macbeth* and *Alexandre* are both studies of how ambition disrupts an established order, and both contain scenes where the violation of social conventions represents disruption in visual terms which would have had an impact upon contemporaries.

Both dramatists use the signifying power of collapse on to a chair:

> Shakespeare picks up Antony's loss of self-control ("he was not his own man"), extends it to his leadership of men, whom he can no longer command, but only entreat, and clinches it by the stage symbol, as Antony collapses in a state of total self-abandonment.
>
> (Slater)

The stage direction here is most probably authorial:

> ANTONY. . . . indeed I have lost command,
> Therefore I pray you. I'll see you by and by.
> *Sits down.*
>
> (*Antony and Cleopatra,* 3.11.23-24)

Racine brings Phèdre on stage only to have her collapse in the same posture:

> PHEDRE. . . . mes genoux tremblants se dérobent
>   sous moi.
> Hélas! *Elle s'assied.*
>
> (*Phèdre,* 1.3.156)

Shakespeare and Racine insist on the humiliation caused by this loss of control. Antony averts his face: "See /

How I convey my shame" (3.11.51). The same gesture is implied for Phèdre as she addresses her confidant: "la rougeur me couvre le visage: / Je te laisse trop voir mes honteuses douleurs" (3.182). Later Phèdre, like Antony, confesses that she is no longer in command:

> Moi régner! Moi ranger un état sous ma loi,
> Quand ma faible raison ne règne plus sur moi.
>   (*Phèdre,* 3.1.759)

Shakespeare employed kneeling in many contexts, to signal order when men kneel in prayer, homage, or supplication, and to signal disorder or deceit when they refuse to kneel or they kneel insincerely. Kneeling can be the pivot of the tragic mechanism. Titus Andronicus's *hamartia* is given visual expression when he is seen rejecting the captive Tamora's pleas to spare her son. Although there is no explicit stage direction, her situation strongly implies that she kneels. The essence of Shakespeare's visual tableau here is paralleled in Racine's *Andromaque* where Hermione, like Titus Andronicus, commits the fatal error of rejecting a kneeling suppliant. Hermione dismisses Andromaque scornfully, sending her to plead with Pyrrhus (3.4). This starts a chain of supplications from which Andromaque eventually emerges victorious, whilst Hermione and Pyrrhus meet their death.

Unconventional kneeling is seen in Shakespeare when Volumnia kneels to her son Coriolanus, or Lear to his daughter Regan. Racine also knew the power of such incongruous actions. Queen Clytemnestre kneels to the subordinate Achille to ask him to protect Iphigénie, who is to be a human sacrifice. Achille is disconcerted; indeed he is struck rigid and says in astonishment: "Madame je me tais et demeure immobile. . . . / Une reine à mes pieds se vient humilier!" (*Iphigénie,* 3.5-6.949, 952). Racine uses Clytemnestre's posture to emphasize the extreme peril of her daughter. It carries the implication that Agamemnon, Iphigénie's father and natural protector, has forfeited his natural protective role because he is to sacrifice his daughter. The scene which Racine has contrived for the kneeling Clytemnestre could well be glossed by Shakespeare's lines in *Coriolanus,* which describe Volumnia's keeling to her son:

> Behold, the heavens do ope,
> The gods look down, and this unnatural scene
> They laugh at.
>
> (5.3.183-85)

Shakespeare's lines are especially apt because Racine's *Iphigénie* is a cruel joke. It turns out that the gods never meant Agamemnon's daughter to be the sacrificial victim, and she is saved at the end after much unnecessary suffering.

The verbal and the visual work in conjunction when characters try to persuade each other to perform actions which will be seen on stage. This is a specifically theatrical way of linking speech and action. In Shakespeare's *King John* a handshake signalling alliance provides the visual focus for a long debate in which the King of France hesitates between alliance with England or Rome. King Philip holds King John by the hand. The conflicting parties try to make them part:

> PANDULPH. Philip of France, on peril of a curse,
> Let go the hand of that arch-heretic,
> And raise the power of France upon his head,
> Unless he do submit himself to Rome.
> ELINOR. Looks't thou pale, France? Do not let
>   go thy hand.
>
> (*King John,* 3.1.191-95)

An analagous effect occurs in **La Thébaïde** when Racine makes a potential embrace the visual focus of the debate between the warring brothers, Polynice and Étéocle. Here Jocaste's arguments are aimed at making her sons embrace. She calls them by name to draw near to each other and then she pauses to focus on the action: "Hé quoi! loin d'approcher, vous reculez tous deux? . . . Commencez, Polynice, embrassez votre frère" (4.3.985, 999). Such examples illustrate the dynamics of persuasive speech combined with the focussing power of bodily movement. Not only does this generate dramatic tension but, as so often, Racine creates a visual image which encapsulates the theme of the tragedy, here the fruitless attempts by a mother to make peace between her two warring sons.

Another technique which combines the verbal and the visual is the use of a stage property as the focus of imaginative speech. One can compare the use of daggers in *Macbeth* and **Bajazet**. "For Shakespeare [wrote J. L. Styan, in his *Shakespeare's Stagecraft* (1967)] a property was a dramatic opportunity—think only of Macbeth's dagger, the real weapon slung at his waist, the 'air-drawn' fantasy a chance to plumb his mind" (Styan 32). The important point here is that although Macbeth is addressing an imaginary dagger, he is prompted by the real one which he wears and which he handles when he says: "I see thee yet, in form as palpable / As this which now I draw" (2.1.40-41). Bajazet's dagger is also the starting point for musings which reveal his state of mind. He has purchased his freedom by accepting marriage with Roxane. Atalide is jealous and Bajazet should be responding to her anxieties. Instead, the concrete reality of his dagger feeds his imagination with thoughts of noble exploits against his brother:

> Mais enfin je me vois les armes à la main;
> Je suis libre, et je puis contre un frère inhumain,
> Non plus, par un silence aidé de votre adresse,
> Disputer en ces lieux le cœur de ma maîtresse,
> Mais par de vrais combats, par de nobles
>   dangers,
> Moi-même le cherchant aux climats étrangers,
> Lui disputer les cœurs du peuple et de l'armée,
> Et pour juge entre nous prendre la renommée.
>
> (**Bajazet,** 3.4.947-54)

In his exultant mood, he fails to see that Atalide does not share his dreams. She weeps. Bajazet's insensitive response to her tears precipitates a crisis which will lead them all to their deaths. It could be called Bajazet's "dagger

speech." Both Racine and Shakespeare weave together material reality, fantasy, and tragedy.

When a hat temporarily functions as a stage property and becomes the focus of attention, the connotations are more light-hearted. In *Hamlet* (5.2) Osric displays excessive deference to Hamlet by refusing to replace his hat after they have exchanged greetings. Hamlet urges him "Put your bonnet to his right use, 'tis for the head" (92-93), and a contest of courtesy ensues, emphasizing the incongruity of Osric's conduct "especially in a creature of the usurping King addressing that King's victim" [wrote Andrew Gurr, in *The Shakespearean Stage,* 2nd ed. (1980)] The porter in **Les Plaideurs,** acting the part of a barrister, does not know that barristers addressed the court wearing their hats. Hence his incongruous contest of courtesy with the judge:

> DANDIN. Couvrez-vous.
> PETIT JEAN.   O! Mes . . .
> DANDIN.
>   Couvrez-vous, vous dis-je.
> PETIT JEAN. Oh! Monsieur, je sais bien à quoi
>   l'honneur m'oblige.
> DANDIN. Ne te couvre donc pas.
> PETIT JEAN. *se couvrant* Messieurs. . . .
>
> (3.3.671-73)

In this manner Racine launches his sparkling parody of legal procedures and forensic oratory.

Romantic praise of Shakespeare and condescension towards Racine led to misconceptions with regard to the tears which are shed copiously in both Racine and Shakespeare. Failure to appreciate this has helped to perpetuate misconceptions concerning Racine's theatricality. Stendhal's spokesman for Romanticism blamed Racine for being the slave of the conventions of his day:

> LE ROMANTIQUE. Racine ne croyait pas que l'on pût faire la tragédie autrement. S'il vivait de nos jours, et qu'il osât suivre les règles nouvelles, il ferait cent fois mieux qu'*Iphigénie*. Au lieu de n'inspirer que de l'admiration, sentiment un peu froid, il ferait couler des torrents de larmes.
>
> (*Racine et Shakespeare*)

There is a double error here in Stendhal's comparison between Racine and Shakespeare. Racine's **Iphigénie** did excite torrents of tears and he did employ the same techniques as Shakespeare. Hermione in *The Winter's Tale* makes an exit under arrest while all her women weep: "My women may be with me, for you see / My plight requires it. Do not weep, good fools" (2.1.117-19). Agamemnon in **Iphigénie** looks around him as he comes to take his daughter to be sacrificed and says: "Ma fille, vous pleurez, . . . Mais tout pleure, et la fille, et la mère." Both plays show several characters on stage weeping together and this was a means of prompting the audience's tears. Racine in his preface to **Iphigénie** congratulated himself on achieving this response, and contemporary evidence confirms the tears that this play generated.

The visual language of Racine and Shakespeare overlaps to a much greater extent than the traditional opposition between them allows for. Although it is true that Racine confines himself to the more subdued visual effects deriving from décor, stage properties, bodily movements and gestures, he generally extracts maximum significance from them and his visual language is nearly always related to a central theme of the play. This same range of effects is found in Shakespeare, though not always with such key significance. But in both there is a weaving together of the material and the intellectual that can disconcert the literary minded critic. In the seventeenth century both were criticized for stage business which was felt to be inconsistent with the dignity of tragedy. Thomas Rymer, in his boisterous diatribe against *Othello,* inveighed against the physical object on which the plot hangs: "So much ado, so much stress, so much passion and repetition about an Handkerchief! Why was this not called the *Tragedy of the Handkerchief?*" He objected to the actors's visual language: "the Mops and Mows, the Grimace, the Grins, and Gesticulation." Subligny, reporting on a performance of Racine's **Phèdre** during its first run, criticized it in similar vein. Racine had invested Phèdre with "trop de fureur, trop d'effronterie"; Oenone, who clasps her mistress's knees "arrache avec trop d'indiscrétion et d'emportement le secret de sa maîtresse." Subligny reserved his fiercest strictures for the snatching of Hippolyte's sword by Phèdre (**Phèdre**, 2.5), and in so doing bears witness to Racine's uncompromising theatricality:

> Cette épée tirée est un incident qui fait pitié . . . si M. Racine a eu quelque sujet d'exposer à nos yeux cette violente action, c'est assurément pour donner un beau jeu à sa piéce . . . mais quand on cherche des jeux de théâtre, il ne faut pas être si critique.

The visual language of the theatre displeased critics like Rymer and Subligny, but it links great dramatists and crosses linguistic frontiers. The divisions symbolized by the doors in *Henry V* and **Bérénice,** the polyvalence of the throne in *Richard II* and **Esther,** the disrupted seating arrangements in *Macbeth* and **Alexandre,** the collapse into a chair in *Antony and Cleopatra* and **Phèdre,** the spurning of a supliant in *Titus Andronicus* and **Andromaque,** the unconventional kneeling in *Coriolanus* and **Iphigénie,** the gestures of alliance in *King John* and **La Thébaïde,** the daggers in *Macbeth* and **Bajazet**—Racine and Shakespeare provide examples of a common visual vocabulary which is the peculiar feature of theatrical language, and which unites dramatists who can exploit its rich potential.

FURTHER READING

Barnwell, H. T. *The Tragic Drama of Corneille and Racine: An Old Parallel Revisited.* Oxford: Clarendon Press, 1982, 275 p.

> Investigates various aspects of plot in the dramas of Racine and Corneille with the aim of seeing more clearly "both the parallels and the divergences between the two dramatists, not only in their technique itself (what they

called their art) but also in its implication in the presentation of their tragic vision."

Barthes, Roland. *On Racine.* Translated by Richard Howard. 1960. Reprint. New York: Octagon Books, 1977, 172 p.

> In-depth examination of each of Racine's dramas, attempting to reconstruct "a kind of Racinian anthropology, both structural and psycholanalytic: structural in content, because tragedy is here treated as a system of units ('figures') and functions; psycholanylitic in form, because only an approach ready to acknowledge the fear of the world, as I believe psychoanalysis is, seems to me suitable for dealing with the image of man confined."

C. M. Bowra. "The Simplicity of Racine." In his *In General and Particular,* pp. 149-72. London: Weidenfeld and Nicolson, 1964.

> Addresses the manner in which Racine trimmed every aspect of his dramas to their essentials to set a new standard of dramatic effectiveness and power in the French theater.

Brereton, Geoffrey. *Jean Racine: A Critical Biography.* London: Cassell & Co., 1951, 362 p.

> Well-received scholarly treatment of Racine's life and works.

Cloonan, William J. *Racine's Theatre: The Politics of Love.* University, Miss.: Romance Monographs, 1977, 149 p.

> A Freudian critique of Racine's canon, which finds that love in Racine's dramas "is a political force because those who love are defying, whether they are completely cognizant of it or not, society's principal ideal and mainstay, namely *gloire*. In a large measure the frenzied, at times destructive expression taken by Racinian love stems not only from unrequited passion, but also from society's inability, because of its obsession with *gloire*, to provide the means for genuine individual fulfillment."

Goodkin, Richard E. *The Tragic Middle: Racine, Aristotle, Euripides.* Madison: University of Wisconsin Press, 1991, 211 p.

> Employs "the 'shared' works of Racine and Euripides—the four pairs of plays in which the two tragedians deal with the same myth—in the elaboration of a tragic discourse, a discourse centered on the problem of the middle," a "crisis which has been building since some undefined cause or 'beginning' and which will subsequently demand some sort of resolution or 'ending'."

Haley, Marie Philip. *Racine and the "Art Poétique" of Boileau.* Baltimore: Johns Hopkins Press, 1938.

> Treats the relationships between the two poets before and during the composition of Boileau's *Art Poétique*, and compares Racine's theoretical writings and the pronouncements of Boileau. Haley seeks to answer the question, "To what extent may Boileau's precepts be considered a summary of Racine's practice?"

Hawcroft, Michael. *Word as Action: Racine, Rhetoric, and Theatrical Language.* Oxford: Clarendon Press, 1992, 275 p.

> Intensive study of Racine's employment of rhetoric, which aims "to make a contribution to an understanding

of how the tragedies of Racine, so often described as predominantly verbal, none the less work well in the theatre."

Lapp, John C. *Aspects of Racinian Tragedy*. Toronto: University of Toronto Press, 1955, 195 p.

Offers "a contribution to the study of Racine's form" to enable the English-speaking reader to better appreciate Racine's accomplishment.

Knapp, Bettina L. *Jean Racine: Mythos and Renewal in Modern Theater*. University: University of Alabama Press, 1967, 278 p.

Psychoanalytical examination of each of Racine's dramas.

Orlando, Francesco. *Toward a Freudian theory of Literature, with an Analysis of Racine's "Phèdre."* Translated by Charmaine Lee. Baltimore and London: Johns Hopkins University Press, 1978.

Intensive Freudian analysis of Racine's most-discussed play.

Tilley, Arthur. "Racine." *Three French Dramatists: Racine, Marivaux, Musset*, pp. 1-77. 1933. Reprint. New York: Russell & Russell, 1967.

Detailed survey which focuses upon the poetic power of Racine's dramas.

Turnell, Martin. "Jean Racine." In his *The Classical Moment: Studies of Corneille, Molière and Racine*, pp. 133-41. 1948. Reprint. Westport, Conn.: Greenwood Press, 1975.

Provides a general account of Racine in relation to the social and literary background of his age, then illustrates what Turnell deems the essential qualities of his poetry by a closer, textual examination of his major works.

Weinbert, Bernard. *The Art of Jean Racine*. Chicago: University of Chicago Press, 1963, 355 p.

Examines Racine's eleven tragedies sequentially, seeking to discern how Racine's dramatic art evolved and developed and noting both innovations and recurrent problems in the dramatist's tragic canon.

Literature
Criticism from
1400 to 1800

Cumulative Indexes

How to Use This Index

The main references

Calvino, Italo
1923-1985.....CLC 5, 8, 11, 22, 33, 39,
73; SSC 3

list all author entries in the following Gale Literary Criticism series:

BLC = *Black Literature Criticism*
CLC = *Contemporary Literary Criticism*
CLR = *Children's Literature Review*
CMLC = *Classical and Medieval Literature Criticism*
DA = *DISCovering Authors*
DC = *Drama Criticism*
HLC = *Hispanic Literature Criticism*
LC = *Literature Criticism from 1400 to 1800*
NCLC = *Nineteenth-Century Literature Criticism*
PC = *Poetry Criticism*
SSC = *Short Story Criticism*
TCLC = *Twentieth-Century Literary Criticism*
WLC = *World Literature Criticism, 1500 to the Present*

The cross-references

See also CANR 23; CA 85-88;
obituary CA 116

list all author entries in the following Gale biographical and literary sources:

AAYA = *Authors & Artists for Young Adults*
AITN = *Authors in the News*
BEST = *Bestsellers*
BW = *Black Writers*
CA = *Contemporary Authors*
CAAS = *Contemporary Authors Autobiography Series*
CABS = *Contemporary Authors Bibliographical Series*
CANR = *Contemporary Authors New Revision Series*
CAP = *Contemporary Authors Permanent Series*
CDALB = *Concise Dictionary of American Literary Biography*
CDBLB = *Concise Dictionary of British Literary Biography*
DLB = *Dictionary of Literary Biography*
DLBD = *Dictionary of Literary Biography Documentary Series*
DLBY = *Dictionary of Literary Biography Yearbook*
HW = *Hispanic Writers*
JRDA = *Junior DISCovering Authors*
MAICYA = *Major Authors and Illustrators for Children and Young Adults*
MTCW = *Major 20th-Century Writers*
NNAL = *Native North American Literature*
SAAS = *Something about the Author Autobiography Series*
SATA = *Something about the Author*
YABC = *Yesterday's Authors of Books for Children*

Literary Criticism Series
Cumulative Author Index

Augier, Emile 1820-1889 . . . . **NCLC 31**

August, John
See De Voto, Bernard (Augustine)

Augustine, St. 354-430 . . . . **CMLC 6**

Aurelius
See Bourne, Randolph S(illiman)

Austen, Jane
1775-1817 . . . . **NCLC 1, 13, 19, 33; DA;**
　　　　　　　　　　　　　　　　　　WLC
See also CDBLB 1789-1832; DLB 116

Auster, Paul 1947- . . . . **CLC 47**
See also CA 69-72; CANR 23

Austin, Frank
See Faust, Frederick (Schiller)

Austin, Mary (Hunter)
1868-1934 . . . . **TCLC 25**
See also CA 109; DLB 9, 78

Autran Dourado, Waldomiro
See Dourado, (Waldomiro Freitas) Autran

Averroes 1126-1198 . . . . **CMLC 7**
See also DLB 115

Avison, Margaret 1918- . . . . **CLC 2, 4**
See also CA 17-20R; DLB 53; MTCW

Axton, David
See Koontz, Dean R(ay)

Ayckbourn, Alan
1939- . . . . **CLC 5, 8, 18, 33, 74**
See also CA 21-24R; CANR 31; DLB 13;
　　MTCW

Aydy, Catherine
See Tennant, Emma (Christina)

Ayme, Marcel (Andre) 1902-1967 . . . **CLC 11**
See also CA 89-92; CLR 25; DLB 72

Ayrton, Michael 1921-1975 . . . . **CLC 7**
See also CA 5-8R; 61-64; CANR 9, 21

Azorin . . . . **CLC 11**
See also Martinez Ruiz, Jose

Azuela, Mariano
1873-1952 . . . . **TCLC 3; HLC**
See also CA 104; 131; HW; MTCW

Baastad, Babbis Friis
See Friis-Baastad, Babbis Ellinor

Bab
See Gilbert, W(illiam) S(chwenck)

Babbis, Eleanor
See Friis-Baastad, Babbis Ellinor

Babel, Isaak (Emmanuilovich)
1894-1941(?) . . . . . **TCLC 2, 13; SSC 16**
See also CA 104

Babits, Mihaly 1883-1941 . . . . **TCLC 14**
See also CA 114

Babur 1483-1530 . . . . **LC 18**

Bacchelli, Riccardo 1891-1985 . . . . . **CLC 19**
See also CA 29-32R; 117

Bach, Richard (David) 1936- . . . . **CLC 14**
See also AITN 1; BEST 89:2; CA 9-12R;
　　CANR 18; MTCW; SATA 13

Bachman, Richard
See King, Stephen (Edwin)

Bachmann, Ingeborg 1926-1973 . . . . . **CLC 69**
See also CA 93-96; 45-48; DLB 85

Bacon, Francis 1561-1626 . . . . '. . . **LC 18**
See also CDBLB Before 1660

Bacon, Roger 1214(?)-1292 . . . . . . **CMLC 14**
See also DLB 115

Bacovia, George . . . . **TCLC 24**
See also Vasiliu, Gheorghe

Badanes, Jerome 1937- . . . . **CLC 59**

Bagehot, Walter 1826-1877 . . . . . . **NCLC 10**
See also DLB 55

Bagnold, Enid 1889-1981 . . . . **CLC 25**
See also CA 5-8R; 103; CANR 5, 40;
　　DLB 13; MAICYA; SATA 1, 25

Bagrjana, Elisaveta
See Belcheva, Elisaveta

Bagryana, Elisaveta
See Belcheva, Elisaveta
See also DLB 147

Bailey, Paul 1937- . . . . **CLC 45**
See also CA 21-24R; CANR 16; DLB 14

Baillie, Joanna 1762-1851 . . . . **NCLC 2**
See also DLB 93

Bainbridge, Beryl (Margaret)
1933- . . . . **CLC 4, 5, 8, 10, 14, 18, 22, 62**
See also CA 21-24R; CANR 24; DLB 14;
　　MTCW

Baker, Elliott 1922- . . . . **CLC 8**
See also CA 45-48; CANR 2

Baker, Nicholson 1957- . . . . **CLC 61**
See also CA 135

Baker, Ray Stannard 1870-1946 . . . **TCLC 47**
See also CA 118

Baker, Russell (Wayne) 1925- . . . . . . **CLC 31**
See also BEST 89:4; CA 57-60; CANR 11,
　　41; MTCW

Bakhtin, M.
See Bakhtin, Mikhail Mikhailovich

Bakhtin, M. M.
See Bakhtin, Mikhail Mikhailovich

Bakhtin, Mikhail
See Bakhtin, Mikhail Mikhailovich

Bakhtin, Mikhail Mikhailovich
1895-1975 . . . . **CLC 83**
See also CA 128; 113

Bakshi, Ralph 1938(?)- . . . . **CLC 26**
See also CA 112; 138

Bakunin, Mikhail (Alexandrovich)
1814-1876 . . . . **NCLC 25**

Baldwin, James (Arthur)
1924-1987 . . . . . . **CLC 1, 2, 3, 4, 5, 8, 13,**
　　　　　　　15, 17, 42, 50, 67; BLC; DA; DC 1;
　　　　　　　　　　　　　　　　SSC 10; WLC
See also AAYA 4; BW 1; CA 1-4R; 124;
　　CABS 1; CANR 3, 24;
　　CDALB 1941-1968; DLB 2, 7, 33;
　　DLBY 87; MTCW; SATA 9;
　　SATA-Obit 54

Ballard, J(ames) G(raham)
1930- . . . . **CLC 3, 6, 14, 36; SSC 1**
See also AAYA 3; CA 5-8R; CANR 15, 39;
　　DLB 14; MTCW

Balmont, Konstantin (Dmitriyevich)
1867-1943 . . . . **TCLC 11**
See also CA 109

Balzac, Honore de
1799-1850 . . . . **NCLC 5, 35; DA; SSC 5;**
　　　　　　　　　　　　　　　　　　WLC
See also DLB 119

Bambara, Toni Cade
1939- . . . . **CLC 19; BLC; DA**
See also AAYA 5; BW 2; CA 29-32R;
　　CANR 24; DLB 38; MTCW

Bamdad, A.
See Shamlu, Ahmad

Banat, D. R.
See Bradbury, Ray (Douglas)

Bancroft, Laura
See Baum, L(yman) Frank

Banim, John 1798-1842 . . . . **NCLC 13**
See also DLB 116

Banim, Michael 1796-1874 . . . . . . **NCLC 13**

Banks, Iain
See Banks, Iain M(enzies)

Banks, Iain M(enzies) 1954- . . . . **CLC 34**
See also CA 123; 128

Banks, Lynne Reid . . . . **CLC 23**
See also Reid Banks, Lynne
See also AAYA 6

Banks, Russell 1940- . . . . **CLC 37, 72**
See also CA 65-68; CAAS 15; CANR 19;
　　DLB 130

Banville, John 1945- . . . . **CLC 46**
See also CA 117; 128; DLB 14

Banville, Theodore (Faullain) de
1832-1891 . . . . **NCLC 9**

Baraka, Amiri
1934- . . . . **CLC 1, 2, 3, 5, 10, 14, 33;**
　　　　　　　　　　　　　　　　BLC; DA; PC 4
See also Jones, LeRoi
See also BW 2; CA 21-24R; CABS 3;
　　CANR 27, 38; CDALB 1941-1968;
　　DLB 5, 7, 16, 38; DLBD 8; MTCW

Barbellion, W. N. P. . . . . **TCLC 24**
See also Cummings, Bruce F(rederick)

Barbera, Jack (Vincent) 1945- . . . . . . **CLC 44**
See also CA 110; CANR 45

Barbey d'Aurevilly, Jules Amedee
1808-1889 . . . . **NCLC 1; SSC 17**
See also DLB 119

Barbusse, Henri 1873-1935 . . . . **TCLC 5**
See also CA 105; DLB 65

Barclay, Bill
See Moorcock, Michael (John)

Barclay, William Ewert
See Moorcock, Michael (John)

Barea, Arturo 1897-1957 . . . . **TCLC 14**
See also CA 111

Barfoot, Joan 1946- . . . . **CLC 18**
See also CA 105

Baring, Maurice 1874-1945 . . . . **TCLC 8**
See also CA 105; DLB 34

Barker, Clive 1952- . . . . **CLC 52**
See also AAYA 10; BEST 90:3; CA 121;
　　129; MTCW

Barker, George Granville
1913-1991 . . . . **CLC 8, 48**
See also CA 9-12R; 135; CANR 7, 38;
　　DLB 20; MTCW

Barker, Harley Granville
See Granville-Barker, Harley
See also DLB 10

Bertrand, Aloysius 1807-1841 . . . . **NCLC 31**

Bertran de Born c. 1140-1215 . . . . . **CMLC 5**

Besant, Annie (Wood) 1847-1933 . . . **TCLC 9**
See also CA 105

Bessie, Alvah 1904-1985 . . . . **CLC 23**
See also CA 5-8R; 116; CANR 2; DLB 26

Bethlen, T. D.
See Silverberg, Robert

Beti, Mongo . . . . **CLC 27; BLC**
See also Biyidi, Alexandre

Betjeman, John
1906-1984 . . . . **CLC 2, 6, 10, 34, 43**
See also CA 9-12R; 112; CANR 33;
CDBLB 1945-1960; DLB 20; DLBY 84;
MTCW

Bettelheim, Bruno 1903-1990 . . . . . . **CLC 79**
See also CA 81-84; 131; CANR 23; MTCW

Betti, Ugo 1892-1953 . . . . **TCLC 5**
See also CA 104

Betts, Doris (Waugh) 1932- . . . . **CLC 3, 6, 28**
See also CA 13-16R; CANR 9; DLBY 82

Bevan, Alistair
See Roberts, Keith (John Kingston)

Bialik, Chaim Nachman
1873-1934 . . . . **TCLC 25**

Bickerstaff, Isaac
See Swift, Jonathan

Bidart, Frank 1939- . . . . **CLC 33**
See also CA 140

Bienek, Horst 1930- . . . . **CLC 7, 11**
See also CA 73-76; DLB 75

Bierce, Ambrose (Gwinett)
1842-1914(?) . . . . . . **TCLC 1, 7, 44; DA;**
SSC 9; WLC
See also CA 104; 139; CDALB 1865-1917;
DLB 11, 12, 23, 71, 74

Billings, Josh
See Shaw, Henry Wheeler

Billington, (Lady) Rachel (Mary)
1942- . . . . **CLC 43**
See also AITN 2; CA 33-36R; CANR 44

Binyon, T(imothy) J(ohn) 1936- . . . . **CLC 34**
See also CA 111; CANR 28

Bioy Casares, Adolfo
1914- . . . . . . **CLC 4, 8, 13; HLC; SSC 17**
See also CA 29-32R; CANR 19, 43;
DLB 113; HW; MTCW

Bird, Cordwainer
See Ellison, Harlan (Jay)

Bird, Robert Montgomery
1806-1854 . . . . **NCLC 1**

Birney, (Alfred) Earle
1904- . . . . **CLC 1, 4, 6, 11**
See also CA 1-4R; CANR 5, 20; DLB 88;
MTCW

Bishop, Elizabeth
1911-1979 . . . . . **CLC 1, 4, 9, 13, 15, 32;**
DA; PC 3
See also CA 5-8R; 89-92; CABS 2;
CANR 26; CDALB 1968-1988; DLB 5;
MTCW; SATA-Obit 24

Bishop, John 1935- . . . . **CLC 10**
See also CA 105

Bissett, Bill 1939- . . . . **CLC 18**
See also CA 69-72; CAAS 19; CANR 15;
DLB 53; MTCW

Bitov, Andrei (Georgievich) 1937- . . . **CLC 57**
See also CA 142

Biyidi, Alexandre 1932-
See Beti, Mongo
See also BW 1; CA 114; 124; MTCW

Bjarme, Brynjolf
See Ibsen, Henrik (Johan)

Bjornson, Bjornstjerne (Martinius)
1832-1910 . . . . **TCLC 7, 37**
See also CA 104

Black, Robert
See Holdstock, Robert P.

Blackburn, Paul 1926-1971 . . . . . . **CLC 9, 43**
See also CA 81-84; 33-36R; CANR 34;
DLB 16; DLBY 81

Black Elk 1863-1950 . . . . **TCLC 33**
See also CA 144; NNAL

Black Hobart
See Sanders, (James) Ed(ward)

Blacklin, Malcolm
See Chambers, Aidan

Blackmore, R(ichard) D(oddridge)
1825-1900 . . . . **TCLC 27**
See also CA 120; DLB 18

Blackmur, R(ichard) P(almer)
1904-1965 . . . . **CLC 2, 24**
See also CA 11-12; 25-28R; CAP 1; DLB 63

Black Tarantula, The
See Acker, Kathy

Blackwood, Algernon (Henry)
1869-1951 . . . . **TCLC 5**
See also CA 105

Blackwood, Caroline 1931- . . . . **CLC 6, 9**
See also CA 85-88; CANR 32; DLB 14;
MTCW

Blade, Alexander
See Hamilton, Edmond; Silverberg, Robert

Blaga, Lucian 1895-1961 . . . . **CLC 75**

Blair, Eric (Arthur) 1903-1950
See Orwell, George
See also CA 104; 132; DA; MTCW;
SATA 29

Blais, Marie-Claire
1939- . . . . **CLC 2, 4, 6, 13, 22**
See also CA 21-24R; CAAS 4; CANR 38;
DLB 53; MTCW

Blaise, Clark 1940- . . . . **CLC 29**
See also AITN 2; CA 53-56; CAAS 3;
CANR 5; DLB 53

Blake, Nicholas
See Day Lewis, C(ecil)
See also DLB 77

Blake, William
1757-1827 . . . . . **NCLC 13, 37; DA; WLC**
See also CDBLB 1789-1832; DLB 93;
MAICYA; SATA 30

Blasco Ibanez, Vicente
1867-1928 . . . . **TCLC 12**
See also CA 110; 131; HW; MTCW

Blatty, William Peter 1928- . . . . **CLC 2**
See also CA 5-8R; CANR 9

Bleeck, Oliver
See Thomas, Ross (Elmore)

Blessing, Lee 1949- . . . . **CLC 54**

Blish, James (Benjamin)
1921-1975 . . . . **CLC 14**
See also CA 1-4R; 57-60; CANR 3; DLB 8;
MTCW; SATA 66

Bliss, Reginald
See Wells, H(erbert) G(eorge)

Blixen, Karen (Christentze Dinesen)
1885-1962
See Dinesen, Isak
See also CA 25-28; CANR 22; CAP 2;
MTCW; SATA 44

Bloch, Robert (Albert) 1917-1994 . . . **CLC 33**
See also CA 5-8R; 146; CAAS 20; CANR 5;
DLB 44; SATA 12

Blok, Alexander (Alexandrovich)
1880-1921 . . . . **TCLC 5**
See also CA 104

Blom, Jan
See Breytenbach, Breyten

Bloom, Harold 1930- . . . . **CLC 24**
See also CA 13-16R; CANR 39; DLB 67

Bloomfield, Aurelius
See Bourne, Randolph S(illiman)

Blount, Roy (Alton), Jr. 1941- . . . . . **CLC 38**
See also CA 53-56; CANR 10, 28; MTCW

Bloy, Leon 1846-1917 . . . . **TCLC 22**
See also CA 121; DLB 123

Blume, Judy (Sussman) 1938- . . . **CLC 12, 30**
See also AAYA 3; CA 29-32R; CANR 13,
37; CLR 2, 15; DLB 52; JRDA;
MAICYA; MTCW; SATA 2, 31, 79

Blunden, Edmund (Charles)
1896-1974 . . . . **CLC 2, 56**
See also CA 17-18; 45-48; CAP 2; DLB 20,
100; MTCW

Bly, Robert (Elwood)
1926- . . . . **CLC 1, 2, 5, 10, 15, 38**
See also CA 5-8R; CANR 41; DLB 5;
MTCW

Boas, Franz 1858-1942 . . . . **TCLC 56**
See also CA 115

Bobette
See Simenon, Georges (Jacques Christian)

Boccaccio, Giovanni
1313-1375 . . . . **CMLC 13; SSC 10**

Bochco, Steven 1943- . . . . **CLC 35**
See also AAYA 11; CA 124; 138

Bodenheim, Maxwell 1892-1954 . . . **TCLC 44**
See also CA 110; DLB 9, 45

Bodker, Cecil 1927- . . . . **CLC 21**
See also CA 73-76; CANR 13, 44; CLR 23;
MAICYA; SATA 14

Boell, Heinrich (Theodor)
1917-1985 . . . . **CLC 2, 3, 6, 9, 11, 15, 27,**
32, 72; DA; WLC
See also CA 21-24R; 116; CANR 24;
DLB 69; DLBY 85; MTCW

Boerne, Alfred
See Doeblin, Alfred

Bogan, Louise 1897-1970 . . . . . **CLC 4, 39, 46**
See also CA 73-76; 25-28R; CANR 33;
DLB 45; MTCW

Bogarde, Dirk . . . . CLC 19
See also Van Den Bogarde, Derek Jules
    Gaspard Ulric Niven
See also DLB 14

Bogosian, Eric 1953- . . . . CLC 45
See also CA 138

Bograd, Larry 1953- . . . . CLC 35
See also CA 93-96; SATA 33

Boiardo, Matteo Maria 1441-1494 . . . . LC 6

Boileau-Despreaux, Nicolas
    1636-1711 . . . . LC 3

Boland, Eavan (Aisling) 1944- . . . CLC 40, 67
See also CA 143; DLB 40

Bolt, Lee
See Faust, Frederick (Schiller)

Bolt, Robert (Oxton) 1924- . . . . CLC 14
See also CA 17-20R; CANR 35; DLB 13;
    MTCW

Bombet, Louis-Alexandre-Cesar
See Stendhal

Bomkauf
See Kaufman, Bob (Garnell)

Bonaventura . . . . NCLC 35
See also DLB 90

Bond, Edward 1934- . . . . CLC 4, 6, 13, 23
See also CA 25-28R; CANR 38; DLB 13;
    MTCW

Bonham, Frank 1914-1989 . . . . CLC 12
See also AAYA 1; CA 9-12R; CANR 4, 36;
    JRDA; MAICYA; SAAS 3; SATA 1, 49;
    SATA-Obit 62

Bonnefoy, Yves 1923- . . . . CLC 9, 15, 58
See also CA 85-88; CANR 33; MTCW

Bontemps, Arna(ud Wendell)
    1902-1973 . . . . CLC 1, 18; BLC
See also BW 1; CA 1-4R; 41-44R; CANR 4,
    35; CLR 6; DLB 48, 51; JRDA;
    MAICYA; MTCW; SATA 2, 44;
    SATA-Obit 24

Booth, Martin 1944- . . . . CLC 13
See also CA 93-96; CAAS 2

Booth, Philip 1925- . . . . CLC 23
See also CA 5-8R; CANR 5; DLBY 82

Booth, Wayne C(layson) 1921- . . . . . CLC 24
See also CA 1-4R; CAAS 5; CANR 3, 43;
    DLB 67

Borchert, Wolfgang 1921-1947 . . . . . TCLC 5
See also CA 104; DLB 69, 124

Borel, Petrus 1809-1859 . . . . NCLC 41

Borges, Jorge Luis
    1899-1986 . . . CLC 1, 2, 3, 4, 6, 8, 9, 10,
        13, 19, 44, 48, 83; DA; HLC; SSC 4;
                                            WLC
See also CA 21-24R; CANR 19, 33;
    DLB 113; DLBY 86; HW; MTCW

Borowski, Tadeusz 1922-1951 . . . . . . TCLC 9
See also CA 106

Borrow, George (Henry)
    1803-1881 . . . . NCLC 9
See also DLB 21, 55

Bosman, Herman Charles
    1905-1951 . . . . TCLC 49

Bosschere, Jean de 1878(?)-1953 . . . TCLC 19
See also CA 115

Boswell, James
    1740-1795 . . . . LC 4; DA; WLC
See also CDBLB 1660-1789; DLB 104, 142

Bottoms, David 1949- . . . . CLC 53
See also CA 105; CANR 22; DLB 120;
    DLBY 83

Boucicault, Dion 1820-1890 . . . . . . NCLC 41

Boucolon, Maryse 1937-
See Conde, Maryse
See also CA 110; CANR 30

Bourget, Paul (Charles Joseph)
    1852-1935 . . . . TCLC 12
See also CA 107; DLB 123

Bourjaily, Vance (Nye) 1922- . . . . CLC 8, 62
See also CA 1-4R; CAAS 1; CANR 2;
    DLB 2, 143

Bourne, Randolph S(illiman)
    1886-1918 . . . . TCLC 16
See also CA 117; DLB 63

Bova, Ben(jamin William) 1932- . . . . CLC 45
See also CA 5-8R; CAAS 18; CANR 11;
    CLR 3; DLBY 81; MAICYA; MTCW;
    SATA 6, 68

Bowen, Elizabeth (Dorothea Cole)
    1899-1973 . . . . . . CLC 1, 3, 6, 11, 15, 22;
                                            SSC 3
See also CA 17-18; 41-44R; CANR 35;
    CAP 2; CDBLB 1945-1960; DLB 15;
    MTCW

Bowering, George 1935- . . . . CLC 15, 47
See also CA 21-24R; CAAS 16; CANR 10;
    DLB 53

Bowering, Marilyn R(uthe) 1949- . . . CLC 32
See also CA 101

Bowers, Edgar 1924- . . . . CLC 9
See also CA 5-8R; CANR 24; DLB 5

Bowie, David . . . . CLC 17
See also Jones, David Robert

Bowles, Jane (Sydney)
    1917-1973 . . . . CLC 3, 68
See also CA 19-20; 41-44R; CAP 2

Bowles, Paul (Frederick)
    1910- . . . . CLC 1, 2, 19, 53; SSC 3
See also CA 1-4R; CAAS 1; CANR 1, 19;
    DLB 5, 6; MTCW

Box, Edgar
See Vidal, Gore

Boyd, Nancy
See Millay, Edna St. Vincent

Boyd, William 1952- . . . . CLC 28, 53, 70
See also CA 114; 120

Boyle, Kay
    1902-1992 . . . . . CLC 1, 5, 19, 58; SSC 5
See also CA 13-16R; 140; CAAS 1;
    CANR 29; DLB 4, 9, 48, 86; DLBY 93;
    MTCW

Boyle, Mark
See Kienzle, William X(avier)

Boyle, Patrick 1905-1982 . . . . CLC 19
See also CA 127

Boyle, T. C.
See Boyle, T(homas) Coraghessan

Boyle, T(homas) Coraghessan
    1948- . . . . CLC 36, 55; SSC 16
See also BEST 90:4; CA 120; CANR 44;
    DLBY 86

Boz
See Dickens, Charles (John Huffam)

Brackenridge, Hugh Henry
    1748-1816 . . . . NCLC 7
See also DLB 11, 37

Bradbury, Edward P.
See Moorcock, Michael (John)

Bradbury, Malcolm (Stanley)
    1932- . . . . CLC 32, 61
See also CA 1-4R; CANR 1, 33; DLB 14;
    MTCW

Bradbury, Ray (Douglas)
    1920- . . . CLC 1, 3, 10, 15, 42; DA; WLC
See also AITN 1, 2; CA 1-4R; CANR 2, 30;
    CDALB 1968-1988; DLB 2, 8; MTCW;
    SATA 11, 64

Bradford, Gamaliel 1863-1932 . . . . . TCLC 36
See also DLB 17

Bradley, David (Henry, Jr.)
    1950- . . . . CLC 23; BLC
See also BW 1; CA 104; CANR 26; DLB 33

Bradley, John Ed(mund, Jr.)
    1958- . . . . CLC 55
See also CA 139

Bradley, Marion Zimmer 1930- . . . . . CLC 30
See also AAYA 9; CA 57-60; CAAS 10;
    CANR 7, 31; DLB 8; MTCW

Bradstreet, Anne
    1612(?)-1672 . . . . LC 4; DA; PC 10
See also CDALB 1640-1865; DLB 24

Brady, Joan 1939- . . . . CLC 86
See also CA 141

Bragg, Melvyn 1939- . . . . CLC 10
See also BEST 89:3; CA 57-60; CANR 10;
    DLB 14

Braine, John (Gerard)
    1922-1986 . . . . CLC 1, 3, 41
See also CA 1-4R; 120; CANR 1, 33;
    CDBLB 1945-1960; DLB 15; DLBY 86;
    MTCW

Brammer, William 1930(?)-1978 . . . . CLC 31
See also CA 77-80

Brancati, Vitaliano 1907-1954 . . . . . TCLC 12
See also CA 109

Brancato, Robin F(idler) 1936- . . . . . CLC 35
See also AAYA 9; CA 69-72; CANR 11,
    45; CLR 32; JRDA; SAAS 9; SATA 23

Brand, Max
See Faust, Frederick (Schiller)

Brand, Millen 1906-1980 . . . . CLC 7
See also CA 21-24R; 97-100

Branden, Barbara . . . . CLC 44

Brandes, Georg (Morris Cohen)
    1842-1927 . . . . TCLC 10
See also CA 105

Brandys, Kazimierz 1916- . . . . CLC 62

Branley, Franklyn M(ansfield)
    1915- . . . . CLC 21
See also CA 33-36R; CANR 14, 39;
    CLR 13; MAICYA; SAAS 16; SATA 4,
    68

Brathwaite, Edward Kamau 1930-... **CLC 11**
See also BW 2; CA 25-28R; CANR 11, 26, 47; DLB 125

Brautigan, Richard (Gary)
1935-1984 .... **CLC 1, 3, 5, 9, 12, 34, 42**
See also CA 53-56; 113; CANR 34; DLB 2, 5; DLBY 80, 84; MTCW; SATA 56

Braverman, Kate 1950- .... **CLC 67**
See also CA 89-92

Brecht, Bertolt
1898-1956 ...... **TCLC 1, 6, 13, 35; DA; DC 3; WLC**
See also CA 104; 133; DLB 56, 124; MTCW

Brecht, Eugen Berthold Friedrich
See Brecht, Bertolt

Bremer, Fredrika 1801-1865 ..... **NCLC 11**

Brennan, Christopher John
1870-1932 .... **TCLC 17**
See also CA 117

Brennan, Maeve 1917-............. **CLC 5**
See also CA 81-84

Brentano, Clemens (Maria)
1778-1842 .... **NCLC 1**
See also DLB 90

Brent of Bin Bin
See Franklin, (Stella Maraia Sarah) Miles

Brenton, Howard 1942-.......... **CLC 31**
See also CA 69-72; CANR 33; DLB 13; MTCW

Breslin, James 1930-
See Breslin, Jimmy
See also CA 73-76; CANR 31; MTCW

Breslin, Jimmy .... **CLC 4, 43**
See also Breslin, James
See also AITN 1

Bresson, Robert 1907- .... **CLC 16**
See also CA 110

Breton, Andre 1896-1966... **CLC 2, 9, 15, 54**
See also CA 19-20; 25-28R; CANR 40; CAP 2; DLB 65; MTCW

Breytenbach, Breyten 1939(?)- .. **CLC 23, 37**
See also CA 113; 129

Bridgers, Sue Ellen 1942- .... **CLC 26**
See also AAYA 8; CA 65-68; CANR 11, 36; CLR 18; DLB 52; JRDA; MAICYA; SAAS 1; SATA 22

Bridges, Robert (Seymour)
1844-1930 .... **TCLC 1**
See also CA 104; CDBLB 1890-1914; DLB 19, 98

Bridie, James.................... **TCLC 3**
See also Mavor, Osborne Henry
See also DLB 10

Brin, David 1950-................ **CLC 34**
See also CA 102; CANR 24; SATA 65

Brink, Andre (Philippus)
1935- .... **CLC 18, 36**
See also CA 104; CANR 39; MTCW

Brinsmead, H(esba) F(ay) 1922- .... **CLC 21**
See also CA 21-24R; CANR 10; MAICYA; SAAS 5; SATA 18, 78

Brittain, Vera (Mary)
1893(?)-1970 .... **CLC 23**
See also CA 13-16; 25-28R; CAP 1; MTCW

Broch, Hermann 1886-1951....... **TCLC 20**
See also CA 117; DLB 85, 124

Brock, Rose
See Hansen, Joseph

Brodkey, Harold 1930-............ **CLC 56**
See also CA 111; DLB 130

Brodsky, Iosif Alexandrovich 1940-
See Brodsky, Joseph
See also AITN 1; CA 41-44R; CANR 37; MTCW

Brodsky, Joseph .. **CLC 4, 6, 13, 36, 50; PC 9**
See also Brodsky, Iosif Alexandrovich

Brodsky, Michael Mark 1948- ..... **CLC 19**
See also CA 102; CANR 18, 41

Bromell, Henry 1947-............. **CLC 5**
See also CA 53-56; CANR 9

Bromfield, Louis (Brucker)
1896-1956 .... **TCLC 11**
See also CA 107; DLB 4, 9, 86

Broner, E(sther) M(asserman)
1930- .... **CLC 19**
See also CA 17-20R; CANR 8, 25; DLB 28

Bronk, William 1918-............. **CLC 10**
See also CA 89-92; CANR 23

Bronstein, Lev Davidovich
See Trotsky, Leon

Bronte, Anne 1820-1849......... **NCLC 4**
See also DLB 21

Bronte, Charlotte
1816-1855 ... **NCLC 3, 8, 33; DA; WLC**
See also CDBLB 1832-1890; DLB 21

Bronte, (Jane) Emily
1818-1848 .... **NCLC 16, 35; DA; PC 8; WLC**
See also CDBLB 1832-1890; DLB 21, 32

Brooke, Frances 1724-1789 .... **LC 6**
See also DLB 39, 99

Brooke, Henry 1703(?)-1783 .... **LC 1**
See also DLB 39

Brooke, Rupert (Chawner)
1887-1915 .... **TCLC 2, 7; DA; WLC**
See also CA 104; 132; CDBLB 1914-1945; DLB 19; MTCW

Brooke-Haven, P.
See Wodehouse, P(elham) G(renville)

Brooke-Rose, Christine 1926- ...... **CLC 40**
See also CA 13-16R; DLB 14

Brookner, Anita 1928- ...... **CLC 32, 34, 51**
See also CA 114; 120; CANR 37; DLBY 87; MTCW

Brooks, Cleanth 1906-1994 ..... **CLC 24, 86**
See also CA 17-20R; 145; CANR 33, 35; DLB 63; MTCW

Brooks, George
See Baum, L(yman) Frank

Brooks, Gwendolyn
1917- ...... **CLC 1, 2, 4, 5, 15, 49; BLC; DA; PC 7; WLC**
See also AITN 1; BW 2; CA 1-4R; CANR 1, 27; CDALB 1941-1968; CLR 27; DLB 5, 76; MTCW; SATA 6

Brooks, Mel.................... **CLC 12**
See also Kaminsky, Melvin
See also AAYA 13; DLB 26

Brooks, Peter 1938-.............. **CLC 34**
See also CA 45-48; CANR 1

Brooks, Van Wyck 1886-1963...... **CLC 29**
See also CA 1-4R; CANR 6; DLB 45, 63, 103

Brophy, Brigid (Antonia)
1929-.................. **CLC 6, 11, 29**
See also CA 5-8R; CAAS 4; CANR 25; DLB 14; MTCW

Brosman, Catharine Savage 1934-.... **CLC 9**
See also CA 61-64; CANR 21, 46

Brother Antoninus
See Everson, William (Oliver)

Broughton, T(homas) Alan 1936- ... **CLC 19**
See also CA 45-48; CANR 2, 23

Broumas, Olga 1949- .... **CLC 10, 73**
See also CA 85-88; CANR 20

Brown, Charles Brockden
1771-1810 .... **NCLC 22**
See also CDALB 1640-1865; DLB 37, 59, 73

Brown, Christy 1932-1981........ **CLC 63**
See also CA 105; 104; DLB 14

Brown, Claude 1937- .... **CLC 30; BLC**
See also AAYA 7; BW 1; CA 73-76

Brown, Dee (Alexander) 1908- .. **CLC 18, 47**
See also CA 13-16R; CAAS 6; CANR 11, 45; DLBY 80; MTCW; SATA 5

Brown, George
See Wertmueller, Lina

Brown, George Douglas
1869-1902 .... **TCLC 28**

Brown, George Mackay 1921-.... **CLC 5, 48**
See also CA 21-24R; CAAS 6; CANR 12, 37; DLB 14, 27, 139; MTCW; SATA 35

Brown, (William) Larry 1951-...... **CLC 73**
See also CA 130; 134

Brown, Moses
See Barrett, William (Christopher)

Brown, Rita Mae 1944-..... **CLC 18, 43, 79**
See also CA 45-48; CANR 2, 11, 35; MTCW

Brown, Roderick (Langmere) Haig-
See Haig-Brown, Roderick (Langmere)

Brown, Rosellen 1939-............ **CLC 32**
See also CA 77-80; CAAS 10; CANR 14, 44

Brown, Sterling Allen
1901-1989 .... **CLC 1, 23, 59; BLC**
See also BW 1; CA 85-88; 127; CANR 26; DLB 48, 51, 63; MTCW

Brown, Will
See Ainsworth, William Harrison

Brown, William Wells
1813-1884 .... **NCLC 2; BLC; DC 1**
See also DLB 3, 50

Browne, (Clyde) Jackson 1948(?)-... **CLC 21**
See also CA 120

Browning, Elizabeth Barrett
1806-1861 ..... **NCLC 1, 16; DA; PC 6; WLC**
See also CDBLB 1832-1890; DLB 32

Browning, Robert
    1812-1889 . . . . NCLC 19; DA; PC 2
    See also CDBLB 1832-1890; DLB 32;
    YABC 1

Browning, Tod   1882-1962 . . . . CLC 16
    See also CA 141; 117

Bruccoli, Matthew J(oseph)   1931- . . CLC 34
    See also CA 9-12R; CANR 7; DLB 103

Bruce, Lenny . . . . CLC 21
    See also Schneider, Leonard Alfred

Bruin, John
    See Brutus, Dennis

Brulard, Henri
    See Stendhal

Brulls, Christian
    See Simenon, Georges (Jacques Christian)

Brunner, John (Kilian Houston)
    1934- . . . . CLC 8, 10
    See also CA 1-4R; CAAS 8; CANR 2, 37;
    MTCW

Bruno, Giordano   1548-1600 . . . . LC 27

Brutus, Dennis   1924- . . . . CLC 43; BLC
    See also BW 2; CA 49-52; CAAS 14;
    CANR 2, 27, 42; DLB 117

Bryan, C(ourtlandt) D(ixon) B(arnes)
    1936- . . . . CLC 29
    See also CA 73-76; CANR 13

Bryan, Michael
    See Moore, Brian

Bryant, William Cullen
    1794-1878 . . . . NCLC 6, 46; DA
    See also CDALB 1640-1865; DLB 3, 43, 59

Bryusov, Valery Yakovlevich
    1873-1924 . . . . TCLC 10
    See also CA 107

Buchan, John   1875-1940 . . . . TCLC 41
    See also CA 108; 145; DLB 34, 70; YABC 2

Buchanan, George   1506-1582 . . . . LC 4

Buchheim, Lothar-Guenther   1918- . . . CLC 6
    See also CA 85-88

Buchner, (Karl) Georg
    1813-1837 . . . . NCLC 26

Buchwald, Art(hur)   1925- . . . . CLC 33
    See also AITN 1; CA 5-8R; CANR 21;
    MTCW; SATA 10

Buck, Pearl S(ydenstricker)
    1892-1973 . . . . CLC 7, 11, 18; DA
    See also AITN 1; CA 1-4R; 41-44R;
    CANR 1, 34; DLB 9, 102; MTCW;
    SATA 1, 25

Buckler, Ernest   1908-1984 . . . . CLC 13
    See also CA 11-12; 114; CAP 1; DLB 68;
    SATA 47

Buckley, Vincent (Thomas)
    1925-1988 . . . . CLC 57
    See also CA 101

Buckley, William F(rank), Jr.
    1925- . . . . CLC 7, 18, 37
    See also AITN 1; CA 1-4R; CANR 1, 24;
    DLB 137; DLBY 80; MTCW

Buechner, (Carl) Frederick
    1926- . . . . CLC 2, 4, 6, 9
    See also CA 13-16R; CANR 11, 39;
    DLBY 80; MTCW

Buell, John (Edward)   1927- . . . . CLC 10
    See also CA 1-4R; DLB 53

Buero Vallejo, Antonio   1916- . . . CLC 15, 46
    See also CA 106; CANR 24; HW; MTCW

Bufalino, Gesualdo   1920(?)- . . . . CLC 74

Bugayev, Boris Nikolayevich   1880-1934
    See Bely, Andrey
    See also CA 104

Bukowski, Charles
    1920-1994 . . . . CLC 2, 5, 9, 41, 82
    See also CA 17-20R; 144; CANR 40;
    DLB 5, 130; MTCW

Bulgakov, Mikhail (Afanas'evich)
    1891-1940 . . . . TCLC 2, 16; SSC 18
    See also CA 105

Bulgya, Alexander Alexandrovich
    1901-1956 . . . . TCLC 53
    See also Fadeyev, Alexander
    See also CA 117

Bullins, Ed   1935- . . . . CLC 1, 5, 7; BLC
    See also BW 2; CA 49-52; CAAS 16;
    CANR 24, 46; DLB 7, 38; MTCW

Bulwer-Lytton, Edward (George Earle Lytton)
    1803-1873 . . . . NCLC 1, 45
    See also DLB 21

Bunin, Ivan Alexeyevich
    1870-1953 . . . . TCLC 6; SSC 5
    See also CA 104

Bunting, Basil   1900-1985 . . . . CLC 10, 39, 47
    See also CA 53-56; 115; CANR 7; DLB 20

Bunuel, Luis   1900-1983 . . CLC 16, 80; HLC
    See also CA 101; 110; CANR 32; HW

Bunyan, John   1628-1688 . . LC 4; DA; WLC
    See also CDBLB 1660-1789; DLB 39

Burford, Eleanor
    See Hibbert, Eleanor Alice Burford

Burgess, Anthony
    . CLC 1, 2, 4, 5, 8, 10, 13, 15, 22, 40, 62,
                                                            81
    See also Wilson, John (Anthony) Burgess
    See also AITN 1; CDBLB 1960 to Present;
    DLB 14

Burke, Edmund
    1729(?)-1797 . . . . LC 7; DA; WLC
    See also DLB 104

Burke, Kenneth (Duva)
    1897-1993 . . . . CLC 2, 24
    See also CA 5-8R; 143; CANR 39; DLB 45,
    63; MTCW

Burke, Leda
    See Garnett, David

Burke, Ralph
    See Silverberg, Robert

Burney, Fanny   1752-1840 . . . . NCLC 12
    See also DLB 39

Burns, Robert
    1759-1796 . . . . . . LC 3; DA; PC 6; WLC
    See also CDBLB 1789-1832; DLB 109

Burns, Tex
    See L'Amour, Louis (Dearborn)

Burnshaw, Stanley   1906- . . . . . CLC 3, 13, 44
    See also CA 9-12R; DLB 48

Burr, Anne   1937- . . . . CLC 6
    See also CA 25-28R

Burroughs, Edgar Rice
    1875-1950 . . . . TCLC 2, 32
    See also AAYA 11; CA 104; 132; DLB 8;
    MTCW; SATA 41

Burroughs, William S(eward)
    1914- . . . . CLC 1, 2, 5, 15, 22, 42, 75;
                                                        DA; WLC
    See also AITN 2; CA 9-12R; CANR 20;
    DLB 2, 8, 16; DLBY 81; MTCW

Burton, Richard F.   1821-1890 . . . . NCLC 42
    See also DLB 55

Busch, Frederick   1941- . . . CLC 7, 10, 18, 47
    See also CA 33-36R; CAAS 1; CANR 45;
    DLB 6

Bush, Ronald   1946- . . . . CLC 34
    See also CA 136

Bustos, F(rancisco)
    See Borges, Jorge Luis

Bustos Domecq, H(onorio)
    See Bioy Casares, Adolfo; Borges, Jorge
    Luis

Butler, Octavia E(stelle)   1947- . . . . . CLC 38
    See also BW 2; CA 73-76; CANR 12, 24,
    38; DLB 33; MTCW

Butler, Robert Olen (Jr.)   1945- . . . . . CLC 81
    See also CA 112

Butler, Samuel   1612-1680 . . . . LC 16
    See also DLB 101, 126

Butler, Samuel
    1835-1902 . . . . . . TCLC 1, 33; DA; WLC
    See also CA 143; CDBLB 1890-1914;
    DLB 18, 57

Butler, Walter C.
    See Faust, Frederick (Schiller)

Butor, Michel (Marie Francois)
    1926- . . . . CLC 1, 3, 8, 11, 15
    See also CA 9-12R; CANR 33; DLB 83;
    MTCW

Buzo, Alexander (John)   1944- . . . . . . CLC 61
    See also CA 97-100; CANR 17, 39

Buzzati, Dino   1906-1972 . . . . CLC 36
    See also CA 33-36R

Byars, Betsy (Cromer)   1928- . . . . CLC 35
    See also CA 33-36R; CANR 18, 36; CLR 1,
    16; DLB 52; JRDA; MAICYA; MTCW;
    SAAS 1; SATA 4, 46, 80

Byatt, A(ntonia) S(usan Drabble)
    1936- . . . . CLC 19, 65
    See also CA 13-16R; CANR 13, 33;
    DLB 14; MTCW

Byrne, David   1952- . . . . CLC 26
    See also CA 127

Byrne, John Keyes   1926-
    See Leonard, Hugh
    See also CA 102

Byron, George Gordon (Noel)
    1788-1824 . . . . . . NCLC 2, 12; DA; WLC
    See also CDBLB 1789-1832; DLB 96, 110

C. 3. 3.
    See Wilde, Oscar (Fingal O'Flahertie Wills)

Caballero, Fernan   1796-1877 . . . . . NCLC 10

Cabell, James Branch   1879-1958 . . . TCLC 6
    See also CA 105; DLB 9, 78

Cable, George Washington
     1844-1925 . . . . **TCLC 4; SSC 4**
     See also CA 104; DLB 12, 74

Cabral de Melo Neto, Joao   1920- . . . **CLC 76**

Cabrera Infante, G(uillermo)
     1929- . . . . **CLC 5, 25, 45; HLC**
     See also CA 85-88; CANR 29; DLB 113;
     HW; MTCW

Cade, Toni
     See Bambara, Toni Cade

Cadmus and Harmonia
     See Buchan, John

Caedmon   fl. 658-680 . . . . **CMLC 7**
     See also DLB 146

Caeiro, Alberto
     See Pessoa, Fernando (Antonio Nogueira)

Cage, John (Milton, Jr.)   1912- . . . . . **CLC 41**
     See also CA 13-16R; CANR 9

Cain, G.
     See Cabrera Infante, G(uillermo)

Cain, Guillermo
     See Cabrera Infante, G(uillermo)

Cain, James M(allahan)
     1892-1977 . . . . **CLC 3, 11, 28**
     See also AITN 1; CA 17-20R; 73-76;
     CANR 8, 34; MTCW

Caine, Mark
     See Raphael, Frederic (Michael)

Calasso, Roberto   1941- . . . . **CLC 81**
     See also CA 143

Calderon de la Barca, Pedro
     1600-1681 . . . . **LC 23; DC 3**

Caldwell, Erskine (Preston)
     1903-1987 . . . . **CLC 1, 8, 14, 50, 60**
     See also AITN 1; CA 1-4R; 121; CAAS 1;
     CANR 2, 33; DLB 9, 86; MTCW

Caldwell, (Janet Miriam) Taylor (Holland)
     1900-1985 . . . . **CLC 2, 28, 39**
     See also CA 5-8R; 116; CANR 5

Calhoun, John Caldwell
     1782-1850 . . . . **NCLC 15**
     See also DLB 3

Calisher, Hortense
     1911- . . . . **CLC 2, 4, 8, 38; SSC 15**
     See also CA 1-4R; CANR 1, 22; DLB 2;
     MTCW

Callaghan, Morley Edward
     1903-1990 . . . . **CLC 3, 14, 41, 65**
     See also CA 9-12R; 132; CANR 33;
     DLB 68; MTCW

Calvino, Italo
     1923-1985 . . . . . **CLC 5, 8, 11, 22, 33, 39,**
                                                      73; SSC 3
     See also CA 85-88; 116; CANR 23; MTCW

Cameron, Carey   1952- . . . . **CLC 59**
     See also CA 135

Cameron, Peter   1959- . . . . **CLC 44**
     See also CA 125

Campana, Dino   1885-1932 . . . . **TCLC 20**
     See also CA 117; DLB 114

Campbell, John W(ood, Jr.)
     1910-1971 . . . . **CLC 32**
     See also CA 21-22; 29-32R; CANR 34;
     CAP 2; DLB 8; MTCW

Campbell, Joseph   1904-1987 . . . . . . **CLC 69**
     See also AAYA 3; BEST 89:2; CA 1-4R;
     124; CANR 3, 28; MTCW

Campbell, Maria   1940- . . . . **CLC 85**
     See also CA 102; NNAL

Campbell, (John) Ramsey   1946- . . . . **CLC 42**
     See also CA 57-60; CANR 7

Campbell, (Ignatius) Roy (Dunnachie)
     1901-1957 . . . . **TCLC 5**
     See also CA 104; DLB 20

Campbell, Thomas   1777-1844 . . . . **NCLC 19**
     See also DLB 93; 144

Campbell, Wilfred . . . . **TCLC 9**
     See also Campbell, William

Campbell, William   1858(?)-1918
     See Campbell, Wilfred
     See also CA 106; DLB 92

Campos, Alvaro de
     See Pessoa, Fernando (Antonio Nogueira)

Camus, Albert
     1913-1960 . . . . **CLC 1, 2, 4, 9, 11, 14, 32,**
                        63, 69; DA; DC 2; SSC 9; WLC
     See also CA 89-92; DLB 72; MTCW

Canby, Vincent   1924- . . . . **CLC 13**
     See also CA 81-84

Cancale
     See Desnos, Robert

Canetti, Elias
     1905-1994 . . . . . . **CLC 3, 14, 25, 75, 86**
     See also CA 21-24R; 146; CANR 23;
     DLB 85, 124; MTCW

Canin, Ethan   1960- . . . . **CLC 55**
     See also CA 131; 135

Cannon, Curt
     See Hunter, Evan

Cape, Judith
     See Page, P(atricia) K(athleen)

Capek, Karel
     1890-1938 . . . . . **TCLC 6, 37; DA; DC 1;**
                                                                   WLC
     See also CA 104; 140

Capote, Truman
     1924-1984 . . . . . . **CLC 1, 3, 8, 13, 19, 34,**
                              38, 58; DA; SSC 2; WLC
     See also CA 5-8R; 113; CANR 18;
     CDALB 1941-1968; DLB 2; DLBY 80,
     84; MTCW

Capra, Frank   1897-1991 . . . . **CLC 16**
     See also CA 61-64; 135

Caputo, Philip   1941- . . . . **CLC 32**
     See also CA 73-76; CANR 40

Card, Orson Scott   1951- . . . . **CLC 44, 47, 50**
     See also AAYA 11; CA 102; CANR 27, 47;
     MTCW

Cardenal (Martinez), Ernesto
     1925- . . . . **CLC 31; HLC**
     See also CA 49-52; CANR 2, 32; HW;
     MTCW

Carducci, Giosue   1835-1907 . . . . **TCLC 32**

Carew, Thomas   1595(?)-1640 . . . . **LC 13**
     See also DLB 126

Carey, Ernestine Gilbreth   1908- . . . . **CLC 17**
     See also CA 5-8R; SATA 2

Carey, Peter   1943- . . . . **CLC 40, 55**
     See also CA 123; 127; MTCW

Carleton, William   1794-1869 . . . . . **NCLC 3**

Carlisle, Henry (Coffin)   1926- . . . . . . **CLC 33**
     See also CA 13-16R; CANR 15

Carlsen, Chris
     See Holdstock, Robert P.

Carlson, Ron(ald F.)   1947- . . . . **CLC 54**
     See also CA 105; CANR 27

Carlyle, Thomas   1795-1881 . . **NCLC 22; DA**
     See also CDBLB 1789-1832; DLB 55; 144

Carman, (William) Bliss
     1861-1929 . . . . **TCLC 7**
     See also CA 104; DLB 92

Carnegie, Dale   1888-1955 . . . . **TCLC 53**

Carossa, Hans   1878-1956 . . . . **TCLC 48**
     See also DLB 66

Carpenter, Don(ald Richard)
     1931- . . . . **CLC 41**
     See also CA 45-48; CANR 1

Carpentier (y Valmont), Alejo
     1904-1980 . . . . **CLC 8, 11, 38; HLC**
     See also CA 65-68; 97-100; CANR 11;
     DLB 113; HW

Carr, Caleb   1955(?)- . . . . **CLC 86**

Carr, Emily   1871-1945 . . . . **TCLC 32**
     See also DLB 68

Carr, John Dickson   1906-1977 . . . . . . **CLC 3**
     See also CA 49-52; 69-72; CANR 3, 33;
     MTCW

Carr, Philippa
     See Hibbert, Eleanor Alice Burford

Carr, Virginia Spencer   1929- . . . . **CLC 34**
     See also CA 61-64; DLB 111

Carrier, Roch   1937- . . . . **CLC 13, 78**
     See also CA 130; DLB 53

Carroll, James P.   1943(?)- . . . . **CLC 38**
     See also CA 81-84

Carroll, Jim   1951- . . . . **CLC 35**
     See also CA 45-48; CANR 42

Carroll, Lewis . . . . **NCLC 2; WLC**
     See also Dodgson, Charles Lutwidge
     See also CDBLB 1832-1890; CLR 2, 18;
     DLB 18; JRDA

Carroll, Paul Vincent   1900-1968 . . . . **CLC 10**
     See also CA 9-12R; 25-28R; DLB 10

Carruth, Hayden
     1921- . . . . . . **CLC 4, 7, 10, 18, 84; PC 10**
     See also CA 9-12R; CANR 4, 38; DLB 5;
     MTCW; SATA 47

Carson, Rachel Louise   1907-1964 . . . **CLC 71**
     See also CA 77-80; CANR 35; MTCW;
     SATA 23

Carter, Angela (Olive)
     1940-1992 . . . . . . **CLC 5, 41, 76; SSC 13**
     See also CA 53-56; 136; CANR 12, 36;
     DLB 14; MTCW; SATA 66;
     SATA-Obit 70

Carter, Nick
     See Smith, Martin Cruz

Carver, Raymond
     1938-1988 . . . **CLC 22, 36, 53, 55; SSC 8**
     See also CA 33-36R; 126; CANR 17, 34;
     DLB 130; DLBY 84, 88; MTCW

Clemens, Samuel Langhorne 1835-1910
See Twain, Mark
See also CA 104; 135; CDALB 1865-1917;
DA; DLB 11, 12, 23, 64, 74; JRDA;
MAICYA; YABC 2

Cleophil
See Congreve, William

Clerihew, E.
See Bentley, E(dmund) C(lerihew)

Clerk, N. W.
See Lewis, C(live) S(taples)

Cliff, Jimmy..................... CLC 21
See also Chambers, James

Clifton, (Thelma) Lucille
1936- .... CLC 19, 66; BLC
See also BW 2; CA 49-52; CANR 2, 24, 42;
CLR 5; DLB 5, 41; MAICYA; MTCW;
SATA 20, 69

Clinton, Dirk
See Silverberg, Robert

Clough, Arthur Hugh 1819-1861.. NCLC 27
See also DLB 32

Clutha, Janet Paterson Frame 1924-
See Frame, Janet
See also CA 1-4R; CANR 2, 36; MTCW

Clyne, Terence
See Blatty, William Peter

Cobalt, Martin
See Mayne, William (James Carter)

Coburn, D(onald) L(ee) 1938- ...... CLC 10
See also CA 89-92

Cocteau, Jean (Maurice Eugene Clement)
1889-1963 .... CLC 1, 8, 15, 16, 43; DA;
WLC
See also CA 25-28; CANR 40; CAP 2;
DLB 65; MTCW

Codrescu, Andrei 1946- .... CLC 46
See also CA 33-36R; CAAS 19; CANR 13,
34

Coe, Max
See Bourne, Randolph S(illiman)

Coe, Tucker
See Westlake, Donald E(dwin)

Coetzee, J(ohn) M(ichael)
1940- .... CLC 23, 33, 66
See also CA 77-80; CANR 41; MTCW

Coffey, Brian
See Koontz, Dean R(ay)

Cohen, Arthur A(llen)
1928-1986 .... CLC 7, 31
See also CA 1-4R; 120; CANR 1, 17, 42;
DLB 28

Cohen, Leonard (Norman)
1934- .... CLC 3, 38
See also CA 21-24R; CANR 14; DLB 53;
MTCW

Cohen, Matt 1942- .... CLC 19
See also CA 61-64; CAAS 18; CANR 40;
DLB 53

Cohen-Solal, Annie 19(?)- .... CLC 50

Colegate, Isabel 1931- .... CLC 36
See also CA 17-20R; CANR 8, 22; DLB 14;
MTCW

Coleman, Emmett
See Reed, Ishmael

Coleridge, Samuel Taylor
1772-1834 .. NCLC 9; DA; PC 11; WLC
See also CDBLB 1789-1832; DLB 93, 107

Coleridge, Sara 1802-1852...... NCLC 31

Coles, Don 1928- .... CLC 46
See also CA 115; CANR 38

Colette, (Sidonie-Gabrielle)
1873-1954 ...... TCLC 1, 5, 16; SSC 10
See also CA 104; 131; DLB 65; MTCW

Collett, (Jacobine) Camilla (Wergeland)
1813-1895 .... NCLC 22

Collier, Christopher 1930-......... CLC 30
See also AAYA 13; CA 33-36R; CANR 13,
33; JRDA; MAICYA; SATA 16, 70

Collier, James L(incoln) 1928- ..... CLC 30
See also AAYA 13; CA 9-12R; CANR 4,
33; CLR 3; JRDA; MAICYA; SATA 8,
70

Collier, Jeremy 1650-1726.......... LC 6

Collins, Hunt
See Hunter, Evan

Collins, Linda 1931-.............. CLC 44
See also CA 125

Collins, (William) Wilkie
1824-1889 .... NCLC 1, 18
See also CDBLB 1832-1890; DLB 18, 70

Collins, William 1721-1759 .... LC 4
See also DLB 109

Colman, George
See Glassco, John

Colt, Winchester Remington
See Hubbard, L(afayette) Ron(ald)

Colter, Cyrus 1910- .... CLC 58
See also BW 1; CA 65-68; CANR 10;
DLB 33

Colton, James
See Hansen, Joseph

Colum, Padraic 1881-1972........ CLC 28
See also CA 73-76; 33-36R; CANR 35;
CLR 36; MAICYA; MTCW; SATA 15

Colvin, James
See Moorcock, Michael (John)

Colwin, Laurie (E.)
1944-1992 .... CLC 5, 13, 23, 84
See also CA 89-92; 139; CANR 20, 46;
DLBY 80; MTCW

Comfort, Alex(ander) 1920-........ CLC 7
See also CA 1-4R; CANR 1, 45

Comfort, Montgomery
See Campbell, (John) Ramsey

Compton-Burnett, I(vy)
1884(?)-1969 ...... CLC 1, 3, 10, 15, 34
See also CA 1-4R; 25-28R; CANR 4;
DLB 36; MTCW

Comstock, Anthony 1844-1915 .... TCLC 13
See also CA 110

Conan Doyle, Arthur
See Doyle, Arthur Conan

Conde, Maryse 1937-............. CLC 52
See also Boucolon, Maryse
See also BW 2

Condillac, Etienne Bonnot de
1714-1780 .... LC 26

Condon, Richard (Thomas)
1915- .... CLC 4, 6, 8, 10, 45
See also BEST 90:3; CA 1-4R; CAAS 1;
CANR 2, 23; MTCW

Congreve, William
1670-1729 ... LC 5, 21; DA; DC 2; WLC
See also CDBLB 1660-1789; DLB 39, 84

Connell, Evan S(helby), Jr.
1924-.................... CLC 4, 6, 45
See also AAYA 7; CA 1-4R; CAAS 2;
CANR 2, 39; DLB 2; DLBY 81; MTCW

Connelly, Marc(us Cook)
1890-1980 .... CLC 7
See also CA 85-88; 102; CANR 30; DLB 7;
DLBY 80; SATA-Obit 25

Connor, Ralph .... TCLC 31
See also Gordon, Charles William
See also DLB 92

Conrad, Joseph
1857-1924 .... TCLC 1, 6, 13, 25, 43, 57;
DA; SSC 9; WLC
See also CA 104; 131; CDBLB 1890-1914;
DLB 10, 34, 98; MTCW; SATA 27

Conrad, Robert Arnold
See Hart, Moss

Conroy, Pat 1945-.............. CLC 30, 74
See also AAYA 8; AITN 1; CA 85-88;
CANR 24; DLB 6; MTCW

Constant (de Rebecque), (Henri) Benjamin
1767-1830 .... NCLC 6
See also DLB 119

Conybeare, Charles Augustus
See Eliot, T(homas) S(tearns)

Cook, Michael 1933- .... CLC 58
See also CA 93-96; DLB 53

Cook, Robin 1940-............... CLC 14
See also BEST 90:2; CA 108; 111;
CANR 41

Cook, Roy
See Silverberg, Robert

Cooke, Elizabeth 1948- .... CLC 55
See also CA 129

Cooke, John Esten 1830-1886..... NCLC 5
See also DLB 3

Cooke, John Estes
See Baum, L(yman) Frank

Cooke, M. E.
See Creasey, John

Cooke, Margaret
See Creasey, John

Cooney, Ray .... CLC 62

Cooper, Douglas 1960-........... CLC 86

Cooper, Henry St. John
See Creasey, John

Cooper, J. California.............. CLC 56
See also AAYA 12; BW 1; CA 125

Cooper, James Fenimore
1789-1851 .... NCLC 1, 27
See also CDALB 1640-1865; DLB 3;
SATA 19

Coover, Robert (Lowell)
1932- .. CLC 3, 7, 15, 32, 46, 87; SSC 15
See also CA 45-48; CANR 3, 37; DLB 2;
DLBY 81; MTCW

Copeland, Stewart (Armstrong)
1952- .... CLC 26

Coppard, A(lfred) E(dgar)
1878-1957 .... TCLC 5
See also CA 114; YABC 1

Coppee, Francois 1842-1908 ...... TCLC 25

Coppola, Francis Ford 1939-....... CLC 16
See also CA 77-80; CANR 40; DLB 44

Corbiere, Tristan 1845-1875 ..... NCLC 43

Corcoran, Barbara 1911-.......... CLC 17
See also AAYA 14; CA 21-24R; CAAS 2;
CANR 11, 28; DLB 52; JRDA; SATA 3,
77

Cordelier, Maurice
See Giraudoux, (Hippolyte) Jean

Corelli, Marie 1855-1924........ TCLC 51
See also Mackay, Mary
See also DLB 34

Corman, Cid..................... CLC 9
See also Corman, Sidney
See also CAAS 2; DLB 5

Corman, Sidney 1924-
See Corman, Cid
See also CA 85-88; CANR 44

Cormier, Robert (Edmund)
1925- .... CLC 12, 30; DA
See also AAYA 3; CA 1-4R; CANR 5, 23;
CDALB 1968-1988; CLR 12; DLB 52;
JRDA; MAICYA; MTCW; SATA 10, 45

Corn, Alfred (DeWitt III) 1943-.... CLC 33
See also CA 104; CANR 44; DLB 120;
DLBY 80

Corneille, Pierre 1606-1684........ LC 28

Cornwell, David (John Moore)
1931- .... CLC 9, 15
See also le Carre, John
See also CA 5-8R; CANR 13, 33; MTCW

Corso, (Nunzio) Gregory 1930-... CLC 1, 11
See also CA 5-8R; CANR 41; DLB 5, 16;
MTCW

Cortazar, Julio
1914-1984 ...... CLC 2, 3, 5, 10, 13, 15,
33, 34; HLC; SSC 7
See also CA 21-24R; CANR 12, 32;
DLB 113; HW; MTCW

Corwin, Cecil
See Kornbluth, C(yril) M.

Cosic, Dobrica 1921- .... CLC 14
See also CA 122; 138

Costain, Thomas B(ertram)
1885-1965 .... CLC 30
See also CA 5-8R; 25-28R; DLB 9

Costantini, Humberto
1924(?)-1987 .... CLC 49
See also CA 131; 122; HW

Costello, Elvis 1955-............. CLC 21

Cotter, Joseph Seamon Sr.
1861-1949.......... TCLC 28; BLC
See also BW 1; CA 124; DLB 50

Couch, Arthur Thomas Quiller
See Quiller-Couch, Arthur Thomas

Coulton, James
See Hansen, Joseph

Couperus, Louis (Marie Anne)
1863-1923 .... TCLC 15
See also CA 115

Coupland, Douglas 1961-.......... CLC 85
See also CA 142

Court, Wesli
See Turco, Lewis (Putnam)

Courtenay, Bryce 1933-........... CLC 59
See also CA 138

Courtney, Robert
See Ellison, Harlan (Jay)

Cousteau, Jacques-Yves 1910-...... CLC 30
See also CA 65-68; CANR 15; MTCW;
SATA 38

Coward, Noel (Peirce)
1899-1973 .... CLC 1, 9, 29, 51
See also AITN 1; CA 17-18; 41-44R;
CANR 35; CAP 2; CDBLB 1914-1945;
DLB 10; MTCW

Cowley, Malcolm 1898-1989 .... CLC 39
See also CA 5-8R; 128; CANR 3; DLB 4,
48; DLBY 81, 89; MTCW

Cowper, William 1731-1800....... NCLC 8
See also DLB 104, 109

Cox, William Trevor 1928- ... CLC 9, 14, 71
See also Trevor, William
See also CA 9-12R; CANR 4, 37; DLB 14;
MTCW

Coyne, P. J.
See Masters, Hilary

Cozzens, James Gould
1903-1978 .... CLC 1, 4, 11
See also CA 9-12R; 81-84; CANR 19;
CDALB 1941-1968; DLB 9; DLBD 2;
DLBY 84; MTCW

Crabbe, George 1754-1832....... NCLC 26
See also DLB 93

Craig, A. A.
See Anderson, Poul (William)

Craik, Dinah Maria (Mulock)
1826-1887 .... NCLC 38
See also DLB 35; MAICYA; SATA 34

Cram, Ralph Adams 1863-1942.... TCLC 45

Crane, (Harold) Hart
1899-1932 .... TCLC 2, 5; DA; PC 3;
WLC
See also CA 104; 127; CDALB 1917-1929;
DLB 4, 48; MTCW

Crane, R(onald) S(almon)
1886-1967 .... CLC 27
See also CA 85-88; DLB 63

Crane, Stephen (Townley)
1871-1900 ...... TCLC 11, 17, 32; DA;
SSC 7; WLC
See also CA 109; 140; CDALB 1865-1917;
DLB 12, 54, 78; YABC 2

Crase, Douglas 1944-............. CLC 58
See also CA 106

Crashaw, Richard 1612(?)-1649...... LC 24
See also DLB 126

Craven, Margaret 1901-1980....... CLC 17
See also CA 103

Crawford, F(rancis) Marion
1854-1909 .... TCLC 10
See also CA 107; DLB 71

Crawford, Isabella Valancy
1850-1887 .... NCLC 12
See also DLB 92

Crayon, Geoffrey
See Irving, Washington

Creasey, John 1908-1973.......... CLC 11
See also CA 5-8R; 41-44R; CANR 8;
DLB 77; MTCW

Crebillon, Claude Prosper Jolyot de (fils)
1707-1777 .... LC 28

Credo
See Creasey, John

Creeley, Robert (White)
1926- ..... CLC 1, 2, 4, 8, 11, 15, 36, 78
See also CA 1-4R; CAAS 10; CANR 23, 43;
DLB 5, 16; MTCW

Crews, Harry (Eugene)
1935- .... CLC 6, 23, 49
See also AITN 1; CA 25-28R; CANR 20;
DLB 6, 143; MTCW

Crichton, (John) Michael
1942-..................... CLC 2, 6, 54
See also AAYA 10; AITN 2; CA 25-28R;
CANR 13, 40; DLBY 81; JRDA;
MTCW; SATA 9

Crispin, Edmund .... CLC 22
See also Montgomery, (Robert) Bruce
See also DLB 87

Cristofer, Michael 1945(?)-........ CLC 28
See also CA 110; DLB 7

Croce, Benedetto 1866-1952 ...... TCLC 37
See also CA 120

Crockett, David 1786-1836 .... NCLC 8
See also DLB 3, 11

Crockett, Davy
See Crockett, David

Crofts, Freeman Wills
1879-1957 .... TCLC 55
See also CA 115; DLB 77

Croker, John Wilson 1780-1857 .. NCLC 10
See also DLB 110

Crommelynck, Fernand 1885-1970 .. CLC 75
See also CA 89-92

Cronin, A(rchibald) J(oseph)
1896-1981 .... CLC 32
See also CA 1-4R; 102; CANR 5; SATA 47;
SATA-Obit 25

Cross, Amanda
See Heilbrun, Carolyn G(old)

Crothers, Rachel 1878(?)-1958..... TCLC 19
See also CA 113; DLB 7

Croves, Hal
See Traven, B.

Crowfield, Christopher
See Stowe, Harriet (Elizabeth) Beecher

Crowley, Aleister.................. TCLC 7
See also Crowley, Edward Alexander

Crowley, Edward Alexander 1875-1947
See Crowley, Aleister
See also CA 104

Crowley, John 1942-.............. CLC 57
See also CA 61-64; CANR 43; DLBY 82;
SATA 65

Day Lewis, C(ecil)
1904-1972 . . . . **CLC 1, 6, 10; PC 11**
See also Blake, Nicholas
See also CA 13-16; 33-36R; CANR 34;
CAP 1; DLB 15, 20; MTCW

Dazai, Osamu . . . . **TCLC 11**
See also Tsushima, Shuji

de Andrade, Carlos Drummond
See Drummond de Andrade, Carlos

Deane, Norman
See Creasey, John

**de Beauvoir, Simone (Lucie Ernestine Marie
Bertrand)**
See Beauvoir, Simone (Lucie Ernestine
Marie Bertrand) de

de Brissac, Malcolm
See Dickinson, Peter (Malcolm)

de Chardin, Pierre Teilhard
See Teilhard de Chardin, (Marie Joseph)
Pierre

Dee, John 1527-1608 . . . . **LC 20**

Deer, Sandra 1940- . . . . **CLC 45**

De Ferrari, Gabriella . . . . **CLC 65**

Defoe, Daniel
1660(?)-1731 . . . . **LC 1; DA; WLC**
See also CDBLB 1660-1789; DLB 39, 95,
101; JRDA; MAICYA; SATA 22

de Gourmont, Remy
See Gourmont, Remy de

de Hartog, Jan 1914- . . . . **CLC 19**
See also CA 1-4R; CANR 1

de Hostos, E. M.
See Hostos (y Bonilla), Eugenio Maria de

de Hostos, Eugenio M.
See Hostos (y Bonilla), Eugenio Maria de

Deighton, Len . . . . **CLC 4, 7, 22, 46**
See also Deighton, Leonard Cyril
See also AAYA 6; BEST 89:2;
CDBLB 1960 to Present; DLB 87

Deighton, Leonard Cyril 1929-
See Deighton, Len
See also CA 9-12R; CANR 19, 33; MTCW

Dekker, Thomas 1572(?)-1632 . . . . **LC 22**
See also CDBLB Before 1660; DLB 62

de la Mare, Walter (John)
1873-1956 . . **TCLC 4, 53; SSC 14; WLC**
See also CDBLB 1914-1945; CLR 23;
DLB 19; SATA 16

Delaney, Franey
See O'Hara, John (Henry)

Delaney, Shelagh 1939- . . . . **CLC 29**
See also CA 17-20R; CANR 30;
CDBLB 1960 to Present; DLB 13;
MTCW

Delany, Mary (Granville Pendarves)
1700-1788 . . . . **LC 12**

Delany, Samuel R(ay, Jr.)
1942- . . . . **CLC 8, 14, 38; BLC**
See also BW 2; CA 81-84; CANR 27, 43;
DLB 8, 33; MTCW

De La Ramee, (Marie) Louise 1839-1908
See Ouida
See also SATA 20

de la Roche, Mazo 1879-1961 . . . . . . **CLC 14**
See also CA 85-88; CANR 30; DLB 68;
SATA 64

Delbanco, Nicholas (Franklin)
1942- . . . . **CLC 6, 13**
See also CA 17-20R; CAAS 2; CANR 29;
DLB 6

del Castillo, Michel 1933- . . . . **CLC 38**
See also CA 109

Deledda, Grazia (Cosima)
1875(?)-1936 . . . . **TCLC 23**
See also CA 123

Delibes, Miguel . . . . **CLC 8, 18**
See also Delibes Setien, Miguel

Delibes Setien, Miguel 1920-
See Delibes, Miguel
See also CA 45-48; CANR 1, 32; HW;
MTCW

DeLillo, Don
1936- . . . . . **CLC 8, 10, 13, 27, 39, 54, 76**
See also BEST 89:1; CA 81-84; CANR 21;
DLB 6; MTCW

de Lisser, H. G.
See De Lisser, Herbert George
See also DLB 117

De Lisser, Herbert George
1878-1944 . . . . **TCLC 12**
See also de Lisser, H. G.
See also BW 2; CA 109

Deloria, Vine (Victor), Jr. 1933- . . . . **CLC 21**
See also CA 53-56; CANR 5, 20; MTCW;
NNAL; SATA 21

Del Vecchio, John M(ichael)
1947- . . . . **CLC 29**
See also CA 110; DLBD 9

de Man, Paul (Adolph Michel)
1919-1983 . . . . **CLC 55**
See also CA 128; 111; DLB 67; MTCW

De Marinis, Rick 1934- . . . . **CLC 54**
See also CA 57-60; CANR 9, 25

Demby, William 1922- . . . . **CLC 53; BLC**
See also BW 1; CA 81-84; DLB 33

Demijohn, Thom
See Disch, Thomas M(ichael)

de Montherlant, Henry (Milon)
See Montherlant, Henry (Milon) de

Demosthenes 384B.C.-322B.C. . . . **CMLC 13**

de Natale, Francine
See Malzberg, Barry N(athaniel)

Denby, Edwin (Orr) 1903-1983 . . . . . **CLC 48**
See also CA 138; 110

Denis, Julio
See Cortazar, Julio

Denmark, Harrison
See Zelazny, Roger (Joseph)

Dennis, John 1658-1734 . . . . **LC 11**
See also DLB 101

Dennis, Nigel (Forbes) 1912-1989 . . . . **CLC 8**
See also CA 25-28R; 129; DLB 13, 15;
MTCW

De Palma, Brian (Russell) 1940- . . . . **CLC 20**
See also CA 109

De Quincey, Thomas 1785-1859 . . . **NCLC 4**
See also CDBLB 1789-1832; DLB 110; 144

Deren, Eleanora 1908(?)-1961
See Deren, Maya
See also CA 111

Deren, Maya . . . . **CLC 16**
See also Deren, Eleanora

Derleth, August (William)
1909-1971 . . . . **CLC 31**
See also CA 1-4R; 29-32R; CANR 4;
DLB 9; SATA 5

Der Nister 1884-1950 . . . . **TCLC 56**

de Routisie, Albert
See Aragon, Louis

Derrida, Jacques 1930- . . . . **CLC 24, 87**
See also CA 124; 127

Derry Down Derry
See Lear, Edward

Dersonnes, Jacques
See Simenon, Georges (Jacques Christian)

Desai, Anita 1937- . . . . **CLC 19, 37**
See also CA 81-84; CANR 33; MTCW;
SATA 63

de Saint-Luc, Jean
See Glassco, John

de Saint Roman, Arnaud
See Aragon, Louis

Descartes, Rene 1596-1650 . . . . **LC 20**

De Sica, Vittorio 1901(?)-1974 . . . . . **CLC 20**
See also CA 117

Desnos, Robert 1900-1945 . . . . **TCLC 22**
See also CA 121

Destouches, Louis-Ferdinand
1894-1961 . . . . **CLC 9, 15**
See also Celine, Louis-Ferdinand
See also CA 85-88; CANR 28; MTCW

Deutsch, Babette 1895-1982 . . . . **CLC 18**
See also CA 1-4R; 108; CANR 4; DLB 45;
SATA 1; SATA-Obit 33

Devenant, William 1606-1649 . . . . **LC 13**

Devkota, Laxmiprasad
1909-1959 . . . . **TCLC 23**
See also CA 123

De Voto, Bernard (Augustine)
1897-1955 . . . . **TCLC 29**
See also CA 113; DLB 9

De Vries, Peter
1910-1993 . . . . **CLC 1, 2, 3, 7, 10, 28, 46**
See also CA 17-20R; 142; CANR 41;
DLB 6; DLBY 82; MTCW

Dexter, Martin
See Faust, Frederick (Schiller)

Dexter, Pete 1943- . . . . **CLC 34, 55**
See also BEST 89:2; CA 127; 131; MTCW

Diamano, Silmang
See Senghor, Leopold Sedar

Diamond, Neil 1941- . . . . **CLC 30**
See also CA 108

di Bassetto, Corno
See Shaw, George Bernard

Dick, Philip K(indred)
1928-1982 . . . . **CLC 10, 30, 72**
See also CA 49-52; 106; CANR 2, 16;
DLB 8; MTCW

Dickens, Charles (John Huffam)
1812-1870 ..... **NCLC 3, 8, 18, 26, 37;
DA; SSC 17; WLC**
See also CDBLB 1832-1890; DLB 21, 55,
70; JRDA; MAICYA; SATA 15

Dickey, James (Lafayette)
1923- .... **CLC 1, 2, 4, 7, 10, 15, 47**
See also AITN 1, 2; CA 9-12R; CABS 2;
CANR 10; CDALB 1968-1988; DLB 5;
DLBD 7; DLBY 82, 93; MTCW

Dickey, William 1928-1994 ..... **CLC 3, 28**
See also CA 9-12R; 145; CANR 24; DLB 5

Dickinson, Charles 1951- .... **CLC 49**
See also CA 128

Dickinson, Emily (Elizabeth)
1830-1886 .. **NCLC 21; DA; PC 1; WLC**
See also CDALB 1865-1917; DLB 1;
SATA 29

Dickinson, Peter (Malcolm)
1927- .... **CLC 12, 35**
See also AAYA 9; CA 41-44R; CANR 31;
CLR 29; DLB 87; JRDA; MAICYA;
SATA 5, 62

Dickson, Carr
See Carr, John Dickson

Dickson, Carter
See Carr, John Dickson

Diderot, Denis 1713-1784 .... **LC 26**

Didion, Joan 1934- ..... **CLC 1, 3, 8, 14, 32**
See also AITN 1; CA 5-8R; CANR 14;
CDALB 1968-1988; DLB 2; DLBY 81,
86; MTCW

Dietrich, Robert
See Hunt, E(verette) Howard, (Jr.)

Dillard, Annie 1945- .... **CLC 9, 60**
See also AAYA 6; CA 49-52; CANR 3, 43;
DLBY 80; MTCW; SATA 10

Dillard, R(ichard) H(enry) W(ilde)
1937- .... **CLC 5**
See also CA 21-24R; CAAS 7; CANR 10;
DLB 5

Dillon, Eilis 1920- .... **CLC 17**
See also CA 9-12R; CAAS 3; CANR 4, 38;
CLR 26; MAICYA; SATA 2, 74

Dimont, Penelope
See Mortimer, Penelope (Ruth)

Dinesen, Isak .... **CLC 10, 29; SSC 7**
See also Blixen, Karen (Christentze
Dinesen)

Ding Ling .... **CLC 68**
See also Chiang Pin-chin

Disch, Thomas M(ichael) 1940- ... **CLC 7, 36**
See also CA 21-24R; CAAS 4; CANR 17,
36; CLR 18; DLB 8; MAICYA; MTCW;
SAAS 15; SATA 54

Disch, Tom
See Disch, Thomas M(ichael)

d'Isly, Georges
See Simenon, Georges (Jacques Christian)

Disraeli, Benjamin 1804-1881 .. **NCLC 2, 39**
See also DLB 21, 55

Ditcum, Steve
See Crumb, R(obert)

Dixon, Paige
See Corcoran, Barbara

Dixon, Stephen 1936- ..... **CLC 52; SSC 16**
See also CA 89-92; CANR 17, 40; DLB 130

Dobell, Sydney Thompson
1824-1874 .... **NCLC 43**
See also DLB 32

Doblin, Alfred .... **TCLC 13**
See also Doeblin, Alfred

Dobrolyubov, Nikolai Alexandrovich
1836-1861 .... **NCLC 5**

Dobyns, Stephen 1941- .... **CLC 37**
See also CA 45-48; CANR 2, 18

Doctorow, E(dgar) L(aurence)
1931- ..... **CLC 6, 11, 15, 18, 37, 44, 65**
See also AITN 2; BEST 89:3; CA 45-48;
CANR 2, 33; CDALB 1968-1988; DLB 2,
28; DLBY 80; MTCW

Dodgson, Charles Lutwidge 1832-1898
See Carroll, Lewis
See also CLR 2; DA; MAICYA; YABC 2

Dodson, Owen (Vincent)
1914-1983 .... **CLC 79; BLC**
See also BW 1; CA 65-68; 110; CANR 24;
DLB 76

Doeblin, Alfred 1878-1957 .... **TCLC 13**
See also Doblin, Alfred
See also CA 110; 141; DLB 66

Doerr, Harriet 1910- .... **CLC 34**
See also CA 117; 122; CANR 47

Domecq, H(onorio) Bustos
See Bioy Casares, Adolfo; Borges, Jorge
Luis

Domini, Rey
See Lorde, Audre (Geraldine)

Dominique
See Proust, (Valentin-Louis-George-Eugene-)
Marcel

Don, A
See Stephen, Leslie

Donaldson, Stephen R. 1947- .... **CLC 46**
See also CA 89-92; CANR 13

Donleavy, J(ames) P(atrick)
1926- .... **CLC 1, 4, 6, 10, 45**
See also AITN 2; CA 9-12R; CANR 24;
DLB 6; MTCW

Donne, John
1572-1631 .... **LC 10, 24; DA; PC 1**
See also CDBLB Before 1660; DLB 121

Donnell, David 1939(?)- .... **CLC 34**

Donoghue, P. S.
See Hunt, E(verette) Howard, (Jr.)

Donoso (Yanez), Jose
1924- .... **CLC 4, 8, 11, 32; HLC**
See also CA 81-84; CANR 32; DLB 113;
HW; MTCW

Donovan, John 1928-1992 .... **CLC 35**
See also CA 97-100; 137; CLR 3;
MAICYA; SATA 72; SATA-Brief 29

Don Roberto
See Cunninghame Graham, R(obert)
B(ontine)

Doolittle, Hilda
1886-1961 ..... **CLC 3, 8, 14, 31, 34, 73;
DA; PC 5; WLC**
See also H. D.
See also CA 97-100; CANR 35; DLB 4, 45;
MTCW

Dorfman, Ariel 1942- .... **CLC 48, 77; HLC**
See also CA 124; 130; HW

Dorn, Edward (Merton) 1929- ... **CLC 10, 18**
See also CA 93-96; CANR 42; DLB 5

Dorsan, Luc
See Simenon, Georges (Jacques Christian)

Dorsange, Jean
See Simenon, Georges (Jacques Christian)

Dos Passos, John (Roderigo)
1896-1970 ...... **CLC 1, 4, 8, 11, 15, 25,
34, 82; DA; WLC**
See also CA 1-4R; 29-32R; CANR 3;
CDALB 1929-1941; DLB 4, 9; DLBD 1;
MTCW

Dossage, Jean
See Simenon, Georges (Jacques Christian)

Dostoevsky, Fedor Mikhailovich
1821-1881 ...... **NCLC 2, 7, 21, 33, 43;
DA; SSC 2; WLC**

Doughty, Charles M(ontagu)
1843-1926 .... **TCLC 27**
See also CA 115; DLB 19, 57

Douglas, Ellen .... **CLC 73**
See also Haxton, Josephine Ayres;
Williamson, Ellen Douglas

Douglas, Gavin 1475(?)-1522 .... **LC 20**

Douglas, Keith 1920-1944 .... **TCLC 40**
See also DLB 27

Douglas, Leonard
See Bradbury, Ray (Douglas)

Douglas, Michael
See Crichton, (John) Michael

Douglass, Frederick
1817(?)-1895 .... **NCLC 7; BLC; DA;
WLC**
See also CDALB 1640-1865; DLB 1, 43, 50,
79; SATA 29

Dourado, (Waldomiro Freitas) Autran
1926- .... **CLC 23, 60**
See also CA 25-28R; CANR 34

Dourado, Waldomiro Autran
See Dourado, (Waldomiro Freitas) Autran

Dove, Rita (Frances)
1952- .... **CLC 50, 81; PC 6**
See also BW 2; CA 109; CAAS 19;
CANR 27, 42; DLB 120

Dowell, Coleman 1925-1985 .... **CLC 60**
See also CA 25-28R; 117; CANR 10;
DLB 130

Dowson, Ernest Christopher
1867-1900 .... **TCLC 4**
See also CA 105; DLB 19, 135

Doyle, A. Conan
See Doyle, Arthur Conan

Doyle, Arthur Conan
1859-1930 . . . . . . TCLC 7; DA; SSC 12;
WLC
See also AAYA 14; CA 104; 122;
CDBLB 1890-1914; DLB 18, 70; MTCW;
SATA 24

Doyle, Conan
See Doyle, Arthur Conan

Doyle, John
See Graves, Robert (von Ranke)

Doyle, Roddy 1958(?)- . . . . CLC 81
See also AAYA 14; CA 143

Doyle, Sir A. Conan
See Doyle, Arthur Conan

Doyle, Sir Arthur Conan
See Doyle, Arthur Conan

Dr. A
See Asimov, Isaac; Silverstein, Alvin

Drabble, Margaret
1939- . . . . CLC 2, 3, 5, 8, 10, 22, 53
See also CA 13-16R; CANR 18, 35;
CDBLB 1960 to Present; DLB 14;
MTCW; SATA 48

Drapier, M. B.
See Swift, Jonathan

Drayham, James
See Mencken, H(enry) L(ouis)

Drayton, Michael 1563-1631 . . . . LC 8

Dreadstone, Carl
See Campbell, (John) Ramsey

Dreiser, Theodore (Herman Albert)
1871-1945 . . . . . . TCLC 10, 18, 35; DA;
WLC
See also CA 106; 132; CDALB 1865-1917;
DLB 9, 12, 102, 137; DLBD 1; MTCW

Drexler, Rosalyn 1926- . . . . CLC 2, 6
See also CA 81-84

Dreyer, Carl Theodor 1889-1968. . . . CLC 16
See also CA 116

Drieu la Rochelle, Pierre(-Eugene)
1893-1945 . . . . TCLC 21
See also CA 117; DLB 72

Drinkwater, John 1882-1937 . . . . . . TCLC 57
See also CA 109; DLB 10, 19

Drop Shot
See Cable, George Washington

Droste-Hulshoff, Annette Freiin von
1797-1848 . . . . NCLC 3
See also DLB 133

Drummond, Walter
See Silverberg, Robert

Drummond, William Henry
1854-1907 . . . . TCLC 25
See also DLB 92

Drummond de Andrade, Carlos
1902-1987 . . . . CLC 18
See also Andrade, Carlos Drummond de
See also CA 132; 123

Drury, Allen (Stuart) 1918- . . . . CLC 37
See also CA 57-60; CANR 18

Dryden, John
1631-1700 . . . LC 3, 21; DA; DC 3; WLC
See also CDBLB 1660-1789; DLB 80, 101,
131

Duberman, Martin 1930- . . . . CLC 8
See also CA 1-4R; CANR 2

Dubie, Norman (Evans) 1945- . . . . . . CLC 36
See also CA 69-72; CANR 12; DLB 120

Du Bois, W(illiam) E(dward) B(urghardt)
1868-1963 . . . . . . CLC 1, 2, 13, 64; BLC;
DA; WLC
See also BW 1; CA 85-88; CANR 34;
CDALB 1865-1917; DLB 47, 50, 91;
MTCW; SATA 42

Dubus, Andre 1936- . . . CLC 13, 36; SSC 15
See also CA 21-24R; CANR 17; DLB 130

Duca Minimo
See D'Annunzio, Gabriele

Ducharme, Rejean 1941- . . . . CLC 74
See also DLB 60

Duclos, Charles Pinot 1704-1772 . . . . . LC 1

Dudek, Louis 1918- . . . . CLC 11, 19
See also CA 45-48; CAAS 14; CANR 1;
DLB 88

Duerrenmatt, Friedrich
1921-1990 . . . . . . CLC 1, 4, 8, 11, 15, 43
See also CA 17-20R; CANR 33; DLB 69,
124; MTCW

Duffy, Bruce (?)- . . . . CLC 50

Duffy, Maureen 1933- . . . . CLC 37
See also CA 25-28R; CANR 33; DLB 14;
MTCW

Dugan, Alan 1923- . . . . CLC 2, 6
See also CA 81-84; DLB 5

du Gard, Roger Martin
See Martin du Gard, Roger

Duhamel, Georges 1884-1966 . . . . CLC 8
See also CA 81-84; 25-28R; CANR 35;
DLB 65; MTCW

Dujardin, Edouard (Emile Louis)
1861-1949 . . . . TCLC 13
See also CA 109; DLB 123

Dumas, Alexandre (Davy de la Pailleterie)
1802-1870 . . . . NCLC 11; DA; WLC
See also DLB 119; SATA 18

Dumas, Alexandre
1824-1895 . . . . NCLC 9; DC 1

Dumas, Claudine
See Malzberg, Barry N(athaniel)

Dumas, Henry L. 1934-1968 . . . . . CLC 6, 62
See also BW 1; CA 85-88; DLB 41

du Maurier, Daphne
1907-1989 . . . . . . CLC 6, 11, 59; SSC 18
See also CA 5-8R; 128; CANR 6; MTCW;
SATA 27; SATA-Obit 60

Dunbar, Paul Laurence
1872-1906 . . . . . . TCLC 2, 12; BLC; DA;
PC 5; SSC 8; WLC
See also BW 1; CA 104; 124;
CDALB 1865-1917; DLB 50, 54, 78;
SATA 34

Dunbar, William 1460(?)-1530(?) . . . . LC 20
See also DLB 132, 146

Duncan, Lois 1934- . . . . CLC 26
See also AAYA 4; CA 1-4R; CANR 2, 23,
36; CLR 29; JRDA; MAICYA; SAAS 2;
SATA 1, 36, 75

Duncan, Robert (Edward)
1919-1988 . . . . CLC 1, 2, 4, 7, 15, 41, 55;
PC 2
See also CA 9-12R; 124; CANR 28; DLB 5,
16; MTCW

Dunlap, William 1766-1839 . . . . NCLC 2
See also DLB 30, 37, 59

Dunn, Douglas (Eaglesham)
1942- . . . . CLC 6, 40
See also CA 45-48; CANR 2, 33; DLB 40;
MTCW

Dunn, Katherine (Karen) 1945- . . . . . CLC 71
See also CA 33-36R

Dunn, Stephen 1939- . . . . CLC 36
See also CA 33-36R; CANR 12; DLB 105

Dunne, Finley Peter 1867-1936 . . . . TCLC 28
See also CA 108; DLB 11, 23

Dunne, John Gregory 1932- . . . . CLC 28
See also CA 25-28R; CANR 14; DLBY 80

Dunsany, Edward John Moreton Drax
Plunkett 1878-1957
See Dunsany, Lord
See also CA 104; DLB 10

Dunsany, Lord . . . . TCLC 2
See also Dunsany, Edward John Moreton
Drax Plunkett
See also DLB 77

du Perry, Jean
See Simenon, Georges (Jacques Christian)

Durang, Christopher (Ferdinand)
1949- . . . . CLC 27, 38
See also CA 105

Duras, Marguerite
1914- . . . . . . CLC 3, 6, 11, 20, 34, 40, 68
See also CA 25-28R; DLB 83; MTCW

Durban, (Rosa) Pam 1947- . . . . CLC 39
See also CA 123

Durcan, Paul 1944- . . . . CLC 43, 70
See also CA 134

Durkheim, Emile 1858-1917 . . . . . . TCLC 55

Durrell, Lawrence (George)
1912-1990 . . . . CLC 1, 4, 6, 8, 13, 27, 41
See also CA 9-12R; 132; CANR 40;
CDBLB 1945-1960; DLB 15, 27;
DLBY 90; MTCW

Durrenmatt, Friedrich
See Duerrenmatt, Friedrich

Dutt, Toru 1856-1877 . . . . NCLC 29

Dwight, Timothy 1752-1817 . . . . . . NCLC 13
See also DLB 37

Dworkin, Andrea 1946- . . . . CLC 43
See also CA 77-80; CANR 16, 39; MTCW

Dwyer, Deanna
See Koontz, Dean R(ay)

Dwyer, K. R.
See Koontz, Dean R(ay)

Dylan, Bob 1941- . . . . . . CLC 3, 4, 6, 12, 77
See also CA 41-44R; DLB 16

Eagleton, Terence (Francis) 1943-
See Eagleton, Terry
See also CA 57-60; CANR 7, 23; MTCW

Eagleton, Terry . . . . CLC 63
See also Eagleton, Terence (Francis)

Emecheta, (Florence Onye) Buchi
1944- . . . . CLC 14, 48; BLC
See also BW 2; CA 81-84; CANR 27;
DLB 117; MTCW; SATA 66

Emerson, Ralph Waldo
1803-1882 . . . . . . NCLC 1, 38; DA; WLC
See also CDALB 1640-1865; DLB 1, 59, 73

Eminescu, Mihail 1850-1889 . . . . . NCLC 33

Empson, William
1906-1984 . . . . CLC 3, 8, 19, 33, 34
See also CA 17-20R; 112; CANR 31;
DLB 20; MTCW

Enchi Fumiko (Ueda) 1905-1986. . . . CLC 31
See also CA 129; 121

Ende, Michael (Andreas Helmuth)
1929- . . . . CLC 31
See also CA 118; 124; CANR 36; CLR 14;
DLB 75; MAICYA; SATA 61;
SATA-Brief 42

Endo, Shusaku 1923- . . . . . CLC 7, 14, 19, 54
See also CA 29-32R; CANR 21; MTCW

Engel, Marian 1933-1985 . . . . CLC 36
See also CA 25-28R; CANR 12; DLB 53

Engelhardt, Frederick
See Hubbard, L(afayette) Ron(ald)

Enright, D(ennis) J(oseph)
1920- . . . . CLC 4, 8, 31
See also CA 1-4R; CANR 1, 42; DLB 27;
SATA 25

Enzensberger, Hans Magnus
1929- . . . . CLC 43
See also CA 116; 119

Ephron, Nora 1941- . . . . CLC 17, 31
See also AITN 2; CA 65-68; CANR 12, 39

Epsilon
See Betjeman, John

Epstein, Daniel Mark 1948- . . . . CLC 7
See also CA 49-52; CANR 2

Epstein, Jacob 1956- . . . . CLC 19
See also CA 114

Epstein, Joseph 1937- . . . . CLC 39
See also CA 112; 119

Epstein, Leslie 1938- . . . . CLC 27
See also CA 73-76; CAAS 12; CANR 23

Equiano, Olaudah
1745(?)-1797 . . . . LC 16; BLC
See also DLB 37, 50

Erasmus, Desiderius 1469(?)-1536. . . . LC 16

Erdman, Paul E(mil) 1932- . . . . CLC 25
See also AITN 1; CA 61-64; CANR 13, 43

Erdrich, Louise 1954- . . . . CLC 39, 54
See also AAYA 10; BEST 89:1; CA 114;
CANR 41; MTCW; NNAL

Erenburg, Ilya (Grigoryevich)
See Ehrenburg, Ilya (Grigoryevich)

Erickson, Stephen Michael 1950-
See Erickson, Steve
See also CA 129

Erickson, Steve . . . . CLC 64
See also Erickson, Stephen Michael

Ericson, Walter
See Fast, Howard (Melvin)

Eriksson, Buntel
See Bergman, (Ernst) Ingmar

Eschenbach, Wolfram von
See Wolfram von Eschenbach

Eseki, Bruno
See Mphahlele, Ezekiel

Esenin, Sergei (Alexandrovich)
1895-1925 . . . . TCLC 4
See also CA 104

Eshleman, Clayton 1935- . . . . CLC 7
See also CA 33-36R; CAAS 6; DLB 5

Espriella, Don Manuel Alvarez
See Southey, Robert

Espriu, Salvador 1913-1985 . . . . CLC 9
See also CA 115; DLB 134

Espronceda, Jose de 1808-1842 . . . NCLC 39

Esse, James
See Stephens, James

Esterbrook, Tom
See Hubbard, L(afayette) Ron(ald)

Estleman, Loren D. 1952- . . . . CLC 48
See also CA 85-88; CANR 27; MTCW

Eugenides, Jeffrey 1960(?)- . . . . CLC 81
See also CA 144

Euripides c. 485B.C.-406B.C. . . . . DC 4
See also DA

Evan, Evin
See Faust, Frederick (Schiller)

Evans, Evan
See Faust, Frederick (Schiller)

Evans, Marian
See Eliot, George

Evans, Mary Ann
See Eliot, George

Evarts, Esther
See Benson, Sally

Everett, Percival L. 1956- . . . . CLC 57
See also BW 2; CA 129

Everson, R(onald) G(ilmour)
1903- . . . . CLC 27
See also CA 17-20R; DLB 88

Everson, William (Oliver)
1912-1994 . . . . CLC 1, 5, 14
See also CA 9-12R; 145; CANR 20; DLB 5,
16; MTCW

Evtushenko, Evgenii Aleksandrovich
See Yevtushenko, Yevgeny (Alexandrovich)

Ewart, Gavin (Buchanan)
1916- . . . . CLC 13, 46
See also CA 89-92; CANR 17, 46; DLB 40;
MTCW

Ewers, Hanns Heinz 1871-1943 . . . TCLC 12
See also CA 109

Ewing, Frederick R.
See Sturgeon, Theodore (Hamilton)

Exley, Frederick (Earl)
1929-1992 . . . . CLC 6, 11
See also AITN 2; CA 81-84; 138; DLB 143;
DLBY 81

Eynhardt, Guillermo
See Quiroga, Horacio (Sylvestre)

Ezekiel, Nissim 1924- . . . . CLC 61
See also CA 61-64

Ezekiel, Tish O'Dowd 1943- . . . . CLC 34
See also CA 129

Fadeyev, A.
See Bulgya, Alexander Alexandrovich

Fadeyev, Alexander . . . . TCLC 53
See also Bulgya, Alexander Alexandrovich

Fagen, Donald 1948- . . . . CLC 26

Fainzilberg, Ilya Arnoldovich 1897-1937
See Ilf, Ilya
See also CA 120

Fair, Ronald L. 1932- . . . . CLC 18
See also BW 1; CA 69-72; CANR 25;
DLB 33

Fairbairns, Zoe (Ann) 1948- . . . . CLC 32
See also CA 103; CANR 21

Falco, Gian
See Papini, Giovanni

Falconer, James
See Kirkup, James

Falconer, Kenneth
See Kornbluth, C(yril) M.

Falkland, Samuel
See Heijermans, Herman

Fallaci, Oriana 1930- . . . . CLC 11
See also CA 77-80; CANR 15; MTCW

Faludy, George 1913- . . . . CLC 42
See also CA 21-24R

Faludy, Gyoergy
See Faludy, George

Fanon, Frantz 1925-1961 . . . . . CLC 74; BLC
See also BW 1; CA 116; 89-92

Fanshawe, Ann 1625-1680 . . . . LC 11

Fante, John (Thomas) 1911-1983 . . . CLC 60
See also CA 69-72; 109; CANR 23;
DLB 130; DLBY 83

Farah, Nuruddin 1945- . . . . CLC 53; BLC
See also BW 2; CA 106; DLB 125

Fargue, Leon-Paul 1876(?)-1947 . . . TCLC 11
See also CA 109

Farigoule, Louis
See Romains, Jules

Farina, Richard 1936(?)-1966 . . . . CLC 9
See also CA 81-84; 25-28R

Farley, Walter (Lorimer)
1915-1989 . . . . CLC 17
See also CA 17-20R; CANR 8, 29; DLB 22;
JRDA; MAICYA; SATA 2, 43

Farmer, Philip Jose 1918- . . . . CLC 1, 19
See also CA 1-4R; CANR 4, 35; DLB 8;
MTCW

Farquhar, George 1677-1707 . . . . LC 21
See also DLB 84

Farrell, J(ames) G(ordon)
1935-1979 . . . . CLC 6
See also CA 73-76; 89-92; CANR 36;
DLB 14; MTCW

Farrell, James T(homas)
1904-1979 . . . . CLC 1, 4, 8, 11, 66
See also CA 5-8R; 89-92; CANR 9; DLB 4,
9, 86; DLBD 2; MTCW

Farren, Richard J.
See Betjeman, John

Farren, Richard M.
See Betjeman, John

Folke, Will
See Bloch, Robert (Albert)

Follett, Ken(neth Martin) 1949- . . . . **CLC 18**
See also AAYA 6; BEST 89:4; CA 81-84;
CANR 13, 33; DLB 87; DLBY 81;
MTCW

Fontane, Theodor 1819-1898 . . . . . **NCLC 26**
See also DLB 129

Foote, Horton 1916- . . . . **CLC 51**
See also CA 73-76; CANR 34; DLB 26

Foote, Shelby 1916- . . . . **CLC 75**
See also CA 5-8R; CANR 3, 45; DLB 2, 17

Forbes, Esther 1891-1967 . . . . **CLC 12**
See also CA 13-14; 25-28R; CAP 1;
CLR 27; DLB 22; JRDA; MAICYA;
SATA 2

Forche, Carolyn (Louise)
1950- . . . . **CLC 25, 83, 86; PC 10**
See also CA 109; 117; DLB 5

Ford, Elbur
See Hibbert, Eleanor Alice Burford

Ford, Ford Madox
1873-1939 . . . . **TCLC 1, 15, 39, 57**
See also CA 104; 132; CDBLB 1914-1945;
DLB 34, 98; MTCW

Ford, John 1895-1973 . . . . **CLC 16**
See also CA 45-48

Ford, Richard 1944- . . . . **CLC 46**
See also CA 69-72; CANR 11, 47

Ford, Webster
See Masters, Edgar Lee

Foreman, Richard 1937- . . . . **CLC 50**
See also CA 65-68; CANR 32

Forester, C(ecil) S(cott)
1899-1966 . . . . **CLC 35**
See also CA 73-76; 25-28R; SATA 13

Forez
See Mauriac, Francois (Charles)

Forman, James Douglas 1932- . . . . . . **CLC 21**
See also CA 9-12R; CANR 4, 19, 42;
JRDA; MAICYA; SATA 8, 70

Fornes, Maria Irene 1930- . . . . . . **CLC 39, 61**
See also CA 25-28R; CANR 28; DLB 7;
HW; MTCW

Forrest, Leon 1937- . . . . **CLC 4**
See also BW 2; CA 89-92; CAAS 7;
CANR 25; DLB 33

Forster, E(dward) M(organ)
1879-1970 . . . . . **CLC 1, 2, 3, 4, 9, 10, 13,**
15, 22, 45, 77; DA; WLC
See also AAYA 2; CA 13-14; 25-28R;
CANR 45; CAP 1; CDBLB 1914-1945;
DLB 34, 98; DLBD 10; MTCW;
SATA 57

Forster, John 1812-1876 . . . . **NCLC 11**
See also DLB 144

Forsyth, Frederick 1938- . . . . . . **CLC 2, 5, 36**
See also BEST 89:4; CA 85-88; CANR 38;
DLB 87; MTCW

Forten, Charlotte L. . . . . **TCLC 16; BLC**
See also Grimke, Charlotte L(ottie) Forten
See also DLB 50

Foscolo, Ugo 1778-1827 . . . . **NCLC 8**

Fosse, Bob . . . . **CLC 20**
See also Fosse, Robert Louis

Fosse, Robert Louis 1927-1987
See Fosse, Bob
See also CA 110; 123

Foster, Stephen Collins
1826-1864 . . . . **NCLC 26**

Foucault, Michel
1926-1984 . . . . **CLC 31, 34, 69**
See also CA 105; 113; CANR 34; MTCW

Fouque, Friedrich (Heinrich Karl) de la Motte
1777-1843 . . . . **NCLC 2**
See also DLB 90

Fournier, Henri Alban 1886-1914
See Alain-Fournier
See also CA 104

Fournier, Pierre 1916- . . . . **CLC 11**
See also Gascar, Pierre
See also CA 89-92; CANR 16, 40

Fowles, John
1926- . . . . . . **CLC 1, 2, 3, 4, 6, 9, 10, 15,**
33, 87
See also CA 5-8R; CANR 25; CDBLB 1960
to Present; DLB 14, 139; MTCW;
SATA 22

Fox, Paula 1923- . . . . **CLC 2, 8**
See also AAYA 3; CA 73-76; CANR 20,
36; CLR 1; DLB 52; JRDA; MAICYA;
MTCW; SATA 17, 60

Fox, William Price (Jr.) 1926- . . . . . **CLC 22**
See also CA 17-20R; CAAS 19; CANR 11;
DLB 2; DLBY 81

Foxe, John 1516(?)-1587 . . . . **LC 14**

Frame, Janet . . . . **CLC 2, 3, 6, 22, 66**
See also Clutha, Janet Paterson Frame

France, Anatole . . . . **TCLC 9**
See also Thibault, Jacques Anatole Francois
See also DLB 123

Francis, Claude 19(?)- . . . . **CLC 50**

Francis, Dick 1920- . . . . **CLC 2, 22, 42**
See also AAYA 5; BEST 89:3; CA 5-8R;
CANR 9, 42; CDBLB 1960 to Present;
DLB 87; MTCW

Francis, Robert (Churchill)
1901-1987 . . . . **CLC 15**
See also CA 1-4R; 123; CANR 1

Frank, Anne(lies Marie)
1929-1945 . . . . **TCLC 17; DA; WLC**
See also AAYA 12; CA 113; 133; MTCW;
SATA-Brief 42

Frank, Elizabeth 1945- . . . . **CLC 39**
See also CA 121; 126

Franklin, Benjamin
See Hasek, Jaroslav (Matej Frantisek)

Franklin, Benjamin 1706-1790 . . . **LC 25; DA**
See also CDALB 1640-1865; DLB 24, 43,
73

Franklin, (Stella Maraia Sarah) Miles
1879-1954 . . . . **TCLC 7**
See also CA 104

Fraser, (Lady) Antonia (Pakenham)
1932- . . . . **CLC 32**
See also CA 85-88; CANR 44; MTCW;
SATA-Brief 32

Fraser, George MacDonald 1925- . . . . **CLC 7**
See also CA 45-48; CANR 2

Fraser, Sylvia 1935- . . . . **CLC 64**
See also CA 45-48; CANR 1, 16

Frayn, Michael 1933- . . . . . . **CLC 3, 7, 31, 47**
See also CA 5-8R; CANR 30; DLB 13, 14;
MTCW

Fraze, Candida (Merrill) 1945- . . . . . **CLC 50**
See also CA 126

Frazer, J(ames) G(eorge)
1854-1941 . . . . **TCLC 32**
See also CA 118

Frazer, Robert Caine
See Creasey, John

Frazer, Sir James George
See Frazer, J(ames) G(eorge)

Frazier, Ian 1951- . . . . **CLC 46**
See also CA 130

Frederic, Harold 1856-1898 . . . . . . **NCLC 10**
See also DLB 12, 23

Frederick, John
See Faust, Frederick (Schiller)

Frederick the Great 1712-1786 . . . . . . **LC 14**

Fredro, Aleksander 1793-1876 . . . . . **NCLC 8**

Freeling, Nicolas 1927- . . . . **CLC 38**
See also CA 49-52; CAAS 12; CANR 1, 17;
DLB 87

Freeman, Douglas Southall
1886-1953 . . . . **TCLC 11**
See also CA 109; DLB 17

Freeman, Judith 1946- . . . . **CLC 55**

Freeman, Mary Eleanor Wilkins
1852-1930 . . . . **TCLC 9; SSC 1**
See also CA 106; DLB 12, 78

Freeman, R(ichard) Austin
1862-1943 . . . . **TCLC 21**
See also CA 113; DLB 70

French, Albert 1943- . . . . **CLC 86**

French, Marilyn 1929- . . . . . . **CLC 10, 18, 60**
See also CA 69-72; CANR 3, 31; MTCW

French, Paul
See Asimov, Isaac

Freneau, Philip Morin 1752-1832 . . **NCLC 1**
See also DLB 37, 43

Freud, Sigmund 1856-1939 . . . . **TCLC 52**
See also CA 115; 133; MTCW

Friedan, Betty (Naomi) 1921- . . . . . . **CLC 74**
See also CA 65-68; CANR 18, 45; MTCW

Friedman, B(ernard) H(arper)
1926- . . . . **CLC 7**
See also CA 1-4R; CANR 3

Friedman, Bruce Jay 1930- . . . . **CLC 3, 5, 56**
See also CA 9-12R; CANR 25; DLB 2, 28

Friel, Brian 1929- . . . . **CLC 5, 42, 59**
See also CA 21-24R; CANR 33; DLB 13;
MTCW

Friis-Baastad, Babbis Ellinor
1921-1970 . . . . **CLC 12**
See also CA 17-20R; 134; SATA 7

Frisch, Max (Rudolf)
1911-1991 . . . . . **CLC 3, 9, 14, 18, 32, 44**
See also CA 85-88; 134; CANR 32;
DLB 69, 124; MTCW

Fromentin, Eugene (Samuel Auguste)
1820-1876 . . . . **NCLC 10**
See also DLB 123

Frost, Frederick
See Faust, Frederick (Schiller)

Frost, Robert (Lee)
1874-1963 . . . . **CLC 1, 3, 4, 9, 10, 13, 15,**
26, 34, 44; DA; PC 1; WLC
See also CA 89-92; CANR 33;
CDALB 1917-1929; DLB 54; DLBD 7;
MTCW; SATA 14

Froude, James Anthony
1818-1894 . . . . **NCLC 43**
See also DLB 18, 57, 144

Froy, Herald
See Waterhouse, Keith (Spencer)

Fry, Christopher 1907- . . . . **CLC 2, 10, 14**
See also CA 17-20R; CANR 9, 30; DLB 13;
MTCW; SATA 66

Frye, (Herman) Northrop
1912-1991 . . . . **CLC 24, 70**
See also CA 5-8R; 133; CANR 8, 37;
DLB 67, 68; MTCW

Fuchs, Daniel 1909-1993 . . . . **CLC 8, 22**
See also CA 81-84; 142; CAAS 5;
CANR 40; DLB 9, 26, 28; DLBY 93

Fuchs, Daniel 1934- . . . . **CLC 34**
See also CA 37-40R; CANR 14

Fuentes, Carlos
1928- . . . . . . **CLC 3, 8, 10, 13, 22, 41, 60;**
DA; HLC; WLC
See also AAYA 4; AITN 2; CA 69-72;
CANR 10, 32; DLB 113; HW; MTCW

Fuentes, Gregorio Lopez y
See Lopez y Fuentes, Gregorio

Fugard, (Harold) Athol
1932- . . . . **CLC 5, 9, 14, 25, 40, 80; DC 3**
See also CA 85-88; CANR 32; MTCW

Fugard, Sheila 1932- . . . . **CLC 48**
See also CA 125

Fuller, Charles (H., Jr.)
1939- . . . . **CLC 25; BLC; DC 1**
See also BW 2; CA 108; 112; DLB 38;
MTCW

Fuller, John (Leopold) 1937- . . . . **CLC 62**
See also CA 21-24R; CANR 9, 44; DLB 40

Fuller, Margaret . . . . **NCLC 5**
See also Ossoli, Sarah Margaret (Fuller
marchesa d')

Fuller, Roy (Broadbent)
1912-1991 . . . . **CLC 4, 28**
See also CA 5-8R; 135; CAAS 10; DLB 15,
20

Fulton, Alice 1952- . . . . **CLC 52**
See also CA 116

Furphy, Joseph 1843-1912 . . . . **TCLC 25**

Fussell, Paul 1924- . . . . **CLC 74**
See also BEST 90:1; CA 17-20R; CANR 8,
21, 35; MTCW

Futabatei, Shimei 1864-1909 . . . . . . **TCLC 44**

Futrelle, Jacques 1875-1912 . . . . . . **TCLC 19**
See also CA 113

Gaboriau, Emile 1835-1873 . . . . . . **NCLC 14**

Gadda, Carlo Emilio 1893-1973 . . . . **CLC 11**
See also CA 89-92

Gaddis, William
1922- . . . . . **CLC 1, 3, 6, 8, 10, 19, 43, 86**
See also CA 17-20R; CANR 21; DLB 2;
MTCW

Gaines, Ernest J(ames)
1933- . . . . **CLC 3, 11, 18, 86; BLC**
See also AITN 1; BW 2; CA 9-12R;
CANR 6, 24, 42; CDALB 1968-1988;
DLB 2, 33; DLBY 80; MTCW

Gaitskill, Mary 1954- . . . . **CLC 69**
See also CA 128

Galdos, Benito Perez
See Perez Galdos, Benito

Gale, Zona 1874-1938 . . . . **TCLC 7**
See also CA 105; DLB 9, 78

Galeano, Eduardo (Hughes) 1940- . . . **CLC 72**
See also CA 29-32R; CANR 13, 32; HW

Galiano, Juan Valera y Alcala
See Valera y Alcala-Galiano, Juan

Gallagher, Tess 1943- . . . . **CLC 18, 63; PC 9**
See also CA 106; DLB 120

Gallant, Mavis
1922- . . . . **CLC 7, 18, 38; SSC 5**
See also CA 69-72; CANR 29; DLB 53;
MTCW

Gallant, Roy A(rthur) 1924- . . . . **CLC 17**
See also CA 5-8R; CANR 4, 29; CLR 30;
MAICYA; SATA 4, 68

Gallico, Paul (William) 1897-1976 . . . **CLC 2**
See also AITN 1; CA 5-8R; 69-72;
CANR 23; DLB 9; MAICYA; SATA 13

Gallup, Ralph
See Whitemore, Hugh (John)

Galsworthy, John
1867-1933 . . . . **TCLC 1, 45; DA; WLC 2**
See also CA 104; 141; CDBLB 1890-1914;
DLB 10, 34, 98

Galt, John 1779-1839 . . . . **NCLC 1**
See also DLB 99, 116

Galvin, James 1951- . . . . **CLC 38**
See also CA 108; CANR 26

Gamboa, Federico 1864-1939 . . . . . . **TCLC 36**

Gann, Ernest Kellogg 1910-1991 . . . . **CLC 23**
See also AITN 1; CA 1-4R; 136; CANR 1

Garcia, Cristina 1958- . . . . **CLC 76**
See also CA 141

Garcia Lorca, Federico
1898-1936 . . . . **TCLC 1, 7, 49; DA;**
DC 2; HLC; PC 3; WLC
See also CA 104; 131; DLB 108; HW;
MTCW

Garcia Marquez, Gabriel (Jose)
1928- . . . . **CLC 2, 3, 8, 10, 15, 27, 47, 55,**
68; DA; HLC; SSC 8; WLC
See also AAYA 3; BEST 89:1, 90:4;
CA 33-36R; CANR 10, 28; DLB 113;
HW; MTCW

Gard, Janice
See Latham, Jean Lee

Gard, Roger Martin du
See Martin du Gard, Roger

Gardam, Jane 1928- . . . . **CLC 43**
See also CA 49-52; CANR 2, 18, 33;
CLR 12; DLB 14; MAICYA; MTCW;
SAAS 9; SATA 28, 39, 76

Gardner, Herb . . . . **CLC 44**

Gardner, John (Champlin), Jr.
1933-1982 . . . . . **CLC 2, 3, 5, 7, 8, 10, 18,**
28, 34; SSC 7
See also AITN 1; CA 65-68; 107;
CANR 33; DLB 2; DLBY 82; MTCW;
SATA 40; SATA-Obit 31

Gardner, John (Edmund) 1926- . . . . . **CLC 30**
See also CA 103; CANR 15; MTCW

Gardner, Noel
See Kuttner, Henry

Gardons, S. S.
See Snodgrass, W(illiam) D(e Witt)

Garfield, Leon 1921- . . . . **CLC 12**
See also AAYA 8; CA 17-20R; CANR 38,
41; CLR 21; JRDA; MAICYA; SATA 1,
32, 76

Garland, (Hannibal) Hamlin
1860-1940 . . . . **TCLC 3; SSC 18**
See also CA 104; DLB 12, 71, 78

Garneau, (Hector de) Saint-Denys
1912-1943 . . . . **TCLC 13**
See also CA 111; DLB 88

Garner, Alan 1934- . . . . **CLC 17**
See also CA 73-76; CANR 15; CLR 20;
MAICYA; MTCW; SATA 18, 69

Garner, Hugh 1913-1979 . . . . **CLC 13**
See also CA 69-72; CANR 31; DLB 68

Garnett, David 1892-1981 . . . . **CLC 3**
See also CA 5-8R; 103; CANR 17; DLB 34

Garos, Stephanie
See Katz, Steve

Garrett, George (Palmer)
1929- . . . . **CLC 3, 11, 51**
See also CA 1-4R; CAAS 5; CANR 1, 42;
DLB 2, 5, 130; DLBY 83

Garrick, David 1717-1779 . . . . **LC 15**
See also DLB 84

Garrigue, Jean 1914-1972 . . . . **CLC 2, 8**
See also CA 5-8R; 37-40R; CANR 20

Garrison, Frederick
See Sinclair, Upton (Beall)

Garth, Will
See Hamilton, Edmond; Kuttner, Henry

Garvey, Marcus (Moziah, Jr.)
1887-1940 . . . . **TCLC 41; BLC**
See also BW 1; CA 120; 124

Gary, Romain . . . . **CLC 25**
See also Kacew, Romain
See also DLB 83

Gascar, Pierre . . . . **CLC 11**
See also Fournier, Pierre

Gascoyne, David (Emery) 1916- . . . . **CLC 45**
See also CA 65-68; CANR 10, 28; DLB 20;
MTCW

Gaskell, Elizabeth Cleghorn
1810-1865 . . . . **NCLC 5**
See also CDBLB 1832-1890; DLB 21, 144

Gass, William H(oward)
1924- . . . **CLC 1, 2, 8, 11, 15, 39; SSC 12**
See also CA 17-20R; CANR 30; DLB 2;
MTCW

Gasset, Jose Ortega y
See Ortega y Gasset, Jose

Gates, Henry Louis, Jr. 1950-...... **CLC 65**
See also BW 2; CA 109; CANR 25; DLB 67

Gautier, Theophile 1811-1872..... **NCLC 1**
See also DLB 119

Gawsworth, John
See Bates, H(erbert) E(rnest)

Gaye, Marvin (Penze) 1939-1984 ... **CLC 26**
See also CA 112

Gebler, Carlo (Ernest) 1954-....... **CLC 39**
See also CA 119; 133

Gee, Maggie (Mary) 1948-......... **CLC 57**
See also CA 130

Gee, Maurice (Gough) 1931-....... **CLC 29**
See also CA 97-100; SATA 46

Gelbart, Larry (Simon) 1923- ... **CLC 21, 61**
See also CA 73-76; CANR 45

Gelber, Jack 1932-........ **CLC 1, 6, 14, 79**
See also CA 1-4R; CANR 2; DLB 7

Gellhorn, Martha (Ellis) 1908- .. **CLC 14, 60**
See also CA 77-80; CANR 44; DLBY 82

Genet, Jean
1910-1986 ... **CLC 1, 2, 5, 10, 14, 44, 46**
See also CA 13-16R; CANR 18; DLB 72;
DLBY 86; MTCW

Gent, Peter 1942-................. **CLC 29**
See also AITN 1; CA 89-92; DLBY 82

Gentlewoman in New England, A
See Bradstreet, Anne

Gentlewoman in Those Parts, A
See Bradstreet, Anne

George, Jean Craighead 1919-...... **CLC 35**
See also AAYA 8; CA 5-8R; CANR 25;
CLR 1; DLB 52; JRDA; MAICYA;
SATA 2, 68

George, Stefan (Anton)
1868-1933 .... **TCLC 2, 14**
See also CA 104

Georges, Georges Martin
See Simenon, Georges (Jacques Christian)

Gerhardi, William Alexander
See Gerhardie, William Alexander

Gerhardie, William Alexander
1895-1977 .... **CLC 5**
See also CA 25-28R; 73-76; CANR 18;
DLB 36

Gerstler, Amy 1956-.............. **CLC 70**

Gertler, T. .... **CLC 34**
See also CA 116; 121

Ghalib 1797-1869 .... **NCLC 39**

Ghelderode, Michel de
1898-1962 .... **CLC 6, 11**
See also CA 85-88; CANR 40

Ghiselin, Brewster 1903- .... **CLC 23**
See also CA 13-16R; CAAS 10; CANR 13

Ghose, Zulfikar 1935-............. **CLC 42**
See also CA 65-68

Ghosh, Amitav 1956- .... **CLC 44**

Giacosa, Giuseppe 1847-1906 ...... **TCLC 7**
See also CA 104

Gibb, Lee
See Waterhouse, Keith (Spencer)

Gibbon, Lewis Grassic .... **TCLC 4**
See also Mitchell, James Leslie

Gibbons, Kaye 1960- .... **CLC 50**

Gibran, Kahlil
1883-1931 .... **TCLC 1, 9; PC 9**
See also CA 104

Gibson, William 1914-........ **CLC 23; DA**
See also CA 9-12R; CANR 9, 42; DLB 7;
SATA 66

Gibson, William (Ford) 1948- ... **CLC 39, 63**
See also AAYA 12; CA 126; 133

Gide, Andre (Paul Guillaume)
1869-1951 .... **TCLC 5, 12, 36; DA;
SSC 13; WLC**
See also CA 104; 124; DLB 65; MTCW

Gifford, Barry (Colby) 1946-....... **CLC 34**
See also CA 65-68; CANR 9, 30, 40

Gilbert, W(illiam) S(chwenck)
1836-1911 .... **TCLC 3**
See also CA 104; SATA 36

Gilbreth, Frank B., Jr. 1911-....... **CLC 17**
See also CA 9-12R; SATA 2

Gilchrist, Ellen 1935-.. **CLC 34, 48; SSC 14**
See also CA 113; 116; CANR 41; DLB 130;
MTCW

Giles, Molly 1942- .... **CLC 39**
See also CA 126

Gill, Patrick
See Creasey, John

Gilliam, Terry (Vance) 1940-....... **CLC 21**
See also Monty Python
See also CA 108; 113; CANR 35

Gillian, Jerry
See Gilliam, Terry (Vance)

Gilliatt, Penelope (Ann Douglass)
1932-1993 .... **CLC 2, 10, 13, 53**
See also AITN 2; CA 13-16R; 141; DLB 14

Gilman, Charlotte (Anna) Perkins (Stetson)
1860-1935 .... **TCLC 9, 37; SSC 13**
See also CA 106

Gilmour, David 1949-............. **CLC 35**
See also CA 138

Gilpin, William 1724-1804...... **NCLC 30**

Gilray, J. D.
See Mencken, H(enry) L(ouis)

Gilroy, Frank D(aniel) 1925-........ **CLC 2**
See also CA 81-84; CANR 32; DLB 7

Ginsberg, Allen
1926- ...... **CLC 1, 2, 3, 4, 6, 13, 36, 69;
DA; PC 4; WLC 3**
See also AITN 1; CA 1-4R; CANR 2, 41;
CDALB 1941-1968; DLB 5, 16; MTCW

Ginzburg, Natalia
1916-1991 .... **CLC 5, 11, 54, 70**
See also CA 85-88; 135; CANR 33; MTCW

Giono, Jean 1895-1970......... **CLC 4, 11**
See also CA 45-48; 29-32R; CANR 2, 35;
DLB 72; MTCW

Giovanni, Nikki
1943- ...... **CLC 2, 4, 19, 64; BLC; DA**
See also AITN 1; BW 2; CA 29-32R;
CAAS 6; CANR 18, 41; CLR 6; DLB 5,
41; MAICYA; MTCW; SATA 24

Giovene, Andrea 1904-............. **CLC 7**
See also CA 85-88

Gippius, Zinaida (Nikolayevna) 1869-1945
See Hippius, Zinaida
See also CA 106

Giraudoux, (Hippolyte) Jean
1882-1944 .... **TCLC 2, 7**
See also CA 104; DLB 65

Gironella, Jose Maria 1917-....... **CLC 11**
See also CA 101

Gissing, George (Robert)
1857-1903 .... **TCLC 3, 24, 47**
See also CA 105; DLB 18, 135

Giurlani, Aldo
See Palazzeschi, Aldo

Gladkov, Fyodor (Vasilyevich)
1883-1958 .... **TCLC 27**

Glanville, Brian (Lester) 1931-...... **CLC 6**
See also CA 5-8R; CAAS 9; CANR 3;
DLB 15, 139; SATA 42

Glasgow, Ellen (Anderson Gholson)
1873(?)-1945 .... **TCLC 2, 7**
See also CA 104; DLB 9, 12

Glaspell, Susan (Keating)
1882(?)-1948 .... **TCLC 55**
See also CA 110; DLB 7, 9, 78; YABC 2

Glassco, John 1909-1981 .... **CLC 9**
See also CA 13-16R; 102; CANR 15;
DLB 68

Glasscock, Amnesia
See Steinbeck, John (Ernst)

Glasser, Ronald J. 1940(?)-........ **CLC 37**

Glassman, Joyce
See Johnson, Joyce

Glendinning, Victoria 1937-........ **CLC 50**
See also CA 120; 127

Glissant, Edouard 1928-........ **CLC 10, 68**

Gloag, Julian 1930- .... **CLC 40**
See also AITN 1; CA 65-68; CANR 10

Glowacki, Aleksander
See Prus, Boleslaw

Glueck, Louise (Elisabeth)
1943- .... **CLC 7, 22, 44, 81**
See also CA 33-36R; CANR 40; DLB 5

Gobineau, Joseph Arthur (Comte) de
1816-1882 .... **NCLC 17**
See also DLB 123

Godard, Jean-Luc 1930-.......... **CLC 20**
See also CA 93-96

Godden, (Margaret) Rumer 1907-... **CLC 53**
See also AAYA 6; CA 5-8R; CANR 4, 27,
36; CLR 20; MAICYA; SAAS 12;
SATA 3, 36

Godoy Alcayaga, Lucila 1889-1957
See Mistral, Gabriela
See also BW 2; CA 104; 131; HW; MTCW

Godwin, Gail (Kathleen)
1937- .... **CLC 5, 8, 22, 31, 69**
See also CA 29-32R; CANR 15, 43; DLB 6;
MTCW

Godwin, William 1756-1836...... **NCLC 14**
See also CDBLB 1789-1832; DLB 39, 104,
142

Goethe, Johann Wolfgang von
1749-1832 .... **NCLC 4, 22, 34; DA;
PC 5; WLC 3**
See also DLB 94

Gogarty, Oliver St. John
1878-1957 .... **TCLC 15**
See also CA 109; DLB 15, 19

Gogol, Nikolai (Vasilyevich)
1809-1852 .... **NCLC 5, 15, 31; DA;
DC 1; SSC 4; WLC**

Goines, Donald
1937(?)-1974 .... **CLC 80; BLC**
See also AITN 1; BW 1; CA 124; 114;
DLB 33

Gold, Herbert 1924- .... **CLC 4, 7, 14, 42**
See also CA 9-12R; CANR 17, 45; DLB 2;
DLBY 81

Goldbarth, Albert 1948- .... **CLC 5, 38**
See also CA 53-56; CANR 6, 40; DLB 120

Goldberg, Anatol 1910-1982 .... **CLC 34**
See also CA 131; 117

Goldemberg, Isaac 1945- .... **CLC 52**
See also CA 69-72; CAAS 12; CANR 11,
32; HW

Golding, William (Gerald)
1911-1993 .... **CLC 1, 2, 3, 8, 10, 17, 27,
58, 81; DA; WLC**
See also AAYA 5; CA 5-8R; 141;
CANR 13, 33; CDBLB 1945-1960;
DLB 15, 100; MTCW

Goldman, Emma 1869-1940 ...... **TCLC 13**
See also CA 110

Goldman, Francisco 1955- .... **CLC 76**

Goldman, William (W.) 1931- .... **CLC 1, 48**
See also CA 9-12R; CANR 29; DLB 44

Goldmann, Lucien 1913-1970 ...... **CLC 24**
See also CA 25-28; CAP 2

Goldoni, Carlo 1707-1793 .... **LC 4**

Goldsberry, Steven 1949- .... **CLC 34**
See also CA 131

Goldsmith, Oliver
1728-1774 .... **LC 2; DA; WLC**
See also CDBLB 1660-1789; DLB 39, 89,
104, 109, 142; SATA 26

Goldsmith, Peter
See Priestley, J(ohn) B(oynton)

Gombrowicz, Witold
1904-1969 .... **CLC 4, 7, 11, 49**
See also CA 19-20; 25-28R; CAP 2

Gomez de la Serna, Ramon
1888-1963 .... **CLC 9**
See also CA 116; HW

Goncharov, Ivan Alexandrovich
1812-1891 .... **NCLC 1**

Goncourt, Edmond (Louis Antoine Huot) de
1822-1896 .... **NCLC 7**
See also DLB 123

Goncourt, Jules (Alfred Huot) de
1830-1870 .... **NCLC 7**
See also DLB 123

Gontier, Fernande 19(?)- .... **CLC 50**

Goodman, Paul 1911-1972 .... **CLC 1, 2, 4, 7**
See also CA 19-20; 37-40R; CANR 34;
CAP 2; DLB 130; MTCW

Gordimer, Nadine
1923- .... **CLC 3, 5, 7, 10, 18, 33, 51, 70;
DA; SSC 17**
See also CA 5-8R; CANR 3, 28; MTCW

Gordon, Adam Lindsay
1833-1870 .... **NCLC 21**

Gordon, Caroline
1895-1981 ... **CLC 6, 13, 29, 83; SSC 15**
See also CA 11-12; 103; CANR 36; CAP 1;
DLB 4, 9, 102; DLBY 81; MTCW

Gordon, Charles William 1860-1937
See Connor, Ralph
See also CA 109

Gordon, Mary (Catherine)
1949- .... **CLC 13, 22**
See also CA 102; CANR 44; DLB 6;
DLBY 81; MTCW

Gordon, Sol 1923- .... **CLC 26**
See also CA 53-56; CANR 4; SATA 11

Gordone, Charles 1925- .... **CLC 1, 4**
See also BW 1; CA 93-96; DLB 7; MTCW

Gorenko, Anna Andreevna
See Akhmatova, Anna

Gorky, Maxim .... **TCLC 8; WLC**
See also Peshkov, Alexei Maximovich

Goryan, Sirak
See Saroyan, William

Gosse, Edmund (William)
1849-1928 .... **TCLC 28**
See also CA 117; DLB 57, 144

Gotlieb, Phyllis Fay (Bloom)
1926- .... **CLC 18**
See also CA 13-16R; CANR 7; DLB 88

Gottesman, S. D.
See Kornbluth, C(yril) M.; Pohl, Frederik

Gottfried von Strassburg
fl. c. 1210- .... **CMLC 10**
See also DLB 138

Gould, Lois .... **CLC 4, 10**
See also CA 77-80; CANR 29; MTCW

Gourmont, Remy de 1858-1915 .... **TCLC 17**
See also CA 109

Govier, Katherine 1948- .... **CLC 51**
See also CA 101; CANR 18, 40

Goyen, (Charles) William
1915-1983 .... **CLC 5, 8, 14, 40**
See also AITN 2; CA 5-8R; 110; CANR 6;
DLB 2; DLBY 83

Goytisolo, Juan
1931- .... **CLC 5, 10, 23; HLC**
See also CA 85-88; CANR 32; HW; MTCW

Gozzano, Guido 1883-1916 .... **PC 10**
See also DLB 114

Gozzi, (Conte) Carlo 1720-1806 .. **NCLC 23**

Grabbe, Christian Dietrich
1801-1836 .... **NCLC 2**
See also DLB 133

Grace, Patricia 1937- .... **CLC 56**

Gracian y Morales, Baltasar
1601-1658 .... **LC 15**

Gracq, Julien .... **CLC 11, 48**
See also Poirier, Louis
See also DLB 83

Grade, Chaim 1910-1982 .... **CLC 10**
See also CA 93-96; 107

Graduate of Oxford, A
See Ruskin, John

Graham, John
See Phillips, David Graham

Graham, Jorie 1951- .... **CLC 48**
See also CA 111; DLB 120

Graham, R(obert) B(ontine) Cunninghame
See Cunninghame Graham, R(obert)
B(ontine)
See also DLB 98, 135

Graham, Robert
See Haldeman, Joe (William)

Graham, Tom
See Lewis, (Harry) Sinclair

Graham, W(illiam) S(ydney)
1918-1986 .... **CLC 29**
See also CA 73-76; 118; DLB 20

Graham, Winston (Mawdsley)
1910- .... **CLC 23**
See also CA 49-52; CANR 2, 22, 45;
DLB 77

Grant, Skeeter
See Spiegelman, Art

Granville-Barker, Harley
1877-1946 .... **TCLC 2**
See also Barker, Harley Granville
See also CA 104

Grass, Guenter (Wilhelm)
1927- ..... **CLC 1, 2, 4, 6, 11, 15, 22, 32,
49; DA; WLC**
See also CA 13-16R; CANR 20; DLB 75,
124; MTCW

Gratton, Thomas
See Hulme, T(homas) E(rnest)

Grau, Shirley Ann
1929- .... **CLC 4, 9; SSC 15**
See also CA 89-92; CANR 22; DLB 2;
MTCW

Gravel, Fern
See Hall, James Norman

Graver, Elizabeth 1964- .... **CLC 70**
See also CA 135

Graves, Richard Perceval 1945- .... **CLC 44**
See also CA 65-68; CANR 9, 26

Graves, Robert (von Ranke)
1895-1985 ...... **CLC 1, 2, 6, 11, 39, 44,
45; PC 6**
See also CA 5-8R; 117; CANR 5, 36;
CDBLB 1914-1945; DLB 20, 100;
DLBY 85; MTCW; SATA 45

Gray, Alasdair (James) 1934- ...... **CLC 41**
See also CA 126; CANR 47; MTCW

Gray, Amlin 1946- .... **CLC 29**
See also CA 138

Gray, Francine du Plessix 1930- .... **CLC 22**
See also BEST 90:3; CA 61-64; CAAS 2;
CANR 11, 33; MTCW

Gray, John (Henry) 1866-1934 .... **TCLC 19**
See also CA 119

Gray, Simon (James Holliday)
1936- .... **CLC 9, 14, 36**
See also AITN 1; CA 21-24R; CAAS 3;
CANR 32; DLB 13; MTCW

Harris, Christie (Lucy) Irwin
1907- .... **CLC 12**
See also CA 5-8R; CANR 6; DLB 88;
JRDA; MAICYA; SAAS 10; SATA 6, 74

Harris, Frank 1856(?)-1931 ...... **TCLC 24**
See also CA 109

Harris, George Washington
1814-1869 .... **NCLC 23**
See also DLB 3, 11

Harris, Joel Chandler 1848-1908 ... **TCLC 2**
See also CA 104; 137; DLB 11, 23, 42, 78,
91; MAICYA; YABC 1

Harris, John (Wyndham Parkes Lucas)
Beynon 1903-1969
See Wyndham, John
See also CA 102; 89-92

Harris, MacDonald .... **CLC 9**
See also Heiney, Donald (William)

Harris, Mark 1922- .... **CLC 19**
See also CA 5-8R; CAAS 3; CANR 2;
DLB 2; DLBY 80

Harris, (Theodore) Wilson 1921-.... **CLC 25**
See also BW 2; CA 65-68; CAAS 16;
CANR 11, 27; DLB 117; MTCW

Harrison, Elizabeth Cavanna 1909-
See Cavanna, Betty
See also CA 9-12R; CANR 6, 27

Harrison, Harry (Max) 1925- ...... **CLC 42**
See also CA 1-4R; CANR 5, 21; DLB 8;
SATA 4

Harrison, James (Thomas)
1937- .... **CLC 6, 14, 33, 66**
See also CA 13-16R; CANR 8; DLBY 82

Harrison, Jim
See Harrison, James (Thomas)

Harrison, Kathryn 1961- .... **CLC 70**
See also CA 144

Harrison, Tony 1937-............. **CLC 43**
See also CA 65-68; CANR 44; DLB 40;
MTCW

Harriss, Will(ard Irvin) 1922-...... **CLC 34**
See also CA 111

Harson, Sley
See Ellison, Harlan (Jay)

Hart, Ellis
See Ellison, Harlan (Jay)

Hart, Josephine 1942(?)- .... **CLC 70**
See also CA 138

Hart, Moss 1904-1961 .... **CLC 66**
See also CA 109; 89-92; DLB 7

Harte, (Francis) Bret(t)
1836(?)-1902 .... **TCLC 1, 25; DA;**
SSC 8; WLC
See also CA 104; 140; CDALB 1865-1917;
DLB 12, 64, 74, 79; SATA 26

Hartley, L(eslie) P(oles)
1895-1972 .... **CLC 2, 22**
See also CA 45-48; 37-40R; CANR 33;
DLB 15, 139; MTCW

Hartman, Geoffrey H. 1929-........ **CLC 27**
See also CA 117; 125; DLB 67

Haruf, Kent 19(?)- .... **CLC 34**

Harwood, Ronald 1934-........... **CLC 32**
See also CA 1-4R; CANR 4; DLB 13

Hasek, Jaroslav (Matej Frantisek)
1883-1923 .... **TCLC 4**
See also CA 104; 129; MTCW

Hass, Robert 1941-............ **CLC 18, 39**
See also CA 111; CANR 30; DLB 105

Hastings, Hudson
See Kuttner, Henry

Hastings, Selina.................. **CLC 44**

Hatteras, Amelia
See Mencken, H(enry) L(ouis)

Hatteras, Owen .... **TCLC 18**
See also Mencken, H(enry) L(ouis); Nathan,
George Jean

Hauptmann, Gerhart (Johann Robert)
1862-1946 .... **TCLC 4**
See also CA 104; DLB 66, 118

Havel, Vaclav 1936-........ **CLC 25, 58, 65**
See also CA 104; CANR 36; MTCW

Haviaras, Stratis .... **CLC 33**
See also Chaviaras, Strates

Hawes, Stephen 1475(?)-1523(?) ..... **LC 17**

Hawkes, John (Clendennin Burne, Jr.)
1925- ...... **CLC 1, 2, 3, 4, 7, 9, 14, 15,**
27, 49
See also CA 1-4R; CANR 2, 47; DLB 2, 7;
DLBY 80; MTCW

Hawking, S. W.
See Hawking, Stephen W(illiam)

Hawking, Stephen W(illiam)
1942-....................... **CLC 63**
See also AAYA 13; BEST 89:1; CA 126;
129

Hawthorne, Julian 1846-1934 ..... **TCLC 25**

Hawthorne, Nathaniel
1804-1864 ...... **NCLC 39; DA; SSC 3;**
WLC
See also CDALB 1640-1865; DLB 1, 74;
YABC 2

Haxton, Josephine Ayres 1921-
See Douglas, Ellen
See also CA 115; CANR 41

Hayaseca y Eizaguirre, Jorge
See Echegaray (y Eizaguirre), Jose (Maria
Waldo)

Hayashi Fumiko 1904-1951...... **TCLC 27**

Haycraft, Anna
See Ellis, Alice Thomas
See also CA 122

Hayden, Robert E(arl)
1913-1980 ...... **CLC 5, 9, 14, 37; BLC;**
DA; PC 6
See also BW 1; CA 69-72; 97-100; CABS 2;
CANR 24; CDALB 1941-1968; DLB 5,
76; MTCW; SATA 19; SATA-Obit 26

Hayford, J(oseph) E(phraim) Casely
See Casely-Hayford, J(oseph) E(phraim)

Hayman, Ronald 1932-............ **CLC 44**
See also CA 25-28R; CANR 18

Haywood, Eliza (Fowler)
1693(?)-1756 .... **LC 1**

Hazlitt, William 1778-1830 ...... **NCLC 29**
See also DLB 110

Hazzard, Shirley 1931- .... **CLC 18**
See also CA 9-12R; CANR 4; DLBY 82;
MTCW

Head, Bessie 1937-1986... **CLC 25, 67; BLC**
See also BW 2; CA 29-32R; 119; CANR 25;
DLB 117; MTCW

Headon, (Nicky) Topper 1956(?)- ... **CLC 30**

Heaney, Seamus (Justin)
1939- .... **CLC 5, 7, 14, 25, 37, 74**
See also CA 85-88; CANR 25;
CDBLB 1960 to Present; DLB 40;
MTCW

Hearn, (Patricio) Lafcadio (Tessima Carlos)
1850-1904 .... **TCLC 9**
See also CA 105; DLB 12, 78

Hearne, Vicki 1946-.............. **CLC 56**
See also CA 139

Hearon, Shelby 1931-............. **CLC 63**
See also AITN 2; CA 25-28R; CANR 18

Heat-Moon, William Least.......... **CLC 29**
See also Trogdon, William (Lewis)
See also AAYA 9

Hebbel, Friedrich 1813-1863..... **NCLC 43**
See also DLB 129

Hebert, Anne 1916- .... **CLC 4, 13, 29**
See also CA 85-88; DLB 68; MTCW

Hecht, Anthony (Evan)
1923-.................. **CLC 8, 13, 19**
See also CA 9-12R; CANR 6; DLB 5

Hecht, Ben 1894-1964 .... **CLC 8**
See also CA 85-88; DLB 7, 9, 25, 26, 28, 86

Hedayat, Sadeq 1903-1951........ **TCLC 21**
See also CA 120

Hegel, Georg Wilhelm Friedrich
1770-1831 .... **NCLC 46**
See also DLB 90

Heidegger, Martin 1889-1976 ...... **CLC 24**
See also CA 81-84; 65-68; CANR 34;
MTCW

Heidenstam, (Carl Gustaf) Verner von
1859-1940 .... **TCLC 5**
See also CA 104

Heifner, Jack 1946-.............. **CLC 11**
See also CA 105; CANR 47

Heijermans, Herman 1864-1924 ... **TCLC 24**
See also CA 123

Heilbrun, Carolyn G(old) 1926-..... **CLC 25**
See also CA 45-48; CANR 1, 28

Heine, Heinrich 1797-1856 .... **NCLC 4**
See also DLB 90

Heinemann, Larry (Curtiss) 1944- .. **CLC 50**
See also CA 110; CANR 31; DLBD 9

Heiney, Donald (William) 1921-1993
See Harris, MacDonald
See also CA 1-4R; 142; CANR 3

Heinlein, Robert A(nson)
1907-1988 ...... **CLC 1, 3, 8, 14, 26, 55**
See also CA 1-4R; 125; CANR 1, 20;
DLB 8; JRDA; MAICYA; MTCW;
SATA 9, 69; SATA-Obit 56

Helforth, John
See Doolittle, Hilda

Hellenhofferu, Vojtech Kapristian z
See Hasek, Jaroslav (Matej Frantisek)

Heller, Joseph
1923- .... CLC 1, 3, 5, 8, 11, 36, 63; DA;
WLC
See also AITN 1; CA 5-8R; CABS 1;
CANR 8, 42; DLB 2, 28; DLBY 80;
MTCW

Hellman, Lillian (Florence)
1906-1984 ...... CLC 2, 4, 8, 14, 18, 34,
44, 52; DC 1
See also AITN 1, 2; CA 13-16R; 112;
CANR 33; DLB 7; DLBY 84; MTCW

Helprin, Mark 1947- ..... CLC 7, 10, 22, 32
See also CA 81-84; CANR 47; DLBY 85;
MTCW

Helvetius, Claude-Adrien
1715-1771 .... LC 26

Helyar, Jane Penelope Josephine 1933-
See Poole, Josephine
See also CA 21-24R; CANR 10, 26

Hemans, Felicia 1793-1835 ...... NCLC 29
See also DLB 96

Hemingway, Ernest (Miller)
1899-1961 .... CLC 1, 3, 6, 8, 10, 13, 19,
30, 34, 39, 41, 44, 50, 61, 80; DA; SSC 1;
WLC
See also CA 77-80; CANR 34;
CDALB 1917-1929; DLB 4, 9, 102;
DLBD 1; DLBY 81, 87; MTCW

Hempel, Amy 1951- .... CLC 39
See also CA 118; 137

Henderson, F. C.
See Mencken, H(enry) L(ouis)

Henderson, Sylvia
See Ashton-Warner, Sylvia (Constance)

Henley, Beth .... CLC 23
See also Henley, Elizabeth Becker
See also CABS 3; DLBY 86

Henley, Elizabeth Becker 1952-
See Henley, Beth
See also CA 107; CANR 32; MTCW

Henley, William Ernest
1849-1903 .... TCLC 8
See also CA 105; DLB 19

Hennissart, Martha
See Lathen, Emma
See also CA 85-88

Henry, O. .... TCLC 1, 19; SSC 5; WLC
See also Porter, William Sydney

Henry, Patrick 1736- .... LC 25
See also CA 145

Henryson, Robert 1430(?)-1506(?). ... LC 20
See also DLB 146

Henry VIII 1491-1547 .... LC 10

Henschke, Alfred
See Klabund

Hentoff, Nat(han Irving) 1925- ..... CLC 26
See also AAYA 4; CA 1-4R; CAAS 6;
CANR 5, 25; CLR 1; JRDA; MAICYA;
SATA 27, 42, 69

Heppenstall, (John) Rayner
1911-1981 .... CLC 10
See also CA 1-4R; 103; CANR 29

Herbert, Frank (Patrick)
1920-1986 ...... CLC 12, 23, 35, 44, 85
See also CA 53-56; 118; CANR 5, 43;
DLB 8; MTCW; SATA 9, 37;
SATA-Obit 47

Herbert, George 1593-1633 .... LC 24; PC 4
See also CDBLB Before 1660; DLB 126

Herbert, Zbigniew 1924- .... CLC 9, 43
See also CA 89-92; CANR 36; MTCW

Herbst, Josephine (Frey)
1897-1969 .... CLC 34
See also CA 5-8R; 25-28R; DLB 9

Hergesheimer, Joseph
1880-1954 .... TCLC 11
See also CA 109; DLB 102, 9

Herlihy, James Leo 1927-1993 ...... CLC 6
See also CA 1-4R; 143; CANR 2

Hermogenes fl. c. 175- .... CMLC 6

Hernandez, Jose 1834-1886...... NCLC 17

Herrick, Robert
1591-1674 .... LC 13; DA; PC 9
See also DLB 126

Herring, Guilles
See Somerville, Edith

Herriot, James 1916- .... CLC 12
See also Wight, James Alfred
See also AAYA 1; CANR 40

Herrmann, Dorothy 1941-......... CLC 44
See also CA 107

Herrmann, Taffy
See Herrmann, Dorothy

Hersey, John (Richard)
1914-1993 .... CLC 1, 2, 7, 9, 40, 81
See also CA 17-20R; 140; CANR 33;
DLB 6; MTCW; SATA 25;
SATA-Obit 76

Herzen, Aleksandr Ivanovich
1812-1870 .... NCLC 10

Herzl, Theodor 1860-1904 .... TCLC 36

Herzog, Werner 1942- .... CLC 16
See also CA 89-92

Hesiod c. 8th cent. B.C.- .... CMLC 5

Hesse, Hermann
1877-1962 .... CLC 1, 2, 3, 6, 11, 17, 25,
69; DA; SSC 9; WLC
See also CA 17-18; CAP 2; DLB 66;
MTCW; SATA 50

Hewes, Cady
See De Voto, Bernard (Augustine)

Heyen, William 1940- .... CLC 13, 18
See also CA 33-36R; CAAS 9; DLB 5

Heyerdahl, Thor 1914-............. CLC 26
See also CA 5-8R; CANR 5, 22; MTCW;
SATA 2, 52

Heym, Georg (Theodor Franz Arthur)
1887-1912 .... TCLC 9
See also CA 106

Heym, Stefan 1913- .... CLC 41
See also CA 9-12R; CANR 4; DLB 69

Heyse, Paul (Johann Ludwig von)
1830-1914 .... TCLC 8
See also CA 104; DLB 129

Hibbert, Eleanor Alice Burford
1906-1993 .... CLC 7
See also BEST 90:4; CA 17-20R; 140;
CANR 9, 28; SATA 2; SATA-Obit 74

Higgins, George V(incent)
1939- ....CLC 4, 7, 10, 18
See also CA 77-80; CAAS 5; CANR 17;
DLB 2; DLBY 81; MTCW

Higginson, Thomas Wentworth
1823-1911 .... TCLC 36
See also DLB 1, 64

Highet, Helen
See MacInnes, Helen (Clark)

Highsmith, (Mary) Patricia
1921- .... CLC 2, 4, 14, 42
See also CA 1-4R; CANR 1, 20; MTCW

Highwater, Jamake (Mamake)
1942(?)- .... CLC 12
See also AAYA 7; CA 65-68; CAAS 7;
CANR 10, 34; CLR 17; DLB 52;
DLBY 85; JRDA; MAICYA; SATA 30,
32, 69

Hijuelos, Oscar 1951- ...... CLC 65; HLC
See also BEST 90:1; CA 123; DLB 145; HW

Hikmet, Nazim 1902(?)-1963....... CLC 40
See also CA 141; 93-96

Hildesheimer, Wolfgang
1916-1991 .... CLC 49
See also CA 101; 135; DLB 69, 124

Hill, Geoffrey (William)
1932- ....CLC 5, 8, 18, 45
See also CA 81-84; CANR 21;
CDBLB 1960 to Present; DLB 40;
MTCW

Hill, George Roy 1921- .... CLC 26
See also CA 110; 122

Hill, John
See Koontz, Dean R(ay)

Hill, Susan (Elizabeth) 1942- .... CLC 4
See also CA 33-36R; CANR 29; DLB 14,
139; MTCW

Hillerman, Tony 1925-............ CLC 62
See also AAYA 6; BEST 89:1; CA 29-32R;
CANR 21, 42; SATA 6

Hillesum, Etty 1914-1943 .... TCLC 49
See also CA 137

Hilliard, Noel (Harvey) 1929-...... CLC 15
See also CA 9-12R; CANR 7

Hillis, Rick 1956-............... CLC 66
See also CA 134

Hilton, James 1900-1954........ TCLC 21
See also CA 108; DLB 34, 77; SATA 34

Himes, Chester (Bomar)
1909-1984 .... CLC 2, 4, 7, 18, 58; BLC
See also BW 2; CA 25-28R; 114; CANR 22;
DLB 2, 76, 143; MTCW

Hinde, Thomas .... CLC 6, 11
See also Chitty, Thomas Willes

Hindin, Nathan
See Bloch, Robert (Albert)

Hine, (William) Daryl 1936-....... CLC 15
See also CA 1-4R; CAAS 15; CANR 1, 20;
DLB 60

Hinkson, Katharine Tynan
See Tynan, Katharine

Hinton, S(usan) E(loise)
1950- . . . . CLC 30; DA
See also AAYA 2; CA 81-84; CANR 32;
CLR 3, 23; JRDA; MAICYA; MTCW;
SATA 19, 58

Hippius, Zinaida . . . . TCLC 9
See also Gippius, Zinaida (Nikolayevna)

Hiraoka, Kimitake   1925-1970
See Mishima, Yukio
See also CA 97-100; 29-32R; MTCW

Hirsch, E(ric) D(onald), Jr.   1928-. . . CLC 79
See also CA 25-28R; CANR 27; DLB 67;
MTCW

Hirsch, Edward   1950- . . . . CLC 31, 50
See also CA 104; CANR 20, 42; DLB 120

Hitchcock, Alfred (Joseph)
1899-1980 . . . . CLC 16
See also CA 97-100; SATA 27;
SATA-Obit 24

Hitler, Adolf   1889-1945 . . . . TCLC 53
See also CA 117

Hoagland, Edward   1932-. . . . . CLC 28
See also CA 1-4R; CANR 2, 31; DLB 6;
SATA 51

Hoban, Russell (Conwell)   1925- . . CLC 7, 25
See also CA 5-8R; CANR 23, 37; CLR 3;
DLB 52; MAICYA; MTCW; SATA 1,
40, 78

Hobbs, Perry
See Blackmur, R(ichard) P(almer)

Hobson, Laura Z(ametkin)
1900-1986 . . . . CLC 7, 25
See also CA 17-20R; 118; DLB 28;
SATA 52

Hochhuth, Rolf   1931-. . . . . . . CLC 4, 11, 18
See also CA 5-8R; CANR 33; DLB 124;
MTCW

Hochman, Sandra   1936-. . . . . CLC 3, 8
See also CA 5-8R; DLB 5

Hochwaelder, Fritz   1911-1986. . . . . . CLC 36
See also CA 29-32R; 120; CANR 42;
MTCW

Hochwalder, Fritz
See Hochwaelder, Fritz

Hocking, Mary (Eunice)   1921- . . . . . CLC 13
See also CA 101; CANR 18, 40

Hodgins, Jack   1938-. . . . . CLC 23
See also CA 93-96; DLB 60

Hodgson, William Hope
1877(?)-1918 . . . . TCLC 13
See also CA 111; DLB 70

Hoffman, Alice   1952-. . . . . CLC 51
See also CA 77-80; CANR 34; MTCW

Hoffman, Daniel (Gerard)
1923- . . . . CLC 6, 13, 23
See also CA 1-4R; CANR 4; DLB 5

Hoffman, Stanley   1944-. . . . . CLC 5
See also CA 77-80

Hoffman, William M(oses)   1939- . . . CLC 40
See also CA 57-60; CANR 11

Hoffmann, E(rnst) T(heodor) A(madeus)
1776-1822 . . . . NCLC 2; SSC 13
See also DLB 90; SATA 27

Hofmann, Gert   1931-. . . . . CLC 54
See also CA 128

Hofmannsthal, Hugo von
1874-1929 . . . . TCLC 11; DC 4
See also CA 106; DLB 81, 118

Hogan, Linda   1947-. . . . . CLC 73
See also CA 120; CANR 45; NNAL

Hogarth, Charles
See Creasey, John

Hogg, James   1770-1835. . . . . NCLC 4
See also DLB 93, 116

Holbach, Paul Henri Thiry Baron
1723-1789 . . . . LC 14

Holberg, Ludvig   1684-1754 . . . . LC 6

Holden, Ursula   1921-. . . . . CLC 18
See also CA 101; CAAS 8; CANR 22

Holderlin, (Johann Christian) Friedrich
1770-1843 . . . . NCLC 16; PC 4

Holdstock, Robert
See Holdstock, Robert P.

Holdstock, Robert P.   1948-. . . . . CLC 39
See also CA 131

Holland, Isabelle   1920- . . . . CLC 21
See also AAYA 11; CA 21-24R; CANR 10,
25, 47; JRDA; MAICYA; SATA 8, 70

Holland, Marcus
See Caldwell, (Janet Miriam) Taylor
(Holland)

Hollander, John   1929-. . . . . . CLC 2, 5, 8, 14
See also CA 1-4R; CANR 1; DLB 5;
SATA 13

Hollander, Paul
See Silverberg, Robert

Holleran, Andrew   1943(?)-. . . . . CLC 38
See also CA 144

Hollinghurst, Alan   1954-. . . . . CLC 55
See also CA 114

Hollis, Jim
See Summers, Hollis (Spurgeon, Jr.)

Holmes, John
See Souster, (Holmes) Raymond

Holmes, John Clellon   1926-1988. . . . CLC 56
See also CA 9-12R; 125; CANR 4; DLB 16

Holmes, Oliver Wendell
1809-1894 . . . . NCLC 14
See also CDALB 1640-1865; DLB 1;
SATA 34

Holmes, Raymond
See Souster, (Holmes) Raymond

Holt, Victoria
See Hibbert, Eleanor Alice Burford

Holub, Miroslav   1923-. . . . . CLC 4
See also CA 21-24R; CANR 10

Homer   c. 8th cent. B.C.-. . . . . CMLC 1; DA

Honig, Edwin   1919-. . . . . CLC 33
See also CA 5-8R; CAAS 8; CANR 4, 45;
DLB 5

Hood, Hugh (John Blagdon)
1928- . . . . CLC 15, 28
See also CA 49-52; CAAS 17; CANR 1, 33;
DLB 53

Hood, Thomas   1799-1845. . . . . NCLC 16
See also DLB 96

Hooker, (Peter) Jeremy   1941-. . . . . . CLC 43
See also CA 77-80; CANR 22; DLB 40

Hope, A(lec) D(erwent)   1907-. . . . CLC 3, 51
See also CA 21-24R; CANR 33; MTCW

Hope, Brian
See Creasey, John

Hope, Christopher (David Tully)
1944-. CLC 52
See also CA 106; CANR 47; SATA 62

Hopkins, Gerard Manley
1844-1889 . . . . NCLC 17; DA; WLC
See also CDBLB 1890-1914; DLB 35, 57

Hopkins, John (Richard)   1931-. . . . . . CLC 4
See also CA 85-88

Hopkins, Pauline Elizabeth
1859-1930 . . . . TCLC 28; BLC
See also BW 2; CA 141; DLB 50

Hopkinson, Francis   1737-1791 . . . . . . LC 25
See also DLB 31

Hopley-Woolrich, Cornell George   1903-1968
See Woolrich, Cornell
See also CA 13-14; CAP 1

Horatio
See Proust, (Valentin-Louis-George-Eugene-)
Marcel

Horgan, Paul   1903- . . . . CLC 9, 53
See also CA 13-16R; CANR 9, 35;
DLB 102; DLBY 85; MTCW; SATA 13

Horn, Peter
See Kuttner, Henry

Hornem, Horace Esq.
See Byron, George Gordon (Noel)

Horovitz, Israel (Arthur)   1939-. . . . . CLC 56
See also CA 33-36R; CANR 46; DLB 7

Horvath, Odon von
See Horvath, Oedoen von
See also DLB 85, 124

Horvath, Oedoen von   1901-1938. . . TCLC 45
See also Horvath, Odon von
See also CA 118

Horwitz, Julius   1920-1986. . . . . CLC 14
See also CA 9-12R; 119; CANR 12

Hospital, Janette Turner   1942-. . . . . CLC 42
See also CA 108

Hostos, E. M. de
See Hostos (y Bonilla), Eugenio Maria de

Hostos, Eugenio M. de
See Hostos (y Bonilla), Eugenio Maria de

Hostos, Eugenio Maria
See Hostos (y Bonilla), Eugenio Maria de

Hostos (y Bonilla), Eugenio Maria de
1839-1903 . . . . TCLC 24
See also CA 123; 131; HW

Houdini
See Lovecraft, H(oward) P(hillips)

Hougan, Carolyn   1943- . . . . CLC 34
See also CA 139

Household, Geoffrey (Edward West)
1900-1988 . . . . CLC 11
See also CA 77-80; 126; DLB 87; SATA 14;
SATA-Obit 59

Housman, A(lfred) E(dward)
1859-1936 . . . . . . TCLC 1, 10; DA; PC 2
See also CA 104; 125; DLB 19; MTCW

Housman, Laurence   1865-1959. . . . . TCLC 7
See also CA 106; DLB 10; SATA 25

Immermann, Karl (Lebrecht)
1796-1840 .... **NCLC 4**
See also DLB 133

Inclan, Ramon (Maria) del Valle
See Valle-Inclan, Ramon (Maria) del

Infante, G(uillermo) Cabrera
See Cabrera Infante, G(uillermo)

Ingalls, Rachel (Holmes) 1940- ..... **CLC 42**
See also CA 123; 127

Ingamells, Rex '13-1955 .... **TCLC 35**

Inge, William M( )er
1913-1973 . . .. **CLC 1, 8, 19**
See also CA 9- R; CDALB 1941-1968;
DLB 7; MTCW

Ingelow, Jean 1820-1897 .... **NCLC 39**
See also DLB 35; SATA 33

Ingram, Willis J.
See Harris, Mark

Innaurato, Al ert (F.) 1948(?)- .. **CLC 21, 60**
See also CA 115; 122

Innes, Michael
See Stewart, J(ohn) I(nnes) M(ackintosh)

Ionesco, Eugene
1909-1994 .... **CLC 1, 4, 6, 9, 11, 15, 41,**
86; DA; WLC
See also CA 9-12R; 144; MTCW; SATA 7;
SATA-Obit 79

Iqbal, Muhammad 1873-1938 ..... **TCLC 28**

Ireland, Patrick
See O'Doherty, Brian

Iron, Ralph
See Schreiner, Olive (Emilie Albertina)

Irving, John (Winslow)
1942- .... **CLC 13, 23, 38**
See also AAYA 8; BEST 89:3; CA 25-28R;
CANR 28; DLB 6; DLBY 82; MTCW

Irving, Washington
1783-1859 .... **NCLC 2, 19; DA; SSC 2;**
WLC
See also CDALB 1640-1865; DLB 3, 11, 30,
59, 73, 74; YABC 2

Irwin, P. K.
See Page, P(atricia) K(athleen)

Isaacs, Susan 1943- .... **CLC 32**
See also BEST 89:1; CA 89-92; CANR 20,
41; MTCW

Isherwood, Christopher (William Bradshaw)
1904-1986 .... **CLC 1, 9, 11, 14, 44**
See also CA 13-16R; 117; CANR 35;
DLB 15; DLBY 86; MTCW

Ishiguro, Kazuo 1954- ...... **CLC 27, 56, 59**
See also BEST 90:2; CA 120; MTCW

Ishikawa Takuboku
1886(?)-1912 .... **TCLC 15; PC 10**
See also CA 113

Iskander, Fazil 1929- .... **CLC 47**
See also CA 102

Ivan IV 1530-1584 .... **LC 17**

Ivanov, Vyacheslav Ivanovich
1866-1949 .... **TCLC 33**
See also CA 122

Ivask, Ivar Vidrik 1927-1992....... **CLC 14**
See also CA 37-40R; 139; CANR 24

Jackson, Daniel
See Wingrove, David (John)

Jackson, Jesse 1908-1983 .... **CLC 12**
See also BW 1; CA 25-28R; 109; CANR 27;
CLR 28; MAICYA; SATA 2, 29;
SATA-Obit 48

Jackson, Laura (Riding) 1901-1991
See Riding, Laura
See also CA 65-68; 135; CANR 28; DLB 48

Jackson, Sam
See Trumbo, Dalton

Jackson, Sara
See Wingrove, David (John)

Jackson, Shirley
1919-1965 .... **CLC 11, 60, 87; DA;**
SSC 9; WLC
See also AAYA 9; CA 1-4R; 25-28R;
CANR 4; CDALB 1941-1968; DLB 6;
SATA 2

Jacob, (Cyprien-)Max 1876-1944 ... **TCLC 6**
See also CA 104

Jacobs, Jim 1942-................ **CLC 12**
See also CA 97-100

Jacobs, W(illiam) W(ymark)
1863-1943 .... **TCLC 22**
See also CA 121; DLB 135

Jacobsen, Jens Peter 1847-1885 .. **NCLC 34**

Jacobsen, Josephine 1908-........ **CLC 48**
See also CA 33-36R; CAAS 18; CANR 23

Jacobson, Dan 1929- .... **CLC 4, 14**
See also CA 1-4R; CANR 2, 25; DLB 14;
MTCW

Jacqueline
See Carpentier (y Valmont), Alejo

Jagger, Mick 1944-............... **CLC 17**

Jakes, John (William) 1932- .... **CLC 29**
See also BEST 89:4; CA 57-60; CANR 10,
43; DLBY 83; MTCW; SATA 62

James, Andrew
See Kirkup, James

James, C(yril) L(ionel) R(obert)
1901-1989 .... **CLC 33**
See also BW 2; CA 117; 125; 128; DLB 125;
MTCW

James, Daniel (Lewis) 1911-1988
See Santiago, Danny
See also CA 125

James, Dynely
See Mayne, William (James Carter)

James, Henry
1843-1916 ...... **TCLC 2, 11, 24, 40, 47;**
DA; SSC 8; WLC
See also CA 104; 132; CDALB 1865-1917;
DLB 12, 71, 74; MTCW

James, M. R.
See James, Montague (Rhodes)

James, Montague (Rhodes)
1862-1936 .... **TCLC 6; SSC 16**
See also CA 104

James, P. D. .... **CLC 18, 46**
See also White, Phyllis Dorothy James
See also BEST 90:2; CDBLB 1960 to
Present; DLB 87

James, Philip
See Moorcock, Michael (John)

James, William 1842-1910..... **TCLC 15, 32**
See also CA 109

James I 1394-1437 .... **LC 20**

Jameson, Anna 1794-1860 .... **NCLC 43**
See also DLB 99

Jami, Nur al-Din 'Abd al-Rahman
1414-1492 .... **LC 9**

Jandl, Ernst 1925- .... **CLC 34**

Janowitz, Tama 1957- .... **CLC 43**
See also CA 106

Jarrell, Randall
1914-1965 .... **CLC 1, 2, 6, 9, 13, 49**
See also CA 5-8R; 25-28R; CABS 2;
CANR 6, 34; CDALB 1941-1968; CLR 6;
DLB 48, 52; MAICYA; MTCW; SATA 7

Jarry, Alfred 1873-1907....... **TCLC 2, 14**
See also CA 104

Jarvis, E. K.
See Bloch, Robert (Albert); Ellison, Harlan
(Jay); Silverberg, Robert

Jeake, Samuel, Jr.
See Aiken, Conrad (Potter)

Jean Paul 1763-1825 .... **NCLC 7**

Jefferies, (John) Richard
1848-1887 .... **NCLC 47**
See also DLB 98, 141; SATA 16

Jeffers, (John) Robinson
1887-1962 .... **CLC 2, 3, 11, 15, 54; DA;**
WLC
See also CA 85-88; CANR 35;
CDALB 1917-1929; DLB 45; MTCW

Jefferson, Janet
See Mencken, H(enry) L(ouis)

Jefferson, Thomas 1743-1826 .... **NCLC 11**
See also CDALB 1640-1865; DLB 31

Jeffrey, Francis 1773-1850....... **NCLC 33**
See also DLB 107

Jelakowitch, Ivan
See Heijermans, Herman

Jellicoe, (Patricia) Ann 1927-...... **CLC 27**
See also CA 85-88; DLB 13

Jen, Gish .... **CLC 70**
See also Jen, Lillian

Jen, Lillian 1956(?)-
See Jen, Gish
See also CA 135

Jenkins, (John) Robin 1912-....... **CLC 52**
See also CA 1-4R; CANR 1; DLB 14

Jennings, Elizabeth (Joan)
1926- .... **CLC 5, 14**
See also CA 61-64; CAAS 5; CANR 8, 39;
DLB 27; MTCW; SATA 66

Jennings, Waylon 1937-.......... **CLC 21**

Jensen, Johannes V. 1873-1950.... **TCLC 41**

Jensen, Laura (Linnea) 1948- ...... **CLC 37**
See also CA 103

Jerome, Jerome K(lapka)
1859-1927 .... **TCLC 23**
See also CA 119; DLB 10, 34, 135

Jerrold, Douglas William
1803-1857 .... **NCLC 2**

Jewett, (Theodora) Sarah Orne
1849-1909 . . . . TCLC 1, 22; SSC 6
See also CA 108; 127; DLB 12, 74;
SATA 15

Jewsbury, Geraldine (Endsor)
1812-1880 . . . . NCLC 22
See also DLB 21

Jhabvala, Ruth Prawer
1927- . . . . CLC 4, 8, 29
See also CA 1-4R; CANR 2, 29; DLB 139;
MTCW

Jiles, Paulette 1943- . . . . CLC 13, 58
See also CA 101

Jimenez (Mantecon), Juan Ramon
1881-1958 . . . . TCLC 4; HLC; PC 7
See also CA 104; 131; DLB 134; HW;
MTCW

Jimenez, Ramon
See Jimenez (Mantecon), Juan Ramon

Jimenez Mantecon, Juan
See Jimenez (Mantecon), Juan Ramon

Joel, Billy . . . . CLC 26
See also Joel, William Martin

Joel, William Martin 1949-
See Joel, Billy
See also CA 108

John of the Cross, St. 1542-1591 . . . . LC 18

Johnson, B(ryan) S(tanley William)
1933-1973 . . . . CLC 6, 9
See also CA 9-12R; 53-56; CANR 9;
DLB 14, 40

Johnson, Benj. F. of Boo
See Riley, James Whitcomb

Johnson, Benjamin F. of Boo
See Riley, James Whitcomb

Johnson, Charles (Richard)
1948- . . . . CLC 7, 51, 65; BLC
See also BW 2; CA 116; CAAS 18;
CANR 42; DLB 33

Johnson, Denis 1949- . . . . CLC 52
See also CA 117; 121; DLB 120

Johnson, Diane 1934- . . . . CLC 5, 13, 48
See also CA 41-44R; CANR 17, 40;
DLBY 80; MTCW

Johnson, Eyvind (Olof Verner)
1900-1976 . . . . CLC 14
See also CA 73-76; 69-72; CANR 34

Johnson, J. R.
See James, C(yril) L(ionel) R(obert)

Johnson, James Weldon
1871-1938 . . . . TCLC 3, 19; BLC
See also BW 1; CA 104; 125;
CDALB 1917-1929; CLR 32; DLB 51;
MTCW; SATA 31

Johnson, Joyce 1935- . . . . CLC 58
See also CA 125; 129

Johnson, Lionel (Pigot)
1867-1902 . . . . TCLC 19
See also CA 117; DLB 19

Johnson, Mel
See Malzberg, Barry N(athaniel)

Johnson, Pamela Hansford
1912-1981 . . . . CLC 1, 7, 27
See also CA 1-4R; 104; CANR 2, 28;
DLB 15; MTCW

Johnson, Samuel
1709-1784 . . . . LC 15; DA; WLC
See also CDBLB 1660-1789; DLB 39, 95,
104, 142

Johnson, Uwe
1934-1984 . . . . CLC 5, 10, 15, 40
See also CA 1-4R; 112; CANR 1, 39;
DLB 75; MTCW

Johnston, George (Benson) 1913- . . . CLC 51
See also CA 1-4R; CANR 5, 20; DLB 88

Johnston, Jennifer 1930- . . . . CLC 7
See also CA 85-88; DLB 14

Jolley, (Monica) Elizabeth 1923- . . . CLC 46
See also CA 127; CAAS 13

Jones, Arthur Llewellyn 1863-1947
See Machen, Arthur
See also CA 104

Jones, D(ouglas) G(ordon) 1929- . . . . CLC 10
See also CA 29-32R; CANR 13; DLB 53

Jones, David (Michael)
1895-1974 . . . . CLC 2, 4, 7, 13, 42
See also CA 9-12R; 53-56; CANR 28;
CDBLB 1945-1960; DLB 20, 100; MTCW

Jones, David Robert 1947-
See Bowie, David
See also CA 103

Jones, Diana Wynne 1934- . . . . CLC 26
See also AAYA 12; CA 49-52; CANR 4,
26; CLR 23; JRDA; MAICYA; SAAS 7;
SATA 9, 70

Jones, Edward P. 1950- . . . . CLC 76
See also BW 2; CA 142

Jones, Gayl 1949- . . . . CLC 6, 9; BLC
See also BW 2; CA 77-80; CANR 27;
DLB 33; MTCW

Jones, James 1921-1977 . . . . CLC 1, 3, 10, 39
See also AITN 1, 2; CA 1-4R; 69-72;
CANR 6; DLB 2, 143; MTCW

Jones, John J.
See Lovecraft, H(oward) P(hillips)

Jones, LeRoi . . . . CLC 1, 2, 3, 5, 10, 14
See also Baraka, Amiri

Jones, Louis B. . . . . CLC 65
See also CA 141

Jones, Madison (Percy, Jr.) 1925- . . . CLC 4
See also CA 13-16R; CAAS 11; CANR 7

Jones, Mervyn 1922- . . . . CLC 10, 52
See also CA 45-48; CAAS 5; CANR 1;
MTCW

Jones, Mick 1956(?)- . . . . CLC 30

Jones, Nettie (Pearl) 1941- . . . . CLC 34
See also BW 2; CA 137; CAAS 20

Jones, Preston 1936-1979 . . . . CLC 10
See also CA 73-76; 89-92; DLB 7

Jones, Robert F(rancis) 1934- . . . . . . CLC 7
See also CA 49-52; CANR 2

Jones, Rod 1953- . . . . CLC 50
See also CA 128

Jones, Terence Graham Parry
1942- . . . . CLC 21
See also Jones, Terry; Monty Python
See also CA 112; 116; CANR 35; SATA 51

Jones, Terry
See Jones, Terence Graham Parry
See also SATA 67

Jones, Thom 1945(?)- . . . . CLC 81

Jong, Erica 1942- . . . . . CLC 4, 6, 8, 18, 83
See also AITN 1; BEST 90:2; CA 73-76;
CANR 26; DLB 2, 5, 28; MTCW

Jonson, Ben(jamin)
1572(?)-1637 . . . . LC 6; DA; DC 4; WLC
See also CDBLB Before 1660; DLB 62, 121

Jordan, June 1936- . . . . CLC 5, 11, 23
See also AAYA 2; BW 2; CA 33-36R;
CANR 25; CLR 10; DLB 38; MAICYA;
MTCW; SATA 4

Jordan, Pat(rick M.) 1941- . . . . CLC 37
See also CA 33-36R

Jorgensen, Ivar
See Ellison, Harlan (Jay)

Jorgenson, Ivar
See Silverberg, Robert

Josephus, Flavius c. 37-100 . . . . . . CMLC 13

Josipovici, Gabriel 1940- . . . . CLC 6, 43
See also CA 37-40R; CAAS 8; CANR 47;
DLB 14

Joubert, Joseph 1754-1824 . . . . NCLC 9

Jouve, Pierre Jean 1887-1976 . . . . . . CLC 47
See also CA 65-68

Joyce, James (Augustine Aloysius)
1882-1941 . . . . . . TCLC 3, 8, 16, 35; DA;
SSC 3; WLC
See also CA 104; 126; CDBLB 1914-1945;
DLB 10, 19, 36; MTCW

Jozsef, Attila 1905-1937 . . . . TCLC 22
See also CA 116

Juana Ines de la Cruz 1651(?)-1695 . . . LC 5

Judd, Cyril
See Kornbluth, C(yril) M.; Pohl, Frederik

Julian of Norwich 1342(?)-1416(?) . . . . LC 6
See also DLB 146

Just, Ward (Swift) 1935- . . . . CLC 4, 27
See also CA 25-28R; CANR 32

Justice, Donald (Rodney) 1925- . . CLC 6, 19
See also CA 5-8R; CANR 26; DLBY 83

Juvenal c. 55-c. 127 . . . . CMLC 8

Juvenis
See Bourne, Randolph S(illiman)

Kacew, Romain 1914-1980
See Gary, Romain
See also CA 108; 102

Kadare, Ismail 1936- . . . . CLC 52

Kadohata, Cynthia . . . . CLC 59
See also CA 140

Kafka, Franz
1883-1924 . . . . TCLC 2, 6, 13, 29, 47, 53;
DA; SSC 5; WLC
See also CA 105; 126; DLB 81; MTCW

Kahanovitsch, Pinkhes
See Der Nister

Kahn, Roger 1927- . . . . CLC 30
See also CA 25-28R; CANR 44; SATA 37

Kain, Saul
See Sassoon, Siegfried (Lorraine)

Kaiser, Georg 1878-1945 . . . . TCLC **9**
See also CA 106; DLB 124

Kaletski, Alexander 1946- . . . . CLC **39**
See also CA 118; 143

Kalidasa fl. c. 400- . . . . CMLC **9**

Kallman, Chester (Simon)
1921-1975 . . . . CLC **2**
See also CA 45-48; 53-56; CANR 3

Kaminsky, Melvin 1926-
See Brooks, Mel
See also CA 65-68; CANR 16

Kaminsky, Stuart M(elvin) 1934- . . . CLC **59**
See also CA 73-76; CANR 29

Kane, Paul
See Simon, Paul

Kane, Wilson
See Bloch, Robert (Albert)

Kanin, Garson 1912- . . . . CLC **22**
See also AITN 1; CA 5-8R; CANR 7;
DLB 7

Kaniuk, Yoram 1930- . . . . CLC **19**
See also CA 134

Kant, Immanuel 1724-1804 . . . . . . NCLC **27**
See also DLB 94

Kantor, MacKinlay 1904-1977 . . . . . . CLC **7**
See also CA 61-64; 73-76; DLB 9, 102

Kaplan, David Michael 1946- . . . . . . CLC **50**

Kaplan, James 1951- . . . . CLC **59**
See also CA 135

Karageorge, Michael
See Anderson, Poul (William)

Karamzin, Nikolai Mikhailovich
1766-1826 . . . . NCLC **3**

Karapanou, Margarita 1946- . . . . CLC **13**
See also CA 101

Karinthy, Frigyes 1887-1938 . . . . . . TCLC **47**

Karl, Frederick R(obert) 1927- . . . . . CLC **34**
See also CA 5-8R; CANR 3, 44

Kastel, Warren
See Silverberg, Robert

Kataev, Evgeny Petrovich 1903-1942
See Petrov, Evgeny
See also CA 120

Kataphusin
See Ruskin, John

Katz, Steve 1935- . . . . CLC **47**
See also CA 25-28R; CAAS 14; CANR 12;
DLBY 83

Kauffman, Janet 1945- . . . . CLC **42**
See also CA 117; CANR 43; DLBY 86

Kaufman, Bob (Garnell)
1925-1986 . . . . CLC **49**
See also BW 1; CA 41-44R; 118; CANR 22;
DLB 16, 41

Kaufman, George S. 1889-1961 . . . . . CLC **38**
See also CA 108; 93-96; DLB 7

Kaufman, Sue . . . . CLC **3, 8**
See also Barondess, Sue K(aufman)

Kavafis, Konstantinos Petrou 1863-1933
See Cavafy, C(onstantine) P(eter)
See also CA 104

Kavan, Anna 1901-1968 . . . . . . CLC **5, 13, 82**
See also CA 5-8R; CANR 6; MTCW

Kavanagh, Dan
See Barnes, Julian

Kavanagh, Patrick (Joseph)
1904-1967 . . . . CLC **22**
See also CA 123; 25-28R; DLB 15, 20;
MTCW

Kawabata, Yasunari
1899-1972 . . . . . CLC **2, 5, 9, 18; SSC 17**
See also CA 93-96; 33-36R

Kaye, M(ary) M(argaret) 1909- . . . . . CLC **28**
See also CA 89-92; CANR 24; MTCW;
SATA 62

Kaye, Mollie
See Kaye, M(ary) M(argaret)

Kaye-Smith, Sheila 1887-1956 . . . . . TCLC **20**
See also CA 118; DLB 36

Kaymor, Patrice Maguilene
See Senghor, Leopold Sedar

Kazan, Elia 1909- . . . . CLC **6, 16, 63**
See also CA 21-24R; CANR 32

Kazantzakis, Nikos
1883(?)-1957 . . . . TCLC **2, 5, 33**
See also CA 105; 132; MTCW

Kazin, Alfred 1915- . . . . CLC **34, 38**
See also CA 1-4R; CAAS 7; CANR 1, 45;
DLB 67

Keane, Mary Nesta (Skrine) 1904-
See Keane, Molly
See also CA 108; 114

Keane, Molly . . . . CLC **31**
See also Keane, Mary Nesta (Skrine)

Keates, Jonathan 19(?)- . . . . CLC **34**

Keaton, Buster 1895-1966 . . . . CLC **20**

Keats, John
1795-1821 . . . NCLC **8; DA; PC 1; WLC**
See also CDBLB 1789-1832; DLB 96, 110

Keene, Donald 1922- . . . . CLC **34**
See also CA 1-4R; CANR 5

Keillor, Garrison . . . . CLC **40**
See also Keillor, Gary (Edward)
See also AAYA 2; BEST 89:3; DLBY 87;
SATA 58

Keillor, Gary (Edward) 1942-
See Keillor, Garrison
See also CA 111; 117; CANR 36; MTCW

Keith, Michael
See Hubbard, L(afayette) Ron(ald)

Keller, Gottfried 1819-1890 . . . . . . NCLC **2**
See also DLB 129

Kellerman, Jonathan 1949- . . . . CLC **44**
See also BEST 90:1; CA 106; CANR 29

Kelley, William Melvin 1937- . . . . . . CLC **22**
See also BW 1; CA 77-80; CANR 27;
DLB 33

Kellogg, Marjorie 1922- . . . . CLC **2**
See also CA 81-84

Kellow, Kathleen
See Hibbert, Eleanor Alice Burford

Kelly, M(ilton) T(erry) 1947- . . . . . . CLC **55**
See also CA 97-100; CANR 19, 43

Kelman, James 1946- . . . . CLC **58, 86**

Kemal, Yashar 1923- . . . . CLC **14, 29**
See also CA 89-92; CANR 44

Kemble, Fanny 1809-1893 . . . . . . NCLC **18**
See also DLB 32

Kemelman, Harry 1908- . . . . CLC **2**
See also AITN 1; CA 9-12R; CANR 6;
DLB 28

Kempe, Margery 1373(?)-1440(?) . . . . . LC **6**
See also DLB 146

Kempis, Thomas a 1380-1471 . . . . LC **11**

Kendall, Henry 1839-1882 . . . . NCLC **12**

Keneally, Thomas (Michael)
1935- . . . . . . CLC **5, 8, 10, 14, 19, 27, 43**
See also CA 85-88; CANR 10; MTCW

Kennedy, Adrienne (Lita)
1931- . . . . CLC **66; BLC; DC 5**
See also BW 2; CA 103; CAAS 20; CABS 3;
CANR 26; DLB 38

Kennedy, John Pendleton
1795-1870 . . . . NCLC **2**
See also DLB 3

Kennedy, Joseph Charles 1929-
See Kennedy, X. J.
See also CA 1-4R; CANR 4, 30, 40;
SATA 14

Kennedy, William 1928- . . . CLC **6, 28, 34, 53**
See also AAYA 1; CA 85-88; CANR 14,
31; DLB 143; DLBY 85; MTCW;
SATA 57

Kennedy, X. J. . . . . CLC **8, 42**
See also Kennedy, Joseph Charles
See also CAAS 9; CLR 27; DLB 5

Kenny, Maurice (Francis) 1929- . . . . CLC **87**
See also CA 144; NNAL

Kent, Kelvin
See Kuttner, Henry

Kenton, Maxwell
See Southern, Terry

Kenyon, Robert O.
See Kuttner, Henry

Kerouac, Jack . . . . . CLC **1, 2, 3, 5, 14, 29, 61**
See also Kerouac, Jean-Louis Lebris de
See also CDALB 1941-1968; DLB 2, 16;
DLBD 3

Kerouac, Jean-Louis Lebris de 1922-1969
See Kerouac, Jack
See also AITN 1; CA 5-8R; 25-28R;
CANR 26; DA; MTCW; WLC

Kerr, Jean 1923- . . . . CLC **22**
See also CA 5-8R; CANR 7

Kerr, M. E. . . . . CLC **12, 35**
See also Meaker, Marijane (Agnes)
See also AAYA 2; CLR 29; SAAS 1

Kerr, Robert . . . . CLC **55**

Kerrigan, (Thomas) Anthony
1918- . . . . CLC **4, 6**
See also CA 49-52; CAAS 11; CANR 4

Kerry, Lois
See Duncan, Lois

Kesey, Ken (Elton)
1935- . . . . . . CLC **1, 3, 6, 11, 46, 64; DA;**
WLC
See also CA 1-4R; CANR 22, 38;
CDALB 1968-1988; DLB 2, 16; MTCW;
SATA 66

Kesselring, Joseph (Otto)
1902-1967 . . . . CLC **45**

Kessler, Jascha (Frederick) 1929-.... CLC 4
See also CA 17-20R; CANR 8

Kettelkamp, Larry (Dale) 1933- .... CLC 12
See also CA 29-32R; CANR 16; SAAS 3;
SATA 2

Keyber, Conny
See Fielding, Henry

Keyes, Daniel 1927-......... CLC 80; DA
See also CA 17-20R; CANR 10, 26;
SATA 37

Khanshendel, Chiron
See Rose, Wendy

Khayyam, Omar
1048-1131 .... CMLC 11; PC 8

Kherdian, David 1931-.......... CLC 6, 9
See also CA 21-24R; CAAS 2; CANR 39;
CLR 24; JRDA; MAICYA; SATA 16, 74

Khlebnikov, Velimir .... TCLC 20
See also Khlebnikov, Viktor Vladimirovich

Khlebnikov, Viktor Vladimirovich 1885-1922
See Khlebnikov, Velimir
See also CA 117

Khodasevich, Vladislav (Felitsianovich)
1886-1939 .... TCLC 15
See also CA 115

Kielland, Alexander Lange
1849-1906 .... TCLC 5
See also CA 104

Kiely, Benedict 1919-......... CLC 23, 43
See also CA 1-4R; CANR 2; DLB 15

Kienzle, William X(avier) 1928- .... CLC 25
See also CA 93-96; CAAS 1; CANR 9, 31;
MTCW

Kierkegaard, Soren 1813-1855.... NCLC 34

Killens, John Oliver 1916-1987..... CLC 10
See also BW 2; CA 77-80; 123; CAAS 2;
CANR 26; DLB 33

Killigrew, Anne 1660-1685.......... LC 4
See also DLB 131

Kim
See Simenon, Georges (Jacques Christian)

Kincaid, Jamaica 1949- ... CLC 43, 68; BLC
See also AAYA 13; BW 2; CA 125;
CANR 47

King, Francis (Henry) 1923-..... CLC 8, 53
See also CA 1-4R; CANR 1, 33; DLB 15,
139; MTCW

King, Martin Luther, Jr.
1929-1968 .... CLC 83; BLC; DA
See also BW 2; CA 25-28; CANR 27, 44;
CAP 2; MTCW; SATA 14

King, Stephen (Edwin)
1947-...... CLC 12, 26, 37, 61; SSC 17
See also AAYA 1; BEST 90:1; CA 61-64;
CANR 1, 30; DLB 143; DLBY 80;
JRDA; MTCW; SATA 9, 55

King, Steve
See King, Stephen (Edwin)

Kingman, Lee.................... CLC 17
See also Natti, (Mary) Lee
See also SAAS 3; SATA 1, 67

Kingsley, Charles 1819-1875 ..... NCLC 35
See also DLB 21, 32; YABC 2

Kingsley, Sidney 1906-........... CLC 44
See also CA 85-88; DLB 7

Kingsolver, Barbara 1955-...... CLC 55, 81
See also CA 129; 134

Kingston, Maxine (Ting Ting) Hong
1940- .... CLC 12, 19, 58
See also AAYA 8; CA 69-72; CANR 13,
38; DLBY 80; MTCW; SATA 53

Kinnell, Galway
1927-........... CLC 1, 2, 3, 5, 13, 29
See also CA 9-12R; CANR 10, 34; DLB 5;
DLBY 87; MTCW

Kinsella, Thomas 1928-......... CLC 4, 19
See also CA 17-20R; CANR 15; DLB 27;
MTCW

Kinsella, W(illiam) P(atrick)
1935-................... CLC 27, 43
See also AAYA 7; CA 97-100; CAAS 7;
CANR 21, 35; MTCW

Kipling, (Joseph) Rudyard
1865-1936 ...... TCLC 8, 17; DA; PC 3;
SSC 5; WLC
See also CA 105; 120; CANR 33;
CDBLB 1890-1914; DLB 19, 34, 141;
MAICYA; MTCW; YABC 2

Kirkup, James 1918- .... CLC 1
See also CA 1-4R; CAAS 4; CANR 2;
DLB 27; SATA 12

Kirkwood, James 1930(?)-1989 ...... CLC 9
See also AITN 2; CA 1-4R; 128; CANR 6,
40

Kis, Danilo 1935-1989 .... CLC 57
See also CA 109; 118; 129; MTCW

Kivi, Aleksis 1834-1872 .... NCLC 30

Kizer, Carolyn (Ashley)
1925-................. CLC 15, 39, 80
See also CA 65-68; CAAS 5; CANR 24;
DLB 5

Klabund 1890-1928.............. TCLC 44
See also DLB 66

Klappert, Peter 1942-............. CLC 57
See also CA 33-36R; DLB 5

Klein, A(braham) M(oses)
1909-1972 .... CLC 19
See also CA 101; 37-40R; DLB 68

Klein, Norma 1938-1989 .... CLC 30
See also AAYA 2; CA 41-44R; 128;
CANR 15, 37; CLR 2, 19; JRDA;
MAICYA; SAAS 1; SATA 7, 57

Klein, T(heodore) E(ibon) D(onald)
1947-..................... CLC 34
See also CA 119; CANR 44

Kleist, Heinrich von
1777-1811 .... NCLC 2, 37
See also DLB 90

Klima, Ivan 1931-................. CLC 56
See also CA 25-28R; CANR 17

Klimentov, Andrei Platonovich 1899-1951
See Platonov, Andrei
See also CA 108

Klinger, Friedrich Maximilian von
1752-1831 .... NCLC 1
See also DLB 94

Klopstock, Friedrich Gottlieb
1724-1803 .... NCLC 11
See also DLB 97

Knebel, Fletcher 1911-1993........ CLC 14
See also AITN 1; CA 1-4R; 140; CAAS 3;
CANR 1, 36; SATA 36; SATA-Obit 75

Knickerbocker, Diedrich
See Irving, Washington

Knight, Etheridge
1931-1991 .... CLC 40; BLC
See also BW 1; CA 21-24R; 133; CANR 23;
DLB 41

Knight, Sarah Kemble 1666-1727 ..... LC 7
See also DLB 24

Knister, Raymond 1899-1932...... TCLC 56
See also DLB 68

Knowles, John
1926-........... CLC 1, 4, 10, 26; DA
See also AAYA 10; CA 17-20R; CANR 40;
CDALB 1968-1988; DLB 6; MTCW;
SATA 8

Knox, Calvin M.
See Silverberg, Robert

Knye, Cassandra
See Disch, Thomas M(ichael)

Koch, C(hristopher) J(ohn) 1932- ... CLC 42
See also CA 127

Koch, Christopher
See Koch, C(hristopher) J(ohn)

Koch, Kenneth 1925-......... CLC 5, 8, 44
See also CA 1-4R; CANR 6, 36; DLB 5;
SATA 65

Kochanowski, Jan 1530-1584........ LC 10

Kock, Charles Paul de
1794-1871 .... NCLC 16

Koda Shigeyuki 1867-1947
See Rohan, Koda
See also CA 121

Koestler, Arthur
1905-1983 .... CLC 1, 3, 6, 8, 15, 33
See also CA 1-4R; 109; CANR 1, 33;
CDBLB 1945-1960; DLBY 83; MTCW

Kogawa, Joy Nozomi 1935-........ CLC 78
See also CA 101; CANR 19

Kohout, Pavel 1928-.............. CLC 13
See also CA 45-48; CANR 3

Koizumi, Yakumo
See Hearn, (Patricio) Lafcadio (Tessima
Carlos)

Kolmar, Gertrud 1894-1943...... TCLC 40

Komunyakaa, Yusef 1947-........ CLC 86
See also DLB 120

Konrad, George
See Konrad, Gyoergy

Konrad, Gyoergy 1933-...... CLC 4, 10, 73
See also CA 85-88

Konwicki, Tadeusz 1926-..... CLC 8, 28, 54
See also CA 101; CAAS 9; CANR 39;
MTCW

Koontz, Dean R(ay) 1945-........ CLC 78
See also AAYA 9; BEST 89:3, 90:2;
CA 108; CANR 19, 36; MTCW

Kopit, Arthur (Lee) 1937- .... **CLC 1, 18, 33**
See also AITN 1; CA 81-84; CABS 3;
DLB 7; MTCW

Kops, Bernard 1926-.............. **CLC 4**
See also CA 5-8R; DLB 13

Kornbluth, C(yril) M. 1923-1958.... **TCLC 8**
See also CA 105; DLB 8

Korolenko, V. G.
See Korolenko, Vladimir Galaktionovich

Korolenko, Vladimir
See Korolenko, Vladimir Galaktionovich

Korolenko, Vladimir G.
See Korolenko, Vladimir Galaktionovich

Korolenko, Vladimir Galaktionovich
1853-1921 .... **TCLC 22**
See also CA 121

Kosinski, Jerzy (Nikodem)
1933-1991 .... **CLC 1, 2, 3, 6, 10, 15, 53,
70**
See also CA 17-20R; 134; CANR 9, 46;
DLB 2; DLBY 82; MTCW

Kostelanetz, Richard (Cory) 1940- .. **CLC 28**
See also CA 13-16R; CAAS 8; CANR 38

Kostrowitzki, Wilhelm Apollinaris de
1880-1918
See Apollinaire, Guillaume
See also CA 104

Kotlowitz, Robert 1924-............ **CLC 4**
See also CA 33-36R; CANR 36

Kotzebue, August (Friedrich Ferdinand) von
1761-1819 .... **NCLC 25**
See also DLB 94

Kotzwinkle, William 1938- ... **CLC 5, 14, 35**
See also CA 45-48; CANR 3, 44; CLR 6;
MAICYA; SATA 24, 70

Kozol, Jonathan 1936-............ **CLC 17**
See also CA 61-64; CANR 16, 45

Kozoll, Michael 1940(?)-.......... **CLC 35**

Kramer, Kathryn 19(?)-.......... **CLC 34**

Kramer, Larry 1935- .... **CLC 42**
See also CA 124; 126

Krasicki, Ignacy 1735-1801 .... **NCLC 8**

Krasinski, Zygmunt 1812-1859 .... **NCLC 4**

Kraus, Karl 1874-1936............ **TCLC 5**
See also CA 104; DLB 118

Kreve (Mickevicius), Vincas
1882-1954 .... **TCLC 27**

Kristeva, Julia 1941- .... **CLC 77**

Kristofferson, Kris 1936-.......... **CLC 26**
See also CA 104

Krizanc, John 1956-.............. **CLC 57**

Krleza, Miroslav 1893-1981........ **CLC 8**
See also CA 97-100; 105; DLB 147

Kroetsch, Robert 1927- ...... **CLC 5, 23, 57**
See also CA 17-20R; CANR 8, 38; DLB 53;
MTCW

Kroetz, Franz
See Kroetz, Franz Xaver

Kroetz, Franz Xaver 1946- .... **CLC 41**
See also CA 130

Kroker, Arthur 1945-............ **CLC 77**

Kropotkin, Peter (Aleksieevich)
1842-1921 .... **TCLC 36**
See also CA 119

Krotkov, Yuri 1917-.............. **CLC 19**
See also CA 102

Krumb
See Crumb, R(obert)

Krumgold, Joseph (Quincy)
1908-1980 .... **CLC 12**
See also CA 9-12R; 101; CANR 7;
MAICYA; SATA 1, 48; SATA-Obit 23

Krumwitz
See Crumb, R(obert)

Krutch, Joseph Wood 1893-1970.... **CLC 24**
See also CA 1-4R; 25-28R; CANR 4;
DLB 63

Krutzch, Gus
See Eliot, T(homas) S(tearns)

Krylov, Ivan Andreevich
1768(?)-1844 .... **NCLC 1**

Kubin, Alfred 1877-1959 .... **TCLC 23**
See also CA 112; DLB 81

Kubrick, Stanley 1928-............ **CLC 16**
See also CA 81-84; CANR 33; DLB 26

Kumin, Maxine (Winokur)
1925- .... **CLC 5, 13, 28**
See also AITN 2; CA 1-4R; CAAS 8;
CANR 1, 21; DLB 5; MTCW; SATA 12

Kundera, Milan
1929- .... **CLC 4, 9, 19, 32, 68**
See also AAYA 2; CA 85-88; CANR 19;
MTCW

Kunene, Mazisi (Raymond) 1930-... **CLC 85**
See also BW 1; CA 125; DLB 117

Kunitz, Stanley (Jasspon)
1905- .... **CLC 6, 11, 14**
See also CA 41-44R; CANR 26; DLB 48;
MTCW

Kunze, Reiner 1933-.............. **CLC 10**
See also CA 93-96; DLB 75

Kuprin, Aleksandr Ivanovich
1870-1938 .... **TCLC 5**
See also CA 104

Kureishi, Hanif 1954(?)-.......... **CLC 64**
See also CA 139

Kurosawa, Akira 1910-............ **CLC 16**
See also AAYA 11; CA 101; CANR 46

Kushner, Tony 1957(?)- .... **CLC 81**
See also CA 144

Kuttner, Henry 1915-1958........ **TCLC 10**
See also CA 107; DLB 8

Kuzma, Greg 1944-.............. **CLC 7**
See also CA 33-36R

Kuzmin, Mikhail 1872(?)-1936 .... **TCLC 40**

Kyd, Thomas 1558-1594....... **LC 22; DC 3**
See also DLB 62

Kyprianos, Iossif
See Samarakis, Antonis

La Bruyere, Jean de 1645-1696...... **LC 17**

Lacan, Jacques (Marie Emile)
1901-1981 .... **CLC 75**
See also CA 121; 104

Laclos, Pierre Ambroise Francois Choderlos
de 1741-1803 .... **NCLC 4**

Lacolere, Francois
See Aragon, Louis

La Colere, Francois
See Aragon, Louis

La Deshabilleuse
See Simenon, Georges (Jacques Christian)

Lady Gregory
See Gregory, Isabella Augusta (Persse)

Lady of Quality, A
See Bagnold, Enid

**La Fayette, Marie (Madelaine Pioche de la
Vergne Comtes** 1634-1693....... **LC 2**

Lafayette, Rene
See Hubbard, L(afayette) Ron(ald)

Laforgue, Jules 1860-1887........ **NCLC 5**

Lagerkvist, Paer (Fabian)
1891-1974 .... **CLC 7, 10, 13, 54**
See also Lagerkvist, Par
See also CA 85-88; 49-52; MTCW

Lagerkvist, Par
See Lagerkvist, Paer (Fabian)
See also SSC 12

Lagerloef, Selma (Ottiliana Lovisa)
1858-1940 .... **TCLC 4, 36**
See also Lagerlof, Selma (Ottiliana Lovisa)
See also CA 108; SATA 15

Lagerlof, Selma (Ottiliana Lovisa)
See Lagerloef, Selma (Ottiliana Lovisa)
See also CLR 7; SATA 15

La Guma, (Justin) Alex(ander)
1925-1985 .... **CLC 19**
See also BW 1; CA 49-52; 118; CANR 25;
DLB 117; MTCW

Laidlaw, A. K.
See Grieve, C(hristopher) M(urray)

Lainez, Manuel Mujica
See Mujica Lainez, Manuel
See also HW

Lamartine, Alphonse (Marie Louis Prat) de
1790-1869 .... **NCLC 11**

Lamb, Charles
1775-1834 .... **NCLC 10; DA; WLC**
See also CDBLB 1789-1832; DLB 93, 107;
SATA 17

Lamb, Lady Caroline 1785-1828.. **NCLC 38**
See also DLB 116

Lamming, George (William)
1927- .... **CLC 2, 4, 66; BLC**
See also BW 2; CA 85-88; CANR 26;
DLB 125; MTCW

L'Amour, Louis (Dearborn)
1908-1988 .... **CLC 25, 55**
See also AITN 2; BEST 89:2; CA 1-4R;
125; CANR 3, 25, 40; DLBY 80; MTCW

Lampedusa, Giuseppe (Tomasi) di ... **TCLC 13**
See also Tomasi di Lampedusa, Giuseppe

Lampman, Archibald 1861-1899 .. **NCLC 25**
See also DLB 92

Lancaster, Bruce 1896-1963........ **CLC 36**
See also CA 9-10; CAP 1; SATA 9

Landau, Mark Alexandrovich
See Aldanov, Mark (Alexandrovich)

Landau-Aldanov, Mark Alexandrovich
See Aldanov, Mark (Alexandrovich)

Lewisohn, Ludwig 1883-1955...... **TCLC 19**
See also CA 107; DLB 4, 9, 28, 102

Lezama Lima, Jose 1910-1976 ... **CLC 4, 10**
See also CA 77-80; DLB 113; HW

L'Heureux, John (Clarke) 1934-.... **CLC 52**
See also CA 13-16R; CANR 23, 45

Liddell, C. H.
See Kuttner, Henry

Lie, Jonas (Lauritz Idemil)
1833-1908(?) .... **TCLC 5**
See also CA 115

Lieber, Joel 1937-1971............ **CLC 6**
See also CA 73-76; 29-32R

Lieber, Stanley Martin
See Lee, Stan

Lieberman, Laurence (James)
1935-.................... **CLC 4, 36**
See also CA 17-20R; CANR 8, 36

Lieksman, Anders
See Haavikko, Paavo Juhani

Li Fei-kan 1904-
See Pa Chin
See also CA 105

Lifton, Robert Jay 1926-.......... **CLC 67**
See also CA 17-20R; CANR 27; SATA 66

Lightfoot, Gordon 1938-.......... **CLC 26**
See also CA 109

Lightman, Alan P. 1948- .... **CLC 81**
See also CA 141

Ligotti, Thomas 1953- .... **CLC 44; SSC 16**
See also CA 123

Liliencron, (Friedrich Adolf Axel) Detlev von
1844-1909 .... **TCLC 18**
See also CA 117

Lilly, William 1602-1681.......... **LC 27**

Lima, Jose Lezama
See Lezama Lima, Jose

Lima Barreto, Afonso Henrique de
1881-1922 .... **TCLC 23**
See also CA 117

Limonov, Eduard................. **CLC 67**

Lin, Frank
See Atherton, Gertrude (Franklin Horn)

Lincoln, Abraham 1809-1865..... **NCLC 18**

Lind, Jakov .... **CLC 1, 2, 4, 27, 82**
See also Landwirth, Heinz
See also CAAS 4

Lindbergh, Anne (Spencer) Morrow
1906-...................... **CLC 82**
See also CA 17-20R; CANR 16; MTCW;
SATA 33

Lindsay, David 1878-1945....... **TCLC 15**
See also CA 113

Lindsay, (Nicholas) Vachel
1879-1931 .... **TCLC 17; DA; WLC**
See also CA 114; 135; CDALB 1865-1917;
DLB 54; SATA 40

Linke-Poot
See Doeblin, Alfred

Linney, Romulus 1930- .... **CLC 51**
See also CA 1-4R; CANR 40, 44

Linton, Eliza Lynn 1822-1898.... **NCLC 41**
See also DLB 18

Li Po 701-763 .... **CMLC 2**

Lipsius, Justus 1547-1606 .... **LC 16**

Lipsyte, Robert (Michael)
1938- .... **CLC 21; DA**
See also AAYA 7; CA 17-20R; CANR 8;
CLR 23; JRDA; MAICYA; SATA 5, 68

Lish, Gordon (Jay) 1934-.. **CLC 45; SSC 18**
See also CA 113; 117; DLB 130

Lispector, Clarice 1925-1977...... **CLC 43**
See also CA 139; 116; DLB 113

Littell, Robert 1935(?)- .... **CLC 42**
See also CA 109; 112

Little, Malcolm 1925-1965
See Malcolm X
See also BW 1; CA 125; 111; DA; MTCW

Littlewit, Humphrey Gent.
See Lovecraft, H(oward) P(hillips)

Litwos
See Sienkiewicz, Henryk (Adam Alexander
Pius)

Liu E 1857-1909............... **TCLC 15**
See also CA 115

Lively, Penelope (Margaret)
1933-.................. **CLC 32, 50**
See also CA 41-44R; CANR 29; CLR 7;
DLB 14; JRDA; MAICYA; MTCW;
SATA 7, 60

Livesay, Dorothy (Kathleen)
1909-................ **CLC 4, 15, 79**
See also AITN 2; CA 25-28R; CAAS 8;
CANR 36; DLB 68; MTCW

Livy c. 59B.C.-c. 17 .... **CMLC 11**

Lizardi, Jose Joaquin Fernandez de
1776-1827 .... **NCLC 30**

Llewellyn, Richard
See Llewellyn Lloyd, Richard Dafydd
Vivian
See also DLB 15

Llewellyn Lloyd, Richard Dafydd Vivian
1906-1983 .... **CLC 7, 80**
See also Llewellyn, Richard
See also CA 53-56; 111; CANR 7;
SATA 11; SATA-Obit 37

Llosa, (Jorge) Mario (Pedro) Vargas
See Vargas Llosa, (Jorge) Mario (Pedro)

Lloyd Webber, Andrew 1948-
See Webber, Andrew Lloyd
See also AAYA 1; CA 116; SATA 56

Llull, Ramon c. 1235-c. 1316..... **CMLC 12**

Locke, Alain (Le Roy)
1886-1954 .... **TCLC 43**
See also BW 1; CA 106; 124; DLB 51

Locke, John 1632-1704 .... **LC 7**
See also DLB 101

Locke-Elliott, Sumner
See Elliott, Sumner Locke

Lockhart, John Gibson
1794-1854 .... **NCLC 6**
See also DLB 110, 116, 144

Lodge, David (John) 1935-........ **CLC 36**
See also BEST 90:1; CA 17-20R; CANR 19;
DLB 14; MTCW

Loennbohm, Armas Eino Leopold 1878-1926
See Leino, Eino
See also CA 123

Loewinsohn, Ron(ald William)
1937-...................... **CLC 52**
See also CA 25-28R

Logan, Jake
See Smith, Martin Cruz

Logan, John (Burton) 1923-1987..... **CLC 5**
See also CA 77-80; 124; CANR 45; DLB 5

Lo Kuan-chung 1330(?)-1400(?)...... **LC 12**

Lombard, Nap
See Johnson, Pamela Hansford

London, Jack.. **TCLC 9, 15, 39; SSC 4; WLC**
See also London, John Griffith
See also AAYA 13; AITN 2;
CDALB 1865-1917; DLB 8, 12, 78;
SATA 18

London, John Griffith 1876-1916
See London, Jack
See also CA 110; 119; DA; JRDA;
MAICYA; MTCW

Long, Emmett
See Leonard, Elmore (John, Jr.)

Longbaugh, Harry
See Goldman, William (W.)

Longfellow, Henry Wadsworth
1807-1882 .... **NCLC 2, 45; DA**
See also CDALB 1640-1865; DLB 1, 59;
SATA 19

Longley, Michael 1939-.......... **CLC 29**
See also CA 102; DLB 40

Longus fl. c. 2nd cent. - .... **CMLC 7**

Longway, A. Hugh
See Lang, Andrew

Lopate, Phillip 1943- .... **CLC 29**
See also CA 97-100; DLBY 80

Lopez Portillo (y Pacheco), Jose
1920-...................... **CLC 46**
See also CA 129; HW

Lopez y Fuentes, Gregorio
1897(?)-1966 .... **CLC 32**
See also CA 131; HW

Lorca, Federico Garcia
See Garcia Lorca, Federico

Lord, Bette Bao 1938-............ **CLC 23**
See also BEST 90:3; CA 107; CANR 41;
SATA 58

Lord Auch
See Bataille, Georges

Lord Byron
See Byron, George Gordon (Noel)

Lorde, Audre (Geraldine)
1934-1992 .... **CLC 18, 71; BLC**
See also BW 1; CA 25-28R; 142; CANR 16,
26, 46; DLB 41; MTCW

Lord Jeffrey
See Jeffrey, Francis

Lorenzo, Heberto Padilla
See Padilla (Lorenzo), Heberto

Loris
See Hofmannsthal, Hugo von

Loti, Pierre . . . . TCLC 11
See also Viaud, (Louis Marie) Julien
See also DLB 123

Louie, David Wong   1954- . . . . CLC 70
See also CA 139

Louis, Father M.
See Merton, Thomas

Lovecraft, H(oward) P(hillips)
1890-1937 . . . . TCLC 4, 22; SSC 3
See also AAYA 14; CA 104; 133; MTCW

Lovelace, Earl   1935-. . . . . CLC 51
See also BW 2; CA 77-80; CANR 41;
DLB 125; MTCW

Lovelace, Richard   1618-1657. . . . . . . LC 24
See also DLB 131

Lowell, Amy   1874-1925 . . . . TCLC 1, 8
See also CA 104; DLB 54, 140

Lowell, James Russell   1819-1891 . . NCLC 2
See also CDALB 1640-1865; DLB 1, 11, 64,
79

Lowell, Robert (Traill Spence, Jr.)
1917-1977 . . . CLC 1, 2, 3, 4, 5, 8, 9, 11,
15, 37; DA; PC 3; WLC
See also CA 9-12R; 73-76; CABS 2;
CANR 26; DLB 5; MTCW

Lowndes, Marie Adelaide (Belloc)
1868-1947 . . . . TCLC 12
See also CA 107; DLB 70

Lowry, (Clarence) Malcolm
1909-1957. . . . . TCLC 6, 40
See also CA 105; 131; CDBLB 1945-1960;
DLB 15; MTCW

Lowry, Mina Gertrude   1882-1966
See Loy, Mina
See also CA 113

Loxsmith, John
See Brunner, John (Kilian Houston)

Loy, Mina . . . . CLC 28
See also Lowry, Mina Gertrude
See also DLB 4, 54

Loyson-Bridet
See Schwob, (Mayer Andre) Marcel

Lucas, Craig   1951-. . . . . CLC 64
See also CA 137

Lucas, George   1944-. . . . . CLC 16
See also AAYA 1; CA 77-80; CANR 30;
SATA 56

Lucas, Hans
See Godard, Jean-Luc

Lucas, Victoria
See Plath, Sylvia

Ludlam, Charles   1943-1987. . . . . CLC 46, 50
See also CA 85-88; 122

Ludlum, Robert   1927- . . . . CLC 22, 43
See also AAYA 10; BEST 89:1, 90:3;
CA 33-36R; CANR 25, 41; DLBY 82;
MTCW

Ludwig, Ken. CLC 60

Ludwig, Otto   1813-1865. . . . . NCLC 4
See also DLB 129

Lugones, Leopoldo   1874-1938 . . . . . TCLC 15
See also CA 116; 131; HW

Lu Hsun   1881-1936 . . . . TCLC 3

Lukacs, George . . . . CLC 24
See also Lukacs, Gyorgy (Szegeny von)

Lukacs, Gyorgy (Szegeny von)   1885-1971
See Lukacs, George
See also CA 101; 29-32R

Luke, Peter (Ambrose Cyprian)
1919-. . . . . CLC 38
See also CA 81-84; DLB 13

Lunar, Dennis
See Mungo, Raymond

Lurie, Alison   1926-. . . . . CLC 4, 5, 18, 39
See also CA 1-4R; CANR 2, 17; DLB 2;
MTCW; SATA 46

Lustig, Arnost   1926-. . . . . CLC 56
See also AAYA 3; CA 69-72; CANR 47;
SATA 56

Luther, Martin   1483-1546 . . . . LC 9

Luzi, Mario   1914-. . . . . CLC 13
See also CA 61-64; CANR 9; DLB 128

Lynch, B. Suarez
See Bioy Casares, Adolfo; Borges, Jorge
Luis

Lynch, David (K.)   1946-. . . . . CLC 66
See also CA 124; 129

Lynch, James
See Andreyev, Leonid (Nikolaevich)

Lynch Davis, B.
See Bioy Casares, Adolfo; Borges, Jorge
Luis

Lyndsay, Sir David   1490-1555 . . . . . . LC 20

Lynn, Kenneth S(chuyler)   1923-. . . . CLC 50
See also CA 1-4R; CANR 3, 27

Lynx
See West, Rebecca

Lyons, Marcus
See Blish, James (Benjamin)

Lyre, Pinchbeck
See Sassoon, Siegfried (Lorraine)

Lytle, Andrew (Nelson)   1902-. . . . . . CLC 22
See also CA 9-12R; DLB 6

Lyttelton, George   1709-1773. . . . . . . LC 10

Maas, Peter   1929- . . . . CLC 29
See also CA 93-96

Macaulay, Rose   1881-1958 . . . . . TCLC 7, 44
See also CA 104; DLB 36

Macaulay, Thomas Babington
1800-1859 . . . . NCLC 42
See also CDBLB 1832-1890; DLB 32, 55

MacBeth, George (Mann)
1932-1992 . . . . CLC 2, 5, 9
See also CA 25-28R; 136; DLB 40; MTCW;
SATA 4; SATA-Obit 70

MacCaig, Norman (Alexander)
1910-. . . . . CLC 36
See also CA 9-12R; CANR 3, 34; DLB 27

MacCarthy, (Sir Charles Otto) Desmond
1877-1952 . . . . TCLC 36

MacDiarmid, Hugh
. . . . CLC 2, 4, 11, 19, 63; PC 9
See also Grieve, C(hristopher) M(urray)
See also CDBLB 1945-1960; DLB 20

MacDonald, Anson
See Heinlein, Robert A(nson)

Macdonald, Cynthia   1928-. . . . . . CLC 13, 19
See also CA 49-52; CANR 4, 44; DLB 105

MacDonald, George   1824-1905. . . . . TCLC 9
See also CA 106; 137; DLB 18; MAICYA;
SATA 33

Macdonald, John
See Millar, Kenneth

MacDonald, John D(ann)
1916-1986 . . . . CLC 3, 27, 44
See also CA 1-4R; 121; CANR 1, 19;
DLB 8; DLBY 86; MTCW

Macdonald, John Ross
See Millar, Kenneth

Macdonald, Ross. . . . . CLC 1, 2, 3, 14, 34, 41
See also Millar, Kenneth
See also DLBD 6

MacDougal, John
See Blish, James (Benjamin)

MacEwen, Gwendolyn (Margaret)
1941-1987 . . . . CLC 13, 55
See also CA 9-12R; 124; CANR 7, 22;
DLB 53; SATA 50; SATA-Obit 55

Macha, Karel Hynek   1810-1846. . NCLC 46

Machado (y Ruiz), Antonio
1875-1939 . . . . TCLC 3
See also CA 104; DLB 108

Machado de Assis, Joaquim Maria
1839-1908 . . . . TCLC 10; BLC
See also CA 107

Machen, Arthur. . . . . TCLC 4
See also Jones, Arthur Llewellyn
See also DLB 36

Machiavelli, Niccolo   1469-1527 . . LC 8; DA

MacInnes, Colin   1914-1976. . . . . . CLC 4, 23
See also CA 69-72; 65-68; CANR 21;
DLB 14; MTCW

MacInnes, Helen (Clark)
1907-1985 . . . . CLC 27, 39
See also CA 1-4R; 117; CANR 1, 28;
DLB 87; MTCW; SATA 22;
SATA-Obit 44

Mackay, Mary   1855-1924
See Corelli, Marie
See also CA 118

Mackenzie, Compton (Edward Montague)
1883-1972 . . . . CLC 18
See also CA 21-22; 37-40R; CAP 2;
DLB 34, 100

Mackenzie, Henry   1745-1831 . . . . NCLC 41
See also DLB 39

Mackintosh, Elizabeth   1896(?)-1952
See Tey, Josephine
See also CA 110

MacLaren, James
See Grieve, C(hristopher) M(urray)

Mac Laverty, Bernard   1942-. . . . . . . CLC 31
See also CA 116; 118; CANR 43

MacLean, Alistair (Stuart)
1922-1987 . . . . CLC 3, 13, 50, 63
See also CA 57-60; 121; CANR 28; MTCW;
SATA 23; SATA-Obit 50

Maclean, Norman (Fitzroy)
1902-1990 . . . . CLC 78; SSC 13
See also CA 102; 132

MacLeish, Archibald
 1892-1982 .... CLC **3, 8, 14, 68**
 See also CA 9-12R; 106; CANR 33; DLB 4,
 7, 45; DLBY 82; MTCW

MacLennan, (John) Hugh
 1907-1990 .... CLC **2, 14**
 See also CA 5-8R; 142; CANR 33; DLB 68;
 MTCW

MacLeod, Alistair 1936- .... CLC **56**
 See also CA 123; DLB 60

MacNeice, (Frederick) Louis
 1907-1963 .... CLC **1, 4, 10, 53**
 See also CA 85-88; DLB 10, 20; MTCW

MacNeill, Dand
 See Fraser, George MacDonald

Macpherson, (Jean) Jay 1931- ...... CLC **14**
 See also CA 5-8R; DLB 53

MacShane, Frank 1927- .... CLC **39**
 See also CA 9-12R; CANR 3, 33; DLB 111

Macumber, Mari
 See Sandoz, Mari(e Susette)

Madach, Imre 1823-1864 .... NCLC **19**

Madden, (Jerry) David 1933- .... CLC **5, 15**
 See also CA 1-4R; CAAS 3; CANR 4, 45;
 DLB 6; MTCW

Maddern, Al(an)
 See Ellison, Harlan (Jay)

Madhubuti, Haki R.
 1942- .... CLC **6, 73; BLC; PC 5**
 See also Lee, Don L.
 See also BW 2; CA 73-76; CANR 24;
 DLB 5, 41; DLBD 8

Maepenn, Hugh
 See Kuttner, Henry

Maepenn, K. H.
 See Kuttner, Henry

Maeterlinck, Maurice 1862-1949 ... TCLC **3**
 See also CA 104; 136; SATA 66

Maginn, William 1794-1842 ...... NCLC **8**
 See also DLB 110

Mahapatra, Jayanta 1928- .... CLC **33**
 See also CA 73-76; CAAS 9; CANR 15, 33

Mahfouz, Naguib (Abdel Aziz Al-Sabilgi)
 1911(?)-
 See Mahfuz, Najib
 See also BEST 89:2; CA 128; MTCW

Mahfuz, Najib .... CLC **52, 55**
 See also Mahfouz, Naguib (Abdel Aziz
 Al-Sabilgi)
 See also DLBY 88

Mahon, Derek 1941- .... CLC **27**
 See also CA 113; 128; DLB 40

Mailer, Norman
 1923- ...... CLC **1, 2, 3, 4, 5, 8, 11, 14,
 28, 39, 74; DA**
 See also AITN 2; CA 9-12R; CABS 1;
 CANR 28; CDALB 1968-1988; DLB 2,
 16, 28; DLBD 3; DLBY 80, 83; MTCW

Maillet, Antonine 1929- .... CLC **54**
 See also CA 115; 120; CANR 46; DLB 60

Mais, Roger 1905-1955 .... TCLC **8**
 See also BW 1; CA 105; 124; DLB 125;
 MTCW

Maistre, Joseph de 1753-1821 .... NCLC **37**

Maitland, Sara (Louise) 1950- ...... CLC **49**
 See also CA 69-72; CANR 13

Major, Clarence
 1936- .... CLC **3, 19, 48; BLC**
 See also BW 2; CA 21-24R; CAAS 6;
 CANR 13, 25; DLB 33

Major, Kevin (Gerald) 1949- .... CLC **26**
 See also CA 97-100; CANR 21, 38;
 CLR 11; DLB 60; JRDA; MAICYA;
 SATA 32

Maki, James
 See Ozu, Yasujiro

Malabaila, Damiano
 See Levi, Primo

Malamud, Bernard
 1914-1986 ...... CLC **1, 2, 3, 5, 8, 9, 11,
 18, 27, 44, 78, 85; DA; SSC 15; WLC**
 See also CA 5-8R; 118; CABS 1; CANR 28;
 CDALB 1941-1968; DLB 2, 28;
 DLBY 80, 86; MTCW

Malaparte, Curzio 1898-1957 ..... TCLC **52**

Malcolm, Dan
 See Silverberg, Robert

Malcolm X .... CLC **82; BLC**
 See also Little, Malcolm

Malherbe, Francois de 1555-1628 ..... LC **5**

Mallarme, Stephane
 1842-1898 .... NCLC **4, 41; PC 4**

Mallet-Joris, Francoise 1930- ...... CLC **11**
 See also CA 65-68; CANR 17; DLB 83

Malley, Ern
 See McAuley, James Phillip

Mallowan, Agatha Christie
 See Christie, Agatha (Mary Clarissa)

Maloff, Saul 1922- .... CLC **5**
 See also CA 33-36R

Malone, Louis
 See MacNeice, (Frederick) Louis

Malone, Michael (Christopher)
 1942- .... CLC **43**
 See also CA 77-80; CANR 14, 32

Malory, (Sir) Thomas
 1410(?)-1471(?) .... LC **11; DA**
 See also CDBLB Before 1660; DLB 146;
 SATA 33, 59

Malouf, (George Joseph) David
 1934- .... CLC **28, 86**
 See also CA 124

Malraux, (Georges-)Andre
 1901-1976 ...... CLC **1, 4, 9, 13, 15, 57**
 See also CA 21-22; 69-72; CANR 34;
 CAP 2; DLB 72; MTCW

Malzberg, Barry N(athaniel) 1939- ... CLC **7**
 See also CA 61-64; CAAS 4; CANR 16;
 DLB 8

Mamet, David (Alan)
 1947- .... CLC **9, 15, 34, 46; DC 4**
 See also AAYA 3; CA 81-84; CABS 3;
 CANR 15, 41; DLB 7; MTCW

Mamoulian, Rouben (Zachary)
 1897-1987 .... CLC **16**
 See also CA 25-28R; 124

Mandelstam, Osip (Emilievich)
 1891(?)-1938(?) .... TCLC **2, 6**
 See also CA 104

Mander, (Mary) Jane 1877-1949 ... TCLC **31**

Mandiargues, Andre Pieyre de .... CLC **41**
 See also Pieyre de Mandiargues, Andre
 See also DLB 83

Mandrake, Ethel Belle
 See Thurman, Wallace (Henry)

Mangan, James Clarence
 1803-1849 .... NCLC **27**

Maniere, J.-E.
 See Giraudoux, (Hippolyte) Jean

Manley, (Mary) Delariviere
 1672(?)-1724 .... LC **1**
 See also DLB 39, 80

Mann, Abel
 See Creasey, John

Mann, (Luiz) Heinrich 1871-1950 ... TCLC **9**
 See also CA 106; DLB 66

Mann, (Paul) Thomas
 1875-1955 .... TCLC **2, 8, 14, 21, 35, 44;
 DA; SSC 5; WLC**
 See also CA 104; 128; DLB 66; MTCW

Manning, David
 See Faust, Frederick (Schiller)

Manning, Frederic 1887(?)-1935 ... TCLC **25**
 See also CA 124

Manning, Olivia 1915-1980 ...... CLC **5, 19**
 See also CA 5-8R; 101; CANR 29; MTCW

Mano, D. Keith 1942- .... CLC **2, 10**
 See also CA 25-28R; CAAS 6; CANR 26;
 DLB 6

Mansfield, Katherine
 .... TCLC **2, 8, 39; SSC 9; WLC**
 See also Beauchamp, Kathleen Mansfield

Manso, Peter 1940- .... CLC **39**
 See also CA 29-32R; CANR 44

Mantecon, Juan Jimenez
 See Jimenez (Mantecon), Juan Ramon

Manton, Peter
 See Creasey, John

Man Without a Spleen, A
 See Chekhov, Anton (Pavlovich)

Manzoni, Alessandro 1785-1873 .. NCLC **29**

Mapu, Abraham (ben Jekutiel)
 1808-1867 .... NCLC **18**

Mara, Sally
 See Queneau, Raymond

Marat, Jean Paul 1743-1793 .... LC **10**

Marcel, Gabriel Honore
 1889-1973 .... CLC **15**
 See also CA 102; 45-48; MTCW

Marchbanks, Samuel
 See Davies, (William) Robertson

Marchi, Giacomo
 See Bassani, Giorgio

Margulies, Donald .... CLC **76**

Marie de France c. 12th cent. -.... CMLC **8**

Marie de l'Incarnation 1599-1672.... LC **10**

Mariner, Scott
 See Pohl, Frederik

Marinetti, Filippo Tommaso
 1876-1944 .... TCLC **10**
 See also CA 107; DLB 114

Marivaux, Pierre Carlet de Chamblain de
1688-1763 .... LC 4

Markandaya, Kamala .... CLC 8, 38
See also Taylor, Kamala (Purnaiya)

Markfield, Wallace 1926-.......... CLC 8
See also CA 69-72; CAAS 3; DLB 2, 28

Markham, Edwin 1852-1940 ...... TCLC 47
See also DLB 54

Markham, Robert
See Amis, Kingsley (William)

Marks, J
See Highwater, Jamake (Mamake)

Marks-Highwater, J
See Highwater, Jamake (Mamake)

Markson, David M(errill) 1927- .... CLC 67
See also CA 49-52; CANR 1

Marley, Bob..................... CLC 17
See also Marley, Robert Nesta

Marley, Robert Nesta 1945-1981
See Marley, Bob
See also CA 107; 103

Marlowe, Christopher
1564-1593 ..... LC 22; DA; DC 1; WLC
See also CDBLB Before 1660; DLB 62

Marmontel, Jean-Francois
1723-1799 .... LC 2

Marquand, John P(hillips)
1893-1960 .... CLC 2, 10
See also CA 85-88; DLB 9, 102

Marquez, Gabriel (Jose) Garcia
See Garcia Marquez, Gabriel (Jose)

Marquis, Don(ald Robert Perry)
1878-1937 .... TCLC 7
See also CA 104; DLB 11, 25

Marric, J. J.
See Creasey, John

Marrow, Bernard
See Moore, Brian

Marryat, Frederick 1792-1848 .... NCLC 3
See also DLB 21

Marsden, James
See Creasey, John

Marsh, (Edith) Ngaio
1899-1982 .... CLC 7, 53
See also CA 9-12R; CANR 6; DLB 77;
MTCW

Marshall, Garry 1934-........... CLC 17
See also AAYA 3; CA 111; SATA 60

Marshall, Paule
1929- .... CLC 27, 72; BLC; SSC 3
See also BW 2; CA 77-80; CANR 25;
DLB 33; MTCW

Marsten, Richard
See Hunter, Evan

Martha, Henry
See Harris, Mark

Martial c. 40-c. 104 .... PC 10

Martin, Ken
See Hubbard, L(afayette) Ron(ald)

Martin, Richard
See Creasey, John

Martin, Steve 1945- .... CLC 30
See also CA 97-100; CANR 30; MTCW

Martin, Violet Florence
1862-1915 .... TCLC 51

Martin, Webber
See Silverberg, Robert

Martindale, Patrick Victor
See White, Patrick (Victor Martindale)

Martin du Gard, Roger
1881-1958 .... TCLC 24
See also CA 118; DLB 65

Martineau, Harriet 1802-1876.... NCLC 26
See also DLB 21, 55; YABC 2

Martines, Julia
See O'Faolain, Julia

Martinez, Jacinto Benavente y
See Benavente (y Martinez), Jacinto

Martinez Ruiz, Jose 1873-1967
See Azorin; Ruiz, Jose Martinez
See also CA 93-96; HW

Martinez Sierra, Gregorio
1881-1947 .... TCLC 6
See also CA 115

Martinez Sierra, Maria (de la O'LeJarraga)
1874-1974 .... TCLC 6
See also CA 115

Martinsen, Martin
See Follett, Ken(neth Martin)

Martinson, Harry (Edmund)
1904-1978 .... CLC 14
See also CA 77-80; CANR 34

Marut, Ret
See Traven, B.

Marut, Robert
See Traven, B.

Marvell, Andrew
1621-1678 ..... LC 4; DA; PC 10; WLC
See also CDBLB 1660-1789; DLB 131

Marx, Karl (Heinrich)
1818-1883 .... NCLC 17
See also DLB 129

Masaoka Shiki................... TCLC 18
See also Masaoka Tsunenori

Masaoka Tsunenori 1867-1902
See Masaoka Shiki
See also CA 117

Masefield, John (Edward)
1878-1967 .... CLC 11, 47
See also CA 19-20; 25-28R; CANR 33;
CAP 2; CDBLB 1890-1914; DLB 10, 19;
MTCW; SATA 19

Maso, Carole 19(?)- .... CLC 44

Mason, Bobbie Ann
1940- .... CLC 28, 43, 82; SSC 4
See also AAYA 5; CA 53-56; CANR 11,
31; DLBY 87; MTCW

Mason, Ernst
See Pohl, Frederik

Mason, Lee W.
See Malzberg, Barry N(athaniel)

Mason, Nick 1945- .... CLC 35

Mason, Tally
See Derleth, August (William)

Mass, William
See Gibson, William

Masters, Edgar Lee
1868-1950 ...... TCLC 2, 25; DA; PC 1
See also CA 104; 133; CDALB 1865-1917;
DLB 54; MTCW

Masters, Hilary 1928- .... CLC 48
See also CA 25-28R; CANR 13, 47

Mastrosimone, William 19(?)-...... CLC 36

Mathe, Albert
See Camus, Albert

Matheson, Richard Burton 1926- ... CLC 37
See also CA 97-100; DLB 8, 44

Mathews, Harry 1930-.......... CLC 6, 52
See also CA 21-24R; CAAS 6; CANR 18,
40

Mathews, John Joseph 1894-1979... CLC 84
See also CA 19-20; 142; CANR 45; CAP 2;
NNAL

Mathias, Roland (Glyn) 1915-...... CLC 45
See also CA 97-100; CANR 19, 41; DLB 27

Matsuo Basho 1644-1694........... PC 3

Mattheson, Rodney
See Creasey, John

Matthews, Greg 1949- .... CLC 45
See also CA 135

Matthews, William 1942-.......... CLC 40
See also CA 29-32R; CAAS 18; CANR 12;
DLB 5

Matthias, John (Edward) 1941-...... CLC 9
See also CA 33-36R

Matthiessen, Peter
1927- .... CLC 5, 7, 11, 32, 64
See also AAYA 6; BEST 90:4; CA 9-12R;
CANR 21; DLB 6; MTCW; SATA 27

Maturin, Charles Robert
1780(?)-1824 .... NCLC 6

Matute (Ausejo), Ana Maria
1925- .... CLC 11
See also CA 89-92; MTCW

Maugham, W. S.
See Maugham, W(illiam) Somerset

Maugham, W(illiam) Somerset
1874-1965 ...... CLC 1, 11, 15, 67; DA;
SSC 8; WLC
See also CA 5-8R; 25-28R; CANR 40;
CDBLB 1914-1945; DLB 10, 36, 77, 100;
MTCW; SATA 54

Maugham, William Somerset
See Maugham, W(illiam) Somerset

Maupassant, (Henri Rene Albert) Guy de
1850-1893 .... NCLC 1, 42; DA; SSC 1;
WLC
See also DLB 123

Maurhut, Richard
See Traven, B.

Mauriac, Claude 1914-............ CLC 9
See also CA 89-92; DLB 83

Mauriac, Francois (Charles)
1885-1970 .... CLC 4, 9, 56
See also CA 25-28; CAP 2; DLB 65;
MTCW

Mavor, Osborne Henry 1888-1951
See Bridie, James
See also CA 104

Melanter
See Blackmore, R(ichard) D(oddridge)

Melikow, Loris
See Hofmannsthal, Hugo von

Melmoth, Sebastian
See Wilde, Oscar (Fingal O'Flahertie Wills)

Meltzer, Milton 1915- . . . . **CLC 26**
See also AAYA 8; CA 13-16R; CANR 38;
CLR 13; DLB 61; JRDA; MAICYA;
SAAS 1; SATA 1, 50, 80

Melville, Herman
1819-1891 . . . . **NCLC 3, 12, 29, 45; DA;**
SSC 1, 17; WLC
See also CDALB 1640-1865; DLB 3, 74;
SATA 59

Menander
c. 342B.C.-c. 292B.C. . . . . **CMLC 9; DC 3**

Mencken, H(enry) L(ouis)
1880-1956 . . . . **TCLC 13**
See also CA 105; 125; CDALB 1917-1929;
DLB 11, 29, 63, 137; MTCW

Mercer, David 1928-1980 . . . . **CLC 5**
See also CA 9-12R; 102; CANR 23;
DLB 13; MTCW

Merchant, Paul
See Ellison, Harlan (Jay)

Meredith, George 1828-1909 . . . **TCLC 17, 43**
See also CA 117; CDBLB 1832-1890;
DLB 18, 35, 57

Meredith, William (Morris)
1919- . . . . **CLC 4, 13, 22, 55**
See also CA 9-12R; CAAS 14; CANR 6, 40;
DLB 5

Merezhkovsky, Dmitry Sergeyevich
1865-1941 . . . . **TCLC 29**

Merimee, Prosper
1803-1870 . . . . **NCLC 6; SSC 7**
See also DLB 119

Merkin, Daphne 1954- . . . . **CLC 44**
See also CA 123

Merlin, Arthur
See Blish, James (Benjamin)

Merrill, James (Ingram)
1926- . . . . **CLC 2, 3, 6, 8, 13, 18, 34**
See also CA 13-16R; CANR 10; DLB 5;
DLBY 85; MTCW

Merriman, Alex
See Silverberg, Robert

Merritt, E. B.
See Waddington, Miriam

Merton, Thomas
1915-1968 . . **CLC 1, 3, 11, 34, 83; PC 10**
See also CA 5-8R; 25-28R; CANR 22;
DLB 48; DLBY 81; MTCW

Merwin, W(illiam) S(tanley)
1927- . . . . . . **CLC 1, 2, 3, 5, 8, 13, 18, 45**
See also CA 13-16R; CANR 15; DLB 5;
MTCW

Metcalf, John 1938- . . . . **CLC 37**
See also CA 113; DLB 60

Metcalf, Suzanne
See Baum, L(yman) Frank

Mew, Charlotte (Mary)
1870-1928 . . . . **TCLC 8**
See also CA 105; DLB 19, 135

Mewshaw, Michael 1943- . . . . **CLC 9**
See also CA 53-56; CANR 7, 47; DLBY 80

Meyer, June
See Jordan, June

Meyer, Lynn
See Slavitt, David R(ytman)

Meyer-Meyrink, Gustav 1868-1932
See Meyrink, Gustav
See also CA 117

Meyers, Jeffrey 1939- . . . . **CLC 39**
See also CA 73-76; DLB 111

Meynell, Alice (Christina Gertrude Thompson)
1847-1922 . . . . **TCLC 6**
See also CA 104; DLB 19, 98

Meyrink, Gustav . . . . **TCLC 21**
See also Meyer-Meyrink, Gustav
See also DLB 81

Michaels, Leonard
1933- . . . . **CLC 6, 25; SSC 16**
See also CA 61-64; CANR 21; DLB 130;
MTCW

Michaux, Henri 1899-1984 . . . . . . **CLC 8, 19**
See also CA 85-88; 114

Michelangelo 1475-1564 . . . . **LC 12**

Michelet, Jules 1798-1874 . . . . . . **NCLC 31**

Michener, James A(lbert)
1907(?)- . . . . **CLC 1, 5, 11, 29, 60**
See also AITN 1; BEST 90:1; CA 5-8R;
CANR 21, 45; DLB 6; MTCW

Mickiewicz, Adam 1798-1855 . . . . . **NCLC 3**

Middleton, Christopher 1926- . . . . . . **CLC 13**
See also CA 13-16R; CANR 29; DLB 40

Middleton, Richard (Barham)
1882-1911 . . . . **TCLC 56**

Middleton, Stanley 1919- . . . . **CLC 7, 38**
See also CA 25-28R; CANR 21, 46;
DLB 14

Middleton, Thomas 1580-1627 . . . . **DC 5**
See also DLB 58

Migueis, Jose Rodrigues 1901- . . . . . **CLC 10**

Mikszath, Kalman 1847-1910 . . . . . **TCLC 31**

Miles, Josephine
1911-1985 . . . . **CLC 1, 2, 14, 34, 39**
See also CA 1-4R; 116; CANR 2; DLB 48

Militant
See Sandburg, Carl (August)

Mill, John Stuart 1806-1873 . . . . . **NCLC 11**
See also CDBLB 1832-1890; DLB 55

Millar, Kenneth 1915-1983 . . . . **CLC 14**
See also Macdonald, Ross
See also CA 9-12R; 110; CANR 16; DLB 2;
DLBD 6; DLBY 83; MTCW

Millay, E. Vincent
See Millay, Edna St. Vincent

Millay, Edna St. Vincent
1892-1950 . . . . . . **TCLC 4, 49; DA; PC 6**
See also CA 104; 130; CDALB 1917-1929;
DLB 45; MTCW

Miller, Arthur
1915- . . . . **CLC 1, 2, 6, 10, 15, 26, 47, 78;**
DA; DC 1; WLC
See also AITN 1; CA 1-4R; CABS 3;
CANR 2, 30; CDALB 1941-1968; DLB 7;
MTCW

Miller, Henry (Valentine)
1891-1980 . . . . **CLC 1, 2, 4, 9, 14, 43, 84;**
DA; WLC
See also CA 9-12R; 97-100; CANR 33;
CDALB 1929-1941; DLB 4, 9; DLBY 80;
MTCW

Miller, Jason 1939(?)- . . . . **CLC 2**
See also AITN 1; CA 73-76; DLB 7

Miller, Sue 1943- . . . . **CLC 44**
See also BEST 90:3; CA 139; DLB 143

Miller, Walter M(ichael, Jr.)
1923- . . . . **CLC 4, 30**
See also CA 85-88; DLB 8

Millett, Kate 1934- . . . . **CLC 67**
See also AITN 1; CA 73-76; CANR 32;
MTCW

Millhauser, Steven 1943- . . . . **CLC 21, 54**
See also CA 110; 111; DLB 2

Millin, Sarah Gertrude 1889-1968 . . **CLC 49**
See also CA 102; 93-96

Milne, A(lan) A(lexander)
1882-1956 . . . . **TCLC 6**
See also CA 104; 133; CLR 1, 26; DLB 10,
77, 100; MAICYA; MTCW; YABC 1

Milner, Ron(ald) 1938- . . . . **CLC 56; BLC**
See also AITN 1; BW 1; CA 73-76;
CANR 24; DLB 38; MTCW

Milosz, Czeslaw
1911- . . . **CLC 5, 11, 22, 31, 56, 82; PC 8**
See also CA 81-84; CANR 23; MTCW

Milton, John 1608-1674 . . . **LC 9; DA; WLC**
See also CDBLB 1660-1789; DLB 131

Min, Anchee 1957- . . . . **CLC 86**

Minehaha, Cornelius
See Wedekind, (Benjamin) Frank(lin)

Miner, Valerie 1947- . . . . **CLC 40**
See also CA 97-100

Minimo, Duca
See D'Annunzio, Gabriele

Minot, Susan 1956- . . . . **CLC 44**
See also CA 134

Minus, Ed 1938- . . . . **CLC 39**

Miranda, Javier
See Bioy Casares, Adolfo

Mirbeau, Octave 1848-1917 . . . . . . **TCLC 55**
See also DLB 123

Miro (Ferrer), Gabriel (Francisco Victor)
1879-1930 . . . . **TCLC 5**
See also CA 104

Mishima, Yukio
. . . . . . **CLC 2, 4, 6, 9, 27; DC 1; SSC 4**
See also Hiraoka, Kimitake

Mistral, Frederic 1830-1914 . . . . . . **TCLC 51**
See also CA 122

Mistral, Gabriela . . . . **TCLC 2; HLC**
See also Godoy Alcayaga, Lucila

Mistry, Rohinton 1952- . . . . **CLC 71**
See also CA 141

Mitchell, Clyde
See Ellison, Harlan (Jay); Silverberg, Robert

Mitchell, James Leslie 1901-1935
See Gibbon, Lewis Grassic
See also CA 104; DLB 15

Mitchell, Joni 1943-............. CLC 12
See also CA 112

Mitchell, Margaret (Munnerlyn)
1900-1949 .... TCLC 11
See also CA 109; 125; DLB 9; MTCW

Mitchell, Peggy
See Mitchell, Margaret (Munnerlyn)

Mitchell, S(ilas) Weir 1829-1914 .. TCLC 36

Mitchell, W(illiam) O(rmond)
1914- .... CLC 25
See also CA 77-80; CANR 15, 43; DLB 88

Mitford, Mary Russell 1787-1855.. NCLC 4
See also DLB 110, 116

Mitford, Nancy 1904-1973........ CLC 44
See also CA 9-12R

Miyamoto, Yuriko 1899-1951 ..... TCLC 37

Mo, Timothy (Peter) 1950(?)-...... CLC 46
See also CA 117; MTCW

Modarressi, Taghi (M.) 1931-...... CLC 44
See also CA 121; 134

Modiano, Patrick (Jean) 1945- .... CLC 18
See also CA 85-88; CANR 17, 40; DLB 83

Moerck, Paal
See Roelvaag, O(le) E(dvart)

Mofolo, Thomas (Mokopu)
1875(?)-1948 .... TCLC 22; BLC
See also CA 121

Mohr, Nicholasa 1935-...... CLC 12; HLC
See also AAYA 8; CA 49-52; CANR 1, 32;
CLR 22; DLB 145; HW; JRDA; SAAS 8;
SATA 8

Mojtabai, A(nn) G(race)
1938- .... CLC 5, 9, 15, 29
See also CA 85-88

Moliere 1622-1673 .... LC 28; DA; WLC

Molin, Charles
See Mayne, William (James Carter)

Molnar, Ferenc 1878-1952....... TCLC 20
See also CA 109

Momaday, N(avarre) Scott
1934- .... CLC 2, 19, 85; DA
See also AAYA 11; CA 25-28R; CANR 14,
34; DLB 143; MTCW; NNAL; SATA 30,
48

Monette, Paul 1945-............. CLC 82
See also CA 139

Monroe, Harriet 1860-1936....... TCLC 12
See also CA 109; DLB 54, 91

Monroe, Lyle
See Heinlein, Robert A(nson)

Montagu, Elizabeth 1917-........ NCLC 7
See also CA 9-12R

Montagu, Mary (Pierrepont) Wortley
1689-1762 .... LC 9
See also DLB 95, 101

Montagu, W. H.
See Coleridge, Samuel Taylor

Montague, John (Patrick)
1929- .... CLC 13, 46
See also CA 9-12R; CANR 9; DLB 40;
MTCW

Montaigne, Michel (Eyquem) de
1533-1592 .... LC 8; DA; WLC

Montale, Eugenio 1896-1981... CLC 7, 9, 18
See also CA 17-20R; 104; CANR 30;
DLB 114; MTCW

Montesquieu, Charles-Louis de Secondat
1689-1755 .... LC 7

Montgomery, (Robert) Bruce 1921-1978
See Crispin, Edmund
See also CA 104

Montgomery, L(ucy) M(aud)
1874-1942 .... TCLC 51
See also AAYA 12; CA 108; 137; CLR 8;
DLB 92; JRDA; MAICYA; YABC 1

Montgomery, Marion H., Jr. 1925-.. CLC 7
See also AITN 1; CA 1-4R; CANR 3;
DLB 6

Montgomery, Max
See Davenport, Guy (Mattison, Jr.)

Montherlant, Henry (Milon) de
1896-1972 .... CLC 8, 19
See also CA 85-88; 37-40R; DLB 72;
MTCW

Monty Python
See Chapman, Graham; Cleese, John
(Marwood); Gilliam, Terry (Vance); Idle,
Eric; Jones, Terence Graham Parry; Palin,
Michael (Edward)
See also AAYA 7

Moodie, Susanna (Strickland)
1803-1885 .... NCLC 14
See also DLB 99

Mooney, Edward 1951-
See Mooney, Ted
See also CA 130

Mooney, Ted .... CLC 25
See also Mooney, Edward

Moorcock, Michael (John)
1939- .... CLC 5, 27, 58
See also CA 45-48; CAAS 5; CANR 2, 17,
38; DLB 14; MTCW

Moore, Brian
1921- .... CLC 1, 3, 5, 7, 8, 19, 32
See also CA 1-4R; CANR 1, 25, 42; MTCW

Moore, Edward
See Muir, Edwin

Moore, George Augustus
1852-1933 .... TCLC 7
See also CA 104; DLB 10, 18, 57, 135

Moore, Lorrie .... CLC 39, 45, 68
See also Moore, Marie Lorena

Moore, Marianne (Craig)
1887-1972 .... CLC 1, 2, 4, 8, 10, 13, 19,
47; DA; PC 4
See also CA 1-4R; 33-36R; CANR 3;
CDALB 1929-1941; DLB 45; DLBD 7;
MTCW; SATA 20

Moore, Marie Lorena 1957-
See Moore, Lorrie
See also CA 116; CANR 39

Moore, Thomas 1779-1852........ NCLC 6
See also DLB 96, 144

Morand, Paul 1888-1976 .... CLC 41
See also CA 69-72; DLB 65

Morante, Elsa 1918-1985........ CLC 8, 47
See also CA 85-88; 117; CANR 35; MTCW

Moravia, Alberto ...... CLC 2, 7, 11, 27, 46
See also Pincherle, Alberto

More, Hannah 1745-1833 .... NCLC 27
See also DLB 107, 109, 116

More, Henry 1614-1687............. LC 9
See also DLB 126

More, Sir Thomas 1478-1535 .... LC 10

Moreas, Jean................... TCLC 18
See also Papadiamantopoulos, Johannes

Morgan, Berry 1919-.............. CLC 6
See also CA 49-52; DLB 6

Morgan, Claire
See Highsmith, (Mary) Patricia

Morgan, Edwin (George) 1920-..... CLC 31
See also CA 5-8R; CANR 3, 43; DLB 27

Morgan, (George) Frederick
1922- .... CLC 23
See also CA 17-20R; CANR 21

Morgan, Harriet
See Mencken, H(enry) L(ouis)

Morgan, Jane
See Cooper, James Fenimore

Morgan, Janet 1945- .... CLC 39
See also CA 65-68

Morgan, Lady 1776(?)-1859...... NCLC 29
See also DLB 116

Morgan, Robin 1941-.............. CLC 2
See also CA 69-72; CANR 29; MTCW;
SATA 80

Morgan, Scott
See Kuttner, Henry

Morgan, Seth 1949(?)-1990 .... CLC 65
See also CA 132

Morgenstern, Christian
1871-1914 .... TCLC 8
See also CA 105

Morgenstern, S.
See Goldman, William (W.)

Moricz, Zsigmond 1879-1942 ..... TCLC 33

Morike, Eduard (Friedrich)
1804-1875 .... NCLC 10
See also DLB 133

Mori Ogai .... TCLC 14
See also Mori Rintaro

Mori Rintaro 1862-1922
See Mori Ogai
See also CA 110

Moritz, Karl Philipp 1756-1793 ...... LC 2
See also DLB 94

Morland, Peter Henry
See Faust, Frederick (Schiller)

Morren, Theophil
See Hofmannsthal, Hugo von

Morris, Bill 1952-............... CLC 76

Morris, Julian
See West, Morris L(anglo)

Morris, Steveland Judkins 1950(?)-
See Wonder, Stevie
See also CA 111

Morris, William 1834-1896 .... NCLC 4
See also CDBLB 1832-1890; DLB 18, 35, 57

Morris, Wright 1910-... **CLC 1, 3, 7, 18, 37**
See also CA 9-12R; CANR 21; DLB 2;
DLBY 81; MTCW

Morrison, Chloe Anthony Wofford
See Morrison, Toni

Morrison, James Douglas 1943-1971
See Morrison, Jim
See also CA 73-76; CANR 40

Morrison, Jim .... **CLC 17**
See also Morrison, James Douglas

Morrison, Toni
1931- .... **CLC 4, 10, 22, 55, 81, 87;**
BLC; DA
See also AAYA 1; BW 2; CA 29-32R;
CANR 27, 42; CDALB 1968-1988;
DLB 6, 33, 143; DLBY 81; MTCW;
SATA 57

Morrison, Van 1945- .... **CLC 21**
See also CA 116

Mortimer, John (Clifford)
1923- .... **CLC 28, 43**
See also CA 13-16R; CANR 21;
CDBLB 1960 to Present; DLB 13;
MTCW

Mortimer, Penelope (Ruth) 1918-.... **CLC 5**
See also CA 57-60; CANR 45

Morton, Anthony
See Creasey, John

Mosher, Howard Frank 1943-...... **CLC 62**
See also CA 139

Mosley, Nicholas 1923-........ **CLC 43, 70**
See also CA 69-72; CANR 41; DLB 14

Moss, Howard
1922-1987 .... **CLC 7, 14, 45, 50**
See also CA 1-4R; 123; CANR 1, 44;
DLB 5

Mossgiel, Rab
See Burns, Robert

Motion, Andrew 1952-............. **CLC 47**
See also DLB 40

Motley, Willard (Francis)
1909-1965 .... **CLC 18**
See also BW 1; CA 117; 106; DLB 76, 143

Motoori, Norinaga 1730-1801 .... **NCLC 45**

Mott, Michael (Charles Alston)
1930-.................... **CLC 15, 34**
See also CA 5-8R; CAAS 7; CANR 7, 29

Mowat, Farley (McGill) 1921- ..... **CLC 26**
See also AAYA 1; CA 1-4R; CANR 4, 24,
42; CLR 20; DLB 68; JRDA; MAICYA;
MTCW; SATA 3, 55

Moyers, Bill 1934-............... **CLC 74**
See also AITN 2; CA 61-64; CANR 31

Mphahlele, Es'kia
See Mphahlele, Ezekiel
See also DLB 125

Mphahlele, Ezekiel 1919-..... **CLC 25; BLC**
See also Mphahlele, Es'kia
See also BW 2; CA 81-84; CANR 26

Mqhayi, S(amuel) E(dward) K(rune Loliwe)
1875-1945 .... **TCLC 25; BLC**

Mr. Martin
See Burroughs, William S(eward)

Mrozek, Slawomir 1930-........ **CLC 3, 13**
See also CA 13-16R; CAAS 10; CANR 29;
MTCW

Mrs. Belloc-Lowndes
See Lowndes, Marie Adelaide (Belloc)

Mtwa, Percy (?)-................ **CLC 47**

Mueller, Lisel 1924-.......... **CLC 13, 51**
See also CA 93-96; DLB 105

Muir, Edwin 1887-1959 .... **TCLC 2**
See also CA 104; DLB 20, 100

Muir, John 1838-1914 .... **TCLC 28**

Mujica Lainez, Manuel
1910-1984 .... **CLC 31**
See also Lainez, Manuel Mujica
See also CA 81-84; 112; CANR 32; HW

Mukherjee, Bharati 1940-........ **CLC 53**
See also BEST 89:2; CA 107; CANR 45;
DLB 60; MTCW

Muldoon, Paul 1951-.......... **CLC 32, 72**
See also CA 113; 129; DLB 40

Mulisch, Harry 1927-............. **CLC 42**
See also CA 9-12R; CANR 6, 26

Mull, Martin 1943-............. **CLC 17**
See also CA 105

Mulock, Dinah Maria
See Craik, Dinah Maria (Mulock)

Munford, Robert 1737(?)-1783 .... **LC 5**
See also DLB 31

Mungo, Raymond 1946-........... **CLC 72**
See also CA 49-52; CANR 2

Munro, Alice
1931- .... **CLC 6, 10, 19, 50; SSC 3**
See also AITN 2; CA 33-36R; CANR 33;
DLB 53; MTCW; SATA 29

Munro, H(ector) H(ugh) 1870-1916
See Saki
See also CA 104; 130; CDBLB 1890-1914;
DA; DLB 34; MTCW; WLC

Murasaki, Lady................. **CMLC 1**

Murdoch, (Jean) Iris
1919- ...... **CLC 1, 2, 3, 4, 6, 8, 11, 15,**
22, 31, 51
See also CA 13-16R; CANR 8, 43;
CDBLB 1960 to Present; DLB 14;
MTCW

Murnau, Friedrich Wilhelm
See Plumpe, Friedrich Wilhelm

Murphy, Richard 1927-........... **CLC 41**
See also CA 29-32R; DLB 40

Murphy, Sylvia 1937-............. **CLC 34**
See also CA 121

Murphy, Thomas (Bernard) 1935-... **CLC 51**
See also CA 101

Murray, Albert L. 1916- .... **CLC 73**
See also BW 2; CA 49-52; CANR 26;
DLB 38

Murray, Les(lie) A(llan) 1938- ..... **CLC 40**
See also CA 21-24R; CANR 11, 27

Murry, J. Middleton
See Murry, John Middleton

Murry, John Middleton
1889-1957 .... **TCLC 16**
See also CA 118

Musgrave, Susan 1951- .... **CLC 13, 54**
See also CA 69-72; CANR 45

Musil, Robert (Edler von)
1880-1942 .... **TCLC 12; SSC 18**
See also CA 109; DLB 81, 124

Musset, (Louis Charles) Alfred de
1810-1857 .... **NCLC 7**

My Brother's Brother
See Chekhov, Anton (Pavlovich)

Myers, Walter Dean 1937- ... **CLC 35; BLC**
See also AAYA 4; BW 2; CA 33-36R;
CANR 20, 42; CLR 4, 16, 35; DLB 33;
JRDA; MAICYA; SAAS 2; SATA 27, 41,
71

Myers, Walter M.
See Myers, Walter Dean

Myles, Symon
See Follett, Ken(neth Martin)

Nabokov, Vladimir (Vladimirovich)
1899-1977 ..... **CLC 1, 2, 3, 6, 8, 11, 15,**
23, 44, 46, 64; DA; SSC 11; WLC
See also CA 5-8R; 69-72; CANR 20;
CDALB 1941-1968; DLB 2; DLBD 3;
DLBY 80, 91; MTCW

Nagai Kafu..................... **TCLC 51**
See also Nagai Sokichi

Nagai Sokichi 1879-1959
See Nagai Kafu
See also CA 117

Nagy, Laszlo 1925-1978........... **CLC 7**
See also CA 129; 112

Naipaul, Shiva(dhar Srinivasa)
1945-1985 .... **CLC 32, 39**
See also CA 110; 112; 116; CANR 33;
DLBY 85; MTCW

Naipaul, V(idiadhar) S(urajprasad)
1932-.......... **CLC 4, 7, 9, 13, 18, 37**
See also CA 1-4R; CANR 1, 33;
CDBLB 1960 to Present; DLB 125;
DLBY 85; MTCW

Nakos, Lilika 1899(?)-............ **CLC 29**

Narayan, R(asipuram) K(rishnaswami)
1906-................... **CLC 7, 28, 47**
See also CA 81-84; CANR 33; MTCW;
SATA 62

Nash, (Frediric) Ogden 1902-1971 .. **CLC 23**
See also CA 13-14; 29-32R; CANR 34;
CAP 1; DLB 11; MAICYA; MTCW;
SATA 2, 46

Nathan, Daniel
See Dannay, Frederic

Nathan, George Jean 1882-1958 ... **TCLC 18**
See also Hatteras, Owen
See also CA 114; DLB 137

Natsume, Kinnosuke 1867-1916
See Natsume, Soseki
See also CA 104

Natsume, Soseki .... **TCLC 2, 10**
See also Natsume, Kinnosuke

Natti, (Mary) Lee 1919-
See Kingman, Lee
See also CA 5-8R; CANR 2

Nye, Robert 1939- .... CLC **13, 42**
See also CA 33-36R; CANR 29; DLB 14;
MTCW; SATA 6

Nyro, Laura 1947- .... CLC **17**

Oates, Joyce Carol
1938- ...... CLC **1, 2, 3, 6, 9, 11, 15, 19,**
33, 52; DA; SSC 6; WLC
See also AITN 1; BEST 89:2; CA 5-8R;
CANR 25, 45; CDALB 1968-1988;
DLB 2, 5, 130; DLBY 81; MTCW

O'Brien, Darcy 1939- .... CLC **11**
See also CA 21-24R; CANR 8

O'Brien, E. G.
See Clarke, Arthur C(harles)

O'Brien, Edna
1936- ... CLC **3, 5, 8, 13, 36, 65; SSC 10**
See also CA 1-4R; CANR 6, 41;
CDBLB 1960 to Present; DLB 14;
MTCW

O'Brien, Fitz-James 1828-1862... NCLC **21**
See also DLB 74

O'Brien, Flann .... CLC **1, 4, 5, 7, 10, 47**
See also O Nuallain, Brian

O'Brien, Richard 1942- .... CLC **17**
See also CA 124

O'Brien, Tim 1946-......... CLC **7, 19, 40**
See also CA 85-88; CANR 40; DLBD 9;
DLBY 80

Obstfelder, Sigbjoern 1866-1900... TCLC **23**
See also CA 123

O'Casey, Sean
1880-1964 .... CLC **1, 5, 9, 11, 15**
See also CA 89-92; CDBLB 1914-1945;
DLB 10; MTCW

O'Cathasaigh, Sean
See O'Casey, Sean

Ochs, Phil 1940-1976............ CLC **17**
See also CA 65-68

O'Connor, Edwin (Greene)
1918-1968 .... CLC **14**
See also CA 93-96; 25-28R

O'Connor, (Mary) Flannery
1925-1964 .... CLC **1, 2, 3, 6, 10, 13, 15,**
21, 66; DA; SSC 1; WLC
See also AAYA 7; CA 1-4R; CANR 3, 41;
CDALB 1941-1968; DLB 2; DLBD 12;
DLBY 80; MTCW

O'Connor, Frank .... CLC **23; SSC 5**
See also O'Donovan, Michael John

O'Dell, Scott 1898-1989........... CLC **30**
See also AAYA 3; CA 61-64; 129;
CANR 12, 30; CLR 1, 16; DLB 52;
JRDA; MAICYA; SATA 12, 60

Odets, Clifford 1906-1963 ...... CLC **2, 28**
See also CA 85-88; DLB 7, 26; MTCW

O'Doherty, Brian 1934- .... CLC **76**
See also CA 105

O'Donnell, K. M.
See Malzberg, Barry N(athaniel)

O'Donnell, Lawrence
See Kuttner, Henry

O'Donovan, Michael John
1903-1966 .... CLC **14**
See also O'Connor, Frank
See also CA 93-96

Oe, Kenzaburo 1935-....... CLC **10, 36, 86**
See also CA 97-100; CANR 36; MTCW

O'Faolain, Julia 1932-....... CLC **6, 19, 47**
See also CA 81-84; CAAS 2; CANR 12;
DLB 14; MTCW

O'Faolain, Sean
1900-1991 .... CLC **1, 7, 14, 32, 70;**
SSC 13
See also CA 61-64; 134; CANR 12;
DLB 15; MTCW

O'Flaherty, Liam
1896-1984 .... CLC **5, 34; SSC 6**
See also CA 101; 113; CANR 35; DLB 36;
DLBY 84; MTCW

Ogilvy, Gavin
See Barrie, J(ames) M(atthew)

O'Grady, Standish James
1846-1928 .... TCLC **5**
See also CA 104

O'Grady, Timothy 1951- .... CLC **59**
See also CA 138

O'Hara, Frank
1926-1966 .... CLC **2, 5, 13, 78**
See also CA 9-12R; 25-28R; CANR 33;
DLB 5, 16; MTCW

O'Hara, John (Henry)
1905-1970 .... CLC **1, 2, 3, 6, 11, 42;**
SSC 15
See also CA 5-8R; 25-28R; CANR 31;
CDALB 1929-1941; DLB 9, 86; DLBD 2;
MTCW

O Hehir, Diana 1922- .... CLC **41**
See also CA 93-96

Okigbo, Christopher (Ifenayichukwu)
1932-1967 ..... CLC **25, 84; BLC; PC 7**
See also BW 1; CA 77-80; DLB 125;
MTCW

Okri, Ben 1959- .... CLC **87**
See also BW 2; CA 130; 138

Olds, Sharon 1942-........ CLC **32, 39, 85**
See also CA 101; CANR 18, 41; DLB 120

Oldstyle, Jonathan
See Irving, Washington

Olesha, Yuri (Karlovich)
1899-1960 .... CLC **8**
See also CA 85-88

Oliphant, Laurence
1829(?)-1888 .... NCLC **47**
See also DLB 18

Oliphant, Margaret (Oliphant Wilson)
1828-1897 .... NCLC **11**
See also DLB 18

Oliver, Mary 1935-........... CLC **19, 34**
See also CA 21-24R; CANR 9, 43; DLB 5

Olivier, Laurence (Kerr)
1907-1989 .... CLC **20**
See also CA 111; 129

Olsen, Tillie
1913- .... CLC **4, 13; DA; SSC 11**
See also CA 1-4R; CANR 1, 43; DLB 28;
DLBY 80; MTCW

Olson, Charles (John)
1910-1970 ..... CLC **1, 2, 5, 6, 9, 11, 29**
See also CA 13-16; 25-28R; CABS 2;
CANR 35; CAP 1; DLB 5, 16; MTCW

Olson, Toby 1937- .... CLC **28**
See also CA 65-68; CANR 9, 31

Olyesha, Yuri
See Olesha, Yuri (Karlovich)

Ondaatje, (Philip) Michael
1943- .... CLC **14, 29, 51, 76**
See also CA 77-80; CANR 42; DLB 60

Oneal, Elizabeth 1934-
See Oneal, Zibby
See also CA 106; CANR 28; MAICYA;
SATA 30

Oneal, Zibby .... CLC **30**
See also Oneal, Elizabeth
See also AAYA 5; CLR 13; JRDA

O'Neill, Eugene (Gladstone)
1888-1953 ...... TCLC **1, 6, 27, 49; DA;**
WLC
See also AITN 1; CA 110; 132;
CDALB 1929-1941; DLB 7; MTCW

Onetti, Juan Carlos 1909-1994 ... CLC **7, 10**
See also CA 85-88; 145; CANR 32;
DLB 113; HW; MTCW

O Nuallain, Brian 1911-1966
See O'Brien, Flann
See also CA 21-22; 25-28R; CAP 2

Oppen, George 1908-1984 .... CLC **7, 13, 34**
See also CA 13-16R; 113; CANR 8; DLB 5

Oppenheim, E(dward) Phillips
1866-1946 .... TCLC **45**
See also CA 111; DLB 70

Orlovitz, Gil 1918-1973 .... CLC **22**
See also CA 77-80; 45-48; DLB 2, 5

Orris
See Ingelow, Jean

Ortega y Gasset, Jose
1883-1955 .... TCLC **9; HLC**
See also CA 106; 130; HW; MTCW

Ortiz, Simon J(oseph) 1941-....... CLC **45**
See also CA 134; DLB 120; NNAL

Orton, Joe .... CLC **4, 13, 43; DC 3**
See also Orton, John Kingsley
See also CDBLB 1960 to Present; DLB 13

Orton, John Kingsley 1933-1967
See Orton, Joe
See also CA 85-88; CANR 35; MTCW

Orwell, George
.... TCLC **2, 6, 15, 31, 51; WLC**
See also Blair, Eric (Arthur)
See also CDBLB 1945-1960; DLB 15, 98

Osborne, David
See Silverberg, Robert

Osborne, George
See Silverberg, Robert

Osborne, John (James)
1929- .... CLC **1, 2, 5, 11, 45; DA; WLC**
See also CA 13-16R; CANR 21;
CDBLB 1945-1960; DLB 13; MTCW

Osborne, Lawrence 1958- .... CLC **50**

Oshima, Nagisa 1932- .... CLC **20**
See also CA 116; 121

Oskison, John Milton
1874-1947 .... TCLC **35**
See also CA 144; NNAL

Ossoli, Sarah Margaret (Fuller marchesa d')
1810-1850
See Fuller, Margaret
See also SATA 25

Ostrovsky, Alexander
1823-1886 . . . . **NCLC 30**

Otero, Blas de 1916-1979 . . . . **CLC 11**
See also CA 89-92; DLB 134

Otto, Whitney 1955- . . . . **CLC 70**
See also CA 140

Ouida . . . . **TCLC 43**
See also De La Ramee, (Marie) Louise
See also DLB 18

Ousmane, Sembene 1923- . . . . **CLC 66; BLC**
See also BW 1; CA 117; 125; MTCW

Ovid 43B.C.-18(?) . . . . **CMLC 7; PC 2**

Owen, Hugh
See Faust, Frederick (Schiller)

Owen, Wilfred (Edward Salter)
1893-1918 . . . . . . **TCLC 5, 27; DA; WLC**
See also CA 104; 141; CDBLB 1914-1945;
DLB 20

Owens, Rochelle 1936- . . . . **CLC 8**
See also CA 17-20R; CAAS 2; CANR 39

Oz, Amos 1939- . . . **CLC 5, 8, 11, 27, 33, 54**
See also CA 53-56; CANR 27, 47; MTCW

Ozick, Cynthia
1928- . . . . **CLC 3, 7, 28, 62; SSC 15**
See also BEST 90:1; CA 17-20R; CANR 23;
DLB 28; DLBY 82; MTCW

Ozu, Yasujiro 1903-1963 . . . . **CLC 16**
See also CA 112

Pacheco, C.
See Pessoa, Fernando (Antonio Nogueira)

Pa Chin . . . . **CLC 18**
See also Li Fei-kan

Pack, Robert 1929- . . . . **CLC 13**
See also CA 1-4R; CANR 3, 44; DLB 5

Padgett, Lewis
See Kuttner, Henry

Padilla (Lorenzo), Heberto 1932- . . . **CLC 38**
See also AITN 1; CA 123; 131; HW

Page, Jimmy 1944- . . . . **CLC 12**

Page, Louise 1955- . . . . **CLC 40**
See also CA 140

Page, P(atricia) K(athleen)
1916- . . . . **CLC 7, 18**
See also CA 53-56; CANR 4, 22; DLB 68;
MTCW

Paget, Violet 1856-1935
See Lee, Vernon
See also CA 104

Paget-Lowe, Henry
See Lovecraft, H(oward) P(hillips)

Paglia, Camille (Anna) 1947- . . . . **CLC 68**
See also CA 140

Paige, Richard
See Koontz, Dean R(ay)

Pakenham, Antonia
See Fraser, (Lady) Antonia (Pakenham)

Palamas, Kostes 1859-1943 . . . . **TCLC 5**
See also CA 105

Palazzeschi, Aldo 1885-1974 . . . . **CLC 11**
See also CA 89-92; 53-56; DLB 114

Paley, Grace 1922- . . . . **CLC 4, 6, 37; SSC 8**
See also CA 25-28R; CANR 13, 46;
DLB 28; MTCW

Palin, Michael (Edward) 1943- . . . . . **CLC 21**
See also Monty Python
See also CA 107; CANR 35; SATA 67

Palliser, Charles 1947- . . . . **CLC 65**
See also CA 136

Palma, Ricardo 1833-1919 . . . . **TCLC 29**

Pancake, Breece Dexter 1952-1979
See Pancake, Breece D'J
See also CA 123; 109

Pancake, Breece D'J . . . . **CLC 29**
See also Pancake, Breece Dexter
See also DLB 130

Panko, Rudy
See Gogol, Nikolai (Vasilyevich)

Papadiamantis, Alexandros
1851-1911 . . . . **TCLC 29**

Papadiamantopoulos, Johannes 1856-1910
See Moreas, Jean
See also CA 117

Papini, Giovanni 1881-1956 . . . . . . **TCLC 22**
See also CA 121

Paracelsus 1493-1541 . . . . **LC 14**

Parasol, Peter
See Stevens, Wallace

Parfenie, Maria
See Codrescu, Andrei

Parini, Jay (Lee) 1948- . . . . **CLC 54**
See also CA 97-100; CAAS 16; CANR 32

Park, Jordan
See Kornbluth, C(yril) M.; Pohl, Frederik

Parker, Bert
See Ellison, Harlan (Jay)

Parker, Dorothy (Rothschild)
1893-1967 . . . . **CLC 15, 68; SSC 2**
See also CA 19-20; 25-28R; CAP 2;
DLB 11, 45, 86; MTCW

Parker, Robert B(rown) 1932- . . . . . . **CLC 27**
See also BEST 89:4; CA 49-52; CANR 1,
26; MTCW

Parkin, Frank 1940- . . . . **CLC 43**

Parkman, Francis, Jr.
1823-1893 . . . . **NCLC 12**
See also DLB 1, 30

Parks, Gordon (Alexander Buchanan)
1912- . . . . **CLC 1, 16; BLC**
See also AITN 2; BW 2; CA 41-44R;
CANR 26; DLB 33; SATA 8

Parnell, Thomas 1679-1718 . . . . **LC 3**
See also DLB 94

Parra, Nicanor 1914- . . . . **CLC 2; HLC**
See also CA 85-88; CANR 32; HW; MTCW

Parrish, Mary Frances
See Fisher, M(ary) F(rances) K(ennedy)

Parson
See Coleridge, Samuel Taylor

Parson Lot
See Kingsley, Charles

Partridge, Anthony
See Oppenheim, E(dward) Phillips

Pascoli, Giovanni 1855-1912 . . . . . . **TCLC 45**

Pasolini, Pier Paolo
1922-1975 . . . . **CLC 20, 37**
See also CA 93-96; 61-64; DLB 128;
MTCW

Pasquini
See Silone, Ignazio

Pastan, Linda (Olenik) 1932- . . . . . . **CLC 27**
See also CA 61-64; CANR 18, 40; DLB 5

Pasternak, Boris (Leonidovich)
1890-1960 . . . . . . **CLC 7, 10, 18, 63; DA;
PC 6; WLC**
See also CA 127; 116; MTCW

Patchen, Kenneth 1911-1972 . . . **CLC 1, 2, 18**
See also CA 1-4R; 33-36R; CANR 3, 35;
DLB 16, 48; MTCW

Pater, Walter (Horatio)
1839-1894 . . . . **NCLC 7**
See also CDBLB 1832-1890; DLB 57

Paterson, A(ndrew) B(arton)
1864-1941 . . . . **TCLC 32**

Paterson, Katherine (Womeldorf)
1932- . . . . **CLC 12, 30**
See also AAYA 1; CA 21-24R; CANR 28;
CLR 7; DLB 52; JRDA; MAICYA;
MTCW; SATA 13, 53

Patmore, Coventry Kersey Dighton
1823-1896 . . . . **NCLC 9**
See also DLB 35, 98

Paton, Alan (Stewart)
1903-1988 . . . . . . **CLC 4, 10, 25, 55; DA;
WLC**
See also CA 13-16; 125; CANR 22; CAP 1;
MTCW; SATA 11; SATA-Obit 56

Paton Walsh, Gillian 1937-
See Walsh, Jill Paton
See also CANR 38; JRDA; MAICYA;
SAAS 3; SATA 4, 72

Paulding, James Kirke 1778-1860 . . **NCLC 2**
See also DLB 3, 59, 74

Paulin, Thomas Neilson 1949-
See Paulin, Tom
See also CA 123; 128

Paulin, Tom . . . . **CLC 37**
See also Paulin, Thomas Neilson
See also DLB 40

Paustovsky, Konstantin (Georgievich)
1892-1968 . . . . **CLC 40**
See also CA 93-96; 25-28R

Pavese, Cesare 1908-1950 . . . . **TCLC 3**
See also CA 104; DLB 128

Pavic, Milorad 1929- . . . . **CLC 60**
See also CA 136

Payne, Alan
See Jakes, John (William)

Paz, Gil
See Lugones, Leopoldo

Paz, Octavio
1914- . . . . **CLC 3, 4, 6, 10, 19, 51, 65;
DA; HLC; PC 1; WLC**
See also CA 73-76; CANR 32; DLBY 90;
HW; MTCW

Peacock, Molly 1947-............. **CLC 60**
See also CA 103; DLB 120

Peacock, Thomas Love
1785-1866 .... **NCLC 22**
See also DLB 96, 116

Peake, Mervyn 1911-1968 ...... **CLC 7, 54**
See also CA 5-8R; 25-28R; CANR 3;
DLB 15; MTCW; SATA 23

Pearce, Philippa .... **CLC 21**
See also Christie, (Ann) Philippa
See also CLR 9; MAICYA; SATA 1, 67

Pearl, Eric
See Elman, Richard

Pearson, T(homas) R(eid) 1956- .... **CLC 39**
See also CA 120; 130

Peck, Dale 1968(?)- .... **CLC 81**

Peck, John 1941- .... **CLC 3**
See also CA 49-52; CANR 3

Peck, Richard (Wayne) 1934- ...... **CLC 21**
See also AAYA 1; CA 85-88; CANR 19,
38; CLR 15; JRDA; MAICYA; SAAS 2;
SATA 18, 55

Peck, Robert Newton 1928-.... **CLC 17; DA**
See also AAYA 3; CA 81-84; CANR 31;
JRDA; MAICYA; SAAS 1; SATA 21, 62

Peckinpah, (David) Sam(uel)
1925-1984 .... **CLC 20**
See also CA 109; 114

Pedersen, Knut 1859-1952
See Hamsun, Knut
See also CA 104; 119; MTCW

Peeslake, Gaffer
See Durrell, Lawrence (George)

Peguy, Charles Pierre
1873-1914 .... **TCLC 10**
See also CA 107

Pena, Ramon del Valle y
See Valle-Inclan, Ramon (Maria) del

Pendennis, Arthur Esquir
See Thackeray, William Makepeace

Penn, William 1644-1718 .... **LC 25**
See also DLB 24

Pepys, Samuel
1633-1703 .... **LC 11; DA; WLC**
See also CDBLB 1660-1789; DLB 101

Percy, Walker
1916-1990 .... **CLC 2, 3, 6, 8, 14, 18, 47,**
65
See also CA 1-4R; 131; CANR 1, 23;
DLB 2; DLBY 80, 90; MTCW

Perec, Georges 1936-1982 .... **CLC 56**
See also CA 141; DLB 83

Pereda (y Sanchez de Porrua), Jose Maria de
1833-1906 .... **TCLC 16**
See also CA 117

Pereda y Porrua, Jose Maria de
See Pereda (y Sanchez de Porrua), Jose
Maria de

Peregoy, George Weems
See Mencken, H(enry) L(ouis)

Perelman, S(idney) J(oseph)
1904-1979 ... **CLC 3, 5, 9, 15, 23, 44, 49**
See also AITN 1, 2; CA 73-76; 89-92;
CANR 18; DLB 11, 44; MTCW

Peret, Benjamin 1899-1959 .... **TCLC 20**
See also CA 117

Peretz, Isaac Loeb 1851(?)-1915... **TCLC 16**
See also CA 109

Peretz, Yitzkhok Leibush
See Peretz, Isaac Loeb

Perez Galdos, Benito 1843-1920 ... **TCLC 27**
See also CA 125; HW

Perrault, Charles 1628-1703 .... **LC 2**
See also MAICYA; SATA 25

Perry, Brighton
See Sherwood, Robert E(mmet)

Perse, St.-John .... **CLC 4, 11, 46**
See also Leger, (Marie-Rene Auguste) Alexis
Saint-Leger

Peseenz, Tulio F.
See Lopez y Fuentes, Gregorio

Pesetsky, Bette 1932-............. **CLC 28**
See also CA 133; DLB 130

Peshkov, Alexei Maximovich 1868-1936
See Gorky, Maxim
See also CA 105; 141; DA

Pessoa, Fernando (Antonio Nogueira)
1888-1935 .... **TCLC 27; HLC**
See also CA 125

Peterkin, Julia Mood 1880-1961.... **CLC 31**
See also CA 102; DLB 9

Peters, Joan K. 1945-............. **CLC 39**

Peters, Robert L(ouis) 1924-........ **CLC 7**
See also CA 13-16R; CAAS 8; DLB 105

Petofi, Sandor 1823-1849 .... **NCLC 21**

Petrakis, Harry Mark 1923-........ **CLC 3**
See also CA 9-12R; CANR 4, 30

Petrarch 1304-1374 .... **PC 8**

Petrov, Evgeny .... **TCLC 21**
See also Kataev, Evgeny Petrovich

Petry, Ann (Lane) 1908- ...... **CLC 1, 7, 18**
See also BW 1; CA 5-8R; CAAS 6;
CANR 4, 46; CLR 12; DLB 76; JRDA;
MAICYA; MTCW; SATA 5

Petursson, Halligrimur 1614-1674 .... **LC 8**

Philipson, Morris H. 1926-........ **CLC 53**
See also CA 1-4R; CANR 4

Phillips, David Graham
1867-1911 .... **TCLC 44**
See also CA 108; DLB 9, 12

Phillips, Jack
See Sandburg, Carl (August)

Phillips, Jayne Anne
1952-........... **CLC 15, 33; SSC 16**
See also CA 101; CANR 24; DLBY 80;
MTCW

Phillips, Richard
See Dick, Philip K(indred)

Phillips, Robert (Schaeffer) 1938-... **CLC 28**
See also CA 17-20R; CAAS 13; CANR 8;
DLB 105

Phillips, Ward
See Lovecraft, H(oward) P(hillips)

Piccolo, Lucio 1901-1969......... **CLC 13**
See also CA 97-100; DLB 114

Pickthall, Marjorie L(owry) C(hristie)
1883-1922 .... **TCLC 21**
See also CA 107; DLB 92

Pico della Mirandola, Giovanni
1463-1494 .... **LC 15**

Piercy, Marge
1936- .... **CLC 3, 6, 14, 18, 27, 62**
See also CA 21-24R; CAAS 1; CANR 13,
43; DLB 120; MTCW

Piers, Robert
See Anthony, Piers

Pieyre de Mandiargues, Andre 1909-1991
See Mandiargues, Andre Pieyre de
See also CA 103; 136; CANR 22

Pilnyak, Boris .... **TCLC 23**
See also Vogau, Boris Andreyevich

Pincherle, Alberto 1907-1990 ... **CLC 11, 18**
See also Moravia, Alberto
See also CA 25-28R; 132; CANR 33;
MTCW

Pinckney, Darryl 1953-........... **CLC 76**
See also BW 2; CA 143

Pindar 518B.C.-446B.C......... **CMLC 12**

Pineda, Cecile 1942-............. **CLC 39**
See also CA 118

Pinero, Arthur Wing 1855-1934 ... **TCLC 32**
See also CA 110; DLB 10

Pinero, Miguel (Antonio Gomez)
1946-1988 .... **CLC 4, 55**
See also CA 61-64; 125; CANR 29; HW

Pinget, Robert 1919- .... **CLC 7, 13, 37**
See also CA 85-88; DLB 83

Pink Floyd
See Barrett, (Roger) Syd; Gilmour, David;
Mason, Nick; Waters, Roger; Wright,
Rick

Pinkney, Edward 1802-1828 ..... **NCLC 31**

Pinkwater, Daniel Manus 1941- .... **CLC 35**
See also Pinkwater, Manus
See also AAYA 1; CA 29-32R; CANR 12,
38; CLR 4; JRDA; MAICYA; SAAS 3;
SATA 46, 76

Pinkwater, Manus
See Pinkwater, Daniel Manus
See also SATA 8

Pinsky, Robert 1940-........ **CLC 9, 19, 38**
See also CA 29-32R; CAAS 4; DLBY 82

Pinta, Harold
See Pinter, Harold

Pinter, Harold
1930- ..... **CLC 1, 3, 6, 9, 11, 15, 27, 58,**
73; DA; WLC
See also CA 5-8R; CANR 33; CDBLB 1960
to Present; DLB 13; MTCW

Pirandello, Luigi
1867-1936 ..... **TCLC 4, 29; DA; DC 5;**
WLC
See also CA 104

Pirsig, Robert M(aynard)
1928- .... **CLC 4, 6, 73**
See also CA 53-56; CANR 42; MTCW;
SATA 39

Pisarev, Dmitry Ivanovich
1840-1868 .... **NCLC 25**

Pix, Mary (Griffith)   1666-1709 . . . . . . **LC 8**
See also DLB 80

Pixerecourt, Guilbert de
   1773-1844 . . . . **NCLC 39**

Plaidy, Jean
See Hibbert, Eleanor Alice Burford

Planche, James Robinson
   1796-1880 . . . . **NCLC 42**

Plant, Robert   1948- . . . . **CLC 12**

Plante, David (Robert)
   1940- . . . . **CLC 7, 23, 38**
See also CA 37-40R; CANR 12, 36;
   DLBY 83; MTCW

Plath, Sylvia
   1932-1963 . . . . . **CLC 1, 2, 3, 5, 9, 11, 14,
   17, 50, 51, 62; DA; PC 1; WLC**
See also AAYA 13; CA 19-20; CANR 34;
   CAP 2; CDALB 1941-1968; DLB 5, 6;
   MTCW

Plato   428(?)B.C.-348(?)B.C. . . . . **CMLC 8; DA**

Platonov, Andrei . . . . **TCLC 14**
See also Klimentov, Andrei Platonovich

Platt, Kin   1911- . . . . **CLC 26**
See also AAYA 11; CA 17-20R; CANR 11;
   JRDA; SAAS 17; SATA 21

Plick et Plock
See Simenon, Georges (Jacques Christian)

Plimpton, George (Ames)   1927- . . . . . **CLC 36**
See also AITN 1; CA 21-24R; CANR 32;
   MTCW; SATA 10

Plomer, William Charles Franklin
   1903-1973 . . . . **CLC 4, 8**
See also CA 21-22; CANR 34; CAP 2;
   DLB 20; MTCW; SATA 24

Plowman, Piers
See Kavanagh, Patrick (Joseph)

Plum, J.
See Wodehouse, P(elham) G(renville)

Plumly, Stanley (Ross)   1939- . . . . . . **CLC 33**
See also CA 108; 110; DLB 5

Plumpe, Friedrich Wilhelm
   1888-1931 . . . . **TCLC 53**
See also CA 112

Poe, Edgar Allan
   1809-1849 . . . . . **NCLC 1, 16; DA; PC 1;
   SSC 1; WLC**
See also AAYA 14; CDALB 1640-1865;
   DLB 3, 59, 73, 74; SATA 23

Poet of Titchfield Street, The
See Pound, Ezra (Weston Loomis)

Pohl, Frederik   1919- . . . . **CLC 18**
See also CA 61-64; CAAS 1; CANR 11, 37;
   DLB 8; MTCW; SATA 24

Poirier, Louis   1910-
See Gracq, Julien
See also CA 122; 126

Poitier, Sidney   1927- . . . . **CLC 26**
See also BW 1; CA 117

Polanski, Roman   1933- . . . . **CLC 16**
See also CA 77-80

Poliakoff, Stephen   1952- . . . . **CLC 38**
See also CA 106; DLB 13

Police, The
See Copeland, Stewart (Armstrong);
   Summers, Andrew James; Sumner,
   Gordon Matthew

Pollitt, Katha   1949- . . . . **CLC 28**
See also CA 120; 122; MTCW

Pollock, (Mary) Sharon   1936- . . . . . . **CLC 50**
See also CA 141; DLB 60

Pomerance, Bernard   1940- . . . . **CLC 13**
See also CA 101

Ponge, Francis (Jean Gaston Alfred)
   1899-1988 . . . . **CLC 6, 18**
See also CA 85-88; 126; CANR 40

Pontoppidan, Henrik   1857-1943 . . . **TCLC 29**

Poole, Josephine . . . . **CLC 17**
See also Helyar, Jane Penelope Josephine
See also SAAS 2; SATA 5

Popa, Vasko   1922- . . . . **CLC 19**
See also CA 112

Pope, Alexander
   1688-1744 . . . . **LC 3; DA; WLC**
See also CDBLB 1660-1789; DLB 95, 101

Porter, Connie (Rose)   1959(?)- . . . . . **CLC 70**
See also BW 2; CA 142; SATA 81

Porter, Gene(va Grace) Stratton
   1863(?)-1924 . . . . **TCLC 21**
See also CA 112

Porter, Katherine Anne
   1890-1980 . . . . . . **CLC 1, 3, 7, 10, 13, 15,
   27; DA; SSC 4**
See also AITN 2; CA 1-4R; 101; CANR 1;
   DLB 4, 9, 102; DLBD 12; DLBY 80;
   MTCW; SATA 39; SATA-Obit 23

Porter, Peter (Neville Frederick)
   1929- . . . . **CLC 5, 13, 33**
See also CA 85-88; DLB 40

Porter, William Sydney   1862-1910
See Henry, O.
See also CA 104; 131; CDALB 1865-1917;
   DA; DLB 12, 78, 79; MTCW; YABC 2

Portillo (y Pacheco), Jose Lopez
See Lopez Portillo (y Pacheco), Jose

Post, Melville Davisson
   1869-1930 . . . . **TCLC 39**
See also CA 110

Potok, Chaim   1929- . . . . **CLC 2, 7, 14, 26**
See also AITN 1, 2; CA 17-20R; CANR 19,
   35; DLB 28; MTCW; SATA 33

Potter, Beatrice
See Webb, (Martha) Beatrice (Potter)
See also MAICYA

Potter, Dennis (Christopher George)
   1935-1994 . . . . **CLC 58, 86**
See also CA 107; 145; CANR 33; MTCW

Pound, Ezra (Weston Loomis)
   1885-1972 . . . . . . **CLC 1, 2, 3, 4, 5, 7, 10,
   13, 18, 34, 48, 50; DA; PC 4; WLC**
See also CA 5-8R; 37-40R; CANR 40;
   CDALB 1917-1929; DLB 4, 45, 63;
   MTCW

Povod, Reinaldo   1959-1994 . . . . **CLC 44**
See also CA 136; 146

Powell, Anthony (Dymoke)
   1905- . . . . **CLC 1, 3, 7, 9, 10, 31**
See also CA 1-4R; CANR 1, 32;
   CDBLB 1945-1960; DLB 15; MTCW

Powell, Dawn   1897-1965 . . . . **CLC 66**
See also CA 5-8R

Powell, Padgett   1952- . . . . **CLC 34**
See also CA 126

Powers, J(ames) F(arl)
   1917- . . . . **CLC 1, 4, 8, 57; SSC 4**
See also CA 1-4R; CANR 2; DLB 130;
   MTCW

Powers, John J(ames)   1945-
See Powers, John R.
See also CA 69-72

Powers, John R. . . . . **CLC 66**
See also Powers, John J(ames)

Pownall, David   1938- . . . . **CLC 10**
See also CA 89-92; CAAS 18; DLB 14

Powys, John Cowper
   1872-1963 . . . . **CLC 7, 9, 15, 46**
See also CA 85-88; DLB 15; MTCW

Powys, T(heodore) F(rancis)
   1875-1953 . . . . **TCLC 9**
See also CA 106; DLB 36

Prager, Emily   1952- . . . . **CLC 56**

Pratt, E(dwin) J(ohn)
   1883(?)-1964 . . . . **CLC 19**
See also CA 141; 93-96; DLB 92

Premchand . . . . **TCLC 21**
See also Srivastava, Dhanpat Rai

Preussler, Otfried   1923- . . . . **CLC 17**
See also CA 77-80; SATA 24

Prevert, Jacques (Henri Marie)
   1900-1977 . . . . **CLC 15**
See also CA 77-80; 69-72; CANR 29;
   MTCW; SATA-Obit 30

Prevost, Abbe (Antoine Francois)
   1697-1763 . . . . **LC 1**

Price, (Edward) Reynolds
   1933- . . . . **CLC 3, 6, 13, 43, 50, 63**
See also CA 1-4R; CANR 1, 37; DLB 2

Price, Richard   1949- . . . . **CLC 6, 12**
See also CA 49-52; CANR 3; DLBY 81

Prichard, Katharine Susannah
   1883-1969 . . . . **CLC 46**
See also CA 11-12; CANR 33; CAP 1;
   MTCW; SATA 66

Priestley, J(ohn) B(oynton)
   1894-1984 . . . . **CLC 2, 5, 9, 34**
See also CA 9-12R; 113; CANR 33;
   CDBLB 1914-1945; DLB 10, 34, 77, 100,
   139; DLBY 84; MTCW

Prince   1958(?)- . . . . **CLC 35**

Prince, F(rank) T(empleton)   1912- . . **CLC 22**
See also CA 101; CANR 43; DLB 20

Prince Kropotkin
See Kropotkin, Peter (Aleksieevich)

Prior, Matthew   1664-1721 . . . . **LC 4**
See also DLB 95

Pritchard, William H(arrison)
   1932- . . . . **CLC 34**
See also CA 65-68; CANR 23; DLB 111

Pritchett, V(ictor) S(awdon)
1900-....... **CLC 5, 13, 15, 41; SSC 14**
See also CA 61-64; CANR 31; DLB 15,
139; MTCW

Private 19022
See Manning, Frederic

Probst, Mark 1925-............. **CLC 59**
See also CA 130

Prokosch, Frederic 1908-1989.... **CLC 4, 48**
See also CA 73-76; 128; DLB 48

Prophet, The
See Dreiser, Theodore (Herman Albert)

Prose, Francine 1947-............ **CLC 45**
See also CA 109; 112; CANR 46

Proudhon
See Cunha, Euclides (Rodrigues Pimenta) da

Proulx, E. Annie 1935-.......... **CLC 81**

Proust, (Valentin-Louis-George-Eugene-)
Marcel
1871-1922 ... **TCLC 7, 13, 33; DA; WLC**
See also CA 104; 120; DLB 65; MTCW

Prowler, Harley
See Masters, Edgar Lee

Prus, Boleslaw 1845-1912 .... **TCLC 48**

Pryor, Richard (Franklin Lenox Thomas)
1940-...................... **CLC 26**
See also CA 122

Przybyszewski, Stanislaw
1868-1927 .... **TCLC 36**
See also DLB 66

Pteleon
See Grieve, C(hristopher) M(urray)

Puckett, Lute
See Masters, Edgar Lee

Puig, Manuel
1932-1990 ... **CLC 3, 5, 10, 28, 65; HLC**
See also CA 45-48; CANR 2, 32; DLB 113;
HW; MTCW

Purdy, Al(fred Wellington)
1918-................ **CLC 3, 6, 14, 50**
See also CA 81-84; CAAS 17; CANR 42;
DLB 88

Purdy, James (Amos)
1923-............ **CLC 2, 4, 10, 28, 52**
See also CA 33-36R; CAAS 1; CANR 19;
DLB 2; MTCW

Pure, Simon
See Swinnerton, Frank Arthur

Pushkin, Alexander (Sergeyevich)
1799-1837 .... **NCLC 3, 27; DA; PC 10;**
WLC
See also SATA 61

P'u Sung-ling 1640-1715 .... **LC 3**

Putnam, Arthur Lee
See Alger, Horatio, Jr.

Puzo, Mario 1920-........ **CLC 1, 2, 6, 36**
See also CA 65-68; CANR 4, 42; DLB 6;
MTCW

Pym, Barbara (Mary Crampton)
1913-1980 .... **CLC 13, 19, 37**
See also CA 13-14; 97-100; CANR 13, 34;
CAP 1; DLB 14; DLBY 87; MTCW

Pynchon, Thomas (Ruggles, Jr.)
1937-..... **CLC 2, 3, 6, 9, 11, 18, 33, 62,**
72; DA; SSC 14; WLC
See also BEST 90:2; CA 17-20R; CANR 22,
46; DLB 2; MTCW

Qian Zhongshu
See Ch'ien Chung-shu

Qroll
See Dagerman, Stig (Halvard)

Quarrington, Paul (Lewis) 1953-.... **CLC 65**
See also CA 129

Quasimodo, Salvatore 1901-1968 ... **CLC 10**
See also CA 13-16; 25-28R; CAP 1;
DLB 114; MTCW

Queen, Ellery.................. **CLC 3, 11**
See also Dannay, Frederic; Davidson,
Avram; Lee, Manfred B(ennington);
Sturgeon, Theodore (Hamilton); Vance,
John Holbrook

Queen, Ellery, Jr.
See Dannay, Frederic; Lee, Manfred
B(ennington)

Queneau, Raymond
1903-1976 .... **CLC 2, 5, 10, 42**
See also CA 77-80; 69-72; CANR 32;
DLB 72; MTCW

Quevedo, Francisco de 1580-1645.... **LC 23**

Quiller-Couch, Arthur Thomas
1863-1944 .... **TCLC 53**
See also CA 118; DLB 135

Quin, Ann (Marie) 1936-1973 .... **CLC 6**
See also CA 9-12R; 45-48; DLB 14

Quinn, Martin
See Smith, Martin Cruz

Quinn, Simon
See Smith, Martin Cruz

Quiroga, Horacio (Sylvestre)
1878-1937 .... **TCLC 20; HLC**
See also CA 117; 131; HW; MTCW

Quoirez, Francoise 1935-.......... **CLC 9**
See also Sagan, Francoise
See also CA 49-52; CANR 6, 39; MTCW

Raabe, Wilhelm 1831-1910 .... **TCLC 45**
See also DLB 129

Rabe, David (William) 1940-... **CLC 4, 8, 33**
See also CA 85-88; CABS 3; DLB 7

Rabelais, Francois
1483-1553 .... **LC 5; DA; WLC**

Rabinovitch, Sholem 1859-1916
See Aleichem, Sholom
See also CA 104

Racine, Jean 1639-1699 .... **LC 28**

Radcliffe, Ann (Ward) 1764-1823 .. **NCLC 6**
See also DLB 39

Radiguet, Raymond 1903-1923 .... **TCLC 29**
See also DLB 65

Radnoti, Miklos 1909-1944 .... **TCLC 16**
See also CA 118

Rado, James 1939-.............. **CLC 17**
See also CA 105

Radvanyi, Netty 1900-1983
See Seghers, Anna
See also CA 85-88; 110

Rae, Ben
See Griffiths, Trevor

Raeburn, John (Hay) 1941-........ **CLC 34**
See also CA 57-60

Ragni, Gerome 1942-1991 .... **CLC 17**
See also CA 105; 134

Rahv, Philip 1908-1973 .... **CLC 24**
See also Greenberg, Ivan
See also DLB 137

Raine, Craig 1944-............... **CLC 32**
See also CA 108; CANR 29; DLB 40

Raine, Kathleen (Jessie) 1908- ... **CLC 7, 45**
See also CA 85-88; CANR 46; DLB 20;
MTCW

Rainis, Janis 1865-1929 .... **TCLC 29**

Rakosi, Carl..................... **CLC 47**
See also Rawley, Callman
See also CAAS 5

Raleigh, Richard
See Lovecraft, H(oward) P(hillips)

Rallentando, H. P.
See Sayers, Dorothy L(eigh)

Ramal, Walter
See de la Mare, Walter (John)

Ramon, Juan
See Jimenez (Mantecon), Juan Ramon

Ramos, Graciliano 1892-1953 ..... **TCLC 32**

Rampersad, Arnold 1941-......... **CLC 44**
See also BW 2; CA 127; 133; DLB 111

Rampling, Anne
See Rice, Anne

Ramuz, Charles-Ferdinand
1878-1947 .... **TCLC 33**

Rand, Ayn
1905-1982 ...... **CLC 3, 30, 44, 79; DA;**
WLC
See also AAYA 10; CA 13-16R; 105;
CANR 27; MTCW

Randall, Dudley (Felker)
1914-.................... **CLC 1; BLC**
See also BW 1; CA 25-28R; CANR 23;
DLB 41

Randall, Robert
See Silverberg, Robert

Ranger, Ken
See Creasey, John

Ransom, John Crowe
1888-1974 .... **CLC 2, 4, 5, 11, 24**
See also CA 5-8R; 49-52; CANR 6, 34;
DLB 45, 63; MTCW

Rao, Raja 1909-.............. **CLC 25, 56**
See also CA 73-76; MTCW

Raphael, Frederic (Michael)
1931-.................... **CLC 2, 14**
See also CA 1-4R; CANR 1; DLB 14

Ratcliffe, James P.
See Mencken, H(enry) L(ouis)

Rathbone, Julian 1935-.......... **CLC 41**
See also CA 101; CANR 34

Rattigan, Terence (Mervyn)
1911-1977 .... **CLC 7**
See also CA 85-88; 73-76;
CDBLB 1945-1960; DLB 13; MTCW

Riefenstahl, Berta Helene Amalia   1902-
See Riefenstahl, Leni
See also CA 108

Riefenstahl, Leni . . . . CLC 16
See also Riefenstahl, Berta Helene Amalia

Riffe, Ernest
See Bergman, (Ernst) Ingmar

Riggs, (Rolla) Lynn   1899-1954 . . . . TCLC 56
See also CA 144; NNAL

Riley, James Whitcomb
1849-1916 . . . . TCLC 51
See also CA 118; 137; MAICYA; SATA 17

Riley, Tex
See Creasey, John

Rilke, Rainer Maria
1875-1926 . . . . TCLC 1, 6, 19; PC 2
See also CA 104; 132; DLB 81; MTCW

Rimbaud, (Jean Nicolas) Arthur
1854-1891 . . . . . NCLC 4, 35; DA; PC 3;
WLC

Rinehart, Mary Roberts
1876-1958 . . . . TCLC 52
See also CA 108

Ringmaster, The
See Mencken, H(enry) L(ouis)

Ringwood, Gwen(dolyn Margaret) Pharis
1910-1984 . . . . CLC 48
See also CA 112; DLB 88

Rio, Michel   19(?)- . . . . CLC 43

Ritsos, Giannes
See Ritsos, Yannis

Ritsos, Yannis   1909-1990 . . . . . CLC 6, 13, 31
See also CA 77-80; 133; CANR 39; MTCW

Ritter, Erika   1948(?)- . . . . CLC 52

Rivera, Jose Eustasio   1889-1928 . . . TCLC 35
See also HW

Rivers, Conrad Kent   1933-1968 . . . . . . CLC 1
See also BW 1; CA 85-88; DLB 41

Rivers, Elfrida
See Bradley, Marion Zimmer

Riverside, John
See Heinlein, Robert A(nson)

Rizal, Jose   1861-1896 . . . . NCLC 27

Roa Bastos, Augusto (Antonio)
1917- . . . . CLC 45; HLC
See also CA 131; DLB 113; HW

Robbe-Grillet, Alain
1922- . . . . . . CLC 1, 2, 4, 6, 8, 10, 14, 43
See also CA 9-12R; CANR 33; DLB 83;
MTCW

Robbins, Harold   1916- . . . . CLC 5
See also CA 73-76; CANR 26; MTCW

Robbins, Thomas Eugene   1936-
See Robbins, Tom
See also CA 81-84; CANR 29; MTCW

Robbins, Tom . . . . CLC 9, 32, 64
See also Robbins, Thomas Eugene
See also BEST 90:3; DLBY 80

Robbins, Trina   1938- . . . . CLC 21
See also CA 128

Roberts, Charles G(eorge) D(ouglas)
1860-1943 . . . . TCLC 8
See also CA 105; CLR 33; DLB 92;
SATA 29

Roberts, Kate   1891-1985 . . . . CLC 15
See also CA 107; 116

Roberts, Keith (John Kingston)
1935- . . . . CLC 14
See also CA 25-28R; CANR 46

Roberts, Kenneth (Lewis)
1885-1957 . . . . TCLC 23
See also CA 109; DLB 9

Roberts, Michele (B.)   1949- . . . . CLC 48
See also CA 115

Robertson, Ellis
See Ellison, Harlan (Jay); Silverberg, Robert

Robertson, Thomas William
1829-1871 . . . . NCLC 35

Robinson, Edwin Arlington
1869-1935 . . . . TCLC 5; DA; PC 1
See also CA 104; 133; CDALB 1865-1917;
DLB 54; MTCW

Robinson, Henry Crabb
1775-1867 . . . . NCLC 15
See also DLB 107

Robinson, Jill   1936- . . . . CLC 10
See also CA 102

Robinson, Kim Stanley   1952- . . . . . . CLC 34
See also CA 126

Robinson, Lloyd
See Silverberg, Robert

Robinson, Marilynne   1944- . . . . CLC 25
See also CA 116

Robinson, Smokey . . . . CLC 21
See also Robinson, William, Jr.

Robinson, William, Jr.   1940-
See Robinson, Smokey
See also CA 116

Robison, Mary   1949- . . . . CLC 42
See also CA 113; 116; DLB 130

Rod, Edouard   1857-1910 . . . . TCLC 52

Roddenberry, Eugene Wesley   1921-1991
See Roddenberry, Gene
See also CA 110; 135; CANR 37; SATA 45;
SATA-Obit 69

Roddenberry, Gene . . . . CLC 17
See also Roddenberry, Eugene Wesley
See also AAYA 5; SATA-Obit 69

Rodgers, Mary   1931- . . . . CLC 12
See also CA 49-52; CANR 8; CLR 20;
JRDA; MAICYA; SATA 8

Rodgers, W(illiam) R(obert)
1909-1969 . . . . CLC 7
See also CA 85-88; DLB 20

Rodman, Eric
See Silverberg, Robert

Rodman, Howard   1920(?)-1985 . . . . . CLC 65
See also CA 118

Rodman, Maia
See Wojciechowska, Maia (Teresa)

Rodriguez, Claudio   1934- . . . . CLC 10
See also DLB 134

Roelvaag, O(le) E(dvart)
1876-1931 . . . . TCLC 17
See also CA 117; DLB 9

Roethke, Theodore (Huebner)
1908-1963 . . . . . CLC 1, 3, 8, 11, 19, 46
See also CA 81-84; CABS 2;
CDALB 1941-1968; DLB 5; MTCW

Rogers, Thomas Hunton   1927- . . . . . CLC 57
See also CA 89-92

Rogers, Will(iam Penn Adair)
1879-1935 . . . . TCLC 8
See also CA 105; 144; DLB 11; NNAL

Rogin, Gilbert   1929- . . . . CLC 18
See also CA 65-68; CANR 15

Rohan, Koda . . . . TCLC 22
See also Koda Shigeyuki

Rohmer, Eric . . . . CLC 16
See also Scherer, Jean-Marie Maurice

Rohmer, Sax . . . . TCLC 28
See also Ward, Arthur Henry Sarsfield
See also DLB 70

Roiphe, Anne (Richardson)
1935- . . . . CLC 3, 9
See also CA 89-92; CANR 45; DLBY 80

Rojas, Fernando de   1465-1541 . . . . . . LC 23

**Rolfe, Frederick (William Serafino Austin
Lewis Mary)**   1860-1913 . . . . . . TCLC 12
See also CA 107; DLB 34

Rolland, Romain   1866-1944 . . . . TCLC 23
See also CA 118; DLB 65

Rolvaag, O(le) E(dvart)
See Roelvaag, O(le) E(dvart)

Romain Arnaud, Saint
See Aragon, Louis

Romains, Jules   1885-1972 . . . . CLC 7
See also CA 85-88; CANR 34; DLB 65;
MTCW

Romero, Jose Ruben   1890-1952 . . . TCLC 14
See also CA 114; 131; HW

Ronsard, Pierre de
1524-1585 . . . . LC 6; PC 11

Rooke, Leon   1934- . . . . CLC 25, 34
See also CA 25-28R; CANR 23

Roper, William   1498-1578 . . . . LC 10

Roquelaure, A. N.
See Rice, Anne

Rosa, Joao Guimaraes   1908-1967 . . . CLC 23
See also CA 89-92; DLB 113

Rose, Wendy   1948- . . . . CLC 85
See also CA 53-56; CANR 5; NNAL;
SATA 12

Rosen, Richard (Dean)   1949- . . . . . . CLC 39
See also CA 77-80

Rosenberg, Isaac   1890-1918 . . . . . . TCLC 12
See also CA 107; DLB 20

Rosenblatt, Joe . . . . CLC 15
See also Rosenblatt, Joseph

Rosenblatt, Joseph   1933-
See Rosenblatt, Joe
See also CA 89-92

Rosenfeld, Samuel   1896-1963
See Tzara, Tristan
See also CA 89-92

Rosenthal, M(acha) L(ouis)   1917- . . . CLC 28
See also CA 1-4R; CAAS 6; CANR 4;
DLB 5; SATA 59

Salamanca, J(ack) R(ichard)
1922- .... CLC 4, 15
See also CA 25-28R

Sale, J. Kirkpatrick
See Sale, Kirkpatrick

Sale, Kirkpatrick 1937- .... CLC 68
See also CA 13-16R; CANR 10

Salinas (y Serrano), Pedro
1891(?)-1951 .... TCLC 17
See also CA 117; DLB 134

Salinger, J(erome) D(avid)
1919- ...... CLC 1, 3, 8, 12, 55, 56; DA;
SSC 2; WLC
See also AAYA 2; CA 5-8R; CANR 39;
CDALB 1941-1968; CLR 18; DLB 2, 102;
MAICYA; MTCW; SATA 67

Salisbury, John
See Caute, David

Salter, James 1925- .... CLC 7, 52, 59
See also CA 73-76; DLB 130

Saltus, Edgar (Everton)
1855-1921 .... TCLC 8
See also CA 105

Saltykov, Mikhail Evgrafovich
1826-1889 .... NCLC 16

Samarakis, Antonis 1919- .... CLC 5
See also CA 25-28R; CAAS 16; CANR 36

Sanchez, Florencio 1875-1910 ..... TCLC 37
See also HW

Sanchez, Luis Rafael 1936- .... CLC 23
See also CA 128; DLB 145; HW

Sanchez, Sonia 1934- ... CLC 5; BLC; PC 9
See also BW 2; CA 33-36R; CANR 24;
CLR 18; DLB 41; DLBD 8; MAICYA;
MTCW; SATA 22

Sand, George
1804-1876 ...... NCLC 2, 42; DA; WLC
See also DLB 119

Sandburg, Carl (August)
1878-1967 .... CLC 1, 4, 10, 15, 35; DA;
PC 2; WLC
See also CA 5-8R; 25-28R; CANR 35;
CDALB 1865-1917; DLB 17, 54;
MAICYA; MTCW; SATA 8

Sandburg, Charles
See Sandburg, Carl (August)

Sandburg, Charles A.
See Sandburg, Carl (August)

Sanders, (James) Ed(ward) 1939- ... CLC 53
See also CA 13-16R; CANR 13, 44;
DLB 16

Sanders, Lawrence 1920- .... CLC 41
See also BEST 89:4; CA 81-84; CANR 33;
MTCW

Sanders, Noah
See Blount, Roy (Alton), Jr.

Sanders, Winston P.
See Anderson, Poul (William)

Sandoz, Mari(e Susette)
1896-1966 .... CLC 28
See also CA 1-4R; 25-28R; CANR 17;
DLB 9; MTCW; SATA 5

Saner, Reg(inald Anthony) 1931- .... CLC 9
See also CA 65-68

Sannazaro, Jacopo 1456(?)-1530 ..... LC 8

Sansom, William 1912-1976 .... CLC 2, 6
See also CA 5-8R; 65-68; CANR 42;
DLB 139; MTCW

Santayana, George 1863-1952 ..... TCLC 40
See also CA 115; DLB 54, 71

Santiago, Danny .... CLC 33
See also James, Daniel (Lewis); James,
Daniel (Lewis)
See also DLB 122

Santmyer, Helen Hoover
1895-1986 .... CLC 33
See also CA 1-4R; 118; CANR 15, 33;
DLBY 84; MTCW

Santos, Bienvenido N(uqui) 1911- ... CLC 22
See also CA 101; CANR 19, 46

Sapper .... TCLC 44
See also McNeile, Herman Cyril

Sappho fl. 6th cent. B.C.- .... CMLC 3; PC 5

Sarduy, Severo 1937-1993 .... CLC 6
See also CA 89-92; 142; DLB 113; HW

Sargeson, Frank 1903-1982 .... CLC 31
See also CA 25-28R; 106; CANR 38

Sarmiento, Felix Ruben Garcia
See Dario, Ruben

Saroyan, William
1908-1981 ..... CLC 1, 8, 10, 29, 34, 56;
DA; WLC
See also CA 5-8R; 103; CANR 30; DLB 7,
9, 86; DLBY 81; MTCW; SATA 23;
SATA-Obit 24

Sarraute, Nathalie
1900- .... CLC 1, 2, 4, 8, 10, 31, 80
See also CA 9-12R; CANR 23; DLB 83;
MTCW

Sarton, (Eleanor) May
1912- .... CLC 4, 14, 49
See also CA 1-4R; CANR 1, 34; DLB 48;
DLBY 81; MTCW; SATA 36

Sartre, Jean-Paul
1905-1980 .... CLC 1, 4, 7, 9, 13, 18, 24,
44, 50, 52; DA; DC 3; WLC
See also CA 9-12R; 97-100; CANR 21;
DLB 72; MTCW

Sassoon, Siegfried (Lorraine)
1886-1967 .... CLC 36
See also CA 104; 25-28R; CANR 36;
DLB 20; MTCW

Satterfield, Charles
See Pohl, Frederik

Saul, John (W. III) 1942- .... CLC 46
See also AAYA 10; BEST 90:4; CA 81-84;
CANR 16, 40

Saunders, Caleb
See Heinlein, Robert A(nson)

Saura (Atares), Carlos 1932- .... CLC 20
See also CA 114; 131; HW

Sauser-Hall, Frederic 1887-1961 .... CLC 18
See also CA 102; 93-96; CANR 36; MTCW

Saussure, Ferdinand de
1857-1913 .... TCLC 49

Savage, Catharine
See Brosman, Catharine Savage

Savage, Thomas 1915- .... CLC 40
See also CA 126; 132; CAAS 15

Savan, Glenn 19(?)- .... CLC 50

Sayers, Dorothy L(eigh)
1893-1957 .... TCLC 2, 15
See also CA 104; 119; CDBLB 1914-1945;
DLB 10, 36, 77, 100; MTCW

Sayers, Valerie 1952- .... CLC 50
See also CA 134

Sayles, John (Thomas)
1950- .... CLC 7, 10, 14
See also CA 57-60; CANR 41; DLB 44

Scammell, Michael .... CLC 34

Scannell, Vernon 1922- .... CLC 49
See also CA 5-8R; CANR 8, 24; DLB 27;
SATA 59

Scarlett, Susan
See Streatfeild, (Mary) Noel

Schaeffer, Susan Fromberg
1941- .... CLC 6, 11, 22
See also CA 49-52; CANR 18; DLB 28;
MTCW; SATA 22

Schary, Jill
See Robinson, Jill

Schell, Jonathan 1943- .... CLC 35
See also CA 73-76; CANR 12

Schelling, Friedrich Wilhelm Joseph von
1775-1854 .... NCLC 30
See also DLB 90

Schendel, Arthur van 1874-1946 ... TCLC 56

Scherer, Jean-Marie Maurice 1920-
See Rohmer, Eric
See also CA 110

Schevill, James (Erwin) 1920- .... CLC 7
See also CA 5-8R; CAAS 12

Schiller, Friedrich 1759-1805 .... NCLC 39
See also DLB 94

Schisgal, Murray (Joseph) 1926- ..... CLC 6
See also CA 21-24R

Schlee, Ann 1934- .... CLC 35
See also CA 101; CANR 29; SATA 36, 44

Schlegel, August Wilhelm von
1767-1845 .... NCLC 15
See also DLB 94

Schlegel, Friedrich 1772-1829 .... NCLC 45
See also DLB 90

Schlegel, Johann Elias (von)
1719(?)-1749 .... LC 5

Schlesinger, Arthur M(eier), Jr.
1917- .... CLC 84
See also AITN 1; CA 1-4R; CANR 1, 28;
DLB 17; MTCW; SATA 61

Schmidt, Arno (Otto) 1914-1979 .... CLC 56
See also CA 128; 109; DLB 69

Schmitz, Aron Hector 1861-1928
See Svevo, Italo
See also CA 104; 122; MTCW

Schnackenberg, Gjertrud 1953- ..... CLC 40
See also CA 116; DLB 120

Schneider, Leonard Alfred 1925-1966
See Bruce, Lenny
See also CA 89-92

Schnitzler, Arthur
1862-1931 .... TCLC 4; SSC 15
See also CA 104; DLB 81, 118

Schor, Sandra (M.) 1932(?)-1990 ... CLC 65
See also CA 132

Shaffer, Peter (Levin)
1926- . . . . **CLC 5, 14, 18, 37, 60**
See also CA 25-28R; CANR 25, 47;
CDBLB 1960 to Present; DLB 13;
MTCW

Shakey, Bernard
See Young, Neil

Shalamov, Varlam (Tikhonovich)
1907(?)-1982 . . . . **CLC 18**
See also CA 129; 105

Shamlu, Ahmad 1925- . . . . **CLC 10**

Shammas, Anton 1951- . . . . **CLC 55**

Shange, Ntozake
1948- . . . . **CLC 8, 25, 38, 74; BLC; DC 3**
See also AAYA 9; BW 2; CA 85-88;
CABS 3; CANR 27; DLB 38; MTCW

Shanley, John Patrick 1950- . . . . **CLC 75**
See also CA 128; 133

Shapcott, Thomas William 1935- . . . **CLC 38**
See also CA 69-72

Shapiro, Jane . . . . **CLC 76**

Shapiro, Karl (Jay) 1913- . . **CLC 4, 8, 15, 53**
See also CA 1-4R; CAAS 6; CANR 1, 36;
DLB 48; MTCW

Sharp, William 1855-1905 . . . . **TCLC 39**

Sharpe, Thomas Ridley 1928-
See Sharpe, Tom
See also CA 114; 122

Sharpe, Tom . . . . **CLC 36**
See also Sharpe, Thomas Ridley
See also DLB 14

Shaw, Bernard . . . . **TCLC 45**
See also Shaw, George Bernard
See also BW 1

Shaw, G. Bernard
See Shaw, George Bernard

Shaw, George Bernard
1856-1950 . . . . **TCLC 3, 9, 21; DA; WLC**
See also Shaw, Bernard
See also CA 104; 128; CDBLB 1914-1945;
DLB 10, 57; MTCW

Shaw, Henry Wheeler
1818-1885 . . . . **NCLC 15**
See also DLB 11

Shaw, Irwin 1913-1984 . . . . **CLC 7, 23, 34**
See also AITN 1; CA 13-16R; 112;
CANR 21; CDALB 1941-1968; DLB 6,
102; DLBY 84; MTCW

Shaw, Robert 1927-1978 . . . . **CLC 5**
See also AITN 1; CA 1-4R; 81-84;
CANR 4; DLB 13, 14

Shaw, T. E.
See Lawrence, T(homas) E(dward)

Shawn, Wallace 1943- . . . . **CLC 41**
See also CA 112

Shea, Lisa 1953- . . . . **CLC 86**

Sheed, Wilfrid (John Joseph)
1930- . . . . **CLC 2, 4, 10, 53**
See also CA 65-68; CANR 30; DLB 6;
MTCW

Sheldon, Alice Hastings Bradley
1915(?)-1987
See Tiptree, James, Jr.
See also CA 108; 122; CANR 34; MTCW

Sheldon, John
See Bloch, Robert (Albert)

Shelley, Mary Wollstonecraft (Godwin)
1797-1851 . . . . **NCLC 14; DA; WLC**
See also CDBLB 1789-1832; DLB 110, 116;
SATA 29

Shelley, Percy Bysshe
1792-1822 . . . . **NCLC 18; DA; WLC**
See also CDBLB 1789-1832; DLB 96, 110

Shepard, Jim 1956- . . . . **CLC 36**
See also CA 137

Shepard, Lucius 1947- . . . . **CLC 34**
See also CA 128; 141

Shepard, Sam
1943- . . . . **CLC 4, 6, 17, 34, 41, 44; DC 5**
See also AAYA 1; CA 69-72; CABS 3;
CANR 22; DLB 7; MTCW

Shepherd, Michael
See Ludlum, Robert

Sherburne, Zoa (Morin) 1912- . . . . . . **CLC 30**
See also AAYA 13; CA 1-4R; CANR 3, 37;
MAICYA; SAAS 18; SATA 3

Sheridan, Frances 1724-1766 . . . . **LC 7**
See also DLB 39, 84

Sheridan, Richard Brinsley
1751-1816 . . . **NCLC 5; DA; DC 1; WLC**
See also CDBLB 1660-1789; DLB 89

Sherman, Jonathan Marc . . . . **CLC 55**

Sherman, Martin 1941(?)- . . . . **CLC 19**
See also CA 116; 123

Sherwin, Judith Johnson 1936- . . . **CLC 7, 15**
See also CA 25-28R; CANR 34

Sherwood, Frances 1940- . . . . **CLC 81**

Sherwood, Robert E(mmet)
1896-1955 . . . . **TCLC 3**
See also CA 104; DLB 7, 26

Shestov, Lev 1866-1938 . . . . **TCLC 56**

Shiel, M(atthew) P(hipps)
1865-1947 . . . . **TCLC 8**
See also CA 106

Shiga, Naoya 1883-1971 . . . . **CLC 33**
See also CA 101; 33-36R

Shilts, Randy 1951-1994 . . . . **CLC 85**
See also CA 115; 127; 144; CANR 45

Shimazaki Haruki 1872-1943
See Shimazaki Toson
See also CA 105; 134

Shimazaki Toson . . . . **TCLC 5**
See also Shimazaki Haruki

Sholokhov, Mikhail (Aleksandrovich)
1905-1984 . . . . **CLC 7, 15**
See also CA 101; 112; MTCW;
SATA-Obit 36

Shone, Patric
See Hanley, James

Shreve, Susan Richards 1939- . . . . . . **CLC 23**
See also CA 49-52; CAAS 5; CANR 5, 38;
MAICYA; SATA 46; SATA-Brief 41

Shue, Larry 1946-1985 . . . . **CLC 52**
See also CA 145; 117

Shu-Jen, Chou 1881-1936
See Hsun, Lu
See also CA 104

Shulman, Alix Kates 1932- . . . . . . **CLC 2, 10**
See also CA 29-32R; CANR 43; SATA 7

Shuster, Joe 1914- . . . . **CLC 21**

Shute, Nevil . . . . **CLC 30**
See also Norway, Nevil Shute

Shuttle, Penelope (Diane) 1947- . . . . . **CLC 7**
See also CA 93-96; CANR 39; DLB 14, 40

Sidney, Mary 1561-1621 . . . . **LC 19**

Sidney, Sir Philip 1554-1586 . . . . **LC 19; DA**
See also CDBLB Before 1660

Siegel, Jerome 1914- . . . . **CLC 21**
See also CA 116

Siegel, Jerry
See Siegel, Jerome

Sienkiewicz, Henryk (Adam Alexander Pius)
1846-1916 . . . . **TCLC 3**
See also CA 104; 134

Sierra, Gregorio Martinez
See Martinez Sierra, Gregorio

Sierra, Maria (de la O'LeJarraga) Martinez
See Martinez Sierra, Maria (de la
O'LeJarraga)

Sigal, Clancy 1926- . . . . **CLC 7**
See also CA 1-4R

Sigourney, Lydia Howard (Huntley)
1791-1865 . . . . **NCLC 21**
See also DLB 1, 42, 73

Siguenza y Gongora, Carlos de
1645-1700 . . . . **LC 8**

Sigurjonsson, Johann 1880-1919 . . . **TCLC 27**

Sikelianos, Angelos 1884-1951 . . . . **TCLC 39**

Silkin, Jon 1930- . . . . **CLC 2, 6, 43**
See also CA 5-8R; CAAS 5; DLB 27

Silko, Leslie (Marmon)
1948- . . . . **CLC 23, 74; DA**
See also AAYA 14; CA 115; 122;
CANR 45; DLB 143; NNAL

Sillanpaa, Frans Eemil 1888-1964 . . . **CLC 19**
See also CA 129; 93-96; MTCW

Sillitoe, Alan
1928- . . . . **CLC 1, 3, 6, 10, 19, 57**
See also AITN 1; CA 9-12R; CAAS 2;
CANR 8, 26; CDBLB 1960 to Present;
DLB 14, 139; MTCW; SATA 61

Silone, Ignazio 1900-1978 . . . . **CLC 4**
See also CA 25-28; 81-84; CANR 34;
CAP 2; MTCW

Silver, Joan Micklin 1935- . . . . **CLC 20**
See also CA 114; 121

Silver, Nicholas
See Faust, Frederick (Schiller)

Silverberg, Robert 1935- . . . . **CLC 7**
See also CA 1-4R; CAAS 3; CANR 1, 20,
36; DLB 8; MAICYA; MTCW; SATA 13

Silverstein, Alvin 1933- . . . . **CLC 17**
See also CA 49-52; CANR 2; CLR 25;
JRDA; MAICYA; SATA 8, 69

Silverstein, Virginia B(arbara Opshelor)
1937- . . . . **CLC 17**
See also CA 49-52; CANR 2; CLR 25;
JRDA; MAICYA; SATA 8, 69

Sim, Georges
See Simenon, Georges (Jacques Christian)

Smith, Woodrow Wilson
　　See Kuttner, Henry

Smolenskin, Peretz 1842-1885. . . . **NCLC 30**

Smollett, Tobias (George) 1721-1771 . . **LC 2**
　　See also CDBLB 1660-1789; DLB 39, 104

Snodgrass, W(illiam) D(e Witt)
　　1926- . . . . **CLC 2, 6, 10, 18, 68**
　　See also CA 1-4R; CANR 6, 36; DLB 5;
　　　MTCW

Snow, C(harles) P(ercy)
　　1905-1980 . . . . . . **CLC 1, 4, 6, 9, 13, 19**
　　See also CA 5-8R; 101; CANR 28;
　　　CDBLB 1945-1960; DLB 15, 77; MTCW

Snow, Frances Compton
　　See Adams, Henry (Brooks)

Snyder, Gary (Sherman)
　　1930- . . . . **CLC 1, 2, 5, 9, 32**
　　See also CA 17-20R; CANR 30; DLB 5, 16

Snyder, Zilpha Keatley 1927- . . . . . . **CLC 17**
　　See also CA 9-12R; CANR 38; CLR 31;
　　　JRDA; MAICYA; SAAS 2; SATA 1, 28,
　　　75

Soares, Bernardo
　　See Pessoa, Fernando (Antonio Nogueira)

Sobh, A.
　　See Shamlu, Ahmad

Sobol, Joshua. . . . . **CLC 60**

Soderberg, Hjalmar 1869-1941 . . . . **TCLC 39**

Sodergran, Edith (Irene)
　　See Soedergran, Edith (Irene)

Soedergran, Edith (Irene)
　　1892-1923 . . . . **TCLC 31**

Softly, Edgar
　　See Lovecraft, H(oward) P(hillips)

Softly, Edward
　　See Lovecraft, H(oward) P(hillips)

Sokolov, Raymond 1941- . . . . **CLC 7**
　　See also CA 85-88

Solo, Jay
　　See Ellison, Harlan (Jay)

Sologub, Fyodor . . . . **TCLC 9**
　　See also Teternikov, Fyodor Kuzmich

Solomons, Ikey Esquir
　　See Thackeray, William Makepeace

Solomos, Dionysios 1798-1857 . . . **NCLC 15**

Solwoska, Mara
　　See French, Marilyn

Solzhenitsyn, Aleksandr I(sayevich)
　　1918- . . . . . . **CLC 1, 2, 4, 7, 9, 10, 18, 26,**
　　　　　　　　　　　　　　34, 78; DA; WLC
　　See also AITN 1; CA 69-72; CANR 40;
　　　MTCW

Somers, Jane
　　See Lessing, Doris (May)

Somerville, Edith 1858-1949 . . . . . **TCLC 51**
　　See also DLB 135

Somerville & Ross
　　See Martin, Violet Florence; Somerville,
　　　Edith

Sommer, Scott 1951- . . . . **CLC 25**
　　See also CA 106

Sondheim, Stephen (Joshua)
　　1930- . . . . **CLC 30, 39**
　　See also AAYA 11; CA 103; CANR 47

Sontag, Susan 1933-. . . **CLC 1, 2, 10, 13, 31**
　　See also CA 17-20R; CANR 25; DLB 2, 67;
　　　MTCW

Sophocles
　　496(?)B.C.-406(?)B.C. . . . . **CMLC 2; DA;**
　　　　　　　　　　　　　　　　　　DC 1

Sorel, Julia
　　See Drexler, Rosalyn

Sorrentino, Gilbert
　　1929- . . . . **CLC 3, 7, 14, 22, 40**
　　See also CA 77-80; CANR 14, 33; DLB 5;
　　　DLBY 80

Soto, Gary 1952-. . . . . . . **CLC 32, 80; HLC**
　　See also AAYA 10; CA 119; 125; DLB 82;
　　　HW; JRDA; SATA 80

Soupault, Philippe 1897-1990 . . . . . . **CLC 68**
　　See also CA 116; 131

Souster, (Holmes) Raymond
　　1921- . . . . **CLC 5, 14**
　　See also CA 13-16R; CAAS 14; CANR 13,
　　　29; DLB 88; SATA 63

Southern, Terry 1926- . . . . **CLC 7**
　　See also CA 1-4R; CANR 1; DLB 2

Southey, Robert 1774-1843 . . . . **NCLC 8**
　　See also DLB 93, 107, 142; SATA 54

Southworth, Emma Dorothy Eliza Nevitte
　　1819-1899 . . . . **NCLC 26**

Souza, Ernest
　　See Scott, Evelyn

Soyinka, Wole
　　1934- . . . . **CLC 3, 5, 14, 36, 44; BLC;**
　　　　　　　　　　　　　　　　DA; DC 2; WLC
　　See also BW 2; CA 13-16R; CANR 27, 39;
　　　DLB 125; MTCW

Spackman, W(illiam) M(ode)
　　1905-1990 . . . . **CLC 46**
　　See also CA 81-84; 132

Spacks, Barry 1931-. . . . . **CLC 14**
　　See also CA 29-32R; CANR 33; DLB 105

Spanidou, Irini 1946- . . . . **CLC 44**

Spark, Muriel (Sarah)
　　1918- . . . . **CLC 2, 3, 5, 8, 13, 18, 40;**
　　　　　　　　　　　　　　　　　　SSC 10
　　See also CA 5-8R; CANR 12, 36;
　　　CDBLB 1945-1960; DLB 15, 139; MTCW

Spaulding, Douglas
　　See Bradbury, Ray (Douglas)

Spaulding, Leonard
　　See Bradbury, Ray (Douglas)

Spence, J. A. D.
　　See Eliot, T(homas) S(tearns)

Spencer, Elizabeth 1921-. . . . . **CLC 22**
　　See also CA 13-16R; CANR 32; DLB 6;
　　　MTCW; SATA 14

Spencer, Leonard G.
　　See Silverberg, Robert

Spencer, Scott 1945-. . . . . **CLC 30**
　　See also CA 113; DLBY 86

Spender, Stephen (Harold)
　　1909- . . . . **CLC 1, 2, 5, 10, 41**
　　See also CA 9-12R; CANR 31;
　　　CDBLB 1945-1960; DLB 20; MTCW

Spengler, Oswald (Arnold Gottfried)
　　1880-1936 . . . . **TCLC 25**
　　See also CA 118

Spenser, Edmund
　　1552(?)-1599 . . . . **LC 5; DA; PC 8; WLC**
　　See also CDBLB Before 1660

Spicer, Jack 1925-1965 . . . . . . **CLC 8, 18, 72**
　　See also CA 85-88; DLB 5, 16

Spiegelman, Art 1948-. . . . . **CLC 76**
　　See also AAYA 10; CA 125; CANR 41

Spielberg, Peter 1929- . . . . **CLC 6**
　　See also CA 5-8R; CANR 4; DLBY 81

Spielberg, Steven 1947- . . . . **CLC 20**
　　See also AAYA 8; CA 77-80; CANR 32;
　　　SATA 32

Spillane, Frank Morrison 1918-
　　See Spillane, Mickey
　　See also CA 25-28R; CANR 28; MTCW;
　　　SATA 66

Spillane, Mickey . . . . **CLC 3, 13**
　　See also Spillane, Frank Morrison

Spinoza, Benedictus de 1632-1677 . . . . **LC 9**

Spinrad, Norman (Richard) 1940-. . . **CLC 46**
　　See also CA 37-40R; CAAS 19; CANR 20;
　　　DLB 8

Spitteler, Carl (Friedrich Georg)
　　1845-1924 . . . . **TCLC 12**
　　See also CA 109; DLB 129

Spivack, Kathleen (Romola Drucker)
　　1938- . . . . **CLC 6**
　　See also CA 49-52

Spoto, Donald 1941-. . . . . **CLC 39**
　　See also CA 65-68; CANR 11

Springsteen, Bruce (F.) 1949- . . . . . . **CLC 17**
　　See also CA 111

Spurling, Hilary 1940-. . . . . **CLC 34**
　　See also CA 104; CANR 25

Spyker, John Howland
　　See Elman, Richard

Squires, (James) Radcliffe
　　1917-1993 . . . . **CLC 51**
　　See also CA 1-4R; 140; CANR 6, 21

Srivastava, Dhanpat Rai 1880(?)-1936
　　See Premchand
　　See also CA 118

Stacy, Donald
　　See Pohl, Frederik

Stael, Germaine de
　　See Stael-Holstein, Anne Louise Germaine
　　　Necker Baronn
　　See also DLB 119

Stael-Holstein, Anne Louise Germaine Necker
　　Baronn 1766-1817 . . . . **NCLC 3**
　　See also Stael, Germaine de

Stafford, Jean 1915-1979 . . . **CLC 4, 7, 19, 68**
　　See also CA 1-4R; 85-88; CANR 3; DLB 2;
　　　MTCW; SATA-Obit 22

Stafford, William (Edgar)
　　1914-1993 . . . . **CLC 4, 7, 29**
　　See also CA 5-8R; 142; CAAS 3; CANR 5,
　　　22; DLB 5

Staines, Trevor
　　See Brunner, John (Kilian Houston)

Stairs, Gordon
See Austin, Mary (Hunter)

Stannard, Martin 1947- . . . . **CLC 44**
See also CA 142

Stanton, Maura 1946- . . . . **CLC 9**
See also CA 89-92; CANR 15; DLB 120

Stanton, Schuyler
See Baum, L(yman) Frank

Stapledon, (William) Olaf
1886-1950 . . . . **TCLC 22**
See also CA 111; DLB 15

Starbuck, George (Edwin) 1931- . . . . **CLC 53**
See also CA 21-24R; CANR 23

Stark, Richard
See Westlake, Donald E(dwin)

Staunton, Schuyler
See Baum, L(yman) Frank

Stead, Christina (Ellen)
1902-1983 . . . . **CLC 2, 5, 8, 32, 80**
See also CA 13-16R; 109; CANR 33, 40;
MTCW

Stead, William Thomas
1849-1912 . . . . **TCLC 48**

Steele, Richard 1672-1729 . . . . **LC 18**
See also CDBLB 1660-1789; DLB 84, 101

Steele, Timothy (Reid) 1948- . . . . **CLC 45**
See also CA 93-96; CANR 16; DLB 120

Steffens, (Joseph) Lincoln
1866-1936 . . . . **TCLC 20**
See also CA 117

Stegner, Wallace (Earle)
1909-1993 . . . . **CLC 9, 49, 81**
See also AITN 1; BEST 90:3; CA 1-4R;
141; CAAS 9; CANR 1, 21, 46; DLB 9;
DLBY 93; MTCW

Stein, Gertrude
1874-1946 . . . . . . **TCLC 1, 6, 28, 48; DA;
WLC**
See also CA 104; 132; CDALB 1917-1929;
DLB 4, 54, 86; MTCW

Steinbeck, John (Ernst)
1902-1968 . . . . . . **CLC 1, 5, 9, 13, 21, 34,
45, 75; DA; SSC 11; WLC**
See also AAYA 12; CA 1-4R; 25-28R;
CANR 1, 35; CDALB 1929-1941; DLB 7,
9; DLBD 2; MTCW; SATA 9

Steinem, Gloria 1934- . . . . **CLC 63**
See also CA 53-56; CANR 28; MTCW

Steiner, George 1929- . . . . **CLC 24**
See also CA 73-76; CANR 31; DLB 67;
MTCW; SATA 62

Steiner, K. Leslie
See Delany, Samuel R(ay, Jr.)

Steiner, Rudolf 1861-1925 . . . . **TCLC 13**
See also CA 107

Stendhal
1783-1842 . . . . . **NCLC 23, 46; DA; WLC**
See also DLB 119

Stephen, Leslie 1832-1904 . . . . **TCLC 23**
See also CA 123; DLB 57, 144

Stephen, Sir Leslie
See Stephen, Leslie

Stephen, Virginia
See Woolf, (Adeline) Virginia

Stephens, James 1882(?)-1950 . . . . . . **TCLC 4**
See also CA 104; DLB 19

Stephens, Reed
See Donaldson, Stephen R.

Steptoe, Lydia
See Barnes, Djuna

Sterchi, Beat 1949- . . . . **CLC 65**

Sterling, Brett
See Bradbury, Ray (Douglas); Hamilton,
Edmond

Sterling, Bruce 1954- . . . . **CLC 72**
See also CA 119; CANR 44

Sterling, George 1869-1926 . . . . . . **TCLC 20**
See also CA 117; DLB 54

Stern, Gerald 1925- . . . . **CLC 40**
See also CA 81-84; CANR 28; DLB 105

Stern, Richard (Gustave) 1928- . . . **CLC 4, 39**
See also CA 1-4R; CANR 1, 25; DLBY 87

Sternberg, Josef von 1894-1969 . . . . . **CLC 20**
See also CA 81-84

Sterne, Laurence
1713-1768 . . . . **LC 2; DA; WLC**
See also CDBLB 1660-1789; DLB 39

Sternheim, (William Adolf) Carl
1878-1942 . . . . **TCLC 8**
See also CA 105; DLB 56, 118

Stevens, Mark 1951- . . . . **CLC 34**
See also CA 122

Stevens, Wallace
1879-1955 . . . . **TCLC 3, 12, 45; DA;
PC 6; WLC**
See also CA 104; 124; CDALB 1929-1941;
DLB 54; MTCW

Stevenson, Anne (Katharine)
1933- . . . . **CLC 7, 33**
See also CA 17-20R; CAAS 9; CANR 9, 33;
DLB 40; MTCW

Stevenson, Robert Louis (Balfour)
1850-1894 . . . . **NCLC 5, 14; DA;
SSC 11; WLC**
See also CDBLB 1890-1914; CLR 10, 11;
DLB 18, 57, 141; JRDA; MAICYA;
YABC 2

Stewart, J(ohn) I(nnes) M(ackintosh)
1906- . . . . **CLC 7, 14, 32**
See also CA 85-88; CAAS 3; CANR 47;
MTCW

Stewart, Mary (Florence Elinor)
1916- . . . . **CLC 7, 35**
See also CA 1-4R; CANR 1; SATA 12

Stewart, Mary Rainbow
See Stewart, Mary (Florence Elinor)

Stifle, June
See Campbell, Maria

Stifter, Adalbert 1805-1868 . . . . . . **NCLC 41**
See also DLB 133

Still, James 1906- . . . . **CLC 49**
See also CA 65-68; CAAS 17; CANR 10,
26; DLB 9; SATA 29

Sting
See Sumner, Gordon Matthew

Stirling, Arthur
See Sinclair, Upton (Beall)

Stitt, Milan 1941- . . . . **CLC 29**
See also CA 69-72

Stockton, Francis Richard 1834-1902
See Stockton, Frank R.
See also CA 108; 137; MAICYA; SATA 44

Stockton, Frank R. . . . . **TCLC 47**
See also Stockton, Francis Richard
See also DLB 42, 74; SATA-Brief 32

Stoddard, Charles
See Kuttner, Henry

Stoker, Abraham 1847-1912
See Stoker, Bram
See also CA 105; DA; SATA 29

Stoker, Bram . . . . **TCLC 8; WLC**
See also Stoker, Abraham
See also CDBLB 1890-1914; DLB 36, 70

Stolz, Mary (Slattery) 1920- . . . . **CLC 12**
See also AAYA 8; AITN 1; CA 5-8R;
CANR 13, 41; JRDA; MAICYA;
SAAS 3; SATA 10, 71

Stone, Irving 1903-1989 . . . . **CLC 7**
See also AITN 1; CA 1-4R; 129; CAAS 3;
CANR 1, 23; MTCW; SATA 3;
SATA-Obit 64

Stone, Oliver 1946- . . . . **CLC 73**
See also CA 110

Stone, Robert (Anthony)
1937- . . . . **CLC 5, 23, 42**
See also CA 85-88; CANR 23; MTCW

Stone, Zachary
See Follett, Ken(neth Martin)

Stoppard, Tom
1937- . . . . . . **CLC 1, 3, 4, 5, 8, 15, 29, 34,
63; DA; WLC**
See also CA 81-84; CANR 39;
CDBLB 1960 to Present; DLB 13;
DLBY 85; MTCW

Storey, David (Malcolm)
1933- . . . . **CLC 2, 4, 5, 8**
See also CA 81-84; CANR 36; DLB 13, 14;
MTCW

Storm, Hyemeyohsts 1935- . . . . **CLC 3**
See also CA 81-84; CANR 45; NNAL

Storm, (Hans) Theodor (Woldsen)
1817-1888 . . . . **NCLC 1**

Storni, Alfonsina
1892-1938 . . . . **TCLC 5; HLC**
See also CA 104; 131; HW

Stout, Rex (Todhunter) 1886-1975 . . . **CLC 3**
See also AITN 2; CA 61-64

Stow, (Julian) Randolph 1935- . . **CLC 23, 48**
See also CA 13-16R; CANR 33; MTCW

Stowe, Harriet (Elizabeth) Beecher
1811-1896 . . . . **NCLC 3; DA; WLC**
See also CDALB 1865-1917; DLB 1, 12, 42,
74; JRDA; MAICYA; YABC 1

Strachey, (Giles) Lytton
1880-1932 . . . . **TCLC 12**
See also CA 110; DLBD 10

Strand, Mark 1934- . . . . . . **CLC 6, 18, 41, 71**
See also CA 21-24R; CANR 40; DLB 5;
SATA 41

Straub, Peter (Francis) 1943- . . . . . . **CLC 28**
See also BEST 89:1; CA 85-88; CANR 28;
DLBY 84; MTCW

Strauss, Botho 1944- .... CLC **22**
See also DLB 124

Streatfeild, (Mary) Noel
1895(?)-1986 .... CLC **21**
See also CA 81-84; 120; CANR 31;
CLR 17; MAICYA; SATA 20;
SATA-Obit 48

Stribling, T(homas) S(igismund)
1881-1965 .... CLC **23**
See also CA 107; DLB 9

Strindberg, (Johan) August
1849-1912 ...... TCLC **1, 8, 21, 47; DA;**
WLC
See also CA 104; 135

Stringer, Arthur 1874-1950 .... TCLC **37**
See also DLB 92

Stringer, David
See Roberts, Keith (John Kingston)

Strugatskii, Arkadii (Natanovich)
1925-1991 .... CLC **27**
See also CA 106; 135

Strugatskii, Boris (Natanovich)
1933- .... CLC **27**
See also CA 106

Strummer, Joe 1953(?)- .... CLC **30**

Stuart, Don A.
See Campbell, John W(ood, Jr.)

Stuart, Ian
See MacLean, Alistair (Stuart)

Stuart, Jesse (Hilton)
1906-1984 .... CLC **1, 8, 11, 14, 34**
See also CA 5-8R; 112; CANR 31; DLB 9,
48, 102; DLBY 84; SATA 2;
SATA-Obit 36

Sturgeon, Theodore (Hamilton)
1918-1985 .... CLC **22, 39**
See also Queen, Ellery
See also CA 81-84; 116; CANR 32; DLB 8;
DLBY 85; MTCW

Sturges, Preston 1898-1959 .... TCLC **48**
See also CA 114; DLB 26

Styron, William
1925- .... CLC **1, 3, 5, 11, 15, 60**
See also BEST 90:4; CA 5-8R; CANR 6, 33;
CDALB 1968-1988; DLB 2, 143;
DLBY 80; MTCW

Suarez Lynch, B.
See Bioy Casares, Adolfo; Borges, Jorge
Luis

Su Chien 1884-1918
See Su Man-shu
See also CA 123

Suckow, Ruth 1892-1960
See also CA 113; DLB 9, 102; SSC 18

Sudermann, Hermann 1857-1928 .. TCLC **15**
See also CA 107; DLB 118

Sue, Eugene 1804-1857 .... NCLC **1**
See also DLB 119

Sueskind, Patrick 1949- .... CLC **44**
See also Suskind, Patrick

Sukenick, Ronald 1932- ..... CLC **3, 4, 6, 48**
See also CA 25-28R; CAAS 8; CANR 32;
DLBY 81

Suknaski, Andrew 1942- .... CLC **19**
See also CA 101; DLB 53

Sullivan, Vernon
See Vian, Boris

Sully Prudhomme 1839-1907 ...... TCLC **31**

Su Man-shu .... TCLC **24**
See also Su Chien

Summerforest, Ivy B.
See Kirkup, James

Summers, Andrew James 1942- ..... CLC **26**

Summers, Andy
See Summers, Andrew James

Summers, Hollis (Spurgeon, Jr.)
1916- .... CLC **10**
See also CA 5-8R; CANR 3; DLB 6

Summers, (Alphonsus Joseph-Mary Augustus)
Montague 1880-1948 .... TCLC **16**
See also CA 118

Sumner, Gordon Matthew 1951-.... CLC **26**

Surtees, Robert Smith
1803-1864 .... NCLC **14**
See also DLB 21

Susann, Jacqueline 1921-1974 ...... CLC **3**
See also AITN 1; CA 65-68; 53-56; MTCW

Suskind, Patrick
See Sueskind, Patrick
See also CA 145

Sutcliff, Rosemary 1920-1992 ...... CLC **26**
See also AAYA 10; CA 5-8R; 139;
CANR 37; CLR 1; JRDA; MAICYA;
SATA 6, 44, 78; SATA-Obit 73

Sutro, Alfred 1863-1933 .... TCLC **6**
See also CA 105; DLB 10

Sutton, Henry
See Slavitt, David R(ytman)

Svevo, Italo .... TCLC **2, 35**
See also Schmitz, Aron Hector

Swados, Elizabeth 1951- .... CLC **12**
See also CA 97-100

Swados, Harvey 1920-1972 .... CLC **5**
See also CA 5-8R; 37-40R; CANR 6;
DLB 2

Swan, Gladys 1934- .... CLC **69**
See also CA 101; CANR 17, 39

Swarthout, Glendon (Fred)
1918-1992 .... CLC **35**
See also CA 1-4R; 139; CANR 1, 47;
SATA 26

Sweet, Sarah C.
See Jewett, (Theodora) Sarah Orne

Swenson, May
1919-1989 .... CLC **4, 14, 61; DA**
See also CA 5-8R; 130; CANR 36; DLB 5;
MTCW; SATA 15

Swift, Augustus
See Lovecraft, H(oward) P(hillips)

Swift, Graham (Colin) 1949- .... CLC **41**
See also CA 117; 122; CANR 46

Swift, Jonathan
1667-1745 ...... LC **1; DA; PC 9; WLC**
See also CDBLB 1660-1789; DLB 39, 95,
101; SATA 19

Swinburne, Algernon Charles
1837-1909 ...... TCLC **8, 36; DA; WLC**
See also CA 105; 140; CDBLB 1832-1890;
DLB 35, 57

Swinfen, Ann .... CLC **34**

Swinnerton, Frank Arthur
1884-1982 .... CLC **31**
See also CA 108; DLB 34

Swithen, John
See King, Stephen (Edwin)

Sylvia
See Ashton-Warner, Sylvia (Constance)

Symmes, Robert Edward
See Duncan, Robert (Edward)

Symonds, John Addington
1840-1893 .... NCLC **34**
See also DLB 57, 144

Symons, Arthur 1865-1945 .... TCLC **11**
See also CA 107; DLB 19, 57

Symons, Julian (Gustave)
1912- .... CLC **2, 14, 32**
See also CA 49-52; CAAS 3; CANR 3, 33;
DLB 87; DLBY 92; MTCW

Synge, (Edmund) J(ohn) M(illington)
1871-1909 .... TCLC **6, 37; DC 2**
See also CA 104; 141; CDBLB 1890-1914;
DLB 10, 19

Syruc, J.
See Milosz, Czeslaw

Szirtes, George 1948- .... CLC **46**
See also CA 109; CANR 27

Tabori, George 1914- .... CLC **19**
See also CA 49-52; CANR 4

Tagore, Rabindranath
1861-1941 .... TCLC **3, 53; PC 8**
See also CA 104; 120; MTCW

Taine, Hippolyte Adolphe
1828-1893 .... NCLC **15**

Talese, Gay 1932-................. CLC **37**
See also AITN 1; CA 1-4R; CANR 9;
MTCW

Tallent, Elizabeth (Ann) 1954- ..... CLC **45**
See also CA 117; DLB 130

Tally, Ted 1952-.................. CLC **42**
See also CA 120; 124

Tamayo y Baus, Manuel
1829-1898 .... NCLC **1**

Tammsaare, A(nton) H(ansen)
1878-1940 .... TCLC **27**

Tan, Amy 1952- .... CLC **59**
See also AAYA 9; BEST 89:3; CA 136;
SATA 75

Tandem, Felix
See Spitteler, Carl (Friedrich Georg)

Tanizaki, Jun'ichiro
1886-1965 .... CLC **8, 14, 28**
See also CA 93-96; 25-28R

Tanner, William
See Amis, Kingsley (William)

Tao Lao
See Storni, Alfonsina

Tarassoff, Lev
See Troyat, Henri

Tarbell, Ida M(inerva)
1857-1944 .... TCLC **40**
See also CA 122; DLB 47

Tarkington, (Newton) Booth
1869-1946 .... **TCLC 9**
See also CA 110; 143; DLB 9, 102;
SATA 17

Tarkovsky, Andrei (Arsenyevich)
1932-1986 .... **CLC 75**
See also CA 127

Tartt, Donna 1964(?)- .... **CLC 76**
See also CA 142

Tasso, Torquato 1544-1595 .... **LC 5**

Tate, (John Orley) Allen
1899-1979 .... **CLC 2, 4, 6, 9, 11, 14, 24**
See also CA 5-8R; 85-88; CANR 32;
DLB 4, 45, 63; MTCW

Tate, Ellalice
See Hibbert, Eleanor Alice Burford

Tate, James (Vincent) 1943- ... **CLC 2, 6, 25**
See also CA 21-24R; CANR 29; DLB 5

Tavel, Ronald 1940- .... **CLC 6**
See also CA 21-24R; CANR 33

Taylor, C(ecil) P(hilip) 1929-1981... **CLC 27**
See also CA 25-28R; 105; CANR 47

Taylor, Edward 1642(?)-1729.... **LC 11; DA**
See also DLB 24

Taylor, Eleanor Ross 1920- .... **CLC 5**
See also CA 81-84

Taylor, Elizabeth 1912-1975 ... **CLC 2, 4, 29**
See also CA 13-16R; CANR 9; DLB 139;
MTCW; SATA 13

Taylor, Henry (Splawn) 1942- ...... **CLC 44**
See also CA 33-36R; CAAS 7; CANR 31;
DLB 5

Taylor, Kamala (Purnaiya) 1924-
See Markandaya, Kamala
See also CA 77-80

Taylor, Mildred D. .... **CLC 21**
See also AAYA 10; BW 1; CA 85-88;
CANR 25; CLR 9; DLB 52; JRDA;
MAICYA; SAAS 5; SATA 15, 70

Taylor, Peter (Hillsman)
1917- ...... **CLC 1, 4, 18, 37, 44, 50, 71;**
SSC 10
See also CA 13-16R; CANR 9; DLBY 81;
MTCW

Taylor, Robert Lewis 1912- .... **CLC 14**
See also CA 1-4R; CANR 3; SATA 10

Tchekhov, Anton
See Chekhov, Anton (Pavlovich)

Teasdale, Sara 1884-1933.......... **TCLC 4**
See also CA 104; DLB 45; SATA 32

Tegner, Esaias 1782-1846........ **NCLC 2**

Teilhard de Chardin, (Marie Joseph) Pierre
1881-1955 .... **TCLC 9**
See also CA 105

Temple, Ann
See Mortimer, Penelope (Ruth)

Tennant, Emma (Christina)
1937- .... **CLC 13, 52**
See also CA 65-68; CAAS 9; CANR 10, 38;
DLB 14

Tenneshaw, S. M.
See Silverberg, Robert

Tennyson, Alfred
1809-1892 .. **NCLC 30; DA; PC 6; WLC**
See also CDBLB 1832-1890; DLB 32

Teran, Lisa St. Aubin de .... **CLC 36**
See also St. Aubin de Teran, Lisa

Terence 195(?)B.C.-159B.C...... **CMLC 14**

Teresa de Jesus, St. 1515-1582 ...... **LC 18**

Terkel, Louis 1912-
See Terkel, Studs
See also CA 57-60; CANR 18, 45; MTCW

Terkel, Studs .... **CLC 38**
See also Terkel, Louis
See also AITN 1

Terry, C. V.
See Slaughter, Frank G(ill)

Terry, Megan 1932- .... **CLC 19**
See also CA 77-80; CABS 3; CANR 43;
DLB 7

Tertz, Abram
See Sinyavsky, Andrei (Donatevich)

Tesich, Steve 1943(?)-.......... **CLC 40, 69**
See also CA 105; DLBY 83

Teternikov, Fyodor Kuzmich 1863-1927
See Sologub, Fyodor
See also CA 104

Tevis, Walter 1928-1984 .... **CLC 42**
See also CA 113

Tey, Josephine................... **TCLC 14**
See also Mackintosh, Elizabeth
See also DLB 77

Thackeray, William Makepeace
1811-1863 .... **NCLC 5, 14, 22, 43; DA;**
WLC
See also CDBLB 1832-1890; DLB 21, 55;
SATA 23

Thakura, Ravindranatha
See Tagore, Rabindranath

Tharoor, Shashi 1956- .... **CLC 70**
See also CA 141

Thelwell, Michael Miles 1939- ..... **CLC 22**
See also BW 2; CA 101

Theobald, Lewis, Jr.
See Lovecraft, H(oward) P(hillips)

Theodorescu, Ion N. 1880-1967
See Arghezi, Tudor
See also CA 116

Theriault, Yves 1915-1983........ **CLC 79**
See also CA 102; DLB 88

Theroux, Alexander (Louis)
1939- .... **CLC 2, 25**
See also CA 85-88; CANR 20

Theroux, Paul (Edward)
1941- ...... **CLC 5, 8, 11, 15, 28, 46**
See also BEST 89:4; CA 33-36R; CANR 20,
45; DLB 2; MTCW; SATA 44

Thesen, Sharon 1946-............. **CLC 56**

Thevenin, Denis
See Duhamel, Georges

Thibault, Jacques Anatole Francois
1844-1924
See France, Anatole
See also CA 106; 127; MTCW

Thiele, Colin (Milton) 1920- .... **CLC 17**
See also CA 29-32R; CANR 12, 28;
CLR 27; MAICYA; SAAS 2; SATA 14,
72

Thomas, Audrey (Callahan)
1935- .... **CLC 7, 13, 37**
See also AITN 2; CA 21-24R; CAAS 19;
CANR 36; DLB 60; MTCW

Thomas, D(onald) M(ichael)
1935- .... **CLC 13, 22, 31**
See also CA 61-64; CAAS 11; CANR 17,
45; CDBLB 1960 to Present; DLB 40;
MTCW

Thomas, Dylan (Marlais)
1914-1953 ... **TCLC 1, 8, 45; DA; PC 2;**
SSC 3; WLC
See also CA 104; 120; CDBLB 1945-1960;
DLB 13, 20, 139; MTCW; SATA 60

Thomas, (Philip) Edward
1878-1917 .... **TCLC 10**
See also CA 106; DLB 19

Thomas, Joyce Carol 1938-........ **CLC 35**
See also AAYA 12; BW 2; CA 113; 116;
CLR 19; DLB 33; JRDA; MAICYA;
MTCW; SAAS 7; SATA 40, 78

Thomas, Lewis 1913-1993 .... **CLC 35**
See also CA 85-88; 143; CANR 38; MTCW

Thomas, Paul
See Mann, (Paul) Thomas

Thomas, Piri 1928- .... **CLC 17**
See also CA 73-76; HW

Thomas, R(onald) S(tuart)
1913- .... **CLC 6, 13, 48**
See also CA 89-92; CAAS 4; CANR 30;
CDBLB 1960 to Present; DLB 27;
MTCW

Thomas, Ross (Elmore) 1926- ...... **CLC 39**
See also CA 33-36R; CANR 22

Thompson, Francis Clegg
See Mencken, H(enry) L(ouis)

Thompson, Francis Joseph
1859-1907 .... **TCLC 4**
See also CA 104; CDBLB 1890-1914;
DLB 19

Thompson, Hunter S(tockton)
1939- .... **CLC 9, 17, 40**
See also BEST 89:1; CA 17-20R; CANR 23,
46; MTCW

Thompson, James Myers
See Thompson, Jim (Myers)

Thompson, Jim (Myers)
1906-1977(?) .... **CLC 69**
See also CA 140

Thompson, Judith .... **CLC 39**

Thomson, James 1700-1748........ **LC 16**

Thomson, James 1834-1882...... **NCLC 18**

Thoreau, Henry David
1817-1862 ...... **NCLC 7, 21; DA; WLC**
See also CDALB 1640-1865; DLB 1

Thornton, Hall
See Silverberg, Robert

Thurber, James (Grover)
1894-1961 ... **CLC 5, 11, 25; DA; SSC 1**
See also CA 73-76; CANR 17, 39;
CDALB 1929-1941; DLB 4, 11, 22, 102;
MAICYA; MTCW; SATA 13

Thurman, Wallace (Henry)
1902-1934 .... **TCLC 6; BLC**
See also BW 1; CA 104; 124; DLB 51

Ticheburn, Cheviot
See Ainsworth, William Harrison

Tieck, (Johann) Ludwig
1773-1853 .... **NCLC 5, 46**
See also DLB 90

Tiger, Derry
See Ellison, Harlan (Jay)

Tilghman, Christopher 1948(?)-..... **CLC 65**

Tillinghast, Richard (Williford)
1940- .... **CLC 29**
See also CA 29-32R; CANR 26

Timrod, Henry 1828-1867 .... **NCLC 25**
See also DLB 3

Tindall, Gillian 1938-............. **CLC 7**
See also CA 21-24R; CANR 11

Tiptree, James, Jr. .... **CLC 48, 50**
See also Sheldon, Alice Hastings Bradley
See also DLB 8

Titmarsh, Michael Angelo
See Thackeray, William Makepeace

Tocqueville, Alexis (Charles Henri Maurice
Clerel Comte) 1805-1859..... **NCLC 7**

Tolkien, J(ohn) R(onald) R(euel)
1892-1973 ...... **CLC 1, 2, 3, 8, 12, 38;
DA; WLC**
See also AAYA 10; AITN 1; CA 17-18;
45-48; CANR 36; CAP 2;
CDBLB 1914-1945; DLB 15; JRDA;
MAICYA; MTCW; SATA 2, 32;
SATA-Obit 24

Toller, Ernst 1893-1939 .... **TCLC 10**
See also CA 107; DLB 124

Tolson, M. B.
See Tolson, Melvin B(eaunorus)

Tolson, Melvin B(eaunorus)
1898(?)-1966 .... **CLC 36; BLC**
See also BW 1; CA 124; 89-92; DLB 48, 76

Tolstoi, Aleksei Nikolaevich
See Tolstoy, Alexey Nikolaevich

Tolstoy, Alexey Nikolaevich
1882-1945 .... **TCLC 18**
See also CA 107

Tolstoy, Count Leo
See Tolstoy, Leo (Nikolaevich)

Tolstoy, Leo (Nikolaevich)
1828-1910 ...... **TCLC 4, 11, 17, 28, 44;
DA; SSC 9; WLC**
See also CA 104; 123; SATA 26

Tomasi di Lampedusa, Giuseppe 1896-1957
See Lampedusa, Giuseppe (Tomasi) di
See also CA 111

Tomlin, Lily...................... **CLC 17**
See also Tomlin, Mary Jean

Tomlin, Mary Jean 1939(?)-
See Tomlin, Lily
See also CA 117

Tomlinson, (Alfred) Charles
1927- .... **CLC 2, 4, 6, 13, 45**
See also CA 5-8R; CANR 33; DLB 40

Tonson, Jacob
See Bennett, (Enoch) Arnold

Toole, John Kennedy
1937-1969 .... **CLC 19, 64**
See also CA 104; DLBY 81

Toomer, Jean
1894-1967 ..... **CLC 1, 4, 13, 22; BLC;
PC 7; SSC 1**
See also BW 1; CA 85-88;
CDALB 1917-1929; DLB 45, 51; MTCW

Torley, Luke
See Blish, James (Benjamin)

Tornimparte, Alessandra
See Ginzburg, Natalia

Torre, Raoul della
See Mencken, H(enry) L(ouis)

Torrey, E(dwin) Fuller 1937-....... **CLC 34**
See also CA 119

Torsvan, Ben Traven
See Traven, B.

Torsvan, Benno Traven
See Traven, B.

Torsvan, Berick Traven
See Traven, B.

Torsvan, Berwick Traven
See Traven, B.

Torsvan, Bruno Traven
See Traven, B.

Torsvan, Traven
See Traven, B.

Tournier, Michel (Edouard)
1924- .... **CLC 6, 23, 36**
See also CA 49-52; CANR 3, 36; DLB 83;
MTCW; SATA 23

Tournimparte, Alessandra
See Ginzburg, Natalia

Towers, Ivar
See Kornbluth, C(yril) M.

Towne, Robert (Burton) 1936(?)-.... **CLC 87**
See also CA 108; DLB 44

Townsend, Sue 1946- .... **CLC 61**
See also CA 119; 127; MTCW; SATA 55;
SATA-Brief 48

Townshend, Peter (Dennis Blandford)
1945- .... **CLC 17, 42**
See also CA 107

Tozzi, Federigo 1883-1920....... **TCLC 31**

Traill, Catharine Parr
1802-1899 .... **NCLC 31**
See also DLB 99

Trakl, Georg 1887-1914.......... **TCLC 5**
See also CA 104

Transtroemer, Tomas (Goesta)
1931- .... **CLC 52, 65**
See also CA 117; 129; CAAS 17

Transtromer, Tomas Gosta
See Transtroemer, Tomas (Goesta)

Traven, B. (?)-1969............ **CLC 8, 11**
See also CA 19-20; 25-28R; CAP 2; DLB 9,
56; MTCW

Treitel, Jonathan 1959- .... **CLC 70**

Tremain, Rose 1943-............. **CLC 42**
See also CA 97-100; CANR 44; DLB 14

Tremblay, Michel 1942-.......... **CLC 29**
See also CA 116; 128; DLB 60; MTCW

Trevanian...................... **CLC 29**
See also Whitaker, Rod(ney)

Trevor, Glen
See Hilton, James

Trevor, William
1928- .... **CLC 7, 9, 14, 25, 71**
See also Cox, William Trevor
See also DLB 14, 139

Trifonov, Yuri (Valentinovich)
1925-1981 .... **CLC 45**
See also CA 126; 103; MTCW

Trilling, Lionel 1905-1975 .... **CLC 9, 11, 24**
See also CA 9-12R; 61-64; CANR 10;
DLB 28, 63; MTCW

Trimball, W. H.
See Mencken, H(enry) L(ouis)

Tristan
See Gomez de la Serna, Ramon

Tristram
See Housman, A(lfred) E(dward)

Trogdon, William (Lewis) 1939-
See Heat-Moon, William Least
See also CA 115; 119; CANR 47

Trollope, Anthony
1815-1882 ...... **NCLC 6, 33; DA; WLC**
See also CDBLB 1832-1890; DLB 21, 57;
SATA 22

Trollope, Frances 1779-1863 ..... **NCLC 30**
See also DLB 21

Trotsky, Leon 1879-1940........ **TCLC 22**
See also CA 118

Trotter (Cockburn), Catharine
1679-1749 .... **LC 8**
See also DLB 84

Trout, Kilgore
See Farmer, Philip Jose

Trow, George W. S. 1943-........ **CLC 52**
See also CA 126

Troyat, Henri 1911-.............. **CLC 23**
See also CA 45-48; CANR 2, 33; MTCW

Trudeau, G(arretson) B(eekman) 1948-
See Trudeau, Garry B.
See also CA 81-84; CANR 31; SATA 35

Trudeau, Garry B................. **CLC 12**
See also Trudeau, G(arretson) B(eekman)
See also AAYA 10; AITN 2

Truffaut, Francois 1932-1984...... **CLC 20**
See also CA 81-84; 113; CANR 34

Trumbo, Dalton 1905-1976 .... **CLC 19**
See also CA 21-24R; 69-72; CANR 10;
DLB 26

Trumbull, John 1750-1831 .... **NCLC 30**
See also DLB 31

Trundlett, Helen B.
See Eliot, T(homas) S(tearns)

Tryon, Thomas 1926-1991 .... **CLC 3, 11**
See also AITN 1; CA 29-32R; 135;
CANR 32; MTCW

Tryon, Tom
See Tryon, Thomas

Ts'ao Hsueh-ch'in 1715(?)-1763...... **LC 1**

Tsushima, Shuji 1909-1948
See Dazai, Osamu
See also CA 107

Tsvetaeva (Efron), Marina (Ivanovna)
1892-1941 .... **TCLC 7, 35**
See also CA 104; 128; MTCW

Tuck, Lily 1938-................. **CLC 70**
See also CA 139

Tu Fu 712-770.................... **PC 9**

Tunis, John R(oberts) 1889-1975 ... **CLC 12**
See also CA 61-64; DLB 22; JRDA;
MAICYA; SATA 37; SATA-Brief 30

Tuohy, Frank.................... **CLC 37**
See also Tuohy, John Francis
See also DLB 14, 139

Tuohy, John Francis 1925-
See Tuohy, Frank
See also CA 5-8R; CANR 3, 47

Turco, Lewis (Putnam) 1934- ... **CLC 11, 63**
See also CA 13-16R; CANR 24; DLBY 84

Turgenev, Ivan
1818-1883 ...... **NCLC 21; DA; SSC 7;
WLC**

Turgot, Anne-Robert-Jacques
1727-1781 .... **LC 26**

Turner, Frederick 1943-.......... **CLC 48**
See also CA 73-76; CAAS 10; CANR 12,
30; DLB 40

Tutu, Desmond M(pilo)
1931- .... **CLC 80; BLC**
See also BW 1; CA 125

Tutuola, Amos 1920- ... **CLC 5, 14, 29; BLC**
See also BW 2; CA 9-12R; CANR 27;
DLB 125; MTCW

Twain, Mark
... **TCLC 6, 12, 19, 36, 48; SSC 6; WLC**
See also Clemens, Samuel Langhorne
See also DLB 11, 12, 23, 64, 74

Tyler, Anne
1941- .... **CLC 7, 11, 18, 28, 44, 59**
See also BEST 89:1; CA 9-12R; CANR 11,
33; DLB 6, 143; DLBY 82; MTCW;
SATA 7

Tyler, Royall 1757-1826......... **NCLC 3**
See also DLB 37

Tynan, Katharine 1861-1931 .... **TCLC 3**
See also CA 104

Tyutchev, Fyodor 1803-1873 ..... **NCLC 34**

Tzara, Tristan .... **CLC 47**
See also Rosenfeld, Samuel

Uhry, Alfred 1936-.............. **CLC 55**
See also CA 127; 133

Ulf, Haerved
See Strindberg, (Johan) August

Ulf, Harved
See Strindberg, (Johan) August

Ulibarri, Sabine R(eyes) 1919- ..... **CLC 83**
See also CA 131; DLB 82; HW

Unamuno (y Jugo), Miguel de
1864-1936 .... **TCLC 2, 9; HLC; SSC 11**
See also CA 104; 131; DLB 108; HW;
MTCW

Undercliffe, Errol
See Campbell, (John) Ramsey

Underwood, Miles
See Glassco, John

Undset, Sigrid
1882-1949 .... **TCLC 3; DA; WLC**
See also CA 104; 129; MTCW

Ungaretti, Giuseppe
1888-1970 .... **CLC 7, 11, 15**
See also CA 19-20; 25-28R; CAP 2;
DLB 114

Unger, Douglas 1952-............. **CLC 34**
See also CA 130

Unsworth, Barry (Forster) 1930-.... **CLC 76**
See also CA 25-28R; CANR 30

Updike, John (Hoyer)
1932- .... **CLC 1, 2, 3, 5, 7, 9, 13, 15,
23, 34, 43, 70; DA; SSC 13; WLC**
See also CA 1-4R; CABS 1; CANR 4, 33;
CDALB 1968-1988; DLB 2, 5, 143;
DLBD 3; DLBY 80, 82; MTCW

Upshaw, Margaret Mitchell
See Mitchell, Margaret (Munnerlyn)

Upton, Mark
See Sanders, Lawrence

Urdang, Constance (Henriette)
1922- .... **CLC 47**
See also CA 21-24R; CANR 9, 24

Uriel, Henry
See Faust, Frederick (Schiller)

Uris, Leon (Marcus) 1924-...... **CLC 7, 32**
See also AITN 1, 2; BEST 89:2; CA 1-4R;
CANR 1, 40; MTCW; SATA 49

Urmuz
See Codrescu, Andrei

Ustinov, Peter (Alexander) 1921-.... **CLC 1**
See also AITN 1; CA 13-16R; CANR 25;
DLB 13

Vaculik, Ludvik 1926-............. **CLC 7**
See also CA 53-56

Valdez, Luis (Miguel)
1940-................. **CLC 84; HLC**
See also CA 101; CANR 32; DLB 122; HW

Valenzuela, Luisa 1938-... **CLC 31; SSC 14**
See also CA 101; CANR 32; DLB 113; HW

Valera y Alcala-Galiano, Juan
1824-1905 .... **TCLC 10**
See also CA 106

Valery, (Ambroise) Paul (Toussaint Jules)
1871-1945 .... **TCLC 4, 15; PC 9**
See also CA 104; 122; MTCW

Valle-Inclan, Ramon (Maria) del
1866-1936 .... **TCLC 5; HLC**
See also CA 106; DLB 134

Vallejo, Antonio Buero
See Buero Vallejo, Antonio

Vallejo, Cesar (Abraham)
1892-1938 .... **TCLC 3, 56; HLC**
See also CA 105; HW

Valle Y Pena, Ramon del
See Valle-Inclan, Ramon (Maria) del

Van Ash, Cay 1918-.............. **CLC 34**

Vanbrugh, Sir John 1664-1726 ...... **LC 21**
See also DLB 80

Van Campen, Karl
See Campbell, John W(ood, Jr.)

Vance, Gerald
See Silverberg, Robert

Vance, Jack .... **CLC 35**
See also Vance, John Holbrook
See also DLB 8

Vance, John Holbrook 1916-
See Queen, Ellery; Vance, Jack
See also CA 29-32R; CANR 17; MTCW

**Van Den Bogarde, Derek Jules Gaspard Ulric
Niven** 1921-
See Bogarde, Dirk
See also CA 77-80

Vandenburgh, Jane .... **CLC 59**

Vanderhaeghe, Guy 1951- .... **CLC 41**
See also CA 113

van der Post, Laurens (Jan) 1906- ... **CLC 5**
See also CA 5-8R; CANR 35

van de Wetering, Janwillem 1931- .. **CLC 47**
See also CA 49-52; CANR 4

Van Dine, S. S. .... **TCLC 23**
See also Wright, Willard Huntington

Van Doren, Carl (Clinton)
1885-1950 .... **TCLC 18**
See also CA 111

Van Doren, Mark 1894-1972..... **CLC 6, 10**
See also CA 1-4R; 37-40R; CANR 3;
DLB 45; MTCW

Van Druten, John (William)
1901-1957 .... **TCLC 2**
See also CA 104; DLB 10

Van Duyn, Mona (Jane)
1921- .... **CLC 3, 7, 63**
See also CA 9-12R; CANR 7, 38; DLB 5

Van Dyne, Edith
See Baum, L(yman) Frank

van Itallie, Jean-Claude 1936-....... **CLC 3**
See also CA 45-48; CAAS 2; CANR 1;
DLB 7

van Ostaijen, Paul 1896-1928 ..... **TCLC 33**

Van Peebles, Melvin 1932- ...... **CLC 2, 20**
See also BW 2; CA 85-88; CANR 27

Vansittart, Peter 1920-............ **CLC 42**
See also CA 1-4R; CANR 3

Van Vechten, Carl 1880-1964 ...... **CLC 33**
See also CA 89-92; DLB 4, 9, 51

Van Vogt, A(lfred) E(lton) 1912-..... **CLC 1**
See also CA 21-24R; CANR 28; DLB 8;
SATA 14

Varda, Agnes 1928- .... **CLC 16**
See also CA 116; 122

Vargas Llosa, (Jorge) Mario (Pedro)
1936- .... **CLC 3, 6, 9, 10, 15, 31, 42, 85;
DA; HLC**
See also CA 73-76; CANR 18, 32, 42;
DLB 145; HW; MTCW

Vasiliu, Gheorghe 1881-1957
See Bacovia, George
See also CA 123

Vassa, Gustavus
See Equiano, Olaudah

Vassilikos, Vassilis 1933-......... **CLC 4, 8**
See also CA 81-84

Vaughan, Henry 1621-1695 . . . . LC **27**
 See also DLB 131

Vaughn, Stephanie . . . . CLC **62**

Vazov, Ivan (Minchov)
 1850-1921 . . . . TCLC **25**
 See also CA 121; DLB 147

Veblen, Thorstein (Bunde)
 1857-1929 . . . . TCLC **31**
 See also CA 115

Vega, Lope de 1562-1635 . . . . LC **23**

Venison, Alfred
 See Pound, Ezra (Weston Loomis)

Verdi, Marie de
 See Mencken, H(enry) L(ouis)

Verdu, Matilde
 See Cela, Camilo Jose

Verga, Giovanni (Carmelo)
 1840-1922 . . . . TCLC **3**
 See also CA 104; 123

Vergil 70B.C.-19B.C. . . . . CMLC **9**; DA

Verhaeren, Emile (Adolphe Gustave)
 1855-1916 . . . . TCLC **12**
 See also CA 109

Verlaine, Paul (Marie)
 1844-1896 . . . . NCLC **2**; PC **2**

Verne, Jules (Gabriel)
 1828-1905 . . . . TCLC **6, 52**
 See also CA 110; 131; DLB 123; JRDA;
 MAICYA; SATA 21

Very, Jones 1813-1880 . . . . NCLC **9**
 See also DLB 1

Vesaas, Tarjei 1897-1970 . . . . CLC **48**
 See also CA 29-32R

Vialis, Gaston
 See Simenon, Georges (Jacques Christian)

Vian, Boris 1920-1959 . . . . TCLC **9**
 See also CA 106; DLB 72

Viaud, (Louis Marie) Julien 1850-1923
 See Loti, Pierre
 See also CA 107

Vicar, Henry
 See Felsen, Henry Gregor

Vicker, Angus
 See Felsen, Henry Gregor

Vidal, Gore
 1925- . . . . . CLC **2, 4, 6, 8, 10, 22, 33, 72**
 See also AITN 1; BEST 90:2; CA 5-8R;
 CANR 13, 45; DLB 6; MTCW

Viereck, Peter (Robert Edwin)
 1916- . . . . CLC **4**
 See also CA 1-4R; CANR 1, 47; DLB 5

Vigny, Alfred (Victor) de
 1797-1863 . . . . NCLC **7**
 See also DLB 119

Vilakazi, Benedict Wallet
 1906-1947 . . . . TCLC **37**

Villiers de l'Isle Adam, Jean Marie Mathias
 Philippe Auguste Comte
 1838-1889 . . . . NCLC **3**; SSC **14**
 See also DLB 123

Vinci, Leonardo da 1452-1519 . . . . . . LC **12**

Vine, Barbara . . . . CLC **50**
 See also Rendell, Ruth (Barbara)
 See also BEST 90:4

Vinge, Joan D(ennison) 1948- . . . . . . CLC **30**
 See also CA 93-96; SATA 36

Violis, G.
 See Simenon, Georges (Jacques Christian)

Visconti, Luchino 1906-1976 . . . . CLC **16**
 See also CA 81-84; 65-68; CANR 39

Vittorini, Elio 1908-1966 . . . . . CLC **6, 9, 14**
 See also CA 133; 25-28R

Vizinczey, Stephen 1933- . . . . CLC **40**
 See also CA 128

Vliet, R(ussell) G(ordon)
 1929-1984 . . . . CLC **22**
 See also CA 37-40R; 112; CANR 18

Vogau, Boris Andreyevich 1894-1937(?)
 See Pilnyak, Boris
 See also CA 123

Vogel, Paula A(nne) 1951- . . . . CLC **76**
 See also CA 108

Voight, Ellen Bryant 1943- . . . . CLC **54**
 See also CA 69-72; CANR 11, 29; DLB 120

Voigt, Cynthia 1942- . . . . CLC **30**
 See also AAYA 3; CA 106; CANR 18, 37,
 40; CLR 13; JRDA; MAICYA;
 SATA 48, 79; SATA-Brief 33

Voinovich, Vladimir (Nikolaevich)
 1932- . . . . CLC **10, 49**
 See also CA 81-84; CAAS 12; CANR 33;
 MTCW

Voloshinov, V. N.
 See Bakhtin, Mikhail Mikhailovich

Voltaire
 1694-1778 . . . LC **14**; DA; SSC **12**; WLC

von Daeniken, Erich 1935- . . . . CLC **30**
 See also AITN 1; CA 37-40R; CANR 17,
 44

von Daniken, Erich
 See von Daeniken, Erich

von Heidenstam, (Carl Gustaf) Verner
 See Heidenstam, (Carl Gustaf) Verner von

von Heyse, Paul (Johann Ludwig)
 See Heyse, Paul (Johann Ludwig von)

von Hofmannsthal, Hugo
 See Hofmannsthal, Hugo von

von Horvath, Odon
 See Horvath, Oedoen von

von Horvath, Oedoen
 See Horvath, Oedoen von

von Liliencron, (Friedrich Adolf Axel) Detlev
 See Liliencron, (Friedrich Adolf Axel)
 Detlev von

Vonnegut, Kurt, Jr.
 1922- . . . . . . CLC **1, 2, 3, 4, 5, 8, 12, 22,**
 40, 60; DA; SSC **8**; WLC
 See also AAYA 6; AITN 1; BEST 90:4;
 CA 1-4R; CANR 1, 25;
 CDALB 1968-1988; DLB 2, 8; DLBD 3;
 DLBY 80; MTCW

Von Rachen, Kurt
 See Hubbard, L(afayette) Ron(ald)

von Rezzori (d'Arezzo), Gregor
 See Rezzori (d'Arezzo), Gregor von

von Sternberg, Josef
 See Sternberg, Josef von

Vorster, Gordon 1924- . . . . CLC **34**
 See also CA 133

Vosce, Trudie
 See Ozick, Cynthia

Voznesensky, Andrei (Andreievich)
 1933- . . . . CLC **1, 15, 57**
 See also CA 89-92; CANR 37; MTCW

Waddington, Miriam 1917- . . . . CLC **28**
 See also CA 21-24R; CANR 12, 30;
 DLB 68

Wagman, Fredrica 1937- . . . . CLC **7**
 See also CA 97-100

Wagner, Richard 1813-1883 . . . . NCLC **9**
 See also DLB 129

Wagner-Martin, Linda 1936- . . . . CLC **50**

Wagoner, David (Russell)
 1926- . . . . CLC **3, 5, 15**
 See also CA 1-4R; CAAS 3; CANR 2;
 DLB 5; SATA 14

Wah, Fred(erick James) 1939- . . . . . . CLC **44**
 See also CA 107; 141; DLB 60

Wahloo, Per 1926-1975 . . . . CLC **7**
 See also CA 61-64

Wahloo, Peter
 See Wahloo, Per

Wain, John (Barrington)
 1925-1994 . . . . CLC **2, 11, 15, 46**
 See also CA 5-8R; 145; CAAS 4; CANR 23;
 CDBLB 1960 to Present; DLB 15, 27,
 139; MTCW

Wajda, Andrzej 1926- . . . . CLC **16**
 See also CA 102

Wakefield, Dan 1932- . . . . CLC **7**
 See also CA 21-24R; CAAS 7

Wakoski, Diane
 1937- . . . . CLC **2, 4, 7, 9, 11, 40**
 See also CA 13-16R; CAAS 1; CANR 9;
 DLB 5

Wakoski-Sherbell, Diane
 See Wakoski, Diane

Walcott, Derek (Alton)
 1930- . . . . CLC **2, 4, 9, 14, 25, 42, 67, 76**;
 BLC
 See also BW 2; CA 89-92; CANR 26, 47;
 DLB 117; DLBY 81; MTCW

Waldman, Anne 1945- . . . . CLC **7**
 See also CA 37-40R; CAAS 17; CANR 34;
 DLB 16

Waldo, E. Hunter
 See Sturgeon, Theodore (Hamilton)

Waldo, Edward Hamilton
 See Sturgeon, Theodore (Hamilton)

Walker, Alice (Malsenior)
 1944- . . . . CLC **5, 6, 9, 19, 27, 46, 58**;
 BLC; DA; SSC **5**
 See also AAYA 3; BEST 89:4; BW 2;
 CA 37-40R; CANR 9, 27;
 CDALB 1968-1988; DLB 6, 33, 143;
 MTCW; SATA 31

Walker, David Harry 1911-1992 . . . . CLC **14**
 See also CA 1-4R; 137; CANR 1; SATA 8;
 SATA-Obit 71

Walker, Edward Joseph 1934-
 See Walker, Ted
 See also CA 21-24R; CANR 12, 28

Welch, (Maurice) Denton
1915-1948 . . . . **TCLC 22**
See also CA 121

Welch, James 1940- . . . . **CLC 6, 14, 52**
See also CA 85-88; CANR 42; NNAL

Weldon, Fay
1933- . . . . **CLC 6, 9, 11, 19, 36, 59**
See also CA 21-24R; CANR 16, 46;
CDBLB 1960 to Present; DLB 14;
MTCW

Wellek, Rene 1903- . . . . **CLC 28**
See also CA 5-8R; CAAS 7; CANR 8;
DLB 63

Weller, Michael 1942- . . . . **CLC 10, 53**
See also CA 85-88

Weller, Paul 1958- . . . . **CLC 26**

Wellershoff, Dieter 1925- . . . . **CLC 46**
See also CA 89-92; CANR 16, 37

Welles, (George) Orson
1915-1985 . . . . **CLC 20, 80**
See also CA 93-96; 117

Wellman, Mac 1945- . . . . **CLC 65**

Wellman, Manly Wade 1903-1986 . . **CLC 49**
See also CA 1-4R; 118; CANR 6, 16, 44;
SATA 6; SATA-Obit 47

Wells, Carolyn 1869(?)-1942 . . . . . . **TCLC 35**
See also CA 113; DLB 11

Wells, H(erbert) G(eorge)
1866-1946 . . . . **TCLC 6, 12, 19; DA;
SSC 6; WLC**
See also CA 110; 121; CDBLB 1914-1945;
DLB 34, 70; MTCW; SATA 20

Wells, Rosemary 1943- . . . . **CLC 12**
See also AAYA 13; CA 85-88; CLR 16;
MAICYA; SAAS 1; SATA 18, 69

Welty, Eudora
1909- . . . . . . **CLC 1, 2, 5, 14, 22, 33; DA;
SSC 1; WLC**
See also CA 9-12R; CABS 1; CANR 32;
CDALB 1941-1968; DLB 2, 102, 143;
DLBD 12; DLBY 87; MTCW

Wen I-to 1899-1946 . . . . **TCLC 28**

Wentworth, Robert
See Hamilton, Edmond

Werfel, Franz (V.) 1890-1945 . . . . . . **TCLC 8**
See also CA 104; DLB 81, 124

Wergeland, Henrik Arnold
1808-1845 . . . . **NCLC 5**

Wersba, Barbara 1932- . . . . **CLC 30**
See also AAYA 2; CA 29-32R; CANR 16,
38; CLR 3; DLB 52; JRDA; MAICYA;
SAAS 2; SATA 1, 58

Wertmueller, Lina 1928- . . . . **CLC 16**
See also CA 97-100; CANR 39

Wescott, Glenway 1901-1987 . . . . . . **CLC 13**
See also CA 13-16R; 121; CANR 23;
DLB 4, 9, 102

Wesker, Arnold 1932- . . . . **CLC 3, 5, 42**
See also CA 1-4R; CAAS 7; CANR 1, 33;
CDBLB 1960 to Present; DLB 13;
MTCW

Wesley, Richard (Errol) 1945- . . . . . . **CLC 7**
See also BW 1; CA 57-60; CANR 27;
DLB 38

Wessel, Johan Herman 1742-1785 . . . . **LC 7**

West, Anthony (Panther)
1914-1987 . . . . **CLC 50**
See also CA 45-48; 124; CANR 3, 19;
DLB 15

West, C. P.
See Wodehouse, P(elham) G(renville)

West, (Mary) Jessamyn
1902-1984 . . . . **CLC 7, 17**
See also CA 9-12R; 112; CANR 27; DLB 6;
DLBY 84; MTCW; SATA-Obit 37

West, Morris L(anglo) 1916- . . . . . **CLC 6, 33**
See also CA 5-8R; CANR 24; MTCW

West, Nathanael
1903-1940 . . . . . **TCLC 1, 14, 44; SSC 16**
See also CA 104; 125; CDALB 1929-1941;
DLB 4, 9, 28; MTCW

West, Owen
See Koontz, Dean R(ay)

West, Paul 1930- . . . . **CLC 7, 14**
See also CA 13-16R; CAAS 7; CANR 22;
DLB 14

West, Rebecca 1892-1983 . . **CLC 7, 9, 31, 50**
See also CA 5-8R; 109; CANR 19; DLB 36;
DLBY 83; MTCW

Westall, Robert (Atkinson)
1929-1993 . . . . **CLC 17**
See also AAYA 12; CA 69-72; 141;
CANR 18; CLR 13; JRDA; MAICYA;
SAAS 2; SATA 23, 69; SATA-Obit 75

Westlake, Donald E(dwin)
1933- . . . . **CLC 7, 33**
See also CA 17-20R; CAAS 13; CANR 16,
44

Westmacott, Mary
See Christie, Agatha (Mary Clarissa)

Weston, Allen
See Norton, Andre

Wetcheek, J. L.
See Feuchtwanger, Lion

Wetering, Janwillem van de
See van de Wetering, Janwillem

Wetherell, Elizabeth
See Warner, Susan (Bogert)

Whalen, Philip 1923- . . . . **CLC 6, 29**
See also CA 9-12R; CANR 5, 39; DLB 16

Wharton, Edith (Newbold Jones)
1862-1937 . . . . . . **TCLC 3, 9, 27, 53; DA;
SSC 6; WLC**
See also CA 104; 132; CDALB 1865-1917;
DLB 4, 9, 12, 78; MTCW

Wharton, James
See Mencken, H(enry) L(ouis)

Wharton, William (a pseudonym)
. . . . **CLC 18, 37**
See also CA 93-96; DLBY 80

Wheatley (Peters), Phillis
1754(?)-1784 . . . . **LC 3; BLC; DA; PC 3;
WLC**
See also CDALB 1640-1865; DLB 31, 50

Wheelock, John Hall 1886-1978 . . . . **CLC 14**
See also CA 13-16R; 77-80; CANR 14;
DLB 45

White, E(lwyn) B(rooks)
1899-1985 . . . . **CLC 10, 34, 39**
See also AITN 2; CA 13-16R; 116;
CANR 16, 37; CLR 1, 21; DLB 11, 22;
MAICYA; MTCW; SATA 2, 29;
SATA-Obit 44

White, Edmund (Valentine III)
1940- . . . . **CLC 27**
See also AAYA 7; CA 45-48; CANR 3, 19,
36; MTCW

White, Patrick (Victor Martindale)
1912-1990 . . **CLC 3, 4, 5, 7, 9, 18, 65, 69**
See also CA 81-84; 132; CANR 43; MTCW

White, Phyllis Dorothy James 1920-
See James, P. D.
See also CA 21-24R; CANR 17, 43; MTCW

White, T(erence) H(anbury)
1906-1964 . . . . **CLC 30**
See also CA 73-76; CANR 37; JRDA;
MAICYA; SATA 12

White, Terence de Vere
1912-1994 . . . . **CLC 49**
See also CA 49-52; 145; CANR 3

White, Walter F(rancis)
1893-1955 . . . . **TCLC 15**
See also White, Walter
See also BW 1; CA 115; 124; DLB 51

White, William Hale 1831-1913
See Rutherford, Mark
See also CA 121

Whitehead, E(dward) A(nthony)
1933- . . . . **CLC 5**
See also CA 65-68

Whitemore, Hugh (John) 1936- . . . . . **CLC 37**
See also CA 132

Whitman, Sarah Helen (Power)
1803-1878 . . . . **NCLC 19**
See also DLB 1

Whitman, Walt(er)
1819-1892 . . . . . **NCLC 4, 31; DA; PC 3;
WLC**
See also CDALB 1640-1865; DLB 3, 64;
SATA 20

Whitney, Phyllis A(yame) 1903- . . . . **CLC 42**
See also AITN 2; BEST 90:3; CA 1-4R;
CANR 3, 25, 38; JRDA; MAICYA;
SATA 1, 30

Whittemore, (Edward) Reed (Jr.)
1919- . . . . **CLC 4**
See also CA 9-12R; CAAS 8; CANR 4;
DLB 5

Whittier, John Greenleaf
1807-1892 . . . . **NCLC 8**
See also CDALB 1640-1865; DLB 1

Whittlebot, Hernia
See Coward, Noel (Peirce)

Wicker, Thomas Grey 1926-
See Wicker, Tom
See also CA 65-68; CANR 21, 46

Wicker, Tom . . . . **CLC 7**
See also Wicker, Thomas Grey

Wideman, John Edgar
1941- . . . . **CLC 5, 34, 36, 67; BLC**
See also BW 2; CA 85-88; CANR 14, 42;
DLB 33, 143

Wittlin, Jozef 1896-1976 . . . . **CLC 25**
See also CA 49-52; 65-68; CANR 3

Wodehouse, P(elham) G(renville)
1881-1975 . . . **CLC 1, 2, 5, 10, 22; SSC 2**
See also AITN 2; CA 45-48; 57-60;
CANR 3, 33; CDBLB 1914-1945;
DLB 34; MTCW; SATA 22

Woiwode, L.
See Woiwode, Larry (Alfred)

Woiwode, Larry (Alfred) 1941- . . . **CLC 6, 10**
See also CA 73-76; CANR 16; DLB 6

Wojciechowska, Maia (Teresa)
1927- . . . . **CLC 26**
See also AAYA 8; CA 9-12R; CANR 4, 41;
CLR 1; JRDA; MAICYA; SAAS 1;
SATA 1, 28

Wolf, Christa 1929- . . . . **CLC 14, 29, 58**
See also CA 85-88; CANR 45; DLB 75;
MTCW

Wolfe, Gene (Rodman) 1931- . . . . **CLC 25**
See also CA 57-60; CAAS 9; CANR 6, 32;
DLB 8

Wolfe, George C. 1954- . . . . **CLC 49**

Wolfe, Thomas (Clayton)
1900-1938 . . . **TCLC 4, 13, 29; DA; WLC**
See also CA 104; 132; CDALB 1929-1941;
DLB 9, 102; DLBD 2; DLBY 85; MTCW

Wolfe, Thomas Kennerly, Jr. 1931-
See Wolfe, Tom
See also CA 13-16R; CANR 9, 33; MTCW

Wolfe, Tom . . . . **CLC 1, 2, 9, 15, 35, 51**
See also Wolfe, Thomas Kennerly, Jr.
See also AAYA 8; AITN 2; BEST 89:1

Wolff, Geoffrey (Ansell) 1937- . . . . . **CLC 41**
See also CA 29-32R; CANR 29, 43

Wolff, Sonia
See Levitin, Sonia (Wolff)

Wolff, Tobias (Jonathan Ansell)
1945- . . . . **CLC 39, 64**
See also BEST 90:2; CA 114; 117; DLB 130

Wolfram von Eschenbach
c. 1170-c. 1220 . . . . **CMLC 5**
See also DLB 138

Wolitzer, Hilma 1930- . . . . **CLC 17**
See also CA 65-68; CANR 18, 40; SATA 31

Wollstonecraft, Mary 1759-1797 . . . . . . **LC 5**
See also CDBLB 1789-1832; DLB 39, 104

Wonder, Stevie . . . . **CLC 12**
See also Morris, Steveland Judkins

Wong, Jade Snow 1922- . . . . **CLC 17**
See also CA 109

Woodcott, Keith
See Brunner, John (Kilian Houston)

Woodruff, Robert W.
See Mencken, H(enry) L(ouis)

Woolf, (Adeline) Virginia
1882-1941 . . . . . . **TCLC 1, 5, 20, 43, 56;**
DA; SSC 7; WLC
See also CA 104; 130; CDBLB 1914-1945;
DLB 36, 100; DLBD 10; MTCW

Woollcott, Alexander (Humphreys)
1887-1943 . . . . **TCLC 5**
See also CA 105; DLB 29

Woolrich, Cornell 1903-1968 . . . . . . **CLC 77**
See also Hopley-Woolrich, Cornell George

Wordsworth, Dorothy
1771-1855 . . . . **NCLC 25**
See also DLB 107

Wordsworth, William
1770-1850 . . . . **NCLC 12, 38; DA; PC 4;**
WLC
See also CDBLB 1789-1832; DLB 93, 107

Wouk, Herman 1915- . . . . **CLC 1, 9, 38**
See also CA 5-8R; CANR 6, 33; DLBY 82;
MTCW

Wright, Charles (Penzel, Jr.)
1935- . . . . **CLC 6, 13, 28**
See also CA 29-32R; CAAS 7; CANR 23,
36; DLBY 82; MTCW

Wright, Charles Stevenson
1932- . . . . **CLC 49; BLC 3**
See also BW 1; CA 9-12R; CANR 26;
DLB 33

Wright, Jack R.
See Harris, Mark

Wright, James (Arlington)
1927-1980 . . . . **CLC 3, 5, 10, 28**
See also AITN 2; CA 49-52; 97-100;
CANR 4, 34; DLB 5; MTCW

Wright, Judith (Arandell)
1915- . . . . **CLC 11, 53**
See also CA 13-16R; CANR 31; MTCW;
SATA 14

Wright, L(aurali) R. 1939- . . . . **CLC 44**
See also CA 138

Wright, Richard (Nathaniel)
1908-1960 . . . . **CLC 1, 3, 4, 9, 14, 21, 48,**
74; BLC; DA; SSC 2; WLC
See also AAYA 5; BW 1; CA 108;
CDALB 1929-1941; DLB 76, 102;
DLBD 2; MTCW

Wright, Richard B(ruce) 1937- . . . . . . **CLC 6**
See also CA 85-88; DLB 53

Wright, Rick 1945- . . . . **CLC 35**

Wright, Rowland
See Wells, Carolyn

Wright, Stephen Caldwell 1946- . . . . **CLC 33**
See also BW 2

Wright, Willard Huntington 1888-1939
See Van Dine, S. S.
See also CA 115

Wright, William 1930- . . . . **CLC 44**
See also CA 53-56; CANR 7, 23

Wu Ch'eng-en 1500(?)-1582(?) . . . . **LC 7**

Wu Ching-tzu 1701-1754 . . . . **LC 2**

Wurlitzer, Rudolph 1938(?)- . . . **CLC 2, 4, 15**
See also CA 85-88

Wycherley, William 1641-1715 . . . . **LC 8, 21**
See also CDBLB 1660-1789; DLB 80

Wylie, Elinor (Morton Hoyt)
1885-1928 . . . . **TCLC 8**
See also CA 105; DLB 9, 45

Wylie, Philip (Gordon) 1902-1971 . . . **CLC 43**
See also CA 21-22; 33-36R; CAP 2; DLB 9

Wyndham, John . . . . **CLC 19**
See also Harris, John (Wyndham Parkes
Lucas) Beynon

Wyss, Johann David Von
1743-1818 . . . . **NCLC 10**
See also JRDA; MAICYA; SATA 29;
SATA-Brief 27

Yakumo Koizumi
See Hearn, (Patricio) Lafcadio (Tessima
Carlos)

Yanez, Jose Donoso
See Donoso (Yanez), Jose

Yanovsky, Basile S.
See Yanovsky, V(assily) S(emenovich)

Yanovsky, V(assily) S(emenovich)
1906-1989 . . . . **CLC 2, 18**
See also CA 97-100; 129

Yates, Richard 1926-1992 . . . . . **CLC 7, 8, 23**
See also CA 5-8R; 139; CANR 10, 43;
DLB 2; DLBY 81, 92

Yeats, W. B.
See Yeats, William Butler

Yeats, William Butler
1865-1939 . . . . . **TCLC 1, 11, 18, 31; DA;**
WLC
See also CA 104; 127; CANR 45;
CDBLB 1890-1914; DLB 10, 19, 98;
MTCW

Yehoshua, A(braham) B.
1936- . . . . **CLC 13, 31**
See also CA 33-36R; CANR 43

Yep, Laurence Michael 1948- . . . . . . **CLC 35**
See also AAYA 5; CA 49-52; CANR 1, 46;
CLR 3, 17; DLB 52; JRDA; MAICYA;
SATA 7, 69

Yerby, Frank G(arvin)
1916-1991 . . . . **CLC 1, 7, 22; BLC**
See also BW 1; CA 9-12R; 136; CANR 16;
DLB 76; MTCW

Yesenin, Sergei Alexandrovich
See Esenin, Sergei (Alexandrovich)

Yevtushenko, Yevgeny (Alexandrovich)
1933- . . . . **CLC 1, 3, 13, 26, 51**
See also CA 81-84; CANR 33; MTCW

Yezierska, Anzia 1885(?)-1970 . . . . . **CLC 46**
See also CA 126; 89-92; DLB 28; MTCW

Yglesias, Helen 1915- . . . . **CLC 7, 22**
See also CA 37-40R; CAAS 20; CANR 15;
MTCW

Yokomitsu Riichi 1898-1947 . . . . . . **TCLC 47**

Yonge, Charlotte (Mary)
1823-1901 . . . . **TCLC 48**
See also CA 109; DLB 18; SATA 17

York, Jeremy
See Creasey, John

York, Simon
See Heinlein, Robert A(nson)

Yorke, Henry Vincent 1905-1974 . . . **CLC 13**
See also Green, Henry
See also CA 85-88; 49-52

Yosano Akiko 1878-1942 . . . . **PC 11**

Yoshimoto, Banana . . . . **CLC 84**
See also Yoshimoto, Mahoko

Yoshimoto, Mahoko 1964-
See Yoshimoto, Banana
See also CA 144

Literary Criticism Series
Cumulative Topic Index

This index lists all topic entries in the Gale Literary Criticism Series *Classical and Medieval Literature Criticism, Contemporary Literary Criticism, Literature Criticism from 1400 to 1800, Nineteenth-Century Literature Criticism,* and *Twentieth-Century Literary Criticism.*

LC Cumulative Nationality Index

LC Cumulative Title Index

Title Index

Title Index

Title Index

Title Index

Title Index

Ju-lin wai-shih (*The Forest of Scholars*) (Wu Ching-tzu) **2**:511-38

Julius Excluded from Heaven (Erasmus)
See *Julius secundus exlusus*

Julius exclusus (Erasmus)
See *Julius secundus exlusus*

Julius secundus exlusus (*Julius Excluded from Heaven*; *Julius exclusus*) (Erasmus) **16**:132, 169, 172, 175-76, 182, 191-92

Der junge Gelehrte (*The Young Savant*) (Lessing) **8**:63, 94, 98, 113

Jungfer-Hobel (Beer)
See *Der neu ausgefertigte Jungfer-Hobel*

"Jupiter et Europe" (Rousseau) **9**:341

Jure Divino (Defoe) **1**:162

"Justice II" (Herbert) **24**:257-59, 266

The Justice of God in the Damnation of Sinners (Edwards) **7**:98, 117

Justice without Revenge (Vega)
See *El castigo sin venganza*

Justification of Andromeda Liberata (Chapman) **22**:51,73-4

Justi Lipsii Diva Sichemiensis sive Aspricollis: nova ejus beneficia & admiranda (Lipsius) **16**:253

Justi Lipsii Diva Virgo Hallensis: beneficia ejus & miracula fide atque ordine descripta (Lipsius) **16**:253

The Just Italian (Davenant) **13**:175

A Just Rebuke (Penn) **25**:290-91

"Juvenilia" **16**:418

Juvenilia; or, Certaine paradoxes, and problems (*Paradoxes and Problems*) (Donne) **10**:76, 95-6; **24**:151, 205

"Kalendae Maiae" (Buchanan) **4**:120, 122-23

"K'ao-pi ssu" ("The Bureau of Frauds") (P'u Sung-ling) **3**:354

Katharine and Petruchio (Garrick) **15**:94

Keep the Widow Waking (Dekker) **22**:107

Der keusche Joseph (*Chaste Joseph*) (Grimmelshausen) **6**:247-48

"Kew Gardens" (Chatterton) **3**:125-26, 132, 134-35

A Key Opening a Way (Penn) **25**:334

Khátimat al-hayát (*End of Life*) (Jami) **9**:65, 68

Khirad-náma-yi Iskandarí (*Wisdom of Alexander*) (Jami) **9**:68, 70-1

Kierlighed uden strømper (*Kjælighed uden Strömper*) (Wessel) **7**:388-92

Kildereisen (*Journey to the Spring*) (Holberg) **6**:259, 277

Kinderlogik (Moritz)
See *Versuch einer kleinen praktischen Kinderlogik*

The Kind Keeper; or, Mr. Limberham (*Mr. Limberham*) (Dryden) **3**:222, 229-30; **21**:55

"The King and His Three Daughters" (Walpole) **2**:500, 507

"King Arthur; or, The British Worthy" (Dryden) **3**:222; **21**:88

King Charles's Works (Charles I) **13**:134

The King is the Best Judge (Vega)
See *El mejor alcalde, el rey*

The King is the Best Magistrate (Vega)
See *El mejor alcalde, el rey*

King Peter in Madrid and the Liege Lord of Illescas (Vega)
See *El reydon Pedro en Madrid y el infazón de Illescas*

King's Book (Henry VIII)

See *A Necessary Doctrine and Erudition for any Christen Man, Sette Furthe by the Kynges Majestie of Englande*

King Vamba (Vega) **23**:348

The King without a Kingdom (Vega)
See *El rey sin reino*

"The Kirk's Alarm" (Burns) **3**:71, 78, 96

Kjælighed uden Strömper (Wessel)
See *Kierlighed uden strømper*

Der kleine Catechismus (*Small Catechism*) (Luther) **9**:151

Kleine Schriften (Lessing) **8**:82

Kleine Schriften, die deutsche Sprache betreffend (Moritz) **2**:241

Kleonnis (Lessing) **8**:109

"Knave" (Butler) **16**:52, 55

The Knight-Commanders of Cordova (Vega)
See *Los commendadores de Cordoba*

The Knight from Olmedo (Vega)
See *El cabalero de Olmedo*

"Knight's" (Chaucer)
See "Knight's Tale"

A Knight's Conjuring, done in earnest, discovered in jest (Dekker) **22**:95

"Knight's Tale" ("Knight's"; "Palamon and Arcite") (Chaucer) **17**:49, 53, 55, 69-70, 72, 117, 123-28, 130-31, 133-36, 149, 183-84, 195, 202, 205, 214, 218, 226-27, 230, 232-35, 237, 243

"Knight's Tale" ("Palamon and Arcite") (Dryden) **3**:184-85, 187, 196, 204, 243

The Knowledge that Maketh a Wise Man (Elyot)
See *Of the Knowledge Which Maketh a Wise Man*

Know Yourself (Arbuthnot) **1**:19

Korte Verhandeling van God, de Mensch und deszelhs Welstand (*Short Treatise*) (Spinoza) **9**:423

Kritische Briefe (Lessing) **8**:112

"Kung-sun Hsia" (P'u Sung-ling) **3**:352

Der kurtzweilige Bruder Blau-Mantel (*Bruder Blau-Mantel*) (Beer) **5**:56

Die kurtzweiligen Sommer-Täge (Beer) **5**:46, 48, 50-2, 57-60

El laberinto de amor (Cervantes) **6**:180-81; **23**:101-02, 143, 147

El laberinto de Creta (Vega) **23**:393

"A la Bourbon" (Lovelace) **24**:327

Le labyrinthe de Versailles (Perrault) **2**:266, 280

Labyrinthus medicorum (Paracelsus) **14**:200

De la causa, principio et uno (*Concerning the Cause, Principle, and One*; *On Cause, the Principle, and the One*) (Bruno) **27**:83, 86, 90, 96-97, 104

"A la Chabot" (Lovelace) **24**:327

Ladies' Library (Steele) **18**:347, 349-50, 380

The Ladies Subscription (Cleland) **2**:51, 53

"The Ladle" (Prior) **4**:455, 461, 467, 473

"The Lady A. L., My Asylum in a Great Extremity" (Lovelace) **24**:304

"The Lady Cornelia" (Cervantes)
See "La Señora Cornelia"

The Lady in Child-bed (Holberg) **6**:259

Lady Juliet Catesby (Brooke)
See *Letters from Juliet, Lady Catesby, to Her Friend, Lady Henrietta Campley*

"The Lady Knight-Errant" (P'u Sung-ling)
See "Hsia-nü"

The Lady of May (Sidney) **19**:328-29, 374, 391, 393, 396-98, 400, 409-10, 421

"The Lady's Answer To The Knight" (Butler) **16**:30, 39, 49

"The Lady's Dressing Room" (Swift) **1**:453, 461, 483-84, 502, 510

The Lady's Pacquet of Letters Broke Open (Manley)
See *The New Atalantis*

The Lady's Tale (Davys) **1**:97, 100, 102-03

"A Lady with a Falcon in Her Fist" (Lovelace) **24**:336, 346

Lágrimas de un penitente (Quevedo) **23**:176-77

Lailá u Majnún (*Laylá and Majnún*) (Jami) **9**:66, 70-1

"The Lament" (Burns) **3**:48, 52, 86

"Lament I" (Kochanowski) **10**:166-68

"Lament II" (Kochanowski) **10**:165-67

"Lament III" (Kochanowski) **10**:153, 166

"Lament IV" (Kochanowski) **10**:153, 166-68, 170

"Lament V" (Kochanowski)
See "Threnody V"

"Lament VI" (Kochanowski) **10**:153, 157, 166, 170

"Lament VII" (Kochanowski)
See "Tren VII"

"Lament VIII" (Kochanowski)
See "Tren VIII"

"Lament IX" (Kochanowski)
See "Tren IX"

"Lament X" (Kochanowski) **10**:157-58, 166, 170

"Lament XI" (Kochanowski)
See "Threnody XI"

"Lament XII" (Kochanowski) **10**:153, 157-58,166-67

"Lament XIII" (Kochanowski) **10**:153, 166-67

"Lament XIV" (Kochanowski) **10**:153, 159, 165, 169

"Lament XV" (Kochanowski) **10**:153, 165-66, 170

"Lament XVI" (Kochanowski)
See "Tren XVI"

"Lament XVII" (Kochanowski)
See "Tren XVII"

"Lament XVII" (Kochanowski)
See "Threnody XVII"

"Lament XIX" (Kochanowski)
See "Tren XIX"

Lament and Exhortation aginst the excessive un-Christian Power of the Bishop of Rome and the unministerial Ministers (*A Remonstrance and a Warning against the Presumptuous, Unchristian Power of the Bishop of Rome and the Unspiritual Spiritual Estate*) (Hutten) **16**:225, 234

"Lamentation for the Queen" (More) **10**:430

"The Lamentations of Jeremy, for the most part according to Tremelius" (Donne) **10**:84

"Lament for Creech" (Burns)
See "Burlesque Lament for Creech"

"Lament for Glencairn" (Burns)
See "Lament for James, Earl of Glencairn"

"Lament for James, Earl of Glencairn" ("Lament for Glencairn") (Burns) **3**:84

Laments (Kochanowski)
See *Treny*

Lamon's Tale (Sidney) **19**:422

De lampade combinatoria Lulliana (Bruno) **27**:119

Title Index

Title Index

Title Index

See "Epistle to William Simpson of
Ochiltree, May 1785"

Town Eclogues (Montagu)
See *Court Poems*

The Town Fop; or, Sir Timothy Tawdrey
(Behn) **1**:33, 39, 46-7

Los trabajos de Persiles y Sigismunda (*Persiles y
Sigismunda*) (Cervantes) **6**:142-43, 151,
169-70, 174-76, 178, 180; **23**:94-99, 111, 115,
120-21, 132-34, 143-44

*Tractatus theologico-politicus continens
dissertationes all quot,quibus ostenditur
libertatem philosophandi non tantum salva
pietate, & reipublicae* (*Theological-Political
Treatise*) (Spinoza) **9**:393, 397-98, 402, 408-
09, 418-19, 423-24, 431, 436, 438-40

"Tract on the Popery Laws" (Burke) **7**:46

La tragedia por los celos (Castro) **19**:7-8

The Tragedie of Soliman and Perseda (*Hamlet*)
(Kyd) **22**:254, 259

Tragedy (*Pompey the Great; his faire Cornelias
Tragedie; effected by her Father and
Husbands downe-cast death and fortune;
Solyman and Perseda*) (Kyd) **22**:246, 254

The Tragedy of Bussy D'Ambois
(*BussyD'Ambois*; *D'Ambois*) (Chapman)
22:3, 5, 7-8, 11, 15, 18-19, 20-2, 30-1, 34,
36-9, 40, 42, 44, 52, 54, 56, 57, 78-9, 80-1

The Tragedy of Caesar and Pompey (*Caesar
and Pompey*) (Chapman) **22**:7, 12-13, 15,
30, 34, 46-7, 54

Tragedy of Cato (Addison) **18**:7, 10-11, 14-15,
17-19, 31-2, 46-7, 76-7

The Tragedy of Chabot, Admiral of France
(*Chabot*; *Philip Chabot, Admiral of France*)
(Chapman) **22**:7, 13, 15, 45-6

The Tragedy of Cleopatra (*Cleopatra*) (Daniel)
24:85, 89, 98, 107, 112-15, 118, 122, 130-31,
134

The Tragedy of Dido, Queen of Carthage (*Dido,
Queen of Carthage*) (Marlowe) **22**:362

The Tragedy of Jane Shore (*Jane Shore*)
(Rowe) **8**:285, 287, 292-97, 299-302, 304-
08, 314, 316

The Tragedy of Lady Jane Gray (*Jane*) (Rowe)
8:293, 297, 300, 302, 305, 307-08

The Tragedy of Philotas (*Philotas*) (Daniel)
24:85, 89, 90, 98, 122, 128, 134, 141-42, 145

The Tragedy of Sophonisba (*Sophonisba*)
16:387

The Tragedy of the Horatii (Aretino)
See *Orazia*

The Tragedy of Tom Thumb (Fielding) **1**:203,
239

The Tragicall History(Marlowe) **22**:380-2, 385

*The Tragicall History of the Life and Death of
Doctor Faustus* (*Doctor Faustus*) (Marlowe)
22:328, 338, 371, 378-81, 384-5

Tragicomedia de Calisto y Melibea (Rojas)
See *La Celestina*

The Tragicomedy of Calisto and Melibea
(Rojas)
See *La Celestina*

A Tragic Play in the Christian World **23**:65

Traité de métaphysique (Voltaire) **14**:339,
366-67, 379

Traité des animaux (*Treatise on the Animals*)
(Condillac) **26**:45, 47, 50, 53

Traité des devoirs (Montesquieu) **7**:339, 356,
360

Traité des sensations (*Treatise on the
Sensations*) (Condillac) **26**:6, 8, 10, 12-15,
23, 27-9,44, 47, 50-3, 55-6, 59-60

Traité des systèmes (*Treatise on Systems*)
(Condillac) **26**:6, 8, 11-12, 17, 38, 44,47

Traité sur la tolérance (Voltaire) **14**:370, 379,
402

Le Traître puni (Lesage) **28**:199, 206, 208,
210

Trampagos, the Pimp Who Lost His Moll
(Cervantes) **6**:190-92

"The Transfiguration" (Herrick) **13**:353, 403

*Translation of the Latter Part of the Third
Book of Lucretius: Against the Fear of Death*
(*Against the Fear of Death*) (Dryden)
21:72-4, 76-7

*A Translation of the Psalms of David,
Attempted in the Spirit of Christianity, and
Adapted to the Divine Service* ("*Psalms*")
(Smart) **3**:371, 376-78, 382, 395, 398

"Transmigrations of Pug the Monkey"
(Addison) **18**:28

El trato de Argel (*Los tratos de Argel*)
(Cervantes) **6**:177-78, 180-81; **23**:100

Los tratos de Argel (Cervantes)
See *El trato de Argel*

Trattato della Pittura (*Treatise on Painting*)
(Vinci) **12**:384, 391, 393-96, 406, 412, 417-
18, 420-21, 423-25, 427

Travel Journal (Montaigne)
See *Journal du voyage de Michel de
Montaigne en Italie par la Suisse et
l'Allemagne en 1580 et 1581*

The Traveller (Goldsmith) **2**:66, 68, 71-5,
80-2, 94-5, 97, 102, 104-05, 112-15, 128-31

"The Traveller Benighted and Lost"
(Hopkinson) **25**:250-51

Travels (Addison) **18**:30

*Travels, Chiefly on Foot, through Several Parts
of England in 1782* (Moritz)
See *Reisen eines Deutschen in England im
Jahr 1782*

*Travels into Several Remote Nations of the
World, in Four Parts; By Lemuel Gulliver*
(Swift) **1**:426-29, 432-37, 439-42, 444-52,
456, 460-79, 483-91, 497-502, 504-10, 513-
17, 519, 527-29

Travels through France and Italy (Smollett)
2:322,329, 331, 344, 363, 365-67

The Treasure (Lessing) **8**:112

*The Treasure of the City of Ladies, or, The
Book of the Three Virtues* (Christine de
Pizan)
See *La trésor de la cité des dames; or, Le
livre des trois vertus*

Treatise (Taylor)
See *Treatise Concerning the Lord's Supper*

Treatise Concerning Enthusiasm (More) **9**:318

A Treatise concerning Religious Affections
(*Religious Affections*) (Edwards) **7**:94, 96,
101-02, 118-21

Treatise Concerning the Lord's Supper
(*Treatise*) (Taylor) **11**:373, 385-86

*A Treatise Historical containing the Bitter
Passion of our Saviour Christ* (More) **10**:370

Treatise of Civil Government (Locke) **7**:269,
273

*A Treatise of Human Nature: Being an Attempt
to Introduce the Experimental Method of
Reasoning into Moral Subjects* (Hume)
7:136-41, 154-55, 157-58, 160-61, 163, 165-
66, 168, 171, 174, 176, 178, 183, 188, 197-
99, 202

A Treatise of the Art of Political Lying
(Arbuthnot) **1**:15

"Treatise on Charity" (Crashaw) **24**:16

Treatise on Painting (Vinci)
See *Trattato della Pittura*

A Treatise on Polite Conversation (Swift)
1:437

Treatise on Religion and the State (Spinoza)
9:421

Treatise on Shadows (Vinci) **12**:405

Treatise on Systems (Condillac)
See *Traité des systèmes*

Treatise on the Animals (Condillac)
See *Traité des animaux*

A Treatise on the Astrolabe (Chaucer) **17**:214-
15

Treatise on the Fable (Lessing) **8**:104

Treatise on the New Testament (Luther) **9**:140

*A Treatise on the Nobilitie and excellencye of
woman kynde* (Agrippa von Nettesheim)
See *De nobilitate et praeccelentia foeminei
sexus*

Treatise on the Sensations (Condillac)
See *Traité des sensations*

A Treatise to Receaue the Blessed Sacrament
(More) **10**:367

Treatise upon the Christian Religion (Addison)
18:8

A Treatise upon the Passion (More) **10**:367,
399-400, 405, 436, 440

"The Tree" (Winchilsea) **3**:442, 444, 451, 454

The Tree of the Choicest Fruit (Calderon dela
Barca) **23**:9

"Tren VII" ("Lament VII") (Kochanowski)
10:153, 157, 166-67, 170

"Tren VIII" ("Lament VIII"; "Threnody
VIII") (Kochanowski) **10**:153, 157, 159,
163, 166-67, 170

"Tren IX" ("Lament IX") (Kochanowski)
10:158, 170, 174

"Tren XVI" ("Lament XVI") (Kochanowski)
10:153, 158, 165, 170, 174

"Tren XVII" ("Lament XVII"; "Threnody
XVII") (Kochanowski) **10**:153, 157-59,
165, 173-74

"Tren XIX" ("The Dream";"Lament XIX")
(Kochanowski) **10**:153, 157-58, 165, 170,
173

Treny (*Laments*; *The Threnodies*)
(Kochanowski) **10**:151-53, 156-59, 162,
164-65, 167-76

*La trésor de la cité des dames; or, Le livre des
trois vertus* (*The Treasure of the City of
Ladies, or, The Book of the Three Virtues*)
(Christine de Pizan) **9**:25, 33-5, 38-9, 45,
47

"The Trials of a Noble House" (Juana Ines de
la Cruz)
See *Los empeños de una casa*

Trias Romana (Hutten)
See *Vadiscus, sive Trias Romana*

De tribus tabernaculis (Kempis) **11**:411

The Tricks of Scapin (Moliere)
See *Les fourberies de Scapin*

Trifles (Kochanowski)
See *Fraski*

Title Index

ISBN 0-8103-8944-4